The Handbook of Forensic Psychology

Third Edition

Edited by
Irving B. Weiner
Allen K. Hess

WILEY

John Wiley & Sons, Inc.

For general information on our other products and services please contact our Customer Care Department within the United States at (800) 762-2974, outside the United States at (317) 572-3993 or fax (317) 572-4002.

Wiley also publishes its books in a variety of electronic formats. Some content that appears in print may not be available in electronic books. For more information about Wiley products, visit our web site at www.wiley.com.

ISBN-13 978-0-471-69232-4

ISBN-10 0-471-69232-8

Printed in the United States of America.

10   9   8   7   6   5   4   3   2   1

Contributors

Pedro M. Paz Alonso, PhD
University of California
Davis, California

Anne M. Bartol, PhD
Bartol Consulting and Writing Group
Castleton, Vermont

Curt R. Bartol, PhD
Bartol Consulting and Writing Group
Castleton, Vermont

James N. Butcher, PhD
University of Minnesota
Minneapolis, Minnesota

Paola Castelli, MA
University of California
Davis, California

Charles R. Clark, PhD
Independent Practice
Ann Arbor, Michigan

Tyler L. Cox, MS, JD
Cox & Day, PC
Montgomery, Alabama

Robin S. Edelstein, MA
University of California
Davis, California

Sheila French, MA
University of New Brunswick
Fredericton, New Brunswick,
   Canada

Michele Galietta, PhD
John Jay College of Criminal Justice
New York, New York

Paul Gendreau, PhD
University of New Brunswick
Fredericton, New Brunswick,
   Canada

Claire Goggin, MA
University of New Brunswick
Fredericton, New Brunswick,
   Canada

Stephen L. Golding, PhD
University of Utah
Salt Lake City, Utah

Gail S. Goodman, PhD
University of California
Davis, California

Jennifer L. Groscup, JD, PhD
John Jay College of Criminal Justice
New York, New York

Stephen D. Hart, PhD
Simon Fraser University
Burnaby, British Columbia, Canada

Allen K. Hess, PhD
Auburn University at Montgomery
Montgomery, Alabama

Kathryn D. Hess, MS, MPA
Montgomery, Alabama

William G. Iacono, PhD
University of Minnesota
Minneapolis, Minnesota

Daniel A. Krauss, JD, PhD
Claremont McKenna College
Claremont, California

Thomas R. Litwack, PhD, JD
John Jay College of Criminal Justice
New York, New York

Kristen E. Lyons, BS
University of California
Davis, California

William L. Marshall, PhD
Queen's University
Kingston, Ontario, Canada

Joan McCord, PhD
Temple University
Philadelphia, Pennsylvania

Kathryn B. Miller, PhD
University of Minnesota
Minneapolis, Minnesota

Emilie B. Mitchell, MA
University of California
Davis, California

Max J. Mobley, PhD
Department of Corrections
Pine Bluff, Arkansas

Jeremy W. Newton, MA
University of California
Davis, California

David Nussbaum, PhD
Whitby Mental Health Centre
Whitby, Ontario, Canada

Christopher J. Patrick, PhD
University of Minnesota
Minneapolis, Minnesota

Steven Penrod, JD, PhD
John Jay College of Criminal Justice
New York, New York

Daniel J. Reschly, PhD
Vanderbilt University
Nashville, Tennessee

Jennifer K. Robbennolt, JD, PhD
University of Missouri-Columbia
School of Law
Columbia, Missouri

Ronald Roesch, PhD
Simon Fraser University
Burnaby, British Columbia, Canada

Bruce D. Sales, PhD, JD
University of Arizona
Tucson, Arizona

Alan W. Scheflin, LLM
Santa Clara University School of Law
Santa Clara, California

Ellen Scrivner, PhD
Chicago Police Department
Chicago, Illinois

Ralph Slovenko, JD
Wayne University Law School
Detroit, Michigan

Paula Smith, MA
University of Cincinnati
Cincinnati, Ohio

Barbara Stanley, PhD
John Jay College of Criminal Justice
and New York State Psychiatric
Institute
New York, New York

Steven Walfish, PhD
Georgia State University and Atlanta
Center for Cognitive Therapy
Atlanta, Georgia

Irving B. Weiner, PhD
University of South Florida
Tampa, Florida

Patricia A. Zapf, PhD
John Jay College of Criminal Justice
New York, New York

Preface

THIS THIRD edition of *The Handbook of Forensic Psychology* provides an authoritative and comprehensive resource for understanding the theoretical foundations of forensic psychology, becoming familiar with the expanding research base in this specialty, and learning to apply forensic concepts artfully in everyday practice. With two decades having passed since the first edition of the *Handbook,* some comparison with the two previous editions may be helpful.

The preface for the first edition described forensic psychology as a "rapidly emerging professional specialty," noted that "an increasing number of practitioners . . . are being called upon for opinions concerning questions of child custody, competency, criminal responsibility, personal injury or handicaps, suitability to working in law enforcement, and candidacy for probation or parole," and observed that "developmental and experimental psychologists have come into demand for their expert opinions on such matters as the reliability of eyewitness testimony and lie detection."

The preface for the second edition identified professionals, scholars, and students as the three intersecting audiences for the *Handbook.* We reported that an increasing number of psychologists were not only providing forensic services but also identifying themselves specifically as forensic psychologists. With respect to scholarship, we pointed out that the literature in forensic psychology and psychological research journals was calling attention to an increasing number of legal issues that psychologists can address as research questions having empirical answers (e.g., "What are the memory capabilities of children and adults for adults recalling childhood experiences?" "How can we assess violence risk?"). Adoption of the *Handbook* as a text to meet student demand was anticipated in relation to a growing number of forensic courses being offered in universities and in continuing education workshops.

This third edition of the *Handbook* was undertaken with the same premises as its predecessors, but with even stronger conviction. The interrelationship and interpenetration of law and psychology have accelerated exponentially in the past several years, in terms of public issues and professional developments. Print and electronic media offer a drumbeat of news concerning various domestic law-psychology issues, including parental and grandparental rights to child custody, options for interstate and international custody, child rights to privacy from parental control, and who can marry or adopt, particularly with respect to gay and lesbian adults. As for criminal law, occasional television programs like *Dragnet* 40 years ago have been succeeded by a flood of such TV dramas as *NYPD Blue, Law and Order,* and a group of *CSI* shows and their permutations. Each of these programs features psychologists appearing regularly or detectives who use psychology in obvious and pointed ways. The public, along with our students, are rapidly becoming amateur forensic psychologists.

In terms of professional developments, numerous events have captured our attention in recent years. We have seen various effects of the *Daubert-Joiner-Kumho* trilogy, the three decisions that were supposed to stem the flow of "junk science" into the courtroom. We have seen the maturation of forensic assessment in such areas as estimating violence risk assessment and determining suitability for probation and parole. Recent laws concerning educational disability, the acceptability of forensic hypnosis, and the reliability of lie detection have resulted in procedural changes in each of these areas. Our decision to organize and edit this third edition of the *Handbook* was also prompted by developments in rehabilitation and other emerging areas of practice that expose psychologists to new kinds of ethical considerations.

The contributors to this volume are accomplished scholars and practitioners in their respective areas. Some are prominent academicians who conduct research and offer consultation as well. Others are actively engaged service providers who also make significant contributions to the literature. These authors were asked to delineate the enduring issues in an area of their specialty and to frame these issues in the light of recent research findings and currently prevalent conceptual formulations. The overall objective for the chapters was to provide a useful guide for practitioners, a sophisticated review for scholars, and an informative text for students.

The third edition of the *Handbook* comprises seven parts. Part One begins with an account of the history of forensic psychology, following which Chapter 2 traces the emergence of three current psychology-law interactions: psychology *by* the law, which refers to the necessity of psychologists being informed about laws bearing on their daily practice, whether academic or applied; psychology *in* the law, which refers to the practice of forensic psychology in civil and criminal cases; and psychology *of* the law, which refers to legal issues that psychologists address with empirical research. To assist readers in assessing the legal literature, Chapter 3 then describes how various publications concerning statutes and litigations are structured.

Part Two concerns applying psychology to civil proceedings and begins with two chapters on family matters. Chapter 4 takes up adult issues related to marriage, divorce, and domestic violence, and Chapter 5 addresses child-related issues of custody, adoptions, and abuse. These two chapters expand a single chapter that was devoted to family matters in the previous edition of the *Handbook.* The next two chapters also expand on a single chapter from the previous edition, in this instance on personal injury, with Chapter 6 discussing personal injury litigation and Chapter 7 focusing on personality assessment in personal injury cases. Chapter 8 reviews the impact of recent congressional legislation on identifying and treating educational disabilities. Chapter 9 then examines issues of civil competency as they pertain to the family, personal injury, and educational disabilities issues discussed in Chapters 4 through 8. Part Two concludes with a newly written discussion of the important issue of informed consent in treatment and research, which was not covered in the second edition.

Part Three deals with applying psychology to criminal proceedings and begins in Chapter 11 with an updated review of developments related to child and adult eyewitness testimony. Chapter 12 provides guidelines for assessing competence to stand trial, Chapter 13 traces the development and current applications of the concepts of criminal responsibility and legal insanity, and Chapter 14 delineates the related nuances of criminal intent and diminished capacity. Chapter 15 reviews research on jury selection and offers guidance for making recommendations in this regard, and Chapter 16 deals similarly with research and recommendations concerning probation and parole.

Part Four presents information on four special applications of forensic psychology. Chapter 17 leads off with a discussion of violence risk research and practical aspects of assessing dangerousness, and Chapter 18 follows with an overview of emerging roles for psychologists in law enforcement. Chapters 19 and 20 then provide accounts of the development of lie detection and hypnosis and describe current and emerging trends in forensic use of these procedures.

Part Five of the *Handbook* looks at effective communication of expert opinion in forensic cases. Chapter 21 focuses on the essentials of writing appropriate and useful reports, and Chapter 22 discusses the admissibility of expert witness testimony and key considerations in preparing for a courtroom appearance.

Part Six takes up some important aspects of crime prevention and the treatment of offenders. Chapter 23 is published posthumously and was Joan McCord's last writing on a topic central to her career, the prevention of delinquency. Chapter 24 discusses principles of effective correctional rehabilitation in both prison settings and the community, and Chapter 25 provides a behind-the-bars guide to conducting psychotherapy with criminal offenders. Chapter 26 continues this theme with specific attention to diagnostic and treatment procedures useful in working with sexual offenders.

Part Seven concludes the *Handbook* with chapters on ethical and training issues in forensic psychology. Chapter 27 presents an aspirational approach to defining proper professional conduct and alerts forensic psychologists to legal jeopardies they may encounter and to the implications for their work of the 2002 American Psychological Association ethics code. Chapter 28 describes training models and resources in forensic psychology for the information of faculty developing programs of instruction and students and general practitioners seeking specialized education or supervised experience in forensic psychology.

We have been gratified by a positive response to the first two editions of the *Handbook,* and we look forward to hearing from readers of this third edition about what they find useful and what they would like to see in future editions. The growth of forensic psychology over the years and whatever part our volume may have played in this growth has been richly rewarding to us. We have also appreciated the opportunity to work with our informed, talented, and personable chapter authors, who have taught us much during this collaboration. We thank as well our spouses, Frances Weiner and Kathryn Hess, for their support during this project, and AKH adds that Tanya, Clara, and Joel Hess continue to make life ever more meaningful and valuable.

IRVING B. WEINER
Tampa, Florida
iweiner@hsc.usf.edu

ALLEN K. HESS
Montgomery, Alabama
ahess@mail.aum.edu

Contents

PART ONE

THE CONTEXT OF FORENSIC PSYCHOLOGY

CHAPTER 1

History of Forensic Psychology

CURT R. BARTOL and ANNE M. BARTOL

IN HIS presidential address to the American Psychological Association (APA) in 1898, Hugo Münsterberg remarked "Peoples [*sic*] never learn from history" (Münsterberg, 1899/1994, p. 234). In similar fashion, in the introductory paragraph to this chapter in the first edition of this *Handbook,* we asserted that psychologists do not care about the history of their profession. Instead, we said, they are drawn to contemporary issues and theories, even fads. In the second edition, we acknowledged that our initial statement had been somewhat rash. Indeed, we reassert now that psychologists do indeed care, as is apparent from numerous articles published in professional journals reviewing historical trends, as well as the continuing publication of a journal exclusively devoted to the history of psychology. Nevertheless, many psychologists today doubtlessly would still share the sentiments of Stanley Brodsky, who candidly began an article with the comment, "I am a dreadful historian" (1996, p. 5). Brodsky proceeded to demonstrate, however, through his insights into earlier events, that he was not a dreadful historian at all.

Psychology, like other disciplines, needs historical insights. It needs to understand whence it came in order to assess where it is going. A perusal of journals and books published at the turn of the twentieth century, for example, may spark interest in a concept long forgotten or a predecessor whose theories and research deserve to be revisited. On the other hand, delving into early works reminds us of false starts and the occasional damage they did, such as the work of Henry H. Goddard on feeblemindedness during the early 1900s and the self-promotion of Münsterberg, who is sometimes called the father of applied psychology.

In these early years of the twenty-first century, forensic psychology holds claim as the newest branch of applied psychology, having been recognized by the APA as a specialization in 2001. In this chapter, though, forensic psychology is being viewed broadly. It is both (1) the *research endeavor* that examines aspects of human behavior directly related to the legal process (e.g., eyewitness memory and testimony, jury decision making, and criminal behavior) and (2) the *professional practice* of psychology within or in consultation with a legal system that encompasses both criminal and civil law and the numerous areas where they intersect. Therefore, forensic psychology refers broadly to the *production* of psychological knowledge and its *application* to the civil and criminal justice systems. It includes activities as varied as the following: courtroom testimony, child custody evaluations, law enforcement candidate screening, treatment of offenders in correctional facilities, assessment of plaintiffs in disability claims, research and theory building in the area of criminal behavior, and the design and implementation of intervention and prevention programs for youthful offenders. It should be noted that Hess also defines forensic psychology broadly in the following chapter, as he did in the two earlier editions of the *Handbook* (Hess, 1987, 1999).

Others have adopted a more narrow view. According to Ronald Roesch, for example (cited in Brigham, 1999, p. 279), "Most psychologists define the area more narrowly to refer to clinical psychologists who are engaged in clinical practice within the legal system." In addition, in recognizing forensic psychology as a specialty in 2001, the APA itself adopted the narrow approach, to include "the primarily clinical aspects of forensic assessment, treatment, and consultation" (Otto & Heilbrun, 2002, p. 8). Although we appreciate the rationale behind this more limited definition, we continue to see the merits of a more inclusive approach. Consequently, this history chapter embraces areas of forensic psychology that may not be considered relevant by those who share the more narrow view.

It should be noted, also, that the term "legal psychology" is sometimes used interchangeably with this narrower view of forensic psychology. However, it is also sometimes used in a slightly more expanded sense, to include not only clinical practice but also theory and research relating to the law. Our own conception of legal psychology is closer to this second view. It is a subset of forensic psychology, referring to psychological theory, research, and practice that is *directly* pertinent to the law and legal issues. Thus, legal psychology focuses on psycholegal research and contacts with judges and lawyers in a wide range of contexts.

In the pages to follow, after an introductory section covering seminal contributions, we review developments in four major areas of forensic psychology. They are legal psychology (with subheadings for expert testimony and assessment), correctional psychology, police psychology, and criminal psychology. Readers will undoubtedly recognize that there is considerable overlap in these categories and in the subheadings. Correctional psychology, for example, presupposes some understanding of criminal psychology. Assessment, both cognitive and personality, is an essential tool of the trade for psychologists, and it underlies each area of practice. Nonetheless, for purposes of identifying historical trends and landmarks, discussion of these four major areas is warranted.

We focus, of course, on forensic psychology distinguished from forensic psychiatry, which has its own well-documented, rich history. In addition, we focus on the work of forensic psychologists in North America, although we give due recognition to the work of European psychologists, who dominated the field prior to World War I. We review the achievements of psychologists from the end of the nineteenth century and extend our discussion into the 1970s, when forensic psychology came of age (Loh, 1981). The reader interested in more detail about the issues and individuals discussed might check landmark summaries of psychology and law published by Whipple (1909–1915, 1917), Hutchins and Slesinger (1929), Louisell (1955, 1957), Tapp (1976), Loh (1981), and Monahan and Loftus (1982). Developments after the 1970s will be addressed in the works of other contributors to this *Handbook*.

LEGAL PSYCHOLOGY

Do chestnut or oak trees lose their leaves earlier in autumn?
Do horses in the field stand with head or tail to the wind?
In which direction do the seeds of an apple point?
What was the weather one week ago today?

When J. McKeen Cattell posed these questions to 56 college students at Columbia University in March 1893, he was probably conducting one of the first studies, albeit an informal one, on the psychology of testimony. The questions he asked his students were similar to those that "might naturally be asked in a court of justice" (Cattell, 1895, p. 761). His subjects were allowed 30 seconds to consider their answers, then told to write their responses. They were also asked to indicate their degree of confidence in each answer.

When Cattell conducted his informal study, it was reasonably well established that courtroom eyewitness testimony was unreliable and incomplete. Both French and German psychologists were familiar with the powerful influence of suggestion over sensation and perception, having conducted substantial research in these areas. The specific conditions under which testimony was inaccurate were not known, however. Furthermore, as Cattell noted, "An unscrupulous attorney can discredit the statements of a truthful witness by cunningly selected questions. The jury, or at least the judge, should know how far errors in recollection are normal and how they vary under different conditions" (p. 761). But Cattell himself was surprised at both the degree of inaccuracy he uncovered and the wide range of individual differences in the levels of confidence expressed by the students. Answers to the weather question, for example, were "equally distributed over all kinds of weather which are possible at the beginning of March" (p. 761). Some students were nearly always sure they were correct, even when they were not, while others were consistently uncertain and hesitant in their answers, even when they were correct.

Cattell's study probably was the genesis of modern forensic psychology, because it sparked the interest of other researchers in the psychology of testimony. Joseph Jastrow immediately replicated Cattell's "experiment" at the University of Wisconsin and obtained similar results (Bolton, 1896). Aside from this brief flirtation, however, American psychologists did not immediately embrace the study of legal issues.

Psychologists in Europe seemed more intrigued. First, Alfred Binet (1900) replicated Cattell's project in France. In addition, he summarized relevant experiments on the psychology of testimony that were being conducted in Europe and called for a "science psycho-judiciaire" (Binet, 1905; Binet & Clarparede, 1906). Most significant for the historical development of forensic psychology, however, was the apparent fascination Cattell's experiment and Binet's work held for (Louis) William Stern, who had received his PhD in psychology at the University of Berlin under the tutelage of H. Ebbinghaus. In 1901, Stern collaborated with the criminologist F. V. Liszt in an attempt to lend realism to the Cattell design. Stern and Liszt conducted a "reality experiment" in a law class, staging a bogus quarrel between two students over a scientific controversy. The argument accelerated until one student drew a revolver (Stern, 1939). At this point, the professor intervened and asked for written and oral reports from the class about aspects of the dispute. Although the witnesses were law students who, Stern asserted, should have known the pitfalls of testifying, none could give a faultless report. The number of errors per individual ranged from 4 to 12. Moreover, the researchers found that inaccuracies increased with respect to the second half of the scenario, when excitement and tension were at their peak. They concluded—tentatively—that "emotions reduce accuracy of recall."

Stern became an active researcher in the psychology of testimony over the next few years (1906, 1910). He also helped establish the first journal on the psychology of testimony, *Betrage zur Psychologie der Aussage (Contributions to the Psychology of Testimony)*, which he edited and which was published at Leipzig. The journal was superseded in 1908 by the much broader *Zeitschrift fur Angewande Psychologie (Journal of Applied Psychology)*, the first of its kind. In his *Aussage* research Stern concluded, among other things, that "subjective sincerity" does not guarantee "objective truthfulness"; that leading and suggestive questions contaminate the accuracy of eyewitness accounts of critical events; that there are important differences between adult and child witnesses; that lineups are of limited value when the members are not matched for age and physical appearance; and that interceding events between an initial event and its recall can have drastic effects on memory. It can be concluded, therefore, that modern forensic psychology began as legal psychology with empirical research on the psychology of testimony.

As a parallel phenomenon, European, particularly German, psychologists at the turn of the century were beginning to be used as "expert witnesses" in criminal cases, often applying the knowledge gained from the newly established psychological laboratory. They offered both factual testimony, such as reporting the results of an experiment, and opinion testimony. Perhaps the earliest such testimony, an example of opinion testimony, occurred in 1896, when Albert von Schrenck-Notzing testified at the trial of a Munich man accused of murdering three women (Hale, 1980). The murders had received extensive and sensational press coverage in the months prior to the trial, and Schrenck-Notzing (1897) opined that this pretrial publicity, through a process of suggestion, probably led numerous witnesses to "retroactive memory-falsification." Witnesses could not distinguish between what they had seen and what the press reported had happened. He supported his opinion with factual testimony in the form of accounts of laboratory research on memory and suggestibility. Although the accused was convicted on the basis of solid evidence, Schrenck-Notzing's direct application of the psychology of suggestion to court processes helped stimulate the interest of both German jurists and psychologists (Hale, 1980).

European psychologists at the turn of the twentieth century and until World War I also were delving into the area of guilt deception, the precursor of the lie detection of today. In 1904, psychologists in Germany, Austria, and Switzerland were busy developing a lie detection test for use in criminal investigations. The test was a word association/reaction time task where key words were embedded in a list of innocuous words. Presumably, the slower the reaction time in recognizing the key words, the more likely the respondent was lying. Barland (1988), who has reviewed this history in impressive detail, notes that this approach did not catch on because it was inefficient, time-consuming, and often yielded inconclusive results.

With the exception of this work on guilt deception, early forensic psychology first made its mark in the courtroom, where psychologists in Europe both consulted with judges and lawyers and offered testimony. American psychologists, though, did not become firmly established in this arena until well into the twentieth century. However, in both Europe and the United States, psychologists became involved in conducting research that was relevant to the legal process, although most did not promote it as such.

At the turn of the century, psychologists remained comparatively uninterested in applying research on topics related to law. First, they were just beginning to explore the broad psychological landscape and had little inclination to specialize in law-related matters. This reticence was probably also due to the influence of Wilhelm Wundt, who had trained many of the American pioneers in his Leipzig laboratory (Cattell being the first). Wundt, a philosopher and an experimentalist, was wary of applying psychology until sufficient research had been conducted. He believed that the premature use of partial information could be disastrous. His students often took this caveat quite seriously, although some, like Cattell, eventually began to link the laboratory to the world outside.

One of Wundt's not-so-cautious students was the German psychologist Hugo Münsterberg, who arrived in the United States in 1892 at the invitation of William James to direct the psychology laboratory at Harvard University. Münsterberg spent 24 years trying to persuade the public that psychology had something to offer virtually every area of human endeavor. Now acknowledged by many as the father of applied psychology, he believed psychological knowledge could be applied to education, industry, advertising, music, art, and, of course, law. His claims were often exaggerated, however, and his proposals were rarely empirically based. He usually published in popular magazines rather than scholarly journals (some of his colleagues called his a "Sunday-supplement psychology"). He also incessantly promoted himself and his native Germany, a practice that alienated him increasingly from his colleagues and the public as World War I approached. In fact, this ardent pro-German stance may have had as much to do with the public's antipathy toward him as his abrasive personality.

Not surprisingly, the legal community vehemently resisted his intrusion into its territory (Hale, 1980). Even before the eve of World War I, the great legal commentator Wigmore (1909) found it necessary to assail Münsterberg in a satirical and devastating law review article. Wigmore's attack was prompted by the publication of Münsterberg's (1908) controversial best-seller *On the Witness Stand*, in which he proclaimed that the time was ripe to apply psychology to the practical needs of the legal system. The book dealt with a wide spectrum of topics, ranging from witness accuracy and jury persuasion to hypnosis and lie detection.

In 1914, Münsterberg published a study of group decision making, using Harvard and Radcliffe students as subjects, which he titled "The Mind of the Juryman." In a conclusion not atypical of the times, he commented that "the psychologist has every reason to be satisfied with the jury system as long as the women are kept out of it" (p. 202, cited in Moskowitz, 1977). He based his conclusion on a finding that the female students in his study were less accurate in their final decisions than the male students. Interestingly, as will be noted shortly, one of his own students later arrived at a very different conclusion.

Münsterberg, always willing to give speeches, gave his inaugural lecture at Radcliffe College in 1894 and his last at the same location in 1916, when he suddenly died of a heart attack at midsentence while lecturing his general psychology class (Landy, 1992). Landy writes that "at the time of his death . . . Münsterberg was an object of public scorn and was well on the way to professional ostracism. By 1919, less than three years after his death, there was hardly any reference to any of his more than 10 books and dozens of articles in basic and applied psychology" (p. 787). Benjamin (2003, p. 734) notes that Münsterberg "was one of the most despised individuals in America."

In sum, then, Münsterberg has been accused of being more an opportunist than trailblazing (Kuna, 1978). It is tempting to blame his brashness, his apparent despicable demeanor, and his pro-German views for the tenuous and occasionally hostile initial relationship between psychology and law. Nonetheless, he undeniably pushed his reluctant American colleagues into the practical legal arena and made a seminal contribution to forensic psychology. Readers are left to make their own judgments as to whether his contributions represent a false start.

During these early years, European psychologists continued to interact much more regularly with the courts than their American counterparts did. In 1911, several psychologists testified at a Belgian murder trial in which a man was accused of raping and killing a 9-year-old girl. Two of the child's playmates had apparently seen the murderer but gave inconsistent and contradictory accounts. Among the psychologists retained by the defense was J. Varendonck, who designed a series of experiments based on questions suggested by information obtained at the preliminary hearing. Varendonck's subjects were children of approximately the same age as the two witnesses (8 to 10). He found that they were inaccurate in their recall of important events. Over the objection of the prosecution, he was allowed to present the results of these experiments as well as the general research on the psychology of testimony that was available at that time. The jury found the defendant not guilty.

Varendonck, it should be noted, was vehemently opposed to *any* use of child witnesses in the courtroom. In contrast, both Binet (1900) and Stern (1939) believed that errors in recollection, whether by children or adults, were more a reflection of leading, suggestive courtroom questioning than of any "natural" tendency to distort reality.

In 1922, Karl Marbe, a psychology professor at the University of Wurzburg, became one of the earliest European psychologists to testify at a civil trial, offering expert opinion on the psychological issue of reaction times as applied to a train wreck near Mullheim. Professor Marbe was asked to testify as to the probable effect of alcohol both on the mental status of the engineer and on the reaction time of the fireman and guard applying the breaks. Based on reaction-time experiments, Marbe testified that the train could not have been stopped in time to avert a disaster. During the same year, Marbe also testified in a criminal trial similar to the one in which Varendonck had challenged the credibility of child witnesses. Several German adolescent girls had accused their teacher of sexually molesting them. Marbe persuaded the jury that the statement of the girls was unreliable, and the teacher was exonerated.

World War I placed in abeyance most of the exploration in applying psychology to law, although the war and early postwar years saw a few landmarks in American forensic psychology, including the gradual acceptance of psychologists as expert witnesses, particularly on matters of fact. The first psychologists were also appointed to law school faculties during these years.

Psychologist Donald Slesinger, a protégé of Robert M. Hutchins, made his mark during the years immediately following World War I. Although he had no formal legal training, Slesinger was appointed by Acting Dean Hutchins as a one-year Sterling Fellow to the Yale Law School in 1927. The following year he became a research assistant. In 1929, he was appointed associate professor, teaching a course in the psychology of evidence, which appears to qualify him as the first psychologist granted faculty status in an American law school. In 1930, Slesinger followed Hutchins to the University of Chicago, where he served as professor of law and, briefly, as dean of the Law School.

Several years earlier, psychologist William Marston had been the first to receive a faculty appointment as professor of legal psychology. He joined the faculty at American University in 1922. Marston was by far the most influential psychologist associated with the legal system during this era. He was a student of Münsterberg but did not have his mentor's penchant for alienating the legal community and much of the American public. He received a law degree in 1918 and a PhD in 1921, both from Harvard. Marston's interests were multifaceted. (He was even the originator, cartoonist, and producer of the successful comic strip *Wonder Woman*, under the pen name Charles Moulton—a dubious distinction to be sure.) Although admitted to the Massachusetts bar, Marston soon gave up his law practice to concentrate on psychology.

As a laboratory assistant in psychology at Radcliffe College, Marston (1917) had discovered a significant positive correlation between systolic blood pressure and lying, which became the basis of the modern polygraph. In fact, Marston was the psychologist who testified in the landmark case *Frye v. U.S.* (1923), the case that set the original standard for the acceptance of expert testimony in federal courts. Although his continuing work in lie detection (Marston 1920, 1921, 1925) represents one of his major contributions to the forensic area, it was by no means the only one. He frequently consulted with attorneys, police, and other criminal justice personnel, and his evidence was determinative in the acquittals of several defendants accused of murder. It is likely, therefore, that Marston—along with Lewis Terman and psychologists associated with the New York City Psychopathic Clinic (both to be discussed later in the chapter)—qualifies as one of the first psychological consultants to the criminal justice system in the United States.

Marston also conducted the first serious research on the jury system (Winick, 1961). Using subjects in simulated jury conditions, he found in a series of studies (Marston, 1924) that written evidence was superior to oral evidence; that free narration, though less complete, was more accurate than cross-examination or direct questioning; that a witness's caution in answering was a good indicator of accuracy; and that female jurors considered evidence more carefully than male jurors (compare with Münsterberg's conclusions about female jurors, mentioned earlier). Because of his legal background and his cautious style, Marston's ideas and research were more acceptable to the legal community than Münsterberg's had been, although there is little evidence that the legal system put his findings to extensive use. This is not surprising because some of his recommendations (e.g., free recall rather than directed questions and cross-examinations) were inapposite to the adversarial process, and others would have required fundamental changes in court procedures.

Also during this time period, various reviewers took on the task of documenting the progress of legal psychology. Hutchins and Slesinger, for example, coauthored numerous summary articles on its status (1927, 1928a, 1928b, 1928c, 1929). Slesinger wrote another with Marion Pilpel in 1929, surveying 48 articles written by psychologists on issues relating to the law that had appeared in professional journals up to that time. Eleven were concerned with the psychology of testimony, ten with deception, seven with intelligence and crime, and six with criminal behavior. The remainder focused on general topics such as the scientific method or legal research. Fifteen of the 48 articles had been written by German psychologists.

Like applied psychology in general, legal psychology was somewhat dormant between the two World Wars and did not recoup its energy until the late 1940s and 1950s. In addition to Marston's work, the period did see scattered research by Weld (Weld & Danzig, 1940; Weld & Roff, 1938) on how juries formed opinions and verdicts, a master's thesis on the relationship between narrative and interrogative methods of questioning (Cady, 1924), another study on questioning and testimony (Snee & Lush, 1941), and a survey of legal and psychological opinions about the validity of some of Wigmore's rules of evidence (Britt, 1940).

According to Loh (1981), there was interest in psychology and law during the late 1920s and the 1930s. However, the interest was almost exclusively on the part of lawyers, who produced such books as *Legal Psychology* (Brown, 1926), *Psychology for the Lawyer* (McCarty, 1929), and *Law and the Social Sciences* (Cairns, 1935). Wigmore (1940), the foremost authority on rules of evidence, paved the way for the use of test data in the courtroom. He observed that the psychometrist introducing test evidence would stand "on the same footing as the expert witness to insanity" (cited by McCary, 1956, p. 9), as long as such tests are recognized as valid and feasible by the general scientific community.

In 1931, Howard Burtt (who was also a former student of Münsterberg) wrote *Legal Psychology*, the first textbook in the area written by a psychologist. Burtt's primary interest was industrial psychology, however, and he himself did not conduct much research on legal issues. Although the book made a valuable contribution to the academic psychological literature, it had little discernible influence on the legal profession or on applied psychology in general. In 1935, Edward S. Robinson published *Law and the Lawyers*, that predicted that jurisprudence would become one of the family of social sciences and argued that all of its fundamental concepts must be brought into line with psychological knowledge. The book was lambasted by lawyers and essentially ignored by psychologists. In hindsight, contemporary scholars have found Robinson's ideas much more palatable (e.g., Loh, 1981; Horowitz & Willging, 1984).

ACCEPTANCE OF PSYCHOLOGISTS AS EXPERT WITNESSES

It is generally believed that American psychologists have served as expert witnesses since the early 1920s (Comment, 1979), but as we have seen they clearly provided information to the courts, particularly the civil courts, before that time. According to Rogers (1910, 1918), the results of experimental research on visual perception were routinely accepted in trademark infringement cases. In *Coca-Cola Company v. Chero-Cola Company* (1921), for example, an experimental psychologist was asked whether the trademarks used by the two companies were so similar as to be likely to cause confusion in the public mind and ultimately deceive the consumer. This was apparently considered a "safe" undertaking, as the psychologists were not infringing on the territory of the "medical experts"—physicians and psychiatrists—who routinely testified on matters of criminal responsibility. As Louisell (1955) notes, however, because trial court records are generally unavailable and only appellate decisions are published, the testimony of psychologists, particularly in civil cases, may have been less rare than the paucity of documentation would indicate. We do know that psychological testimony was almost inevitably *rejected* in criminal cases involving the defendant's mental state. "As a general rule, only medical men—that is, persons licensed by law to practice the profession of medicine—can testify as experts on the question of insanity; and the propriety of this general limitation is too patent to permit discussion" (*Odom v. State*, 1911; cited in Comment, 1979, fn. 14).

The first published case in which an American psychologist qualified as an expert appears to be *State v. Driver* in 1921. The occasion was only a partial victory for forensic psychology, however. A West Virginia trial court accepted the chief psychologist of the State Bureau of Juvenile Research as an expert on the matter of juvenile delinquency. However, it rejected his testimony, based on psychological test data, that a 12-year-old alleged victim of an attempted rape was a "moron" (an unfortunate term coined by Henry H. Goddard, who is discussed later) and could not be presumptively believed. In agreeing with the trial court, the West Virginia Supreme Court noted, "It is yet to be demonstrated that psychological and medical tests are practical, and will detect the lie on the witness stand" (*State v. Driver*, 1921, p. 488). Although some commentators interpreted *Driver* as a major loss for psychologists wishing to achieve status as expert witnesses, Louisell (1955) noted that the decision was not a rejection of psychologists per se, only of the particular evidence offered by one psychologist. Nevertheless, it was not until much later, in the 1940s and 1950s, that psychologists testified in courts of law on a regular basis, at least in some jurisdictions. They offered opinions and presented data relevant to subjects as diverse as the influence of pretrial publicity on potential witnesses and juries, the effects of pornography on adolescents, the effect of certain educational practices on children, and the likely influence of advertisements on consumers (Greenberg, 1956; Loh, 1981; Louisell, 1955). This is not to say that there was widespread acceptance of the idea that psychologists deserved a niche in the courtroom. Resistance to the idea, or at best a cautious approach, consistently characterized much of the legal literature (Comment, 1979).

In the early 1940s and the postwar era, appellate courts also began to allow qualified psychologists as expert witnesses on the issue of mental responsibility for criminal and tortious conduct. Loh (1981) attributes this eventual acceptance to an increase in professionalization, "the rapid growth of mental health professions during this period, and the formulation of legal doctrines of insanity consistent with modern psychiatry" (1981, p. 323).

The first influential decision was *People v. Hawthorne* (1940), a Michigan case. Hawthorne had been tried for the murder of his wife's lover and had pleaded not guilty by reason of insanity. The trial court refused to qualify as an expert witness a professor of psychology from Michigan State Normal College who had a PhD and an impressive list of credentials. In finding that the trial court had erred in not accepting the psychologist as an expert, the Michigan Supreme Court ruled that the standard for determining expert status was not a medical degree but the extent of the witness's knowledge. It advised trial courts to evaluate carefully the merits of a potential witness's claim to expertise, noting that a psychologist's ability to detect insanity could not be presumed inferior to that of a "medical man." The dissenters, however, believed that insanity is a disease and therefore only a person with medical training should qualify as an expert.

Later, in *Hidden v. Mutual Life Insurance Co.* (1954), the 4th Circuit Court of Appeals allowed psychological expertise to be applied to a *civil* case relating to mental status. The insured argued that a disabling nervous condition prevented him from engaging in any gainful occupation and entitled him to disability benefits. A clinical psychologist with a doctoral degree administered a battery of projective tests and testified on his behalf. Not only did he report on the test results, but he also gave the opinion that the plaintiff deserved the benefits. When the lawyer for the insurance company objected, the trial judge instructed the jury to disregard the entire opinion testimony on the grounds that the psychologist did not qualify as an expert. The circuit court of appeals ruled that the psychologist should have been qualified as an expert to express his opinion about the plaintiff's mental condition.

While some psychologists were struggling to be accepted as experts on questions of mental status, competence, and criminal responsibility, others during this era were joining the crucial legal battle against school segregation by testifying and consulting with attorneys in the state cases that would ultimately culminate in the 1954 landmark ruling, *Brown v. Board of Education* (Kluger, 1975). David Krech and Helen Trager, social psychologists who had published articles on racial attitude tests, and Horace B. English, an expert on child psychology, were among many who testified for the plaintiffs at some of the school segregation trials. On the other hand, psychologist Henry Garrett, a former president of the APA, testified on behalf of the state (Jackson, 2000). Perhaps the most widely publicized—and since then highly critiqued—contribution on behalf of the plaintiffs was that of Kenneth Clark and Mamie Clark, who conducted the now-famous "doll research" to gauge the effects of segregation. Kenneth Clark then gave factual testimony reporting the results of this research (Kluger, 1975). When the NAACP appealed *Brown* and three other segregation cases to the U.S. Supreme Court, Kenneth Clark, Isidor Chein, and Stuart W. Cook wrote the Social Science Statement that included signatures of 32 eminent social scientists (Jackson, 2000).

History has not been kind to these early scientists, as has been demonstrated in a recent article by John P. Jackson (2000). They were faulted by later social scientists for naïve methodology, lack of objectivity, and faulty conclusions based on insufficient scientific evidence. In his historiographical inquiry, however, Jackson notes that the doll experiments were but one prong of many studies that psychologists and other social scientists referenced in their trial testimony and in the brief submitted to the Supreme Court. He also argues convincingly that critiques of these social scientists reflected a misreading of their testimony, their research, and their evaluation of relevant evidence.

During the same era, psychologists were continuing to make enough inroads testifying on the issue of criminal responsibility that psychiatrists felt the need to protect their turf. In 1954, the Council of the American Psychiatric Association, the Executive Council of the American Psychoanalytical Association, and the American Medical Association joined in a resolution stating that only physicians were legitimate experts in the field of mental illness for purposes of courtroom testimony. Other individuals could participate only if their testimony was coordinated by medical authority. The resolution greatly influenced trial courts (Miller, Lower, & Bleechmore, 1978), which became reluctant to accept independent psychological testimony.

Finally, in *Jenkins v. United States* (1962), the Court of Appeals for the District of Columbia gave its own direct, although conditional, support to the use of psychologists as experts on the issue of mental illness. Although the court was sharply divided, its decision remains the predominant authority for the use of psychologists in the area of criminal responsibility. Following that opinion, federal courts and increasingly more state courts certified psychologists as expert witnesses in both criminal and civil courts.

COGNITIVE AND PERSONALITY ASSESSMENT

During the years in which Münsterberg was proselytizing about psychology's usefulness in the courtroom, particularly involving expert testimony, another American psychologist was more quietly making inroads into a different forensic area, one specifically related to juvenile courts. In 1909, clinical psychologist Grace M. Fernald worked with psychiatrist William Healy to establish the first clinic designed for youthful offenders, the Juvenile Psychopathic Institute. It was initially developed to serve the newly established Juvenile Court of Chicago by offering clinical diagnoses of "problem" children. Fernald, who received her doctorate from the University of Chicago in 1907, was probably the first clinical psychologist to work under the supervision of a psychiatrist (Napoli, 1981), as well as one of the earliest psychologists to specialize in the diagnosis and treatment of juvenile delinquency. The Institute, which extended its services rapidly to include treatment and research as well as diagnosis, became a public agency in 1914, the Institute for Juvenile Research. Arguably, it also provided the earliest formal internships in forensic psychology in the country (Resnick, 1997).

Fernald and Healy used the relatively new Stanford-Binet Intelligence Scale to test delinquents, but they soon realized the importance of obtaining "performance" measures as well. This prompted them to develop the Healy-Fernald series of 23 performance tests, which they began to use in 1911. The two eventually went their separate ways. Fernald became a specialist in mental deficiency and testing and taught psychology at UCLA for 27 years, until her retirement in 1948.

Healy, along with psychologist Augusta Bronner, went on to establish the Judge Baker Clinic (Boston) in 1917. Healy (who was a former undergraduate psychology student of William James at Harvard) gained considerable attention in 1924, when he evaluated Nathan Leopold and Richard Loeb in a famous juvenile case sweeping the country at the time (Fass, 1993; Herman, 2001). "According to Healy, teenagers Nathan Leopold and Richard Loeb were not cold-blooded murderers; they were deeply troubled youngsters, whose tragic murder of a neighbor was attributable to undiagnosed developmental difficulties" (Herman, 2001, pp. 304–305).

During the first third of the twentieth century, most psychologists providing services to the courts were psychometrists associated with clinics. It appears that much of the forensic work of psychologists during this period consisted of cognitive and personality assessments of individuals, both juveniles and adults, who were to come before the courts. The drudgery of day-to-day testing (often under the watchful eyes of a physician or psychiatrist) made applied psychology, as it was then known, less than appealing as a profession. Often, however, it was where female psychologists were most accepted. In the 1930s, for example, fewer than one-third of all American psychologists were women, but women made up over 60% of all applied psychologists (Napoli, 1981).

In one of the first published accounts of the work of these early psychometrists, E. I. Keller (1918) described some of the challenges they faced. He noted that in December 1916, a psychopathic laboratory was established at the New York City Police Department for the express purpose of examining persons detained before trial. The staff included psychiatrists, neurologists, social workers, and psychologists, whose task was to conduct hasty pretrial evaluations. (Because these psychologists worked out of the police department but conducted evaluations for the courts, they could be considered both legal and police psychologists.) According to Keller, who was a consulting psychologist to the clinic, detainees arrived for testing at 9 A.M. "The disadvantage is the lack of time, for all prisoners [*sic*] must be examined in time to get them to court by noon or earlier, and many courts are situated in distant parts of the city" (p. 85). Staff members had little time in which to conduct the evaluation and prepare a report that would help the court in its decision making.

The work of Henry H. Goddard during this time must be regarded with embarrassment. A student of G. Stanley Hall, Goddard paved the way for the massive intelligence testing of immigrants and residents of mental institutions, prisons, and juvenile training schools. His followers consulted with the juvenile courts and dutifully administered these tests to the children of the poor who arrived at their door. Goddard's warning that "feeble-minded" individuals should not be allowed to roam about freely in society because of their innate proclivity toward antisocial behavior contributed significantly to the incarceration of individuals during their reproductive periods as well as to the sterilization of residents in both juvenile and adult facilities (Kelves, 1984).

Psychologists continued to work in court clinics during the second third of the twentieth century, performing a variety of tasks that related to the assessment process (see Box 1.1). In addition, as we described earlier, they gradually became more involved in providing expert testimony, not only on the results of their assessments but also on research that was relevant to legal issues. Other psychologists continued to offer services to inmates and staff of jails and prisons, an endeavor that apparently began early in the twentieth century. It is to this second aspect of forensic psychology that we now turn.

BOX 1.1
Help Wanted: Court Psychologist

An article in Volume 1 of *The American Psychologist* (Shartle, 1946) carried the following job description for a court psychologist.

COURT PSYCHOLOGIST
(Clinical Psychologist)

Duties

Interviews offenders referred by the court to determine the causes of the crime, the attitudes and conflicts, and the educational, vocational, and social background of the client. Also may interview parents and guardians.

Administers and interprets individual intelligence, performance, and personality tests including projective techniques.

Writes complete case histories including interview information and test interpretations. Presents case histories and recommended treatment to colleagues including medical and other officers of the court. May testify in court.

Qualifications include MA in psychology with a PhD preferred, relevant course work (e.g., abnormal, clinical, psychometrics, criminology, medical subjects), previous experience, and emotional maturity.

Interestingly, Shartle noted that, though few psychologists were employed in such positions, there was indication that employment in the field would increase. However, "higher positions" in the court were not usually open to psychologists.

CORRECTIONAL PSYCHOLOGY

Lindner (1955) pinpoints 1913 as the first instance of psychological services being offered in a U.S. correctional facility, specifically a women's reformatory in the state of New York. The precise nature of the services and the identity of the psychologist(s) who provided them are not known.

The main function of psychologists employed in some capacity in the state and federal correctional systems during the 1910s and early 1920s was apparently the detection of "feeblemindedness" among offenders, a condition thought to lead to a life of crime (Giardini, 1942; Watkins, 1992). Again, the work of Goddard and his followers is relevant.

Concurrently, however, some psychologists became involved in a different endeavor, the classification of inmates into various groups for determining where they were to be placed. The first prison classification system developed by psychologists was apparently instituted in New Jersey in 1918 (Barnes & Teeters, 1959; Watkins, 1992). New Jersey also became the first state to hire a full-time correctional psychologist. The first state in the United States to provide comprehensive psychological examinations of all admissions to its prison system and applications for parole was Wisconsin, in 1924 (Bodemar, 1956).

In the late 1930s, Darley and Berdie (1940) surveyed 13 federal and 123 state prisons and learned that they employed a total of 64 psychologists who called themselves "prison psychologists." Although all considered themselves clinical psychologists, only about half had PhDs in psychology. Later, Raymond Corsini (1945) expressed concern that there was as yet "no history of prison psychology." He estimated that during the 1940s there were approximately 200,000 individuals confined in U.S. correctional facilities who were served by a mere 80 psychologists. Their work consisted of (1) testing (personality, aptitude, and academic progress); (2) giving educational, vocational, and personal guidance (usually at the inmate's request); and (3) maintaining working relationships with all members of the prison staff (see Box 1.2). In one of the most comprehensive surveys undertaken during the early 1940s, the Office of Psychological Personnel sent questionnaires to 4,580 psychologists (3,209 men and 1,371 women) in an effort to discover the nature of the profession (Bryan & Boring, 1946). Of the 3,241 questionnaires returned in 1940, 76 men and 20 women indicated they were employed as full-time psychologists in prisons or correctional institutions. Of the 3,106 questionnaires returned by the same group in 1944, 53 men and 27 women said they were employed in prisons or correctional institutions. Although these data support Corsini's estimation that between 80 and 100 psychologists were employed in the nation's correctional facilities during the early to mid-1940s, it is interesting to note that, by the mid-1940s, approximately one-third of prison psychologists were women.

Psychological services to corrections in Canada appeared much later, perhaps as late as the early 1950s. Watkins (1992) notes that Canadian correctional psychology made its first appearance in the literature in 1952 in a series of newsletters published by the Ontario Psychological Association. The newsletters focused on psychology in the Ontario provincial corrections programs and the federal correctional service. The first correctional psychologist in the fed-

---

BOX 1.2
Help Wanted: Correctional Psychologist

1940S VERSION

In Volume 1 of *The American Psychologist,* Shartle (1946) described the work of a prison psychologist.

PSYCHOLOGIST, PENAL INSTITUTION
(Prison Psychologist)

Duties

Administers intelligence, aptitude, and other tests to either all inmates or certain groups depending on institutional policy. Writes an interpretation of test results for the prisoner's records.

Interviews each prisoner to determine background, attitudes, and personality traits for use in guidance, education, possibilities for parole, and placement. Results of interview are written and may be submitted in form of case study with test results or other reports.

Makes recommendations for parole and supplies technical information at staff meetings. Gives information in consultation with administrative officers or with specialists in the field of medicine, psychiatry, sociology, education, occupational training, or parole.

Assists in planning or revising programs for medically sponsored cases including psychiatric and severe physical disability cases.

Participates in research. Investigates problems of penal psychology or test construction and prepares reports of finding.

Again it was noted that opportunities in the field were limited and the number of openings not numerous. However, several states were planning postwar expansion in buildings and services.

---

eral system in Canada was employed in 1955 at St. Vincent de Paul Penitentiary (later renamed Laval Institution) in the province of Quebec (Watkins, 1992). Interestingly, correctional psychologists in Canada were employed primarily to classify inmates for security placement and were usually not a component of the mental health treatment afforded to inmates. In the United States, their role appears to have been broader (see Box 1.2).

This is not to suggest that classification was not an important enterprise. To the contrary, reliable offender classification was (and is) both an important service to offer to correctional administrators and in many respects a prerequisite to effective treatment. In both the United States and Canada, psychologists became more involved in developing and testing classification systems that went far beyond the crude versions of the early twentieth century. One of the earliest of these "modern" systems was the Jesness (1971) Classification System. Most well-known, however, was the system proposed by Edwin Megargee and based on the Minnesota Multiphasic Personality Inventory (MMPI). Megargee (1977), using his research on overcontrolled and undercontrolled personalities as a springboard, identified 10 "inmate types." Prison officials then made use of these groupings to assign inmates to custody levels, job assignments, and rehabilitation programs. According to Clements (1996, p. 132), Megargee's system has held up "reasonably well" and is still in use in some prison systems. However, he adds that Megargee also should be credited for providing correctional psychologists with an excellent list of seven criteria for a good classification system.

In the 1960s and early 1970s, correctional psychology as a subdiscipline of forensic psychology began to expand. Until then, and although there were exceptions, psychologists in correctional facilities focused more on classification than on treatment, both because the demand for diagnostic services was great and the obstacles relative to respecting confidentiality and achieving the trust of inmates were difficult to surmount. In the 1960s, rehabilitation as a correctional goal gained favor, and psychologists spent more time working directly with offenders and providing treatment services. Although positions were plentiful, the turnover rate was high, primarily because psychologists often had not received the preparation for this environment (Watkins, 1992).

One noteworthy innovation that was introduced in federal prisons during this era was the unit management system that was initially conceptualized by Daniel Glaser (1964) and later promoted by Robert Levinson (Toch, 1992). Unit management divided prison populations into small groups of prisoners and staff members based on the programming needs of the former and the expertise of the latter. Some units—those in which more intensive treatment services could be provided—became "therapeutic communities." Other units provided education, training, or work experiences, together with some counseling (Toch, 1992). Although unit management lost favor during the punitive 1980s and 1990s (with overcrowding having its obvious effects), the concept survives in some state and federal facilities, particularly where substance abuse treatment is provided.

Many correctional psychologists worked in the trenches during the 1960s and early 1970s and made significant contributions. However, Stan Brodsky, probably more than any other single individual, was the most instrumental in launching modern correctional psychology. His two-year term as president of the American Association for Correctional Psychology (AACP) helped provide the impetus to move correctional psychology into a recognized and viable profession. (The AACP was actually born in 1953 under the name Society of Correctional Psychologists and underwent several name changes during the late 1950s through the early 1970s; Bartol & Freeman, 2005.) During 1972 and 1973, with Brodsky at the helm, the AACP played a key role in setting up a series of conferences on psychology in the criminal justice system, with emphasis on corrections. The proceedings were published in a volume edited by Brodsky (1973), *Psychologists in the Criminal Justice System*. The publication of this influential book could arguably be called the official launch date of modern correctional psychology, even though the AACP itself predated Brodsky's book. Brodsky also became the founding editor of the international journal *Criminal Justice and Behavior*, launched in 1974 and sponsored by the AACP. Brodsky's leadership and enthusiasm also helped build one of the earliest doctoral programs specifically designed to prepare clinical psychologists to work in the criminal justice system, particularly corrections, at the University of Alabama.

POLICE PSYCHOLOGY

Those who favor the more narrow definition of forensic psychology do not typically include police psychology in its purview. We have done so because police are sworn to uphold the law and are in many cases the gatekeepers to entry into criminal and juvenile courts, if not civil courts.

It is difficult to pinpoint precisely when police psychology began, primarily because individual psychologists have provided a variety of services to law enforcement without their work being formally recognized. Viteles (1929) noted that police departments in Germany were using psychologists in a variety of capacities as early as 1919. In the United States, in keeping with the psychometric movement of that era, early contributions centered around assessment, particularly cognitive assessment administered to candidates for law enforcement positions.

Four discernible but *overlapping* historical trends in American police psychology can be identified: (1) cognitive and aptitude screening, (2) personality assessment and the search for the "police personality," (3) stress management and other clinical services, and (4) fairness in screening and selection (Bartol & Bartol, 2004). The first trend (1916 to 1960) is characterized by attempts of psychologists to assess the intellectual skills required to be an effective police officer. The second trend (1952 to 1975) focused on the development of personality measures capable of distinguishing effective from less effective officers. During the second trend, there also were many unsuccessful attempts to identify a "police personality." The third trend (1974 to 1994) is characterized by psychologists becoming increasingly involved in the identification and treatment of stress and other emotional reactions often experienced by police officers. Such topics of interest included the use of excessive force, police decision making, postshooting traumatic reaction, fitness for duty evaluations, and police suicide. The fourth trend (1980 to the present) refers to the legal requirements that all persons should have an equal chance of being selected on the basis of individual merit and qualifications. Topics during this trend include the Americans with Disabilities Act of 1990, gender issues in policing, and minority/ethnic/racial composition of law enforcement agencies. Because this chapter focuses on early history, we only briefly sketch the first two trends.

TREND ONE

Lewis Terman (1917) was the first American psychologist to use "mental tests" as screening devices in the selection of law enforcement personnel. On October 31, 1916, at the request of the city manager of San Jose, California, he administered an abbreviated form of the Stanford-Binet to 30 police and fire department applicants. They ranged in age from 21 to 38, with a median age of 30. Only four had attended high school, and none had gone beyond the sophomore year. Terman found that most of the applicants functioned near the dull-normal range of intelligence (68 to 84 on the Stanford revision of the Binet-Simon Intelligence Scale); only three obtained an IQ over 100, the score considered average for the general population. Based on his experience with the intellectual capabilities of school-age children, Terman suggested, somewhat arbitrarily, that applicants with an IQ under 80 were not fit for police work or firefighting. The city manager agreed, and 10 applicants were immediately excluded from further consideration.

A contemporary of Terman, psychologist Louis Thurstone, was also interested in the value of mental testing to police screening. Thurstone (1922) administered the newly developed Army Intelligence Examination (Army Alpha) to 358 male members of the Detroit Police Department. The Army Alpha, developed by Robert Yerkes, E. L. Thorndike, and Lewis Terman and adopted by the U.S. Army in 1917, was probably the first exclusively American test of intelligence (Resnick, 1997). Police officers at all ranks scored below average on the Army Alpha; in fact, the more experienced the police officer, the lower was his intelligence score. The average score for the 307 patrol officers was 71.44; the sergeants averaged 54.71, and the 17 lieutenants 57.80 (Army Alpha mean = 100, standard deviation of 15). Thurstone concluded that law enforcement did not attract intelligent individuals. He also surmised that the more intelligent individuals who entered police service left for other occupations where their abilities and intelligence were better utilized.

Law enforcement officers were vindicated somewhat, however, when Maude A. Merrill (1927) administered the Army Alpha to a group of already employed officers and applicants. They scored at the average level (the sample's mean IQ was 104). The differences between her findings and those of Terman and Thurstone were probably due to department leadership factors, recruitment procedures, and selection ratios (Terrio, Swanson, & Chambelin, 1977).

TREND TWO

In the years between the two World Wars psychologists gradually became more involved in the screening of law enforcement personnel and began to incorporate personality assessment into that enterprise. Wilmington, Delaware, and Toledo, Ohio, appear to share the distinction of being the first two cities to require ongoing psychological screening for use in police selection, in the form of mental and personality tests (Gottesman, 1975; Oglesby, 1957). The year was 1938. Thus, personality tests came on the scene at about this time. It was not until the late 1950s and 1960s, though, that personality assessment overtook cognitive tests in the screening of law enforcement personnel. While the aforementioned psychologists were among the first to study the cognitive capacities of police officers and candidates, there is no indication that they *consistently* participated in the screening and selection of law enforcement personnel. At this point, we have no information about who might have been the first psychologist to assume this regular role. As late as 1939, Donald Paterson (1940) could identify only one professional psychologist, L. J. O'Rourke, who had actively investigated the validity of the civil service examination system, even though the Civil Service Commission had adopted routine competitive exams as far back as 1883.

During the late 1940s and the 1950s, psychologists continued to consult with police departments. The psychological screening initiated by the Wilmington and Toledo police departments was adopted by other cities; Jacksonville in 1947, Berkeley in 1949, Oakland in 1950, New Orleans in 1952, and Pasadena, Philadelphia, Milwaukee, and Cleveland in 1953 (Gottesman, 1975; Oglesby, 1957). In June 1952, the Los Angeles Police Department began to administer a battery of psychological tests (MMPI, Rorschach, and a psychological interview; Rankin, 1957, 1959). The 1957 Rankin article was the first to appear in the literature attesting to any ongoing program of psychological assessment for police applicants (Gottesman, 1975).

During the late 1960s, personality assessment, psychological screening, and police psychology in general received an immense boost when the President's Commission on Law Enforcement and the Administration of Justice (1967) strongly recommended widespread use of psychological measures to determine the emotional stability of all potential officers. This recommendation was followed by the strong endorsement in 1968 by the National Advisory Commission on Civil Disorder that psychological screening would improve the emotional quality of individuals entering law enforcement (Scrivner, 1994). In keeping with Commission recommendations, Congress provided Law Enforcement Assistance Administration funds for law enforcement agencies to retain the services of mental health professionals. In 1973, the Police Task Force Report of the National Commission on Criminal Justice Standards and Goals encouraged the establishment of a behavioral sciences unit or consultant for all law enforcement agencies.

Shortly before then, in December 1968, Martin Reiser was hired by the Los Angeles Police Department as a full-time police psychologist. The evidence to date indicates that Reiser was the first full-time psychologist whose responsibilities were strictly police-related. Reiser (1982) himself is not entirely certain he was the first full-time police psychologist in the country. In 1969, he presented a paper at the Western Psychological Association Convention in Vancouver entitled "The Police Department Psychologist." This presentation may represent the "official" launch of contemporary North American police psychology. The paper was published in 1972. Reiser continued to be the most prolific writer on police psychology during the early 1970s. In 1972, in cooperation with the California School of Professional Psychology and the Los Angeles Police Department, he helped establish what is believed to be the first clinical internship in police psychology in the United States. By 1977, at least six other law enforcement agencies had hired full-time psychologists (Reese, 1986, 1987).

CRIMINAL PSYCHOLOGY

In the early years of the twentieth century, psychologists began to offer psychological perspectives on criminal behavior and to speculate about the causes of crime. Like the police psychology discussed earlier, criminal psychology is typically not considered in the narrow definitions of forensic psychology, primarily because it appears more theoretical than clinical in nature. However, in its youth, criminal psychology was essentially clinical in nature, as the theories often centered on the measurable mental capacities of offenders.

Psychologists like Goddard had repeatedly found that most juvenile and adult offenders were mentally deficient, which led to the conclusion that a primary "cause" of crime and delinquency was intellectual limitation. In large part, this belief reflected the pervasive influence of Darwinism, which contended that humans differ only in degree from their animal brethren (and that some humans are closer to their animal ancestry than others). The mentally deficient were considered both intellectually and morally less capable of adapting to modern society. They presumably resorted to more "primitive" ways of meeting their needs, such as crime. These unfortunate conclusions, which did not take into account social conditions, cultural differences, or socialization processes, lent support to unconscionable practices such as lengthy incarceration of the disadvantaged, confused, and powerless.

In the history of psychology, few scholars have ventured to offer comprehensive theories on crime or delinquent behavior. Those who have (e.g., Eysenck, 1964) have often been strongly influenced by Darwinian thinking. Therefore, theoretical orientations focusing on mental deficiency or biological and constitutional dispositions have dominated early psychological criminology.

In the early 1960s, a psychological criminology distinct from psychiatric and more extensive than psychometrics began to show signs of life. Hans Toch (1961), who was also making significant contributions to correctional psychology, edited one of the first books on psychological criminology, *Legal and Criminal Psychology*. Some may argue that Hans Gross published the first criminal psychology book in 1898 (*Kriminal psychologie*), the same year in which he was appointed professor in ordinary for criminal law and justice administration at the University of Czernowitz in Austria. However, Gross was a lawyer by training, in practice, and in spirit and eventually became a successful judge. His book details his observations of offenders, witnesses, jurors, and judges but relies very little on psychological research. This is not surprising, of course, because psychology in 1898 was far from being an integrated discipline with a rich body of knowledge. Nevertheless, it is significant that Toch's book, published over 60 years later, represents the earliest attempt to integrate, in an interdisciplinary fashion, the empirical research of psychologists relevant to criminal behavior and legal issues.

British psychologist Hans J. Eysenck (1964), in *Crime and Personality*, formulated the first comprehensive theoretical statement on criminal behavior advanced by a psychologist. Shortly afterward, Edwin Megargee (1966) put forth his own heuristic statements regarding undercontrolled and overcontrolled personalities and their relationships to violence, a theory that then served as a basis for his classification system referred to earlier. Toch (1969) followed with *Violent Men*. The relationship between aggression and violence was studied seriously under the leadership of Leonard Berkowitz (1962), Albert Bandura (1973; Bandura & Walters, 1959), and later Robert Baron (1977). The psychopath became the subject of vigorous theory building and research in the hands of

Robert Hare (1970) and others (e.g., Quay, 1965) and continues as a rich research area to this day.

THE 1970S AND BEYOND

Since the 1970s, we have witnessed a literature and research explosion in all areas of forensic psychology. At this point, as Loh (1981) observed, forensic psychology had "come of age." In 1965, just over 100 English-language articles and books related to forensic psychology had been published (Tapp, 1976). By the mid-1970s, the numbers were well into the thousands. Professional journals exclusively devoted to forensic psychological research and issues were beginning to emerge in North America. *Criminal Justice and Behavior* led the way in 1974, followed by *Law and Psychology Review* (a journal published by law students and graduate psychology students at the University of Alabama) beginning in 1975, *Law and Human Behavior* in 1977, *Behavioral Sciences & the Law* in 1982, and *Psychology, Public Policy, and Law* in 1995. Great Britain followed suit with *Criminal Behavior and Mental Health* (launched in 1990), *Psychology, Crime, & Law* (1994), the British Psychological Society's *Legal and Criminological Psychology* (1996), and the *Journal of Forensic Psychology Practice* (2001). In addition to these, other interdisciplinary scholarly and scientific journals relevant to forensic psychology have emerged in recent years (e.g., *Journal of Forensic Sciences, American Journal of Forensic Psychiatry, Journal of Psychiatry and Law*).

During the 1970s, interdisciplinary and specialized training in forensic psychology was introduced at the doctoral, master's, internship, postdoctoral, and continuing education levels (Ogloff, Tomkins, & Bersoff, 1996). The first interdisciplinary, successful psychology and law program was developed by Bruce Sales at the University of Nebraska-Lincoln in 1974 (Ogloff et al., 1996). Other universities soon followed in this endeavor, some more successfully than others. Another indication of the growth in forensic psychology is professional certification of practitioners in the field, a development that began in the late 1970s. Beginning in 1978, board certification in forensic psychology was provided by the American Board of Forensic Psychology (Otto & Heilbrun, 2002). In recent years, other board certifications have emerged, such as the American College and Board of Forensic Examiners. In 2001, as noted earlier, the APA voted to recognize forensic psychology as a specialty. Forensic psychology has seen a rapid expansion in other parts of the globe besides North America, particularly in Europe and Australia. Blackburn (1996, p. 3), in the first issue of *Legal and Criminological Psychology*, asserted, "The growth in the number of forensic psychologists has been among the most prominent developments in the burgeoning application of psychology to law during the last two decades." He notes that, although the growth has been most apparent in the United States, there has been a parallel growth throughout Europe over the past 20 years.

After an uncertain beginning and some stagnation between the two World Wars, it is clear that forensic psychology is now well established. All indicators suggest that forensic psychology, whether viewed as a broad or a narrow field of research and practice, has an extremely promising future as we continue into the twenty-first century. In the following chapters, other contributors assess forensic psychology's current status and the promise it holds for a future generation of researchers, practicing psychologists, theorists, and legal practitioners.

REFERENCES

Bandura, A. (1973). *Aggression: A social learning analysis.* Englewood Cliffs, NJ: Prentice-Hall.

Bandura, A., & Walters, R. H. (1959). *Adolescent aggression.* New York: Ronald Press.

Barland, G. H. (1988). The polygraph test in the U.S.A. and elsewhere. In A. Gale (Ed.), *The polygraph test: Lies, truth and science* (pp. 73–96). London: Sage.

Barnes, H. E., & Teeters, N. K. (1959). *New horizons in criminology* (2nd ed.). New York: Prentice-Hall.

Baron, R. A. (1977). *Human aggression.* New York: Plenum Press.

Bartol, C. R., & Bartol, A. M. (2004). *Introduction to forensic psychology.* Thousand Oaks, CA: Sage.

Bartol, C. R., & Freeman, N. (2005). History of the American Association for Correctional Psychology. *Criminal Justice and Behavior, 32,* 123–142.

Benjamin, L. T. (2003). Behavioral science and the Nobel prize: A history. *American Psychologist, 58,* 731–741.

Berkowitz, L. (1962). *Aggression: A social-psychological analysis.* New York: McGraw-Hill.

Binet, A. (1900). *La suggestibilite.* Paris: Schleicher.

Binet, A. (1905). La science du termoignage [The science of testimony]. *L'Annee Psychologique, 11,* 128–137.

Binet, A., & Clarparede, E. (1906). La psychologie judiciaire [Legal psychology]. *L'Anne Psychologique, 12,* 274–302.

Blackburn, R. (1996). What *is* forensic psychology? *Legal and Criminological Psychology, 1,* 3–16.

Bodemar, O. A. (1956). Correctional psychology in Wisconsin. *Journal of Correctional Psychology, 1,* 7–15.

Bolton, F. E. (1896). The accuracy of recollection and observation. *Psychological Review, 3,* 286–295.

Brigham, J. C. (1999). What is forensic psychology anyway? *Law and Human Behavior, 23,* 273–278.

Britt, S. H. (1940). The rules of evidence: An empirical study in psychology and law. *Cornell Law Quarterly, 25,* 556–580.

Brodsky, S. L. (1973). *Psychologists in the criminal justice system.* Urbana: University of Illinois Press.

Brodsky, S. L. (1996). Twenty years of criminal justice and behavior: An observation from the beginning. *Criminal Justice and Behavior, 23,* 5–11.

Brown, M. (1926). *Legal psychology.* Indianapolis, IN: Bobbs-Merrill.

Brown v. Board of Education, 347 U.S. 483 (1954).

Bryan, A. I., & Boring, E. G. (1946). Women in American psychology: Statistics from the OPP questionnaire. *American Psychologist, 1,* 71–79.

Burtt, H. E. (1931). *Legal psychology.* New York: Prentice-Hall.

Cady, H. M. (1924). On the psychology of testimony. *American Journal of Psychology, 35,* 110–112.

Cairns, H. (1935). *Law and the social sciences.* New York: Harcourt, Brace.

Cattell, J. M. (1895). Measurements of the accuracy of recollection. *Science, 2,* 761–766.

Clements, C. B. (1996). Offender classification: Two decades of progress. *Criminal Justice and Behavior, 23,* 121–143.

Coca-Cola Company v. Chero-Cola Company. 273 Fed. 755 (App. D.C. 1921).

Comment. (1979). The psychologist as expert witness: Science in the courtroom? *Maryland Law Review, 38,* 539–615.

Corsini, R. (1945). Functions of the prison psychologist. *Journal of Consulting Psychology, 9,* 101–104.

Darley, J. G., & Berdie, R. (1940). The fields of applied psychology. *Journal of Consulting Psychology, 4,* 41–52.

Eysenck, H. J. (1964). *Crime and personality.* London: Routledge & Kegan Paul.

Fass, P. (1993). Making and remaking an event: The Leopold and Loeb case in American culture. *Journal of American History, 80,* 919–951.

Frye v. United States, 54 App. D.C. 46, 47 293 F. 1013, 1014 (1923).

Giardini, G. I. (1942). The place of psychology in penal and correctional institutions. *Federal Probation, 6,* 29–33.

Glaser, D. (1964). *The effectiveness of a prison and parole system.* Indianapolis, IN: Bobbs-Merrill.

Goddard, H. H. (1914). *Feeblemindedness: Its causes and consequences.* New York: Macmillan.

Gottesman, J. (1975). *The utility of the MMPI in assessing the personality patterns of urban police applicants.* Hoboken, NJ: Stevens Institute of Technology.

Greenberg, J. (1956). Social scientists take the stand: A review and appraisal of their testimony in litigation. *Michigan Law Review, 54,* 953–970.

Hale, M. (1980). *Human science and social order: Hugo Münsterberg and origins of applied psychology.* Philadelphia: Temple University Press.

Hare, R. D. (1970). *Psychopathy: Theory and research.* New York: Wiley.

Herman, E. (2001). How children turn out and how psychology turns them out. *History of Psychology, 4,* 297–316.

Hess, A. (1987). Dimensions of forensic psychology. In I. B. Weiner & A. K. Hess (Eds.), *Handbook of forensic psychology* (pp. 22–49). New York: Wiley.

Hess, A. (1999). Defining forensic psychology. In A. K. Hess & I. B. Weiner (Eds.), *Handbook of forensic psychology* (2nd ed., pp. 24–47). New York: Wiley.

Hidden v. Mutual Life Insurance Co., 217 F.2d 818 (4th Cir. 1954).

Horowitz, I. A., & Willging, T. E. (1984). *The psychology of law: Integration and applications.* Boston: Little, Brown.

Hutchins, R. M., & Slesinger, D. (1927). Some observations on the law of evidence: Consciousness of guilt. *University of Pennsylvania Law Review, 77,* 725–740.

Hutchins, R. M., & Slesinger, D. (1928a). Some observations on the law of evidence: The competency of witnesses. *Yale Law Journal, 37,* 1017–1028.

Hutchins, R. M., & Slesinger, D. (1928b). Some observations of the law of evidence: Memory. *Harvard Law Review, 41,* 860–873.

Hutchins, R. M., & Slesinger, D. (1928c). Some observations of the law of evidence: Spontaneous exclamations. *Columbia Law Review, 28,* 432–440.

Hutchins, R. M., & Slesinger, D. (1929). Legal psychology. *Psychological Review, 36,* 13–26.

Jackson, J. P. (2000). The triumph of the segregationists? A historiographical inquiry into psychology and the *Brown* litigation. *History of Psychology, 3,* 239–261.

Jenkins v. United States, 307 F.2d 637 (D.C. Cir. 1962) *en banc.*

Jesness, C. (1971). Jesness Inventory Classification System. *Criminal Justice and Behavior, 15,* 78–91.

Keller, E. I. (1918). Psychopathic laboratory at police headquarters, New York City. *Journal of Applied Psychology, 2,* 84–88.

Kelves, D. J. (1984, October 15). Annals of eugenics, II. *New Yorker,* 52–125.

Kluger, R. (1975). *Simple justice.* New York: Knopf.

Kuna, D. P. (1978). One-sided portrayal of Münsterberg. *American Psychologist, 33,* 700.

Landy, F. J. (1992). Hugo Münsterberg: Victim or visionary? *Journal of Applied Psychology, 77,* 787–802.

Lindner, H. (1955). The work of court and prison psychologists. In G. J. Dudycha (Ed.), *Psychology for law enforcement officers.* Springfield, IL: Charles C. Thomas.

Loh, W. D. (1981). Perspectives on psychology and law. *Journal of Applied Social Psychology, 11,* 314–355.

Louisell, D. W. (1955). The psychologist in today's legal world: Part I. *Minnesota Law Review, 39,* 235–260.

Louisell, D. W. (1957). The psychologist in today's legal world: Part II. *Minnesota Law Review, 41,* 731–750.

Marston, W. M. (1917). Systolic blood pressure changes in deception. *Journal of Experimental Psychology, 2,* 117–163.

Marston, W. M. (1920). Reaction-time symptoms of deception. *Journal of Experimental Psychology, 3,* 72–87.

Marston, W. M. (1921). Psychological possibilities in deception tests. *Journal of the American Institute of Criminal Law and Criminology, 11,* 551–570.

Marston, W. M. (1924). Studies in testimony. *Journal of Criminal Law and Criminology, 15,* 5–32.

Marston, W. M. (1925). Negative type reaction-time symptoms of deception. *Psychological Review, 32,* 241–247.

McCary, J. L. (1956). The psychologist as an expert witness in court. *American Psychologist, 11,* 8–13.

McCarty, D. G. (1929). *Psychology for the lawyer.* New York: Prentice-Hall.

Megargee, E. I. (1977). A new classification system for criminal offenders. *Criminal Justice and Behavior, 4,* 107–114.

Merrill, M. A. (1927). Intelligence of policemen. *Journal of Personnel Research, 5,* 511–515.

Miller, H. L., Lower, J. S., & Bleechmore, J. (1978). The clinical psychologist as an expert witness on questions of mental illness and competency. *Law and Psychology Review, 4,* 115–125.

Monahan, J., & Loftus, E. F. (1982). The psychology of law. *Annual Review of Psychology, 33,* 441–475.

Moskowitz, M. J. (1977). Hugo Münsterberg: A study in the history of applied psychology. *American Psychologist, 32*, 824–842.

Münsterberg, H. (1899/1994). Psychology and history. *Psychological Review, 101*, 230–236.

Münsterberg, H. (1908). *On the witness stand: Essays on psychology and crime.* New York: McClure.

Münsterberg, H. (1914). *Psychology and social sanity.* New York: Doubleday, Page.

Napoli, D. S. (1981). *Architects of adjustment.* Port Washington, NY: Kennikat.

Odom v. State, 174 Ala. 4, 7, 56 So. 913, 914 (1911).

Oglesby, T. W. (1957). Use of emotional screening in the selection of police applicants. *Public Personnel Review, 18*, 228–231, 235.

Ogloff, J. R. P., Tomkins, A. J., & Bersoff, D. N. (1996). Education and training in psychology and law/criminal justice. *Criminal Justice and Behavior, 23*, 200–235.

Otto, R. K., & Heilbrun, K. (2002). The practice of forensic psychology: A look toward the future in light of the past. *American Psychologist, 57*, 5–19.

Paterson, D. G. (1940). Applied psychology comes of age. *Journal of Consulting Psychology, 4*, 1–9.

People v. Hawthorne, 293 Mich. 15, 291 N.W. 205 (1940).

President's Commission on Law Enforcement and the Administration of Justice. (1967). *Task force report: The police.* Washington, DC: USGPO.

Quay, H. C. (1965). Psychopathic personality: Pathological stimulation-seeking. *American Journal of Psychiatry, 122*, 180–183.

Rankin, J. H. (1957). Preventive psychiatry in the Los Angeles Police Department. *Police, 2*, 24–29.

Rankin, J. H. (1959). Psychiatric screening of police recruits. *Public Personnel Review, 20*, 191–196.

Reese, J. T. (1986). Foreward. In J. T. Reese & H. Goldstein (Eds.), *Psychological services for law enforcement* (p. v). Washington, DC: USGPO.

Reese, J. T. (1987). *A history of police psychological services.* Washington, DC: USGPO.

Reiser, M. (1972). *The police psychologist.* Springfield, IL: Charles C. Thomas.

Reiser, M. (1982). *Police psychology: Collected papers.* Los Angeles: LEHI.

Resnick, R. J. (1997). A brief history of practice—expanded. *American Psychologist, 52*, 463–468.

Robinson, E. S. (1935). *Law and the lawyers.* New York: Macmillan.

Rogers, O. (1910). The unwary purchaser: A study in the psychology of trademark infringement. *Michigan Law Review, 8*, 613–644.

Rogers, O. (1918). An account of some psychological experiments on the subject of trademark infringements. *Michigan Law Review, 18*, 75–95.

Schrenck-Notzing, A. (1897). *Uber suggestion und erinnerungsfalschung im berchtholdprocess.* Leipzig: Johann Ambrosius Barth.

Scrivner, E. M. (1994). *The role of police psychology in controlling excessive forces.* Washington, DC: National Institute of Justice.

Shartle, C. L. (1946). Occupations in psychology. *American Psychologist, 1*, 559–582.

Slesinger, D., & Pilpel, M. E. (1929). Legal psychology: A bibliography and a suggestion. *Psychological Bulletin, 12*, 677–692.

Snee, T. J., & Lush, D. E. (1941). Interaction of the narrative and interrogatory methods of obtaining testimony. *Journal of Psychology, 11*, 225–236.

State v. Driver, 88 W. Va. 479, 107 S. E. 189 (1921).

Stern, L. W. (1906). Zur psychologie der aussage. *Zeitschrift fur die gesamte Strafrechswissenschaft, 23*, 56–66.

Stern, L. W. (1910). Abstracts of lectures on the psychology of testimony. *American Journal of Psychology, 21*, 273–282.

Stern, L. W. (1939). The psychology of testimony. *Journal of Abnormal and Social Psychology, 40*, 3–20.

Tapp, J. L. (1976). Psychology and the law: An overture. *Annual Review of Psychology, 27*, 359–404.

Terman, L. M. (1917). A trial of mental and pedagogical tests in a civil service examination for policemen and firemen. *Journal of Applied Psychology, 1*, 17–29.

Terrio, L., Swanson, C. R., Jr., & Chambelin, N. C. (1977). *The police personnel selection process.* Indianapolis, IN: Bobbs-Merrill.

Thurstone, L. L. (1922). The intelligence of policemen. *Journal of Personnel Research, 1*, 64–74.

Toch, H. (Ed.). (1961). *Legal and criminal psychology.* New York: Holt, Rinehart & Winston.

Toch, H. (1969). *Violent men: An inquiry into the psychology of violence.* Chicago: Aldine.

Toch, H. (1992). Functional unit management: An unsung achievement. *Federal Prisons Journal, 2*, 15–19.

Viteles, M. S. (1929). Psychological methods in the selection of patrolmen in Europe. *Annals of the American Academy, 146*, 160–165.

Watkins, R. E. (1992). *An historical review of the role and practice of psychology in the field of corrections.* Ottawa: Correctional Service of Canada.

Weld, H. P., & Danzig, E. R. (1940). A study of the way in which a verdict is reached by a jury. *American Journal of Psychology, 53,* 518–536.

Weld, H. P., & Roff, M. (1938). A study in the formation of opinion based upon legal evidence. *American Journal of Psychology, 51,* 609–628.

Whipple, G. M. (1909). The observer as reporter: A survey of the "psychology of testimony." *Psychological Bulletin, 6,* 153–170.

Whipple, G. M. (1910). Recent literature on the psychology of testimony. *Psychological Bulletin, 7,* 365–368.

Whipple, G. M. (1911). Psychology of testimony. *Psychological Bulletin, 8,* 307–309.

Whipple, G. M. (1912). Psychology of testimony and report. *Psychological Bulletin, 9,* 264–269.

Whipple, G. M. (1913). Psychology of testimony and report. *Psychological Bulletin, 10,* 264–268.

Whipple, G. M. (1914). Psychology of testimony and report. *Psychological Bulletin, 11,* 245–250.

Whipple, G. M. (1915). Psychology of testimony. *Psychological Bulletin, 12,* 221–224.

Whipple, G. M. (1917). Psychology of testimony. *Psychological Bulletin, 14,* 234–236.

Wigmore, J. H. (1909). Professor Münsterberg and the psychology of testimony: Being a report of the case of *Cokestone v. Münsterberg. Illinois Law Review, 3,* 399–445.

Wigmore, J. H. (1940). *Evidence in trials at common law.* Boston: Little, Brown.

Winick, C. (1961). The psychology of juries. In H. Toch (Ed.), *Legal and criminal psychology* (pp. 96–120). New York: Holt, Rinehart and Winston.

CHAPTER 2

Defining Forensic Psychology

ALLEN K. HESS

Alberto Flores, 19-years of age, raped and killed a six-year-old Italian girl. When caught for another sexual assault, questioning elicited a confession from Mr. Flores. His mentality became in issue almost immediately, displaying a concreteness that beggared for an intellectual assessment. The Stanford-Binet revealed a mental age of 7 years, 6 months, and was replicated twice. Test results on other intelligence scales were consistent with his S-B test results and with his third grade education, which terminated when he was 13 or 14 years old. (condensed from Terman, 1918)

THERE IS nothing surprising in this account. Regrettably, such cases are neither unusual nor uncommon. Similar scenes may have been played out as you read the account and as I typed it. But the interesting feature is that the author is Lewis Terman and the date of publication is 1918. As soon as the Stanford-Binet was translated into English and normed, it found forensic applications. Indeed, law and psychology participate in each other, as the term is used in philosophy, as red and apple participate. That is, red is a part of what many apples are and apples are a prototypic example of a red item. One is tied acausally to the other, just as psychology and law, as illustrated in this chapter, participate in each other.

In the past several decades, collaboration between psychology and law has grown prodigiously. The number of journals, textbooks, and continuing education workshops available in forensic psychology has increased; the American Psychological Association (APA) Division 41, the American Psychology-Law Society, has more than 2,000 members; and postdoctoral credentialing boards offer diplomate status in forensic psychology.

In recent years, there has been a shift in the focus of clinical psychology from investigating anxiety (neurotic) and schizophrenic conditions to studying character disorders, examining externalizing versus internalizing styles of personality, generally, and criminal and violent behavior specifically. As the public's interest in crime increased, clinical psychologists broadened their interests to include forensic questions and criminal behavior. Journals such as

Behavioral Sciences and the Law, Criminal Justice and Behavior, Law and Human Behavior, Journal of Personality Disorders, and *Psychology, Public Policy and Law* are devoted to forensic psychology. Increasingly, *Ethics & Behavior, Journal of Abnormal Psychology, Journal of Consulting and Clinical Psychology, Professional Psychology: Research and Practice,* and the APA newsletter *Monitor on Psychology* publish articles devoted to forensic psychology concerns. Given the growth in collaboration, it is important to examine both the ways psychology and law relate to each other and the ways they differ. The two disciplines have much to offer each other. However, they have differing philosophical assumptions that need to be described in order that collaborative efforts are not stymied by conflicts due to a failure to understand these differences.

The first section of this chapter describes three ways psychology and law interact: the practice of psychology in legal settings, the effects of the law on the practice of psychology, and research and scholarly inquiry as applied to legal issues. The second section describes epistemological differences between law and psychology. Both lawyers and psychologists need to understand these differences for their collaborations to meet with success. The third section provides a brief prospectus for future work in the theory, research, and practice of forensic psychology.

Legal issues extend to all psychologists' practices, whether they occur in academia, in business, on the lecture circuit, or in the clinical office. Some might feel "belegaled" by the growing legal strictures concerning psychological practice (Simon, 1987), but increased sensitivity to various interests and issues should help practitioners elevate their professional functioning, not limit it. Practitioners are advised not to become quasi attorneys but rather to be aware of legal issues to remain current in their practice. Practitioners should hone their skills by keeping up with the literature, seeking consultation and supervision before questions become critical (an ongoing peer supervision group can be inestimably helpful), and practicing as if a videotape of their activities will be reviewed in court (Weiner, 2002). The best safeguard from legal troubles is to be constantly mindful of the best standards of care and practice in one's profession, to be aware of relevant state and case law, and to try to anticipate the consequences of one's activities.

THREE WAYS PSYCHOLOGY AND LAW INTERACT

We can establish a functional definition of forensic psychology by describing the three ways psychology and law interact: psychology in the law, psychology by the law, and psychology of the law.

PSYCHOLOGY IN THE LAW

Some psychologists practice in a legal setting and must be aware of and knowledgeable about legal issues; expert witnesses are an example. Expert witnesses must be familiar with legal standards, definitions, and tests and the procedures by which the law operates (e.g., see Clark, Chapter 14; A. K. Hess, Chapters 22; K. D. Hess, Chapters 4, 5; Zapf, Golding, & Roesch, Chapter 13; Zapf &

Roesch, Chapter 12, in this volume). They must be aware of specific ethical parameters that govern forensic psychology practice, particularly where such practice differs from traditional clinical or experimental practices (see A. K. Hess, Chapter 27, in this volume).

For example, psychologists who conduct research in prison settings need to know that prison officials have total authority to restrict access to prisoners except for approved family and friends and legal and spiritual counsel (*Pell v. Procunier*, 1974). Ethically informed psychologists realize the strictures of working with incarcerated populations and inform their research team about the protocol for conducting research in the prison. The psychologist must educate subordinates and student aides and provide continual monitoring concerning issues such as what constitutes contraband (flowing in either direction, in or out of the facility) and what constitutes forbidden contact. For example, students working with a responsible psychologist are allowed no contact with prisoners or prison authorities outside of those regulated by the professional.

Psychologists may find their clinical research applicable to legal questions. For example, Eisendrath (1996) ably distinguishes among factitious disorders, malingering, and other forms of abnormality such as conversion, hypochondriasis, and somatization in Munchausen cases. Traditionally, such distinctions help clinicians develop treatment plans. However, distinctions such as Eisendrath's have important implications for legal questions such as disability determination, for competency and sanity questions, and for testimonial reliability (credibility).

Many of the following chapters involve the artful application of psychology in legal contexts. These chapters illustrate the advances in research and practice in such areas as domestic law, child eyewitness competence, lie detection, assessing jury competence, predicting violence and recommending parole, psychotherapeutic intervention, assessing disabilities, applying hypnosis, and police psychology.

PSYCHOLOGY BY THE LAW

Psychologists must be aware of the way law has increased its influence on their daily functioning, whether in clinical practice, in academia, or in research contexts. For example, the *Tarasoff* (1976) decision had a major impact on the conditions of confidentiality clinicians could offer clients. In the decades since *Tarasoff*, the law has refined the duty to warn third parties of a client's threats of violence (*Perreira v. State*, 1989), established a "zone of danger" regarding who might be a foreseeable victim (*Hamman v. County of Maricopa*, 1989), and identified what determines the remoteness of time between a threat and an overtly violent act (*In re* Hofmaster, 1989).

The psychologist must continue to follow refinements in the law as they affect practice and, because state law and local custom shape legal and ethical practice, to learn about the law as applicable where the psychologist practices. For example, recently the number of disciplines that offer psychotherapy and counseling to the public has multiplied; the psychologist who receives or makes referrals needs to know about relevant law such as *Jaffee v. Redmond*

(1996), which defined which professions can offer the protection of privilege to clients. With respect to the public's understanding of confidentiality, Knowles and McMahon (1995) found an Australian sample in accord with the need for privacy in psychotherapy yet having an expectation for suspension of privacy in murder, suicide, child abuse, and treason situations or when a child is younger than 13 years. Parents felt more strongly about being informed than nonparents in questions concerning drug use and child abuse.

As clinical practices involve greater numbers of personnel such as secretaries, billing clerks, office managers, psychological assistants, associates, and partners, practitioners need to know the degree to which their staff is covered by the practitioner's ability to offer privilege. *Oregon v. Miller* (1985) described both the umbrella of privilege that covers a professional's support staff (nurses, receptionists, typists) and the time when privilege begins. In *Oregon v. Miller,* Miller's brother advised him to talk with mental health professionals after Miller had strangled his allegedly homosexual partner. Miller told the secretary-receptionist answering his phone call that he had killed someone and needed to talk with a professional. The attending psychiatrist, a Dr. Saville, then talked with him for 10 to 15 minutes, assuring him that the conversation was confidential. Then Miller gave his name and the professional stalled while police traced the phone number from which he was calling. Absent a clear and present danger (the victim was dead by then), psychotherapist privilege began when the circumstances showed that Miller held the belief that the communication was made for the purposes of diagnosis and treatment, even in the first minutes of the initial and sole conversation.

When hiring personnel, psychologists functioning as employers need to know about employment law; when managing a suicidal client, they need to know what constitutes the appropriate standard of care; when terminating psychotherapy, the clinician needs to know what would be actionable as patient abandonment; and when teaching, the instructor needs to know about issues such as what constitutes grounds for student or professor misconduct and what are the parameters of disclosure of student records (Office of Juvenile Justice and Delinquency Prevention, 1997). Psychologists as employers, clinicians, and teachers need to know about the Americans with Disabilities Act (1990) so they can better serve prisoners, students, faculty, staff members, and clients who need reasonable accommodations for their impairments (Greenlaw & Kohl, 1992). Although practicing in a legal manner does not constitute a forensic psychology practice, psychologists who become expert in legal parameters of practice to the degree that they offer consulting services to other psychologists regarding legal practice questions are practicing forensic psychology.

There are many resources to guide the psychologist interested in the ethical, moral, and lawful practice of forensic psychology. Several chapters concern writing reports (see Weiner, Chapter 21, in this volume), practicing principled forensic psychology (see A. K. Hess, Chapter 27, in this volume), treatment (see Gendreau, Coggin, French, & Smith, Chapter 24; Marshall, Chapter 26; McCord, Chapter 23; Mobley, Chapter 25, in this volume), assessing competence (see Slovenko, Chapter 9; Zapf & Roesch, Chapter 12, in this volume), and using legal source materials to answer particular questions (see

Cox, Chapter 3, in this volume). There are other excellent sources to answer legal questions about practice issues, including journals (e.g., *Professional Psychology; Ethics and Behavior; Psychology, Public Policy and Law*); books by Bersoff (1995), Corey, Corey, and Callanan (1993), Keith-Spiegel and Koocher (1985), Rinas and Clyne-Jackson (1988), Steininger, Newell, and Garcia (1984), and Swenson (1993); codes of professional conduct (e.g., APA, 2002; Committee on Ethical Guidelines for Forensic Psychologists, 1991); newsletters and reports (e.g., *Appelbaum/Grisso Report, Mental Health Report, Register Report of the National Register of Health Service Providers*, and the APA Monitor's *Judicial Notebook*); and legal sources.

Academicians have been drawn into the legal arena regarding their rights to conduct research and to disseminate their findings. For example, the case of Dr. Paul Fischer should alert psychologists to the degree that legal parameters can affect research. At dinner, Fischer's 2-year-old son sucked on a straw pretending it was a cigarette and told his father how he was going to puff away when he was older. Fischer, a family medicine practitioner, constructed a little card game and tested it on 229 3- to 6-year-old children in day care, having obtained parental consent with the usual provision that neither the parent nor the child would be identified. Fischer found that 33% of the 3-year-old children and 91% of the 6-year-old children correctly placed Joe Camel on the picture of cigarettes. In contrast, fewer than 61% of the 6-year-old children whom Fischer studied correctly identified the Marlboro Man ("Doctors Whose Study," 1997). The *Journal of the American Medical Association* published Fischer's paper. R. J. Reynolds (RJR) subpoenaed Fischer's records and notes and the names, addresses, and telephone numbers of the 229 children and their parents in the course of their defense in a lawsuit in which Fischer's research was mentioned in passing. A series of legal actions followed, with RJR asserting the need for the raw research data, Fischer asserting the need to preserve the promised confidentiality, and the Medical School of Georgia and Georgia state attorney failing to back Fischer. Under Georgia's open records law, Fischer was deemed a public employee and his records considered public records. This leads to a number of questions:

> Do researchers who guarantee confidentiality stand on solid ground when relying on professional codes of ethics rather than the state law and the policies of the institution in which they work?
>
> Can researchers and their professional associations influence state law and institutional policy?
>
> Can the researcher separate the identification information of research participants from the raw data to assure the confidentiality of the participants?

In a case involving lecturing about controversial issues, a Dr. Whitfield publicly taught about recovered memory of sexual abuse, using the case of Jennifer Freyd as an example. Her parents sued Whitfield for defamation, claiming that his intent was malicious, that his information was erroneous, and that his professional degree should have made him aware of the falsity of their adult daughter's claims about them. The judge held that such a guarantee of the truth of their hypotheses would stifle the very debate that leads to scientific knowledge ("Judge Protects," 1997, p. AB). Lecturers have a broad freedom to express their views, but this freedom needs to be weighed against legal limitations such as defamation and the personal destructiveness their statements might have. Could Whitfield's points in his lecture be made without distressing the Freyds? What may be legally permissible may not always be right.

Psychology of the Law: Psychological Research on Legal Issues and Processes

The third area that is subsumed under forensic psychology concerns scholarly inquiry into what has been termed "psycholegal issues." For example, Saks, Hollinger, Wissler, Evans, and Hart (1997) address the important issue of variability of civil jury awards, a synonym for tort reform, a burning issue for legislatures and media across the country but an issue that has received little scientific study. In Saks et al.'s experiment, mock jurors were presented six different ways of awarding damages: a cap condition indicating the maximum amount allowed by law, an average award information cue, an award interval or range cue, an average-plus-interval condition, an exemplar condition, and a control condition, all presented over the three injury-severity levels. The researchers found that the cap condition, advocated by many who want to limit awards, actually increased both the variability of awards at the three levels of injury severity and the size of awards in low and intermediate levels of injury cases, the very cases that make up the bulk of civil injury litigation. The authors consider the adverse effect on distributive justice and the way anchoring and assimilation theory would result in a more just system of civil injury awards.

Greene, Coon, and Bronstein (2001) hypothesized that capping punitive awards (money awarded to punish the offender and serve as a warning for other potential offenders) would inflate compensatory awards (awards given to compensate the victim for the damages). In their analogue study, this effect was not found. However, they found jurors with no option to award any punitive damages did increase compensatory awards. In fact, the award by juries is rarely the last word. Hallinan (2004) points out two interesting facts regarding malpractice awards: 4% of medical malpractice payments result from jury awards (contrast this with the public's perception influenced by media reports); and 2% of health care spending is accounted for by malpractice costs. He describes the New York State jury award of $112 million that made the news; the actual award of $6 million did not garner headlines. The area of tort reform, the public's perception, and determining fairness in the award system merits continued research attention by forensic psychologists.

Stinson, Devenport, Cutler, and Kravitz (1996) applied psychology to study the question of whether the presence of lawyers provided a safeguard for the defendant at lineups. They used videotaped lineups and found that public defenders were sensitive to the use of foils (people known to be innocent) but were less sensitive to instructional bias, where the witness is led to understand that the perpetrator is among the lineup members (a biasing factor). Attorneys rated simultaneous lineups (having four, five, or six people viewed at the same time) as less biased than sequential lineups (having the people viewed one at a time); this is in contrast to the literature that holds that sequential lineups, though not often used, are less biasing than simultaneous lineups.

A key assumption in a jury case is that jurors will weigh the evidence against legal standards issued in the instructions by the judge. Smith (1991) found that when uninstructed people hold incorrect legal information, these misunderstandings influence their verdicts, and that this prototype information is resistant to change by typical instruction. Smith asserts that for our legal system to function according to the law rather than by lay (mis)conceptions of the law, instruction must be effective in changing prototype information.

Psychologists have applied research methodologies to a number of legal questions and practices. Literature concerning juror selection and jury dynamics, privacy, and discretion show applications of psychology studying the law.

Jury Processes and Juror Competence

Attorneys have long held that a trial verdict may have been determined before the opening statements are uttered if the attorney has wisely selected the jurors. In the 1970s, two brothers named Berrigan were accused of antiwar activities and conspiring to kidnap Secretary of State Henry Kissinger. Their trial established the practice of scientific jury selection (SJS) by social scientists (Diamond, 1990). Despite efforts and expenses devoted to SJS, Diamond concluded that research shows from 16% to fewer than 5% of trial outcomes can be attributed to SJS. Perhaps SJS continues to be used because of attorney anxiety and because it shows that the attorney left no stone unturned in his or her client's advocacy, but it may leave the psychologist offering a service without any demonstrated validity.

Diamond (1990) suggests that social scientists may be making a more substantive, and ethical, contribution if they explore such issues as the possibility of community bias that can support a motion for a change of venue or if consultants help attorneys identify the presentation of arguments that may be more effective with jurors. For example, Diamond, Casper, Heiert, and Marshall (1996) showed that jurors did not spend much time talking about the attorneys, and that they did focus on attorney behavior, were affected by what the witnesses presented, were persuaded by the strength and effectiveness of cross-examination, and were open to changing their verdicts as the trial unfolded.

How can psychological research inform the legal system about jurors and juries? Kuhn, Weinstock, and Flaton (1994) showed that there are significant individual differences among jurors in reasoning skills, showed how juror reasoning processes are activated, and showed that competent jurors choose moderate verdicts and are less certain in their judgments than less competent jurors. Kuhn et al. offered suggestions for training jurors to be competent because competent jurors follow the judicial instructions by weighing alternatives. Forsterlee and Horowitz (1997) found that note takers, in contrast to non-note-taking jurors, demonstrated better cognitive performance, were more effective decision makers, and were less distracted by nonprobative evidence. Cooper et al. (1996) showed that mock jurors were more persuaded by highly expert witnesses than less expert witnesses when testimony was highly complex, but when testimony was simpler, the content of the testimony was telling in contrast to the expertise level of the witnesses. They demonstrated the Rosenthal expectancy effect, wherein judges' biases were transmitted to mock student and nonstudent jurors but that this biasing effect was titrated when simplified jury instructions were given.

Jurors are exposed to stress both in the juror selection process and in the trial process. Hafemeister, Ventis, Levine, Constanza, and Constanza (reported by DeAngelis, 1995) showed that a juror might be exposed to graphic and grue-some evidence, and sequestered, and that these stresses can affect verdicts. Towell et al. (1996) showed that masking affected the nonverbal communica-tion between witness and juror and reduced juror recall of information in pixilated and shadowed masks but not in photo-negative masks. Yet juror cer-tainty remained high even when jurors' recall was reduced.

Kagehiro (1990a) examined the objections to quantifying the standards of proof in instructing juries. She found no basis to the objections that jurors would be overly certain and prone to conviction if the standards of proof em-ployed statistical anchors and that such instructions would weaken the legal definition. In fact, Kagehiro found that quantifying the standards of proof—greater than 90% certainty for "beyond a reasonable doubt," 75% certainty for "clear and convincing" evidence, and more than 50% of the evidence for a "pre-ponderance of the evidence"—was consistent with the law's intended effect in setting legal standards; further, juries' findings for the plaintiffs decrease as the standards of proof became stricter. Statistical instruction alone and in com-bination with legal definitions were superior to the traditional definition alone in achieving the law's purpose, the increased comprehension of the legal in-structions on which verdicts are based. It seems that the standards of liability, ranging from "reckless indifference," "reckless disregard," and "callous disre-gard" to "gross negligence," "outrageous conduct," and "a shock to the con-science" would be more easily understood with more metric definition. Thus, justice will be better served if legislation is informed by psychological research concerning scaling techniques as a way to clarify jury instructions.

Training jurors to be more competent would address an important societal problem, that of the perception of jury incompetence that has contributed to the erosion of trust in the jury system. Moreover, the jury research just re-viewed shows that juror selection might be a dead end, but there are much more exciting and useful lines of research that psychologists are developing to improve jury performance (see Robbennolt, Groscup, & Penrod, Chapter 15, in this volume).

Privacy and Identity

Psychological and legal concerns about questions of privacy are becoming in-creasingly important. Electronic information bases are compounding the prob-lem of identity theft.

Bronti Kelly's life was tormented. Despite a resume, replete with sales expe-rience, he was rejected hundreds of times in a four-year search for a sales job. When Kelly was hired, the employer would terminate him within days to re-turn Kelly to the treadmill of the job seekers. He lost his apartment, filed for bankruptcy, lived in a parking garage to shield himself from the elements, and was rejected by welfare because he had no permanent address. Despondent, he blamed himself (Kalish, 1997). Kelly reported losing his wallet in 1990; this resulted in his identification papers being used by someone who engaged in arson, burglary, and shoplifting. Although Kelly was on active military duty when he was alleged to have committed the crimes, his record was never cleared. He was ensnared in the Kafkaesque world of being punished and not even knowing why. Eventually, the identity theft was discovered, although the records of his putative criminal activity seem to persist in the "system" long after the discovery.

Since the previous edition containing this chapter, congressional hearings have been held and government reports have been issued on the increasing scale of identity theft and its devastating emotional impact on the victims. As the information age speeds along, the need for psychological research on its impact will grow accordingly.

Pedersen (1997) examined aspects of the concept of privacy and found that people use solitude for creative efforts, to secure personal information, and to contemplate who they are, what they want to be, how to experiment with new behaviors without social condemnation, and for rejuvenation. Sex differences in privacy needs can account for differences in how males and females experience intrusion (Pedersen, 1987). Sheffey and Tindale (1992) found that female-dominated work situations (termed "traditional") compared with male-dominated or mixed work settings (termed "nontraditional" and "integrated") differed in the threshold for a determination of appropriate versus harassing sexual behavior. Larger status discrepancies produced more severe judgments of inappropriateness. Stockdale (1993) reviewed research showing that men perceive women's friendliness as more sexually charged than women intend and examined factors contributing to these differences. Sheffey and Tindale (1992) warn about the complexities in litigating charges based on complex subjective judgments and urged managers to be mindful of these factors in constructing their sexual harassment policies and training programs.

Kagehiro (1990b) wondered whether people understood their Fourth Amendment consent rights: that voluntariness for consent means absence of governmental coercion and not informed consent, that such consent waives the requirement of a warrant, and that consent can be waived by a third party without an individual's permission or knowledge when the premises are in possession and control of another (as often happens with a roommate or suite mate). Furthermore, she wanted to know how a third party, such as a judge reviewing a motion to dismiss evidence, would perceive the degree to which a person who waived his or her rights against search and seizure was free from coercion and acted voluntarily.

Kagehiro (1990b) found that observers attributed more voluntariness than did nonconsenters in waiving the consenter's rights to the ability of the consenter to revoke consent, to ask for information during the entry and search process, and for these judgments to be affected by the formality of the request (e.g., "Why don't you let me take a peek in your purse so we can resolve this problem easily" versus "Empty the contents of your purse on the floor now"). These results are consistent with the actor-observer bias that has been well established in attribution theory research. Kagehiro's subjects did understand that civil and criminal justice authorities had no more right of entry than did social or commercial parties, but their view of "common authority" and "exclusive use" differed from legal rulings. The subjects perceived coresidents' right to consent as more circumscribed than the courts have held and that the parties' presence influenced these judgments, whereas the courts have held a person's presence as less telling when someone who has access to the area waives the person's rights while he or she is present.

Finally, courts hold that a wider range of people can waive privacy rights than subjects believe. Kagehiro (1990b) found that students view both the suspect's relationship to a third party and the third party's control over the space to be important, but the courts emphasize the third party's place control or control of the residence even momentarily as primary in importance. This means that a person's house sitter, babysitter, house painter, or even a visitor with place control has more authority over our privacy than most of us assume. Interestingly, responses from a police detective sample were more similar to the students' views than they were to the court's holdings, perhaps demonstrating an intuitive sense of privacy consistent with lay expectations. Kagehiro further cautions that the court's understanding of privacy holds a more concrete view of the world than reality suggests when one considers the cultural differences in privacy among many of our ethnic groups and the nontraditional constitution of the American household.

Bomser et al. (1995) ramble down the information superhighway in their review of the legal issues concerning privacy and security of copyrighted and trademarked work, personal communications, defamation, and even the antitrust impact on access, privacy, and security of our business and personal data. Tracey (1998) cautions the clinician against the perils of electronic devices such as cellular and cordless phones, fax machines, photocopiers, answering machines, and pagers as threats to our clients' confidentiality. Who we are, how we determine our lives, and the penetrability of our identities are crucial issues affected by judgments regarding privacy. Vitek (1997) described privacy and civility as linked within "placed communities." For Vitek, the people who share an event in time, place, and emotional commitment constitute a placed community, defined by shared values and a sense of civility. For example, a community that celebrates a marriage knows that the married couple will be sexually engaged later that evening; nonetheless, the act remains private. The sense of being in a placed community involves the shared values of affection, restraint, and propriety. Vitek's concern is that as modern life involves greater rootlessness, leading to a lessened sense of community ties, there is an attenuation of shared values and the respect for privacy that we need (Vitek & Jackson, 1996).

Discretion

Shaver, Gilbert, and Williams (1975) described the concept of discretion. At every step in the legal system, decisions are made that involve a complex of factors described by Konecni and Ebbesen (1982). This subjectivity is trenchantly captured by Goble (1955, p. 403): "Facts are true only as judged by a selected system of references." Figure 2.1 shows the choice points in the processing of a criminal case: the decision by the perpetrator to commit an offense, the victim's recognition and subsequent declaration to authorities (a separate decision) to report the offense, the police's decision to make an arrest, the prosecutor's decision to pursue charges, the grand jury's bringing an indictment, the arraignment, the trial, sentencing, and finally the system's disposition of an imposed sentence.

Let us examine discretion at two points in Figure 2.1: (1) factors influencing how people determine that they are victims and (2) dimensions of judicial discretion. If people do not perceive that they were crime victims, there will most likely be no crime reported, as depicted on the left side of Figure 2.1. The veracity of memory and the effects of repression, particularly of childhood sexual offenses, is a highly controversial issue. Positions include the view that all memory is a contemporary reconstruction of events, the idea that memory can be distorted, and the notion that memory is recorded almost as a mechanical process (the last view is largely archaic and mostly held by the lay public).

Brainerd, Reyna, and Bradnse (1995) use fuzzy trace theory to show that in certain circumstances, false memories can be more firmly established than true memories because the implanted memory might be better embedded in a supporting set of memory traces. That is, there are two parallel processes used to store and retrieve memories. The more surface or verbally mediated process and the "gist" or meaningful content process work in parallel fashion (Brainerd & Reyna, 2002). For example, if you read "Coffee is hotter than tea" and "Tea is hotter than cocoa" and are then asked whether you read "Coffee is hotter than cocoa," you will likely falsely report having read the third statement. The surface or factual information becomes subsidiary to the essential information of the coffee being hotter than cocoa, or the gist of the information. This scenario can easily be transposed to recall of crime scene information.

Pezdek, Finger, and Hodge (1997) show that false memories can be successfully embedded when the event is plausible or consistent with the person's experience. Tromp, Koss, Figueredo, and Tharan (1995) found that rape memories were less clear and vivid, were less meaningfully ordered, were less well remembered, and were less often thought of or discussed in contrast with unpleasant and pleasant memories. Tromp et al.'s findings have implications for both testimony and psychotherapeutic intervention. Dissociative disorders are often implicated as trauma's consequences. Eich, Macaulay, Loewenstein, and Dihle (1997) studied nine dissociative identity disordered people and found that priming with word-stem completion occurred in the same personality state, and priming in a picture-fragment completion was robust between personalities; thus, we must be sensitive to the conditions under which memory is assessed. Karon and Widener (1997) review the arguments of those skeptical about recalled memory (e.g., Newman & Baumeister, 1996) and a well-documented body of clinical findings about repressed memories of World War II, which are now more than 50 years old (Viederman, 1995).

Holmes, Offen, and Waller (1997) tackle the question of why so few male victims of childhood sexual abuse receive help for abuse-related issues in adulthood. They conclude that society's perception that few males are sexually abused and that those who are do not show much of an adverse effect are incorrect. Instead, Holmes et al. see society as having no legitimizing social construct regarding male sexual abuse, so that the clinician does not see, hear, or ask about male sexual abuse; nor does the victim feel any legitimacy in either recognizing or discussing the abuse. Discretion operates through what society construes as legitimate: in this case, that girls are sexual abuse targets but boys are not.

Blumenthal (1998) reviewed gender differences in the perception of sexual harassment, a difference that can affect the victim's reporting of a purported event, the investigator's filing of a complaint, the prosecutor's arraigning of an alleged perpetrator, a judge's acceptance of charges, and the jurors' determination of guilt. Memory and social perception play crucial roles in the criminal justice system, invite more research (see Castelli, Goodman, Edelstein, Mitchell, Paz Alonso, et al., Chapter 11, in this volume), and illustrate the complexities of the psychological processes mediating discretion.

Before leaving discretion, let us briefly examine judicial discretion, a topic receiving attention in *General Electric Company v. Joiner* (1997). Figure 2.1 on page 40 shows that judges have wide latitude in handling charges. They can exercise discretion in granting or denying bail; in assigning counsel for indigents and in accepting counsel; in limiting, reducing, or dismissing charges; in admitting or dismissing evidence; in accepting or rejecting a jury's verdict; and in sentencing. *General Electric Company v. Joiner* serves as an example of judicial discretion. *Joiner* affirmed the judge's role as the gatekeeper who applies the law in determining what constitutes admissible scientific evidence. The standard for such judgments is that of "abuse of discretion." Such abuse occurs only when the judge acts with disregard to logic and with disregard to settled law in the application of the law to the offered testimony. Discretion is broadly defined and exercised with regard to nonscientific testimony, too. Is the following an abuse of discretion?

JUDGE: Mr. G. cooperated with you in every way?
OFFICER: Very cooperative.
JUDGE: And you had your gun out during the entire period?
OFFICER: That is correct, sir.
JUDGE: Where was the gun pointed, sir? At his stomach, mid-section, head?
OFFICER: It was nestled right down the back of his neck.
JUDGE: Did you say anything to Mr. G., by the way, sir, concerning what would happen if he tried to move or get away?
OFFICER: I said I would blow his head off.
JUDGE: It was during this time, when Mr. G. had that .38 special cradled on the back of his neck, that you told him his rights under Miranda? Is that correct?
OFFICER: Yes, sir.
THE JUDGE'S RULING: I think it is a very unusual circumstance to have a gun pointed at the back of someone's head during the course of statement. No question . . . that it raises substantial question as to whether any statement was voluntary; however . . . I think the officer acted reasonably under the circumstances. . . . The defendant could have just as well said, "I have nothing to say," and that would have been the end of it. . . . So I would not find

What is the sequence of events in the criminal justice system?

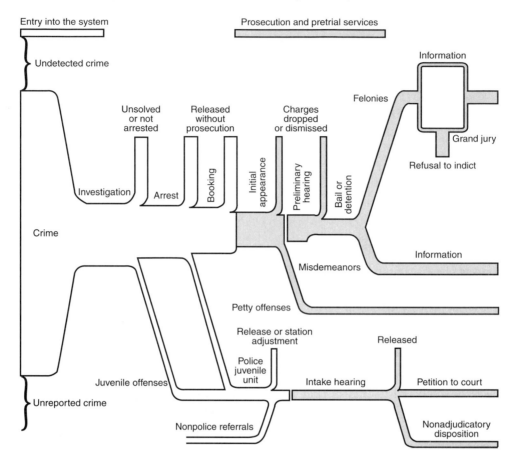

Note: This chart gives a simplified view of caseflow through the criminal justice system. Procedures vary among jurisdictions. The weights of the lines are not intended to show the actual size of caseloads.

Figure 2.1 Discretionary Points in the Criminal Justice System.

Source: From Report to the Nation and Justice, Bureau of Justice Statistics, U.S. Department of Justice, October 1983, pp. 42–45.

the statement involuntary, even though a gun was pointed at the back of the defendant's head. (*Harper's,* 1987, p. 26)

As mentioned earlier, discretion permeates the legal system, has received attention by psychologists, and remains an area richly deserving of more attention. Discretion is seen as sound when it appears reasonable or tied to logical application of the law in weighing evidence. Let us consider this fundamental concept of the law, reasonableness, and how psychological inquiry can help explicate reasonableness.

Reasonable Man Hypothesis

The law's benchmark is cognitive: What would we expect of the "reasonable man"? Redmount (1965) claims that psychologists should contribute to defining reasonableness. Consider three cases. In the first, a woman strikes a man on the

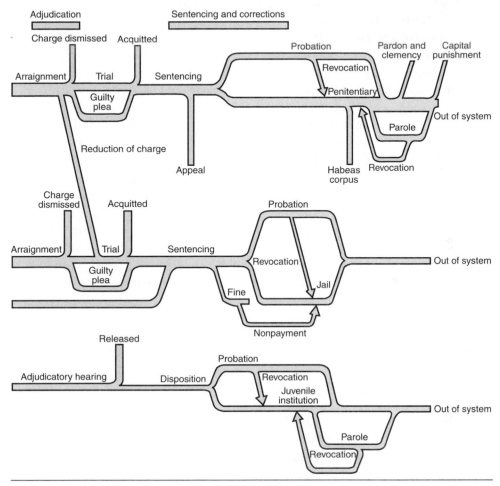

Figure 2.1 *(Continued)*

jaw so hard that she knocks him out. Did she act unreasonably? If she were an airline flight attendant and a sudden drop during the flight caused the man to panic, start screaming, and lose control to the point that the other passengers began to panic, then she might have acted not only reasonably but heroically.

Courtney Love, a rock music star, was charged with slugging two fans at her concert in Orlando, Florida, in 1995. The judge dismissed the two counts of battery because the fans were not exposed to any more violence than one should expect at a rock concert. What is a reasonable risk of exposure to violence seems to depend on the setting or context. What normative expectation does the public or the reasonable man have regarding risk in various settings? Are decisions regarding the definition of a social situation at least in part psychologically determined?

Have times changed? The 2004 "Throw-down in Motown" during which the Detroit Piston and Indiana Pacer National Basketball Association teams fought with fans in the stands might lead to a different decision. The fans did not expect to be attacked by highly trained athletes. Would such expectations differ at a hockey game, at which fighting is usual and increasingly involves fans? Psychologists have yet to provide a research base regarding what reasonable fans might expect when they attend a professional (or college) game. The day after the "Throw-down," the Clemson and University of South Carolina football teams fought twice. The presidents of both universities immediately banned their team from bowl games that season, and the president of South Carolina banned this year's team from accepting a bowl game. Will these sanctions prove effective in preventing further college sports conflagrations?

Louise Woodward was tried for causing the death of a child in her care. Much was made of the fact that the British-born and raised 19-year-old Woodward did not display appropriate emotion during the police interrogation, the prosecutors' questioning, or the trial itself. Television commentators riveted viewers' attention to this "insight." However, they did not take into account cultural differences in emotional expression; they did not include in their commentary her reaction to the guilty verdict, instead attributing her emotion to that of a person reacting not to the crime but to her conviction; and they did not attend to Woodward's parents' seemingly stoic reaction to their daughter's wailing at the verdict. What would have been a reasonable response by Louise Woodward? What expectations for emotional display did the jurors hold, and to what would they have attributed her emotional response had she displayed any? Was her stoicism judged within the jurors' or the media commentators' particular cultural emotional histories with little regard to Woodward's upbringing in a culture given to little public emotional expression? Could consulting forensic psychologists have been useful to Woodward's attorneys in witness preparation and in constructing their presentation to the jury in light of their client's seeming lack of emotion?

Contrast Louise Woodward with the demeanor of Scott Peterson. Here a man's pregnant wife disappeared on Christmas Eve, yet he was planning a date with his mistress the next day rather than expressing concern for his wife and child-to-be. His apparent callousness contributed to the jury's finding of guilt. Attribution theory has great application to the justice system in helping attorneys understand the thought processes of fact finders.

A Functional Definition of Forensic Psychology

Forensic psychology can be defined by the functions described earlier: providing psychological services in the justice or legislative system, developing a specialized knowledge of legal issues as they affect the practice of psychology, and conducting research on legal questions involving psychological processes. But defining forensic psychology using these three functions has limitations. Any typology serves at best as a guide and has two weaknesses: the cases on the border between types and complex cases that amalgamate two or more categories in the typology.

Walzer and Miltimore (1993) address the specific case in which disciplined health care professionals are mandated to enter controlled supervision, monitoring, and psychotherapy. Would the treating psychotherapist be practicing in a legal arena? Practicing psychology in accord with legal mandates? Engaging in a rich research area, as Conner (1996) has done in concluding that the willing client is not a precondition for successful psychotherapy? Or blending all three categories? Psychology in the law, psychology by the law, and psychology of the law together constitute forensic psychology.

FUNDAMENTAL DISTINCTIONS BETWEEN PSYCHOLOGY AND LAW

As psychologists and lawyers work together with greater frequency, there are more chances for misunderstandings to occur. It is useful to consider distinctions that can become troublesome if not recognized. These differences arise from historical and philosophical sources that shaped the two professions. They are summarized in Table 2.1 and explicated in this section.

Table 2.1
Epistemological Differences between Psychology and Law

Dimension	Psychology	Law
Epistemology	Objectivity: Psychologists presume to progressively approach an ultimate truth. Any bias in theory or research is assumed to be balanced by competing theories, discovered by rigorous critique and determined true or false by replication.	Advocacy: Truth in a case will be determined by the vigorous advocacy of the "stronger" facts that are more consistent with the prevailing law.
Nature of "Law"	Descriptive: Research will reveal the underlying natural order or lawful relationships between variables, ideally realized in a formula, such as the relationship between anxiety and performance, or by typologies that are predictive of behavior, such as the type of person who would succeed in police work or on parole.	Prescriptive: Law directs behavior, clearly states what is proscribed or banned, and authorizes punishment to enforce the prescriptions.
Knowledge	Empirical: Based on nomothetic or normative data gathered through methodologies described with sufficient detail to enable replication of the findings.	Rational: Based on idiographic or detailed case data from which similarities to other cases and to compelling logic from the law supports one's argument.

(continued)

Table 2.1 *(Continued)*

Dimension	Psychology	Law
Methodology	Experimental: Control through experimental design or statistical regression allows the scientist to eliminate rival hypotheses so that conclusions can be deduced about the main variables under investigation.	Case Method: Analyses of the particulars in a case allows the investigator to draw parallels to other cases or to construct a narrative that encompasses the details into a tightly woven whole.
Criterion	Conservative: The usual criterion is $p < .05$, or that results must occur fewer than one time in twenty to be accepted.	Expedient: To resolve the case at hand, the criterion may be a "preponderance" or more than 50%, "clear and convincing" or more that 75%, or "beyond a reasonable doubt" or more than 90% of the weight of the evidence to produce a verdict.
Principles	Exploratory: Encourages a multiplicity of theories that are falsifiable or that can be tested and found wanting.	Conservative: The predominant theory in a case prevails based on the coherence of the facts to statutes and to stare decisis or precedent cases.
Latitude of Courtroom Behavior	Limited: Restricted to the rules of evidence and the attorney's questions or, in amicus curiae briefs, to the questions posed by the attorneys or judge.	Broad: Within the rules of procedure and evidence, and within courtroom decorum, can introduce a wide variety of evidence in a desired sequence with as vigorous a style as befits a successful presentation of the case.

EPISTEMOLOGY: OBJECTIVITY VERSUS ADVOCACY

The task of the psychologist offering expert testimony is to seek the truth. The scientist is supposed to be as delighted in the disproof as in the proof of a favored theory, because then science will be closer to finding law describing the nature of and mechanisms underlying the phenomenon in question. The law recognizes this goal of science, as can be seen in one of the four prongs of the *Daubert v. Merrill* (1993) decision that replaced the *Frye* test regarding admissibility of expert testimony (see A. K. Hess, Chapter 22, in this volume, for greater treatment of *Frye* and *Daubert*). The prong relies on Karl Popper's (1989) criterion of falsifiability of scientific theories; that is, a theory should be so operationally specific that it can be tested and found false. (This is an interesting example of the penetration of the philosophy of science into the court's thinking; Levine & Howe, 1985.) The goal of science, for Popper, is the construction of theories that are successively more accurate representations of nature. Cacioppo, Semin, and Berntson (2004) draw contrasts between the idealized Science they term "scientific realism," by which ultimate truths are to be discovered, and "scientific instrumentalism," by which we learn about empirical relationships that reflect some approximation of realism. Cacioppo et al.'s goal is integration. This is a healthy antidote to deconstructionism, in which knowledge is wholly attributable to context, and which has held sway for a few decades; it is also a way for law and psychology to share an approach to knowledge.

On the other hand, the Anglo-American concept of law grew out of the trial by ordeal; that is, if one party were not telling the truth or did not have God on his or her side, then trial and tribulation would reveal which party was on the side of Right and which was in league with the Devil. Thus, the combat between good and evil was replayed in the adversarial trial. As we were being weaned from the rack and the dunking chair between the fifteenth and nineteenth centuries, advocates in courts replaced these physical tests with argumentation. It is now the task of the attorney to present the most telling case for his or her client (Stern, 1998). This advocacy proceeds through carefully crafted rules and procedures. The search for justice is more important than truth in the particular case. Stern writes, "*Fair* refers to a case well tried by both parties with an opportunity to present evidence and arguments. It is hoped that from such fairness the truth will emerge—but this is not always the case" (p. 103). For example, the basis for the exclusionary rule, and the public's angst over this rule, is founded on the idea that excluding evidence obtained in a way that violated the rules of evidence and procedure is better than including it, no matter how probative, compelling, or definitive that evidence is regarding the guilt of an alleged perpetrator. The law is structured so that it does not reward violation of the rules of justice.

CAUSATION OF BEHAVIOR

The task of behavioral science is to find causes for actions. These causes can be internal, as in the case of biological factors, or external, as in the case of environmental influences. In both cases, the scientist seeks deterministic explanations. From a legal perspective, one cannot be held accountable for a cause beyond one's control. A biologically based failing or a social learning regimen that compromised the individual's ability to control his or her own decision making would be deterministic in the sense that free will could not be exercised and individual legal responsibility would be negated. The law holds a person with moral sense legally responsible. Definitions of moral sense most often involve the cognitive ability to understand moral issues and the freedom from defects to exercise that understanding. If the law is to work, it must hold individuals responsible or there would be an excuse for every human action. Just as a person may attribute positive actions to his or her own traits, negative events could be externally attributed.

Lawyers and the public share the assumption that people exercise free will. Such attributions influence life-or-death determinations, as shown in Sundby's (1997) research. He studied the effects of expert witnesses, lay experts, and friends and family members as witnesses in the penalty phase of capital murder cases. Professional experts were viewed negatively by jurors in two-thirds of the cases but mentioned as positively influential by one-fifth of the juror references, a difference more pronounced in defense witnesses seeking to help avoid the death penalty for the guilty party than in prosecution expert witnesses. Consider a juror's reaction to an anthropologist's testimony that the defendant's background impelled his violence when he found someone else had fathered his daughter. The juror exclaimed, "Give me a break! Like we're supposed to believe it was just one of those macho things" (p. 1133). Another juror reacted to a social scientist's explanation about eyewitness identification errors, which are instances of external factors affecting a person's sincerely felt judgments, as "insulting"; another called the expert a "charlatan. . . [who said] you can't trust your own perceptions" (p. 1133). Even jurors who had similar drug experiences, described during the juror selection process and probably accepted by the defense as potentially empathic, said, "Yeah, well, I went through that and I didn't end up a killer," and "I've done this stuff. . . . I've used it. . . . Even so, when you do the drugs you know it's illegal, you know it's wrong, so I just believe you're responsible for your actions" (p. 1137). The presumption of personal responsibility seems augmented by what social psychologists term the "fundamental attribution error." Suffice it to say, "experts' explanations of human behavior that run contrary to notions of free will are hard to sell to the jury" (p. 1139).

THE NATURE OF "LAW"

Psychology uses the term "law" in the sense of descriptive laws. Law is something hidden in nature, a truth to be discovered, as with the law of gravity. For example, Latane (1981) wondered whether the failure of people to report a crime they witness can be understood in social psychological terms. Intrigued by the Kitty Genovese case in which at least 39 people heard her screams as she was being murdered, Latane wanted to see whether the witnesses' failure to report a crime followed a lawful relationship. He found that the diffusion of responsibility, or the impact of the victim's entreaty, was a function of the message's strength, immediacy, and the number of other potential interveners present. This multiplicative function is expressed by the psychophysical power function where the nth (e.g., sixth) person has less impact on the witness than the nth −1 (fifth) person present at a crime scene, accounting for the diffusion of responsibility phenomenon. The task of science is to find such lawful relationships, or empirical generalizations.

   After research establishes lawful relationships, the practitioner fits the relevant scientific findings to the specific case. For the forensic psychologist this means determining, for example, whether cross-racial eyewitness identification research findings are applicable to the particulars in the specific case, or whether the expert witness's perception that a parent's temper in a particular case renders him or her less fit to discharge parental responsibilities than other alternatives or whether the clinical judgment is inadequate because it is based on speculation rather than established empirical foundations.

Lawyers use the term "law" in a prescriptive sense. Behavior has a value that calls for its elicitation or, more often, its inhibition. For example, society values charity, so it codifies charity as meriting a tax deduction; if an HIV carrier knowingly has sex with unsuspecting partners, we codify and prosecute such activity because we deem it harmful. Codification is what the law needs because it deals with specific cases. For larger unresolved issues, the law often waits for science to develop methods such as DNA testing or truth-detecting devices. The courts can wait for social changes; this is happening in the case of workplace sexual relations, which became an issue with the advent of women's ascending organizational hierarchies. The court waits for the ripening of cases that lead to changes in the law by legislative means or by landmark court decisions.

KNOWLEDGE

Knowledge is justified belief that is normative and replicable. The laws are public, and the method section in research reports should be detailed enough to allow for others to repeat the experiment or to confirm or fail to find the phenomenon at issue. Although the single case study can reveal a phenomenon's existence or help us see the process underlying the phenomenon, the law of large numbers helps us increase the power of our statistical analyses in a nomothetic study, enabling us to reveal the generalizability of an effect.

In contrast, the law is based on statutes covering classes of behaviors, but it operates through the single case. The application of the law is doctrinal, operates on a case-by-case basis, and relies on settled law, *stare decisis* (stand by a decided matter), or the previously decided case. The law must decide the case, whereas the psychologist can defer a decision in the face of ambiguous results in favor of conducting more research.

The goal of the law is closure on important issues. Judge Brandeis wrote: "It is more important that the applicable rule of law be settled than it be settled right" (cited in Wrightsman, Nietzel, & Fortune, 1994, p. 18). The law, or certainly its portrayal on televised courtroom proceedings and the incessant drumbeat of the talk shows, is contemporary society's version of the Middle Ages' morality plays. Plea bargaining is an example of the law's satisfaction with a case being closed, although many people feel justice was violated by the "cutting of a deal." A sense of veridicality or of a just world with a balance of crime and punishment seems to underlie this feeling people hold about plea bargaining.

Currently, psychology and law are sharing more from each other's traditional knowledge bases. Psychologists in the legal arena increasingly rely on the case method, as can be seen in the following chapters that cite cases with the same ease as they cite empirical studies. Increasingly, courts have admitted research findings from social scientists as evidence, and lawyers are learning about experimental design and statistical analysis just as psychologists are learning about case citations. Still, there is a fundamental difference in what psychologists and lawyers consider an adequate basis for knowledge.

Methodology is tied to knowledge. Psychology has roots in both philosophy and science, but the latter has been its dominant model. Like the physical and biological sciences, psychology studies phenomena through the use of controls, be they experimental or statistical. The critical difference between science and art is that science can use controlled studies, or hold certain conditions constant while varying other conditions. Historians can speculate about counterfactual conditions, such as what might have happened if Cleopatra did not have her alluring charms or if Hitler had listened to Rommel about the Calais versus Normandy landing site for the D-day invasion of continental Europe. A lawyer can wonder about whether his or her client would have killed someone but for the alcohol and work stress the client experienced that presumably led to the murder. Neither the historian nor the lawyer can replicate the conditions and use a control group to see whether their alternative hypothesis is correct. However, psychologists can conduct studies to determine the effects of punishment on group performance or the effectiveness of a Minnesota Multiphasic Personality Inventory or an inkblot indicator in predicting suicide, or, in the case of counterfactual conditions, set up studies on the effects of hindsight bias (Roese, 1997).

Benjamin, Rogers, and Rosenbaum (1991) provide an early and exemplary example of psychological research in the court. The Coca-Cola Company was charged under the then new Federal Food and Drug Act of 1906 with marketing and selling an adulterated beverage containing an ingredient harmful to health, caffeine. The government and Coca-Cola both assembled an array of medical expert witnesses, but because the charges involved caffeine's role as "a drug that makes one forget he is tired" (p. 596) and previous research was confined to motor responses and lacked experimental controls, Coca-Cola sought a psychologist's services. Hollingworth, lacking money and because he "had as yet no sanctity to preserve" (p. 593), accepted the assignment with several conditions. Aware of the suspicions with which people view privately sponsored research, of the "unclean" or nature of applied research (p. 594), and of the potential for the misuse of the research in advertising, Hollingworth structured the agreement so that he could publish the research in academic journals whatever the results and that Coca-Cola could not use the research in its advertising.

Hollingworth used a multimethod approach, testing several cognitive processes alone and in combination, including perception, association, attention, motor speed and steadiness, and judgment and discrimination, assessed by color naming, identifying word opposites, daily diary records of sleep, health and alertness, mental calculations, and discrimination reaction times as dependent measures. He hired his wife, Leta Stigger Hollingworth, to conduct the research (as a married woman, she was ineligible for work in her profession, teaching children). She ran blind testing sessions: examiners did not know the caffeine dosages that they gave to the subjects, and subjects did not know what dosage they ingested. Using placebos, employing counterbalanced administrations of dosages, controlling for diet, and measuring the effects of the caffeine through the course of the day, the Hollingworths generated some 64,000 data points.

In contrast to the Hollingworths' research, one of the government's medical witnesses testified that caffeine produces congested cerebral arteries in rabbits. Cross-examination revealed that the researcher killed his test animals by hitting them on the head with a stick, "congesting" the arteries. Research presented by the government and by Coca-Cola, excepting the Hollingworths', was replete with flawed experimental designs, misinterpreted results, failure to use quantitative measures where possible, use of excessive quantities of caffeine atypical of customary use, and administering caffeine with other drugs, confounding the caffeine effect! (The perspicacious reader will note that the same arguments and errors are made in more contemporary cases, such as whether massive doses of saccharine were fed to mice in the 1970s controversy concerning a saccharine-cancer causal relationship or whether the Cox-2 inhibitor pain relief drug, Vioxx, was taken off the market because of research that was based on biased subject samples, heavy and constant dosing of the drug, and unwarranted interpretations of the research.) Observers of the trial and leading medical journals hailed the Hollingworth research for its rigor, scope, and findings. It was still being cited 22 times in a literature search of the Science Citation Index and Social Science Citation Index for the 1983 to 1988 period (Benjamin et al., 1991, fn. 48).

Those familiar with court cases will not be surprised that the case did not go to the jury. The judge ruled that caffeine was not an added, adulterated ingredient but was natural to the drink, directing a verdict in favor of the defendant.

Harry Hollingworth was elected president of the APA in 1927. He helped industrial psychology shed some of academia's scorn and contributed to industrial-organizational psychology's uninterrupted involvement with the law to this day. Leta Stetter Hollingworth (1928) wrote the classic text on adolescent psychology, following G. S. Hall's (1904) two-volume classic and helping to establish the developmental perspective in psychology.

CRITERIA

Changes in systems are costly. Consequently, psychological research adopted a standard that calls for results so unusual that only 1 time in 20 can we attribute the differences obtained to a chance occurrence and then require replication of the results. Of course, many factors affect this standard, including faulty research design, inclusion of so many variables that significant findings are inevitable (family-wise error rates), serendipitous findings, and unscrupulous researchers who falsify data, making replication another touchstone for psychological research. Psychologists presenting research or clinical findings in legal arenas parenthesize their work by citing limiting conditions, or they will be highly vulnerable on cross-examination and may be misrepresenting both their work and the state of certainty in the field.

Whereas the legal system needs the immediate resolution of the case at issue, a decision resulting from research in science often requires expensive retooling of a system. For example, research that showed student ratings of their professors highly correlated with the ease of the professors' grades and lax course requirements may require reconsideration of the value of student ratings in determining promotion, tenure, and salary, as well as the development of alternative measurement strategies (Greenwald, 1997). Research showing the superiority of a method of teaching children to read requires expensive retraining of teachers; if the research is flawed, a generation of children may suffer. Consequently, research uses conservative statistical criteria.

The law requires resolution in the particular case. Shorn of the luxury of deferring a decision, the courts established standards for cases based on the gravity of the charges and outcomes. Consequently, legal thresholds consist of a preponderance of the evidence in favor of one side (more than 50%), clear and convincing evidence (what Kagehiro, 1990a, equates to 75% certainty), and evidence beyond a reasonable doubt (Kagehiro's 90% level of certainty). Note that the most compelling level of legal evidence approaches only the minimal level of difference that psychological research accepts.

PRINCIPLES

In some ways, the principles undergirding law and psychology are reciprocal to their respective criteria. The conservative scientific criteria are balanced by the encouragement of alternative hypotheses and a multiplicity of theories that vie to explain phenomena. The law, too, is an exercise in developing alternative hypotheses to explain the facts and matters of law in a way that is compatible with victory for the side propounding each theory. Although encouraging alternative explanations on the individual case level, the law tends to be conservative with regard to legal principles. The law moves when circumstances are compelling. Otherwise, stare decisis, or the precedent, rules. Appellate courts may elect not to hear a case because the issues are not yet "ripe"; they await more case law, law review papers, and discussion in other forums before considering an issue ripe. For example, commentators have speculated that the number of Blacks on the Nicolle Simpson-Ron Goldman murder trial jury led to the acquittal of O. J. Simpson, a Black man accused of killing two White people. However, if the jury did engage in nullification, or the ruling by a jury on their sense of justice gainsaying the law, this issue has not ripened enough for the U.S. Supreme Court to hear. Whether jury nullification occurred, how often it occurs, whether there are concrete cases available to consider, and whether jury discretion is adequately defined are questions that could gather momentum and call for the law's attention.

LATITUDE OF COURTROOM BEHAVIOR

The forensic psychologist's practice encompasses three roles: the expert witness, the consultant, and the amicus curiae, or friend of the court. As an expert witness, the psychologist is confined to presenting evidence through questioning by the attorney retaining the expert and through cross-examination by the opposing counsel. The opposing counsel tries to diminish the impact of the expert's testimony or even to use it to discredit the side that hired the expert. The consulting psychologist can help an attorney build a case, select jurors, and prepare materials for motions or strategies of presenting evidence (including witness preparation) and attacking adverse evidence. The psychologist serving as an amicus curiae might conduct research, review literature, conduct attitude surveys in cases involving change of venue due to a prejudiced jury pool, or help construct briefs to persuade the court regarding a psychological issue. Occasionally, the judge will hire a consulting psychologist, as in the case of a court monitor who examines whether a school or prison under court order is meeting the court's edicts. Each of these roles serves the attorney or the judge who retained the psychologist and requires the psychologist to work within the parameters established by the rules of evidence and procedure, the attorney's direction, and the judge's wishes.

The attorney, on the other hand, has great latitude to gather evidence to the limits of the client's resources, to develop a theory most favorable to the client to secure witnesses, to file motions, to conduct voir dire (to determine witness or juror competence), to order the sequence of presentation of witnesses and evidence, and to choose the tone of the advocacy. The psychologist may advise, but the attorney controls the decisions in managing the legal case.

PROSPECTUS FOR A VIGOROUS FORENSIC PSYCHOLOGY

The interaction between psychology and law, or forensic psychology, over the past century can be described in several ways. Certainly, forensic psychology as *psychology in the law* has a continual history of contributions. Psychologists have been working with delinquents and with families in distress and determining competence and sanity for over a century. If one considers forensic psychology as *psychology by the law,* or the regulation of practice by various statutes, laws, ordinances, and regulations, then psychological practice, as with the rest of our society, has developed with an eye to legal issues. Simply consider the impact of employment law (hiring office help or taking in a partner or psychological assistant), the Health Insurance Portability and Accountability Act, Americans with Disabilities Act, or licensing issues (the changing nature of continuing education or the licensing concerns of the psychologists testifying in a case in a state or province in which they are not licensed) to realize the penetration of legal issues into one's daily practice.

Forensic psychology has become an interstate practice as trials in one state employ expert witnesses imported from other states (see A. K. Hess, Chapter 22, in this volume). This raises questions about the portability of the psychologist's license. In McLuhan's "global village," in which electronic communication has shrunk distances and times, the expert witness may be called on to testify in another country. This raises interesting questions in addition to licensure issues. It makes knowledge of laws in other national jurisdictions important. Thus, the forensic psychologist from the United States might benefit from knowing *Regina v. Mohan* (1994), *Regina v. Lavallee* (1990), and *Syndicat Northcrest v. Anselem* (2004), just as the Canadian psychologist would benefit from knowing the *Daubert-Joiner-Kumho* trilogy. Each set of cases describes the entry of the expert witness and defines expert testimony in, respectively, Canadian and U.S. courts. For both practical purposes and for one's intellectual growth, developing an international forensic psychology perspective may become another aspect of psychology by the law and psychology of the law.

However, it is in *psychology of the law* that we have seen the most explosive growth. Münsterberg's and Marston's initial forays into "legal psychology" may have been met with frustration and failure, but as much as the law has penetrated into psychology's practice, so has psychology penetrated the law, and this penetration will accelerate in the near term. There are a number of exciting areas worthy of exploration. Consider several examples.

COGNITIVE PSYCHOLOGY AND TRADEMARK AND COPYRIGHT INFRINGEMENT

A baby clothing store opened call "Gnu 4 U." They have not advertised, relying on word of mouth to establish their reputation. If another store opened called "New for ewe" selling animal feed, or lambskin coats, would this constitute trademark infringement? Would a kosher French restaurant called "Nu, for Vous" be different enough in product and signage to avoid trademark infringement? These are questions a cognitive forensic psychologist might explore.

EXPERIMENTAL DESIGN BIAS AND DEMAND CHARACTERISTICS

DNA testing has been in the news because it is a tool used to free people condemned to the death sentence. It received iconic status on the *CSI* (crime scene investigation) television shows as conclusive beyond doubt. Yet, consider that DNA evidence is merely a set of markings that require a trained technician to read the squiggles. Thompson (1999) has shown how biased such a reading can be: Consider, for example, the following notation I recently observed in the laboratory notes of a forensic DNA analyst.

> [Detective] phoned—suspect know crip gang member—keeps "skating" on charges—never serves time—this robbery he gets hit in head w/Barstool—left blood trail. [Detective] wants to connect his guy to the scene—DNA—if Blood on swab. (p. 313)

This is a virtual textbook definition of demand characteristics. The technician has but one sample and the excerpted description. Would a methodologist help develop a procedure, perhaps with five samples of which one is the suspected one, which would cut down on the biasing effects of the traditional laboratory testing? Of course, there would be added expense, but one can ask, What is a wrongful conviction worth? And how many of those released from death row are wrongfully released, as well as wrongfully convicted? If this example is not compelling enough, consider that fingerprinting requires the same type of inference, and it, too, has been recently examined for the same biasing effects as described for DNA (Begley, 2004). We are not suggesting that either method is invalid, just not infallible. And both are in need of examination concerning the fact that neither is collected in controlled laboratory conditions but in the chaos of a crime scene, both are analyzed without checks we would use in a social psychology experiment for biasing effects, and both rely on "magical numbers" such as a "match on nine points" of fingerprint whorls that might need more verification.

DETECTING DECEPTION

Exciting developments in detection of deception such as use of brain imaging (Windham, 2004) involve what might be termed forensic neuropsychology. More fruitful research concerning brain imaging and voice stress analysis might replace the seemingly interminable quest for a lie detector. Work by Ekman (Ekman & O'Sullivan, 1991) on facial expression as a means to detect deception continues to be a rich resource for criminal investigators and intelligence agencies. Consider how more enriching is Griffin's (2004) research that shows the "eyes are right when the mouth is wrong," a study in discrepant modes of emotional expression.

EMOTIONAL SUPPRESSION

Emotional suppression, or not responding or muting a response to an emotionally charged situation, is a phenomenon with import for forensic psychology. For example, the expert witness may be challenged as follows:

ATTORNEY: Doctor, is it? Can you prescribe medicine?
PSYCHOLOGIST: No, sir. I am a doctorate of philosophy in clinical psychology.
ATTORNEY: So you run rats or something like that but would not know a cadaver from a candle holder!

At this point, the successful psychologist would engage emotional suppression and respond educationally, telling the court and jury about how psychology can bring something of probative value to deciding the case at hand. On the other hand, if psychologists did not engage in emotional suppression, they might get temporary satisfaction by a retort such as "We run rats, but we do not run after ambulances." The psychologist who replies in this way might best reconsider further forensic work. In one case, an attorney during voir dire whispered in my ear, "Hess, Hess. Isn't that a Nazi name?" expecting me to respond to what the court did not hear. Richards (2004) describes the cognitive consequences of concealing feelings. The successful witness will discover ways to reframe the situation and avoid the negative consequences, such as stressful physiological responses and temporary cognitive declines (Richards & Gross, 2000), of suppressed emotion.

It is common for the expert witness to be privy to information that would help the other side by virtue of being involved in planning conferences. The psychologist must engage in withholding that information, requiring emotional suppression. As psychology has turned from behavioral and cognitive eras to entering an era in which we will be focusing on emotions, it is interesting to see DePrince and Freyd's (2004) work on how we handle traumatic stimuli, and Bonnano, Papa, Lalande, Westphal, and Coifman (2004) show that the flexible use of emotional suppression is superior to its blanket use or failure to be used.

Emotional suppression has been shown to block recall (Richards & Gross, 2000), which has implications for both witnesses and jurors who are exposed to gruesome crime scene evidence and reconstructions. Although there are costs to emotional suppression, there are also benefits and ways of using emotional suppression that merit attention. For example, if one reappraises the traumatic event and uses various distancing procedures, the impairment of cognitive processes may be limited or even eliminated. Perhaps this is the wisdom behind analyzing a patient's hostility toward a psychotherapist as actually being directed toward a person from the patient's past; thus, the analyst can distance himself or herself from the hostile attack. Similarly, accepting that the cross-examining attorney's job is to impeach the witness's testimony, sometimes by hook or by crook, will bleach out the emotional aspects of the attack. With the advent of the era of emotions in psychology, many exciting avenues for both basic and applied research, with particular relevance to forensic psychology, await us.

DISCRETION: AN ONGOING CONCERN

Discretion is woven into the justice system. It will be an area of continual concern. Recently, Fields (2004b) reported the U.S. Sentencing Commission, designed in the mid-1980s to eliminate capricious sentencing disparities, found that minorities serve longer sentences than their White counterparts. He found that prosecutors and judges cooperate in setting charges in such a way as to induce suspected conspirators to testify on their partners in crime. This can result in huge disparities in sentences, based on which criminal rushes to take the deal first. While such plea bargaining may be a necessary investigative and prosecutorial tool, it does result in a type of justice that leads to inequities. How such decisions are made will continue to be a fruitful line of research by forensic psychologists.

TERRORISM

Only since the World Trade Center and Pentagon terror attacks has terrorism captured the public's attention. However, social scientists such as Lopez (1979; Garrigan & Lopez, 1977), who assembled learning packets to educate professionals about terrorism, and Paust (1984), who examined the types of terrorism-specific statutes that might impact potential terrorist acts have been concerned about terrorism for decades. Terrorism poses some interesting questions for forensic psychologists. As more aggressive tactics are used to extort information from captured terrorists, questions are raised as to the use of force. Parkes's (2000) work concerning sudden death in mental patients when restraint force is used is applicable to interrogation techniques. Corrado (1981) criticizes the mental disorder model often invoked to explain terrorists. The correctional psychologist will be called on to face immense challenges in managing mental health issues because the detained terrorists will become the charges of the prisons and the correctional psychologist (Summerill, 2004).

METHODOLOGY

As discussed earlier, law and psychology have different approaches to methodology, with law using the case and psychology using more nomothetic methods.

Fishman (2004) tackled this question and has proposed a journal in which forensic cases are collected and aggregated data can be used. Thus, a case involving whether a mentally retarded murderer could form intent might be compared to a set of cases that are similar on various parameters. In this way, Fishman, much like Westen and Weinberger's (2004) more general proposal for clinical psychology, would combine the best of the idiographic (case) and nomothetic (group data) approaches.

On a more molecular level, Mumma (2004) proposed an intraindividual idiographic approach to case data collection that allows measurement, with error estimates that are crucial to the *Daubert* criteria, over time to see fluctuations in cognitive measures (and extendable to emotional and psychopathological assessments). His method allows for factor analysis, reminiscent of both Cattell's (1966) P-technique and Kelly's (1955) individual factor structure method. Of course, these are empirical and not experimental approaches in the sense that no controls are invoked and cause and effect cannot be asserted. Psychology still faces the desire for thickly textured and ecologically grounded individual cases with the equally appealing discovery of laws of behavior applicable across individuals. It is exciting to see these new attempts to close the chasm between methodologies.

CODA

Münsterberg presented psychology as having an immense contribution to make to the courts; Wigmore disabused Münsterberg and psychology of the idea that either one was ready to make an impact on the justice system (see Bartol & Bartol, Chapter 1, in this volume). The question facing us is not whether psychology and the law are ready for psychology to have an influence throughout the legal system. Research reviewed in this chapter and in this volume makes clear that the science and artful application of psychology to legal issues has matured to the point where it would be remiss of society, of the law, and of attorneys to ignore these developments. The questions facing us concern how such collaborations are to be managed: How do we promote psycholegal research? How do we establish relationships with appropriate bodies so that legal practice and legislation can be informed by psychological research? How can we improve the standards of practice of forensic psychology? All of these activities we should do in the service of making ours a more just society.

> Justice, justice shall you pursue, that you may thrive and occupy the Land the Lord your God is giving you. (Deuteronomy 16:20, Hertz 1981)

REFERENCES

Begley, S. (2004, June 4). Despite its reputation, fingerprint evidence isn't really infallible. *Wall Street Journal*, p. B1.

Benjamin, L. T., Rogers, A. M., & Rosenbaum, A. (1991). Coca-Cola, caffeine, and mental deficiency: Harry Hollingworth and the Chattanooga Trial of 1911. *Journal of the History of the Behavioral Sciences, 27*, 42–55.

Bersoff, D. N. (1995). *Ethical conflicts in psychology.* Washington, DC: American Psychological Association.

Blumenthal, J. A. (1998). The reasonable women standard: A meta-analytic review of gender differences in the perceptions of sexual harassment. *Law and Human Behavior, 22*, 33–58.

Bomser, A. H., Costa, J. G., Friedman, J. R., Pomerantz, S. A., Post, J. A., Prowda, J. B., et al. (1995). A lawyer's ramble down the information superhighway. *Fordham Law Review, 64,* 697–850.

Bonnano, G. A., Papa, A., Lalande, K., Westphal, M., & Coifman, K. (2004). The importance of being flexible: The ability to both enhance and suppress emotional expression predicts long-term adjustment. *Psychological Science, 15,* 482–487.

Brainerd, C. J., & Reyna, V. F. (2002). Fuzzy trace and false memory. *Current Directions in Psychological Science, 11,* 164–169.

Brainerd, C. J., Reyna, V. F., & Brandse, E. (1995). Are children's false memories more persistent than their true memories? *Psychological Science, 6,* 359–364.

Cacioppo, J. T., Semin, G. R., & Berntson, G. G. (2004). Realism, instrumentalism, and scientific symbiosis: Psychological theory as a search for truth and the discovery of solutions. *American Psychologist, 59,* 214–223.

Cattell, R. B. (1966). *The scientific analysis of personality.* Chicago: Aldine.

Committee on Ethical Guidelines for Forensic Psychologists. (1991). Specialty guidelines for forensic psychologists. *Law and Human Behavior, 15,* 655–665.

Conner, T. A. (1996). Ethical and clinical issues in involuntary psychotherapy. *Psychotherapy, 33,* 587–592.

Cooper, J., Bennett, E. A., & Sukel, H. L. (1996). Complex scientific testimony: How do jurors make decisions? *Law and Human Behavior, 20,* 379–394.

Corey, G., Corey, M. S., & Callanan, P. (1993). *Issues and ethics in the helping professions* (4th ed.). Monterey, CA: Brooks/Cole.

Corrado, R. R. (1981). A critique of the metal disorder perspective of political terrorism. *International Journal of Law and Psychiatry, 4,* 203–309.

Daubert v. Merrell Dow Pharmaceuticals, Inc., 113 S. Ct. 2786 (1993).

DeAngelis, T. (1995, June). Juror stress can influence final verdict. *APA Monitor,* 5–6.

DePrince, A. P., & Freyd, J. J. (2004). Forgetting trauma stimuli. *Psychological Science, 15,* 488–497.

Diamond, S. S. (1990). Scientific jury selection: What social scientists know and do not know. *Judicature, 73,* 178–183.

Diamond, S. S., Casper, J. D., Heiert, C. L., & Marshall, A. (1996). Juror reactions to attorneys at trial. *Journal of Criminal Law and Criminology, 87,* 17–47.

Doctor whose study tied Joe Camel to kids goes on an odd journey. (1997, February 21). *Wall Street Journal,* p. A1.

Eich, E., Macaulay, D., Loewenstein, R. J., & Dihle, P. H. (1997). Memory, amnesia and dissociative identity disorder. *Psychological Science, 8,* 417–422.

Eisendrath, S. J. (1996). When Munchausen becomes malingering: Factitious disorders that penetrate the legal system. *Bulletin of the American Academy of Psychiatry and Law, 24,* 471–481.

Ekman, P., & O'Sullivan, M. (1991). Who can catch a liar? *American Psychologist, 46,* 913–920.

Exner, J. E., Jr. (1993). *The Rorschach: A comprehensive system: Vol. 1. Basic foundations* (3rd ed.). New York: Wiley.

Fields, G. (2004a, December 2). In drug sentences, guesswork often plays heavy role. *Wall Street Journal,* p. A1, A8.

Fields, G. (2004b, November 24). Commission finds racial disparity in jail sentences. *Wall Street Journal,* p. A4.

Fishman, D. B. (2004). Background on the "Psycholegal Lexis Proposal": Exploring the potential for a systematic case study database in forensic psychology. *Psychology, Publica Policy, and Law, 9,* 267–274.

Foley, L. A. (1993). *A psychological view of the legal system.* Madison, WI: Benchmark & Brown.

Forsterlee, L., & Horowitz, I. A. (1997). Enhancing juror competence in a complex trial. *Applied Cognitive Psychology, 11,* 305–319.

Garrigan, T. B., & Lopez, G. A. (1977, June). *Terrorism: A problem of political violence.* Presented at the Summer Institute of Consortium for International Studies Education, Colorado Springs, CO.

General Electric Company v. Joiner, 118 U.S. Ct. 512 (1997).

Goble, G. W. (1955). Nature, man and law. *American Bar Association Journal, 41,* 403.

Greene, E., Coon, D., & Bornstein, B. (2001). The effects of limiting punitive damage awards. *Law and Human Behavior, 25,* 217–234.

Greenlaw, P. S., & Kohl, J. P. (1992). The ADA: Public personnel management, reasonable accommodation and undue hardship. *Public Personnel Management, 21,* 411–427.

Greenwald, A. G. (1997). Validity concerns and usefulness of student ratings of instruction. *American Psychologist, 52,* 1182–1186.

Griffin, Z. M. (2004). The eyes are right when the mouth is wrong. *Psychological Science, 15,* 814–821.

Hall, G. S. (1904). *Adolescence, Its Psychology and Its Relation to Physiology, Anthropology, Sociology, Sex, Crime, Religion and Education, two volumes.* New York: D. Appleton.

Hallinan, J. T. (2004, November 30). In malpractice trials, juries rarely have the last word. *Wall Street Journal*, p. A1.

Hamman v. County of Maricopa, No. CV-87-0070-PR, Arizona Supreme Court, January 15, 1989.

Harper's. (1987, April). p. 6. (Excerpted from, C. M. Sevilla's "Great moments in courtroom history," Champion, December 1986.)

Hollingworth, L. S. (1928). *The psychology of the adolescent*. New York: D. Appleton.

Hertz, J. H. (1981). *The Pentateuch and Maftorahs* (2nd ed.). London: Soncino Press.

Holmes, G. R., Offen, L., & Waller, G. (1997). See no evil, hear no evil, speak no evil: Why do relatively few male victims of childhood sexual abuse receive help abuse-related issues in adulthood? *Clinical Psychology Review, 17*, 69–88.

In re Hofmaster, No. Cl-88-2177, Minnesota Court of Appeals, January 17, 1989.

Jaffee v. Redmond, 116 S. Ct. 1923, 1996 WL 315841 (U.S. Ill.). June 13, 1996.

Judge protects scientists' statements. (1997, August 8). *Chronicle of Higher Education*, p. i.

Kagehiro, D. (1990a). Defining the standard of proof in jury instructions. *Psychological Science, 1*, 194–200.

Kagehiro, D. (1990b). Psycholegal research on the fourth amendment. *Psychological Science, 1*, 187–193.

Kalish, D. E. (1997, September 24). Thief tainted man's identity: Dogged by bogus data computers bred years of stigma. *Record*, p. B1.

Karon, B. P., & Widener, A. J. (1997). Repressed memories and World War II: Lest forget! *Professional Psychology, 28*, 338–340.

Kelly, G. A. (1955). *The psychology of personal constructs*. New York: Norton.

Knowles, A. D., & McMahon, M. (1995). Expectations and preferences regarding confidentiality in the psychologist-client relationship. *Australian Psychologist, 30*, 175–178.

Konecni, V. J., & Ebbesen, E. B. (1982). *The criminal justice system: A social psychological analysis*. San Francisco: Freeman.

Koocher, G. P., & Keith-Spiegel, P. (1998). *Ethics in psychology: Professional standards and cases*. New York: Oxford University Press.

Kuhn, D., Weinstock, M., & Flaton, R. (1994). How well do jurors reason? Competence dimensions of individual variation in a juror reasoning task. *Psychological Science, 5*, 289–296.

Latane, B. (1981). The psychology of social impact. *American Psychologist, 36*, 343–356.

Levine, M., & Howe, B. (1985). The penetration of social science into legal culture. *Law and Policy, 7*, 173–198.

Lopez, G. A. (1979). Teaching about terrorism: Notes on methods and material. *Terrorism, 3*, 10–25.

Mumma, G. H. (2004). Validation of idiosyncratic cognitive schema in cognitive case formulations: An intraindiviudal idiographic approach. *Psychological Assessment, 16*, 211–230.

Newman, L. S., & Baumeister, R. F. (1996). Toward an explanation of the UFO abduction phenomenon: Hypnotic elaboration, extraterrestrial sadomasochism, and sirious memories. *Psychological Inquiry, 7*, 99–126.

Office of Juvenile Justice and Delinquency Prevention. (1997). *Sharing information: A guide to the Family Educational Rights and Privacy Act and Participation in Juvenile Justice Programs*. Washington, DC: U.S. Department of Justice.

Oregon v. Miller, 300 Or. 203, 709 P. 2d 225. Decided November 5, 1985.

Parkes, J. (2000). Sudden death during restraint: A study to measure the effect of restraint positions on the rate of recovery from exercise. *Medical Science and the Law, 40*, 39–44.

Paust, J. J. (1984). Terrorism and "terrorism-specific" statutes. *Terrorism: An International Journal, 7*, 233–239.

Pedersen, D. M. (1987). Sexual differences in privacy preferences. *Perceptual and Motor Skills, 64*, 1239–1242.

Pedersen, D. M. (1997). Psychological functions of privacy. *Journal of Environmental Psychology, 17*, 147–156.

Pell v. Procunier, 417 US 817 (June 24, 1974).

Perreira v. State, No. 87SC75, Colorado Supreme Court, February 6, 1989.

Pezdek, K., Finger, K., & Hodge, D. (1997). Planting false childhood memories: The role of event plausibility. *Psychological Science, 8*, 437–441.

Popper, K. (1989). *Conjectures and refutations: The growth of scientific knowledge* (5th ed.). London: Routledge.

Redmount, R. S. (1965). The use of psychologists in legal practice. *Practical Lawyer, 11*, 23–38.

Regina v. Lavellee. (1990). 1 S.C.R. 852.

Regina v. Mohan. (1994). 2 S.C.R. 9.

Richards, J. M. (2004). The cognitive consequences of concealing feelings. *Current Directions in Psychological Science, 13*, 131–134.

Richards, J. M., & Gross, J. J. (2000). Emotional regulation and memory: The cognitive costs of keeping one's cool. *Journal of Personality and Social Psychology, 79,* 410–424.

Rinas, J., & Clyne-Jackson, S. (1988). *Professional conduct and legal concerns in mental health practice.* Norwalk, CT: Appleton & Lange.

Roese, N. J. (1997). Counterfactual thinking. *Psychological Bulletin, 121,* 133–148.

Saks, M. J., Hollinger, L. A., Wissler, R. L., Evans, D. L., & Hart, A. J. (1997). Reducing variability in civil jury awards. *Law and Human Behavior, 21,* 243–256.

Shaver, K. G., Gilbert, M. A., & Williams, M. C. (1975). Social psychology, criminal justice, and the principle of discretion: A selective review. *Personality and Social Psychology Bulletin, 1,* 471–484.

Sheffey, S., & Tindale, R. S. (1992). Perceptions of sexual harassment in the workplace. *Journal of Applied Social Psychology, 22,* 1502–1520.

Simon, R. I. (1987). Epilogue: We are belegaled. In *Clinical psychiatry and the law* (pp. 467–487). Washington, DC: American Psychiatric Association.

Smith, V. L. (1991). Prototypes in the courtroom: Lay representations of legal concepts. *Journal of Personality and Social Psychology, 61,* 857–872.

Steininger, M., Newell, J. D., & Garcia, L. T. (1984). *Ethical issues in psychology.* Homewood, IL: Dorsey Press.

Stern, P. (1998). *Preparing and presenting expert testimony in child abuse litigation: A guide for expert witnesses and attorneys.* Thousand Oaks, CA: Sage.

Stinson, V., Devenport, I. L., Cutler, B. L., & Kravitz, D. A. (1996). How effective is the presence-of-counsel safeguard? Attorney perceptions of suggestiveness, fairness, and correctability of biased lineup procedures. *Journal of Applied Psychology, 81,* 64–75.

Stockdale, M. S. (1993). The role of sexual misperceptions of women's friendliness in an emerging theory of sexual harassment. *Journal of Vocational Behavior, 42,* 84–101.

Summerall, J. (2004). Detention and the war on terrorism: How far can the government go? *Corrections Today, 66,* 20–31.

Sundby, S. E. (1997). The jury as critic: An empirical look at how capital juries perceive expert and lay testimony. *Virginia Law Review, 83,* 1109–1188.

Swenson, L. C. (1993). *Psychology and law for the helping professions.* Belmont, CA: Brooks/Cole.

Syndicat Northcrest v. Anselem. (2004). S.C.C. 47.

Tarasoff v. Regents of the University of California, Supp. 131. California Reporter, 14 (1976).

Terman, L. M. (1918). Expert testimony in the case of Alberto Flores. *Journal of Delinquency, 3,* 145–164.

Thompson, W. C. (1999). Examiner bias in forensic DNA testing. In *Psychological expertise and criminal justice.* Washington, DC: American Psychological Association.

Towell, N. A., Kemp, R. I., & Pike, G. E. (1996). The effects of witness identification masking on memory and person perception. *Psychology, Crime & Law, 2,* 333–346.

Tracey, M. (1998, January/February). Be aware of malpractice risks when using electronic office devices. *National Psychologist,* p. 17.

Tromp, S., Koss, M. P., Figueredo, A. I., & Tharan, M. (1995). Are rape memories different? A comparison of rape, other unpleasant, and pleasant memories among employed women. *Journal of Traumatic Stress, 8,* 607–627.

Viederman, M. (1995). The reconstruction of a repressed sexual molestation fifty years later. *Journal of the American Psychoanalytic Association, 43,* 1169–1195.

Vitek, W. (1997). Privacy's place: The role of civility and community in a technological culture. *Ethics and Behavior, 7,* 265–270.

Vitek, W., & Jackson, W. (Eds.). (1996). *Rooted in the land: Essays on community and place.* New Haven, CT: Yale University Press.

Walzer, R. S., & Miltimore, S. (1993). Mandated supervision, monitoring, and therapy of disciplined health care professionals: Implementation and model regulations. *Journal of Legal Medicine, 14,* 565–596.

Weiner, I. B. (2002). How to anticipate ethical and legal challenges in personality assessments. In I. N. Butcher (Ed.), *Clinical personality assessment: Practical applications* (2nd ed., pp. 126–134). New York: Oxford University Press.

Westen, D., & Weinberger, J. (2004). When clinical description becomes statistical prediction. *American Psychologist, 59,* 595–613.

Windham, C. (2004, November 30). Brain activity shows who is telling lies, new study indicates. *Wall Street Journal,* D-4.

Wrightsman, L. S., Nietzel, M. T., & Fortune, W. H. (1994). *Psychology and the legal system* (3rd ed.). Monterey, CA: Brooks/Cole.

CHAPTER 3

Legal Research for the Social Scientist

TYLER L. COX

SOCIAL SCIENTISTS today face an ever-expanding legal arena reaching every facet of our society. This chapter provides the novice legal researcher with a working knowledge of our judicial system, commonly used research techniques, and various legal resources available.

AMERICAN JUDICIAL SYSTEM

The American judicial system is a collective of constitutions, statutes, administrative regulations, executive decrees, and court rulings, each interacting with the others to various degrees and with various consequences. It is the Constitution of the United States that provides the foundation of our legal system and therefore serves as an important starting point for any legal researcher.

PREEMPTION DOCTRINE

The Tenth Amendment of the U.S. Constitution specifies that those powers not delegated to the United States by the Constitution, or specifically prohibited to the states by it, are reserved to the states or to the people. Therefore, issues that have not been preempted by the U.S. Constitution or federal law are reserved to the state constitutions. The preemption doctrine is a very important step to consider when conducting legal research because it allows researchers to refine their search between federal and state law.

The preemption doctrine can also be applied to the state constitutional level, but to a greater extent. Counties and municipalities are generally organized under charters that serve as their constitutions and are superior to all ordinances enacted by these entities. However, charters are inferior and subject to state and federal law, and many state constitutions severely limit the amount of authority counties and municipalities may have.

LEGISLATIVE ENACTMENTS

Statutes are formal written enactments of a legislative body, whether federal, state, county, or city. Basically, statutes are the laws of the land for which that legislative body has authority. The U.S. Congress, for example, enacts federal statutes that are superior to state statutes enacted by state legislatures.

Statutory law is important for the legal researcher because statutes are the law from which our legal system functions. It is also important to note that statutes not only address criminal and civil law, but they include other enactments that guide our judicial system, such as court procedures and professional privileging.

AGENCY REGULATIONS

The U.S. Congress and state legislatures often need detailed guidance regarding the implementation and enforcement of statutes and therefore delegate some of their power to administrative agencies. For example, President Truman established the National Institute of Mental Health, but during the Kennedy administration, Congress granted the agency authority to monitor the nation's community mental health centers. Congress, however, retains oversight responsibility and budgetary power over the agency.

The president of the United States and state governors can direct an agency within their respective authority by issuing executive orders and proclamations that have the effect of law. Sometimes, chief executives seek advice from their attorneys general regarding an area of law, and the resulting opinion may offer the legal researcher insight into the rationale and fundamental argument for or against an executive order.

Regulations issued by administrative agencies, such as tax regulations issued by the Internal Revenue Service, are legally binding and considered administrative law. Agency functions are commonly referred to as *quasi-judicial* because they hold hearings, issue orders, and offer advisory opinions similar to the actions of a court.

CASE LAW

The aggregate of reported cases interpreting statutes, regulations, and constitutional provisions form a body of jurisprudence called case law. Once a court has laid down a principle of law, its decision becomes authority, or binding precedent, in the same court and in other courts of equal or lower jurisdiction in subsequent cases where the same principle of law is again in controversy. This policy of precedent is referred to as *stare decisis* and forms the foundation of the American common law system.

State and federal court systems have their own common law and case law histories. Therefore, it is important to note that what may be a recognized principle of law in one system may not be as strongly recognized in another. For example, the federal common law has not recognized a general physician-patient privilege but has indicated a disposition to recognize a psychotherapist-patient privilege. State legislatures adopting statutory law recognizing the physician- and psychotherapist-patient privileges have mostly circumvented recognition of the privilege by state courts.

Courts can only function within the jurisdiction that grants them authority to decide a matter in controversy. Jurisdiction not only refers to geographic location but also to subject matter, such as bankruptcy and probate courts. Generally, state courts have jurisdiction to decide issues regarding state law and conflicts arising within their physical borders. Federal courts have jurisdiction over federal laws, constitutional issues, conflicts where the federal government is a party, and controversies between citizens of different states. Court systems, whether state or federal, are divided into districts based on jurisdictional authority.

Federal Court System

The federal court system is divided into 13 circuits below the U.S. Supreme Court. Federal courts of appeals, or circuit courts, have jurisdiction to hear appeals of decisions from federal administrative agencies and district courts, commonly referred to as trial courts. The current federal judicial circuit is as follows:

First Circuit: Maine, Massachusetts, New Hampshire, Puerto Rico.

Second Circuit: Connecticut, New York, Vermont.

Third Circuit: Delaware, New Jersey, Pennsylvania.

Fourth Circuit: Maryland, North Carolina, South Carolina, Virginia, West Virginia.

Fifth Circuit: Louisiana, Mississippi, Texas.

Sixth Circuit: Kentucky, Michigan, Ohio, Tennessee.

Seventh Circuit: Illinois, Indiana, Wisconsin.

Eighth Circuit: Arkansas, Iowa, Minnesota, Missouri, Nebraska, North Dakota, South Dakota.

Ninth Circuit: Alaska, Arizona, California, Guam, Hawaii, Idaho, Montana, Nevada, Northern Mariana Islands, Oregon, Washington.

Tenth Circuit: Colorado, Kansas, New Mexico, Oklahoma, Utah, Wyoming.

Eleventh Circuit: Alabama, Florida, Georgia.

D.C. Circuit: Washington, D.C.

Federal Circuit: Washington, D.C.

LEGAL RESEARCH STRATEGIES

Generally, research sources can be categorized into two types: primary sources and secondary sources. Secondary sources are summaries, discussions, characterizations, and even restatements of primary sources of authority. Treatises, restatements, legal encyclopedias, law journals, and law reviews are all secondary sources that provide legal information known as secondary authority and offer an effective starting point for legal research. However, it is important to remember that secondary authority is not the law and therefore not binding on the courts. Never limit your legal research to secondary authority.

Secondary sources are an important step in the legal research process because they frequently provide numerous citations to primary authority. Constitutional law, statutory law, administrative law, and case law are considered primary sources or authority because our law is derived from them.

ANALYZING LEGAL ISSUES

When first approaching a legal research problem, it is important to gather as much information as possible about the issue in order to define the structure of your search. Finding the best terms to describe a legal question will save time and resources that could otherwise be spent preparing your case.

A common method used to gather key terms about a legal issue is to categorize information based on parties involved, facts of the case, legal theory forming the basis of the action, defense to the action, and relief sought. For example, consider an issue where an individual was civilly committed to a state psychiatric hospital and subjected to medical restraint without consent. A legal researcher may categorize information in these terms:

- *Parties involved:* psychiatric patient, state commissioner of mental health, psychiatrist, psychologist.
- *Facts of the case (including where the action arose and matters involved):* state psychiatric hospital, psychotropic medication, treatment, medical restraint, mental illness.
- *Legal theory forming the basis of the action* (including state or federal law): state administrative agency law on treatment of the civilly committed, state seclusion and restraint policy, due process, equal protection, cruel and unusual punishment, Eighth and Fourteenth Amendments to the U.S. Constitution.
- *Defense to the action:* state police power, sovereign immunity.
- *Relief sought:* individual liberty, damages.

Some category systems also address jurisdiction when that issue becomes difficult to determine or when federal and state law share jurisdictional authority. For example, some environmental and tax conflicts are regulated by both state and federal law.

GENERAL REFERENCE SOURCES

Once key words and phrases have been identified and categorized, legal researchers must then determine the applicable resource material. Given that there are millions of cases, with thousands being added each year, beginning a search with case law would be tedious and time-consuming. Additionally, some questions about the law can be answered without searching through several resource materials, and in some circumstances all that may be needed is a legal treatise or encyclopedia.

Legal treatises offer a general overview of a specific area of law, such as health law, criminal law, and probate law. *Hornbooks* and the *Nutshell Series* published by West Group are a couple of the most commonly used series of treatises and can be found at most law libraries and some computer-assisted research services. Treatises are very helpful for a legal researcher who is searching for a basic foundation of an area of law, but because the law constantly changes they should not be relied on as the only source for specific information.

Legal encyclopedias are similar to general encyclopedias in that both contain alphabetically arranged summaries of topics with an index provided for easy access. The difference between treatises and legal encyclopedias is that encyclopedias tend to concentrate on case law and offer references to case authority, whereas treatises provide only a general overview of an area of law.

Corpus Juris Secundum (*CJS*), *American Jurisprudence 2d* (*Am Jur 2d*), and *American Law Reports* (*ALR*) are three of the most commonly used legal encyclopedias. The philosophical approach subscribed to by *CJS* presents the legal researcher with an extensively cited description of a wide variety of legal topics. In fact, most pages contain few lines of text with many lines of citations to cases and materials arranged by state. *Am Jur 2d* has a similar format but limits citations to emphasize leading decisions. *ALR*'s approach is to emphasize the development of a point of law across jurisdictions while providing extensive annotations to primary sources of law. All three sets include an index for easy reference and remain current with replacement volumes and pocket supplements that are located in the back covers of each volume.

Most legal resources contain pocket supplements inserted in the back covers to account for the constantly changing legal system. When using these legal resources, it is extremely important to check the pocket supplements or the applicable replacement volumes to ensure that the material reviewed is current.

JOURNALS, REVIEWS, AND RESTATEMENTS

Social scientists are familiar with scholarly journals devoted to specific areas of research and social concern. Legal periodicals are similar in format, with a focus on a specific area of law; due to a relatively short publication cycle, they cover current topics in the law. Generally published by private companies or law schools, legal periodicals are aimed toward practicing attorneys specializing in particular fields of law. The *Journal of Psychiatry and Law* and the *American Journal of Law and Medicine* are examples of journals devoted to a specific area of law.

Bar association periodicals such as the American Bar Association's *ABA Journal*, privately published periodicals such as Lawyers Weekly, Inc.'s *Lawyers Weekly United States*, and online periodicals such as American Lawyers Media's *Law.com* offer articles focusing on a variety of legal issues. Internet legal news and resource sites such as West Group's *FindLaw.com* also offer articles on current legal topics but with an integrated Web-based search engine geared specifically for legal research.

Law reviews are a special type of legal periodical where the editorial management is controlled by student editors. Most law schools have at least one law review. Some law reviews are oriented toward a specific area of law or practice, such as the University of Alabama's *Law and Psychology Review.* Law reviews generally contain detailed discussions and analysis of aspects of the law that may not be covered in other sources. Additionally, legal researchers benefit greatly from the extensive footnotes and citations to primary sources most law review articles contain.

Comprehensive periodical indexes or digests are available for assisting with researching law reviews, bar association journals, and legal newspapers. The most frequently used index is H. W. Wilson Company's *Index to Legal Periodicals.* The *Index* contains references to articles from more that 850 journals and 300 law reviews from the United States, Canada, Great Britain, Ireland, New Zealand, and Australia. Legal indexing systems are comparable to general indexing systems in that they are arranged alphabetically by both topic (e.g., mental health, civil rights) and author. As with all legal resources, it is important to research more than one topic or key word within a given area. For example, articles regarding mental capacity may be found under "Mental Health," "Psychiatry," "Psychology," and "Insanity."

In 1923, a group of prominent American judges, lawyers, and teachers established the American Law Institute (ALI) with the purpose of promoting clarification and simplification of the law through a restatement of basic legal subjects. The *Restatements* series covers 12 fields of law, such as torts and contracts. The ALI also publishes the *Model Code* series that has a great deal of prestige among judges and scholars. Since the *Model Code* series was developed to assist legislatures with establishing statutory law, several areas of the series, such as the *Model Penal Code* and the *Model Code of Evidence*, provide the novice legal researcher with the essential principles that form the foundation of our judicial system as well as possible future trends in statutory law.

STATUTES AND REGULATIONS

Statutory law, a source of primary authority, is codified in one of two ways. Some states use a subject matter organization system, but most use a numbering system with a topical index arranged alphabetically by subject matter. For example, consider the issue of involuntary treatment of the mentally ill in Wisconsin. Key terms such as "mental capacity," "treatment," and "psychotropic medication" should be compiled. Under "treatment" in the topical index of West Group's *Wisconsin Statutes Annotated* is found "Mentally Deficient and Mentally Ill Persons, this index." Under "Mentally Deficient and Mentally Ill Persons," the researcher will find "Psychotropic medication, guardian and ward, consent or refusal" along with the numbered reference to the particular statutes.

When conducting statutory research, novice legal researchers should remember that each state legislature has adopted a statutory code for its own state. Therefore, a statutory requirement or exception for New York child custody cases may differ slightly, or greatly, from requirements found in California statutes.

Most states provide access to their statutes and constitutions on the Internet but with little commentary and even fewer citations to case law than their paper counterparts. Online research services such as Westlaw.com, Lexis.com, and VersusLaw.com offer comprehensive case summaries and citations interpreting each statute. Cornell Law School's Legal Information Institute located at www.law.cornell.edu offers nonsubscription access to online statutes and constitutions for all 50 states, the District of Columbia, and the federal government with additional access to administrative codes and some case law.

Federal statutory law can be found online and in an official code published by the U.S. government entitled the *United States Code* (U.S.C.). Two unofficial annotated codes are the *United States Code Service* (U.S.C.S.), published by Lexis-Nexis, and the *United States Code Annotated* (U.S.C.A.), published by West. Federal administrative law can also be found online or in an official code entitled the *Code of Federal Regulations* (C.F.R.), published annually, and the *Federal Register*, published daily. The *Federal Register* also publishes some documents issued by the Office of the President, such as presidential proclamations and executive orders. State administrative materials, however, are more difficult to find than federal materials and may not be updated as frequently. Sometimes, the best source for state regulations is the administrative agency itself.

The rules for citing statutes, as well as case law, are too extensive for a general overview of legal research. However, knowledge of the basic citation form will be beneficial when a legal researcher has a citation to a particular statute without a copy of the actual text. Basic federal statute citations follow the title, code, and section format. For example, 42 U.S.C. § 1983 would read: Title 42 of the *United States Code*, section 1983. For additional legal citation formats, novice legal researchers should consult *The Bluebook: A Uniform System of Citation*, published by the Harvard Law Review Association in conjunction with the *Columbia Law Review,* the *University of Pennsylvania Law Review,* and the *Yale Law Journal.* The *Bluebook* is considered the handbook for legal citations.

CASE LAW

With the number of decided cases in the millions and more being added each year, legal researchers would benefit from a working ability to find and read case law.

Court Reports

Court reporters are a series of books that contain the full text of judicial opinions. These reports are primarily decisions of federal and state appellate courts. Trial court decisions, for the most part, are generally not published because they may lack precedential value or simply be redundant. In fact, the current trend has been to report fewer opinions on a percentage basis, leading some jurisdictions to establish court rules indicating when reporting is necessary.

Many nonreported opinions are available online or in print form. The problem with these opinions is that most jurisdictions either do not permit them to be used as precedent or may allow them to be used only after the court and opposing counsel have been given notice. Whether or not nonreported opinions are allowed as precedential authority, they may help the legal researcher develop a feel for the current judicial thinking within a certain jurisdiction.

The *United States Reports* (U.S.) is the official reporter for the U.S. Supreme Court. The Supreme Court generally has only one term each year, beginning in October and ending around June. This is known as the October Term. The opinions are initially issued separately as "slip" opinions immediately after being handed down. They are subsequently published in "advance sheets" presented in reporter format before sufficient opinions accumulate to form a bound volume. As this reporting process can take several months or years, it is important to always check advance sheets and slip opinions when researching a legal issue.

The *Supreme Court Reporter* (S. Ct.), published by West, and the *United States Supreme Court Reports, Lawyers' Edition* (L. Ed. and L. Ed. 2d), published by LexisNexis, are the most commonly used unofficial reporters that publish decisions of the U.S. Supreme Court. Another source for Supreme Court opinions is the *United States Law Week* (USLW), published on a weekly basis by the Bureau of National Affairs. The USLW is a two-volume set containing complete decisions of the Court in one volume and abstracts of many lower federal and state court opinions in another.

Decisions of the federal courts of appeals can be found in the *Federal Reporter* (F., F.2d., and F.3d.), and federal district court opinions are published in the *Federal Supplement* (F. Supp. and F. Supp 2d.). Both reporter series are published by West.

State court decisions are similarly published in official and unofficial reports. Some states publish their own reports, such as New York's *New York Reports* and *New York Miscellaneous Reports;* other states rely on the National Reporter System published by West. The National Reporter System covers the opinions of the courts of last resort and intermediate appellate courts. These opinions are divided into seven regional reporters arranged by geographic divisions:

- *Atlantic Reporter* (A. or A.2d): Connecticut, Delaware, Maine, Maryland, New Hampshire, New Jersey, Pennsylvania, Rhode Island, Vermont, District of Columbia (Court of Appeals).
- *North Eastern Reporter* (N.E. or N.E.2d): Illinois, Indiana, Massachusetts, New York (Court of Appeals), Ohio.
- *North Western Reporter* (N.W. or N.W.2d): Iowa, Michigan, Minnesota, Nebraska, North Dakota, South Dakota, Wisconsin.
- *Pacific Reporter* (P. or P.2d): Alaska, Arizona, California (Supreme Court), Colorado, Hawaii, Idaho, Kansas, Montana, New Mexico, Oklahoma, Oregon, Utah, Washington, Wyoming.

- *South Eastern Reporter* (S.E. or S.E.2d): Georgia, North Carolina, South Carolina, Virginia, West Virginia.
- *South Western Reporter* (S.W. or S.W.2d): Arkansas, Kentucky, Missouri, Tennessee, Texas.
- *Southern Reporter* (So. or So.2d): Alabama, Florida, Louisiana, Mississippi.
- *New York Supplement* (N.Y.S.2d): New York.
- *California Reporter* (Cal. Rptr. or Cal. Rptr. 2d): California.

FINDING THE LAW

The citation of a case published in a reporter includes the name of the case, the volume of the reporter, the name of the reporter, the page number in the reporter on which the case begins, and the year the case was decided. For example, *Washington v. Harper,* 494 U.S. 210, 110 S. Ct. 1028 (1990) would be found in volume 494 of the *United States Reports* on page 210. Because the *United States Reports* is the official publication of U.S. Supreme Court decisions, it appears first in the citation followed by the unofficial reporter. Therefore, *Washington v. Harper* can also be found in volume 110 of the *Supreme Court Reporter* beginning on page 1028; the decision was handed down in 1990. Consult *The Bluebook: A Uniform System of Citation* for more formal rules of case citation.

When a legal researcher has only a list of topics and no case citations, a good starting point is a legal digest. Digests are a series of books containing abstracts of cases organized by subject with an index provided for easy access. The most commonly used digest system is published by West and offers individual state, regional, federal, and state/federal digests. The American Digest System published by West covers all cases from all jurisdictions, both state and federal, and includes the *Century Digest* (1658–1896), the *Decennial Digest,* and the *General Digest.* Most states have their own digest and are included in the regional digests. The *Federal Digest* includes federal cases and the *United States Supreme Court Digest* covers U.S. Supreme Court decisions.

Once a specific case has been located that addresses the researcher's topic, the next step is to make sure that the decision has not been overruled and is still good law. Citations found in legal digests often include case history if the case has been overturned. *Shepard's Citations,* published by LexisNexis, is the most comprehensive system used by legal researchers to determine whether a case has been affirmed, reversed, or overruled. The process for verifying the authority of a citation is commonly referred to as "Shepardizing."

Using *Shepard's Citations* can be cumbersome for novice legal researchers because its abbreviations and case citations are not commonly used by other legal publications. For example, federal cases found in the *Federal Supplement* are designated in *Shepard's* as "FS," not "F. Supp."

When Shepardizing a citation, the appropriate *Shepard's Citations* publication must be selected. There are specific *Shepard's* publications for each reporter in the National Reporter System, including every state reporter, federal reporter, and U.S. Supreme Court reporter. Volumes covering federal administrative rules and regulations, law review articles, state and federal statutes, and court rules are also available. Each volume includes a date on the spine or inside its cover that should correspond with the year the case being Shepardized was decided.

Once the appropriate *Shepard's Citations* volume has been selected, find the appropriate reporter series within the publication, for example, *South Eastern Reporter* or *South Eastern Reporter 2d*. The names of the reporter series and the volume numbers for that series appear at the top of each page. Page numbers that correspond to citations located in the specific reporter volume are presented in boldface on each page of the appropriate *Shepard's* publication. For example, *Washington v. Harper*, 494 U.S. 210 (1990) is found in *Shepard's United States Reporter Citations* for 1990 on a page that has volume 494 at the top and number 210 in boldface in one of the columns.

After a case citation has been located in the appropriate *Shepard's* publication, the legal researcher will notice a list of citations directly under the case notation. Citations shown in parentheses are additional reporters in which the case appears. These citations are generally referred to as parallel citations. Citations without parentheses are listed in reverse chronological order and refer to other cases citing the original researched case. Letter abbreviations may precede some citations, giving the history and treatment of the case. Use the tables of abbreviations at the front of each volume to decipher each treatment letter, such as "o" for overruled and "d" for distinguished.

When Shepardizing a case, remember that a decision may be upheld one year and overruled another. Therefore, following a case through all subsequent *Shepard's* volumes and supplements is important.

LAW LIBRARIES AND ONLINE SERVICES

Law libraries can be found on law school campuses and are generally open to the public and offer the widest variety of resource material. Although law librarians are usually not allowed to provide legal advice, they can offer information and assistance about navigating the legal research process. Most university and larger public libraries contain some primary sources but may offer limited support materials and lack experienced law librarians. State and federal courthouses generally contain law libraries but usually limit access to judges, attorneys, and law students. Historically, law firms contained small law libraries, and some still do, but the current trend for firms and attorneys has been the ease and convenience of online legal research.

Internet-based legal research systems, such as Westlaw.com, Lexis.com, and VersusLaw.com, have simplified the research process by providing most of the previously discussed material online. For example, Westlaw offers an online citation research service called KeyCite that functions similarly to *Shepard's Citations*, which is offered online by Lexis. All three services offer extensive search engines that allow legal researchers broader access to the law while decreasing the amount of time conducting research. However, these services are subscription-based and can be costly for a novice legal researcher.

STOPPING

The key to legal research is to know when to stop. When novice legal researchers face volumes of reporters containing an enormous amount of case law addressing several points within a single topic, they can easily become frustrated, intimidated, and discouraged. They tend to spend many hours in the law library on an endless search for that perfect case. Rarely is there a perfect case. Familiarity with the research materials and techniques previously discussed will provide skills to narrow the search, and persistence along with experience will eliminate time-consuming mistakes. Also, remember the Loop Rule: When you start to see the same information over and over again—the same cases, the same statutes, the same regulations, the same law review articles, the same citations—then it is probably time to stop.

PART TWO

APPLYING PSYCHOLOGY TO CIVIL PROCEEDINGS

CHAPTER 4

Understanding Adult Domestic Law Issues: Marriage, Divorce, and Domestic Violence

KATHRYN D. HESS

DAILY WE are exposed to the issues surrounding our domestic laws. One cannot read a newspaper or magazine or view a television news broadcast without seeing both discussion of the current issues in family law policy and the impact of those policies on family members. Political party platforms in the 2004 presidential campaigns expounded on who had the right to marry, on abortion rights, and on stem cell research prerogatives. Current legislation, both federal and state, aims to define and redefine marriage. New laws affecting prenuptial agreements (Silverman, 2003), restrictions on custody agreements (McGrew, 2004), methods of obtaining a divorce (Silverman, 2004), and types of adoptions (Hwang, 2004) abound in the general media. Similarly, each day psychological practitioners deal with a plethora of changing domestic law issues.

This chapter and the next intend to provide a general working knowledge of domestic and juvenile laws and an understanding of the issues and values around which these laws and procedures evolved, without which a clinician cannot practice in domestic issues. The focus of this chapter is on specific issues of interest to the clinician in dealing with marriage, divorce, and domestic violence; Chapter 5 discusses child custody, adoptions, child abuse, and child sexual abuse. Differences in adult and juvenile court systems and domestic violence are explored in both chapters. The chapters provide a practical framework on which a clinician can develop an evaluation and a treatment plan or testimony. Finally, these chapters provide the psychologist with both a knowledge base and an agenda to develop domestic and family policy.

HOW THE DOMESTIC COURTS FUNCTION

Increasingly, the architects of our most intimate family life are no longer family and kinship ties but federal legislative statutes and the domestic courts

(Elrod, 1995). Through their judgments, domestic courts often define who will be a child's parents, as well as who is the most fit to provide the child's intimate social context and value system. Parental or custodial rights may be terminated and family relationships extensively restructured on the premise that the judge or various experts know best how a family should function, despite the fact that satisfactory family functioning cannot be dictated. In recognition of the fallacy of omniscience of experts, domestic courts in the past few years have become increasingly reluctant to intervene in ongoing family relationships any more than necessary to resolve the issues at hand. Rather, the courts are now encouraging families to reorganize themselves. Acknowledging the domestic court's conservative view toward intervention in domestic matters, it is incumbent on the clinician to formulate opinions and responses in conservative terms, sensitive to his or her personal biases and recognizing the family's essential right to self-determination.

While society generally recognizes the family's right to self-determination, a breakdown in the family structure or function can trigger court involvement. In the event that the requisite threshold of disruption occurs, the courts will intervene to mediate the family's difficulties. In these cases, the court's intervention is usually intended to minimize the disruption of the ongoing functions of the family, and the court is generally willing to allow families the opportunity to resolve their differences through negotiation and on their own terms. In the event the family members are unable or unwilling to negotiate an agreement, the court will provide a final decision that is presumably consistent with the values of the broader community. The goals of domestic jurisprudence are to achieve efficiency, harmony, and balance in the family order.

Mermin (1982) suggests a number of important services offered to society and the family by domestic jurisprudence. These services include the definition of a status in society, including minority, marriage, legitimacy, domains of responsibility, and immunity from responsibility; the settlement of domestic disputes through arbitration or negotiation and as a final authority in reaching a decision; the maintenance of order through policing, protection, and definition of the relationships between family members; the protection of the family against the exercise of excessive or unfair government power; and assurances that family members enjoy the minimum decencies of life, such as economic protection, preservation of social status, and maintenance of the individual's physical and psychological well-being.

The central purpose of the domestic court is protection. The court has traditionally executed its responsibility through a determination of fault or failure to fulfill contractual marital responsibilities, agreements for custody and visitation following the dissolution of a marriage, and provision for the support and maintenance of those deemed unable to support themselves. With the formation of the juvenile court system in the United States in the late nineteenth century, the state extended its responsibility to dominion over delinquent children and their subsequent rehabilitation. More recently, the domestic courts have begun to intervene in support of children's relationships with grandparents and other significant family members. There has also been further development of policy regarding abused and neglected children, the termination of parental rights, abortion, and foster or adoptive placement.

The domestic court's two primary values center on community standards and the continuity of family relationships. Rather than fact-finding, the court seeks remedies that assure a child's basic economic needs, with the exception of the child's safety in cases of child abuse and maltreatment (Aldous, 1997; Mermin, 1982). The domestic court is permitted broad dispositional powers and procedural limitations, especially in regard to its treatment of juveniles. The domestic court judge, more often than a judge in other courts, enlists the advice of professionals from other disciplines in identifying problems, recommending courses of action, and interpreting facts presented to the court. It is in this dynamic arena for the resolution of some of life's most intense problems that a psychologist may be asked to offer professional input.

CLINICAL CONTRIBUTIONS TO DOMESTIC COURT

The development of the family court and juvenile justice system over the past 150 years has paralleled the growth in influence of psychologists and the social sciences. Indeed, the juvenile justice system grew out of cooperative efforts of social workers and the court system to rehabilitate juvenile offenders and the identity of children in need of care. Thus, the clinician in domestic court finds clinical and judicial purposes closely tied in helping to realize the potential of the family to function in its own behalf.

In the past, input from the social sciences to the domestic court has primarily been limited to clinical input (Goldzband, 1983; Underwager & Wakefield, 1992), frequently reflecting the judgment and personal bias of the psychologist rather than scientific fact. Recent flagrant abuses by mental health professionals, centered around charges of abuse in child care facilities, raised questions about the expert's role (Wakefield & Underwager, 1992). As *Daubert* replaces the *Frye* standard for admissibility of evidence or expert testimony, the nature of psychological evidence should become more empirically oriented (Bala, 1994a, 1994b; A. Hess, Chapter 22, in this volume).

In contrast to juvenile court issues, the domestic courts have done little to solicit empirical input from psychologists on domestic issues. Melton (1984) pointed out that Chief Justice Burger cited "common sense and intuition" as his primary authority on domestic issues. The reliance of the court on common sense and intuition is consistent with the "reasonable man hypothesis" and "rule of reason" concepts, both foundations of our jurisprudence. Melton points out that the use of intuition and unsupportable clinical lore represents a major threat to the application of empirical information in the courtroom because the legal system traditionally relies on previous case law and decisions as a basis for current decisions. Grossman and Okun (2003) write that for legal professionals to attend to what psychologists have to offer, the work must be framed in legal terms. Legal professionals employ a case approach rather than the nomothetic approach of scientific psychology. Therefore, one of the psychologist's tasks is to present empirical findings in a way that can be understood by the court.

TRADITIONAL AND CONSTITUTIONAL PRINCIPLES RELATED TO DOMESTIC JURISPRUDENCE

With these points in mind, the question arises: What does the psychologist have to offer beyond common sense and clinical lore? For the psychologist to effectively contribute to the domestic courtroom, he or she first needs to know how the court functions.

PHILOSOPHICAL UNDERPINNINGS OF DOMESTIC COURT

Traditionally, the domestic court protected and supported the integrity of the family unit. Domestic jurisprudence relied on common law concepts of the family as the basis for decisions in domestic proceedings. Common law, or English case law, enforces long-standing customs and traditions. The focus of the contemporary domestic court has shifted in the past 150 years from the extended family to the family in society. The former educational, social, and economic safety nets of the extended family are now the province of social agencies and government.

Simultaneously, the Industrial Revolution, changing concepts regarding the roles of women, children, and families, and efforts to establish a more pluralistic democracy mark changes in domestic law. As society became more integrated with a philosophical and economic stake in the child, changes occurred in the role of education and equal participation in social institutions, and the perception of children as under the dominion of parents shifted to the family as a socializing agent of the greater society. This shift can be seen in the decreased reliance on common law theory and the increase in statutory provisions.

PRINCIPLES GOVERNING THE DOMESTIC COURT

Broadly speaking, the principles and doctrines governing the domestic court are subsumed under three areas: jurisdiction, procedures, and disposition. Issues of jurisdiction relate to the basis by which the court is empowered to act in a given circumstance. Procedures reflect the judicial processes, such as giving testimony, and serve as the vehicle for offering the protection of individual rights from undue state interference. Disposition refers to the range of alternatives the court has at its disposal to implement its decisions.

Jurisdiction

Domestic court emerged from the English common law and operates because of the doctrine of *parens patriae*. The contemporary domestic courts are the direct descendants of the English chauncery court or "common court" and have responsibility for the resolution of disputes rising out of a marriage or issues involving the care or behavior of minor children.

The U.S. Constitution's Ninth and Tenth Amendments specify that functions not expressly federal are state functions. Historically, the federal courts avoided becoming involved in domestic issues. Yet, as traced earlier, when society assumed more safety net functions, a number of cases and laws show the growing federal role in family relations, for example, in decisions such as *In re*

Gault (1967) and legislation such as the Uniform Marriage and Divorce Act (UMDA; 1979), the Uniform Services Former Spouses Protection Act (USFSPA; 1990), the Civil Service Retirement Spouse Equity Act (1984), the Child Support Recovery Act (1992), the Uniform Child Custody Jurisdiction Act (UCCJA; 1979), the Parental Kidnapping Prevention Act (PKPA; 1980), the International Parental Kidnapping Crime Act (1993), and the Family and Medical Leave Act (FMLA; 1993). The increased federal activity has primarily centered around constitutional issues of due process and rights to privacy. For example, the UMDA, the UCCJA, and the PKPA are federal responses to the growing problems of interstate disputes regarding marriage, child custody, and the removal of children by noncustodial parents. These acts are essentially recommended statutory legislation, which individual states are encouraged to enact in an effort to create a uniform set of laws regarding marriage, child custody, and the interstate transportation of children of disputed custody. On an international level, the Hague Conference on Private International Law adopted the Hague International Child Abduction Convention (1980), the Hague Convention on Protection of Children and Cooperation in Respect of Intercountry Adoption (1993), and the Hague Convention on Protection of Minors, a revision of the 1961 Hague Convention concerning jurisdiction and law regarding minors (2000).

Many have argued for the removal of domestic issues from the court system and greater use of the less adversarial administrative processes, such as arbitration, collaboration, conciliation, mediation, and education. But there has been little change in the domestic court's jurisdictional rights. On the contrary, the courts have vigorously defended their jurisdiction as the final arbiter of domestic issues. Yet, the courts seek psychological help to strengthen and improve their decisions. In California, for example, family law attorneys who have been granted the designation "specialist in family law" by the state bar must include courses in psychology in their continuing legal education (Kirkland, 2003).

In contrast to the common law basis for the jurisdiction of the domestic court, the juvenile justice system is a relatively novel judicial program. The juvenile justice system clearly relies on the parens patriae concept. It developed from social and psychological theories in the late nineteenth and early twentieth centuries and operates in the interests of the children brought before the court.

The parens patriae concept casts issues as more civil than criminal in nature. A child may have come to the court's attention due to criminal activities, but the psychologist needs to know that the court's thrust is more civil, more rehabilitative toward the child, and more informal on connecting the circumstances that caused the child to be brought before the court. Consequently, the juvenile court is not bound by many of the due process issues, rules of evidence, and right to representation that govern adults in criminal courts. From its inception, the juvenile court was intended to be rehabilitative in purpose and to focus on correcting the circumstances antecedent to the child's appearance before the court. The procedures in juvenile court are generally informal and closed to public observation, and they invest broad discretionary powers in the juvenile court judge.

Procedures

Procedures within domestic jurisprudence, exclusive of the juvenile court, are similar to other jurisdictions (civil or criminal), facilitating the presentation and illustration of relevant facts while protecting the rights of the individuals from undue government intrusion. The domestic court follows such standard evidentiary rules in the presentation of testimony as due process procedures, rights of appeal, and other procedures protected by the Constitution or by precedent. Because the juvenile court system provides guidance and rehabilitation for the child rather than assessing responsibility and punishment, state courts have often held that the procedural safeguards enjoyed by adults are unnecessary to protect the interests of the child. The reasoning is that under the parens patriae doctrine, the court is charged with protecting the interests of the child; therefore, there is presumed to be no conflict of interest between the needs of the state and the needs of the minor in question.

Because the state's needs and the child's needs are presumed to be the same, procedures in juvenile court are relatively unstructured, informal, and directed toward the clinical needs of the children it serves, as opposed to being more procedure bound. The unstructured nature of the procedures of the juvenile court has been justified by the need to protect children from the stress of traditional court procedures as well as to shield their juvenile records from others, such as adult criminal justice system agents.

Disposition

The court acts to protect vulnerable family members and to see that children are placed in a setting assuring their well-being. Thus, the court assumes or assigns custody or guardianship of the children involved, establishes responsibilities, and makes judgments regarding financial arrangements for the interests of the children and other family members.

The court can encourage parental participation with the child through the assignment of custody and visitation and in programs such as counseling or therapy. The court can terminate parental rights if, in the court's opinion, the present living conditions are a threat to the life or well-being of the child. In the disposition of a case, the clinician can be of particular service to the court by evaluating workable possibilities and suggesting alternatives that foster the reorganization of the family. That is, in a custody agreement between two parents who have trouble agreeing or are very hostile to each other, the court can order very structured visitation, spelling out when and where each visit will occur, who will provide transportation to and from the visits, and under what conditions exceptions can be made. Or, if the findings of the consultant warrant, the arrangements can be flexible and open-ended with few guidelines.

Summary

In each of these areas, jurisdiction, procedures, and disposition, the court may call on the advice of expert witnesses such as social workers and psychologists. The psychologist may be asked to assess the present living conditions and emotional atmosphere of the home, the competency of a minor, the legitimate religious beliefs of a parent refusing medical treatment of a child's illness, the suitability of prospective parents or children for adoption or foster placement, grounds for termination of parental rights, determination for treatment as a juvenile or an adult in a criminal case, and the ability of parents to act in the best interest of their children.

GUIDELINES FOR THE PSYCHOLOGIST IN DOMESTIC COURT

When working with domestic law cases, the practitioner must be knowledgeable regarding a number of professional guidelines. Depending on the case, the psychologist in domestic court may need to consult the following:

- "Guidelines for Child Custody Evaluations in Divorce Procedures" (American Psychological Association [APA], 1994).
- *Guidelines for Psychological Evaluations in Child Protection Matters* (APA, 1998).
- "Ethical Guidelines for Forensic Psychologists" (Committee on Ethical Guidelines for Forensic Psychologists, 1991).
- "Ethical Principles of Psychologists and Code of Conduct" (APA, 2002).
- *Record Keeping Guidelines* (APA, 1993).
- "Specialty Guidelines for the Delivery of Services" (APA, 1981).
- *Standards for Educational and Psychological Testing* (APA, 1999).
- *Standards for Providers of Psychological Services* (APA, 1977).
- Additionally, child custody guidelines have been developed in some states and should be consulted if practicing in such a state.

Following these general guidelines, reports and testimony to the court should be conservative, comprehensive, and concise and should demonstrate a sensitivity to the complex emotional, psychological, and personal rights of all individuals and family members involved. Clinicians need to remember that they are not called on by the court to render a decision, but to offer an evaluation and interpretation of the psychological issues presented as relevant to the questions before the court.

Contributions by Blau (1984, 1985, 1994), Grisso (2003), Hess (1985), Melton, Petrila, Poythress, and Slobogin (1997), Shapiro (1984), Weiner (1985; Chapter 21, in this volume), and Ziskin and Faust (1988) are useful in developing forensic reports and courtroom testimony.

THEMES IN FAMILY LAW

Themes such as *parens patriae,* the basic right of people to marry, the contractual nature of marriage, competency or fitness as a parent, and the obligations existing between parents and children are woven throughout domestic law. An awareness of how these themes contribute to the normative family and the laws regarding proper relationships between family members is useful for the practitioner.

THE CONTRACTUAL NATURE OF MARRIAGE

Marriage is recognized under common law as a contract or civil partnership in which each member of the marriage is granted certain rights and charged with responsibilities, either implied or stated. Because marriage, as the fundamental family unit, is of vital importance to society, the state takes an active and continuing role in defining the expectations and relationship between marital partners and family members. Consistent with its esteemed social status, marriage is protected and regulated by statutes in all jurisdictions (Ehrlich, 1997).

As a contract, the marriage is unique, in that it not only defines a relationship between a man and a woman, it extends beyond to establish rights and obligations evolving from a person's status as a married man or woman. Marriage, usually viewed sacramentally, is a civil contract in most civilized nations and regulated by law. Society builds the family unit on it, and from it springs social relations and social obligations and duties.

Several specific conditions have been presumed to be implicit within the marital contract. The court recognizes marriage as a singular relationship between a man and a woman, and though not all jurisdictions specifically limit marriage to heterosexual unions, until recently all cases that have come before the court have restricted marriage to individuals of the opposite sex. In all jurisdictions, the courts have defined marriage between men and women of certain blood relationships as incestuous and therefore prohibited. But although statutes in all jurisdictions prohibit incestuous marriages, they differ as to what degree of consanguinity constitutes incest.

Marriage is formed by a contract and is subject to a number of conditions. These include age, competence to enter the marriage contract, full disclosure and absence of fraud, and entering the contract with free choice. If any of these conditions are not met, the marriage may be voided, annulled, or dissolved.

Psychologists have interests in marriage both as practitioners who offer marital and family therapy and as researchers who contribute to debate on public policy. An examination of marriage laws shows them to be in a state of flux. The Federal Defense of Marriage Act (1996) defines marriage as a legal union between a man and a woman and gives states the right to refuse to recognize same-sex marriages in other states. Plans are currently underway for a possible constitutional amendment banning same-sex marriages. As of March 2004, California, Connecticut, Hawaii, New Jersey, and the District of Columbia have passed domestic partnership laws which allow many of the same state benefits and protections given to married couples, such as hospital visitation rights (Swisher, 2004). Vermont has allowed civil unions since 2000. Massachusetts; San Francisco; Multnomah County, Oregon; New Paltz, New York; and the provinces of British Columbia and Ontario in Canada have recently allowed same-sex marriages. The U.S. Supreme Court has declined to review a challenge to the 2003 Massachusetts Supreme Court ruling legalizing gay marriage in that state (Greenberger, 2004).

Internationally, in 2001 the Netherlands extended full marriage rights to same-sex couples who are citizens or residents of the Netherlands (Swisher,

2004). In *Goodridge v. Department of Public Health* (2003), the supreme court of Massachusetts struck down that state's marriage law as "failing to meet the rational basis test for either due process or equal protection" (George, 2003, p. A-8). On November 2, 2004, 11 states approved bans on gay marriage. In less than one week lawsuits were filed challenging those bans. Exit polls from the 2004 elections found that although many voters opposed gay marriage, they were not opposed to civil unions or domestic partner arrangements. Most of the lawsuits center on the marriage-like benefits that are currently offered to unmarried couples, which many of the new laws restrict. The U.S. Supreme Court may ultimately rule on the marriage question, but that ruling may be years away (Rayburn, 2004).

While some jurisdictions are considering reducing premarital requirements, such as blood and health tests and residency requirements (Maclean, 1997), others are attempting to modify divorce rates by making it more difficult to get married or to obtain a divorce. Louisiana established a two-tier system of marriage licenses in 1997. The "regular" marriage license allows the couple a no-fault divorce after a six-month separation, whereas a covenant marriage license requires premarital counseling and either a two-year separation or proof of abuse, adultery, or felony prior to divorce (Goodman, 1997). Continued changes in marital laws are expected, and the marriage and couples therapist must know the current statues where he or she is practicing.

Individual Rights and Family Rights

Psychologists and the public at large recognize the legitimacy of differing statuses for groups and their subsequent differential treatment rights, depending on their present status. For example, married persons and single persons are treated differently for tax purposes, adults and minors are treated differently in terms of ability to make binding contracts, and mentally competent and mentally incompetent individuals have differing legal responsibilities. Prior to the mid-nineteenth century, domestic law decisions were generally based on civil precepts of property, with children as chattel and men as sole proprietors of the family's wealth and relationships.

With the advent of the Civil War and the equality provisions of the Fourteenth Amendment, the issue of different treatment for individuals of differing status and the whole concept of people as property became a problem for the courts. Along with such issues as civil rights, women's rights, and the availability of abortion as birth control, psychology developed with its emphasis on individual identity and personality. Drawing on this emergence of the individual, the courts reexamined questions such as rights to custody, individual and children's rights, the natural bonds between family members, and the proper developmental environment for children. Domestic rulings now implicitly address questions regarding the competency of parents to act in the interests of their children or the child's ability to act in his or her own behalf. As the child was seen as a person with emerging cognitive and emotional competencies, the courts began to take the child's wishes and even testimony into greater account.

In divorce and custody suits, this has led to the court's giving weight to the child's interest and welfare. Under the mantle of parens patriae and guided by the best interests of the child doctrine, the court acts to ensure the interests of any children involved. In the past, this has resulted in the court's radically restructuring parent-child relationships through custody, visitation, and support. In apparent recognition of the court's inability to dictate family relationships in all cases, several alternative arrangements have been developed. The courts now assign joint custody and protection of rights to visitation for the noncustodial parent and even nonparental relationships (e.g., grandparents) if they benefit the child. As has become a mantra in the quirky status of domestic law, these considerations are continually changing.

MARITAL AND FAMILY PRIVACY

Several landmark cases have redefined the concept of marital and family privacy and parents' rights to control of their children (e.g., *Pierce v. Society of Sisters*, 1925). English common law viewed a husband and a wife as "being of one body." Consequently, there developed presumptions regarding the sacredness of the marital unit and the need for protection of this unit from undue interference. In the case of *Griswold v. Connecticut* (1965), Justice Douglas drew on specified provisions from the Fourteenth Amendment prohibiting undue governmental interference:

> Specific guarantees in the Bill of Rights have penumbras, formed by emanations from those guarantees that give them life and substance. . . . Various guarantees create zones of privacy. . . . We deal with a right of privacy older than the Bill of Rights—older than our political parties, older than our school system. Marriage is a coming together for better or for worse, hopefully enduring, and intimate to the degree of being sacred. It is an association that promotes a way of life, not causes. (p. 4)

While the specifics of the *Griswold* case affirm the right of married couples to use contraceptives, its more important impact is to acknowledge realms of married life as so sacred and private that the state may not intrude.

Children are generally protected under the same rights to privacy as adults, although in some cases the courts have gone further, finding that under certain circumstances, the child's right to privacy may be superior to the interests of his or her parents (*Planned Parenthood v. Danforth*, 1976). The support for children's rights to privacy has been particularly evident in cases where children have attempted to avail themselves of community resources, such as contraception (*Carey v. Population Services International*, 1972), family planning (*Planned Parenthood v. Danforth*, 1976), and drug abuse programs and psychological testing (*Merriken v. Cressman*, 1973).

Stanton (1982) points out that when the question arises as to who controls the rights to privacy, the family or the children, the courts have generally supported a family-based theory of privacy and integrity over the individual and autonomous rights of children. Notable exceptions have occurred in situations where children, either by their actions or petition, demonstrate competency in making their own decisions (*Planned Parenthood v. Danforth*, 1976).

The courts have generally recognized a number of areas of family life as so intimate that they are protected by provisions of the Constitution and the Bill of Rights. Specifically, the courts have ruled in favor of marital privacy in areas of abortion (*Roe v. Wade*, 1973), procreation (*Skinner v. State of Oklahoma*, 1942), the marital couple's right to use contraception (*Eisendtadt v. Baird*, 1967; *Griswold v. Connecticut*, 1965), and family relationships and rearing and educating children (*Pierce v. Society of Sisters*, 1925; *Whalen v. Row*, 1977; *Planned Parenthood of Southeastern Pennsylvania v. Casey*, 1990).

PRIVILEGED COMMUNICATION AMONG FAMILY MEMBERS

Privileged communication refers to the common law or statutory rights granted to specified individuals that preserve communications from being compelled in testimony. Privileged communication is permitted in specified circumstances because the disclosure of designated information would frustrate a relationship that society has determined to be worthy of fostering and preserving. Communications between spouses enjoy the status of privilege, and consequently marital partners cannot be compelled to provide testimony regarding private communications between them. On the other hand, marital partners are not foreclosed from giving testimony if they should so elect.

Although the privacy of communications between parents and their children has generally been supported by the courts, there is no common law provision granting privileged communication to family members beyond the spouses. The defense of privacy of communication among family members has typically fallen under the scope of rights to privacy rather than of privileged communication (see *In re* A&M, 1978; Stanton, 1982). This becomes relevant in the case where a child, under no coercion, discloses a parent's drug abuse to the authorities.

A significant issue facing the clinician arises out of the common law provisions necessary to assure the status of privileged communication. Under common law, for a communication to be considered private, it must occur only between the parties involved. A third party, such as a child or other family member, being present or information relayed among parties, such as that among child-parent-therapist, may invalidate the provisions necessary for privileged communication. Because the statutes regarding privileged communication are derived through the state legislatures, clinicians should become familiar with their local statutes to assure their clients the extent and nature of the protection available under the scope of privileged communication. In particular, some jurisdictions provide that all competent and relevant evidence, unless specifically excluded by privilege, may become compelled testimony.

MARRIAGE

Marriage is a social institution, universally recognized across all cultures, although it may take various forms in different parts of the world. In Western cultures, marriage has been primarily governed by religious precepts. The early church held that marriage was a sacrament ordained by God and consummated by His hand. Ecclesiastical doctrine specified the nature and conditions necessary for the marital contract, including who could marry, the minimum age for marriage, the need for mutual consent, the purpose of marriage (procreation), and the conditions under which a marriage could be voided. These early doctrines, specified in the *Casti Connubi* and other church proclamations, were adopted with some statutory modification into English common law and the Anglican Church upon its formation by Henry VIII.

In England, the church maintained control over marriage until 1857, when jurisdiction was transferred to the statutory domestic courts. The transfer of jurisdiction from the ecclesiastical courts to domestic courts did not promote much change in the law regarding marriage. Indeed, the legislation effecting the transfer of authority stipulated that the courts base their decisions on precedents formulated in the ecclesiastical courts. In continental Europe, the Protestant clergy rejected the concept of marriage as a religious sacrament, insisting that it be honored as a contract based on civil law.

In the United States, marriage has always been considered a civil contract with special statutory status, governed by the domestic courts. All jurisdictions in the United States accept marriages performed by recognized clergy, and some jurisdictions still recognize common law marriages. The civil foundation for marriage in the United States should not imply the absence of religious influences. On the contrary, the civil statutes governing marriage reflect the adoption of virtues originating in traditional religious thought, only now adopted and administered by the civil courts.

In the United States, jurisdiction over marriage rests with the various states; consequently, a wide range of legislation has developed over the years governing marriage. These laws, particularly those concerning divorce and child custody, have frequently conflicted with one another, causing confusion when decisions in one state's jurisdiction are argued in another state. In an effort to reduce the number of conflicting statutes, the federal government has proposed several comprehensive laws for implementation in the various states, including the aforementioned UMDA, UCCJA, FMLA, USFSPA, CSREA, and PKPA statutes.

Although the U.S. Constitution does not specifically deal with marriage, the Supreme Court recognized in *Meyer v. Nebraska* (1923) that the right "to marry, establish a home and bring up children" was an essential part of the liberty guaranteed by the Fourteenth Amendment. This judgment was strengthened in *Skinner v. State of Oklahoma* (1942), in which the Supreme Court extended its view on the right to marry, writing, "Marriage is one of the 'basic rights of man,' fundamental to our very existence and survival, therefore the state cannot force sterilization since a basic premise of marriage is procreation."

Marriage has generally been viewed as a contract, relation, or condition existing between one man and one woman. In the case of *Reynolds v. United States* (1878), the court held that polygamy is not legal, although it may be permitted by religious institutions. Marriage is a contract for life that may only be terminated by the court following a formal hearing of the facts presented for divorce (*Popham v. Duncan*, 1930). Consistent with this concept of marriage for life, marriage cannot be performed for a period of time or in degrees of involvement. Although persons planning to marry may enter into antenuptial agreements regarding a broad range of property issues, the court retains the privilege of examination to verify that certain minimal provisions of disclosure, consideration, and support have been given. Individuals may not contract away the legitimate power of the court to rule in marital issues (*Popham v. Duncan*, 1930). Thus, it might be said that marriage is a partnership between two people and the state, with the state being the senior partner in the contract.

Through its statutory provisions for marriage, the state stipulates the antecedent conditions necessary for a valid marriage to take place. These qualifications to marry generally include minimum age, general physical and mental conditions, presence of voluntary consent, absence of a presently valid marriage, and limitations on consanguinity.

Dissolution of Marriage: Void and Voidable

Marriages are considered void, voidable, or valid and may be dissolved through annulment, divorce, or death of a spouse. Conditions necessary for each action to dissolve a marriage are generally specified in individual state codes regarding marriage and divorce.

A void marriage is one that is forbidden by common law or statute, or would have been forbidden had the facts been known at the time of the marriage. Some marriages are void from the outset and are never recognized. Other marriages may be voidable but are not considered void until some protest is made regarding the validity of the marriage. A marriage may be void for a number of reasons, including presence of a currently valid marriage, consanguinity or other relationships specified by statute, and, more pertinent to clinicians, violations of the presumptions governing contracts, such as competency, consent to the marriage under duress, or failure to provide full disclosure of relevant facts or medical condition prior to the marriage.

Voidable marriages generally require a petition to the court to effect an annulment. A marriage may be voidable for a number of reasons, usually reasons that violate conditions of status or the basic conditions necessary for a valid marital contract. Violations of the premises of a valid contract include incompetence or failure to understand the nature and implications of the marital contract, marriage below minimum age requirements, duress, failure to disclose material information that may be relevant to the basis or purpose of the marriage, and presence of a medical or psychiatric condition such as venereal disease, impotency, or genetic disorders that would incapacitate the individual from fulfilling the implied obligations of the marital contract.

Physical or mental difficulties having an onset following the marriage are not considered a basis for annulment (Ehrlich, 1997, p. 125). The mentally retarded may be permitted to marry provided they are competent to give consent to the marriage and the cause of their difficulties is unlikely to be genetically transmitted. The presence of a mental disorder (e.g., Schizophrenia) is not necessarily a condition for voiding a marriage. For example, if it was understood between the parties that one had a history of mental illness, and if the disorder was in a state of remission at the time of entering into the marital agreement, then the contract is valid.

A number of other conditions have been found to be a satisfactory basis for nullifying a marriage. Impotency, regardless of cause, physical or psychological, is considered a basis for nullifying a marriage (Krause, 1977). In one case, intoxication was found as a basis for nullifying a marriage on the grounds of incapacity to consent to a binding agreement, thus illustrating the need for knowledgeable consent for a contract to be binding (*Parken v. Saileau,* 1968). In specific regard to the medical or psychological basis for annulment, the courts have held that the condition in question must have existed prior to the marriage and been concealed from the spouse.

ANNULMENT

Annulment is a legal process terminating and invalidating a void or voidable marriage. The major difference between an annulment and a divorce is that an annulment is retroactive to the inception of the marriage, and a divorce is effective from the date of the decree forward, a point laden with important implications for inheritance. Consequently, the partners or heirs in an annulled marriage may have substantially different rights than in a marriage ended by a divorce.

Generally, for an annulment to be granted, the contested circumstances must have existed at the initiation of the marriage and have been concealed from the spouse. Annulment usually does not provide for permanent alimony or support obligations, although temporary support provisions may be granted, depending on the local statutes. The grounds for an annulment are similar to grounds for a divorce and include impotency, fraud, dare or jest, prior existing marriage, mental incapacity, and duress. Defenses to an annulment include continuing to live with the person after learning of the grounds for annulment, antenuptial knowledge of the contested condition, and *res judicata,* or expiration of the statute of limitations.

DIVORCE

Divorce is the most common form of dissolution of a marriage and represents the legal termination of a valid marriage. Divorce must be concluded under the auspices of the court following a formal hearing. This degree of formality is necessary because the state is presumed to have a vital interest in the marriage. Further, it is presumed that the material interests of the estranged couple and any children of the marriage are at risk. Divorce stands in marked contrast to the relatively informal procedural requirements for initiating a marriage. The procedural differences in treatment of marriage and divorce arise out of differing perceptions regarding the interests of the parties involved. In the case of marriage, it is presumed that the parties define their interests as similar and not conflictual; in the case of divorce, the parties define their interests as different and unresolvably in conflict, and thus a state of risk exists.

Under common law, prior to granting a divorce, some basis or fault must be demonstrated in justification of the divorce. These grounds were typically presented as breaches of the implicit provisions of the marital contract, including adultery, desertion, mental cruelty or inhumane treatment, abuse, insanity, drug addiction, and gross neglect, any of which could call for psychological expertise in presenting to a court. During the 1970s and 1980s, there was a shift in focus from fault finding to expeditious decisions regarding marital property, support, and custodial issues. Most states enacted no-fault divorce statutes, which permit a divorce without proof of wrongdoing. In the 1990s, some states began a return to "fault" divorces and requirements of increasing time living apart (Walker, 1992). As mentioned earlier, Louisiana was the first state in the United States to institute two separate marriage licenses, one in which the couple is entitled to a no-fault divorce after a six-month separation and a covenant marriage license, which can be dissolved only after a two-year separation or proven "grounds"(Goodman, 1997).

There are several important points to consider regarding no-fault divorce statutes. In particular, note the conditions necessary to justify the divorce action: a determination of complete incompatibility of temperament, a determination of an irretrievable breakdown of the marriage, and an unwillingness to reconcile differences between the estranged spouses. Generally, the court will accept statements from the parties of the necessary conditions, and the divorce will be granted forthwith.

The courts have attempted to objectify the decision-making process in no-fault divorces by defining the phrases "incompatibility of temperament," "irretrievable breakdown in the marriage," and "failure to reconcile." For example, in *Phillips v. Phillips* (1973), the court stated that incompatibility refers to conflicts in personalities and disposition so deep as to be irreconcilable and rendering it impossible for the parties to continue a normal marital relationship with each other. In the case of *Rikard v. Rikard* (1980), reconciliation was defined as a resumption of marital cohabitation in the fullest sense of living together as husband and wife, having sexual relations, and, where possible, joint domicile. The intentions of the parties must be to resume their married life entirely and not merely to enjoy each other's company temporarily, for limited purposes, or as a trial reconciliation. The length of their cohabitation is not material in determining whether there has been a reconciliation sufficient to deny the cause of action in the divorce.

In the event that the divorce is contested, a number of actions may invalidate claims of an irretrievable breakdown in the marriage. For example, should the spouses continue actions traditionally reserved for married couples, such as cohabitation or continued sexual relations, the court may justifiably question the basis for granting a no-fault divorce. In some jurisdictions, the courts have reserved the option to recommend counseling or mediation in an attempt to clarify the present state and condition of the marriage prior to granting a no-fault divorce. The clinician involved in marital counseling and likely to be drawn into the courtroom to testify must be informed about the law. For example, operating according to accepted treatment practices and with the best of intentions, the clinician might recommend graduated sexual or other relations. This intervention could have a legal impact on the marriage or divorce outcome. There is no stipulation for the clinician to be held harmless no matter how accepted his or her practice or intervention.

By submitting to the jurisdiction of the court for a determination of custody, the divorcing spouses implicitly state that they are unable to resolve their differences and therefore submit their problem to the court for a decision. But does the fact that a couple seeks a divorce necessarily imply that their conflicts are unresolvable? The court's general tendency to go along with negotiated agreements worked out between the divorce attorneys for the division of property, custody arrangements, and the provisions for support indicates that the courts recognize the right of the couple to decide for themselves how to best carry their family forward following divorce. The court decides only when no agreement can be reached.

ALTERNATIVE DISPUTE RESOLUTION

Beginning in the 1980s, developments in the psychological and legal literature regarding divorce promoted several novel approaches to negotiating divorce and conflict resolution. These approaches have been variously called conciliation, mediation, arbitration, and parent education, depending on the specific goal and circumstances under which they are employed. The broad goal of these approaches to negotiation is to facilitate communication and increased understanding between the estranged parties. Negotiation is favored as an alternative because it is rooted in the concepts of individual choice and the couple's right to effect their own resolution to their differences. Further, many advocates of these negotiating strategies suggest that negotiated settlements are likely to be less expensive, more permanent, and more likely to reduce the stress of divorce and family reorganization on all family members, particularly children.

Conciliation

The goal of formal conciliation processes is the reorganization and preservation of the marital unit. Conciliation may be initiated at any point in the negotiating process, from the first recognition of difficulty through the first several weeks following the filing of a divorce petition. In the event that a conciliation is brought about, the marriage is reaffirmed and the court ceases action in the matter. In this sense, conciliation is similar to marital therapy in its goals and methods (Sprenkle & Storm, 1983).

As an aspect of the court's support for marriage, conciliation programs have been adopted by many jurisdictions as a prerequisite or adjunctive process to petitions for a divorce. In these cases, the courts often employ staff clinicians and social workers to meet with the divorcing couple and assess the likelihood of a reconciliation. In some states, the meeting with the couple and the court worker is considered confidential and the court worker does not make recommendations to the court; in other states, the clinician may report back to the judge on the contents of the session, make recommendations, and participate in the court hearing—another instance of the need to know your state's laws.

Mediation

Divorce mediation is intended to be a nonadversarial means of conflict resolution in contested areas of the divorce action such as financial, property, and custodial issues. The goal of mediation is to forge an agreement that fairly meets the needs of all the parties, thereby avoiding litigation. Mediation is an attempt to arrive at a mutually satisfactory agreement regarding property and custodial issues, thereby encouraging a family to arrive at their own solution to the conflicting issues surrounding divorce. The assumption is that a settlement in which the parties have taken an active role is more likely to be successful in resolving differences and encourages the development of a successful foundation for the resolution of postdivorce differences. Beck and Sales (2000, 2001) have found that, on the basis of current research, these claims may be overly optimistic. They offer methodological suggestions for further research so that the claims for mediation's value can be fairly evaluated.

A satisfactory divorce is the presumed outcome of the mediation process. Mediation stands in stark contrast to the conciliation process, for which the goal is the reaffirmation of the marriage. In both conciliation and mediation, the family members are encouraged to articulate their differences and reorganize their relationships toward each other (Foster & Freed, 1983; Irving, 1980).

Arbitration

Arbitration is a negotiating strategy in which the parties agree to present their case to a neutral third party, who then renders a decision that is binding on both of the parties to implement. Arbitration is most closely aligned with traditional jurisprudence, in which the neutral judge renders a binding verdict. Arbitration is generally faster, less costly, and more private than court proceedings (Silverman, 2004). Not all states, however, have accepted the use of arbitration, and some have ruled that the rulings may be overturned if they are not in the best interest of the child.

In all three of these approaches, the divorcing couple is permitted the opportunity to appeal for a court judgment should they disagree with the negotiated settlement. Arbitration is most difficult to appeal.

Collaboration

In a collaborative divorce, the spouses sign a contract with their lawyers agreeing not to litigate. The couple, with their lawyers, then seek to negotiate a settlement. If the parties cannot reach agreement, they then must find new lawyers and start over (Silverman, 2004).

Parent Education Programs

The most recent trend for family courts is education programming for separated and divorcing parents established as a result of state legislation or court rules. The first court-affiliated programs began in the 1970s; their numbers grew in the early 1990s as either a form of premediation orientation or as a voluntary or court-mandated parent education program. In 1996, there were more than 560 programs in more than 40 states, and they seemed to be evolving into a distinct field of practice (Salem, Schepard, & Schlissel, 1996). The programs are offered by family courts, private and public mental health agencies, community-based agencies, and educational institutions. And while presenters come from varied backgrounds, often, due to the emotionally charged content, mental health professionals serve as group facilitators. Most programs emphasize (1) postdivorce reactions of parents, (2) postdivorce reactions of children, (3) children's developmental needs, and (4) the benefit of cooperative postdivorce parenting (Braver, Salem, Pearson, & DeLusé, 1996). For further information see the "Special Issue on Parent Education in Divorce and Separation" of *Family and Conciliation Courts Review* (McIsaac, 1996).

PROBLEMS ASSOCIATED WITH ALTERNATIVE DISPUTE RESOLUTIONS: ETHICAL ISSUES

Divorce mediation represents an area of intervention that creates complex ethical questions. While the role of peacemaker is attractive, the mediator's role is fraught with confusion because he or she is presumed to be a neutral third party but one who has an ambiguous purpose, methods, and ethical boundaries. A psychologist conducting divorce mediation needs to be aware of differences in his or her view of the process from that of other professionals. For example, a lawyer may view mediation as more desirable than litigation due to its effectiveness in improving the family's functioning (Lee, Beauregard, & Hunsley, 1998).

Becker (1996) discusses the ethical conflicts deriving from the role of lawyer/mediator. They include fraudulent contracts and disclosure of confidential information that arises from the relationships of the mediator and the family members. For example, the participants may not realize that their communications with a court worker are not necessarily confidential and may be reported back to the judge. In cases involving domestic violence, requiring a victim to sit with her or his abuser in a spirit of conciliation and cooperation may be counterproductive and inappropriate. If the mediator is a nonlawyer, the question arises of whether the mediator is engaging in unauthorized practice of law (Girdner, 1985b, 1986). Regardless of the professional orientation of the mediator, Girdner (1985a) and Manocherian (1985) have written on the difficulty of determining who the mediator represents: the mother, the father, or the child.

Sprenkle and Storm (1983) reviewed 22 studies in the areas of mediation and conciliation divorce groups, separation techniques, and marriage counseling with divorce as an unintended outcome. They concluded that among couples who resolved their differences regarding child custody, mediation facilitated high rates of pretrial agreements, high levels of satisfaction with their mediated agreements as compared with resolutions imposed by courts, a reduction in the amount of litigation following final order, an increase in joint custody arrangements, and a decrease in expenses frequently associated with court resolutions of custodial differences. They found that conditions favoring the mediation efforts included a moderate level of conflict between divorcing parties, acceptance by both parties of the divorce, the absence of third parties involving themselves in the dispute, a willingness to communicate by both parties, the absence of money as a major issue, and the acceptance and support by the opposing attorney of the mediation process. As noted earlier, Beck and Sales (2000) encourage research to substantiate the efficacy and use of mediation.

In assessing a couple for suitability for clinical interventions such as conciliation or mediation, professionals must evaluate the couple's specified goals for the resolution of the marriage and the present status of the marriage and conflict resolution abilities, including perceptions of the marriage, perceptions of divorce actions to date, perceptions of default, and desires for reconciliation. Additionally, both individual characteristics, such as cognitive and emotional maturity levels of both partners, and family characteristics, such as length of marriage, age of children, and typical problem resolution strategies, should be assessed.

DOMESTIC VIOLENCE

Family violence as discussed in this chapter includes spouse abuse, parent abuse, and incestuous relationships. Child abuse is discussed in Chapter 5. Although domestic violence seems to have been present in both Eastern and Western cultures since recorded time, the amount of attention being paid to it in the past 20 years has increased dramatically. Similarly, the legal system, in recognizing the convergence of family problems and criminal behavior, is developing new strategies for coping with abuse.

The U.S. Bureau of Justice Statistics (2003) report on the rates of family violence found that when family violence occurred, about 85% of the violent behaviors were assaults, 7% were robberies, and 7% were rapes. They report that although the number of violent crimes by intimate partners against females declined from 1.1 million in 1993, there were still more than 588,000 experiences of such crimes in 2001. Rates of violent crimes by an intimate partner for males dropped from 162,870 to 103,220 over the same time span. In 2000, 1,247 women and 440 men were killed by an intimate partner. About 33% of female murder victims and 4% of male murder victims were killed by a current or former partner (U.S. Department of Justice, 2003). Obviously, domestic violence is still a problem.

Incidence of domestic violence tends to be cyclical. Widom (1989) discussed the intergenerational patterns and the variety of forms the abuses can take over the life cycle of the family. Kaufman and Zigler (1987) reviewed the literature on intergenerational violence and concluded that the best estimate was a rate of about 30%, which is considerably higher than the 2% to 4% rate found in the general population. Although this chapter and the next separate the issues, spouse and child abuse are believed to be variations of family violence rather than individual entities.

SPOUSE ABUSE

Over the past 25 years, numerous books and articles have been written on the etiology of spouse abuse (Dobash & Dobash, 1979; Gelles & Straus, 1988; Jacobson & Gottman, 1998; Martin, 1976; Moore, 1979; Straus & Gelles, 1990; Straus, Gelles, & Steinmetz, 1980; Walker, 1979, 1984, 1989). Domestic violence has been explored from a variety of views, such as psychoanalytic, sociological, economic, and spousal interaction. Initial research consisted of surveys identifying the prevalence, extent, and types of violence; more recent studies have focused on interpersonal variables. These include women's new status at the societal level, marital inequality, violence (Yllo, 1984), the effect of domestic violence legislation on police intervention disposition (Bell, 1985), and the effects on mental and physical health of the women and children (Campbell & Lewandowski, 1997; Follette, Polusny, Bechtle, & Naugle, 1996). Emery and Billings (1998) reviewed research on the etiology of abuse and found a number of factors contributing to the development of family violence. They looked at both multiple risk factors and multiple pathways to family violence and arrived at the following conclusions:

1. Individual factors such as low self-esteem, poor impulse control, external locus of control, negative affectivity, and heightened response to stress have all been found to increase the probability of abusing.
2. Immediate context, such as size and structure of the family, family conflict resolution style, and acute stressors, increase the likelihood of abuse.
3. Societal or community factors such as poverty, social isolation, lack of community services, and unemployment add to the risk of abuse.
4. The cultural context of a community such as use of physical punishment and violence in the media may condone family violence.

Initially, researchers had difficulty obtaining accurate statistics on all areas of domestic violence due to unreliable record keeping from many sources of statistics and differences in defining the issue. Police tend to define domestic violence by its effect, legal systems by degree of severity, and social science researchers by degree of acceptance within the community. After 25 years of empirical research, estimates of the number of women abused by their partner each year range from 2.1 million (Langan & Innes, 1986) to more than 12 million (Loue, 2000). Obviously, other parametric and causal questions also remain unresolved.

TREATMENT AND REDUCTION OF DOMESTIC VIOLENCE

As the police change their role in investigating and disposing of family disputes, there is a need for consultation in areas such as defusing violence, problem resolution, mediation, and appropriate referral, as well as in basic in-service information identifying abuse and the characteristics of the abused and the abusers. Bell (1984), Brown (1984), and Dutton (1984) describe early attempts by various communities to provide more appropriate police services. Hirschel, Hutchison, and Dean (1992) discuss the effectiveness of several possible police responses: providing advice to the couple, separating the couple, issuing a citation to the offender, and arresting the offender.

In addition to consulting with police, a second avenue for input in the legal system is through the courts. Both judges and lawyers are increasingly aware of the issues involved in the battered wife syndrome (American Bar Association, 1997; Duryee, 1995; Follingstad, 2003; Frazier & Borgida, 1985; Special Issue on Domestic Violence, 1995; Walker, 1984) and are accepting exculpatory testimony of expert witnesses in cases where the battered wife victims have fought back and incurred assault or homicide charges. Consultation with lawyers is important in educating them about the apparent inconsistencies in their abused female client's behavior, such as the fear of filing for divorce from a battering spouse, leaving and returning to an abusive situation several times, and returning to request alimony and/or child support. Changes in statutes have encouraged police and court interventions.

Treatment of both the abused and the abuser often begins with legal interventions. In many families, the first step to resolving the abuse is contacting a crisis hotline or shelter where information regarding local legal alternatives is provided. For the abuser, the first contact with any external party may begin as a result of a legal intervention or at the suggestion of a divorce judge or lawyer who discovers the abuse in legal proceedings.

Treatment approaches may include individual, group, or marital sessions. Walker (1979) discussed the use of individual sessions for both partners in an abusive situation. Neidig (1984), in working with military families, developed a treatment program for couples. Bograd (1984) examined the biases that may arise from family systems approaches and the implications these biases have on joint treatment. Many clinicians decline to see abusive couples jointly due to inequality between the partners and for safety concerns for the abused spouse. Menard and Salius (1990) discussed the judicial response to violence. Bourne (1995) and Gottlieb (1995) discussed the ethical and legal issues in the management of domestic violence. Babcock and La Taillade (2000) reviewed current treatment models that have been empirically tested: psychoeducational (Duluth model), cognitive-behavioral groups, and couples therapy. Although treatment effects are not large, all three models show a small reduction in recidivism though the multimodal modified psychoeducational approach may be more effective than more circumscribed skills training.

Recent research on domestic violence has also included classification of both victims and batterers. A tripartite typology of batterers has been developed by Holtzworth-Munroe and Stuart (1994) identifying generally violent/antisocial, dysphoric/borderline, and family-only types. This typology was validated by Waltz, Babcock, Jacobson, and Gottman (2000) on a community sample, and suggestions were made for developing treatments for the various typologies. For example, treatment for the generally violent and pathological is unlikely to be successful unless it takes into account the Axis II pathology. For a family-only batterer showing little pathology, a treatment with a focus on violence, abusive behavior, and relationship problems may be successful. Heyman, Feldbau-Kohn, Ehrensaft, Langhinrichsen-Rohling, and O'Leary (2001) have begun working to establish diagnostic criteria that will be reliable across questionnaires and interview methods. Comparisons of structured diagnostic interviews with a modified version of a standard scale for assessing relationship aggression, the Conflicts Tactics Scale (Straus, 1979), found that spouses do not report the same information on occurrence or impact of violence in the two formats. Recommendations are made for continuing to develop diagnostic criteria of abuse and for increasing testing of questionnaires against the criterion.

In terms of public policy, the Violence Against Women Act (VAWA; 1994), a part of the 1994 crime bill, attempts to make crimes against women considered in the same manner as those motivated by religion, racial, or political bias. VAWA also provides for a national telephone hotline to assist victims and requires states to recognize protection orders of other states (Klein, 1995). The states are continuing to develop their responses to comply with VAWA (Loue, 2000).

CONCLUSIONS

A number of issues involving current domestic law have been surveyed and references for further study have been provided. Although much has been accomplished in improving the statutes ensuring the rights of individuals and families, it is apparent that the job is not yet complete. The clinician needs to be aware of changes in the literature, in the availability of local resources, and of local, state, and national legal and policy developments.

Psychological findings have influenced policy, legislation, and police training. Psychological research on parenting, bonding, effects of various custodial arrangements, and violent behavior have become part of clinical training and practice. Through the collaborative efforts of lawyers and psychologists, we can continue to profoundly and beneficially affect the lives of our most vulnerable fellow humans.

REFERENCES

Aldous, J. (1997). The political process and the failure of the child labor amendment. *Journal of Family Issues, 18,* 71–91.

American Bar Association. (1997). *When will they ever learn? Education to end domestic violence.* Washington, DC: U.S. Department of Justice.

American Psychological Association. (1977). *Standards for providers of psychological services* (revised). Washington, DC: Author.

American Psychological Association. (1981). Specialty guidelines for the delivery of services by counseling psychologists. *American Psychologist, 36,* 652–663.

American Psychological Association. (1993). *Record keeping guidelines.* Washington, DC: Author.

American Psychological Association. (1994). Guidelines for child custody evaluations in divorce proceedings. *American Psychologist, 49,* 677–680.

American Psychological Association. (2002). Ethical principles of psychologists and code of conduct. *American Psychologist, 57,* 1060–1073.

American Psychological Association, American Educational Research Association, & National Council on Measurement in Education. (1999). *Standards for educational and psychological testing.* Washington, DC: Author.

American Psychological Association Committee on Professional Practice and Standards. (1998). *Guidelines for psychological evaluations in child protection matters.* Washington, DC: American Psychological Association.

Babcock, J. C., & La Taillade, J. J. (2000). Evaluating interventions for men who batter. In J. Vincent & E. Jourices (Eds.), *Domestic violence: Guidelines for research-informed practice* (pp. 37–77). Philadelphia: Jessica Kingley.

Bala, N. (1994a). Children, psychiatrists and the courts: Understanding the ambivalence of the legal profession. *Canadian Journal of Psychiatry, 39,* 526–530.

Bala, N. (1994b). Children, psychiatrists and the courts: Understanding the ambivalence of the legal profession, II. *Canadian Journal of Psychiatry, 39,* 531–539.

Beck, C. A., & Sales, B. D. (2000). A critical reappraisal of divorce meditation research and policy. *Psychology, Public Policy, and Law, 6,* 989–1056.

Beck, C. A., & Sales, B. D. (2001). *Family mediation: Facts, myths, and future prospects.* Washington, DC: American Psychological Association.

Becker, L. (1996). Ethical concerns in negotiating family law agreements. *Family Law Quarterly, 30,* 587–659.

Bell, D. J. (1984). The police response to domestic violence: An exploratory study. *Police Studies: The International Review of Police Development, 7,* 23–30.

Bell, D. J. (1985). Domestic violence: Victimization, police intervention, and disposition. *Journal of Criminal Justice, 13,* 525–534.

Blau, T. H. (1984). *The psychologist as expert witness.* New York: Wiley.

Blau, T. H. (1985). The psychologist as expert in the courts. *Clinical Psychologist, 38,* 76.

Blau, T. H. (1994). Expert testimony. In R. J. Corsini (Ed.), *Encyclopedia of psychology* (2nd ed., Vol. 1, pp. 539–540). New York: Wiley.

Bograd, M. (1984). Family systems approaches to wife batterings: A feminist critique. *American Journal of Orthopsychiatry, 54,* 558–568.

Bourne, R. (1995). Ethical and legal dilemmas in the management of family violence. *Ethics and Behavior, 5,* 261–271.

Braver, S. L., Salem, P., Pearson, J., & DeLusé, S. R. (1996). Content of divorce programs: Result of a survey. *Family and Conciliation Courts Review, 34,* 41–59.

Brown, S. E. (1984). Police responses to wife beating: Neglect of a crime of violence. *Journal of Criminal Justice, 12,* 277–288.

Campbell, J. C., & Lewandowski, L. A. (1997). Mental and physical health effects of intimate partner violence on women and children. *Psychiatric Clinics of North America, 20,* 353–374.

Carey v. Population Services International, 438 U.S. 678 (1972).

Child Support Recovery Act. 18 U.S.C.A. § 228 (1992).

Civil Service Retirement Equity Act. Act, 5 C.F.R. 831 (1984).

Committee on Ethical Guidelines for Forensic Psychologists. (1991). Specialty guidelines for forensic psychologists. *Law and Human Behavior, 6,* 655–665.

Dobash, R. E., & Dobash, R. (1979). *Violence against wives.* New York: Free Press.

Duryee, M. A. (1995). Guidelines for family court services intervention when there are allegations of domestic violence Special issue: Domestic violence. *Family and Concilliation Courts Review, 33,* 79–86.

Dutton, D. C. (1984). Interventions into the problem of wife assault: Therapeutic policy and research implications. *Canadian Journal of Behavioral Science, 16,* 281–297.

Ehrlich, J. S. (1997). *Family law for paralegals.* New York: Aspen Law and Business.

Eisendtadt v. Baird, 405 U.S. 438, 453 (1967).

Elrod, L. D., & Spector, R. G. (1996). A review of the year in family law: Children's issues take spotlight. *Family Law Quarterly, 29,* 741–769.

Emery, R. E., & Billings, L. L. (1998). An overview of the nature, causes, and consequences of abusive family relationships. *American Psychologist,* 121–135.

Family and Medical Leave Act. (FMLA), 29 U.S.C. § 2601 *et seq.* (1993).

Federal Defense of Marriage Act. HR 3396, May 7 (1996).

Follette, V. M., Polusny, M. A., Bechtle, A. E., & Naugle, A. E. (1996). Cumulative trauma: The impact of child sexual abuse, adult sexual assault, and spouse abuse. *Journal of Traumatic Stress, 9,* 25–35.

Follingstad, D. R. (2003). Battered women syndrome in the courts. In A. M. Goldstein (Ed.), *Forensic psychology* (pp. 485–507). Vol. 11 in, I. B. Weiner (Editor-in-Chief), *Handbook of psychology.* Hoboken, NJ: Wiley.

Foster, H. H., & Freed, D. J. (1983). Child custody and the adversary process: Forum conveniens? *Family Law Quarterly, 17,* 133–150.

Frazier, P., & Borgida, E. (1985). Rape trauma syndrome evidence in court. *American Psychologist, 40,* 984–993.

Gelles, R. J., & Straus, M. A. (1988). *Intimate violence.* New York: Simon & Schuster.

George, R. P. (2003, November 28). One man one woman. *Wall Street Journal,* p. A-8.

Girdner, L. K. (1985a). Adjudication and mediation: A comparison of custody decision-making processes involving third parties. *Journal of Divorce, 8,* 33–47.

Girdner, L. K. (1985b). Strategies of conflict: Custody litigation in the United States. *Journal of Divorce, 9,* 1–15.

Girdner, L. K. (1986). Child custody determination. In E. Seidman & J. Rappaport (Eds.), *Redefining social problems* (pp. 165–183). New York: Plenum Press.

Goldzband, M. G. (1983). Current trends affecting family law and child custody. *Psychiatric Clinics of North America, 6,* 683–693.

Goodman, E. (1997, August 12). When people get married they believe theirs will last. *Montgomery Advertiser*, p. A-6.

Goodridge v. Department of Public Health. SCJ 08860, November 18 (2003).

Gottlieb, M. C. (1995). Family violence and family systems: Who is the patient? *Ethics and Behavior, 5,* 273–277.

Greenberger, R. S. (2004, November 30). High court won't review challenge to gay marriage. *Wall Street Journal*, pp. A-2, A-12.

Grisso, T. (2003). *Evaluating competencies: Forensic assessments and instruments* (2nd ed.). New York: Kluwer Academic/Plenum Press.

Griswold v. State of Connecticut, 381 U.S. 479, 85 S. Ct. 1678. 14 L.Ed.2d 510 (1965).

Grossman, N. S., & Okun, B. F. (2003). Family psychology and family law: Introduction to the special issue. *Journal of Family Psychology, 17,* 163–168.

Hague Convention on the Protection of children and Cooperation in respect of Intercountry Adoption. (1993, May 29). The Hague Conference on private international law, final act of the seventeenth session.

Hague Convention on the Protection of Minors Act. (2000, December 16). Number 37 of 2000.

Hague International Child Abduction Convention S. Treaty Doc. No. 11, 99th Cong., 1st Sess., Reprinted in 19 I.L.M. 1501 (1980).

Hess, A. K. (1985). The psychologist as expert witness: A guide to the courtroom arena. *Clinical Psychologist, 38,* 75–76.

Heyman, R. E., Feldbau-Kohn, S. R., Ehrenstaft, M. K., Langhinrichsen-Rohling, J., & O'Leary, K. D. (2001). Can Questionnaire Reports correctly classify relationship distress and partner physical abuse? *Journal of Family Psychology, 15,* 334–346.

Hirschel, J. D., Hutchison, I. W., & Dean, C. W. (1992). The failure of arrest to deter spouse abuse. *Journal of Research in Crime and Delinquency, 29,* 7–33.

Holtzworth-Munroe, A., & Stuart, G. L. (1994). Typologies of male batters: Three subtypes and the differences among them. *Psychological Bulletin, 116,* 476–497.

Hwang, S. (2004, September 28). U.S. adoptions get easier. *Wall Street Journal*, p. D-1.

In re A & M, No. 61 A.D. 2d. 426, 403 (New York State, 2d. 375, 381, 1978).

In re Gault, 387 U.S. 1 (1967).

International Parental Kidnapping Crime Act, Pub.L. No. 103-173 December 2 (1993).

Irving, H. H. (1980). *Divorce mediation: A rational alterative to the adversary systems.* New York: Universe.

Jacobson, N. S., & Gottman, J. M. (1998). *When men batter women: New insights into ending abusive relationships.* New York: Simon & Schuster.

Kaufman, J., & Zigler, E. (1987). Do abused children become abusive parents? *American Journal of Orthopsychiatry, 57,* 186–192.

Kirkland, K. (2003). A legal perspective on family psychology and family law: Comment on the special issue. *Journal of Family Psychology, 17,* 263–266.

Klein, C. F. (1995). Full faith and credit: Interstate enforcement of protection orders under the Violence Against Women Act of 1994. *Family Law Quarterly, 29,* 253–271.

Krause, H. D. (1977). *Family law in a nutshell.* St. Paul, MN: West.

Langan, P., & Innes, C. (1986). *U.S. Bureau of Justice statistics special report: Preventing domestic violence against women.* Washington, DC: U.S. Bureau of Justice Statistics.

Lee, C. M., Beauregard, C. P. M., & Hunsley, J. (1998). Lawyer's opinions regarding child custody mediation and assessment services: Implications for psychological practice. *Professional Psychology: Research and Practice, 29,* 115–120.

Loue, S. (2000). Intimate partner violence: Bridging the gap between law and science. *Journal of Legal Medicine, 21,* 1–34.

Maclean, J. F. (1997, November 4). Area, state figures show popularity of matrimony. *Montgomery Advertiser*, pp. A1–A2.

Manocherian, J. (1985). Family mediation: A descriptive case study. *Journal of Divorce, 8,* 97–118.

Martin, D. (1976). *Battered wives.* San Francisco: Glide.

McGrew, J. (2004, November 20). Lawsuit thrown out of court. *Montgomery Advertiser*, p. A-1.

McIsaac, H. (Ed.). (1996). Parent education in divorce and separation [Special issue]. *Family and Conciliation Courts Review, 34*(1).

Melton, G. B. (1984). Developmental psychology and the law: The state of the art. *Journal of Family Law, 22,* 445–482.

Melton, G. B., Petrila, J., Poythress, N. G., & Slobogin, C. (1997). *Psychological evaluations for the courts* (2nd ed.). New York: Guilford Press.

Menard, A. E., & Salius, A. J. (1990). Judicial response to family violence: The importance of message. *Mediation Quarterly, 7,* 293–302.

Mermin, S. (1982). *Law and the legal system.* Boston: Little, Brown.

Merriken v. Cressman, 354 F. Supp. 913 (E.D. Penn. 1973).

Meyer v. Nebraska, 262 U.S. 390 (1923).

Moore, D. M. (1979). *Battered women.* Beverly Hills, CA: Sage.

Neidig, P. H. (1984). *Spouse abuse: A treatment program for couples.* Champaign, IL: Research Press.

Parental Kidnapping Prevention Act of 1980, Pub. L. § 96-611.

Parken v. Saileau, 213 So. 2d. 190 (1968).

Phillips v. Phillips, 274 So. 2d. 71 (1973).

Pierce v. Society of Sisters, 268 U.S. 510 (1925).

Planned Parenthood v. Danforth, 423 U.S. 52, 75 (1976).

Planned Parenthood of Southern Pennsylvania v. Casy, 744 F. Supp. 1323 (E.D. Pa. 1990).

Popham v. Duncan, 87 Colo. 149, 285 p. 757, 70 A. L.R. 824 (1930).

Rayburn, K. (2004, November 18). Gay-marriage bans face suits. *Wall Street Journal,* p. A-4.

Reynolds v. United States, 98 U.S. 145 (1878).

Rikard v. Rikard, 378 So. 2d. (1980).

Roe v. Wade, 409 U.S.817 (1973).

Salem, P., Schepard, A., & Schlissel, S. W. (1996). Parent education as a distinct field of practice: The agenda for the future. *Family and Concilation Courts Reveiw, 34,* 9–22.

Shapiro, D. L. (1984). *Psychological evaluation and expert testimony.* New York: Van Nostrand Reinhold.

Silverman, R. E. (2003, April 9). Don't like you prenup? Blame Barry Bonds. *Wall Street Journal.* p. D-1.

Silverman, R. E. (2004, October 28). Making a divorce easier, less costly. *Wall Street Journal,* p. D-2.

Skinner v. State of Oklahoma, 316 U.S. 535, 541, 62 S.Ct. 1100, 1113. 86 L.Ed. 1655 (1942).

Special issue on domestic violence. (1995). *Family Law Quarterly, 29*(2).

Sprenkle, D. H., & Storm, C. L. (1983). Divorce therapy outcome research: A substantium and methodological review. *Journal of Marital and Family Therapy, 9,* 239–258.

Stanton, A. M. (1982). Child-parent privilege for confidential communications: An examination and proposal. *Family Law Quarterly, 16,* 1–67.

Straus, M. A. (1979). Measuring intrafamily conflict and violence: The Conflict Tactics (CT) Scales. *Journal of Marriage and the Family, 41,* 75–78.

Straus, M. A., & Gelles, R. J. (1990). *Physical violence in American families.* New Brunswick, NJ: Transaction Press.

Straus, M. A., Gelles, R., & Steinmetz, S. K. (1980). *Behind closed doors: Violence in the American family.* Garden City, NY: Anchor.

Swisher, K. (2004, March 11). Cashing in on gay marriage. *Wall Street Journal,* pp. D-1, D-6.

Underwager, R., & Wakefield, H. (1992). Poor psychology produces poor law. *Law and Human Behavior, 16,* 233–243.

Uniform Child Custody Jurisdiction Act, 9 U.C.A. § III (1979).

Uniform Marriage and Divorce Act, 402, 9A U.C.A. §§ 197–198 (1979).

Uniform Services Former Spouse Act, DL 101–510 (1990).

U.S. Department of Justice, Bureau of Justice Statistics. (2003, February). *Crime data brief: Intimate partner violence, 1993–2001.* Washington. DC: Author.

Violence Against Women. 18 U.S.C.A § 2265 (1994) Pub. L. No. 103-322, Title IV, 108 Stat. 1902-55.

Wakefield, H., & Underwager, R. (1992). Assessing credibility of children's testimony in ritual sexual abuse allegations. *Issues in Child Abuse Accusations, 4,* 32–44.

Walker, L. E. (1979). *The battered woman.* New York: Harper & Row.

Walker, L. E. (1984). *The battered woman syndrome.* New York: Springer.

Walker, L. E. (1989). *Terrifying love.* New York: Harper Perennial.

Walker, T. B. (1992). Family law in the fifty states: An overview. *Family Law Quarterly, 25,* 417–520.

Waltz, J., Babcock, J. C., Jacobson, N. S., & Gottsman, J. M. (2000). Testing a typology of batterers. *Journal of Consulting and Clinical, 68,* 658–669.

Weiner, I. B. (1985). Preparing forensic reports and testimony. *Clinical Psychologist, 38,* 78–80.

Whalen v. Row, 429 U.S. 589. 599 (1977).

Widom, C. S. (1989, April 14). The cycle of violence. *Science, 244,* 160–166.

Yllo, K. (1984). The status of women, marital equality, and violence against wives. *Journal of Family Issues, 5,* 307–320.

Ziskin, J., & Faust, D. (1988). *Coping with psychiatric and psychological testimony* (5th ed.). Los Angeles: Law and Psychology Press.

CHAPTER 5

Understanding Child Domestic Law Issues: Custody, Adoptions, and Abuse

KATHRYN D. HESS

TODAY'S FAMILY is not the same as the family of the 1950s or 1990s. The 2003 U.S. Census Bureau Report notes that people are waiting until later to marry. In 2003, the average age at time of first marriage for women in the United States was 25 years and for men 27 (Armas, 2004). There has been an increase of 23% among women and 33% among men age 30 through 40 who have never been married compared to 1970, when only 6% of females and 9% of males age 30 to 34 had never been married. Nearly half of all marriages end in divorce, although, at last, the percentage has leveled off. Thirty-one percent of U.S. children live in single-parent families, with 4% living with their father only (U.S. Census Bureau, 2003). Of the U.S. children born in 2002, 34% were born to a mother who never married. Considering the delay in age of first marriage, it is not surprising that teenage mothers are especially likely to be unmarried; 88% of the children born to teens age 15 through 17 were born to unmarried mothers, as were 75% of those born to 18- and 19-year-olds. These are seismic, cataclysmic, and potentially devastating changes.

Daily, the media report on changes in U.S. and international laws regarding such issues as same-sex marriage, international custody guidelines, grandparents' rights, custody of frozen ovum, and adoptions. This chapter reviews the domestic and juvenile law issues that a practitioner must know and understand in order to be useful to clients dealing with child custody, adoption, child abuse, and child sexual abuse.

THEMES IN FAMILY LAW

Several themes are woven throughout family law: the natural, basic right of all people to marry (*Loving v. Virginia*, 1967); the contractual or partnership nature of marriage; and competency or fitness as a parent. Overlying these themes are concepts about the nature and competency of minor children, responsibility and dependency, *parens patriae,* the best interests of the child doctrine, and concepts regarding the natural relationship and obligations existing between parents and their children. Most of these legal concepts have their origins in Roman law, common law, or ecclesiastical doctrines regarding the nature and purpose of marriage and the proper relationship between husbands and wives and between parents and their children. Collectively, these themes contribute to the normative model of the family, its character, and the proper relationships among family members.

PARENS PATRIAE

The doctrine of *parens patriae* is central to domestic law. This doctrine, passed down from Roman law and adopted into English common law in about the eleventh century, presumes the state as protector and trustee for those persons who cannot help themselves, usually children. Under parens patriae, the state, represented by the courts, is responsible for securing the property rights of minor children and members of other classes presumed incompetent to administer their own affairs against possible loss if, in the case of children, their rights cannot be protected by the natural parents or guardians. Under common law, this threshold is presumed to have been crossed when the family is presented to the court as disrupted and unable to continue as an intact unit.

Can the state's abil. y to guard the child's interest exceed the parent's ability? The court typic ily presumes that the natural parent-child bonds in an intact family are sufficiently strong to assure the protection of a minor's interest. This fundamental assumption is overturned in a disrupted family and the natural bonds between parent and child no longer exert sufficient force of responsibility to assure the protection of the child's interest. Can the court balance the demands of the general public against the needs of the child in question? The needs of the parents, child, and the public are mutually exclusive and represent possible conflicts of interest. It stretches the limits of reason to assume that the interests of the larger society are synonymous with the interests of the individual, yet this is precisely the task before the juvenile judge. Some jurisdictions have addressed this problem by providing for a guardian ad litem. The court appoints a competent neutral party (e.g., an attorney or psychologist) to the ad litem ("during the interim") role who is competent to pursue the minor's interests, thus freeing the court from a conflict of interest.

Implicit within the parens patriae doctrine is the assumption that in matters concerning children, the court is the guardian of the well-being of any minor children involved. In fulfilling this role, the court is presumed to act in the best interests of the child and as such cannot have a conflict of interest with the child's interests. Because it is the presumption that the wishes of the court are for the child's best interest, domestic courts cannot delegate their jurisdiction in matters involving children. Although the court is forbidden to delegate this responsibility to outside agencies, it can, through its broad discretionary powers, employ a wide range of means to achieve its goals, including requesting intervention and input from psychologists.

Competency, Responsibility, Dependency, and the Best Interests of the Child Doctrine

Children have traditionally been viewed by the courts as dependent and incapable of making sound, independent judgments. They are treated differently from adults with respect to statutory law, representation in court, treatment in juvenile court, and issues of parental responsibility for the child. The court recognizes the natural bond between parent and child and in almost all but the most extreme circumstances strives to maintain and support the parent-child relationship. The best interest of the child doctrine implies that the responsibility of the court is first to protect the interests of the child. Yet, just as there are possible conflicts of interest when considering the rights of parents and the rights of children, so, too, there are serious questions about whether or not the interests of the child are synonymous with the court's interest. Under the parens patriae concept, the court has been put into the final role of mediating the needs of the social order and the needs of the child. Clearly, these needs are not always the same.

Under English common law, children under the age of majority are considered incapable of sound, independent judgment and therefore must look to their parents or guardian for direction and decision making. Thus, the normative model presupposes an intact family system, with dependent children, who rely on their parents for support, care, and protection. This relationship among family members transcends individual needs and possible conflicts of interest. English common law presupposes that the interests of the children are consonant with the interests of their parents, who will execute their trust to the benefit of their children. This model of mutual responsibility (of parents' caretaking and children's obeisance) and the inalienable right of parents to execute this responsibility have been repeatedly supported in court.

What exactly is the nature of the legal concept of minority and of competence, and at what point does a child become competent to make his or her own decisions? There are no simple answers to the latter question, but the courts have laid down a fairly clear framework for determining competence. According to one court's reasoning, competence represents "the capacity for individual choice" (*Ginsberg v. N.Y.*, 1968). This description may not appear to be particularly illuminating, but implicit within it is the understanding that "individual choice" requires an understanding on the part of the individual of the possible consequences of various alternative choices.

In her investigation into children's decision-making competence, Weithorn (1982, p. 89) defines competence as "an individual's skills, abilities, knowledge or experience or a capacity to perform in a certain manner." While it is felt that not all persons less than 18 years of age are incompetent to make decisions regarding their welfare, states have strongly supported parents' rights to provide consent or refusal for actions of their children (Weithorn, 1982). This right to privacy in decision making on behalf of children has repeatedly been supported through the decisions in the courts (*Parham v. J. L. & J. R.*, 1979; *Prince v. Massachusetts*, 1944; *Wisconsin v. Yoder*, 1972).

CUSTODY

Custody issues have been explored extensively in both legal and psychological literature in the past 25 years. Standards for conducting custody evaluations have been developed (American Psychological Association [APA], 1994). The *Family Law Quarterly* has presented an annual review of federal and state changes in family law since 1992 (Walker, 1992) and has published special issues on topics such as custody and working with mental health professionals (American Bar Association, 1995).

A clinician may be asked to serve as a consultant to the court in several types of custody disputes. Consider a private dispute between the parents or between a parent and other family member or third party following a divorce. In these cases, the court is involved because there has been a breakdown in the individuals' ability to solve the custody issue among themselves. A second kind of dispute involves issues such as assisted conception, surrogate parents, and unwed fathers contesting adoptions. In the third type of custody issue, the parties involve the parent and the state (usually the Division of Child Welfare or Department of Human Resources) in cases where there has been an allegation of parental abuse or neglect and may involve the attenuation or termination of parental rights.

As of 2004, all states have enacted a version of the Uniform Child Custody Jurisdiction Act (UCCJA), and nearly all of the states have adopted some version of the Parental Kidnapping Prevention Act, making child abduction by a noncustodial parent a felony. The Hague Convention on International Child Abduction is useful in returning children to their country of habitual residence for resolution of any custody dispute (Silberman, 1994).

The UCCJA (1979) provides a uniform framework within which custodial issues may be developed, thereby encouraging consistency in rulings across jurisdictions. In establishing criteria for determination of custody, the UCCJA suggests consideration of the following: (1) the age and sex of the child; (2) the wishes of the child as to choice of custodian; (3) the interactions and interrelationships of the child with parents, siblings, and significant others; (4) the child's adjustment to home, school, and community; and (5) the mental and physical health of all parties involved.

Standards for a Determination of Custody

In divorces prior to the late 1800s, fathers almost always retained custody of their children. However, with the shift in family work patterns, mothers were presumed to be more satisfactory caretakers for young children, particularly children under the age of 6 or 7 years. The presumption in favor of mothers retaining custody became formalized in the "tender years" doctrine. The tender years doctrine was supported by theories of personality development that discounted the influence of the father in favor of the child's relationship with the mother during the formative tender years. The influence of these mother-centered theories is exemplified in the research of John Bowlby, who as late as the 1950s made the statement that there was no point in investigating the father-child relationship as it was, in his opinion, of no consequence to the development of children (Bowlby, 1969). Indeed, typical studies of father-child interaction in the period prior to the late 1960s involved questionnaires given to mothers, who were asked to describe the relationships between fathers and their children.

More recent research has indicated that fathers and mothers are equally capable of fulfilling the needs of their children (Lamb, 1996). Changing attitudes about child rearing, coupled with the movement of women into the full-time workforce outside of the home, culminated in changes in family law that have encouraged the development of a variety of custodial arrangements. In 2003, the U.S. Census Bureau reported 5.5 times more single mothers than single fathers with custody of children under the age of 18. Two recent controversial cases involved mothers who worked or attended school. In the first, a Washington, D.C., lawyer working long hours lost custody to her unemployed husband (Clay, 1995). In a Michigan case (*Ireland v. Smith*, 1994), a teenage mother temporarily lost custody when the child's father petitioned that his mother would watch the child while he worked rather than place the child in child care while the mother attended college classes.

Since the 1980s much has been written on the role of psychology in custody disputes and the assessment of parenting (Brodzinsky, 1993; Clark, 1995; Heilbrun, 1995; Jameson, Ehrenberg, & Hunter, 1997; Krauss & Sales, 2000: Stahl, 1994; Weithorn, 1987; Zarski, Knight, & Zarski, 1985). Otto, Buffington-Vollum, and Edens (2003, chap. 11) reviewed current practices and research on child custody evaluations.

The American Psychological Association (1994) developed 16 guidelines for child custody evaluations. The first three guidelines emphasize (1) that the primary purpose of a custody evaluation is to assess the best psychological interests of the child, (2) that the child's well-being and interests are paramount, and (3) that the focus is on the needs of the child, the parenting capacity, and the resulting fit. The next four focus on preparing for the evaluation and specify that (4) the role of the psychologist is that of an objective, impartial professional expert; (5) the psychologist has obtained specialized competence in the areas needed; (6) the psychologist recognizes personal and societal biases and strives to overcome such biases; and (7) the psychologist avoids multiple relationships. The third section of the guidelines concerns conducting the evaluation and includes items such as (8) the scope of the evaluation; (9) informed consents; (10) information to the participants regarding limits of confidentiality and disclosure of information; (11) use of multiple methods of data gathering; (12) conservative interpretation of the assessment data; (13) limits of opinions; (14) recommendations, if any, based on the best interests of the child; (15) clarification of financial arrangements; and (16) record keeping.

Morris (1997) notes that participation in custody evaluations may lead to malpractice claims and ethical complaints filed against the evaluator. This is partially due to the nature of the evaluations (parents unhappy with final custody arrangements) and partially to the number of ethical standards that have direct relevance to the conduct of the evaluations. Bow and Quinnell (2001) found that 10% of their respondents had malpractice suits filed against them, and 35% had an ethics board complaint. However, many of the respondents noted in the margin of the survey that the complaints or suits had been dismissed.

Writing about preventing and managing ethics complaints, Glassman (1998) lists a number of strategies to reduce the likelihood of incurring a complaint. For example, he suggests obtaining a court appointment when accepting a referral to conduct a custody evaluation and to obtain informed consent from all parties clarifying the limits of confidentiality and disclosure of records even though the assessment was court ordered. Clients may not realize that privilege is waived when they speak to the evaluator or that any information provided to the evaluator or used in making the custody determination is potentially discoverable. The evaluator needs to be familiar with the "Specialty Guidelines for Forensic Psychologists" (APA, 1991) and the *Record Keeping Guidelines* (APA, 1993). Glassman also recommends avoiding one-party evaluations and spending more time with one party than the other to avoid the appearance of partiality or bias. Documentation of all details of the evaluation is advisable to meet the higher standards of documentation required of forensic assessments. Step-by-step guidelines are provided by Glassman regarding how to respond if you receive an ethics complaint.

CURRENT PRACTICES

While there is no disagreement that the best interests of the child are the heart of custody determination, there is variation both in how best to assess the child's best interest and in court guidelines for children of different ages. Ackerman and Ackerman (1997) surveyed 201 psychologists who had participated in at least 10 custody evaluations. All of the respondents preferred to be retained by the court or jointly by both attorneys. Almost all respondents used testing as part of their assessment procedure and tended to administer four to five tests per person being evaluated.

A survey of 198 psychologists in the child custody field explored current practices and procedures used in making custody evaluations and to what degree the 1994 APA Guidelines were being met (Bow & Quinnell, 2001). An eight-page questionnaire was developed addressing all aspects of child custody work. The average number of custody evaluations completed by each psychologist was 254, with a median of 120 evaluations. The average time spent on an evaluation involving two parents and one child was 24.5 hours, with a range of 5 to 90 hours. Most of the clinicians had training with adults, children, and adolescents and had received their custody evaluation training primarily through seminars. This type of postdoctoral training is not surprising as the average age of the respondents was 51 and university and internship programs focusing on child custody are recent.

When asked about their practices, 99.5% of Bow and Quinell's (2001) respondents reported that they did a psychosocial interview and a clinical interview with each parent, 98% reviewed documents, 97% conducted a clinical interview with the child, 92% took psychosocial histories of the child by the parent and observed parent-child interaction, 91% used psychological testing with the parents, and 61% did psychological testing with the child. Ninety-two percent of the respondents provided a written custody report involving over seven hours of the practitioner's time. Thus, there appears to be a highly uniform procedure that has evolved in child custody evaluations. As one defense to an ethics or legal complaint against a professional is the "usual and customary" or "accepted standard" of practice, child custody evaluators should make exceptions to this procedure only for good and justifiable reasons.

The Michigan Best Interests of the Child Criteria (Michigan Child Custody Act of 1970, 1993), a set of criteria that is often used as a model, were rated by the respondents on a 9-point Likert scale from totally unimportant to extremely important. All were rated as 6 or higher, meaning that all of the items were felt to be at least moderately important. When Bow and Quinnell (2001) asked if the respondents would make explicit recommendations regarding the "ultimate issue," custody and visitation, 94% said yes. Although this is still a topic of ongoing controversy, the evaluators in the study were more willing than those in the Ackerman and Ackerman (1997) survey (65%) to make specific custody and visitation recommendations to the court.

When Horvath, Logan, and Walker (2002) reviewed court records rather than asking evaluators what their practices were, they found wide variability in the actual documented practices, with the friend of the court evaluations being more likely to follow the custody evaluation guidelines (APA, 1994; Clark, 1995; Association of Family and Conciliation Courts, 1994) than the private practitioners. The evaluators in the study often skipped the assessment of domestic violence, child abuse, parenting skills, health status of all parties, and formal psychological testing, a practice fraught with peril if the practitioner faces a searching cross-examination. In 40% of the cases, the evaluations relied on only two methods of assessment. When the evaluators were divided by professional subtype, it was observed that neither PhD nor EdD psychologists made home visits, whereas the MSWs conducted them 37.5% of the time. The EdD psychologists were more likely to test the child, but not likely to observe the mother and child together. Despite the variability in the evaluations, the judges and attorneys tended to place importance on the findings. In fewer than 10% of the cases was the final decision counter to the evaluators' recommendations.

Heinze and Grisso (1996) reviewed five assessment procedures that are currently used in assessing parenting capacity. These measures use a variety of methods, including observation of parents, parental preferences of the child, stress levels of parents, and child abuse potential of parents. As can be seen from the variety of assessments used, no one test currently available would be appropriate in all custody evaluations. In addition to intelligence measures and projective techniques, some of the newer techniques used include the Ackerman-Schoendorf Scales for Parent Evaluation of Custody (ASPECT; Ackerman & Schoendorf, 1992), Bricklin Perceptual Scales (BPS; Bricklin, 1984), Parent-Child Relationship Inventory (PCRI; Gerard, 1994), and the Parenting Stress Index (Abidin, 1990).

In the Quinnell and Bow (2001) survey of custody evaluation practices, their respondents used IQ tests in about 30% of their evaluations and achievement tests with children about as often. The Wide Range Achievement Test was the most frequently used achievement test. Among the adult objective personality tests, the Minnesota Multiphasic Personality Inventory (MMPI-2) was the most frequently used, at 88% of the time, with the Millon Clinical Multiaxial Inventory, the Sixteen Personality Factors, and the California Personality Inventory being used less often. For adolescents, the Minnesota Multiphasic Personality Inventory-Adolescent Version was the most commonly used, with the Millon Adolescent Clinical Inventory being used about half as often.

The most popular projective test remains the Rorschach Ink Blot test, followed by the Thematic Apperception Test. In the assessment of children and adolescents, the use of family drawings, or Kinetic Family Drawing, has shown an increase, with 45% of the evaluators now using this projective device.

The most dramatic change in practice over the past five years was in the use of parent rating scales: 31% of the evaluators now use them, as contrasted with 4% in the Ackerman and Ackerman (1997) survey. The Achenbach Child Behavior Checklist was the most commonly used, followed by the Conner's Parent Rating Scale. Parenting inventories introduced in the early 1990s have also increased in usage, with more than 40% of the evaluators reporting using the PCRI and Parenting Stress Inventory (also known as Parenting Stress Index), contrasted with 10% in the 1997 survey. Relatively low usage of some tests designed for child custody evaluations was found. For example, fewer than 30% of the evaluators used the BPS, the Perception of Relationship Test, or the Parent Awareness Skills Survey. Similarly, custody batteries were seldom used. ASPECT was used by only 16% of the evaluators, and Bricklin's ACCESS: A Comprehensive Custody Evaluation Standard System and the Uniform Custody Evaluation System were used by fewer than 10%. Thus, although psychological testing is widely used in custody evaluations, it is not considered as important as clinical interviews with parents, children, and parent-child observations.

As noted earlier, the court may request a written report or an appearance. In a courtroom handbook for mental health professionals, Tsushima and Anderson (1996, chap. 5) provide examples of courtroom examinations of a custody evaluator witness and alternative ways of responding. One needs to know not only the material one is testifying about but also how to appropriately present the material to the court. Krauss and Sales (1999, 2000) write that under *Daubert v. Merrell Dow Pharmaceuticals* (1993) the Federal Rules of Evidence may in the future block the admission of current child assessment instruments. Although they meet the first three criteria of *Daubert* (i.e., they are testable and tested, the basis for the evidence is published and subject to peer review, and procedures are generally accepted), the high error rate of the tests might preclude their admissibility in courts that follow a *Daubert* standard.

TYPES OF CUSTODY ARRANGEMENTS

Traditionally, custody was a unitary concept: One parent was responsible for child rearing and making all decisions regarding the child's life. By 1990, most jurisdictions had amended their custody laws to include joint custody and to make a distinction between physical and legal custody (Ehrlich, 1997). Physical custody refers to where the child lives and includes authority regarding day-to-day decisions. Legal custody refers solely to decision-making authority on major life events, such as where the child goes to school, religious instruction, and health care.

Currently, custody arrangements tend to fall into one of four patterns: sole custody, divided custody, split custody, and joint custody. These may encompass physical and/or legal custody. *Sole physical and legal custody* is the most commonly approved form of custody upon the dissolution of a marriage. In this form, custody is awarded to one parent, with visitation rights to the noncustodial parent. While the noncustodian may have authority over some decisions concerning the child by informal agreement, the ultimate control and legal responsibility remain with the custodial parent. There are emotional costs to both the custodial and noncustodial parents: Noncustodial parents often experience feelings of loss of their children similar to bereavement, and custodial parents often feel overwhelmed, overburdened, and trapped by the responsibility. Hyde (1984) points out that it is difficult for a mother to establish a career, to earn a living for her family, to become financially independent, and to establish a social life as well as provide the child care normally provided by two parents. Perhaps the most negative indictment of sole custody is that it tends to indicate to a child that one parent is right and one is wrong regarding divorce and custody.

Divided or alternating custody allows each parent to have the child for a part of the year, exercising full control over the child while the child is in his or her custody and having visitation rights for the period of time that the child is in the other parent's custody. Critics of divided custody generally believe that it creates confusion for the child with regard to authority and that shifting the child from home to home results in an unstable environment with lack of permanent associations for the child.

Split custody occurs when custody of one or more of the children is awarded to one parent with the remaining children being awarded to the other. As this arrangement may tend to further disrupt the family unit, it is not generally approved unless there are compelling circumstances to indicate that it would be in the best interest of the children.

The fourth type of custody is *joint or shared custody*, which is defined as a sharing of legal and/or physical custody by both parents so as to assure the access of the child to both parents in a frequent and continuing manner. There seems to be increasing support for joint custody in those cases where there is a willingness of both parties to carry out such a plan.

There have been a number of arguments for and against joint custody, ranging from attempting to make Solomonic decisions and the likelihood of continuing strife between the parents, to the opportunity of preserving the functional integrity of the various parent-child relationships. The issue at hand is not to arrive at one state of law applicable to everyone; rather, the goal is to develop a repertoire of custodial arrangements that might be applied to foster the best interests of the children and to encourage continued relationships between the parents and children, as well as with the broader social support network of the child.

A large number of psychologists and practitioners in domestic legal issues encourage placement of a child with the parent who seems most likely to encourage and foster the continued contact between the child and the noncustodial parent. Indeed, the California statutes favoring joint custody also provide that, in the event sole custody is determined to be in the child's best interest, the placement is made with the parent who evidences a willingness to share residential time as well as decision making with the other parent (Foster & Freed, 1983).

Weiner (1985) noted that in the past decade there have been numerous changes in family law in response to the evolving role of women, increased interest in parenting on the part of fathers, and interest in the rights of the children caught as unwitting third parties in the conflict. This trend has continued. Elrod and Spector (1996), in an annual review of family law, noted that 1994 through 1995 was a period in which children's issues of child custody and support dominated the arena of family law on national, state, and local levels, indicating the unsettled state of affairs in determining optimal custody policy. Each state is continuing to modify its custody laws, requiring practitioners to stay updated on the changes in their location. For example, several states no longer presume that a physical move (job relocation, remarriage) that benefits the custodial parent will benefit the child (Higgins, 2004). Child development research can assist the courts in determining what is in the best interest of an individual child (Kelly & Lamb, 2003). In a sample of college students from divorced families, Braver, Ellman, and Fabricius (2003) found that negative effects were associated with parental moves by mother or father with or without the child when compared to divorced families in which neither parent moved.

EFFECTS OF DIVORCE ON CHILDREN

The past 45 years have shown a dramatic increase in the number of children affected by divorce. Each year more than 1 million children in the United States experience the divorce of their parents (U.S. Bureau of the Census, 1999). While these families have been studied regarding the effects of divorce since the early 1970s, the earlier studies tended to focus on the effect of divorce on clinical cases. More recently, families not in the clinical population have also been studied, leading to slightly different findings.

Early studies of divorced families revealed that a number of changes were generally common to these families. Typically, divorced families experienced lowered economic stability, higher levels of interpersonal stress, loyalty conflicts, and an increased reliance on external support systems such as relatives and institutional and social service providers to aid in meeting familial needs. In addition, children frequently experienced major shifts in the amount and quality of parental contact available to them from both the custodial and noncustodial parents. Although the detrimental effects of these shifts in circumstances are often ameliorated by the second or third year following the divorce (Hetherington, 1979; Hetherington, Cox, & Cox, 1979;

Wallerstein & Kelly, 1980), the family may develop chronically inadequate means of meeting their needs. Some of the research suggested that these adjustment problems decrease significantly with time and assistance from external sources.

Generally, the most pervasive changes found in the early studies of children from divorced families were disruptions in their academic achievement and social relationships. Research indicated that although divorced families were generally stabilized by the second or third year following the divorce, the performance of children from divorced families continues to lag behind that of children from intact families (Lamb, 1977). Atkeson, Forehand, and Rickard (1982) further cite the parents' personal adjustment and the postdivorce relationship between parents and between parents and their children as material factors affecting the child's adjustment.

As samples of children experiencing divorce became more representative of all children experiencing divorce, fewer negative consequences were found than in the earlier studies. Amato and Keith (1991b) performed a meta-analysis of 92 comparative studies of children living in divorced single-parent families and children in continuously intact families. In general, they found that children from divorced families were less well-adjusted than their intact family counterparts but that the differences were small, with the most recent studies finding even smaller differences between groups. Amato and Keith found only moderate support for theories regarding the effect of parental absence and economic disadvantage, but the effect of continued family conflict was strongly supported.

Amato (2001) updated the Amato and Keith (1991b) meta-analysis with a new analysis of 67 studies published in the 1990s. Compared with children of continuously married parents, children of divorced parents continued to score significantly lower on measures of academic achievement, conduct, psychological adjustment, self-concept, and social relations. Although small, the differences in the scores of children of continuously married parents and divorced parents were greater in the 1990s. Amato points out that these are average differences and, depending on the particular constellation of factors surrounding the divorce, such as level of conflict between parents before and after the separation, the quality of parenting from both custodial and noncustodial parents, and changes in life stresses the individual child may show varying effects.

However, knowledge of the group averages cannot predict for an individual child. Bauserman (2002) meta-analyzed eight studies comparing child adjustment in joint physical or joint legal custody with sole custody arrangements. He found that children in joint legal or physical custody were better adjusted than children in sole custody settings but no different from those in intact families when looking at general adjustment, family relationships, self-esteem, and behavioral adjustment. Joint custody parents reported less current and past conflict than did sole custody parents. Similar findings were obtained by Gunnoe and Braver (2001) in a study of the effects of joint legal custody. They also found more frequent father-child visitation and fewer child adjustment problems in the joint legal custody families.

Additional research is needed on evaluating the various types of therapeutic and educational programs for divorcing families. One emerging model is that of a parent coordinator, appointed by the court, who can help parents resolve day-to-day conflicts. A parent coordinator project in Washington, D.C., is currently evaluating the kinds of interventions needed and whether the use of a parent coordinator can reduce the number of court appearances, improve the children's view of the family situation, and make an impact from the judge's point of view (Bailey, 2004).

Cherlin et al. (1991) found in a follow-up study that there was little difference in the adjustment of postdivorce 11-year-olds 5 years after the divorce. A longitudinal study by Chase-Lansdale, Cherlin, and Kiernan (1995) found long-term negative effects when the participants were 23 years of age, effects that were not displayed when they were 11 years of age. There may be some stressors in late adolescence or early adulthood that are not revealed by the cross-sectional studies.

A review of the literature of adult children of divorce supports the view that parental divorce has lasting implications for their achievement level and quality of life (Amato & Keith, 1991a). While we do not know all of the parameters for maximizing a successful adjustment following divorce, it does seem that a crucial factor promoting the success of a child's postdivorce adjustment is the quality of the relationship that develops between the child and the divorced parents.

A large body of research indicates that the circumstances that foster the most positive social, intellectual, and moral development are high levels of contact with both parents, provided the parents are able to minimize their personal conflicts (Kelly, 2000; Kurdek & Berg, 1983; Kurdek, Blisk, & Siesky, 1981; Wallerstein & Kelly, 1980). By the same token, no research supports the presumption that the child benefits from minimizing contact with the noncustodial parent, except in cases where the family is continually disrupted by verbal and/or physical conflict. In these cases, exposure to continued conflict is detrimental to the child's well-being in both divorced and intact families (Amato & Keith, 1991b).

As divorce mediation has grown into a widely used alternative for custody disputes over the past 20 years, research is appearing that contrasts mediated and litigated child custody arrangements. Emery, Laumann-Billings, Waldron, Sbarra, and Dillon (2001) studied 71 families who had been randomly assigned either to attempt mediation or to continue with an adversary procedure at the time of their first custody hearing. Twelve years after the resolution of their custody dispute, it was found that compared to families who litigated, nonresidential parents who mediated were more involved with their child, had more contact with their children, and had a greater influence in coparenting. Fathers who had mediated were more satisfied with the arrangements after 12 years than fathers who had litigated, but there were no differences in satisfaction in the two groups of mothers.

Finally, parents should be supported in their efforts to initiate independent lifestyles that recognize their status as functional parents. The stabilization process may be expected to take from 2 to 5 years, depending on the level of conflict, economic changes, and development of a viable social network outside of the marriage. It is unreasonable to assume that interruption of parental contact with the children of the marriage will encourage a reorganization and stabilization that includes the children. Both parents need the active support of the court and broader social system during the process of reorganization.

STEPPARENTS AND STEPFAMILIES

Because 75% of divorced mothers and 83% of divorced fathers remarry within 5 years, most children who experience divorce will also experience the remarriage of at least one of their parents (Fine, 1997). Under common law and current domestic law, stepparents do not enjoy the same privileges regarding stepchildren as natural parents. Much recent legislation has been directed toward considering on a case-by-case basis visitation rights of divorcing stepparents, as well as grandparents and other nonparent relatives, such as second cousins who had functioned as de facto parents. Questions about the current law regarding the status of visitation rights of relatives should be referred to lawyers in the psychologist's state.

Typically, the remarriage of a person paying child support or alimony does not change the individual's obligation to pay. The court assumes that the person marries with a full understanding of these obligations. Further, child support and alimony may not be discharged under bankruptcy proceedings. Whether or not the support payments are affected by pensions or retirement savings is currently being decided in the courts. Alimony customarily stops when the receiver remarries. Women have typically been the recipients of alimony, but recent court decisions have awarded men alimony. Other arrangements reflect a shift toward remedial alimony, or alimony that continues for a period while the recipient is retrained for employment so that the recipient can support himself or herself in the interim. In the past, the marriage of the individual receiving alimony was the criterion under which alimony would stop, encouraging nonmarital cohabitation so as not to terminate the alimony payments. This status is contrary to public policy. Thus, recent court decisions have changed the criteria for cessation of alimony payments somewhat by including the condition of residing with another man or woman for a period of time as sufficient reason to stop payments.

Visitation is a right rather than an obligation and needs to be considered when either of the divorced parents remarries. Many problems between divorced spouses do not arise until one or the other remarries. The unmarried former spouse may react with jealousy and anger and, if that person has custody, may prevent the other former spouse from seeing the children. By the same token, the new stepparent, confused about his or her role with the stepchildren or resentful of the continued influence of the former spouse, may disrupt the status quo that had been achieved between the divorced couple.

The noncustodial parent may react to the marriage of a former spouse by a cessation of visitation or support payments. Clinicians should be aware of the potential problems with the advent of a marriage within the divorced family, be aware of the legal responsibilities associated with the children, and be prepared to counsel their clients accordingly in an effort to reestablish a balance within the new family structure.

BLENDED FAMILIES

The blended family may be thought of as a family involving children from prior marriages as well as from the current marriage and involving several sets of interacting parents. Premarital counseling to address the financial and emotional shifts resulting from blending families may be useful in avoiding some of the destructive stress associated with joining two and three families. In some cases, it might be helpful for the clinician to work with all of the parties—former spouses and new family members—to facilitate the adjustment of all concerned.

Fine and Kurdek (1992) note that just as parenting practices and family climate affect intact and single-parent families, they affect children's adjustment in stepfamilies. A finding unique to stepfamilies, however, is that parents develop more positive relationships with their stepchildren when they do not initially assume an active role in discipline but wait until a trusting relationship has developed.

An important area for consideration in working with blended families is the issue of discipline and the rights of stepparents with regard to their stepchildren. Typically, custodial and noncustodial parents have the right and responsibility to invoke appropriate disciplinary procedures when dealing with their children and are protected from abuse or liability statutes so long as their behavior and discipline fall within the broad disciplinary mores of the greater community. In addition, natural parents have rights with regard to visitation and contact with their children that are substantially different from rights for stepparents and other persons significant to the child.

A stepparent has no disciplinary or visitation rights regarding a stepchild. His or her status is essentially that of any other nonfamily member. The result of this condition is that, should a stepparent threaten or harm a stepchild, a reasonable parental act may turn into an assault or battery, subjecting the stepparent to both civil and criminal liability. Likewise, reasonable touching by a biological parent to medicate or inspect a tender area, when done by a stepparent might be taken out of context and viewed as sexual assault or fondling (Bernstein & Haberman, 1981). On the other hand, a stepparent who has adopted a stepchild is accorded the full rights of the natural parents.

In the event of the failure of the blended family, it is important to consider that contracts between parents or between parents and stepparents regarding the care and custody of children might well be held invalid, as parents may not contract away the right of the court to rule on a custodial issue.

BONDING IN THE STEPFAMILY

Stepparents' fears about establishing a sound parental relationship with their stepchildren may be complicated by their limited rights of access to that child in the event of a divorce. As many laws stand now, in the event of a subsequent divorce within a blended family, the stepparent or foster parent would enjoy no rights toward the former spouse's children. A petition to the court to continue contact with the child following the divorce would be unsupportable under extant law. This condition would also hold true in most states in the event of the death of a spouse in that the children would likely be remanded to the surviving natural parent. Texas has given stepparents standing to seek custody if a child's natural parent dies (Elrod, 1995).

This issue becomes doubly complicated in the case of multiple sets of children: mine, yours, and ours. Since this issue of the rights of stepparents toward their stepchildren has become a significant litigation issue, there has been some impetus toward recognizing the possible relationships between stepparents and children. "Psychological parentage" represents the pivotal issue promulgated by Goldstein, Freud, and Solnit (1979) and is a substantial factor in determining the best interests of the child. Again, as this issue is currently in a state of flux, a good working relationship with a family lawyer in the party's jurisdiction is necessary to stay abreast of the changes.

ADOPTION

Adoption issues center on consent to adoption, eligibility to adopt, and effects of adoption. An additional arena of concern is that of the legal, ethical, and psychological issues involved in the alternative reproductive technologies.

CONSENT TO ADOPT

The best interests of the child and rights of the adults are sometimes in conflict. "Baby Jessica" (*In re* Clausen, 1993) and "Baby Richard" (*In re* Kirchner, 1995), are two of the more visible cases that have granted biological fathers custody even though the children had been in adoptive families for several years. Both cases involved the need for consent from biological parents. Some states have established laws narrowing the time frame for unwed fathers to show their commitment by requiring support for the mother during pregnancy or maintaining a relationship with the child. In cases where the fathers have abandoned their parental rights or not maintained a relationship, or where conception resulted from a rape, courts have allowed adoption without the biological father's consent. Some of these cases can be quite complex, and case law is now being established on those cases where the biological parents differ in the sequence of events, degree of relationship, or two or more states or countries are involved.

ALTERNATIVE REPRODUCTIVE TECHNOLOGIES AND ADOPTION

A California appellate court has ruled that people who contract to create a child through new technology (a child who would never have existed if they had not arranged for his or her "creation") become the child's legal parents and are responsible for child support (*Buzzanca v. Buzzanca*, 1998). In this case, the contractual parents, who divorced before her birth, had arranged for the creation of JayCee, the child of anonymous sperm and egg donors, arranging for her to be implanted and carried to term by a surrogate mother. The child thus had five potential or actual parents, but because the Buzzancas had subsequently divorced, she had no '"actual" parents. As the Buzzancas had no genetic ties to the child, they tried to walk away. This ruling sends the message that people cannot create babies without accepting the consequences and also supports those who want to be declared parents but fear that the courts will find surrogates or sperm or egg donors legal parents of the children they arranged to create.

Although it is unlikely that JayCee will remain unaware of the origins of her birth, due to the nationwide media coverage, there are many questions regarding the effect of revealing the specifics to children who were the products of alternative reproductive technologies (ART). Schwartz (2003) wrote that, as in other cases of adoption, how involved the extended family/community was in the parents' decision to use ART will affect the disclosure and source of disclosure. There is a need not only for a solid research base on the relationships formed by ART adoptions, but also for mental health professionals to provide counseling to the families. Counseling should begin prior to conception, progress through the child's learning how he or she came to be in the family, and assist children in dealing with such adoption issues as their unmet siblings, biological parents, or surrogates.

The first cohort of in vitro fertilization children have now reached adolescence. Golombok, MacCallum, and Goodman (2001) found that, when compared to naturally conceived children on measures of parent-child relationships and child's psychological well-being, the few differences that occurred were associated with the experience of infertility rather than the in vitro fertilization. Schwartz (2003) writes that other Western countries have more specific laws regarding the rights and responsibilities of all involved in ART, thus reducing the number of court contests that ultimately have psychological impact on those involved.

Who Can Adopt

Who can adopt is also being challenged. A Florida case is questioning the statute that bars homosexual partners from adopting (*Cox v. Florida Department of Health and Rehabilitation Services*, 1995). The District of Columbia has found that homosexual partners may jointly adopt a child previously adopted by one of the partners (*In re* M.M.D., 1995). Lesbian partners may adopt a child conceived by artificial insemination in some states, with both mothers' names being on the birth certificate. Tye (2003) reports that although a majority of states place considerable legal hurdles in the way of lesbian, gay, bisexual, and transgender individuals who want to adopt, research has demonstrated that the sexual orientation of a parent is irrelevant with respect to ability to parent or the psychological adjustment of the children. In addition to legal hurdles, Crawford, McLeod, Zamboni, and Jordan (1999) found that psychologists in the United States were less likely to recommend custody to couples who were identified in vignettes as gay or lesbian rather than heterosexual. The American

Psychological Association has filed *amicus curiae* briefs attesting to the fitness of lesbian and gay parents and the absence of negative effects on their children's development and adjustment (APA, 1998, n.d.).

Open adoptions, adoptions in which there is communication between birth and adoptive parents, are now recognized and protected by 18 states (Hwang, 2004). The New York State Supreme Court (*In re* Gerald, 1995) allowed a parent to include visitation and communication rights in the document surrendering the child if the adopting parents agree. While arrangements vary widely, examples of contact between birth parents and an adoptive family might be a monthly e-mail and an annual visit, or pictures from the adoptive family and occasional calls or visits. It is estimated that, in 2003, 80% of the adoptions in Minnesota were open and that open adoptions are growing faster in the midwestern and western parts of the country. They are still less common on the East Coast and parts of the South. A longitudinal study of open adoptions (Siegel, 2003) found that after 7 years, although the contact between families may have changed, the parents' enthusiasm for the openness remained.

In the United States each year, approximately 17,000 children are adopted from overseas. Weitzman (2003) writes that most of these children have been reared in orphanages and have suffered varying amounts of deprivation and neglect. They may have received substandard nutrition and health care.

LEGAL INTERVENTION IN ADOPTIONS

Adoption may affect grandparents' rights. For example, adoption by a stepfather may terminate the visitation rights of the paternal grandparents (*Hawk v. Hawk*, 1993), or parents may not want step-grandparents to have visitation rights (Associated Press, 2001). Although historically grandparents have lacked legal standing, all 50 states have passed some type of visitation act and the Grandparents for Children's Rights organization estimates more than 250 calls weekly from grandparents concerned about access to their grandchildren (Singhania, 1997). As in other areas, the courts come into play only when family members are unable to resolve the relationships on their own.

National and state courts have been active in adoptions in the 1990s. The Uniform Adoption Act (UAA; 1995) distinguished different types of adoptions, including agency, independent, and stepparent. UAA also set up standardized procedures for consents and relinquishments. Some of the procedures include a 30-day claim period following a proposed adoption for biological fathers, 8 days for a birth mother to change her mind, evaluation of all prospective parents, and open adoptions (Elrod, 1995). As a result of UAA, many states are reevaluating their adoption statues both for intrastate and interstate adoptions.

In May 1993, the Hague Conference on Private International Law proposed the Convention on Protection of Children and Cooperation in Respect of Intercountry Adoption (1993). The Convention endorsed intercountry adoptions, created rules of procedure and recognition of international adoption decrees, and established a central agency in each country to evaluate the suitability of adoptive parents and children. Hollingsworth (2003) cautions us to be aware of a number of issues in international adoptions. These include the risk to the children's rights to knowledge of their birth history, parentage, ethnic background, and cultural and national origins as well as the possibility of abduction, deceit, and trafficking in children. We await the results of this effort.

CHILD ABUSE

In 1874, the Society for Prevention of Cruelty to Children was established as an appendage to the American Society for the Prevention of Cruelty to Animals and came to be a determining force in obtaining child protective laws. Presently, although there is no official definition of maltreatment, all states have had child abuse and neglect protection laws since the 1960s. The Juvenile Justice Standards Project (1981) is the first set of legal definitions that explicitly state that harm to a child, not the characteristics of the abuser (individuals having poor parenting skills) or the acts of mistreatment (physical force or neglect), should serve as the determining factor in defining child abuse and neglect.

Kempe's recognition of the battered child syndrome sparked the public's attention to the issue (Kempe, Silverman, Steele, Droemueller, & Silverman, 1962). The practitioner needs to be familiar with the developments concerning the etiology, treatment, and prognosis in the ensuing four decades (Belsky, 1993; Dubowitz, Black, Starr, & Zuravin, 1993; Melton & Barry, 1994; Milner, 1991; Starr & Wolfe, 1991).

Because of the prevalence and effects of abuse on cognitive, emotional, and social development, the American Psychological Association (1996) has developed a guide for including information on child abuse and child neglect in graduate professional training. The guide contains information on (1) the prevalence of child abuse and neglect, (2) the consequences of abuse and neglect, (3) theories about the development of abusive and neglectful behaviors in adults, (4) the recognition and referral of abused and neglected children and adults, (5) the responses to abuse and neglect (child protection system, legal involvement, and mental health interventions), and (6) the prevention of child abuse and neglect. It also provides resources concerning ethical issues, involvement with other professionals, assessment of victims and their families, and interventions with both victims and perpetrators for trainees in clinical, counseling, and school psychology.

ASSESSMENT OF CHILD ABUSE

Clinicians are often called on to testify as expert witnesses regarding child abuse and neglect. They also are called on as material witnesses concerning abuse or neglect by parents or others when their clients are involved in litigation. Barth and Sullivan (1985) provide information on obtaining evidence that is useful when one is called as a material or fact witness rather than as an expert witness. A fact witness presents observations rather than opinions that have been derived from observations or from test and secondary data. Being a fact witness may occur when the clinician (or teacher or physician or school bus driver) observes fresh welts or bruises, a child sent out in snowstorms inadequately clothed, or acts of violence. Sagatun (1991) addresses the admissibility of expert testimony on child abuse and child sexual abuse. Only when someone has challenged the assertion that the child has been abused is expert testimony admitted that addresses the characteristics of an abused child, the characteristics of a class of victims, and observed behavior of the child in question.

Sattler (1997) provides comprehensive guidelines for assessment and clinical and forensic report writing in child maltreatment cases. Blau and Alberts (2004) have provided a documentation sourcebook containing suggested forms for forensic evaluations. Ellis (2001) has also provided guidelines for conducting parental fitness evaluations. Ellis recommends evaluating 10 areas: clinical history, level of involvement as a parent, parenting competence, mental status, home environment, parent-child interactions, child's needs and stressors, allegations of unfitness, compliance with rehabilitation plan, and summary for the court. Budd, Felix, Poindexter, Naik-Polan, and Sloss (2002) reviewed assessments provided to an urban court system. They found that psychological, developmental, and parent bonding assessments were completed in one office session, whereas parenting assessment team evaluations averaged nearly five sessions and included visits in the clinic and home visits. The assessments often fell short of the multisource, multisession approach recommended by the American Psychological Association Committee on Professional Practice and Standards (1998) for evaluations in child protection matters.

REPORTING CHILD ABUSE OR NEGLECT

Professionals may come into contact with an abused child through many different avenues. Physical abuse, neglect, and sexual abuse may occur as a direct action of parents, siblings, and extended family. Reporting laws in all 50 states have made it mandatory for professionals, including psychologists, to report suspected abuse. Liability provisions in the reporting statutes involve three elements: (1) immunity from criminal and civil liability, (2) criminal liability for failure to report, and (3) criminal liability for making a false report (Small, Lyons, & Guy, 2002).

Surveys of licensed psychologists have revealed that the laws are not adhered to 100% of the time. Brosig and Kalichman (1992b), reviewing earlier literature, found that between 30% and 40% of practicing psychologists are noncompliant. Furthermore, they found that the wording of the law affected the likelihood of reporting, in that professionals were more likely to report when the legal requirements were clear and specific (Brosig & Kalichman, 1992a). Professionals were less likely to report when they did not feel that they had enough evidence. In cases involving clients, some practitioners are concerned that reporting may harm the therapeutic relationship. It is important to assess and repair the breach in trust between therapist and client in order to reaffirm the therapeutic relationship after the necessary break in confidentiality.

Renninger, Veach, and Bagdade (2002), assessing knowledge of the reporting law and compliance with the law, found that professionals felt they had a better understanding of the reporting law than they actually did, and that they actually tended to overreport. Concerns about reporting were similar to those in the earlier Brosig and Kalichman (1992b) study.

Institutional abuse is too often the outcome for child victims who are removed from their family's neglect or abuse and are placed in a foster care system only to be further abused. Davidson (1983) considers keeping children in foster care for prolonged periods to be an abuse per se. The Adoption Assistance and Child Welfare Act of 1980 was designed to provide funding for services that would facilitate a speedy return of children to their parents or to assist in the adoption of those who are not able to return to their family of origin.

CHILD SEXUAL ABUSE

Child sexual abuse (CSA) is defined by Browne and Finkelhor (1986) as any forced or coerced sexual behavior imposed on a child, and/or sexual activity between a child and a much older person, whether or not obvious coercion is involved. The prevalence of CSA has been estimated at 15% to 33% among females in the general population and 35% to 75% in clinical populations, and for males at 13% to 16% in the general population and 13% to 23% in clinical populations (Polusny & Follette, 1995). Finkelhor (1979), studying the incidence of incest and child abuse through a survey of students, reported finding that most sexual victimization of children was incestuous. Mullen, King, and Tonge (2000), reviewing 20 years of research, found that the perpetrators were predominantly male, but that natural parents were the abusers in only 3% of the cases. Strangers were perpetrators in 23% of the cases, and acquaintances, at 48%, were the most frequent group. The risk of a stepparent abusing a child, however, is 10 times higher than for a natural parent, and intrafamilial abuse is more likely to be repeated than nonfamilial abuse.

The 1980s and 1990s saw a flood of research (with a wide range of populations and methodological problems) on the effects of sexual abuse. Surveys concerning the sequelae of sexual abuse by Browne and Finkelhor (1986) and Polusny and Follette (1995) identified initial reactions of fear, anxiety, depression, anger, hostility, and inappropriate sexual behavior and long-term effects for both females and males. They found higher levels of general psychological distress, including depression and anxiety disorders, suicidal behaviors, self-mutilation, somatic complaints, and substance abuse. A practitioner working with either a child or an adult survivor needs to be knowledgeable about the etiology, treatment, and legal resources for dealing with incest and sexual abuse. Toward building a firm knowledge base, the reader is well advised to consult Briere (1991), Burgess, Groth, Holstrom, and Sgroi (1978), Finklehor (1990), Kempe and Kempe (1984), Kendall-Tackett, Williams, and Finkelhor (1993), Kuehnle (1996), and Milner (1992).

Following the disclosure of CSA, the child may experience turmoil. That is, the child and family will come into contact with a number of institutions, such as child protective services, medical institutions, law enforcement social service agencies, and court systems, that may not be responsive to the child's psychological needs. Each agency may reopen wounds by having the child relive the abuse. Wakefield and Underwager (1992) focus on ways that interviews with children can be biased unknowingly by the interviewers (interrogators), who are trying to elicit as much information as possible from the child in anticipation of adjudication.

Concerning the veracity of child witnesses in sexual abuse cases, Meyer and Geis (1994) write that rather than discussing the virtues and demerits of anatomically correct dolls and the suggestibility of children, we should conduct research on how to determine which children are unreliable witnesses. Bruck and Ceci (2004) focus on urban legends regarding the reliability of children's reports of sexual abuse in an attempt to encourage conducting interviews with possible abuse victims using scientifically validated methods. The myths are (1) that sexually abused children do not disclose their abuse, (2) that the number of leading statements influence the child's report, (3) that suggestibility is primarily a problem for preschoolers, and (4) that multiple suggestive interviews are needed to taint a report. Interviewers of children of all ages need to take care not to bias, lead, or shape the responses. Kuehnle (2003, chap. 22) describes the use of assessment tools such as anatomical dolls, projective tests, and figure drawings in evaluating alleged sexual abuse victims.

The question of what kinds of expert testimony will be allowed in CSA cases is still unanswered. In *In re* Amber (1987), a trial court found that a child had been abused based on a psychologist's testimony regarding the alleged victim's play with anatomically correct dolls. Because it needed to and did not meet the *Frye* test, the appellate court excluded the testimony and reversed the trial court judgment (Sagatun, 1991). Garb, Wood, and Nezworski (2000) questioned the validity of using projective techniques in the detection of sexual abuse of children, and authorities on these methods generally concur that they are not appropriate for this purpose (Kelly, 1999; Kuehnle, 1996; Meyer & Archer, 2001; Weiner, in press).

CHILD SEXUAL ABUSE AND THE INTERNET

As children and child molesters become more Internet-savvy, the risk for children increases. Children have been lured across state lines and across national borders. Workshops for professionals on characterizing the susceptible child victim, online child abuse indicators, and interview techniques for online victims and online abusers are being developed. Research on incidence, treatment for online victims, and prevention techniques is needed.

CONCLUSIONS

There are few areas of forensic psychology practice encompassing as vast and as emotionally charged an area as child domestic law issues. Part of the complexity stems from the quickly changing laws, cases, statutes, and regulations as well as from a burgeoning and vibrant psychological literature. Competent practice involves knowing the local, state, and jurisdictional laws and practices and keeping abreast of relevant research, theory, and assessment methods.

REFERENCES

Abidin, R. R. (1990). *Parenting Stress Index* (3rd ed.). Odessa, FL: Psychological Assessment Resources.

Ackerman, M. J., & Ackerman, M. C. (1997). Custody evaluation practices: A survey of experienced professionals (revisited). *Professional Psychology: Research and Practice, 28,* 137–145.

Ackerman, M. J., & Schoendorf, K. (1992). *Ackerman-Schoendorf Scales for Parent Evaluation of Custody* (ASPECT). Los Angeles: Western Psychological Services.

Adoption Assistance and Child Welfare Act of 1980, Pub. L. No. 96-272.

Amato, P. R. (2001). Children of divorce in the 1990s: An update of the Amato and Keith (1991). Meta-analysis. *Journal of Family Psychology, 15,* 355–370.

Amato, P. R., & Keith, B. (1991a). Parental divorce and adult well being. *Journal of Marriage and Family, 53,* 43–58.

Amato, P. R., & Keith, B. (1991b). Parental divorce and the well being of children: A meta-analysis. *Psychological Bulletin, 110,* 26–46.

American Bar Association. (1995, Spring). Special symposium on working with mental health professionals. *Family Law Quarterly, 29.*

American Psychological Association. (n.d.). Brief of *Amicus curiae* (in the Supreme Court of the State of Missouri, Delong v. Delong).

American Psychological Association. (1991). Specialty guidelines for forensic psychologists. *Law and Human Behavior, 6,* 655–665.

American Psychological Association. (1993). *Record keeping guidelines.* Washington, DC: Author.

American Psychological Association. (1994). Guidelines for child custody evaluations in divorce proceedings. *American Psychologist, 49,* 677–680.

American Psychological Association. (1996). *Agenda for including information in child abuse and neglect in graduate and professional education and training.* American Psychological Association Public Interest Directorate. Washington, DC: Author.

American Psychological Association. (1998). Brief of *Amicus curiae* (In the Court of Appeals of Tennessee. In the Court of Appeals of Maryland, Boswell v. Boswell).

American Psychological Association Committee on Professional Practice and Standards. (1998). *Guidelines for psychological evaluations in child protection matters.* Washington, DC: American Psychological Association.

Armas, G. C. (2004, December 2). Many Americans wed for first time after 30. *Montgomery Advertiser,* p. A-4.

Associated Press. (2001, September 2). Grandparent visitation nixed. *Montgomery Advertiser,* p. 11-B.

Association of Family and Conciliation Courts. (1994). Model standards of practice for child custody evaluation. *Family and Conciliation Courts Review, 32,* 504.

Atkeson, B. M., Forehand, R. L., & Rickard, K. M. (1982). The effect of divorce on children. In B. B. Lahey & A. E. Kazdin (Eds.), *Advances in clinical child psychology* (Vol. 5, pp. 255–279). New York: Plenum Press.

Bailey, D. S. (2004). Reconceptualizing custody. *Monitor on Psychology, 35,* 44–45.

Barth, R. P., & Sullivan, R. (1985). Competent evidence in behalf of children. *Social Work, 30,* 130–136.

Bauserman, R. (2002). Child adjustment in joint custody arrangements: A meta-analytic review. *Journal of Family Psychology, 16,* 91–102.

Belsky, J. (1993). Etiology of child maltreatment: A developmental analysis. *Psychological Bulletin, 114,* 413–434.

Bernstein, B. E., & Haberman, B. G. (1981). Lawyer and counselor as a team: Problem awareness in the blended family. *Child Welfare, 60,* 211–219.

Blau, T. H., & Alberts, F. L. (2004). *Forensic documentation sourcebook.* Hoboken, NJ: Wiley.

Bow, J. N., & Quinnell, F. A. (2001). Psychologists' current practices and procedures in child custody evaluations: Five years after American Psychological Association Guidelines. *Professional Psychology: Research and Practice, 32,* 261–268.

Bowlby, J. (1969). *Attachment.* New York: Basic Books.

Braver, S. L., Ellman, I. M., & Fabricius, W. V. (2003). Relocation of children after divorce and children's best interest: New evidence and legal considerations. *Journal of Family Psychology, 17,* 206–219.

Bricklin, B. (1984). *Brickin Perceptual Scales*. Furlong, PA: Village.

Briere, J. (Ed.). (1991). *Treating victims of child sexual abuse*. New York: Jossey Bass.

Brodzinsky, D. M. (1993). On the use and misuse of psychological testing in child custody evaluations. *Professional Psychology: Research and Practice, 24,* 213–219.

Brosig, C. L., & Kalichman, S. C. (1992a). Child abuse reporting decisions: Effects of statutory wording of reporting requirements. *Professional Psychology: Research and Practice, 23,* 486–492.

Brosig, C. L., & Kalichman, S. C. (1992b). Clinicians' reporting of suspected child abuse: A review of the empirical literature. *Clinical Psychology Review, 12,* 155–168.

Browne, A., & Finkelhor, D. (1986). Impact of child sexual abuse. *Psychological Bulletin, 99,* 66–77.

Bruck, M., & Ceci, S. (2004). Forensic developmental psychology: Unveiling four common misconceptions. *Current Directions in Psychological Science, 13,* 229–232.

Budd, K. S., Felix, E. D., Poindexter, L. M., Naik-Polan, A. T., & Sloss, C. F. (2002). Clinical assessment of children in child protection cases: An empirical analysis. *Professional Psychology: Research and Practice, 33,* 3–12.

Burgess, A. W., Groth, A. N., Holstrom, L. L., & Sgroi, S. M. (1978). *Sexual assault of children and adolescents*. Lexington, MA: Lexington.

Buzzanca v. Buzzanca (*In re* Marriage of Buzzanca), 72 Cal. Rpt 2d. 280, 293 (Ct. App.1998).

Chase-Lansdale, P. L., Cherlin, A. J., & Kiernan, K. E. (1995). The long-term effects of parental divorce on the mental health of young adults: A developmental perspective. *Child Development, 66,* 1614–1634.

Cherlin, A. J., Furstenberg, F. F., Jr., Chase-Lansdale, P. L., Kiernan, K. E., Robbins, P. K., Morrison, D. R., et al. (1991). Longitudinal studies of the effects of divorce on children in Great Britain and the United States. *Science, 252,* 1386–1389.

Clark, B. K. (1995). Acting in the best interests of the child: Essential components of a child custody evaluation. *Family Law Quarterly, 29,* 19–38.

Clay, R. A. (1995, December). Courts reshape image of "the good mother." *APA Monitor,* 31.

Cox v. Florida Department of Health and Rehabilitation Services, 656 So. 2nd 902 (Fla., 1995).

Crawford, I., McLeod, A., Zamboni, B. D., & Jordan, M. B. (1999). Psychologists' attitudes toward gay and lesbian parenting. *Professional Psychology: Research and Practice, 30,* 394–401.

Daubert v. Merrell Dow Pharmaceuticals, 509 U.S. 579 (1993).

Davidson, H. A. (1983, December). Children's rights: Emerging trends for the 1980s. *Trial,* 44–48.

Dubowitz, H., Black, M., Starr, R., & Zuravin, S. (1993). *A conceptual definition of child neglect: Foundations for a new national strategy*. New York: Guilford Press.

Ehrlich, J. S. (1997). *Family law for paralegals*. New York: Aspen Law and Business.

Ellis, E. M. (2001). Guidelines for conducting parental fitness evaluations. *American Journal of Forensic Psychology, 19,* 5–40.

Elrod, L. D. (1995). A review of the year in family law. *Family Law Quarterly, 28,* 541–557.

Elrod, L. D., & Spector, R. G. (1996). A review of the year in family law: Children's issues take spotlight. *Family Law Quarterly, 29,* 741–769.

Emery, R. E., Laumann-Billings, L., Waldron, M. C., Sbarra, D. A., & Dillon P. (2001). Child custody mediation and litigation: Custody, contact, and coparenting 12 years after initial dispute resolution. *Journal of Consulting and Clinical Psychology, 69,* 323–332.

Fine, M. A. (1997). Helping children cope with marital conflict, divorce, and remarriage. *In Session: Psychotherapy in Practice, 3,* 55–67.

Fine, M. A., & Kurdek, L. A. (1992). The adjustment of adolescents in stepfather and stepmother families. *Journal of Marriage and the Family, 54,* 725–736.

Finkelhor, D. (1979). *Sexually victimized children*. New York: Free Press.

Finkelhor, D. (1990). Early and longterm effects of child sexual abuse: An update. *Professional Psychology: Research and Practice, 21,* 325–330.

Foster, H. H., & Freed, D. J. (1983). Child custody and the adversary process: Forum convenient? *Family Law Quarterly, 17,* 133–150.

Garb, H. N., Wood, J. M., & Nezworski, M. T. (2000). Projective techniques and the detection of child sexual abuse. *Child Abuse and Neglect, 24,* 437–438.

Gerard, A. B. (1994). *Parent-Child Relationship Inventory (PCRI): Manual*. Los Angeles: Western Psychological Services.

Ginsberg v. N.Y., 390 U.S. 629, 649–650 (1968).

Glassman, J. B. (1998). Preventing and managing board complaints: The downside risk of custody evaluation. *Professional Psychology: Research and Practice, 29,* 121–124.

Goldstein, J., Freud, A., & Solnit, A. J. (1979). *Beyond the best interest of the child*. New York: Free Press.

Golombok, S., MacCallum, F., & Goodman, E. (2001). The test-tube generation: Parent-child relationships and the psychological well-being of in vitro fertilization children at adolescence. *Child Development, 72,* 599–608.

Gunnoe, M. L., & Braver, S. L. (2001). The Effects of joint legal custody on mothers, fathers, and children controlling for factors that predispose a sole maternal versus joint legal award. *Law and Human Behavior, 25,* 25–43.

Hague Convention on the Protection of Children and Cooperation in Respect of Intercountry Adoption. (1993, May 29). The Hague Conference on private international law, final act of the seventeenth session.

Hague International Child Abduction Convention S. Treaty Doc. No 11, 99th Cong., 1st Sess., Reprinted in 19 I. L. M. 1501 (1980).

Hawk v. Hawk, 855 S. W.2d. 573, 579–580 (Tenn. 1993).

Heilbrun, K. (1995). Child custody evaluation: Critically assessing mental health experts and psychological tests. *Family Law Quarterly, 29,* 63–78.

Heinze, M. C., & Grisso, T. (1996). Review of instruments assessing parenting capacities used in child custody evaluations. *Behavioral Sciences and the Law, 14,* 293–313.

Hetherington, E. M. (1979). Divorce: A child's perspective. *American Psychologist, 34,* 851–852.

Hetherington, E. M., Cox, M., & Cox, R. (1979). Play and social interaction in children following divorce. *Journal of Social Issues, 35,* 26–49.

Higgins, M. (2004, Jan. 22). Divorced parents face new legal hurdles. *Wall Street Journal,* pp. D-1, D-2.

Hollingsworth, L. D. (2003). International adoption among families in the United States: Considerations of social justice. *Social Work, 48,* 209–217.

Horvath, L. S., Logan, T. K., & Walker, R. (2002). Child custody cases: A content analysis of evaluations in practice. *Professional Psychology Research and Practice, 33,* 557–565.

Hwang, S. (2004, September 28). U.S. adoptions get easier. *Wall Street Journal.* p. D-1.

Hyde, L. M. (1984). Child custody in divorce. *Juvenile and Family Court Journal, 35,* 1–72.

In re Amber B., 191 Cal. App. 3d. 682, 236 Cal. Rptr 623 (1987).

In re Clausen, 505 N. W.2d. 575 (Mich.1993).

In re Gerald (Cindy W.), 625N. Y. S. 2d. 509 (App. Div. 1995).

In re Kirchner, 649 N.E.2d. 324 (Ill.1995).

In re M.M.D., 662 A.2d. 837 (D.C. Ct. App. 1995).

Ireland v. Smith, Michigan Cir. Ct., Macomb County June 27, 1994 Docket no. 93–385.

Jameson, B. J., Ehrenberg, M. F., & Hunter, M. A. (1997). Psychologists' rating of the best-interest-of-the-child custody and access criterion: A family system assessment model. *Professional Psychology: Research and Practice, 28,* 253–262.

Juvenile Justice Standards Project, Institute of Judicial Administration, American Bar Association. (1981). *Standards relating to abuse and neglect.* Cambridge, MA: Ballinger.

Kelly, F. D. (1999). *The psychological assessment of abused and traumatized children.* Mahwah, NJ: Erlbaum.

Kelly, J. B. (2000). Children's adjustment in conflicted marriage and divorce: A decade review of research. *Journal of the American Academy of Child and Adolescent Psychiatry, 39,* 963–973.

Kelly, J. B., & Lamb, M. E. (2003). Developmental issues in relocation cases involving young children: When, whether, and how? *Journal of Family Psychology, 17,* 193–205.

Kempe, C. H., Silverman, F., Steele, B., Droemueller, W., & Silverman, H. (1962). The battered child syndrome. *Journal of the American Medical Association, 181,* 17–24.

Kempe, R., & Kempe, C. (1984). *The common secret: Sexual abuse of children and adolescents.* New York: Freeman.

Kendall-Tackett, K. A., Williams, L. M., & Finkelhor, D. (1993). Impact of sexual abuse in children: A review and synthesis of recent empirical studies. *Psychological Bulletin, 113,* 164–180.

Krauss, D. A., & Sales, B. D. (1999). The problem of "helpfulness" in applying Daubert to expert testimony: Child custody determinations in family law as an exemplar. *Psychology, Public Policy and the Law, 5,* 78–99.

Krauss, D. A., & Sales, B. D. (2000). Legal standards, expertise, and experts in the resolution of contested child custody cases. *Psychology, Public Policy and the Law, 6,* 843–879.

Kuehnle, K. (1996). *Assessing allegations of child sexual abuse.* Sarasota, FL: Professional Resource Press.

Kuehnle, K. (2003). Child sexual abuse evaluations. In A. M. Goldstein (Ed.), *Forensic psychology* (pp. 437–460). Volume 11 in, I. B. Weiner (Editor-in-Chief), *Handbook of psychology.* Hoboken, NJ: Wiley.

Kurdek, L. A., & Berg, B. (1983). Correlates of children's adjustments to their parents' divorces. *New Directions for Child Development, 19,* 47–60.

Kurdek, L. A., Blisk, D., & Siesky, A. E. (1981). Correlates of children's long-term adjustment to their parents' divorce. *Developmental Psychology, 17,* 565–579.

Lamb, M. E. (1977). The effects of divorce on children's personality development. *Journal of Divorce, 1,* 163–174.

Lamb, M. E. (Ed.). (1996). *The role of the father in child development* (3rd ed.). New York: Wiley.

Loving v. Virginia, 388 U.S. 1 (1967).

Melton, G. B., & Barry, F. (1994). *Protecting children from abuse and neglect: Foundations for a new national strategy.* New York: Guilford Press.

Meyer, G. J., & Archer, R. (2001). The hard science of Rorschach research: What do we know and where do we go? *Psychological Assessment, 13,* 486–502.

Meyer, J. F., & Geis, G. (1994). Psychological research on child witnesses in sexual abuse cases: Fine answers to mostly wrong questions. *Child and Adolescent Social Work Journal, 11,* 209–220.

Michigan Child Custody Act of 1970, M.C.L. 722.23 (1993, amended).

Milner, J. S. (Ed.). (1991). Physical child abuse [Special issue]. *Criminal Justice and Behavior, 18.*

Milner, J. S. (Ed.). (1992). Sexual child abuse [Special issue]. *Criminal Justice and Behavior, 19.*

Morris, R. J. (1997). Child custody evaluations: A risky business. *Register Report, 23,* 6–7.

Mullen, P. E., King, N. J., & Tonge, B. J. (2000). Child sexual abuse: An overview. *Behavior Change, 17,* 2–14.

Otto, R. K., Buffington-Vollum, J. K., & Edens, J. F. (2003). Child custody evaluation. In A. M. Goldstein (Ed.), *Forensic psychology* (pp. 179–298). Vol. 11 in, I. B. Weiner (Editor-in-Chief), *Handbook of psychology.* Hoboken, NJ: Wiley.

Parental Kidnapping Prevention Act of 1980, Pub. L. No. 96-611 December 28.

Parham v. J. L. & J. R., 422 U.S. 584 (1979).

Polusny, M. A., & Follette, V. M. (1995). Long term correlates of child sexual abuse: Theory and review of the empirical literature. *Applied and Preventive Psychology: Current Scientific Perspectives, 4,* 143–166.

Prince v. Massachusetts, 321 U.S. 158 (1944).

Quinnell, F. A., & Bow, J. N. (2001). Psychological tests used in child custody evaluations. *Behavioral Sciences and the Law, 19,* 491–501.

Renninger, S. M., Veach, P. M., & Bagdade, P. (2002). Psychologists' knowledge, opinions, and decision-making process regarding child abuse and neglect reporting laws. *Professional Psychology: Research and Practice, 33,* 19–23.

Sagatun, I. J. (1991). Expert witnesses in child abuse cases. *Behavioral Science and the Law, 9,* 201–215.

Sattler, J. M. (1997). *Clinical and forensic interviewing of children and families.* San Diego, CA: Jerome Sattler.

Schwartz, L. L. (2003). A nightmare for King Solomon: The new reproductive technologies. *Journal of Family Psychology, 17,* 229–237.

Siegel, D. H. (2003). Open adoption of infants: Adoptive parents' feelings seven years later. *Social Work, 48,* 409–419.

Silberman L. (1994). Hague convention on international child abduction: A brief overview and case law analysis. *Family Law Quarterly, 28,* 9–34.

Singhania, L. (1997, November 3). Laws back grandparents who sue their children for visitation rights. *Montgomery Advertiser,* p. E-6.

Small, M. A., Lyons, P. M., & Guy, L. S. (2002). Liability issues in child abuse and neglect reporting statutes. *Professional Psychology: Research and Practice, 33,* 13–18.

Stahl, P. M. (1994). *Conducting child custody evaluations: A comprehensive guide.* Thousand Oaks, CA: Sage.

Starr, R. H., & Wolfe, D. A. (Eds.). (1991). *The effect of child abuse and neglect: Issues and research.* New York: Guilford Press.

Tsushima, W. T., & Anderson, R. M. (1996). *Mastering expert testimony.* Mahwah, NJ: Erlbaum.

Tye, M. C. (2003). Lesbian, gay, bisexual, and transgender parents: Special considerations for the custody and adoption evaluator. *Family Court Review, 41,* 92–103.

Uniform Adoption Act, 9 U.L.A. § 1 (West Supp. 1995).

Uniform Child Custody Jurisdiction Act, 9 U.S.C.A. § III (1979).

United States Bureau of the Census. (1999). *Statistical abstract of the United States: 1999.* (119th ed.). Washington, DC: Author.

U.S. Census Bureau. (2003). http://www.childstats.gov/ac2003/indicators.asp?104$id=1.

Wakefield, H., & Underwagner, R. (1992). Assessing credibility of children's testimony in ritual sexual abuse allegations. *Issues in Child Abuse Accusations, 4,* 32–44.

Walker, T. B. (1992). Family law in the fifty states: An overview. *Family Law Quarterly, 25,* 417–520.

Wallerstein, J. S., & Kelly, J. B. (1980). *Surviving the breakup: How children and parents cope with divorce.* New York: Basic Books.

Weiner, B. A. (1985). An overview of child custody laws. *Hospital and Community Psychiatry, 36,* 838–843.

Weiner, I. B. (in press). Rorschach assessment in child custody cases. *Journal of Child Custody.*

Weithorn, L. A. (1982). Developmental factors and competence to make informed treatment decisions. *Child and Youth Services, 4,* 85–100.

Weithorn, L. A. (Ed.). (1987). *Psychology and child custody determinations.* Lincoln: University of Nebraska Press.

Weitzman, C. C. (2003). Developmental assessment of the internationally adopted child: Challenges and rewards. *Clinical Child Psychology and Psychiatry, 8,* 303–313.

Wisconsin v. Yoder, 406 U.S. (1972).

Zarski, L. P., Knight, R., & Zarski, J. J. (1985). Child custody disputes: A review of legal and clinical resolution methods. *International Journal of Family Therapy, 7,* 96–106.

CHAPTER 6

Conducting Personal Injury Evaluations

STEVEN WALFISH

PERSONAL INJURY litigations are based on the law of torts. Tort law posits four requirements for demonstrating a personal injury that entitles a plaintiff to some compensation from a defendant. First, there must be a clear and specific duty or obligation owed to the plaintiff in a personal injury case by the defendant in the case, whether a person or some corporate or organizational entity. Second, there must have been some demonstrable dereliction in that duty by act of omission or commission on the part of the defendant. Third, the plaintiff must give evidence of some damage or disability that represents a decline in functioning capacity or peace of mind from some earlier point in time. Fourth, there must be good reason to believe that the plaintiff's damage or disability resulted from or was exacerbated by the defendant's dereliction of duty, which therefore constituted a "proximate cause" of the damage. Whether the defendant in fact had an obligation and was derelict in meeting it are legal matters that are beyond the purview of psychology and for the courts to decide. Whether a plaintiff is mentally or emotionally damaged, the severity of this damage, and the extent to which it can be attributed to actions or inactions of the defendant are the aspects of personal injury litigation in which forensic psychologists are likely to become involved.

When conducting personal injury evaluations, psychologists are accordingly faced with answering three basic questions:

1. Does the person being evaluated have a psychological injury?
2. If so, what is the extent of this injury?
3. How much of the injury present can be attributed on a "more likely than not" basis to the event claimed to have caused it?

I gratefully acknowledge the generosity of Steve Bloomfield, Vicki Campagna, Jonathan Gould, David Kazar, and Jodi Sabatino in providing examples.

These questions may appear straightforward, yet answering them in a way that meets the standard of a competent forensic evaluation may be complicated and labor-intensive. In addition to these basic questions, Blau (1998, p. 215) indicates that expert witnesses are asked to render an opinion regarding "permanence, replacement or remediation," that is, the degree to which the injured person will recover, the individual's future capacity to function, and the likely requirements for rehabilitation to be achieved.

Personal injury lawsuits are not limited in scope to a narrow type of injury such as being involved in a motor vehicle accident or medical malpractice. Rather, personal injury occurs in a number of life events and scenarios, and a psychologist may be called on to assess and render an opinion on myriad types of cases. Blau (1998, pp. 212–213) identifies the most common areas that may support a claim for personal injury: (1) negligence, simple or gross, (2) willful or wanton misconduct, (3) nuisance, (4) breach of warranty, (5) strict liability, (6) defamation, (7) fraud, (8) intentional acts, (9) breach of contract, and (10) the effect of a statute regulation, or ordinance. For further descriptions of each of these categories, please refer to this work.

To illustrate Blau's (1998) point regarding the array of cases psychologists might become involved in with this type of clinical work, I sought to explore the experiences of forensic psychologists on the PsyLaw listserve. A solicitation was posted on this listserv asking these individuals to describe the assortment of cases they have been involved with related to civil law suits. These cases are presented in Table 6.1. As can be seen, these cases are not limited to

Table 6.1
Examples of Personal Injury Cases

A wrongful termination due to age discrimination.

A rape in an apartment complex.

A slip and fall in a grocery store.

A rape in a hospital.

Sexual abuse in a juvenile detention facility.

The loss of an eye due to a toy that malfunctioned.

Mugging in a business's parking lot.

An unnecessary hysterectomy and subsequent loss of consortium.

Claustrophobic individual twice stuck in an apartment elevator.

Patient was in an MRI tube and technician left the room. Patient had a panic attack and subsequently developed other generalized fears.

Sexual harassment by a supervisor.

Bodily disfigurement due to product negligence that caused a fire.

Patient was sexually assaulted by plastic surgeon under anesthesia.

A wrongful job termination due to gender discrimination.

Cruise ship almost sinking.

Physical assault by a supervisor on the job.

A psychologist having sexual relations with one of his patients.

motor vehicle accidents or simple slip and fall accidents. At times, the cases even become unusual.

Case 6.1

A young college student was working a summer job in a rural area selling books from door to door. He obtained a permit to do this work. One day he knocked on a door and there was no answer. He left and returned the next day. Once again he knocked and there was no answer; he returned to his car. A pickup truck came to a screeching halt in front of him and the driver jumped out, waving a gun and telling the young man to get out of the car. Stunned and frightened, he followed the directive. The wild man put a gun to his head and said, "I know what you've done. You make one move before the cops get here and I will kill you!" The police arrived and arrested the young man. After six hours in jail with no Miranda rights being read to him and no call to anyone, the police looked into the young man's story and his identity. It was a case of mistaken identity and the young man was released. Since that time, he has suffered from Posttraumatic Stress Disorder (PTSD), and his eligibility as a scholar-athlete was in peril due to poor grades secondary to the emotional trauma of this event.

*   *   *

Entire volumes of work have been dedicated to the topic of mental health professionals completing personal injury evaluations in a forensic context (Foote & Goodman-Delahunty, 2004; Greenberg & Brodsky, 2001; Murrey, 2001; Simon, 2003). Those wanting to learn about this area in greater depth are encouraged to seek out this body of work. In the following pages, I present a framework for the mental health professional to consider when completing these types of evaluations: (1) consideration of who is making the referral for the evaluation and the resulting relationship between the interested parties (e.g., physician, attorney, client); (2) making a decision on the methodology as to how to answer the referral question(s); (3) the role that existing literature on both the tests instruments utilized and the specific problem area being addressed plays in drawing conclusions; and (4) the importance of ruling out malingering. Two specific types of cases, motor vehicle accidents and worker's compensation, will be utilized to highlight the issues being presented.

THE REFERRAL

In this volume, A. K. Hess (Chapter 22) elaborates on issues for the psychologist to consider when accepting a referral for a forensic evaluation. If followed, this advice will clarify the questions to be addressed in the evaluation and help the psychologist to decide whether or not to accept the referral.

In personal injury evaluations, referrals come from two primary sources: attending physicians and personal injury attorneys. Each has different implications for the role the psychologist will play in the evaluation and to whom the psychologist is responsible for reporting the results of the evaluation.

Attending physicians primarily tend to the physical needs of an individual who has been injured. That is, they fix broken bones, heal burns that may have been inflicted, or prescribe medicines to help the patient deal with pain. In addition, the attending physician is in a prime position to notice the presence of cognitive and emotional aspects of an injury. If a patient is not responding to initial medical care, or if the patient reports persistent difficulties with memory and concentration, the physician may consider further diagnostic evaluation by a psychologist to address these problem areas. In these instances, the physician, acting as a gatekeeper and coordinator of services for the patient, is primarily seeking information from the psychologist to help better understand what emotional or cognitive difficulties may be present in the patient. With such diagnostic information, appropriate treatment planning may take place.

CASE 6.2

Mr. Jones was employed as a warehouse worker for an office supply chain. One day, several boxes filled with legal pads of paper accidentally fell on his shoulder, causing severe bruising. He also developed low back pain as a result of his falling to the ground with the boxes on top of him. He went to his primary care physician and received medicines and a prescription for a course of physical therapy. Although he experienced some improvement, later discussions with his physician found Mr. Jones having difficulty sleeping and intrusive flashbacks of the experience. He was referred to a psychologist for an evaluation and was diagnosed as having an Adjustment Disorder with Anxious Mood. His primary care physician then prescribed a course of psychotropic medication to address his symptoms and a course of psychotherapy. In 6 weeks, Mr. Jones improved in both his physical and emotional functioning.

*   *   *

In this instance, the primary care physician made the referral directly to the psychologist and had diagnosis and treatment in mind, not a forensic evaluation. The physician makes a note in the patient's chart requesting the referral and the psychologist responds with a written report addressed to the physician. A patient may share this evaluation with a representing attorney; however, the contract for services is between the patient and the psychologist. Fees may be paid directly by the patient or through a third party such as an auto insurance policy, regular health insurance policy, or worker's compensation fund on behalf of the patient. At a later date, the attorney for the patient may ask for the records of the psychologist and the information may be used in a forensic case should the attorney believe it in the patient's best interest to do so.

Personal injury attorneys may also make a direct referral to a psychologist for an evaluation. In my experience, they do so for three reasons: (1) They want their client to have the benefit of all relevant diagnostic services that may be related to their health care; (2) if a mental health injury is present, they want their client to receive treatment for these difficulties; and (3) it might add to the dollar amount of any settlement or damage award in the case.

CASE 6.3

Ms. Smith was driving on the interstate in the middle of the city and noted that traffic ahead had slowed down. She then slightly applied the brakes so as not to hit the car in front of her. Unfortunately, the cement truck driver who had been behind her was not as attentive to the flow of traffic as she had been. This resulted in the cement truck smashing into the rear of her car. Despite wearing a seat belt and shoulder harness, Ms. Smith's head did hit the windshield. In addition to her physical injuries, she subsequently experienced a persistent loss of concentration, an increase in her level of anxiety, and a fear of driving. Her attorney referred Ms. Smith to a psychologist, who completed an assessment. She was diagnosed with both Posttraumatic Stress Disorder and Postconcussion Syndrome. The psychologist made recommendations to address these problem areas.

*   *   *

In this case, the attorney was requesting services from the psychologist on behalf of her client. As such, no outside party was privy to the results of the evaluation, or even that it had taken place at all, unless the attorney advised the client to make the information available to other parties. The costs of the evaluation were borne by the attorney directly (though passed on to the client), and no third parties, such as an auto insurance company or personal health insurance policy, were involved in payment to the psychologist.

CHOOSING THE EVALUATION METHODOLOGY

The personal injury evaluation completed by the psychologist should first and foremost be comprehensive, with the goal of answering the referral question. At the end of the evaluation, the psychologist must feel confident in drawing conclusions regarding the presence or absence of a psychological injury and the proximate causes of such an injury if present. To draw a compelling conclusion, the psychologist must review all relevant medical, educational, and vocational data that are available. At times, this may be as little as 10 to 20 pages. At other times, data may exceed 2,000 pages. Without such a review, the psychologist may miss pertinent information in drawing conclusions about the psychological injury in question and runs the risk of being embarrassed on cross-examination.

The psychologist should conduct a thorough client history that includes both interview data and a review of all available documentation (e.g., school records, medical chart notes). This information might be crucial in attributing causation of the psychological injury. Such a thorough history can be important depending on the jurisdiction and purpose of the evaluation. In a personal injury evaluation, the question to be answered is whether, on a more likely than not basis, the individual would be experiencing these difficulties had the particular incident not occurred. Often, the psychologist will be cross-examined regarding the possibility that preexisting conditions (e.g., history of abuse, prior treatment of depression or anxiety, previous accidents) caused the current psychological injury. The psychologist should naturally be aware of preexisting conditions and their impact on the later development of psychological problems, but also be familiar with the "eggshell skull" rule. This refers to the fact that a preexisting condition was present (and dormant) but was "lit up" by the current injury; that is, although the client may have had a previous history of depressive episodes, the symptoms were absent at the time of the injury, and if not for the injury, it could be presumed that the symptoms would have remained in remission or dormant. In some jurisdictions, in certain types of cases, this history may not be relevant. In other jurisdictions, this information may be relevant in the types of monetary awards as well as services that can be offered to treat the present mental health condition. For example, in one case, the psychologist determined that the present accident could account for only 25% of the current emotional symptoms, with the other 75% being due to factors outside of the accident. As such, the worker's compensation wage losses were limited to 25% of the individual's previous salary.

In addition to a thorough interview and review of relevant historical documents, standardized psychological tests should also be administered. This is the unique contribution that psychology brings to the arena of personal injury evaluation, as compared to psychiatry, social work, and mental health counseling. These professionals must rely solely on record review and a clinical interview. The objectivity of psychological assessment, especially the inclusion of measures to rule out the feigning of a mental illness or malingering (described in more detail later), sets the psychological evaluation apart. Psychologists present normative data for attorneys and juries to consider in making their decisions about accountability related to the psychological injury.

In choosing standardized tests, it is recommended that the psychologist not rely on any one measure (e.g., Minnesota Multiphasic Personality Inventory [MMPI], Personality Assessment Inventory [PAI]), but include multiple measures before drawing conclusions. No one psychometric instrument measuring personality or psychopathology is sufficient to meet all of the standards necessary for reliability and validity across the variety of situations and types of people the psychologist may be asked to evaluate. Weiner (1995), while pointing out the strengths of the MMPI-2, also notes its limitations in a forensic context: "The MMPI-2 can be used most effectively . . . when combined with other sound instruments to provide opportunities to compare and contrast indications of problems, complaints, and characteristics" (p. 78). He concludes:

> The issues considered in arriving at these conclusions are by no means unique to the MMPI-2; rather, they are applicable to all psychological assessment procedures, each of which has its own particular blend of strengths, applications, limitations, and aspects in need of further study. (p. 79)

The psychologist must carefully choose instruments that will stand the test of rigorous cross-examination. Individual psychologists have several catalogues full of interesting tests to choose from that have been developed and marketed by major companies. These include tests of personality and level of psychological functioning, cognitive abilities and deficits, and vocational interests. From these options, the psychologist must carefully choose a battery of tests that are psychometrically sound and that target aspects of the referral question to be addressed in the evaluation. For example, I recently considered adding a particular psychological test to my previously chosen battery of tests in completing presurgical evaluations. I then consulted the latest edition of *Buros' Mental Measurements Yearbook* to view independent reviews of this particular instrument. I found that two of the subscales of most interest to me were considered to have inadequate reliability coefficients. Thus, I did not add this test to the battery.

As Weiner (1995) cautioned, the psychologist has the responsibility to be aware of the strengths and limitations of each instrument. In the context of a forensic evaluation, psychologists should be discouraged from using their own "pet tests" or unusual methodologies for assessing psychological difficulties that may not meet the standards necessary for the forensic question being addressed. To do so opens the possibility of exposing the entire evaluation to attack, particularly in light of *Daubert* challenges (see Litwack, Zapf, Groscup, & Hart, Chapter 17, this volume). For example, I am aware that some psychologists have used the Bender-Gestalt Visual-Motor Test as a projective instrument to make clinical interpretations about individuals they are evaluating in a clinical context. To do so in a forensic evaluation would likely not hold up in cross-examination.

It is also important for the psychologist to be aware of his or her own limitations in competence in completing the evaluation and when to make an appropriate referral for further consultation or diagnostic testing. For example, in completing an evaluation with an individual who has been involved in a motor vehicle accident, a psychologist may administer standard tests of cognitive functioning such as the Wechsler scales of intelligence and memory. Other measures often used for screening of neuropsychological difficulties, such as Trails A and Trails B or the Stroop Neuropsychological Screening Test, may also be administered. However, when administering such tests, patterns of concern may emerge (e.g., significant split between Verbal IQ and Performance IQ), or clear deficiencies on specific tests or subtests may be noted (e.g., Trails B score at the 15th percentile for an individual with above-average IQ). At that point, the psychologist must determine if further neuropsychological testing is needed beyond the screening completed in the initial part of the test battery.

Not all psychologists are skilled in neuropsychological assessment. If the psychologist does not possess advanced training in this area, then it is incumbent upon him or her to refer to a colleague who does have such specialized skills and experiences. In my evaluations, as I am not a qualified neuropsychologist, I refer cases to colleagues when I have suspicions that further cognitive testing would yield important information about a client. The same principle holds true if the psychologist determines that projective testing might yield important information beyond what is learned about the client through a clinical interview and objective personality testing. Projective testing is a controversial issue, and not all psychologists are equally skilled in administering and interpreting these types of data. Both Hess, Zachar, & Kramer (2001) and

Weiner (2001) note that in the hands of skilled evaluators, projective test data can yield important and valid information in answering referral questions.

THE IMPORTANCE OF KNOWING THE LITERATURE

Not enough can be said regarding the importance of the psychologist's being both generally well informed and current on the literature relevant to the case at hand. This entails current knowledge about the test instruments being used in the evaluation, as well as the literature that may be specifically related to the type of personal injury at hand.

The strength of our psychological test instruments lies in the large body of research that is completed with the goal of developing a better understanding of the instrument itself (e.g., reliability, validity, factor structure) and the validity of its use for understanding the psychological status of individual clients and predicting their behavior. Knowledge of these instruments is generated in large quantities each year. It is imperative that psychologists using these tests in a forensic context render opinions and conclusions from a data-based perspective and have weighed the strengths and limitations of each instrument. Using outdated instruments or overlook recent research on the integrity of the psychometric instruments may leave the psychologist's credibility vulnerable during cross-examination.

As noted earlier, psychologists may be called on to complete evaluations related to personal injuries from a wide context. Some of these situations may be unique, and a reliable body of literature may not exist in the specific problem area being assessed. On the other hand, some areas have been well researched and may have implications for developing a better understanding of the individual client who is being evaluated. For example, trauma is an area of psychology that has received considerable attention. In their meta-analysis, Ozer, Best, Lipsey, and Weiss (2003) attempted to identify predictors of the development of PTSD after an individual has been exposed to a traumatic event. On average, those who had previously experienced a traumatic event reported somewhat higher levels of PTSD symptoms. The relationship between prior trauma and the development of PTSD was stronger when the previous experience involved non-combat-related interpersonal violence such as assault, rape, or domestic violence. Pretrauma psychological problems (e.g., depression) were also related to the development of PTSD, as was having a family history of psychopathology, especially when the traumatic experience involved noncombatant interpersonal violence. Individuals reporting lower levels of perceived social support after the traumatic event reported higher levels of PTSD symptoms or rates of current PTSD.

This type of data can be important for the psychologist in completing the personal injury evaluation, especially when the issue of causation of the emotional injury is being addressed in the assessment. Similarly, in neuropsychological evaluations it is important to understand the cognitive, emotional, and behavioral changes that may follow the occurrence of a traumatic brain injury (Murrey, 2000). In areas in which a significant body of literature exists that may affect one's clinical opinion, the psychologist must be cognizant of this work. In competent expert testimony, a battle of the literature is more mature, helpful, and beneficial than a battle of experts as hired guns.

MALINGERING

When completing the psychological evaluation, it is important to determine the client's test-taking attitude in approaching the evaluation. This attitude can either be on a conscious basis, meaning he or she means to do it on purpose, or an unconscious basis, which means the attitude is not intentional but is reflected in the test responses nonetheless. Attorneys on both sides will always want to know how confident the psychologist is that the client being evaluated is being truthful. Although the concept of "compensation neurosis" (Blanchard & Hickling, 2004; Cunnien, 1997; Resnick, 1997) has been dismissed as empirically nonexistent, the psychologist should always be prepared to answer the question, How do you know that this person is really traumatized, because if he has this disorder called PTSD, he will come away with a bigger wad of cash from this accident?

CASE 6.4

An individual involved in a motorcycle accident was referred to a psychologist by a personal injury attorney to evaluate for the presence of PTSD. As part of the psychometric test battery, the psychologist included the administration of three separate tests targeting the possible presence of defensiveness or malingering. Although the results did not definitely indicate the presence of malingering on the part of the client, the psychologist could not rule out this possibility. These results were communicated to the referring attorney by telephone. The attorney thanked the psychologist, requested the evaluation results not be put in written form, and indicated that this would remain a private consultation between the attorney and the psychologist.

*   *   *

This may be contrasted with another case.

CASE 6.5

An individual involved in a motor vehicle accident was referred to a psychologist by a personal injury attorney to evaluate for the presence of PTSD. The same three separate tests targeting the possible presence of defensiveness or malingering were administered as part of the assessment. In the written report, the psychologist concluded, "The results of these three indices suggest that there is no reason to suspect that the symptoms that he is reporting are exaggerated for the purpose of secondary gain."

*   *   *

Naturally, the referring attorney was pleased with this conclusion. The attorney defending the auto insurance company was informed that the possibility of malingering was considered and investigated in the examination.

The *Diagnostic and Statistical Manual of Mental Disorders IV (DSM-IV)* refers to malingering as "the intentional production of false or grossly exaggerated physical or psychological symptoms, motivated by external incentives" (American Psychiatric Association, 1994, p. 296). Due to the possibility of secondary gain (usually financial), it is essential that the validity of the injured party's psychological injuries pass a scrutiny test. Rosen (1995) cites the case of individuals involved in a fishing boat accident in which the ship went down and there were 22 survivors. Of these, 19 were referred to a psychologist or psychiatrist for evaluation. Of these, 86% were later diagnosed as having chronic PTSD, a level far exceeding what the trauma literature would suggest. The sole source of data in the vast majority of these cases was the client's self-report of symptoms. In only four of these cases were psychometric tests (e.g., MMPI) administered. Regarding deception, Wiley (1998, p. 870) contends, "If you do not look for it, you will not find it; and if you do not find it, you are going to miss a lot." Resnick (1997) cautions clinicians to diagnose malingering only when strong evidence is available. He cites far-ranging effects of misclassification related to health care, financial, and legal consequences. In terms of personal injury evaluations, Rogers (1997) makes an important and helpful point. He notes that historically, malingering and defensiveness have been treated as if they were dichotomous variables. However, he believes that conceptualizing "gradations of malingering" is of "considerable importance in addressing dispositional issues or treatment recommendations" (p. 13).

Whereas malingering refers to direct deception and manufacturing of symptoms, what sometimes occurs, whether it is conscious or unconscious, is an exaggeration of symptoms on the part of the injured party. Why this is the case can only be speculated. One reason may be that the individual is in acute emotional pain, and thus response on psychological tests may reflect "a cry for help." Another reason may lie in a romanticization of the life that was prior to the accident. In an interesting study, Lees-Haley, et al. (1997) compared perceived quality of life ratings prior to the injury of parties involved in litigation with a sample of individuals who had not been injured. The injured workers rated their premorbid quality of life as having been higher than the nonclinical sample from the community. There is no reason for these ratings to have been statistically different; injured workers may be overestimating how happy and functional they were prior to the injury, thus suggesting the limited reliability of such preinjury self-report ratings.

In discussing the high incidence of the diagnosis of PTSD in the ship accident, Rosen (1995) partially attributes these findings to "attorney advice and symptom sharing amongst the survivors." Victor and Abeles (2004) present a review of the effects of attorneys' "coaching of clients" who are going to undergo a psychological evaluation. These authors point to the need for better collaboration between psychologists and attorneys, as well as the need for better methods for detecting that coaching has taken place.

Clinicians should be aware of an excellent resource on research related to malingering provided by Kenneth Pope on his Web site, kspope.com. He presents citations and brief summaries of studies and review articles that have been published since January 2001 on this topic. These articles examine tests and approaches developed specifically to identify malingering, other tests that include subscales or indices to identify malingering, and tests and approaches that are vulnerable to malingering.

MOTOR VEHICLE ACCIDENTS

In an epidemiological study, Norris (1992) examined the incidence and prevalence rates of traumatic events. She presented data suggesting that trauma secondary to involvement in a motor vehicle accident (MVA) is common. A sizable portion (2%) of the population is likely to experience an injury-causing MVA during the course of a given year. However, almost 25% of individuals can expect this event to take place sometime during their lifetime.

My interest in developing this aspect of my clinical practice grew after becoming familiar with the research program of Edward Blanchard and Edward Hickling and their colleagues. The first paper of theirs that I read examined the psychological morbidity of involvement in MVAs (Blanchard, Hickling, Taylor, Loos, & Gerardi, 1994). They examined individuals 1 to 4 months following the MVA who had sought medical attention (e.g., emergency room, visit to family physician or chiropractor) within one week of the incident. They found an astounding 46% incidence for the diagnosis of PTSD in this population, with another 20% having a subsyndromal form of this disorder (meeting branch B or branch C but not both in the *DSM-IV* diagnostic criteria). As the authors followed these individuals for one year, the incidence of PTSD was reduced to 23%, a significant reduction but a high incidence nonetheless. These numbers stood out to me as a way to fill a service need for physicians and personal injury attorneys. These researchers developed a comprehensive assessment, treatment, and follow-up program with two cohorts of MVA victims; their work is summarized in Blanchard and Hickling (2004) and serves as the model for the types of evaluations that I complete with this clinical population.

CASE 6.6

Ms. Chrysler was driving her son to an appointment and sitting at a red light when a car rear-ended them because the driver was not paying attention to the traffic light. She and her son were taken separately by ambulance to the emergency room of the local hospital. They were kept for observation and both discharged to home the same day. For 6 months, Dr. X treated her and her son for physical injuries secondary to their involvement in the MVA. However, she was not progressing in her physical recovery as expected. She reported to her physician excessive amounts of anxiety, poor sleep, and an avoidance of driving, except when absolutely necessary to accomplish household tasks for her family. Being suspicious that other than physical factors might be involved in her lack of progress, he referred her to a psychologist for an evaluation. The psychological evaluation consisted of a clinical interview, a review of medical records, and a battery of tests, including the Shipley Institute of Living Scale, Beck Depression Inventory, Trait Anxiety Scale, Trauma Symptom Inventory,

MMPI-2, Clinician Administered PTSD Scale, the Motor Vehicle Accident Interview, and the Structured Interview of Reported Symptoms. There was no suggestion of the presence of cognitive difficulties, so traditional measures in this area (Wechsler Adult Intelligence Scales [WAIS], neuropsychological screening measures) were not administered. The results of the evaluation led to a diagnosis of PTSD and that, on a more likely than not basis, this diagnosis could be attributed to the MVA of 6 months earlier. Her perceived failure to protect her son (obviously an irrational belief, but based on her belief that mothers are supposed to protect their children regardless of the situation) also contributed to her emotional reaction to the MVA. She was referred for a medication evaluation and a course of cognitive-behavioral therapy to help address her symptoms.

*   *   *

This case example also illustrates the importance of knowing the research literature in this area. It has been found that individuals are more likely to develop a diagnosis of PTSD following an MVA if the fault of the accident lies with the other driver rather than with themselves (Delahanty, et al., 1997). It is an issue of personal control: If one made a mistake, one can correct that particular behavior during future driving; however, there is no controlling the behavior or mistakes of all other drivers on the road, and therefore a heightened sense of fear and anxiety may be present when driving. This client also had a history of previous trauma. Research has suggested that this may place individuals at higher risk to develop PTSD when they are exposed to traumatic events at a later time in their lives (Blanchard & Hickling, 2004; Ozer et al., 2003).

CASE 6.7

Mr. Cadillac was referred for evaluation by his primary care physician. He had been involved in an MVA in which he had run a red light and was then sideswiped by another vehicle that had legally entered the intersection. He was fortunate in that his physical injuries were moderate and he had only some lingering chronic pain. However, 3 months following the MVA, he had poor concentration, poor memory, was highly anxious and frequently irritable, and often had headaches. He was administered the same battery of tests as Ms. Chrysler in the earlier case. In addition, he was also administered the WAIS-III, Wechsler Memory Scale-Revised, and three neuropsychological screening tests, Visual Search and Attention Test, Color Trails A and Trails B, and the Stroop Neuropsychological Screening Tests. The results indicated that although he had an above-average IQ, his subtest pattern of responses on the WAIS-III and low percentile scores on the other tests suggested the presence of neuropsychological difficulties. He was diagnosed as having an Adjustment Disorder with Anxious Mood (he was not significantly avoidant and thus did not qualify for a diagnosis of PTSD) and Cognitive Disorder, Not Otherwise Specified. He was referred for a full neuropsychological evaluation; pending the results of the evaluation, further treatment recommendations (e.g., medication management, psychotherapy) would be made.

WORKER'S COMPENSATION

Psychologists are often asked to evaluate individuals who have experienced an industrial injury. There is no lack of individuals who become injured on the job. For this reason, independent practitioners wanting to reduce their financial dependence on managed care organizations have suggested that providing services to clients involved in the worker's compensation system is a viable alternative (Walfish, 2001).

It should be pointed out that worker's compensation rules and policies are set by statute. These statutes, and the accompanying policies, vary in each of the states. As such, the laws governing worker's compensation in Washington State are different from the laws in Georgia. The role that mental health professionals play in each of these systems will thus be different and so may the questions psychologists will be asked to answer in their evaluations. One example relates to the role of preexisting conditions. In one state, a preexisting condition is not a major consideration in assigning mental health benefits if the condition was dormant or in arrest at the time of the industrial injury. Full benefits are provided to the injured worker in this case. In another state, the psychologist is asked to estimate what percentage of the present emotional injury could be attributed to the preexisting condition; benefits to the injured worker are then reduced by this percentage. This illustrates the importance of psychologists becoming thoroughly familiar with the statutes covering the mental health component of worker's compensation law in their municipality. In describing the role of the psychologist in this section, I have based my discussion on worker's compensation law in Washington State, where I practiced for 10 years. A significant portion of my practice was related to assessment and treatment of injured workers.

The questions to be answered in a psychological evaluation of an injured worker are similar to those in other civil evaluations as described earlier: Is there a mental health injury present, and if present, on a more likely than not basis, is the emotional injury attributable to the event(s) that occurred in the workplace? There are three circumstances in which workers may qualify for psychological services as a result of an industrial injury: (1) emotional injury as a direct result of a physical industrial injury, (2) emotional injury due to a nonroutine stressful event in the workplace, and (3) an emotional injury that interferes with improvement in physical recovery of a physical industrial injury. The most common scenario for an individual to be referred for a psychological evaluation is when he or she has experienced an emotional injury (e.g., depression, anxiety, PTSD) secondary to having experienced a physical injury.

Case 6.8

Mr. North was employed as a logger in the forests of the Pacific Northwest. While working, he slipped and injured his back. Two surgeries followed and left him with chronic pain and an inability to remain employed in his previous position. He had no other marketable skills, and his inability to sit or stand for long periods of time precluded his being able to successfully work at any other job in a regular and reliable manner. He was referred for evaluation and diagnosed with Major Depression and Psychological Factors Affecting a Medical Condition. A course of psychotherapy and pain management was recommended.

CASE 6.9

Mr. South was employed as a roofer and slipped off the roof of a house on which he was working. He went from being a big, strapping, self-sufficient man to one who lived much of his life in chronic pain. He developed a Panic Disorder with Agoraphobia as a result of the sequelae of his inability to work and his overconcern with other people's judgments of him. A course of cognitive therapy was recommended, along with a medical evaluation by a psychiatrist to address these symptoms.

*   *   *

In these cases, the emotional symptoms that emerged would not have been present if not for the occurrence of the emotional injury. As such, the employees were entitled to have mental health services paid for by their worker's compensation system. Cleveland and Packer (2003) describe a case in which the Wyoming State Supreme Court ruled in favor of compensating an injured worker who had attempted suicide. In this case, the court reasoned that the self-inflicted gunshot was proximately caused by a mental disorder resulting from a compensable physical injury.

Many people have stressful jobs and develop mental health symptoms as a result of remaining in this emotionally difficult environment. For example, having an employer that yells, coworkers who are unsupportive and backstabbing, and the pressure of deadlines to meet can all contribute to the development of a diagnosable mental health problem for an employee. However, worker's compensation laws do not apply to emotional injuries resulting from having a stressful job. But in the routine performance of one's work duties, an emotional injury may result from a nonroutine event. In these cases, worker's compensation benefits may be available to the worker. MacDonald, Colotta, Flamer, and Karlinsky (2003) completed a retrospective analysis of worker's compensation benefits for the diagnosis of PTSD. They found the majority (82%) to have directly experienced a traumatic event, and a significant portion (18%) had witnessed such an event. Two such cases, where the worker's compensation system did allow a valid claim, are described next.

CASE 6.10

Mr. East was employed in a store as a cashier. While on duty one evening, a car came crashing through the storefront window and narrowly missed hitting him by a few feet. Glass shattered everywhere and the store was in an upheaval. He kept on replaying this event in his mind and was unable to return to the workplace without experiencing an overwhelming sense of anxiety. He was referred for evaluation and diagnosed with PTSD secondary to this event. A course of psychotherapy and biofeedback was recommended to address his symptoms.

CASE 6.11

Ms. West was employed as a social worker in the inner-city projects. While making a home visit to a client, she witnessed a murder. As a result of this event, she began to fear for her own life, became avoidant, was unable to sleep, developed a startle response, and was chronically anxious. She was referred for evaluation and diagnosed with PTSD from witnessing this event. A course of psychotherapy and medication management was recommended.

*   *   *

Research suggests that emotional issues may hamper recovery from a physical injury. Colorado psychologist Kevin Gaffney (healthpsych.com, 1997) refers to this as "delayed recovery." He suggests that this occurs when an injured worker is not responding to medical treatment within the expected time frame. He contends that psychosocial factors are usually the main contributing factors at these times. As an example, he cites clinical depression as compromising motivation to recover.

CASE 6.12

Ms. Northeast injured her shoulder and back when several boxes of supplies fell on top of her while she was working in an auto parts store. She received medical treatment from both a chiropractor and a physiatrist. She was not improving medically. While she returned to work in a light duty position, she described feeling mistreated by her employers who thought she was faking and exaggerating her injury. Her emotional reaction to this perceived treatment at work was to withdraw and become vegetatively depressed. This further hampered her ability to recover from the physical injuries, as she did not have the energy to participate in physical therapy and had poor concentration and memory lapses resulting in her not taking the medication as prescribed by her physician. She was referred for a psychological evaluation and was prescribed a course of medication management and individual and family therapy.

CONCLUSIONS

Psychologists have an important role to play in a personal injury case. Physicians can describe to a jury the medical injuries incurred and physical limitations that remain as a result of being involved in an MVA. An economist can calculate the loss of future earning potential. By being aware of the literature and being skilled in psychometric testing, psychologists can attest to the extent of emotional and/or functional cognitive damages as a result of being involved in the accident and make recommendations to restore the person to emotional health. This skill set is highly valued by both clients and attorneys in the civil justice system.

REFERENCES

American Psychiatric Association. (1994). *Quick reference to the diagnostic criteria from* DSM-IV. Washington, DC: American Psychiatric Association.

Blanchard, E., & Hickling, E. (2004). *After the crash: Psychological assessment and treatment of survivors of motor vehicle accidents.* Washington, DC: American Psychological Association.

Blanchard, E., Hickling, E., Taylor, A., Loos, W., & Gerardi, R. (1994). Psychological morbidity associated with motor vehicle accidents. *Behaviour Research and Therapy, 32,* 283–290.

Blau, T. (1998). *The psychologist as expert witness* (2nd ed.). New York: Wiley.

Cleveland, J., & Packer, I. (2003). Mental injury and worker's compensation. *Journal of the American Academy of Psychiatry and the Law, 31,* 259–261.

Colorado Compensation Insurance Authority. (1997). *Understanding the injured worker: Psychology's role in worker's comp.* Retrieved October 25, 2004, from http://www.healthpsych.com /articles/ccia.html.

Cunnien, A. (1997). Psychiatric and medical syndromes associated with deception. In R. Rogers (Ed.), *Clinical assessment of malingering and deception* (2nd ed., pp. 23–46). New York: Guilford Press.

Delahanty, D., Herberman, H., Craig, K., Hayward, M., Fullerton, C., Ursano, R., et al. (1997). Acute and chronic distress and PTSD as a function of responsibility for serious motor vehicle accidents. *Journal of Consulting and Clinical Psychology, 65,* 560–567.

Foote, W., & Goodman-Delahunty, J. (2004). *Evaluating sexual harassment: Psychological, social, and legal considerations in forensic examinations.* Washington, DC: American Psychological Association.

Greenberg, S. A., & Brodsky, S. (2001). *The practice of civil forensic psychology.* Washington, DC: American Psychological Association.

Healthpsych.com. (1997). *Understanding the injured worker: Psychology's role in worker's comp.* Retrieved October 30, 2004, from http://www.healthpsych.com/articles/ccia.html.

Hess, A., Zachar, P., & Kramer, J. (2001). Rorschach [Test review]. In B. S. Plake & J. C. Impara (Eds.), *Buros' mental measurements yearbook* (Vol. 14, pp. 1033–1038). Lincoln, NB: Buros Institute.

Lees-Haley, P., Williams, C., Zasler, N., Margulies, S., English, L., & Stevens, K. (1997). Response bias in plaintiff's histories. *Brain Injury, 11,* 791–799.

MacDonald, H., Colotta, V., Flamer, S., & Karlinsky, H. (2003). PTSD in the workplace: A descriptive study of workers experiencing PTSD from work injury. *Journal of Occupational Rehabilitation, 13,* 63–77.

Murrey, G. (2000). *The forensic evaluation of traumatic brain injury: A handbook for clinicians and attorneys.* Boca Raton, FL: CRC Press.

Norris, F. (1992). Epidemiology of trauma: Frequency and impact of different potentially traumatic events on different demographic groups. *Journal of Consulting and Clinical Psychology, 60,* 409–418.

Ozer, E., Best, S., Lipsey, T., & Weiss, D. (2003). Predictors of PTSD and symptoms in adults: A meta-analysis. *Psychological Bulletin, 129,* 52–73.

Resnick, P. (1997). Malingering of posttraumatic stress disorders. In R. Rogers (Ed.), *Clinical assessment of malingering and deception* (2nd ed., pp. 130–152). New York: Guilford Press.

Rogers, R. (Ed.). (1997). *Clinical assessment of malingering and deception* (2nd ed.). New York: Guilford Press.

Rosen, G. (1995). The Aleutian Enterprise sinking and posttraumatic stress disorder: Misdiagnosis in clinical and forensic settings. *Professional Psychology: Research and Practice, 26,* 82–87.

Simon, R. (2003). *Posttraumatic stress disorder in litigation: Guidelines for forensic assessment.* Washington, DC: American Psychiatric Association.

Victor, T., & Abeles, N. (2004). Coaching clients to take psychological and neuropsychological tests: A clash of ethical obligations. *Professional Psychology: Research and Practice, 35,* 373–379.

Walfish, S. (2001, August). *Clinical practice strategies outside the realm of managed care.* Paper presented at the meetings of the American Psychological Association, San Francisco, CA.

Weiner, I. (1995). Psychometric issues in forensic applications of the MMPI-2. In Y. Ben-Porath, J. Graham, G. Hall, R. Hirschman, & M. Zaragoza (Eds.), *Forensic applications of the MMPI-2* (pp. 48–81). Thousand Oaks, CA: Sage.

Weiner, I. (2001). Advancing the science of psychological assessment: The Rorschach Inkblot Method as exemplar. *Psychological Assessment, 13,* 423–432.

Wiley, S. (1998). Deception and detection in psychiatric diagnosis. *Psychiatric Clinics of North America, 21,* 869–893.

CHAPTER 7

Personality Assessment in Personal Injury Litigation

JAMES N. BUTCHER and KATHRYN B. MILLER

PSYCHOLOGISTS ARE becoming increasingly involved in personal injury litigation cases as expert witnesses. Their expanded involvement in the courtroom comes, in part, from the greater number of cases that incorporate a mental health or "pain and suffering" component to damage claims. It has also resulted from maturation of the field of psychological assessment, as many attorneys understand that psychologists now use objective evaluation methods that can provide valuable testimony about the mental health status of litigants.

THE ROLE OF PSYCHOLOGISTS IN PERSONAL INJURY LITIGATION

There are a number of considerations that are important to understanding the role of a psychologist in conducting psychological evaluations in personal injury cases.

THE ADVERSARIAL CONTEXT OF PERSONAL INJURY ASSESSMENTS

Most psychologists involved in personal injury assessments are persons originally trained in clinical psychology, counseling, or neuropsychology and who entered the field as a helping professional. Their venturing into forensic assessment, with its high potential for challenge, represents a different type of psychological assessment context than most are accustomed to experiencing. They may find themselves consulting or providing test interpretations that actually work against the wishes and intent of the individuals being tested. Psychologists who wander from the relatively safe environment of clinical assessment may find the often confrontational nature of legal challenge in forensic assessment quite difficult, particularly if their academic background is spotty or incomplete or if they employ assessment methods that cannot withstand the harsh scrutiny of sharp cross-examination. Expert witnesses need to assure that they have the necessary expertise for personal injury litigation consultation and need to employ the most objective methods available in their assessments.

APPROPRIATE BACKGROUND FOR PERSONAL INJURY CASE EXPERTISE

Psychologists conducting forensic examinations should have appropriate background and relevant experience as follows.

Educational Requirements

It is extremely important for psychologists to have an appropriate educational background that provides sufficient focus for using psychological tests in forensic settings. A doctoral degree in a mental health field is a minimum requirement; for example, a PhD or PsyD in clinical, counseling, or health psychology with an appropriate clinical internship is desirable. This education should be obtained in an academic program approved by the American Psychological Association. The psychologist should also hold appropriate licensure, which is often a requirement for purchasing psychological tests (American Psychological Association, 1986).

Experience Requirements

An expert witness should also have work-related experiences in health or mental health settings pertinent to the case, whether in mental health centers, hospitals, rehabilitation, or neuropsychology settings. For example, if the case being tried is one that involves alleged physical injury, the psychologist should have substantial professional experience evaluating similar cases in a medical setting; if the case being tried involves assessing posttraumatic symptoms, the psychologist should have relevant experience evaluating or treating individuals in crisis or posttraumatic situations.

Expertise in Procedures Being Employed

To be a credible witness, the psychologist needs to demonstrate expertise in the techniques being used to assess the litigant. A history of graduate-level coursework in the psychological procedures being used is important. It is also desirable for the psychologist to demonstrate extensive current experience through postdoctoral professional experiences, continuing education experience, teaching graduate courses, or publishing relevant research articles in peer-reviewed resources. Ultimately, each case will determine which, if any, of the experts submitted by counsel will be allowed to testify.

Documentation of Expertise

It is valuable for the forensic practitioner to be able to document expertise in testifying about psychological procedures used in the case. Prior testimony, or having been admitted by other courts to testify in similar cases, can serve to establish one as a qualified expert. It is important for psychologists to

keep a record of previous cases in which they have testified in personal injury litigation.

Measuring Instruments in Forensic Assessment

Psychologists testifying in personal injury cases should employ procedures
that can be objectively interpreted because of the need to defend one's conclusions in an adversarial environment. Any objective psychological test used
should (1) be psychometrically structured to allow for appropriate discrimina-
tions in forensic assessment and (2) have an appropriate research base supporting its use in forensic assessment. Currently, the personality assessment
instrument that most clearly meets these two criteria is the Minnesota Multiphasic Personality Inventory (MMPI-2). The MMPI-2 is the most widely used
and objective method of evaluating a litigant's mental health status in court
cases (Boccaccini & Brodsky, 1999; Watkins, Campbell, Niebirding, & Hallmark, 1995). It is also the most widely used instrument in forensic assessment
(Borum & Grisso, 1995; Keilen & Bloom, 1986; Lees-Haley, Smith, Williams, &
Dunn, 1995) and in personality-clinical research (Butcher & Rouse, 1996).

When the MMPI-2 is administered and used in a standardized manner, supported by research, expert testimony based on the results is usually accepted
in legal proceedings (Otto, 2002). The MMPI-2 is a paper-and-pencil questionnaire comprising 567 symptoms, beliefs, and attitudes that reflect potential
mental health problems in test takers who respond frankly to the items.

The MMPI was originally developed in the 1940s as an objective measure of
personality and symptomatic behavior. Since that time, an extensive amount
of empirical research has been published documenting and detailing the
meaning of the empirical scales of the inventory. When the MMPI was revised
in 1989, the MMPI Re-standardization Committee made efforts to maintain the
continuity of the original clinical scales because of their rich database. The traditional scales are essentially the same in the MMPI-2 as in the original instrument. The MMPI committee also developed a number of new measures for the
revised test, which provide information with respect to other clinical problem
areas, such as substance abuse and marital problems.

The inventory contains a number of measures that address test-taking attitudes, perhaps the most important factor to evaluate in individuals being assessed in forensic settings. In court cases, litigants often possess the
motivation to present themselves in a particular way, to either appear free of
psychological disturbance or severely disabled and deserving of compensation. Any psychological assessment procedure, if it is to shed light on the test
taker, needs to have a means of appraising the varying motivations of litigants.
The revised version of the inventory contains several indexes to assess clients'
self-presentation styles. These are addressed later in this chapter.

ASSESSING PSYCHOLOGICAL ISSUES IN PERSONAL INJURY CLAIMS USING THE MMPI-2

Research on the impact of psychological factors in the manifestation of physical illness has yielded varying results depending on the specific area studied.

We review current research on the role that personality factors play in the presentation and maintenance of physical symptoms.

As in any MMPI-2-based assessment, the way the individual presents himself or herself is a crucial consideration for interpretation. A valid, interpretable protocol is necessary for personality and symptomatic appraisal. One study (Lees-Haley, 1997) found that for 492 personal injury plaintiffs, 70% to 80% of their MMPI-2 profiles were valid. Research on disability determination cases typically does not find extremely exaggerated MMPI-2 profiles but instead shows F scale elevations clearly within an interpretable range (Flamer & Birch, 1992; Long, Rouse, Nelson, & Butcher, 2004). Some individuals involved in personal injury cases, however, may present an extreme and hardly credible set of mental health symptoms in order to be viewed as psychologically disabled (Butcher, 1997a, 1997b, 1997c). This type of profile is not consistent with valid profiles.

Low Back Injury and Pain

Low back pain (LBP) is one of the most costly problems in the American workplace today. Billions of dollars are lost each year through workers' compensation claims around LBP and lost earnings. Of particular concern are the statistics suggesting that the longer someone is out of work, the lower his or her probability of returning to work, even over short periods (Gallagher et al., 1989). Studies assessing determinants of returning to work after LBP injury have found that several factors are predictive. Gallagher et al. found that psychosocial as opposed to physical symptoms predicted return to work 6 months after initial assessment in a combined sample of clinic patients and applicants for Social Security Administration compensation. Significant predictors of return-to-work status were length of time out of work, ease of changing occupations, score on the MMPI Hy scale, locus of health control, and ability to perform daily tasks. Gatchel, Polatin, and Mayer (1995) found that score on the MMPI Hy scale, self-reported pain and disability, and litigation status were important in differentiating those who returned to work within 1 year from those who did not. In this follow-up study, severity of initial low back injury and physical demands of the job were not found to be predictive of subsequent return-to-work status.

Prospective studies are advantageous because they allow researchers to determine the relative contributions of premorbid personality characteristics and postinjury factors in the manifestation of back pain. Fordyce, Bigos, Batti'e, and Fisher (1992) assessed 3,020 industrial employees using a variety of instruments, including the MMPI. The workers were followed for an average of 3 years, during which time 117 employees reported back injury. Initial score on the MMPI Hy scale was a significant predictor of later back injury. In particular, the lassitude/malaise, denial of social anxiety, and need for affection Harris-Lingoes scales from the Hy scale were found to be predictive. In general, psychological variables had greater predictive power than biomechanical variables, suggesting that emotional or psychological factors may play a key role in the development of physical symptoms. In another prospective study, depression predicted application for early retirement in a 6-month follow-up of 111 patients with acute back pain (Hasenbring, Marienfeld, Kuhlendahl, & Soyka, 1994). Overall, there appears to be an interaction between psychological factors and LBP such that those who are more depressed and more likely to respond to psychological problems physically have a greater likelihood of developing and maintaining chronic back pain.

HEAD INJURY

In forensic evaluation, personality assessments of individuals claiming head injury should always be accompanied by medical and/or neuropsychological information about the veracity of the claim. Head injury is a particularly difficult area to assess with the MMPI-2 because symptoms commonly associated with it can be found in other types of psychopathology. Standard indicators of malingering such as F and Fp need to be evaluated differently when assessing a head injury case because individuals may elevate these scales when reporting valid symptoms. Alfano, Neilson, Paniak, and Finlayson (1992) conducted a profile analysis of 103 patients judged by a neurosurgical team to have moderate to severe closed-head injuries (CHI). Overall, the subjects showed elevations on all MMPI clinical scales except Si. The most frequent 2-point code for men was 8 to 2, and the most frequent for women was 1 to 3.

Several correction methods have been developed in an attempt to facilitate interpretation of valid elevated CHI profiles on the MMPI. Gass (1992) proposed a 14-item correction factor that reflects the physical and cognitive symptoms frequently seen in CHI patients. The items load most heavily on the Pt and Sc scales. In a cross-validation study, Gass and Wald (1997) found that this correction factor discriminated 54 closed-head trauma individuals from 2,600 normals. None of the closed-head trauma individuals were involved in litigation, nor did they have any premorbid history of psychiatric disorders or alcohol dependence.

Recent research, however, has raised several concerns about such correction methods. One concern is that correction factors are not specific to CHI. Glassmire et al. (2003) tested three separate correction methods and found that they were sensitive in discriminating CHI patients from normal individuals but were not specific in differentiating CHI patients from psychiatric patients. Similarly, Edwards et al. (2003) applied three neurocorrection methods to both a CHI population and a psychiatric population. They found that the groups did not significantly differ in the number of corrective items endorsed or the way their profiles changed when the corrective methods were applied.

A second concern is how valid the corrective methods are in relation to the severity of the head injury. Rayls, Mittenberg, Burns, and Theroux (2000) found that individuals with mild head injury differed from a control sample on the number of correction factor items endorsed when they were acutely hospitalized, but not at 3-month follow-up. The authors concluded that extended endorsement of correction factor items in mild head injury is more likely due to psychological than physical variables. Brulot, Strauss, and Spellacy (1997) compared endorsement of corrective factor items to other measures of head injury severity. The results showed no significant associations between the correction factors and duration of loss of consciousness, posttraumatic amnesia, or performance on neuropsychological tests. There were, however, significant associations between depression content scale and correction factors, suggesting that correction factors may be more sensitive to depression than severity of head injury. These studies raise questions about the validity of neurocorrective methods. At this point, it is unclear whether they are measuring deficits caused by head injury or more global psychological symptoms.

POSTTRAUMATIC STRESS DISORDER

Emotional damage or distress is increasingly being claimed by litigators against defendants such as employers. Specifically, people may claim that they have developed Posttraumatic Stress Disorder (PTSD) as a result of harassment, difficult work conditions, or an accident. This poses a problem for attorneys because it is extremely difficult to determine the change in a person's emotional functioning without premorbid data. Lack of premorbid data precludes determining a causal relationship between the event and current functioning because it is unknown whether or not the person had preexisting emotional problems. Blanchard et al. (1996) looked at the development of PTSD after a motor vehicle accident (MVA) and found that 70% of the people who developed PTSD symptoms within 4 months of the accident could be predicted using four variables: prior Major Depression, extent of physical injury sustained, fear of dying in the accident, and the initiation of litigation. Mayou, Bryant, and Duthie (1993), however, did not find that premorbid psychopathology, baseline depression, or neuroticism was predictive of the later development of PTSD after an MVA. Other investigations have found that attributional or coping style is important in moderating the effects of stress on the individual (Hovanitz & Kozora, 1989; McCormick, Taber, & Krudelback, 1989).

There has been debate in the literature as to whether the MMPI accurately assesses PTSD as opposed to a more general form of emotional distress (Lees-Haley, 1997; Miller, Goldberg, & Streiner, 1995). The MMPI posttraumatic stress scales, PK and PS, were originally designed using samples of armed services veterans. Some studies have found that Keane's subscale (PK) does not discriminate PTSD veterans from non-PTSD veterans very well (Silver & Salamone-Genovese, 1991; Vanderploeg, Sison, & Hickling, 1987), but other studies suggest better discrimination (Keane, Malloy, & Fairbank, 1984; Munley, Bains, Bloem, & Busby, 1995; Watson et al., 1994). Studies assessing the efficacy of the MMPI PTSD scale in civilian populations have also yielded mixed results. Neal et al. (1994), using a sample of 70 civilians in the United Kingdom, concluded that the MMPI PTSD scale was useful in quantifying PTSD symptom severity but cautioned against using it as a dichotomous indicator of PTSD. Overall, high elevations on the PK and PS scales should be interpreted with caution because they may indicate PTSD or they may indicate more general mental health problems. For a broader discussion of the use of the MMPI-2 in assessing clients with PTSD, see Penk, Rierdan, Losardo, and Robinowitz (in press).

FACTORS TO CONSIDER WHEN CONDUCTING PERSONALITY ASSESSMENTS WITH THE MMPI-2

In forensic settings, it is difficult to determine whether an individual claiming problems as a result of an injury or stressful experience or exposure to a toxic substance is manifesting symptoms consistent with such injuries or whether other factors such as psychological adjustment are contributing to his or her problems. In these situations, the professionals involved may be asked to render an opinion or evaluate:

- Whether there is a possibility that the individual's physical complaints are due to actual organic changes.
- Whether the symptoms of disability result from a psychological disorder such as traumatic reaction to stress or "traumatic neurosis."
- Whether the pattern of symptoms may be neither physical nor "psychological," but are instead contrived to gain compensation or to obtain special services or considerations, such as job transfer or reduced workload. It has been noted that malingering is difficult to determine without direct objective evidence (Marcus, 1983).

Psychological evaluation may prove valuable in appraising personality factors contributing to an individual's symptom pattern or appraising the dynamics of an individual's response to an acquired physical disability. However, psychological evaluations in disability determinations have some inherent limitations. It is not possible to determine, on the basis of the MMPI-2, or any psychological test for that matter, whether a claimant's injuries are actually based on organic conditions or derive from personality factors. It is also not possible, with confidence, to determine on the basis of a psychological test alone whether the patient is malingering. It is not possible to establish with any degree of certainty the nature of an individual's premorbid personality and its influence on current functioning unless psychological testing was conducted at a point in time prior to the present disability. There are no foolproof ways of detecting premorbid personality or preinjury functioning with only present-time measurement.

Nevertheless, psychological testing can be of value in disability determinations in a number of ways (see discussion by Shaffer, Nussbaum, & Little, 1972). If the psychological tests provide, as the MMPI-2 does, scales that measure response attitudes, the individual's cooperation with the assessment, and "believability," then the results can be reliably assessed. Psychological assessment instruments, if they are objectively derived and validated, can provide a comparison of the client's symptomatic status with that of numerous other cases. Psychological testing can also provide some indication of the severity and long-term stability of the individual's problems.

In assessing the behavior of litigants in personal injury assessments, a psychologist needs to be aware of a number of factors that could impact the evaluation.

ATTORNEY BRIEFINGS PRIOR TO TEST ADMINISTRATION

One of the most problematic factors encountered in forensic assessment is the tendency of many attorneys to guide their clients through a desired strategy for responding to psychological test items. MMPI-2 interpretation is based on the assumption that standard administration procedures have been followed and the client received the same instructions as the normative sample. Some attorneys may try to aid their clients in producing a desired clinical pattern, for example, to emphasize a problem area while not getting tripped up by the validity indicators. When conducting assessments of clients who may have been coached, it is important to determine the extent and nature of the information they were provided about the testing. In a survey of attorneys, 63% reported that they give clients information about psychological test validity measures (Wetter & Corrigan, 1995). The assessment psychologist should inquire as to what the client has been told in order to determine if there were any potentially test-spoiling conditions.

IMPORTANCE OF ASSESSING PROFILES AGAINST POPULATION BASE RATES

In interpreting MMPI-2 patterns for a given population, it is often useful to determine what typical or modal profiles exist in similar samples. For example, among samples of alcoholic patients, the most frequent profiles contain Pd scale elevations, and among chronic pain samples, the dominant profile pattern usually involves the 1-3 code. Knowing, for example, that a client's profile deviates substantially from the base rate might provide interpretive insights about the client. Several studies have described extensive base rate information that can be employed to provide an appropriate context for forensic MMPI-2 profile interpretation (Ben-Porath, McNulty, Watt, & McCormick, 1997; Butcher, 1997a, 1997b, 1997c; Lees-Haley, 1997; Long et al., 2004; Putnam, Kurtz, Millis, & Adams, 1995). The frequency data are made available in the Pearson Assessments (National Computer Systems) computer-based interpretive program (the Minnesota Report) for forensic settings (Butcher, 1997c).

Butcher (1997c) examined the major self-presentation styles of personal injury litigants by grouping profiles according to the following categories: the defensive claimant, the exaggerated problem presentation, and the honest self-portrayal. He then developed base rate information for this sample ($N = 157$) of personal injury litigants and presented profile frequency information for different response styles. It was not possible to group cases into actual versus feigned records or type of personal injury because only the profiles were available for evaluation. Therefore, the group mean profiles of all cases were divided into groups based on whether the validity pattern reflected an essentially normal response approach, a highly defensive protocol, or a highly exaggerated pattern.

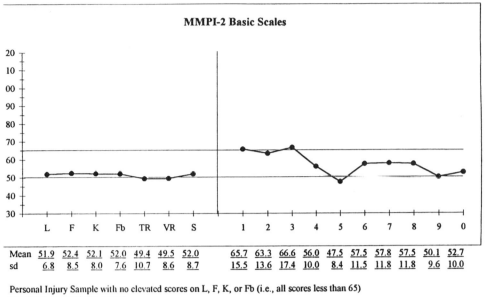

MMPI-2 Basic Scales

	L	F	K	Fb	TR	VR	S		1	2	3	4	5	6	7	8	9	0
Mean	51.9	52.4	52.1	52.0	49.4	49.5	52.0		65.7	63.3	66.6	56.0	47.5	57.5	57.8	57.5	50.1	52.7
sd	6.8	8.5	8.0	7.6	10.7	8.6	8.7		15.5	13.6	17.4	10.0	8.4	11.5	11.8	11.8	9.6	10.0

Personal Injury Sample with no elevated scores on L, F, K, or Fb (i.e., all scores less than 65)
N=80 (33 men and 47 women)

Figure 7.1   Mean MMPI-2 Profile of Personal Injury Litigants Who Presented a Credible Validity Scale Performance (*N* = 33 men; 47 women).

The three group mean profiles shown in Figures 7.1, 7.2, and 7.3 are informative. The first profile (the clearly valid cases) shows a pattern of somatic symptoms in the context of a validity pattern that is credible. The second profile (the defensive records) shows a presentation of self as experiencing somatic problems but in a context of problem denial or claiming of excessive virtue. The third profile presents a rather different pattern, one in which the individual is likely to be exaggerating symptoms. In this pattern, the litigant is asserting great psychological disability and symptoms of distress but in the context of an exaggerated or low credible response pattern.

IMPORTANCE OF ASSESSING PRIOR MENTAL HEALTH HISTORY

For cases in which a litigant alleges mental health problems as a result of an accident or circumstance such as workplace harassment, it is assumed that the individual was not experiencing mental health problems prior to the incident. The veracity of the claim rests on whether the incident actually occurred and whether it was powerful enough to have caused the alleged mental health problems. The defense (usually a corporation or an insurance carrier) may attempt to establish that the alleged injury likely existed prior to the incident and therefore the claimed damages cannot be the sole responsibility of the defendant. Efforts to establish the existence of prior mental health problems can involve procedures such as obtaining preaccident medical records or psychological testing or having witnesses testify that the problems actually preceded the alleged incident. At times, it may be possible for the defense attorneys to

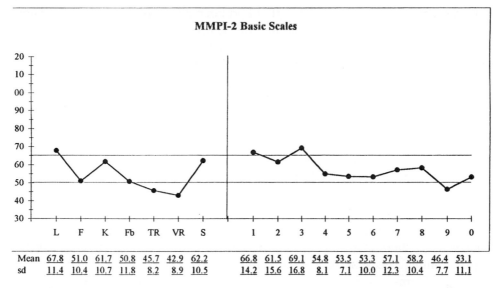

	L	F	K	Fb	TR	VR	S		1	2	3	4	5	6	7	8	9	0
Mean	67.8	51.0	61.7	50.8	45.7	42.9	62.2		66.8	61.5	69.1	54.8	53.5	53.3	57.1	58.2	46.4	53.1
sd	11.4	10.4	10.7	11.8	8.2	8.9	10.5		14.2	15.6	16.8	8.1	7.1	10.0	12.3	10.4	7.7	11.1

Personal Injury Sample with elevations on L or K (i.e., L or K greater than 65 and greater than F and Fb)
N=36 (9 men and 27 women)

Figure 7.2 Mean MMPI-2 Profile of Personal Injury Litigants Who Presented a Highly Defensive and Overly Virtuous Validity Scale Performance (*N* = 9 men; 27 women).

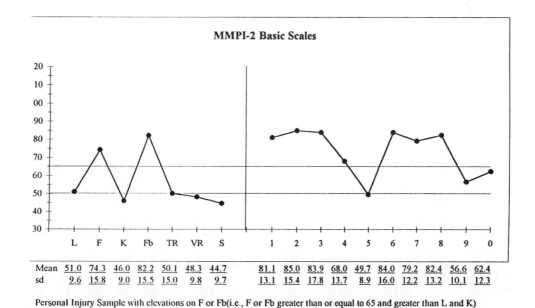

	L	F	K	Fb	TR	VR	S		1	2	3	4	5	6	7	8	9	0
Mean	51.0	74.3	46.0	82.2	50.1	48.3	44.7		81.1	85.0	83.9	68.0	49.7	84.0	79.2	82.4	56.6	62.4
sd	9.6	15.8	9.0	15.5	15.0	9.8	9.7		13.1	15.4	17.8	13.7	8.9	16.0	12.2	13.2	10.1	12.3

Personal Injury Sample with elevations on F or Fb(i.e., F or Fb greater than or equal to 65 and greater than L and K)
N=41 (12 men and 29 women)

Figure 7.3 Mean MMPI-2 Profile of Personal Injury Litigants Who Presented a Highly Exaggerated Validity Scale Performance (*N* = 12 men; 9 women).

obtain records such as an MMPI-2 that had been administered when the client was in marital therapy or seeking mental heath services for other reasons. In such cases, it may be possible to learn whether or not the client's mental health problems resulted from the claimed incident. The following case illustrates the value of obtaining mental health records for problems that actually occurred before the accident in question.

CASE 7.1

Ms. X, age 35, alleged that she had suffered psychological and neurological damage as a result of an incident in which she claimed to have been injured when a rental car, with a stuck accelerator, chased her around a rental car lot. Witnesses testified that she was not actually hit by the car.

Attorneys for the plaintiff introduced into evidence an evaluation conducted after the incident that suggested she had suffered irreparable psychological damage because of the incident and was experiencing severe mental health problems as a result. She claimed to be so impaired cognitively that she could not perform even simple mental tasks such as reading bedtime stories to her children.

Her MMPI-2 profile (shown in Figure 7.4) suggested that she was experiencing substantial mental health problems in the context of a valid but somewhat exaggerated test performance.

Psychological testing conducted prior to the incident, however, indicated that the mental health disability that she claimed actually preceded her acci-

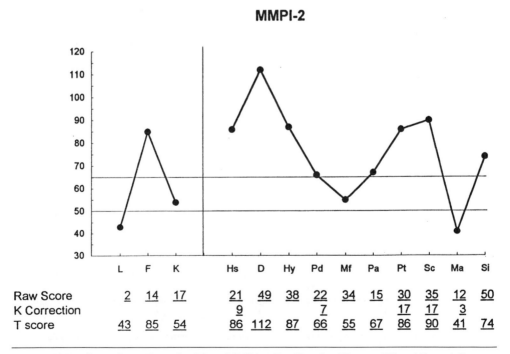

Figure 7.4 Case One: Post-Accident MMPI-2 Profile of a Woman Who Alleged Severe Damages Following a Minimal Accident.

MMPI-2

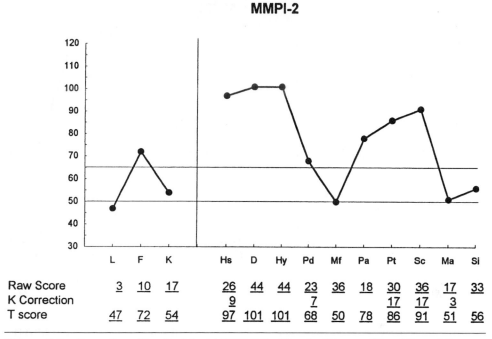

	L	F	K		Hs	D	Hy	Pd	Mf	Pa	Pt	Sc	Ma	Si
Raw Score	3	10	17		26	44	44	23	36	18	30	36	17	33
K Correction					9			7			17	17	3	
T score	47	72	54		97	101	101	68	50	78	86	91	51	56

Figure 7.5 Case One: Pre-Accident MMPI-2 Profile of a Woman Who Alleged Severe Damages Following a Minimal Accident.

dent. Ms. X had been evaluated about 1 month prior to the incident as part of a different lawsuit in which she was allegedly rear-ended by a garbage truck. She had litigation pending from this incident as well. The MMPI-2 evaluation in this earlier litigation showed that she was experiencing a pattern of severe emotional disturbance at the time the second accident occurred (see MMPI-2 pattern in Figure 7.5).

The jury in this case found for the defense. They did not believe that the incident in the rental car lot had caused the mental damages that the plaintiff claimed, in large part because the problems preexisted the incident.

ANALYSIS OF POSTACCIDENT ADJUSTMENT

Attorneys might attempt to clarify the extent of psychological damage to litigants by conducting postaccident assessments. For instance, a defense team might conduct a psychological evaluation at different points after the incident to determine whether the client is showing physical or psychological symptoms consistent with the claimed disability. The MMPI-2 can be helpful in making this determination. Extreme elevations on F, Fb, or Fp scales are signals that the individual is not selectively responding to symptoms but is instead indiscriminately exaggerating symptoms.

The MMPI profile shown in Figure 7.6 on page 152 illustrates this problem. The litigant claimed disabling ear damage after a sudden change in cabin

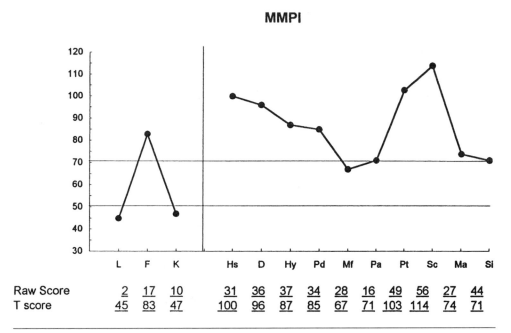

MMPI

	L	F	K		Hs	D	Hy	Pd	Mf	Pa	Pt	Sc	Ma	Si
Raw Score	2	17	10		31	36	37	34	28	16	49	56	27	44
T score	45	83	47		100	96	87	85	67	71	103	114	74	71

Figure 7.6 Case Two Post-Accident MMPI-2 Profile of a Litigant Who Alleged Severe Inner Ear Damage Following an In-Flight Change in Altitude on a Commercial Airliner.

pressure, which occurred when an aircraft was descending. As shown in Figure 7.6, the litigant produced a highly exaggerated F scale score, greater than a T of 80, and a clinical profile that showed no selective responding. Unlike most genuine patients, he responded in the clinical range across all of the traditional MMPI clinical scales; all clinical scale scores were T > 70. He showed no specific pattern of symptoms as one would find in clients who are accurately reporting their internal state. Instead, the litigant simply endorsed all or most symptoms without specificity.

Clients who are alleging posttraumatic stress from interpersonal situations such as workplace harassment may also exaggerate and present an extreme pattern of symptoms that they believe reflects their anguish and "disability" but that appear on the testing to be extreme, even malingered, because they are not a specific symptom review.

The profile shown in Figure 7.7 clearly shows this feigned traumatic distress in a case where the litigant alleged PTSD after being fired from his job for sexually harassing several women. Clients who are experiencing genuine PTSD tend to present more specific psychological symptoms with a credible validity pattern.

In another case, a woman who filed a suit against the owner of the apartment building in which she was living produced the MMPI-2 profile shown in Figure 7.8. A few months earlier, she had experienced a traumatizing sexual assault because the apartment compound's security system had been breached. After the sexual assault, she experienced considerable PTSD symptoms.

MMPI-2

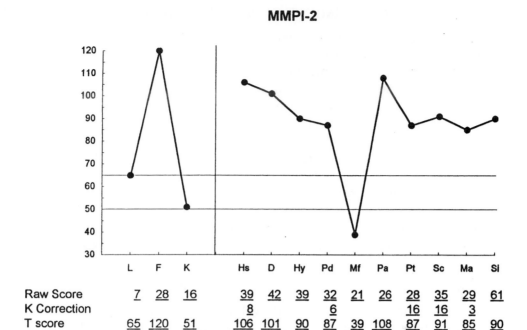

	L	F	K		Hs	D	Hy	Pd	Mf	Pa	Pt	Sc	Ma	Si
Raw Score	7	28	16		39	42	39	32	21	26	28	35	29	61
K Correction					8			6			16	16	3	
T score	65	120	51		106	101	90	87	39	108	87	91	85	90

Figure 7.7 Case Three: Likely Malingered MMPI-2 Profile a Sexual-Harassment Perpetrator Who Claimed PTSD Symptoms after Being Fired from His Job.

MMPI-2

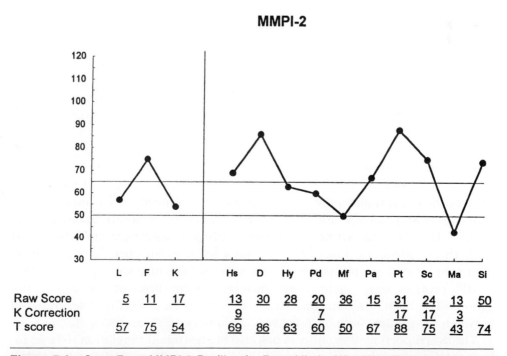

	L	F	K		Hs	D	Hy	Pd	Mf	Pa	Pt	Sc	Ma	Si
Raw Score	5	11	17		13	30	28	20	36	15	31	24	13	50
K Correction					9			7			17	17	3	
T score	57	75	54		69	86	63	60	50	67	88	75	43	74

Figure 7.8 Case Four: MMPI-2 Profile of a Rape Victim Who Was Experiencing Posttraumatic Stress Disorder.

ASSESSMENT OF MALINGERING

Because of the potential financial reward, individuals involved in litigation are frequently motivated to exaggerate symptoms or personality characteristics in either a positive or negative direction on the MMPI. For instance, people alleging work-related back pain may want to make their physical symptoms look worse than they are while simultaneously making their mental health look better than it actually is. An advantage of using the MMPI-2 is that it has several validity indicators designed to detect instances of exaggeration and defensiveness. The success of both the standard validity scales (F, Fb, L, K) and additional scales (F-K, Fp, S, Mp) at detecting malingerers has been widely reviewed in the literature, both in forensic settings and in analogue studies using college students. It is important for a forensic psychologist to know the strengths and limitations of the MMPI-2 validity indicators at detecting malingering (see, e.g., Bagby, Buis, & Nicholson, 1995; Berry, Baer, & Harris, 1991).

Detection of Symptom Exaggeration, or Faking Bad

The fake-bad literature suggests that the validity indicators are usually effective at distinguishing malingerers from nonmalingerers. The validity scales, which are most effective, however, may vary according to the sample characteristics and diagnosis. Studies asking clinical populations to either answer honestly or fake bad have generally found that the standard validity scales accurately distinguish the two groups (Bagby et al., 1995; Berry et al., 1996; Rogers, Sewell, & Ustad, 1995). Graham, Watts, and Timbrook (1991) found that the F, Fb, and F-K scales were successful at discriminating between honest versus faking-bad college samples and college students faking bad versus psychiatric patients.

Information about specific disorders such as Schizophrenia, Major Depression, and PTSD has been supplied to normal adult populations to see if their faking of these disorders can be detected. Respondents have also received information about the validity indicators to see if that improves their ability to reliably fake disorders. Cramer (1995), using psychology students, found that students given specific information about either Major Depression or Paranoid Schizophrenia produced more valid profiles than individuals simply told to fake either disorder without any additional information. Although the informed versus uninformed groups produced significantly different profiles, the F and Fb validity indicators were still able to discriminate these groups from authentic responders. Wetter, Baer, Berry, Robinson, and Sumpter (1993) found similar results when comparing the profiles of adults asked to fake either PTSD or Paranoid Schizophrenia with psychiatric patients diagnosed with those disorders. Even though fakers were given specific information about the disorders and monetary incentives to produce valid profiles, their MMPI profiles were significantly different from those of the psychiatric groups. The F, Fb, F-K, and Ds validity indicators successfully discriminated between the groups, with hit rates varying between 73% and 95%.

The overreporting of symptoms has also been studied in relation to head injuries. In a comprehensive review of the literature, Berry and Butcher (1998) analyzed the effectiveness of the MMPI-2 in detecting feigned head injury. Overall, they found most support for the use of the F scale in detecting overreporting, with the F-K, Ds/Ds2, and Fb scales also receiving some support. F scale T scores above 80 may be indicative of an exaggerated profile, and T scores above 90 should definitely raise suspicions. An additional complicating factor in assessing feigned head injury is that individuals may not universally feign symptoms; for instance, they may feign cognitive symptoms but not psychological symptoms. Therefore, these two domains should be viewed independently, without assuming that feigning in one invariably leads to feigning in the other.

In conclusion, the fake-bad literature finds good support for the ability of the standard MMPI-2 validity indicators to discriminate between valid and feigned profiles. Although several new scales have been developed for the purposes of detecting malingering, the empirical literature is overwhelmingly in favor of the standard validity indicators.

The Fake Bad Scale

The Fake Bad Scale (FBS) was designed as a means of assessing malingering in personal injury cases with the MMPI-2 (Lees-Haley, English, & Glenn, 1991). The scale developers claim that the scale assesses an invalid response style pertinent to personal injury cases that could be viewed as somatic malingering in cases in which physical injuries or pain are involved. Several investigators have reported the utility of the scale in assessing malingering of pain (Greiffenstein, Baker, Gola, Donders, & Miller, 2002; Larrabee, 1998, 2000; Martens, Donders, & Millis, 2001; Slick, Hopp, Strauss, & Spellacy, 1996; and Tsushima & Tsushima, 2001).

A recent article by Larrabee (2003) attempted to confirm the validity of the FBS. However, several methodological problems with the study limit its utility. Larrabee used a small sample of patients from his clinical practice to verify the predictive power of the FBS against several other malingering tests (e.g., the Test of Malingering Memory indexes from the Wechsler Adult Intelligence Scales-Revised; and Rey's Portland Digit Recognition Test or the Warrington Recognition Memory Test) as a means of establishing malingering for clients. Larabee did not utilize an external method to determine malingering other than the test results. He concluded that 33 patients (20 females and 13 males) had engaged in cognitive malingering in this sample of convenience. However, according to Larrabee's results, using a conservative cut-off on FBS (23 for men and 25 for women) classified only 54% of the sample of suspected malingerers as malingering. This is not a particularly effective result for an assessment scale.

A number of published studies have not supported the use of the FBS in identifying malingering of psychopathology (Greiffenstein et al., 2002). In one recent meta-analysis of the detection of malingering of psychiatric illness with the MMPI-2, the FBS performed poorly at detecting malingering (Rogers, Sewell, Martin, & Vitacco, 2003). In other studies, the FBS has not effectively identified individuals who are instructed to feign PTSD as a result of work-related injuries, childhood sexual abuse, or combat-related trauma (Bury & Bagby, 2002; Elhai, Gold, Frueh, & Gold, 2000; Elhai, Gold, Sellers, & Dorfman, 2001). These studies indicate that the FBS is not suited to the detection of malingering of psychopathology even in the context of compensation seeking (Elhai et al., 2000).

The most compelling reason for not using the FBS for assessing clients in personal injury litigation evaluations is the fact that the scale overpredicts malingering in groups of patients with likely genuine problems (Butcher, Arbisi, Atlis, & McNulty, 2003). Butcher et al. evaluated the performance of the FBS for assessing clients in various settings in several ways. First, an item analysis was conducted revealing that the FBS did not operate as do other malingering or exaggeration measures on the MMPI-2, by assessing rare or unusual symptom expression; instead, the FBS comprised a number of items that are actually scored on scales that assess health or mental health problems for example, the Hs, Hy, and HEA content scale. Consequently, patients who endorse such symptoms as part of their clinical pattern are classified by the FBS as malingering. This situation was verified by examining the percentages of FBS elevations in various mental health and health settings (e.g., chronic pain programs).

Second, the FBS was also shown to have an unacceptably high rate of false positives, especially among woman and patients with psychiatric illness. In several large health and mental health settings, the FBS was found to overpredict malingering, in some settings calling malingering as high as 65% of patients. The FBS is accordingly more likely to be used by defense-oriented practitioners in personal injury assessments given the proclivity of the scale finding malingering in a large number of cases.

DETECTION OF SYMPTOM UNDERREPORTING, OR FAKING GOOD

Individuals involved in personal injury litigation may be motivated to downplay any preexisting psychological problems while exaggerating symptoms caused by the alleged accident. They want to portray themselves in the best light possible to convince people that their problems are real. The validity indicators on the MMPI are also designed to detect these faking-good individuals. The standard validity scales L and K as well as some newer scales, Mp, Sd, and S, have been found to effectively discriminate those who underreport symptoms from honest responders. Baer, Wetter, and Berry (1992) conducted a meta-analysis of 25 studies assessing the ability of the MMPI to detect underreporting of symptoms. The optimal cut-off scores used to discriminate those underreporting symptoms compared to those answering honestly varied among studies. Overall, however, the mean effects for the L, K, and L+K scales averaged approximately 1.0, suggesting a difference of about 1 standard deviation between the underreporters and honest reporters. The mean effects for the positive malingering (Mp) and social desirability (Sd) scales were 1.59 and 1.60, respectively. Bagby et al. (1995) also found that the Mp and L scales effectively discriminated between those college students told to fake good versus those given standard instructions.

The S scale has been shown to detect persons motivated to fake good. This scale has five different factors: belief in human goodness, serenity, contentment with life, patience and denial of irritability and anger, and denial of moral flaws. The S scale effectively distinguished between the MMPIs of male pilots seeking a job with a major airline and the MMPI-2 restandardization sample. People with high S scores reported fewer clinical problems and presented fewer negative personality traits than normals (Butcher & Han, 1993). Baer, Wetter, Nichols, Greene, and Berry (1995) applied the S scale to a sample of participants told to either fake good or answer in the standard manner. They found that the S scale and Wiggin's social desirability scale (Wsd) added incremental validity above and beyond the L and K scales to the detection of faking-good responders. In regression analyses on the data, the L and K scales did not add any predictive power beyond that of the S and Wsd scales. The authors concluded that the S and Wsd scales may be the most effective scales for detecting underreporting of symptoms. These data, of course, must be interpreted with caution until subsequent studies replicate these results. However, they do suggest that the S scale shows promise as a method for detecting underreporting of psychopathology.

Although many studies have advocated the success of the obvious-subtle scales in detecting both faking good and faking bad, they have not been included in this review because of their questionable validity. The subtle items on some of the MMPI clinical scales were included largely as a result of chance and do not relate significantly to external criteria. That is, these subtle items are essentially an artifact of empirical scale construction and were originally included on the clinical scales as a result of incomplete cross-validation (see discussion in Pope, Butcher, & Seelen, 2000). Although some investigators have attempted to employ these subtle measures as indices of test validity (Greene, 1991; Wiener, 1948), these items have been pretty well discredited (Nelson, 1987; Weed, Ben-Porath, & Butcher, 1990) and have been dropped from the test publisher's list of recommended MMPI-2 scales. Therefore, we recommend against using the obvious-subtle scales as a method for discriminating between malingerers and honest responders.

THE EFFECTS OF LITIGATION ON THE CLAIMANT

The litigation process can have a strong impact on psychological test results.

MMPI PROFILES OF LITIGANTS

When personality profiles of pending disability claimants are studied, the response pattern appears to be more exaggerated and generally more pathological than in the general population (Pollack & Grainey, 1984; Sternbach, Wolf, Murphy, & Akeson, 1973). Whether these differences reflect acute/situational symptoms or chronic mental health problems or whether there is a trend toward excessive symptom claiming to emphasize perceived disability is not known. Most of the MMPI research involving workers' compensation cases, however, reflects this increased level of psychological symptoms. Workers' compensation claimants have been studied descriptively by a number of authors. In cases where physical injury is believed to be involved, the MMPI profile of workers' compensation cases usually involves extreme scale elevations on Hs, D, and Hy (Hersch & Alexander, 1990; Repko & Cooper, 1983). Iverson, King, Scott, and Adams (2001) found that litigating workers' compensation claimants with pain complaints reported higher levels of cognitive symptoms than nonlitigating head injury patients. These results suggest that litigating individuals may produce exaggeration of a variety of symptoms in addition to their primary complaint.

Regardless of the type of claim being made, litigants generally display elevations on the clinical scales of the MMPI. Gandolfo (1995) compared workers' compensation claimants alleging harassment to those making a claim for something other than harassment. He found similar profile elevations with regard to scales 1, 2, 3, 7, and 8 between the groups. The main difference was that harassment claimants also elevated scale 6, indicating that they felt angry, mistreated, and suspicious, which is consistent with their claim of harassment. Overall, however, their MMPI profile patterns resembled other workers' compensation claimants. Similarly, Snibbe, Peterson, and Sosner (1980) found that workers' compensation applicants had generally similar and rather disturbed MMPI profiles (with high elevations on scales F, 1, 2, 3, 4, 8) regardless of the reason for the claim—psychiatric, low back pain, or head injury.

THE IMPACT OF LITIGATION ON TREATMENT OUTCOME

Historically, people have referred to "compensation neurosis" or "litigation neurosis" as if it were a condition that claimants had until litigation was settled. Inherent in these terms is the assumption that a claimant's behavior is somehow changed during the course of litigation and that it miraculously improves when litigation terminates. Unfortunately, the belief in this pattern of behavior has led some pain clinics to deny treatment to those clients involved in litigation, with the assumption that they would be difficult clients and not make great improvements during litigation. This denial of treatment shortly after an accident may actually do more harm to clients than their involvement in litigation. Literature reviews have found that litigation status does not appear to consistently impact treatment outcome regardless of the type of injury the person claimed, whether neck injury, low back injury, head injury, or chronic pain (Evans, 1994; Mendelson, 1982, 1995).

In fact, Evans (1994) concluded that one of the greatest predictors of successful outcome was the inclusion of psychological services in the treatment plan. It was also important that individuals received immediate intervention with the goal of returning them to work as quickly as possible, even if their work functioning was at a lower level than before. Binder, Trimble, and McNiel (1991) assessed individuals 1 and 2 years after litigation settlement and found significantly less psychiatric impairment among individuals who had shorter durations between injury and settlement, suggesting that rapid settlement was most beneficial to the mental health of the litigants.

Mendelson (1995) studied a group of 264 respondents who had not yet returned to work at the time of litigation settlement. The subjects were a heterogeneous group whose claims included industrial, automobile, and other accidents. A follow-up study a mean of 23.1 months after litigation settlement found that 75% of the subjects remained unemployed. Contrary to the compensation neurosis hypothesis, these data suggest that the majority of individuals not working at the end of litigation will also not be working 2 years later. In general, the longer people are out of work, the less likely they are to return. This may be one way the process of litigation impacts people's functioning: Litigation may prevent them from receiving immediate treatment and prevent them from returning to work promptly, both of which are negatively correlated with long-term outcomes.

There is some evidence that litigation status affects MMPI-2 profiles in head injury cases. Youngjohn, Davis, and Wolf (1997) assessed 30 minor/mild head injury patients involved in litigation and 30 moderate/severe head injury patients, 18 of whom were involved in litigation. They found that the minor/mild head injury group had significantly higher scale scores on Hs, D, Hy, and Pt than either the litigating or nonlitigating severe head injury group. In addition, the severe head injury litigating group reported significantly higher scale scores on Hs, Hy, Sc, and health concerns than the severe nonlitigating group. The authors conclude that premorbid emotional and personality difficulties may influence who decides to pursue litigation.

Hoffman, Scott, Emick, and Adams (1999) found that in a nonlitigating group, MMPI-2 profile elevations on Hs, D, Hy, and Pt were inversely related to head injury severity. This was not true, however, for severe head injury patients who were litigating. The authors conclude that litigation moderates MMPI-2 item endorsement. Without prospective studies, it is impossible to know whether genuine premorbid problems account for elevations in litigating patients or whether litigation itself prompts MMPI-2 scale elevations. Both of these studies, however, suggest that the MMPI-2 profiles of litigating mild and severe head injury patients are elevated relative to nonlitigating head injury patients.

Evans (1994) surveyed personal injury patients involved in automobile accidents about their impression of the most difficult stressor related to the accident at 1, 3, 4, 12, 18, and 24 months postaccident. After the first month, 78% reported that their medical symptoms were the most stressful. Surprisingly, at 6 months and each time period thereafter, the most frequent stressful event reported was the uncooperativeness of medical insurance carriers in promptly paying medical bills. By 24 months, nearly all respondents reported that failure of the insurance companies to honor financial obligations was the greatest stressor remaining from their accident. Of particular interest is their finding from a subgroup of the patients that 97% of the people whose insurance carriers paid their bills promptly (within 30 days) had returned to work compared to only 4% of the subgroup whose insurance carriers were taking more than 90 days to make payments.

These results indicate that there may be myriad factors impacting any individual's return to work after an accident. Most previous studies have focused on the characteristics of the individual, such as premorbid psychopathology and personality, which contribute to postaccident functioning. Although these individual factors certainly play a role in the course of the individual's recovery, it is also likely that they interact with external factors. As the studies detailed earlier have found, the legal and insurance systems are not designed to maximize an individual's recovery. The excessive paperwork and delays associated with these systems are likely to contribute to litigants' stress and thereby detrimentally impact their long-term recovery.

NONSTANDARD INTERPRETIVE STRATEGIES: SENIOR-DOUGLAS

A recent article published by Senior and Douglas (2001) questioned traditional MMPI-2 interpretive strategies and provided what they considered a new and more effective approach to test interpretation. However, in a recent evaluation of the Senior-Douglas data set and the conclusions they derived from it, Butcher and Ben-Porath (2004) pointed out that the Senior and Douglas critique of the MMPI-2 in medical and legal settings stems largely from an opinion-driven rather than a data-driven perspective. Butcher and Ben-Porath provided a critique of the Senior-Douglas article, offering a perspective on the importance of using the extensive research base on the MMPI-2 to provide a more effective interpretive and less idiosyncratic strategy for interpretation. The Senior-Douglas article was shown to be an idiosyncratic interpretative approach that is not supported by the data reported in the Senior-Douglas paper. An examination of the data from which Senior and Douglas drew their conclusions indicated that the sample was ill-defined and insufficiently described; the authors drew conclusions that were not supported by the data; they generalized from a rather weak database and failed to take into consideration standard and well-established interpretation strategies and provided no effective alternative strategies for interpreting MMPI-2 scales and indices.

CAUTIONS IN USING MMPI-2 MEASURES NOT YET VALIDATED IN FORENSIC ASSESSMENT: THE RESTRUCTURED CLINICAL SCALES (RC)

Newly introduced measures that may have been derived from MMPI-2 items have not been sufficiently studied or validated with forensic clients to incorporate in forensic evaluations. The Restructured Clinical Scales (RC scales) by Tellegen et al. (2003) were developed to improve the traditional clinical scales by reducing item overlap, lowering scale intercorrelation, and eliminating subtle items to improve convergent and discriminant validity of the scales. In the test manual, the RC scales were recommended as supplemental measures and not considered to be replacements for the original clinical scales. The scales were developed through psychometric analyses of responses of psychiatric patients as follows.

Initially, the authors developed a "Demoralization Scale" to measure the general factors that were considered to run through the existing scales. They then removed items from the eight clinical scales that they believed might be influenced by this set of general maladjustment items. The initial construction was aimed at capturing a demoralization factor that was viewed as common to most clinical scales and produced construct overlap. The authors then constructed "seed" scales for the eight clinical scales by removing the demoralization component from them. They next broadened these residual items on the original clinical scales by including other items from the MMPI-2 item pool that correlated with the seed constructs. They conducted both internal and external validity analyses to further understand the operation of the scales. Finally, the authors provided analyses of the RC scales' internal validity and predictive validity using mental health patients from the Portage Path Outpatient Sample (Graham, Ben-Porath, & McNulty, 1999) and two inpatient samples (Arbisi, Ben-Porath, & McNulty, 2003). These analyses showed that the RC scales have a degree of association comparable to external behavioral correlates and to the traditional clinical scales.

The initial publication on the RC scales did not present information on the relationships of the RC scales and other widely used MMPI-2 measures such as the MMPI-2 content scales. However, the correlational scale construction strategies used in the development of the RC scales assured that the scales were unidimensional in character and homogeneous in content, similar to the MMPI-2 content scales. It is not known at this point the extent to which the RC scales operate like the MMPI-2 content scales; it is known, however, that there are some RC scales that have significantly higher item overlap with MMPI-2 content scales (e.g., RC3 has 80% overlap with the CYN content scale) than with the clinical scales from which they were derived. If the RC scales turn out to operate in a manner similar to the MMPI-2 content scales, then they might have more limited applicability in settings like personal injury evaluations in which the obvious item content is somewhat transparent and clearly avoided by persons wishing to present a picture of extremely virtuous personal qualities.

The RC scales likely would not function in the manner of the original clinical scales in personal injury evaluations. For example, the RC3 scale has little to do with the Hy scale, one of the most frequent high points in medical and forensic applications, in terms of item overlap and content. Nichols (in press) has referred to the apparent scale changes between Hy and RC3 as "construct drift." This change in measurement focus between the two measures is illustrated by the negative correlation between them (−.42), suggesting that the RC3 scale is not measuring traditional Hy constructs—those personality features that are often so pronounced in medical settings and that the MMPI-2 clinical scales address well. In addition, RC3 appears to be measuring only cynicism, as noted by the extreme item sharing with the CYN content scale, over 80% of the items. It appears as though RC3 is an alternate form of the content scale CYN—which has not necessarily been a historically powerful scale in medical applications. It should also be noted that the Hy scale is frequently the highest point among medical clients, yet the Hy scale constructs are not represented in the RC scales.

The extent to which these seemingly unrelated modified measures can add to the interpretation of the original scales needs to be determined by further research, particularly in diverse settings such as medical and forensic populations. When used in medical settings, the profile high points for the RC scales will likely be quite noncongruent. So when a patient has a high Hy on the clinical scales, the RC3 is not likely to be prominent; therefore, it is not likely to be a factor in the interpretive process. As noted earlier, Tellegen et al. (2003) pointed out that the RC scales are not to be viewed as replacements for the

MMPI-2 clinical scales but as a means of refining their interpretation. Exactly what the scales assess in forensic settings needs to be established through empirical research.

The initial publication of the RC scales provided information on the use of the scales in severely disturbed and hospitalized psychiatric patients. Research has not been conducted, however, on other samples, such as personal injury cases, chronic pain or other medical patients, or personnel evaluations. Consequently, at this point, the use of the RC scales in assessing persons involved in litigation is not recommended.

SUMMARY

Currently, workers' compensation and personal injury litigation are multi-billion-dollar businesses involving legal, medical, psychological, industrial, union, insurance, and government personnel in increasingly heated opposition. Concern over fraud and claim exaggeration has grown as economic retrenchment and policy liberalization have increased incentives for claims falsification. In addition, conditions that are difficult to verify, such as psychological and stress-induced disability, are increasingly being claimed in compensation cases. Consequently, psychological professionals are being asked to make determinations about possible exaggeration, malingering, and exacerbation of physical problems claimed by litigants.

The psychologist faced with such evaluations may be asked to assess whether a plaintiff's complaints are possibly due to stress or malingering. Clearly, no foolproof method of determining such distinctions is available at this time. However, by selecting the most objective, valid, and reliable tests appropriate to the complaints, conducting thorough interviews, and carefully recording case notes and test reports, clinicians can be helpful in clarifying the extent to which psychological factors may be involved in personal injury cases.

Assessment for court testimony poses some unique challenges to the psychologist, which requires consideration of a variety of factors. One of the most significant is the extent to which the client has been coached by an attorney. Attorney coaching might produce invalid profiles, which are exaggerated in either a positive or a negative direction. Most research has found that, even with coaching, the MMPI-2 validity indicators are still able to detect malingering. There is some indication, however, that explicit knowledge about the validity indicators can reduce their effectiveness. For detecting exaggeration or overreporting of symptoms, the F, Fb, and F-K scales are most effective. In addition, the new Fp scale has shown some promising results. For detecting underreporting of symptoms, the L and K standard validity indicators are effective. Recent studies have also found the Mp and S scales to be effective at detecting fake-good profiles. More research is needed, however, to confirm these preliminary findings.

Despite considerable research and debate, assessment of malingering on the MMPI-2 is often inconclusive. Researchers have hypothesized that elevated scores on the Hs, D, and Hy scales are indicative of psychological contributions to physical ailments at the least and possibly malingering. Psychological contributions are posited to result in more chronic and exaggerated forms of physical problems. And while this hypothesis appears to be true in a general sense, it should be interpreted with caution because there are instances when nonmalingerers also elevate these scales. For instance, most individuals with low back pain or head injury elevate these scales above average. Therefore, the classic conversion V profile (with elevated Hs and Hy scales) cannot automatically be interpreted as a malingered profile. The psychologist must incorporate all relevant data, including premorbid personality functioning, type of injury, and validity scale indices, to make a determination about the likelihood of malingering.

Personality assessment in personal injury cases is a growing field in need of more research on the true psychological sequelae to injury. To date, research has largely focused on the differences between those who are obviously attempting to malinger their symptoms and the actual symptoms of real sufferers. Continued research should attempt to build on and refine our knowledge about malingered symptoms using valid, objective, standardized instruments, such as the MMPI-2. This will ultimately allow psychologists to provide more accurate testimony on the personality characteristics and motivation of litigants.

REFERENCES

Alfano, D. P., Neilson, P. M., Paniak, C. E., & Finlayson, M. A. J. (1992). The MMPI and closed-head injury. *The Clinical Neuropsychologist, 6*(2), 134–142.

American Psychological Association. (1986). *American Psychological Association guidelines for computer-based tests and interpretations.* Washington, DC: Author.

Arbisi, P. A., Ben-Porath, Y. S., & McNulty, J. L. (2003). Empirical correlates of common MMPI-2 two-point codes in male psychiatric inpatients. *Assessment, 10*(3), 237–247.

Baer, R. A., Wetter, M. W., & Berry, D. T. R. (1992). Detection of underreporting of psychopathology on the MMPI: A meta-analysis. *Clinical Psychology Review, 12,* 509–525.

Baer, R. A., Wetter, M. W., Nichols, D. S., Greene, R., & Berry, D. T. R. (1995). Sensitivity of MMPI-2 validity scales to underreporting of symptoms. *Psychological Assessment, 7*(4), 419–423.

Bagby, R. M., Buis, T., & Nicholson, R. A. (1995). Relative effectiveness of the standard validity scales in detecting fake-bad and fade-good responding: Replication and extension. *Psychological Assessment, 7*(1), 84–92.

Ben-Porath, Y. S., McNulty, J. L., Watt, M., & McCormick, R. A. (1997). Unpublished data from a substance abuse program at the Cleveland VAMC.

Berry, D. T. R., Adams, J. J., Borden, J. W., Clark, C. D., Thacker, S. R., Burger, T. L., et al. (1996). Detection of a cry for help in the MMPI-2: An analog investigation. *Journal of Personality Assessment, 67*(1), 26–35.

Berry, D. T. R., Baer, R. A., & Harris, M. J. (1991). Detection of malingering on the MMPI: A meta-analysis. *Clinical Psychology Review, 11,* 585–598.

Berry, D. T. R., & Butcher, J. N. (1998). Detection of feigning of head injury symptoms on the MMPI-2. In C. Reynolds (Ed.), *Detection of malingering in head injury litigation* (pp. 209–238). New York: Plenum Press.

Binder, R. L., Trimble, M. R., & McNiel, D. E. (1991). The course of psychological symptoms after resolution of lawsuits. *Journal of Psychiatry, 148*(8), 1073–1075.

Blanchard, E. B., Hickling, E. J., Taylor, A. E., Loos, W. R., Forneris, C. A., & Jaccard, J. (1996). Who develops PTSD from motor vehicle accidents? *Behavioral Research and Therapy, 34*(1), 1–10.

Boccaccini, T. M., & Brodsky, S. L. (1999). Diagnostic test use by forensic psychologists in emotional injury cases. *Professional Psychology: Research and Practice, 31*(1), 251–259.

Borum, R., & Grisso, T. (1995). Psychological test use in criminal forensic evaluations. *Professional Psychology: Research and Practice, 26,* 465–473.

Brulot, M. M., Strauss, E., & Spellacy, F. (1997). Validity of the Minnesota Multiphasic Personality Inventory-2 correction factors for use with patients with suspected head injury. *Clinical Neuropsychologist, 4,* 391–401.

Bury, A. S., & Bagby, R. M. (2002). The detection of feigned uncoached and coached posttraumatic stress disorder with the MMPI-2 in a sample of workplace accident victims. *Psychological Assessment, 14*, 472–484.

Butcher, J. N. (1997a). *Base-rate information for the personal injury samples in the Minnesota forensic study.*

Butcher, J. N. (1997b, August). Frequency of MMPI-2 scores in forensic evaluations. *MMPI-2 News & Profiles, 8*, 1–2.

Butcher, J. N. (1997c). *User's guide to the Minnesota report: Forensic system.* Minneapolis, MN: National Computer Systems.

Butcher, J. N., Arbisi, P. A., Atlis, M. M., & McNulty, J. L. (2003). The construct validity of the Lees-Haley Fake Bad Scale (FBS): Does this scale measure malingering and feigned emotional distress? *Archives of Clinical Neuropsychology, 18*, 473–485.

Butcher, J. N., & Ben-Porath, Y. S. (2004). Use of the MMPI-2 in medico legal evaluations: An alternative interpretation for the Senior & Douglas (2001) Critique. *Australian Psychologist, 39*, 44–50.

Butcher, J. N., & Han, K. (1993). Development of an MMPI-2 scale to assess the presentation of self in a superlative manner: The S scale. In James N. Butcher & C. D. Spielberger (Eds.), *Advances in personality assessment* (Vol. 10, pp. 25–50). Hillsdale, NJ: Erlbaum.

Butcher, J. N., & Rouse, S. (1996). Clinical personality assessment. *Annual Review of Psychology, 47*, 87–111.

Cramer, K. M. (1995). The effects of description clarity and disorder type on MMPI-2 fake-bad validity indices. *Journal of Clinical Psychology, 51*(6), 831–839.

Edwards, D. W., Dahmen, B. A., Wanlass, R. L., Homquist, L. A., Wicks, J. J., Davis, C., et al. (2003). Personality assessment in neuropsychology: The nonspecificity of MMPI-2 neurocorrection methods. *Assessment, 10*(3), 222–227.

Elhai, J. D., Gold, P. B., Frueh, B. C., & Gold, S. N. (2000). Cross-validation of the MMPI-2 in detecting malingered posttraumatic stress disorder. *Journal of Personality Assessment, 75*(3), 449–463.

Elhai, J. D., Gold, S. N., Sellers, A. H., & Dorfman, W. I. (2001). The detection of malingered posttraumatic stress disorder with MMPI-2 fake bad indices. *Assessment, 8*(2), 221–236.

Evans, R. W. (1994). The effects of litigation on treatment outcome with personal injury patients. *American Journal of Forensic Psychology, 12*(4), 19–34.

Flamer, S., & Birch, W. (1992, May). *Differential diagnosis of post-traumatic stress disorder in injured workers; Evaluating the MMPI-2.* Paper presented at the 27th Annual Symposium on Recent Developments in the Use of the MMPI (MMPI-2), Minneapolis, MN.

Fordyce, W. E., Bigos, S. J., Batti'e, M. C., & Fisher, L. D. (1992). MMPI scale 3 as a predictor of back injury report: What does it tell us? *Clinical Journal of Pain, 8*, 222–226.

Gallagher, R. M., Rauh, V., Haugh, L. D., Milhous, R., Callas, P. W., Langelier, R., et al. (1989). Determinants of return-to-work among low back pain patients. *Pain, 39*, 55–67.

Gandolfo, R. (1995). MMPI-2 profiles of worker's compensation claimants who present with complaints of harassment. *Journal of Clinical Psychology, 51*(5), 711–715.

Gass, C. S. (1992). MMPI-2 interpretation of patients with cerebrovascular disease: A correction factor. *Archives of Neuropsychology, 7*, 17–27.

Gass, C. S., & Wald, H. S. (1997). MMPI-2 interpretation and closed-head trauma: Cross-validation of a correction factor. *Archives of Clinical Neuropsychology, 12*, 199–205.

Gatchel, R. J., Polatin, P. B., & Mayer, T. G. (1995). The dominant role of psychosocial risk factors in the development of chronic low back pain disability. *Spine, 20*(24), 2702–2709.

Glassmire, D. M., Kinney, D. I., Greene, R. L., Stolberg, R. A., Berry, D. T. R., & Cripe, L. (2003). Sensitivity and specificity of MMPI-2 neurologic correction factors: Receiver operating characteristic analysis. *Assessment, 10*(3), 299–309.

Graham, J. R., Ben-Porath, Y. S., & McNulty, J. L. (1999). *MMPI-2 correlates for outpatient mental health settings.* Minneapolis: University of Minnesota Press.

Graham, J. R., Watts, D., & Timbrook, R. E. (1991). Detecting fake-good and fake-bad MMPI-2 profiles. *Journal of Personality Assessment, 57*(2), 264–277.

Greene, R. L. (1991). *MMPI-2/MMPI: An interpretive manual.* Boston: Allyn & Bacon.

Greiffenstein, M. F., Baker, W. J., Gola, T., Donders, J., & Miller, L. J. (2002). The FBS in atypical and severe closed head injury litigants. *Journal of Clinical Psychology, 58*, 1591–1600.

Hasenbring, M., Marienfeld, G., Kuhlendahl, D., & Soyka, D. (1994). Risk factors of chronicity in lumbar disc patients: A prospective investigation of biologic, psychologic, and social predictors of therapy outcome. *Spine, 19*(24), 2759–2765.

Hersch, P. D., & Alexander, R. W. (1990). MMPI profile patterns of emotional disability claimants. *Journal of Clinical Psychology, 46*(6), 798–799.

Hoffman, R. G., Scott, J. G., Emick, M. A., & Adams, R. L. (1999). The MMPI-2 and closed head injury: Effects of litigation and head injury severity. *Journal of Forensic Neuropsychology, 1,* 3–13.

Hovanitz, C. A., & Kozora, E. (1989). Life stress and clinically elevated MMPI scales: Gender differences in the moderating influence of coping. *Journal of Clinical Psychology, 45,* 766–777.

Iverson, G. L., King, R. J., Scott, J. G., & Adams, R. L. (2001). Cognitive complaints in litigating patients with head injuries or chronic pain. *Journal of Forensic Neuropsychology, 2,* 19–30.

Keane, T. M., Malloy, P. F., & Fairbank, J. A. (1984). Empirical development of an MMPI subscale for assessment combat related posttraumatic stress disorder. *Journal of Consulting and Clinical Psychology, 52,* 888–891.

Keilen, W. G., & Bloom, L. J. (1986). Child custody evaluation practices: A survey of experienced professionals. *Professional Psychology: Research and Practice, 17,* 338–346.

Larrabee, G. J. (1998). Somatic malingering on the MMPI and MMPI-2 in personal injury litigants. *Clinical Neuropsychologist, 12,* 179–188.

Larrabee, G. J. (2000, February 11). *Exaggerated MMPI-2 symptom report in probable malingerers.* Paper presented at the 28th annual meeting of the International Neuropsychological Society, Denver, CO.

Larrabee, G. J. (2003). Exaggerated MMPI-2 symptom report in personal injury litigants with malingered neurocognitve deficit. *Archives of Clinical Neuropsychology, 18*(6), 673–686.

Lees-Haley, P. R. (1997). MMPI-2 base rates for 492 personal injury plaintiffs: Implications and challenges for forensic assessment. *Journal of Clinical Psychology, 53*(7), 745–755.

Lees-Haley, P. R., English, L. T., & Glenn, W. J. (1991). A Fake Bad Scale on the MMPI-2 for personal injury claimants. *Psychological Reports, 68,* 203–210.

Lees-Haley, P. R., Smith, H. H., Williams, C. W., & Dunn, J. T. (1995). Forensic neuropsychological test usage: An empirical survey. *Archives of Clinical Neuropsychology, 11,* 45–51.

Long, B., Rouse, S. V., Nelson, R. O., & Butcher, J. N. (2004). The MMPI-2 in sexual harassment and discrimination litigants. *Journal of Clinical Psychology, 60,* 643–658.

Marcus, E. H. (1983, Spring). Causation in psychiatry: Realities and speculations. *Medical Trial Technical Quarterly, 29,* 424–433.

Martens, M., Donders, J., & Millis, S. R. (2001). Evaluation of invalid response sets after traumatic head injury. *Journal of Forensic Neuropsychology, 2,* 1–18.

Mayou, R., Bryant, B., & Duthie, R. (1993). Psychiatric consequences of road traffic accidents. *British Medical Journal, 307,* 647–651.

McCormick, R. A., Taber, J. I., & Krudelback, N. (1989). The relationship between attributional style and posttraumatic stress disorder in addicted patients. *Journal of Traumatic Stress, 2,* 477–487.

Mendelson, G. (1982). Not "cured by a verdict." *Medical Journal of Australia, 2,* 132–134.

Mendelson, G. (1995). "Compensation neurosis" revisited: Outcome studies of the effects of litigation. *Journal of Psychosomatic Research, 39*(6), 695–706.

Miller, H. R., Goldberg, J. O., & Streiner, D. L. (1995). What's in a name? The MMPI-2 PTSD Scales. *Journal of Clinical Psychology, 51*(5), 626–631.

Munley, P. H., Bains, D. S., Bloem, W. D., & Busby, R. M. (1995). Post-traumatic stress disorder and the MMPI-2. *Journal of Traumatic Stress, 8*(1), 171–178.

Neal, L. A., Busuttil, W., Rollins, J., Herepath, R., Strike, P., & Turnbull, G. (1994). Convergent validity of measures of post-traumatic stress disorder in a mixed military and civilian population. *Journal of Traumatic Stress, 7*(3), 447–455.

Nelson, L. (1987). Measuring depression in a clinical population using the MMPI. *Journal of Consulting and Clinical Psychology, 35,* 788–790.

Nichols, D. (in press). Old wine in new bottles? A review and critique of the MMPI-2 Restructured Clinical Scales. *Journal of Personality Assessment.*

Otto, R. K. (2002). Use of the MMPI-2 in forensic settings. *Journal of Forensic Psychology Practice, 2,* 71–92.

Penk, W. E., Rierdan, J., Losardo, M., & Robinowitz, R. (in press). Using the MMPI-2 for assessing post-traumatic stress disorder (PTSD). In J. N. Butcher (Ed.), *MMPI-2: A practitioner's guide.* Washington, DC: APA Books.

Pollack, D. R., & Grainey, T. F. (1984). A comparison of MMPI profiles for state and private disability insurance applicants. *Journal of Personality Assessment, 48*(2), 121–125.

Pope, K. S., Butcher, J. N., & Seelen, J. (2000). *The MMPI/MMPI-2/MMPI-A in court* (2nd ed.). Washington, DC: American Psychological Association.

Putnam, S. H., Kurtz, J. E., Millis, S. R., & Adams, K. M. (1995, March). *Prevalence and correlates of MMPI-2 codetypes in patients with traumatic brain injury.* Paper presented at the 30th Annual Symposium on Research Developments in the Use of the MMPI-2, St. Petersburg, FL.

Rayls, K. R., Mittenberg, W., Burns, W. J., & Theroux, S. (2000). Prospective study of the MMPI-2 correction factor after mild head injury. *Clinical Neuropsychologist, 14*(4), 546–550.

Repko, G. R., & Cooper, R. (1983). A study of the average workers' compensation case. *Journal of Clinical Psychology, 39,* 287–295.

Rogers, R., Sewell, K. W., Martin, M. A., & Vitacco, M. J. (2003). Detection of Feigned Mental Disorders: A Meta-analysis of the MMPI-2 and Malingering. *Assessment, 10*(2), 160–177.

Rogers, R., Sewell, K. W., & Ustad, K. L. (1995). Feigning among chronic outpatients on the MMPI-2: A systematic examination of fake-bad indicators. *Psychological Assessment, 2*(1), 81–89.

Senior, G., & Douglas, L. (2001). Misconceptions and misuse of the MMPI-2 in assessing personal injury claimants. *Neurorehabilitation, 16*(4), 203–213.

Shaffer, J. W., Nussbaum, K., & Little, J. M. (1972). MMPI profiles of disability insurance claimants. *American Journal of Psychiatry, 129*(4), 64–67.

Silver, S. M., & Salamone-Genovese, L. (1991). A study of the MMPI clinical and research scales for post-traumatic stress disorder diagnostic utility. *Journal of Traumatic Stress, 4*(4), 533–548.

Slick, D. J., Hopp, G., Strauss, E., & Spellacy, F. J. (1996). Victoria Symptom Validity Test: Efficiency for detecting feigned memory impairment and relationship to neuropsychological tests and MMPI-2 validity scales. *Journal of Clinical and Experimental Neuropsychology, 18,* 911–922.

Snibbe, J. R., Peterson, P. J., & Sosner, B. (1980). Study of psychological characteristics of a worker's compensation sample using the MMPI and Millon Clinical Multiaxial Inventory. *Psychological Reports, 47,* 959–966.

Sternbach, R. A., Wolf, S. R., Murphy, R. W., & Akeson, W. H. (1973). Traits of pain patients: The low back "loser." *Psychosomatics, 14,* 226–229.

Tellegen, A., Ben-Porath, Y. S., McNulty, J. L., Arbisi, P. A., Graham, J. R., & Kaemmer, B. (2003). *The MMPI-2 Restructured Clinical (RC) Scales: Development, Validation, and Interpretation.* Minneapolis: University of Minnesota Press.

Tsushima, W. T., & Tsushima, V. G. (2001). Comparison of the Fake Bad Scale and other MMPI-2 validity scales with personal injury litigants. *Assessment, 8*(2), 205–212.

Vanderploeg, R. D., Sison, G. F., & Hickling, E. J. (1987). A reevaluation of the use of the MMPI in the assessment of combat-related posttraumatic stress disorder. *Journal of Personality Assessment, 51,* 140–150.

Watkins, C. E., Campbell, V. L., Niebirding, R., & Hallmark, R. (1995). Contemporary practice of psychological assessment by clinical psychologists. *Professional Psychology, 26,* 54–60.

Watson, G., Plemel, D., DeMotts, J., Howard, M. T., Tuorila, J., Moog, R., et al. (1994). A comparison of four PTSD measures' convergent validities in Vietnam veterans. *Journal of Traumatic Stress, 7,* 75–82.

Weed, N., Ben-Porath, Y. S., & Butcher, J. N. (1990). Failure of the Weiner-Harmon MMPI subtle scales as predictors of psychopathology and as validity indicators. *Psychological Assessment, 2,* 281–283.

Wetter, M. W., Baer, D. T. R., Berry, D., Robinson, L. H., & Sumpter, J. (1993). MMPI-2 profiles of motivated fakers given specific symptom information: A comparison to matched patients. *Psychological Assessment, 5*(3), 317–323.

Wetter, M. W., & Corrigan, S. K. (1995). Providing information to clients about psychological tests: A survey of attorneys' and law students' attitudes. *Professional Psychology: Research and Practice, 26,* 474–477.

Wiener, D. (1948). Subtle and obvious keys for the Minnesota Multiphasic Personality Inventory. *Journal of Consulting Psychology, 12,* 164–170.

Youngjohn, J. R., Davis, D., & Wolf, I. (1997). Head injury and the MMPI-2: Paradoxical severity effects and the influence of litigation. *Psychological Assessment, 9,* 177–184.

CHAPTER 8

Legal Influences on the Identification and Treatment of Educational Disabilities

DANIEL J. RESCHLY

ASSESSMENT OF educational disabilities is a major and sometimes controversial role of psychologists in the United States. Although many kinds of psychologists may be involved with the identification and treatment of children and youth with disabilities, this is the primary role for the approximately 30,000 school psychologists employed by educational agencies in the United States. This chapter discusses the legal influences on the identification and treatment of disabilities in educational settings, including the nature of these disabilities, classification systems, and public policy changes that may affect current practices significantly.

GROWTH OF PSYCHOLOGISTS IN ASSESSMENT OF EDUCATIONAL DISABILITIES

Assessment of educational disabilities has been prominent in school psychology since its earliest days. Arnold Gesell, most likely the first person to use the title of school psychologist, was hired by the Connecticut State Department of Education in 1913 to examine school-age children suspected of being mentally retarded (Fagan, 1987a, 1987b). Throughout the twentieth century, the expansion of special education services for students with disabilities (SWD) and the employment of school psychologists was parallel. By 1975 there were at least a few school psychologists in every state and, although the national ratio was in excess of 4,500 students per school psychologist, some states had achieved ratios in the 2,000 to 3,000 students per psychologist range (Kicklighter, 1976).

In 1975, a federal law was established requiring states to provide special education services that met specific requirements to qualify for federal funding

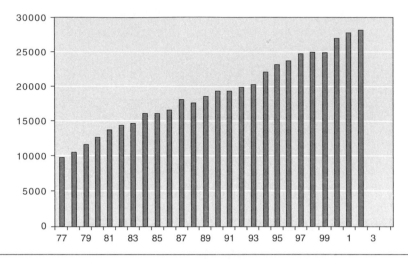

Figure 8.1   Growth of Psychologists Employed in Schools Serving Students with Disabilities from Annual Reports to Congress on the Implementation of the Individuals with Disabilities Education Act, www.ideadata.org.

(Education of the Handicapped Act [EHA], 1975, 1977). There is no federal special education legal mandate per se because a state can decline the federal funding, but all states have chosen to implement the law to receive the funding. EHA and the state mandates regarding special education were enacted in the mid-1970s as a response to litigation in the federal courts that established the right of students with disabilities to an appropriate education at public expense and other protections (see later section; Reschly & Bersoff, 1999). Among those rights was an individual assessment that met certain requirements and, in most states, was conducted primarily by school psychologists.

Together, the federal and state legislation led to an increase from about 3.3 million between 1976 and 1977 to approximately 6.7 million SWD age 6 to 17 identified and placed in special education programs (U.S. Department of Education [USDE], www.ideadata.org, November 29, 2004). As special education enrollments grew over the past 25 years, so, too, did the employment of school psychologists (see Figure 8.1). The USDE has collected information since 1977/1978 on the employment of personnel providing services to SWD (see www.ideadata.org). From the first year these data were collected until the most recent year for which results are reported (2002), the number of psychologists serving SWD employed by public educational agencies grew from approximately 9,500 to approximately 28,500, a threefold increase. Clearly, the growth of psychologists serving SWD in schools is closely related to the expansion of the number of identified SWD and special education programs.

Although the growth of the employment of psychologists serving SWD in the schools clearly parallels the growth of SWD and special education, there is no federal mandate regarding employment of school or other type of psychologists. State legal requirements vary significantly; most require that school psychologists licensed or certified by their state education agency conduct certain evaluations and provide specific services; others are silent or permit other professionals (e.g., educational diagnosticians) to provide these services.

In the Individuals with Disabilities Education Act (IDEA; 1997, 1999), the successor to the EHA, *psychological services* is listed in the Code of Federal Regulations (C.F.R.) as a related service at 34 C.F.R. 300.24 b, 9 and defined as (1) administering psychological and educational tests and other assessment procedures; (2) interpreting assessment results; (3) obtaining, integrating, and interpreting information about child behavior and conditions relating to learning; (4) consulting with other staff members in planning school programs to meet the special needs of children as indicated by psychological tests, interviews, and behavioral evaluations; (5) planning and managing a program of psychological services, including psychological counseling for children and parents; and (6) assisting in developing positive behavioral intervention strategies.

EVOLUTION OF LEGAL INFLUENCES

Multiple layers of legal influence on the assessment of educational disabilities have evolved over the past 35 years through litigation, state and federal statute and regulations, and best practices guidelines developed by federal and state authorities. Although most areas of psychological practice are to varying degrees influenced by legal requirements, the assessment of educational disabilities as a prerequisite to the provision of mandated accommodations and special education and related services clearly is one of the most heavily regulated. These legal requirements have developed through dynamic and continuing cycles of litigation, legislation, and regulation, each exerting reciprocal influences on the other (Prasse, 2002; Reschly & Bersoff, 1999).

PRE-1975 LITIGATION: RIGHT TO EDUCATION

Although a number of court cases dealing with testing and educational assessment issues appeared before 1970, major cases dealing directly with individual assessment of students with disabilities did not appear until the early 1970s. Two cases in the federal district courts (*Mills v. Board of Education*, 1972; *Pennsylvania Association for Retarded Children (PARC) v. Commonwealth of Pennsylvania*, 1972) established the right of disabled students to educational services. Prior to these landmark cases, many SWD were either excluded entirely from the public schools by local, district, and state policies or were provided educational services that were not individually tailored to their unique needs. The plaintiffs asked federal district courts to apply the Fourteenth Amendment concepts of equal protection and due process and to force the states to provide appropriate educational services to *all* students. The courts agreed with the parental claims, deciding that exclusion of SWD students from public schools constituted a violation of the concept of equal protection of the laws and the concept of due process. Further discussion of the early legal cases can be found in Reschly and Bersoff (1999).

The major impact of these cases was the advancement of the rights of SWD to educational services and to due process protections in educational decisions made about them. These court precedents in the early 1970s were used by parent advocacy groups throughout the United States in efforts to convince state legislatures to pass mandatory special education legislation. In fact, every state passed such mandates between about 1972 and 1977, largely in response to the court precedents.

PRE-1975 LITIGATION: PLACEMENT BIAS

A second kind of case, also applying the concepts of equal protection and due process but advocating *fewer,* rather than more, special education services, appeared in the federal district courts in the late 1960s and early 1970s. Cases alleging discriminatory assessment practices and improper special education placement and programming profoundly influenced subsequent legislation and professional practices regarding the identification of SWD with minority status, and ultimately all SWD regardless of race or ethnicity. Three cases (*Diana v. State Board of Education*, 1970; *Guadalupe Organization v. Tempe Elementary School District No. 3*, 1972; *Larry P. v. Riles*, 1972, 1974) were filed on behalf of minority students placed in special class programs for students with mild mental retardation (MMR). The three districts and minority students involved were Hispanic students in Monterey County, California (*Diana*), Native American Indian students in Tempe, Arizona (*Guadalupe*), and Black students in San Francisco (later extended to all of California; *Larry P.*). Minority students were placed in MMR programs at 1.5 to 3 times the rate of placement for nonminority students.

The *Diana* and *Guadalupe* cases were settled by consent decrees, establishing a number of safeguards in the identification of SWD that applied to all students, including determination of primary language, assessment instruments administered using procedures consistent with the student's primary language, reliance on nonverbal rather than on verbal ability measures with language-minority children, greater reliance on adaptive behavior measures in diagnosis of MMR, and due process protections. Some of the phrases that appeared in the *Diana* and *Guadalupe* consent decrees appear verbatim today in federal regulations and the special education rules of state education agencies (see later section).

The *Larry P.* case was somewhat different in that the primary language of the home was not a central issue. The plaintiffs were Black students, and intelligence tests became the central issue in the case. *Larry P.* resulted in injunctions in 1972 and 1974, restraining, first, the San Francisco Unified School District and, later, the entire State of California from using IQ tests with Black students.

There is a clear irony in the pre-1975 litigation. In one type of case, school districts were cited by the federal courts for violation of equal protection and due process rights because special education services were *not* provided (*Mills,* 1972; *PARC,* 1972), and in another, the same constitutional principles were the basis for ruling that special education with minority students was used excessively and inappropriately (*Diana,* 1972; *Guadalupe,* 1972; *Larry P.,* 1972, 1974).

STATE AND FEDERAL LEGISLATION

State legislatures had passed mandatory special education bills in every state by the mid-1970s. SWD had to be served by the public schools and the educational programs had to meet certain standards. Generally, the legislation provided state monies for these programs, thus alleviating part of the burden of providing expensive special education and related services incurred by local educational agencies. Rather than attempting further discussion of state legislative mandates, the key principles in a subsequent federal law with which all states now comply will be discussed. This federal law also incorporated the major principles from the pre-1975 litigation.

The federal EHA (1975, 1977), reauthorized in 1991, 1997, and 2004 as IDEA, provides federal monies to assist state and local education agencies in educating SWD. To receive federal funding, state education agencies are required to monitor implementation of these regulations in local education agencies. To qualify for this assistance, the educational services for disabled students must meet the requirements detailed in the following sections.

Free, Appropriate Education

The first and most important of the general principles is the right of all students with disabilities to free, appropriate, publicly supported education programs. Subsequent interpretation of EHA/IDEA by the courts has established that this right truly does apply to all students, even those who have no apparent learning ability (*Timothy W. v. Rochester*, 1988, 1989). The effect of this principle is that many more students are now diagnosed as disabled and provided special education services and that students with more severe disabilities, previously excluded from public schools, were present in school settings where they receive a full range of assessment and programming services. The implications for assessment of this principle were a greatly increased need for individual psychoeducational assessment services as well as the need for specialized skills not previously emphasized in graduate programs, for example, assessment of communication skills with autism or functional analyses of the ecological conditions maintaining severe self-injurious behaviors.

Least Restrictive Environment

A second important EHA/IDEA principle is that of the least restrictive environment:

> That to the maximum extent appropriate, children with disabilities . . . are educated with children who are nondisabled. That special classes, separate schooling or other removal of children with disabilities from the regular educational environment occurs only when the nature or severity of the disability is such that education in regular classes with the use of supplementary aids and services cannot be achieved satisfactorily. (C.F.R. 34.300.550)

The principle of least restrictive environment had the effect of greater integration of students with disabilities with general education students and greatly increasing the complexity of psychological assessment. It is important to note that neither the law nor any court pronounces a full inclusion requirement, mandating that all students with disabilities be educated in general education environments.

Individualized Education Program

Students with disabilities also were guaranteed an individualized educational program (IEP) that was to be reviewed annually and modified as appropriate. The emphasis on greater individualization increased demands for criterion-referenced assessment, leading to clear specification of strengths and weaknesses and the development of assessment information useful in designing and evaluating instructional interventions and psychological treatments.

Additional IEP requirements (IDEA, 1997, 1999, 2004) have been established mandating assessment of progress in the general educational curriculum and participation of SWD in state and federally mandated achievement testing (34 C.F.R. 300. 137–139). A small proportion, up to 3% of the general student population under circumstances, can be excused from the mandated achievement testing due to the severity of their disabilities. Excused students must be given alternative assessments that are aligned with the general education curriculum in the areas of communication, mathematics, social studies, and science. Life skills can be part of the alternative assessments.

Development and alignment of the alternative assessments with the general education curriculum is extraordinarily difficult. For example, consider the scaling and construct validity problems in representing achievement in communication skills from extremely low (e.g., eye movements in response to social stimuli) to extremely high (e.g., advanced written composition) levels. Scale integration algorithms can be applied to this problem, but the critical issue is whether the same construct is being measured. Much work remains to be done to develop the underlying conceptual and technological basis for the alternative assessments (Elliott, Kratochwill, & McKevitt, 2001; Elliott, McKevitt, & Kettler, 2002; Fuchs, 2002; McDonnell, McLaughlin, & Morison, 1997; Ysseldyke & Olsen, 1999).

In the mandate requiring participation of all SWD in standards-based achievement assessments, accommodations are allowed in scheduling, response mode, setting, and presentation of tests. The accommodations must be tailored individually, stated in the IEP, and designed to facilitate participation, but, at the same time, they must not undermine the validity of the test. Some examples of accommodations are larger print on a reading test for students with visual impairments, more time on a science test for students with poor reading fluency, and a separate quiet setting with a proctor for students who are highly distractible (Elliott et al., 2001, 2002; Fuchs, 2002). Concerns about the effects and effectiveness of accommodations have been expressed, at the same time that efforts are being made to develop tests along universal design principles that permit participation by virtually all persons regardless of disabilities (e.g., markedly expanding the amount of time allowed for all participants to complete tests).

Due Process

The due process protections established in the courts, then mandated in state and federal legislation, guaranteed the rights of children with disabilities to (1) advance notice of decisions a school is contemplating, (2) information in an understandable form, (3) reasons the decision is contemplated, (4) names of decision-making participants, and (5) discretion to approve or reject decisions. Complex hearing procedures are available to schools and parents to resolve disputes.

Children with disabilities have access to nearly everything a psychologist might do as part of the assessment of educational disabilities, including the right to review (but not necessarily copy) copyrighted test protocols. These rights mean that the work of psychologists can be scrutinized by students, parents, and their legal advocates and challenged in a legal proceeding. The legal rights of children can establish legal and ethical dilemmas for psychologists who are mandated by IDEA and the Family Education Rights and Privacy Act (34 C.F.R. 99) to share their findings, including the documents and procedures used to produce the findings. Other legal requirements mandate that they conform to laws regarding the nondisclosure of copyrighted materials such as test protocols and ethical principles concerning maintaining test security and confidentiality of information. Easy resolutions to these dilemmas do not exist. Psychologists must study the available ethical codes as well as materials from professional associations on the resolution of such dilemmas (American Psychological Association, 2002).

Protection in Evaluation and Determination of Eligibility

The legal requirements that have the greatest influence on assessment appear in the Protection in Evaluation and Determination of Eligibility (PEDE) regulations at 34 C.F.R. 300.530 to 543. These regulations were renamed in IDEA (1999) from Protection in Evaluation Procedures to the current title and expanded significantly. The special regulations in PEDE regarding specific learning disabilities are discussed in a later section. The key provisions of these regulations that are applicable to all evaluations of students referred for consideration of disability status are as follows:

- Full and individual evaluation must occur before special education or related services are provided.
- "Tests and other evaluation materials used to assess a child are selected and administered so as not to be discriminatory on a racial or cultural basis; and are provided and administered in the child's native language or other mode of communication, unless it is clearly not feasible to do so." The law does not provide a definition of discrimination, nor are there guidelines on the feasibility of testing children in their native language. Both are considerable challenges. An implicit definition of discrimination that was added to IDEA (1997, 1999) is discussed later.
- A variety of assessment tools and strategies are used to gather relevant functional and developmental information about the child from multiple sources that are relevant to determination of disability status and formulation of the IEP.
- Tests and other assessment procedures are valid for the purpose for which they are used and administered by appropriately trained personnel.

- Tests and evaluation materials are appropriate to determine specific educational needs, not just "a single intelligence quotient," and are selected and administered to assess the domain of behavior intended, not the effects of the disability on the domain. For example, this provision would protect visually impaired and blind children from being administered an individual IQ test that requires visual spatial reasoning using visual stimuli.
- "The child is assessed in all areas related to the suspected disability, including, *if appropriate,* health, vision, hearing, social and emotional status, general intelligence, academic performance, communicative status, and motor abilities" (emphasis added).
- The evaluation must be sufficiently comprehensive to identify all the child's special education and related services needs.
- Technically sound instruments and strategies are used that may assess the relative contribution of cognitive and behavioral factors, in addition to physical or developmental factors, and provide relevant information that directly assists in determining the educational needs of the child.
- In IDEA (1997, 1999) the mandatory triennial reevaluation of disability status was made optional depending on a determination of the need for additional data through an extensive review involving parents and professionals.
- Initial evaluations and, if needed, reevaluations of disability status must be based on consideration of classroom-based assessments and observations, eligibility for disability status, present levels of performance and educational needs, documented need for special education, and, in a reevaluation, whether additions or changes in special education and related services are needed for the student to participate in the general education curriculum.
- Eligibility decisions must be based on the individual evaluation made by a group of persons, including parents, using the categories of disability defined in the law at 34 C.F.R. 300.7 (see later discussion on classification system). The disability cannot be due to lack of instruction in reading or mathematics or limited English proficiency.
- The educational agency must document careful consideration of information from a variety of sources, including "aptitude and achievement tests, parent input, teacher recommendations, physical condition, social or cultural background, and adaptive behavior." If the child is determined to be eligible for disability classification and needs special education, an IEP must be developed that meets extensive requirements (34 C.F.R. 300.340–350).

A virtual revolution in rights of SWD has occurred over the past 25 years and conceptions of best practices continue to evolve (Thomas & Grimes, 2002). Numerous legal requirements have been established where relatively little legal influence existed previously that directly affect psychological services in schools. Many of these requirements, as noted before, are ambiguous and subject to different interpretations. The general effect, however, is clear. The work of psychologists in the schools regarding assessment of educational disabilities is governed by extensive legal requirements, especially in the diagnosis of disability status and in the determination of special education needs.

COMPLIANCE MONITORING

Implementation of the EHA/IDEA statutes is monitored by federal and state authorities with the ultimate sanction of denying funding to state and local education agencies that fail to implement the law adequately. In fact, withholding or withdrawing funding rarely occurs, and the amounts involved typically are a small portion of overall federal or state support. Moreover, federal monitoring of state and local education agencies since 1975 has resulted in findings of numerous flaws in the implementation of the EHA/IDEA, a pattern that continues today; however, no state education agency has ever been found to fail completely or to defy the IDEA principles. The main influence of compliance monitoring comes not from withholding funds, but through public embarrassment of state and local authorities through public disclosure of violations. This mechanism is highly motivating to education officials.

The cycles vary, but monitoring usually occurs at 3- to 5-year intervals. The USDE Office of Special Education Programs (OSEP) is responsible for monitoring implementation of IDEA. Until recently, OSEP compliance monitoring focused primarily on the *processes* involved with implementing the key IDEA principles. Implementation of the due process and IEP principles were monitored most closely, producing similar practices across the United States. Compliance monitoring of the other principles was less precise and rigorous, leading to significant variations across the states. Recent OSEP compliance monitoring procedures shift the focus from process to *child outcomes*, with "focused monitoring" regarding key outcomes such as improvements in educational achievement, dropout rates, and overrepresentation of minority students. Focused monitoring is likely to have the greatest impact on psychological assessment in situations involving minority overrepresentation.

The USDE Office of Civil Rights (OCR) monitors compliance with several federal laws. Section 504 of the Rehabilitation Act of 1973 (20 U.S.C. Sec. 794. 34 C.F.R. 104) is particularly relevant to educational agencies. This law requires reasonable accommodations for persons with disabilities, using broader criteria than IDEA to define who is eligible, and protects individuals from discrimination based on race, ethnicity, gender, and age. OCR typically investigates complaints from individuals or groups. OCR agreements have been particularly important in changing assessment requirements by state and local education agencies associated with overrepresentation of minority children in special education. For example, an agreement with South Carolina required the reevaluation of all students diagnosed with MMR using more stringent criteria for eligibility on the adaptive behavior criterion. A similar agreement in Alabama produced a decline of about 50% in mental retardation prevalence over a 3-year period. The OCR agreements can change psychological assessment requirements with little consideration for best practices or involvement of psychologists. Generally, these agreements are not available in easily recoverable sources, although most are posted for at least a few years on state education agency Web sites.

Post-1975 Litigation

Over the past 25 years, the right to education and placement bias litigation have continued, with the primary effects of clarifying and elaborating the fundamental principles established in pre-1975 litigation and the EHA/IDEA statutes. Although its influence is still significant, litigation's impact on the psychological services provided to SWD has declined somewhat.

Right to Education

The principles of free, appropriate, publicly supported education programs in a least restrictive environment are particularly ambiguous. What is the standard for an "appropriate" education? Is it an opportunity to learn equal to that of other students, or the best educational opportunity possible? In *Board of Education v. Rowley* (1982), "appropriateness" was defined as "reasonable educational benefit" rather than ideal, most effective, or best educational program. The assessment data indicating that the plaintiff, Amy Rowley, a deaf youngster, was achieving at or above grade level in all of her school subjects were a key factor in the court's determination that an appropriate education in this instance did not require the employment by the district of a sign language interpreter. The concept of appropriateness has been further elaborated in numerous cases since 1982.

What is the meaning of the phrase, "To the maximum extent appropriate, children with disabilities . . . are educated with children who are nondisabled?" The courts established the following criteria to determine whether a school can place a student with a disability outside the general education classroom in a more restrictive setting such as a special class:

1. The educational benefits available to the child in a regular classroom supplemented with appropriate aids and services, as compared to the educational benefits of a more restrictive special education placement.
2. The nonacademic benefits to the handicapped child of interaction with nonhandicapped children.
3. The effect of the presence of the handicapped child on the teacher and other children in the regular classroom.
4. The costs of supplementary aids and services necessary to mainstream the handicapped child in the regular classroom setting. (*Board of Education v. Holland*, 1992, 1994)

Decisions regarding the least restrictive environment must be data-based, establishing the need for more behavioral assessment through observation of natural environments to determine the effects of a student with a disability on other students and the degree to which that student profits from being in the general education environment.

Placement Bias Cases

A second major kind of litigation, based primarily on the EHA/IDEA principle of nondiscrimination, continues to be refined in the federal courts and in other legal and quasi-legal processes. The placement bias litigation that resulted in either court-approved consent degrees or judicial opinions from 1975 to 2000 is discussed briefly here because relatively little activity has occurred over the past 10 years. Thorough discussions appeared elsewhere (Reschly & Bersoff, 1999).

The two fundamental questions in the placement bias litigation from 1975 to 2000 addressed (1) the appropriateness of conventional measures of intelligence with Black students and (2) the acceptability of disproportionate placement of minority students in programs for students with MMR. These questions are adjudicated under the IDEA nondiscrimination clause as well as the constitutional principles of due process and equal protection.

The most famous of these cases, *Larry P. v. Riles* (1979), resulted in sharply varying rulings that have little effect on assessment of disabilities today. In a 1979 opinion by a federal district court for northern California, Judge Peckham ruled that IQ tests were biased against Black students and that IQ test use was primarily responsible for the overrepresentation of Black students in special classes for MMR. Peckham then banned the use of IQ tests if the outcome of such testing was a diagnosis of MMR and placement in special education programs that he regarded as "dead-end" and inferior.

In 1986, Peckham expanded the original injunction to all uses of intelligence tests with Black children in California schools. This comprehensive ban was challenged by another plaintiff group, *Crawford v. Honig* (1988). The plaintiff's challenge was combined with the ongoing *Larry P.* litigation, resulting in these rulings by Peckham in 1992:

- The 1979 *Opinion* was "clearly limited to the use of IQ tests in the assessment and placement of African American students in dead end programs such as MMR" (*Crawford et al. v. Honig* and *Larry P. v. Riles,* 1992, p. 15).
- "Despite the Defendants' attempts to characterize the court's 1979 order as a referendum on the discriminatory nature of IQ testing, this court's review of the decision reveals that the decision was largely concerned with the harm to African American children resulting from improper placement in dead-end educational programs" (*Crawford* and *Larry P.,* 1992, p. 23).

Judge Peckham then ordered the California State Education Agency to inform him of the current special education programs that were equivalent to the dead-end programs that existed in 1979, when his trial opinion was rendered. Instead, the agency appealed the decision, Judge Peckham passed away, and the Ninth Circuit upheld the 1992 order (*Crawford* and *Larry P.,* 1994). No further action has occurred in the case. IQ tests no longer are banned in California, and the California State Education Agency has never informed the court of current dead-end special education programs. The issues in *Larry P.* now appear to be moot.

Other federal court judges reached markedly different conclusions on essentially the same set of facts as those in *Larry P.* (*Parents in Action on Special Education (PASE) v. Hannon*, 1980; *Marshall v. Georgia*, 1984, 1985; *S-1 v. Turlington*, 1986). In these cases, patterns of Black student overrepresentation in MMR and the use of IQ tests were permitted because defendant schools convinced the courts that (1) rigorous due process protections were carefully implemented, (2) IQ tests were used with a wide variety of other measures that were more important than IQ in determining diagnosis and placement decisions, (3) multidisciplinary teams of professionals and parents made the decisions, (4) special education was a last resort as a means to cope with chronic and severe achievement deficits, and (5) the special education programs expanded opportunities for academic and social development.

Concepts of Fairness

The conception of fairness adopted by a court has a profound impact on decisions dealing with disproportionate representation. Two competing conceptions of fairness create enormous tensions that are apparent in the placement bias litigation and in other judicial analyses of disproportionate representation (e.g., *Gratz v. Bollinger*, 2003; *Grutter v. Bollinger et al.*, 2003). *Equal results* means that the same outcomes have to be achieved for all sociocultural groups. To achieve equal results, differential treatment of individuals often is necessary (e.g., adding points for diversity, consideration of a broad set of criteria that values minority status as part of a diversity goal, changing requirements for disability identification with minority students). The main alternative is an *equal treatment* conception of fairness, which requires that all individuals with similar characteristics be treated in the same way regardless of race, ethnicity, social class, or gender. Equal treatment allows disproportionate outcomes by race, ethnicity, social class, or gender as long as individuals are treated in comparable ways.

The inherent weakness of equal treatment is that long-standing patterns of disproportionate outcomes continue to exist, including, for example, differential placement of students by race in special education and admission to university professional schools. There is no easy solution to the problems of disproportionate representation in several domains of public and private life in the United States, but recognizing the tension between competing notions of fairness and the inherent importance of both conceptions is important to understanding legal analyses and public policy. These tensions significantly affect current legal interventions regarding special education disability diagnosis.

Research on equal treatment in the assessment of disabilities is rarely conducted due to the reluctance of state and local education agencies to allow collection of data. The few rigorous studies that exist indicate that equal treatment criteria are met in current assessment services with Black and White students suspected of being disabled or who are disabled (*Coalition to Save Our Children v. State Board of Education*, 1995; MacMillan, Gresham, Lopez, & Bocian, 1996; Reschly & Kicklighter, 1985; Reschly & Ward, 1991). Of course, the null hypothesis of equal treatment cannot be proven because of the impossibility of conducting research in all possible situations.

Changing Legal Analysis of Disproportionality

An influential provision was added to IDEA (1997, 1999) regarding disproportionality that appears to adopt an equal results conception of fairness. The IDEA (1999) regulations state:

> Each State that receives assistance . . . shall provide for the collection and examination of data to determine if significant disproportionality based on race is occurring in the State . . . with respect to the identification of children as children with disabilities . . . and the placement in particular educational settings of these children. . . . In the case of a determination of significant disproportionality with respect to the identification . . . or the placement . . . the state . . . shall provide for the review and, if appropriate, revision of the policies, procedures, and practices used in the identification or placement.

These regulations are the closest provision in the law to date for defining the concept of and criteria for nondiscriminatory assessment and placement. I suspect that these criteria will be challenged in federal courts. Guidance on what accounts for "significant disproportionality" has been discussed extensively, but OSEP officials have not announced specific criteria. Court-approved consent decrees applying these criteria have established narrow ranges for differences in disability identification rates between minority and nonminority groups (e.g., *Mattie T. v. Holliday*, 2003).

Legal Basis for Classification of Students with Disabilities

Legal requirements determine the criteria used to assess disability eligibility and special education need. *Conceptual definitions* specifying the key domains of behavior for 13 disabilities are provided in IDEA at 34 C.F.R. 300.7. States have discretion in whether to use the exact nomenclature in IDEA, but all state and local education agencies must ensure that students with these kinds of disabilities are provided appropriate educations that meet IDEA requirements. For example, the term "mental retardation" is used in IDEA. All state and local education agencies serve this population, but some use the term "mental disability" or "mental handicap" instead. The general trend is toward more consistent adoption of federal conceptual definitions in state special education rules (Reschly & Hosp, 2004).

Classification criteria specifying the pattern and levels of performance for disability diagnosis are provided for only one of the IDEA disabilities in federal statute or regulations: specific learning disabilities (LD; 34 C.F.R. 300.540–543). The LD regulations will be changed soon in response to changes in the IDEA (2004) statute. For example, classification criteria in mental retardation indicate the cutoff scores for general intellectual functioning and adaptive behavior as well as other features that guide the assessment services and decision making regarding eligibility. States are allowed enormous discretion in determination of classification criteria for each of the disabilities, producing a situation whereby a child may be eligible in one state but not in another for disability diagnoses such as mental retardation or LD (Reschly & Hosp, 2004).

The IDEA disability conceptual definitions reflect a mixture of medical and social system models as well as the disability conceptions from other sources such as the American Association on Mental Retardation (Luckasson et al., 2002) and the American Psychiatric Association (1994; e.g., Autism spectrum disorders). In all cases, there is an educational component in that eligibility does not depend exclusively on meeting the classification criteria, but also on documenting need for special education.

Medical model disabilities are defined by the existence of an identifiable underlying biological deficit that can be viewed as causing the disability, although, of course, the behavioral symptoms may vary significantly. Medical model disabilities occur at a low incidence (generally less than 0.3% of the general population) and typically are diagnosed by medical personnel during the preschool years. In contrast, the social system model uses an ecological perspective (Mercer, 1979; Reschly, 1996), wherein deviant behavior or abnormal patterns of development are seen *not* as inherent characteristics of the individual, but as reflecting a discrepancy between what the individual has learned in a cultural context and the expectations for normal behavior in a specific social role and social setting. IDEA disabilities reflecting the social system model occur at approximately 1% or more of the general population. These disabilities typically are diagnosed after school entrance by psychologists, speech clinicians, and others on the basis of language, intellectual, achievement, and behavioral characteristics. A critical step is teacher referral due to low classroom performance in achievement, behavior, or emotional regulation. SWD with social system kinds of disabilities were the subject of placement bias litigation.

The following examples may be useful to illustrate the distinction between social system and medical model disabilities. Most children with LD have difficulties with reading. Often, there is no evidence of other significant difficulties at school, in the home, or in the community. Would a youngster with that pattern of development be regarded as disabled in a society that did not have compulsory school attendance and strong expectations for the acquisition of literacy skills between the ages of 5 and 17? On the other hand, a youngster with cerebral palsy, which usually involves easily observed muscular difficulties, would likely be regarded as disabled regardless of the time, place, or nature of society. In a real sense, social system model disabilities are created by the demands we place on children and youth in a complex, rapidly changing, technologically sophisticated society. To attribute the etiology of these disabilities to societal expectations does not, however, make them or their consequences any less real or any less serious for individuals involved.

DISTRIBUTION OF DISABILITIES AND MODELS OF DISABILITIES

The prevalence of disabilities in the 13 categories recognized in federal legislation is summarized in Table 8.1. Several important trends are revealed in these

Table 8.1
Number and Proportion of Students Age 6–17
with Educational Disabilities, by Category

Category	Number	Percent of Disabled	Percent of Population	Range among States
LD	2,712,475	47.3	5.4	2.53 (KY) to 8.02 (RI)
SL	1,122,346	19.6	2.4	0.61 (HI) to 4.05 (WV)
MR	511,170	8.9	1.0	0.37 (NJ, NH) to 3.07 (WV)
ED	455,348	7.9	0.9	0.13 (AR) to 1.89 (VT, MN)
OHI	436,374	7.6	0.9	0.00 (CO) to 2.17 (RI)
Low incidence	489,937	8.6	1.0	
TOTAL	5,727,650	99.9	11.46	9.01 (CO) to 16.51 (RI)

Note: Based on an age 6–17 population estimate of 49,975,000. ED = Emotional Disability; LD = Specific Learning Disability; Low incidence = Multiple Disabilities, Deaf, Hard of Hearing, Orthopedic Impairments, Visual Impairments, Deaf-Blindness, Autism, and Traumatic Brain Injury; MR = Mental Retardation; OHI = Other Health Impaired; SL = Speech/Language Disability.
Source: U.S. Department of Education, www.ideadata.org, December 3, 2004, Table AA3.

prevalence data. First, the vast majority of the students with disabilities are in the categories of specific learning disability (LD; accounting for nearly 50%), followed by speech-language (SL), mental retardation (MR), emotionally disturbed (ED), and other health impaired (OHI). These four disabilities account for more than 90% of the students with disabilities in U.S. schools. Students with disabilities in the other eight categories account for less than 10% of the population with disabilities and about 1% of the total population.

Some specific disability categories include SWD with biologically based disabilities and others with social system kinds of disabilities. MR and OHI are both good examples of this mixture. Some students with MR have clearly identifiable biological anomalies, whereas others, particularly the MMR, have no evidence of a biological anomaly. OHI involves a broad spectrum of children and youth, some with health conditions that make them fragile (e.g., some form of cancer). Many others in OHI, in fact most, depending on the state, are diagnosed as having Attention-Deficit/Hyperactivity Disorder (ADHD). OHI is used in many states for students with ADHD who need special education but are not eligible in other categories such as LD or ED.

Practices vary dramatically across states in disability classification criteria and in practices involving diagnosis of disabilities. First, prevalence varies significantly (see Table 8.1); for example, Colorado does not use OHI, but Rhode Island identifies slightly more than 2% of its population of children age 6 to 17 as OHI, most of whom are ADHD. Little is understood about the correlates and causes of state prevalence differences (Reschly & Hosp, 2004). It is essential, however, for psychologists diagnosing educational disabilities, whether practicing in a public agency such as a school or in private, independent practice, to use the classification criteria that are specified in the State Education Agency Rules of Special Education. The classification criteria for each educational disability category are nearly always found online at the state department of education Web site under the category of special education.

ELIGIBILITY DECISIONS

Classification-placement decisions involve the application of federal and state laws that establish a two-pronged criterion for eligibility: Can the student be classified as disabled? and Does the student need special education or related services (e.g., counseling) to receive an appropriate education? Affirmative answers to these questions establish the child's eligibility for important legal protections and, typically, the expenditure of markedly increased monies for special education and related services (Parrish, Chambers, & Guarino, 1999). Eligibility decisions have high-stakes consequences that are important to the individual, family, school, and community.

SYSTEM REFORM TRENDS AND ASSESSMENT IMPLICATIONS

In prior versions of this chapter, reform trends were discussed that I thought would markedly influence future legal requirements and professional practices related to assessment of SWD. These trends have continued and are now increasingly reflected in federal statutes and regulations. The reform trends were identified in several publications (Reschly, 1980, 1988; Reschly & Ysseldyke, 2002) and are discussed briefly here. Negative and positive factors drove the system reform agenda and changes in legal requirements. Negative factors included the absence of documented benefits of special education programs, heavy reliance on assessment measures such as IQ tests, the use of nonfunctional and stigmatizing categories such as MR, and lack of relevance of most of the data collected in the initial evaluation for design, implementation, monitoring, and evaluation of treatments. Further, data on referrals indicated that large proportions of students were found to be eligible for special education, raising questions about the importance of the psychoeducational evaluation (Ysseldyke, Vanderwood, & Shriner, 1997).

A major shift to a focus on *outcomes* rather than intervention inputs or processes is apparent in the reform literature. Recently enacted federal general and special education legislation emphasizes the application of scientifically based instructional and behavioral interventions and high levels of achievement for all students, including SWD. Models have been developed that eliminate much of the traditional assessment and establish functional, noncategorical concepts as the foundation for the delivery of services to SWD and other students with at-risk characteristics (Reschly, Tilly, & Grimes, 1999). These models have been implemented successfully as a basis for disability identification and the provision of special education. Psychologists' roles are changed significantly and the assessment that is conducted involves far less use of standardized tests of ability and achievement and far more use of direct measures of skills in natural settings that are useful for determining educational need, designing interventions, monitoring progress, evaluating outcomes, and determining eligibility if the interventions are unsuccessful. Recent legal changes facilitate the broader use of functional assessment approaches.

Problem-solving systems using response-to-intervention (RTI) criteria focus on behavioral definitions of presenting problems, direct measures of behaviors in natural settings, design of interventions, monitoring progress with intervention revisions as necessary, and evaluating outcomes. All are more consistent with the experimental than the correlational tradition in psychology as well as the short-run empiricism described by Cronbach (1975) as a promising replacement for interventions guided by aptitude and treatment interactions. Problem solving depends heavily on curriculum-based and behavioral assessment measures that are developed and applied in the natural settings of classrooms, playgrounds, homes, and communities.

Significant advances in assessment technology permit greater emphasis on measures functionally related to interventions. Most of these advances can be classified as behavioral assessment procedures (Shapiro & Kratochwill, 2000). The knowledge base for practice has improved substantially with the development of curriculum-based assessment, a technology that fosters a close relationship between assessment and treatment (Deno, 1985; Howell & Nolet, 2000; Shapiro, 1996; Shinn, 1998).

INSTRUCTIONAL DESIGN

Behavior assessment and instructional analysis are inextricably related in functional assessment of academic behaviors. The marriage of instructional design principles (e.g., Englemann & Carnine, 1982) with behavioral intervention technologies has produced impressive outcomes for students (Kavale & Forness, 1999). Meta-analysis evidence indicates that interventions driven by behavioral assessment of social or emotional domains or curriculum-based assessment of academic skills domains have effect sizes that are two to three times the effect sizes associated with traditional, largely norm-referenced, standardized assessment practices (Kavale & Forness, 1999). These superior results likely will create the dynamics for assessment practices to change rapidly in the 2005 to 2015 period. Use of this knowledge base produces results that are potentially markedly superior to traditional special education programs or instruction based on matching teaching methods to presumed strengths in cognitive style, information processing, or neuropsychological status.

BEHAVIOR CHANGE

Behavior change principles are well established (Shinn, Stoner, & Walker, 2002; Sulzer-Azaroff & Mayer, 1991). In addition, characteristics of effective schools and effective teaching are well represented in the school psychology and special education literature (e.g., Foorman, 1995; Vaughn, Gersten, & Chard, 2000). There is a solid knowledge base for alternative approaches to assessment and intervention; however, the assessment services and special education for most children and youth with disabilities do not apply all, or even most, of this knowledge base.

The continuing education needs of psychologists who provide assessment services to students with disabilities have arguably never been greater. Much of what is in current programs regarding standardized, norm-referenced assessment is of declining importance. Preservice and continuing education opportunities to acquire the new set of skills are expanding but, to date, are inadequate to meet the needs of personnel in systems undergoing rapid changes. Meeting these continuing education needs is one of the largest current challenges to university graduate programs and to professional associations.

The traditional training of psychologists continues to provide a solid foundation for the competencies needed in the delivery system of the future. The knowledge base in learning, normal and exceptional patterns of development, sensitivity to cultural differences, measurement, assessment, counseling methods, and relationship skills is unique among the professionals in schools involved with providing assessment and intervention services to SWD. These foundation competencies need to be supplemented with skills in functional assessment and effective interventions that are crucial to improved assessment of children with disabilities.

LEGAL CHANGES IN LEARNING DISABILITIES CLASSIFICATION CRITERIA

IDEA was reauthorized and signed by President Bush in November/December 2004. Implementing regulations are scheduled for publication by early December 2005. The language in the statute forces a markedly different approach to LD identification, changing the focus from standardized tests to assessing RTI. The current LD regulations at 34 C.F.R. 300.540 to 543 essentially establish three broad classification criteria: (1) low achievement in at least one of eight specified areas, (2) severe discrepancy between intellectual ability and achievement, and (3) exclusion of other plausible causes of low achievement such as MR or ED. Assessment of ability and achievement using individually administered, standardized tests has been a major role of school psychologists and many other psychologists in clinics and private practice. The following language that appears in IDEA (2004) is intended to change these practices:

> When determining whether a child has a specific learning disability . . . the local educational agency shall *not* be required to take into consideration whether the child has a severe discrepancy between achievement and intellectual ability in oral expression, listening comprehension, written expression, basic reading skill, reading comprehension, mathematical calculation, or mathematical reasoning. In determining whether a child has a specific learning disability, a local educational agency may use a process that determines if a child responds to scientific, research-based intervention. (IDEA; 2004, Section 614, emphasis added)

The effect of this change is to eliminate current federal and state LD requirements regarding the identification of a severe discrepancy between ability and achievement and to encourage a problem-solving approach that uses RTI criteria. IQ-achievement as a major component of LD identification has been sharply criticized because of poor validity, questionable reliability, and failure to identify problems at early grade levels where treatment is more effective. (Fletcher et al., 2002; Gresham, 2002; Reschly, in press). There now is a broad consensus that greater emphasis on primary and secondary interventions in general education will be an essential prerequisite to LD diagnoses.

Moreover, IQ and cognitive processing tests will be used far less frequently, changing the assessment practices of psychologists diagnosing LD. Many questions remain about the exact procedures that will be used in LD diagnosis and the role of psychological assessment. The stakes are high for psychologists, but significant changes likely will be necessary.

The LD changes are consistent with the system reform trends identified earlier. In fact, where problem-solving systems have been implemented using RTI criteria for eligibility determination, psychologists administer few standardized tests of ability and achievement. Assessment continues to play a key role, but with a shift toward behavior assessment procedures (behavior observation, checklists, rating scales, curriculum-based measurement of academic skills, monitoring the effects of interventions and changing the interventions if goals are not accomplished). Slightly more time is devoted to problem-solving consultation and direct interventions such as counseling and social skills groups. Psychologists continue to have crucial roles in the assessment of educational disabilities, but the kind of assessment and roles changes significantly (Reschly et al., in preparation).

PSYCHOLOGICAL TESTIMONY IN LEGAL PROCEEDINGS

Use of psychoeducational assessment in legal or quasi-legal proceedings such as due process hearings has usually been restricted to the testimony of expert witnesses or examination of the results from standardized tests. It is crucial to note that typical school psychology practitioners meet the criteria for court recognition as expert witnesses. Moreover, most psychologists will appear one or more times in their career as expert witnesses in an administrative hearing or in court. Although testimony and standardized test results are acceptable kinds of evidence, their impact often is diminished by attacks on the tests and the nearly inevitable appearance of contradictory testimony from other experts representing the other side. Furthermore, the highly inferential court testimony that psychologists sometimes provide is quite vulnerable to impeachment during cross-examination (Faust & Ziskin, 1988; Ziskin & Faust, 1988).

Psychologists often experience frustration in attempting to explain complex patterns of behavior with imprecise but intricate diagnostic constructs and complicated classification criteria. Explanations of these matters in legal proceedings can be particularly trying when cross-examination may be devoted to undermining the salience and credibility of the testimony. Sattler's (1982) account of his experiences in *Larry P.* is an excellent illustration of this problem.

Although sound testimony from genuine experts is probably essential and irreplaceable, this testimony can be significantly enhanced if supported by a variety of more tangible forms of evidence. In the *S-1 v. Turlington* (1986) trial, a videotape was shown in which Black and White regular education students of approximately average ability were contrasted with Black and White students classified as MMR and placed in special education programs. The children were about 10 years old. Each child was shown in a brief interview and then asked to perform such common, everyday cognitive skills as telling time, performing simple computations, and reading a brief passage. Differences among these students were not apparent in the interview or from casual observation. However, dramatic differences among the students on these relatively simple cognitive tasks were obvious to everyone in the court. The critical differences among disabled and nondisabled were exemplified far better by the videotape than any expert witness using protocols from standardized tests, normal curve distributions, and deviation IQ scores could ever have shown. The videotape provided a means whereby far more tangible examples of the basic issue in the litigation could be presented. Similar uses of videotape would seem appropriate and desirable in due process hearings and civil court proceedings concerning disabled students.

In addition to videotape, a variety of other kinds of evidence, such as audiotape, samples of daily work, observation protocols, and interview schedules, can be used to support expert testimony. A major problem with some of the previous placement bias cases, *Larry P.* and *PASE,* is the relatively sparse use of these alternative kinds of evidence, which left federal district court judges with the unenviable tasks of determining item bias and whether certain students were truly retarded. Psychologists can best serve the courts by presenting tangible evidence that reflects the basic phenomena rather than relying only on testimony.

CONCLUSIONS

Legal influences on school psychology and other professions associated with assessment of educational disabilities have expanded enormously over the past three decades. Further influence through the gradual evolution of case law and the enactment of legislation should be anticipated in the future. Legislative changes in 2004 may have the greatest impact of any legal influence since the establishment of mandatory special education programs and the requirements regarding individual evaluations prior to disability diagnosis and special education placement. The traditional use of standardized ability tests is likely to decline as alternative LD criteria are implemented. The need for changes in graduate training and continuing education programs is substantial and challenging.

The uneasy relationship between the courts and psychologists and the occasional misuse and distortion of psychological evidence by the courts require substantial additional efforts toward mutual understanding. Greater appreciation on the part of psychologists for the essential role of the courts in determining the educational rights of SWD is needed as well as greater understanding by the courts of the strengths and limitations of psychoeducational assessment. Better assessment can produce better evidence, which, in turn, will improve legal decisions that affect the lives of children and youth.

REFERENCES

American Psychiatric Association. (1994). *Diagnostic and statistical manual of mental disorders* (4th ed.). Washington, DC: Author.

American Psychological Association. (2002). *Ethical principles of psychologists and code of conduct.* Washington, DC: Author.

Board of Education v. Holland, 786 F. Supp. 874 (E.D. CA 1992) (9th Cir. 1994).

Board of Education v. Rowley, 102 S. Ct. 3034 (1982).

Coalition to Save Our Children v. State Board of Education (1995), Civil Action Nos. 56-1816-1822-SLR, U.S. District Court for the District of Delaware.

Crawford et al. v. Honig No. C-89-0014 RFP U.S. District Court, Northern District of California, Complaint for Declaratory Judgment, May 1988; Order, September 29, 1989; Memorandum and Order, August 31, 1992.

Cronbach, L. J. (1975). Beyond the two disciplines of scientific psychology. *American Psychologist, 30,* 116–127.

Deno, S. L. (1985). Curriculum-based measurement: The emerging alternative. *Exceptional Children, 52,* 219–232.

Diana v. State Board of Education, No. C-70-37 RFP U.S. District Court, Northern District of California, Consent Decree, February 3, 1970.

Education of the Handicapped Act. (1975, 1977). 20 U.S.C. 1400–1485, 34 C.F.R.-300.

Elliott, S. N., Kratochwill, T. R., & McKevitt, B. C. (2001). Experimental analysis of the effects of testing accommodations on the scores of students with and without disabilities. *Journal of School Psychology, 39,* 3–24.

Elliott, S. N., McKevitt, B. C., & Kettler, R. (2002). Testing accommodations research and decision-making: The case of "good" scores being highly valued but difficult to achieve for all students. *Measurement and Evaluation in Counseling and Development, 35,* 153–166.

Englemann, S., & Carnine, D. (1982). *Theory of instruction: Principles and applications.* New York: Irvington.

Fagan, T. K. (1987a). Gesell: The first school psychologist: Part I: The road to Connecticut. *School Psychology Review, 16,* 103–107.

Fagan, T. K. (1987b). Gesell: The first school psychologist: Part II: Practice and significance. *School Psychology Review, 16,* 399–409.

Faust, D., & Ziskin, J. (1988). The expert witness in psychology and psychiatry. *Science, 241,* 31–35.

Fletcher, J. M., Lyon, G. R., Barnes, M., Stuebing, K. K., Francis, D. J., Olson, R. K., et al. (2002). Classification of Learning Disabilities: An evidence-based evaluation. In R. Bradley, L. Danielson, & D. P. Hallahan (Eds.), *Identification of learning disabilities: Research to practice* (pp. 185–250). Mahwah, NJ: Erlbaum.

Foorman, B. R. (1995). Research on the great debate: Code-oriented versus whole-language approaches to reading instruction. *School Psychology Review, 24,* 376–392.

Fuchs, L. S. (2002). Best practices in providing accommodations for assessment. In A. Thomas & J. Grimes (Eds.), *Best practices in school psychology IV* (pp. 899–909). Bethesda, MD: National Association of School Psychologists.

Gratz et al. v. Bollinger et al., No. 02-516, U.S. Supreme Court, Opinion, June 23, 2003.

Gresham, F. M. (2002). Responsiveness to intervention: An alternative approach to the identification of learning disabilities. In R. Bradley, L. Danielson, & D. P. Hallahan (Eds.), *Identification of learning disabilities: Research to practice* (pp. 467–519). Mahwah, NJ: Erlbaum.

Grutter v. Bollinger et al., No. 02-241. U.S. Supreme Court, Opinion, June 23, 2003.

Guadalupe Organization v. Tempe Elementary School District No. 3, No. 71-435 (D. Ariz., January 24, 1972) (consent decree).

Howell, K., & Nolet, V. (2000). *Curriculum-based evaluation: Teaching and decision making* (3rd ed.). Atlanta, GA: Wadsworth.

Individuals with Disabilities Education Act. (1997, 1999, 2004), 20 U.S.C. Chapter 33, Sections 1400–1485 (Statute).

Kavale, K. A., & Forness, S. R. (1999). Effectiveness of special education. In C. R. Reynolds & T. B. Gutkin (Eds.), *The handbook of school psychology* (3rd ed., pp. 984–1024). New York: Wiley.

Kicklighter, R. H. (1976). School psychology in the U.S.: A quantitative survey. *Journal of School Psychology, 14,* 151–156.

Larry P. v. Riles (1972, 1974, 1979, 1984, 1986, 1992), 343 F. Supp. 1306 (N.D. Cal. 1972) (preliminary injunction); aff'd 502 F. 2d 963 (9th cir. 1974); 495 F. Supp. 926 (N.D. Cal. 1979) (decision on merits); aff'd (9th cir. no. 80-427, Jan. 23, 1984). Order modifying judgment, C-71-2270 RFP, September 25, 1986. Memorandum and Order, August 31, 1992, aff'd F. (9th Cir. 1994).

Luckasson, R., Coulter, D. L., Polloway, E. A., Reiss, S., Schalock, R. L., Snell, M. E., et al. (1992). *Mental retardation: Definition, classification, and systems of support* (9th ed.). Washington, DC: American Association on Mental Retardation.

Marshall et al. v. Georgia (1984, 1985). U.S. District Court for the Southern District of Georgia, CV482-233, June 28, 1984; Affirmed (11th Cir. No. 84-8771, Oct. 29, 1985). (Appealed as NAACP v. Georgia). Note: the court of appeals decision was published as Georgia State Conference of Branches of NAACP v. State of Georgia.

MacMillan, D. L., Gresham, F. M., Lopez, M. F., & Bocian, K. M. (1996). Comparison of students nominated for prereferral interventions by ethnicity and gender. *Journal of Special Education, 30*, 133–151.

Mattie T., et al. v. Johnson, et al., Consent Decree, U.S. District Court, Northern District of Mississippi, No. DC-75-31-S, December 23, 2003.

McDonnell, L. M., McLaughlin, M. J., & Morison, P. (1997). *Educating one and all: Students with disabilities and standards-based reform.* Washington, DC: National Academy Press.

Mercer, J. (1979). In defense of racially and culturally nondiscriminatory assessment. *School Psychology Digest, 8*, 89–115.

Mills v. Board of Education, 348 F. Supp. 866 (D.D.C. 1972).

Parents in Action on Special Education (PASE) v. Joseph P. Hannon, U.S. District Court, Northern District of Illinois, Eastern Division, No. 74 (3586), July, 1980.

Parrish, T. B., Chambers, J. G., & Guarino, C. M. (Eds.). (1999). *Funding special education.* Thousand Oaks, CA: Corwin Press.

Pennsylvania Association for Retarded Children (PARC) v. Commonwealth of Pennsylvania, 343 F. Supp. 279 (E.D. Pa. 1972).

Prasse, D. P. (2002). School psychology and the law. In A. Thomas & J. Grimes (Eds.), *Best practices in school psychology IV* (4th ed., pp. 57–75). Washington, DC: National Association of School Psychologists.

Reschly, D. J. (1980). School psychologists and assessment in the future. *Professional Psychology, 11*, 841–848.

Reschly, D. J. (1988). Special education reform: School psychology revolution. *School Psychology Review, 17*, 459–475.

Reschly, D. J. (1996). Identification and assessment of children with disabilities. *The Future of Children: Special Education for Children with Disabilities, 6*(1), 40–53.

Reschly, D. J. (in press). LD identification: Primary intervention, secondary intervention, then what? *Journal of Learning Disabilities.*

Reschly, D. J., & Bersoff, D. N. (1999). Law and school psychology. In C. R. Reynolds & T. B. Gutkin (Eds.), *The handbook of school psychology* (3rd ed., pp. 1077–1112). New York: Wiley.

Reschly, D. J., & Hosp, J. L. (2004). State SLD policies and practices. *Learning Disability Quarterly, 27*, 197–213.

Reschly, D. J., Ikeda, M. J., Tilly, W. D. III., Allison, R., Grimes, J. P., & Upah, K. F. (in preparation). *School psychologists in problem solving-RTI systems: Roles, assessment, satisfaction, supervision, and evaluation.*

Reschly, D. J., & Kicklighter, R. J. (1985). *Comparison of black and white EMR students from Marshall v. Georgia.* Paper presented at the Annual Convention of the American Psychological Association, Los Angeles, ERIC ED 271 911.

Reschly, D. J., Tilly, W. D. III., & Grimes, J. P. (Eds.). (1999). *Special education in transition: Functional assessment and noncategorical programming.* Longmont, CO: Sopris West.

Reschly, D. J., & Ward, S. M. (1991). Use of adaptive measures and overrepresentation of black students in programs for students with mild mental retardation. *American Journal of Mental Retardation, 96*, 257–268.

Reschly, D. J., & Ysseldyke, J. E. (2002). Paradigm shift: The past is not the future. In A. Thomas & J. Grimes (Eds.), *Best practices in school psychology IV* (4th ed., pp. 3–20). Bethesda, MD: National Association of School Psychologists.

S-1 v. Turlington, Preliminary Injunction, U.S. District Court, Southern District of Florida, Case No. 79-8020-Civ-CA WPB, June 15, 1979. Affirmed United States Court of Appeals, 5th Circuit, January 26, 1981, 635 F 2d 342 (1981). Trial on Merits, May 19–June 4, 1986. Order on Motion to Dismiss, No. 79-8020-Civ-Atkins, U.S. District Court, Southern District of Florida, October 9, 1986.

Sattler, J. (1982). The psychologist in court: Personal reflections of one expert witness in the case of Larry P. *School Psychology Review, 11*, 306–319.

Shapiro, E. S. (Ed.). (1996). *Academic skills problems: Direct assessment and intervention* (2nd ed.). New York: Guilford Press.

Shapiro, E. S., & Kratochwill, T. R. (Eds.). (2000). *Behavioral assessment in schools: Theory, research, and clinical applications* (2nd ed.). New York: Guilford Press.

Shinn, M. R. (Ed.). (1998). *Advanced applications of curriculum-based measurement*. New York: Guilford Press.

Shinn, M. R., Stoner, G., & Walker, H. M. (2002). *Interventions for academic and behavioral problems II: Preventive and remedial approaches*. Bethesda, MD: National Association of School Psychologists.

Sulzer-Azaroff, B., & Mayer, G. R. (1991). *Behavior analysis for lasting change*. Fort Worth, TX: Holt, Rinehart and Winston.

Thomas, A., & Grimes, J. (Eds.). (2002). *Best practices in school psychology IV* (4th ed.). Bethesda, MD: National Association of School Psychologists.

Timothy W. v. Rochester, Sch. Dist., IDELR, 559:480 (D.N.H., 1988, Case No. C-84-733-L); IDELR 441:393 (1st Cir., 1989, Case No. 88-1847).

Vaughn, S., Gersten, R., & Chard, D. J. (2000). The underlying message in LD intervention research: Findings from research syntheses. *Exceptional Children, 67*, 99–114.

Ysseldyke, J. E., & Olsen, K. (1999). Putting alternate assessments into practice: What to measure and possible sources of data. *Exceptional Children, 65*, 175–186.

Ysseldyke, J. E., Vanderwood, M. L., & Shriner, J. (1997). Changes over the past decade in special education referral to placement probability: An incredibly reliable practice. *Diagnostique, 23*, 193–201.

Ziskin, J., & Faust, D. (1988). *Coping with psychiatric and psychological testimony* (Vols. 1–3, 4th ed.). Los Angeles: Law and Psychology Press.

CHAPTER 9

Civil Competency

RALPH SLOVENKO

THE TERM *competency* refers to a person's ability to act or make decisions in a particular context. This chapter discusses competency in the contexts in which the issue most often arises in law: employment and professional competency, witness competency, competency to make a will, competency to contract, competency to obtain medical care, and competency of a minor in that regard. A person lacking competency may not only be excluded from certain activities but may be subjected to certain legal proceedings, such as the appointment of a guardian.

As the enumerated situations would indicate, the test of competency depends on the activity or task; its connotation is contextual, relating to a specific task. The test of competency is not global. Thus, an elderly man may be found competent to marry though lacking in testamentary capacity (*In re* McElroy, 1978). There is a functional explanation for the varying standards of competency: Different types of transactions or decisions entail different consequences.

COMPETENCY IN EMPLOYMENT

In his now famous book *The Peter Principle,* Laurence J. Peter wrote that in a hierarchy, employees tend to rise to their level of incompetence (Peter & Hull, 1969). Peter observed that employees start off competent, then rise, through promotion, to a position where they are not competent to perform the job. In other words, cream rises until it sours. Peter later wrote that this principle applies as well to all or at least most professions (*The Peter Prescription,* 1972).

Various techniques may be used to protect or enhance competence. Israeli kibbutzniks rotate jobs every 3 or 4 years. At its Saturn plant in Tennessee, General Motors inaugurated a series of work rules to enhance morale and productivity. Instead of performing a single repetitive task, employees work together in self-directing teams of 6 to 15 people; each team is responsible for large sections of the car, and its members have the latitude to reach a consensus on how to divide and rotate job assignments. The workers receive a salary instead of an hourly wage, their pay directly based on performance (Alexander, 1985).

In an application for employment, there is no legal obligation to disclose a disability or history of disability. The law prohibits a prospective employer from inquiring during an interview about an applicant's health status (though there are exceptions to this rule for bona fide occupational qualifications; for instance, applicants seeking employment on a loading dock may be asked if they can lift at least 50 lbs.). Following a conditional job offer or once on the job, an employer is permitted, in limited circumstances, to make medical inquiries and examinations. Under the Americans With Disabilities Act, enacted in 1990, an employer must reasonably accommodate a disabled employee where (1) the employer knows of the disability; (2) the individual satisfies all of the skill, experience, education, and licensing requirements of the job; and (3) the individual can perform the essential functions of the job if a reasonable accommodation is made.

It can be difficult to determine whether incompetence rests with the person, with others, or with the system. The legal standard for measuring incompetence is related to vocational, social, educational, and other circumstances. Custom or state of the art can be a measure of competency or negligence. Thus, in *Stepakoff v. Kantar* (1985), where it was alleged that the psychiatrist's negligence led to the patient's suicide, the court held that the psychiatrist was required to exercise only the care and skill customarily exercised by an average qualified psychiatrist. In a malpractice (professional negligence) action, the complainant is obliged as a matter law to call as an expert witness a member of the profession (or one familiar with the profession) to testify as to the standard of care of the profession.

Age is increasingly viewed as a discriminatory basis for mandatory retirement. With more and more elderly people continuing to work, the question of their competency increasingly arises in the context of determining safety to others or competence to perform certain operations that require unusual physical or mental skills. Boards of medicine frequently refer elderly physicians for mandatory psychological evaluations to determine continued competency to practice with the requisite degree of skill and care. However, the examiner must be careful in evaluating the exam results as emotional arousal of the client can lead to atypical performance that does not accurately reflect actual capacity (Aldridge, 2003).

COMPETENCY OF A PROFESSIONAL

The word "profession" comes from the Latin *profiteri*, "to profess," meaning to make a public dedication to the ideals and practices associated with a learned calling. Professionalism involves several elements: fidelity to ethics and integrity as a meaningful commitment, service with competence and dedication, meaningful education, and civility. Most of the current law on professional competence concerns physicians and lawyers, but the general standards gleaned from those contexts apply to psychologists as well.

Every professional organization, in one way or another, must face up to the incompetency of a member. Exclusion or discipline of a member may be based either on emotional instability or on professional misconduct. However, the degree of proof necessary to justify loss of membership or suspension varies from state to state and from profession to profession. In some states, professional misconduct must be shown by a preponderance of the evidence; in others, by clear and convincing evidence. Seldom does a malpractice suit trigger a hearing by a disciplinary board, though some professional organizations, such as those governing psychologists, now track the filing of suits as part of their licensing renewal process. Yet, negligence as established in litigation is not equated with incompetency to practice or even with a presumption of incompetency.

A licensing board may withdraw a license, or find that a professional lacks competence, when the practitioner is found to have violated an ethical or legal norm. In a first-of-its-kind ruling, the U.S. Seventh Circuit Court of Appeals ruled that a professional society may discipline a member on account of testimony presented at trial that is deemed not up to standard. In *Austin v. American Association of Neurological Surgeons* (2001) the court said:

> Although [the expert witness] did not treat the malpractice plaintiff for whom he testified, his testimony at her trial was a type of medical service, and if the quality of his testimony reflected the quality of his medical judgment, he is probably a poor physician. His discipline by the Association therefore served an important public policy exemplified by the federal Health Care Quality Improvement Act.

Some years earlier, the Mississippi Supreme Court upheld the withdrawal of a license on account of breach of confidentiality (*Mississippi State Board of Psychological Examiners v. Hosford*, 1987).

Generally, acts or omissions, which themselves would be grounds for discipline, bring to light mental or emotional problems. Often, the issue of mental instability is raised in mitigation of the wrongful conduct. In a few cases, however, the petition for suspension is based on a rule that provides for the suspension of individuals who are mentally or emotionally unstable.[1]

Substance abuse may be a factor in determining professional competency. A status report from the American Bar Association asserts that 13 of every 100 students who graduate from an accredited law school show signs of drug or alcohol dependency. A report by the National Transportation Safety Board cites alcohol use as a common denominator in fatal commercial aviation accidents. In a survey of 9,000 physicians, 8% admitted to having abused or been dependent on alcohol or other drugs during their lives. A report by the American Nurses Association links 68% of all state board actions against nurses to substance abuse (Coombs, 1997).

Over time, the standards by which professionals are judged change. For example, in the case of lawyer competency in criminal cases, until the 1970s, the prevailing standard of effective assistance of counsel was the mockery-of-justice test, under which representation was considered ineffective or incompetent only when it was so poor as to "reduce the trial to a farce" or render it a "mockery of justice." Under this test, lawyers could appear in court drunk or could fall asleep during trial and still not be found ineffective. (Disciplinary action, however, could be brought against an attorney for appearing in court intoxicated.) The test required "such minimal level of performance from counsel" that it was called "a mockery of the Sixth Amendment" (Bazelon, 1973, p. 20). It was feared that honoring such claims would force trial judges to intervene whenever a possible error was being committed, lead appellate courts to second-guess defense tactics with the benefit of hindsight, make lawyers more reluctant to accept court assignments, and encourage lawyers with desperate cases to commit errors deliberately. In the early 1970s, the U.S. Supreme Court approached the issue of ineffective counsel in terms of whether counsel fell "within the range of competence demanded of attorneys in criminal cases" (*McMann v. Richardson*, 1970). The Supreme Court subsequently ruled that reversal of a conviction will be required only when the defendant shows that the attorney acted improperly in a way that directly and adversely affected the result at trial (*Strickland v. Washington*, 1984).

However, even where the standard of care is settled law, disclosure requirements may not be. Given that the informed consent doctrine calls for the disclosure of risks, and given that the competency of the health care provider is a risk, it is now contended that failure to disclose the provider's competency may result in liability in the event of poor outcome even though standard of care was followed. The decisions are mixed (Petrila, 2003). The Louisiana Court of Appeals in *Hidding v. Williams* (1991) ruled that a physician's failure to disclose his chronic alcohol abuse vitiated the patient's consent to surgery. There was a poor outcome, but no evidence that the physician was under the influence of alcohol at the time of surgery, or that his hands trembled, or that the care fell below acceptable standards. Nonetheless, the court said:

> Because this condition creates a material risk associated with the surgeon's ability to perform, which if disclosed would have obliged the patient to have elected another course of treatment, the fact-finder's conclusion that nondisclosure is a violation of the informed consent doctrine is entirely correct. (p. 470)

In contrast, in *Reaves v. Bergsrud* (1999), the Arizona Court of Appeals declined to allow evidence as to alcoholism of an anesthesiologist as a separate claim of negligence, absent a showing that he was intoxicated or impaired at the time of the surgery. The plaintiff argued that alcoholism diminishes a physician's capacity to render the proper standard of care. The plaintiff cited legislation regulating the medical profession wherein unprofessional conduct is defined to include habitual intemperance in the use of alcohol. The court recognized that an alcoholic doctor might present a danger to the public if allowed to continue to practice medicine, but that, it said, is a matter for the medical board in deciding whether to revoke a license to practice. In a tort case such as this, on the other hand, where a plaintiff is bringing a malpractice suit against a physician for damages, the issue is simply, the court said, whether the physician exercised the proper standard of care in treating a particular patient at a particular time.

If a patient suffers a poor outcome and then learns that the physician was inexperienced, the patient may bring suit against the physician for failure to disclose that lack of experience. Often, hospital patients are unaware that they are being treated by a medical student or resident or possibly a psychologist rather than a fully trained physician. Psychologists use the honorific "Dr." often without clarification, and many patients come to believe that the individual is a medical doctor. Because Phillip C. McGraw (known as "Dr. Phil") carries the honorific "Dr."—though he is a clinical psychologist, not a physician—his critics say that consumers are more likely to trust his recommendations (Day, 2003). London's *Financial Times* has the policy to use the honorific only when referring to a medical doctor.

In *Johnson v. Kokemoor* (1996), a Wisconsin case, the plaintiff sued her physician for failure to inform her that he had very little experience in performing an operation on an aneurysm. The plaintiff was rendered a quadriplegic by the surgery. It was discovered that the physician had never performed surgery on a large basilar bifurcation aneurysm such as the plaintiff's. The Wisconsin Supreme Court stated that the duty to disclose information that is "material" to a patient's decision must be decided on a case-by-case basis. A bright-line rule, that physicians must always give their qualifications to every patient, would be impossible, the court said. The court held that in this particular case, the plaintiff introduced enough evidence that, had a reasonable patient in her position been made aware that the physician lacked experience with this surgery, it likely would not have been undergone with him. "A reasonable person in the plaintiff's position would have considered such information material in making an intelligent and informed decision about the surgery."

In *Whiteside v. Lukson* (1996), the Washington Court of Appeals held that a surgeon's duty to obtain informed consent did not require him to disclose his lack of experience in performing a particular surgical procedure. In this case, the plaintiff needed to have her gallbladder removed. The plaintiff's physician had never performed a gallbladder removal at the time he obtained the plaintiff's consent. The surgery was delayed, however, and during the delay, the physician performed a gallbladder removal on two patients. During the plaintiff's surgery, the physician misidentified and damaged her bile duct and, as a result, she suffered numerous complications after the surgery. The Washington Court of Appeals stated that the duty to disclose material facts include only those facts that relate to the proposed treatment. The court declined to follow those cases applying a broader construction of material fact. Applying the traditional approach, the court held that a physician's lack of experience in performing a surgical procedure is not a material fact for purposes of finding liability predicated on failure to secure an informed consent.

The consensus that physicians do not have to disclose their experience or qualifications to a patient apparently has a major exception. In a situation involving high-risk treatment, such as brain surgery, a patient's right to know the doctor's experience becomes more important than a physician's right to privacy (*Johnson v. Kokemoor*, 1996). Although this rule is not a bright-line rule, it does set forth a guideline that physicians should follow. In routine, low-risk procedures, physicians do not have a duty to disclose that they are not experienced with the particular procedure, yet in situations where experience may determine life or death, the issue of the doctor's experience is critical. Quite likely, in these high-risk situations, physicians have a duty to disclose the fact that they have not performed the procedure or have less experience than someone else who could perform the procedure. Often, hospital patients are unaware that they are being treated by a medical student or resident rather than a fully trained physician.

According to a report of the National Conference of State Legislatures, at least 11 states have enacted laws to make physician profiles available to the public. Physicians have managed to keep similar laws from being passed in eight other states. In 1996, Massachusetts became the first state to publish physician malpractice histories and hospital disciplinary records on the Internet. Under the Physician Profile Act, the state now provides information on a physician's number of malpractice suits and settlements, warnings by the medical board, and hospital disciplinary measures. The Ohio State Medical Board Web site currently lists about 32,000 physicians' ages, education, medical specialties, official reprimands, and license suspensions and revocations. Proposed legislation would add the following physician information to the site: malpractice settlements and awards, felony and some misdemeanor convictions, and any restrictions on hospital admitting privileges.

Psychologists are not yet subject to such public scrutiny, but they should be aware that the public and the courts may require disclosure of a lack of experience or previous malpractice claims in some circumstances. Moreover, they should be aware that what they say in court may later be used against them by the licensing board.

COMPETENCY OF A WITNESS

As a general rule, in civil and criminal cases, every adult witness is presumed competent to testify unless it can be shown that the witness does not have personal knowledge of the matters about which he or she is to testify, that he or she does not have the ability to recall the subject matter, or that he or she does not understand the duty to testify truthfully (Rule 601 of the Federal Rules of Evidence). Any objection to the competency of a witness must be raised at the time the party is presented as a witness; absent objection at that time, the claim of incompetency is waived.

Generally, the decision whether or not to hold a competency hearing is a matter entirely within the discretion of the trial judge. A witness may be found competent despite the fact that in another case, the witness may have been found criminally insane or incompetent to stand trial. In these and other cases, a psychiatrist or psychologist may be called to testify whether the witness has sufficient memory, understands the oath, and has the ability to communicate (Slovenko, 1995). Among the considerations to be taken into account in deciding whether to order a psychiatric examination, many courts include protection of privacy and not deterring complaints and lawsuits of certain kinds. As one court put it, "It is unpleasant enough to have to testify in a public trial subject to cross-examination the results of which will be spread on the record in open court to disqualify you, or at least to spice up your cross-examination" (*United States v. Gutman*, 1984).

The rule that allows an individual deemed insane to testify assumes that jurors are capable of evaluating a witness's testimony. "If a lunatic takes the stand and babbles gibberish, the jury will ignore it and the defendant will not be harmed," said the court in *Gutman*. In this case, the witness had been hospitalized 13 months earlier and was described as "highly depressed" with "some psychiatric thought disorder in addition to the difficulty he has in organizing and being relevant." This witness for the state was again hospitalized some 2 months after testifying. The court listed several factors in its decision not to order an examination of the witness's ability to testify: (1) protection of the witness's privacy interests, (2) potential for harassment of witnesses, (3) the possibility that a mental exam will hamper law enforcement by deterring potential witnesses from coming forward, (4) whether the witness was a key to the case, and (5) whether there are substantial indications that the witness is suffering from a mental abnormality at the time of trial.

It has long been established that age alone is not determinative of competency to testify (Myers, 1993). The issue of competency of a child to testify came before the U.S. Supreme Court in 1895 in an oft-cited case, *Wheeler v. United States*. The question was whether the 5-year-old son of a murder victim could testify. The homicide took place on June 12, 1894; the case was tried on December 21 of that year. (In those days, trials took place soon after the event.) In reply to questions put to him on his voir dire, the boy said that he knew the difference between the truth and a lie, that if he told a lie the bad man would get him, and that he was going to tell the truth. When asked what they would do with him in court if he told a lie, he replied that they would put him in jail. He also said that his mother had told him that morning to "tell no lie," and when asked what the clerk had said to him when he was told to hold up his hand, he answered, "Don't you tell no story." He was asked about his residence, his relationship to the deceased, and whether he had ever been to school, to which he responded in the negative. The Supreme Court said:

> That the boy was not by reason of his youth, as a matter of law, absolutely disqualified as a witness, is clear. While no one would think of calling as a witness an infant only two or three years old, there is no precise age which determines the question of competency. This depends on the capacity and intelligence of the child, his appreciation of the difference between truth and falsehood, as well as of his duty to tell the former. The decision of this question rests primarily with the trial judge, who sees the proposed witness, notices his manner, his apparent possession or lack of intelligence, and may resort to any examination which will tend to disclose his capacity and intelligence as well as his understanding of the obligations of an oath. As many of these matters cannot be photographed into the record, the decision of the trial judge will not be disturbed on review unless from that which is preserved it is clear that it was erroneous. . . . The boy was intelligent, understood the difference between truth and falsehood, and the consequences of telling the latter, and also what was required by the oath which he had taken. At any rate, the contrary does not appear. Of course, care must be taken by the trial judge, especially where, as in this case, the question is one of life or death. On the other hand, to exclude from the witness stand one who shows himself capable of understanding the difference between truth and falsehood, and who does not appear to have been simply taught to tell a story, would sometimes result in staying the hand of justice. (pp. 524–525)

In early law, a child or adult could be automatically barred from testifying because of insufficient religious training. John Wigmore, the leading authority on evidence, in 1935 recommended that there be no requirement of competency of a child witness (Wigmore, 1979). He argued against the qualifying of witnesses by judges because of the judiciary's lack of expertise in this area. He argued for permitting children to testify and allowing the jury or judge to assess the overall credibility of the testimony. Although Wigmore's view has not been entirely adopted, numerous studies support the competency of child witnesses. However, lawyers do not like to put children on the stand and usually will do so only if their testimony is necessary. Jurors usually want medical evidence to corroborate a child's story of sexual abuse (Survey, 1997).

Psychological research confirms the popular view that children are more subject to suggestion than adults, but Loftus and Davies (1984, p. 63) observe:

> Perhaps age alone is the wrong focus for these studies. Whether children are more susceptible to suggestive information than adults probably depends on the interaction of age with other factors. If an event is understandable and interesting to both children and adults, and if their memory for it is still equally strong, age differences in suggestibility may not be found. But if the event is not encoded well to begin with, or if a delay weakens the child's memory relative to an adult's, then age differences may emerge.

To obtain accurate information from young children, the danger of suggestion must be taken into account as well as the fact that children have greater communication difficulties than adults and are often in need of assistance in this regard.

In common law, it was presumed that a child under age 14 was not competent. At present, there is no fixed age below which a witness is deemed incompetent, although children under age 10 are routinely examined by the court. The question in each case is whether the witness understands the obligations of the oath and has sufficient intelligence to give evidence. Age is considered along with the child's understanding of all the facts and circumstances of the case. It is often essential that the child have an understanding of the obligation of an oath and the obligation to tell the truth. For these purposes, it is generally sufficient if the child knows it is wrong to lie and that lying will be punished. In this regard, it was significant in *State v. Green* (1976) that a child witness said he would be spanked if he lied.

The level of suggestibility of a witness is an important factor in determining competence. Of particular concern is the nature of certain kinds of evidence. For instance, sex offense cases are particularly difficult when they involve children or individuals with a mental disability. In recent years, considerable attention has been paid to the subject of children as witnesses in sexual abuse cases. The methods of questioning children have been widely discredited (Rabinowitz, 2003), yet, in some jurisdictions, legislation has lowered the threshold on competency of children to testify in sexual abuse cases. For example, a Colorado statute provides:

> [While] the following persons shall not be witnesses: . . . (b) (1) Children under ten years of age who appear incapable of receiving just impressions of the facts respecting which they are examined or of relating them truly, (II) [t]his proscription does not apply to a child under ten years of age, in any civil or criminal

proceeding for child abuse, sexual abuse, sexual assault, or incest, when the
child is able to describe or relate in language appropriate for a child of that age
the events or facts respecting which the child is examined. (Colo. Stat., 1995)

This statute has been interpreted to render a child competent even though the
child did not know the difference between telling the truth and lying (*People v.
District Court*, 1990). In some jurisdictions in sex offense cases, corroboration of
the minor's allegations is required as a matter of law (Margolick, 1984; Melton,
1981; see also Press, 1985; Renshaw, 1985).

Under the law of evidence, the courts recognize that leading questions are
undesirable; courts make an exception in the case of children, yet it is the child
witness who is probably most easily misled by a suggestive question. Children
are especially suggestible and compliant with parents and those adults whom
they seek to please and protect. Thus, the child's suggestibility very much depends on the examiner. On cross-examination, attorneys ask questions that
confuse the child; they confuse adults, too. Children tend to speak and think
slowly, and the adult world gets impatient with them; they take longer to understand questions and to give answers. An adult may try to elicit a story that
makes sense from one point of view. Children may have only one word for an
object; they may not know the meaning of words such as penis, vagina, and
anus. They may not have the same sense of time and chronology as adults, thus
confusing lunch and dinner, for example.

By and large, judges and juries view the testimony of child witnesses with
suspicion. Over 60% of juries and over 80% of health professionals believe children are unreliable (Goodman, Golding, Helgeson, Haith, & Michelli, 1987).
Children fidget, their voices drop, they look down or away, and this can be interpreted as their not telling the truth or being less effective. For security, a
child may hug a doll while testifying, and that action may impugn credibility
(see Goodman & Michelli, 1981).

The competency of elderly witnesses has also been questioned. Research
shows that the elderly experience a decline in episodic memory (which affects
specific events like what happened at yesterday's meeting) but not in implicit
memory (which affects the large variety of mental activities that occur sponta-
neously, without having to make an intentional effort, such as driving a car) or
semantic memory (the overall store of information and experience people accumulate over a lifetime). The elderly also tend to suffer from source amnesia,
when they know something but cannot remember when or where they learned it
(Coleman, 1990).

COMPETENCY TO MAKE A WILL

A will or testament is a legal document describing a person's wishes regarding the disposition of his or her property upon the person's death. At the time
of the making of the will, testators must have "testamentary capacity," which
is the capacity to understand and remember the nature and extent of their
property, the persons who are the natural objects of their bounty, and the disposition that they desire to make of the property. It is not necessary that a person desiring to make a will have the capacity to make a contract and do

business generally or to engage in complex and intricate business matters (*Petterson v. Imbsen*, 1923). A guardian may not make a will for a ward, but the fact that a guardian was appointed does not of itself invalidate a will for lack of testamentary capacity.

Making a will actually requires only minimal competency, for it is an easy task. Moreover, whereas the terms of the disposition in the will are the testator's, the actual writing of the will is usually done by a lawyer. Though estate planning is complex, the formalities in making a will are simple. Even a considerable degree of eccentricity will not incapacitate a person in making a will. However, despite the language of courts upholding freedom of testation, the testamentary capacity concept has been used at times to undo the testamentary act in furthering society's interests in family maintenance. But generally speaking, a will is difficult to overturn.

Usually, the only way a disappointed heir can contest a will is on the grounds of a lack of testamentary capacity at the time of the making of the will or on the grounds that the testator was susceptible, because of mental condition, to undue influence or duress in the making of the will. These challenges most frequently focus on some sort of bodily disease or infirmity, alcohol or drug use, or cerebral arteriosclerosis. To establish either capacity or incapacity or undue influence, psychiatric testimony is usually presented. Often, because the testator has died prior to the contesting of the will, this testimony must be based on medical records, the recollections of associates, and the circumstances of the execution of the instrument in question (Spiegle & Crona, 2003). A presumption of undue influence arises when the beneficiary actively participated in the preparation and execution of the will and unduly profited from it (*In re* Estate of Anders, 1975).

A person who is addicted to drugs or liquor does not lack testamentary capacity if he or she is lucid and sober when the will is made. One who contests the will must establish that the influence of the drugs or liquor negated the "calm judgment" that the law requires. That is, the burden of proof is on the contestant of the will to establish that the testator was not lucid at the time of the making of the will. It is a heavy and difficult burden. Proof of addiction alone, for example, is not sufficient to carry the burden. The contestant must affirmatively show that the testator was intoxicated, affecting lucidity, at the time the will was made (an early case illustrating this point is *Elkinton v. Brick,* 1888).

Proof that the testator suffered from an insane delusion when making the will may also be enough to render the act invalid. An insane delusion is defined as a belief in things that do not exist and that no rational mind would believe to exist. The subject matter of the delusion must have no foundation in fact, be unable to be dispelled by reason, and be the product of mental disorder or the product or offspring of delusion. Delusional religious beliefs are a common source of litigation but do not generally affect capacity unless the mind of the believer assumes a chronic delusional state that controls and dictates the conduct of the testamentary act. A belief in witchcraft is not necessarily conclusive on the issue of insanity (*Rice v. Henderson*, 1954).

The effect of a lack of testamentary capacity is to invalidate the entire will. In general, one part of the will cannot be rejected for lack of capacity while another part, written at the same time, is acceptable as the decedent's will. However, in cases where a part of the will is affected by an insane delusion, there is a growing trend to strike out that particular provision if in doing so there is no effect on the other parts of the will that are not a result of the delusion.[2]

A will expresses a relationship between an individual and the people he or she loves or hates. As one author put it, "Perhaps more than any other human document [wills] reflect the character of the writer and reveal his relationship with family, friends, and the world at large. His nature, his prejudice, his interests, his eccentricities, and the full range of man's virtues and vices can be found in the pages of wills" (Menchin, 1963, p. 12). A lawyer in Washington, D.C., provided the proper levity to an otherwise mundane legacy:

> As for my debts, just and unjust,
> And to many creditors who did me trust,
> I hereby direct my executor to tell
> Them all kindly to go to hell.
> Then posthumously in court we will fight:
> For litigation is a lawyer's delight.

COMPETENCY TO CONTRACT

Competency to contract calls for an understanding of the nature of the contract and its consequences. A determination by a court that an individual requires psychiatric treatment does not constitute a finding of legal incompetence. Only the appointment of a guardian operates as an adjudication of legal incompetence (Michigan Compiled Laws 330.1489). It is to be noted that a guardian not only may not write a will for the ward but also may not commit the ward to a psychiatric facility (and thereby circumvent the law on civil commitment) or on behalf of the ward consent to an abortion, sterilization, psychosurgery, electroconvulsive therapy, or removal of a healthy body organ (Pennsylvania Statute 20:5521(d)(1)(2002)). A guardian may file for divorce on behalf of a ward where the ward "is capable of exercising reasonable judgment as to the personal decision, understands the nature of the action and is able to express unequivocally a desire to dissolve the marriage" (*Syno v. Syno*, 1991).

If the individual is actually incompetent at the time of entering into the contract but has not been declared legally incompetent, the contract is usually considered voidable rather than void. That is, the impaired individual has the option of affirming the contract, but if he or she wishes to nullify it, court action will be necessary. The interests of commerce dictate preserving the validity of contracts, but at the same time, society has a *parens patriae* (father of the people) interest in protecting the welfare of impaired individuals. In the case of contracting for basic necessities—shelter, clothes, food, and medical services—the policy of protecting the mentally incompetent is less critical than in other cases because there is usually a fair trade in these matters. On the other hand, the highest level of capacity is required for entering into a business contract (Knaver, 2003). To constitute incompetency to contract, cognitive and not merely affective deficits usually are necessary. Sometimes courts also apply an insane delusion test, which is a belief in the reality of facts that do not exist and that no rational person could believe, which motivates the making of the contract.

In the criminal law, impulsivity is not a defense under the M'Naghten test of criminal responsibility; neither in the law of sales is it a basis for voiding a contract. Indeed, merchants encourage impulsive buying. Likewise, compulsive buying is not a basis for voiding a contract. Contrary to a number of reports, the American Psychiatric Association at this time is not planning on adding "compulsive shopping disorder" to the list of mental disorders in its *Diagnostic and Statistical Manual of Mental Disorders.*

A consumer, however greedy, stupid, and gullible, does have protection from fraud. Customers are smarter than ever, but good judgment is often overcome by greed or gullibility. While looking for good buys at an antique show situated on the grounds of an old farm, one woman commented, "One hundred years ago, they used to milk cows here. Now they milk people." U.S. law enforcement officials report that letter scams from Nigeria rake in $250 million a year from Americans. The Nigeria letter scams hook victims by playing on their greed or gullibility. In such cases, the legal concept of vice or consent (error or fraud) rather than contractual incompetency may come into play.

The most common reason for initiating a guardianship or conservatorship proceeding is the concern of family members who have noticed changes in the judgment of an aged person and his or her dissipating money (many states distinguish between guardianship of the person and guardianship of property, or conservatorship). In that event, a guardian or conservator (usually a family member or an attorney) is appointed to handle the person's affairs. Because the percentage of the U.S. population 80 years and older has tripled since 1950, there are more cases of impaired capacity, notably due to Alzheimer's disease. In January 1996, at the urging of the elderly, a comprehensive competency law went into effect in California; the Due Process in Competence Determinations Act requires clear and convincing evidence of inability to appreciate the consequences of one's acts before appointing a conservator. Many states use some version of the Uniform Probate Code, which includes a list of partial competencies.

In some states, the determination of incompetency is a blanket incompetency ruling, which deprives the individual of any contractual capacity, including (theoretically) even buying groceries. In other states, a determination of incompetency may be limited, for example, to the managing of business affairs (Note, 1959; Slovenko, 2002; Weihofen, 1966). In the ordinary course of events, a merchant would find it awkward and time-consuming to go to the courthouse to check on the legal status of every contracting party. People do not wear badges indicating competency; hence, one contracts at a risk.

For centuries, there have been calls to simplify language in commercial transactions as well as in the law generally. (Napoleon simplified the French Civil Code to make it more understandable.) However, the devotion to archaic language is rooted in a desire for well-settled meaning, and the use of seemingly redundant terms stems from a prudent effort to cover every contingency. The informed consent form used by physicians and hospitals in medical care likewise tends to be boilerplate or so highly detailed that almost no one bothers to read it. In recent years, there has been a crescendo of voices calling for plain and readable language. Some legislatures have enacted "plain English" laws calling for simple language in contractual forms in sales, mortgages, and leases.

COMPETENCY REGARDING MEDICAL CARE

In the ordinary course of medical practice, the physician discusses the illness and proposed treatment with the patient. The informed consent form is usually distributed by the nurse or administrator shortly before the procedure is to take place. Researchers have noted that these consent forms are written at a level too difficult for most people to understand (Mariner & McArdle, 1985). To protect the patient's rights to make a voluntary and knowledgeable (informed) decision about treatment, the law imposes a correlative duty on the physician to disclose the relevant risks and benefits that the patient might be expected not to know. Actually, the informed consent document is designed to provide evidence of consent rather than to help a patient make a decision about treatment. In any event, the document as evidence may backfire under the theory, as commonly said, that "if contracting parties write at all they must write it all because the law presumes they wrote it all if and when they write at all."

Health care providers may act in the absence of express consent if (1) the patient is unable to give consent (because unconscious, intoxicated, mentally ill, incompetent); (2) there is a risk of serious bodily harm if treatment is delayed; (3) a reasonable person would consent to treatment under the circumstances; and (4) this patient would consent to treatment under the circumstances. In general, the courts have upheld the ability of a competent adult to refuse medical treatment, even if that care is deemed necessary to save or sustain life. The New York Court of Appeals upheld the termination of respiratory capabilities by a patient who previously, while competent, had manifested a desire not to be placed on a respirator. The rule is more sparingly applied in the case of incompetent patients, however. In a companion case, the court refused to terminate treatment of a patient who had never been competent (*Matter of Storar,* 1981).

Competency to consent to medical care involves several considerations: the ability to communicate and sustain a choice, the ability to understand relevant information, the ability to appreciate the situation and its consequences, and the ability to handle the information rationally. According to a study by the MacArthur Research Network, most patients hospitalized with serious mental illness have abilities similar to persons without mental illness for making treatment decisions (Appelbaum & Grisso, 2001). In practice, differing levels of competency are considered depending on the decision that must be made. When the risk of a treatment is low and the benefit is high and the patient refuses treatment, frequently a somewhat knowledgeable patient may be found incompetent so that consent may be sought from a substitute decision maker and treatment administered despite the patient's refusal (Roth, Meisel, & Lidz, 1977). The appointment of a guardian is called for when the patient is deemed incompetent.

The doctrine of substituted judgment is often used as a method by which the court may substitute its own judgment for that of the incompetent person. Originally, in the appointment of a guardian, the doctrine was used as a method for authorizing the disposition of an incompetent's property. Then it came to be employed in deciding whether to authorize withholding medical treatment for persons deemed incompetent. The goal of the doctrine is to make the decision that incompetent persons would make were they capable. It is often put in language that emphasizes the best interests of the person affected. For instance, sterilization proceedings may be included in some jurisdictions under the broad equity powers of probate courts to act for incompetent persons. The rationale is that all persons have a privacy right to choose to be sterilized, and incompetent persons must be afforded a means for making such a decision. In general, however, a guardian's decision as to what is in the person's best interests is granted only on a showing of clear and convincing evidence.

Decisions concerning euthanasia or the termination of life-support systems raise even more serious questions about competency. The failure of a person to establish and make known his or her choices regarding medical treatment prior to a finding of legal incompetence can result in long court battles over what the person would have wanted (*In re* Guardianship of Schiavo, 2003). Yet, can one ever be competent to make a decision about death? The New York cases draw a distinction between competent and incompetent decisions about death, although it is difficult to explain the difference. Ernest Becker wrote in his book *The Denial of Death* (1973, p. 361) that "the idea of death, the fear of it, haunts the human animal like nothing else, it is a mainspring of human activity—activity designed largely to avoid the fatality of death, to overcome it by denying in some way that it is the final destiny of man" (see Haber, 1982). Becker's thesis is that under no condition can one make a rational decision about one's own death; rather, one is always in extremis, hence *noncompos mentis*, on this matter.

Because individuals in medical care are often exceedingly vulnerable and dependent, the informed consent document is regarded much like a contract of adhesion—one that is looked on with a great deal of circumspection. An adhesion contract is a contract drafted by one party on a take-it-or-leave-it basis and is heavily restrictive of one party and nonrestrictive of another; because of the grave inequality of bargaining power, doubts arise as to its representation as a voluntary and uncoerced agreement.

Relationships between patients—in business parlance, consumers—and physicians are becoming increasingly depersonalized. Health maintenance organizations and managed care corporations pose ethical dilemmas where profit and the provision of quality medical care are often in conflict. Then, too, the physician's integrity is compromised by gifts from pharmaceutical companies (Anstett, 1997).

The U.S. Supreme Court has ruled that decisionally incompetent individuals cannot consent to voluntary hospitalization, as this requires informed consent (*Zinermon v. Burch*, 1990). They must be admitted by way of an involuntary commitment that affords them the procedural safeguards set out in the mental health code (Winick, 1997). In *Kennedy v. Schafer* (1995), the Eighth Circuit

Court of Appeals considered whether the state's failure to supervise the patient adequately to protect her from harming herself amounted to a deprivation of her constitutional rights. Although the Fourteenth Amendment does not generally impose a duty on a state to protect its citizens, the state may incur an affirmative obligation to provide safe and humane conditions of confinement when it assumes custodial control over the care of an individual such as a prisoner or an involuntarily committed mentally ill or retarded patient. Because the individual in this case was voluntarily admitted to the state facility by her parents, the court held that she was not entitled to the same due process right to a safe and humane environment as would a patient under the same circumstances who had been involuntarily committed to the facility.

Involuntary commitment to a mental hospital of itself, as noted, is neither a determination of incompetency nor a deprivation of civil or political rights. Hence, the status of a mental patient is—or should be—the same as that of any individual, and he or she should have all the rights listed in the mental patient's bill of rights without their enumeration (Saks, 2002). Identification of commitment with incompetency proceedings, which is still sometimes done in some jurisdictions, stems from the time when commitment spelled the end of an individual's contact with the outside world. The prevailing view today is that commitment, even without a competency hearing, entitles the hospital to use nonintrusive therapies in the case of a nonconsenting patient.

COMPETENCY OF A MINOR TO CONSENT TO TREATMENT

Minors (typically under age 18) are not considered legally competent to act on their own. The consent, express or implied, of a parent or guardian is necessary to authorize treatment or services. Absent that consent, treatment in law regardless of the outcome constitutes a battery (if there is physical contact) or possibly negligence. To this general rule, however, there are a number of exceptions: (1) parens patriae, (2) emergencies, (3) emancipated minors, (4) mature minors, and (5) certain types of care.

The state, as parens patriae, may protect the best interests of a minor in the face of parental refusal to consent to treatment deemed necessary to preserve the life or health of the minor. Under this authority, for example, the state can compel vaccination or fluoridation. And the state may override parental consent. Even with parental consent, sterilization or transplantation involving a minor is a procedure fraught with legal hazards, so court authorization is required or at least warranted (*Hart v. Brown*, 1972). Some states by legislation forbid a minor under 18 from getting a tattoo with or without parental permission. When a parent refuses on religious or other grounds to provide medical treatment for a child, courts are likely to grant an application to overrule the parent if the illness is life-threatening (*In re* Sampson, 1992), but not if it will only improve the child's comfort or appearance (*In re* Green, 1972). In the case of mental health hospitalization, the responsibility for the care and treatment of the patient becomes invested in the hospital or court, so a parent has no right of access to the minor's records (*In re* J.C.G., 1976). Additionally, under federal regulations, a parent's permission may not be required for a minor to participate in research on abused or neglected children (Rubinstein, 2003; 45 C.F.R. § 46.408(c) (1994)).

In an emergency where delay would produce serious risks for the minor, a physician may proceed with treatment without awaiting parental consent. Consent is implied from the emergency, defined as

> a situation wherein, in competent medical judgment, the proposed surgical or medical treatment or procedures are immediately or imminently necessary and any delay occasioned by an attempt to obtain a consent would reasonably jeopardize the life, health or limb of the person affected, or would reasonably result in disfigurement or impairment of faculties. (Mo. Stat.)

When the question arises, the courts give a broad interpretation to what constitutes an emergency. Thus, the treatment of a fracture was deemed an emergency, though it was not life-saving but done to stop pain and suffering (*Greenspan v. Slate*, 1953; *Sullivan v. Montgomery*, 1935). The Michigan Supreme Court (*Luka v. Lowrie*, 1912) had this to say about implied consent in emergency situations:

> The fact that surgeons are called upon daily, in our large cities, to operate instantly in emergency cases in order that life may be preserved, should be considered. Many small children are injured upon the streets in large cities. To hold that a surgeon must wait until perhaps he may be able to secure the consent of the parents before giving to the injured one the benefit of his skill and learning, to the end that life may be preserved, would, we believe, result in the loss of many lives which might otherwise be saved. It is not to be presumed that competent surgeons will want only to operate, nor that they will fail to obtain the consent of parents to operations where such consent may be reasonably obtained in view of the exigency. Their work, however, is highly humane and very largely charitable in character, and no rule should be announced which would tend in the slightest degree to deprive sufferers of the benefit of their services.

An emancipated minor—a minor who is legally free from the care, custody, and control of his or her parents—may give a legally valid consent. By dint of certain legislation, pregnancy amounts to emancipation. Alabama's statute, for example, provides: "Any minor who is married, or having been married is divorced, or has borne a child may give effective consent to any legally authorized medical, dental, health or mental health services for himself, his child or for herself or her child" (Alabama Code, 1973). More generally, in most states, minors can become emancipated by marrying or enlisting in the armed services. Some also allow for a judicial determination of emancipation (Michigan Compiled Laws 722.1 *et seq.*).

Under the mature minor doctrine, minors are permitted to consent to medical treatment if they are sufficiently mature to understand the nature of the procedure and its consequences and the alternatives to that treatment. But maturity is a matter of dispute. It is a behavioral test. One pediatrician suggested that any child who could get to the doctor's Greenwich Village office by subway from the Bronx was, in her eyes, an adult. The mature minor doctrine has found application in cases where the minor is at least 15 years of age, the treatment is for the benefit of the minor, and the procedure is something less than major or serious in nature. There is apparently only one case (*Bonner v. Moran*, 1941) where liability has been imposed on a doctor for treating a minor without parental consent. The operation in this case, however, was not for the benefit of the minor, a 15-year-old, but was a transplant operation for the benefit of a cousin (consent was by an aunt), yet the case has been cited and relied on in discussions of the need for parental consent in every situation.

In recent years, ad hoc exceptions (characterized as "general medical emancipation" statutes) have been made to parents' authority to consent, usually to help deal with problems that have high social costs, such as venereal disease, drug or alcohol abuse, contraception, and pregnancy. Underlying psychodynamics may be identical among individuals showing different symptoms or behavior, but it is only the named symptom or behavior that opens the door to care or treatment without parental consent. Some states set a minimum age for consent in these treatments or procedures. Many people—for example, Eunice Kennedy Shriver ("Sex Values," 1981), who suggested that programs involving parents in their children's lives are more worthy of support than those that isolate them—argue that such services should not be provided without parental consent, notice, or consultation. In any event, a number of state statutes authorize minors to receive mental health treatment without parental consent. For example, an Illinois statute provides: "Any minor fourteen years of age or older may request and receive counseling services or psychotherapy on an outpatient basis. The consent of the parent, guardian, or person in *loco parentis* shall not be necessary to authorize outpatient counseling or psychotherapy" (Ill. Stat).

The majority of states have enacted statutes permitting minors to consent without parental notice or consultation to receive treatment for venereal disease and drug or alcohol abuse and to seek and receive counseling on and devices for contraception. In *Carey v. Populations Services* (1977), the U.S. Supreme Court upheld the right of minors to obtain contraceptives without parental consent. In the wake of that decision, the Sixth Circuit Court of Appeals in *Doe v. Irwin* (1980) ruled that contraceptives may be provided to minors also without the knowledge of their parents. A number of state statutes specifically provide that records concerning the treatment of a minor for venereal disease or the performance of an abortion shall not be released or in any manner be made available to the parent (N.Y. Public Health Law, 1977). However, in the event the minor is using a family insurance plan to pay for service, the parents may learn about it when they receive a benefit report from the insurer.

As a tangential observation, it may be noted that the Georgia Supreme Court ruled the state's seduction statute unconstitutional; the statute gave the parent of a daughter a cause of action against anyone who seduced the daughter. The court said the statute was outmoded, harking back to the time when parents "had property interests in the bodies of their children" (*Franklin v. Hill*, 1994).

The U.S. Supreme Court in 1976 in *Planned Parenthood of Missouri v. Danforth* ruled that a parent may not veto a minor's decision to have an abortion, but the Court went on to say, "We emphasize that our holding . . . does not suggest every minor regardless of age or maturity, may give effective consent for termination of her pregnancy." This language might imply that immature or in-competent minors are required to obtain parental consent to abortion, even in the first trimester, just as they must for any other procedure. That issue came to the Supreme Court in 1979 in *Bellotti v. Baird.* In that case, the Court said that every minor has the right to go directly to a court without consulting her par-ents. Justice Powell wrote:

> A pregnant minor is entitled in such a proceeding to show either: (1) that she is mature enough, well enough informed to make her abortion decision, in consul-tation with her physician, independently of her parents' wishes; or (2) that even if she is not able to make this decision independently, the desired abortion would be in her best interests.

In many contexts, the scope and application of a state constitutional right of privacy may be broader and more protective of privacy than the federal consti-tutional right of privacy as interpreted by the federal courts. After nearly a decade of legal battles and a crucial change in court membership, the Califor-nia Supreme Court in 1997 struck down as a violation of privacy a law that would have required an unmarried minor either to obtain consent from one parent for an abortion or, as an alternative, to persuade a judge, in a confiden-tial hearing, that she was mature enough to make the decision or that an abor-tion was in her best interests. The court said:

> The statute denies a pregnant minor, who believes it is in her best interest to ter-minate her pregnancy rather than have a child at such a young age, control over her own destiny. In addition, the statutory requirement that the minor obtain parental consent or judicial authorization will delay the minor's access to a med-ically safe abortion in many instances, and thereby will increase, at least to some extent, the health risks posed by an abortion. Finally, in some instances, a minor who does not wish to continue her pregnancy but who is too frightened to tell her parents about her condition or go to court may be led by the statutory restrictions to attempt to terminate the pregnancy herself or seek a "back-alley abortion," courses of conduct that in the past have produced truly tragic results—or, alter-natively, to postpone action until it is too late to terminate her pregnancy, leaving her no choice but to bear an unwanted child. Of course, such consequences un-questionably would represent a most significant intrusion on the minor's pro-tected privacy interest. (*American Academy of Pediatrics v. Lungren,* 1997)

The question has been raised whether a state may impose a requirement of parental notice (as opposed to consent or consultation) as a condition of a minor's receiving an abortion. Given notice, parents may dissuade their minor from having an abortion. Justice Stevens in *Bellotti* remarked in a footnote: "[Our previous decisions do not determine] the constitutionality of a statute which does no more than require notice to the parents, without affording them or any other third party an absolute veto." Two years later, in 1981, in *H.L. v. Matheson,* the Supreme Court by a 6–3 vote upheld a Utah parental notification law. The Court said: "A statute setting out a 'mere requirement of parental no-tice' does not violate the constitutional rights of an immature, dependent minor. The Utah statute gives neither parents nor judges a veto power over the minor's abortion decision." The Supreme Court's decision does not make parental notification mandatory nationwide but leaves it up to each state to decide whether to impose the requirement.

As a matter of practice, the procedure set out by the Court in *Bellotti* has been and continues to be ignored. Abortion clinics around the country are carrying out abortions on minors just as they are on adults. No path is beaten to the courthouse door for a determination of maturity or best interests. Should there be complications, however, the minor will usually find that a hospital will not admit her without parental consent. Emergency care in a clearly life-saving situation may be available, but even then the hospital (while administering such care) will as a matter of practice attempt to contact a parent or guardian.

What actually is the hazard in treating a minor without parental consent? In general, physicians and other therapists appear to be overly fearful in the care and treatment of minors, leading quite often to tragic results. Although the law defines an emergency broadly, many physicians and hospitals define it very narrowly. One publicized case (Ramos, 1981) involved a minor who slit his lip and was spurting blood, but the doctor in the emergency room refused to suture it without parental consent. In actual fact, there has not been a reported case in any state since the aforementioned 1941 transplant case in which a physician or health facility has been held liable for treating a minor over age 15 without parental consent (Pilpel, 1972).

Parental consent is no insulation against liability in the case of faulty treatment. Consent protects from a charge of battery, but not from negligence or malpractice. In a case where the treatment measures up to acceptable standards of care but there is no parental consent or applicable exception, the parents may claim that their expenses for the support and maintenance of their child were increased by an unfavorable result of the treatment, but that is not likely.

CONCLUSION

In law, competency depends on the context and is defined in relation to a particular act: writing a will, entering into a contract, or testifying in court. Even then, it depends on the nature of the will or contract or type of case. Rarely is a person totally incompetent to carry out any type of act. Incompetency may be the symptom of an illness and, like other symptoms, may respond to treatment.

NOTES

1. "Validity and Application of Regulation Requiring Suspension of Disbarment of Attorney Because of Mental or Emotional Illness," 50 A.L.R.3d 1259.
2. "Partial Invalidity of a Will," 64 A.L.R.3d 261.

REFERENCES

Ala. Code title 22, § I04 (16)(Supp. 1973).
Aldridge, R. L. (2003, June). Capacity, competency, and other cans of worms. *Advocate (State Bar of Idaho), 46,* 9.
Alexander, C. P. (1985, August 5). GM picks the winner. *Time,* 42.

American Academy of Pediatrics v. Lungren, 66 Cal. Rptr.2d 210, 940 P.2d 797 (1997).

Anstett, P. (1997, August 19). Prescription for trouble. *Detroit Free Press*, p. F-6.

Appelbaum, P. S., & Grisso, T. (2001, February). MacArthur Research Network on Mental Health and the Law. The MacArthur Treatment Competence Study Executive Summary, at http://www.macarthur.Virginia.edu.treatment.htm1.

Austin v. American Association of Neurological Surgeons, 253 F.3d 967 (7th Cir. 2001).

Bazelon, D. (1973). The defective assistance of counsel. *University of Cincinnati Law Review, 42,* 1.

Becker, E. (1973). *The denial of death.* New York: Free Press.

Bellotti v. Baird, 428 U.S. 132 (1979).

Bonner v. Moran, 75 U.S. App, D.C. 156, 126 F.2d 121 (1941).

Carey v. Population Services International, 431 U.S. 678 (1977).

Coleman, D. (1990, March 27). Studies offer fresh clues to memory. *New York Times*, p. C-1.

Colo. Stat. § 13-90-106 (1995).

Coombs, R. H. (1997). *Drug-impaired professionals.* Cambridge, MA: Harvard University Press.

Day, S. (2003, October 27). Dr. Phil, medicine man. *New York Times*, p. C-1.

Doe v. Irwin, 615 F.2d 1162 (6th Cir. 1980).

Elkinton v. Brick, 44 N.J. Eq. 154, 15 Atl. 391 (1888).

Franklin v. Hill, 264 Ga. 302, 444 S.E.2d 778 (1994).

Goodman, G. S., Golding, J. M., Helgeson, V. S., Haith, M. M., & Michelli, J. (1987). When a child takes the stand/jurors' perceptions of children's eyewitness testimony. *Law and Human Behavior, 11,* 27.

Goodman, G. S., & Michelli, J. A. (1981, November). Would you believe a child witness? *Psychology Today,* 82.

Greenspan v. Slate, 12 N.J. 426, 97 A.2d 390 (1953).

Haber, H. G. (1982). In re Storar: Euthanasia for incompetent patients, a proposed model. *Pace Law Review, 3,* 351.

Hart v. Brown, 29 Conn. Sup. 368, 289 A.2d 386 (1972).

Hidding v. Williams, 578 So.2d 1192 (La. App. 1991).

H.L. v. Matheson, 450 U.S. 398 (1981).

Ill. Stat. ch. 91, § 3-5016(a).

In re Estate of Anders, 226 N. W.2d 170 (S.D. 1975).

In re Green, 448 Pa. 338, 292 A.2d 387 (1972).

In re Guardianship of Schiavo, 851 So.2d 182 (Fla. App. 2003).

In re J.C.G., 144 N.J. Super. 579, 366 A.2d 733 (1976).

In re Lanning, 565 N.W.2d 794 (S.D. 1997).

In re McElroy (1978), 93 D.L.R. (3d) 522.

In re Sampson, 29 N.Y.2d 900, 328 N.Y.S.2d 686, 278 N.E.2d 918 (1972).

In re Storar, 52 N.Y.2d 363, 420 N.E.2d 64, 438 N.Y.S.2d 266 (1981).

Johnson v. Kokemoor, 545 N. W.2d 495 (Wis. 1996).

Kennedy v. Schafer, 71 F.3d 292 (8th Cir. 1995).

Knaver, N. J. (2003). Defining capacity: Balancing the competing interests of autonomy and need. *Temple Political and Civil Rights Law Review, 12,* 321.

Loftus, E., & Davies, G. M. (1984). Distortions in the memory of children. *Journal of Social Issues, 40,* 51.

Luka v. Lowrie, 171 Mich. 122, 136 N.W. 1106 (1912).

Margolick, D. (1984, September 22). The corroboration requirement in prosecuting sexual abuse. *New York Times*, p. 13.

Mariner, W. K., & McArdle, P. A. (1985). Consent forms, readability, and comprehension: The need for new assessment tools. *Law, Medicine and Health Care, 12,* 68.

McMann v. Richardson, 397 U.S. 759 (1970).

Melton, G. B. (1981). Children's competency to testify. *Law and Human Behavior, 5,* 73.

Menchin, R. S. (1963). *The last caprice.* New York: Simon & Schuster.

Mo. Stat. title 28 sec. 431,063.

Mississippi State Board of Psychological Examiners v. Hosford, 508 So.2d 1049 (Miss. 1987).

Myers, J. E. B. (1993). The competence of young children to testify in legal proceedings. *Behavioral Sciences and the Law, 11,* 121.

N.Y. Public Health Law ch. 763 (McKinney 1971).

Note. (1959). Mental illness and the law of contracts. *Michigan Law Review, 57,* 1020.

People v. District Court, 791 P.2d 682 (Colo. 1990).

Peter, L. J. (1972). *The Peter prescription.* New York: Morrow.

Peter, L. J., & Hull, R. (1969). The Peter principle. New York: Morrow.

Petrila, J. (2003). The emerging debate over the shape of informed consent: Can the doctrine bear the weight? *Behavioral Sciences and the Law, 21,* 121.

Petterson v. Imbsen, 46 S.D. 540, 194 N.W. 842 (1923).

Pilpel, H. (1972). Minor's rights to medical care. *Albany Law Review, 36,* 462.

Planned Parenthood of Missouri v. Danforth, 428 U.S. 52 (1976).

Press, A. (1985, February 18). The youngest witness: Is there a "witch hunt" mentality in sex-abuse cases? *Newsweek,* 72.

Rabinowitz, D. (2003). *No crueler tyrannies: Accusation, false witness, and other terrors of our times.* New York: Free Press.

Ramos, S. (1981, January 22). Insuring medical aid if parents are away. *New York Times,* p. 15.

Reaves v. Bergsrud, 982 P.2d 497 (N.M. App. 1999).

Renshaw, D. C. (1985, July). When sex abuse is falsely charged. *Medical Aspects of Human Sexuality,* 116.

Rice v. Henderson, 140 W. Va. 284, 83 S.E.2d 762 (1954).

Roth, L., Meisel, A., & Lidz, C. W. (1977). Tests of competency to consent to treatment. *American Journal of Psychiatry, 134,* 279.

Rubinstein, E. (2003). Going beyond parents and institutional review boards in protecting children involved in nontherapeutic research. *Golden Gate University Law Review, 33,* 251.

Rule 601, Federal Rules of Evidence.

Saks, E. R. (2002). *Refusing care: Forced treatment and the rights of the mentally ill.* Chicago: University of Chicago Press.

Sex values for teens. (1981, March 1). *New York Times,* p. E-21.

Slovenko, R. (1995). Psychiatry and criminal culpability. New York: Wiley.

Slovenko, R. (2002). *Psychiatry in law/Law in psychiatry.* New York: Brunner-Routledge.

Spiegle, R. F., & Crona, S. J. (2003, June). Legal guidelines and methods for evaluating capacity. *Colorado Lawyer, 32,* 65.

State v. Green, 267 S.C. 599, 230 S.E.3d 618 (1976).

Stepakoff v. Kantar, 393 Mass. 836, 473, N.E.2d 1131 (1985).

Strickland v. Washington, 104 S. Ct. 2052 (1984).

Sullivan v. Montgomery, 155 Misc. 418, 279 N.Y.S. 575 (1935).

Survey. (1997, July 3). Lawyers find children can make very difficult witnesses. *Detroit Legal News,* p. 1.

Syno v. Syno, 406 Pa. Super. 218 (1991).

United States v. Gutman, 725 F.2d 417 at 420 (7th Cir. 1984).

Weihofen, H. (1966). Mental incompetence to contract or convey. *Southern California Law Review, 39,* 211.

Wheeler v. United States, 159 U.S. 523 (1985).

Whiteside v. Lukson, 947 P.2d 1263 (Wash. App. 1996).

Wigmore, J. (1979). *Evidence* (Rev. ed.). Boston: Little, Brown.

Winick, B. J. (1997). *The right to refuse treatment.* Washington, DC: American Psychological Association.

Zinermon v. Burch, 494 U.S. 113 (1990).

CHAPTER 10

Informed Consent in Treatment and Research

BARBARA STANLEY and MICHELE GALIETTA

THE DOCTRINE of informed consent has been well integrated into all biomedical research and most forms of other research over the past two decades. Similarly, obtaining informed consent to standard treatments, particularly medical procedures and surgery, is the accepted and required practice. Practice guidelines, ethical codes, and federal and state regulations cover what should be included in the consent process and how it should be conducted. This chapter places informed consent to treatment and research in its historical context, describes the elements of informed consent, and reviews empirical research that addresses consent issues.

HISTORICAL CONTEXT

The doctrine of informed consent is derived from two sources. Informed consent to treatment has primarily been influenced by litigation and subsequent case law. Although the doctrine of informed consent emerged only in the past half century, informed consent has existed in legal doctrine for several centuries. It grew out of common law that an unauthorized operation will subject the physician to liability in tort to the patient, with negligence as the cause for action (Ludlum, 1972; Rovosky, 1990). In contrast, the doctrine of informed consent to research evolved through a series of policies, regulations, and professional codes. The first guidelines and standards for human experimentation were developed in response to the atrocities perpetrated by Nazi experimenters during World War II (National Research Council [NRC], 2003, p. 60). Perhaps one of the most significant developments in the area of scientific research was the crafting of the Nuremberg Code in 1949 by the judges for the

---

Technical assistance provided by Abbie Kwitel.

second Nuremberg military tribunal. This document established a set of principles essential to the conduct of ethical research with human subjects. The first principle in the Nuremberg Code (1949–1953) unequivocally stated that research participants must give voluntary, informed consent. The Code also specified that researchers must be appropriately skilled and that designs must be scientifically appropriate, and it outlined the process of weighing risks and benefits involved in the research.

In 1964, the World Health Organization saw a need to clarify and expand the protections established in the Nuremberg Code. The result was the Declaration of Helsinki (1964), which placed substantial emphasis on the need for fully informing research participants of the "aims, methods, anticipated benefits and potential hazards of the study and the discomfort it may entail." Furthermore, it emphasized the voluntary nature of research participation and the need for consent by an individual who is competent. The researcher was also cautioned that requesting research participation may place subtle pressure on the individual when that individual is in some way dependent on the investigator, for example, when the researcher is also the patient's primary care physician.

In the next few decades, scientific research increased, and federal funding for such research increased as well. By this time, many organizations (both governmental and professional) involved in research had voluntarily established ethical research review procedures based on the Nuremberg Code (NRC, 2003, p. 60). Despite such procedures, unethical and ethically troubling practices were apparently fairly commonplace, even in prestigious research institutions (Beecher, 1966). Concern over such practices prompted the U.S. Public Health Service to create a policy on human research participant protection in 1966 (NRC, 2003, p. 61).

Problems with the implementation of the 1966 policy and media coverage of several instances of abuses of participants in biomedical research led to the development of additional federal guidelines and regulations protecting human research participants (Department of Health, Education and Welfare [DHEW], 1973; Department of Health and Human Services [DHHS], 1981). Some of the abuses stemmed from the fact that individuals were either unaware that they were research subjects or were only partially informed about the experiment in which they were participating. The Jewish Chronic Disease Hospital and the Tuskegee syphilis experiments (Levine, 1981) were two of the most publicized abuse cases. The Tuskegee experiment, which began in 1932, was designed to determine the natural course of syphilis. More than 400 men were recruited without their informed consent and were left untreated even after it became clear in the 1940s that penicillin was an effective treatment for syphilis. It was not until 1972, when the facts of the study became known to the public, that the study was halted (Brandt, 1978; for a detailed review of this case, see Beecher, 1966; Katz, 1972; Brandt, 1978). In the Jewish Chronic Disease Hospital study, chronically ill patients were injected with live cancer cells without their permission.

Not all cases with a lack of consent were biomedical studies. Difficulties also came to light in the social sciences. Among the most well-known of these is the Tearoom Trade studies. The purpose of these studies (Humphreys, 1970) was to develop a sociological description of homosexual practices in public restrooms. To accomplish this, the investigator either disguised or misrepresented himself at various points in the study; thus, in addition to the lack of fully informed consent, these studies involved the use of deception.

To prevent ethically unsound research practices and to clarify and expand existing government policy on research with human subjects, DHEW (1973) created a "Yellow Book," shorthand for the "Institutional Guide to DHEW Policy on Protection of Human Subjects." This guide reaffirmed the need for voluntary informed consent and specified particulars related to informed consent (e.g., consent for secondary analysis of data; NRC, 2003, p. 62). In addition, professional organizations drafted ethical principles with special relevance to human experimentation. The American Psychological Association (1972) was a forerunner in this regard. Subsequently, Congress passed the National Research Act of 1974 (NRC, 2003), which established a national commission charged with investigating the Institutional Review Board (IRB) system and making recommendations for additional safeguards for human protections.

Perhaps the most important achievement of the commission was the creation and publication of the Belmont Report in 1979. The Belmont Report presented the philosophical basis for ethical treatment of individuals and outlined the three principles to be considered in conducting research: respect for persons, beneficence, and justice. This report has become the foundation for contemporary IRBs and human subject protections. Also at this time, in response to recommendations from the National Commission for the protection of Human Subjects of Biomedical and Behavioral Research, the federal policies concerning human research participants were revised again. In 1981, the policies became regulations (DHHS, 1981). These regulations defined in precise detail what informed consent entailed.

Government regulation of research has continued to grow, becoming more expansive and complex. In 1991, a common rule was developed by an interagency government task force to standardize protections for research conducted or regulated by 15 government departments or agencies (NCR, 2003). Most recently, in 2002, the Office for Human Research Protections (OHRP) was established and charged with oversight of IRBs as well as providing education and guidance on human research participant protection to both federal and nonfederal bodies and institutions (NRC, 2003, p. 76). The OHRP offers Web-based education on human research participant protection currently required at most institutions for those conducting or working on research projects (see http://www.nihtraining.com/ohsrsite/index.html). Establishment of the OHRP has resulted in increased attention to various aspects of research ethics and participant protections. With regard to informed consent, the issue of vulnerability of special populations is currently in the forefront of ethical debates and is addressed later in this chapter.

WHAT IS INFORMED CONSENT?

Although the informed consent doctrine has evolved over several decades and from a variety of sources, there is consensus on the three major elements of the doctrine: adequate disclosure of information, voluntariness, and competency (Meisel, Roth, & Lidz, 1977; Melton, Petrila, Poythress, & Slobogin, 1997; Roberts, 2002). Both case law developments and expanded federal regulations have resulted in increased scrutiny of treatment providers and researchers with regard to the presence and adequacy of informed consent procedures. While empirical studies have indicated that informed consent in the real world is often far from optimal, it is generally agreed that informed consent must be solicited for all treatments and research studies.

A signed consent form is written documentation that an informed consent to the proposed procedure has taken place; however, a signed form is not all that is involved in obtaining consent. A process takes place during which the caregiver or researcher provides (usually orally) the patient or subject with the information relevant to the treatment or research decision at hand; the individual weighs that information and reaches a decision based on an adequate understanding of the information. The consent form ideally serves the function of documenting that this process has taken place.

ADEQUATE DISCLOSURE

Patients require adequate information to determine which course of treatment to choose (Culver & Gert, 1982; Stanley & Stanley, 1981). The same need applies to the decision to participate in research. With regard to what is considered sufficient information, federal regulations indicate that the following should be included: (1) a statement that the study involves research and a description of the purposes, procedures, and duration of the research; (2) a description of the foreseeable risks and discomforts; (3) explanation of potential benefits to the participant; (4) available alternatives; (5) the extent of confidentiality; (6) the extent of compensation and treatment for injuries; (7) the name of an appropriate contact person in case questions or problems arise; and (8) a statement that participation is voluntary and that participants may withdraw at any time without penalty or loss of benefits to which they are otherwise entitled (NRC, 2003, p. 82; 45 CFR 46.116(a)). In the treatment setting, usually the first four items (i.e., purposes and procedures, risks, benefits, and alternatives) are thought to be the most important pieces of information.

Integral to this element of informed consent is the notion that the information should be provided in a way that is understandable to the patient. This means that consent documents should describe the study in simple, nontechnical language and that researchers must be available to answer questions as well as assess whether the individual comprehends the information presented adequately enough to make a reasoned decision. It has been noted, however, that such disclosure requirements are frequently unmet (Melton et al., 1997).

VOLUNTARINESS

The second element of informed consent is voluntariness. This requires that the individual be free from coercive influences and undue pressure in reaching the decision to participate in treatment or research (Meisel et al., 1977; Culver & Gert, 1982; Roberts, 2002). Research in this area suggests that this principle may be compromised by factors such as the power differential between professionals and patients, fear of having services withheld, and subtly coercive behavior on the part of professionals (Melton et al., 1997). Coercion exists on a continuum, from cajoling to forced treatment and explicit threats if the patient does not comply with the proposed procedure. Some suggest that coercion in psychiatry may be greater than in other fields of medicine because the psychiatrist has available the threat of involuntary hospitalization and treatment (Culver & Gert, 1982).

Suggestions have been made about ways to minimize coercion in arriving at treatment decisions (President's Commission, 1982). These include allowing a certain amount of time to elapse between the doctor-patient discussion and the patient's actual decision; giving patients the opportunity to temporarily remove themselves from the environment that may be exerting influence; and, for research, making available a professional not directly involved in the research project for patient consultation. Many IRBs ensure that such techniques are employed in the informed consent process.

COMPETENCY

The third element of informed consent, competency, is the most problematic. Competency is specific to a particular decision embedded in a unique context and rooted in a point in time. Thus, whereas someone might be competent to make a relatively simple decision with few alternatives, he or she might be incompetent to make a more complex decision. Similarly, competence may fluctuate over time.

It is often assumed that there is a consensually agreed to or legally defined means for determining competency to give consent. However, this is a misconception. Despite general agreement on the existence of various tests of competence, professionals often disagree with regard to which of these tests should be utilized and how much competence is sufficient to make an informed decision. This is further complicated by the fact that although there have been improvements in standardized instruments to assess competence, these have not been widely adopted in clinical use.

Although there is no universal standard for competence, most definitions include some combination of the following: ability to communicate a choice, ability to understand relevant information, ability to provide rational reasons for one's decision, ability to appreciate the situation and probable consequences associated with various options, and ability to manipulate relevant information in a rational manner (Appelbaum & Grisso, 1988). Many authors have advocated the use of a sliding scale for competence whereby decisions with little risk would require a lower threshold for competence, and important decisions such as participating in a clinical research study or refusing life-sustaining treatment would require a higher level of decision-making competence (Cassel, 1988; Fellows, 1998; Ryan, 1996).

Ryan (1996) has advocated for the use of a three-part competence classification system in which patients who meet minimum standards of understanding would be classified as "fully competent," those who fail to meet standards for competency but who are capable of expressing a choice consistent with their long-standing values would be classified as "partially competent," and those who lack even that capacity would be classified as "fully incompetent." However, others warn against using a lower threshold for cognitively impaired individuals regardless of the level of risk inherent in the decision, given the potential harm that might result (Rovosky, 1990).

Legal Standards of Competence

Legal standards of competence are most clearly differentiated by the level of protection they provide to the individual and can be arranged in a hierarchical order. The protection inherent in each test is inversely related to the degree of independence granted to the patient or research subject. In reviewing the standards, the level of protection that each test affords is discussed.

In 1977, Roth, Meisel, and Lidz outlined five basic functional tests of competency: (1) evidencing a choice, (2) factual comprehension, (3) rational reasoning, (4) appreciation of the nature of the situation, and (5) reasonable outcome of choice. The first four are widely accepted as constituting the construct of competence (Melton et al., 1997). Except for reasonable outcome of choice, these tests are ordered according to the level of protection they provide, ranging from the lowest to the highest level. The reasonable outcome test does not fit comfortably at any one point in the hierarchy. This test evaluates the individual's capacity to reach a reasonable result. The person who fails to make a decision that is roughly congruent with the decision that a reasonable person would have made is viewed as incompetent (Friedman, 1975).

This standard has been strongly criticized for its paternalistic orientation and, hence, lack of respect for the individual's rights. Any decision with which the reviewer disagreed might provide a basis for judging the individual incompetent. Its relevance to competency to consent to research can be problematic because research projects are, by their very nature, experimental. Thus, it is difficult to know what is reasonable. It has been suggested that this standard could be adapted in such a way as to tap "capacity to reach reasonable decisions" about treatment, independent of the decision at hand (Stanley & Stanley, 1981). This test is seldom used because of autonomy concerns.

Perhaps more appropriately, perceived unreasonableness often functions as a trigger for a competence assessment using some or all of the following widely used tests. Although these standards are presented separately here, they are not necessarily mutually exclusive, and two or more of the tests are often combined during a single assessment. The first four tests of competence identified by Roth, Meisel, and Lidz (1977) are as follows:

1. *Evidencing a choice:* This test focuses only on the presence or absence of a decision: If a person makes a decision, he or she is judged competent. This test is the least protective of the individual because assessment is minimal. Actually, this test is rarely used. It has been criticized on the grounds that the decision does not assure that the individual has a good understanding of the

proposed treatment or experiment. However, in this regard, it has been argued that evaluation of the person's rationality and ability to comprehend is inappropriate in a competency test because it is too paternalistic.

In assessing competency for research participation according to this standard, the relevant information is simply presented to the prospective participant, and he or she either agrees or declines to become a subject. No effort is made to determine whether the information was understood or if rational reasoning was employed to reach the decision. The yes or no response by the individual is taken as enough to determine competency. Despite some arguments in favor of this test, it is generally agreed that the standard is too lenient.

2. *Factual comprehension:* This test requires that the individual understand the information relevant to the proposed treatment or research (e.g., the procedures, risks, benefits, and alternatives available). This standard does not take into account how reasonable the decision is or how rational the thought processes were in arriving at the decision. As a result, it is fairly respectful of the individual's independence. Probably the most commonly used standard, degree of understanding has been measured in most empirical studies of competency and informed consent (Bergler, Pennington, Metcalfe, & Freis, 1980; Cassileth, Zupkis, Sutton-Smith, & March, 1980). Despite its widespread acceptance, however, it presents a major difficulty in that it relies heavily on the individual's verbal skills, particularly verbal expression. As a result, there is a potential for a biasing of competency findings against the less verbally skilled. Some studies have shown that comprehension of consent information increases with the subject's intelligence (Stanley & Stanley, 1981). While this is not surprising, the policy implications are striking; individuals with lower IQs are less likely to be judged competent and thereby are subject to exclusion from research.

Comprehension can be subdivided into understanding of the consent information at the moment of consent and retention of that information over a period of time. Retention, however, has been justifiably criticized as an invalid criterion (Stanley & Stanley, 1981). Although it is important that a research subject remember that he or she can withdraw from an experiment, it may be completely unnecessary that he or she keep all the consent information in mind several weeks or months after the initial decision. The fact that an individual forgets information following a decision does not mean that he or she did not use that information in making the decision.

3. *Rational reasoning:* Under this standard, competency is defined as the capacity to understand the nature of the procedure, to weigh the risks and benefits, and to reach a decision for rational reasons (Friedman, 1975; Roth et al., 1977). This test focuses on the overall pattern of thought rather than on the particular result of the decision. It asks whether the individual has used a rational or logical decision-making process. It offers a high degree of protection to the subjects, but its application may express a bias toward a particular type of reasoning. In comparison with other competency tests, it is fairly paternalistic. Some authors have suggested that the rationality of the individual's entire reasoning process be assessed under this standard (Appelbaum & Roth, 1982);

others have recommended that assessment be tied more directly to the decision to participate in the research (Friedman, 1975; Stanley & Stanley, 1981) or undergo the treatment. The former would be tested with a typical mental status examination designed to elicit the presence of severe impairment in judgment, thought disorder, hallucinations, and delusions. Actual judgment in daily life activities may also be assessed. The major problem with this sort of generalized testing is that we cannot be certain that when judgment is impaired in relation to some decisions it is also impaired with respect to decisions in an unrelated area of functioning.

This brings us to the second form of rationality assessment: rationality with respect to the decision. In this instance, the individual's reasoning about his or her decision is directly elicited. The doctor or researcher must assess whether the patient's or subject's reasons make sense. The problem with this test is that the assessor's view of what is rational often becomes the standard rather than some objective determinant of rationality.

4. *Appreciation of the nature of the situation:* This standard of competency to give consent is closely aligned to the type of assessment that is performed when determining whether an individual was responsible for a criminal act. When applied to competency to give consent, subjects are tested to determine whether they appreciate their situation (Appelbaum & Roth, 1982). Do they understand the consequences of consenting or not consenting? Do they understand what information is relevant to the decision and what is not? Under this standard, comprehension of the consent information is a prerequisite, with the additional requirement that the individual must be able to use that information in a rational manner. This test is highly protectionistic in that the demands placed on the subject are stringent. For example, it is not sufficient that a potential subject understand the risks, benefits, and alternatives to the research; he or she must also "appreciate" the implications of acceptance or refusal. This involves the ability not only to appreciate alternatives, but to manipulate and weigh options as they apply to a person's unique context. Even "nonvulnerable" populations have a difficult time appreciating that fact (McCullum & Schwartz, 1969).

INSTRUMENTS TO ASSESS COMPETENCE

For many years, the sole instrument used in the assessment of decision-making capacity was the Mini-Mental State Examination (MMSE; Folstein, Folstein, & McHugh, 1975). Originally developed as a brief screening measure for cognitive impairment, the MMSE taps orientation, memory, and concentration but provides no formal assessment of reasoning abilities or decision-making capacity. Further, studies have found no relationship between MMSE scores and measures of decision-making ability (Barton, Mallik, & Orr, 1996; Etchells et al., 1997; Janofsky, McCarthy, & Folstein, 1992).

Similar criticisms apply to the two measures developed by Tobacyk, Dixon, and Dixon (1983) that were specifically designed to aid in screening for impaired decision-making capacity in the elderly. Their measures were based on the hypothesis that decision-making capacity reflected a single, unitary construct and did not need to be tailored to treatment decisions per se. Hence, they constructed two rating scales, one to measure orientation and short-term recall (e.g., "What day of the week is it today?") and a second to measure functional behaviors (e.g., "Follows current events"). They found that scores on this measure were significantly associated with clinical ratings of impairment as well as with performance on several neuropsychological tests.

As a result of these shortcomings and the growing awareness that competence determinations must be specific to a particular decision situation (rather than a global assessment of cognitive functioning), a number of researchers have developed more specialized instruments designed to more accurately quantify decision-making capacity with respect to treatment decisions (Appelbaum & Grisso, 1998; Janofsky et al., 1992; Joffe, Cook, Cleary, Clark, & Weeks, 2001; Marson, Ingram, Cody, et al., 1995a; Miller, O'Donnell, Searight, et al., 1996).

The first such instrument developed, the Hopkins Competency Assessment Test (HCAT), was designed to assess patient capacity to provide informed consent to treatment and advance directives (Janofsky et al., 1992). The HCAT requires patients to read or listen to a short essay describing informed consent and durable power of attorney and then answer six questions about the information provided (e.g., "What are the four things a doctor must tell a patient before beginning a procedure?"). The HCAT typically requires only 10 minutes to complete and, in preliminary research, has demonstrated a high degree of accuracy in distinguishing competent and incompetent individuals. Janofsky and colleagues found that a cutoff score of 4 (out of 10 possible points) correctly classified all of the research subjects in their pilot study (compared to decisions reached by an experienced clinician blind to the subjects' performance on the HCAT).

Despite these seemingly strong findings, this measure has not been widely accepted by either clinicians or researchers. One possible reason for this lack of popularity is the general nature of information disclosed and assessed by the HCAT. Patients are provided with only general information regarding the nature of informed consent and durable power of attorney rather than specific information about particular medical decisions they may be facing. Thus, the HCAT may overestimate the ability of some patients to fully appreciate the implications of various treatment options, particularly if they have limited abstract reasoning abilities or the decisions in question are particularly complex. On the other hand, the HCAT may underestimate the decision-making capacity of individuals with impaired short-term recall, who might be capable of making adequate decisions with the use of memory aids or carefully presented material but who nevertheless perform poorly on a standardized test of recall.

Grisso and Appelbaum (1995, 1998) addressed many of these concerns in the development of the MacArthur Competence Assessment Tool, Treatment (MacCAT-T). Unlike the HCAT, the MacCAT-T assesses decision making for a particular decision rather than general informed consent issues. The MacCAT-T is administered in a semistructured interview that is tailored to the specific decision the patient faces, allowing the instrument to be used for an unlimited range of decisions.

Because the MacCAT-T is rooted in Grisso and Appelbaum's (1995) theoretical conceptualization of competence, the authors allowed for the possibility that deficits in one domain of decision-making capacity may lead one to consider a patient incompetent even if other domains of cognitive functioning are intact. Hence, rather than generating a total score, the MacCAT-T yields separate ratings for each of four aspects of decision making: ability to express a choice, ability to understand treatment-related information, appreciation of the significance of the information for the patient's particular situation, and ability to rationally compare alternatives in light of their relative consequences.

The authors recommend that information about each domain of decision making be considered in conjunction with clinical and background data in order to determine a patient's decision-making capacity. Research with the MacCAT-T has demonstrated a high degree of reliability as well as strong validity data (e.g., a high degree of consistency with expert opinions regarding decision-making capacity, some of which are described later). Because of these features, the MacCAT-T has rapidly gained popularity among both clinicians and researchers for use in a wide range of clinical and research settings.

Another measure of decision making, developed by Marson and his colleagues, the Capacity to Consent to Treatment Instrument (CCTI), was specifically designed to assess decision-making capacity in older adults (Marson, Ingram, Cody, et al., 1995a, 1995b). The instrument utilizes two hypothetical vignettes, one related to neoplasm (i.e., cancer) and the second describing cardiac problems, to rate patients on five different legal standards considered to reflect an ascending level of difficulty. The five standards assessed by the CCTI are ability to make a treatment choice, ability to make a reasonable choice, appreciating the consequences involved with various choices, ability to provide rational reasons for choosing a particular decision, and the capacity to understand the treatment situation and choices. This last standard requires synthesis of treatment information as well as a fairly sophisticated, contextualized understanding of each treatment choice.

The authors have published a number of studies comparing the performance of cognitively intact older individuals with demented patients on this measure and correlating performance on the CCTI with various neuropsychological measures. Although the authors have observed a high degree of reliability and validity with this measure, the CCTI has not been adopted by clinicians or used by other researchers interested in the study of decision-making capacity, perhaps because it is less widely known and is not commercially available (unlike the MacArthur instruments, which are sold by several psychological test publishers).

Recently, a number of other measures have been developed to assess competence to consent to clinical research, including a version of the MacArthur Competence Assessment Tool (the MacCAT-CR; Applebaum & Grisso, 2001). This measure utilizes the same model as the MacCAT-T, enabling the investigator to customize the information disclosed to fit the study characteristics. Other research groups have offered their own such instruments, but like the

HCAT and CCTI, these measures have not been made commercially available and to date have been utilized only by the scale authors (Joffe et al., 2001; Miller et al., 1996).

INFORMED CONSENT, CONFIDENTIALITY, AND PSYCHOTHERAPY

While professional codes (e.g., Committee on Scientific and Professional Ethics and Conduct, 1984) stress the importance of informed consent with a clear delineation of the limits of confidentiality, it is unclear how often the doctrine of informed consent is followed in psychotherapeutic practice. The emphasis on achieving change in psychotherapy can come at the expense of respecting an individual's autonomy and privacy needs.

The ethical guidelines from the American Psychological Association (APA; 2002) mandate full informed consent to treatment. This becomes particularly important in the era of empirically supported or evidence-based treatments. If a client with Panic Disorder approaches a clinician, informed consent to treatment may include information about the fact that behavioral therapies have demonstrated effectiveness and relatively quick changes in the treatment of panic. It is unclear to what extent fully informed consent such as this occurs in the community.

Most discussion of informed consent to psychotherapy has centered on the bounds of confidentiality in therapy. This discussion arose in large part as the aftermath to the *Tarasoff* decision (Noll, 1976). In *Tarasoff v. Regents of University of California,* the court held that if a patient expresses a death threat toward a third party, it is the responsibility of the therapist to inform, in some way, that third party of the threat. Later cases have both modified and diverged from the *Tarasoff* decision. In *Thompson v. Alameda* (1980) it was decided that the need to notify held only when there was an identifiable victim. However, other cases have broadened the identifiable clause (*Davis v. Lhim,* 1983).

Whether *Tarasoff* is interpreted broadly or narrowly, it has made an impact on informed consent in psychotherapy. Noll (1976) has stated that the *Tarasoff* decision imposes a social control role on psychotherapists. In another article, he suggests that psychotherapists ought to disclose to prospective patients the "material risks" of psychotherapy (No. 11, 1981). These risks include:

- Informing employers (present or potential) or insurers that psychiatric treatment may lead to a negative outcome such as loss of a job or denial of insurance.
- Using a third-party payer could lead to the information being recorded in a centralized computer bank (i.e., Medical Information Bureau) and thus become available to other insurers.
- Responding affirmatively to questions on insurance or application forms regarding previous psychotherapy can lead to further questioning by prospective employers or insurers.

- The information revealed by the patient may lead to his or her hospitalization (either voluntary or involuntary) or to disclosure to the potential victims of violence.
- Records maintained by the therapist may not be completely inaccessible to others. Access can be gained either by robbery or subpoena.

In addition to informing patients of the material risks posed by psychotherapy, the APA's (2002) ethical guidelines require that psychologists inform patients about the nature and anticipated course of therapy, fees, involvement of third parties (including supervisors and consultants), and the limits of confidentiality. This information needs to be presented in a manner that is easily understood. In addition, the potential patient must have the opportunity to ask questions and receive answers.

The issue of informed consent is particularly problematic in the criminal justice system. In the forensic setting, the issue of informed consent has several dimensions.

There is a complicated body of case law dealing with the ability of patients to refuse to accept treatment and conditions under which they can and cannot be forced to accept treatment over their objections (see Perlin, 1994). Thus, in certain circumstances, clinicians in forensic settings may be expected to treat clients over their objections pursuant to court orders. Individuals in forensic settings may choose not to comply with court-ordered treatment; however, consequences will ensue (e.g., revocation of probation, forced administration of medication). In such cases, some version of informed consent still needs to take place whereby consequences of refusal to cooperate are discussed in a nonthreatening way (Clingempeel, Mulvey, & Reppucci, 1980).

The second dimension of informed consent concerns the limits of confidentiality in forensic settings. For example, to what extent should patients be informed if the information obtained in therapy sessions is to be used in parole decisions, decisions about privileges, or the like? Monahan (1980) has framed this issue in terms of the mixed loyalties of the therapist, which may not be amenable to simple solutions. In general, informed consent for treatment or assessment in forensic settings includes a statement to the effect that anything the client says may be documented and thus has potential to affect the client's case or prospects for discharge.

More recently, the Health Insurance Portability and Accountability Act was enacted and required implementation by October 2003 (Office for Civil Rights, 1996) by the federal government. This act applies to both the treatment and research settings. It is a complex rule that describes the disclosure of limits of confidentiality and the procedures for protecting privacy of patients particularly with respect to electronic transmission and records.

EMPIRICAL RESEARCH

Over the past 50 years, interest in informed consent in medical treatment and research has burgeoned. Evidence of this growing concern is the large number of published articles on consent during this period. Woodward (1979) reports that the number of articles about human experimentation and informed consent increased sixfold after 1960, as contrasted with the 20-year period prior to 1960. Kaufmann (1983), in a review of articles relative to informed consent, found that medical journals published far more articles on informed consent than did either law or social science journals. In addition, she found that the social sciences lagged behind the other disciplines in both the point at which it began to study informed consent and the quantity of articles it produced.

A review of the published articles on the consent process shows that the majority of early publications were opinion or position papers (Burra, Kimberley, & Miura, 1980; Culver, Ferrell, & Green, 1980; Loftus & Fries, 1979; Vaccarino, 1978). They serve to clarify the issues (Gray, 1978) involved in obtaining consent and aid in the development of a uniform doctrine. The opinions expressed in these articles ran the gamut from the view that informed consent is the "absolute right" of the patient and is in no way detrimental to the goals of treatment and research (McLean, 1980; Park, Covi, & Uhlenhuth, 1967) to the opinion that informing the patient serves only to terrify him or her and cause undue anxiety, destroys the nature of the doctor-patient relationship, and may severely impede the progress of research (Coleman, 1974; Park, Slaughter, Cori, & Kniffin, 1966). Some authors suggest that truly informed consent is a myth (Leeb, Bowers, & Lynch, 1976), a fiction, or an illusion (Goin, Burgoyne, & Goin, 1976; Hirsch, 1977; Laforet, 1976). Others believe that a reasonable consent can be obtained (Alfidi, 1971).

This diversity of opinion is also expressed with respect to obtaining consent from patients whose competence is suspect, as in the case of severely disturbed psychiatric patients. Some view the presence of mental illness as limiting the possibility of obtaining a competent consent (Pryce, 1978). Others believe consent can be meaningfully obtained from many patients afflicted with psychiatric illness.

While opinion plays an important role in identifying and clarifying the issues, it is rather disappointing that many position papers that address ability to give consent do so without an empirical base substantiating their views. The questions surrounding informed consent remain in need of empirical investigation (Stanley & Stanley, 1981), and the social sciences could make contributions in this direction.

The available empirical research on consent falls into four major areas: (1) disclosure and comprehension of consent information, (2) individuals' subjective reactions to consent information, (3) methods of decision making in the consent process, and (4) competence of the patient or research participant to give consent. Competence is closely related to comprehension, but, for purposes of this chapter, studies that address populations of questionable competence are reviewed separately. Furthermore, studies that investigate consent to treatment are reviewed along with those that examine consent to research.

COMPREHENSION AND DISCLOSURE

Early studies focused primarily on comprehension of consent information by patients. Medical patients are the most frequently investigated. More than 20 studies have assessed understanding of consent information by patients (cf. Appelbaum & Grisso, 1997; Bergler et al., 1980; Cassileth et al., 1980; Hasser &

Weintraub, 1976; Kennedy & Lillehaugen, 1979; Marini, Sheard, & Bridges, 1976; Penman et al., 1980; Robinson & Merav, 1976; Schultz, Pardee, & Ensinck, 1975; Singer, 1978). The prototype of these studies is as follows. Individuals are given a consent form for either a research protocol or standard treatment, and the form is usually read to them by a physician or investigator. They are then asked questions regarding their knowledge of the consent information. The point in time that they are asked these questions varies from immediately afterward to several months later. In the latter case, the study becomes one of testing recall instead of comprehension.

Although it is difficult to make comparisons across studies due to their different methodologies, it is generally concluded that comprehension of consent information—irrespective of assessment time—is poor. Overall comprehension ranges from approximately 35% to 80% of the total information conveyed. Patients tend to be best informed about their diagnosis and the proposed treatment (e.g., the name of the drug they were to take) and least knowledgeable about alternative treatments available and risks, including side effects of drugs and possible complications of surgical procedures. In addition, some studies of research subjects demonstrate that many were not aware or did not acknowledge that they were, in fact, participating in a research study (McCullum & Schwartz, 1969; Park, Slaughter, Cori, & Kniffin, 1966).

While results of these studies are, at first glance, discouraging about the prospects of obtaining a fully informed consent, most of the studies have limitations that make it difficult to consider them conclusive (Meisel & Roth, 1981). First, in several studies, it is not clear exactly what information was conveyed to the patients (Cassileth et al., 1980; Goin et al., 1976; Priluck, Robertson, & Buettner, 1979). Second, because some studies gave patients the consent form to read and then tested knowledge of this form, it is not known whether all patients actually read the form (Olin & Olin, 1975). In this same vein, the amount of instruction given to patients varied from study to study. In some, instruction was minimal, with no particular effort made to convey the consent information (Benson, Gordon, Mitchell, & Place, 1977). In other studies, investigators went through a good deal of instruction with patients (Faden & Beauchamp, 1980).

Across studies, in general, greater instruction appears to be associated with greater understanding. This conclusion must be tentative, however, as most studies investigated only one level of instruction (e.g., consent form, videotape aids), and differences among sample characteristics and medical procedures for which consent was to be obtained vary greatly (Arluke, 1980; Muss et al., 1979; Stuart, 1978).

Another factor that makes it difficult to draw generalizable conclusions is that in many of the studies we do not know the level of complexity of the language of the consent form that was related in the consent session. Grundner (1980) and Morrow (1980) suggest that most consent forms are written in highly technical language. This may account for some of the poor comprehension attained in the empirical studies. However, this is a speculation because most studies do not report the readability of their consent material.

Epstein and Lasagna (1969) conducted one of the only studies that systematically varied complexity of consent material. They presented three different consent forms of varying length to normal volunteers. They found that comprehension was inversely related to the length of the consent form. Therefore, greater comprehension may be achieved by increasing instruction and decreasing the complexity of material. As simple a technique as giving the patient a consent form to take home prior to signing it increases knowledge (Morrow, Gootnick, & Schmale, 1978). Also suggested are bifurcated consent forms, objective tests, and videotape aids (Barbour & Blumenkrantz, 1978; Grabowski & Mintz, 1979; Schwartz, 1978; Silberstein, 1974; Stuart, 1978; Williams et al., 1977).

Other studies have investigated the modality of disclosure (i.e., how the information is conveyed to the patient) to determine if comprehension systematically varies according to type of presentation: written information, videotape, discussion groups (Faden, 1977; Faden & Beauchamp, 1980). These initial studies show that modality does not seem to make a difference in level of comprehension.

Comparing studies of comprehension of consent information is further complicated when the methods for assessing comprehension are examined. Some investigators use multiple-choice or true-false tests as a means of assessment; others use open-ended questions with coded responses. Relevant literature on learning and psychological testing has shown that tests of recognition, such as multiple-choice tests, are easier than tests of recall using open-ended questions. Therefore, comparing results of studies that use open-ended questions with objective questions is problematic.

A further difficulty in comparing these studies lies in the fact that immediate understanding and recall at some later point in time are often treated interchangeably. Not surprisingly, however, results show that retention of information declines over time. The utility of assessing retention of all consent information must be questioned. Certainly, it is important that research subjects remember that they have the freedom to withdraw from an experiment, but it may not be necessary that they keep all the consent information in mind several weeks or months after the initial decision. Further, the fact that an individual forgets information does not mean that it was not used at the time of the decision and then forgotten as part of the normal forgetting process.

It must be noted that in the studies reviewed here, most of the investigators assumed that knowledge of the consent information as measured by some form of objective test is equated with comprehension of that information. However, individuals' ability to repeat what they have been told does not necessarily mean they understand that information. In other words, knowledge is a necessary but not sufficient condition for understanding. A novel approach such as that taken by Mellinger, Huffine, and Balter (1980) seems to be called for. They developed an assessment of comprehension that includes an objective test requiring subjects to make judgments about a series of statements in addition to a standard evaluation of comprehension. Illogical judgments indicate a lack of comprehension.

Finally, the sample characteristics of the patients or subjects must be taken into account when examining comprehension. Many of the studies examined understanding of consent information by medical patients who have serious illnesses; others looked at the less seriously ill; and some examined normal volunteers (i.e., those without medical illness). Further, hospitalized and non-hospitalized patients have been studied. Comparability of these subject groups cannot be assumed. The ill patient is under more emotional stress than the healthy volunteer, and this stress may interfere with comprehension of consent information. Further, differences may be found between the hospital-ized and nonhospitalized patients; some research suggests that hospitaliza-tion itself makes an individual feel more vulnerable, and this in turn may influence comprehension of consent information. Cassileth and associates (1980) found that ambulatory patients demonstrated greater comprehension of consent information for cancer treatment than those who were bedridden. Perhaps bedridden patients were preoccupied with more serious illness. Fur-ther, educational level and intelligence have shown some relationship with comprehension of consent information (Cassileth et al., 1980), although this is not a consistent finding.

Overall, the comprehension level of consent information is poor. However, instructional aids seem to increase comprehension. In general, conclusions from these studies of comprehension must be drawn with caution because of their limitations.

DECISION MAKING

Several studies have investigated factors that influence patient decision mak-ing in the consent process. Some studies have shown that people feel that they have no choice and must participate (McCullum & Schwartz, 1969). Other studies do not find this; their primary focus has been to determine whether disclosure of risks discourages patients and research subjects from giving con-sent (Alfidi, 1971; Lankton, Batchelder, & Ominslay, 1977).

In a study of risk disclosure for anesthesia, patients did not refuse the pro-cedure following detailed information about the risks (Lankton et al., 1977). Similarly, in two studies, only a few patients refused angiography following detailed risk disclosure (Alfidi, 1971). Perhaps the best-known study in this area was conducted on kidney donors (Fellner & Marshall, 1970). This study was designed to determine whether kidney donors utilized risk information in their decision to donate a kidney. It was found that decisions were made long before any detailed risk disclosure and that disclosure had little impact on the donors. However, other research (Stanley, Stanley, Schwartz, Lautin, & Kane, 1980; Stanley, Stanley, Lautin, Kane, & Schwartz, 1981) has shown that participation in hypothetical research projects varies according to the risk of the project.

A few studies have attempted to relate comprehension of consent informa-tion to decision making (Epstein & Lasagna, 1969; Stuart, 1978). Findings seem to indicate that higher levels of comprehension are associated with a higher rate of agreement to the proposed procedure by the patient. However, interpre-tation of these findings is problematic because the risk-benefit ratios of the procedures must be known in order to determine whether the patients' affir-mative decisions were sensible.

As an outgrowth of the studies showing that risk disclosure does not seem to influence decision making with regard to medical procedures, some investigators have begun to identify factors that do influence decisions. In a study of participation in psychology experiments (Geller & Faden, 1979), the relative influence of standard consent information versus personal testimony of one individual was examined. Whereas recall of consent information was affected by personal testimonials that contradicted information presented in the informed consent process, the decision to participate was not affected. In another study, subjects reported that disclosed information was not the primary determinant in decisions regarding contraception. Instead, personal feelings about the study were reported to have a greater influence on the decision (Faden & Beauchamp, 1980).

COMPETENCY

Research on competency has burgeoned in the past 20 years despite the fact that there are major difficulties inherent in researching this topic: There is no standard definition of competence (Meisel et al., 1977; Roth et al., 1977), no accepted test of competency (Appelbaum & Bateman, 1979; Appelbaum, Mirkin, & Bateman, 1981; Dabrowski, Gerald, Walczak, Wororiowicz, & Zakowska-Dabrowski, 1978), and no clear agreement on the appropriate dividing line between competence and incompetence. Often, data that one investigator believes signify competence (Woodward, 1979), another believes indicate incompetence (Bergler et al., 1980). Further, agreement is lacking on which groups of patients should be suspect as having "uncertain competence." Mentally ill patients have been identified as one such group and there have been several empirical studies on competency focused on the mentally ill. However, other populations may also fall into this category of "questionable competence." These groups are the elderly, children, the mentally retarded, and those patients with dementia or other cognitive impairments.

Mentally Ill Individuals

The empirical evidence available with respect to the mentally ill presents a somewhat mixed picture. Under the rubric of mentally ill are primarily schizophrenic and psychotically depressed patients. One conclusion that can be safely drawn with respect to the mentally ill is that they certainly do no better than medical patients in the consent process. The evidence that they are less able to give consent is somewhat equivocal and to a certain extent depends on the definition of competency that is used.

With respect to comprehension of consent information, a few studies have assessed psychiatric patients' ability to understand consent information (Appelbaum et al., 1981; Grossman & Summers, 1980; Soskis & Jaffe, 1979; Roth et al., 1982). In general, these patients do not have a very high level of understanding of consent information. However, when comparing studies of medical patients' comprehension with studies of psychiatric patients' comprehension, understanding in both groups seems to be fairly equal (Grossman & Summers, 1980; Soskis & Jaffe, 1979). An example of this is seen in a study that found that schizophrenic patients understood about 50% of the material on a consent form that was read to them (Grossman & Summers, 1980). In a direct comparison of psychiatric and medical patients, it was found that schizophrenic patients were more aware of the risks and side effects of their medication than were medical patients (Soskis, 1978).

On the other hand, medical patients were better informed about the name and dosage of their medication as well as their diagnosis. The poor knowledge of diagnosis by psychiatric patients may be partly the result of a general reluctance by hospital staff to tell patients that they have, for instance, schizophrenia.

Related to the comprehension level of psychiatric patients are studies that examined the literacy skills of these patients. Despite the fact that psychiatric patients' comprehension of consent information seems to be equal to that of medical patients, research indicates that their reading comprehension scores were only at the 5th-grade level (Berg & Hammit, 1980; Coles, Roth, & Pollack, 1978). As a result, Berg and Hammit (1980) suggested that hospital documents be simplified for psychiatric patients, as others have suggested for medical patients.

In studies of psychiatric patients' ability to consent to hospitalization, the results indicate that level of knowledge of patient rights is relatively poor (Applebaum et al., 1981; Palmer & Wohl, 1972). However, it is important to determine whether medical patients would score higher than psychiatric patients, and also to separate patients' inabilities from deficient information giving on the part of the hospital admissions service. In contrast to the studies concluding that psychiatric patients may not be competent to give consent, one study concludes that 93% of the patients gave a valid consent (Dabrowski et al., 1978). However, the standard for competency was set much lower than the standard in other studies described here.

In a study of consent to electroconvulsive therapy (Roth et al., 1982), about 25% of the patients were found to be incompetent based on their understanding of consent information and independent judges' opinions about their comprehension. This study is the first to take a comprehensive approach by coordinating objective information (i.e., patient comprehension) with legal judgments and psychiatric opinions and seems to be a fruitful direction for further research.

A few studies of psychiatric patients have examined the relationship between understanding and the decision to consent to or refuse the proposed procedure (Grossman & Summers, 1980; Roth et al., 1982). These studies found that, like medical patients, psychiatric patients who understood more of the consent information tended to agree to the procedure more often. Several studies found that depression may influence such decision making (Lockwood, Alexopoulos, & van Gorp, 2002; M. D. Sullivan & Youngner, 1994; Ganzini, Lee, Heintz, Bloom, & Fenn, 1994). For instance, Ganzini and colleagues found that patients who refused life-saving measures while depressed changed their preferences after their depression was treated and remitted. Personality disorders, in particular, Borderline Personality Disorder, have also been raised as an impediment to competent decision making (Ganzini, Lee, & Heintz, 1994; Gutheil & Bursztajn, 1986). Such individuals frequently change their minds in response to vacillating emotional states.

Overall, the empirical research on informed consent shows that psychiatric patients do have some impairment in their abilities. However, research also shows that in some respects, they do not differ from medical patients. As a result, further studies involving comparison groups, particularly medical patients, are vital if conclusions are to be drawn about any one group of patients. In addition, it is also important to state precisely the standards used for determining competency so that comparisons can be more readily made from study to study. Conclusions such as only a quarter of the patients could give true consent (Pryce, 1978) are helpful only if the criteria for true consent are disclosed.

More recent research supports the notion that, given appropriate procedures for the consent process (Roberts, Warner, et al., 2002, 2003), most individuals with psychiatric disorders have the capacity to consent to research (Moser, Schultz, et al., 2002). Further, research has shown that individuals with psychiatric disorders often get satisfaction out of participation in research, believe that psychiatric research is important, and believe that such studies ought to be conducted (Roberts, Warner, & Brody, 2000).

Children and Adolescents

Experts have argued that research with children and adolescents requires additional protections because they may not have the legal right to consent, they may be cognitively less sophisticated than adults, and they may have less perceived or actual power to refuse to participate in social science experiments (Fisher, Hoagwood, et al., 2002). Usually, both parental consent and the child's assent is required (APA, 2002). In cases where it would not be in the best interests of the child or adolescent to inform a parent, independent parties may be appointed to act as advocates (Fisher, Hoagwood, et al., 2002). However, the child's assent is still required. Assent procedures need to be appropriate to the child's age, comprehension skills, and maturity level.

Research has indicated that children as young as 9 years reached treatment decisions the same way adults do (Weithorn & Campbell, 1982), although they did not understand consent information as well as adults. By the age of 14, children do not appear to differ in competency from the adult population (Weithorn & Campbell, 1982). In a conceptual analysis of adolescents' competency to make informed birth control and pregnancy decisions, Carter and St. Lawrence (1985) suggest that adolescents generally have the cognitive capacities necessary to make competent decisions. Currently, much research on informed consent with children and adolescents is focused on investigating enhancements to the informed consent process designed to maximize comprehension and adequate decision making (e.g., Bruzzese & Fisher, 2003).

Individuals with Developmental Disabilities

Research relating to the capacity of mentally retarded individuals to consent to research is similar to the body of research relating to children and informed consent. To a large extent, the particular abilities of the individual dictate his or her ability to provide informed consent. It has been argued, however, that individual decisional capacities interact with the consent context and that modifications to consent procedures or context may affect the individual's abilities to provide meaningful informed consent (Fisher, 2003a, 2003b). Thus, future research should continue to focus on the types of enhancements that will protect participants with mental retardation and developmental disabilities and allow their participation in research studies.

The Elderly

As the population of the United States has aged, research on decision making in the elderly has increased dramatically. With respect to the elderly, studies have shown some impairment in their ability to comprehend consent information (Stanley, Guido, Stanley, & Shortell, 1984). Impaired recall of consent information has been noted in those elderly who have poorer verbal skills. It appears that although comprehension and recall may be affected by age, the overall quality of decision making is not (Stanley, Guido, et al., 1984). In other words, the elderly typically reach similar decisions regarding agreement to proposed procedures in the same manner as their younger counterparts.

Taub and his colleagues have conducted the first systematic studies of the impact of aging on capacity to provide informed consent and exemplify the limitations of these early study methods (Taub, 1981; Taub, Baker, & Sturr, 1986; Taub, Kline, & Baker, 1981). In their first study, they compared 56 elderly adults recruited from a community center and 34 "housewives" in terms of their recall of information contained in an informed consent document that subjects had been asked to read and sign (Taub, 1981). Not surprisingly, both younger and older subjects made numerous errors when asked to recall the content of the consent form several weeks later, but the older sample made significantly more of these errors. Further, Taub found that less educated subjects and those with poorer verbal abilities made even more errors even after adjusting for age group. Similar findings emerged from their subsequent studies, with higher levels of verbal abilities and education predicting retention of consent information (Taub, Baker, & Sturr, 1986; Taub, Kline, & Baker, 1981). Reliance on simple tests of recall of information as the sole indicator of capacity to provide informed consent limits the relevance of these results for the assessment of competence. Further, this limitation is even more pronounced given the inconsequential nature of the study to which subjects had consented. Because the consent form that participants read and signed had so little personal importance, there is little reason to believe that even high-functioning, cognitively intact individuals would bother to remember this information (as evidenced by the numerous errors made by the younger samples).

Stanley and colleagues (1984) utilized a somewhat more sophisticated measure of decision making in their comparison of older and younger patients. They presented subjects with hypothetical consent information to assess patients' abilities to comprehend this information. In addition, they rated patients on the quality of their reasoning and on whether or not they made reasonable choices. Interestingly, although older subjects had significantly poorer comprehension of the information presented, there was no difference between older and younger patients with regard to the selection of reasonable choices. The researchers also noted that some subgroups, such as elderly patients with Alzheimer's disease, were at even greater risk for impaired decision making relative to cognitively intact elderly subjects.

Tymchuck and colleagues expanded on Stanley's model, using a series of hypothetical vignettes describing high- and low-risk procedures to assess decision making in a sample of elderly residents of a long-term care facility (Tymchuck, Ouslander, Rahbar, & Fitten, 1988). Decision-making abilities were based on subjects' comprehension of the information disclosed, as well as a 4-point rating of the quality of their reasoning. In addition, the vignettes were presented via three different methods: a standard disclosure, a simplified version, and through the use of a storybook. They found that presentation method significantly influenced subjects' comprehension of consent information, particularly as the complexity of the scenario increased (i.e., involving high-risk procedures). On the other hand, presentation format had relatively little influence on the quality of decisions made by this sample, suggesting that quality of reasoning may be separate from memory abilities.

Because many questions of decision-making capacity arise in the context of medical treatment decisions, it is perhaps only natural that researchers would question whether medical illness adversely impacts decision making beyond the effects of natural aging. One such study, conducted by Fitten and Waite (1990), compared 25 hospitalized elderly patients with a comparison group of community residents matched on age and education level. The authors utilized three hypothetical vignettes to assess decision-making capacity and found that the hospitalized patients evidenced significantly poorer understanding and reasoning than the community sample. On the basis of their measure, they concluded that 7 of the 25 hospitalized patients "had significant decisional impairments" that had not been detected by their physicians. Interestingly, they found no relationship between cognitive functioning (as assessed by the MMSE) and decision-making ability. Nevertheless, Fitten and Waite concluded that medically ill older persons are at increased risk for impaired decision-making capacity when hospitalized for an acute medical illness.

Dellasega, Frank, and Smyer (1996) also studied capacity to make medical treatment decisions in a sample of elderly hospitalized patients, but unfortunately they did not recruit a healthy elderly sample against whom to compare these patients. The authors administered several measures to these subjects, including an early version of the MacCAT-T (the Understanding of Treatment Disclosures or UTD), to assess decision-making abilities at two time points: shortly after admission and immediately prior to discharge. They found evidence of impairment in capacity to make decisions in many subjects and the impairments were consistent across time, although the assessment of decision making was primarily based on recall of disclosed information.

At both time points, their sample of elderly subjects performed markedly more poorly on the UTD than did the normative sample for the UTD (a sample of middle-aged angina patients). The authors noted that performance improved considerably when they used a simpler disclosure method (disclosing information in small segments and testing recall after each brief disclosure rather than after the entire disclosure had been presented). The authors suggested that similar procedural modifications, breaking up information into smaller segments, might be useful for improving informed consent in clinical practice with older patients.

Cognitively Impaired Individuals

The most recent surge in capacity-related research has focused on decision-making capacity in individuals with cognitive impairment, most of it involving patients diagnosed with dementia. The impact of dementia on decisional capacity can be profound, even in relatively mild cases of Alzheimer's Dementia (AD; Marson, Hawkins, McInturff, & Harrell, 1997; Stanley, Stanley, & Guido, 1988). Nevertheless, researchers have consistently found that some individuals with cognitive impairment due to AD are able to consistently express choices in response to questions about daily living, as well as choices about participation in hypothetical research scenarios (Feinberg & Whitlatch, 2001; Stanley, Stanley, Guido, & Garvin, 1988).

Stanley and colleagues conducted the first systematic study of decision-making capacity in elderly individuals with cognitive impairment, comparing 38 psychiatric patients with early- to moderate-stage Alzheimer's disease to 45 depressed elderly psychiatric patients and 20 elderly comparison subjects (Stanley, Stanley, & Guido, 1988). Decision-making capacity was assessed by reading to the subjects a description of a proposed drug treatment and rating them on their comprehension of the information and the quality of their reasoning (based on a 5-point scale, ranging from "no evidence of weighing or identification of risks and benefits" to "weighs both risks and benefits explicitly"). Interestingly, they found no group differences in quality of reasoning, and all three groups showed considerable limitations in their ability to weigh the risks and benefits of the proposed treatment. Understanding and retention of the information disclosed, on the other hand, differed significantly across the three groups, with the cognitively impaired subjects demonstrating significantly poorer comprehension than the other two groups. Further, depressed patients performed comparably to the healthy comparison subjects with respect to both comprehension and reasoning.

Marson, Ingram, Cody, and Harrell (1995a) evaluated a sample of 29 patients with probable Alzheimer's disease and compared these individuals to 15 elderly adults with no apparent cognitive impairment. Their measure of decision-making capacity (the CCTI) utilized two vignettes to assess decision making with regard to five different legal standards of competence (evidencing a choice, reasonableness of that choice, appreciation of the consequences of the decision, expressing rational reasons for the decision, and general understanding of treatment situation and choices). Further, they divided AD patients into those with mild impairment (based on an MMSE score of 20 or greater) and moderate impairment (MMSE score less than 20). Interestingly, no differences were found between any of the groups with regard to their ability to express a choice or make reasonable choices (as opposed to unreasonable alternatives). However, on the more difficult tests of competence (appreciation, rational reasons, understanding the situation), both mildly and moderately impaired AD patients demonstrated impaired decision-making capacity compared to the cognitively intact sample. Further, decision-making abilities appeared to deteriorate with dementia severity, as moderately impaired AD patients performed significantly worse than mildly impaired patients.

Although it is noteworthy that all but the most severely demented individuals retained some ability to express a reasonable choice, this finding is perhaps troublesome for clinicians faced with cognitively impaired patients as these individuals might express reasonable treatment preferences yet have relatively little genuine understanding of the basis for their decisions. Moreover, the finding that almost all of the AD patients, including those with relatively mild levels of impairment, demonstrated serious impairment in decision-making abilities, substantially hindering their ability to make medical treatment decisions, has important implications for the assessment of decision-making capacity in elderly patients with cognitive impairment.

In a subsequent study, Marson and colleagues (Marson, Chatterjee, Ingram, & Harrell, 1996) attempted to identify specific cognitive deficits that impaired decision-making ability in terms of the various legal conceptualizations of competence. They administered an extensive battery of neuropsychological tests assessing attention, expressive and receptive language abilities, short-term and delayed verbal memory, abstraction ability, social comprehension and judgment, executive functioning, and overall dementia level. When comparing performance on these neuropsychological tests to performance on the CCTI, Marson et al. found no specific cognitive functions that corresponded to impaired decision making among the healthy comparison sample (despite some variation in both decision-making and cognitive abilities). However, they found that deficits in abstraction ability and semantic knowledge were strongly associated with impairment in the ability to understand treatment situation and choices (the highest standard of decision-making competence in their model), and measures of executive functioning were strongly associated with ability to appreciate the decision situation. Based on the pattern of results they observed, Marson et al. posited that as AD progresses and severity of cognitive impairment increases, impaired decision making progresses from the highest legal standard to the lower standards (i.e., that patients fail successively easier tests of decision-making capacity as their impairment increases). Further, in a subsequent analysis, this research group concluded that deteriorating executive functioning appears to be the single most important aspect of cognitive functioning heralding impaired decision making (Marson, Annis, McInturff, Bartolucci, & Harrell, 1999).

More recently, Kim, Caine, Currier, Leibovici, and Ryan (2001) used Grisso and Appelbaum's MacCAT-CR to assess decision making in 37 patients with mild to moderate AD, comparing these patients to a sample of 15 elderly subjects with no identified cognitive impairment. Like Marson's studies, this group found significant impairments in decision-making ability even among patients with relatively mild levels of dementia. Roughly half of their sample obtained high scores on the MacCAT-CR Appreciation and Reasoning subscales (compared to virtually all of the elderly comparison subjects), indicating adequate decision-making abilities. Performance on the Understanding subscale, however, was considerably poorer, with only a handful of AD patients obtaining high scores on this measure (again, compared to virtually all the comparison subjects). Further, they reported high levels of classification accuracy when performance on the MacCAT-CR was compared to clinical ratings of incapacity, suggesting that this instrument might be a useful adjunct to the evaluation process. Nevertheless, they concluded that even with improved (i.e., structured and standardized) measures for assessing decision-making capacity, distinguishing competent from incompetent individuals remains a difficult task.

One problem arising in this area is the issue of how to conduct research on those unable to give consent. Ethical arguments about vulnerable populations often take place in the absence of research with and input from members of those populations. Constraints on participation may not reflect the population's wishes. For instance, research conducted on individuals in the last weeks of life found that participants reported direct benefits in the form of enjoying the activity of research interviews and obtaining satisfaction from contributing to society (Galietta & Pessin, 2002).

Novel consent procedures such as developing advanced informed consent (prior to cognitive deterioration) or using substituted consent may be options. However, there is much work to be done in this area. Legal and political realities make research with vulnerable populations, including cognitively impaired and terminally ill individuals, difficult. The remedies that have been proposed include discussions with stakeholders and additional research focused on values related to surrogate research as well as decision making and ways to preserve decisional abilities (Kim & Karlawish, 2003).

CONCLUSION

Informed consent to treatment and research has received considerable attention in the legal, ethics, and psychiatric literature over the past two decades. Much empirical research has been conducted, yet many issues remain partially unaddressed, such as development of well-validated and practical tools for evaluation of competency. Legal doctrine, federal and state regulations, and professional codes have defined the ideal in doctor-patient and researcher-participant communication with regard to consent procedures, but the clinical utility and practical reality of this ideal have been relatively unexplored.

REFERENCES

Alfidi, R. J. (1971). Informed consent: A study of patient reaction. *Journal of the American Medical Association, 216,* 1325–1329.

American Psychological Association. (1972). *Ethical principles in the conduct of research with human participants.* Washington, DC: Author.

American Psychological Association. (1982). *Ethical principles in the conduct of research with human participants.* Washington, DC: Author.

American Psychological Association. (2002). *Ethical principles of psychologists and code of conduct.* Available from http://www.apa.org/ethics/code2002.pdf.

Appelbaum, P. S., & Bateman, A. (1979). Competency to consent to voluntary psychiatric hospitalization: A theoretical approach. *Bulletin of the American Academy of Psychiatry and the Law, 7,* 390–399.

Applebaum, P. S., & Grisso, T. (1988). Assessing patients' capacities to consent to treatment. *New England Journal of Medicine, 319,* 315–336.

Appelbaum, P. S., & Grisso, T. (1997). Capacities of hospitalized, medically-ill patients to consent to treatment. *Psychosomatics, 38*(2), 119–125.

Appelbaum, P. S., & Grisso, T. (2001). *MacCAT-CR: MacArthur Competence Assessment Tool for Clinical Research.* Sarasota, FL: Professional Resource Press.

Appelbaum, P. S., Mirkin, S., & Bateman, A. (1981). Competency to consent to psychiatric hospitalization: An empirical assessment. *American Journal of Psychiatry, 138,* 170–176.

Appelbaum, P., & Roth, L. (1982). Competency to consent to research: A psychiatric overview. *Archives of General Psychiatry, 39,* 951–958.

Arluke, A. (1980). Judging drugs: Patients' conceptions of therapeutic efficacy in the treatment of arthritis. *Human Organization, 39*(1), 84–88.

Barbour, G. L., & Blumenkrantz, M. J. (1978). Videotape aids informed consent decisions. *Journal of the American Medical Association, 240,* 2741–2742.

Barton, C. D., Mallik, H. S., & Orr, W. B. (1996). Clinicians judgment of capacity of nursing home patients to give informed consent. *Psychiatric Services, 47*(9), 956–960.

Beecher, H. K. (1966). Ethics and clinical research. *New England Journal of Medicine, 274,* 1354–1360.

Benson, H., Gordon, L., Mitchell, C., & Place, V. (1977). Patient education and intrauterine conception: A study of two package inserts. *American Journal of Public Health, 67,* 446–449.

Berg, A., & Hammit, K. B. (1980). Assessing the psychiatric patient's ability to meet the literacy demands of hospitalization. *Hospital and Community Psychiatry, 31*(4), 266.

Bergler, J., Pennington, C., Metcalfe, M., & Freis, E. (1980). Informed consent: How much does the patient understand? *Clinical Pharmacology and Therapeutics, 27,* 435–439.

Brandt, A. M. (1978). Racism and research: The case of the Tuskegee syphilis study. *Hastings Center Report, 8*(6), 21–29.

Bruzzese, J., & Fisher, C. B. (2003). Assessing and enhancing the research consent capacity of children and youth. *Applied Developmental Science, 7,* 13–26.

Burra, P., Kimberley, R., & Miura, C. (1980). Mental competence and consent to treatment. *Canadian Journal of Psychiatry, 25,* 251–253.

Carter, P., & St. Lawrence, J. (1985). Adolescents' competency to make informed birth control and pregnancy decisions: An interface for psychology and the law. *Behavioral Sciences and the Law, 3,* 309–319.

Cassel, C. (1988). Ethical issues in the conduct of research in long-term care. *Gerontologist, 28*(3 Suppl.), 90–96.

Cassileth, B. R., Zupkis, R. B., Sutton-Smith, K., & March, V. (1980). Informed consent: Why are its goals imperfectly realized? *New England Journal of Medicine, 302*(16), 896–900.

Clingenpeel, W., Mulvey, E., & Reppucci, N. (1980). A national study of ethical dilemmas of psychologists in the criminal justice system. In J. Monahan (Ed.), *Who is the client?* Washington, DC: American Psychological Association.

Coleman, L. (1974). The patient-physician relationship: Terrified consent. *Physician's World, 607.*

Coles, G., Roth, L., & Pollack, I. (1978). Literacy skills of long-term hospitalized mental patients. *Hospital and Community Psychiatry, 29,* 512–516.

Committee on Scientific and Professional Ethics and Conduct. (1984, Spring). Policy statement on informed consent and supervision. *Clinical Psychologist, 67.*

Culver, C. M., Ferrell, R. B., & Green, R. M. (1980). ECT and special problems of informed consent. *American Journal of Psychiatry, 137,* 5.

Culver, C. M., & Gert, B. (1982). *Philosophy in medicine: Conceptual and ethical issues in medicine and psychiatry.* New York: Oxford Press.

Dabrowski, S., Gerald, K., Walczak, S., Woronowicz, B., & Zakowska-Dabrowski, T. (1978). Inability of patients to give valid consent to psychiatric hospitalization. *International Journal of Law and Psychiatry, 1*(4), 437–443.

Davis v. Lhim, 335 N.W. 2d 481 Michigan Ct. App. (1983.)

Declaration of Helsinki: Recommendations guiding medical doctors in biomedical research involving human subjects. Adopted by the 18th World Medical Assembly, Helsinki, Finland, 1964, and as revised by the 29th World Medical Assembly, Tokyo, 1975.

Dellasega, C., Frank, L., & Smyer, M. (1996). Medical decision-making capacity in elderly hospitalized patients. *Journal of Ethics on Law Aging, 2*(2), 65–74.

Department of Health, Education, and Welfare. (1973). National Institute of Health. *Protection of Human Subjects: Policies and Procedures, 38*(221), 31, 738–749.

Department of Health and Human Services. (1981). *Federal Register, 46*(16), 8366–8391.

Epstein, L., & Lasagna, L. (1969). Obtaining informed consent: Form or substance. *Archives of Internal Medicine, 123,* 682–685.

Etchells, E., Katz, M., Shuchman, M., Wong, G., Workman, S., Choudry, N., et al. (1997). Accuracy of clinical impressions and Mini-Mental-State Exam scores for assessing capacity to consent to major medical treatment: Comparison with criterion-standard psychiatric assessments. *Psychosomatics, 38*(3), 239–245.

Faden, R. (1977). Disclosure and informed-consent: Does it matter how we tell it? *Health Education Monographs, 5,* 198–214.

Faden, R., & Beauchamp, T. (1980). Decision-making and informed consent: A study of the impact of disclosed information. *Social Indicators Research, 7,* 13–36.

Feinberg, L., & Whitlatch, C. J. (2001). Are persons with cognitive impairment able to state consistent choices? *Gerontologist, 41,* 374–382.

Fellner, C., & Marshall, J. (1970). Kidney donors: The myth of informed consent. *American Journal of Psychiatry, 126,* 1245–1251.

Fellows, L. K. (1998). Competency and consent in dementia. *Journal of the American Geriatrics Society, 46,* 922–926.

Fisher, C. B. (2003a). *Decoding the Ethics Code: A practical guide for psychologists.* Thousand Oaks, CA: Sage.

Fisher, C. B. (2003b). Goodness of-fit ethic for informed consent to research involving adults with mental retardation and developmental disabilities. *Mental Retardardation and Developmental Disabilities Research Review, 9*(1), 27–31.

Fisher, C. B., Hoagwood, K., Boyces, C., Duster, T., Frank, D. A., Grisso, T., et al. (2002). Research ethics for mental health science involving ethnic minority children and youths. *American Journal of Psychology, 57*(12), 1024–1040.

Fitten, L. J., & Waite, M. S. (1990). Impact of medical hospitalization on treatment decision-making capacity in the elderly. *Archives of Internal Medicine, 150*(8), 1717–1721.

Folstein, M. F., Folstein, S. E., & McHugh, P. R. (1975). Mini-mental state. A practical method for grading the cognitive state of patients for the clinician. *Journal of Psychiatric Research, 12*(3), 189–198.

Friedman, P. (1975). Legal regulation of applied behavior analysis in mental institutions and prisons. *Arizona Law Review, 17,* 39–104.

Galietta, M., & Pessin, H. (2002, May). *Burdens and benefits of research with terminally ill cancer patients.* Paper presented at the European Association for Palliative Care, 2nd Research Congress, Lyon, France.

Ganzini, L., Lee, M. A., & Henitz, R. T. (1994). The capacity to make decisions in advance borderline personality disorder. *Journal of Clinical Ethics, 5*(4), 360–364. Ganzini, L., Lee, M. A., Heintz, R. T., Bloom, J. D., & Fenn, D. S. (1994). The effect of depression on elderly patients' preferences for life-sustaining medical therapy. *American Journal of Psychiatry, 51,* 1631–1636.

Geller, D., & Faden, R. (1979). *Decision-making in informed consent: Base rate and individuating information.* Paper presented at the annual meeting of the American Psychological Association.

Goin, M., Burgoyne, R., & Goin, J. (1976). Facelift operation: The patient's secret motivations and reactions to "informed consent." *Plastic and Reconstructive Surgery, 58,* 273–279.

Grabowski, J., & Mintz, J. (1979). Increasing the likelihood that consent is informed. *Journal of Applied Behavior Analysis, 12,* 283–284.

Gray, B. (1978). Complexities of informed consent. *Annals of the American Academy of Political and Social Sciences, 437,* 37–48.

Grisso, T., & Appelbaum, P. S. (1995). The MacArthur Treatment Competence Study III: Abilities of patients to consent psychiatric and medical treatments. *Law and Human Behavior, 19*(2), 149–174.

Grisso, T., & Applebaum, P. S. (1998). *Assessing competence to consent to treatment: A guide for physicians and other health professionals.* New York: Oxford University.

Grossman, L., & Summers, F. (1980). A study of the capacity of schizophrenic patients to give informed consent. *Hospital and Community Psychiatry, 31*(3), 205–207.

Grundner, T. M. (1980). On the readability of surgical consent forms. *New England Journal of Medicine, 302,* 900–902.

Gutheil, T., & Bursztajn, H. (1986). Clinician's guidelines for assessing and presenting subtle forms of patient incompetence in legal settings. *American Journal of Psychiatry, 43*(8), 1020–1023.

Hassar, M., & Weintraub, M. (1976). "Uninformed" consent and the wealthy volunteer: An analysis of patient volunteers in a clinical trial of a new anti-inflammatory drug. *Clinical Pharmacology and Therapeutics, 20,* 379–386.

Hirch, H. R. (1977). Informed consent: Fact or fiction. *Journal of Legal Medicine, 5,* 25.

Humphreys, L. (1970). *Tearoom trade: Impersonal sex in public places.* Chicago: Aldine.

Janofsky, J. S., McCarthy, R. T., & Folstein, M. F. (1992). The Hopkins Competency Assessment Test: A brief method for evaluating patients' capacity to give informed consent. *Hospital and Community Psychiatry, 43*(2), 132–136.

Joffe, S., Cook, E. F., Cleary, P. D., Clark, J. W., & Weeks, J. C. (2001). Quality of informed consent: A new measure of understanding among research subjects. *Journal of the National Cancer Institute, 93*(2), 139–147.

Katz, J. (1972). *Experimentation with human beings.* New York: Russell Sage Foundations.

Kennedy, B. J., & Lillenhaugen, A. (1979). Patient recall of informed consent. *Medical and Pediatric Oncology, 7*(2), 173–178.

Kim, S. Y., Caine, E. D., Currier, G. W., Leibovici, A., & Ryan, J. M. (2001). Assessing the competence of person's with Alzheimer's disease in providing informed consent for participation in research. *American Journal of Psychiatry, 158*(5), 712–717.

Kim, S. Y., & Karlawish, J. (2003). Ethics and politics of research involving subjects with impaired decision-making abilities. *Neurology, 61*(12), 1645–1646.

Laforet, E. G. (1976). The fiction of informed consent. *Journal of the American Medical Association, 235*, 1579–1585.

Lankton, J., Batchelder, B., & Ominslay, A. (1977). Emotional responses to detailed risk disclosure for anesthesia. *Anesthesiology, 46*, 294–296.

Leeb, D., Bowers, D. G., Jr., & Lynch, J. B. (1976). Observation on the myth of "informed consent." *Plastic and Reconstructive Surgery, 58*, 280–282.

Levine, R. J. (1981). *Ethics and regulation of clinical research.* Baltimore: Urban & Schwarzenberg.

Lockwood, K. A., Alexopoulos, G. S., & van Gorp, W. G. (2002). Executive dysfunction in geriatric depression. *American Journal of Psychiatry, 159*(7), 1119–1126.

Loftus, E. G., & Fries, J. F. (1979). Informed consent may be hazardous to health. (Editorial.) *Science, 204*, 4388.

Ludlum, J. (1972). *Informed consent.* Chicago: American Hospital Association.

Marini, J. L., Shreard, M. H., & Bridges, C. I. (1976). An evaluation of "informed consent" with volunteer prisoner subjects. *Yale Journal of Biology and Medicine, 49*, 427–437.

Marson, D. C., Annis, S. M., McInturff, B., Bartolucci, A., & Harrell, L. E. (1999). Error behaviors associated with loss of competency in Alzheimer's disease. *Neurology, 53*(9), 1983–1992.

Marson, D. C., Chatterjee, A., Ingram, K. K., & Harrell, L. E. (1996). Toward a neurologic model of competency: Cognitive predictors of capacity to consent in Alzheimer's disease using three different legal standards. *Neurology, 46*(3), 666–672.

Marson, D. C., Hawkins, L., McInturff, B., & Harrell, L. E. (1997). Cognitive models that predict physician judgments of capacity to consent in mild Alzheimer's disease. *Journal of the American Geriatrics Society, 45*(4), 458–464.

Marson, D. C., Ingram, K. K., Cody, H. A., & Harrell, L. E. (1995a). Assessing the competency of patients with Alzheimer's disease under different legal standards. A prototype instrument. *Archives of Neurology, 52*(10), 949–954.

Marson, D. C., Ingram, K. K., Cody, H. A., & Harrell, L. E. (1995b). Neuropsychologic predictors of competency in Alzheimer's disease using a rational reasons legal standard. *Archives of Neurology, 52*(10), 955–959.

McCullum, A., & Schwartz, A. (1969). Pediatric research hospitalization: Its meaning to parents. *Pediatric Research, 3*, 199–204.

Mclean, P. D. (1980). The effect of informed consent on the acceptance of random treatment assignment in a clinical population. *Behavior Research and Therapy, 11*, 29–133.

Meisel, A., & Roth, L. (1981). What we do and do not know about informed consent. *Journal of the American Medical Association, 246*(21), 2473–2477.

Meisel, A., Roth, L., & Lidz, C. (1977). Towards a model of the legal doctrine of informed consent. *American Journal of Psychiatry, 134*(3), 285–289.

Mellinger, G. D., Huffine, C. L., & Balter, M. B. (1980). Assessing compression in a survey of public reactions to complex issues. Institute for Research in Social Behavior.

Melton, G., Petrila, R., Poythress, N., & Slobogin C. (1997). *Psychological evaluations for the courts* (2nd ed.). New York: Guilford Press.

Miller, C. K., O'Donnell, D. C., Searight, H. R., & Barbarash, R. A. (1996). The Deaconess Informed Consent Comprehension Test: An assessment tool for clinical research subjects. *Pharmacotherapy, 16*(5), 872–878.

Monahan, J. (Ed.). (1980). *Who is the client?* Washington, DC: American Psychological Association.

Morrow, G. (1980). How readable are subject consent forms? *Journal of the American Medical Association, 244,* 56–58.

Morrow, G., Gootnick, J., & Schmale, A. (1978). A simple technique for increasing cancer patients' knowledge of informed consent to treatment. *Cancer, 42,* 793–799.

Moser, D. J., Schultz, S. K., Arndt, S., Benjamin, M. L., Fleming, F. W., Brems, C. S., et al. (2002). Capacity to provide informed consent for participation in schizophrenia and HIV research. *American Journal of Psychiatry, 159*(7), 1201–1207.

Muss, H. B., White, D. R., Michielutte, R., Richards, F., II, Cooper, M. R., Williams, S., et al. (1979). Written informed consent in patients with breast cancer. *Cancer, 43,* 1549–1556.

National Research Council Committee of National Statistics. (2003). *Protecting participants and facilitating social and behaviorial science research.* Washington, DC: National Academics Press.

Noll, J. (1976). The psychotherapist and informed consent. *American Journal of Psychiatry, 33,* 1451–1453.

Noll, J. (1981). Material risks and informed consent to psychotherapy. *American Psychologist, 36,* 915–916.

Nuremberg Code. (1949–1953). *Trials of war criminals before the Nuremberg Military Tribunals under Control Council Law No. 10. Nuremberg, October 1946–April 1949.* Washington, DC: U.S. Government Printing Office.

Office for Civil Rights. (1996). HIPAA, Department of Health and Human Services, Washington, DC: Available from: http://www.hhs.gov/ocr/hipaa.

Olin, G. B., & Olin, H. S. (1975). Informed consent in voluntary mental hospital admissions. *American Journal of Psychiatry, 132,* 938–941.

Palmer, A., & Wohl, J. (1972). Voluntary admission forms: Does the patient know what he's signing? *Hospital and Community Psychiatry, 23,* 250–252.

Park, L., Covi, L., & Uhlenhuth, E. (1967). Effects of informed consent on research patients and study results. *Journal of Nervous and Mental Diseases, 145,* 349–357.

Park, L., Slaughter, R., Cori, L., & Kniffin, H. G. (1966). The subjective experience of the research patient. *Journal of Nervous and Mental Diseases, 143,* 199–206.

Penman, D., Bahna, G., Holland, J., Morrow, G., Morse, I., Schmale, A., et al. (1980). *Patients' perceptions of giving informed consent for investigational chemotherapy.* Paper presented at the annual meeting of the American Psychological Association.

Perlin, M. L. (1994). *Law and Mental Disability.* Charlottesville, VA: Michie Company.

President's Commission for the Study of Ethical Problems in Medicine and Biomedical and Behavioral Research. (1982). *Making health care decisions.* Washington, DC: U.S. Government Printing Office.

Priluck, I. A., Robertson, D. M., & Buettner, H. (1979). What patients recall of the preoperative discussion after retinal detachment surgery. *American Journal of Ophthalmology, 87,* 620–623.

Pryce, I. G. (1978). Clinical research upon mentally ill subjects who cannot give informed consent. *British Journal of Psychiatry, 22,* 209.

Roberts, L. W. (2002). Informed consent and the capacity for voluntarism. *American Journal of Psychiatry, 159*(5), 705–712.

Roberts, L. W., Warner, T. D., & Brody, J. L. (2000). Perspectives of patients with schizophrenia and psychiatrists regarding ethically important aspects of research participation. *American Journal of Psychiatry, 157*(1), 67–74.

Roberts, L. W., Warner, T. D., Brody, J. L., Roberts, B., Laureillo, J., & Lyketsos, C. (2002). Patient and psychiatrist ratings of hypothetical schizophrenia research protocols: Assessment of harm potential and factors influencing participation decisions. *American Journal of Psychiatry, 159*(4), 573–584.

Robinson, G., & Merav, A. (1976). Informed consent: Recall by patients tested post-operatively. *Annals of Thoracic Surgery, 22,* 209.

Roth, L., Lidz, C., Meisel, A., Soloff, P., Kaufman, K., Spikers, D., et al. (1982). Competency to decide about treatment or research. *International Journal of Law and Psychiatry, 5,* 29–50.

Roth, L. H., Meisel, A., & Lidz, C. W. (1977). Tests of competency to consent to treatment. *American Journal of Psychiatry, 134*(3), 279–284.

Rovosky, F. A. (1990). *Consent to treatment: A practical guide* (2nd ed.). Boston: Little, Brown.

Ryan, S. P. (1996). Competence and the elderly patient with cognitive impairments. *Australian and New Zealand Journal of Psychiatry, 30,* 768–773.

Schultz, A. L., Pardee, G. P., & Ensinck, J. W. (1975). Are research subjects really informed? *Western Journal of Medicine, 123,* 76–80.

Schwartz, E. (1978). The use of a checklist in obtaining informed consent for treatment with medication. *Hospital and Community Psychiatry, 29,* 97, 100.

Silberstein, E. (1974). Extension of two part consent form. *New England Journal of Medicine, 291*, 155–156.

Singer, E. (1978). The effects of informed consent procedures on respondents' reactions to surveys. *Journal of Consumer Research, 5*(1), 49–57.

Soskis, D. A. (1978). Schizophrenic and medical inpatients as informed drug consumers. *Archives of General Psychiatry, 35*, 645–647.

Soskis, D. A., & Jaffe, R. L. (1979). Communicating with patients about antipsychotic drugs. *Comprehensive Psychiatry, 20*, 126–131.

Stanley, B., Guido, J., Stanley, M., & Shortell, D. (1984). The elderly patient and informed consent. *Journal of the American Medical Association, 252*, 1302–1306.

Stanley, B., & Stanley, M. (1981). Psychiatric patients and research: Protecting their autonomy. *Comprehensive Psychiatry, 22*(4), 420–427.

Stanley, B., Stanley, M., Guido, J., & Garvin, L. (1988). The functional competency of elderly at risk. *The Gerontologist, 28*(Suppl.), 53–58.

Stanley, B., Stanley, M., Lautin, A., Kane, J., & Schwartz, N. (1981). Preliminary findings on psychiatric patients as research participants: A population at risk? *American Journal of Psychiatry, 138*(5), 669–671.

Stanley, B., Stanley, M., Schwartz, N., Lautin, A., & Kane, J. (1980). The ability of the mentally ill to evaluate research risks. IRCS Medical Science: *Clinical Pharmacology and Therapeutics; Psychology and Psychiatry; Surgery and Transplantation, 8*, 657–658.

Stuart, R. B. (1978). Protection of the right to informed consent to participate in research. *Behaviour Research and Therapy, 9*(1), 73–82.

Sullivan, M. D., & Youngner, S. J. (1994). Depression, competence, and the right to refuse life-saving medical treatment. *American Journal of Psychiatry, 151*(7), 971–978.

Taub, H., Kline, G., & Baker, M. (1981). The elderly and informed consent: Effects of vocabulary level and corrected feedback. *Experimental Aging Research, 7*, 137–146.

Taub, H. A. (1981). Informed consent, memory and age. *Gerontologist, 20*, 686–690.

Taub, H. A., Kline, G. E., & Baker, M. T. (1981). The elderly and informed consent: Effects of vocabulary level and corrected feedback. *Experimental Aging Research, 7*, 137–146.

Thompson v. County of Alameda, 614 P.2d 728 (California 1980).

Tobacyk, J., Dixon, J. C., & Dixon, J. S. (1983). Two brief measures for assessing mental competence in the elderly. *Journal of Personality Assessment, 47*(6), 648–655.

Tymchuck, A. J., Ouslander, J. G., Rahbar, B., & Fitten, J. (1988). Medical decision-making among elderly people in long-term care. *Gerontologist, 28*(3 Suppl.), 59–63.

Vaccarino, J. M. (1978). Consent, informed consent and the consent form. (Editorial.) *New England Journal of Medicine, 298*(8), 455.

Weithorn, L., & Campbell, S. (1982). The competency of children and adolescents to make informed treatment decisions. *Child Development, 53*, 1589–1598.

Williams, R. L., Rieckmann, K. H., Trenholme, G. M., Frischer, H., & Carson, P. E. (1977). The use of a test to determine that consent is informed. *Military Medicine, 1*(42), 542–545.

Woodward, W. E. (1979). Informed consent of volunteers: A direct measurement of comprehension and retention of information. *Clinical Research, 27*, 248–252.

PART THREE

APPLYING PSYCHOLOGY TO CRIMINAL PROCEEDINGS

CHAPTER 11

Evaluating Eyewitness Testimony in Adults and Children

PAOLA CASTELLI, GAIL S. GOODMAN, ROBIN S. EDELSTEIN, EMILIE B. MITCHELL, PEDRO M. PAZ ALONSO, KRISTEN E. LYONS, and JEREMY W. NEWTON

How accurate is eyewitness testimony? Part of the fascination with this question derives from the fact that people's fate may hang on human memory, which is known to be fallible. A report issued by the National Institute of Justice (Connors, Lundregan, Miller, & McEwan, 1996), reviewing 28 cases in which defendants were wrongfully convicted by juries but later exonerated by DNA evidence, concluded that in the majority of the cases, the most compelling evidence presented at trial was (inaccurate) eyewitness testimony. To date, the number of convicted individuals exonerated by DNA evidence exceeds 100. It has been estimated that about 75% of these individuals were mistakenly identified by eyewitnesses (Scheck, Neufeld, & Dwyer, 2000; Wells et al., 1998).

Not only the fate of the accused rests on witness accuracy, but so may the fate of the victim; for instance, if an accurate victim is not believed, the victim may endure further assaults by the perpetrator and disillusionment with the legal system. Nevertheless, our legal system necessarily relies on witness testimony, making its study of substantial practical importance. It has profound theoretical significance as well. Research on eyewitness testimony informs theories of memory and has led to new insights about the workings of the human mind. Given the crucial nature of these issues, it is not surprising that the study of eyewitness memory is an active and at times controversial endeavor.

Courts currently show a surprising inclination to permit psychologists to educate judges and jurors about eyewitness testimony. In educating the court, psychologists may testify as expert witnesses about relevant research findings or provide an evaluation of a specific witness. In either case, a firm grounding in current knowledge about eyewitness reports is essential.

In this chapter, we examine issues and research findings of importance to psychologists who serve as expert witnesses on eyewitness testimony. The

243

literature in this field is extensive; rather than reviewing it all, we focus on key issues. (For more in-depth coverage, several recent books and review articles on specific eyewitness memory issues are available: e.g., Eisen, Quas, & Goodman, 2002; Goodman, Emery, & Haugaard, 1997; Sporer, Malpass, & Koehnken, 1996.) Our goal is to present a more balanced view than is common in discussions of eyewitness testimony. Most research in this area, and consequently most reviews, focus on the inaccuracies of human memory. In contrast, we present evidence relevant to both accuracies and inaccuracies. We also review research literature on both adult and child witnesses.

We first discuss factors known to affect memory acquisition, storage, and retention. In the course of doing so, we discuss research on eyewitness memory and identification generally, for both adults and children. We next address a number of special topics of particular importance to experts who testify about eyewitness memory. These topics include face recognition, individual differences in eyewitness memory ability, "repressed/recovered memory," memory in abuse victims, and child and elderly witnesses. Our discussion of special topics adds to the more general review of research on memory and identification presented first. We close with a consideration of ecological validity, that is, the generalizabilty of research findings to actual forensic situations, and with a few comments on the role of expert witnesses who educate the court about eyewitness testimony in children and adults.

HUMAN MEMORY

The scientific study of eyewitness testimony capitalizes on a simple fact: An objective record of the original event is available against which to evaluate the witness's report. Without this, the validity of a witness's statements cannot be determined. For actual crimes, the availability of an objective record is extremely unlikely. There is usually no definitive way to know whether the witness's report—even a detailed report given with great confidence—is correct or not. Many clinical discussions of memory for traumatic events, although valuable as sources of anecdotal information, are problematic because no objective record is available. In contrast, scientific studies of eyewitness testimony, although sometimes lacking in ecological validity (i.e., in the realism and trauma of real crime), provide many replicable findings that can be helpful in evaluating a witness's report.

When a record of the original event is available, one finds that memory is not perfect. Eyewitness reports contain accuracies, but also inaccuracies. The presence of accuracies and inaccuracies is consistent with theories of memory that emphasize its reconstructive nature (e.g., Bartlett, 1932; Loftus, 1979a). A reconstructive approach proposes that memory is not like a videotape recorder that stores all information encountered. Instead, forgetting may occur, and human memory becomes an amalgamation of what actually happened (the main source of accuracies) and what a person intuits, hears, or infers must have happened, sometimes inaccurately (one source of inaccuracies).

The reconstructive view of memory is generally accepted among psychologists who study human memory and eyewitness testimony. But an important debate exists about whether memory for events can change irreversibly (as implied by the reconstructive view) or whether memories are more permanent (see Alba & Hasher, 1983; McCloskey & Egeth, 1983). Under the latter view, forgetting does not occur, but retrieval failures do. That is, the original memory is retained but cannot be retrieved unless the right retrieval cue can be found. Without attempting to resolve this controversy here, we take the view that, for all practical purposes, memories may be permanently lost or changed because retrieval conditions may not be found—if they indeed exist—that can provide the cues needed to unleash the "true" memory.

According to a reconstructive approach, memory can be divided into three stages: acquisition, retention, and retrieval. Acquisition refers to the encoding of information into memory. Retention refers to the storage of information over time. Retrieval refers to the witness's ability to access what has been retained. Many factors, to be reviewed here, affect each of these stages and consequently affect witnesses' reports.

When a complex event such as a crime occurs (the encoding stage), it is impossible to attend to all of it, much less remember every detail of the incident. Instead, people form a general interpretation of the event (e.g., "I'm being robbed") and encode what they can based on what seems most important, novel, and salient to them at the time (e.g., "He has a gun"). If a detail is only glimpsed but not thoroughly examined, a witness's expectations may distort what is seen; for example, a stick in an assailant's hand might be encoded as a gun. Thus, even at this early stage, a totally complete and accurate representation of the event is unlikely to be stored. During the retention stage, the interpretation of the event may be retained relatively well, but details may be readily forgotten or undergo further change and distortion. One source of memory change is misleading postevent information offered by other witnesses or interviewers (Loftus, 1979a). Finally, during the retrieval stage, when a witness tries to communicate his or her memory of what happened, the conditions of retrieval will have an important influence on what is remembered.

When psychologists testify in courts of law about eyewitness testimony, they often begin by explaining that memory can be divided into the three stages just described. We have therefore organized this chapter by first discussing factors that affect these three stages.

ACQUISITION

When a crime takes place, many factors affect how well a witness can encode the event. The crime (e.g., a mugging) may last only a few seconds, occur once, and be violent. On the other hand, the crime (e.g., incest) might last minutes or hours, take place repeatedly, and be committed with minimal force. Factors such as these will affect how well the witness can encode and later remember what happened.

Temporal Factors

A number of temporal factors influence a witness's ability to encode an event. One of the most significant is the length of time a witness has to view it. Studies on face recognition suggest that, in general, the longer the exposure, the more accurate the witness's testimony (Brewer, Gordon, & Bond, 2000; Memon, Hope, & Bull, 2003).

Although longer exposures lead to increased accuracy, the duration of an event must often be judged by the witness's report. This can be problematic as there is a human tendency to overestimate or "telescope" the duration of criminal events (Buckhout, 1974). Time markers may serve as aids for reporting durations, however. If the witness was watching a half-hour TV show during the time of a robbery, that show can be used to help gauge how long the event lasted or the approximate time it occurred. Similarly, people also show a systematic error of underestimating how long ago events occurred, and landmarks (e.g., the witness's birthday, presidential elections) can help date when an incident took place (Loftus & Margurger, 1983). Such telescoping of memory is not as problematic for events in which individuals have participated (Betz & Skowronski, 1997), however.

Although exposure duration constrains encoding, the type of information processing a witness performs during the exposure period is also important. For example, laboratory studies on face recognition indicate that, given the same exposure period, people who engage in deeper processing (e.g., semantic judgments such as those about a person's personality) are later more likely to recognize the person's face than are people who engage in more shallow processing (e.g., structural judgments such as focusing on a specific facial feature) (Bloom & Mudd, 1991; Burgess & Weaver, 2003; McKelvie, 1985; but see Wells & Hryciw, 1984). However, these effects need to be replicated in field research to ensure their generalizability to actual eyewitness situations that find their way into the legal system.

How frequently an event was experienced is another temporal factor likely to affect eyewitness reports. Traditional laboratory studies indicate that the more frequently an item is experienced, the better it is retained (e.g., Ebbinghaus, 1885/1964). Also, as one might expect, the more often a person is seen, the easier he or she is to identify (Sanders & Warnick, 1979). But one difference between laboratory and real-life events is that, whereas the former can be repeated in an identical fashion, no two real-life events will be the same. Also, real-life events are more complicated and detailed than stimuli used in traditional laboratory studies. Although the gist of repeated events may be remembered quite well, details may begin to blur. For instance, children who are victims of incest or repeated sexual assault are not always able to remember the details of each incident or whether a certain act occurred during the first or fifteenth assault. Such examples are consistent with results of studies of repeated, realistic incidents, which indicate that as an event recurs, it may become difficult to remember exactly when a specific detail or act was experienced (Farrar & Boyer-Pennington, 1999; Fivush, 1984; Fivush, Hudson, & Nelson, 1984), even though what is recalled is quite accurate.

Although some crimes do reoccur, many criminal events are novel, if not startling, one-time incidents. For these kinds of events, memory—even children's memory—can be quite accurate and fairly detailed (e.g., D. A. Brown et al., 1999; Eisen, Qin, Goodman, & Davis, 2002; Rudy & Goodman, 1991). However, many factors impinge on memory for one-time or repeated events, making it impossible to base predictions of memory accuracy simply on how often an event was experienced.

The Core Event versus Peripheral Detail

Crime witnesses are most likely to encode and remember what is often called the core event, for example, that they experienced a robbery, a kidnapping, or a sexual assault, compared to more peripheral details. This trend holds for stressful as well as nonstressful events and for adult and child witnesses. The cue-utilization hypothesis set forth by Easterbrook (1959) is one classic, though not undisputed, explanation of the reason the core events of emotional experiences are better remembered.

Easterbrook (1959) proposed that arousal has the effect of limiting the range of attention and hence the number of cues that can be used in performing a task. Under moderate levels of stress, when attentional resources are limited, the emotional content of an event may draw attention to central information of the traumatic event, to the detriment of more peripheral aspects that are left outside the focus of attention. As a consequence of such differential encoding, memory for central contents of the emotional situation would be relatively good, whereas memory for peripheral details would be impaired. Under high levels of arousal, however, the range of attention is further narrowed so that even some relevant cues are ignored, causing performance to decline. Although the attentional narrowing proposed by Easterbrook has received some research support, the more favored theoretical account currently is that stress enhances the encoding of central stressors without an encoding decrement for such information at high stress levels (Christianson, 1992), findings confirmed in both laboratory (J. M. Brown, 2003; Christianson & Loftus, 1991; Wessel & Merckelbach, 1997) and field studies (Christianson & Hübinette, 1993; Christianson & Loftus, 1990).

Christianson and Loftus (1991), for example, had adults view a thematic series of slides. The content of one critical slide in the middle of the series was varied as either emotional or neutral. Their findings indicate that when the critical slide was emotional, participants were better at remembering central than peripheral details. The same results were replicated by J. M. Brown (2003), who examined the influence of contextual reinstatement (CR) procedures on adults' memories for arousing slides (see also Berntsen, 2002).

In another intriguing study, Wessel and Merckelbach (1997) had spider phobic patients confront the object of their fear (a large live spider). On a later cued recall test, spider phobics were less likely to remember the peripheral details of the experimental situation compared to control subjects, while no difference in the amount of central information reported emerged between the groups. Similar results have also been obtained with children (e.g., Goodman, Hirschman, Hepps, & Rudy, 1991; Peterson & Whalen, 2001).

When attention is focused on core events, witnesses are also more likely to encode and retain the actions related to the event compared to the surrounding details (Migueles & Garcia-Bajos, 1999; Woolnough & MacLeod, 2001). Migueles and Garcia-Bajos, for example, found that participants reported more actions than details when referring to the central events of a witnessed (i.e., videotaped) kidnapping attempt, but no difference in the quality of information reported emerged for peripheral events.

Although central actions are more likely to be encoded and remembered, witnesses may still be able to recall many other features of the core event that are important to police investigation or courtroom testimony. However, because attention is selective, witnesses will still be more likely to attend to and retain the most salient details of the event (Marquis, Marshall, & Oskamp, 1972). As we discuss later (see section on "Violence and Stress"), a gun pointed at the witness, for example, is likely to be better attended to than the color of the culprit's shirt. However, if a witness intentionally focuses attention on a specific detail with the goal of remembering it, presumably that attentional strategy will aid subsequent memory.

People often assume that someone who can provide testimony about peripheral detail must have been paying close attention to the central events as well or must have an exceptional memory. But a person's testimony can be accurate about central issues without including peripheral detail, and vice versa. Wells and Leippe (1981), for example, reported that participants who accurately identified the culprit of a staged theft were less likely to remember minor details about the room where the theft occurred. Unfortunately, jurors are often impressed by memory for peripheral detail and may be less willing to believe a witness who cannot remember such information (Bell & Loftus, 1989; but see Borckardt, Sprohge, & Nash, 2003).

Expectations

A person's expectations can either enhance or impede accurate perception and memory. When an event is predictable, expectations support rapid encoding and recall. A classic study by Zadny and Gerard (1974) exemplified this point: Adults were asked to observe a skit involving a student registering for classes. The adults were led to believe that the student was either a chemistry, psychology, or music major, and the student carried items relevant to all three of these fields. Those biased to believe that the student was a chemistry major recalled proportionally more chemistry-related items than those biased to believe the student was a psychology or music major; adults in the latter two groups recalled more psychology- and music-related items, respectively. The authors concluded that biasing information affected the encoding stage because subjects who were biased *after* viewing the event recalled items relevant to all three majors.

Accurate recall of expected information, however, can be accompanied by "memory" of expected information not actually encountered (Garcia-Bajos & Migueles, 2003; Greenberg, Westcott, & Bailey, 1998; Holst & Pezdek, 1992). These schema-consistent intrusions are especially likely when an event is viewed under ambiguous or fast-moving circumstances (Loftus, 1979a; Tuckey & Brewer, 2003). When longer processing time is possible, however, expectations can increase the attention paid to unexpected details. Expected information serves this function because it defines what is unexpected. To interpret the unexpected event, attention may quickly shift to detailed encoding of the novel event. As a consequence, unexpected information may later be recognized with heightened accuracy (Friedman, 1979; Maki, 1990).

Violence and Stress

Many criminal events are violent in nature and therefore traumatic or, because of their potential for violence, cause witnesses anxiety. Thus, research investigating the impact of violence and stress on memory is of crucial importance for eyewitness testimony. This topic has been addressed both by field studies, in which police reports of actual crimes were analyzed or witnesses of actual crimes were interviewed (e.g., Bidrose & Goodman, 2000; Orbach & Lamb, 1999; Woolnough & MacLeod, 2001), and laboratory studies, where witnesses' emotional responses to and memories of more standardized incidents (e.g., stressful medical procedures, slide-depicted or staged events) were examined. Overall, from this array of studies, controversy exists over the effects of stress on memory. In particular, questions arise concerning how well laboratory researchers are able to mimic the levels of stress induced by criminal events and how well field research can pin down cause-effect relationships. For both types of research, the extent to which findings can be generalized to witnesses in specific real-life crimes can be questioned (Deffenbacher, 1983; Egeth & McCloskey, 1984; Tollestrup, Turtle, & Yuille, 1994).

Results from field studies tend to show that witnesses can retain information about stressful events well, although findings may depend on the type of stressful event experienced and whether the event is personally experienced or merely witnessed. Bidrose and Goodman (2000) analyzed eyewitness reports of four child sexual abuse victims. The girls, who ranged in age from 8 to 15 years at time of interview, had been photographed and audiotaped during sexual acts with adult males, providing an objective record of many of the sexual assaults. In the girls' reports to the police and to the courts, substantial accuracy was maintained. Studies of eyewitness accounts of adult rape victims also suggest that memories for such experiences are reasonably accurate and well retained for long periods, especially for central details, whereas inaccuracies are found mainly for peripheral details (Tromp, Koss, Figueredo, & Tharan, 1995; Wagstaff et al., 2003). Similar results are obtained in studies examining bystanders' memories for traumatic events (Yuille & Cutshall, 1986), although when compared to that of actual victims, bystanders' reports tend to be less accurate (Christianson & Hübinette, 1993).

Evidence in support of a positive relationship between stress and memory also comes from research addressing the phenomenon of "flashbulb memory" (R. Brown & Kulik, 1977), a type of particularly vivid memory people often report following experience of highly charged emotional events (e.g., assassination of President Kennedy, the September 11 terrorist attack). Research indicates that these memories appear to contain vivid and durable information about specific circumstances surrounding the events (Bohannon, 1988; Christianson & Engelberg, 1999). Furthermore, higher levels of emotional responses at the time of the event appear to be associated with better recollection of the flashbulb circumstances (Christianson, 1989). To account for the flashbulb memory phenomenon, some proposed a special "Now print!" neuropsychological mechanism that "freezes" the exact details of a scene in memory (R. Brown & Kulik, 1977). Others have argued that special memory mechanisms for traumatic memories are not necessary at all (Hembrooke & Ceci, 1995). Evidence suggests that flashbulb memories can be accurate or at least more accurate than more mundane events (Christianson, 1989; Er, 2003; Hornstein, Brown, & Mulligan, 2003), but they are not immune from forgetting or distortion (Christianson, 1989; Curci, Luminet, Finkenauer, & Gisle, 2001; Neisser & Harsch, 1992).

In summary, studies based on field methods that have examined memory for actual crimes or that have lacked an objective record of the to-be-remembered event seem to indicate that stress at the time of the event does not impair witnesses' memory. However, such studies are limited in number and are often problematic from a scientific perspective. Laboratory-based studies and field studies of noncrime events—studies that often have certain scientific advantages over those concerning actual crimes—yield a somewhat more complex picture.

Some studies reveal a negative impact of stress on adults' and children's reports (e.g., D. A. Brown et al., 1999; Eisen, Goodman, Qin, & Davis, 2004; Loftus & Burns, 1982). For example, in the study by Loftus and Burns, participants were asked to view a film depicting a bank robbery. At the end of the film, the robbers, chased by guards, turn and shoot. In the nonviolent version, no one is hit. In the violent version, a bullet hits a young boy in the face. The boy covers his face in pain as he falls to the ground bleeding. Participants who viewed the violent version remembered less about the film than those who saw the nonviolent version. However, it can be argued that only participants' memory for details that were not directly associated with the shooting was impaired. Their memories of the central information (e.g., the shooting and the boy falling to the ground bleeding) may have been well retained. Moreover, a number of studies indicate errors of omission (e.g., failing to report true information) rather than commission (e.g., reporting false information) as a result of stress.

Yet other research points to an enhancing relationship between stress and memory, fails to uncover any relationship at all, or finds both positive and negative effects within the same study (see Pezdek & Taylor, 2002, for a review).

Quas and colleagues (1999), for instance, report that children who were more stressed during a medical procedure were less suggestible. However, the same children also reported less information in free recall and doll reenactment than less stressed children, perhaps because they did not want to talk about or demonstrate the stressful and somewhat embarrassing medical procedure. Peterson and Bell (1996) also found mixed results when interviewing children about their memories for a traumatic injury that brought them to a hospital for emergency treatment.

Contrasting hypotheses about the relationship between stress and memory have been reflected in the theoretical accounts advanced to date. In the early 1900s, the Yerkes-Dodson law depicted the relationship between stress and performance as an inverted-U-shaped function: At low to optimal stress levels, performance improves, but once past the optimal level, stress decreases performance, especially if the task is difficult. Although intuitively appealing, the main problems with the Yerkes-Dodson law are that it is not clear what constitutes the optimal level of stress, and the law fails to address the finding that at high levels of stress, memory for emotionally charged details is enduring, with fear-provoking details being encoded particularly well (Christianson, 1992; Metcalfe & Jacobs, 2000).

An alternative view is offered by the Easterbrook (1959) hypothesis, mentioned earlier, which proposes that, as stress increases, the individual's attention is progressively restricted to the more central features of an event, at the expense of memory for information that falls outside the range of attention. Thus, the Easterbrook hypothesis predicts that the relationship between stress and memory depends on the centrality of information.

This hypothesis, as modified by Christianson (1992), accounts for certain important phenomena, such as "weapon focus." Weapons are one source of stress in many criminal situations. It has been proposed that when a weapon is in view, attention becomes focused on it, resulting in less attention directed to other details, such as the culprit's appearance, especially in settings in which a gun is unexpected (Pickel, 1998, 1999).

Several laboratory studies provide evidence of the occurrence of this phenomenon (e.g., Loftus, Loftus, & Messo, 1987; Maass & Kohnken, 1989). Field studies, however, yield a somewhat different picture (e.g., Tollestrup et al., 1994; Yuille & Cutshall, 1986). In a study based on police reports of a robbery, Tollerstrup et al. found that eyewitnesses to crimes involving a weapon provided more details about clothing and physical appearance compared to those involved in a robbery without a weapon. Although the presence of a weapon did not seem to affect the accuracy of witnesses' reports, it did have a detrimental effect on witnesses' ability to recognize the person who held the weapon. One possible explanation for this mixed finding is that descriptions may be more vigorously pursued from eyewitnesses of crimes involving a weapon, thus accounting for the large number of details reported.

While attempting to comprehend the complex relationship between stress and memory, researchers have begun to investigate other factors that might mediate this association. Attachment style, for example, has been associated with memory for attachment-related stressful events (including situations concerning personal safety) in both adults (e.g., Edelstein et al., in press; Fraley, Garner, & Shaver, 2000; Miller & Noirot, 1999) and children (e.g., Goodman, Quas, Batterman-Faunce, Riddlesberger, & Kuhn, 1997; Quas et al., 1999). Other individual differences explored are dissociation and coping styles (e.g., Briere, 1992; Nemiah, 1998) and, in the child eyewitness memory literature, parent-child interaction style (e.g., Alexander et al., 2002), children's temperament (e.g., Merritt, Ornstein, & Spicker, 1994), and children's physiological reactivity (e.g., Quas, Bauer, & Boyce, 2004) have been identified as potentially important in affecting children's stress levels during the event and their memory performance later. However, these individual difference factors typically account for a relatively small percentage of the variance and thus may or may not be useful forensically.

Summary

In summary, the relationship between stress and memory appears to be a complex one. Whether stress has a positive or negative impact on memory may partly depend on the type of information (e.g., central versus peripheral) being tested. It may also be mediated by individual difference variables. In general, there is growing consensus that negative events of high emotionality are especially well retained (Alexander et al., 2005; Berntsen, 2002; Christianson, 1992). Even when stress inhibits certain aspects of memory or adversely affects memory in certain individuals, which is still open to debate, this does not mean that witnesses to traumatic incidents will remember nothing or that what they do remember will be fraught with error. It may simply mean that their memories will be relatively limited. What they do remember might still be quite accurate.

Because attention is limited, people cannot encode everything about real-life events, particularly those as complex as most crimes. We have reviewed the ways in which temporal factors affect encoding and how our expectations can distort what is encoded, although they usually do not. Violent events may lead to impaired memories for peripheral information, although memories for central information (e.g., the action, the weapon) may still be largely accurate. Acquisition factors influence what is encoded, which in turn determines what can be stored and retained.

Retention

Retention is the second stage of memory. During the retention interval, encoded information may be affected by various factors. The length of time that passes between an event and its attempted retrieval may lead to forgetting. In addition, information acquired during the retention interval can, under some circumstances, distort the original memory (or at least the witness's report of it). We next examine some of the circumstances that can affect forgetting rates and some of the factors that can lead to malleability of memory. We also discuss conditions that make memory relatively resistant to change.

Delay

One of the most replicable findings of memory research is that forgetting increases with time. Ebbinghaus' (1885/1964) famous "forgetting curve" represented the fact that the rate of forgetting of nonsense syllables is steepest during the first few postexposure minutes and then levels off. In the same fashion, after rapid initial forgetting, memory for highly familiar information declines quite slowly as time passes and may still be accurate after long delays. Forgetting also occurs for real-life events, and it would be relevant to examine a possible forgetting curve for different experiences (Rubin, 2000; Wixted & Ebbesen, 1997), given that the rate at which information is lost varies considerably (see Shepherd, 1983, for review). Research on younger and older adults' autobiographical memories, for example, suggests that forgetting of experiences from the most recent 10 years of life follows a power function (e.g., Rubin & Schulkind, 1997) and that fewer memories are reported from childhood than from other years (e.g., Rubin, 2000). However, research on adults' memories for early childhood events suggests that emotions associated with those events may facilitate their long-term retention (e.g., Howes, Siegel, & Brown, 1993).

Memory for highly familiar information may also decline quite slowly. Bahrick and colleagues' studies, for example, showed that retention of a foreign language (Bahrick, 1984) and recognition memory for pictures of high school classmates (Bahrick, Bahrick, & Wittlinger, 1975) remained almost perfect after 35 years and was still quite accurate after an average delay of 45 years, suggesting that the level of initial learning or exposure may be an important factor. Even studies that involve recognition of strangers do not always find a decline in accuracy, at least over the delay intervals tested. In a review of seven roughly comparable eyewitness identification experiments that employed delays ranging from an immediate to a 5-month interval, Shepherd (1983) found no clear relationship between delay and correct recognitions or incorrect choices. These findings led Shepherd to conclude that, at least for face recognition, other factors such as amount of attention paid to the target during encoding may be more important than delay.

After sufficiently long delays, people almost invariably forget some of what was originally encoded. Although the gist of an event may be remembered almost indefinitely, more specific information (e.g., exactly what the suspect looked like or details of exactly how the event unfolded) tends to become lost relatively rapidly (Powell, Roberts, Ceci, & Hembrooke, 1999; Reyna, 1995; Riniolo, Koledin, Drakulic, & Payne, 2003). When adults were exposed to an irate stranger for 45 seconds, their ability to later pick him out of a video lineup dropped considerably over time, from 65% of the adults providing correct recognitions after a 1-week delay to only 10% correct recognitions after an 11-month delay (Shepherd, 1983, Experiment 2). Even when the number of correct recognitions does not decline with time, the number of false recognitions of innocent people can increase dramatically (e.g., Cutler, Penrod, & Martens, 1987; see also Yarmey & Matthys, 1992, for similar findings in voice identification).

In the American justice system, incorrect eyewitness identifications appear to be the leading cause of wrongful criminal convictions. False-positive identification errors or false recognition of an innocent person is considered more grievous than false negatives or failing to identify a true culprit (e.g., Rattner, 1988; Scheck et al., 2000). The consequences of misidentification can be quite serious, and may be magnified in child sexual abuse cases, given that children are more likely than adult to make positive identification errors (e.g., R. C. L. Lindsay, Pozzulo, Craig, Lee, & Corber, 1997). However, again, the familiarity of the person to the victim or witness, including to child victim/witnesses of sexual assault, needs to be considered (Cordon, 2004). For many crimes, the most likely perpetrator is someone known to the victim. Nevertheless, delay may adversely affect children's identification accuracy.

Studies examining the effect of delay on children's memory have found results similar to studies conducted with adults. As with adults, there are circumstances in which length of delay does not significantly influence accuracy of memory reports (Fivush & Hudson, 1990; Jones & Pipe, 2002; see Peterson, 2002, for a review), particularly for personally salient events (e.g., Eisen & Goodman, 1998; Peterson, 1999). Ornstein and colleagues conducted extensive research examining children's recall of a medical examination over delays of up to 1 year. Children in their studies were 3, 5, and 7 years of age. Although 3- and 5-year-olds showed some forgetting compared to older children (see Ornstein, Baker-Ward, Gordon, & Merrit, 1997, for a review), recall for reported features was (arguably) impressive: Preschoolers accurately reported approximately three-quarters of the features of their medical treatment over the tested delay intervals (e.g., Burgwyn-Bailes, Baker-Ward, Gordon, & Ornstein, 2001; see also Cassel & Bjorklund, 1995, and Jones & Pipe, 2002, for similar findings).

With longer delays (e.g., 1 to 6 years), children's forgetting increases (Goodman, Batterman-Faunce, Schaaf, & Kenney, 2002; Pipe, Gee, Wilson, & Egerton, 1999, Experiment 1). In fact, there is evidence to suggest that forgetting occurs more quickly, and stored representations of experiences become more difficult to access over time, in younger children compared to older children and adults (Brainerd, Reyna, Howe, & Kingma, 1990; Flin, Boon, Knox, & Bull, 1992).

Important questions remain regarding children's long-term memory of more stressful, or traumatic, events. Peterson and colleagues (Peterson, 1999; Peterson, Moores, & White, 2001; Peterson, Parsons, & Dean, 2004) investigated reports of an emergency medical treatment following an injury in children age 2 to 13 years. Although a slight decrease in accuracy emerged after a 2-year delay, little evidence was found for differential age-related decrements in memory performance.

Many factors can influence children's recall of traumatic experience. Age at time of the event (e.g., Peterson & Rideout, 1998), language skills (e.g., Bauer & Wewerka, 1995), event understanding or comprehension (e.g., Goodman et al., 1997), and parental variables may all play a facilitative role in children's long-term recall of these experiences (see Peterson, 2002, for a review).

As mentioned earlier (see section on "Violence and Stress"), individual differences, such as parent-child interaction style, may also influence children's long-term recall. For example, parents who spend time discussing salient events with their children, particularly using a more topic-extending or elaborative style, seem to help them recall more, even after relatively long delays (e.g., Goodman et al., 1997; Haden, Haine, & Fivush, 1997). In contrast, children whose parents are more traditional in their parenting practices, or have an avoidant attachment style, tend to show poorer long-term recall (e.g., Quas et al., 1999; Quas, Qin, Schaaf, & Goodman, 1997).

The accuracy of children's (and adults') memory after long delays may also depend on the retrieval cues provided at the time of interview (see Fivush, 1993, and Salmon, 2001, for reviews). For example, Pipe et al. (1999, Experiment 2) reinterviewed children about an event they had experienced 1 year earlier. Results indicated that children interviewed with specific cues reported more items than did those interviewed without cues; in particular, younger children interviewed with cues reported twice as much information as those interviewed with a standard verbal interview. These findings suggest that decrements in recall may be at least partially due to retrieval, rather than storage, failure (Howe, 1991; Wilson & Pipe, 1989). Consistently, research has demonstrated that young children remember more about events than they can actually recall verbally (e.g., Fivush, Kuebli, & Clubb, 1992;

K. Nelson, 1986; Price & Goodman, 1990). Unfortunately, the introduction of some forms of cuing (e.g., dolls and toy props) can also lead to increased errors, especially in young children (e.g., Goodman, Quas, et al., 1997). Thus, although the introduction of cues during forensic interviews may be helpful, caution is also warranted. In any case, it seems that for both children and adults, forgetting of salient aspects of real-life events does not necessarily occur as rapidly as the typical Ebbinghaus forgetting curve for nonsense syllables might imply.

An important factor that may affect the relationship between delay and memory accuracy, even at times producing a "freezing" effect in the normal progress of forgetting, is the act of recalling (e.g., Bjork, 1988). Witnesses are often questioned several times by police officers, attorneys, and others before they give testimony in the courtroom. Some studies have found a positive relationship between the number of interviews (conducted at differing time intervals) and accuracy in remembering (e.g., Goodman, Bottoms, Schwartz-Kenney, & Rudy, 1991; Scrivner & Safer, 1988).

Repeated interviewing appears to keep memories alive and helps inoculate against forgetting, especially if witnesses are tested shortly after the experience (e.g., Brainerd & Ornstein, 1991; Roediger, Wheeler, & Rajaram, 1993). Repeated testing may also facilitate more complete memory accounts across multiple attempts (i.e., hypermnesia), and the retrieval of previously unreported information (i.e., reminiscence; Dunning & Stern, 1992; Payne, Hembrooke, & Anastasi, 1993; Turtle & Yuille, 1994). Nevertheless, with repeated misleading questioning, the potential for increases in inaccuracies also exists (e.g., Cassel, Roebers, & Bjorklund, 1996; Warren & Lane, 1995).

To decrease susceptibility to suggestion, Warren and Lane (1995) recommend interviewing witnesses as soon as possible after an event. However, in rape and child abuse cases, for example, victims are often not interviewed until months or even years have passed since the time of the experience(s) because the crime may not be disclosed before then. Recent research suggests that the core information of such crimes may still be retained accurately, even after delays up to 20 years, especially in more traumatized victims (Alexander et al., 2005).

Malleability of Memory

In evaluating studies of eyewitness testimony, it is important to pay special attention to whether memory merely fades over time or whether inaccuracies begin to appear in witnesses' reports. One source of inaccuracies is misleading postevent information. This information can be introduced during the retention interval in various ways: through discussions held by witnesses after a criminal event (e.g., Gabbert, Memon, & Allan, 2003), questioning by police and attorneys (e.g., Gudjonsson, 2003), exposure to newspaper articles and television news (e.g., Roberts & Blades, 2000), and even through one's own thoughts and dreams (e.g., Loftus, 2000). Although studies of memory malleability often involve both retention and retrieval factors, we focus on memory malleability in this section on retention.

Elizabeth Loftus has demonstrated that, through the use of misleading questioning, witnesses can be made to report such things as barns that were not seen

(Loftus, 1975), an assailant with curly hair whose hair was in fact straight (Loftus & Greene, 1980), broken glass in car accidents that in reality involved no broken glass (Loftus & Palmer, 1974), incorrect colors of objects (Loftus, 1977), and changes in the frequency of one's own headache pain (Loftus, 1979a). Misleading questions are especially effective in altering eyewitness reports when the questions are complex and therefore direct witnesses' attention away from the misleading detail. Timing is also important in evaluating the effects of misleading questioning. The greatest distortion occurs when misleading information is introduced after a delay and just before the final memory test, instead of right after the initial event: Because of the delay, memory may fade to the point where witnesses do not notice that the misleading information is incorrect (Loftus, 1979a; Loftus, Miller, & Burns, 1978, Experiment 3).

Another way to add postevent information to witnesses' reports is to use verbs of different strengths in asking questions. Loftus and Palmer (1974) found that adults who were exposed to stronger verbs in earlier questioning (i.e., "About how fast were the two cars going when they *smashed* into each other?" as compared to when *hit* is used) were more likely to report the presence of broken glass at the accident scene in a later memory test, even though none was present in the film that depicted the accident. Because smashing and broken glass are both associated with severe accidents, the adults apparently inferred that broken glass must have been present and incorporated this inference into their reports (see also Zykowski & Singg, 1999). Even more subtle changes in the wording of a question can significantly alter a witness's report. For example, a yes response is more likely when a witness is asked, "Did you see *the* stop sign?" (even though a stop sign had not been seen) than if the witness is asked, "Did you see *a* stop sign?" (Loftus & Zanni, 1975).

Although the effects of misleading information on eyewitness reports have been clearly established and seem to be more easily obtained in young children (Ceci & Bruck, 1993; Ceci, Ross, & Toglia, 1987; but see Zaragoza, 1991), it is important to note that the majority of these demonstrations involve peripheral detail (Yuille, 1980). It is much more difficult to change a witness's report about central information (Roebers & Schneider, 2000; Schwartz-Kenney & Goodman, 1999; Sutherland & Hayne, 2001), information with high memory strength (Brainerd & Reyna, 1998; Pezdek & Roe, 1995), and negative information with great personal significance (Bruck, Ceci, & Hembrooke, 1998; Ceci & Huffman, 1997). However, if a person's memory is weak enough, for example, because of a long time interval between encoding and retrieval, it is possible that reports might change even for more central information.

As we explain in greater depth later in this chapter (see section on "Recovered Memories of Childhood Abuse"), it is only recently that studies have shown that under certain conditions, adults and children can be led to report entirely fictitious events that never actually occurred (Ghetti & Alexander, 2004; Hyman, Husband, & Billings, 1995; Loftus & Pickrell, 1995). Such "implanted memories" may depend in part on the plausibility of the events suggested (Ghetti & Alexander, 2004; Mazzoni, Loftus, & Kirsch, 2001; Pezdek, Finger, & Hodge, 1997). Similarly, in a study with children, Pezdek and Roe (1997) found that it is easier to obtain memory malleability effects about a plausible change in an action that did occur (i.e., contradictory false item) than to suggest an entirely new action that did not occur (i.e., supplementary false item; see Roberts & Blades, 1998, for similar findings; but see also Gobbo, 2000, Experiment 2).

Originally, Loftus (1979a) interpreted misinformation effects as indicating that a witness's memory can become distorted and, perhaps, irreversibly changed or overwritten. However, memory distortion, such as the misinformation effect, can occur without suggestions erasing memories of the original event. For example, according to trace strength theory (fuzzy trace theory; Brainerd & Reyna, 1998), people store two separate representations of an event: a verbatim trace, which is a representation of the event's surface forms and other event-specific information, and a gist trace that represents the event's semantic, relational, and elaborative properties. These traces are differentially affected by factors such as the length of the retention interval, encoding manipulation, and age. Because verbatim memories, which are the basis for correct recognitions, are subject to more rapid forgetting, presentation of misinformation can interfere with the retrieval of such memories. After a delay, verbatim memories of the original event may in fact have faded and hence be more susceptible to interference by the verbatim trace of the misleading information (e.g., Reyna, 1995; see also Chandler & Gargano, 1995, 1998; Chandler, Gargano, & Holt, 2001). Thus, according to fuzzy trace theory, misinformation effects occur not because the original memory has been erased, but simply because the verbatim trace of the misinformation is more accessible. Both trace alteration and trace strength theories propose that memories for original events will normally become more malleable as they fade, underlining the importance of the timing in which misinformation is presented.

Another interpretation of the misinformation effect is offered by the social demand and response bias approaches (McCloskey & Zaragoza, 1985; Zaragoza, McCloskey, & Jamis, 1987), which highlight the contribution of social-related factors and ease-of-retrieval "gap filling" strategies to the inclusion of misleading information in witnesses' event reports.

Research shows that misleading information is most likely to be accepted if the source of the communication is of high status or appears to be unbiased (Ceci et al., 1987; Lampinen & Smith, 1995). For example, if a person involved in a car accident claimed that the accident occurred in front of a yield sign instead of a stop sign, witnesses would presumably be less likely to change their reports than if a police officer made the same claim. The police officer would be both high in status and relatively unbiased. Consistent with the "sleeper effect," well known in the study of persuasion, susceptibility to suggestion coming from a high-credibility source is also less likely to decrease over time. Underwood and Pezdek (1998) had undergraduates view a series of slides. A narrative containing misinformation about two of four target items was then presented. The source of the narrative was attributed either to a 4-year-old boy (low-credibility source) or a memory psychologist (high-credibility source) who described the slides. Misinformation coming from the low-credibility source was more easily incorporated into participants' accounts when they were tested after a month compared to after a 10-minute delay. On the other hand, for those exposed to the high-credibility source, the misinformation effect did not differ between the delayed and the immediate conditions. Thus, social demand characteristics may influence witnesses to agree with the interviewers' suggestion, even though they remember the original event accurately, and this effect may be persistent over time (e.g., Cassel et al., 1996; McCloskey & Zaragoza, 1985).

Response bias can also account for misinformation effects, especially if the memory test includes the suggested item as an answer option (i.e., standard paradigm; Loftus et al., 1978). Because the misleading information is the most recently presented relevant information, participants who have failed to encode part of the original event may tend to select the misleading information to fill in a gap in their memory (McCloskey & Zaragoza, 1985).

Yet another possible mechanism for misinformation effects involves errors in source monitoring (Johnson, Hashtroudi, & Lindsay, 1993), the process by which people make judgments about when, where, and how a memory was acquired. The model was developed on the basis of a series of studies by Johnson and colleagues (Johnson, 1988; Johnson & Raye, 1981), which concerned the processes involved in distinguishing memories of actual events and memories of prior imaginings and fantasies (i.e., reality monitoring). This line of research has yielded evidence that source monitoring failures (i.e., misremembering the suggested postevent information instead of the original information) play a role in at least some memory distortions following misleading postevent information (Belli, Lindsay, Gales, & McCarthy, 1994; D. S. Lindsay, 1990; D. S. Lindsay & Johnson, 1989; Zaragoza & Lane, 1994). Evidence suggests that when people make errors regarding the source of their memory, they become susceptible to various other kinds of memory distortions and illusions. For example, in a study by Jacoby, Kelley, Brown, and Jasechko (1989), participants who had been exposed to a nonfamous name would later call that name famous if they did not remember that they had seen the name in a previous experimental session after a long delay. The name may have seemed like a familiar one when it was exposed a second time, but because participants failed to recall the source of their knowledge, they mistakenly attributed the name's familiarity to the fame of the nonfamous person (see also Multhaup, 1995). This result highlights the fact that people often make inferences and attributions concerning the source of retrieved knowledge and that these source attributions are prone to error.

Developmental differences in source monitoring may also render young children more susceptible to misinformation effects than older children and adults. Studies suggest that, compared to older children and adults, younger children are less able to accurately monitor the source of suggested information (Ackil & Zaragoza, 1995; Markham, Howie, & Hlavacek, 1999), have more difficulty distinguishing their memory for actions they actually performed from memory for actions they only imagined performing (Foley & Johnson, 1985; Foley & Ratner, 1998; Parker, 1995), and are more vulnerable to the effects of source similarity (Day, Howie, & Markham, 1998; D. S. Lindsay, Johnson, & Kwon, 1991; Roberts & Blades, 1998). In a series of studies, D. S. Lindsay et al. demonstrated that although both children and adults are more likely to confuse sources that are highly similar, source monitoring improves during the preschool and childhood years (see also Poole & Lindsay, 2001, 2002).

Recent studies generally point to a confluence of all or several of these mechanisms in producing memory distortion (see Holliday, Reyna, & Hayes,

2002, for a review). However, at least under certain conditions, such as long retention intervals, memory impairment (i.e., actual memory change) may occur as the result of misinformation (e.g., Belli et al., 1994).

Resistance to Misleading Information

Are there ways to reduce suggestibility and make reports more tamper resistant? As expected, warning people about the possible presence of misinformation helps ward off the ill effects. If a witness is told, for example, "Some of the questions you were asked may have contained incorrect information. Please answer the questions now only on the basis of what you actually experienced during the incident," or if the witness has been educated about the effects of leading questions, he or she may edit from memory much of the incorrect information (Boon & Baxter, 2000; Greene, Flynn, & Loftus, 1982).

A general warning may have a similar effect. In a study by Warren, Hulse-Trotter, and Tubbs (1991), half of the participants in each of three age groups (7-year-olds, 12-year-olds, and adults) received warnings that the questions they were about to be asked were tricky or difficult and that they should answer only what they confidently remembered (see also Chambers & Zaragoza, 2001). Although warnings significantly reduced the effect of misleading questions across all age groups, it seems that the more explicit the warning, the more effective it was (Schaaf, 2001; Weingardt, Loftus, & Lindsay, 1995; Wright, 1993). Warning participants with logic of opposition instructions (Jacoby, Woloshyn, & Kelley, 1989; D. S. Lindsay, Gonzales, & Eso, 1995), which inform participants that postevent information does not provide a correct answer to any question on the memory test, has also been found to induce resistance to misleading information in both adults (D. S. Lindsay, 1990, 1994) and children (Schaaf, 2001).

It is also helpful to provide at least one of the warnings immediately before the witness's report. In this case, the warning can be given as long as 45 minutes after the misleading information and still be effective (Christiaansen & Ochalek, 1983).

Because adults are more resistant to blatant than to subtle misinformation, exposure to blatant misinformation can serve as a warning. If we suggested to a witness that a purple gorilla had been present at the crime scene, the witness would be unlikely to incorporate that information into his or her eyewitness report (see Ornstein, Gordon, & Larus, 1992, for children's acceptance of blatant misinformation). Further, blatantly misleading information has an alerting effect, so that people reject more subtle misinformation as well (Loftus, 1979b). The beneficial effects on subtle misinformation are present, however, only when both kinds of misleading information are presented at the same time, not when the blatant misleading information is delayed.

Witnesses' commitment to their initial report may also make memory more resistant to change, as shown by Bregman and McAllister (1982). In this study, adults viewed a videotaped car accident and then filled out a questionnaire concerning what had happened. Those in the commitment condition were asked to sign their name on the questionnaire before turning it in. After all of the adults were subsequently exposed to misleading information, the committed ones were less likely to change their reports. However, commitment can also make people commit to their earlier mistakes.

Finally, witnesses may be better able to overcome the effects of misleading information if the order of questioning matches the original input sequence. In Loftus's (1975, 1979b) original misinformation studies, adults viewed a criminal incident, received misleading information, and were then questioned about what originally happened. The final memory test consisted of questions presented in random order, and the predicted distortions emerged: A subset of adults incorporated misleading information into their reports. But if the questions on the memory test are given in an order that matches the original event sequence, the misinformation effect can disappear (Bekerian & Bowers, 1983; but see Bowers & Bekerian, 1984), and witnesses' accuracy can improve (Morris & Morris, 1985; Tulving, 1983). Unfortunately, in real criminal investigations, the original order will often be unknown, making it difficult to decide how best to order the questions.

Summary

Memory can suffer during the retention interval because of both forgetting and contamination by postevent information. This decline in quantity and accuracy of report is not inevitable, however. It depends in part on the kind of information encoded: Central, familiar, or well-encoded information is more resistant to forgetting and distortion than is more peripheral, less familiar, or poorly encoded information. It also depends on the credibility and status of the source of misinformation: High-status and unbiased sources are more likely to produce change. It depends on whether warnings were given and whether witnesses committed themselves to an earlier report. As will be seen later, it may also depend on the interviewing technique used and certain individual difference factors.

RETRIEVAL

During retrieval, the information that was encoded and then retained is brought back into the open, or at least back into consciousness. Typical retrieval situations for witnesses include reporting to the police, viewing lineups, recounting to friends, family, and mental health professionals, and testifying in court. We next review the ways in which accuracy and completeness of testimony can depend on the interviewing techniques used and the retrieval environment. We also examine the relationship between witnesses' confidence in their memory and the accuracy of their statements.

Interviewing Techniques

Remembering and recalling specifics in crime situations can differ in several ways from remembering in other situations. Crimes are often witnessed in a state of intense stress, especially when the witness is also the victim or has reason to fear for his or her own safety. In addition, witnesses may focus on certain items that are salient at the time (e.g., weapons) rather than information that may be useful for later investigation of the crime, such as identifying marks on the perpetrator. Certainly, in the pressure of potentially terrifying moments, eyewitnesses are unlikely to deliberately use mnemonic strategies to remember information. Despite the shortcomings that may exist in eyewitness memory, the information that is retained by eyewitnesses is unique and valuable.

In the past 10 years, much research has been driven by the development of interviewing protocols that maximize eyewitness memory reports, and forensic and experimental psychologists have made significant progress in specifying ways to increase both the amount and the accuracy of information that eyewitnesses recall. Most researchers and professionals agree that when an individual, particularly a child, is questioned during a crime investigation, the interviewers should begin with rapport building and then ask open-ended questions. Specific probes may be used later in the session, as necessary, but they should be followed by open-ended questions to elicit narratives that, it is hoped, are freer from the constraints of the direct-question form (Alexander, Redlich, Christian, & Goodman, 2003; Poole & Lamb, 1998). In reality, however, investigative interviewers often fail to follow these recommendations and rely heavily on specific questions to elicit information, even after receiving special training specifically focused on the structure of the interview (e.g., Aldridge & Cameron, 1999; Warren, Woodall, Hunt, & Perry, 1996; but see Orbach, Hershkowitz, Lamb, Esplin, & Horowitz, 2000). It is unclear why this occurs, but it may reflect impatience on the part of the interviewer or, more likely, the need to obtain certain quite specific types of information for a legal case to go forward, information that may be difficult if not impossible to obtain from children when asking them open-ended questions.

Recent research has evaluated the effectiveness of scientifically based interview protocols (e.g., Sternberg, Lamb, Esplin, Orbach, & Hershkowitz, 2002; see Lamb, Sternberg, & Esplin, 1998, for a review). An example is the Cognitive Interview (CI; Fisher & Geiselman, 1992; Geiselman & Fisher, 1989), which can be used with both adults and older children to obtain extensive and accurate reports of events (see Koehnken, Milne, Memon, & Bull, 1999, for a meta-analysis). Based on general principles of memory, cognition, and communication, its instructions require that witnesses (1) mentally reconstruct the personal and environmental context at the time of the crucial event; (2) report everything, including partial information, even though it may be considered unimportant; and (3) recount the event in a variety of orders and from a variety of perspectives. Further, witnesses are given specific directions to facilitate the recall of details, conversations, and names.

Although advantages of the CI seem to be consistently found with adults (e.g., Fisher & Geiselman, 1992), results are somewhat mixed with children. In some studies, the CI improved recall (Hayes & Delamothe, 1997; Larsson, Granhag, & Spjut, 2003; Milne & Bull, 2003), but increased errors were also sometimes noted (Milne, Bull, Koehnken, & Memon, 1995).

The CI may be especially ineffective or detrimental when used with children under 6 years old. Some specific CI techniques, such as the direction to recount the event from a different perspective, may be difficult for young children, and thus this technique is not recommended with this population (Geiselman, 1999; Memon & Bull, 1991). Memon, Cronin, and Bull (1993) hypothesized that some children cannot understand and effectively use the CI instructions. A lack of understanding would account for inconsistent results with children and underline the need to take into consideration the cognitive and linguistic capabilities of an individual child.

A protocol devised by the National Institute of Child Health and Human Development (NICHD; Orbach et al., 2000) represents another promising approach to ensure that interviews are conducted in an effective manner. The aim of the protocol is to translate research-based recommendations into operational guidelines to enhance the retrieval of accurate and complete accounts by young victims/witnesses.

The NICHD protocol is structured to promote a supportive interview environment. Thus, in the introductory phase, the interviewer is instructed to first introduce himself or herself and clarify his or her role to the child. The child is then given an explanation of the interview task and informed about the ground rules and expectations (i.e., that the child can and should say "I don't remember," "I don't know," "I don't understand," or correct the interviewer) as well as the importance of telling the truth. The rapport-building phase then follows; it consists of two parts, both of which rely on open-ended prompts. The aim of the first part is to create a relaxed, supportive environment and to establish rapport with the child. The child is therefore prompted to talk about and describe some positive and negative experienced events in detail. This task is intended to "train" children to provide narrative responses to open-ended interviewer utterances, thus preparing them for the type of prompts they will encounter later in the interview. In the second phase, the interviewer attempts to shift the child's focus to the substantive issue in a nonsuggestive manner ("Tell me why you came to talk to me today") so that the recollection process can begin. More focused prompts can be adopted to identify the alleged abuse only if the child fails to disclose in response to this first open prompt.

Once the allegation has been mentioned, the questioning phase begins, wherein the child is encouraged to report everything that happened ("Tell me everything that happened from the beginning to the end as best you can remember"). When the child's free-recall narrative is completed, the interviewer is allowed to ask whether the incident happened once or more than one time. If the child reports experiencing the abuse once, the interviewer prompts the child about that time in an open-ended way. If the child reports multiple experiences, the interviewer prompts the child to report those events that are most accessible to memory, relying mainly on open-ended questions.

Focused questions are allowed only at the end of the questioning phase to elicit essential information that may still be missing. The interviewer, however, should always return to an open-ended questioning mode following confirmatory responses to focused questions, a practice labeled "pairing." Contextual cuing (references to events, people, places mentioned by the child) may also be used to refocus children on material they have disclosed before requesting additional elaboration using open-ended invitations. At the end, children are asked whether they have any additional information to report, they are thanked for their cooperation, and the discussion is shifted to a neutral topic for closure.

Orbach and collaborators (2000) asked experienced forensic interviewers to participate in a training program and to follow the scripted NICHD protocol when interviewing real alleged victims of sexual offenses. When the protocol interviews were compared with prior interviews by the same investigators, matched with respect to characteristics likely to affect the richness of the children's accounts, the NICHD protocol interview was found to positively affect retrieval conditions.

Specifically, when employing the protocol interview, interviewers made more extensive efforts to explain the rules of communication and to encourage the children to practice retrieving episodic memories. Moreover, although children interviewed using the two protocols provided the same amount of information, more of the details obtained in the protocol interviews were elicited using open-ended prompts compared to directive and option-posing questions, thus suggesting (although not proving) that information of superior quality is likely to have been obtained in these interviews compared to nonprotocol interviews (Hutcheson, Baxter, Telfer, & Warden, 1995; Orbach & Lamb, 2000; Sternberg, Lamb, Orbach, Esplin, & Mitchell, 2001).

Interviewing Considerations: Timing and Atmosphere

The question often arises whether it is best to interview a witness immediately after a stressful event or wait until the stress subsides. Unfortunately, there is little scientific research on this important retrieval issue. Several studies of memory for arousal-producing words or events indicate that memory improves over time (Butters, 1970; Kleinsmith & Kaplan, 1963; Scrivner & Safer, 1988), but the finding is not always replicated. Some of these studies involve repeated interviewing and find that new information is accessed across interviews. Indeed, research findings indicate that repeated interviewing can improve children's accuracy (Brainerd & Ornstein, 1991). Prior interviews may in fact function as cues to the original event, thus facilitating later recall (Goodman, Hirschman, et al., 1991; see Fivush, Peterson, & Schwarzmueller, 2002). However, when such "hypermnesia" is examined by asking for repeated recall of stressful criminal events, increases in the reporting of accurate information are often accompanied by increases in the reporting of inaccuracies, nullifying the beneficial effect (Buckhout, 1974; G. A. Shaw, Bekerian, & McCubbin, 1995). Moreover, being asked to relive the stressful event through multiple interviews can be particularly traumatic for the victims (i.e., retraumatization effect) and can at times have even more severe effects than the stressful event itself (Whitcomb, 1992).

The retrieval atmosphere is also important. Whenever a witness is approached by the police, there may be social pressure to identify a perpetrator or give a lengthy report. As Buckhout (1974) pointed out, the police would hardly bother to have a witness come in for an identification unless they have a suspect in mind. High-status interviewers tend to elicit longer reports from lower-status individuals, but high-status interviewers also produce greater misinformation effects should they introduce false postevent suggestions (Ceci et al., 1987; Marquis et al., 1972). When a retrieval atmosphere is intimidating, one might expect a drop in accuracy. One of the few studies to investigate hostile versus friendly interviewers surprisingly found no difference in accuracy or quantity of report with adults (Marquis et al., 1972), although intimidating interviewers can increase errors in children's reports (Carter, Bottoms, &

Levine, 1996: Goodman, Bottoms, et al., 1991). The retrieval atmosphere has been studied in particular for children's testimony, and several studies have shown that social support promotes better performance in terms of children's accuracy and resistance to suggestion (Carter et al., 1996; Goodman, Bottoms, et al., 1991; Moston, 1992).

Context Reinstatement

The extent to which the retrieval environment matches the encoding situation is an important determinant of a person's ability to provide accurate and complete eyewitness testimony (see Tulving, 1983, for a theoretical account). The more cues shared at acquisition and retrieval, the better retrieval will be. This principle has important implications for interviewers because it implies that testimony may be greatly enhanced as more and more retrieval cues can be found. As we mentioned earlier, context reinstatement techniques are in fact often included in interview protocols as a source of additional cues. The efficacy of such techniques in improving recall has been confirmed by a number of researchers (Bowen & Howie, 2002; Hershkowitz, Orbach, Lamb, Sternberg, & Horowitz, 2001, 2002; Price & Goodman, 1990).

Reinstatement of context can be both physical and mental: Physical context reinstatement (PCR) exposes an individual to the original setting in which the event occurred; mental context reinstatement (MCR) is achieved by guiding the individual to reconstruct that setting in his or her mind.

Hershkowitz and colleagues (2002) compared the effectiveness of these two types of context reinstatement procedures. In their study, alleged victims of sexual abuse were interviewed either at the scene of the incidents (PCR) or in the investigator's room with MCR instructions, or were not provided any contextual cuing. Although more open-ended questions ("invitations") were posed by interviewers in the PCR than in the MCR condition, more details were provided by children following invitations in the MCR condition than in the PCR condition. Moreover, less information was elicited using focused questions in the MCR than in the PCR condition. Although children's accuracy could not be directly assessed in this study, many researchers have shown that open-ended prompts elicit more accurate information than do focused prompts (Dent & Stephenson, 1979; Goodman, Hirschman, et al., 1991; Hutcheson et al., 1995; Peterson & Bell, 1996). Thus, the MCR condition might have been associated with higher-quality information retrieval than was the PCR condition.

Malpass and Devine (1981a) employed MCR procedures to enhance eyewitness identification among adult witnesses who had viewed a staged vandalism 5 months earlier. Adults were instructed to visualize the classroom where the incident took place, their position in it, the suspect, the vandalism itself, and their reaction to it. When presented with a photo lineup that included the culprit, 60% of the witnesses were correct in their identifications. In comparison, only 40% of the witnesses who were not given the guided-memory task correctly identified the culprit. Of importance, the guided-memory procedure did not lead to more false identifications or false rejections of the culprit.

Although MCR procedures may enhance eyewitness recall, some researchers caution against the potential risks of using visualization together with other kinds of "memory work"; namely, certain of these combined techniques seem to enhance the probability of creating false memories in some individuals (e.g., Loftus, 1994; Qin, 2000).

In summary, context reinstatement techniques may improve recall through several kinds of contextual cues, including both environmental and emotional cues, and there is still no clear evidence that a particular kind of cue is superior to another in improving retrieval performance, probably because the effects of context reinstatement interact with other variables (Cutler & Penrod, 1988; Emmett, Clifford, & Gwyer, 2003; McSpadden, Schooler, & Loftus, 1988).

Confidence and Accuracy

At retrieval, some witnesses will seem quite confident of their statements, and others will not. Many studies show that confidence is highly related to jurors' perceptions of the credibility of a witness, regardless of whether the witness is an adult (see Penrod & Cutler, 1995, for a review) or a child (Goodman et al., 1998; Leippe, Manion, & Romanczyk, 1992). Whether confident witnesses are also more accurate is still open to debate.

When Deffenbacher (1980) reviewed the extant literature about 25 years ago, he found 22 independent experiments that indicated a significant positive correlation between confidence and accuracy. At the same time, in 21 studies, nonsignificant or even negative correlations between confidence and accuracy were evident. Deffenbacher attempted to resolve these contradictory results by examining the conditions under which witnesses encoded, stored, and retrieved the crucial information. He concluded that when these conditions were optimal, a positive correlation between confidence and accuracy typically emerged. When they were not, no relationship or a negative relationship existed. This proposition has been traditionally called the optimality hypothesis. Shapiro and Penrod (1986) found evidence in favor of the optimality hypothesis: When individuals in their study were exposed longer to target faces, confidence was more strongly related to accuracy than when individuals viewed faces for less time. The optimality hypothesis, however, has not received consistent support (Egeth & McCloskey, 1984; D. S. Lindsay, Read, & Sharma, 1998; Wells, Rydell, & Seelau, 1993).

The vast majority of studies regarding the confidence-accuracy (CA) relationship have been conducted using recognition memory tasks, particularly face recognition. In 1987, Bothwell and colleagues (Bothwell, Deffenbacher, & Brigham, 1987) conducted the first meta-analysis of 35 staged-event studies examining the CA relationship in identification experiments. They uncovered an overall $r = .25$, with a 95% confidence interval of .08 to .42, thus confirming that confidence should probably not be recommended as a systematic indicator of accuracy.

Research shows that the CA relationship can be affected by several factors. For example, Brigham (1990) tested the hypothesis that the distinctiveness of the target may enhance the CA relationship. Brigham exposed adults to distinctive, unusual faces as opposed to more prototypical faces and also to attractive versus unattractive faces. Consistent with his hypothesis, Brigham found that the CA relationship was higher when the target faces were distinctive on some dimension rather than prototypical and when they were unattractive rather than attractive.

Researchers also investigated the CA relationship by examining factors that differentially affect accuracy and confidence. One such factor is the similarity between the target stimulus and distractors. For instance, Tulving (1981) found what has been termed a "double dissociation" between adults' accuracy on a forced-choice recognition test and the confidence they expressed for their choice. Participants were shown pictures of nature scenes. The recognition test forced participants to choose which of two presented scenes was previously viewed. In each pair was one old scene, paired with either a completely new scene or an unseen portion of an old scene. Adults performed best and had the highest confidence when discriminating between seen and completely new pictures. When the two portions of the picture belonged to different nature scenes (one previously seen portion, one unseen portion of a previously viewed scene), participants had relatively low accuracy but high confidence in their choice. In this case, the familiarity elicited by both pictures may have increased errors. In contrast, when the two portions of the picture belonged to the same nature scene, participants had higher accuracy but low confidence. In this case, probably because participants scrutinized the images more carefully, they were more accurate but, because they were aware of the difficulty of the task, they reported low confidence. These results might have implications in the legal context; for instance, when an eyewitness must identify someone in the legal context, the degree of similarity between individuals included in the lineup may differentially influence accuracy and confidence.

There are other factors that affect accuracy and confidence in different ways and therefore could potentially influence the CA relationship. For instance, Luus and Wells (1994) tested the hypothesis that confidence in an identification task may be affected by knowing the outcome of the identification of another witnesses. In their study, pairs of naïve participants witnessed staged thefts and were then asked to identify the culprit from a lineup. Unknown to the participants, however, the actual thief was not included in the lineup. After each participant made a choice, he or she was told either that the cowitness chose the same person or that the cowitness chose someone else. Results indicated that with accuracy held constant (all the participants who made an identification were by definition inaccurate), confidence could be either augmented or reduced by the type of available information regarding another witness's choice.

Another factor relevant to the CA relationship is postevent questioning. J. S. Shaw (1996) demonstrated that questioning adults after viewing slides of a crime differentially affected accuracy and confidence on a forced-choice recognition task. Postevent questioning did not have a significant influence on accuracy but did produce higher confidence ratings for incorrect responses.

Attempts to increase the CA relationship have resulted in inconsistent results. Factors such as accountability (e.g., adults were led to believe that their decisions were monitored by others) and context reinstatement have been found to have positive influences on the CA relationship (e.g., Kassin, Rigby, & Castillo, 1991; Krafka & Penrod, 1985). However, in Robinson and Johnson's (1996) research, these factors and others (e.g., public self-consciousness, retrospective narration of the event, hypothesis generation, and disconfirmations regarding the goodness of identification) did not produce the expected enhancement of the CA relationship.

In summary, meta-analyses indicate that the CA relationship for recognition memory is fairly low. Although manipulations of factors such as quality of encoding and type of target enhanced the CA relationship in some studies, the magnitude of the CA relationship for recognition is typically not large, certainly not high or reliable enough to justify the use of witness confidence as an indicator of accuracy.

The majority of the research about the CA relationship has been conducted using eyewitness identification paradigms (e.g., Wells, Ferguson, & Lindsay, 1981); fewer studies have concerned the relationship between accuracy of memories for staged events, such as simulated crimes, and confidence about those memories. The few studies that have investigated the CA relationship regarding crime-relevant information indicate a small CA relationship when recognition tests were used, but a substantially higher CA relationship when recall (usually cued recall) was introduced. For example, Robinson and Johnson (1996) conducted an experiment in which memory for details of a simulated crime was measured either with recall or recognition. In both conditions, adults made confidence ratings, thus allowing a comparison of the CA relationship in recognition and recall. The authors found a higher CA correlation in the recall condition compared to the forced-choice recognition condition. They explained this finding by arguing that individuals may rely on the higher cognitive demands associated with recall as an indicator of accuracy. That is, individuals may assess the amount of effort they spend on retrieving information, and the ease with which a memory trace is retrieved is directly reflected in their confidence for that memory.

Even when recall measures are used, however, some factors seemingly have differential influences on accuracy and confidence. One such factor is the acquisition of postevent information. Ryan and Geiselman (1991), for example, studied participants' accuracy and confidence of memory of a videotaped crime scenario. After 1 week, participants received a written passage describing the crime scene and containing either leading, misleading, or no supplemental information. After 1 week, accuracy decreased, particularly for participants who received misleading information. However, participants were more confident when reporting the misinformation received in the written passage than when relying on their own memories.

The salience of information may also interfere with the CA relationship. Weaver (1993) had a group of college students complete a memory questionnaire after being exposed to an ordinary event. On the same day, by coincidence, the Iraq bombing of the Gulf War started. Participants were therefore asked to fill out a similar memory questionnaire about the bombing. After a 3-month interval and 1-year interval, students completed both questionnaires again. The results showed that although the level of accuracy of memories for the two events did not differ, students attributed higher levels of confidence to their memories of the Iraq bombing than to their memories for the ordinary event. Thus, although the CA relationship in recall is usually higher than in recognition, it is still affected by variables that exert a different influence on confidence and accuracy.

Whether information reported more confidently by witnesses is more accurate than information reported less confidently is of interest for applied as well as theoretical reasons. However, despite its intuitive appeal, the relationship between accuracy and confidence is not a simple one: Both eyewitness testimony research (for a review, see Luus & Wells, 1994) and basic memory research (e.g., Tulving, 1981; Weaver, 1993) reveal that confidence and accuracy can be, under certain conditions, dissociated. These results contradict the simplistic view that memory accuracy and confidence directly reflect the strength of a memory trace.

Summary

The retrieval context plays a crucial role in forensic interviews. Research on the optimal forensic interview for a specific situation (e.g., with child victim/witness in sexual abuse cases) is still underway, and new promising approaches are emerging. In principle, retrieval cues can serve a useful role, but misleading retrieval cues raise the specter of suggestibility, as was discussed earlier in the section on memory malleability. Intimidation of witnesses, especially children, can lead to increased error, and witnesses' confidence should not be regarded as a reliable indicator of their accuracy and credibility.

SPECIAL ISSUES

We now turn to a number of special issues in the study of eyewitness memory. We focus on issues that have received considerable attention in recent years, including face recognition, "repressed/recovered memories," eyewitness memory in abuse victims, individual differences in eyewitness ability, the elderly as witnesses, the use of drawing, children's suggestibility, and hearsay testimony.

FACE RECOGNITION

The ability to recognize an unfamiliar face varies considerably depending on the conditions of encoding, retention, and retrieval. Additional factors such as the fairness of identification procedures used by authorities must also be considered (see Levi & Lindsay, 2001, for reviews). Although we have already examined many of the factors that affect eyewitness identification (e.g., encoding opportunity, delay interval), it is worthwhile here to consider several of the topics specific to face recognition (see Sporer et al., 1996, for a review).

Cross-Racial Identification

The majority of studies and meta-analyses to date indicate that cross-race identifications are more difficult than same-race identifications (Malpass & Kravitz, 1969; Sporer, 2001; Wright, Boyd, & Tredoux, 2001; see Meissner & Brigham, 2001, for meta-analysis). For instance, Wright and colleagues conducted studies in South Africa and England. Participants were approached by confederates and later asked to identify the confederate. In both countries, participants were better able to recognize confederates of their own race. The own-race bias is present by 7 to 9 years of age, if not sooner (Pezdek, Blandon-Gitlin, & Moore, 2003), and may actually dissipate somewhat by adulthood (Chance, Turner, & Goldstein, 1982; Goodman et al., 2004). Research shows that the effect is likely to be at least partly a function of meaningful experience with members of different races (Brigham, Maass, Snyder, & Spaulding, 1982; Platz & Hosch, 1988; Sporer, 2001). An example of this would be where individuals of certain ethnic or racial backgrounds are more commonly exposed to individuals of another ethnic/racial background, such as Asian Americans living in a society where Caucasians are the majority (Goodman et al., 2004).

Lineup Fairness

Imagine that you have witnessed a crime, and a week later the police ask you to view a photo lineup of three men. It turns out that two of them are suspects in the crime. If you were randomly guessing when attempting the identification, what would be the chances of selecting one of the two men? The chances are high (66% if you feel you must make a choice, and 50% if you include "none" as an option). What if your instructions included biased statements, such as "We have reason to believe that the culprit is in today's lineup"? What if you were allowed to see that only one lineup member arrived in handcuffs? Most defense attorneys would assert that such lineups were unfair.

Psychologists have devised several ways to evaluate the fairness of a lineup (e.g., Brigham, Meissner, & Wasserman, 1999). It is generally acknowledged that the functional size of a lineup (i.e., the number of viable lineup members) may be much smaller than the nominal size (i.e., the number of members present). If the foils are dissimilar from the suspect, the suspect may be easily picked out by "mock witnesses," that is, people who were not present at the crime but who have heard a description of the suspect. An extreme example of this would be if a witness described the perpetrator as a Caucasian man and in a lineup of six people one was Caucasian and five were African American. The similarity of the foils to the suspect is not the only variable to consider in creating a fair lineup. If the foils are more similar to the suspect than they are to each other, the suspect may stand out (Clark & Tunnicliff, 2001; Wogalter, Marwitz, & Leonard, 1992).

Sequential lineups, in which persons or photographs of persons are presented one at a time, may have advantages over traditional lineup procedures because they discourage witnesses from simply choosing the lineup member most similar to their memory of the suspect (R. C. L. Lindsay, 1999; R. C. L. Lindsay & Wells, 1985). A sequential lineup is especially effective when witnesses are unaware of the total number of persons to be presented (R. C. L. Lindsay, Lea, & Fulford, 1991). Another identification procedure is the showup, in which a single suspect is presented to a witness. Although this procedure has long been criticized as too leading (Sobel, 1985; Steblay, Dysart, Fulero, & Lindsay, 2003), some research indicates it may not be so biasing. Indeed, a witness may be more likely to indicate that the suspect is not present in a showup than in a lineup (Gonzalez, Ellsworth, & Pembroke, 1993; but see Yarmey, Yarmey, & Yarmey, 1996). Showups yield a higher rate of correct rejections than lineup procedures. However, false identifications are higher when an innocent suspect resembles the description of the perpetrator (Steblay et al., 2003). A new and promising lineup procedure is the elimination lineup, which tries to combine the best features of previous lineup tasks (Ogle & Reisberg, 2004). In this procedure, the witness is first asked to eliminate all but one lineup member, and then is asked to identify whether that person is the culprit or not. This approach seems to be particularly beneficial to children's lineup performance (Pozzulo & Lindsay, 1999).

Unconscious Transference

Sometimes a witness recognizes a face but incorrectly identifies the circumstances under which he or she first saw the face. If a face in a lineup looks familiar to the witness, he or she may identify that person as the culprit, even if that person was really an innocent bystander to the crime, or even someone encountered at a completely different time. This is called unconscious transference, and has led to mistaken identification in actual cases (Buckhout, 1984). Although this phenomenon has some experimental support (Loftus, 1976), recent studies indicate that it is not easy to re-create the phenomenon in the laboratory. Read, Tollestrup, Hammersley, McFadzen, and Christensen (1990) found little evidence of unconscious transference across five studies. Dysart, Lindsay, Hammond, and Dupuis (2001) reported that false identification rates in an unconscious transference group were similar to that of the control group. Ross, Ceci, Dunning, and Toglia (1994) suggest that what appeared to be unconscious transference was in reality a by-product of participants' confusion: Many incorrectly believed at the time of the incident that the assailant and a bystander were the same person. In a recent study comparing child (5- to 8-year-olds) and adult witnesses, unconscious transference effects were found for adults but not for children (Ross et al., 1998).

Interference

Seeing other faces does not always result in unconscious transference, but it may still affect retrieval. Searching through mug shots, for example, may make it harder to identify the face of a suspect because the intervening faces may interfere with memory (Laughery, Alexander, & Lane, 1971). Suppose that a witness views many mug shots after the crime and selects no one. Then a lineup is presented that includes a face from the mug shots. The face seen before is selected. It is difficult to know whether this selection was made based on the familiarity of having seen the face in the mug shots, or because that person was the culprit. Viewing mug shots may also be detrimental because it could cause the witness to develop a negative response set, responding "no" to faces even if they have been seen previously.

The "commitment effect" represents another danger. An incorrect identification made in the presence of others stands relatively little chance of being altered at a later time, even if the correct option becomes available (Gorenstein & Ellsworth, 1980). Although a more recent study found that interference from mug shots had little effect on correct decision rates from perpetrator-present and perpetrator-absent lineups, the commitment effect presents a significant threat to identification accuracy from lineups following mug shot searches (Dysart et al., 2001).

Disguises

Sometimes even familiar people can be difficult to recognize because their appearance has changed with a new hairstyle, weight fluctuation, or simply the passage of time. These differences between initial appearance and subsequent identification exacerbate difficulties that witnesses have in identifying criminals, and criminals can capitalize on and extend these difficulties through the use of disguises (Shapiro & Penrod, 1986). Changes in clothing, pose, and expression have all been found to decrease identification accuracy (Davies & Milne, 1982; Sporer, 1993; Wogalter & Laughery, 1987). Upper facial features and hair seem to have particular significance, and disguises that cover them (such as a hat) or distort them (such as glasses) may be especially effective (Cutler et al., 1987; Metzger, 2001). Similarly, a disguised voice makes voice recognition more difficult (see Read & Craik, 1995).

Training

Obviously, it would be advantageous if people could be trained to become better witnesses. Training studies indicate that it is possible to improve adults' ability to recognize "other-race" faces through a variety of techniques (Elliott, Wills, & Goldstein, 1973; Lavrakas, Buri, & Mayznere, 1976), but it is more difficult to improve recognition of "same-race" faces. In any case, it is not clear how long training effects last (Lavrakas et al., 1976).

Psychologists have investigated whether police are more accurate than laypeople in recognition of culprits or in recalling events. Two findings emerge. One is that police officers are more likely than civilians to "see" criminal events in ambiguous circumstances (Verinis & Walker, 1970). The second is that police are generally no better than civilians in recognizing faces (Billig & Milner, 1976) but may remember more information about specific details, such as license plate numbers, dress, and physical appearance, especially if given sufficient time to encode these features (Clifford & Richards, 1977). Thus, training can be helpful, but is not always as helpful as might be hoped, and it is unclear whether these advantages represent training per se or other factors (e.g., knowledge base effects).

There is evidence to indicate that older children may benefit from training on photo identification tasks. In general, children have a more difficult time with target-absent photo lineups and often do not seem to understand that the person of interest (i.e., the perpetrator) may not be present and that it is important not to guess. When 5- to 7-year-old children received practice trials on target-present and target-absent photo lineups, their accuracy on a subsequent lineup identification task was higher than that of children who did not receive the training (Goodman, Bottoms, et al., 1991). However, the use of practice trials did not improve photo lineup accuracy for 3- to 4-year-olds, indicating that this type of training may not be effective for very young children.

Individual Differences

Can we predict who is likely to provide accurate testimony? The answer at this time appears to be no, although a few individual difference measures seem to hold some promise.

Intelligence and Cognitive Abilities

Are more intelligent witnesses also more accurate? The relationship between intelligence and eyewitness testimony has been examined in numerous studies, employing a variety of measures, including standardized intelligence tests, achievement tests, digit span tasks, "social intelligence" tests, and tests of verbal fluency (e.g., D. A. Brown & Pipe, 2003; Geddie, Fradin, & Beer, 2000; Gudjonsson, 1984, 1987; Roebers & Schneider, 2001). For normal adults, no consistent relationship between intelligence and accuracy has been found. Some more recent studies, however, reveal that children's intelligence is positively, although quite moderately, related to their eyewitness memory accuracy (e.g., D. A. Brown & Pipe, 2003; Geddie et al., 2000; Roebers & Schneider, 2001). It is possible that the two tasks—eyewitness reports and intelligence tests—tap somewhat different abilities at different ages.

Findings regarding the relationship between intelligence and susceptibility to suggestion have also been mixed (e.g., Gudjonsson & Henry, 2003; Jaschinski & Wentura, 2002; McFarlane, Powell, & Dudgeon, 2002; Richardson & Kelly, 1995). Jaschinski and Wentura found that adults' working memory capacity, which is related to general fluid intelligence (Engle, Tuholski, Laughlin, & Conway, 1999), was negatively correlated with susceptibility to misleading postevent information. Intelligence has also been negatively associated with suggestibility among children (e.g., Eisen, Winograd, & Qin, 2002; Geddie et al., 2000), including those with cognitive disabilities (Young, Powell, & Dudgeon, 2003). Other studies, however, have found nonsignificant relationships between intelligence and suggestibility among children (e.g., Roebers & Schneider, 2001) and adults (Gudjonsson & Henry, 2003).

Another cognitive individual difference factor that may influence suggestibility and memory performance is metamemory (i.e., beliefs regarding how memory functions and one's own memory capabilities; Henry & Norman, 1996; O'Sullivan, Howe, & Marche, 1996). Children with greater mnemonic knowledge have been found to be more accurate when recounting a past experience (Geddie et al., 2000). Overconfidence in one's memory abilities, however, may negatively affect adults' and children's vulnerability to suggestion (Tousant, 1984, as cited in Loftus, Levidow, & Duensing, 1992).

In addition, there is some evidence that the ability to monitor the sources of one's knowledge is negatively related to suggestibility (e.g., Giles, Gopnik, & Heyman, 2002; Mitchell, Johnson, & Mather, 2003), and that providing children with source-monitoring training can decrease suggestibility and increase memory accuracy (Poole & Lindsay, 2002; Thierry & Spence, 2002). Although further research is needed, other potential predictors of accuracy and suggestibility may include inhibitory skills (Alexander et al., 2002; Ruffman, Rustin, Garnham, & Parkin, 2001), imaginativeness (Shyamalan, Lamb, & Sheldrick, 1995), and language capabilities (Burgwyn-Bailes et al., 2001; Carter et al., 1996). However, these certainly should not be used as single determinants of accuracy. Further, given the limited information currently available for other cognitive factors (e.g., imaginativeness, language abilities), reliance on these factors to predict accuracy is probably unwarranted.

Anxiety

Earlier, we reviewed evidence, pro and con, relevant to the claim that memory is relatively poor for stressful events. In a similar vein, it has been proposed that people who are highly anxious may retain eyewitness information less accurately than their less anxious counterparts, perhaps because anxious individuals are preoccupied with task-irrelevant processing such as noticing their own feelings of nervousness (e.g., Lieberman & Rosenthal, 2001). To examine the influence of anxiety on eyewitness memory, Dobson and Markham (1992) showed high- and low-anxious participants a series of slides depicting a purse-snatching incident. Highly anxious witnesses exhibited poorer recognition memory compared to low-anxiety witnesses; however, these differences were present only when the task contained anxiety-inducing instructions, suggesting that anxiety may impair eyewitness memory only under stressful conditions. Consistent with this idea, Bothwell, Brigham, and Pigott (1987) found that high levels of arousal facilitated memory only for low-anxious participants; for high-anxious participants, high levels of arousal instead impaired memory. Thus, the accuracy of an eyewitness's performance may depend on an interaction between individual and situational factors.

RECOVERED MEMORIES OF CHILDHOOD ABUSE

In the past several years, few topics have been as controversial as repressed and recovered memories of traumatic experiences, especially of child sexual abuse (CSA; e.g., APA Working Group, 1998; Williams & Banyard, 1999). According to Freud (1915/1957), exposure to a traumatic event may initiate unconscious defensive processes that render memory for the event (at least temporarily) repressed, or otherwise inaccessible to conscious awareness. Although the repressed memory is not consciously accessible, it is thought to be expressed indirectly through dreams, flashbacks, or psychological difficulties, with recovery possible under certain conditions (e.g., during psychotherapy).

The validity of recovered memories of CSA, especially those recovered during the process of psychotherapy, remains under heated debate (Alpert, Brown, & Courtois, 1998; Berliner & Williams, 1994; Bottoms, Shaver, & Goodman, 1996; Harvey & Herman, 1994; D. S. Lindsay & Read, 1994; Ornstein, Ceci, & Loftus, 1998). Those who question the validity of such memories contend that many of the factors known to increase memory distortion in laboratory-based studies are also present in some types of psychotherapy sessions. These factors include repeated suggestions from a trusted authority; believing in the plausibility of suggested information (e.g., hidden memories); having strong motivation for memory recovery; searching for long ago, thus often vague memories;

and using techniques such as guided visualization or hypnosis that enhance imagery and lower the response criterion (e.g., Hyman & Pentland, 1996; Read & Lindsay, 2000). Although memory recovery techniques may help genuine survivors of childhood abuse retrieve memories, many argue that such techniques impose a substantial danger of creating false memories among vulnerable adults who do not have an abuse history (D. S. Lindsay & Read, 1994; Loftus, 1993).

Those who believe in the validity of recovered memories argue that a significant proportion of adult survivors of CSA can forget their earlier abuse experiences (e.g., Briere & Conte, 1993; Williams, 1994; see Epstein & Bottoms, 1998, for a review) and that recovering and dealing with memories of CSA are integral parts of psychotherapy (Courtois, 1992; Herman, 1992; Olio, 1994). In addition, proponents of recovered memories argue that laboratory-based research on suggestibility and memory distortion has only limited generalizability to therapeutic situations (e.g., Freyd & Gleaves, 1996) and that the risk of implanting false memories of CSA in clients who do not have such a history is minimal (Alpert et al., 1998; Berliner & Williams, 1994; L. S. Brown, 1996; Pezdek, 1994).

Several related but distinct questions are involved in the recovered-memory controversy. One question is whether memories of traumatic events can be repressed or otherwise lost from consciousness. There are a large number of published case studies and clinical reports on functional amnesias, in which emotionally traumatic events can produce extensive amnesia for much or all of a patient's personal past (see Spiegel, 1995). Although these cases typically involve situations in which a single traumatic experience produced retrograde amnesia for both traumatic and nontraumatic events, they nevertheless show that traumatic memories can be excluded from conscious awareness.

In addition, the results from several studies of adults' memories of CSA clearly indicate that self-reported forgetting or nondisclosure of CSA is not uncommon (e.g., Widom & Morris, 1997; Williams, 1994; Wilsnack, Wonderlich, Kristjanson, Vogeltanz-Holm, & Wilsnack, 2002). In one influential study, Williams interviewed 129 women who had been seen at a hospital in the early 1970s because of alleged sexual abuse. When questioned approximately 17 years later about a variety of personal topics, including CSA, 38% of the women failed to disclose the documented abuse case. Individuals who did not disclose tended to be more closely related to the perpetrator of the abuse than were those who disclosed, consistent with the idea that more traumatic events (e.g., abuse perpetrated by a family member) are more likely to be repressed. Although nondisclosure could reflect psychological processes other than repression, such as reluctance to discuss sensitive topics, nondisclosers were no less likely to report other CSA experiences, leading Williams to conclude that these women had in fact forgotten the abuse. Furthermore, based on the relatively high rate of nondisclosure in her sample, Williams concluded that forgetting of CSA is a relatively common occurrence (see also Widom & Morris, 1997).

In a more recent study, however, Goodman et al. (2003) examined CSA disclosure in a sample of men and women with documented sexual abuse histories, after a delay of approximately 13 years. Only 15.5% of this sample failed to disclose the documented abuse, a rate considerably lower than that obtained by Williams (1994). Moreover, Goodman et al. found that individuals who disclosed had experienced more severe abuse than the nondisclosers, contrary to the notion that more severe trauma is more likely to be forgotten. Instead, the positive relationship between abuse severity and disclosure is consistent with the idea that salient events are more likely to be remembered (Howe, 1997), despite their traumatic nature. In addition, findings from prospective studies (Ghetti et al., 2004; Williams, 1995), in which documentation exists to corroborate participants' CSA histories, suggest that self-reported forgetting rates may be considerably lower than those obtained in retrospective studies (e.g., Briere & Conte, 1993).

Moreover, although researchers generally agree that it is possible for traumatic memories of CSA to become lost, the mechanisms for such memory loss are far from clear (Alpert et al., 1998; Freyd, 1996; Loftus, 1993). Amnesia for CSA may occur either because of special defense mechanisms, such as repression or dissociation (Berliner & Williams, 1994; Briere & Conte, 1993; Freyd, 1996; Terr, 1991), or because of normal memory processes that apply to both traumatic and nontraumatic events, such as decay, interference, inhibition, and intentional or unintentional failure to rehearse an event (Anderson et al., 2004; D. S. Lindsay & Read, 1994; Shobe & Kihlstrom, 1997). To date, available studies do not provide adequate evidence to distinguish among these possibilities. Thus, although researchers agree that victims of childhood trauma may fail to disclose their abuse experiences, the precise cause of this failure to report remains controversial.

A second question concerns the extent to which lost memories can be accurately recovered. Evidence bearing on this question is far from definitive. There are several clinical reports in which patients' recovered abuse memories have been objectively verified and appeared credible (e.g., Martinez-Taboas, 1996; Nash, 1994). In a few notable legal cases, the accused perpetrator corroborated the recovered memory (Horn, 1993). Further, prospective studies suggest that individuals reporting prior periods of amnesia for abuse are no less accurate in their accounts of the incidents than individuals reporting that they had never forgotten the CSA incidents (Ghetti et al., 2004; Williams, 1995). There is currently no solid evidence, however, that people can forget and then recover years of repeated, horrific abuse of the kind that is sometimes described in repressed memory cases (e.g., satanic ritual abuse; Ofshe & Watters, 1994; Qin, Goodman, Bottoms, & Shaver, 1998).

Moreover, certain methodological limitations inherent in retrospective assessments of amnesia (e.g., memory loss is generally based on participants' self-reports) preclude a definitive conclusion regarding the veracity of these reportedly recovered memories. To illustrate the potential fallibility of self-report data on amnesia, Schooler, Ambadar, and Bendiksen (1997) interviewed four women who reported having forgotten a sexual abuse experience. Friends and family members of these women were then questioned, permitting independent corroboration of the abuse and subsequent forgetting. In at least two of the cases, these corroborative interviews suggested that the women had not entirely forgotten the abuse; instead, they appeared to have forgotten having previously remembered it. Perhaps individuals in such studies interpret the term "forget" differently from researchers (e.g., the research participants are thinking of a memory being temporarily out of mind as opposed to an amnesia-like inaccessibility). Also consistent with the idea that retrospective assessments of prior memory states may not reflect genuine forgetting, Ghetti et al. (2004) found that the predictors of such assessments differed from those of objective (i.e., documented) forgetting. For example, although more severe abuse was more likely to be forgotten according to retrospective reports, objective indicators suggested that more severe abuse was more likely to be disclosed (Goodman et al., 2003) and to be recalled accurately (Ghetti et al., 2004).

Can individuals create an entirely false memory of childhood abuse? A number of former psychotherapy patients have come to believe that their recovered memories of CSA were false, suggesting the possibility of false memory formation (Lief & Fetkewicz, 1995; Nelson & Simpson, 1994; Qin, Tyda, & Goodman, 1997). However, subjective experience itself cannot necessarily be taken as definitive evidence of false memory, and empirical evidence unequivocally demonstrating the phenomenon is not yet available (Pope, 1996). Although ethical considerations clearly limit the extent to which direct experimental demonstrations of "implanted memories" are possible, suggestive findings are abundant. Aside from evidence that memory distortion about certain details of events can occur as a result of suggestion (see Ceci & Bruck, 1993, and D. S. Lindsay & Read, 1994, for reviews), a number of studies conducted in recent years demonstrate that, under certain conditions, a significant minority of adults can provide detailed reports of recollections about childhood events that did not occur (e.g., Ghetti & Alexander, 2004; Loftus & Pickrell, 1995; Porter, Yuille, & Lehman, 1999; but see Pezdek et al., 1997). For example, in a study conducted by Loftus and Pickrell, participants were led to believe that several specific events had happened to them when they were around 5 years old, although one particular event (being lost in a shopping mall) had not actually happened. Participants were asked to try to remember the events and provide details about them during two interviews. As a result, 6 out of 24 participants claimed that they had fully or partially remembered the false event. Comparable results have been obtained by several researchers using a similar paradigm (Hyman et al., 1995; Hyman & Pentland, 1996), including with children (e.g., Ghetti & Alexander, 2004). The limited ecological validity of these studies, however, raises doubts about the generalizability of the findings to the memory recovery process that occurs during psychotherapy (e.g., Alpert et al., 1998; L. S. Brown, 1996; Freyd & Gleaves, 1996).

In summary, there is yet no definitive answer to many questions central to the repressed-memory debate. On the one hand, studies show that real victims of childhood abuse may at times fail to report the abuse (e.g., Goodman et al., 2003), may forget the abuse for some period of time (e.g., Ghetti et al., 2004), and may then remember it again (e.g., Williams, 1995). Delayed memories cannot necessarily be dismissed. On the other hand, there is accumulating evidence that false memories can be created, at least in a minority of adults under certain conditions (e.g., Loftus & Pickrell, 1995). Without independent corroborative evidence, we cannot yet determine which of these two phenomena is the most frequent, or whether and how true and false memories can be differentiated. One can, however, keep in mind the circumstances under which memory may be more or less veridical.

MEMORY IN ABUSE VICTIMS

The debate about repressed and recovered memories raises the issue of memory in abuse victims more generally. Abuse and neglect are associated, at least under certain circumstances, with detrimental effects on children's emotional and cognitive development (see Cicchetti & Toth, 1995, for a review), which may, in turn, influence children's memory and suggestibility. A history of maltreatment or other trauma may also lead to the development of heightened dissociative tendencies or Posttraumatic Stress Disorder (PTSD) symptoms (Chu, 1998; Feeny, Zoellner, & Foa, 2000; Van der Kolk & Fisler, 1995), both of which may influence mnemonic processes. For instance, in one study, maltreated children who scored higher on measures of dissociation and lower on a measure of global adaptive functioning tended to exhibit poorer memory for a personally experienced stressful event (Eisen, Goodman, Qin, & Davis, 1998; Eisen, Qin, et al., 2002).

In a similar vein, there is some evidence of long-term memory deficits, particularly for emotional stimuli, among dissociative adults (e.g., DePrince & Freyd, 1999; Goodman et al., 2003). Goodman et al. found that former CSA victims with higher scores on the Dissociative Experiences Scale (DES; Bernstein & Putnam, 1986) were less likely to disclose their documented abuse experiences during an interview about childhood trauma. One potential explanation for this finding is that highly dissociative individuals had poorer memory for the experience. Consistent with this idea, DePrince and Freyd found that DES scores (among nontraumatized individuals) were negatively associated with the number of trauma related words (e.g., "incest," "victim") remembered in a free-recall task. Memory for neutral words, however, was unrelated to DES scores, suggesting that dissociation may function primarily to limit the processing of threatening (or emotional) material.

PTSD has also been associated with long-term memory deficits, although primarily for trauma-related information (e.g., Jenkins, Langlais, Delis, & Cohen, 1998; Moradi, Taghavi, Neshat-Doost, Yule, & Dalgleish, 2000; Vrana, Roodman, & Beckham, 1995). In fact, there is some evidence that PTSD symptomatology may facilitate, rather than impair, memory when the to-be-recalled information is trauma related. Vrana et al., for instance, found that participants with PTSD had better memory for trauma-related words than did non-PTSD participants; however, there was no difference in memory between groups for the neutral words. These findings are consistent with the idea that individuals with PTSD have a memory bias in favor of trauma-related stimuli (Coles & Heimberg, 2002; McNally, 1998). Along these lines, Alexander et al. (2005) found that PTSD symptomatology positively predicted the accuracy of long-term memory for documented CSA incidents.

The physiology of trauma and trauma-related sequelae may also influence subsequent memory. Specifically, there is some evidence that the hippocampus, a brain region centrally involved in memory consolidation, is reduced in volume among adults with PTSD and dissociative tendencies (e.g., Bremner et al., 1995; Villarreal et al., 2002; see Hull, 2002, for a review), including among abuse victims (e.g., Bremner et al., 1997). Although further research is needed, these findings suggest that the experience of trauma can lead to physiological processes (e.g., stress-related release of cortisol) that may influence neurological functioning (Magarinos, McEwen, Fluegge, & Fuchs, 1996; McEwen & Magarinos, 1997).

THE CHILD WITNESS

A number of issues that are either unique or particularly important regarding child witnesses are dealt with next. Increased reporting of crimes against children (e.g., sexual assault and child physical abuse) has brought more and more children into contact with the legal system. As a result, in recent years, research on the eyewitness abilities of children has blossomed (see Goodman, Emery, et al., 1997, and Melton et al., 1995, for reviews) and has helped spawn modifications in the legal system's response to children. Here we focus on three issues of special interest: children's suggestibility when repeatedly interviewed, the use of drawing to increase children's accurate recall of information, and the use of hearsay testimony in lieu of or in addition to children's testimony in court.

Children's Suggestibility When Repeatedly Interviewed

Children are, at least under some circumstances, more suggestible than adults (see Ceci & Bruck, 1993, and Goodman, Emery, et al., 1997, for reviews). Two of these circumstances seem to be the same as those that lead to heightened suggestibility in adults: a relatively weak memory and a high-status interviewer (Ceci et al., 1987; Goodman, 1984; Loftus, 1979a). When children's and adults' memory is equivalent in strength, age differences in suggestibility are less likely to occur and may at times even be reversed (Duncan, Whitney, & Kunen, 1982). Although 3-year-olds have been found to be more suggestible than older children and adults generally, they are still capable of resisting some false suggestions.

Of particular interest to the field of forensic psychology is the effect of repeated interviewing on children's suggestibility. When children enter the legal system as victims or witnesses, there is the potential for them to be repeatedly interviewed about the crime events. This may be particularly true in child sexual abuse cases, in which there is often little physical evidence and children may be interviewed by parents, mental health professionals, police officers, and ultimately the attorneys and judge involved in the case. Theoretically, one might assume that repeated interviewing would in fact reduce children's suggestibility and increase the accuracy of their memories because repeated interviews provide opportunities to rehearse the information. Indeed, research indicates that repeated nonmisleading interviewing helps to maintain accurate memory (Brainerd & Ornstein, 1991), but repeated suggestive interviewing can have an adverse effect on preschoolers' reports (Bruck,

Ceci, Francouer, & Barr, 1995; Bruck, Ceci, & Hembrooke, 2002; but see Goodman, Bottoms, et al., 1991). Ironically, in some studies, when the interviewing starts soon after the event, repeated misleading questions actually improved children's accuracy (Goodman, Bottoms, et al., 1991; Quas et al., 2004). It should be noted that research on the detrimental effects of repeated interviews is sometimes confounded by having the inclusion of repeated interviews as well as suggestive and often coercive interviewing techniques. In the Bruck et al. (2002) study, for example, preschoolers were asked over the course of five interviews about true and false events. In addition to simply asking the children about the events, the researchers also employed peer pressure, leading questions, imagining, encouragement, and praise for talking. Their results indicate that many of the youngest children assented to true and false events by the fifth interview. However, use of multiple suggestive techniques, rather than the repeated questioning alone, may account for the impressive assent rates obtained.

In another study, Garven, Wood, Malpass, and Shaw (1998) reported that 58% of preschool-age children interviewed with a combination of multiple suggestive techniques falsely assented to witnessing acts committed by a stranger during his visit to their preschool. In contrast, when suggestive questioning alone was employed, only 17% of children assented. In a similar fashion, Malloy, Quas, Melinder, D'Mello, and Goodman (2004) found that repeated interviewing per se did not lead to increased false assents; rather, the suggestive interviewing techniques, when used after a long delay since the event, were sufficient to induce preschool children to falsely claim that events happened when they did not.

Despite research emphasizing children's suggestibility, children's false reports to abuse-related questions are surprisingly low in most studies, at least for children of 4 or 5 years of age or older (Goodman, Bottoms, Rudy, Davis, & Schwartz-Kenney, 2001; Krackow & Lynn, 2003; Saywitz, Goodman, Nicholas, & Moan, 1991). For example, Saywitz and colleagues showed that 5- and 7-year-old children who did not experience genital touch during a physical exam did not readily claim that they had been touched when asked about it. This may or may not be true, however, for younger children.

Recent research supports the notion that children are far less likely to assent to abuse-related questions than some prior research would indicate. Krackow and Lynn (2003) had children experience either innocuous touching (e.g., placing a hand over the child's hand) or no touching at all during the course of a game. Children were then asked both direct abuse-related questions ("Did Amy hug you?") or tag questions ("Amy hugged you, didn't she?"). They reported that although tag questions increased children's assent rates, the overwhelming majority of children accurately rejected the direct abused-related questions (98% in the touch condition, and 88% in the no touch condition).

Although it seems likely that repeated misleading suggestions can contribute to false memory formation in children (and adults), including false memories of traumatic events, researchers are still working to pinpoint precisely the conditions under which false memories of CSA are formed and the precise conditions under which children and adults resist false-memory formation (Ghetti & Alexander, 2004).

Drawing and Memory

Another topic of considerable interest is children's use of drawings to facilitate their memory. Allowing children to draw a depiction of the event they are being asked to remember during an interview may facilitate young children's accurate recollections of the past (Butler, Gross, & Hayne, 1995; Gross & Hayne, 1999; Wesson & Salmon, 2001). Drawing may in fact allow children to develop concrete cues of the event that may facilitate their recall by extending the child's memory search (Butler et al., 1995). Moreover, interviews in which children draw tend to be longer than those in which children simply tell what happened (Butler et al., 1995); the longer nature of these interviews may encourage children to spend more time searching their memory and increasing their reminiscence about the event (Roediger & Thorpe, 1978; Wixted & Rohrer, 1994).

Several studies have indicated the usefulness of drawing for children's ability to accurately recall information. Butler et al. (1995) found that 3- to 6-year-olds recalled significantly more information about a trip to a fire station if they were allowed to draw and tell what happened compared to when they were merely asked to verbally recount the details of their trip. Similar results have been found for emotionally salient experiences (Drucker, Greco-Vigorito, Moore-Russell, Alvaltroni, & Ryan, 1997; Gross & Hayne, 1998). For example, the children of substance abusers who were asked to "draw and tell" reported three times the amount of information about a parent's most recent drinking and drug-taking episode than those who were simply asked to tell (Drucker et al., 1997).

Research also indicates that drawing may help children to accurately recall information about events after a delay (Butler et al., 1995; Gross & Hayne, 1999). In the Gross and Hayne study, children reported significantly more information about a trip to a chocolate factory after a year's delay when allowed to "draw and tell" versus just "tell." Of potential interest to the field of forensic interviewing of child victims, the authors found that children reported more than twice as much new as old information about the target event at the 1-year delay. Contrary to research indicating that new information reported by children tends to be inaccurate (Pipe, 1996), Gross and Hayne found that the accuracy of the reports after the 1-year delay was extremely high (96.9%) and nearly identical to the accuracy rates of the information recalled after 1 day (99.6%).

Although drawing may facilitate memory reports for unique and novel events, it may be less useful when children are reporting routine or highly scripted events. Salmon and Pipe (2000), for example, interviewed children about a routine medical exam 3 days as well as 1 year after the exam took place. Children in the drawing condition reported no more information than the verbal group after a 3-day delay and were the most inaccurate after a 1-year delay. These researchers reasoned that drawing may help children develop their own retrieval cues in unique or novel situations, but in more routine or frequently occurring events drawings cue the gist or scripted knowledge about these types of activities, making children's recollection of the actual events less accurate over time.

Recent research by Bruck and her colleagues further highlights the potential deleterious effects of using drawings in forensic evaluations. Specifically, in Bruck, Melnyk, and Ceci's (2000) study, young children interacted with a magician who performed two magic tricks. After the event, all the children were given both true and false reminders of the act. Half of the children were asked to draw the reminders (both true and false), and the other half solely answered questions about the reminders. The results indicated that drawing facilitated the accurate recall of true information, but it also encouraged the acceptance of false information. That is, when children drew false reminders of the magician's visit, they were more likely to claim that these events had actually occurred. Bruck et al.'s results suggest that when drawings are used as a rehearsal strategy rather than as a recall aid, they may be more likely to produce false information (see Strange, Garry, & Sutherland, 2003).

A related topic is the use of human figure drawings during the forensic interview. Human figure drawings are often employed to attempt to elicit additional relevant information from children during a forensic interview or to clarify a child's verbal report; however, the effect of these figures on the quantity and quality of the information elicited has hardly been studied (Poole & Lamb, 1998).

Although substantial research has been conducted on the use of anatomically detailed dolls in forensic interviews (see Everson & Boat, 2002, and Koocher et al., 1995, for reviews), little research has specifically addressed the use of human figure drawings as an aid to children's memory. Steward et al. (1996) used anatomically detailed pictures to query children about medical procedures that for some children included genital touch. The results indicated that children who were exposed to the drawings and had experienced genital touch during their exam were significantly more likely to report the touch than those who were only verbally queried. However, some children incorrectly reported genital touching when none had occurred.

Lamb and his colleagues (Aldridge et al., 2004) have also recently begun to examine the use of anatomically detailed drawings in actual sexual abuse investigations. In their study, children ranging in age from 4 to 13 were presented with an unclothed, gender-neutral outline drawing and asked a series of structured questions about information that they had already disclosed during the course of the interview. Interviewers did not present the drawings until the children had exhausted their memories for the events. When the children were presented with the figure drawings, interviewers were able to elicit a substantial amount of forensically relevant details that were not mentioned during the preceding interview. This effect was most substantial for young children (4 to 7 years old): For this age group, 27% of the total number of details elicited was educed after the presentation of the drawing. It is possible, however, that the number of details elicited increased at the expense of accuracy. Although it is impossible to establish the objective accuracy of the information provided (i.e., children were interviewed about real-life events for which the interviewer was unlikely to have proof of what really happened), after the drawing was introduced the proportion of option-posing prompts increased ("Did he touch you here?" pointing to the figure), while free-recall prompts, which are most likely to elicit accurate, albeit limited, information, were utilized less.

Hearsay Testimony

In sexual abuse cases, a child's initial disclosure of the abuse to a parent, teacher, or other trusted adult may be a more detailed account than the testimony that the child gives in court months or even years later. Certainly, the admission of this type of information would bolster a prosecutor's case and presumably increase the chances of a guilty verdict. As Whitcomb (1992, p. 85) states, "In cases of child sexual abuse, the child's out-of-court statements may be the most compelling evidence available. Indeed, these statements may be the only evidence, since child sexual abuse frequently occurs in the absence of other witnesses or physical trauma to the child." Any information that is expressed outside of the courtroom, however, is considered hearsay and can be admitted only under a strict set of exceptions (e.g., see *Crawford v. Washington*, 2004).

Recently, social scientists have become interested in the controversies surrounding the admittance of hearsay testimony and its influence on jurors' decision making (e.g., Ross, Warren, & McGough, 1999; Schuller, 1995). Whereas studies of jurors' perceptions suggest that adult eyewitnesses tend to be viewed more favorably (e.g., as more accurate) than adult hearsay witnesses (Bull Kovera, Park, & Penrod, 1992; Miene, Park, & Borgida, 1992), findings on the influence of hearsay testimony in CSA cases are not fully consistent. Some studies indicate that hearsay compared to child testimony does not differentially affect jurors' decisions of defendant guilt in mock CSA trial scenarios (Golding, Sanchez, & Sego, 1997; Tubb, Wood, & Hosch, 1999).

The same pattern of results emerged in research involving actual jurors in criminal court trials, although jurors rated adult hearsay witnesses as significantly more accurate, consistent, and confident than child witnesses (Myers, Redlich, Goodman, Prizmich, & Imwinkelried, 1999). Warren and colleagues (Warren, Nunez, Keeney, Buck, & Smith, 2002) also failed to uncover significant effects of hearsay on verdicts. However, they consistently found that adult hearsay witnesses were rated as more accurate and truthful than child witnesses. Thus, somewhat ironically, it appears that adult second-hand testimony of what children say out of court is viewed as more credible than children's first-hand testimony in court.

An important issue in the area of forensic psychology is how accurate individuals are at reporting what children tell them. In one of the first studies to examine individuals' accuracy in reporting conversations with young children, Bruck and Ceci (1999) found that mothers who interviewed their preschool children about an activity that had occurred without the mother being present were particularly good at recalling the gist of the information that their children had provided to them (88% accuracy).

Other research indicates that individuals are not very good at accurately reporting the exact details of what the child has disclosed and the questions used to elicit the information (Lamb, Orbach, Sternberg, Hershkowitz, & Horowitz, 2000; Warren & Woodall, 1999). For example, Lamb et al. compared audiotape recordings of forensic interviews of alleged victims of sexual abuse with the forensic interviewers' verbatim notes of the same interview. They found that interviewers generally failed to report many of the details provided by children and many of the utterances used to elicit them; almost 25% of the forensically relevant details provided by children were not represented in the interviewers' notes. Moreover, 18% of details considered central to the abuse allegation were omitted from the verbatim reports.

Research also shows that individuals tend to misremember what prompted the elicitation of the information from the children, often reporting that children's utterances had been spontaneous when in fact they had been the result of prompted questioning (Bruck & Ceci, 1999), or misattributing children's details to more open rather than more focused prompts (Lamb et al., 2000). Although more research is needed on the accuracy and reliability of hearsay accounts, these studies raise a serious issue, especially in the light of research showing that adults' second-hand accounts of children's report are deemed by jurors to be more accurate and credible than the child's own testimony (e.g., Myers et al., 1999; Warren et al., 2002).

In summary, the courts grapple with the dilemma of ensuring defendants' rights while accommodating child witnesses' special needs. In recent years, there have been attempts to implement courtroom reforms to foster children's eyewitness accuracy and even to spare them the need to testify, but the reforms have often met with legal and empirical challenges.

THE ELDERLY WITNESS

When the first edition of this *Handbook* was published, relatively little research existed on the testimony of elderly witnesses. Almost 20 years later, this deficit persists.

Research generally reveals that the elderly, compared to younger adults, recall less about events (Brimacombe, Jung, Garrioch, & Allison, 2003; Yarmey, 1996), tend to make more memory errors (Loftus & Doyle, 1987), and have more difficulty recognizing faces shown from a single perspective (Deffenbacher, 1991). Older witnesses are sometimes less and sometimes equally accurate in identifying targets in a lineup (Memon et al., 2003; Searcy, Bartlett, Memon, & Swanson, 2001) and tend to show similar hit rates but higher false alarm rates than younger adults in studies of lineup accuracy (Memon & Bartlett, 2002; Searcy et al., 2001). In addition, several phenomena (e.g., mild confidence-accuracy correlations and negative correlations between identification time and accuracy) found for younger adults have not been found for older populations (Searcy et al., 2001).

The elderly may also have more difficulty remembering the source of their information (Coxon & Valentine, 1997). Mitchell et al. (2003) found that elderly subjects were more confident in their incorrect source attributions compared to younger adults. Moreover, older adults tended to be more confident in their incorrect than in their correct source attributions. The poor performance of the elderly in source monitoring may underlie their higher vulnerability to suggestion (Coxon & Valentine, 1997; D. S. Lindsay, 1994; Loftus et al., 1992; Mitchell et al., 2003).

It must be noted, however, that findings of impaired performance among elderly witnesses do not hold true for all elderly persons. That is, some older people's memory abilities do not decline with age and may match those of younger adults (Loftus & Doyle, 1987). Finding differences between older and younger seniors in their research, Memon et al. (2003) caution against casting too wide an age net. They warn that in doing so, one might miss subtle differences between different age groups among the elderly. In this light, Nunez, McCoy, Clark, and Shaw (1999) found that descriptions of elderly witnesses meant to elicit different "elderly" stereotypes yielded varying proportions of guilty verdicts in mock trials, thus acknowledging that there may be considerable variation in the perception of people categorized as "elderly."

Further research is necessary to make more definitive conclusions about elderly witnesses' accuracy and suggestibility. Moreover, it would be particularly useful for future research to investigate elderly witnesses' abilities in light of their psychological age (Birren & Schaie, 2001), a concept that is gathering increasing attention and is slowly replacing that of chronological age in many other fields of study.

ECOLOGICAL VALIDITY

In this chapter, we have reviewed a wealth of research on eyewitness testimony, most of it based on scientific laboratory studies. One frequently asked question about research on eyewitness testimony concerns ecological validity: How much do findings from the laboratory apply to forensic situations? Problems of ecological validity may be especially important in regard to the mock witness paradigm; research efforts have recently focused on increasing external validity in this area (Clark & Tunnicliff, 2001; Corey, Malpass, & McQuiston, 1999; McQuiston & Malpass, 2002).

Yuille and Wells (1991) assert that the criterion of ecological validity is fulfilled if the results can be extended to the real situation. This requires researchers to show that the two contexts (the experimental setting and the criminal and/or forensic situation) elicit the same cognitive, social, and emotional processes.

In an attempt to improve external validity, researchers have followed different paths. In some studies, researchers tried to re-create conditions more similar to real criminal situations (Brigham et al., 1982; Malpass & Devine, 1981b; Murray & Wells, 1982), with some surprising results. For example, it might be argued that the rate of false identification in eyewitness research is often high because participants know that their responses will not result in arrest. In real life, witnesses might be more cautious. Yet, when a realistic vandalism was staged (Malpass & Devine, 1981b), those adults believing the perpetrator would face more serious compared to less serious consequences attempted more identifications, although no differences in the accuracy rates emerged between the two groups. In Murray and Wells's study, on the other hand, being informed that a crime was staged did not affect the number of attempted identifications. Specifically, the uninformed group was more likely than the informed group to pick foils in a target-present lineup.

Other researchers have relied on actual witnesses and victims of crimes to improve external validity (e.g., Christianson & Hübinette, 1993; Lamb & Garretson, 2003). Yuille and Cutshall (1986), for example, investigated the relationship between stress and memory in witnesses to a shooting. No negative effects of stress on witness accuracy emerged, and researchers failed to alter witnesses' memory through suggestive questioning.

Another approach makes use of archival police data to analyze eyewitness performance (e.g., Farrington & Lambert, 1997). Based on those data, Tollestrup and colleagues (1994), for example, found that the accuracy of witness reports depended on the type of crime (robbery versus fraud), hair color was remembered more accurately than other physical characteristics, and weapon-focus effects were evident. Findings from this more ecologically valid type of research can stand alone. They can also be used to validate or question laboratory conclusions.

Over the years, researchers have gone to considerable effort to make their studies of eyewitness testimony as ecologically valid as possible. However, ethical considerations limit the degree of ecological validity that can be achieved, while still maintaining rigorous scientific control of variables and adequate internal validity. More ecologically valid field studies severely limit the element of control achieved in the laboratory. Thus, although the scientific study of eyewitness testimony has come a long way, there may always be questions about the generalizability of the results.

THE PSYCHOLOGIST AS EXPERT WITNESS

Having completed our review of the literature, we would like to comment briefly on the role of the expert witness on eyewitness testimony. Psychologists may be asked to provide expert testimony to the courts about the eyewitness abilities of children or adults. When psychologists provide such testimony, they typically describe the findings of relevant studies, as we have done in this chapter. Expert testimony by psychologists has, at times, been criticized for bias or exceeding scientifically verifiable bounds (e.g., Lyon, 1995; Mason, 1991). However, there is general agreement among a subset of experts in the field that several phenomena, including the effects of stress and weapon focus, as well as many other lab findings, are reliable enough to testify about in court (Kassin, Tubb, Hosch, & Memon, 2001), although such expert testimony is typically provided for the defense.

A leading argument for the admissibility of expert testimony in the courtroom concerns jurors' potential lack of knowledge about the factors that may affect the accuracy of eyewitness testimony. Several survey and mock trial studies have found that prospective jurors hold numerous erroneous beliefs about what factors can impact accuracy (Durham & Dane, 1999; R. C. L. Lindsay, 1994; Quas, Thompson, & Clarke-Stewart, 2004; Shaw, Garcia, & McClure, 1999).

According to the U.S. Supreme Court decision in *Daubert v. Merrell Dow Pharmaceuticals* (1993), a federal judge may admit expert testimony if it pertains to "scientific knowledge" and will "assist the trier of fact." The judge is given the discretion to decide if the expert's testimony is based on a reliable foundation of information (e.g., the methodology is scientifically valid, the theory or technique has been tested and subjected to peer review, the findings have attracted widespread attention within the relevant scientific community; Penrod, Fulero, & Cutler, 1995). Some state court systems have criticized *Daubert*, others have adopted it, and others appear to follow it, though not explicitly (Penrod et al., 1995).

Initially, there was debate over the extent of *Daubert*, specifically whether it encompassed clinical evidence. Recently, the U.S. Supreme Court extended the *Daubert* criteria to include such evidence (*Kumho Tire Co. v. Carmichael*, 1999). The decision declares that under Federal Evidentiary Rule 702, even if "soft" sciences do not qualify as "scientific" knowledge, they qualify as "technical or other specialized knowledge" and are therefore subject to *Daubert* criteria.

Several ethical concerns must also be addressed. What role should the expert assume: advocate for one party or educator for the court? What unexpected or unintended consequences might result? What should the basis for one's remarks be (i.e., how reliable is reliable enough to discuss in court; McCloskey, Egeth, & McKenna, 1986)? Psychologists who serve as expert witnesses should hold themselves to a higher ethical standard than the minimal standards set by the legal system and have a responsibility to recognize the limits of their own expertise (Ornstein & Gordon, 1998; for more in depth coverage on ethical issues, see A. K. Hess, Chapter 27, in this volume).

Regarding testimony in court, experts generally are not permitted to testify as to the credibility of a particular witness (*State v. Milbradt*, 1988). Many psychological commentators argue that psychologists should not testify in court as to the "ultimate legal issue" (Melton & Limber, 1989; see Myers et al., 1989). Complicating the issue, expert testimony may not have an impact on jurors' deliberations unless the testimony is case-specific (Geiselman et al., 2002). Experts who testify about eyewitness memory should be mindful of such restrictions and controversies.

CONCLUSION

Research on the psychology of testimony began about 100 years ago, and research on human memory began even earlier. Looking at the many years of accumulated research, we know that eyewitness testimony can be far from perfect, although in many cases it likely to be accurate enough that justice is served, and we have identified numerous factors that affect eyewitness reports. We still have more to learn about the accuracies and inaccuracies of human memory. In particular, more realistic ecologically valid yet scientifically sound research is needed. Nevertheless, professionals who study eyewitness memory can provide valuable information to the courts.

REFERENCES

Ackil, J. K., & Zaragoza, M. S. (1995). Developmental differences in eyewitness suggestibility and memory for source. *Journal of Experimental Child Psychology, 60*, 57–83.

Alba, J. W., & Hasher, L. (1983). Is memory schematic? *Psychological Bulletin, 93*, 203–231.

Aldridge, J., & Cameron, S. (1999). Interviewing child witnesses: Questioning techniques and the role of training. *Applied Developmental Science, 3,* 136–147.

Aldridge, J., Lamb, M. E., Sternberg, K. J., Orbach, Y., Esplin, P. W., & Bowler, L. (2004). Using a human figure drawing to elicit information from alleged victims of child sexual abuse. *Journal of Consulting and Clinical Psychology, 72,* 304–316.

Alexander, K. W., Goodman, G. S., Schaaf, J. M., Edelstein, R. S., Quas, J. A., & Shaver, P. R. (2002). The role of attachment and cognitive inhibition in children's memory and suggestibility for a stressful event. *Journal of Experimental Child Psychology, 83,* 262–290.

Alexander, K. W., Quas, J. A., Ghetti, S., Goodman, G. S., Edelstein, R. S., Redlich, A. D., et al. (2005). Traumatic impact predicts long-term memory for documented child sexual abuse. *Psychological Science, 16,* 33–40.

Alexander, K. W., Redlich, A. D., Christian, P., & Goodman, G. S. (2003). Interviewing children. In M. Peterson & M. Durfee (Eds.), *Child abuse and neglect: Guidelines for the identification, assessment, and case management* (pp. 17–19). Volcano, CA: Volcano Press.

Alpert, J. L., Brown, L. S., & Courtois, C. A. (1998). Symptomatic clients and memories of childhood abuse: What the trauma and child sexual abuse literature tells us. *Psychology, Public Policy, and Law, 4,* 941–995.

Anderson, M. C., Ochsner, K. N., Kuhl, B., Cooper, J., Robertson, E., Gabrieli, S. W., et al. (2004). Neural systems underlying the suppression of unwanted memories. *Science, 303,* 232–235.

APA Working Group on Investigation of Memories of Childhood Abuse. (1998, December). *Final conclusions of the American Psychological Association Working Group on Investigation of Memories of Child Abuse.* Washington, DC.

Bahrick, H. P. (1984). Semantic memory content in permastore: Fifty years of memory for Spanish learned in school. *Journal of Experimental Psychology, 113,* 1–29.

Bahrick, H. P., Bahrick, P. O., & Wittlinger, R. P. (1975). Fifty years of memory for names and faces: A cross-sectional approach. *Journal of Experimental Psychology: General, 104,* 54–75.

Bartlett, F. C. (1932). *Remembering.* Cambridge, England: Cambridge University Press.

Bauer, P. J., & Wewerka, S. S. (1995). One- to two-year-olds' recall of events: The more expressed, the more impressed. *Journal of Experimental Child Psychology, 59,* 475–496.

Bekerian, D. A., & Bowers, J. M. (1983). Eyewitness testimony: Were we misled? *Journal of Experimental Psychology: Learning, Memory, and Cognition, 9,* 139–145.

Bell, B. E., & Loftus, E. F. (1989). Trivial persuasion in the courtroom: The power of (a few) minor details. *Journal of Personality and Social Psychology, 56,* 669–679.

Belli, R. F., Lindsay, D. S., Gales, M. S., & McCarthy, T. T. (1994). Memory impairment and source misattribution in postevent misinformation experiments with short retention intervals. *Memory and Cognition, 22,* 40–54.

Berliner, L., & Williams, L. M. (1994). Memories of child sexual abuse: A response to Lindsay and Read. *Applied Cognitive Psychology, 8,* 379–388.

Bernstein, E. M., & Putnam, F. W. (1986). Development, reliability, and validity of a dissociation scale. *Journal of Nervous and Mental Diseases, 174,* 727–735.

Berntsen, D. (2002). Tunnel memories for autobiographical events: Central details are remembered more frequently from shocking than from happy experiences. *Memory and Cognition, 30,* 1010–1020.

Betz, A. L., & Skowronski, J. J. (1997). Self-events and other events: Temporal dating and event memory. *Memory and Cognition, 25,* 710–714.

Bidrose, S., & Goodman, G. S. (2000). Testimony and evidence: A scientific case study of memory for child sexual abuse. *Applied Cognitive Psychology, 14,* 197–213.

Billig, M., & Milner, D. (1976). A spade is a spade in the eyes of the law. *Psychology Today, 2,* 13–15, 62.

Birren, J. E., & Schaie, K. W. (Eds.). (2001). *Handbook of the psychology of aging* (5th ed.). San Diego, CA: Academic Press.

Bjork, R. A. (1988). Retrieval practice and the maintenance of knowledge. In M. M. Gruneberg & P. E. Morris (Eds.), *Practical aspects of memory: Current research and issues: Memory in everyday life* (pp. 396–401). Oxford: Wiley.

Bloom, L. C., & Mudd, S. A. (1991). Depth of processing approach to face recognition: A test of two theories. *Journal of Experimental Psychology: Learning, Memory, and Cognition, 17,* 556–565.

Bohannon, J. N. (1988). Flashbulb memories for the space shuttle disaster: A tale of two theories. *Cognition, 29,* 179–196.

Boon, J. C., & Baxter, J. S. (2000). Minimizing interrogative suggestibility. *Legal and Criminological Psychology, 5,* 273–284.

Borckardt, J. J., Sprohge, E., & Nash, M. (2003). Effects of the inclusion and refutation of periph- eral details on eyewitness credibility. *Journal of Applied Social Psychology, 33,* 2187–2197.

Bothwell, R. K., Brigham, J. C., & Pigott, M. A. (1987). An exploratory study of personality dif- ferences in eyewitness memory. *Journal of Social Behavior and Personality, 2,* 335–343.

Bothwell, R. K., Deffenbacher, K. A., & Brigham, J. C. (1987). Correlation of eyewitness accuracy and confidence: Optimality hypothesis revisited. *Journal of Applied Psychology, 72,* 691–695.

Bottoms, B. L., Shaver, P. R., & Goodman, G. S. (1996). An analysis of ritualistic and religion- related child abuse allegations. *Law and Human Behavior, 20,* 1–34.

Bowen, C. J., & Howie, P. M. (2002). Context and cue cards in young children's testimony: A comparison of brief narrative elaboration and context reinstatement. *Journal of Applied Psy- chology, 87,* 1077–1085.

Bowers, J. M., & Bekerian, D. A. (1984). When will postevent information distort eyewitness tes- timony? *Journal of Applied Psychology, 69,* 466–472.

Brainerd, C. J., & Ornstein, P. A. (1991). Children's memory for witnessed events: The develop- mental backdrop. In J. Doris (Ed.), *The suggestibility of children's recollections* (pp. 10–20). Washington, DC: American Psychological Association.

Brainerd, C. J., & Reyna, V. F. (1998). Fuzzy-trace theory and children's false memory. *Journal of Experimental Child Psychology, 71,* 81–129.

Brainerd, C. J., Reyna, V., Howe, M., & Kingma, J. (1990). The development of forgetting and reminiscence. *Monographs of Society for Research in Child Development, 55,* 1–113.

Bregman, N. J., & McAllister, H. A. (1982). Eyewitness testimony: The role of commitment in in- creasing reliability. *Social Psychology Quarterly, 45,* 466–472.

Bremner, J. D., Randall, P., Scott, T. M., Bronen, R. A., Seibyl, J. P., Southwick, S. M., et al. (1995). MRI-based measurement of hippocampal volume in combat-related posttraumatic stress dis- order. *American Journal of Psychiatry, 152,* 973–981.

Bremner, J. D., Randall, P., Vermetten, E., Staib, L., Bronen, R. A., Mazure, C., et al. (1997). Mag- netic resonance imaging-based measurement of hippocampal volume in posttraumatic stress disorder related to childhood physical and sexual abuse: A preliminary report. *Biological Psychiatry, 41,* 23–32.

Brewer, N., Gordon, M., & Bond, N. (2000). Effect of photoarray exposure duration on eyewit- ness identification accuracy and processing strategy. *Psychology, Crime, and Law, 6,* 21–32.

Briere, J. N. (1992). *Child abuse trauma: Theory and treatment of the lasting effects.* Thousand Oaks, CA: Sage.

Briere, J. N., & Conte, J. (1993). Self-reported amnesia for abuse in adults molested as children. *Journal of Traumatic Stress, 6,* 21–31.

Brigham, J. C. (1990). Target person distinctiveness and attractiveness as moderator variables in the confidence-accuracy relationship in eyewitness identifications. *Basic and Applied Social Psychology, 11,* 101–115.

Brigham, J. C., Maass, A., Snyder, L. D., & Spaulding, K. (1982). Accuracy of eyewitness identifi- cations in a field setting. *Journal of Personality and Social Psychology, 42,* 673–681.

Brigham, J. C., Meissner, C. A., & Wasserman, A. W. (1999). Applied issues in the construction and expert assessment of photo lineups. *Applied Cognitive Psychology, 13,* S73–S92.

Brimacombe, C. A. E., Jung, S., Garrioch, L., & Allison, M. (2003). Perceptions of older adult eye- witnesses: Will you believe me when I'm 64? *Law and Human Behavior, 27,* 507–522.

Brown, D. A., & Pipe, M. (2003). Individual differences in children's event memory reports and the narrative elaboration technique. *Journal of Applied Psychology, 88,* 195–206.

Brown, D. A., Salmon, K., Pipe, M., Rutter, M., Craw, S., & Taylor, B. (1999). Children's recall of medical experiences: The impact of stress. *Child Abuse and Neglect, 23,* 209–216.

Brown, J. M. (2003). Eyewitness memory for arousing events: Putting things into context. *Ap- plied Cognitive Psychology, 17,* 93–106.

Brown, L. S. (1996). On the construction of truth and falsity: Whose memory, whose history. In K. Pezdek & W. P. Banks (Eds.), *The recovered memory/false memory debate* (pp. 341–353). San Diego, CA: Academic Press, Inc.

Brown, R., & Kulik, J. (1977). Flashbulb memories. *Cognition, 5,* 73–99.

Bruck, M., & Ceci, S. J. (1999). The suggestibility of children's memory. *Annual Review of Psy- chology, 50,* 419–439.

Bruck, M., Ceci, S. J., Francoeur, E., & Barr, R. (1995). "I hardly cried when I got my shot": Influ- encing children's reports about a visit to their pediatrician. *Child Development, 66,* 193–208.

Bruck, M., Ceci, S. J., & Hembrooke, H. (1998). Reliability and credibility of young children's re- ports: From research to policy and practice. *American Psychologist, 53,* 136–151.

Bruck, M., Ceci, S. J., & Hembrooke, H. (2002). The nature of children's true and false narratives [Special issue: Forensic developmental psychology]. *Developmental Review, 22,* 520–554.

Bruck, M., Melnyk, L., & Ceci, S. J. (2000). Draw it again Sam: The effect of drawing on children's suggestibility and source monitoring ability. *Journal of Experimental Child Psychology, 77,* 169–196.

Buckhout, R. (1974). Eyewitness testimony. *Scientific American, 231,* 23–31.

Buckhout, R. (1984). Double mistaken identification in Dallas: Texas v. Lenell Geter and Anthony Williams. *Social Action and the Law, 10,* 3–11.

Bull Kovera, M., Park, R. C., & Penrod, S. D. (1992). Jurors' perceptions of eyewitness and hearsay evidence. *Minnesota Law Review, 76,* 703–722.

Burgess, M. C. R., & Weaver, G. E. (2003). Interest and attention in facial recognition. *Perceptual and Motor Skills, 96,* 467–480.

Burgwyn-Bailes, E., Baker-Ward, L., Gordon, B. N., & Ornstein, P. A. (2001). Children's memory for emergency medical treatment after one year: The impact of individual difference variables on recall and suggestibility [Special issue: Trauma, stress, and autobiographical memory]. *Applied Cognitive Psychology, 15,* S25–S48.

Butler, S., Gross, J., & Hayne, H. (1995). The effect of drawing on memory performance in young children. *Developmental Psychology, 31,* 597–608.

Butters, M. J. (1970). Differential recall of paired associates as a function of arousal and concreteness-imagery levels. *Journal of Experimental Psychology, 84,* 252–256.

Carter, C. A., Bottoms, B. L., & Levine, M. (1996). Linguistic and socioemotional influences on the accuracy of children's reports. *Law and Human Behavior, 20,* 335–358.

Cassel, W. S., & Bjorklund, D. F. (1995). Developmental patterns of eyewitness memory and suggestibility: An ecologically based short-term longitudinal study. *Law and Human Behavior, 19,* 507–532.

Cassel, W. S., Roebers, C. M., & Bjorklund, D. F. (1996). Developmental patterns of eyewitness responses to repeated and increasingly suggestive questions. *Journal of Experimental Child Psychology, 61,* 116–133.

Ceci, S. J., & Bruck, M. (1993). Suggestibility of the child witness: A historical review and synthesis. *Psychological Bulletin, 113,* 403–439.

Ceci, S. J., & Huffman, M. L. C. (1997). How suggestible are preschool children? Cognitive and social factors. *Journal of the American Academy of Child and Adolescent Psychiatry, 36,* 948–958.

Ceci, S. J., Ross, D. F., & Toglia, M. P. (1987). Suggestibility of children's memory: Psycholegal implications. *Journal of Experimental Psychology: General, 116,* 38–49.

Chambers, K. L., & Zaragoza, M. S. (2001). Intended and unintended effects of explicit warnings on eyewitness suggestibility: Evidence from source identification tests. *Memory and Cognition, 29,* 2001.

Chance, J. E., Turner, A. L., & Goldstein, A. G. (1982). Development of differential recognition for own- and other-race faces. *Journal of Psychology, 112,* 29–37.

Chandler, C. C., & Gargano, G. J. (1995). Item-specific interference caused by cue-dependent forgetting. *Memory and Cognition, 23,* 701–708.

Chandler, C. C., & Gargano, G. J. (1998). Retrieval processes that produce interference in modified forced-choice recognition tests. *Memory and Cognition, 26,* 220–231.

Chandler, C. C., Gargano, G. J., & Holt, B. C. (2001). Witnessing postevents does not change memory traces, but can affect their retrieval. *Applied Cognitive Psychology, 15,* 3–22.

Christiaansen, R. E., & Ochalek, K. (1983). Editing misleading information from memory: Evidence for the coexistence of original and postevent information. *Memory and Cognition, 11,* 467–475.

Christianson, S. A. (1989). Flashbulb memories: Special, but not so special. *Memory and Cognition, 17,* 435–443.

Christianson, S. A. (1992). Emotional stress and eyewitness memory: A critical review. *Psychological Bulletin, 112,* 284–309.

Christianson, S., & Engelberg, E. (1999). Organization of emotional memories. In T. Dalgleish & M. J. Power (Eds.), *Handbook of cognition and emotion* (pp. 211–227). New York: Wiley.

Christianson, S. A., & Hübinette, B. (1993). Hands up: A study of witnesses' emotional reactions and memories associated with bank robberies. *Applied Cognitive Psychology, 7,* 365–379.

Christianson, S. A., & Loftus, E. F. (1990). Some characteristics of people's traumatic memories. *Bulletin of the Psychonomic Society, 28,* 195–198.

Christianson, S. A., & Loftus, E. F. (1991). Remembering emotional events: The fate of detailed information. *Cognition and Emotion, 5,* 81–108.

Chu, J. A. (1998). Dissociative symptomatology in adult patients with histories of childhood physical and sexual abuse. In J. D. Bremner & C. R. Marmar (Eds.), *Trauma, memory, and dissociation* (pp. 179–203). Washington, DC: American Psychiatric Press.

Cicchetti, D., & Toth, S. L. (1995). A developmental psychopathology perspective on child abuse and neglect. *Journal of the American Academy of Child and Adolescent Psychiatry, 34,* 541–565.

Clark, S., & Tunnicliff, J. L. (2001). Selecting lineup foils in eyewitness identification experiments: Experimental control and real-world simulation. *Law and Human Behavior, 25,* 199–216.

Clifford, B. R., & Richards, V. J. (1977). Comparison of recall by policemen and civilians under conditions of long and short durations of exposure. *Perceptual and Motor Skills, 45,* 503–512.

Coles, M. E., & Heimberg, R. G. (2002). Memory biases in the anxiety disorders: Current status. *Clinical Psychology Review, 22,* 587–627.

Connors, E., Lundregan, T., Miller, N., & McEwan, T. (1996). *Convicted by juries, exonerated by science: Case studies in the use of DNA evidence to establish innocence after trial.* Alexandria, VA: National Institute of Justice.

Cordon, I. (2004). *"Who spilled the jelly at Camp Ingrid?": Effects of familiarity and stereotypes on children's memory.* Dissertation submitted to the University of California, Davis.

Corey, D., Malpass, R. S., & McQuiston, D. E. (1999). Parallelism in eyewitness and mock witness identification [Special issue: Measuring lineup fairness]. *Applied Cognitive Psychology, 13,* 41–58.

Courtois, C. A. (1992). The memory retrieval process in incest survivor therapy. *Journal of Child Sexual Abuse, 1,* 15–31.

Coxon, P., & Valentine, T. (1997). The effects of the age of eyewitnesses on the accuracy and suggestibility of their testimony. *Applied Cognitive Psychology, 11,* 415–430.

Crawford v. Washington, 541 U.S. 02-9410 (2004).

Curci, A., Luminet, O., Finkenauer, C., & Gisle, L. (2001). Flashbulb memories in social groups: A comparative test-retest study of memory of French President Mitterrand's death in a French and a Belgian group. *Memory, 9,* 81–101.

Cutler, B. L., & Penrod, S. D. (1988). Improving the reliability of eyewitness identification: Lineup construction and presentation. *Journal of Applied Psychology, 71,* 281–290.

Cutler, B. L., Penrod, S. D., & Martens, T. K. (1987). Improving the reliability of eyewitness identification: Putting context into context. *Journal of Applied Psychology, 72,* 629–637.

Daubert v. Merrell Dow Pharmaceuticals, 509 U.S. 579 (1993).

Davies, G. M., & Milne, A. (1982). Recognizing faces in and out of context. *Current Psychological Research, 2,* 235–246.

Day, K., Howie, P., & Markham, R. (1998). The role of similarity in developmental differences in source monitoring. *British Journal of Developmental Psychology, 16,* 219–232.

Deffenbacher, K. A. (1980). Eyewitness accuracy and confidence: Can we infer anything about their relationship? *Law and Human Behavior, 4,* 243–260.

Deffenbacher, K. A. (1983). The influence of arousal on reliability of testimony. In S. Lloyd-Bostock & B. R. Clifford (Eds.), *Evaluating witness evidence* (pp. 235–254). Chichester, England: Wiley.

Deffenbacher, K. A. (1991). A maturing of research on the behaviour of eyewitnesses. *Applied Cognitive Psychology, 5,* 377–402.

Dent, H. R., & Stephenson, G. M. (1979). An experimental study of the effectiveness of different techniques of questioning child witnesses. *British Journal of Social and Clinical Psychology, 18,* 41–51.

DePrince, A. P., & Freyd, J. J. (1999). Dissociative tendencies, attention, and memory. *Psychological Science, 10,* 449–452.

Dobson, M., & Markham, R. (1992). Individual differences in anxiety level and eyewitness memory. *Journal of General Psychology, 119,* 343–350.

Drucker, P. M., Greco-Vigorito, C., Moore-Russell, M., Alvaltroni, J., & Ryan, E. (1997, April). *Drawing facilitates recall of traumatic past events in young children of substance abusers.* Paper presented at the biennial meeting of the Society for Research in Child Development, Washington, DC.

Duncan, E. M., Whitney, P., & Kunen, S. (1982). Integration of visual and verbal information in children's memories. *Child Development, 53,* 1215–1233.

Dunning, D., & Stern, L. B. (1992). Examining the generality of eyewitness hypermnesia: A close look at time delay and questions type. *Applied Cognitive Psychology, 6,* 643–657.

Durham, M. D., & Dane, F. C. (1999). Juror knowledge of eyewitness behavior: Evidence for the necessity of expert testimony. *Journal of Social Behavior and Personality, 14,* 299–308.

Dysart, J. E., Lindsay, R. C. L., Hammond, R., & Dupuis, P. (2001). Mug shot exposure prior to lineup identification: Interference, transference, and commitment effects. *Journal of Applied Psychology, 86,* 1280–1284.

Easterbrook, J. A. (1959). The effect of emotion on the utilization and organization of behavior. *Psychology Review, 66,* 183–201.

Ebbinghaus, H. E. (1885/1964). *Memory: A contribution to experimental psychology.* New York: Dover.

Edelstein, R. S., Ghetti, S., Quas, J. A., Goodman, G. S., Alexander, K. W., Redlich, A. D., et al. (in press). Individual differences in emotional memory: Adult attachment and long-term memory for child sexual abuse. Personality and Social Psychology Bulletin.

Egeth, H. E., & McCloskey, M. (1984). The jury is still out: A reply to Deffenbacher. *American Psychologist, 39,* 1068–1069.

Eisen, M. L., & Goodman, G. S. (1998). Trauma, memory, and suggestibility in children. *Development and Psychopathology, 10,* 717–738.

Eisen, M. L., Goodman, G. S., Qin, J. J., & Davis, S. L. (1998). Memory and suggestibility in maltreated children: New research relevant to evaluating allegations of abuse. In S. J. Lynn & K. M. McConkey (Eds.), *Truth in memory* (pp. 163–189). New York: Guilford Press.

Eisen, M. L., Goodman, G. S., Qin, J. J., & Davis, S. L. (2004). *Maltreatment and children's memory: Accuracy, suggestibility and psychopathology.* Unpublished manuscript.

Eisen, M. L., Qin, J., Goodman, G. S., & Davis, S. (2002). Memory and suggestibility in maltreated children: Age, stress arousal, dissociation, and psychopathology. *Journal of Experimental Child Psychology, 83,* 167–212.

Eisen, M. L., Quas, J. A., & Goodman, G. S. (2002). *Memory and suggestibility in the forensic interview: Personality and clinical psychology series.* Mahwah, NJ: Erlbaum.

Eisen, M., Winograd, E., & Qin, J. (2002). Individual differences in adults' suggestibility and memory performance. In M. Eisen, J. A. Quas, & G. S. Goodman (Eds.), *Memory and suggestibility in the forensic interview* (pp. 205–234). Mahwah, NJ: Erlbaum.

Elliott, E. S., Wills, E. J., & Goldstein, A. G. (1973). The effects of discrimination training on the recognition of White and Oriental faces. *Bulletin of the Psychonomic Society, 2,* 71–73.

Emmett, D., Clifford, B. R., & Gwyer, P. (2003). An investigation of the interaction between cognitive style and context reinstatement on the memory performance of eyewitnesses. *Personality and Individual Differences, 34,* 1495–1508.

Engle, R. W., Tuholski, S. W., Laughlin, J. E., Conway, A. R. A. (1999). Working memory, short-term memory, and general fluid intelligence: A latent-variable approach. *Journal of Experimental Psychology: General, 128,* 309–331.

Epstein, M. A., & Bottoms, B. L. (1998). Memories of childhood sexual abuse: A survey of young adults. *Child Abuse and Neglect, 22,* 1217–1238.

Er, N. (2003). A new flashbulb memory model applied to the Marmara earthquake. *Applied Cognitive Psychology, 17,* 503–517.

Everson, M. D., & Boat, B. W. (2002). The utility of anatomical dolls and drawings in child forensic interviews. In M. Eisen, J. A. Quas, & G. S. Goodman (Eds.), *Memory and suggestibility in the forensic interview* (pp. 383–408). Mahwah, NJ: Erlbaum.

Farrar, M. J., & Boyer-Pennington, M. (1999). Remembering specific episodes of a scripted event. *Journal of Experimental Child Psychology, 73,* 266–288.

Farrington, D. P., & Lambert, S. (1997). Predicting offender profiles from victim and witness descriptions. In J. L. Jackson & D. A. Bekerian (Eds.), *Offender profiling: Theory, research and practice* (pp. 133–158). New York: Wiley.

Feeny, N. C., Zoellner, L. A., & Foa, E. B. (2000). Anger, dissociation, and posttraumatic stress disorder among female assault victims. *Journal of Traumatic Stress, 13,* 89–100.

Fisher, R. P., & Geiselman, R. E. (1992). *Memory-enhancing techniques for investigative interviewing: The cognitive interview.* Springfield, IL: Charles Thomas.

Fivush, R. (1984). Learning about school: The development of kindergartners' school scripts. *Child Development, 55,* 1697–1709.

Fivush, R. (1993). Developmental perspectives on autobiographical recall. In G. S. Goodman & B. L. Bottoms (Eds.), *Child victims, child witnesses: Understanding and improving testimony* (pp. 1–24). New York: Guilford Press.

Fivush, R., & Hudson, J. A. (1990). *Knowing and remembering in young children.* New York: Cambridge University Press.

Fivush, R., Hudson, J., & Nelson, K. (1984). Children's long-term memory for a novel event: An exploratory study. *Merrill-Palmer Quarterly, 30,* 303–316.

Fivush, R., Kuebli, J., & Clubb, P. A. (1992). The structure of events and event representations: A microdevelopmental analysis. *Child Development, 63,* 188–201.

Fivush, R., Peterson, C., & Schwarzmueller, A. (2002). Questions and answers: The credibility of child witnesses in the context of specific questioning techniques. In M. Eisen, J. A. Quas, & G. S. Goodman (Eds.), *Memory and suggestibility in the forensic interview* (pp. 331–354). Mahwah, NJ: Erlbaum.

Flin, R. H., Boon, J., Knox, A., & Bull, R. (1992). The effect of five-month delay on children's and adult's eyewitness memory. *British Journal of Psychology, 83,* 323–336.

Foley, M. A., & Johnson, M. K. (1985). Confusion between memories for performed and imagined actions. *Child Development, 56,* 1145–1155.

Foley, M. A., & Ratner, H. H. (1998). Distinguishing between memories for thoughts and deeds: The role of prospective processing in children's source monitoring. *British Journal of Developmental Psychology, 16,* 465–484.

Fraley, R. C., Garner, J. P., & Shaver, P. R. (2000). Adult attachment and the defensive regulation of attention and memory: Examining the role of preemptive and postemptive defensive processes. *Journal of Personality and Social Psychology, 79,* 816–826.

Freud, S. (1957). Repression. In J. Strachey (Ed. & Trans.), *The standard edition of the complete psychological works of Sigmund Freud* (Vol. 14, pp. 146–158). London: Hogarth Press. (Original work published 1915)

Freyd, J. J. (1996). *Betrayal trauma: The logic of forgetting childhood abuse.* Cambridge, MA: Harvard University Press.

Freyd, J. J., & Gleaves, D. H. (1996). Remembering words not presented in lists: Implications for the recovered/false memory controversy? *Journal of Experimental Psychology: Learning, Memory, and Cognition, 22,* 811–813.

Friedman, A. (1979). Framing pictures: The role of default knowledge in automatized encoding and memory for gist. *Journal of Experimental Psychology: General, 108,* 315–355.

Gabbert, F., Memon, A., & Allan, K. (2003). Memory conformity: Can eyewitnesses influence each other's memories for an event? *Applied Cognitive Psychology, 17,* 533–543.

Garcia-Bajos, E., & Migueles, M. (2003). False memories for script actions in a mugging account. *European Journal of Cognitive Psychology, 15,* 195–208.

Garven, S., Wood, J. M., Malpass, R. S., & Shaw, J. S. (1998). More than suggestion: The effect of interviewing techniques from the McMartin Preschool case. *Journal of Applied Psychology, 83,* 347–359.

Geddie, L., Fradin, S., & Beer, J. (2000). Child characteristics which impact accuracy of recall and suggestibility in preschoolers: Is age the best predictor? *Child Abuse and Neglect, 24,* 223–235.

Geiselman, R. E. (1999). Commentary on recent research with the cognitive interview [Special issue: The cognitive interview: Current research and applications]. *Psychology, Crime, and Law, 5,* 197–202.

Geiselman, R. E., & Fisher, R. P. (1989). The cognitive interview technique for victims and witnesses of crime. In D. C. Raskin (Ed.), *Psychological methods in criminal investigation and evidence* (pp. 191–215). New York: Springer.

Geiselman, R. E., Putman, C., Korte, R., Shahriary, M., Jachimowicz, G., & Irzhevsky, V. (2002). Eyewitness expert testimony and juror decisions. *American Journal of Forensic Psychology, 20,* 21–36.

Ghetti, S., & Alexander, K. W. (2004). "If it happened, I would remember it": Strategic use of event memorability in the rejection of false autobiographical events. *Child Development, 75,* 542–561.

Ghetti, S., Edelstein, R. S., Cordon, I. M., Goodman, G. S., Quas, J. A., Alexander, K. W., et al. (2004). *What can subjective forgetting tell us about memory for childhood trauma?* Unpublished manuscript.

Giles, J. W., Gopnik, A., & Heyman, G. D. (2002). Source monitoring reduces the suggestibility of preschool children. *Psychological Science, 13,* 288–291.

Gobbo, C. (2000). Assessing the effects of misinformation on children's recall: How and when makes a difference. *Applied Cognitive Psychology, 14,* 163–182.

Golding, J. M., Sanchez, R. P., & Sego, S. A. (1997). The believability of hearsay testimony in a child sexual assault trial. *Law and Human Behavior, 21,* 299–325.

Gonzalez, R., Ellsworth, P. C., & Pembroke, M. (1993). Response biases in lineups and showups. *Journal of Personality and Social Psychology, 64,* 525–537.

Goodman, G. S. (1984). The child witness: Conclusions and future directions for research and legal practice. *Journal of Social Issues, 40,* 157–175.

Goodman, G. S., Batterman-Faunce, J. M., Schaaf, J. M., & Kenney, R. (2002). Nearly 4 years after an event: Children's eyewitness memory and adults' perception of children's accuracy. *Child Abuse and Neglect, 26,* 849–884.

Goodman, G. S., Bottoms, B. L., Rudy, L., Davis, S. L., & Schwartz-Kenney, B. M. (2001). Effects of past abuse experiences on children's eyewitness memory. *Law and Human Behavior, 25*, 269–298.

Goodman, G. S., Bottoms, B. L., Schwartz-Kenney, B. M., & Rudy, L. (1991). Children's testimony about a stressful event: Improving children's reports. *Journal of Narrative and Life History, 1*, 69–99.

Goodman, G. S., Emery, R. E., & Haugaard, J. J. (1997). Developmental psychology and law: Divorce, child maltreatment, foster care, and adoption. In I. Sigel & A. Renninger (Eds.), *Handbook of child psychology: Vol. 4. Child psychology in practice* (5th ed., pp. 775–874). New York: Wiley.

Goodman, G. S., Ghetti, S., Quas, J. A., Edelstein, R. S., Alexander, K. W., Redlich, A. D., et al. (2003). A prospective study of memory for child sexual abuse: New findings relevant to the repressed-memory controversy. *Psychological Science, 14*, 113–118.

Goodman, G. S., Hirschman, J. E., Hepps, D., & Rudy, L. (1991). Children's memory for stressful events. *Merrill-Palmer Quarterly, 37*, 109–157.

Goodman, G. S., Quas, J. A., Batterman-Faunce, J. M., Riddlesberger, M., & Kuhn, J. (1997). Children's reactions to and memory for stressful experience: Influence of age, knowledge, anatomical dolls, and parental attachment. *Applied Developmental Science, 1*, 54–75.

Goodman, G. S., Sayfan, L., Lee, J., Sandhei, M., Magnussen, S., Pezdek, K., et al. (2004). *The development of memory for own- and other-race faces.* Paper submitted for publication.

Goodman, G. S., Tobey, A. E., Batterman-Faunce, J. M., Orcutt, H., Thomas, S., & Shapiro, C. (1998). Face-to-face confrontation: Effects of closed-circuit technology on children's eyewitness testimony and jurors' decisions. *Law and Human Behavior, 22*, 165–203.

Gorenstein, G. W., & Ellsworth, P. D. (1980). Effect of choosing an incorrect photograph on a later identification by an eyewitness. *Journal of Applied Psychology, 665*, 616–622.

Greenberg, M. S., Westcott, D. R., & Bailey, S. E. (1998). When believing is seeing: The effect of scripts on eyewitness memory. *Law and Human Behavior, 22*, 685–694.

Greene, E., Flynn, M. B., & Loftus, E. F. (1982). Inducing resistance to misleading information. *Journal of Verbal Learning and Verbal Behavior, 21*, 207–219.

Gross, J., & Hayne, H. (1998). Drawing facilitates children's verbal reports of emotionally laden events. *Journal of Experimental Psychology: Applied, 4*, 163–179.

Gross, J., & Hayne, H. (1999). Drawing facilitates children's verbal reports after long delays. *Journal of Experimental Psychology: Applied, 5*, 265–283.

Gudjonsson, G. H. (1984). A new scale of interrogative suggestibility. *Personality and Individual Differences, 5*, 303–314.

Gudjonsson, G. H. (1987). The relationship between memory and suggestibility. *Social Behavior, 2*, 29–33.

Gudjonsson, G. H. (2003). *The psychology of interrogation and confessions: A handbook.* Hoboken, NJ: Wiley.

Gudjonsson, G. H., & Henry, L. (2003). Child and adult witnesses with intellectual disability: The importance of suggestibility. *Legal and Criminological Psychology, 8*, 241–252.

Haden, C. A., Haine, R. A., & Fivush, R. (1997). Developing narrative structure in parent-child reminiscing across the preschool years. *Developmental Psychology, 33*, 295–307.

Harvey, M. R., & Herman, J. L. (1994). Amnesia, partial amnesia, and delayed recall among adult survivors of childhood trauma. *Consciousness and Cognition, 3*, 295–306.

Hayes, B. K., & Delamothe, K. (1997). Cognitive interviewing procedures and suggestibility in children's recall. *Journal of Applied Psychology, 82*, 562–577.

Hembrooke, H., & Ceci, S. J. (1995). Traumatic memories: Do we need to invoke special mechanisms? *Consciousness and Cognition: An International Journal, 4*, 75–82.

Henry, L. A., & Norman, T. (1996). The relationships between memory performance, use of simple memory strategies and metamemory in young children. *International Journal of Behavioral Development, 19*, 177–199.

Herman, J. L. (1992). *Trauma and recovery.* New York: Basic Books.

Hershkowitz, I., Orbach, Y., Lamb, M. E., Sternberg, K. J., & Horowitz, D. (2001). The effects of mental context reinstatement on children's accounts of sexual abuse. *Applied Cognitive Psychology, 15*, 235–248.

Hershkowitz, I., Orbach, Y., Lamb, M. E., Sternberg, K. J., & Horowitz, D. (2002). A comparison of mental and physical context reinstatement in forensic interviews with alleged victims of sexual abuse. *Applied Cognitive Psychology, 16*, 429–441.

Holliday, R. E., Reyna, V. F., & Hayes, B. K. (2002). Memory processes underlying misinformation effects in child witnesses. *Developmental Review, 22*, 37–77.

Holst, V. F., & Pezdek, K. (1992). Scripts for typical crimes and their effects on memory for eyewitness testimony. *Applied Cognitive Psychology, 6,* 573–587.

Horn, M. (1993, November 29). Memories, lost and found. *U.S. News and World Report,* 52–63.

Hornstein, S. L., Brown, A. S., & Mulligan, N. W. (2003). Long-term flashbulb memory for learning of Princess Diana's death. *Memory, 11,* 293–306.

Howe, M. L. (1991). Misleading children's story recall: Forgetting and reminiscence of the facts. *Developmental Psychology, 27,* 746–762.

Howe, M. L. (1997). Children's memory for traumatic experiences. *Learning and Individual Differences, 9,* 153–174.

Howes, M., Siegel, M., & Brown, F. (1993). Early childhood memories: Accuracy and affect. *Cognition, 47,* 95–119.

Hull, A. M. (2002). Neuroimaging findings in post-traumatic stress. *British Journal of Psychiatry, 181,* 102–110.

Hutcheson, G. D., Baxter, J. S., Telfer, K., & Warden, D. (1995). Child witness statement quality: Question type and errors of omission. *Law and Human Behavior, 19,* 631–648.

Hyman, I. E., Jr., Husband, T. H., & Billings, F. J. (1995). False memories of childhood experiences. *Applied Cognitive Psychology, 9,* 181–197.

Hyman, I. E., Jr., & Pentland, J. (1996). The role of mental imagery in the creation of false childhood memories. *Journal of Memory and Language, 35,* 101–117.

Jacoby, L. L., Kelley, C. M., Brown, J., & Jasechko, J. (1989). Becoming famous overnight: Limits on the ability to avoid unconscious influences of the past. *Journal of Personality and Social Psychology, 56,* 326–338.

Jacoby, L. L., Woloshyn, V., & Kelley, C. M. (1989). Becoming famous without being recognized: Unconscious influences of memory produced by divided attention. *Journal of Experimental Psychology: General, 118,* 115–125.

Jaschinski, U., & Wentura, D. (2002). Misleading postevent information and working memory capacity: An individual differences approach to eyewitness memory. *Applied Cognitive Psychology, 16,* 223–231.

Jenkins, M. A., Langlais, P. J., Delis, D., & Cohen, R. (1998). Learning and memory in rape victims with posttraumatic stress disorder. *American Journal of Psychiatry, 155,* 278–279.

Johnson, M. K. (1988). Reality monitoring: An experimental phenomenological approach. *Journal of Experimental Psychology: General, 117,* 390–394.

Johnson, M. K., Hashtroudi, S., & Lindsay, D. S. (1993). Source monitoring. *Psychological Bulletin, 114,* 3–28.

Johnson, M. K., & Raye, C. L. (1981). Reality monitoring. *Psychological Review, 88,* 67–85.

Jones, C. H., & Pipe, M. E. (2002). How quickly do children forget events? A systematic study of children's event reports as a function of delay. *Applied Cognitive Psychology, 16,* 755–768.

Kassin, S. M., Rigby, S., & Castillo, S. R. (1991). The accuracy-confidence correlation in eyewitness testimony: Limits and extensions of the retrospective self-awareness effect. *Journal of Personality and Social Psychology, 61,* 698–707.

Kassin, S. M., Tubb, V. A., Hosch, H. M., & Memon, A. (2001). On the general acceptance of eyewitness testimony research: A new survey of the experts. *American Psychologist, 56,* 405–416.

Kleinsmith, L. J., & Kaplan, S. (1963). Paired associated learning as a function of arousal and interpolated interval. *Journal of Experimental Psychology, 65,* 190–193.

Koehnken, G., Milne, R., Memon, A., & Bull, R. (1999). The cognitive interview: A meta-analysis [Special issue: The cognitive interview: Current research and applications]. *Psychology, Crime, and Law, 5,* 3–27.

Koocher, G. P., Goodman, G. S., White, C. S., Friedrich, W. N., Sivan, A. B., & Reynolds, C. R. (1995). Psychological science and the use of anatomically detailed dolls in child sexual-abuse assessments. *Psychological Bulletin, 118,* 199–222.

Krackow, E., & Lynn, S. J. (2003). Is there touch in the game of Twister®? The effects of innocuous touch and suggestive questions on children's eyewitness memory. *Law and Human Behavior, 27,* 589–604.

Krafka, C., & Penrod, S. (1985). Reinstatement of context in a field experiment on eyewitness identification. *Journal of Personality and Social Psychology, 49,* 58–69.

Kumho Tire Co. v. Carmichael, 526 U.S. 137 (1999).

Lamb, M. E., & Garretson, M. E. (2003). The effects of interviewer gender and child gender on the informativeness of alleged child sexual abuse victims in forensic interviews. *Law and Human Behavior, 27,* 157–171.

Lamb, M. E., Orbach, Y., Sternberg, K. J., Hershkowitz, I., & Horowitz, D. (2000). Accuracy of investigators' verbatim notes of their forensic interviews with alleged child abuse victims. *Law and Human Behavior, 24,* 699–708.

Lamb, M. E., Sternberg, K. J., & Esplin, P. W. (1998). Conducting investigative interviews of alleged sexual abuse victims. *Child Abuse and Neglect, 22,* 813–823.

Lampinen, J. M., & Smith, V. L. (1995). The incredible (and sometimes incredulous) child witness: Child eyewitnesses' sensitivity to source credibility cues. *Journal of Applied Psychology, 80,* 621–627.

Larsson, A. S., Granhag, P. A., & Spjut, E. (2003). Children's recall and the Cognitive Interview: Do the positive effects hold over time? *Applied Cognitive Psychology, 17,* 203–214.

Laughery, K. R., Alexander, J. F., & Lane, A. B. (1971). Recognition of human faces: Effects of target exposure time, target position, pose position, and type of photograph. *Journal of Applied Psychology, 51,* 477–483.

Lavrakas, P., Buri, J., & Mayznere, M. (1976). A perspective on the recognition of other-race faces. *Perception and Psychophysics, 20,* 475–481.

Leippe, M. R., Manion, A. P., & Romanczyk, A. (1992). Eyewitness persuasion: How and how well do fact finders judge the accuracy of adults' and children's memory reports? *Journal of Personality and Social Psychology, 63,* 181–197.

Levi, A. M., & Lindsay, R. C. L. (2001). Lineup and photo spread procedures: Issues concerning policy recommendations. *Psychology, Public Policy, and Law, 7,* 776–790.

Lieberman, M. D., & Rosenthal, R. (2001). Why introverts can't always tell who likes them: Multitasking and nonverbal decoding. *Journal of Personality and Social Psychology, 80,* 294–310.

Lief, H. I., & Fetkewicz, J. (1995). Retractors of false memories: The evolution of pseudomemories. *Journal of Psychiatry and Law, 23,* 411–435.

Lindsay, D. S. (1990). Misleading suggestions can impair eyewitnesses' ability to remember event details. *Journal of Experimental Psychology: Learning, Memory, and Cognition, 16,* 1077–1083.

Lindsay, D. S. (1994). Memory source monitoring and eyewitness testimony. In D. F. Ross, J. D. Read, & M. P. Toglia (Eds.), *Adult eyewitness testimony: Current trends and developments* (pp. 27–55). Cambridge, England: Cambridge University Press.

Lindsay, D. S., Gonzales, V., & Eso, K. (1995). Aware and unaware uses of memories of postevent suggestions. In M. S. Zaragoza, J. R. Graham, G. N. C. Hall, R. Hirschman, & Y. S. Ben-Porath (Eds.), *Memory and testimony in the child witness* (pp. 86–108). Thousand Oaks, CA: Sage.

Lindsay, D. S., & Johnson, M. K. (1989). The eyewitness suggestibility effect and memory for source. *Memory and Cognition, 17,* 349–358.

Lindsay, D. S., Johnson, M. K., & Kwon, P. (1991). Developmental changes in memory source monitoring. *Journal of Experimental Child Psychology, 52,* 297–318.

Lindsay, D. S., & Read, J. D. (1994). Psychotherapy and memories of childhood sexual abuse: A cognitive perspective. *Applied Cognitive Psychology, 8,* 281–338.

Lindsay, D. S., Read, J. D., & Sharma, K. (1998). Accuracy and confidence in person identification: The relationship is strong when witnessing conditions vary widely. *Psychological Science, 9,* 215–218.

Lindsay, R. C. L. (1994). Expectations of eyewitness performance: Jurors' verdicts do not follow from their beliefs. In D. F. Ross, J. D. Read, & M. P. Toglia (Eds.), *Adult eyewitness testimony: Current trends and developments* (pp. 362–384). New York: Cambridge University Press.

Lindsay, R. C. L. (1999). Applying applied research: Selling the sequential line-up. *Applied Cognitive Psychology, 13,* 219–225.

Lindsay, R. C. L., Lea, J. A., & Fulford, J. A. (1991). Sequential lineup presentation: Technique matters. *Journal of Applied Psychology, 76,* 741–745.

Lindsay, R. C. L., Pozzulo, J. D., Craig, W., Lee, K., & Corber, S. (1997). Simultaneous lineups, sequential lineups, and showups: Eyewitness identification decisions of adults and children. *Law and Human Behavior, 21,* 391–404.

Lindsay, R. C. L., & Wells, G. L. (1985). Improving eyewitness identifications from lineups: Simultaneous versus sequential lineup presentation. *Journal of Applied Psychology, 70,* 556–564.

Loftus, E. F. (1975). Leading questions and the eyewitness report. *Cognitive Psychology, 7,* 560–572.

Loftus, E. F. (1976). Unconscious transference in eyewitness identification. *Law and Psychology Review, 2,* 93–98.

Loftus, E. F. (1977). Shifting human color memory. *Memory and Cognition, 5,* 696–699.

Loftus, E. F. (1979a). *Eyewitness testimony.* Cambridge, MA: Harvard University Press.

Loftus, E. F. (1979b). Reactions to blatantly contradictory information. *Memory and Cognition, 7,* 368–374.

Loftus, E. F. (1993). The reality of repressed memories. *American Psychologist, 48,* 518–537.

Loftus, E. F. (1994). The repressed memory controversy. *American Psychologist, 49,* 443–445.

Loftus, E. F. (2000). Suggestion, imagination, and transformation of reality. In A. A. Stone, J. S. Turkkan, C. A. Bachrach, J. B. Jobe, H. S. Kurtzman, & V. S. Cain (Eds.), *The science of self-report: Implications for research and practice* (pp. 201–210). Mahwah, NJ: Erlbaum.

Loftus, E. F., & Burns, T. E. (1982). Mental shock can produce retrograde amnesia. *Memory and Cognition, 10,* 318–323.

Loftus, E. F., & Doyle, J. M. (1987). *Eyewitness testimony: Civil and criminal.* New York: Kluwer Law Book Publishers.

Loftus, E. F., & Greene, E. (1980). Warning: Even memory for faces may be contagious. *Law and Human Behavior, 4,* 323–334.

Loftus, E. F., Levidow, B., & Duensing, S. (1992). Who remembers best? Individual differences in memory for events that occurred in a science museum. *Applied Cognitive Psychology, 6,* 93–107.

Loftus, E. F., Loftus, G. R., & Messo, J. (1987). Some facts about "weapon focus." *Law and Human Behavior, 11,* 55–62.

Loftus, E. F., & Margurger, W. (1983). Since the eruption of Mt. St. Helens, has anyone beaten you up? Improving the accuracy of retrospective reports with landmark events. *Memory and Cognition, 11,* 114–120.

Loftus, E. F., Miller, D. G., & Burns, H. J. (1978). Semantic integration of verbal information into a visual memory. *Journal of Experimental Psychology: Human Learning and Memory, 4,* 19–31.

Loftus, E. F., & Palmer, J. C. (1974). Reconstruction of automobile destruction: An example of the interaction between language and memory. *Journal of Verbal Learning and Verbal Behavior, 13,* 585–589.

Loftus, E. F., & Pickrell, J. E. (1995). The formation of false memories. *Psychiatric Annals, 25,* 720–725.

Loftus, E. F., & Zanni, G. (1975). Eyewitness testimony: The influence of the wording of a question. *Bulletin of the Psychnomonic Society, 5,* 86–88.

Luus, C. A. E., & Wells, G. L. (1994). Eyewitness identification confidence. In D. F. Ross, J. D. Read, & M. P. Toglia (Eds.), *Adult eyewitness testimony: Current trends and developments* (pp. 348–361). New York: Cambridge University Press.

Lyon, T. D. (1995). False allegations and false denials in child sexual abuse. *Psychology, Public Policy, and Law, 1,* 429–437.

Maass, A., & Kohnken, G. (1989). Eyewitness identification: Simulating the "weapon effect." *Law and Human Behavior, 13,* 397–408.

Magarinos, A. M., McEwen, B. S., Fluegge, G., & Fuchs, E. (1996). Chronic psychosocial stress causes apical dendritic atrophy of hippocampal CA3 pyramidal neurons in subordinate tree shrews. *Journal of Neuroscience, 16,* 3534–3540.

Maki, R. H. (1990). Memory for script actions: Effects of relevance and detail expectancy. *Memory and Cognition, 18,* 5–14.

Malloy, L., Quas, J. A., Melinder, A., D'Mello, M., & Goodman, G. S. (2004, March). The effects of repeated interviewing and leading instructions on young children's event reports. In M. E. Pipe (Chair), *Repeated interviews in forensic contexts.* Symposium presented at the American Psychology-Law Society biennial meeting, Scottsdale, AZ.

Malpass, R. S., & Devine, P. G. (1981a). Guided memory in eyewitness identification. *Journal of Applied Psychology, 66,* 343–350.

Malpass, R. S., & Devine, P. G. (1981b). Realism and eyewitness identification research. *Law and Human Behavior, 4,* 347–358.

Malpass, R. S., & Kravitz, J. (1969). Recognition for faces of own and other race. *Journal of Personality and Social Psychology, 13,* 330–334.

Markham, R., Howie, P., & Hlavacek, S. (1999). Reality monitoring in auditory and visual modalities: Developmental trends and effects of cross-modal imagery. *Journal of Experimental Child Psychology, 72,* 51–70.

Marquis, K. H., Marshall, J., & Oskamp, S. (1972). Testimony validity as a function of question form, atmosphere, and item difficulty. *Journal of Applied Social Psychology, 2,* 167–186.

Martinez-Taboas, A. (1996). Repressed memories: Some clinical data contributing toward its elucidation. *American Journal of Psychotherapy, 50,* 217–230.

Mason, M. A. (1991). A judicial dilemma: Expert witness testimony in child sex abuse cases. *Journal of Psychiatry and Law, 19,* 185–219.

Mazzoni, G. A., Loftus, E. F., & Kirsch, I. (2001). Changing beliefs about implausible autobiographical events: A little plausibility goes a long way. *Journal of Experimental Psychology: Applied, 7,* 51–59.

McCloskey, M., & Egeth, H. E. (1983). Eyewitness identification: What can a psychologist tell a jury? *American Psychologist, 38,* 550–563.

McCloskey, M., Egeth, H., & McKenna, J. (1986). The experimental psychologist in court: The ethics of expert testimony [Special issue: The ethics of expert testimony]. *Law and Human Behavior, 10,* 1–13.

McCloskey, M., & Zaragoza, M. (1985). Misleading postevent information and memory for events: Arguments and evidence against memory impairment hypotheses. *Journal of Experimental Psychology: General, 117,* 171–181.

McEwen, B. S., & Magarinos, A. M. (1997). Stress effects on morphology and function of the hippocampus. In R. Yehuda & A. C. McFarlane (Eds.), *Psychobiology of posttraumatic stress disorder* (pp. 271–284). New York: New York Academy of Sciences.

McFarlane, F., Powell, M. B., & Dudgeon, P. (2002). An examination of the degree to which IQ, memory performance, socio-economic status and gender predict young children's suggestibility. *Legal and Criminological Psychology, 7,* 227–239.

McKelvie, S. J. (1985). Effect of depth of processing on recognition memory for normal and inverted photographs of faces. *Perceptual and Motor Skills, 60,* 503–508.

McNally, R. J. (1998). Experimental approaches to cognitive abnormality in posttraumatic stress disorder. *Clinical Psychology Review, 18,* 971–982.

McQuiston, D. E., & Malpass, R. S. (2002). Validity of the mock witness paradigm: Testing the assumptions. *Law and Human Behavior, 26,* 439–453.

McSpadden, M. D., Schooler, J. W., & Loftus, E. F. (1988). Here today, gone tomorrow: The appearance and disappearance of context effects. In G. M. Davies & D. M. Thomson (Eds.), *Memory in context: Context in memory* (pp. 215–229). Chichester, England: Wiley.

Meissner, C. A., & Brigham, J. C. (2001). Thirty years of investigating the own-race bias memory for faces: A meta-analytic review. *Psychology, Public Policy, and Law, 7,* 3–35.

Melton, G. B., Goodman, G. S., Kalichman, S. C., Levine, M., Saywitz, K. J., & Koocher, G. P. (1995). Empirical research on child maltreatment and the law. *Journal of Clinical Child Psychology, 24,* 47–77.

Melton, G. B., & Limber, S. (1989). Psychologists' involvement in cases of child maltreatment: Limits of role and expertise. *American Psychologist, 44,* 1225–1233.

Memon, A., & Bartlett, J. (2002). The effects of verbalization on face recognition in young and older adults. *Applied Cognitive Psychology, 16,* 635–650.

Memon, A., & Bull, R. (1991). The cognitive interview: Its origins, empirical support, evaluation and practical implications. *Journal of Community and Applied Social Psychology, 1,* 291–307.

Memon, A., Cronin, O., & Bull, R. (1993). The cognitive interview and child witnesses. *Issues in Criminological and Legal Psychology, 22,* 3–9.

Memon, A., Hope, L., & Bull, R. (2003). Exposure duration: Effects on eyewitness accuracy and confidence. *British Journal of Psychology, 94,* 339–354.

Merritt, K. A., Ornstein, P. A., & Spicker, B. (1994). Children's memory for a salient medical procedure: Implications for testimony. *Pediatrics, 94,* 17–23.

Metcalfe, J., & Jacobs, W. J. (2000). "Hot" emotions in human recollection: Toward a model of traumatic memory. In E. Tulving (Ed.), *Memory, consciousness, and the brain: The Tallinn Conference* (pp. 228–242). New York: Psychology Press.

Metzger, M. M. (2001). Which transformations of stimuli are the most disruptive to facial recognition? *Perceptual and Motor Skills, 92,* 517–526.

Miene, P., Park, R. C., & Borgida, E. (1992). Juror decision making and the evaluation of hearsay evidence. *Minnesota Law Review, 76,* 683–701.

Migueles, M., & Garcia-Bajos, E. (1999). Recall, recognition, and confidence patterns in eyewitness testimony. *Applied Cognitive Psychology, 13,* 257–268.

Miller, J. B., & Noirot, M. (1999). Attachment memories, models and information processing. *Journal of Social and Personal Relationships, 16,* 147–173.

Milne, R., & Bull, R. (2003). Does the cognitive interview help children to resist the effects of suggestive questioning? *Legal and Criminological Psychology, 8,* 21–38.

Milne, R., Bull, R., Koehnken, G., & Memon, A. (1995). The cognitive interview and suggestibility. *Issues in Criminological and Legal Psychology, 22,* 21–27.

Mitchell, K. J., Johnson, M. K., & Mather, M. (2003). Source monitoring and suggestibility to misinformation: Adult age-related differences. *Applied Cognitive Psychology, 17,* 107–119.

Moradi, A. R., Taghavi, R., Neshat-Doost, H. T., Yule, W., & Dalgleish, T. (2000). Memory bias for emotional information in children and adolescents with posttraumatic stress disorder: A preliminary study. *Journal of Anxiety Disorders, 14,* 521–534.

Morris, V., & Morris, P. E. (1985). The influence of question order on eyewitness accuracy. *British Journal of Psychology, 76,* 365–371.

Moston, S. (1992). Social support and children's eyewitness testimony. In H. Dent & R. Flin (Eds.), *Children as witnesses* (pp. 33–46). Chichester, England: Wiley.

Multhaup, K. S. (1995). Aging, source, and decision criteria: When false fame errors do and do not occur. *Psychology and Aging, 10,* 492–498.

Murray, D. M., & Wells, G. L. (1982). Does knowledge that a crime was staged affect eyewitness performance? *Journal of Applied Social Psychology, 12,* 42–53.

Myers, J. E. B., Bays, J., Becker, J., Berliner, L., Corwin, D., Saywitz, K. J., et al. (1989). Expert testimony in child sexual abuse litigation. *Nebraska Law Review, 68,* 1–145.

Myers, J. B., Redlich, A. D., Goodman, G. S., Prizmich, L. P., & Imwinkelried, E. (1999). Jurors' perceptions of hearsay in child sexual abuse cases. *Psychology, Public Policy, and Law, 5,* 388–419.

Nash, M. R. (1994). Memory distortion and sexual trauma: The problem of false negatives and false positives. *The International Journal of Clinical and Experimental Hypnosis, 42,* 346–362.

Neisser, U., & Harsch, N. (1992). Phantom flashbulbs: False recollections of hearing the news about Challenger. In E. Winograd & U. Neisser (Eds.), *Emory Symposia in Cognition: Vol. 4. Affect and accuracy in recall: Studies of "flashbulb" memories.* (pp. 9–31). New York: Cambridge University Press.

Nelson, E. L., & Simpson, P. (1994). First glimpse: An initial examination of subjects who have rejected their recovered visualizations as false memories. *Issues in Child Abuse Accusations, 6,* 123–133.

Nelson, K. (1986). *Event knowledge: Structure and function in development.* Hillsdale, NJ: Erlbaum.

Nemiah, J. C. (1998). Early concepts of trauma, dissociation, and the unconscious: Their history and current implications. In J. D. Bremner & C. R. Marmar (Eds.), *Trauma, memory, and dissociation* (pp. 1–16). Washington, DC: American Psychiatric Press Series.

Nunez, N., McCoy, M. L., Clark, H. L., & Shaw, L. A. (1999). The testimony of elderly victim/witnesses and their impact on juror decisions: The importance of examining multiple stereotypes. *Law and Human Behavior, 23,* 413–423.

Ofshe, R. J., & Watters, E. (1994). *Making monsters: False memories, psychotherapy, and sexual hysteria.* New York: Charles Scribner's Sons.

Ogle, C. M., & Reisberg, D. (2004). *A comparison of elimination, sequential and simultaneous lineup procedures.* Manuscript in preparation.

Olio, K. A. (1994). Truth in memory. *American Psychologist, 49,* 442–443.

Orbach, Y., Hershkowitz, I., Lamb, M. E., Esplin, P. W., & Horowitz, D. (2000). Assessing the value of structured protocols for forensic interviews of alleged child abuse victims. *Child Abuse and Neglect, 24,* 733–752.

Orbach, Y., & Lamb, M. E. (1999). Assessing the accuracy of a child's account of sexual abuse: A case study. *Child Abuse and Neglect, 23,* 91–98.

Orbach, Y., & Lamb, M. E. (2000). Enhancing children's narratives in investigative interviews. *Child Abuse and Neglect, 24,* 1631–1648.

Ornstein, P. A., Baker-Ward, L., Gordon, B. N., & Merritt, K. A. (1997). Children's memory for medical experiences: Implications for testimony. *Applied Cognitive Psychology, 11,* 87–104.

Ornstein, P. A., Ceci, S. J., & Loftus, E. F. (1998). Adult recollections of childhood abuse: Cognitive and developmental perspectives. *Psychology, Public Policy, and Law, 4,* 1025–1051.

Ornstein, P. A., & Gordon, B. N. (1998). Risk versus rewards of applied research with children: Comments on "The potential effects of the implanted-memory paradigm on child participants" by Douglas Herrmann and Carol Yoder. *Applied Cognitive Psychology, 12,* 241–244.

Ornstein, P. A., Gordon, B. N., & Larus, D. M. (1992). Children's memory for a personally experienced event: Implications for testimony. *Applied Cognitive Psychology, 6,* 49–60.

O'Sullivan, J. T., Howe, M. L., & Marche, T. A. (1996). Metamemory and memory construction. *Child Development, 67,* 2989–3009.

Parker, J. F. (1995). Age differences in source monitoring of performed and imagined actions on immediate and delayed test. *Journal of Experimental Child Psychology, 60,* 84–101.

Payne, D. G., Hembrooke, H. A., & Anastasi, J. S. (1993). Hypermnesia in free recall and cued recall. *Memory and Cognition, 21,* 48–62.

Penrod, S. D., & Cutler, B. L. (1995). Witness confidence and witness accuracy: Assessing their forensic relation. *Psychology, Public Policy, and Law, 1,* 817–845.

Penrod, S. D., Fulero, S. M., & Cutler, B. L. (1995). Expert psychological testimony in the United States: A new playing field? *European Journal of Psychological Assessment, 11,* 65–72.

Peterson, C. (1999). Children's memory for medical emergencies: 2 years later. *Developmental Psychology, 35,* 1493–1506.

Peterson, C. (2002). Children's long-term memory for autobiographical events. *Developmental Review, 22,* 370–402.

Peterson, C., & Bell, M. (1996). Children's memory for traumatic injury. *Child Development, 67,* 3045–3070.

Peterson, C., Moores, L., & White, G. (2001). Recounting the same events again and again: Children's consistency across multiple interviews. *Applied Cognitive Psychology, 15,* 353–371.

Peterson, C., Parsons, T., & Dean, M. (2004). Providing misleading and reinstatement information a year after it happened: Effects on long-term memory. *Memory, 12,* 1–13.

Peterson, C., & Rideout, R. (1998). Memory for medical emergencies experiences by one and two years olds. *Developmental Psychology, 34,* 1059–1072.

Peterson, C., & Whalen, N. (2001). Five years later: Children's memory for medical emergencies. *Applied Cognitive Psychology, 15,* 7–24.

Pezdek, K. (1994). The illusion of illusory memory. *Applied Cognitive Psychology, 8,* 339–350.

Pezdek, K., Blandon-Gitlin, I., & Moore, C. (2003). Children's face recognition memory: More evidence of the cross-race effect. *Journal of Applied Psychology, 88,* 760–763.

Pezdek, K., Finger, K., & Hodge, D. (1997). Planting false childhood memories: The role of event plausibility. *Psychological Science, 8,* 437–441.

Pezdek, K., & Roe, C. (1995). The effect of memory trace strength on suggestibility. *Journal of Experimental Child Psychology, 60,* 116–128.

Pezdek, K., & Roe, C. (1997). The suggestibility of children's memory for being touched: Planting, erasing, and changing memories. *Law and Human Behavior, 21,* 95–106.

Pezdek, K., & Taylor, J. (2002). Memory for traumatic events in children and adults. In M. L. Eisen, J. A. Quas, & G. S. Goodman (Eds.), *Memory and suggestibility in the forensic interview: Personality and clinical psychology series* (pp. 165–183). Mahwah, NJ: Erlbaum.

Pickel, K. L. (1998). Unusualness and threat as possible causes of "weapon focus." *Memory, 6,* 277–295.

Pickel, K. L. (1999). The influence of context on the "weapon focus" effect. *Law and Human Behavior, 23,* 299–311.

Pipe, M. E. (1996). Children's eyewitness memory. *New Zealand Journal of Psychology, 25,* 36–43.

Pipe, M. E., Gee, S., Wilson, C. J., & Egerton, J. (1999). Children's recall 1 or 2 years after an event. *Developmental Psychology, 35,* 781–789.

Platz, S. J., & Hosch, H. M. (1988). Cross racial/ethnic eyewitness identification: A field study. *Journal of Applied Social Psychology, 18,* 972–984.

Poole, D. A., & Lamb, M. E. (1998). *Investigative interviews of children: A guide for helping professionals.* Washington, DC: American Psychological Association.

Poole, D. A., & Lindsay, D. S. (2001). Children's eyewitness reports after exposure to misinformation from parents. *Journal of Experimental Psychology: Applied, 7,* 27–50.

Poole, D. A., & Lindsay, D. S. (2002). Reducing child witnesses' false reports of misinformation from parents. *Journal of Experimental Child Psychology, 81,* 117–140.

Pope, K. S. (1996). Memory, abuse, and science: Questioning claims about the false memory syndrome epidemic. *American Psychologist, 51,* 957–974.

Porter, S., Yuille, J. C., & Lehman, D. R. (1999). The nature of real, implanted, and fabricated memories for emotional childhood events: Implications for the recovered memory debate. *Law and Human Behavior, 23,* 517–537.

Powell, M. B., Roberts, K. P., Ceci, S. J., & Hembrooke, H. (1999). The effect of repeated experience on children's suggestibility. *Developmental Psychology, 35,* 1462–1477.

Pozzulo, J. D., & Lindsay, R. C. L. (1999). Elimination lineups: An improved identification procedure for child eyewitnesses. *Journal of Applied Psychology, 84,* 167–176.

Price, D. W., & Goodman, G. S. (1990). Visiting the wizard: Children's memory for a recurring event. *Child Development, 61,* 664–680.

Qin, J. (2000). *Adults' memories of childhood: True versus false reports.* Unpublished doctoral dissertation. University of California, Davis.

Qin, J. J., Goodman, G. S., Bottoms, B. L., & Shaver, P. R. (1998). Repressed memory: An inquiry into allegations of ritual abuse. In S. Lynn & K. M. McConkey (Eds.), *Truth in memory* (pp. 260–283). New York: Guilford Press.

Qin, J. J., Tyda, K. S., & Goodman, G. S. (1997). Retractors' experiences: What we can and cannot conclude. *Psychological Inquiry, 8,* 312–317.

Quas, J. A., Bauer, A., & Boyce, W. T. (2004). Physiological reactivity, social support, and memory in early childhood. *Child Development, 75,* 797–814.

Quas, J. A., Goodman, G. S., Bidrose, S., Pipe, M., Craw, S., & Ablin, D. S. (1999). Emotion and memory: Children's long-term remembering, forgetting, and suggestibility. *Journal of Experimental Child Psychology, 72,* 235–270.

Quas, J. A., Qin, J., Schaaf, J. M., & Goodman, G. S. (1997). Individual differences in children's and adult's suggestibility and false event memory. *Learning and Individual Differences, 9,* 359–390.

Quas, J. A., Thompson, W. C., & Clarke-Stewart, A. (2004). *Perceptions of child witnesses: Do jurors know what isn't so?* Manuscript in preparation.

Rattner, A. (1988). Convicted but innocent: Wrongful conviction and the criminal justice system. *Law and Human Behavior, 12,* 283–293.

Read, J. D., & Craik, F. I. M. (1995). Earwitness identification: Some influences on voice recognition. *Journal of Experimental Psychology: Applied, 1,* 6–18.

Read, J. D., & Lindsay, D. S. (2000). "Amnesia" for summer camps and high school graduation: Memory work increases reports of prior periods of remembering less. *Journal of Traumatic Stress, 13,* 129–147.

Read, J. D., Tollestrup, P., Hammersley, R., McFadzen, E., & Christensen, A. (1990). The unconscious transference effect: Are innocent bystanders ever misidentified? *Applied Cognitive Psychology, 4,* 3–31.

Reyna, V. F. (1995). Interference effects in memory and reasoning: A fuzzy-trace theory and analysis. In F. N. Dempster & C. J. Brainerd (Eds.), *Interference and inhibition in cognition* (pp. 29–59). San Diego, CA: Academic Press.

Richardson, G., & Kelly, T. P. (1995). The relationship between intelligence, memory and interrogative suggestibility in young offenders. *Psychology, Crime, and Law, 1,* 283–290.

Riniolo, T. C., Koledin, M., Drakulic, G. M., & Payne, R. A. (2003). An archival study of eyewitness memory of the Titanic's final plunge. *Journal of General Psychology, 130,* 89–95.

Roberts, K. P., & Blades, M. (1998). The effects of interacting in repeated events on children's eyewitness memory and source monitoring. *Applied Cognitive Psychology, 12,* 489–503.

Roberts, K. P., & Blades, M. (2000). Discriminating between memories of television and real life. In K. P. Roberts & M. Blades (Eds.), *Children's source monitoring* (pp. 147–169). Mahwah, NJ: Erlbaum.

Robinson, M. D., & Johnson, J. T. (1996). Recall memory, recognition memory, and the eyewitness confidence-accuracy correlation. *Journal of Applied Psychology, 5,* 587–594.

Roebers, C. M., & Schneider, W. (2000). The impact of misleading questions on eyewitness memory in children and adults. *Applied Cognitive Psychology, 14,* 509–526.

Roebers, C. M., & Schneider, W. (2001). Individual differences in children's eyewitness recall: The influence of intelligence and shyness. *Applied Developmental Science, 5,* 9–20.

Roediger, H. L., & Thorpe, L. A. (1978). The role of recall time in producing hypermnesia. *Memory and Cognition, 6,* 296–304.

Roediger, H. L., Wheeler, M. A., & Rajaram, S. (1993). Remembering, knowing and reconstructing the past. In D. L. Medin (Ed.), *The psychology of learning and motivation: Advances in research and theory* (pp. 97–134). New York: Academic Press.

Ross, D. F., Ceci, S. J., Dunning, D., & Toglia, M. P. (1994). Unconscious transference and mistaken identity: When a witness misidentifies a familiar but innocent person. *Journal of Applied Psychology, 79,* 918–930.

Ross, D. F., Hoffman, R., Warren, A., Burlingham, A., Marsil, D., & Lindsay, R. C. L. (1998, March). *Unconscious transference and mistaken identity in children: Are children more or less susceptible than adults to misidentifying a familiar but innocent person from a lineup?* Paper presented at the American Psychology-Law Society meetings, Redondo Beach, CA.

Ross, D. F., Warren, A. R., & McGough, L. S. (1999). Foreword: Hearsay testimony in trials involving child witnesses [Special issue]. *Psychology, Public Policy, and Law, 5,* 251–254.

Rubin, D. C. (2000). The distribution of early childhood memories. *Memory, 8,* 265–269.

Rubin, D. C., & Schulkind, M. D. (1997). The distribution of autobiographical memories across the lifespan. *Memory and Cognition, 25,* 859–866.

Rudy, L., & Goodman, G. S. (1991). Effects of participation on children's reports: Implications for children's testimony. *Developmental Psychology, 27,* 527–538.

Ruffman, T., Rustin, C., Garnham, W., & Parkin, A. J. (2001). Source monitoring and false memories in children: Relation to certainty and executive functioning. *Journal of Experimental Child Psychology, 80,* 95–111.

Ryan, R. H., & Geiselman, R. E. (1991). Effects of biased information on the relationship between eyewitness confidence and accuracy. *Bulletin of the Psychonomic Society, 29*, 7–9.

Salmon, K. (2001). Remembering and reporting by children: The influence of cues and props. *Clinical Psychology Review, 21*, 267–300.

Salmon, K., & Pipe, M. E. (2000). Recalling an event one year later: The impact of props, drawing, and a prior interview. *Applied Cognitive Psychology, 14*, 99–120.

Sanders, G. S., & Warnick, D. (1979). Some conditions maximizing eyewitness accuracy: A learning/memory model. *Basic and Applied Social Psychology, 2*, 67–69.

Saywitz, K. J., Goodman, G. S., Nicholas, E., & Moan, S. F. (1991). Children's memories of a physical examination involving genital touch: Implications for reports of child sexual abuse. *Journal of Consulting and Clinical Psychology, 59*, 682–691.

Schaaf, J. M. (2001). Do children believe misleading information? Investigating the effects of postevent misinformation using the logic of opposition instruction. *Dissertation Abstracts International: Section B: The Physical Sciences and Engineering, 61*(9-B), 5021.

Scheck, B., Neufeld, P., & Dwyer, J. (2000). *Actual innocence.* New York: Random House.

Schooler, J. W., Ambadar, Z., & Bendiksen, M. (1997). A cognitive corroborative case study approach for investigating discovered memories of sexual abuse. In J. D. Read & D. S. Lindsay (Eds.), *Recollections of trauma: Scientific evidence and clinical practice* (pp. 379–387). New York: Plenum Press.

Schuller, R. A. (1995). Expert evidence and hearsay: The influence of "secondhand" information on jurors' decisions. *Law and Human Behavior, 19*, 345–362.

Schwartz-Kenney, B. M., & Goodman, G. S. (1999). Children's memory of a naturalistic event following misinformation. *Applied Developmental Science, 3*, 34–46.

Scrivner, E., & Safer, M. A. (1988). Eyewitnesses show hypermnesia for details about a violent event. *Journal of Applied Psychology, 73*, 371–377.

Searcy, J. H., Bartlett, J. C., Memon, A., & Swanson, K. (2001). Aging and lineup performance at long retention intervals: Effects of metamemory and context reinstatement. *Journal of Applied Psychology, 86*, 207–214.

Shapiro, P. N., & Penrod, S. D. (1986). Meta-analysis of facial identification studies. *Psychological Bulletin, 100*, 139–156.

Shaw, G. A., Bekerian, D. A., & McCubbin, J. A. (1995). Effects of videotaped violence on hypermnesia for imaginally encoded concrete and abstract words. *Perceptual and Motor Skills, 80*, 467–477.

Shaw, J. S., III. (1996). Increases in eyewitness confidence resulting from postevent questioning. *Journal of Experimental Psychology: Applied, 2*, 26–146.

Shaw, J. S., Garcia, L. A., & McClure, K. A. (1999). A lay perspective on the accuracy of eyewitness testimony. *Journal of Applied Social Psychology, 29*, 52–71.

Shepherd, J. W. (1983). Identification after long delays. In S. Llyod-Bostock & B. R. Clifford (Eds.), *Evaluating witness evidence* (pp. 173–187). Chichester, England: Wiley.

Shobe, K. K., & Kihlstrom, J. F. (1997). Is traumatic memory special? [Special issue: Memory as the theater of the past: The psychology of false memories]. *Current Directions in Psychological Science, 6*, 70–74.

Shyamalan, B., Lamb, S., & Sheldrick, R. (1995, August). *The effects of repeated questioning on preschoolers' reports.* Poster presented at the American Psychological Association Convention, New York.

Sobel, N. R. (1985). *Eyewitness identification: Legal and practical problems* (2nd ed.). New York: Clark & Boardman Co.

Spiegel, D. (1995). Hypnosis and suggestion. In D. L. Schacter, J. T. Coyle, G. D. Fishcback, M. Mesulam, & L. E. Sullivan (Eds.), *Memory distortion* (pp. 129–149). Cambridge, MA: Harvard University Press.

Sporer, S. L. (1993). Clothing as a contextual cue in facial recognition. *German Journal of Psychology, 17*, 183–199.

Sporer, S. L. (2001). Recognizing the faces of other ethnic groups: An integration of theories. *Psychology, Public Policy, and Law, 7*, 36–97.

Sporer, S. L., Malpass, R. S., & Koehnken, G. (Eds.). (1996). *Psychological issues in eyewitness identification.* Hillsdale, NJ: Erlbaum.

State v. Milbradt, 756 P.2d 620 (Or. 1988).

Steblay, N., Dysart, J., Fulero, S., & Lindsay, R. C. L. (2003). Eyewitness accuracy rates in police showup and lineup presentations. *Law and Human Behavior, 27*, 523–540.

Sternberg, K. J., Lamb, M. E., Esplin, P. W., Orbach, Y., & Hershkowitz, I. (2002). Memory and suggestibility in the forensic interview. *Personality and Clinical Psychology Series, 481,* 409–436.

Sternberg, K. J., Lamb, M. E., Orbach, Y., Esplin, P. W., & Mitchell, S. (2001). Use of a structured investigative protocol enhances young children's responses to free-recall prompts in the course of forensic interviews. *Journal of Applied Psychology, 86,* 997–1005.

Steward, M. S., Steward, D. S., Farquhar, L., Myers, J. E. B., Reinhart, M., Walker, J., et al. (1996). Interviewing young children about body touch and handling. *Monographs of the Society for Research in Child Development, 61,*(Serial No. 248).

Strange, D., Garry, M., & Sutherland, R. (2003). Drawing out children's false memories. *Applied Cognitive Psychology, 17,* 607–619.

Sutherland, R., & Hayne, H. (2001). Age-related changes in the misinformation effect. *Journal of Experimental Child Psychology, 79,* 388–404.

Terr, L. C. (1991). Childhood traumas: An outline and overview. *American Journal of Psychiatry, 148,* 10–20.

Thierry, K. L., & Spence, M. J. (2002). Source-monitoring training facilitates preschoolers' eyewitness memory performance. *Developmental Psychology, 38,* 428–437.

Tollestrup, P. A., Turtle, J. W., & Yuille, J. C. (1994). Actual victims and witnesses to robbery and fraud: An archival analysis. In D. F. Ross, J. D. Read, & M. P. Toglia (Eds.), *Adult eyewitness testimony: Current trends and developments* (pp. 144–160). London: Cambridge University Press.

Tromp, S., Koss, M. P., Figueredo, A. J., & Tharan, M. (1995). Are rape memories different? A comparison of rape, other unpleasant, and pleasant memories among employed women. *Journal of Traumatic Stress, 8,* 607–627.

Tubb, V. A., Wood, J. M., & Hosch, H. M. (1999). Effects of suggestive interviewing and indirect evidence on child credibility in a sexual abuse case. *Journal of Applied Social Psychology, 29,* 1111–1127.

Tuckey, M. R., & Brewer, N. (2003). The influence of schemas, stimulus ambiguity, and interview schedule on eyewitness memory over time. *Journal of Experimental Psychology: Applied, 9,* 101–118.

Tulving, E. (1981). Similarity relations in recognition. *Journal of Verbal Learning and Verbal Behavior, 20,* 479–496.

Tulving, E. (1983). *Elements of episodic memory.* Oxford: Clarendon Press.

Turtle, J. W., & Yuille, J. C. (1994). Lost but not forgotten details: Repeated eyewitness recall leads to reminiscence but not hypermnesia. *Journal of Applied Psychology, 79,* 260–271.

Underwood, J., & Pezdek, K. (1998). Memory suggestibility as an example of the sleeper effect. *Psychonomic Bulletin and Review, 5,* 449–453.

Van der Kolk, B. A., & Fisler, R. E. (1995). Dissociation and the fragmentary nature of traumatic memories: Overview and exploratory study. *Journal of Traumatic Stress, 8,* 505–525.

Verinis, J. S., & Walker, V. (1970). Policemen and the recall of criminal details. *Journal of Social Psychology, 81,* 217–221.

Villarreal, G., Hamilton, D. A., Petropoulos, H., Driscoll, I., Rowland, L. M., Griego, J. A., et al. (2002). Reduced hippocampal volume and total white matter volume in posttraumatic stress disorder. *Biological Psychiatry, 52,* 119–125.

Vrana, S. R., Roodman, A., & Beckham, J. C. (1995). Selective processing of trauma-relevant words in posttraumatic stress disorder. *Journal of Anxiety Disorders, 9,* 515–530.

Wagstaff, G. F., MacVeigh, J., Boston, R., Scott, L., Brunas-Wagstaff, J., & Cole, J. (2003). Can laboratory findings on eyewitness testimony be generalized to the real world? An archival analysis of the influence of violence, weapon presence, and age on eyewitness accuracy. *Journal of Psychology, 137,* 17–28.

Warren, A., Hulse-Trotter, K., & Tubbs, E. C. (1991). Inducing resistance to suggestibility in children. *Law and Human Behavior, 15,* 273–285.

Warren, A. R., & Lane, P. (1995). Effects of timing and type of questioning on eyewitness accuracy and suggestibility. In M. S. Zaragoza, J. R. Graham, G. N. C. Hall, R. Hirschman, & Y. S. Ben-Porath (Eds.), *Memory and testimony in the child witness* (pp. 44–60). Thousand Oaks, CA: Sage.

Warren, A. R., Nunez, N., Keeney, J. M., Buck, J. A., & Smith, B. (2002). The believability of children and their interviewer's hearsay testimony: When less is more. *Journal of Applied Psychology, 87,* 846–857.

Warren, A. R., & Woodall, C. E. (1999). The reliability of hearsay testimony: How well do interviewers recall their interviews with children? *Psychology, Public Policy, and Law, 5,* 355–371.

Warren, A. R., Woodall, C. E., Hunt, J. S., & Perry, N. W. (1996). "It sounds good in theory but": Do investigative interviewers follow guidelines based on memory research? *Child Maltreatment, 1,* 231–245.

Weaver, C. A., III. (1993). Do you need a "flash" to form a flashbulb memory? *Journal of Experimental Psychology: General, 122,* 39–46.

Weingardt, K. R., Loftus, E. F., & Lindsay, D. S. (1995). Misinformation revisited: New evidence on the suggestibility of memory. *Memory and Cognition, 23,* 72–82.

Wells, G. L., Ferguson, T. J., & Lindsay, R. C. L. (1981). The tractability of eyewitness confidence and its implications for triers of fact. *Journal of Applied Psychology, 66,* 688–696.

Wells, G. L., & Hryciw, B. (1984). Memory for faces: Encoding and retrieval operations. *Memory and Cognition, 12,* 338–344.

Wells, G. L., & Leippe, M. R. (1981). How do triers of fact infer the accuracy of eyewitness identifications? Using memory for peripheral detail can be misleading. *Journal of Applied Psychology, 66,* 682–687.

Wells, G. L., & Rydell, S. M., & Seelau, E. P. (1993). The selection of distractors for eyewitness lineups. *Journal of Applied Psychology, 78,* 835–844.

Wells, G. L., Small, M., Penrod, S., Malpass, R. S., Fulero, S. M., & Brinacombe, C. A. E. (1998). Eyewitness identification procedures: Recommendations for lineups and photospreads. *Law and Human Behavior, 22,* 603–647.

Wessel, I., & Merckelbach, H. (1997). The impact of anxiety on memory for details in spider phobics. *Applied Cognitive Psychology, 11,* 223–231.

Wesson, M., & Salmon, K. (2001). Drawing and showing: Helping children to report emotionally laden events. *Applied Cognitive Psychology, 15,* 301–320.

Whitcomb, D. (1992). *When the victim is a child* (2nd ed.). Washington, DC: National Institute of Justice, U.S. Department of Justice.

Widom, C. S., & Morris, S. (1997). Accuracy of adult recollections of childhood victimization: Part 2. Childhood sexual abuse. *Psychological Assessment, 9,* 34–46.

Williams, L. M. (1994). Recall of childhood trauma: A prospective study of women's memories of child sexual abuse. *Journal of Consulting and Clinical Psychology, 62,* 1167–1185.

Williams, L. M. (1995). Recovered memories of abuse in women with documented child sexual victimization histories. *Journal of Traumatic Stress, 8,* 649–673.

Williams, L. M., & Banyard, V. L. (Eds.). (1999). *Trauma and memory.* Thousand Oaks, CA: Sage.

Wilsnack, S. C., Wonderlich, S. A., Kristjanson, A. F., Vogeltanz-Holm, N. D., & Wilsnack, R. W. (2002). Self-reports of forgetting and remembering childhood sexual abuse in a nationally representative sample of U.S. women. *Child Abuse and Neglect, 26,* 139–147.

Wilson, J. C., & Pipe, M. (1989). The effects of cues on young children's recall of real events. *New Zealand Journal of Psychology, 18,* 65–70.

Wixted, J. T., & Ebbesen, E. B. (1997). Genuine power curves in forgetting: A quantitative analysis of individual subject forgetting functions. *Memory and Cognition, 25,* 731–739.

Wixted, J. T., & Rohrer, D. (1994). Analyzing the dynamics of free recall: An integrative review of the empirical literature. *Psychonomic Bulletin and Review, 1,* 89–106.

Wogalter, M. S., & Laughery, K. R. (1987). Face recognition: Effects of study to test maintenance and change of photographic mode and pose. *Applied Cognitive Psychology, 1,* 241–253.

Wogalter, M. S., Marwitz, D. B., & Leonard, D. C. (1992). Suggestiveness in photospread lineups: Similarity induces distinctiveness. *Applied Cognitive Psychology, 6,* 443–453.

Woolnough, P. S., & MacLeod, M. D. (2001). Watching the birdie watching you: Eyewitness memory for actions using CCTV recording of actual crimes. *Applied Cognitive Psychology, 15,* 395–411.

Wright, D. B. (1993). Misinformation and warnings in eyewitness testimony: A new testing procedure to differentiate explanations. *Memory, 1,* 153–161.

Wright, D. B., Boyd, C. E., & Tredoux, C. G. (2001). A field study of own-race bias in South Africa and England. *Psychology, Public Policy, and Law, 7,* 119–133.

Yarmey, A. D. (1996). The elderly witness. In S. L. Sporer, R. S. Malpass, & G. Koehnken (Eds.), *Psychological issues in eyewitness identification* (pp. 259–278). Mahwah, NJ: Erlbaum.

Yarmey, A. D., & Matthys, E. (1992). Voice identification of an abductor. *Applied Cognitive Psychology, 6,* 367–377.

Yarmey, A. D., Yarmey, M. J., & Yarmey, A. L. (1996). Accuracy of eyewitness identifications in showups and lineups. *Law and Human Behavior, 20,* 459–477.

Young, K., Powell, M. B., & Dudgeon, P. (2003). Individual differences in children's suggestibility: A comparison between intellectually disabled and mainstream samples. *Personality and Individual Differences, 35,* 31–49.

Yuille, J. C. (1980). A critical examination of the psychological and practical implications of eye-witness research. *Law and Human Behavior, 4,* 335–345.

Yuille, J. C., & Cutshall, J. L. (1986). A case study of eyewitness of a crime. *Journal of Applied Psychology, 71,* 291–301.

Yuille, J. C., & Wells, G. L. (1991). Concerns about the application of research findings: The issue of ecological validity. In J. Doris (Ed.), *The suggestibility of children's recollections* (pp. 118–128). Washington, DC: American Psychological Association.

Zadny, J., & Gerard, H. B. (1974). Attributed intentions and informational selectivity. *Journal of Experimental Social Psychology, 10,* 34–52.

Zaragoza, M. S. (1991). Preschool children's susceptibility to memory impairment. In J. Doris (Ed.), *The suggestibility of children's recollections* (pp. 27–39). Washington, DC: American Psychological Association.

Zaragoza, M. S., & Lane, S. M. (1994). Source misattributions and the suggestibility of eyewitness memory. *Journal of Experimental Psychology: Learning, Memory, and Cognition, 20,* 934–945.

Zaragoza, M. S., McCloskey, M., & Jamis, M. (1987). Misleading postevent information and recall of the original event: Further evidence against the memory impairment hypothesis. *Journal of Experimental Psychology: Learning, Memory, and Cognition, 13,* 36–44.

Zykowski, T., & Singg, S. (1999). Effects of verb and delay on recall of an accident. *Perceptual and Motor Skills, 88,* 1231–1234.

CHAPTER 12

Competency to Stand Trial: A Guide for Evaluators

PATRICIA A. ZAPF and RONALD ROESCH

COMPETENCY TO stand trial is a concept of jurisprudence allowing the post-ponement of criminal proceedings for those defendants who are considered unable to participate in their defense on account of mental or physical disorder or retardation. Because trial competency issues are raised substantially more often than the insanity defense, psychologists involved in forensic assessment and consultation are likely to have frequent experience with it. Recent estimates are that approximately 60,000 competency evaluations are conducted in the United States annually (Bonnie & Grisso, 2000). This number has increased substantially from estimates that as recently as 1997 placed the annual number of competency evaluations somewhere between 25,000 and 39,000 (Hoge et al., 1997). Stated somewhat differently, between 2% and 8% of all felony defendants are referred for competency evaluations (Bonnie, 1992a; Golding, 1993; Hoge, Bonnie, Poythress, & Monahan, 1992). Given a steady increase in felony arrest rates, the rate of competency referrals is increasingly steadily as well.

In this chapter, we present an overview of competency laws, research, and methods of assessment with the aim of providing forensic psychologists with the basic information they need to conduct competency evaluations. We do not believe, however, that this chapter will sufficiently prepare a novice forensic psychologist to carry out such evaluations. As we make clear, the issues surrounding a competency determination are highly complex. An evaluator needs not only a high level of clinical knowledge and skills but also considerable knowledge of the legal system.

We urge the reader interested in pursuing work in the competency area to supplement this chapter with other materials (e.g., Bonnie, 1992a, 1993; Grisso, 2003; Melton, Petrila, Poythress, & Slobogin, 1997; Nicholson & Norwood, 2000; Ogloff, Wallace, & Otto, 1991; Roesch, Ogloff, & Golding, 1993; Roesch, Hart, & Zapf, 1996; Stafford, 2003; Winick, 1995, 1996) as well as workshops and other forms of continuing education. The *Specialty Guidelines for Forensic Psychologists* (Committee on Ethical Guidelines for Psychologists, 1991) also contains important practice standards for competency evaluations.

DEFINING COMPETENCY

Provisions allowing for a delay of trial because a defendant was incompetent to proceed have long been a part of the legal due process. English common law allowed for an arraignment, trial, judgment, or execution of an alleged capital offender to be stayed if he or she "be[came] absolutely mad" (Hale, 1736, cited in Silten & Tulis, 1977, p. 1053). Over time, statutes have been created in the United States and Canada that have further defined and extended the common law practice (Davis, 1994; Rogers & Mitchell, 1991; Verdun-Jones, 1981; and Webster, Menzies, & Jackson, 1982, for reviews of Canadian competency law and practice). The modern standard in U.S. law was established in *Dusky v. United States* (1960). Although the exact wording varies, all states use a variant of the *Dusky* standard to define competency (Favole, 1983). In *Dusky*, the U.S. Supreme Court held:

> It is not enough for the district judge to find that "the defendant is oriented to time and place and has some recollection of events," but that the test must be whether he has sufficient present ability to consult with his lawyer with a reasonable degree of rational understanding—and whether he has a rational as well as factual understanding of the proceedings against him. (p. 402)

Although the concept of competency to stand trial has been long established in law, its definition, as exemplified by the ambiguities of *Dusky*, has never been explicit. What is meant by "sufficient present ability"? How does one determine whether a defendant "has a rational as well as factual understanding"? To be sure, some courts (e.g., *Wieter v. Settle*, 1960) and legislatures (e.g., Utah Code Annotated, § 77-15-1 *et seq.*, 1994) have provided some direction to evaluators in the form of articulated *Dusky* standards (discussed later). But the typical forensic evaluation is left largely unguided except by a common principle, in most published cases, that evaluators cannot reach a finding of incompetency independent of the facts of the legal case (an issue we return to later).

The problems in defining and assessing competency lead to a broad range of interpretations of the *Dusky* standard. Because the courts and legislatures have given mental health professionals a large share of the responsibility for defining and evaluating competency, it should not be surprising to find that mental status issues, such as presence or absence of psychosis, have played (historically at least) a dominant role in the findings of evaluators. In fact, evaluators initially involved in assessing competency seemed to equate psychosis with incompetency (Cooke, 1969; McGarry, 1965; Roesch & Golding, 1980). Furthermore, evaluators in the past rarely took into account the specific demands of a defendant's case.

This has begun to change. In the past, evaluators were employed typically in state mental hospitals (the site of the majority of competency evaluations at that time) and had no training either in the assessment of competency or in matters of law. As a consequence, the evaluations were based on the same standard mental status examinations that had been used with other patients in the hospital. If psychological tests were used at all, they were used as a diagnostic tool to determine presence or absence of psychosis.

Over the past 25 years, these entrenched practices have been challenged and changed. Thus, research provided evidence that the presence of psychosis was not sufficient by itself for a finding of incompetency (Roesch & Golding, 1980), and modern empirical studies of competency reports demonstrate that evaluators rarely make that simple conceptual error (Heilbrun & Collins, 1995; Nicholson, LaFortune, Norwood, & Roach, 1995; Nicholson & Norwood, 2000; Skeem, Golding, Cohn, & Berge, 1998). However, although forensic evaluators today typically have more training than in the past, most states still do not require forensic evaluator training (Farkas, DeLeon, & Newman, 1997), and examiners are usually only "occasional experts" (Grisso, 1987).

The specific psycholegal abilities required of a defendant are the most important aspect for assessing fitness. The contextual nature of competence has been explored by researchers in the area. Some researchers and scholars have argued that competence should be considered within the context in which it is to be used. For example, the abilities required by the defendant in his or her specific case should be taken into account when assessing competence. This contextual perspective was summarized by Golding and Roesch (1988, p. 79) as follows:

> Mere presence of severe disturbance (a psychopathological criterion) is only a threshold issue—it must be further demonstrated that such severe disturbance in *this* defendant, facing *these* charges, *in light of existing* evidence, anticipating the substantial effort of a *particular* attorney with a *relationship of known characteristics,* results in the defendant being unable to rationally assist the attorney or to comprehend the nature of the proceedings and their likely outcome.

The importance of a contextual determination of specific psycholegal abilities has been repeatedly demonstrated by empirical findings that assessed competencies in one area of functioning are rarely homogeneous with competencies in other areas of functioning (Bonnie, 1992a; Golding & Roesch, 1988; Grisso, Appelbaum, Mulvey, & Fletcher, 1995; Skeem et al., 1998).

Recent Supreme Court decisions in both the United States and Canada, however, have confused this issue by finding that the standard by which competency is to be judged is not context-specific. In *Regina v. Whittle* (1994), the Supreme Court of Canada ruled that there is to be only one standard for competency regardless of the specific abilities to be performed by an accused. The Supreme Court of Canada concluded that there is no difference between the essential abilities needed in making active choices about waiving counsel, making decisions at trial, confessing, or pleading guilty. The court ruled that different standards of competency should not be applied for different aspects of criminal proceedings and that the test to be used is one of "limited cognitive capacity" (p. 567) in each of these circumstances. However, unlike *Godinez v. Moran* (1993, discussed next), the forensic examiners had actually evaluated Mr. Whittle in these specific contexts, regardless of whether or not the standard to be applied was the same or different as a function of the context.

In *Godinez v. Moran* (1993), the U.S. Supreme Court held similarly that the standard for the various types of competency (i.e., competency to plead guilty, to waive counsel, to stand trial) should be considered the same. Justice Thomas wrote for the majority:

> The standard adopted by the Ninth Circuit is whether a defendant who seeks to plead guilty or waive counsel has the capacity for "reasoned choice" among the alternatives available to him. How this standard is different from (much less higher than) the Dusky standard—whether the defendant has a "rational under-standing" of the proceedings—is not readily apparent to us. . . . While the deci-sion to plead guilty is undeniably a profound one, it is no more complicated than the sum total of decisions that a defendant may be called upon to make during the course of a trial. . . . Nor do we think that a defendant who waives his right to the assistance of counsel must be more competent than the defendant who does not, since there is no reason to believe that the decision to waive counsel requires an appreciably higher level of mental functioning than the decision to waive other constitutional rights. (p. 2686)

In his dissent, Justice Blackmun noted that the "majority's analysis is con-trary to both common sense and long-standing case law" (p. 2691). He rea-soned that competency cannot be considered in a vacuum, separate from its specific legal context. Justice Blackmun argued that "competency for one pur-pose does not necessarily translate to competency for another purpose" (p. 2694) and noted that prior Supreme Court cases have "required competency evaluations to be specifically tailored to the context and purpose of a proceed-ing" (p. 2694). What is egregiously missing from the majority's opinion in *Godinez* however, is the fact that, unlike Whittle, Moran's competency to waive counsel or plead guilty to death penalty murder charges was never assessed by the forensic examiners, regardless of which standard (rational choice or ratio-nal understanding) was employed.

The *Godinez* holding has been subsequently criticized by legal scholars (Per-lin, 1996) and courts alike. In the words of the Third Circuit Court of Appeals, "This difficult case presents us with a window through which to view the real-world effects of the Supreme Court's decision in Godinez v. Moran, and it is not a pretty sight" (*Government of the Virgin Islands v. Charles*, 1995). The prob-lem is not whether the standards for various psycholegal competencies are higher, different, or the same, but rather, more fundamentally, whether or not the defendant has been examined with respect to these issues in the first place.

Standards of competence are one area of inquiry; the conceptualization of competence is another. Some researchers and scholars have provided reconcep-tualizations of competence to stand trial. Winick (1985, 1995) persuasively ar-gued that in some circumstances it may be in the best interests of the defendant to proceed with a trial, even if he or she is incompetent. Winick pos-tulated that this could take the form of a provisional trial wherein the support of the defense attorney would serve to ensure protection of the defendant. This would allow the defendant to proceed with his or her case while maintaining decorum in the courtroom and without violating the defendant's constitu-tional rights. As well, Bonnie (1992a, 1993) has provided a reformulation of competence to stand trial. Bonnie proposed a distinction between two types of competencies: competence to assist counsel and decisional competence. He ar-gued that defendants found incompetent to assist counsel would be barred from proceeding until they were restored to competence. Defendants found decisionally incompetent, on the other hand, may be able to proceed in certain cases where their lawyer is able to present a defense.

The past 15 years has also seen the development of better training programs for professionals in forensic psychology and psychiatry. Many graduate psychology programs and law schools cooperate to provide instruction in psychology as well as law, and a number of departments of psychology include forensic psychology as an area of expertise (Bersoff et al., 1997; Roesch, Grisso, & Poythress, 1986).

Another major change has been the shift in the location of competency assessments. Roesch and Golding (1980) argued that inpatient evaluation, which was the common practice until recently, is unnecessary in all but perhaps a small percentage of cases as most determinations of competency can easily be made on the basis of brief screening interviews (discussed later in this chapter). Community-based settings, including jails and mental health centers (Fitzgerald, Peszke, & Goodwin, 1978; Melton, Weithorn, & Slobogin, 1985; Ogloff & Roesch, 1992; Roesch & Ogloff, 1996), appear to be increasingly used to conduct evaluations. In 1994, Grisso and his colleagues published the results of a national survey they had conducted to determine the organization of pretrial forensic evaluation services in the United States (Grisso, Coccozza, Steadman, Fisher, & Greer, 1994). These researchers concluded that "the traditional use of centrally located, inpatient facilities for obtaining pretrial evaluations survives in only a minority of states, having been replaced by other models that employ various types of outpatient approaches" (p. 388). One compelling reason for this shift is cost. Laben, Kashgarian, Nessa, and Spencer (1977) estimated that the cost of the community-based evaluations they conducted in Tennessee was one-third the cost of the typical mental hospital evaluation (see also Fitzgerald et al., 1978). Although Winick (1985) estimated that $185 million was spent annually on competency evaluations, more recent estimates are two or three times higher and probably reach $1 billion (annually) if the costs associated with the entire competency evaluation and treatment process are considered.[1]

The widespread use of screening instruments would serve to lower these rising costs as the majority of individuals, for whom incompetence is clearly not an issue, would be screened out. Only those defendants whom the screening instrument has identified as potentially incompetent would then be sent on for a more formal assessment of competence. Screening instruments can be administered in outpatient settings as well as in local jails and courthouses, thereby also serving to eliminate the unnecessary detention of clearly competent individuals.

Base rates for competency referrals (from 2% to 8% of felony arrests) and for incompetency determinations (from 7% to 60%) vary widely across jurisdictions and evaluation settings (Nicholson & Kugler, 1991; Skeem et al., 1998). This occurs for a number of reasons, including variations in examiner training and use of forensically relevant evaluation procedures (Skeem et al., 1998), the availability of pretrial mental health services, the nature of the referral system, inadequate treatment services for the chronically mentally ill and a criminalization of their conduct, and the extent to which judges scrutinize bona fide doubt about a defendant's competency before granting evaluation petitions

(Golding, 1992). Nevertheless, the modal jurisdiction typically finds only 20% of those referred incompetent to proceed with their trial. Precise data are not available, but conservatively, half of those found competent presented little or no reason for doubting their competency and could have been detected by adequate screening procedures. This is true in the United States as well as in other countries. Zapf and Roesch (1998) investigated the rate of (in)competence in individuals remanded to an inpatient setting for an assessment of fitness to stand trial in Canada. Their results indicate that only 11% of the remands were unfit to stand trial and, further, that with the use of a brief screening interview 82% of the remands could have been screened out at some earlier time as they were clearly fit to stand trial (Zapf & Roesch, 1997). Many of the assessment procedures we describe later in this chapter are either explicitly designed for screening or could easily be adapted for use in such settings.

A major change in the past few decades has been the development of a number of instruments specifically designed for assessing competence. This work was pioneered by McGarry and his colleagues (Lipsitt, Lelos, & McGarry, 1971; McGarry, 1965; McGarry & Curran, 1973). Their work was the starting point for a more sophisticated and systematic approach to the assessment of competency. In 1986, Grisso coined the term "forensic assessment instrument" (FAI) to refer to instruments that provide frameworks for conducting forensic assessments. FAIs are typically semistructured elicitation procedures and lack the characteristics of many traditional psychological tests. However, they serve to make forensic assessments more systematic. These instruments help evaluators to collect important and relevant information and to follow the decision-making process that is required under the law. Since the time that the term was coined, a number of assessment instruments have been developed that are designed to work in this way, and it appears that the use of FAIs has been slowly increasing (Borum & Grisso, 1995; but see Skeem et al.'s 1998 finding that few occasional experts use such devices). This trend is encouraging in that empirical data suggest that trained examiners using FAIs achieve the highest levels of interexaminer and examiner-adjudication agreement (Golding, Roesch, & Schreiber, 1984; Nicholson & Kugler, 1991; Skeem et al., 1998).

Before turning to a review of assessment methods, we provide a brief overview of the legal procedures involved in competency questions.

OVERVIEW OF PROCEDURES

Laws regarding competency vary from state to state, although most jurisdictions follow procedures similar to the overview we describe in this section. Clinicians should consult their own statute for the specific law and procedure applicable in each state.

The issue of competency may be raised at any point in the adjudication process (Golding & Roesch, 1988). If a court determines that a bona fide doubt exists as to a defendant's competency, it must consider this issue formally (*Drope v. Missouri*, 1975; *Pate v. Robinson*, 1966), usually after a forensic evaluation, which can take place, as we noted, in the jail or an outpatient facility or in an institutional setting.

One legal issue that may concern evaluators is whether information obtained in a competency evaluation can be used against a defendant during the guilt phase of a trial or at sentencing. While some concerns have been raised about possible self-incrimination (Berry, 1973; Pizzi, 1977), all jurisdictions in the United States and Canada provide either statutorily or through case law that information obtained in a competency evaluation cannot be introduced on the issue of guilt unless the defendant places his or her mental state into evidence at either trial or at sentencing hearings (*Estelle v. Smith*, 1981; Golding & Roesch, 1988).

Once a competency evaluation has been completed and the written report submitted (see Melton et al., 1997; Petrella & Poythress, 1983; Skeem et al., 1998, for a discussion of the content of these reports), the court may schedule a hearing. If, however, both the defense and the prosecution accept the findings and recommendations in the report, a hearing does not have to take place. It is likely that in the majority of the states, a formal hearing is not held for most cases. If a hearing is held, the evaluators may be asked to testify, but most hearings are quite brief and usually only the written report of an evaluator is used. In fact, the majority of hearings last only a few minutes and are held simply to confirm the findings of evaluators (Steadman, 1979). The ultimate decision about competency rests with the court, which is not bound by the evaluators' recommendations (e.g., *North Dakota v. Heger*, 1982). In most cases, however, the court accepts the recommendations of the evaluators (Hart & Hare, 1992; Steadman, 1979; Williams & Miller, 1981; Zapf, Hubbard, Cooper, Wheeles, & Ronan, 2004).

At this point, defendants found competent proceed with their case. For defendants found incompetent, either trials are postponed until competency is regained or the charges are dismissed, usually without prejudice. The disposition of incompetent defendants is perhaps the most problematic area of the competency procedures. Until the case of *Jackson v. Indiana* (1972), virtually all states allowed the automatic and indefinite commitment of incompetent defendants. In *Jackson,* the U.S. Supreme Court held that a defendant committed solely on the basis of incompetency "cannot be held more than the reasonable period of time necessary to determine whether there is a substantial probability that he will attain that capacity in the foreseeable future" (p. 738). The Court did not specify how long a period of time would be reasonable, nor did it indicate how progress toward the goal of regaining competency could be assessed.

The *Jackson* decision led to revisions in state statutes to provide for alternatives to commitment as well as limits on the length of commitment (Roesch & Golding, 1980). The length of confinement varies from state to state, with some states having specific time limits (e.g., 18 months), while other states base length of treatment on a proportion of the length of the sentence that would have been given had the defendant been convicted.

Medication is the most common form of treatment, although some jurisdictions have established treatment programs designed to increase understanding of the legal process (e.g., Pendleton, 1980; Webster, Jenson, Stermac, Gardner, & Slomen, 1985), or that confront problems that hinder a defendant's ability to participate in the defense (Davis, 1985; Siegel & Elwork, 1990). What happens if an incompetent defendant refuses treatment, particularly medications? A recent U.S. Supreme Court case provides at least a partial answer to this question. In *Sell v. United States* (2003), the Court considered the case of Charles Sell, a dentist who was charged with multiple counts of insurance fraud but was incompetent and committed for treatment at a federal medical center. Dr. Sell refused medication, and treatment staff requested involuntary medication. The medical center's review panels found that Sell was mentally ill and dangerous and that medication would be helpful in reducing his symptoms and would also help restore his competence to stand trial. Sell appealed, and the federal magistrate who had ordered Sell's commitment supported the government's position that medication was the best treatment alternative to address the issue of Sell's dangerousness and also restore his competency. The Supreme Court held that antipsychotic drugs could be administered against the defendant's will for the purpose of restoring competency, but only in limited circumstances. The Court noted that this applied only to the issue of competency restoration and indicated that medication could be justified on other grounds, including dangerousness (see *Riggins v. Nevada*, 1992; *Washington v. Harper*, 1990). Writing for the majority, Justice Breyer identified several factors that a court must consider in determining whether a defendant can be forced to take medication. This includes a finding that the medication is likely to restore competence and will not result in side effects that might affect a defendant's ability to assist counsel. The court must also find that alternative and less intrusive methods that would achieve the same result are not available. The *Sell* decision may limit the use of medication as an option for some incompetent defendants who refuse voluntary treatment. Indeed, Justice Breyer commented that instances of forced medication may be rare. As a consequence, the *Sell* case may result in a greater emphasis being placed on the development of alternative forms of treatment for restoring competence.

This brief overview of the competency procedures is intended to provide a basic understanding of the process. For a more complete discussion of the legal issues as well as a review of empirical research on the various aspects of the competency procedures, the reader is referred to reviews by Golding and Roesch (1988), Nicholson and Kugler (1991), Roesch et al. (1993), and Winick (1996).

ASSESSING COMPETENCY

Though there has been some confusion over the definition of competency, there nevertheless appears to be generally good agreement among evaluators about whether a defendant is competent or not. The few studies of reliability that have been completed report that pairs of evaluators agree in 80% or more of the cases (Goldstein & Stone, 1977; Poythress & Stock, 1980; Roesch & Golding, 1980; Skeem et al., 1998). When evaluators are highly trained and use semistructured competence assessment instruments, even higher rates of agreement have been reported (Golding et al., 1984; Nicholson & Kugler, 1991).

When base rates of findings of competency are considered, however, these high levels of agreement are less impressive, and they do not suggest that evaluators are necessarily in agreement about the criteria for a determination of competency. Without even directly assessing a group of defendants, a psychologist could achieve high levels of agreement with an examining clinician simply by calling all defendants competent (base rate decision). Given that, in most jurisdictions, approximately 80% of all referred defendants are competent (for reasons discussed later in this chapter), the psychologist and the examiner would have modest agreement, even with making no decisions at all. (Though the problem of base rates can be corrected through the use of certain statistics, such as Kappa, the studies reporting reliability usually have small samples overall and consequently very few incompetent defendants.) Most disturbing, Skeem and her colleagues (1998) demonstrated that examiner agreement on specific psycholegal deficits (as opposed to overall competency) averaged only 25% across a series of competency domains. It is the more difficult decisions, involving cases where competency is truly a serious question, that are of concern. How reliable are decisions about these cases? To date, no study has examined enough of these cases to answer this question.

High levels of reliability do not, of course, ensure that valid decisions are being made. Two evaluators could agree that the presence of psychosis automatically leads to a finding of incompetency. As long as the evaluators are in agreement about their criteria for determining psychosis, the reliability of their final judgments about competency will be high. As we suggest throughout this chapter, it is quite possible that the criteria used by many evaluators inappropriately rely on traditional mental status issues without considering the functional aspects of a particular defendant's case.

Validity is difficult to assess because of the criterion problem. Criterion-related validity is usually assessed by examining concurrent validity and predictive validity (Messick, 1980). Predictive validity is impossible to assess fully because only defendants who are considered competent are allowed to proceed. It is feasible to look at the predictive validity of decisions about competent defendants, but not possible, of course, to assess the decisions about incompetent defendants, as they are referred for treatment and judicial proceedings are suspended. Concurrent validity is also difficult to determine because it does not make sense to look simply at correlations with other measures (e.g., diagnosis, intelligence) if one adopts a functional, case-by-case assessment of a defendant's competency. For these reasons, then, there is no "correct" decision against which to compare judgments.

As we have indicated, the courts usually accept mental health judgments about competency. Does this mean that the judgments are valid? Not necessarily, as courts often accept the evaluator's definition of competency and his or her conclusions without review, leading to very high levels of examiner-judge agreement (Hart & Hare, 1992; Skeem et al., 1998; Zapf et al., 2004). We have argued (Roesch & Golding, 1980) that the only ultimate way of assessing the validity of decisions about incompetency is to allow defendants who are believed to be incompetent to proceed with a trial anyway. This could be a provisional trial (on the Illinois model) in which assessment of a defendant's performance could continue. If a defendant was unable to participate, then the trial could be stopped. If a verdict had already been reached and the defendant was convicted, the verdict could be set aside.

We suspect that in a significant percentage of trials, alleged incompetent defendants will be able to participate. In addition to the obvious advantages to defendants, the use of a provisional trial could provide valuable information about what should be expected of a defendant in certain judicial proceedings (e.g., the ability to testify, identify witnesses, describe events, evaluate the testimony of other witnesses). Short of a provisional trial, it may be possible to address the validity issue by having independent experts evaluate the information provided by evaluators and other collateral information sources. We have used this technique in our research and discuss it later in the chapter. Next we review various methods for assessing competency.

The Functional Evaluation Approach

We believe the most reasonable approach to the assessment of competency is based on a functional evaluation of a defendant's ability matched to the contextualized demands of the case. Although an assessment of the mental status of a defendant is important, it is not sufficient as a method of evaluating competency. Rather, the mental status information must be related to the specific demands of the legal case, as has been suggested by legal decisions such as those involving amnesia. As in the case of psychosis, a defendant with amnesia is not per se incompetent to stand trial, as has been held in a number of cases (e.g., *Ritchie v. Indiana*, 1984; *Wilson v. United States*, 1968). In *Missouri v. Davis* (1983), the defendant had memory problems due to brain damage. Nevertheless, the Missouri Supreme Court held that amnesia by itself was not a sufficient reason to bar the trial of an otherwise competent defendant. In *Montana v. Austed* (1983), the court held that the bulk of the evidence against the defendant was physical and not affected by amnesia. Finally, in a Maryland decision (*Morrow v. Maryland*, 1982), the court held that, because of the potential for fraud, amnesia does not justify a finding of incompetence. The court also stated that everyone has amnesia to some degree because the passage of time erodes memory. These decisions are of interest because they support the view that evaluators cannot reach a finding of incompetency independent of the facts of the legal case, an issue we return to later. Similarly, a defendant may be psychotic and still be found competent to stand trial if the symptoms do not impair the defendant's functional ability to consult with his or her attorney and otherwise rationally participate in the legal process.

Some cases are more complex than others and, as a result, may require different types of psycholegal abilities. Thus, it may be that the same defendant is competent for one type of legal proceeding but not for others. In certain cases, a defendant may be required to testify. In this instance, a defendant who is likely to withdraw in a catatonic-like state may be incompetent. But the same defendant may be able to proceed if the attorney intends to plea bargain (the way the vast majority of criminal cases are handled).

The functional approach is illustrated in the famous amnesia case of *Wilson v. United States* (1968). In that decision, the Court of Appeals held that six factors should be considered in determining whether a defendant's amnesia impaired the ability to stand trial:

1. The extent to which the amnesia affected the defendant's ability to consult with and assist his lawyer.
2. The extent to which the amnesia affected the defendant's ability to testify in his own behalf.
3. The extent to which the evidence in suit could be extrinsically reconstructed in view of the defendant's amnesia. Such evidence would include evidence relating to the crime itself as well as any reasonable possible alibi.
4. The extent to which the Government assisted the defendant and his counsel in that reconstruction.
5. The strength of the prosecution's case. Most important here will be whether the Government's case is such as to negate all reasonable hypotheses of innocence. If there is any substantial possibility that the accused could, but for his amnesia, establish an alibi or other defense, it should be presumed that he would have been able to do so.
6. Any other facts and circumstances which would indicate whether or not the defendant had a fair trial (pp. 463–464).

One could substitute any symptom for amnesia in this list. If this were done, the evaluation of competency would certainly be based on a determination of the manner in which a defendant's incapacity may have an effect on the legal proceedings. In fact, some states, such as Florida (Florida Rules of Criminal Procedure 3.21(a)(1); see Winick, 1983) and Utah (1994), already specify that the evaluators must relate a defendant's mental condition to clearly defined legal factors, such as the defendant's appreciation of the charges, the range and nature of possible penalties, and capacity to disclose to attorney pertinent facts surrounding the alleged offense (Winick, 1983). Utah's statute goes the furthest in this direction, specifying the most comprehensive range of psycholegal abilities to be addressed by evaluators (including the iatrogenic effects of medication and decisional competencies) and also requiring judges to identify specifically which psycholegal abilities are impaired when a defendant is found incompetent.

The assessment of competency requires consideration of both mental status and psycholegal abilities. Unfortunately, current data indicate that evaluators often do not address an appropriate range of psycholegal abilities and most often do not tie their psychopathological observations to their psycholegal conclusions (Skeem et al., 1998).

MEASURES OF COMPETENCY

Prior to the 1960s, there were no standard methods for assessing competency. One of the first was a checklist developed by Robey (1965), which focuses on court process issues such as understanding of the legal process. Another early procedure used a checklist and a set of interview questions devised by Bukatman, Foy, and de Grazia (1971). Neither of these early measures was used often (Schreiber, 1978). By far the greatest impact on competency assessment came first from the seminal work of A. Louis McGarry and his colleagues at the Harvard Medical School's Laboratory of Community Psychiatry. McGarry, a psychiatrist, was involved in the development of two measures: the Competency Screening Test (CST) and the Competency Assessment Instrument (CAI). We discuss these measures in addition to a number of other measures that have since been developed (see also Zapf & Viljoen, 2003, for a review of competency assessment instruments).

The Competency Screening Test

The CST was created by Lipsitt et al. (1971) as a screening measure to identify clearly competent defendants and thus minimize the need for lengthy inpatient evaluations. Such a screening process was considered important because the vast majority of defendants referred for evaluations are competent as many factors influence referrals, including the use of the evaluation commitment as a method for denying bail, as a tactical maneuver to delay a trial, as a way of providing a basis for a reduction in charges or sentences, and as a means of getting defendants who are seen as in need of mental health treatment out of the jails and into the hospitals (Dickey, 1980; Golding, 1992; Menzies, Webster, Butler, & Turner, 1980; Roesch & Golding 1985; Teplin, 1984).

The CST, however, has not often been used as a screening device because of various validity considerations. The scoring method has been criticized (Brakel, 1974; Roesch & Golding, 1980) because of its idealized perception of the criminal justice system; certain responses may actually reflect a sense of powerlessness in controlling one's outcome in the legal system and may be based on past experiences with the legal system.

The CST has been examined in a number of studies. It has shown high levels of interrater reliability in terms of scoring the incomplete-sentence format (Randolph, Hicks, & Mason, 1981), but studies comparing classification based on CST cutoff scores and hospital evaluation decisions reveal that it has a high false positive rate; that is, it tends to identify many individuals as incompetent who are later determined to be competent in hospital evaluations (Lipsitt et al., 1971; Nottingham & Mattson, 1981; Randolph et al., 1981; Shatin, 1979).

The results of these studies lead one to give a mixed review of the CST. Although it appears that the CST is a reliable instrument, serious questions can be raised about its usefulness as a screening device because of the potential for misclassifying possibly incompetent defendants. At this point, it is not possible to recommend that it be used as a sole method of screening defendants.

The Competency Assessment Instrument

The most important measure developed by McGarry, the CAI, contains 13 items related to legal issues. It has served as the basis for the subsequent forensic assessment instruments. The items include "appraisal of available legal defenses," "quality of relating to attorney," and "capacity to disclose pertinent facts." Each item is scored on a 1 to 5 scale, ranging from "total incapacity" to "no incapacity." The CAI manual contains clinical examples of levels of incapacity as well as suggested interview questions.

The CAI has been used in a number of jurisdictions, although perhaps more as an interview structuring device than in the two-stage screening manner (with the CST), as originally intended by McGarry (Laben et al., 1977; Schreiber, 1978). Unfortunately, there are few studies reporting either reliability or validity data. We used the CAI in a North Carolina study (Roesch & Golding, 1980). Thirty interviews conducted by pairs of interviewers yielded item agreement ranging from 68.8% to 96.7%, with a median of 81.2%. The interviewers were in agreement on the competency status of 29 of the 30 defendants (26 competent, 3 incompetent). The interviewers' decisions were in concordance with the more lengthy hospital evaluation decisions in 27 of 30 cases, or 90%. In subsequent studies (Golding et al., 1984; others summarized Nicholson & Kugler, 1991), the CAI has shown high levels of *trained* interexaminer agreement and examiner-outcome agreement. Obviously, the CAI holds promise as both a screening device and as a full-blown interview. Its primary disadvantage, relative to the instruments discussed next, is in the range of psycholegal abilities articulated and its lack of focus on the nexus between psychopathology and psycholegal impairment.

The Interdisciplinary Fitness Interview

The Interdisciplinary Fitness Interview (IFI) is designed to assess both the legal and the psychopathological aspects of competency (Golding et al., 1984). The original IFI comprised three major sections: legal issues (5 items), psychopathological issues (11 items), and overall evaluation (4 items). The three items in the consensual judgment section reflect postassessment resolution of differences between judges.

Each of the general items represents an organizing scheme for more specific subareas that have been seen to influence competency decisions. For example, six subareas are subsumed under the broad "capacity to appreciate," which forms the core of item 1. These are (1) appreciating the nature of the state's criminal allegation; (2) ability to provide a reasonable account of one's behavior prior to, during, and subsequent to the alleged crime; (3) ability to provide an account of relevant others during the same time period; (4) ability to provide relevant information about one's own state of mind at the time of the alleged crime, including intentions, feelings, and cognitions; (5) ability to provide information about the behavior of the police during apprehension, arrest, and interrogation; and (6) projected ability to provide feedback to an attorney about the veracity of witness testimony during trial, if a trial is likely to be involved. However, in line with the open-textured nature of the competency construct, a complete enumeration is not possible; instead, an attempt is made to summarize the general lay of the land, allowing for specifics to be a matter of personal judgment.

The IFI was designed so that evaluators would have to consider both legal and mental status issues, but neither in isolation. The format of the IFI requires evaluators to relate their observations to the specific demands of the legal situations. For each item, evaluators are asked to rate the degree of incapacity of the defendant, as well as to give the item a score to indicate the influence that the incapacity might have on the overall decision about competency. Thus, a defendant may receive a score indicating the presence of hallucinations (item 10) but receive a low score because the evaluator has determined that the presence of hallucinations would not have much effect on the conduct of the legal case. Another defendant with the same symptom may receive a high score because the hallucinations are considered to be more of a potential problem during the legal proceedings.

A training manual for the IFI has been developed as a guide for evaluators. For each item, the manual provides a set of suggested questions and follow-up probes and also gives clinical guidance for the handling of typical problems.

Golding et al. (1984) used the IFI in a study of pretrial defendants in the Boston area who were referred by court clinics to a state mental hospital for competency evaluation. They were interviewed by teams composed of a lawyer and either a psychologist or a social worker. While the interviews were conducted jointly, each evaluator independently completed the IFI rating form. The results demonstrated that judgments about competency can be made in a reliable manner by lawyers and mental health evaluators. They were in agreement on 97% of their final determinations of competency. By type of decision, the interviewers found 58 defendants to be competent and 17 incompetent, and they disagreed on the remaining 2 cases.

The IFI has been revised (Golding, 1993) to reflect changes in constitutional law and the adoption by many states of articulated competency standards (e.g., Utah, 1994). In its current form, the Interdisciplinary Fitness Interview-Revised (IFI-R) taps 31 relatively specific psycholegal abilities organized into 11 global domains. The IFI-R was developed on the original model used by Golding et al. (1984), but was altered to reflect a decade of experience, numerous court opinions, and the accumulated professional literature on competency assessments. For example, it specifically addresses the issue of the iatrogenic effects of psychotropic medications (*Riggins v. Nevada*, 1992), a defendant's decisional competency to engage in rational choice about trial strategies, proceeding *pro se* or pleading guilty (see discussion of *Godinez v. Moran*, 1993, earlier), and competency to confess. It was developed to mirror Utah's articulated competency code, which mandates that examiners address its 11 global domains. A revised and comprehensive training manual is available (Golding, 1993).

Golding et al. (1984) also commented on one of the research problems inherent in studies of competency assessment. Because most defendants are competent (77% in the study cited earlier), it is difficult to obtain a sufficiently large sample of incompetent defendants. It is clear to us that decisions about most defendants referred for competency evaluations are straightforward; that is, they are competent to stand trial, a finding that is evident regardless of the method of assessment. The potential value of the IFI-R or other structured assessment methods, we believe, is in assessing defendants whose competency is truly questionable.

The Fitness Interview Test

The Fitness Interview Test (FIT; Roesch, Webster, & Eaves, 1984) was originally created in 1984 to assess fitness to stand trial in Canada. It has since been extensively revised, and the current version is referred to as the Fitness Interview Test-revised edition (FIT-R; Roesch, Zapf, Eaves, & Webster, 1998). The FIT-R focuses on the psycholegal abilities of the individual. The scoring system has been changed to a 3-point scale, with a score of 2 meaning definite or serious impairment, 1 meaning possible or mild impairment, and 0 meaning no impairment. As well, the items on the FIT-R were developed to parallel the standards for fitness that were established in section 2 of the 1992 revision of the *Criminal Code of Canada*.

The FIT-R takes approximately 30 minutes to administer and consists of a structured interview that taps into three main areas: (1) the ability to understand the nature or object of the proceedings, or factual knowledge of criminal procedure; (2) the ability to understand the possible consequences of the proceedings, or the appreciation of personal involvement in and importance of the proceedings; and (3) the ability to communicate with counsel, or to participate in the defense. Each of these three sections is broken down into specific questions that tap into different areas involved in fitness to stand trial. The first section assesses the defendant's understanding of the arrest process, the nature and severity of current charges, the role of key players, legal processes, pleas, and court procedure. The second section assesses the defendant's appreciation of the range and nature of possible penalties, appraisal of available legal defenses, and appraisal of likely outcome. The final section assesses the defendant's capacity to communicate facts to the lawyer, relate to the lawyer, plan legal strategy, engage in his or her own defense, challenge prosecution witnesses, testify relevantly, and manage courtroom behavior.

Research indicates that the FIT-R demonstrates excellent utility as a screening instrument (Zapf & Roesch, 1997). In this study, results of the FIT-R and an institution-based fitness assessment were compared for 57 defendants remanded to an inpatient psychiatric institution for an evaluation of fitness. The FIT-R correctly predicted fitness status (i.e., fit or unfit) for 49 of the 57 individuals. The remaining 8 individuals were judged to be unfit by the FIT-R and fit as a result of the inpatient assessment. This was to be expected as a screening instrument should overestimate the rate of unfitness without making any false negative errors. There was 100% agreement between the FIT-R and the institution-based assessment for those individuals deemed fit to stand trial.

Research has also indicated that the FIT-R appears to have adequate psychometric properties. With respect to reliability, Viljoen, Roesch, and Zapf (2002) found that the average interrater reliability of the FIT-R for overall determination of fitness was .98. Reliability for sections was lower, ranging from .54 to .70 for groups of raters. To investigate the predictive validity of the FIT-R, Zapf and colleagues (Zapf & Roesch, 1997; Zapf, Roesch, & Viljoen, 2001) compared decisions made by the FIT-R to decisions made in an institution-based evaluation of fitness in several samples. In the first sample, the overall rate of agreement between the FIT-R and institution-based judgments was 87%, and the false-negative error rate was 2%. The second sample yielded comparable results. Boddy, Roesch, Zapf, and Eaves (2000) compared defendants who were referred for competency evaluations, including those who were eventually found unfit, and defendants who were not referred. Performance on the FIT-R was able to effectively distinguish these groups in that referred defendants demonstrated significantly more impairment. As additional evidence of the construct validity of the FIT-R, Zapf and Roesch (2001) found reasonably high agreement (chance-corrected $\kappa = .51$) between the FIT-R and the MacArthur Competency Assessment Tool-Criminal Adjudication.

The Georgia Court Competency Test

The Georgia Court Competency Test (GCCT) was originally developed by Wildman et al. (1978) and has since gone through a number of revisions (Bagby, Nicholson, Rogers, & Nussbaum, 1992; Johnson & Mullet, 1987; Nicholson, Briggs, & Robertson, 1988; Wildman, White, & Brandenburg, 1990). The original version consisted of 17 items, and the revised version, referred to as the Mississippi State Hospital Revision (GCCT-MSH), consists of 21 items. The first seven items of the GCCT-MSH require the defendant to visually identify the location of certain participants in the courtroom. This is followed by questions related to the function of certain individuals in the courtroom, the charges that the defendant is facing, and his or her relationship with the lawyer.

Recent research on the GCCT-MSH has indicated that this instrument displays high levels of reliability and validity (Nicholson, Robertson, Johnson, & Jensen, 1988). Three factors have been identified by Nicholson et al.: courtroom layout, general legal knowledge, and specific legal knowledge. These same three factors were later replicated by Bagby et al. (1992). It was later suggested that this three-factor solution may be appropriate only for defendants who have been ordered to undergo assessment at the pretrial stage (Ustad, Rogers, Sewell, & Guarnaccia, 1996). These researchers indicated that a two-factor solution (legal knowledge and courtroom layout) may be more appropriate for defendants who have been adjudicated incompetent and who are undergoing inpatient treatment to restore competence.

The major drawback of the GCCT-MSH is that it focuses on foundational competencies and relatively ignores the more important decisional competencies stressed in the IFI and FIT approaches (Bonnie, 1992a).

The MacArthur Competence Assessment Tool-Criminal Adjudication

The MacArthur Competence Assessment Tool-Criminal Adjudication (MacCAT-CA; Hoge, Bonnie, Poythress, & Monahan, 1999; Poythress et al., 1999) was developed between 1989 and 1996 by the MacArthur Foundation Research Network on Mental Health and the Law. After a comprehensive research instrument, the MacArthur Structured Assessment of the Competencies of Criminal Defendants (MacSAC-CD; Hoge, Poythress, et al., 1997) was developed, pilot-tested, and refined, a large field study was conducted (Bonnie et al., 1997; Hoge, Bonnie, et al., 1997; Hoge, Poythress, et al., 1997; Otto et al., 1998). The MacCAT-CA was developed from this comprehensive research instrument to assess three main subconstructs of the psycholegal abilities: understanding, reasoning, and appreciation.

The MacCAT-CA consists of 22 items that are grouped into three sections. The examiner begins by reading a hypothetical vignette to the defendant to ground the first two sections (16 items). The first section (8 items) assesses the defendant's ability to *understand* information about the legal system and the process. For each item, the defendant is asked a question related to the vignette (e.g., "What is the job of the attorney for the defense?") and is awarded 2 points (items are rated 0, 1, 2) if he or she is able to answer the question in a manner that demonstrates full understanding. If the defendant earns less than 2 points, the examiner discloses the answer and asks the defendant to repeat the disclosure in his or her own words. The purpose of the disclosure is to assess separately the defendant's *capacity* to understand and his or her *actual* or pre-existing understanding.

The second section (8 items) assesses the defendant's ability to *reason*. The first five items in this section assess the defendant's ability to consider two pieces of factual information and identify the most important or legally relevant piece of information that one should disclose to a lawyer. The last three items require the defendant to think through mock legal options (relevant to the vignette) and to evaluate them in various ways.

The final section (6 items) assesses the defendant's ability to *appreciate* his or her own legal circumstances and situation. This section departs from the hypothetical vignette format to explore the defendant's beliefs and perceptions about his or her personal role as a defendant and how he or she will be treated during the course of adjudication. These items are scored on the basis of the reasons that the defendant provides for his or her judgment and whether they are plausible or implausible (i.e., grounded in reality or based on delusional beliefs).

It is important to note that the authors of the MacCAT-CA emphasize that this instrument was developed for use as a tool rather than a test of competence. Thus, the scores obtained must be interpreted in the context of the specific defendant's case and integrated with all the other clinically relevant factors that may surround the specific circumstances of the case.

The psychometric properties of the MacCAT-CA were examined based on a sample of 729 felony defendants in eight states (Otto et al., 1998; see also Rogers, Grandjean, Tillbrook, Vitacco, & Sewell, 2001). The results indicated that the MacCAT-CA demonstrated good reliability. For each of the three sections, internal consistency ranged from .81 to .88 (α = .81 for Reasoning, .85 for Understanding, .88 for Appreciation), and interrater reliability ranged from very good to excellent (intraclass R = .75 for Appreciation, .85 for Reasoning, .90 for Understanding).

Otto and colleagues (1998) report that additional support for the construct validity of the MacCAT-CA was "found in the pattern of correlations between the MacCAT-CA measures and select clinical variables" (p. 439). MacCAT-CA Understanding, Reasoning, and Appreciation scores correlated .41, .34, and .14, respectively, with estimated Wechsler Adult Intelligence Scale-Revised full-scale IQ, and −.23, −.29, and −.36, respectively, with Brief Psychiatric Rating Scale (BPRS) total scores (these scores correlated more strongly with BPRS Psychoticism and Emotional Withdrawal than Depression and Hostility scales). Whether such a pattern of relationships with measures of intelligence and psychopathology is a theoretically desirable characteristic of the construct of competency is discussed later. The three MacCAT-CA scales correlated moderately with clinicians' global ratings of competency ($r = .36$, $.42$, and $.49$, respectively).

COMPETENCY IN SPECIAL POPULATIONS

In recent years, specific attention has become focused on two populations for whom issues of competency are especially important for various reasons: individuals with mental retardation (MR) and juveniles. This section examines some of the issues relevant to the assessment of competence for each of these special populations and describes instruments that have been developed to assess competency to stand trial within these populations.

Relatively few researchers and scholars have addressed the problems faced by mentally retarded individuals in the criminal justice system. Bonnie (1992b) noted that one of the biggest problems for these individuals is under-identification; that is, a considerable number of defendants with MR are not referred for psychological evaluations and a general failure to recognize the magnitude and/or existence of the disabilities of MR is a major cause of this low rate of referral. Although the underidentification hypothesis is widely accepted among researchers and scholars, there is little empirical data to support it (Bonnie, 1992b).

Failure to identify mentally retarded individuals and thus to refer them for evaluations of competency is often a consequence of the tendency of these individuals to attempt to hide their limitations. That is, persons with MR are often compliant and cooperative with authority figures, such as judges or lawyers, and are likely to pretend to understand their lawyers when, in fact, they may not (Bonnie, 1992b). In many circumstances, this "cloak of competence" gives these individuals the appearance of normalcy (Edgerton, 1993). Legally significant impairments, then, become visible only when the individual also has a mental illness or acts in a strange or disruptive manner (Bonnie, 1992b). It is common for these individuals to proceed to trial without ever having been identified (Cooper & Grisso, 1997) and, therefore, to proceed through the criminal justice system without understanding "the process or punishment, often unknowingly participating in agreements that can result in grave and long-lasting consequences" (Everington, 1990, p. 148). The misidentification of mentally retarded individuals can result in a loss of liberty and the violation of a right to a fair trial.

Once individuals with MR have been identified, it is important that they are evaluated by an examiner who is familiar with the specific issues relevant to MR. Petrella (1992) noted that the probability of an adequate evaluation of issues involving MR is highly unlikely for several reasons: (1) Many evaluators are not qualified to administer intelligence tests, (2) evaluators may have minimal experience with MR and limited exposure to the unique clinical presentation of individuals manifesting MR, (3) referrals to professionals and experts in the area of MR seldom occur, and (4) MR professionals have minimal experience with forensic issues.

Research that has examined the rates of incompetence of individuals with MR has found wide variation. In Missouri, rates have been reported at 17%; in

Connecticut and Michigan, rates of incompetence have been reported at 12.5% and 33%, respectively. In addition, the probability of being found incompetent also varies by degree of MR. In Virginia, 23% of defendants diagnosed with mild MR were recommended incompetent, whereas 68% of those with moderate MR were found incompetent (Petrella, 1992).

In terms of restoration to competency for individuals with MR, Bonnie (1992b) hypothesized that the possibility of restoration is highly unlikely. In a sample of 38 incompetent defendants with MR in Virginia, only 16% were viewed as likely to be restored, whereas evaluators estimated that restoration was unlikely for approximately 66% of the defendants (Petrella, 1992). In a 1994 study of 271 mentally retarded individuals committed to a competence restoration program designed specifically for defendants with MR, higher IQ was an indicator of competence. That is, individuals with higher IQs were more likely to be found competent or restored to competence (Jones, 1994). In addition, the author concluded that the absence of comorbidity (i.e., presence of a psychiatric disorder in addition to MR) was highly indicative of competence as only 3% of those with comorbid disorders were restored to competence as compared to approximately 20% of those without comorbid disorders (Jones, 1994).

Although this is certainly an area where further research is required, the few research efforts that have examined issues of MR in the criminal justice system beginning in the early 1990s can be viewed as a positive step forward (Fulero & Everington, 1995). Similarly, the 1990s also saw an increase in research examining issues of competency within the juvenile population. Competency has become more important for adolescents because the juvenile justice system has shifted to a punishment-oriented model, and increasing numbers of adolescents are being either waived or transferred to adult court (Salekin, Rogers, & Ustad, 2001).

Research on competency to stand trial in juveniles has begun to examine issues of the evaluation of maturity (Ryba, Cooper, & Zapf, 2003), decision-making abilities (Grisso et al., 2003), and other factors that might account for adjudicative competence (Redlich, Silverman, & Steiner, 2003). In addition, comparisons of juveniles' competence-related abilities with those of adults has been the focus of much research and scholarly writing (Grisso & Schwartz, 2000). A number of studies have reported that age and competency are negatively correlated, with younger children being more likely to be found incompetent (Cooper, 1995; Cowden & McKee, 1995; Grisso, 2003; Redlich et al., 2003). As the focus of this chapter is on competency to stand trial in adults, the reader is referred to additional sources for more complete information on juvenile competency (e.g., Barnum, 2000; Bonnie & Grisso, 2000; Grisso, 1998; Grisso & Schwartz, 2000; Grisso et al., 2003; Woolard, 2002).

Specialized Measures of Competency

In recent years, there has been a move toward the development of competence assessment instruments for specialized populations of defendants, such as defendants with mental retardation and juvenile defendants. We next briefly describe some of the recent advances in these areas.

*Competence Assessment for Standing Trial for Defendants with
Mental Retardation*

Everington (1990) developed an instrument designed to assess competence
with mentally retarded defendants called the Competence Assessment for
Standing Trial for Defendants with Mental Retardation (CAST-MR; Everington & Luckasson, 1992). The items of the CAST-MR were derived from a review of relevant literature, case law, and existing competency to stand trial
assessment instruments (Everington, 1990). The CAST-MR consists of 50 questions, which are administered orally to the defendant. The questions are divided into three sections that address the basic elements of the *Dusky*
standard. Section I, Basic Legal Concepts, includes 25 multiple-choice items
that address concepts related to the criminal trial process (e.g., the roles
of judges, a jury, the prosecutor, and defense attorney) and terms that are critical to the trial process (e.g., felony, plea bargain, and probation). Section II,
Skills to Assist Defense, comprises 15 multiple-choice items that address the
attorney-client relationship. Items on Sections I and II are scored as either correct (1 point) or incorrect (0 points). Section III, Understanding Case Events,
consists of 10 open-ended questions designed to assess the defendant's ability
to describe the relevant circumstances of his or her alleged offense. Items are
scored as 1 point, ½ point, or 0 points based on the ability of the individual to
relay information to his or her case in an accurate and understandable manner
(Everington & Luckasson, 1992).

The CAST-MR was developed to assist in the determination of whether or not
a defendant with MR is competent to stand trial. The authors of the CAST-MR
emphasize its use as only one component of an overall assessment. Results of
the CAST-MR should be considered in the context of other relevant information
(e.g., interviews, observations, social history; Everington & Luckasson, 1992).

Two studies have been conducted to examine the psychometric properties of
the CAST-MR. The results indicated that the instrument has good reliability
and validity. Reliability and validity findings were similar to those found with
other competency assessment instruments (Everington, 1990; Everington &
Dunn, 1995). Results from the first study demonstrated that the internal consistency of the CAST-MR total score was .93 when estimated by Cronbach's
alpha and .92 when estimated by the Kuder-Richardson method (Everington,
1990). The results from the second study were consistent with the previous
study. Internal consistency of the total score using the Kuder-Richardson
method was estimated between .92 for KR formula 20 and .92 for KR formula
21. These findings indicate that the CAST-MR has a high level of homogeneity
(Everington & Dunn, 1995). Using the Pearson product-moment correlation,
test-retest reliability was estimated twice, at .89 and .90 (Everington, 1990;
Everington & Dunn, 1995). Interrater reliability for Section III was estimated
between 80% and 87% (Everington & Dunn, 1995).

Juvenile Measures of Competency

At the time this chapter was being written, an instrument called the
MacArthur Judgment Evaluation (MacJEN; Grisso et al., 2003; Woolard, 1998)

was being developed for use in the assessment of immaturity of judgment in juveniles but was not yet available for use in clinical settings.

GUIDELINES FOR EVALUATORS

We conclude our chapter with a discussion of several issues to which an examiner must pay special attention when conducting an evaluation of competency (see generally, Committee on Ethical Guidelines for Psychologists, 1991). Even before seeing a defendant face-to-face, it is good clinical practice to speak with both the defense and the prosecuting attorneys to determine as accurately as possible why the fitness issue was raised, what evidence was offered, and what sort of trial and dispositional alternatives are being considered by both sides.

All indications of prior mental health contacts should be pursued *before* the interview takes place, so that the examiner has as complete a set of mental health records as possible. Similarly, complete police reports of the alleged crime are necessary and a past criminal history record helpful, particularly if the defendant has cycled through the criminal justice and mental health systems several times. Obviously, if the defendant is an inpatient, observational records should be consulted, as well as all routine psychological test data. Finally, the examiner should maintain an accurate record of when, where, and how information about the defendant was made available, as well as a date and time record of all contacts with the defendant, attorneys, and other mental health professionals. These records are invaluable at later stages if legal tactics designed to confuse or mislead a witness are attempted.

Having prepared for an examination in this fashion, one can conduct an efficient and comprehensive interview in a short period of time: Most delays in conducting an evaluation can be avoided; for the defendant, time spent in an inpatient facility can be minimized; and a more relevant examination can be conducted.

Prior to the interview, the defendant should be fully informed about any limitations on the interview's confidentiality. The possibility of recording the interview should be discussed, although permission should also be obtained from the defendant's attorney. The examiner should be aware of any aspects of the interview and the resulting report that are covered by statute or accepted practice within the jurisdiction. As an example of the former, some states require *Miranda*-like warnings that inform the defendant of the limitations of confidentiality that may apply. Similarly, other states dictate the form of the report to the court, and an examiner's report may be excluded if it does not comply with the required format.

In *People v. Harris* (1983), for example, a psychiatrist's report (that the defendant was competent) was excluded, and the defendant's subsequent conviction was reversed because the opinion was presented in conclusory terms and failed to give the clinical facts and reasons on which it was based, thus precluding the trier of fact from independently assessing the weight to be given such an opinion. The current competency statutes in Illinois (as in Florida and Utah) are in many ways models of this developing trend. They require the examiner to address the facts on which the conclusion is based, to explain how the conclusion was reached, to describe the defendant's mental and physical disabilities and how these impair the ability to understand the proceedings and assist in the defense, to discuss the likelihood that the defendant will respond to a specified course of treatment, and to explain procedures that would be employed to compensate for the defendant's disabilities, if any. We applaud this sort of specification and urge examiners to adopt the practice, even if it is not mandated in their own jurisdiction.

The conduct of a competency evaluation and the reports prepared for court should be in complete accord with both the spirit and the letter of contemporary legal standards. Examiners must therefore be thoroughly acquainted with the legal literature and in some sense anticipate developments in their practice. For example, *Estelle v. Smith* (1981) clearly prohibits the introduction of material obtained under court-ordered competency proceedings at a "critical" (guilt or sentencing) stage of trial. Many states mirror this in their statutes but nevertheless do not regulate the common practice of requesting competency and sanity evaluations at the same time, often resulting in a combined report. We believe this practice is unfortunate and recommend that separate interviews, with distinct reports, be prepared. While a trier of fact is required to separate these issues, it is cognitively almost impossible to do so when the reports are combined. A defendant who is clearly psychotic and "legally insane" at the time of an assault may respond rapidly to treatment upon arrest and be just as nonpsychotic and "legally fit" when actually examined. Caution and fairness dictate keeping the reports separate so that the two issues can be considered independently by the courts.

CONCLUSIONS

This chapter touches on only a small selection of the vast amount of research and writing on competence to stand trial. Our purpose was to give only a brief overview of competency law, research, and assessment. For a comprehensive review of the recent empirical research on competence to stand trial, the reader is referred to Grisso (1992), Cooper and Grisso (1997), and Mumley, Tillbrook, and Grisso (2003). These authors review the research on the evaluation of competence in three 5-year intervals (1986–1990, 1991–1995, and 1996–2000). As well, Nicholson and Kugler (1991) conducted a meta-analysis using 30 studies and more than 8,000 defendants that provides a quantitative review of the comparative research on competence. Finally, Zapf, Viljoen, Whittemore, Poythress, and Roesch (2002) present a review of the past, present, and future of competency research. These references as well as those listed in the introductory paragraph of this chapter will provide the reader with a more in-depth understanding of competency to stand trial.

NOTE

1. Forensic mental health economic estimates vary, depending on jurisdiction. Bonnie and Grisso (2000) estimate that 60,000 competency evaluations are performed each year. If the national average is 20% adjudicated incompetent, there are 12,000 restoration commitments yearly. In a typical jurisdiction, the average cost of a forensic hospital year is $145,000. Blending inpatient and outpatient evaluations, a typical evaluation cost is $5,000 per defendant.

REFERENCES

Bagby, R. M., Nicholson, R. A., Rogers, R., & Nussbaum, D. (1992). Domains of competency to stand trial: A factor analytic study. *Law and Human Behavior, 16,* 491–507.

Barnum, R. (2000). Clinical and forensic evaluation of competence to stand trial in juvenile defendants. In T. Grisso & R. G. Schwartz (Eds.), *Youth on trial: A developmental perspective on juvenile justice* (pp. 193–223). Chicago: University of Chicago Press.

Berry, F. D., Jr. (1973). Self-incrimination and the compulsory mental examination: A proposal. *Arizona Law Review, 15,* 919–950.

Bersoff, D. N., Goodman-Delahunty, J., Grisso, J. T., Hans, V. P., Poythress, N. G., & Roesch, R. (1997). Training in psychology and law: Models from the Villanova conference. *American Psychologist, 52,* 1301–1310.

Boddy, J., Roesch, R., Zapf, P. A., & Eaves, D. (2000, March). *Characteristics of defendants remanded for fitness assessments.* Paper presented at the Biennial meeting of the American Psychology—Law Society, New Orleans, LA.

Bonnie, R. J. (1992a). The competence of criminal defendants: A theoretical reformulation. *Behavioral Sciences and the Law, 10,* 291–316.

Bonnie, R. J. (1992b). The competence of criminal defendants with mental retardation to participate in their own defense. *Journal of Criminal Law and Criminology, 81,* 419–446.

Bonnie, R. J. (1993). The competence of criminal defendants Beyond. *Dusky* and *Drope. University of Miami Law Review, 47,* 539–601.

Bonnie, R. J., & Grisso, T. (2000). Adjudicative competence and youthful offenders. In T. Grisso & R. G. Schwartz (Eds.), *Youth on trial: A developmental perspective on criminal justice.* Chicago: University of Chicago Press.

Bonnie, R. J., Hoge, S. K., Monahan, J., Poythress, N., Eisenberg, M., & Feucht-Haviar, T. (1997). The MacArthur adjudicative competence study: A comparison of criteria for assessing the competence of criminal defendants. *Journal of the American Academy of Psychiatry and the Law, 25,* 249–259.

Borum, R., & Grisso, T. (1995). Psychological test use in criminal forensic evaluations. *Professional Psychology: Research and Practice, 26,* 465–473.

Brakel, S. J. (1974). Presumption, bias, and incompetency in the criminal process. *Wisconsin Law Review,* 1105–1130.

Bukatman, B. A., Foy, J. L., & DeGrazia, E. (1971). What is competency to stand trial? *American Journal of Psychiatry, 127,* 1225–1229.

Committee on Ethical Guidelines for Forensic Psychologists. (1991). Specialty guidelines for forensic psychologists. *Law and Human Behavior, 15,* 655–665.

Cooke, G. (1969). The court study unit: Patient characteristics and differences between patients judged competent and incompetent. *Journal of Clinical Psychology, 25,* 140–143.

Cooper, D. K. (1995). Juvenile competency to stand trial: The effects of age and presentation of factual information in the attainment of competency in juveniles. *Dissertation Abstracts International, 56*(10-B), 5761.

Cooper, D. K., & Grisso, T. (1997). Five-year research update (1991–1995): Evaluations for competence to stand trial. *Behavioral Sciences and the Law, 15,* 347–364.

Cowden, V. L., & McKee, G. R. (1995). Competency to stand trial in juvenile delinquency proceedings: Cognitive maturity and the attorney-client relationship. *University of Louisville Journal of Family Law, 33,* 629–660.

Criminal Code of Canada, R. S. C., C-46 (1992).

Davis, D. L. (1985). Treatment planning for the patient who is incompetent to stand trial. *Hospital and Community Psychiatry, 36,* 268–271.

Davis, S. (1994). Fitness to stand trial in Canada in light of the recent Criminal Code amendments. *International Journal of Law and Psychiatry, 17,* 319–329.

Dickey, W. (1980). Incompetency and the nondangerous mentally ill client. *Criminal Law Bulletin, 16,* 22–40.

Drope v. Missouri, 420 U.S. 162 (1975).

Dusky v. United States, 362 U.S. 402 (1960).

Edgerton, R. B. (1993). Stigma and the Cloak of Competence. *The Cloak of Competence* (2nd ed., pp. 182–195). California: University of California Press.

Estelle v. Smith, 49 U.S. L. W. 4490 (1981).

Everington, C. T. (1990). The Competence Assessment for Standing Trial for Defendants with Mental Retardation (CAST-MR): A validation study. *Criminal Justice and Behavior, 17,* 147–168.

Everington, C., & Dunn, C. (1995). A second validation study of the competence assessment for standing trial for defendants with mental retardation (CAST-MR). *Criminal Justice and Behavior, 22,* 44–59.

Everington, C. T., & Luckasson, R. (1992). *Competence assessment for standing trial for defendants with mental retardation.* Ohio: IDS Publishing Corporation.

Farkas, G., DeLeon, P., & Newman, R. (1997). Sanity examiner certification: An evolving national agenda. *Professional Psychology: Research and Practice, 28,* 73–76.

Favole, R. J. (1983). Mental disability in the American criminal process: A four issue survey. In J. Monahan & H. J. Steadman (Eds.), *Mentally disordered offenders: Perspectives from law and social science* (pp. 247–295). New York: Plenum Press.

Fitzgerald, J. F., Peszke, M. A., & Goodwin, R. C. (1978). Competency evaluations in Connecticut. *Hospital and Community Psychiatry, 29,* 450–453.

Fulero, S., & Everington, C. (1995). Assessing competency to waive. *Miranda* rights in defendants with mental retardation. *Law and Human Behavior, 19,* 533–543.

Godinez v. Moran, 113 S. Ct. 2680 (1993).

Golding, S. L. (1992). Studies of incompetent defendants: Research and social policy implications. *Forensic Reports, 5,* 77–83.

Golding, S. L. (1993). *Interdisciplinary Fitness Interview-Revised: A training manual.* State of Utah Division of Mental Health.

Golding, S. L., & Roesch, R. (1988). Competency for adjudication: An international analysis. In D. N. Weisstub (Ed.), *Law and mental health: International perspectives* (Vol. 4, pp. 73–109). New York: Pergamon Press.

Golding, S. L., Roesch, R., & Schreiber, J. (1984). Assessment and conceptualization of competency to stand trial: Preliminary data on the Interdisciplinary Fitness Interview. *Law and Human Behavior, 8,* 321–334.

Goldstein, R. L., & Stone, M. (1977). When doctors disagree: Differing views on competency. *Bulletin of the American Academy of Psychiatry and the Law, 5,* 90–97.

Government of Virgin Islands v. Charles, No. 94-7638 (US Ct. App. 1996).

Grisso, T. (1986). Evaluating competencies: Forensic assessments and instruments. New York: Plenum Press.

Grisso, T. (1987). The economic and scientific future of forensic psychological assessment. *American Psychologist, 42,* 831–839.

Grisso, T. (1992). Five-year research update (1986–1990): Evaluations for competence to stand trial. *Behavioral Sciences and the Law, 10,* 353–369.

Grisso, T. (1998). *Forensic evaluation of juveniles.* Sarasota, FL: Professional Resource Press.

Grisso, T. (2003). *Evaluating competencies: Forensic assessments and instruments* (2nd ed.). New York: Kluwer Academic/Plenum Press.

Grisso, T., Appelbaum, P., Mulvey, E., & Fletcher, K. (1995). The MacArthur treatment competence study II: Measures of abilities related to competence to consent to treatment. *Law and Human Behavior, 19,* 127–148.

Grisso, T., Coccozza, J. J., Steadman, H. J., Fisher, W. H., & Greer, A. (1994). The organization of pretrial forensic evaluation services: A national profile. *Law and Human Behavior, 18,* 377–393.

Grisso, T., & Schwartz, R. G. (2000). *Youth on trial: A developmental perspective on juvenile justice.* Chicago: University of Chicago Press.

Grisso, T., Steinberg, L., Woolard, J., Cauffman, E., Scott, E., Graham, S., et al. (2003). Juveniles' competence to stand trial: A comparison of adolescents' and adults' capacities as trial defendants. *Law and Human Behavior, 27,* 333–363.

Hart, S. D., & Hare, R. D. (1992). Predicting fitness for trial: The relative power of demographic, criminal and clinical variables. *Forensic Reports, 5,* 53–65.

Heilbrun, K., & Collins, S. (1995). Evaluations of trial competency and mental state at time of offense: Report characteristics. *Professional Psychology: Research and Practice, 26,* 61–67.

Hoge, S. K., Bonnie, R. J., Poythress, N., & Monahan, J. (1992). Attorney-client decision-making in criminal cases: Client competence and participation as perceived by their attorneys. *Behavioral Sciences and the Law, 10,* 385–394.

Hoge, S. K., Bonnie, R. J., Poythress, N., & Monahan, J. (1999). *The MacArthur Competence Assessment Tool: Criminal Adjudication.* Odessa, FL: Psychological Assessment Resources.

Hoge, S. K., Bonnie, R. J., Poythress, N., Monahan, J., Eisenberg, M., & Feucht-Haviar, T. (1997). The MacArthur Adjudicative Competence Study: Development and validation of a research instrument. *Law and Human Behavior, 21,* 141–179.

Hoge, S. K., Poythress, N., Bonnie, R. J., Monahan, J., Eisenberg, M., & Feucht-Haviar, T. (1997). The MacArthur competence study: Diagnosis, psychopathology, and competence-related abilities. *Behavioral Sciences and the Law, 15,* 329–345.

Jackson v. Indiana, 406 U.S. 715 (1972).

Johnson, W. G., & Mullett, N. (1987). Georgia Court Competency Test-R. In M. Hersen & A. S. Bellack (Eds.), *Dictionary of behavioral assessment techniques.* New York: Pergamon Press.

Jones, B. L. (1994). *Factors related to the competency to stand trial of defendants who are mentally retarded.* Unpublished doctoral dissertation, Florida State University, Tallahassee, FL.

Laben, J. K., Kashgarian, M., Nessa, D. B., & Spencer, L. D. (1977). Reform from the inside: Mental health center evaluations of competency to stand trial. *Journal of Clinical Psychology, 5,* 52–62.

Lipsitt, P. D., Lelos, D., & McGarry, A. L. (1971). Competency for trial: A screening instrument. *American Journal of Psychiatry, 128,* 105–109.

McGarry, A. L. (1965). Competency for trial and due process via the state hospital. *American Journal of Psychiatry, 122,* 623–631.

McGarry, A. L., & Curran, W. J. (1973). *Competency to stand trial and mental illness.* Rockville, MD: National Institute of Mental Health.

Melton, G. B., Petrila, J., Poythress, N. G., & Slobogin, C. (1997). *Psychological evaluations for the courts: A handbook for mental health professionals and lawyers* (2nd ed.). New York: Guilford Press.

Melton, G. B., Weithorn, L. A., & Slobogin, L. A. (1985). *Community mental health centers and the courts: An evaluation of community-based forensic services.* Lincoln: University of Nebraska Press.

Menzies, R. J., Webster, C. D., Butler, B. T., & Turner, R. C. (1980). The outcome of forensic psychiatric assessment: A study of remands in six Canadian cities. *Criminal Justice and Behavior, 7,* 471–480.

Messick, S. (1980). Test validity and the ethics of assessment. *American Psychologist, 35,* 1012–1027.

Missouri v. Davis, 653 S. W. 2d. 167 (Mo. Sup. Ct. 1983).

Montana v. Austed, 641 P. 2d. 1373 (Mont. Sup. Ct. 1982).

Morrow v. Maryland, 443 A. 2d. 108 (MD. Ct. App. 1982).

Mumley, D. L., Tillbrook, C. E., & Grisso, T. (2003). Five year research update (1996–2000): Evaluations for competence to stand trial (adjudicative competence). *Behavioral Sciences and the Law, 21,* 329–350.

Nicholson, R. A., Briggs, S. R., & Robertson, H. C. (1988). Instruments for assessing competency to stand trial: How do they work? *Professional Psychology: Research and Practice, 19,* 383–394.

Nicholson, R. A., & Kugler, K. E. (1991). Competent and incompetent criminal defendants: A quantitative review of comparative research. *Psychological Bulletin, 109,* 355–370.

Nicholson, R., LaFortune, K., Norwood, S., & Roach, R. (1995, August). *Pretrial competency evaluations in Oklahoma: Report characteristics and consumer satisfaction.* Paper presented at the American Psychological Association Convention, New York.

Nicholson, R., & Norwood, S. (2000). The quality of forensic psychological assessments, reports, and testimony: Acknowledging the gap between promise and practice. *Law and Human Behavior, 24,* 9–44.

Nicholson, R. A., Robertson, H. C., Johnson, W. G., & Jensen, G. (1988). A comparison of instruments for assessing competency to stand trial. *Law and Human Behavior, 12,* 313–321.

North Dakota v. Heger, 326 N. W.2d 855 (1982).

Nottingham, E. J., & Mattson, R. E. (1981). A validation study of the competency screening test. *Law and Human Behavior, 5,* 329–336.

Ogloff, J. R. P., & Roesch, R. (1992). Using community mental health centers to provide comprehensive mental health services to jails. In J. R. P. Ogloff (Ed.), *Psychology and law: The broadening of the discipline* (pp. 241–260). Durham, NC: Carolina Academic Press.

Ogloff, J. R. P., Wallace, D. H., & Otto, R. K. (1991). Competencies in the criminal process. In D. K. Kagehiro & W. S. Laufer (Eds.), *Handbook of psychology and law* (pp. 343–360). New York: Springer-Verlag.

Otto, R. K., Poythress, N. G., Nicholson, R. A., Edens, J. F., Monahan, J., Bonnie, R. J., et al. (1998). Psychometric properties of the MacArthur Competence Assessment Tool—Criminal Adjudication (MacCAT-CA). *Psychological Assessment, 10,* 435–443.

Pate v. Robinson, 383 U.S. 375 (1966).

Pendleton, L. (1980). Treatment of persons found incompetent to stand trial. *American Journal of Psychiatry, 137,* 1098–1100.

People v. Harris, 133 Ill. App. 3d. 633 (1983).

Perlin, M. L. (1996). "Dignity was the first to leave": *Godinez v. Moran,* Colin Ferguson, and the trial of mentally disabled criminal defendants. *Behavioral Sciences and the Law, 14,* 61–81.

Petrella, R. C. (1992). Defendants with mental retardation in the forensic services system. In R. W. Conley, R. Luckasson, & G. N. Bouthilet (Eds.), *The criminal justice system and mental retardation* (pp. 79–96). Baltimore: Brookes.

Petrella, R. C., & Poythress, N. G. (1983). The quality of forensic evaluations: An interdisciplinary study. *Journal of Consulting and Clinical Psychology, 51,* 76–85.

Pizzi, W. T. (1977). Competency to stand trial in federal courts: Conceptual and constitutional problems. *University of Chicago Law Review, 45,* 20–71.

Poythress, N., Nicholson, R., Otto, R. K., Edens, J. F., Bonnie, R. J., Monahan, J., et al. (1999). *The MacArthur Competence Assessment Tool: Criminal Adjudication* [Professional manual]. Odessa, FL: Psychological Assessment Resources.

Poythress, N. G., & Stock, H. V. (1980). Competency to stand trial: A historical review and some new data. *Psychiatry and Law, 8,* 131–146.

Randolph, J. J., Hicks, T., & Mason, D. (1981). The Competency Screening Test: A replication and extension. *Criminal Justice and Behavior, 8,* 471–482.

Redlich, A. D., Silverman, M., & Steiner, H. (2003). Pre-adjudicative and adjudicative competence in juveniles and young adults. *Behavioral Sciences and the Law, 21,* 393–410.

Regina v. Whittle, 2 S. C. R. 914 (1994).

Riggins v. Nevada, 112 S. Ct. 1810 (1992).

Ritchie v. Indiana, 468 N. E. 2d. 1369 (Ind. Sup. Ct. 1984).

Robey, A. (1965). Criteria for competency to stand trial: A checklist for psychiatrists. *American Journal of Psychiatry, 122,* 616–623.

Roesch, R., & Golding, S. L. (1980). *Competency to stand trial.* Urbana: University of Illinois Press.

Roesch, R., & Golding, S. L. (1985). The impact of deinstitutionalization. In D. P. Farrington & J. Gunn (Eds.), *Current research in forensic psychiatry and psychology* (pp. 209–239). New York: Wiley.

Roesch, R., Grisso, T., & Poythress, N. G., Jr. (1986). Training programs, courses, and workshops in psychology and law. In M. F. Kaplan (Ed.), *The impact of social psychology on procedural justice* (pp. 83–108). Springfield, IL: Charles C. Thomas.

Roesch, R., & Hart, S. D., & Zapf, P. (1996). Conceptualizing and assessing competency to stand trial: Implications and applications of the MacArthur Treatment Competence Model. *Psychology, Public Policy, and Law, 2,* 96–113.

Roesch, R., & Ogloff, J. R. P. (1996). Settings for providing civil and criminal mental health services. In B. D. Sales & S. A. Shah (Eds.), *Mental health and law: Research, policy and services* (pp. 191–218). Durham, NC: Carolina Academic Press.

Roesch, R., Ogloff, J. R. P., & Golding, S. L. (1993). Competency to stand trial: Legal and clinical issues. *Applied and Preventative Psychology, 2,* 43–51.

Roesch, R., Webster, C. D., & Eaves, D. (1984). *The Fitness Interview Test: A method for assessing fitness to stand trial.* Toronto, Ontario, Canada: University of Toronto Centre of Criminology.

Roesch, R., Zapf, P. A., Eaves, D., & Webster, C. D. (1998). *The Fitness Interview Test* (rev. ed.). Burnaby, British Columbia, Canada: Mental Health Law and Policy Institute, Simon Fraser University.

Rogers, R., Grandjean, N., Tillbrook, C. E., Vitacco, M. J., & Sewell, K. W. (2001). Recent interview-based measures of competency to stand trial: A critical review augmented with research data. *Behavioral Sciences and the Law, 19,* 503–518.

Rogers, R. R., & Mitchell, C. N. (1991). *Mental health experts and the criminal courts.* Scarborough, Ontario, Canada: Carswell.

Ryba, N. L., Cooper, V. G., & Zapf, P. A. (2003). Assessment of maturity in juvenile competency to stand trial evaluations: A survey of practitioners. *Journal of Forensic Psychology Practice, 3,* 23–45.

Salekin, R. T., Rogers, R., & Ustad, K. L. (2001). Juvenile waiver to adult criminal courts: Prototypes for dangerousness, sophistication-maturity, and amenability to treatment. *Psychology, Public Policy, and Law, 7,* 381–408.

Schreiber, J. (1978). Assessing competency to stand trial: A case study of technology diffusion in four states. *Bulletin of the American Academy of Psychiatry and the Law, 6,* 439–457.

Sell v. United States, 282 F. 3d 560 (2003).

Shatin, L. (1979). Brief form of the Competency Screening Test for mental competence to stand trial. *Journal of Clinical Psychology, 35,* 464–467.

Siegel, A. M., & Elwork, A. (1990). Treating incompetence to stand trial. *Law and Human Behavior, 14,* 57–65.

Silten, P. R., & Tullis, R. (1977). Mental competency in criminal proceedings. *Hastings Law Journal, 28,* 1053–1074.

Skeem, J., Golding, S. L., Cohn, N., & Berge, G. (1998). Logic and reliability of evaluations of competence to stand trial. *Law and Human Behavior, 22,* 519–547.

Stafford, K. P. (2003). Assessment of competence to stand trial. In A. M. Goldstein (Ed.), *Handbook of psychology: Forensic psychology* (Vol. 11, pp. 359–380). Hoboken, NJ: Wiley.

Steadman, H. J. (1979). *Beating a rap? Defendants found incompetent to stand trial.* Chicago: University of Chicago Press.

Teplin, L. (1984). Criminalizing mental disorder: The comparative arrest rate of the mentally ill. *American Psychologist, 39,* 794–803.

Utah Code Annotated § 77-15-1 et seq. (1994).

Ustad, K. L., Rogers, R., Sewell, K. W., & Guarnaccia, C. A. (1996). Restoration of competency to stand trial: Assessment with the Georgia Court Competency Test and the Competency Screening Test. *Law and Human Behavior, 20,* 131–146.

Verdun-Jones, S. N. (1981). The doctrine of fitness to stand trial in Canada: The forked tongue of social control. *International Journal of Law and Psychiatry, 4,* 363–389.

Viljoen, J. L., Roesch, R., & Zapf, P. A. (2002). Interrater reliability of the Fitness Interview Test across four professional groups. *Canadian Journal of Psychiatry, 47,* 945–952.

Washington v. Harper, 494 U.S. 210 (1990).

Webster, C. D., Jenson, F. A. S., Stermac, L., Gardner, K., & Slomen, D. (1985). Psychoeducational programmes for forensic psychiatric patients. *Canadian Psychology, 26,* 50–53.

Webster, C. D., Menzies, R. J., & Jackson, M. A. (1982). *Clinical assessment before trial.* Toronto, Ontario, Canada: Butterworths.

Wieter v. Settle, 193 F. Supp. 318 (W. D. Mo. 1961).

Wildman, R. W., Batchelor, E. S., Thompson, L., Nelson, F. R., Moore, J. T., Patterson, M. E., et al. (1978). *The Georgia Court Competency Test: An attempt to develop a rapid, quantitative measure of fitness for trial.* Unpublished manuscript, Forensic Services Division, Central State Hospital, Milledgeville, GA.

Wildman, R. W., II, White, P. A., & Brandenburg, C. A. (1990). The Georgia Court Competency Test: The baserate problem. *Perceptual and Motor Skills, 70,* 1055–1058.

Williams, W., & Miller, K. K. (1981). The processing and disposition of incompetent mentally ill offenders. *Law and Human Behavior, 5,* 245–261.

Wilson v. United States, 391 F. 2d. 460 (1968).

Winick, B. J. (1983). Incompetency to stand trial: Developments in the law. In J. Monahan & H. J. Steadman (Eds.), *Mentally disordered offenders* (pp. 3–38). New York: Plenum Press.

Winick, B. J. (1985). Restructuring competency to stand trial. *UCLA Law Review, 32,* 921–985.

Winick, B. J. (1995). Reforming incompetency to stand trial and plead guilty: A restated proposal and a response to Professor Bonnie. *Journal of Criminal Law and Criminology, 85,* 571–624.

Winick, B. J. (1996). Incompetency to proceed in the criminal process: Past, present, and future. In D. B. Wexler & B. J. Winick (Eds.), *Law in a therapeutic key: Developments in therapeutic jurisprudence* (pp. 77–111). Durham, NC: Carolina Academic Press.

Woolard, J. L. (1998). *Developmental aspects of judgment and competence in legally relevant contexts.* Unpublished doctoral dissertation, Psychology Department, University of Virginia.

Woolard, J. L. (2002). Capacity, competence, and the juvenile defendant: Implications for research and policy. In B. L. Bottoms & M. Bull Kovera (Eds.), *Children, social science, and the law* (pp. 270–298). New York: Cambridge University Press.

Zapf, P. A., Hubbard, K. L., Cooper, V. G., Wheeles, M. C., & Ronan, K. A. (2004). Have the courts abdicated their responsibility for determination of competency to stand trial to clinicians? *Journal of Forensic Psychology Practice, 4,* 27–44.

Zapf, P. A., & Roesch, R. (1997). Assessing fitness to stand trial: A comparison of institution-based evaluations and a brief screening interview. *Canadian Journal of Community Mental Health, 16,* 53–66.

Zapf, P. A., & Roesch, R. (1998). Fitness to stand trial: Characteristics of fitness remands since the 1992 Criminal Code amendments. *Canadian Journal of Psychiatry, 43,* 287–293.

Zapf, P. A., & Roesch, R. (2001). A comparison of the MacCAT-CA and the FIT for making determinations of competency to stand trial. *International Journal of Law and Psychiatry, 24,* 81–92.

Zapf, P. A., Roesch, R., & Viljoen, J. L. (2001). Assessing fitness to stand trial: The utility of the Fitness Interview Test-Revised Edition. *Canadian Journal of Psychiatry, 46,* 426–432.

Zapf, P. A., & Viljoen, J. L. (2003). Issues and considerations regarding the use of assessment instruments in the evaluation of competency to stand trial. *Behavioral Sciences and the Law, 21,* 351–367.

Zapf, P. A., Viljoen, J. L., Whittemore, K. E., Poythress, N. G., & Roesch, R. (2002). Competency: Past, present, and future. In J. R. P. Ogloff (Ed.), *Taking psychology and law into the twenty first century* (pp. 171–198). Kluwer Academic/Plenum Press.

CHAPTER 13

Criminal Responsibility and the Insanity Defense

PATRICIA A. ZAPF, STEPHEN L. GOLDING, and RONALD ROESCH

MUCH HAS been written about criminal responsibility and issues of insanity or mental state at the time of the offense. In this chapter, we have chosen to focus on the following three major areas: (1) insanity standards and the construal of criminal responsibility, including a brief review of the historical and jurisprudential roots of culpable *mens rea*, an overview of the evolution of the legal standards for the insanity defense, and an examination of the movement to reform the insanity defense, particularly by adopting "guilty but mentally ill" verdict options; (2) a review of issues related to the assessment of criminal responsibility, including the structure of these evaluations, instruments developed to guide these evaluations, the role of delusions in the evaluation of criminal responsibility, and issues in the treatment and release of insanity acquittees; and (3) an overview of the empirical developments regarding criminal responsibility, including research on NGRI (not guilty by reason of insanity) verdicts, judicial instruction, and jury/juror decision making. As it is impossible to cover everything in one chapter, the interested reader is also referred to additional resources for an in-depth understanding of this topic area (see especially Borum, 2003; Golding, 1992; Golding & Roesch, 1987; Golding, Skeem, Roesch, & Zapf, 1999; Melton, Petrila, Poythress, & Slobogin, 1997; Rogers & Shuman, 2000).

INSANITY STANDARDS AND THE CONSTRUAL OF CRIMINAL RESPONSIBILITY

The complex of arguments, philosophical debate, opinion, and data on the insanity defense (Eigen, 1995; Gray, 1972; Hermann, 1983; Pasewark, 1982; Platt & Diamond, 1965, 1966; R. Smith, 1981; N. Walker, 1978) cannot be approached without a personal decision to accept or reject a rather simple thesis. Belief in this basic thesis is not subject to scientific argument; rather, it is morally axiomatic. That is, one either accepts it as a function of one's fundamental moral, religious, and jurisprudential presuppositions, or one does not. Given the nonprovable nature of this moral thesis, scientific and logical argument about aspects of the insanity defense and the assessment of mental state are possible, but acceptance or rejection of the argument is not a matter of proof or science. This fundamental belief may be stated as follows:

> In cognizing and regulating social interactions in terms of fundamental principles of "fairness" and "justice," we assume that all such social interactions, including the societal judgment of criminal or civil responsibility for certain classes of proscribed behavior, are based upon an ethical calculus that assigns individual blame, culpability, liability, punishability, and moral and criminal responsibility as a function of intentionality and mental capacity. The classical formulation of this moral presupposition is the legal maxim, *Actus nonfacit reum, nisi mens sit rea,* which translates freely into modern English as "An act is not legally cognizable as evil, and hence criminally punishable, unless it is committed by a person who has the capacity to cognize the act as evil and then freely chooses to do it." (Golding & Roesch, 1987, p. 395)

This fundamental belief goes to the heart of the tension in the public's mind, as well as in the criminal and civil law, between strict or objective liability, on the one hand, and subjective liability, on the other. An examination of the history of the criminal law in Western Judeo-Christian cultures clearly demonstrates the nature of this tension (see especially Crotty, 1924; Gray, 1972; LaFave & Scott, 1972; Platt & Diamond, 1965, 1966; Sayre, 1932). The dilemma is simply this: On the one hand, it is clear that when someone performs a heinous or reprehensible act, he or she is guilty in the commonsense meaning of that term (objective liability). On the other hand, to have a theory of action and responsibility that embodies our cultural sense of fairness and justice and that reflects our increasing knowledge of psychological processes in general and psychotic processes in particular, we have to consider the conjunction of the proscribed behavior (*actus reus*) and an appropriate degree and type of intentionality and mental capacity (*mens rea*) in ascribing guilty or culpable ownership of an act (subjective liability).

In this chapter, we do not attempt to address the logically prior moral question about the insanity defense: whether or not it should exist. Our belief, along with most (but not all) scholars who have examined this issue, is that its existence is integral to the fabric of our social structure, which includes, but surely is not limited to, the structure of our criminal law. Rather, we outline issues that are relevant to those mental health professionals who are called on to evaluate defendants and offer expert opinion on the issue of criminal responsibility.

THE CONCEPT OF *MENS REA*

It is well established in the historical and jurisprudential literatures (Gray, 1972; Hermann, 1983; Platt & Diamond, 1966; Pollack & Maitland, 1952; Sayre, 1932; Stroud, 1914) that the fundamental concept of mens rea in Judeo-Christian cultures has been in existence since the earliest recordings of Hebrew law. Platt and Diamond (1966), for example, quote the Babylonian Talmud as observing, "A deaf-mute, an idiot and a minor are awkward to deal with, as he who injures them is liable [to pay], whereas if they injure others they are exempt" (n. 7, p. 1228). This concept may be traced in a continuous line of development through Greek and Roman law, where the concept of *culpa* (negligence) is distinguished from *dolus* (intentional fraud). Children under the age of 7, for example, were considered *doli incapax,* that is, "not possessed of sufficient discretion and intelligence to distinguish between right and wrong" and hence "incapable of criminal intention or malice" (Black, 1979). Children between the ages of 7 and 12 were presumed doli incapax unless evidence of capacity to form culpable intention was presented. Interestingly, the pattern of evidence most frequently adduced to infer such intentionality, such as lying about the crime, concealing the body, or other such after-the-fact actions, is still used in modern insanity trials as evidence that the person was capable of the prerequisite intentionality at the time of the crime. The culmination of this doctrine in more modern (i.e., since the thirteenth century) jurisprudence is presented in *Blackstone's Commentaries* in its classic form:

> All the several pleas and excuses which protect the committer of a forbidden act from the punishment which is otherwise annexed thereto may be reduced to this single consideration, the want or defect of will. An involuntary act, as it has no claim to merit, so neither can it induce any guilt; the concurrence of the will, when it has its choice either to do or to avoid the fact in question, being the only thing that renders human actions either praiseworthy or culpable. Indeed, to make a complete crime cognizable by human laws, there must be both a will and an act. . . . The rule of law as to . . . [lunatics] . . . is *furiosus furore solum punitur* [The madness of the insane is punishment enough]. In criminal cases, therefore, idiots and lunatics are not chargeable for their own acts, if committed when under these incapacities; no, not even for treason itself. (Cited in *State v. Strasburg,* 1910, pp. 1021–1022)

One can show that the entire structure of the criminal law is built on this principle. No society seems ever to have been without such a means, even if archaic. Sayre (1932) observes that while one of the earliest legal texts, *Leges Henrici Primi* (*The Laws of Henry I*), alternates between advocating absolute liability—"he who commits evil unknowingly must pay for it knowingly"—and advocating the principle of mens rea, it was standard practice for the king to either pardon mentally disordered persons found guilty of "absolute liability crimes" or for other financial arrangements to be made. In fact, Sayre's classic review of mens rea argues that the tradition of criminal law in England since Henry I originated in theological opposition to secular laws of absolute responsibility. This theological opposition was based on a belief that God could not properly hold an infant, idiot, or lunatic justly responsible. It is interesting to note that the age at which children are generally assumed to some degree criminally responsible corresponds to the age in all major religions at which they usually pass through a "certification" ritual where they are deemed morally responsible in the eyes of God. Platt and Diamond (1965, 1966) show, in their historical reviews, that the "furiously" insane have been exempted from moral sanction by an extension of the same logic.

Although mens rea has been historically interpreted in a broad fashion, making it roughly synonymous with "culpable intentionality" (Stroud, 1914, p. 13) or with the general mental and emotional capacity prerequisite to choose freely to commit proscribed acts, the modern trend in criminal law has been to construe the mens rea requirement of criminal conduct more narrowly, and to equate it with such phrases as proscribed conduct performed "intentionally," "recklessly," "knowingly," or "purposefully." Discomfort with the insanity defense has been associated historically with attempts to either abolish it outright or to change it drastically by restricting the relevance of mental state to such a narrowly defined mens rea.

The most comprehensive scholarly review of this narrowing approach is Wales (1976), who discusses the problem using the well-known metaphor of squeezing a lemon (i.e., a defendant, under this narrow view, would not be guilty of killing his wife, if, while strangling her, he believes he is merely squeezing a lemon). In other words, the prototypical case envisioned as qualifying for exculpation under the narrow view would be delusional mistake of fact. In discussing the legislative history of narrowing attempts, Wales makes it clear that the underlying motivation is to eliminate the insanity defense without raising constitutional considerations and to assure that more "insanity-like" acquittees are dispositionally dealt with as guilty first and in need of treatment or mentally ill second. Wales argues that the cases most likely to be acted on differently are those involving command hallucinations, affective delusions, and various forms of paranoid processes, where it is clear that the defendant acted "knowingly" in the narrow sense of the term, but the "knowingness" was conditioned on delusional, hallucinatory, or otherwise psychotic belief systems.

In recent times, starting with the first Nixon administration, there have been many attempts in federal and state legislatures to accomplish this shift in the focus of the insanity defense. In addition to the narrowing of the concept of mens rea, some states have experimented with giving decision makers an "in between" verdict, namely, "guilty but mentally ill" (which, in reality, is simply a guilty verdict with no guarantee of differences in sentencing, disposition, or mental health treatment; see Bumby, 1993; Golding, 1992; Golding & Roesch, 1987). Finally, some states continue to experiment with varying levels of abolition. Currently, the modal insanity defense criteria involve either the traditional American Law Institute formulation (with or without the "volitional" prong), or restricted versions of the traditional M'Naghten test.

THE EVOLUTION OF LEGAL STANDARDS FOR CRIMINAL RESPONSIBILITY

> M'Naghten's trial is assumed to be the starting place for the test that to establish a defense on the ground of insanity, it must be clearly proved that, at the time of the committing of the act, the party accused was labouring under such a defect of reason, from disease of the mind, as not to know the nature and quality of the act he was doing; or, if he did know it, that he did not know he was doing what was wrong. (M'Naghten's Case, 1843, p. 722)

However, it is reasonably clear that the knowledge/right-wrong test had already been used implicitly and explicitly in a series of trials in both England

and the United States. In fact, there was already considerable discomfort with the perceived "narrow scope" of the rule. Isaac Ray (1838/1962) had already published his *Treatise on the Medical Jurisprudence of Insanity,* in which he had attacked the narrowness of such formulations as not according with modern knowledge of the forms of mental disorder and their influence on behavior, affect, and cognition. The same debates that rage today over the scope of what should be included under "knowledge," "appreciation," and the like were influential in court decisions of the day.

Although the M'Naghten rules were rapidly adopted in the United States, they were almost immediately subjected to challenge on the narrowness ground and were modified significantly by some jurisdictions. In 1844, Chief Justice Shaw of the Massachusetts Supreme Court held that while the right-wrong test was proper, a defendant who acted under the influence of an irresistible impulse was not a free agent, and hence was included under the rule because he or she could not know right from wrong (*Commonwealth v. Rogers,* 1844). In 1866, this logic was made explicit in Justice Somerville's holding in *Parsons v. State* (1866):

> If therefore, it be true, as a matter of fact, that the disease of insanity can . . . so affect the mind as to subvert the freedom of the will, and thereby destroy the power of the victim to choose between right and wrong, although he perceived it—by which we mean the power of volition to adhere in action to the right and abstain from wrong—is such a one criminally responsible for an act done under the influence of such a controlling disease? We clearly think not. (p. 586)

In 1924, Crotty documented that the jurisdictions in the United States had fragmented into four sets of rules: (1) relatively pure M'Naghten, (2) M'Naghten broadened by interpretation to include irresistible impulse as meeting the test, (3) M'Naghten supplemented by explicit irresistible impulse rules, and (4) the New Hampshire "product" rule, heavily influenced by Isaac Ray and set forth in *State v. Pike* (1869).

Justice Doe, in setting forth New Hampshire's product test, argued that it was a matter of legal fact, to be decided by a judge or jury, whether or not a defendant suffered from a disease of the mind and whether or not the proscribed behavior was a product of that disease. He hence discarded formal rules of specific states of mind and asserted that it was up to the trier of fact to decide "if [the alleged crime] was the offspring or product of mental disease in the defendant, [then] he was not guilty by reason of insanity" (*State v. Pike,* 1869, p. 442). In fact, for a long time following M'Naghten, there was considerable controversy over insanity rules that surfaced repeatedly.

Charles Guiteau's assassination of President Garfield in 1881 gave rise to a highly controversial trial and execution that took place against the background of a strong concern over "irresistible impulses" and a belief that insanity, especially "moral insanity," was all too easy to feign (Rosenberg, 1968). Rosenberg's scholarly analysis draws out these issues in fine detail, documenting public, legislative, and psychiatric reactions that are strong reminders of current debate. Judge Cox's highly elaborate instructions to the jury in Guiteau's trial left little doubt that the central issue before the jury concerned whether the alleged moral insanity and irresistible impulse fit into a straightforward interpretation of the right-wrong test set out in M'Naghten. Whatever the jury may have thought of the "battle of the experts" and the problems of the insanity defense, however, Guiteau placed himself in fatal jeopardy when he exhibited his uncontested egocentrism and interrupted the prosecutor toward the close of the trial, objecting, "That is not the issue. The issue is, was my free agency destroyed? I was overpowered. That is what the jury is to pass on" (cited in Rosenberg, 1968, p. 201). His rational comments may have allowed the jury to focus on his current mental state, a problem that confronts any defendant asserting a retrospective insanity defense.

Controversy surrounding various definitional and procedural aspects of the insanity defense continued over the first half of this century (see, e.g., Ballantine, 1919, and Keedy, 1917, 1920, debating a proposal for limiting the insanity defense to the narrower mens rea conception, and the materials on early abolition attempts reviewed later in this chapter in the context of the "guilty but mentally ill" option). In 1954, Judge Bazelon of the District of Columbia Court of Appeals attempted to correct numerous deficiencies in the combined right-wrong/irresistible impulse test in *Durham v. United States* (1954). In *United States v. Brawner* (1972), which ended the D.C. Court of Appeal's experiments with the *Durham* "product test" and adopted the Model Penal Code recommendations of the American Law Institute (ALI, 1962), Judge Leventhal carefully reviewed the court's logic in adopting *Durham*. First,

> the old right-wrong/irresistible impulse rule for insanity was antiquated, no longer reflecting the community's judgment as to who ought to be held criminally liable for socially destructive acts. We considered the *Durham* rule as restated to have more fruitful, accurate and considered reflection of the sensibilities of the community as revised and expanded in the light of continued study of abnormal human behavior. (p. 976)

Second, the older test forced expert witnesses to testify in uncomfortably narrow terms of right and wrong, making "it impossible to convey to the judge and jury the full range of information material to an assessment of defendant's responsibility" (p. 976). It has been asserted (Goldstein, 1967; Livermore & Meehl, 1967) that the test need not be narrowly cognitive and could include a wider range of affective knowledge and appreciation if interpreted in proper jurisprudential and historical perspective, but the concern of the *Durham* court was that this was not typical practice and therefore needed to be corrected.

The *Durham* product test ("an accused is not criminally responsible if his unlawful act was the product of a mental disease or defect") was intended to remedy these problems. However, it was not perceived as having its intended effect and seemed, rather, to make the problem, of undue dominance by experts testifying in conclusory terms, worse. The majority in *Brawner* therefore adopted the ALI rule and further encouraged judges to adopt instructions that emphasized the importance of nonconclusory testimony and the role of the expert of explaining to the jury the relationship between the defendant's cognitive, behavioral, and affective disturbance and his or her "substantial capacity to appreciate the criminality of his conduct or to conform his conduct to the requirements of the law" (*United States v. Brawner*, 1972, p. 973, restating the ALI Model Penal Code).

Judge Bazelon, in his partial dissent, agreed that the product test needed to be rejected, but he was more pessimistic, viewing the majority's adoption of the ALI rule as a change that was "primarily one of form rather than of substance" (*United States v. Brawner*, 1972, p. 1010). For Judge Bazelon, the purpose of the reformulation should be to "ask the psychiatrist [*sic*] a single question: what is the nature of the impairment of the defendant's mental and emotional processes and behavioral controls?" (p. 1032), leaving "for the jury the question of whether that impairment is sufficient to relieve the defendant of responsibility for the particular act charged" (p. 1032). To emphasize this, Judge Bazelon advocated a version of a test first proposed by the British Royal Commission on Capital Punishment in 1953: "A defendant is not responsible if at the time of his unlawful conduct his mental or emotional processes or behavior controls were impaired to such an extent that he cannot justly be held responsible for his act" (*United States v. Brawner*, 1972, p. 1032). This "justly responsible" test, Judge Bazelon argued, and we agree, has the virtue of making perfectly overt the underlying moral nature of the insanity defense and placing the hot potato aspect of such judgments squarely into the hands of the jury as representatives of the community. Nevertheless, the test has not been adopted except in Rhode Island (*State v. Johnson*, 1979).

While the ALI rule has been widely adopted in federal jurisdictions and many states (Keilitz & Fulton, 1983), the movement to reform the insanity defense, and to limit its perceived abuse, has led to an attempt to eliminate the volitional prong of the test ("to conform his conduct to the requirements of law"). Advocates for this alteration have included the American Bar Association (1983) and the American Psychiatric Association (1982), following Bonnie (1983). This proposal was adopted into the Federal Code by the U.S. Congress in the Insanity Defense Reform Act (1984).

The Court of Appeals for the Fifth Circuit has agreed with this abolition of the volitional prong, arguing that the position of the American Psychiatric Association, that the profession did not possess sufficiently accurate scientific bases to measure a person's capacity for self-control, was persuasive (*United States v. Lyons*, 1984a). A strongly worded dissent (*United States v. Lyons*, 1984b, p. 995) argues that the "potential threat to society [supposedly] created by the volitional prong" ignores "empirical data that . . . provide little or no support for these fearsome perceptions and in many respects refute them." The dissent's argument cites various studies undercutting the perceptions of the misuse of the insanity defense. The dissenters also could have included Rogers, Bloom, and Manson's (1984) finding that personality disordered defendants, the target of the advocates of abolishing the volitional prong, constituted only 18% of the group of successful insanity acquittees. Citing *United States v. Torniero* (1984), where the Second Circuit placed appropriate limits on "creative" uses of the volitional prong for new personality disorders by requiring the defense to show that "respected authorities in the field share the view that the disorder is a disease or defect that could have impaired the defendant's ability to desist from the offense charged" (p. 730), the dissenters argued that the volitional prong was an essential aspect of the concept of guilt, as this concept "presuppose[s] a morally responsible agent to whom guilt can be attributed. By definition, guilt cannot be attributed to an individual unable to refrain from violating the law" (*United States v. Lyons,* 1984b, p. 1000).

THE GUILTY BUT MENTALLY ILL VERDICT

Currently, approximately 13 states have provisions that allow for a defendant to be found guilty but mentally ill (GBMI; see Arrigo, 1996, for a review; see Borum & Fulero, 1999, for a discussion of various proposed insanity defense reforms). The original GBMI legislation in this century was introduced in Michigan in 1975 in the context of *People v. McQuillan* (1974), a case that had found Michigan's automatic commitment of NGRI acquittees unconstitutional. The verdict was also adopted in Indiana in 1979 under similar circumstances. Following John Hinckley's assault on President Reagan, the stage was set for other states to pass GBMI legislation in response to the perceived abuses of the insanity plea. The current GBMI verdict was not intended to replace the verdict of NGRI (except in Utah and Nevada). Although both verdicts were introduced to stem the perceived tide of violence committed by offenders who escape justice, the current form was aimed primarily at jurors, with the hope that it would allow them a middle ground between guilty and NGRI. It was also motivated by knowledge that an elimination of the insanity verdict itself might be considered unconstitutional, as it had been in *Strasburg* (1910) and *Underwood v. State* (1873).

In *Underwood,* Judge Campbell of the Michigan Supreme Court expressed his sympathies with the abolitionist argument. He acknowledged outrage at the "absurd lengths to which the defense of insanity has been allowed to go under the fanciful theories of incompetent and dogmatic witnesses," but he believed that the remedy was to be found elsewhere:

> No doubt many criminals have escaped justice by the weight foolishly given by credulous jurors to evidence which their common sense should have disregarded. But the remedy is to be sought by correcting false notions, and not by destroying the safeguards of private liberty. (Cited in *State v. Strasburg,* 1910, p. 1028)

The GBMI verdict was intended to make it harder to reach a verdict of NGRI (especially in gray area cases of severe personality disorder) with the hope that most jurors would respond to the superficial logic of the verdict ("Okay, he's crazy, but he did it, didn't he?"). Opponents of the GBMI verdict argue that it should be abolished on the grounds that it confuses and deceives jurors (Melville & Naimark, 2002; see also Palmer, 2000). To cover the punitive and abolitionist motivation, defenders of the GBMI legislation added a gloss of rehabilitation by arguing that the new verdict provided an explicit means of recognizing that some of those sent to prison were in need of mental health treatment. Of course, they did not mention that few, if any, new funds were to be appropriated to the prison system to provide more treatment (Beasley, 1983) and that provisions already existed in every state that passed GBMI to laterally transfer a disturbed prisoner into mental hospital settings for treatment if that was necessary. In commenting on this entire enterprise, Professor Richard Bonnie (1983, p. 194) says, bluntly, "[The GBMI verdict] should be rejected as nothing more than moral sleight of hand."

THE ASSESSMENT OF CRIMINAL RESPONSIBILITY

The evaluation process generally includes, broadly, three major components or sources of data: (1) an interview with the defendant, (2) forensic assessment instruments, and (3) third-party information, including (but by no means limited to) collateral reports, witness statements, victim statements, police reports, and records of various sorts (i.e., mental health, treatment, school, medical, crime scene). We review each of these three major sources of data; however, the reader is referred to additional sources for more complete and detailed information about the assessment process (Borum, 2003; Giorgi-Guarnieri et al., 2002; Golding, 1992; Golding & Roesch, 1987; Golding et al., 1999; Goldstein, Morse, & Shapiro, 2003; Gutheil, 2002; Melton et al., 1997; Rogers & Shuman, 2000; Shapiro, 1999). In addition, we include a section on the role of delusions in evaluations of criminal responsibility as the nature and quality of a defendant's delusionality is often central in determining the extent of impairment in mental state at the time of the offense, especially in contested cases.

INTERVIEW

A comprehensive MSO (mental state at the time of the offense) interview can be conceptualized as falling into a series of phases (as per Sullivan's, 1954, scheme): (1) the formal clinical-legal inception, (2) the reconnaissance, (3) the detailed inquiry of present mental state, (4) the detailed inquiry of mental state at the time of the offense, (5) reconciliation with other data sources (including consultation with other professionals that have evaluated the defendant), and (6) the termination.

Inception

In addition to rapport building, the inception requires explaining clearly one's role to the defendant, focusing on why he or she is being evaluated, to whom the report will be sent, and what limits are placed on the confidentiality of information. These confidentiality rules vary widely across jurisdictions and are strongly influenced by the context of the case, so the examiner must be fully informed, as a matter of professional competence. In most jurisdictions, once defendants have entered their mental state into the adjudication process by interposing an insanity defense or some other mental state claim, no information revealed to the examiner that can be construed as relevant to that claim is exempted. Jurisdictions differ widely, however, as to whether indirect fruits of such evidence are admissible, so extreme caution is required in the preparation of a report. The broadest coverage is found in the federal courts:

No statement made by the defendant in the course of any [forensic] examination . . . with or without the consent of the defendant, no testimony by the expert based upon such statement, and no other fruits of the statement shall be admitted in evidence against the defendant . . . in any criminal proceeding except on an issue respecting mental condition on which the defendant has introduced testimony. (*Federal Rules of Criminal Procedure*, 1985)

As indicated, however, jurisdictions vary widely, and the examiner should conform his or her practice to the local rules. It is also good practice to inform a defendant what reports, records, and files have been made available to the examiner, although in cases of suspected malingering, an examiner may choose to do otherwise. This is a matter of judgment, however, as even in nonmalingering situations, it may aid the clinical discovery process to let the defendant tell his or her "filtered version" first. The examiner may then introduce contradictory evidence at a later point to observe the defendant's reaction and to ascertain if the defendant is consciously distorting, having memorial difficulty because of his or her mental state at the time, repressing memories, or suppressing details that are anxiety-arousing, embarrassing, or painful to reveal.

Reconnaissance

Reconnaissance is a forensically oriented review of the defendant's history. It is important to obtain information regarding the defendant's lifetime history of disturbance, treatments received, and general variability in mental condition. Of particular importance are prior episodes that involved criminal charges and/or fitness evaluations, civil commitments, and other such dispositions. The pattern of mental state disturbance and its relationship to psychotherapeutic and psychopharmacological treatment, medical conditions (e.g., hypoglycemia), situational stressors, and alcohol and drug use are particularly important.

Detailed Inquiries: Present Mental State and Mental State at Offense

Typically, it is difficult to separate these because a disturbed defendant will usually be subjected to treatment by rapidly acting psychotropic medications. Nevertheless, it is crucial to bear in mind that these mental states, though related, are separable, albeit with great difficulty. We advise use of sections of structured and semistructured interviews to cover the domain of psychopathology in a relatively standardized fashion to improve interexaminer reliability in the elicitation and coding of information. The detailed inquiry with respect to the mental state at the time of the offense must also focus on the relationship of the psychopathological elements to the criminal conduct charged. This part of the interview resembles a "psychological autopsy." The defendant must be asked to reconstruct his or her thoughts, perceptions, experiences, attitudes, and behavior, as well as that of those in the field of action during the entire legally significant period. Retrospective evaluations are difficult for laypersons, jurors, judges, and examiners alike, so great care must be taken to obtain detailed information and also to avoid, as far as possible, recall-based contamination of the defendant's memories.

Reconciliation and Termination

As emphasized by many advocates and critics of the role of the forensic examiner in the legal process (Bonnie & Slobogin, 1980; Melton et al., 1997; Morse, 1978), the role of the expert is not to present legal conclusions or formal psychopathological diagnoses. Rather, the role of examiner as expert is to import state-of-the-art/science knowledge about the existence of various psychopathological conditions and their relationship to various behavioral, perceptual, cognitive, and judgmental capacities into the legal/moral decisional process. Thus, at the reconciliation or termination phase, the examiner should be prepared to integrate the information available and to inform all parties concerned: the defendant, defense counsel, prosecutor, and other professionals. One advantage of this openness is that it allows the defendant to produce any additional information that might explain or clarify discrepancies or other problems, and it helps prevent an uninformed battle of the experts. In certain gray area cases, there will be legitimate disagreements among experts. It assists the trier of fact if the nature of these disagreements, as well as areas of agreement, are drawn as precisely as possible, with each examiner fully aware and able to comment in advance as to the reasons for disagreement. Such pretestimony consultations also tend to produce higher-quality and more informative strategies for direct and cross-examination.

Forensic Assessment Instruments

There currently exist two specialized forensic assessment instruments that have been developed to assist in the evaluation of mental state at the time of the offense, both of which were developed two decades ago. Given that the standards of forensic practice appear to be moving in the direction of greater reliance on and respect for forensic assessment instruments in the evaluation of psycholegal issues, these two instruments are reviewed next.

Mental State at the Time of Offense Screening Evaluation

The Mental State at the Time of the Offense Screening Evaluation (MSE; Slobogin, Melton, & Showalter, 1984) is a semistructured interview technique that was developed to screen out defendants for whom an insanity defense was clearly not applicable. In addition, the MSE could be used to identify those individuals who were "obviously insane" and thus did not require any further, more comprehensive, evaluation. The MSE comprises three sections: (1) historical information, which assesses a defendant's premorbid psychological and cognitive functioning; (2) offense information, which accumulates information regarding the offense from the defendant and external sources; and (3) present mental status examination.

Although there have not been any published studies of the reliability of the MSE, its validity was evaluated by Slogobin and colleagues (1984). Twenty-four mental health professionals were trained to use the MSE and were then asked to assess 36 cases. They were given only a description of the charge and the preliminary hearing transcript prior to their assessment. Their decisions were then compared to the decisions made by the inpatient forensic evaluation team, which included one psychiatrist, one psychologist, and one social worker. Overall, there was satisfactory agreement (72%, or 26 of 36 cases) between trainees and the evaluation team. There was 44% agreement (16 of 36 cases) on the cases that were screened out. Using the decisions made by the evaluation team as the criterion, the decisions made by the trainees were found to have a 0% false negative rate and a 28% (10 cases) false positive rate (screened-in defendants who were screened out by the evaluation team). Compared to the evaluation team's decisions, the trainees' decisions had less agreement with the court's verdict. Of the 10 defendants for whom the evaluation team suspected some "significant mental abnormality," one was convicted, seven had their charges *nolle prossed* (prosecution decided not to pursue the case), and two were found insane. On the other hand, of the 20 defendants whom the trainees suspected had some "significant mental abnormality," six were convicted as charged, four were convicted of a lesser charge, six had charges nolle prossed, and two were found insane.

The limitations of the MSE have been debated (Poythress, Melton, Petrila, & Slobogin, 2000; Rogers & Shuman, 2000). Given the lack of reliability research and the limited validity data, the MSE should perhaps be most appropriately viewed as a guide for evaluators to ensure that relevant areas are reviewed. Indeed, evaluators can include the MSE (or the Rogers' instrument, discussed next) in a comprehensive evaluation that would include multiple sources of data (e.g., psychological tests, third-party information, defendant's interview).

Rogers Criminal Responsibility Assessment Scales

The Rogers Criminal Responsibility Assessment Scales (R-CRAS; Rogers, 1984) was designed to quantify the elements of the so-called ALI criteria for criminal nonresponsibility; however, Rogers notes that it may be applicable to the M'Naghten standard as well (Rogers & Shuman, 2000). Based on a comprehensive evaluation, the examiner rates a series of scales grouped into five areas: (1) reliability of report, (2) organicity, (3) psychopathology, (4) cognitive control, and (5) behavioral control. For example, the psychopathology section involves ratings of bizarre behavior, anxiety, amnesia, delusions, hallucinations, depressed or elevated mood, verbal coherence, and affective and thought disorder. In addition, there are a series of more global ratings on final judgments of insanity and impairment. Thus, the R-CRAS is an instrument that reflects the relative importance assigned by examiners to the first-order elements of an insanity decision (e.g., the presence and relevance of psychopathology to MSO). It should be noted that these elements are fairly abstract psychological and legal terms (e.g., "delusions at the time of alleged crime") and do not necessarily represent the cues that are actually utilized by professional examiners in making their decisions. This is a major issue of contention between Rogers, Melton et al. (1997), and Golding (1992) in the evaluation of this instrument. Rogers believes it important to quantify the issue, although it would be unfair to assume that he does not recognize the value of more qualitative data (see Rogers & Ewing, 1992). Melton and Golding agree that quantification is essentially illusory at this stage in the development of evaluations of criminal responsibility. Both groups of authors agree, in large measure, on the domain of conceptual elements to be addressed.

Rogers and Sewell (1999) have responded to the criticisms of Melton et al. (1997) by attempting to extend the construct validity of the R-CRAS via the reanalysis of two data sets to address contributions of individual variables to the various components of the decision model. On the basis of discriminant function analysis, the authors conclude that the R-CRAS variables were able to form differentiating patterns (between individuals showing impairment and those not showing impairment) for each of the five components of the decision model. Results indicated average hit rates of 94.3% (ranging from 87.8% for Major Mental Disorder to 97.2% for Cognitive Control) and average variance accounted for of 63.7% (ranging from 38.5% for Malingering to 79.2% for Behavioral Control).

Factor analysis of the R-CRAS items results in three factors—bizarre behavior, high activity, and high anxiety—that do not mirror the five scales (Borum, 2003). Rogers has reported modest interrater reliabilities at the item level (average kappa 0.58), with lower values (0.49) associated with the product question (i.e., "Was the loss of control attributable to underlying psychopathological disturbance?"), one of the most frequent sources of disagreement in contested trials (Rogers & Shuman, 2000; Rogers, Wasyliw, & Cavanaugh, 1984). Final judgments with the R-CRAS also show reasonable levels of agreement between examiners and triers of fact (96% with respect to sanity, with lower levels of agreement on insanity, 70%; Rogers, Cavanaugh, Seman, & Harris, 1984; see Rogers & Shuman, 2000, for a summary). These findings are in general accord with the levels of agreement between clinicians and courts found in other studies of final judgment that use no formalized interviews or rating scales (Golding, 1992). Unfortunately, all studies in this area appear to use criterion-contaminated groups in that the examination process is part of the judicial (criterial) determination.

A number of proposals for semistructured protocols to assist in the evaluation of mental state at time of the offense have been made (e.g., Golding & Roesch, 1987; Melton et al., 1997; Ogloff, Roberts, & Roesch, 1993). They share in common an open-ended structure, with special attention to developing multisource data, identification of legally and psychologically relevant dimensions of the criminal responsibility evaluation, and disclosure of the logical links in an evaluator's reasoning. The need to develop such a comprehensive analysis is clear. These less-structured approaches have been shown to be empirically useful in various contexts (see Melton et al. 1997, for a review), but they have not been studied in the same fashion as the R-CRAS. The R-CRAS and less-structured MSO evaluation techniques make their most important contributions by clarifying for the trier of fact the underlying bases for professional judgment (Golding, 1990, 1992), hence potentially highlighting the areas of disagreement so that expert testimony can be of more assistance to judge or juror. There is strong reason to believe that forensic examiners reach their generally high level of agreement in ultimate opinions by different logical and empirically sustainable routes. The critical issue remains the association between organic or psychopathological disturbance and control/moral judgment capacities; these devices are most useful when they serve the heuristic value of (1) highlighting the aspects of the defendant's psychological state that are relevant, (2) describing a purported relationship to control and judgment capacities, and (3) organizing known data about the empirical relationships between disorder and psychological capacities in various states and situations.

THIRD-PARTY INFORMATION

It is a commonly accepted professional standard of practice that forensic evaluators seek to examine the consistency of mental health history and other archival data along with details of the crime scene and witnesses accounts of the defendant before, during, and after the alleged incident. This "consistency" examination is relevant to issues of malingering and aids in supporting or challenging various psychological interpretations of the defendant's mental state at the time of the offense. The importance of this aspect of a forensic examination at the time of the offense has been discussed in numerous sources (Golding 1992; Heilbrun, Rosenfeld, Warren, & Collins, 1994; Melton et al., 1997; Ogloff et al., 1993; Rogers, 1997; Rogers & Shuman, 2000). Forensic evaluators need to pay close attention to crime scene data, as well as to more traditional sources of third-party information (e.g., mental health and other records, witness statements). All such sources need to be integrated in as straightforward a manner as possible. Where limited scientific data exist to support the inference (e.g., descriptive studies of the characteristics of hallucinations or delusions), they should be referenced, and where otherwise indicated, the evaluator's logical link analysis should be declared and scrutinized.

As Melton et al. (1997, p. 50) note, the role of the forensic evaluator is not to "resolve conclusively all conflicting accounts about the case" but to conduct an evaluation that can be scrutinized in terms of all available evidence, both psychological and behavioral. Modern forensic standards of practice are to address the issue of the consistency of behavioral crime scene evidence with psycholegal formulations and to allow the trier of fact to make the determination of their significance, guided by whatever scientific evidence can be directly or indirectly adduced.

THE ROLE OF DELUSIONS IN ASSESSMENT OF CRIMINAL RESPONSIBILITY

The nature and quality of a defendant's delusions are central in determining the extent of impairment in mental state at the time of the offense. Several issues are involved. In *contested* cases, forensic examiners are particularly apt to encounter defendants with extreme or idiosyncratic beliefs about religion, politics, or personal identity, and questions regarding the delusional basis for those beliefs will arise. Delusionality also enters the adjudicatory process when the issues of intentionality, compulsion, or the reasonableness of the defendant's conduct may be related to a delusion. Finally, delusionality is an important aspect of risk assessment with respect to release decisions.

Although there are surprisingly few studies on the frequency and nature of delusions among NGRI defendants, indirect data, as well as experience, suggest that delusionality is a vital issue (see Litwack, 2003, for a discussion of defendants who refuse to mount an insanity defense on the basis of delusional reasoning). Delusions (especially delusions of reference, persecution, and control, which are particularly relevant to forensic cases) are highly prevalent among individuals who suffer from psychosis (Winters & Neale, 1983); in turn, roughly 50% of those defendants who raise the insanity defense and 70% of insanity acquittees have psychotic diagnoses (Andreasen & Flaum, 1994; Cirincione, Steadman, & McGreevy, 1995; Ogloff, Schweighofer, Turnbull, & Whittemore, 1992; Rice & Harris, 1990; Taylor et al., 1994). Moreover, delusions have been shown to be specifically and substantially related to violence (Taylor et al., 1994).

In an extensive analysis of case records, Häfner and Böker (1982) found that 70% of individuals with Schizophrenia who were accused of homicide had delusional beliefs about their relationship to their victim. Similarly, in an interview study, Taylor (1985) found that 40% of psychotic defendants acted *directly* on delusions during their offenses. The frequency of *nonpathological* but radical, religious, and/or political beliefs and the extent of the relationship between these beliefs and violence has not been systematically studied (Taylor et al., 1994). However, defendants whose criminal acts are related to such fervently held beliefs are clearly plausible candidates for mental state evaluations.

Distinguishing between radical beliefs and delusions is a difficult but critical task in assessing criminal responsibility. Respecting the principles of autonomy and self-determination, our legal system holds responsible the extremist who chooses to act on a radical system of beliefs, expressing his or her desires, values, and personhood through the crime (Hermann, 1990). The basic moral logic of the insanity defense, however, excuses the mentally disordered individual who acts on a pathological, uncontrollable belief system that distorts his or her sense of reality, thereby impairing the capacity for rational choice. Arguably, the same logic also applies to delusions that would "justify" the actions.

Notwithstanding the centrality of this issue in assessing criminal responsibility, there are relatively few data-oriented studies or professional practice standards available in the forensic literature to aid in assessing the delusionality of beliefs. In gray area cases, or cases in which defendants are neither clearly sane nor insane, the classification of beliefs as delusory is presumably a major source of disagreement among examiners. There is no bright line of demarcation between extreme beliefs and delusions (Garety & Hemsley, 1994; Oltmanns, 1988). Moreover, religious and political belief systems, which reference nonphysical entities and events, are not scientifically testable; consequently, there is "no full standard of truth independent of what the [defendant] says" (Taylor et al., 1994, p. 167; Saks, 1991). For these reasons, in this section we review recent progress in defining and assessing delusions and their likely consequences. Our purpose is to introduce readers to the complex issues involved in assessing delusions and to aid clinicians in conducting informed assessments of defendants' beliefs in the context of insanity evaluations. Emphasis is placed on issues relevant to distinguishing between extreme religious or political beliefs and delusions.

Defining and Conceptualizing Delusions

The *DSM-IV-TR* defines a delusion as follows:

> A *false belief* based on incorrect inference about external reality that is *firmly sustained* despite what almost everyone else believes and despite what constitutes incontrovertible and obvious proof or evidence to the contrary. The belief is *not one ordinarily accepted by other members of the person's culture or subculture* (e.g., it is not an article of religious faith). When a false belief involves a value judgment, it is regarded as a delusion only when the judgment is so extreme as to *defy credibility*. (American Psychiatric Association, 2000, p. 821, emphasis added)

Although this definition is adequate for most forensic and clinical purposes, its shortcomings are readily exposed when one attempts to delineate its boundaries (Sedler, 1995). As noted earlier, there is often no standard of proof by which to assess the falsity of beliefs in many religious, political, or identity systems. Similarly, it is difficult to evaluate the incredibility or implausibility of beliefs: Clinicians rarely agree on the extent to which beliefs are bizarre (Flaum, Arndt, & Andreasen, 1991; Oltmanns, 1988; Spitzer, First, Kendler, & Stein, 1993; cf. Mojtabai & Nicholson, 1995). The degree of conviction with which a belief is held also does not clearly distinguish between delusional and nondelusional beliefs. Like delusional beliefs, nondelusional but highly valued beliefs are often held with great zeal and intensity even in the face of contradictory evidence. Moreover, most patients shift between periods in which they are certain about their delusions and periods in which they have partial or full insight (Harrow, Rattenbury, & Stoll, 1988; Sacks, Carpenter, & Strauss, 1974).

These difficulties are "frequently compounded by ambiguity surrounding the presence or absence of cultural support for the person's belief" (Oltmanns, 1988, p. 3). It is difficult to determine the extent to which the nature of a belief, its experience, or its expression must deviate from that accepted by a designated subgroup to classify as delusional. Clearly, examiners must have considerable knowledge of the social, religious, political, and even scientific context of a defendant's belief to adequately assess its delusionality (Barnhouse, 1986; Oltmanns, 1988). Failure to carefully consider patients' subcultural and religious backgrounds often results in misdiagnosis (Lu, Lukoff, & Turner, 1994).

Most current attempts to systematically analyze delusions are based on the seminal work of Jaspers (1963; see Garety & Hemsley, 1994; Mullen, 1979, 1985; Sedler, 1995). Jaspers arguably provides the most comprehensive, enduring, and clinically useful theory for distinguishing among various categories of delusional and nondelusional beliefs. A simplified summary of this theory focused on differentiating delusional from nondelusional beliefs per se is presented here (see C. Walker, 1991, for details).

Jaspers (1963) argued that the criteria of conviction, imperviousness to counterargument and impossibility or bizarreness, were insufficient external criteria that did not capture the essence of delusionality. Rather, "overvalued beliefs" or even "delusion-like ideas" could be distinguished from primary delusions, based on Jaspers's approach, by attention to three fundamental criteria. First, primary delusions are distinguished from secondary delusions and beliefs that are merely overvalued based on the extent and nature of their "un-understandability." Second, primary delusions are "unmediated" by thought, analysis, deduction, or reflection, whereas overvalued ideas and secondary delusions reflect varying degrees of cognitive appraisal and inference. Third, primary delusions reflect a distinctive change in an individual's personality functioning; that is, they are a distinct change in the totality of the individual's personal meanings and ways of construing the world.

An overvalued idea is understandable, the product of cognitive interpretation, and can be viewed in terms of an individual's personality, life experiences, and sociocultural background. Overvalued ideas are relatively easily understood "as exaggerations, diminutions, or combinations of phenomena which we ourselves experience" (Jaspers, 1963, quoted in C. Walker, 1991, p. 100). In contrast, a secondary delusion ("crazy idea") is understandable *only* in the sense that it emerges through one's process of reasoning about psychopathological experiences (e.g., based on the quiet voices and buzzing an individual occasionally hears, she arrives at the conclusion that she is a target of government surveillance). A primary delusion is *not* understandable because it originates in a direct, immediate experience of new meaning unmediated by thought and unconnected to the person's fundamental personality (e.g., one sees a "man in a brown coat . . . he is the dead Archduke"; C. Walker, 1991, p. 99). Thus, whereas overvalued ideas have "clear precedent" in an individual's existing personality and meaningful life events, secondary delusions emerge from other psychopathological experiences, and primary delusions fundamentally change an individual's personality or "way of looking at the world" (C. Walker, 1991). Although Jaspers's classification has been subject to little empirical research and can be criticized for relying heavily on the subjective criterion of "understandability" (Mullen, 1985), his theory provides useful guidance in conceptualizing the key distinctions between delusions and overvalued ideas.

ISSUES IN THE TREATMENT AND RELEASE OF INSANITY ACQUITTEES

Inherent in the original decision to find a defendant NGRI is concern about the ultimate disposition of such acquittees. Jurors place a great deal of emphasis on this issue in their deliberations (Golding, 1992). A comparison of data on the rates and success of insanity pleas and the nature of insanity dispositions with data on public perceptions about these issues clearly reveals that the public overestimates the frequency and successfulness of the insanity plea and underestimates the nature and length of institutionalization following an insanity "acquittal" (Silver, Cirincione, & Steadman, 1994). Curiously, in *Shannon v. United States* (1994), the U.S. Supreme Court held that NGRI defendants have no right to a jury instruction that makes clear the post-"acquittal" commitment process, because such an instruction would violate the long-standing principle that a jury must base its verdict on the evidence before it. This may be correct jurisprudential theory, but it violates commonsense justice in that we have strong reason to believe that jurors do pay attention to this issue and that these assumptions are incorrect (see later section on empirical developments).

Contrary to strong public concerns, NGRI acquittees are not "easily" released. In fact, research indicates that they are more likely to remain institutionalized for longer periods than crime-equivalent guilty persons (Miller, 1994; Silver, 1995). The constitutionality of this has been justified by the U.S. Supreme Court on the grounds that the purpose of their commitment is to treat their dangerousness, not to punish them for a crime for which they were found not guilty (see *Foucha v. Louisiana,* 1992; *Jones v. United States,* 1983). A number of factors contribute to this lengthy treatment and slow release process.

First, NGRI acquittees are likely to be those severely mentally disordered persons for whom currently available treatment, both biochemical and psychosocial, has been ineffective. This is not because they are bad or noncompliant persons, but because, contrary to medical and pharmaceutical company myth, about a third of the severely mentally disordered fail to show meaningful clinical response (Relman & Angell, 2002). Such individuals may also become noncompliant as a result of a complex psychological process. That is, unless clients perceive a subjective benefit from treatment, they are less likely to tolerate unpleasant side effects. Mental health professionals who establish an authoritarian ("You're sick and you need to take your medicine") as opposed to a collaborative ("Let's work together to find a treatment strategy where the benefits outweigh the risks and side effects") relationship are also more likely to produce noncompliance (Appelbaum & Gutheil, 1982). Where such problems in the therapeutic relationship exist, medications are frequently delusionally reinterpreted as the cause for psychotic symptoms. Thus, upon NGRI admission, a typical person has a long track record of unsuccessful treatment, the most recent frequently occurring only months before the index offense (Golding, Eaves, & Kowaz, 1989).

Second, because their dangerousness (manifested by the actus reus) is linked, by virtue of their plea, to their mental disorder, they are unlikely to be released until their mental disorder is quite well under control. Furthermore, as illustrated in *Jones* and *Foucha,* they can be committed and held for what amounts to an indeterminant length of time (i.e., until no longer deemed dangerous).

Third, political realities based on the sensational publicity produced by the media, in large part because they perpetuate insanity defense myths (Silver et al., 1994) in failed NGRI releases, make decision makers quite cautious.

Finally, few jurisdictions have an articulated prerelease risk assessment, postrelease risk management, and intensive case management system capable of more safely handling the community adjustment and supervision needed for such individuals.

An unstudied aspect of the dispositional issue has to do with the ultimate costs and effectiveness of placing prototypical insanity acquittees in forensic treatment contexts versus placement in traditional correctional facilities. Although some data clearly support the monitored release of NGRI acquittees, the larger trend, in those states with either GBMI or highly restricted (or nonexistent) insanity defenses, is to place such defendants in correctional environments for the majority of their sentence or institutionalization. Wiederanders (1992; Wiederanders & Choate, 1994) and Golding and colleagues (1989) have shown that articulated follow-up of insanity acquittees in the community is feasible and worthy of study. What we do not have is informative data on the differences between similar individuals "treated" in correctional versus forensic mental health contexts. We know of no empirical studies of this issue. With respect to mental health economics, the question is whether society eventually pays more or less for treating mentally disordered offenders in prison versus forensic mental health systems. Clearly, the cost per diem while initially incarcerated will favor prison over mental health system dispositions; however, the analysis also needs to include days institutionalized, days in the community at lower cost, and the likelihood and financial, emotional, and moral costs of recidivism. Again, we know of no direct data, but, on logical grounds, we propose that treated and supervised mentally ill and dangerous offenders would cost less, financially and emotionally, than prison-incarcerated mentally ill offenders who receive less mental health treatment and supervision.

As is evident from this discussion, there are a multitude of issues that clinicians face with respect to the assessment and disposition of NGRI defendants. We now turn to a review of empirical research developments that have taken place with respect to many of these issues.

EMPIRICAL DEVELOPMENTS REGARDING CRIMINAL RESPONSIBILITY

Research in the area of insanity and criminal responsibility has taken a number of forms. We have conceptualized this research as falling into three broad areas: research on NGRI verdicts (including the frequency of NGRI verdicts, rates of agreement among experts as well as between experts and the courts with respect to NGRI opinions, and the characteristics of NGRI acquittees); research on judicial instruction (including an examination of various legal standards or tests of insanity); and jury and juror decision making with respect to insanity (including jurors' case-relevant attitudes, case construals, and implicit theories or prototypes regarding insanity). We present a brief overview of each of these three areas. The reader is referred to other sources for a more detailed and comprehensive review of this literature (see especially Finkel, 1995, 2000; Lymburner & Roesch, 1999; Simon, 1999).

RESEARCH ON INSANITY VERDICTS

Research on the empirical realities of the adjudication of criminal responsibility has continued to demonstrate the same basic phenomena since earlier reviews (Golding, 1992; Pasewark, 1986). The research has primarily been directed at describing the NGRI population in traditional demographic and diagnostic terms and at demythologizing public misconceptions of the insanity defense (see Silver, Cirincione, & Steadman, 1994, for a review).

Frequency of Insanity Verdicts

Empirical research indicates that the insanity defense is seldom raised, averaging less than 1% of total felony indictments (Steadman et al., 1993), and is highly variable in its success rate, with that rate modally being 25% of those who raise the issue. Cirincione et al. (1995) surveyed seven states with respect to the frequency of insanity pleas and the likelihood of insanity acquittal and found an inverse relationship between the two factors. That is, states in which the insanity plea rates were high had a lower insanity acquittal rate. These authors found an average rate of insanity pleas of .85 (less than 1%) per 100 felony indictments and an aggregated success rate of 28%. Silver et al. (1994) cite success rates that are highly variable, ranging from 7% to 87% and averaging 26% (for earlier studies and summaries of success rates, see Janofsky, Vandewalle, & Rappaport, 1989; Pasewark, 1986; Steadman & Braff, 1983).

Cirincione and Jacobs (1999) attempted to collect data on each state with respect to the annual number of insanity acquittals; despite valiant efforts, they were able to obtain data from only 36 states. Their results indicated that, for these 36 states, the mean number of insanity acquittals was 33.4 per state per year, with a median of 17.7 and a standard deviation of 41.7. They found that California (134) and Florida (110.5) had the highest average number of insanity acquittals per year and that New Mexico (0) and South Dakota (0.1) had the lowest, with six states reporting no more than 1 insanity acquittal per year.

Rates of Agreement

There is a high rate of agreement among forensic experts of similar levels of training, experience, and methodology, and high levels of agreement between examiner opinions and judge or juror decisions with respect to insanity opinions. Research on the reliability of forensic judgments indicates that the types of cases likely to be contested include issues of comorbidity with personality disorder; highly idiosyncratic and paranoid religious, political, or identity systems; intoxication or failure to take medications; and extremely bizarre conduct (see Golding, 1992; Hoge & Grisso, 1992; Melton et al., 1997; Rogers & Ewing, 1992, for summaries of the reliability research). NGRI verdicts are typically achieved as either a stipulation between defense and prosecution or a bench trial and rarely involve contested battles of experts in front of jurors (Golding, 1992; Melton et al., 1997; Silver et al., 1994).

Research on interexaminer agreement is of limited utility as it focuses on global agreement. Research on the logic and structure of examiner decision making in competency evaluations (Skeem, Golding, Cohn, & Berge, 1998) demonstrates high global agreement in ultimate conclusions but poor agreement in examiner logic, including defendant's particular abilities and incapacities. Logically, we would expect the same in NGRI evaluations. Similarly, we know of no empirical study of the crime characteristics that lead actual judicial decision makers or forensic examiners to conclude that the defendant lacked the legally or morally relevant mental state. This point is particularly critical because few examiners, in our experience, pay close attention to collateral reports or crime scene data with respect to consistency with their inferences about a defendant's mental state (Melton et al., 1997).

Unfortunately, this type of sociodemographic research does not address the more theoretically interesting question: What types of mental disorder characteristics (beyond psychosis) and what aspects of offense incident characteristics (planning, intentionality behaviors, reasonableness of motive) influence expert, judge, and juror decision making?

Characteristics of Insanity Defendants

Finkel (1995) and Roberts and Golding (1991) have argued and presented rather convincing data from analogue studies that major determinants of mock decision making are jurors' individual construal of the case and particular defendant characteristics, along a set of dimensions: the ability to think and reason rationally and clearly; the capacity to perceive and be aware without distortion; the capacity to choose courses of action; rational motivation for actions; the ability to control thoughts, feeling, and behaviors; and responsibility for altering one's mental state by intoxication, noncompliance with medication, and other factors. It would be important for large-scale research on both examiner judgments and the verdicts reached by judges and the rare trial jury to examine what elements or factors they rely on in reaching their decisions.

Some research has focused on the characteristics of defendants who have presented successful insanity defenses and, thus, have been acquitted as NGRI. These defendants typically have major psychotic diagnoses and extensive mental health histories, often with prior civil commitments or prior findings of incompetency (Golding, 1992; Golding et al., 1989; Ogloff et al., 1992; Steadman et al., 1993). A detailed examination of a large NGRI cohort by Golding and colleagues found that 79% had been previously hospitalized, with a mean of 4.11 hospitalizations; 43% of these prior admissions were for forensic reasons. Over 50% of the subjects with prior admissions were discharged within 1 year of their index offense, and 45% committed their index offense within 6 months of their last discharge.

In terms of decisions made regarding the conditional release of those defendants who have been found NGRI, Callahan and Silver (1998a) studied the factors associated with the conditional release of NGRI acquittees across four states (Connecticut, Maryland, Ohio, and New York) and found wide variance in the types of characteristics that are associated with conditional release. In Connecticut, few individuals were likely to be released conditionally, regardless of their characteristics. In New York, however, demographic characteristics were most predictive of conditional release; females, Whites, and high school graduates were most likely to be conditionally released. In Maryland, clinical outlook was the most critical variable, with those defendants having a diagnosis of Schizophrenia being significantly *less* likely than those with other major mental illnesses to be granted conditional release. In Ohio, the nature of the crime was the most significant predictor, with serious offenders being less likely to be released. It is somewhat concerning that in New York, the variables most predictive of conditional release were related neither to crime characteristics nor to psychiatric variables.

With respect to the revocation of conditional release, research has indicated that revocation rates vary widely (e.g., between 35% and 50%; Callahan & Silver, 1998b; Heilbrun & Griffin, 1993; Wiederanders, Bromley, & Choate, 1997) and that variables such as being White, employed, and married are indicative of successful conditional release (Tellefsen, Cohen, Silver, & Dougherty, 1992). Monson and colleagues (Monson, Gunnin, Fogel, & Kyle, 2001) examined the factors that were related to the revocation of conditional release for a sample of 125 NGRI acquittees and found that minority status, prior criminal history, and diagnosis of substance abuse were significantly predictive of revocation of conditional release.

RESEARCH ON JUDICIAL INSTRUCTION

Jurors are expected to determine an appropriate verdict by conscientiously applying the law to a fair evaluation of the evidence (*Wainwright v. Witt*, 1985). As suggested earlier, the effect of specific language differences in legal standards for insanity has been intensely debated for over two centuries. The nature and outcome of these debates, however, have shown either weak or little practical effect on jurors as a main effect. Research repeatedly demonstrates that mock jurors often do *not* apply judicial instruction on various legal definitions of insanity in rendering verdicts (Finkel 1989, 1991, 2000; Finkel, Shaw, Bercaw, & Kock, 1985; Ogloff; 1991; Ogloff et al., 1992; Simon, 1999). For example, the Insanity Defense Reform Act (IDRA, 1984) was formulated after Hinckley's acquittal to narrow the language of the ALI (1962) standard, thereby curbing the number of insanity verdicts (by eliminating the volitional prong). In an analogue study, Finkel (1989) found *no* verdict differences among mock jurors who were given IDRA instructions, ALI instructions, or very narrow "wild beast" instructions (*Arnold's Case*, 1724; cited in N. Walker, 1978).

In fact, Finkel and others have found that it often makes no difference whether jurors are given *any* test or standard: Mock jurors who receive no insanity definitions or who are told to use their "best lights" judgment to decide a case produce verdict patterns indistinguishable from those of mock jurors who receive various insanity test instructions (Finkel, 1989, 1991; Finkel & Duff, 1989; Finkel & Handel, 1988; Ogloff, 1991; Wheatman & Shaffer, 2001; Whittemore & Ogloff, 1995). As Diamond (1997) observes, many of the effects and their strength depend on the way the verdicts are formulated, the alternatives, the existence of contextual effects, and so forth. The fact that jurors determine whether a defendant is sane or insane *without* the guidance of legal instructions suggests that they rely on their own knowledge about insanity and other cognitive structures to make these decisions; it does not imply that they nullify instructions. Rather, their own implicit theories of insanity guide their interpretation of the admittedly vague and nonspecific linguistic terms of insanity standards.

Research has found that mock jurors who opt for the GBMI verdict option (when given three options: NGRI, GBMI, and guilty) tend to be more moderate than mock jurors selecting NGRI or guilty verdicts in their ratings of deserved blame and punishment as well as in their ratings of a defendant's level of mental disorder, capacity to display rational behavior, and capacity to control psychotic beliefs (Roberts, Sargent, & Chan, 1993). Poulson, Wuensch, and Brondino (1998) found that the addition of the GBMI verdict option resulted in a twofold effect: a reduction in guilty verdicts by about two-thirds and a reduction of NGRI verdicts by about half. These authors conclude that the GBMI verdict appears to be used as a compromise verdict.

Poulson and his colleagues (Poulson et al., 1998; Poulson, Braithwaite, Brondino, & Wuensch, 1997) found that mock jurors' attitudes were reflected in their verdict selections. For example, jurors who opted for guilty verdicts (as opposed to GBMI or NGRI verdicts) held a crime control orientation and favorable attitudes toward the death penalty, as well as unfavorable attitudes toward insanity. The opposite was true of those jurors who opted for an NGRI verdict (over guilty or GBMI).

Recent research on judicial instructions has made clear the importance of allowing jurors the opportunity to deliberate. Wheatman and Shaffer (2001) found that dispositional instructions had no effect on the verdict preferences of individual jurors (i.e., individuals who were not given the opportunity to deliberate but rather made verdict decisions immediately after being presented the trial stimuli); however, after given the opportunity to deliberate as a jury, postdeliberation shifts in these initial verdict preferences were evident. These researchers found that *uninstructed* juries (those juries given no information about the treatment and detainment of individuals acquitted by reason of insanity) were more likely to shift toward a harsher verdict after deliberation, whereas *instructed* juries (given dispositional information) were more likely to shift toward more lenient verdicts after deliberation. These results serve to underscore the importance not only of dispositional instructions but of the opportunity for jurors to deliberate as juries.

RESEARCH ON JURY AND JUROR DECISION MAKING

Although data on the reliability and validity of well-founded forensic criminal responsibility opinions are encouraging, there are no modern studies of actual juries or bench trials in terms of the defendant, expert testimony for and against mental state, and case-specific factors that are weighed in accepting or rejecting an insanity claim. Logically, we can place some weight in surveys of attitudes toward insanity and insanity dispositions, and compare that to what is empirically known. Most of what we know is based on jury simulation studies. Although there are problems with this particular methodology, a careful analysis of analogue studies produces a rather consistent set of findings and implications.

Although the legal system implicitly assumes that people are blank slates who can apply the law in a wholly evidence-driven fashion, substantial research indicates that people have "knowledge structures" which reflect their life experiences and guide their behavior (Fiske, 1993; Schneider, 1991). These knowledge structures include constructs such as attitudes, schemas, prototypes, and stereotypes and appear highly relevant to legal decision making (Moran, Cutler, & DeLisa, 1994; Pennington & Hastie, 1986; V. Smith, 1991; Stalans, 1993). Several sources of research in various stages of development suggest that individual differences in these structures are critical in understanding why jurors reach particular verdicts in insanity defense cases.

Jurors' Case-Relevant Attitudes

The insanity defense is controversial and involves scientific as well as political-moral issues. Although public opinion polls and empirical studies often find support for the basic logic of the insanity defense, they consistently reveal powerful negative attitudes toward the defense (Borum & Fulero, 1999; Cutler,

Moran, & Narby, 1992; Ellsworth, Bukaty, Cowan, & Thompson, 1983; Hans, 1986; Hans & Slater, 1984; Homant & Kennedy, 1987; Jeffrey & Pasewark, 1983; Pasewark & Seidenzahl, 1979; Roberts & Golding, 1991; Skeem & Golding, 2001). For example, Roberts, Golding, and Fincham (1987) found that although 78% of their subjects believed that severe mental illness suggested impairment in one's capacity to make rational decisions and form criminal intent, 66% believed that insanity should *not* be allowed as a complete criminal defense. Across studies, results reflect a primary concern that the insanity defense is an easily abused loophole in the law that allows many guilty criminals to escape punishment (Silver et al., 1994). Additional concerns include beliefs that insanity is easily malingered and that the public is poorly protected from dangerous criminals who are adjudicated insane (Golding, 1992; see also Perlin, 1994, chap. 5). Similarly, jurors' case-specific negative attitudes toward both mental health experts and individuals with severe mental illness appear relevant in their decision making in insanity defense cases (Cutler et al., 1992; Perlin, 1994; Skeem & Golding, 2001).

Many of these concerns reflect inaccurate knowledge about the insanity defense. Such myths are not only prevalent, but may also be inflexible. Jeffrey and Pasewark (1984) presented subjects with factual statistics on the frequency and success rates of the insanity defense. Approximately half of subjects maintained their opinion that the insanity defense was overused and abused despite having seen contradictory evidence. Especially troubling is the robust finding that these prevalent, potentially inflexible, negative attitudes toward the insanity defense exert considerable influence on mock jurors' verdicts in insanity cases (Bailis, Darley, Waxman, & Robinson, 1995; Cutler et al., 1992; Ellsworth et al., 1984; Homant & Kennedy, 1987; Roberts et al., 1987; Robinson & Darley, 1995). For example, Roberts and Golding (1991) found that mock jurors' attitudes toward the insanity defense were *more* strongly associated with their verdicts than were the study design variables, which included manipulations of available verdict categories (insanity versus insanity supplemented by GBMI) and case facts (the relationship of the defendant's delusion to the crime and the planfulness of the crime). The most determinative dimension underlying these attitudes was jurors' belief in strict liability (versus a belief that mental state is relevant to a defendant's blameworthiness). In essence, then, jurors' verdicts may depend more on their attitudes and opinions than on case facts and court instruction.

Despite strong evidence on the biasing effect of negative attitudes toward the insanity defense on verdicts, bias may often go undetected based on limitations in current knowledge and legal procedures. First, despite abundant research on insanity defense attitudes, no well-validated measure of these attitudes has yet been developed. Skeem and Golding (2001) present one of the first checklists of jurors' conceptions that, they suggest, could be adapted to a questionnaire to assess prospective jurors' conceptions of the "typical person who is not responsible for his criminal actions due to mental illness" (p. 607). Second, except in cases involving interracial violent crimes, capital punishment, or pretrial publicity, judges are accorded broad discretion in selecting the topics to be addressed during *voir dire* (Johnson & Haney, 1994; Sklansky, 1996). Although insanity defense cases arguably invoke equally powerful biases, the case law reflects a trend in which judges refuse to inquire about bias against the insanity defense or even allow the impanelment of jurors who express biases against the defense or against the mentally ill (Perlin, 1994). In our opinion, the voir dire process would ideally be reformed such that prospective jurors' case-relevant preconceptions and attitudes were routinely examined in insanity defense cases.

Jurors' Case Construals

Other lines of research suggest that jurors' views are critical. In addition to their case-specific attitudes, jurors' individual ways of interpreting evidence are related to their verdicts. Mock jurors draw *different* inferences about defendants' cognitive and volitional impairments when given *identical* case descriptions (Bailis et al., 1995; Roberts & Golding, 1991; Roberts et al., 1987; Roberts et al., 1993; Simon, 1999; Whittemore & Ogloff, 1995). These inferences, in turn, strongly predict their verdicts. For example, Roberts and Golding presented mock jurors with case vignettes in which they manipulated available verdict categories, the relationship of the defendant's paranoid delusion to the crime, and the planfulness of the crime. The attitude-related ways in which mock jurors interpreted the case evidence were the most powerful predictors of verdict choice. For example, individual differences in jurors' perceptions of the extent to which a defendant was mentally disordered, capable of rational behavior, capable of acting differently, or capable of understanding the wrongfulness of the behavior explained substantially more variance in verdicts than did the objective manipulation of case evidence.

Finkel and Handel (1989), using different methodology, also found that jurors actively construct the meaning of case information in rendering verdicts. They presented mock jurors with four vastly different case vignettes and asked them to render a verdict and explain the reasoning underlying their decisions. Using a rationally derived categorization scheme, they found that mock jurors cited multiple, rational reasons for their decisions in each case (the categorization scheme included, for example, capacity-incapacity to make responsible choices, unimpaired-impaired awareness and perceptions, no motive-evil motive for criminal act). The pattern of the cited constructs or reasons systematically differed based on the verdict that mock jurors reached. In essence, then, jurors construed case information in complex, discriminating ways that were consistent with their verdict choices.

Similarly, Whittemore and Ogloff (1995) found that differences in mock jurors' perceptions of a defendant's mental state at the time of his or her trial predicted their verdicts. Despite manipulation of the defendant's mental state at the time of trial (symptom-free, neurotic, or psychotic), mock jurors differed in their perceptions of the extent to which given defendants were mentally disordered. When mock jurors inferred that the defendant was psychotic at the time of the trial, they were more likely to deem him or her insane.

Jurors' Implicit Theories or Prototypes of Insanity

In essence, then, jurors *construct* the meaning of case information. These constructions or interpretations are more strongly associated with jurors' verdicts than the case as objectively given and appear unaffected by judicial instruction. Based on these findings, several authors have argued that jurors render insanity verdicts by carefully resorting to their personal knowledge or implicit theories of insanity (Finkel & Handel, 1989; Roberts & Golding, 1991; Roberts et al., 1987). However, the nature of these theories and the process by which they affect verdicts remains unclear. The studies that have attempted to infer the nature of mock jurors' conceptions of insanity based on jurors' judgments about insanity case vignettes have produced somewhat conflicting results in terms of the relative importance of various construal dimensions (Roberts et al., 1987; cf. Bailis et al., 1995; Finkel & Handel, 1989; Robinson & Darley, 1995). To date, studies that directly analyze what people mean by insane in the context of an analysis of actual jury decisions are virtually nonexistent: "'What everybody knows' about insanity is perilously unchartered" (Perlin, 1994, p. 294).

Finkel (1995) and colleagues have been conducting research examining jurors' conceptions of insanity by using a prototype theory of categorization. Finkel and Groscup (1997) found that undergraduate subjects describe insanity cases as involving young defendants with a history of strain, mental disorder, violence, and abuse, who perpetrate various crimes, including murder, after various precipitating events (including the loss of loved ones) on a stranger. For successful insanity cases, the defendant's motive is related to a grandiose delusion; for unsuccessful cases, revenge is the motive.

Skeem and Golding (2001) identified three prototypes of insanity and found that these prototypes were systematically related to jurors' case-relevant attitudes and demographic characteristics. The three prototypes identified were (1) severe mental disability, the prototype representing the majority (47%) of the jurors and characterized by an emphasis on severe, long-standing, functional impairment and intellectual disability that is resistant to treatment; (2) moral insanity, the prototype representing 33% of the jurors and characterized by an emphasis on traits of psychopathy, psychosis, and violent, unpredictable behavior; and (3) mental state-centered, the prototype representing 21% of the jurors and characterized by a narrow focus on issues relevant to the defendant's impaired mental state at the time of the offense. These prototypes were related to differences in the ways that jurors interpreted case information and rendered verdicts in that the jurors with the mental state-centered prototypes were more likely to render verdicts of NGRI and more likely to perceive defendants as less worthy of punishment, less able to control their beliefs, and more mentally disordered.

Jurors' decisions are not determined solely by subjective factors. Although individual differences in social-moral cognition appear most critical in understanding jurors' verdicts, objective manipulation of case facts does have some impact on jurors' verdicts. For example, the level of a defendant's mental disorder and the planfulness and bizarreness of the crime are associated with jurors' verdicts (Roberts et al., 1987; Roberts & Golding, 1991). As noted earlier, the characteristics of insanity acquittees suggest that juror and judicial decision making is rational and relatively consistent.

SUMMARY AND CONCLUSIONS

This chapter provided a broad overview of a number of issues and considerations regarding empirical, legal, and clinical aspects of criminal responsibility.

It seems apparent that there has been a great deal of discussion and controversy surrounding various legal standards or tests of criminal responsibility and that the available research indicates that this discussion and controversy may be all for naught given that judicial instructions do not appear to have a significant impact on juries' verdicts. This being said, however, we believe that recent research has begun to tap into various issues that require further consideration. Such issues include the role that deliberation plays in juror/jury decision making and verdicts and the impact of juror prototypes on verdicts and the interpretation of case information. Future research that uses samples of jury-eligible adults (as opposed to simple samples of convenience, such as from undergraduate psychology subject pools) will help to further this important body of knowledge. Similarly, clinically oriented research will help to further develop our assessment techniques and interventions for defendants for whom criminal responsibility arises as an issue.

REFERENCES

American Bar Association. (1983). *Recommendations on the insanity defense.* Washington, DC: Author.

American Law Institute. (1962). *Model penal code.* Philadelphia: Author.

American Psychiatric Association. (1982). *Statement on the insanity defense.* Washington, DC: Author.

American Psychiatric Association. (2000). *Diagnostic and statistical manual of mental disorders* (4th ed., text rev.). Washington, DC: Author.

Andreasen, N., & Flaum, M. (1994). Characteristic symptoms of schizophrenia. In T. Widiger, A. Frances, H. Pincus, M. First, R. Ross, & W. Davis (Eds.), *DSM-IV Sourcebook.* Washington, DC: American Psychiatric Association.

Appelbaum, P. S., & Gutheil, T. G. (1982). Clinical aspects of treatment refusal. *Comprehensive Psychiatry, 23,* 550–566.

Arrigo, B. A. (1996). The behavior of law and psychiatry: Rethinking knowledge construction and the guilty-but-mentally-ill verdict. *Criminal Justice and Behavior, 23,* 572–592.

Bailis, D., Darley, J., Waxman, T., & Robinson, P. (1995). Community standards of criminal liability and the insanity defense. *Law and Human Behavior, 19,* 425–446.

Ballantine, H. W. (1919). Criminal responsibility of the insane and feeble-minded. *Journal of the American Institute of Criminal Law and Criminology, 9,* 485–499.

Barnhouse, R. (1986). How to evaluate patients' religious ideation. In L. Robinson (Ed.), *Psychiatry and Religion: Overlapping Concerns.* Washington, DC: American Psychiatric Press.

Beasley, W. R. (1983). An overview of Michigan's guilty but mentally ill verdict. *Michigan Bar Journal, 62,* 204–205, 215–217.

Black, H. C. (1979). *Black's Law Dictionary* (5th ed.). St. Paul, MN: West Company.

Bonnie, R. J. (1983). The moral basis of the insanity defense. *American Bar Association Journal, 69,* 194–197.

Bonnie, R. J., & Slobogin, C. (1980). The role of mental health professionals in the criminal process: The case for informed speculation. *Virginia Law Review, 66,* 427–522.

Borum, R. (2003). Not guilty by reason of insanity. In T. Grisso (Ed.), *Evaluating competencies* (2nd ed.). New York: Kluwer/Plenum Press.

Borum, R., & Fulero, S. (1999). Empirical research on the insanity defense and attempted reforms: Evidence towards informed policy. *Law and Human Behavior, 23,* 375–394.

Bumby, K. M. (1993). Reviewing the guilty but mentally ill alternative: A case of the blind "pleading" the blind. *Journal of Psychiatry and Law, 21,* 191–220.

Callahan, L. A., & Silver, E. (1998a). Factors associated with the conditional release of persons acquitted by reason if insanity: A decision tree approach. *Law and Human Behavior, 22,* 147–163.

Callahan, L. A., & Silver, E. (1998b). Revocation of conditional release: A comparison of individual and program characteristics across four, U.S. states. *International Journal of Law and Psychiatry, 21,* 177–186.

Cirincione, C., & Jacobs, C. (1999). Identifying insanity acquittals: Is it any easier? *Law and Human Behavior, 23,* 487–497.

Cirincione, C., Steadman, H., & McGreevy, M. (1995). Rates of insanity acquittals and the factors associated with successful insanity pleas. *Bulletin of the American Academy of Psychiatry and Law, 23,* 399–409.

Commonwealth v. Rogers, 7 Metc. (Mass.) 500 (1844).

Crotty, H. D. (1924). The history of insanity as a defense to crime in English criminal law. *California Law Review, 12,* 105–123.

Cutler, B., Moran, G., & Narby, D. (1992). Jury selection in insanity defense cases. *Journal of Research in Personality, 26,* 165–182.

Diamond, S. S. (1997). Illuminations and shadows from jury simulations. *Law and Human Behavior, 21,* 561–572.

Durham v. United States, 214 F. 2d 862 (D.C. Cir., 1954).

Eigen, J. P. (1995). *Witnessing insanity: Madness and mad-doctors in the English Court.* New Haven, CT: Yale University Press.

Ellsworth, P., Bukaty, R., Cowan, C., & Thompson, W. (1984). The death-qualified jury and the defense of insanity. *Law and Human Behavior, 8,* 81–93.

Fed, R., Crim, P. 12.2(c) (1985).

Finkel, N. J. (1989). The Insanity Defense Reform Act of 1984: Much ado about nothing. *Behavioral Sciences and the Law, 7,* 403–419.

Finkel, N. J. (1991). The insanity defense: A comparison of verdict schemes. *Law and Human Behavior, 15,* 533–555.

Finkel, N. J. (1995). *Commonsense justice: Jurors' notions of the law.* Cambridge: Harvard University Press.

Finkel, N. J. (2000). Commonsense justice and jury instructions: Instructive and reciprocating connections. *Psychology, Public Policy, and Law, 6,* 591–628.

Finkel, N. J., & Duff, K. B. (1989). The insanity defense: Giving jurors a third option. *Forensic Reports, 2,* 235–263.

Finkel, N., & Groscup, J. (1997). Crime prototypes, objective versus subjective culpability, and a commonsense balance. *Law and Human Behavior, 21,* 209–230.

Finkel, N., & Handel, S. (1988). Jurors and insanity: Do test instructions instruct? *Forensic Reports, 1,* 65–79.

Finkel, N., & Handel, S. (1989). How jurors construe "insanity." *Law and Human Behavior, 13,* 41–59.

Finkel, N., Shaw, R., Bercaw, S., & Kock, J. (1985). Insanity defenses: From the jurors' perspective. *Law and Psychology Review, 9,* 77–92.

Fiske, S. T. (1993). Social cognition and social perception. *Annual Review of Psychology, 44,* 155–194.

Flaum, M., Arndt, S., & Andreasen, N. (1991). The reliability of "bizarre" delusions. *Comprehensive Psychiatry, 32,* 59–65.

Foucha v. Louisiana, 504 U.S. 71 (1992).

Garety, P., & Hemsley, M. (1994). *Delusions: Investigations into the psychology of delusional reasoning.* New York: Oxford University Press.

Giorgi-Guarnieri, D., Janofsky, J., Keram, E., Lawsky, S. M. P., Mossman, D., Schwartz-Watts, D., et al. (2002). AAPL practice guideline for forensic psychiatric evaluation of defendants raising the insanity defense. *Journal of the American Academy of Psychiatry and the Law, 30,* S3–S40.

Golding, S. L. (1990). Mental health professionals and the courts: The ethics of expertise. *International Journal of Law and Psychiatry, 13,* 281–307.

Golding, S. (1992). The adjudication of criminal responsibility: A review of theory and research. In D. Kagehiro & W. Laufer (Eds.), *Handbook of Psychology and Law.* New York: Springer-Verlag.

Golding, S. L., Eaves, D., & Kowaz, A. (1989). The assessment, treatment and community outcome of insanity acquittees: Forensic history and response to treatment. *International Journal of Law and Psychiatry, 12,* 149–179.

Golding, S. L., & Roesch, R. (1987). The assessment of criminal responsibility: A historical approach to a current controversy. In I. B. Weiner & A. K. Hess (Eds.), *Handbook of forensic psychology* (pp. 395–436). New York: Wiley.

Golding, S. L., Skeem, J. L., Roesch, R., & Zapf, P. A. (1999). The assessment of criminal responsibility: Current controversies. In I. B. Weiner & A. K. Hess (Eds.), *Handbook of forensic psychology* (2nd ed., pp. 379–408). New York: Wiley.

Goldstein, A. S. (1967). *The insanity defense.* New Haven, CT: Yale University Press.

Goldstein, A. M., Morse, S. J., & Shapiro, D. L. (2003). Evaluation of criminal responsibility. In A. M. Goldstein (Ed.), *Handbook of psychology: Forensic psychology* (Vol. 11, pp. 381–406). Hoboken, NJ: Wiley.

Gray, S. (1972). The insanity defense: Historical development and contemporary relevance. *American Criminal Law Review, 10,* 559–583.

Gutheil, T. G. (2002). Assessment of mental state at the time of criminal offense: The forensic examination. In R. I. Simon & D. W. Shuman (Eds.), *Retrospective assessment of mental states in litigation: Predicting the past* (pp. 73–99). Washington, DC: American Psychiatric Publishing.

Häfner, H., & Böker, W. (1982). *Crimes of violence by mentally abnormal offenders.* Trans., H. Marshall. Cambridge: Cambridge University Press.

Hans, V. (1986). An analysis of public attitudes toward the insanity defense. *Criminology, 24,* 383–414.

Hans, V., & Slater, D. (1984). "Plain crazy": Lay definitions of legal insanity. *International Journal of Law and Psychiatry, 7,* 105–114.

Harrow, M., Rattenbury, F., & Stoll, F. (1988). Schizophrenic delusions: An analysis of their persistence, of related premorbid ideas, and of three major dimensions. In T. Oltmanns & B. Maher (Eds.), *Delusional Beliefs.* New York: Wiley.

Heilbrun, K., & Griffin, P. A. (1993). Community-based forensic treatment of insanity acquittees. *International Journal of Law and Psychiatry, 16,* 133–150.

Heilbrun, K., Rosenfeld, B., Warren, J., & Collins, S. (1994). The use of third party information in forensic assessments: A two-state comparison. *Bulletin of the American Academy of Psychiatry and Law, 22,* 399–406.

Hermann, D. H. J. (1983). *The insanity defense: Philosophical, historical, and legal perspectives.* Springfield, IL: Charles C. Thomas.

Hermann, D. (1990). Autonomy, self-determination, the right of involuntarily committed persons to refuse treatment, and the use of substituted judgment in medication decisions involving incompetent persons. *International Journal of Law and Psychiatry, 13,* 361–385.

Hoge, S. K., & Grisso, T. (1992). Accuracy and expert testimony. *Bulletin of the American Academy of Psychiatry and Law, 20,* 67–76.

Homant, R., & Kennedy, D. (1987). Subjective factors in clinicians' judgments of insanity: Comparison of a hypothetical case and an actual case. *Professional Psychology: Research and Practice, 5,* 336–439.

Insanity Defense Reform Act of 1984, Public Law 98–473, Sections 401–406 (1984).

Jaspers, K. (1963). *General Psychopathology.* Trans., J. Hoenig & M. Hamilton. Manchester: Manchester University Press.

Janofsky, J. S., Vandewalle, M. B., & Rappaport, J. R. (1989). Defendants pleading insanity: An analysis of outcome. *Bulletin of the American Academy of Psychiatry and Law, 17,* 203–211.

Jeffrey, R., & Pasewark, R. (1984). Altering opinions about the insanity plea. *Journal of Psychiatry and Law, 11,* 29–40.

Johnson, C., & Haney, C. (1994). Felony voir dire: An exploratory study of its content and effect. *Law and Human Behavior, 18,* 487–506.

Jones v. United States, 103 S. Ct. 3043 (1983).

Keedy, E. R. (1917). Insanity and criminal responsibility. *Harvard Law Review, 30,* 535–560, 724–738.

Keedy, E. R. (1920). Criminal responsibility of the insane—A reply to Professor Ballantine Books. *Journal of American Institute of Criminal Law and Criminology, 10,* 14–34.

Keilitz, I., & Fulton, J. P. (1983). *The insanity defense and its alternatives: A guide for policymakers.* Williamsburg, VA: National Center for State Courts.

LaFave, W., & Scott, A. (1972). *Handbook on criminal law.* St. Paul, MN: West Company.

Litwack, T. R. (2003). The competency of criminal defendants to refuse, for delusional reasons, a viable insanity defense recommended by counsel. *Behavioral Sciences and the Law, 21,* 135–156.

Livermore, J. M., & Meehl, P. E. (1967). The virtues of M'Naghten. *Minnesota Law Review, 51,* 789–856.

Lu, F., Lukoff, D., & Turner, R. (1994). Religious or Spiritual Problems. In T. Widiger, A. Frances, H. Pincus, M. First, R. Ross, & W. Davis (Eds.), *DSM-IV Sourcebook.* Washington, DC: American Psychiatric Association.

Lymburner, J. A., & Roesch, R. (1999). The insanity defense: Five years of research (1993–1997). *International Journal of Law and Psychiatry, 22,* 213–240.

Melton, G. B., Petrila, J., Poythress, N. G., & Slogobin, C. (1997). *Psychological evaluations for the courts: A handbook for mental health professionals and lawyers* (2nd ed.). New York: Guilford Press.

Melville, J. D., & Naimark, D. (2002). Punishing the insane: The verdict of guilty but mentally ill. *Journal of the American Academy of Psychiatry and Law, 30,* 553–555.

Miller, R. (1994). Criminal responsibility. In R. Rosner (Ed.), *Principles and practice of forensic psychiatry* (pp. 198–215). New York: Chapman and Hall.

M'Naghten's Case, 8 Eng. Rep. 718 (1843).

Mojtabai, R., & Nicholson, R. (1995). Interrater reliability of ratings of delusions and bizarre delusions. *American Journal of Psychiatry, 152,* 1804–1806.

Monson, C. M., Gunnin, D. D., Fogel, M. H., & Kyle, L. L. (2001). Stopping (or slowing) the revolving door: Factors related to NGRI acquittees' maintenance of a conditional release. *Law and Human Behavior, 25,* 257–267.

Moran, G., Cutler, B., & DeLisa, A. (1994). Attitudes toward tort reform, scientific jury selection, and juror bias: Verdict inclination in criminal and civil trials. *Law and Psychology Review, 18,* 309–328.

Morse, S. J. (1978). Law and mental health professionals: The limits of expertise. *Professional Psychology, 9,* 389–399.

Mullen, P. (1979). Phenomenology of disordered mental functions. In P. Hill, R. Murray, & A. Thorley (Eds.), *Essentials of Postgraduate Psychiatry.* London: Academic Press.

Mullen, P. (1985). The mental state and states of mind. In P. Hill, R. Murray, & A. Thorley (Eds.), *Essentials of Postgraduate Psychiatry, 2nd ed.* London: Grune & Stratton.

Ogloff, J. (1991). A comparison of insanity defense standards on juror decision making. *Law and Human Behavior, 15,* 509–531.

Ogloff, J. R., Roberts, C. F., & Roesch, R. (1993). The insanity defense: Legal standards and clinical assessment. *Applied and Preventative Psychology, 2,* 163–178.

Ogloff, J., Schweighofer, A., Turnbull, S., & Whittemore, K. (1992). Empirical research regarding the insanity defense: How much do we really know. In J. Ogloff (Ed.), *Law and psychology: The broadening of the discipline.* Durham, NC: Carolina Academic Press.

Oltmanns, T. (1988). Approaches to the definition and study of delusions. In T. Oltmanns & B. Maher (Eds.), *Delusional beliefs.* New York: Wiley.

Palmer, C. A. (2000). The guilty but mentally ill verdict: A review and conceptual analysis of intent and impact. *Journal of the American Academy of Psychiatry and the Law, 28,* 47–54.

Parsons v. State, 81 Ala. 577, 2 So. 854 (1866).

Pasewark, R. A. (1982). Insanity plea: A review of the research literature. *Journal of Psychiatry and Law, 9,* 357–401.

Pasewark, R. (1986). A review of research on the insanity defense. In S. A. Shah (Ed.), *The Law and Mental Health: Annals of the American Academy of Political and Social Science, 484,* 100–114.

Pasewark, R., & Seidenzahl, D. (1979). Opinions concerning the insanity plea and criminality among patients. *Bulletin of the American Academy of Psychiatry and Law, 7,* 199–202.

Pennington, N., & Hastie, R. (1986). Evidence evaluation in complex decision making. *Journal of Personality and Social Psychology, 51,* 242–258.

People v. McQuillan, 221 N. W. 2d 569 (Supreme Court of Michigan, 1974).

Perlin, M. (1994). *The jurisprudence of the insanity defense.* Durham, NC: Carolina Academic Press.

Platt, A. M., & Diamond, B. L. (1965). The origins and development of the "wild beast" concept of mental illness and its relation to theories of criminal responsibility. *Journal of the History of the Behavioral Sciences, 1,* 355–367.

Platt, A. M., & Diamond, B. L. (1966). The origins of the "right and wrong" test of criminal responsibility and its subsequent development in the United States: An historical survey. *California Law Review, 54,* 1227–1259.

Pollock, F., & Maitland, F. (1952). *History of English Law* (Vol. I, 2nd ed.). Cambridge: Cambridge University Press.

Poulson, R. L., Braithwaite, R. L., Brondino, M. J., & Wuensch, K. L. (1997). Mock jurors' insanity defense verdict selections: The role of evidence, attitudes, and verdict options. *Social Behavior and Personality, 12,* 743–758.

Poulson, R. L., Wuensch, K. L., & Brondino, M. J. (1998). Factors that discriminate among mock jurors' verdict selections: Impact of the guilty but mentally ill verdict option. *Criminal Justice and Behavior, 25,* 366–381.

Poythress, N., Melton, G. B., Petrila, J., & Slobogin, C. (2000). Commentary on "The Mental State at the Time of the Offense Measure." *Journal of the American Academy of Psychiatry and the Law, 28,* 29–32.

Ray, Isaac. (1962). *A treatise on the medical jurisprudence on insanity.* Cambridge, MA: Belknap Press (Harvard University). (Original work published 1838)

Relman, A. S., & Angell, M. (2002). Resolved: Psychosocial interventions improve clinical outcomes in organic disease (Con). *Psychosomatic Medicine, 64,* 558–563.

Rice, M., & Harris, G. (1990). The predictors of insanity acquittal. *International Journal of Law and Psychiatry, 13,* 217–224.

Roberts, C., & Golding, S. (1991). The social construction of criminal responsibility and insanity. *Law and Human Behavior, 15,* 349–376.

Roberts, C., Golding, G., & Fincham, F. (1987). Implicit theories of criminal responsibility: Decision making and the insanity defense. *Law and Human Behavior, 11,* 207–232.

Roberts, C. F., Sargent, E. L., & Chan, A. S. (1993). Verdict selection processes in insanity defense cases: Juror construals and the effects of the guilty but mentally ill instructions. *Law and Human Behavior, 17,* 261–275.

Robinson, P., & Darley, D. (1995). *Justice, liability and blame: Community views and the criminal law.* San Francisco: Westview Press.

Rogers, J. L., Bloom, J. D., & Manson, S. M. (1984). Insanity defenses: Contested or conceded? *American Journal of Psychiatry, 141,* 885–888.

Rogers, R. (1984). *Rogers criminal responsibility assessment scales (R-CRAS) and test manual.* Odessa, FL: Psychological Assessment Resources.

Rogers, R. (1997). *The clinical assessment of malingering and deception, 2nd ed.* New York: Guilford Press.

Rogers, R., Cavanaugh, J. L., Seman, W., & Harris, M. (1984). Legal outcome and clinical findings: A study of insanity evaluations. *Bulletin of the American Academy of Psychiatry and the Law, 12,* 75–83.

Rogers, R., & Ewing, C. P. (1992). The measurement of insanity: Debating the merits of the R-CRAS and its alternatives. *International Journal of Law and Psychiatry, 15,* 113–123.

Rogers, R., & Sewell, K. W. (1999). The R-CRAS and insanity evaluations: A re-examination of construct validity. *Behavioral Sciences and the Law, 17,* 181–194.

Rogers, R., & Shuman, D. W. (2000). *Conducting insanity evaluations.* New York: Guilford Press.

Rogers, R., Wasyliw, O. E., & Cavanaugh, J. L. (1984). Evaluating insanity: A study of construct validity. *Law and Human Behavior, 8,* 293–303.

Rosenberg, C. E. (1968). *The trial of the assassin Guiteau: Psychiatry and law in the gilded age.* Chicago: University of Chicago Press.

Sacks, M., Carpenter, W., & Strauss, J. (1974). Recovery from delusions: Three phases documented by patient's interpretation of research procedures. *Archives of General Psychiatry, 30,* 117–120.

Saks, E. (1991). Competency to refuse treatment. *North Carolina Law Review, 69,* 945–999.

Sayre, F. B. (1932). Mens rea. *Harvard Law Review, 45,* 974–1026.

Schneider, D. (1991). Social cognition. *Annual Review of Psychology, 42,* 527–561.

Sedler, M. (1995). Understanding delusions. *The Psychiatric Clinics of North America, 18,* 251–262.

Shannon v. United States, 114 S. Ct. 2419 (1994).

Shapiro, D. L. (1999). *Criminal responsibility evaluations: A manual for practice.* Sarasota, FL: Professional Resource Press/Professional Resource Exchange.

Silver, E. (1995). Punishment or treatment?: Comparing the lengths of confinement of successful and unsuccessful insanity defendants. *Law and Human Behavior, 19,* 375–388.

Silver, E., Circincione, C., & Steadman, H. J. (1994). Demythologizing inaccurate perceptions of the insanity defense. *Law and Human Behavior, 18,* 63–70.

Simon, R. J. (1999). *The jury and the defense of insanity.* New Brunswick, NJ: Transaction.

Skeem, J. L., & Golding, S. L. (2001). Describing jurors' personal conceptions of insanity and their relationship to case judgments. *Psychology, Public Policy, and Law, 7,* 561–621.

Skeem, J. L., Golding, S. L., Cohn, N. B., & Berge, G. (1998). Logic and reliability of evaluations of competence to stand trial. *Law and Human Behavior, 22,* 519–547.

Sklansky, J. (1996). Right to a jury trial. [Special issue: 25th Annual Review of Criminal Procedure]. *The Georgetown Law Journal, 84,* 1139–1160.

Slobogin, C., Melton, G. B., & Showalter, C. R. (1984). The feasibility of a brief evaluation of mental state at the time of offense. *Law and Human Behavior, 8,* 305–321.

Smith, R. (1981). *Trial by medicine: Insanity and responsibility in Victorian trials.* Edinburgh: Edinburgh University Press.

Smith, V. (1991). Prototypes in the courtroom: Lay representations of legal concepts. *Journal of Personality and Social Psychology, 76,* 220–228.

Spitzer, R., First, M., Kendler, K., & Stein, D. (1993). The reliability of three definitions of bizarre delusions. *American Journal of Psychiatry, 150,* 880–884.

Stalans, L. (1993). Citizens' crime stereotypes, biased recall and punishment preferences in abstract cases: The educative role of interpersonal sources. *Law and Human Behavior, 17,* 451–470.

State v. Johnson, 399 A. 2d 469 (Supreme Court of Rhode Island, 1979).

State v. Pike, 49 N. H. 399 (1869).

State v. Strasburg, 110 P. 1020 (Supreme Court of Washington, 1910).

Steadman, H. J., & Braff, J. J. (1983). Defendants found not guilty by reason of insanity. In J. Monahan & H. Steadman (Eds.), *Mentally disordered offenders: Perspectives from law and social science.* New York: Plenum Press.

Steadman, H. J., McGreevy, M. A., Morrissey, J., Callahan, L. A., Robins, P. C., & Cirincione, C. (1993). *Before and after Hinckley: Evaluating insanity defense reform.* New York: Guilford Press.

Stroud, D. A. (1914). *Mens rea or imputability under the laws of England.* London: Sweet & Maxwell.

Sullivan, H. S. (1954). The psychiatric interview. Oxford, England: Norton & Co.

Taylor, P. (1985). Motives for offending among violent and psychotic men. *British Journal of Psychiatry, 147,* 491–498.

Taylor, P., Garety, P., Buchanan, A., Reed, A., Wesseley, S., Ray, K., et al. (1994). Delusions and violence. In J. Monahan & H. Steadman (Eds.), *Violence and mental disorder: Developments in risk assessment.* Chicago: University of Chicago Press.

Tellefsen, C., Cohen, M. I., Silver, S. B., & Dougherty, C. (1992). Predicting success on conditional release for insanity acquittees: Regionalized versus nonregionalized hospital patients. *Bulletin of the American Academy of Psychiatry and the Law, 20,* 87–100.

Underwood v. State, 32 Michigan 1 (Supreme Court of Michigan, 1873).

United States v. Brawner, 471 F. 2d 969 (D.C. Cir., 1972).

United States v. Lyons, 731 F. 2d 243 (Fifth Cir., 1984a).

United States v. Lyons, 739 F. 2d 994 (Fifth Cir., 1984b).

United States v. Torniero, 735 F. 2d 725 (Second Circuit, 1984).

Wainwright v. Witt, 105 S. Ct. 844 (1985).

Wales, H. W. (1976). An analysis of the proposal to "abolish" the insanity defense in S. 1: Squeezing a lemon. *University of Pennsylvania Law Review, 124,* 687–712.

Walker, C. (1991). Delusion: What did Jaspers really say? *British Journal of Psychiatry, 159,* 94–103.

Walker, N. (1978). *Crime and insanity in England, Volume I: The historical perspective.* Edinburgh: University of Edinburgh Press.

Wheatman, S. R., & Shaffer, D. R. (2001). On finding for defendants who plead insanity: The crucial impact of dispositional instructions and opportunity to deliberate. *Law and Human Behavior, 25,* 167–183.

Whittemore, K., & Ogloff, J. (1995). Factors that influence jury decision making: Disposition instructions and mental state at the time of the trial. *Law and Human Behavior, 19,* 283–303.

Wiederanders, M. R. (1992). Recidivism of disordered offenders who were conditionally vs. unconditionally released. *Behavioral Sciences and the Law, 10,* 141–148.

Wiederanders, M. R., Bromley, D. L., & Choate, P. A. (1997). Forensic conditional release programs and outcomes in three states. *International Journal of Law and Psychiatry, 20,* 249–257.

Wiederanders, M. R., & Choate, P. A. (1994). Beyond recidivism: Measuring community adjustments of conditionally released insanity acquittees. *Psychological Assessment, 6,* 61–66.

Winters, K. C., & Neale, J. M. (1983). Delusions and delusional thinking in psychotics: A review of the literature. *Clinical Psychology Review, 3,* 227–253.

CHAPTER 14

Specific Intent and Diminished Capacity

CHARLES R. CLARK

WHAT THE defense of diminished capacity is, how it developed, how it relates to other defense strategies focusing on mental state at the time of an offense, and how forensic examiners can best address questions of diminished capacity are the subjects of this chapter. As challenging to forensic examiners as claims of insanity are in terms of adapting techniques of clinical assessment to questions of mental state at the time of an offense, claims of diminished capacity may seem to represent unsolvable conundrums. In actuality, legislatures and courts have largely solved the puzzles presented by the diminished capacity defense, though forensic practitioners are all too often unaware of the solutions that have been reached.

Even more than in the case of insanity, when diminished capacity is claimed it is vital for the examiner to understand the history of the concept, the controversies that have developed about this defense, and the ways those controversies have been resolved in a number of jurisdictions. Although thoughtful ways to infuse more research-based psychology into legal conceptions of intent continue to be proposed (e.g., Barratt & Felthous, 2003; Denno, 2003; Malle & Nelson, 2003), the history of the defense is one of misunderstandings by psychiatrists and psychologists of what their task is and the arrogation to themselves of solutions to what have always been essentially problems of law and public policy. Forensic examiners do not need to repeat the mistakes of the past.

A claim of diminished capacity may be raised in cases in which there is no good reason to believe that a jury would agree that the defendant was grossly disordered with the severe mental disease or defect, mental illness, or mental retardation that is the threshold test of insanity in the particular jurisdiction. Instead, the claim is that the defendant suffered from some disordered state of mind less than psychotic in its severity—perhaps one that was transitory, perhaps one that was induced by drugs or alcohol—and on that account the defendant, though admittedly guilty of something, was unable to form the intent for the major crime being charged.

When diminished capacity is claimed, the question is raised not of the extent to which a defendant to criminal charges should be considered guilty, but of precisely what crime the defendant is guilty. Each such defendant's mental state is at issue, but only for the purpose of determining just what it was that the defendant did. It is necessary to distinguish diminished capacity conceptually from insanity, although the law regarding this quasi-alternative to the insanity defense has historically been muddled and confused until relatively recently. As has been pointed out before (Clark, 1982), to the extent that there has been coherent law with respect to diminished capacity, the defense may make more sense from a legal than from a psychological perspective. More than does insanity, diminished capacity involves prescientific conceptualizations of intentionality. In asking mental health professionals to offer opinions about a defendant's ability to form the intent necessary for conviction, the law proceeds on the assumption that its legal constructs have genuine psychological content that is open to clinical investigation. That this assumption is unwarranted in at least many of the cases in which diminished capacity is raised will become evident from examining the development in the United States of this defense and the sorts of practical issues that arise in forensic evaluations of actual defendants.

ACTUS REUS AND *MENS REA*

In Anglo-American law, two elements must be present for a finding of guilt: a wrongful deed, or *actus reus,* and also a wrongful purpose or criminal intent, *mens rea.* Both of these elements, along with all of the elements of the crime charged, must be established beyond a reasonable doubt to convict (*In re* Winship, 1970).

The person who unwillingly performs an illegal act, whether consciously or unconsciously, is not guilty of the offense. But though volition may be seen to be a mental construct—and it is explicitly included in certain tests of legal insanity—volition has typically not been seen to be relevant to the question of mens rea. The store clerk forced at gunpoint to tie up other employees and open a safe for a robber is not guilty, just as a sleepwalker who exposes himself by walking outside unclothed is not guilty of a crime. The element of actus reus, although always open to question and never assumed in a criminal prosecution, is seldom open to a psychological defense. Except in some cases in which the insanity defense is used—and it continues to be controversial there—questions of voluntariness ordinarily pertain to the issue of actus reus, not mens rea (Morse, 1999). The so-called automaton defense, for instance, in which the defendant asserts a lack of volition and often a lack of consciousness as well, attacks the prosecution claim that there was an actus reus (Melton, Petrila, Poythress, & Slobogin, 1997). It is in respect to the question of whether a defendant formed mens rea that forensic examiners are most likely to be asked to provide an expert opinion.

Insanity is the principal defense approach that challenges the prosecution's claim that the defendant, who usually has not contested the actus reus, behaved with mens rea. Insanity negates mens rea or mental guilt altogether, in a global way, not in terms of particular, specific elements that may make up a crime, for instance the intent to break into a home, but also to steal, or rape, or kill. The individual who meets the test of insanity, regardless of exactly how insanity is defined, is said to be not guilty, not because there was no actus reus or illegal act committed, but because the individual is deemed to have lacked the requisite state of mind, for example, the capacity to appreciate the nature and quality or wrongfulness of the act.

Although insanity is a mens rea defense, some scholars contend that sanity is not a true element of the offense, at least not one that needs to be proven by the prosecution (and in the federal and many state jurisdictions, the burden of proving insanity is borne by defense). Rather, in this view, a defendant is legally insane and not culpable even if he or she formed the intent ordinarily required for conviction (Steadman et al., 1993). The meaning of mens rea has changed over time, from a term encompassing the concept of blameworthiness to one that simply denotes the intent to cause a defined act (Steadman et al., 1993).

In contrast to the wholesale negation of mental guilt and therefore criminal responsibility implicit in the insanity defense, diminished capacity considers mens rea in a piecemeal fashion, as one or another discrete act of intent. In theory, if not in practice, diminished capacity is not generally exculpating and does not lead to outright acquittal of all wrongdoing, but rather to a finding that a person was not capable of forming intent for the particular crime that is charged. What would follow, in theory, is a conviction of some lesser offense included in the crime originally charged. Additionally limiting the scope of diminished capacity is the fact that not all crimes are susceptible to this partial defense.

Central to the diminished capacity approach are the legal distinctions between crimes involving general intent and those involving specific intent. Only specific intent crimes are open to a diminished capacity defense. Confusingly, diminished capacity is often referred to as a mens rea defense, although strictly speaking, mens rea itself includes general intent as well as the more global moral blameworthiness involved in the concept of criminal responsibility or insanity. To add to the confusion, there is no universal agreement as to which crimes involve specific intent as opposed to general intent. The development of the law in this regard had been viewed as more a matter of expediency than the logical result of legal theory (Dix, 1971).

Finally, the essential logic behind diminished capacity or mens rea defenses is virtually identical to that of the so-called intoxication defense, based on voluntary intoxication, which also employs the distinction between general and specific intent. In practice, as in the cases of the store clerk and the sleepwalker, diminished capacity and intoxication defenses may be indistinguishable. In one investigation of sequential pretrial referrals for criminal responsibility and insanity examinations to Michigan's centralized diagnostic facility, the Center for Forensic Psychiatry, it was found that most (77%) of those defendants for whom diminished capacity was raised as a defense reported substance abuse at the time of the offense, in significant contrast to those for whom insanity but not diminished capacity was raised, of whom only 39% reported substance abuse at the time of the offense (Clark, 1988). Because of the essential similarity of its conceptual foundations to diminished capacity, the intoxication defense, as it involves a claim of incapacity to form intent, need not be treated separately. For a broader discussion of other ways in which intoxication or addiction may affect the grading of responsibility or findings of guilt, see Melton et al. (1997).

GENERAL AND SPECIFIC INTENT

The distinctions between general and specific intent follow a ranking of criminal culpability that is perhaps best illustrated by the American Law Institute's (ALI; 1962) Model Penal Code, which included the recommendation that a defendant's level of culpability should be measured by an examination of mental state with respect to all elements of the offense (p. 24). The drafters proposed that liability be assigned depending on whether the offender acted *purposely, knowingly, recklessly,* or *negligently.* Purposeful intent, the highest level of criminal intent, was posited to occur when the offender had the conscious object of committing the act or causing a particular result. Intent that is knowing involves awareness by the perpetrator of the nature of the criminal conduct or its circumstances. By contrast, a reckless intent occurs when the offender consciously disregards the substantial and unjustifiable risks involved in the conduct, and a negligent intent exists when the actor should have been aware of the risk (p. 21).

The term "willfulness," which appears in a number of statute definitions of crimes, was proposed as an intent element corresponding to knowing intent (ALI, 1962, p. 22). In the Model Penal Code hierarchy of intent, specific intent, which involves the imputation of a positive subjective mental state, unlike negligence and possibly recklessness as well, most closely corresponds to purposeful and knowing intent (Melton et al., 1997). The drafters of the Model Penal Code proposed that negligence in any case roughly corresponds to the common law requirement of general intent (p. 23).

In theory, specific intent may be regarded as a higher-order or more seriously criminal purpose than general intent. Another way to understand the distinction is that general intent crimes are seen as those involving the simple intent to commit the illegal act itself, although that illegal act my be quite serious, such as a killing or rape. Persons convicted of general intent crimes should have been conscious of their actions and the expected results (Melton et al., 1997).

By contrast, specific intent crimes usually require the intent to achieve some additional result beyond the consequences of the general intent crime itself. Thus, in some jurisdictions, a person who breaks into a house is guilty of a general intent crime only (perhaps only trespass), whereas breaking and entering with the further intent of committing larceny would always be viewed as a specific intent offense. Similarly, a sexual assault would be a general intent crime in some jurisdictions, whereas breaking and entering with intent to rape, or assault with intent to rape, would be specific intent offenses. In the solitary case of the highest degree of murder, usually designated first-degree murder, specific intent consists of premeditation and deliberation, supposedly greater and more demanding intent elements than mere intent to kill or malice aforethought.

With the exception of first-degree murder, a specific intent offense may entail the actual accomplishment of some effect beyond that of the general intent crime, but it need not do so. The would-be rapist may be stopped before he actually perpetrates the rape, for instance. Theoretically, therefore, an assault or a burglary with intent to commit a rape that was never accomplished might be a more serious offense than the rape itself. In any event, this would seem to be an exception to the general prohibition against criminal sanctions for evil thoughts alone, an instance in which a conviction is possible when the act or actus reus is nothing more than would have been needed for a general intent offense and in which no separate actus reus is accomplished corresponding to the higher and further specific intent. Whether specific intent results in a completed act or not, the specific intent crime may be regarded as more serious than an included general intent offense, for example, in regard to the possible penalty. It is more serious specifically because of the enormity of the act intended.

In some jurisdictions, any crime that by statute incorporates an explicit intent, for example, assault with intent to commit murder, is on that account a specific intent offense. Crimes of larceny are typically viewed as specific intent offenses regardless of their circumstances or the nature and value of what is stolen. Larceny involves not merely unlawfully taking another's property, an act that may be nothing more than a general intent offense or even a misdemeanor as in "joyriding" or the unauthorized use of a vehicle. Larceny is unlawfully taking property with the further intent of carrying it away, converting it to one's own use, or otherwise depriving the owner of it (Black, 1979, pp. 792–793).

In any jurisdiction in which diminished capacity or mens rea defenses are permitted, the highest degree of homicide, usually called first-degree murder, is considered a specific intent crime. In fact, as seen in the discussion of legal developments in this area, much of the focus of case law in respect to diminished capacity has been on murder. In this instance, the specific intent consists of premeditation and deliberation. These elements, operationally unitary in the sense that both need to be present for a first-degree murder to be committed, are subject to somewhat different constructions in various jurisdictions. Generally, however, they refer respectively to plotting, contriving, planning, or thinking about the killing beforehand, and weighing and examining the reasons for and against a contemplated act or course of conduct, acts, or means (Black, 1979, p. 384).

With short-lived exceptions only in California, as discussed later, what is usually called second-degree murder, which requires malice aforethought but not premeditation and deliberation, has been regarded as a general intent offense that is not susceptible to a diminished capacity or mens rea defense. Despite its intuitive connotations of evil intent, malice survives in law as a mental element that is simply a term of art, a shorthand designation for one of a number of mental elements that would satisfy the requirements for a murder conviction, as opposed to a conviction of the lesser offenses of manslaughter or negligent homicide (Morse, 1979, 1984). The malice required for a second-degree murder conviction could involve the intent to kill, but it could also call for no more than the intent to cause great bodily harm, the willful and wanton disregard of risk to life, or simply the commission of another felony during which a homicide occurs (LaFave & Scott, 1972).

To recapitulate, specific intent offenses that potentially are open to a diminished capacity or mens rea defense are somewhat arbitrarily determined, but include at least premeditated and deliberated murder, larceny, and those offenses defined to explicitly incorporate some further intent.

ELABORATION OF DIMINISHED CAPACITY DOCTRINE IN CALIFORNIA

It is always theoretically possible for defendants charged with crimes to claim that they had been incapable of forming the required specific intent, such as premeditation and deliberation of a murder. These claims have always been rare, and like insanity pleas, they have been rarely successful. Legal developments in California may have encouraged more defendants to raise diminished capacity as a defense, even if in general the defense was seldom successful.

The development of mens rea doctrine, prior to the development of modern psychology with its complex hypotheses explaining human behavior and motivation, may be viewed by mental health professionals today as never incorporating more than primitive and simplistic commonsense conceptualizations of intent. Case law in this area did not invite deeper explorations of the dynamics of intentional conduct, such as its developmental origins or its expression of unconscious drives, or from a behavioral perspective, the individual's learning history. The law did not betray any particular concern about factors now ordinarily seen as inextricably involved in intentional conduct, such as mood and its biological concomitants, cognitive expectations, or learned attitudes in gauging whether a person was capable of criminal intent.

Arguably, much of what psychologists would see as pertinent in thinking about intent could be viewed as aspects of volition, but volitional factors constituting free will—the objective or subjective freedom of the individual to form intent and purpose—were not recognized as germane to mens rea. Besides those jurisdictions that employed an insanity test with a volitional prong—some variation of the irresistible impulse test—considerations of volition were judged relevant, if at all, only to the question of whether the actus reus requirement was met (Bonnie & Slobogin, 1980). Conduct that was compelled in some manner might deserve to be excused in some instances, but not because intentionality, conceived of as a purely cognitive process, had not been present or possible. In one view, the lack of volition in committing a crime negated not mens rea but rather the actus reus: There was no criminal act that required explanation (Dix, 1971; Erlinder, 1983). It followed from this strictly limited view of mens rea as an abstract cognitive function that the defense of diminished capacity, on the few occasions it might have been raised, would have involved little need for expert witnesses.

All of this changed over the course of about a quarter-century in California. The changes wrought there and copied elsewhere eventually produced a backlash of public outrage engendered by the deeply unpopular results in certain notorious cases. However, the effects of those changes continued to resonate for a time in jurisdictions outside California.

As was the case with several other states, California dealt with the dilemma of protecting the rights of the accused to avoid self-incrimination when the accused was also raising the insanity defense—an affirmative defense requiring the commission of the crime and usually an acknowledgment by the defendant of having committed the act—by bifurcating the trial in such a case into a guilt phase and an insanity phase. In this way, a determination would be made that the defendant was the one who committed an act before it would be determined if the defendant was culpable or criminally responsible. Of course, some thought, a determination of guilt intrinsically involves a determination that not only the actus reus but also the mens rea were present. Because insanity theoretically negates mens rea, it is natural to ask how evidence of mental abnormality can be excluded from trial at the guilt phase. If guilt as well as criminal responsibility in this sense is mental as well as physical, expert testimony about mental disorder ought to be permitted at the guilt phase. This was the conclusion reached by the California Supreme Court in 1949 in *People v. Wells*, and it made possible a series of decisions expanding the opportunities to provide expert testimony about diminished capacity.

Wells was a convict serving a sentence in a California penitentiary when he allegedly assaulted a prison guard. As this was a capital offense at the time, namely, assault with malice aforethought, at the guilt phase of trial Wells's defense tried to introduce evidence on the question of whether he had entertained malice. Defense experts intended to testify that Wells was under tension resulting from fears for his own safety at the time he assaulted the guard. In line with bifurcation rules, this testimony was barred by the trial court as inadmissible. On appeal of Wells's conviction, the California Supreme Court ultimately held that evidence of Wells's claimed abnormality was material to the question of his guilt and that it had been an error to exclude this evidence from the guilt phase.

By breaching the separation between guilt and culpability, *Wells* influenced the further course of diminished capacity law in California. The real impetus to introduce more frequent testimony about mental state into determinations of guilt, rather than reserving them solely for determinations of insanity, involved what was perceived as the inadequacy of the insanity test itself (Morse, 1979). At the time, California was using the century-old M'Naghten Rule (1843), which holds that to establish insanity it must be proven that at the time of the act, and as a result of mental disease or defect, the individual did not know what he or she was doing or did not know that it was wrong. This seemingly all-or-nothing, black-or-white, and wholly cognitive test of insanity seemed to some to make no allowance for other important mental considerations, such as volition, the ability to resist committing an act disturbed individuals might recognize as wrong but that their mental disorder impelled them to do.

Many felt that the M'Naghten standard for insanity was far too narrow a test to provide a just and humane result in many cases of obviously disordered individuals. The expansion of diminished capacity into areas it had never gone before, in California or anywhere else, seemed apt to fill the gap. As the court admitted in *People v. Henderson* (1963), diminished capacity became the means by which the courts could ameliorate the harshness of the M'Naghten standard that had been imposed by the legislature; the approach came to be seen as the ameliorative defense. Its first application came in the case of *People v. Gorshen* (1959).

Nicholas Gorshen was a Russian immigrant and a longshoreman. He reportedly came to work one day in an intoxicated condition and was sent home by his foreman. He took offense and fought with the man before he went home. He then got a gun, came back to the docks, and shot his foreman dead in front of witnesses, including police officers. In Gorshen's trial for first-degree murder, the noted psychiatrist Bernard Diamond testified on Gorshen's behalf that he was a long-standing schizophrenic who had been hallucinating for years. When his foreman told him to leave work, Diamond testified, Gorshen's precarious psychological equilibrium was threatened, and he viewed the demand as an attack on his manhood. As a result, Diamond offered, Gorshen had been compelled to retaliate against the source of the threat. Diamond did not dispute Gorshen's own admission that he had consciously intended to shoot his foreman, but he testified that in any case, Gorshen did not possess the mental state required for malice aforethought or anything implying intention, premeditation, or deliberation.

No testimony rebutting Diamond's testimony that Gorshen was schizophrenic was offered, but Gorshen was determined by the judge in a bench trial to be sane under the M'Naghten standard, and he was found guilty of first-degree murder. On appeal, the California Supreme Court affirmed Gorshen's conviction but added that the expert testimony that Gorshen would have been incapable of the malice required for murder—testimony considered but rejected by the trial court—had been properly admitted at trial. The court did not provide a clear definition of what malice consisted of, but by its ruling it appeared to open the door to the redefinition of malice that had been offered by the expert witness, one that called for a volitional component (Dix, 1971) previously absent not only from the concept of malice but from the insanity test. The California Supreme Court held that malice exists when an individual commits an act intentionally, of his or her own free will, rather than as a result of an abnormal compulsion. The way seemed clear to provide greater consideration of subjective psychological factors in guilt determinations. If traditional mens rea concepts such as insanity and malice did not permit relevant expert testimony on mental abnormality, those intent elements might be so construed as to permit a judge or jury to weigh the defendant's ability to morally assess or control his or her conduct (Morse, 1979). This process was clearly at work in the next significant case of this type considered by the court, *People v. Wolff* (1964).

Dennis Wolff, charged with murder, was if anything more obviously disturbed than Gorshen, yet like him, he did not seem to qualify for an insanity verdict under the M'Naghten standard. Wolff was only 15 years old when he allegedly developed a plan to kidnap girls and bring them home for sex. For the plan to work, however, he needed to get his mother out of the way. After one failed attempt, he succeeded in this by beating her to death with an ax handle. At his trial, expert testimony was heard that Wolff was schizophrenic and legally insane, but the jury convicted him of first-degree murder.

As in the Gorshen case 5 years earlier, the California Supreme Court in *Wolff* upheld the jury's finding of sanity, but it boldly held that Wolff had not been capable of the mental processes needed to commit first-degree murder, namely, premeditation. It was plain that Wolff had carefully prepared the homicide and had applied considerable thought to it. However, the court held that more was required for premeditation than Wolff, psychotic as he was, had been capable of. The defendant must have been able, the court ruled, to "maturely and meaningfully reflect" on the enormity of the offense contemplated. Accordingly, the court found that Wolff had been guilty only of second-degree murder.

In essence, the court had declared that it was not enough that a defendant engaged in what might resemble commonsense conceptions of premeditation and deliberation. Rather, the "quantum of his moral turpitude and depravity" needed to be ascertained. At issue was not the simple apparent fact of intent, but the quality of whatever intent had been formed. Though mens rea might otherwise be apparent, it could be negated by a finding that the defendant was morally incapable of true intent. This naturally begged the question of just what the real element looked like, but it opened the door to an expanded consideration of expert testimony on the issue.

The growing trend seemed to validate the hope that Bernard Diamond (1961), the defense expert in *Gorshen*, had expressed, that diminished capacity might become a vehicle for the introduction of a richer, expanded view of the role that mental health issues play in criminal behavior. With this new approach, he wrote, society could no longer evade its obligations to provide the defendant with therapeutic help, because the defendant would now officially be labeled as sick and the courts would have publicly acknowledged the need for treatment. Indeed, as time went on and new developments took place, diminished capacity was viewed as having developed into a "finely honed instrument" for the defense (Bird & Vanderet, 1972). Defense attorneys could imagine how such factors as the stress of being a prisoner could be introduced to mitigate guilt (Marx, 1977).

In the decade following *Wolff,* an expanded view of intent elements continued to hold sway in California. *People v. Conley* (1966) saw the *Wolff* logic regarding premeditation applied to the question of malice aforethought. William Conley allegedly had been drinking heavily for a number of days when he killed his estranged lover and her husband. He claimed later that he had no intention to kill anyone and had no memory of having done so. Expert testimony was heard that the amount of alcohol Conley had consumed would have impaired the judgment of an ordinary person. A psychologist testified that in fact Conley was in a dissociative state at the time of the homicides and could not function normally. Arguing that diminished capacity could negate the malice aforethought required for murder, the defense requested that the jury also be instructed that it might find Conley guilty of voluntary manslaughter; this motion was denied, and the jury returned a two-count conviction of first-degree murder.

On appeal, the California Supreme Court reversed Conley's convictions because of the trial court's denial of a motion to instruct the jury on manslaughter in addition to murder. What amounted to a redefinition of malice that had started in *Wells* and continued in *Gorshen* was elaborated on. For malice to have been present, the court held, the person must have been able to comprehend the duty to govern his or her actions in accord with the duty imposed by law. This refinement of malice stood in contrast to more traditional formulations. Although still cast in terms of mens rea, malice under *Conley* actually became a mini-insanity test, a cognitive-affective version of the M'Naghten standard (Morse, 1979). In the process, diminished capacity seemed to have succeeded to some extent to ameliorate the perceived harshness and strictures of the legislated insanity test.

In 1973, in *People v. Cantrell,* the California Supreme Court ruled that irresistible impulse, not recognized in California as a test of legal insanity, could not serve as a complete defense to a crime. For just that reason, however, the court held, a defendant claiming diminished capacity must be permitted at the guilt phase of trial to show by competent evidence that the act alleged was a result of irresistible impulse that had been caused by mental disease. Such testimony, the court held, could bear on issues of intent to kill and malice aforethought.

The continued recognition of a role for volition that was evident in *Conley* and *Cantrell* reached a new point in *People v. Poddar* (1974). Prosenjit Poddar may be familiar to many as the killer of Tatiana Tarasoff and thus a subject of the leading case on the duty of therapists to protect third parties endangered by their patients, *Tarasoff v. Regents of the University of California* (1976). Poddar was an Indian naval architecture student who was rejected by Tarasoff, a fellow student to whom he had formed an attachment. After a period of despondency and emotional distress, during which he reportedly disclosed to a university counseling psychologist that he intended to kill his girlfriend when she returned from abroad, Poddar fatally stabbed Tarasoff after shooting at her with a pellet gun. At trial, expert witnesses presented Poddar as schizophrenic, although prosecution rebutted this testimony. The jury failed to find Poddar legally insane and instead convicted him of first-degree murder. Citing its rulings in *Conley* and *Cantrell,* however, the California Supreme Court overturned the conviction and ruled that Poddar could be convicted at most of voluntary manslaughter unless it could be established that he was both aware of his duty to act within the law and was not incapable of so doing.

Sweeping aside what was thought to be a bar against using a mens rea or diminished capacity approach as a complete defense to a crime, the California Supreme Court ruled in *People v. Wetmore* (1978) that evidence of mental disorder could be used at the guilt phase of trial to negate any mental element even if outright acquittal might result. Wetmore, a chronic psychiatric patient, was charged with burglary after he broke into an apartment with what he claimed was the belief that the apartment was his. As in many other cases of burglary, or breaking and entering with larcenous intent, if the intent to commit larceny could be negated, there would be no lesser included felony of which the defendant could be convicted.

DENOUEMENT: AN END TO CALIFORNIA'S VERSION OF DIMINISHED CAPACITY

In retrospect, such significant changes in the way mental guilt was assessed could not have gone unchallenged forever. California, ever a trend-setter, was a battleground in which advances in the use of diminished capacity—advances that influenced practice in other jurisdictions—were followed by a retrenchment that proved equally influential. The logical results of an expanded or enriched diminished capacity doctrine by the California Supreme Court galvanized opposition and contributed to its demise. As with the closely contemporaneous events regarding the insanity defense following John Hinckley's 1982 acquittal by reason of insanity for his attempt to assassinate President Ronald Reagan, larger social trends were involved in the changes that reversed diminished capacity law.

Certainly, the new view of diminished capacity had its critics even before worse came to worst. Dix (1971) detailed a variety of objections that had been raised to this approach. Among them were fears that the successful use of diminished capacity would yield shorter prison terms for convicted criminals, particularly killers, and that some individuals would win outright acquittal by means of this defense, with no protection for society, even the psychiatric hospitalization mandated for those found legally insane. In a prescient manner, Dix cited fears by some that the issues involved in the new diminished capacity defense were too complex for judges and juries to understand and that by default the question would be turned over to expert witnesses, whose testimony would be admitted despite its unreliability. Echoing this concern, Morse (1979) asserted that California's diminished capacity approach had not provided any clear standards for judges and juries to apply. It was unclear from the *Wolff* decision, for instance, just how to determine whether a murderer's premeditation and deliberation were mature and meaningful.

The growing and crucial role of the psychiatric expert witness in determinations of diminished capacity was in many ways the crux of the problem seen by critics of the expanded diminished capacity defense. Dix (1971) complained that the admission of expert testimony on this issue was an error. The *Wells* decision, he held, leaped from a finding that evidence of psychological abnormality had some logical relevance to the question of guilt to a conclusion that such evidence was therefore admissible. A critical analysis of the way psychiatric testimony was actually used in these cases, Dix offered, indicated that the testimony never actually addressed the question of whether or not some state of mind required for imposition of criminal liability was absent, but instead supported an entirely different claim, namely, that both the defendant's actions and state of mind were the result of unconscious influences. In the view of Dix and others, citing psychological abnormality as a way of disproving intent was a legal fiction that simply permitted a psychological explanation for the behavior to be offered in court. Dix saw this as placing the psychiatric expert witness in an unfair position, playing a ritualistic role in the proceedings and mouthing the magic words that would permit the court to mitigate the defendant's guilt.

Arenella (1977) viewed the California developments similarly. The *Wolff* decision, he wrote, shifted the focus away from the question of whether a defendant entertained the requisite intent to the question of how and why the defendant entertained it. In this manner, diminished capacity, ostensibly an investigation of a defendant's capacity for intent, had become a disguised version of diminished responsibility, an entirely different project. Where diminished responsibility is used, as in Europe, mental abnormality simply mitigates or reduces the level of culpability of a criminal, but it does not do so by seeking to disprove the defendant's ability to form some intent element. If diminished capacity were employed honestly, as the mens rea doctrine it purported to be, Arenella argued, it would involve only evidence that actually had a bearing on whether requisite intent was missing, and it would rarely serve any purpose not already served by the insanity defense.

Morse (1979, 1984) agreed that diminished capacity had come to be treated as diminished responsibility. Indeed, he pointed out, there is no easy way for psychiatric testimony that is strictly confined to questions of mens rea to rule out or negate the capacity of the defendant to form those intent elements. Morse (1984) saw no danger in a strictly applied mens rea approach to diminished capacity, which was unlikely to benefit the defendant in any case. Correctly anticipating the rulings by federal courts in the coming decade, Morse asserted that a strict mens rea defense, challenging the prosecution's claim that all requisite intent elements were present at the time of a crime, is constitutionally protected.

It is not apparent, of course, that the essential rationale behind the progressive expansion of diminished capacity doctrine in California was the provision of greater or more comprehensive psychiatric or psychological explanations for criminal behavior. Nor is it apparent that the increased involvement of mental health experts in court proceedings was seen as desirable, although that was what was happening during this time in respect to a variety of legal issues. The apparent rationale for the expanded diminished capacity approach was the perception that existing statutes inadequately considered the influence of mental abnormality, and that the harshness of the M'Naghten insanity standard in particular needed to be ameliorated.

To the extent that the California diminished capacity approach was based on this perceived need, it was deprived of its rationale when the California Supreme Court, in *People v. Drew* (1974), decided it could bypass the legislature and ruled that the ALI (1962) Model Penal Code insanity test could be used as the insanity test in California. Always before, despite its perception that the M'Naghten standard was inadequate, the court had been unwilling to invade the province of the legislature and set a judicial test of insanity, and its rulings from *Gorshen* on seemed aimed at avoiding any need to do so. The ALI insanity standard differs from M'Naghten in two ways: It provides a volitional as well as a cognitive test of culpability, and its advisedly ambiguous use of the terms "substantial" and "appreciate" grants considerable discretion in determining whether a particular defendant was insane. Under the ALI standard, Gorshen, Wolff, Poddar, and even Conley might have been found legally insane, obviating the need for tortured redefinitions of mens rea requirements.

With the *Drew* decision, the continued relevance of the diminished capacity ameliorative approach was called into question (Waddell, 1979). But that by itself did not bring about the demise of the approach. It was a defense that had outgrown its original mission and had taken on a life of its own. Then, with the Dan White murder trial, the diminished capacity defense went from being well known to lawyers to being notorious with the public, and deeply troubling. It cannot be a coincidence that this reaction took place during a period of general questioning of the expanded use of the insanity defense itself, questioning that following the Hinckley trial in 1982 culminated in an unprecedented wave of insanity reform legislation in Congress and in state legislatures around the country.

Daniel White was 32 years old when he shot and killed San Francisco mayor George Moscone and an openly homosexual city supervisor, Harvey Milk, on November 27, 1978. As later reported by a defense psychiatric expert (Blinder, 1981–1982), White was one of eight children of a firefighter and was himself a firefighter and a former police officer when he decided to run for a post as city supervisor in 1977. After a hard-fought campaign, he was elected to represent his working-class district, but he encountered personal financial problems. After resigning in early November 1978, he reconsidered and asked Mayor Moscone to reappoint him to the supervisor post. Reportedly, Moscone first promised White his support and then withdrew it. On the morning of November 27, White went to City Hall with a loaded handgun and 10 extra rounds of ammunition. He avoided security personnel and metal detectors by entering City Hall through a ground-floor window. White confronted the mayor and shot him four times before reloading his gun. He then encountered Harvey Milk, whom he believed was involved in the mayor's decision not to reappoint him. He shot Milk five times, then left the building, retreated to a church, and ultimately surrendered to police.

Many questioned the remarkable outcome of Dan White's murder trial and how it could be that the killings of two prominent local political figures resulted in a jury verdict only of voluntary manslaughter. There were suggestions (Szasz, 1981–1982) of a politically motivated collusion between the defense and the surprisingly ineffective prosecution, as well as the influence of antihomosexual prejudice. In any event, the ostensible justification for the jury finding seemed to be provided by expert witness testimony on diminished capacity.

The press seized on a point in the trial when defense expert, Dr. Martin Blinder, testified that White was a manic-depressive whose depressive episodes, one of which he said led to the homicides, were exacerbated by his bingeing on "junk food—Twinkies, cupcakes, and Cokes" (Szasz, 1981–1982). Reporters immediately ridiculed diminished capacity as the "Twinkie defense," although the actual effect on the jury verdict of this part of the testimony is uncertain. The jury heard from several defense experts that White had been incapable of forming the intent elements required for first-degree murder, or even second-degree murder.

A defense attorney asked Dr. Donald Lunde on direct examination if there had been premeditation in White's act of killing, despite the evidence that in various ways White seemed at least to have prepared to commit homicide. Echoing the language of the *Wolff* ruling 15 years earlier, Lunde testified that not only had White not premeditated and deliberated the killings, but because of his mental condition—severe depression and a compulsive personality—White was not capable of any sort of mature and meaningful reflection (Szasz, 1981–1982). Dr. George Solomon (1981–1982), also testifying for the defense, similarly testified that to a reasonable degree of medical certainty, White had lacked the capacity to maturely and meaningfully premeditate and deliberate. Reflecting the language of *Conley,* Lunde also testified about the question of malice, declaring that the last thing White was capable of doing was thinking clearly about his "obligations to society, other people, the law and so on" (Szasz, 1981–1982). Blinder (1981–1982) asserted that premeditation and deliberation both require "reasonably clear thinking" and that at the time of the offense White "no longer had his wits about him."

As a footnote to this case, Dan White was sentenced to the maximum term of confinement for voluntary manslaughter and was released on parole when he became eligible in 1984. He quietly returned to San Francisco, where he committed suicide in October 1985.

INSANITY DEFENSE REFORM AND THE FATE OF DIMINISHED CAPACITY

The controversy raised by the Dan White trial contributed to efforts to abolish the diminished capacity defense in California. The verdict was widely viewed as an outrage and an offense to common sense. Closely contemporaneous with the White trial, the California Supreme Court in *People v. Wetmore* (1978), as discussed earlier, conceded that diminished capacity could conceivably result in outright acquittal when the crime charged, such as Wetmore's burglary, permitted no conviction for any lesser included felony. The court in *Wetmore* indicated the need for legislative clarification of diminished capacity procedures (Morse & Cohen, 1982). What the legislature ultimately delivered was nothing short of a repudiation of the entire diminished capacity approach pioneered by the court in the previous three decades.

California Senate Bill 54 (1981a) reversed judicial redefinitions of intent elements and in effect codified the older, once-superseded traditional forms of premeditation, deliberation, and malice. The legislation provided that it would no longer be necessary to prove that a defendant maturely and meaningfully reflected on the depravity of an act to find that a killing was done with premeditation and deliberation. It provided that it would not be necessary to a finding of malice to determine that the defendant was aware of an obligation to act within the body of laws governing society.

In a related development, California Senate Bill 590 (1981b) aimed to restrict the scope of expert testimony in criminal cases by providing that psychiatrists and psychologists would not be presumed to be able to determine sanity or insanity. Finally, a ballot initiative, Proposition 8, entitled "The Victims' Bill of

Rights," was approved by California voters in 1982 and "abolished" diminished capacity as a defense at trial (Kraus, 1983); it also replaced the court-imposed ALI insanity test with a modified but more restrictive M'Naghten test (Steadman et al., 1993).

The Hinckley trial, which resulted in the acquittal by reason of insanity of a would-be assassin of a U.S. president, may well be the defining moment of the previous century's treatment of mental disorder at the time of offense. It is uncannily similar in its impact to Daniel M'Naghten's acquittal 140 years before, after his attempt to assassinate the prime minister of Great Britain. In both instances, an acquittal at trial resulted in public outrage and in restrictive reform. The Dan White trial, in a smaller way, was a defining moment in the brief and more parochial history of diminished capacity in California. It seemed in many ways to exemplify all that was wrong with an overly broad consideration of mental abnormality in adjudicating guilt for criminal acts. Still, it is apparent that at least with respect to diminished capacity and reform measures, larger social forces were at work. Efforts to rescind what was seen as an overly generous treatment of mentally disordered offenders in California were already in train by the time White committed his homicides, just as similar efforts were under way in other states before Hinckley shot President Reagan.

A get-tough attitude in California had already yielded changes in sentencing procedures and provisions for the commitment of insanity acquitees by 1978, and these had begun to yield results. Indeed, a downturn in the numbers of insanity pleas in California preceded the return of the M'Naghten standard to that state and reflected the changes already implemented that made insanity a less attractive defense option (Steadman et al., 1993). That the shift in California from ALI to M'Naghten did not produce any demonstrable effects in either the rate of insanity pleas or the rate of successful insanity pleas (Steadman et al., 1993) suggests that any notion that the strictures of M'Naghten needed to be ameliorated, by an expanded diminished capacity option or by a liberalized insanity test, may have been mistaken in the first place.

In any event, diminished capacity was tarred with the same brush as was insanity during the wave of reform legislation that took place in the late 1970s and early 1980s. Aside from the decisive repudiation in California of its unique approach to diminished capacity, what may have been the strongest blow to an expanded mens rea rationale of diminished capacity as diminished responsibility was delivered by the federal Insanity Defense Reform Act (IDRA; 1984), which responded most immediately to the Hinckley case.

Along with its elimination of the volitional prong of the ALI insanity test then in use in federal courts, its modification of the cognitive prong, its shifting of the burden of proof from prosecution to defense, and its requirement that insanity be proven by clear and convincing evidence, IDRA (1984) sought to eliminate the diminished capacity defense. After delineating the conditions under which a severe mental disease or defect could result in the affirmative defense of insanity, Congress determined that "mental disease or defect does not otherwise constitute a defense."

In conjunction with the passage of IDRA in 1984, the Federal Rules of Evidence were revised to restrict the scope of expert testimony. The revised rule states: "No expert witness testifying with respect to the mental state or condition of a defendant in a criminal case may state an opinion or inference as to whether the defendant did or did not have the mental state or condition constituting an element of the crime charged or of a defense thereto." Rather, "such ultimate issues are matters for the trier of fact alone" (Federal Rules of Evidence, 704(b)). This restriction was intended to limit testimony by expert witnesses to the presentation and explanation of their diagnoses, such as whether the defendant had a severe mental disease or defect and what the characteristics of such a condition may have been (Senate Report, 1984).

Given subsequent federal court rulings, it appears that Congress actually failed to do more than eliminate the possibility of an affirmative California-style diminished capacity defense. As Morse (1984) asserted at the time, the mens rea diminished capacity partial defense, as opposed to the affirmative California defense, is constitutionally protected from legislative reform. But if Congress did nothing more than that, it may have done enough. The expanded diminished capacity defense, already sinking under its own weight in California, was clearly precluded in the federal jurisdictions, even while federal district and appeals courts in most cases affirmed Morse's view that a strict mens rea inquiry, and the defendant's right to dispute prosecution's claim that an act was done with criminal intent, could never be killed.

In two instances (*U.S. v. White*, 1985; *U.S. v. Hood*, 1988), federal circuit courts of appeals, the First and the Fourth, interpreted IDRA as precluding specific psychiatric testimony directed solely at negating an element of intent and establishing that a defendant lacked requisite mens rea, rather than that the defendant was insane. All of the appellate courts that considered the matter (including eventually the First and the Fourth Circuit Courts of Appeal), however, drew the distinction between a strict mens rea approach to diminished capacity and the affirmative defense diminished responsibility approach, à la California, which all federal appeals courts unanimously regarded as having been abolished by IDRA. All of them indicated that IDRA did not establish a general rule that evidence of a mental disorder is always inadmissible except in relation to insanity.

In *U.S. v. Frisbee* (1985), a U.S. district court in California found that a defendant could submit psychiatric testimony in support of his contention that he did not have the specific intent required for first-degree murder. The defendant reportedly was a chronic alcohol abuser who suffered from periodic blackouts or seizures and from amnesia. However, the court also held that the expert witnesses could not state an opinion or inference as to whether the defendant did or did not form the specific intent to kill at the time of the murder. The court reasoned that the IDRA provision that mental disease or defect does not constitute a defense apart from insanity was not intended to limit the admissibility of evidence negating specific intent. Rather, it held that this provision was aimed at eliminating any affirmative defense other than insanity in which mental abnormality is offered in exculpation, as an excuse for an offense. The court drew the distinction between the defense of diminished capacity, which is properly aimed at negating the presence of intent elements, and a diminished responsibility approach, which does not negate elements or deny guilt, but instead merely mitigates guilt.

Citing *Frisbee* and the Senate Report on the change of the Federal Rules of Evidence, the District of Columbia District Court in *U.S. v. Gold* (1987) found that the reform measures did not preclude defense-offered testimony on the capacity of the defendant to formulate specific intent. In a similar way, the Third Circuit Court of Appeals in *U.S. v. Pohlot* (1987) overturned a district court ruling that prevented a defendant from introducing any evidence of mental abnormality. It held that both the wording and the legislative history of IDRA "leave no doubt that Congress intended . . . to bar only alternative 'affirmative defenses' that 'excuse' misconduct but evidence that disproves an element of the crime itself," and that admitting psychiatric evidence to negate mens rea does not constitute a defense but only negates an element of the offense and is therefore not barred.

The court drew the distinction between diminished capacity—focused on the presence of intent elements—and diminished responsibility, which it identified with the California case law. It presented mens rea as an element that is generally established satisfactorily if by any showing of purposeful activity, regardless of the activity's psychological origins. By contrast, the court held that testimony hoping to explain the behavior may mislead a jury. In *Pohlot,* while affirming the right of the defendant to present expert testimony on the question of mens rea—testimony on both the presence or absence of intent and the defendant's capacity to formulate intent—the court barred testimony concerning the defendant's subconscious motivation in attempting to hire a professional killer to murder his wife. The court regarded that testimony as pertaining not to the strict question of mens rea but to the question of why the intent was formed. Regarding evidence bearing on how meaningful the defendant's understanding was of his actions and their consequences, the court wrote, "We often act intending to accomplish the immediate goal of our activity, while not fully appreciating the consequences of our acts. But purposeful activity is all the law requires."

The Ninth Circuit Court of Appeals reached a similar conclusion the following year in *U.S. v. Twine* (1988). Agreeing with the courts in *Frisbee, Gold* and *Pohlot,* it held that IDRA did not abolish the diminished capacity defense as such. However, after finding that the district court judge had considered and was unpersuaded by the defendant's diminished capacity defense, it affirmed Twine's conviction for making telephone and mail threats to kidnap and injure. Similarly, in 1988 the Eighth Circuit Court of Appeals in *U.S. v. Bartlett* held that IDRA did not render inadmissible psychiatric testimony tending to show that the defendant was incapable of forming the requisite intent.

In 1989, the Ninth Circuit, following its decision the previous year in *Twine,* ruled in *U.S. v. Brown* that evidence of mental defense offered to show that the defendant lacked the specific intent to commit first-degree murder could not be excluded on the basis of IDRA. The Sixth Circuit in *U.S. v. Newman* (1989) made a similar ruling in a case focusing on a defendant's claim that alcoholism produced a chronic brain syndrome that precluded the formulation of sufficient mens rea for a crime of transporting stolen property. While upholding the defendant's conviction, the court in that case held that both insanity and diminished capacity are permissible defenses under IDRA.

The following year, the Eleventh Circuit Court of Appeals made the same finding in vacating a conviction for drug offenses in *U.S. v. Cameron* (1990). It held that despite a "semantic war of labels," both Congress and the courts had recognized a distinction between evidence of psychological impairment that supports an affirmative defense and evidence that simply negates an element of the offense charged. Testimony that helps the trier of fact determine the defendant's specific state of mind with regard to actions at the time the alleged offense was committed does not constitute an affirmative defense, but goes instead to the question of whether the prosecution has met its burden of proving all of the essential elements of the crime.

Continuing this chain of findings, the District of Columbia Circuit Court reached a similar conclusion in *U.S. v. Childress* (1995), a case in which a psychologist had been prevented from testifying at trial that the defendant, facing drug conspiracy charges, was in effect mentally retarded. The court held that although the trial court would need to determine whether the intended expert testimony was sufficiently grounded in science to warrant its use in the courtroom, psychological testimony not intended to establish insanity would be admissible providing it was aimed not at providing an insanity-like excuse for illegal conduct, but at addressing the question of whether the defendant had entertained the specific intent alleged, namely, conspiratorial understanding and purpose.

In 1997, the First Circuit Court of Appeals revisited this matter in *U.S. v. Schneider*, reaching the same conclusion as other appellate courts had done. The defendant in that case had been convicted of multiple counts of mail and wire fraud. Testimony was rejected from a medical doctor and a psychiatrist that would have identified the defendant's judgment as impaired by misprescribed and overprescribed drugs and by chemical dependency and Major Depression with probable mania. The proposed testimony, which would not have gone to demonstrate insanity, was rejected by the trial judge as both irrelevant to the task of negating intent and misleading.

The court of appeals agreed that the testimony would have been of only limited relevance and could easily mislead the jury into thinking that the defendant's mental condition amounted to insanity or ameliorated the offense. The court held that a defendant seeking to present evidence of a mental condition short of legal insanity must show that the evidence is relevant to the requisite intent that is at issue, and that its probative valued is not substantially outweighed by confusion or delay, and that if the evidence comes in by way of expert testimony, it is scientifically reliable and helpful to the jury (*Schneider*).

As indicated by *Childress* and *Schneider*, it is one thing for the courts to acknowledge the legal viability of expert testimony on the question of whether the defendant was able to form specific intent or actually did so, and another to find a sound scientific basis for any such testimony. Indeed, a consideration of actual cases indicates that it is most difficult to marshal the clinical evidence needed to support an opinion that the defendant actually had diminished capacity. As Morse (1984) pointed out, if the mens rea approach is applied strictly, and is not simply the vehicle for a proposed excuse, it is unlikely to be of any benefit to the defendant who seeks to use it. If the assumption of sanity is hard to rebut, it is far more difficult to establish that the intent for a crime that appears to have been committed could not have been formed, or if it could have been formed, was not.

It may have been some sense of the great difficulty associated with a strictly applied mens rea defense that encouraged several states in the years surrounding the Hinckley verdict and IDRA to substitute it for insanity, a defense they abolished. Although each of these states ostensibly retained a mental health defense, if strictly applied it is a defense that would avail a defendant little, even in cases of gross mental disorder or disability. The states do not need to provide an insanity defense, or any affirmative defense, but a substitute defense focusing on mens rea elements has been criticized as not fairly responding to the influence that mental disorder actually has on criminal responsibility (Morse, 1999).

Montana was the first state to abolish the insanity defense, in 1979, providing instead for consideration by the court of "whether the defendant had, at the time that the offense was committed, a particular state of mind that is an essential of the offense" and that a defendant's inability "to appreciate the criminality of . . . behavior or to conform the . . . behavior to the requirements of the law" would be considered only at sentencing (Montana Code, 1979, 46-14-101). Idaho abolished its insanity test in 1982, declaring that a "mental condition shall not be a defense to any charge of criminal conduct," even while providing that "nothing herein is intended to prevent the admission of expert evidence on the issue of any state of mind which is an element of the offense" (Idaho Statutes, 1982, 18-207).

In 1990, Utah abolished its insanity defense, declaring, "It is a defense to a prosecution . . . that the defendant, as a result of mental illness, lacked the mental state required as an element of the offense charged," and that "mental illness is not otherwise a defense, but may be evidence of special mitigation reducing the level of a criminal homicide or attempted criminal homicide" (Utah Code, 1990, 76-2-305). Kansas abolished insanity in 1995, providing instead that the only mental state defense is that "the defendant, as a result of mental disease or defect lacked the mental state required as an element of the offense charged" (Kansas Statute, 1995, 22-321).

If the intention of the states abolishing insanity was to reduce the number of insanity acquittals, especially in states with such small populations and already small numbers of successful insanity pleas, it might have been anticipated that a drastic change of the standard for considering mental health evidence would not necessarily produce the desired results. Indeed, in Utah, a study of acquittals due to mental state at time of offense indicated that there were as many in the 2 years following abolition of the traditional insanity defense (seven) as there were during the 9 years preceding the reform (Heinbecker, 1986, cited in Steadman et al., 1993). This is not evidence that the installation of a mens rea test as a substitute for insanity resulted in a greater openness to the impact of mental disorder on criminal conduct.

In Montana, appellate decisions upheld the convictions under the new standard of individuals diagnosed with significant disorders who would previously have had a potentially viable insanity defense (Stimpson, 1993). Systematic study (Steadman et al., 1993) found that with the use of the mens rea alternative to insanity in Montana, in the first 6 years after the law change only five persons in seven Montana counties that were studied succeeded in winning acquittal on the basis of mental state at time of offense, even though the rate at which criminal responsibility pleas were entered was not affected.

Steadman and his colleagues (1993) discovered that another avenue to achieve a result equivalent to acquittal may be to find the mentally disordered defendant incompetent to stand trial. Prior to insanity reform, most of those defendants who had been found incompetent to stand trial were later adjudicated legally insane. With that disposition no longer possible, the vast majority of those found incompetent after reform had their charges dismissed or deferred. Many of those individuals were civilly committed to the same hospital as those previously found not guilty by reason of insanity. Thus, the investigators found, a different legal provision was being used to produce virtually identical results.

To summarize, the general trend in the United States in the last quarter of the twentieth century of restricting the use of mental state evidence in criminal cases led to the curtailment of testimony that serves to explain an offender's mental state, yet leaving intact, in some places as the only option, a defendant's ability to introduce evidence to negate intent. In none of the statutory changes or case law concerning the newly restricted diminished capacity or mens rea approach, however, is there any guidance for the forensic examiner confronted with these questions—or for the judges and juries that must determine guilt or innocence.

FORENSIC EVALUATIONS OF DIMINISHED CAPACITY AND MENS REA

To an extent exceeding cases in which simply insanity is at issue, the forensic examiner who is asked to offer an opinion on the question of a defendant's capacity to formulate the specific intent for an alleged offense is hard put to offer anything relevant and material. Experts could explore how defendants' mental abnormality—if there is any or if any can plausibly be claimed—affected defendants' awareness of what they were doing, their moral evaluation of it, their anticipation of its effects, and the restricted range of alternatives they had to behaving as they did. Experts can, in other words, use the diminished capacity issue as an analogue of the insanity defense, substituting some relatively minor mental abnormality for the severe mental disease or defect required for insanity, thus seeking exculpation by explanation.

If no settled mental abnormality is apparent, the expert can advert to intoxication or even to stress. It is apparent from the history of diminished capacity and mens rea law, however, that this approach to demonstrating an inability to form requisite intent is irrelevant to the issues as the law has defined them.

Since the death of diminished capacity as diminished responsibility in California, there is no jurisdiction that specifically invites an expert witness to hazard a guess as to what psychological elements true criminal intent ought to involve, or what character flaws, attitudes, and emotional or chemical states can spoil what would otherwise constitute requisite mens rea.

Those experts who feel obliged to confine themselves to speaking of intent strictly in the terms laid down by the law often find themselves with little to say. The question of the capacity for intent is only theoretically, and not actually, separate from the question of whether intent was formed. Consideration of psychological factors ordinarily cannot lead to a conclusion that a defendant lacked the capacity to formulate intent for an offense the defendant appears to have committed. In many instances, unless the expert undertakes to redefine what "real" specific intent is—as in the case of the California Supreme Court's holding in *Wolff* that premeditation and deliberation in murder must involve mature and meaningful reflection on the enormity of the offense contemplated—there is not much left to be said.

There is a fundamental difference between a question of whether intent was formed or could have been formed on the one hand, and a question of the quality and characteristics of whatever intent was formed on the other. The law as it has developed is concerned only with the first question, and the expert attempting to address that question is not particularly helped by exploring the second question. The discovery that a mother was depressed and that the intent she formed to smother her child and relieve him of what she viewed as unbearable sorrows may explain how and why the killing took place, but it does not answer the question of whether she premeditated and deliberated a murder. From the point of view of the law's minimal and wholly cognitive construction of intent, the answer to that question—one solely for the trier of fact in any case—will not require any sophisticated analysis of the defendant's psychology or psychopathology. In most instances, if the perpetrator engaged in planning or preparation, especially if he or she announced an intention to kill, it will be impossible from a strict behavioral science viewpoint to refute a prosecution assertion that the person not only had the capacity to premeditate and deliberate a murder but also actually did so.

By comparison, in the usual case, competent opinion testimony on the issue of insanity is much more possible, and plausible. It is easier to demonstrate that as a result of mental disease or defect a defendant lacked the capacity to appreciate the wrongfulness of the conduct, for instance, than it is to demonstrate that a mental disorder, however severe it is, prevented the defendant from doing what he or she seems to have done. Insanity does not invite the expert witness or anyone else to determine precisely what offense was committed; insanity is an affirmative defense in which an exculpating excuse is offered for an offense that is not itself disputed. Yet, this is what a positive opinion with respect to diminished capacity implies: If the defendant could not form the requisite intent elements, those intent elements were not formed, and whatever offense was committed could not have been the specific intent crime charged.

The problem can be illustrated by a case similar to that of *Conley* involving a 40-year-old woman charged with two counts of first-degree murder. She was an alcoholic who had been divorced but never entirely separated from her alcoholic husband. He owned a bar. For nearly 24 hours before the slayings she had been drinking and talking with her ex-husband and his girlfriend in his tavern. Talk turned to the daughter the defendant shared with her ex-husband, the defendant's fitness as a mother, and whether it was right that she should retain custody of the child. Drunk and angry, the defendant left, drove home, and returned to the bar with a loaded shotgun in the trunk of her car. Once back inside, she resumed her hot exchange with her ex-husband's girlfriend, during which she was heard to threaten the woman's life. The defendant again left the bar, this time telling a barmaid on her way out to "hit the floor" when she came back and telling her that she would not like what she was going to do. The defendant presently returned to the locked door of the bar with the shotgun, and when her ex-husband and his girlfriend opened the door for her, she fatally shot each of them in rapid succession. She then drove back to her apartment, hid the shotgun, told her boyfriend to deny that she had gone out, and passed out on her bed.

It may fairly be asked whether any crime would have been committed but for the defendant's drunkenness, and even whether she would have been drunk had she not been an alcoholic. But these are not the questions that must be answered with respect to the diminished capacity question that was raised at trial. It may be fair for the jury to consider whether the defendant was guilty of first-degree murder, specifically whether anyone as thoroughly intoxicated as she was should be held to have engaged in true premeditation and deliberation. But it is not apparent how a mental health expert could answer that question, or at least do so any more validly than could a layperson. From the law's perspective, what looks like premeditation and deliberation, even if infused with alcohol, may be taken to be actual premeditation and deliberation. The jury in this instance agreed with the prosecutor that they were, and the defendant was convicted of first-degree murder.

So what is the responsible expert witness left to say when diminished capacity is raised? There are several options, depending on the circumstance of the offenses and the findings on examination.

TRUE DIMINISHED CAPACITY?

Although genuine cases of diminished capacity should not be expected to occur often, some individuals lack the capacity to form requisite intent and therefore must not have formed it. Because larceny, a specific intent offense, necessitates an understanding of the concept of property, some individuals may be so mentally retarded or otherwise limited cognitively that they are demonstrably incapable of larceny. Such a person walking off with merchandise from a store, for instance, may not have formed any intent to commit larceny because of an inability to comprehend the basic notion of property. Similarly, it may be possible to provide competent expert testimony that an individual is so demented as to be incapable of planning his or her next step, much less premeditating and deliberating a murder.

Although they are theoretically possible, there are probably reasons why it is rare to encounter these types of diminished capacity cases in practice.

Substantially retarded individuals who seem at first blush to be acting like thieves are unlikely to be charged with larceny. If they are, someone in a position to gate them into either the mental health or the criminal justice systems, including the police, prosecutor, or arraigning magistrate, is likely to have formed the impression that they were not so intellectually impaired in the first place. And those who most clearly have diminished capacity because of gross cognitive impairment are as unlikely to commit specific intent offenses as they are to engage in any other sophisticated, purposeful, and goal-directed behavior.

It is possible that in other, more subtle ways a defendant may evidence diminished capacity in the sense of having been incapable of formulating specific intent. A man with a history of epilepsy was charged with two counts of involuntary manslaughter with a motor vehicle and with failure to stop at a personal injury accident. His seizure disorder had never been fully controlled by medication, and he was restricted from driving. Despite this, he acknowledged that sometimes he did drive his mother's car. On one prior occasion, he had a seizure while driving and ran the car into a parked car at low speed; that collision did not cause any injuries and he was not prosecuted.

On this second occasion, however, the defendant, who reported no memory of the accident, was driving some miles over the speed limit in a residential area when he drove over the curb and onto the sidewalk and struck a sign before running into a group of people farther on. The collision killed two young children and injured their mother and grandfather. After the collision, the car driven by the defendant continued on the sidewalk until a tree stopped it. Witnesses reported that once the car was stopped, the rear wheels of the vehicle continued to spin; apparently the driver was continuing to depress the accelerator. A witness related that the defendant continued to sit behind the wheel with a dazed appearance and that he was not responsive to what the angry and excited witness shouted at him, asking him if he did not know what he had just done. That witness and others ran to the aid of the victims, lying injured some distance back down the street. While the victims were being attended to, the defendant was observed to get out of his car, look at the damage to the front end, get back in, and drive away.

Diminished capacity was raised in this man's defense. There was, aside from anything else, a question of whether he had been conscious of what he had done at the time he left the scene of the accident. Leaving the scene of a personal injury accident was viewed as a specific intent offense, as it required knowledge by the individual that he had caused personal injury to others. It appeared likely in that case that the defendant had one of his characteristic seizures at the time of the accident. From the vivid reports of witnesses, particularly one man who observed him just after the fatal collision, the defendant may have been experiencing postictal clouding of consciousness prior to driving off. It is not implausible that he did not comprehend the witness who demanded to know if he understood what he had just done; he was observed to be dazed and unresponsive. Postictal confusion may have prevented him from understanding what had just happened. He would not have remembered it if he had been having a seizure at the moment of the collision, and before he drove away he did not come back or even look toward the crowd gathered around the people he had struck down some distance behind him. Of course, this says nothing about his guilt for the more serious charges of involuntary manslaughter he also faced; those are general intent offenses for which his epilepsy was, if anything, an aggravating factor, as he drove a vehicle when he knew he was restricted from doing so and had even had a prior accident also brought about by a seizure.

ACTUALITY OF INTENT

In some instances, it is possible to offer testimony that pertains to the actuality of intent rather than the capacity for intent, which may be assumed or not in dispute. These are cases in which consideration of a defendant's psychological functioning and the circumstances of the alleged offense suggest a plausible factual alternative to the crime charged.

A case in point involved a man without prior criminal history who had been charged with breaking and entering a department store with intent to commit larceny. He claimed that he had entered the store late at night solely to find some anticonvulsant medication he was afraid he had dropped there the day before. On examination, he proved to be rigidly obsessive and hypochondriacally preoccupied; he had a history of mild neurological impairment. Over the years, he had persistently worried about the health of his daughter and of children in general.

The day before the break-in, he claimed, he had been in the department store cafeteria and had dropped a vial containing his pills. He thought that he had recovered all the pills, but he worried later that some were missing. He became worried, he said, that some child would come into the cafeteria, would pick up the pills, and would be harmed by them. He resolved to get back into the store and search for the pills. He called the now closed store, trying without success to talk with security officers. He assumed that if he called the police, they would simply tell him to wait until morning, but he worried that if he did he might be too late. Finally, with mounting anxiety, he forced a door open; a silent alarm brought the police, who found him in the store and arrested him. He had no store merchandise or other stolen property on his person. Police reported only that an ice machine in the cafeteria had been moved aside.

In this case, it is not likely, despite his history and odd presentation, that the defendant could be said to be incapable of larceny, unless that term were reinterpreted to mean something more than it ordinarily does. The real question in this case was not whether the defendant could have formed the intent to commit larceny, but whether he did so. Because the mens rea question cast in this light necessarily involves a judgment of what occurred in fact, it must in the final analysis be answered by the trier of fact. However, this is a case in which the results of a psychological evaluation lend plausibility to an alternative explanation of the behavior at issue, one that, if true, would mean that even if the defendant had entered the store illegally and might be subject to prosecution for that, he was not guilty of breaking and entering with intent to commit larceny.

It is uncertain to what extent expert testimony bearing on the actuality of intent rather than capacity to form intent would be admissible. In Michigan, for example, when that state was still permitting diminished capacity to be raised at trial (the state supreme court in *People v. Carpenter* effectively moved to abolish it in 2001), appellate decisions indicated that the only question to be considered was whether a defendant was incapable of forming specific intent, not whether he or she did so or not (*People v. Savoie,* 1984). The issue is unclear in federal jurisdictions. For example, the Third Circuit in *Pohlot* (1987), in noting that "evidence of mental abnormality may help indicate lack of mens rea even when a defendant is legally sane," appeared to suggest that such testimony would be acceptable. On the other hand, the revised Federal Rules of Evidence (Rule 704(b)) appears to preclude such testimony in declaring, "No expert witness . . . may state an opinion or inference as to whether the defendant did or did not have the mental state or condition constituting an element of the crime charged or of a defense thereto." The rule identifies these as "ultimate issues" that are matters for the trier of fact alone.

The forensic clinician faced with this issue in an actual case must be aware of the admissibility in that jurisdiction of opinion testimony concerning the actuality of intent. It is not recommended in any case that the expert offer an opinion on the ultimate issue and testify in effect that the defendant is or is not guilty. Opinions of this type exceed the scope of other expert opinions, such as whether a defendant is competent to stand trial or meets the insanity criteria, and should be objectionable to expert witnesses, if not to courts and lawyers. However, there are occasions when the contributions an expert can make to the deliberations by judge or jury may be valuable.

No Opinion or Negative Opinion: The Common Case?

A young man was arrested for armed robbery in the theft of narcotics from a drug store. There was evidence that he was a narcotics addict who had run out of both drugs and money and was in great need. Defense counsel also cited, in support of a claim that on account of his addiction he was not capable of forming the intent for armed robbery, that the man had been under stress from conflict with his wife, including an argument the very morning of the robbery.

In a great many cases in which diminished capacity is at issue, it is not reasonable to offer testimony other than that there is no good or plausible basis for concluding that the defendant was not capable of forming intent; that the defendant was capable of engaging in conscious, goal-directed behavior; and even that the behavior alleged is not consistent with loss of consciousness or inability to make and execute plans. In this instance, if the man was not capable of forming the intent to commit armed robbery—a marriage of assault and larceny—it is entirely unclear what he was doing in the drug store with a gun. If that was not an armed robber, who was that masked man? His narcotics addiction and his need for drugs serve only to explain why he formed the intent to commit a robbery; they do not negate the intent or make it something less than the requisite intent for this specific intent crime. The stress he cited does not do even that much. The defendant in this case provided the examiner with little to work with in terms of identifying a basis for a positive opinion on diminished capacity.

This case is an example of the sort of situation in which a positive opinion on diminished capacity does not seem possible. Most cases in which a defendant appears to meet the criteria to be considered legally insane also fall into this category. Because of the different approaches the two defenses take to the issue of mens rea, it will typically be easier to demonstrate, for example, that a defendant lacked substantial capacity to appreciate the wrongfulness of conduct than that the defendant could not have formed specific intent. A mentally disordered defendant who committed a homicide for delusional reasons, believing, for instance, that the victim was intending to kill him, that God had ordered him to kill, or that not to do so would bring about some calamity, is usually not at all incapable of premeditating and deliberating a murder and will not dispute that he formed the intent to kill in this way.

What Do Lawyers Really Want?

In some cases in which diminished capacity is raised, defense counsel may not be interested in eliciting an opinion on capacity for intent so much as a description or explanation of the defendant's conduct to present to the jury. If that is the point, the forensic expert may have much to contribute. The danger here lies in the possibility that the expert will conflate explanation and exculpation and testify that because the defendant's intentions and conduct may be understood in terms of his or her psychology, they do not meet the criteria for requisite criminal intent. This sort of testimony would recapitulate the diminished capacity as diminished responsibility approach taken in California prior to retrenchment there, and it should be understood as such.

As long as the law defines intent as it does, as a skeletal cognitive affair, testimony of this sort may be misleading to a jury even if courts permit it. Psychologists and psychiatrists are not in a position to define what requisite legal intent must involve, or even what sorts of mental or emotional disorders preclude it. Inevitably, expert testimony that suggests otherwise involves insupportable claims by the expert, for example, a claim that though it appears that a defendant premeditated and deliberated a murder—having thought about it, planned it, and even announced his intentions—he actually could not have formed such intent because of mental abnormality. Psychologists and psychiatrists often have a great deal to offer in terms of delineating data within their purview concerning a defendant and his or her behavior. But they are not capable of transforming what the law considers requisite intent into something less because of unsupported assumptions about the sorts of mental factors that must be involved in a genuine criminal act.

CONCLUSION

The history of diminished capacity and mens rea conceptualizations indicate a potential for contributions to be made by forensic psychologists and psychiatrists to the resolution of questions of intent. The conceptualizations of intent embodied in the law's approach to criminal liability, however, sharply limit the extent to which mental health expert testimony will bear on the ultimate issue to be determined by the judge or jury.

REFERENCES

American Law Institute. (1962). Model Penal Code, Proposed official draft.

Arenella, P. (1977). The diminished capacity and diminished responsibility defenses: Two children of a doomed marriage. *Columbia Law Review, 77*, 827–865.

Barratt, E. S., & Felthous, A. R. (2003). Impulsive versus premeditated aggression: Implications for *mens rea* decisions. *Behavioral Sciences and the Law, 21*, 619–630.

Bird, R. E., & Vanderet, R. C. (1972). Diminished capacity. In R. M. Cipes (Ed.), *Criminal defense techniques*. New York: Binder.

Black, H. C. (1979). *Black's law dictionary* (5th ed.). St. Paul, MN: West.

Blinder, M. (1981–1982). My psychiatric examination of Dan White. *American Journal of Forensic Psychiatry, 2*, 12–27.

Bonnie, R., & Slobogin, C. (1980). The role of mental health professionals in the criminal justice process: The case for informed speculation. *Virginia Law Review, 43*, 427–522.

California Senate Bill No. 54. (1981a).

California Senate Bill No. 590. (1981b).

Clark, C. R. (1982). Clinical limits of expert testimony on diminished capacity. *International Journal of Law and Psychiatry, 5*, 155–170.

Clark, C. R. (1988). *Diminished capacity in Michigan: Factors associated with forensic evaluation referrals*. Paper presented at American Psychology-Law Society conference, Miami Beach.

Denno, D. W. (2003). A mind to blame: New views on involuntary acts. *Behavioral Sciences and the Law, 21*, 601–618.

Diamond, B. (1961). Criminal responsibility of the mentally ill. *Stanford Law Review, 14*, 59–86.

Dix, G. E. (1971). Psychological abnormality as a factor in grading criminal liability: Diminished capacity, diminished responsibility, and the like. *Journal of Criminal Law, Criminology, and Police Science, 62*, 313–334.

Erlinder, C. P. (1983). Post-traumatic stress disorder, Vietnam veterans and the law: A challenge to effective representation. *Behavioral Sciences and the Law, 1*, 25–50.

Federal Rules of Evidence, FRE 704(b), amended by Comprehensive Crime Control Act of 1984, Public Law No 98-473.

Heinbecker, P. (1986). Two years' experience under Utah's mens rea insanity law. *Bulletin of the American Academy of Psychiatry and Law, 14*(2), 185–191.

Idaho Statutes, 18-207 (1982).

In re Winship, 397 U.S. 358 (1970).

Insanity Defense Reform Act of 1984, Public Law 98-473, 18 U.S.C. § 17.

Kansas Statutes, 22-321 (1995).

Kraus, F. R. (1983). The relevance of innocence: Proposition 8 and the diminished capacity defense. *California Law Review, 71*, 1197–1215.

LaFave, W., & Scott, A., Jr. (1972). *Handbook of criminal law*. St. Paul, MN: West.

Malle, B. F., & Nelson, S. E. (2003). Judging mens rea: The tension between folk concepts and legal concepts of intentionality. *Behavioral Sciences and the Law, 21*, 563–580.

Marx, M. L. (1977). Prison conditions and diminished capacity—A proposed defense. *Santa Clara Law Reporter, 17*, 855–883.

Melton, G. B., Petrila, J., Poythress, N. G., & Slobogin, C. (1997). *Psychological evaluations for the courts: A handbook for mental health professionals and lawyers* (2nd ed.). New York: Guilford Press.

M'Naghten's Case, 10 Cl. & F. 200, 8 Eng. Rep. 718 (H.L. 1843).

Montana Code, 46-14-101 (1979).

Morse, S. J. (1979). Diminished capacity: A moral and legal conundrum. *International Journal of Law and Psychiatry, 2*, 271–298.

Morse, S. J. (1984). Undiminished confusion in diminished capacity. *Journal of Criminal Law and Criminology, 75*, 1–55.

Morse, S. J. (1999). Craziness and criminal responsibility. *Behavioral Sciences and the Law, 17*, 147–164.

Morse, S. J. & Cohen, E. (1982, June). Diminishing diminished capacity in California. *California Lawyer*, 24–26.

People v. Cantrell, 8 Cal. 3d 672, 504 P. 2d 1256, 105 Cal. Rptr. 792 (1973).

People v. Carpenter, 464 Mich 223 (2001).

People v. Conley, 64 Cal. 2d 310, 411 P. 2d 911, 49 Cal. Rptr. 815 (1966).

People v. Drew, 22 Cal. 3d 333, 583 P. 2d 1318, 149 Cal. Rptr. 910 (1974).

People v. Gorshen, 51 Cal. 2d 716, 336 P. 2d 492 (1959).

People v. Henderson, 60 Cal. 2d 482, 386 P. 2d 677 (1963).

People v. Poddar, 10 Cal. 3d 750, 518 P. 2d 342, 111 Cal. Rptr. 910 (1974).

People v. Savoie, 419 Mich 118 (1984).

People v. Wells, 33 Cal. 2d 330, 202 P. 2d 53 (1949).

People v. Wetmore, 22 Cal. 3d 318, 583 P. 2d 1308, 149 Cal. Rptr. 264 (1978).

People v. Wolff, 61 Cal. 2d 795, 394 P. 2d 959, 40 Cal. Rptr. 271 (1964).

Senate Report No. 225, 98th Cong., 2d Sess. 230, reprinted in U.S. Code Cong. & Ad. News 3182, 3412 (1984).

Solomon, G. F. (1981–1982). Comments on the case of Dan White. *American Journal of Forensic Psychiatry, 2,* 22–26.

Steadman, H. J., McGreevy, M. A., Morrissey, J. P., Callahan, L. A., Robbins, P. C., & Cirincione, C. (1993). *Before and after Hinckley: Evaluating insanity defense reform.* New York: Guilford Press.

Stimpson, S. (1993). *State v. Cowan:* The consequences of Montana's abolition of the insanity defense. *Montana Law Review, 55,* 503–524.

Szasz, T. (1981–1982). The political use of psychiatry—The case of Dan White. *American Journal of Forensic Psychiatry, 2,* 1–11.

Tarasoff v. Regents of the University of California, 551 P. 2d 334 (1976).

U.S. v. Bartlett, 856 F. 2d 1071 (8th Cir. 1988).

U.S. v. Brown, 880 F. 2d 1012 (9th Cir. 1989).

U.S. v. Cameron, 907 F. 2d 1051 (11th Cir. 1990).

U.S. v. Childress, 58 F. 3d 693 (D.C. Cir. 1995).

U.S. v. Frisbee, 623 F. Supp. 1217 (D.C. Cal. 1985).

U.S. v. Gold, 661 F. Supp. 1127 (D.D.C. 1987).

U.S. v. Hood, 857 F. 2d 1469 (4th Cir. 1988).

U.S. v. Newman, 889 F. 2d 88 (6th Cir. 1989).

U.S. v. Pohlot, 827 F. 2d 889 (3rd Cir. 1987).

U.S. v. Robinson, 804 F. Supp. 830 (W. D.Va. 1992).

U.S. v. Schneider, 111 F. 3d 197 (1st Cir. 1997).

U.S. v. Twine, 853 F. 2d 676 (9th Cir. 1988).

U.S. v. White, 766 F. 2d 22 (1st Cir. 1985).

Utah Code, 76-2-305 (1990).

Waddell, C. W. (1979). Diminished capacity and California's new insanity test. *Pacific Law Journal, 10,* 751–771.

CHAPTER 15

Evaluating and Assisting Jury Competence in Civil Cases

JENNIFER K. ROBBENNOLT, JENNIFER L. GROSCUP, and STEVEN PENROD

IN AN article entitled "Juries: They May Be Broken, but We Can Fix Them," Supreme Court Justice Sandra Day O'Connor (1997, p. 20) observed:

> Juries usually do their job very well. . . . But juries also have the ability to disappoint us, sometimes to the point of forcing us to question whether we should have jury trials at all. One of this country's great observers of human nature, Mark Twain, once complained that juries had become "the most ingenious and infallible agency for defeating justice that human wisdom could contrive."

O'Connor and Twain have respectable company in their criticism of the jury. During the 1996 presidential campaign, candidate Robert Dole observed:

> The legal guardrails that protected our society . . . have in many places been knocked down, even dismantled, often by the very judges and juries who have been entrusted with the sacred duty of upholding the law. (Cited in Tackett, 1996, p. 1)

Richard A. Posner (1995, p. 14), federal court of appeals judge and former University of Chicago law professor, has sounded similar notes of concern about jury decision making:

> In recent years, a series of highly publicized criminal trials in which obviously guilty defendants were acquitted by juries . . . has made the American jury a controversial institution. Civil juries have rendered some astonishing verdicts as well, ladling out billions in other people's money with insouciance and attracting a drumbeat of criticism from the business community.

In recent years, the civil jury, in particular, has come under attack. In civil cases, juries are asked to determine whether the defendant is liable, to award damages intended to compensate the plaintiff for their injuries (compensatory damages), and, sometimes, to award damages intended to punish the defendant for engaging in egregious conduct and deter the defendant and others from engaging in such conduct in the future (punitive damages). Large jury verdicts such as the $2.7 million verdict against McDonald's when a customer was burned by hot coffee, verdicts in the millions, and even billions, against tobacco companies, and the $5 billion in punitive damages levied against Exxon following the Exxon *Valdez* oil spill (Broder, 1997; Kozinski, 1995; Sachdev, 2003) have caused some to conclude that juries are not an effective mechanism for determining liability and awarding damages. Critics of the civil jury contend that juries are arbitrary, capricious, and unprincipled in the manner in which they award damages, particularly punitive damages. Advocates of jury reform argue that civil juries are incompetent to decide the cases before them, biased in favor of plaintiffs, and overgenerous. In addition, they contend that huge damage awards given by juries have fueled a "litigation crisis" and have contributed to crippling delays in the civil justice system (e.g., Frank, 1949; Quayle, 1992; Viscusi, 1998; see review in Daniels, 1989). Justice O'Connor, dissenting in *Pacific Mutual Life Ins. Co. v. Haslip*, commented, "Recent years . . . have witnessed an explosion in the frequency and size of punitive damages awards" (1991, p. 1066). Large damage verdicts stir incredible controversy and are typically the objects of substantial media attention.

In this chapter, we consider the two themes advanced by Justice O'Connor in the title of her commentary. We consider evidence on the question of just how "broken" the civil jury is, focusing in the first part of the chapter on research examining the factors that influence jury decision making and decision-making processes in civil cases. In the second part of the chapter we consider studies that have evaluated several of the mechanisms that have been advanced as fixes for jury problems: juror note taking, juror questioning of witnesses, reformation of jury instructions, and preinstruction of jurors.

CIVIL JURY DECISION MAKING

In fact, there is little empirical evidence that the civil justice system is "out of control." Recent reviews of civil jury decision making conclude that, overall, jurors perform relatively well in determining liability and damages (Greene & Bornstein, 2003; Greene et al., 2002; Robbennolt, 2002a; Vidmar, 1998). Although punitive damage awards, in particular, have garnered much criticism, the empirical studies that have examined the overall pattern of punitive damage awards have generally found that punitive damages are awarded infrequently, are typically not extremely large, and are rarely collected in the amounts awarded (see Daniels & Martin, 1990; Landes & Posner, 1986; Peterson, Sarma, & Shanley, 1987; Rustad, 1991; U.S. General Accounting Office, 1989; see review in Robbennolt, 2002a). However, punitive damages are claimed in more cases than they are awarded and thus remain a threat. In addition, large awards secure substantial media attention, whereas reductions, though common, are not as extensively reported (Garber, 1998).

Nonetheless, there are aspects of jury decisions that are cause for some concern. Studies have found a large degree of unpredictability in jury-determined damage awards such that juries may award differing amounts for seemingly similar injuries (studies reviewed in Saks, 1992; but see Baker, Harel, & Kugler, 2003). Thus, although the overall amount of damages awarded by juries is not out of control, there may be large variability in awards made by juries. Moreover, studies have found that juries tend to overcompensate plaintiffs with relatively small losses but tend to undercompensate plaintiffs with relatively large losses (Conrad & Bernstein, 1964; King & Smith, 1988). In addition, studies have shown that jurors have some difficulty understanding civil jury instructions (Elwork, Sales, & Alfini, 1982; Hastie, Schkade, & Payne, 1998, 1999; see reviews in English & Sales, 1997; Lieberman & Sales, 1997) and in translating their judgments into dollar awards (Kahneman, Sunstein, & Schkade, 1998; Wissler, Hart, & Saks, 1999).

LEGAL REFORM EFFORTS

Over the past twenty-five years, the constitutionality of large punitive damage awards has captured the attention of the U.S. Supreme Court (*BMW of North America v. Gore,* 1996; *Browning-Ferris Ind. v. Kelco Disposal, Inc.,* 1989; *Cooper Industries, Inc. v. Leatherman Tool Group, Inc.,* 2001; *Honda Motor Co. v. Oberg,* 1994; *Pacific Mutual Life Ins. Co. v. Haslip,* 1991; *State Farm v. Campbell,* 2003; *TXO Production Corp. v. Alliance Resources Corp.,* 1993). The Court has held that the traditional method of awarding punitive damages, that is, the determination of the appropriateness and amount of punitive damages by a jury and subsequent review by both trial and appellate courts, is not "so inherently unfair as to deny due process and be *per se* unconstitutional" but has been willing to consider whether specific jury awards are excessive (*Pacific Mutual Life Ins. Co. v. Haslip,* 1991, p. 1043). In 1996, the Court did, for the first time, find a punitive damage award constitutionally excessive (*BMW of North America v. Gore,* 1996). More recently, in *State Farm v. Campbell* (2003), the Court again found that a jury's punitive damage award was constitutionally excessive. However, in practice, the Court has left the primary responsibility for regulating punitive damage awards and civil litigation to the individual states and to the legislative branch.

Advocates of tort reform have pursued nonjudicial avenues in attempts to restrain what they perceive as out-of-control civil juries, turning to the state and federal legislatures. A number of states have enacted and implemented a variety of measures that are aimed at either limiting liability or restricting the incidence or the amount of damage awards (see review in Robbennolt, 2002a). First, a number of states have implemented rules that eliminate liability under certain circumstances (e.g., Texas Civil Practice & Remedies Code § 84.003, limiting the liability of volunteers working for charitable organizations). Second, many states have implemented limitations on joint and several liability (e.g., California Civil Code § 1431.2). Third, a number of states have limited the amount of money that may be awarded either for noneconomic compensatory damages (e.g., pain and suffering) or for punitive damages (e.g., Missouri Revised Statutes § 538.210, limiting noneconomic damages in medical liability cases; North Dakota Cent. Code § 32-03.2-11, limiting punitive damages to the greater of two times the compensatory damages or $250,000). In addition, a number of states have begun to require the jury to be more certain in their damage award decision before they may award punitive damages. Thus, many states require juries to conclude that the evidence is "clear and convincing" that punitive damages are appropriately awarded rather than that the "preponderance of the evidence" indicates that punitive damages ought to be awarded (e.g., Alaska Statutes § 09.17.020; South Carolina Code Annotated § 15-33-135), and they may require that the jury reach a unanimous decision to award punitive damages (e.g., Texas Civil Practice & Remedies Code § 41.003). Other reform efforts would take some decisions out of the hands of the jury altogether. A few states have decided to allow judges to assess the amount of punitive damages to be awarded rather than juries (e.g., Connecticut General Statutes Annotated § 52-40; Kansas Statutes Annotated § 60-3701). All of these reforms raise the dual questions of how juries make decisions in civil cases and whether their decision-making processes signal serious problems.

JURY DECISION-MAKING PROCESSES

There is a growing body of research focusing on the process by which juries make decisions (for reviews, see Greene et al., 2002; MacCoun, 1993a; Vidmar, 1998). There is empirical support for a number of possibilities that have been advanced as methods by which jurors make decisions. In particular, the "story model" of juror decision making proposes that jurors combine the evidence that is presented into a narrative story; they then learn the verdict options and choose the one that best fits the story they have constructed (Pennington & Hastie, 1993). Robbennolt, Darley, and MacCoun (2003) suggest that jurors operate as "goal managers" as they attempt to use the available verdict options to satisfy a number of goals simultaneously. They propose that juror decision making operates through a process of parallel constraint satisfaction in which jurors seek to maximally satisfy, in parallel, a variety of potentially competing goals, such as achieving appropriate compensation, effecting deterrence, exacting retribution, and expressing symbolic values.

Recently, much attention has focused specifically on the processes by which jurors determine damage awards (see review in Greene & Bornstein, 2003). One hypothesis is that jurors anchor on an initial value and then adjust this value as they become aware of more and more new facts; this is termed "anchoring and adjustment" (Tversky & Kahneman, 1982). Consistent with this view, jurors have been found to be influenced by attorney damage award recommendations (Chapman & Bornstein, 1996; Hinsz & Indahl, 1995), exposure to high damage awards in the press (Greene, Goodman, & Loftus, 1991; Viscusi, 2001b), and caps on damage awards (Robbennolt & Studebaker, 1999; Saks, Hollinger, Wissler, Evans, & Hart, 1997). Some interviewed jurors have reported that they arrived at their compensatory damage award by deciding on an amount for each component of damages and then summing to get a total award amount (Goodman, Greene, & Loftus, 1989; Mott, Hans, & Simpson, 2000). An experimental study by Goodman, Greene, and Loftus found that

27% of jury-eligible adults asked to read written vignettes and to award damages reported arriving at their damage award merely by "picking a fair number" rather than engaging in any calculations that would be required by the additive or anchoring and adjustment methods (see also Mott et al., 2000). Interviews with jurors provide some evidence that final punitive damage awards represent a compromise between high and low amounts advocated by different factions of the jury. In addition, Greene (1989) notes that many punitive damage awards are rounded numbers (e.g., $1 million, $500,000), suggesting that minute calculations are likely not taking place.

A study by Kahneman et al. (1998) found that jurors have difficulty translating into a dollar award their outrage at the defendant's conduct and their intent to punish the defendant accordingly. Across a variety of cases, mock jurors were relatively consistent in their ratings of outrage and evaluations of the degree of punishment required. However, the dollar amounts of their punitive damage judgments were less consistent. Wissler et al. (1999) demonstrated a similar difficulty for jurors, attorneys, and judges in translating noneconomic damages into dollar awards. While evaluations of injury severity were highly predictable from participants' ratings of the specific aspects of the injury, damage awards were less predictable.

INFLUENCES ON JURY DECISIONS

Empirical research has identified a variety of factors that play a role in jury decisions about liability or damages, including the nature of the parties' conduct, the severity of the harm, the defendant's wealth, and individual differences among jurors. On the whole, this research indicates that jurors perform their tasks quite well.

NATURE OF DEFENDANT'S (AND PLAINTIFF'S) CONDUCT

As a general rule, conduct is considered legally blameworthy when it is intended to cause harm or involves an undue risk of harm (Prosser & Keeton, 1984). Thus, the intentional or unreasonable nature of the defendant's conduct ought to have some bearing on determinations of civil liability. Consistent with this premise, Greene, Johns, and Bowman (1999) found that in responding to an automobile accident case, mock jurors and juries were more likely to determine that a defendant was negligent when the defendant's conduct was unreasonable than when it was reasonable. In a related study, Greene, Johns, and Smith (2001) found that mock jurors were more likely to determine that the defendant was negligent when the defendant's conduct was more careless than in a version of the case in which the defendant's behavior was less careless.

Discussions of what factors ought to influence punitive damage awards invariably note that the reprehensibility of the conduct complained of is one such relevant factor (Owen, 1994). Indeed, punitive damages may not be awarded at all unless the defendant's conduct is "outrageous, because of the defendant's evil motive or his reckless indifference to the rights of others" (Restatement (Second) of Torts, § 908(2)). Prosser and Keeton have noted that for punitive damages to be awarded there must be circumstances of aggravation or outrage, such as spite or "malice," or a fraudulent or evil motive on the part of the defendant, or such a conscious and deliberate disregard of the interests of others that the conduct may be called willful or wanton. (pp. 9–10)

One of the guideposts identified by the U.S. Supreme Court in *BMW* (1996) was the degree of reprehensibility of the defendant's conduct. The Court noted that the reprehensibility of the defendant's conduct was "perhaps the most important indicium of the reasonableness of a punitive damages award" because a punitive damages award should reflect the "enormity" of the defendant's offense.

Consistent with the legal theory, empirical research has found a positive relationship between the reprehensibility of the defendant's actions and the size of the punitive damage award. Cather, Greene, and Durham (1996) found that participants awarded more in punitive damages in response to the high reprehensibility scenarios than they did in response to the low reprehensibility scenarios. In another study, using 768 jury-eligible adults and an audiotaped trial, Horowitz and Bordens (1990) found that the reprehensibility of the defendant manufacturer's conduct (operationalized as the length of time the defendant was aware of the harmful effects of its product) was not correlated with compensatory damages but was significantly correlated with punitive damages. Relatedly, Robbennolt (2002b) found that jury-eligible citizens and trial court judges who rated a defendant's conduct as more offensive awarded higher amounts of punitive damages.

OUTCOME SEVERITY

One factor thought to be an important consideration in the awarding of damages, but not liability, is the severity of the outcome to the plaintiff (*BMW of North America v. Gore,* 1996). However, the expected relationship between injury severity and damage awards is complex. Compensatory damages logically should be greater when the injuries and other damages are more severe because the resulting medical bills, lost wages, and pain and suffering are increased. However, this is not necessarily the case with punitive damages. Punitive damages are not aimed at compensating the plaintiff and making him or her whole, as are compensatory damages, but are to punish and deter the defendant. In fact, many have argued that punitive damages ought to be scaled to the heinousness of the offense and *not* to the magnitude of the harm (Galanter & Luban, 1993). Nonetheless, the U.S. Supreme Court has concluded that punitive damages ought to have some reasonable relationship to the damage suffered by the plaintiff (*TXO,* 1993; *BMW,* 1996; *State Farm v. Campbell,* 2003).

The empirical findings regarding the influence of injury severity on liability determinations have been mixed. Several studies have found a relationship between the severity of the injury to the plaintiff and determinations of liability (Bornstein, 1998; Greene et al., 1999; Van der Keilen & Garg, 1994); others have found no relationship (Green, 1968; Greene et al., 1999; Peterson, 1984; Taragin, Willett, Wilczek, Trout, & Carson, 1992). A recent meta-analysis

(Robbennolt, 2000) found that injury severity had a small effect ($r = .03$) on whether or not the plaintiff received a payment (including civil liability verdicts and settlements).

A number of studies have shown that more compensatory damages are awarded when injuries are more severe. In a study of 8,231 medical malpractice cases, Taragin and his colleagues (1992) found that both the likelihood that a plaintiff would obtain a payment and the amount of that payment (either settlement or jury verdict) increased with the severity of the injury. Similarly, Peterson (1984) found that damage awards in general were affected by the level of severity of the plaintiff's injuries. In a recent study, Wissler, Evans, Hart, Morry, and Saks (1997) found that pain and suffering awards were strongly influenced by information about the nature, characteristics, and consequences of the injury (see also Robbennolt, 2000).

The evidence with respect to the influence of injury severity on punitive damages is mixed. Several studies of actual cases have found a correlation between the severity of the injury to the plaintiff and punitive damage awards (Eisenberg, Goerdt, Ostrom, Rottman, & Wells, 1997; Rustad, 1992). Experimental studies have also demonstrated this relationship. Cather et al. (1996) investigated the influence of the severity of the injury to the plaintiff on the amounts of compensatory and punitive damages awarded by jury-eligible adults in response to written vignettes. They found that overall, damage awards in a personal injury case were higher when the plaintiff was more severely injured than when the plaintiff was only mildly injured, but did not find this relationship in other types of cases (product liability and insurance bad faith cases). When they examined punitive damages in particular, they did not find significant differences in the amounts awarded to severely injured and mildly injured plaintiffs (see also Kahneman et al., 1998).

The extent of the actual injury suffered by the plaintiff is not the only important factor related to the severity of the harm inflicted by the defendant. Equally important are the injuries that potentially could have resulted from the defendant's conduct. In *TXO* (1993), the Court recognized that the relationship between injury severity and punitive damages could not be quantified in a numerical ratio. The Court cited a common example of circumstances in which punitive damages many times the compensatory damages would be appropriate:

> For instance, a man wildly fires a gun into a crowd. By sheer chance, no one is injured and the only damage is to a $10 pair of glasses. A jury reasonably could find only $10 in compensatory damages, but thousands of dollars in punitive damages to teach a duty of care. We would allow a jury to impose substantial punitive damages in order to discourage future bad acts. (p. 459)

The Court determined that it was appropriate to take into account the harm that could have potentially occurred due to the defendant's actions as well as harm that did indeed occur and to take into account the "possible harm to other victims that might have resulted if similar future behavior were not deterred" (p. 460). This approach to the relationship between the severity of the injury to the plaintiff and the punitive damage award was maintained in *BMW*

(1996), where the Court found that an important guide for the review of punitive damage awards is the ratio of the punitive damage award to the "harm or potential harm" caused by the defendant (see also *State Farm v. Campbell*, 2003).

Karlovac and Darley (1988, p. 289) noted that in determining an actor's negligence, the legal system takes into account not only the severity of the actual outcome, but also "the severity of all the harms that *could* foreseeably have eventuated from a risky action." In a series of studies, Karlovac and Darley investigated the influence of the severity of the potential harms risked by an actor on the judgments of participants. Using undergraduate participants and tape-recorded stories accompanied by slides, they examined the effect on judgments of varying the degree of the maximum possible harm that could have resulted from an actor's risky action. Consistent with legal theory, they found that judgments of negligence were influenced by the severity of the harm risked. Moreover, they found that judgments of the degree of punishment that was perceived as appropriate were determined by the severity of the harm risked. These judgments were similarly affected both before and after participants were informed of the actual outcome.

In another experimental study, Robbennolt (2002b) examined the influence of both the actual severity of the injury to the plaintiff and the severity of the potential harm. She found that the severity of the actual injury influenced mock jurors' compensatory damage awards, but that both the actual and potential injury influenced punitive damage awards.

DEFENDANT'S WEALTH

Another factor thought by some to be influential in juror decision making is the wealth of the defendant. Because the purpose of compensatory damages is to "make the plaintiff whole," that is, to compensate the plaintiff for his or her losses, the wealth of the defendant ought to play no role in the amount of compensatory damages awarded. However, the purposes of punitive damages are different from those of compensatory damages. Punitive damages are intended to punish the defendant and to deter the defendant and others from engaging in similar behavior in the future. To punish or deter a wealthy defendant, the amount of punitive damages awarded must be sufficient to make an impact on him or her (Simpson, 1996; see also Abraham & Jeffries, 1989, and Arlen, 1992; see generally *Pacific Mutual Life Ins. Co. v. Haslip*, 1991; *TXO*, 1993; *State Farm v. Campbell*, 2003).

Hans and Ermann (1989) found that their 201 student respondents to written vignettes were able to differentiate between the financial resources available to Mr. Jones and to the Jones Corporation and also awarded a plaintiff suing the corporation more compensation than a plaintiff suing the individual. However, regression analysis indicated that there was not a consistent effect of the presumed resources of the defendant on awards. Rather, awards were more strongly linked to judgments about the defendant's recklessness, with participants attributing more recklessness to the corporation than to the individual.

A subsequent study attempted to delineate the distinction between the impact of a "corporate identity" on juror decisions from the impact of the defendant's wealth. Using written case materials, MacCoun (1996; see also MacCoun,

1993b) found that jury-eligible adults treated corporations differently from individual defendants such that larger compensatory damage awards were assessed against the corporate defendant than against the wealthy individual defendant. However, MacCoun found that the compensatory damages awarded against the wealthy individual were no greater than those awarded against the poor individual.

Thus, it appears that there is little evidence for a "deep pockets" effect, at least in terms of the impact of the wealth of the defendant on compensatory damage awards. This is as it should be; as noted earlier, the wealth of the defendant does not impact the extent of the plaintiff's damages nor the amount of money it ought to take to compensate the plaintiff. In contrast, wealth arguably should influence punitive damage awards. Several recent experimental studies have found that the wealth of the defendant does influence the punitive damages awarded. Robbennolt (2002b) found that both jury-eligible citizens and trial court judges awarded more in punitive damages against a wealthier defendant than against a less wealthy defendant. Across three different cases, Greene, Woody, and Winter (2000) found that higher amounts of punitive damages were assessed against wealthier defendants. Similarly, Kahneman et al. (1998) found that the size of a corporate defendant's annual profit influenced punitive damage awards.

Individual Characteristics of Decision Makers

A variety of individual difference variables have been explored in an effort to determine their relationship to legal judgments (Ford, 1986; Litigation Sciences, 1993). In general, demographic variables such as age, gender, and social class have proven to be of limited value in predicting judgments. However, some personality and attitudinal variables have proven to be somewhat more useful. Ellsworth (1993) and her colleagues have attempted to determine which components of the juror decision-making process are influenced by juror attitudes. Ellsworth notes that legal decisions are inherently imprecise and require the decision maker to resolve numerous ambiguities and to engage in a great deal of interpretation. Thus, there is ample room for juror attitudes to influence juror decisions. Ellsworth proposed that attitudes might influence verdicts in three distinct ways. First, attitudes may influence jurors' evaluation of the credibility of witnesses. Second, the inferences drawn by jurors, which are based in part on the jurors' attitudes, may influence the jurors' construction of a narrative summary of the evidence. Third, attitudes may influence the manner in which jurors apply the judge's instructions regarding the law to the facts as they have constructed them. Ellsworth found support for the conclusion that attitudes influence verdicts in all three of these ways.

In their investigation of attitudes toward the police and toward due process, Casper, Benedict, and Perry (1989) hypothesized that attitudes might influence damage awards in a civil rights action through their role in shaping the processing of the testimony to which jurors are exposed. They found that attitudes operated to influence damage awards to some extent through their influence on jurors' interpretation of trial testimony, but that the attitudes also retained an independent effect on awards.

A series of studies by Hans and Lofquist (1992, 1994) investigated jurors' attitudes toward civil litigation. They found that jurors in actual tort cases had strong negative views of both the frequency and the legitimacy of civil lawsuits and believed that civil damage awards are too high. However, jurors also agreed that jurors generally do a good job and found their own jury experience to be positive. Hans and Lofquist found that their 7-item scale measuring juror attitudes toward civil litigation comprised two separate factors, one measuring attitudes toward the worth of civil litigation and a second measuring beliefs about the abilities of civil juries. Moreover, they found a significant correlation between the jury members' average scores on the civil litigation scale and the jury's damage awards, such that the more strongly the jurors believed there was a litigation crisis, the lower the damages awarded.

Other researchers have investigated the relationship between various measures of attitudes toward the civil litigation system and legal decisions and have found similar results. In telephone interviews, Moran, Cutler, and De Lisa (1994) found that attitudes toward tort reform predicted verdicts in both civil and criminal fictional cases. Similarly, Greene et al. (1991) found that the scores of jury-eligible adults on a scale measuring attitudes toward tort reform and damages (e.g., whether there is an insurance crisis, the influence of media on attitudes about civil lawsuits, and beliefs about attorney credibility and damage requests) were significantly correlated with damage awards, such that those most supportive of tort reform gave lower damage awards. In addition, they found a significant positive correlation between participants' estimates of the frequency of large damage awards and the amount of damages they awarded. Moreover, they found that such attitudinal measures were more reliable predictors than were demographic variables (see review in Robbennolt & Studebaker, 2003).

JURORS VERSUS JUDGES

It is clear that many believe that judges would engage in qualitatively different kinds of decision making than would jurors. For example, in his concurrence in *BMW of North America v. Gore* (1996, p. 596), Justice Breyer noted that one cannot "expect jurors to interpret law like judges, who work within a discipline and hierarchical organization that normally promotes roughly uniform interpretation and application of the law." However, there is a paucity of research regarding the comparison between the decision making of jurors and the decision making of judges. What we do know suggests that judges and jurors may engage in decision-making processes that are quite similar.

One of the earliest comparisons of judges and jurors was conducted by Kalven and Zeisel (1966; Kalven, 1964). They asked judges to report, for cases tried before them, how the jury decided the case and how they would have decided it had it been a bench trial. Across 4,000 civil cases, they found that judges and juries agreed 78% of the time as to the liability of defendants. In terms of the amount of damage awards, they found that when both the judge and jury decided in favor of the plaintiff, juries would have awarded more damages 52% of the time and judges would have awarded more damages 39% of the time, with approximate agreement in 9% of the cases. On average, Kalven and Zeisel found that juries awarded 20% more in damages than judges would have awarded (see also Heuer & Penrod, 1994b).

More recent research suggests that judges and jurors are similar in a number of aspects of decision making. For example, judges and jurors have been found to react similarly to potentially biasing, but inadmissible, evidence (Landsman & Rakos, 1994), be susceptible to cognitive biases (Guthrie, Rachlinski, & Wistrich, 2001), and have similar difficulties in assessing statistical (Wells, 1992) and scientific (Kovera & McAuliff, 2000; Kovera, McAuliff, & Herbert, 1999) evidence.

The evidence of how jurors and judges compare in their assessments of damages has been somewhat mixed. Archival research and some experimental research has found many similarities in the damage award decision making of judges and jurors (Clermont & Eisenberg, 1992; Eisenberg, LaFountain, Ostrom, & Rottman, 2002; Robbennolt, 2002b; Vidmar, 1995; Wissler et al., 1999; see Robbennolt, 2002a, for a review). However, other experimental research has suggested some differences (Hastie & Viscusi, 1998; Viscusi, 2001a).

SUMMARY

On balance, existing research on jury decision making in civil cases suggests that the process is, if not perfect, at least orderly. Jurors seem to give systematic consideration to factors such as the severity of outcomes and the reprehensibility of the alleged acts and do not seriously misuse information about a defendant's wealth. Furthermore, the decisions of juries seem to stack up reasonably well against the decisions of other, arguably more expert, decision makers. But, these conclusions must be qualified insofar as the body of scientific research on which they are based is not large. Most of the research on civil jury decision making is of quite recent vintage, and it is easy to imagine that our understanding of these processes will be much richer in another decade.

AIDS TO JURY DECISION MAKING

Although our survey of research on jury decision making in civil cases suggests that the civil jury is probably not as "broken" as some critics would like us to believe, many jury critics have nonetheless been quite inventive in advancing recommendations for jury aids (see generally http://crfc.org/americanjury /reform.html and http://www.ncsconline.org/KIS_JurInnStatesPub.pdf). For instance, in her 1997 article, Justice O'Connor recommended:

> In my view, the first level for reform is in the courtroom. . . . Jurors should be allowed, and encouraged, to take notes at trial. I frankly cannot understand the resistance to this practice. . . . Taking notes is a way for a person to make sense of the information being received . . . and perhaps most importantly for the juror, to take an active, rather than a passive, part in what is going on. (pp. 23–24)

Attorney Kenneth Adamo (1996, pp. 354–355) recommends:

> Let Them Take Notes. . . . Allowing note-taking is almost de rigueur if juror comprehension and interest are to be maximized. . . . Allow the Jury to Ask Questions. . . . If you want an interested and knowledgeable jury, especially as trial proceeds, you need to provide for juror questions.

Jason Scully (1996, p. 648) writes:

> With more guidance and increased comprehension, jurors may be able to fulfill their role as accurate decision-makers. . . . Improved trial techniques include . . . allowing jurors to take notes [and] allowing juror questions.

Among the recommendations in the Final Report of the Blue Ribbon Commission on Jury System Improvement for the State of California (Kelso, 1996, p. 1504) are the following:

> Adopt a Rule of court which requires the trial court to inform jurors of their right to take written notes [and] . . . adopt a [rule] recommending that judges permit jurors to submit written questions to the court which, subject to the discretion of the trial judge and the rules of evidence, may be asked of witnesses who are still on the stand.

In their recent volumes on the jury, Abramson (1994) and Adler (1994) also advocated use of these procedures and drew approval from Judge Posner (1995, p. 16):

> For complex modern cases, both Abramson and Adler propose a series of reforms to make the jury's task easier: allowing jurors to take notes and ask questions.

Regarding predeliberation jury discussions, the Honorable B. Michael Dann (1993, p. 1265, citations omitted) observed:

> The "rules for getting the floor" during trial ought to be modified to permit at least limited discussions of the evidence among jurors who wish to participate, thereby establishing a form of "speaking rights" for the decision makers. Persuaded by studies of group psychology and their own experiences, legal commentators argue that the restriction on predeliberation discussions is anti-educational, nondemocratic, and unnecessary to ensure, at least in its present form, an orderly or otherwise fair trial.

In what has been noted as one of the early court decisions to positively evaluate jury discussions during the trial, Judge Ditter in *United States v. Wexler* (1987, p. 969) observed:

> The duty of a juror involves complex thought processes: assimilating and comprehending the evidence, determining credibility issues, recalling the evidence, putting it all into context and relative degrees of reliability, participating in discussions, and making informed decisions. Jurors need all the help they can get and their only source of untainted information and assistance is from those who share with them the responsibility for making the ultimate decisions.

He further noted that predeliberation jury discussions

will make them more attentive, more apt to be interested and involved, more likely to focus on the issues as they unfold. Jurors who have been told, figuratively, to clap their hands over their mouths, who cannot share their ideas and impressions, may tend to clap their hands over their minds as well. (p. 969)

Despite the enthusiasm for jury aids expressed by such authorities as Justice O'Connor and the California Commission, it turns out that these procedures are rather controversial and not universally endorsed. Arguments for and against such aids have been advanced by the courts, legal scholars, and social scientists alike, and the debate over these procedures is far from new. Appellate decisions concerning juror questions date back to as early as 1825 and decisions about note taking to at least 1900. Contemporary commentary is also abundant.

Although many appellate courts have addressed these issues, there is no clear consensus on their advantages and disadvantages. There is some consensus on how the procedures should be evaluated, at least insofar as the same criteria appear across cases repeatedly. Unfortunately, the appellate judges writing these decisions draw on their own experiences as the principal evidence concerning the strengths and weaknesses of the methods. Of course, until recently, there was little in the way of systematic evidence about the impact of the procedures for judges to rely on. Although late to the scene, the social science community has generated some discussion and research on a variety of jury aids in the past quarter-century.

JUROR QUESTIONS

In an early review of the case law on jury questions, Purver (1970) noted that most courts concluded that it is not improper but is a matter within the discretion of the trial judge. However, courts disagreed about whether juror questions should be encouraged or discouraged. In recent years, there have been a large number of federal and state court decisions regarding the propriety of juror question asking, and many courts have only recently addressed the question for the first time, for example, in *State v. Graves* (1995) and *Williams v. Commonwealth* (1997). However, the general conclusion remains the same as that advanced by Purver: Many courts are reluctant to encourage or to discourage juror questions. Some jurisdictions do discourage the procedure, and Texas has even prohibited it (Cano, 2001; Wolff, 1990). Other states provide for juror questions by state law (e.g., *Lawson v. State*, 1996) or by court rule (e.g., *Cohee v. State*, 1997 *State v. Greer*, 1997).

Overall, appellate decisions reflect some disagreement among judges regarding the propriety of this procedure, but it is not difficult to find recent cases in which courts advise caution. The Second Circuit (*United States v. Douglas*, 1996) takes a firmly skeptical view:

In three recent cases, we have considered the issue of juror questioning of witnesses. . . . All three decisions expressed varying degrees of disapproval of juror questioning, though only *[United States v. Ajmal]* concluded that the questioning that occurred warranted reversal of the conviction.

In *United States v. Ajmal* (1995), the court chastised:

The district court's decision to invite juror questioning was not necessitated by the factual intricacies of this banal drug conspiracy, nor was it prompted by the urging of the jurors themselves. . . . Not surprisingly, the jurors took extensive advantage of this opportunity to question witnesses, including Ajmal himself. Such questioning tainted the trial process. (pp. 14–15)

The Seventh Circuit in *United States v. Feinberg* (1996, p. 336) also expressed reservations:

Whether to permit jurors to ask questions is a decision best left to the discretion of the district judge. . . . However, implicit in his exercise of discretion is an obligation to weigh the potential benefit to the jurors against the potential harm to the parties, especially when one of those parties is a criminal defendant. . . In the vast majority of cases the risks outweigh the benefits.

Empirical Research

There is some research discussing the potential advantages and disadvantages of juror questions. In addition to the Purver (1970) piece (which has been updated with cases through 1995), particularly thorough discussions of the impact of juror questions can be found in McLaughlin (1982) and Wolff (1990) and in the Eighth Circuit opinion in *United States v. Johnson* (1989). A field study by Sand and Reiss (1985) allowed jurors in 26 trials to submit questions to the judge to be asked of witnesses. Unfortunately, there was no nonquestion control group. A pilot field experiment in Dane County, Wisconsin, by Penrod, Linz, and Rios (1983) randomly assigned criminal trials in one courtroom to question-asking versus no-question conditions. Trials in the no-question control group were supplemented with trials from a second courtroom in which questions were not permitted (for a total of 31 trials), which created a partial confound between judges and question asking.

Heuer and Penrod (1988, 1989, 1994a, 1994b) conducted two courtroom field experiments that examined the consequences of permitting jurors to direct questions to witnesses during trials and to take notes. Data for the first experiment were obtained from 550 jurors, 29 judges (sitting in 63 different trials), and 95 lawyers—all of whom participated in the same 67 Wisconsin state court trials. Data for the second experiment included 75 civil and 85 criminal trials in courtrooms from 33 states; there were 1,229 jurors, 103 judges, and 220 lawyers. The procedures in the experiments were similar and included approximately equal numbers of criminal and civil trials. In both studies, judges received packets of materials including (1) instructions about the combination of questioning and note-taking procedures they were to employ in their next jury trial, (2) suggestions about how to administer the procedures, and (3) questionnaires to be completed by the judge, the jurors, and the lawyers at the conclusion of the trial. All respondents were questioned about demographic information and asked their general evaluations of the trial, the trial participants, and the experimental procedures. Judges and lawyers were asked to complete questionnaires while the jury was deliberating. In most trials, questionnaires were completed before participants left the courtroom.

Proponents and critics of jury questions have advanced a number of proposals for questioning procedures and advanced numerous hypotheses about the impact of juror questions. These ideas guided the development of the Heuer and Penrod (1988, 1989, 1994a, 1994b) procedures and dependent measures. A number of courts have stated their preference about the procedures to be employed if juror questions are permitted. In *United States v. Polowichak* (1986), the court disapproved allowing juror questions to be stated within the hearing of other jurors and suggested that the district court require jurors to submit questions in writing, without revealing the question to other jurors, at which point the court could pose the question after determining that the question is proper. Similar procedures have been approved in recent state and federal cases, such as *State v. Greer* (1997), *State v. Alexander* (1997), *United States v. Stierwalt* (1994), *United States v. Bush* (1995), *United States v. Feinberg* (1996; where the court disapproved permitting jurors to ask their questions orally but did not overturn the defendant's conviction because the jury asked only "innocuous" questions), *United States v. Richardson* (2000), and *Commonwealth v. Urena* (1994). Courts and commentators have also suggested that both attorneys be allowed to make any objections to a juror's written question at a bench conference and that the judge's ruling on these objections be made outside the hearing of the jury (Cano, 2001; Dann, 1996; *DeBenedetto v. Goodyear*, 1985; *State v. Howard*, 1987).

In the Heuer and Penrod (1988, 1989, 1994a, 1994b) studies, for trials randomly assigned to permit juror questions, judges received instructions much like those outlined earlier and they generally followed the recommendations. In trials assigned not to include juror questions, judges were asked to disallow direct questions to witnesses. In the Wisconsin study, jurors were permitted to pose questions in 33 trials and asked a total of 88 questions (2.3 questions per trial). Two-thirds were directed to prosecution[1] witnesses and one-third to defense witnesses. Fifteen of the 88 questions drew objections from the prosecution, the defense attorney, or both. They displayed considerable agreement about which were objectionable, for both attorneys typically objected to the same questions. These questions frequently concerned evidence that both attorneys knew would not be admissible (e.g., questions about insurance in civil cases).

In the national study, questions were permitted in 71 trials, though questions were posed in only 51 (a finding that suggests that jurors do not necessarily act on their license). Not counting questions submitted but not asked (due to lawyer objections or screening by the judge), jurors asked an average of 4.4 questions per criminal trial (median = 1.3) and 5.1 questions per civil trial (median = 1.8). In both civil and criminal trials, questions were asked at the rate of about 1 question per 2 hours of trial time (the median was only .25 questions per hour, with a modal rate of 0.0).

In the national study, the majority of jury questions were directed to prosecution or plaintiff witnesses (79% in civil trials, 77% in criminal trials). Though this may suggest some disparity in the rate of questions directed to opposing sides, when the amount of time that prosecution and defense witnesses spent on the stand is considered, the rate is fairly evenly distributed: Questions were submitted to prosecution witnesses at a rate of approximately .7 questions per hour of testimony compared with a rate of approximately .5 per hour for defense witnesses. Twenty-four percent of the jurors' questions were objected to by one or both attorneys. As in the Wisconsin study, the attorneys in trials in the national study largely agreed about which questions were objectionable: 44% of the questions that were objected to were challenged by both lawyers. Defense attorneys reported that 81% of their objections were sustained, compared to 79% for prosecutors. The high levels of co-objection and judges' sustaining of those objections reflects the fact that many questions concerned evidence that was not admissible (e.g., questions that would have called for hearsay testimony).

Evaluation of the Major Possible Advantages of Juror Questions

These studies make it possible to evaluate a variety of possible advantages of allowing jurors to ask questions.

Do Juror Questions Promote Juror Understanding of the Evidence and Issues? Scully (1996, pp. 650–651) argued, "[One] method of improving juror understanding is to allow the jurors to ask questions of expert witnesses. This would be helpful because an expert may overlook information that the jurors believe is crucial to making a decision." In *Williams v. Commonwealth* (1997, p. 155, citation omitted), the court similarly observed, "[A] juror may, and often does, ask a very pertinent and helpful question in furtherance of the investigation." Similar arguments have been advanced by courts in *Ratton v. Busby* (1959), *Schaefer v. St. Louis & Suburban R. Co.* (1895), and *Krause v. State* (1942).

Heuer and Penrod's (1988, 1989, 1994a, 1994b) findings generally support the proposition that juror questions enhance juror understanding. In the Wisconsin cases, jurors permitted to ask questions were more satisfied that the questioning of witnesses had been thorough, seldom believed that a witness needed to be further questioned, and were more convinced that they had sufficient information to reach a responsible verdict. In the national study, jurors in question-asking trials were asked how helpful their questions were for clarifying the evidence, clarifying the law, and getting to the truth. Overall, the answers indicated modest but positive appraisals. Jurors in trials in which questions were permitted also indicated that they were somewhat better informed by the evidence and were more confident that they had sufficient information to reach a responsible verdict in trials.

Do Juror Questions Help Jurors Get to the Truth? Some advocates of juror questions believe they can do more than aid understanding. The Supreme Court of Massachusetts observed in *Commonwealth v. Urena* (1994, p. 1205), "Indeed, there are asserted benefits to juror questioning of witnesses, such as the opportunity for jurors to more fully understand the evidence, . . . enhanced attentiveness of jurors, and furtherance of the truth-seeking ideal." McLaughlin (1982, pp. 697–698) observed, "Rather than an indifferent battle of legal minds with jurors as mere spectators, a trial is above all a search for truth . . . while justice is blind, jurors need not also be." In *State v. Kendall* (1907), the court held that there was nothing improper in a juror asking a question with the apparent purpose of discovering the truth. The court pointed out that jurors ask often pertinent questions that help in advancing the investigation. In other cases (e.g., *Hudson v. Markum*, 1997; *Louisville Bridge & Terminal Co. v. Brown*, 1925;

State v. Graves, 1995; *United States v. Callahan,* 1979; *United States v. Thompson,* 1996; *White v. Little,* 1928), courts have observed that juror questions might aid the jury in finding the truth.

Heuer and Penrod's (1988, 1989, 1994a, 1994b) findings do not offer much support for this proposition. In both the Wisconsin and the national studies, judges and attorneys were asked whether they believed juror questions helped get to the truth. Their answers indicated that they did not expect juror questions to help get to the truth, and after participating in a trial in which questions were permitted, both groups reported that the questions were not very helpful.

Do Juror Questions Increase Juror, Attorney, or Judge Satisfaction with the Trial or the Verdict? As Judge B. Michael Dann (1996, p. 6) put it: "The more active jurors are at trial, the more attentive they are to the proceedings. And juror satisfaction with the whole experience is enhanced." Jurors' overall satisfaction with their trials was assessed in both the Wisconsin and the national studies. In both, the conclusion was that jurors were quite satisfied with their experiences, and their assessments were not influenced by the availability or use of juror questions. Jurors' satisfaction with their verdict and attitudes toward jury service were similarly unaffected by their opportunity to ask questions. The lawyers and judges in the national trial were also asked how satisfied they were with the jury's verdict. Overall, lawyers and judges indicated that they were reasonably satisfied (with judges somewhat more satisfied than attorneys); these assessments were also not influenced by the presence or absence of juror questions.

Do Juror Questions Alert Counsel to Issues That Require Further Development? In *United States v. Callahan* (1979, p. 1086), the court observed, "If a juror is unclear as to a point in the proof, it makes good common sense to allow a question to be asked about it. If nothing else, the question should alert trial counsel that a particular factual issue may need more extensive development." In both of Heuer and Penrod's (1988, 1989, 1994a, 1994b) studies, lawyers and judges were asked whether questions had signaled juror confusion about the law or the evidence. Lawyers and judges expected juror questions to provide useful information about the jury's thinking, but after participating in a trial in which questions were allowed, judges and lawyers agreed that questions did not yield these benefits.

Evaluation of Possible Disadvantages of Juror Questions

Several possible disadvantages of allowing jurors to ask questions were also examined in these studies.

When Jurors Are Allowed to Ask Questions Do They Become Advocates Rather Than Neutrals? In *United States v. Johnson* (1989, p. 713), Chief Judge Donald Lay observed:

> The fundamental problem with juror questions lies in the gross distortion of the adversary system and the misconception of the role of the jury as a neutral factfinder in the adversary process. . . . The neutrality and objectivity of the juror must be sacrosanct.

The Second Circuit raised the same concern in several recent cases, including *United States v. Thompson* (1996) and *United States v. Bush* (1995, p. 515), where it said: "Although we reaffirm . . . that juror questioning of witnesses lies within the trial judge's discretion, we strongly discourage its use. The most troubling concern is that the practice risks turning jurors into advocates, compromising their neutrality." McLaughlin (1982) described this phenomenon as the "12 angry men syndrome," in which jurors lose their objectivity and begin to direct accusatorial questions to the witness.

Heuer and Penrod (1988, 1989, 1994a, 1994b) examined several types of evidence that indirectly address this concern. One was the pattern of jury decisions. The verdict pattern in the national study indicated that jury questions did not have a significant effect on the verdicts. Heuer and Penrod also asked the judges what their preferred verdict would have been in those trials. This allowed the researchers to examine the rate of judge and jury agreement. The agreement rate was not affected by juror questions; judges and jurors agreed on the verdict in 69% of the cases. Although the agreement was slightly higher in cases in which questions were permitted (74% versus 65%), this difference was not statistically significant. In addition, there was no evidence that either lawyer was perceived less favorably as a result of the questioning procedure (a result that might be expected if jurors lost their neutrality). In fact, attorneys on both sides were perceived somewhat more favorably in trials where questions were permitted.

Do Jurors Ask Improper Questions?   One concern of trial attorneys is that jurors, because they are untutored in the law, will ask impermissible questions and should therefore be discouraged from asking any questions at all. Chief Judge Donald Lay in *United States v. Johnson* (1989, p. 713) observed, "Because lay jurors will not understand the rules of evidence, they may well ask impermissible questions, such as those directed at the defendant's character." The court in *Day v. Kilgore* (1994, p. 518) expressed the concern this way: "Questions from a jury, untrained in the rules of evidence, may be improper or may solicit information that is either irrelevant or outside of the evidence presented." Examples of jurors asking classically impermissible questions can be found in the case law. For example, in *Maggart v. Bell* (1931), one juror asked the defendant whether he was covered by accident insurance.

Despite these sorts of reservations, Heuer and Penrod (1988, 1989, 1994a, 1994b) found that although jurors do not know the rules of evidence, they nonetheless ask appropriate questions. In the Wisconsin study, both lawyers and judges reported that they did not expect juror questions to be inappropriate or inept, and they did not find them to be so. Lawyers and judges in the national study who participated in a trial with juror questions reported that improper questions were not a problem.

Do Juror Questions Interfere with Attorney Trial Strategies?   Attorneys in the Wisconsin study were also asked whether juror questions brought up information that they had deliberately omitted; this question was asked because preliminary questioning of trial attorneys revealed a fear that juror questions would play havoc with attorney trial strategies: " 'Trials should continue to be what parties deem to present to jurors,' not an extended search by those jurors for an underlying truth," as one attorney quoted by Tripoli (1997, pp. 104–105) put it. However, attorneys who participated in trials in which questions were permitted reported that this was not a problem.

Are Trial Counsel Reluctant to Object to Inappropriate Juror Questions?   Numerous courts have refused to reverse when counsel did not object, during trial, to permitting jurors to ask questions (e.g., *Chicago Hanson Cab Co. v. Havelick*, 1869) or to improper juror questions (e.g., *Louisville Bridge & Terminal Co. v. Brown*, 1925). In considering whether counsel should be *required* to object to improper juror questions in order to preserve the point for appeal, the court in *State v. Sickles* (1926) asked whether this standard was appropriate when objections raise the risk of offending the juror.

In *Day v. Kilgore* (1994, pp. 517–518), the South Carolina Supreme Court expressed the concern and noted the actions of its brethren in Texas:

> When either the judge or the jury departs from their assigned roles, the lawyer is confronted with the dilemma of whether to object and risk alienating the judge or jury, or remain silent and risk waiving the issue for appeal purposes. . . . Confronted with a barrage of appeals where the jury departed from its normal role of passive listeners, the Texas Supreme Court issued an absolute prohibition on the procedure. [*Morrison v. State*, 845 S.W.2d 882 (Tex., 1992)]

Heuer and Penrod's (1988, 1989, 1994a, 1994b) studies show that lawyers are not immobilized by such fears. In the national and Wisconsin studies, lawyers objected to 20% and 17% (respectively) of questions submitted by jurors. In the national study, lawyers objected to at least one question in 40% of the trials in which at least one question was asked. Of course, Heuer and Penrod's practice of suggesting that jurors submit questions in writing (a procedure now formally adopted in some jurisdictions) so that attorneys may object in private offered some protection to an objecting attorney. Furthermore, if an objection was sustained, judges were asked to explain the ruling to the jury to minimize the possibility that jurors would draw an adverse inference.

General Conclusions about Juror Questioning of Witnesses

- Jury questioning promotes juror understanding of the facts and issues.
- Juror questions do not clearly help get to the truth.
- Juror questions do not alert trial counsel that issues require more extensive development.
- Juror questions do not increase participants' satisfaction with the trial, the judge, or the verdict.
- Jurors do not become advocates rather than neutrals.
- Although jurors do not know the rules of evidence, they ask appropriate questions.
- Juror questions do not interfere with attorney trial strategies.
- Counsel are not reluctant to object to inappropriate juror questions.

Juror Note Taking

The courts have frequently considered the merits of permitting jurors to take notes during trials (an exhaustive, 50,000-word review of the case law can be found in Larsen, 1996). Traditionally, courts were cool to the idea because juror literacy was far from uniform and there were reservations about allowing some jurors to rely on memory and others on notes. As the court in *Sligar v. Bartlett* (1996, p. 1385) observed, "The common law rule grew from a suspicion that a 'lettered' juror would be revered, and thus excessively persuasive to the other jurors who could not read or write. To guard against this note taking was prohibited."

The illiteracy objection has largely disappeared (though see *State v. Triplett*, 1992, for a contemporary expression of concern on this matter), but there are other objections to note taking, and the courts in many jurisdictions have not resolved fully their stance on the question. Thus, it is possible to find recent decisions such as the one in *United States v. Darden* (1995, p. 1537) that take a disapproving or cautious approach: "Note taking by jurors is not a favored procedure. As we have stated, trial courts are properly concerned that the juror with the most detailed notes, whether accurate or not, may dominate jury deliberations." In contrast, it is also possible to find recent decisions such as that in *Crum v. State* (1997, p. 15) that take a neutral to approving stance on note taking: "The decision to allow jurors to take notes and consult them during deliberation is within the sound discretion of the trial judge."

Empirical Research

Several studies have examined the advantages and disadvantages of juror note taking. The research methods employed in these studies have varied widely. In a field study, Flango (1980) assigned one civil trial and one criminal trial to a note-taking condition and compared them to two non-note-taking control trials. A field study by Sand and Reiss (1985) permitted jurors to take notes in 14 criminal and 18 civil trials. Neither of these field studies used random assignment of cases. At the other end of the methodological spectrum is a laboratory study by Hastie (1983), who randomly assigned six-person simulated juries to a note-taking or non-note-taking condition, presented a videotape of an actual armed robbery trial, and had them deliberate to a verdict. Rosenhan, Eisner, and Robinson (1994) also conducted a laboratory experiment, in which 144 jury-eligible college students and jurors were randomly assigned to note-taking or no-notes conditions, viewed a 75-minute videotaped simulation of a civil trial, and were tested for recall and comprehension of trial material immediately afterward. Horowitz and colleagues have conducted several studies using a similar experimental methodology (ForsterLee & Horowitz, 1997; ForsterLee, Horowitz, & Bourgeois, 1994; Horowitz & Bordens, 2002; Horowitz & ForsterLee, 2001). In this line of research, the participants were shown a videotaped mock trial of a toxic tort case with multiple and differentially worthy plaintiffs. The presence or absence of note taking was manipulated, in addition to other trial procedures. Liability judgments, compensation awards, and measures of cognitive performance were recorded. ForsterLee et al. and ForsterLee and Horowitz presented the mock trial to individual jurors, and Horowitz and ForsterLee and Horowitz and Bordens tested the effect of note taking on juries. The two Heuer and Penrod (1988, 1989, 1994a, 1994b) field experiments described earlier also manipulated the opportunity for jurors to take notes.

Note-Taking Procedures

In the Heuer and Penrod (1988, 1989, 1994a, 1994b) studies, when a trial was assigned to the note-taking condition, judges were asked to permit jurors to take notes during all phases of the trial and to instruct the jurors about this permission as soon as practicable after the jury was impaneled. Judges were also provided suggested instructions about note taking. In trials assigned to non-note taking, judges were asked to bar notes.

Across Heuer and Penrod's (1988, 1989, 1994a, 1994b) two studies, juror note taking was allowed in 135 trials. When jurors were given the opportunity to take notes, most did so (66% in the Wisconsin study, 87% in the national study), but they did not take extensive notes. In the Wisconsin study, where trials lasted an average of 2.3 days, jurors took an average of 5.4 pages of notes. In the national study, the juror averages for civil trials (which lasted an average of nearly 10 days) were 14.4 pages of notes, and for criminal trials (which lasted an average of nearly 6 days) 7.1 pages of notes. In the national study, Heuer and Penrod estimated that jurors in both types of trials took an average of .6 pages of notes per hour of trial time. ForsterLee and Horowitz (1997) found that jurors' notes ranged in length from a couple of sentences to 7 pages. However, that study was based on an hour-long video, not a full trial, which could explain the less extensive note taking.

Evaluation of the Possible Advantages of Juror Note Taking

Juror note taking is thought to have a number of advantages. Several of the studies examining the practice have examined these potential benefits.

Does Juror Note Taking Improve Decision Making? The primary method of measuring the quality of juror and jury decision making used by Horowitz and colleagues was to present the mock jurors with four differentially worthy plaintiffs and determine if their compensatory damage awards appropriately distinguished among these plaintiffs. ForsterLee et al. (1994) and Horowitz and ForsterLee (2001) found that note-taking jurors were better able to distinguish among these plaintiffs than non-note-taking jurors. ForsterLee and Horowitz (1997) also found that note taking improved jurors' ability to distinguish among plaintiffs with varying levels of injury, especially when the evidence was less complex and preinstructions on the law were provided. Overall, this research indicates that note taking may help improve the quality of jury decision making, at least as measured by the legal appropriateness of compensatory awards.

Does Juror Note Taking Serve as a Memory Aid? Some earlier studies (e.g., Flango, 1980; Sand & Reiss, 1985) reported that jurors found the note-taking procedure helpful as a memory aid, and courts (e.g., *Marbley v. State*, 1984; *Reece v. Simpson*, 1983; *State v. Trujillo*, 1994; *United States v. Carlisi*, 1940) have endorsed this seemingly reasonable proposition, arguing that there is no reason why notes should not be made by jurors, given that judges and lawyers make notes and given the possibility notes might aid jurors' memories and enable them to consider the evidence more intelligently. In *Densen v. Stanley* (1919), the court concluded that note taking can assist the jurors in arriving at a correct and fair verdict. As the Oklahoma Court of Criminal Appeals (*Cohee v. State*, 1997, p. 2) recently observed:

We find that jurors may benefit from notes in several ways: (1) jurors may follow the proceedings more closely and pay more attention as they take notes for later use; (2) jurors' memories may be more easily and reliably refreshed during deliberations; (3) jurors may make fewer requests to have portions of trial transcript read back during deliberations; and (4) the ability to use their notes may result in increased juror morale and satisfaction.

In both of the Heuer and Penrod (1988, 1989, 1994a, 1994b) studies, jurors were asked a variety of questions about their recall of the evidence. In the Wisconsin study, jurors even completed a multiple-choice test of their understanding of the judge's instructions. Heuer and Penrod's conclusion from both studies was that there was no evidence to suggest that note taking produced better recall. Although we believe the evidence from these field studies is more compelling than findings from prior, but weaker, field research, it is still difficult to argue that there is no memory advantage to juror note taking. As in the other field studies, the measures used by Heuer and Penrod may not have been sufficiently sensitive to detect memory benefits. The researchers relied on quite general measures of recall rather than measures tailored to the facts of each case.

In assessing memory enhancement effects, the benefits of experiments in controlled environments (e.g., mock trials) are clear: Such studies are much more powerful test settings because they can easily control the content of the trial, can vary the complexity of the trial, and can directly measure juror performance as a function of their opportunity to take notes. The Rosenhan et al. (1994) laboratory experiment on note taking did test jurors' recall and comprehension. Jurors were asked questions tailored to the particular case they had observed, and they had their notes available for reference while answering the questions. On a measure of recall, note takers outperformed non-note takers by a modest but significant margin. The authors report that 7 of the 10 highest scores on the recall measure were attained by note takers, whereas 8 of the 10 lowest scores were attained by non-note takers. Among note takers, the authors found a positive relationship between the quantity of notes taken and recall and between the degree of organization in notes and recall. The authors found no effect for notes on jurors' verdict preferences.

Horowitz and colleagues also measured recall of trial evidence in a laboratory experiment by having the participants free-recall the evidence they could remember and later coding that evidence as probative, nonprobative, and evaluative. Generally, note taking resulted in an increase in the amount of information recalled (ForsterLee et al., 1994). Note takers reported more probative evidence than non-note takers, and they reported less nonprobative and evaluative evidence than non-note takers (ForsterLee & Horowitz, 1997; ForsterLee et al., 1994; Horowitz & Bordens, 2002). However, this difference was more pronounced when the jurors were preinstructed and when the case was less ambiguous, indicating that notes are more helpful when jurors are given a framework for the evidence and it is easily understood (ForsterLee & Horowitz, 1997). Horowitz and ForsterLee (2001) measured the effect of note taking on memory by presenting mock juries with recognition items containing trial facts and plausible lures of facts not presented in trial. Using this methodology, they found that note-taking juries made fewer recognition errors and fewer false alarms for both pro-plaintiff and pro-defendant lures.

Given these results, it would appear that note taking has the potential to increase accurate recall of trial evidence, but ForsterLee et al. (1994) also investigated *how* note taking improves memory. Jurors' access to their notes was manipulated, in addition to whether or not they were permitted to take notes at all. Although the researchers did observe an improvement in recall for the note-taking jurors, they observed no difference in memory between the note takers with and without access to their notes. Based on this finding, the authors concluded that the aid to memory provided by note taking may occur at the encoding stage.

Does Note Taking Increase Juror Satisfaction with the Trial or the Verdict?   Dann (1996, p. 6) concurs with the Oklahoma court in *Cohee* that note taking can have a salutary effect on jurors: "The more active jurors are at trial, the more attentive they are to the proceedings. And juror satisfaction with the whole experience is enhanced." In the Wisconsin experiment, Heuer and Penrod (1988, 1989, 1994a, 1994b) detected a slight increase in juror satisfaction with trials, but the finding was not replicated in the national experiment, nor did note taking influence jurors' verdict confidence in the national study. Of course, jurors were already quite satisfied with their verdicts and the procedures in their trials (on 9-point scales, with higher scores indicating greater satisfaction, jurors' mean satisfaction with the verdict was 7.0, and their mean satisfaction with the trial procedure was 7.2), so there may be a ceiling effect in operation. In the laboratory experiments measuring satisfaction, Horowitz and ForsterLee (2001) also found that note-taking juries reported more satisfaction with the deliberations, and note-taking juries believed they were more efficient as a group than non-note-taking juries.

Evaluation of the Possible Disadvantages of Juror Note Taking

A variety of possible disadvantages of allowing juror note taking have also been examined.

Do Jurors' Notes Produce a Distorted Record of the Case?   According to the majority in *Thornton v. Weaber* (1955), jurors are unable to distinguish important from unimportant evidence and will therefore miss the important evidentiary points while noting the unimportant ones. These biased notes, according to this analysis, will then distort the jurors' evaluation of the trial evidence. Similarly, the defendant in *State v. Triplett* (1992) argued (unsuccessfully) that juror notes had distorted the evidence. In *United States v. Davis* (1900), the court considered whether it was appropriate for a judge, upon noticing that two jurors had occasionally taken notes, to direct them to discontinue and turn their notes over to the marshal. In ruling that note taking was improper, the appeals court stated, "Without corrupt purpose, [the juror's] notes may be inaccurate, or meager or careless, and loosely deficient, partial, and altogether incomplete" (p. 839). This critique suggests that juror note taking will interfere with the accurate transmission of information from the courtroom to the deliberation room.

In both of Heuer and Penrod's (1988, 1989, 1994a, 1994b) studies, they concluded that notes tended to be a fair and accurate record of the trial proceedings. With respect to the most important trial outcome, Heuer and Penrod found no evidence that verdicts were affected by note taking. In the experimental studies that measured liability verdicts, there was also no evidence that verdicts were affected by note taking (ForsterLee et al., 1994; Horowitz & ForsterLee, 2001). The absence of a main effect for note taking on verdicts clearly indicates that note taking does not systematically favor the defense or prosecution/plaintiff.

There have been mixed results for the effects of note taking on compensatory awards. Some studies have found no effect (ForsterLee et al., 1994); other studies have found that note takers made reduced awards (Horowitz & ForsterLee, 2001). ForsterLee and Horowitz (1997) found that note takers awarded higher compensatory damages than non-note takers. However, they concluded that this was actually a reflection of better discrimination between the plaintiffs and was a positive effect.

Heuer and Penrod (1988, 1989, 1994a, 1994b) also asked jurors whether their notes tended to be valuable records of the trial or mostly doodles, and they reported that they were considerably more likely to be accurate records. More impressive perhaps are the comments from one of the participating judges in this experiment, who was initially quite skeptical about jurors' note-taking abilities. Upon reviewing the notes from eight trials, his report included the following comments:

> Approximately one-third of all the jurors . . . took surprisingly detailed notes. The notes were so clearly written and organized that I had little trouble determining what went on in the case. . . . Many of the notes were extremely articulate and well organized. I concluded that jurors have far better notetaking capacity than I had realized. (as cited in Heuer & Penrod, 1988, p. 250)

ForsterLee and Horowitz (1997) also measured the quality of jurors' notes and observed that as the length of the notes increased, the jurors' ability to correctly recall probative trial evidence and ability to distinguish between plaintiffs also increased.

Is Note Taking Distracting?　In *Fischer v. Fischer* (1966), the court concluded that jurors should not be allowed to take notes because poor note takers are likely to be distracted. A similar argument was made more recently in *Matthews v. Commonwealth Edison Co.* (1995, p. 7): "Unless a case is complex note taking by jurors is unwarranted and may even interfere with the jurors' ability to observe the witness and attend the testimony." Hastie (1983) similarly suggested that note takers might be distracted from assessing witness credibility. Flango (1980) suggests that note takers may distract non-note takers or themselves by doodling. McLaughlin (1982) suggests that jurors making notes on a trivial point will miss important evidence. The majority in *Thornton v. Weaber* (and Flango, 1980) similarly suggested that note takers could not keep pace with the trial and would therefore miss important points. Jurors in note-taking trials in both Heuer and Penrod (1988, 1989, 1994a, 1994b) experiments overwhelmingly reported that the trial did not proceed too quickly for them to keep pace with the proceedings: 85% of the jurors in the Wisconsin study and

87% of the jurors in the national study said this was not a problem. In both studies, note takers and non-note takers in note-taking trials agreed that they were not distracted by note takers. And in the Wisconsin study, the judges and attorneys said they neither expected nor found note taking to be distracting.

Do Note Takers Have an Undue Influence over Non-Note Takers? Several decisions have expressed concern that more prolific note takers might have inappropriate influence on other jurors. The court in *Fischer v. Fischer* (1966) concluded that jurors should not be allowed to take notes because skilled note takers will gain a marked influential advantage over other jurors. In *Thornton v. Weaber* (1955), the court cleverly speculated that note takers might have more influence because they might seem more alert and informed than non-note takers. And in *United States v. Davis* (1900), the court speculated that a juror who can refer to notes could have undue influence in conflicts of memory.

In both of Heuer and Penrod's (1988, 1989, 1994a, 1994b) studies, note takers and non-note takers agreed that note takers should not and did not have an advantage over non-note takers during deliberations. In addition, in the Wisconsin experiment, Heuer and Penrod found no evidence that better-educated jurors participated more in the jury's deliberations when aided by trial notes.

Do Juror Notes Favor One Side or the Other? Flango (1980) suggested that note taking might favor the prosecution or plaintiff if jurors take notes early in the trial but lose their enthusiasm and take fewer notes later in the trial. Neither of the Heuer and Penrod (1988, 1989, 1994a, 1994b) studies found jurors were more diligent note takers during earlier phases of a trial. In the Wisconsin study, jurors in note-taking trials did report slightly less favorable impressions of the defense attorney, but the effect was small and the pattern was not reproduced in the national study. As noted earlier, the national study also revealed no effect of note taking on verdicts. However, ForsterLee and Horowitz (1997) concluded that the increased compensatory awards given by note takers suggested a pro-plaintiff bias. Overall, the majority of the research indicates that note taking does not favor either the prosecution or the defense.

Does Juror Note Taking Consume Too Much Trial Time? Several appellate decisions have indicated that note taking is acceptable only if it does not require substantial court time (e.g., *Cahill v. Baltimore*, 1916; *Tift v. Towns*, 1879). Hastie (1983) speculated that note taking might lengthen jury deliberations as jurors try to resolve discrepancies in their notes. However, Hastie's study came to the same conclusion as Heuer and Penrod's (1988, 1989, 1994a, 1994b): In neither study was deliberation time affected by juror note taking. In the Wisconsin study, the jurors in note-taking trials did not report any increase in the difficulty of agreeing on the meaning of the law on the application of the judge's instructions to trial facts or in acrimonious debate. The jurors in the national study indicated that little deliberation time was devoted to discussions of notes (the median estimate was 1%; the mode was 0%).

General Conclusions about Juror Notes

- Note taking may improve the quality of jury decision making.
- Juror notes probably are a minor memory aid, perhaps at the encoding stage.

- Juror note taking may increase juror satisfaction with the trial, the judge, or the verdict.
- Jurors' notes do not produce a distorted view of the case.
- Note takers can keep pace with the trial.
- Note-taking jurors do not distract other jurors.
- Note takers do not have an undue influence over non-note takers.
- Juror note taking does not favor either the prosecution or the defense.
- Juror note taking does not consume too much time.

PREDELIBERATION JURY DISCUSSIONS

Traditionally, discussion among the jury members has been prohibited until the case is closed and the jury is deliberating. The arguments against permitting jurors to discuss the case prior to deliberation are that jurors will be more likely to prejudge the case prior to the presentation of all evidence, that shared biases among the jurors will be created, and that discussions will result in a pro-plaintiff or pro-prosecution bias. The potential benefits include increased comprehension, increased ability to recall evidence, a reduction in individual biases due to comparison of views with other jurors, and a reduction in inappropriate discussions with other jurors, friends, and family members.

In 1995, Arizona made several reforms to the jury system. One of these reforms made it permissible to instruct civil jurors that they may discuss the case prior to deliberation if all the jury members are present (Ariz. R.Civ.P. 39(f)). Jurors are also instructed to avoid making premature judgments about the verdict. A few other states are also considering such reforms (for a review of these issues, see Diamond, Vidmar, Rose, Ellis, & Murphy, 2003; Hannaford, Hans, & Munsterman, 2000; Hans, Hannaford, & Munsterman, 1999).

Recent research has been conducted on the effects of this procedure. Hannaford et al. (2000) studied the effects of predeliberation jury discussions on jury decision making with real juries in Arizona. One strength of the study was that juries were randomly assigned to either a discussion or no-discussion condition. In the discussion condition, juries were given the Arizona instruction permitting discussions when all jury members were present, and in the no-discussion condition, juries were instructed not to discuss the case prior to deliberation. At the close of each case, all of the trial participants were given questionnaires, including the judge, the attorneys, the parties to the case, and the jurors. Overall, there were few beneficial effects of discussions on jury decision making, but there were also few harmful effects. Jurors reported that they believed the discussions were helpful, but the other trial participants noted few differences between the discussion and no-discussion juries. Although discussions have the potential to increase comprehension of trial evidence and improve decision-making quality, discussions did not significantly improve jurors' comprehension of evidence, nor did they improve the quality of their ultimate decisions. Some results indicated that jurors permitted to discuss the case with other jurors engaged in less discussion of the case with friends and family members, which is a positive effect of permitting discussions. However, the discussion jurors were also more likely to engage in impermissible informal discussions with other jurors than jurors instructed not to discuss the case at all.

As for the potential negative effects of discussions, the main concern over allowing discussions is the potential for prejudgment, but there were no significant differences observed between the discussion and no-discussion juries on their level of prejudgment. A pro-plaintiff bias was observed, but only in one of many counties studied. From these findings, the authors concluded that permitting predeliberation jury discussions did not have a dramatic positive or negative impact on jury decision making (Hannaford et al., 2000).

More recently, the same jury reform was evaluated by observing jury deliberations in actual Arizona trials, in addition to measuring the effect of discussions by surveying the trial participants (Diamond et al., 2003). Diamond and her colleagues randomly assigned 50 juries to either a discussion or no-discussion procedure. The trials were videotaped, and all of the jurors' interactions in the jury room during breaks and deliberation were videotaped. All trial participants were also given a questionnaire about their perceptions of the trial. Jurors permitted to have discussions spent significantly more time discussing the cases than no-discussion jurors, and this discussion tended to improve recall of the evidence. In general, these discussions were appropriately focused on the trial evidence. Statements of prejudgment were made by some jurors, but no jury reached a verdict prior to deliberations and the prejudgments were not necessarily related to the final verdict. Jurors in both conditions were equally likely to discuss the cases with people outside the jury. As was observed by Hannaford and her colleagues (2000), discussion jurors did not strictly adhere to the rule requiring all members of the jury to be present for discussions. The authors suggest that modifications in the procedure permitting jury discussions might improve their effectiveness. Some of the modifications suggested were the appointment of a temporary leader for the jury to ensure that the discussion topics were appropriate, preliminary instructions on the use of jury questions, and a more extensive written instruction regarding discussions.

Overall, permitting jurors to engage in predeliberation discussion of the trial did not have the extremely positive or negative effects that were predicted. There is evidence that discussions increase the jurors' perceptions that they understand the evidence and are performing their duties efficiently. There is also some evidence that it may increase comprehension of the trial evidence. However, there is little evidence that it results in prejudgment of the case, that it reduces the amount of improper discussion, or that it results in an improvement in overall decision-making quality. Additional procedures related to the jury discussions may improve the effectiveness of this aid to jury decision making.

ACCESS TO TRIAL TRANSCRIPTS

Providing jurors access to the trial transcripts could improve juror decision making, and it is generally within the broad discretion of the judge to determine if the jury should have access to transcripts (see, e.g., *Commonwealth v. Richotte*, 2003). One of the judicial concerns in reviewing testimony for the jury upon their specific request is that the jury will unduly rely on the reviewed testimony in reaching a verdict (*Commonwealth v. Bacigalupo*, 2000). However, permitting jurors to review the transcript of the entire case would allow them to refresh their recollection of the testimony and to clarify points of argument over the testimony.

It has been suggested that trial transcript access could increase the chances that jurors will process the trial evidence systematically (Horowitz & Forster-Lee, 2001). Prior research indicates that access to the trial transcript prevents jurors from relying on biased heuristic cues in their decision making. Bourgeois, Horowitz, and ForsterLee (1993) manipulated access to trial transcripts in a medical malpractice case. Mock jurors with access to transcripts made legally correct decisions, whereas mock jurors without the transcripts were more likely to rely on heuristic cues and to make legally incorrect decisions (Bourgeois et al., 1993).

Horowitz and ForsterLee (2001) investigated the effects of trial transcript access on jury decision making. It was hypothesized that access to trial transcripts would result in systematic evidence processing, better discrimination among plaintiffs who should be differentially compensated, and improved recall of probative evidence. Mock juries in a toxic tort case were either given access to the trial transcript on a computer in the deliberation room or were not given access to the transcript. Four differentially worthy plaintiffs were presented to the jurors, and note taking was also manipulated. Access to transcripts did not significantly affect liability verdicts, but it did decrease the level of compensation given to all of the plaintiffs. However, transcript access did not result in better discrimination among the differentially worthy plaintiffs in terms of the compensatory awards. Juries with access to trial transcripts were not more likely to distinguish among the plaintiffs than the juries without access. It is unclear if the jurors who were given access to the transcripts actually reviewed the transcripts, and if they did, to what extent they relied on the transcripts; this could account for their lack of influence in this area. As for positive outcomes, juries with transcript access made fewer recognition errors for the trial evidence. Additionally, jurors given access to transcripts reported being more satisfied with the trial process and were more likely to believe that their jury worked efficiently than jurors without transcript access (Horowitz & ForsterLee, 2001).

Overall, the results of the existing research indicate that transcripts may help jurors process the evidence, as evidenced by fewer errors in recognizing trial evidence. However, the results are mixed as to whether decision making was improved with the access to transcripts.

Written Witness Summaries

Relying on the theory that jurors would better be able to understand and process trial evidence if provided with a schema for the evidence to be presented, ForsterLee, Horowitz, Athaide-Victor, and Brown (2000) examined the effectiveness of giving jurors written summaries of expert testimony. The mock trial presented to participants was a toxic tort case that included complex expert testimony from a medical doctor. The written summary was three pages long and included the credentials of the expert and a short summary of his testimony, but it did not include his conclusions. This summary was presented to the jurors either prior to the trial, after the trial, or not at all. To determine the effectiveness of the expert, four plaintiffs were involved in the lawsuit who had varying degrees of injury about which the expert provided information.

Those participants who were not given a written summary were unable to reliably distinguish between the injury levels of the four plaintiffs. In contrast, the participants receiving the pretrial summary were able to distinguish among all four of the plaintiffs. The participants receiving the posttrial summary were only able to distinguish between the highest and lowest level of injury. Other differences were observed between the pretrial and posttrial groups. Recall of relevant expert information was better for the pretrial group than both the posttrial and the no-summary group, and ratings of the technicality of the expert's testimony were lower for the pretrial group than for both the posttrial group and the no-summary group. Overall, jurors' memory, information processing, and decision making were improved by the presentation of the summary prior to the evidence.

The authors concluded that the pretrial statement provided the jurors with an appropriate schema with which to evaluate the expert evidence. They referred to this as a "bottom-line schema." The use of the schema assisted the jurors in their processing of the evidence and in their decision making. The authors predicted that the observed positive effects on cognitive processing would be even greater in real trials, which include jury deliberations. However, there are several procedural problems with the use of written witness summaries, including court monitoring of the content for accuracy and to prevent improper conclusions from being presented to the jury (ForsterLee et al., 2000).

CONCLUSIONS FROM EMPIRICAL RESEARCH

These procedures deserve consideration as ways to assist jurors with their often complicated task. Commentators, scholars, attorneys, and judges have long complained about jury performance. It is noteworthy that both criticism and jury reforms have been advanced despite the lack of relevant systematic data. This situation is beginning to change as studies such as those discussed in this chapter provide new insights into the strengths and weaknesses of jury decision making and allow us to identify procedural reforms and decision aids that will optimize jury performance.

NOTE

1. In this chapter, "prosecutor" refers to both the prosecuting and plaintiff's attorneys.

REFERENCES

Abraham, K. S., & Jeffries, J. C. (1989). Punitive damages and the rule of law: The role of defendant's wealth. *Journal of Legal Studies, 18,* 415–425.

Abramson, J. (1994). *We, the jury: The jury system and the ideal of democracy.* New York: Basic Books.

Adamo, K. R. (1996). Reforming jury practice in patent cases: Suggestions towards learning to love using an eighteenth century system while approaching the twenty-first century. *Journal of the Patent and Trademark Office Society, 78,* 345–358.

Adler, S. J. (1994). *The jury: Trial and error in the American courtroom.* New York: Times Books.

Alaska Stat. § 09.17.020 (1994).

Arizona Rules of Civil Procedure, Rule 39(f).

Arlen, J. H. (1992). Should defendants' wealth matter? *Journal of Legal Studies, 21,* 413–429.

Baker, T., Harel, A., & Kugler, T. (2003). *The virtues of uncertainty in law: An experimental approach.* Available from http://papers.ssrn.com/sol3/papers.cfm?bstract_id=380302.

BMW of North America, Inc. v. Gore, 517 U.S. 559 (1996).

Bornstein, B. (1998). From compassion to compensation: The effect of injury severity on mock jurors' liability judgments. *Journal of Applied Social Psychology, 28,* 1477–1502.

Bourgeois, M., Horowitz, I., & ForsterLee, L. (1993). The effects of technicality and access to trial transcripts on verdicts and information processing in a civil trial. *Personality and Social Psychology Bulletin, 19,* 200–227.

Broder, J. M. (September 10, 1997). Stares of lawyerly disbelief at a huge civil award. *New York Times,* p. C-1.

Browning-Ferris Ind. v. Kelco Disposal, Inc., 492 U.S. 257 (1989).

Cahill v. Baltimore, 98 A. 235 (Md. 1916).

California Civil Code § 1431.2.

Cano, E. (2001). Speaking out: Is Texas inhibiting the search for truth by prohibiting juror questioning of witnesses in criminal cases? *Texas Tech Law Review, 32,* 1013–1051.

Casper, J. D., Benedict, K., & Perry, J. L. (1989). Juror decision making, attitudes, and the hindsight bias. *Law and Human Behavior, 13,* 291–310.

Cather, C., Greene, E., & Durham, R. (1996). Plaintiff injury and defendant reprehensibility: Implications for compensatory and punitive damage awards. *Law and Human Behavior, 20,* 189–205.

Chapman, G. B., & Bornstein, B. H. (1996). The more you ask for, the more you get: Anchoring in personal injury verdicts. *Applied Cognitive Psychology, 10,* 519–540.

Chicago Hanson Cab Co. v. Havelick, 22 N. E. 797 (Ill. 1869).

Clermont, K. M., & Eisenberg, T. (1992). Trial by jury or judge: Transcending empiricism. *Cornell Law Review, 77,* 1124–1177.

Cohee v. State, 942 P.2d 211 (Okla. 1997).

Commonwealth v. Bacigalupo, 731 N. E.2d 559 (Mass. App. Ct., 2000).

Commonwealth v. Richotte, 796 N. E.2d 890 (Mass. App. Ct., 2003).

Commonwealth v. Urena, 632 N. E.2d 1200 (Mass. 1994).

Connecticut General Statutes Annotated, 52–40 (West 1987).

Conrad, A. F., & Bernstein, H. (1964). *Automobile accident costs and payments: Studies in the economics of injury reparations.* Ann Arbor: University of Michigan Press.

Cooper Industries, Inc. v. Leatherman Tool Group, Inc., 532 U.S. 424 (2001).

Crum v. State, 946 S.W.2d 349 (Tex. App. 1997).

Daniels, S. (1989). The question of jury competence and the politics of civil justice reform: Symbols, rhetoric, and agenda-building. *Law & Contemporary Problems, 52,* 269–298.

Daniels, S., & Martin, J. (1990). Myth and reality in punitive damages. *Minnesota Law Review, 75,* 1–64.

Dann, B. M. (1993). "Learning lessons" and "speaking rights": Creating educated and democratic juries. *Indiana Law Journal, 68,* 1229–1279.

Dann, B. M. (1996). Free the jury. *Litigation, 23,* 5–6, 64–66.

Day v. Kilgore, 444 S. E.2d 515 (S.C. 1994).

DeBenedetto v. Goodyear, 754 F.2d 512 (4th Cir. 1985).

Densen v. Stanley, 84 So. 770 (Ala. Ct. App. 1919).

Diamond, S., Vidmar, N., Rose, M., Ellis, L., & Murphy, B. (2003). Juror discussions during civil trials: Studying an Arizona innovation. *Arizona Law Review, 45,* 1–79.

Eisenberg, T., Goerdt, J., Ostrom, B., Rottman, D., & Wells, M. T. (1997). The predictability of punitive damages. *Journal of Legal Studies, 26,* 623–660.

Eisenberg, T., LaFountain, N., Ostrom, B., & Rottman, D. (2002). Juries, judges, and punitive damages: An empirical study. *Cornell Law Review, 87,* 743–780.

Ellsworth, P. C. (1993). Some steps between attitudes and verdicts. In R. Hastie (Ed.), *Inside the juror: The psychology of juror decision making* (pp. 42–64). Cambridge, England: Cambridge University Press.

Elwork, A., Sales, B. D., & Alfini, J. J. (1982). *Making jury instructions understandable.* Charlottesville, VA: Michie.

English, P., & Sales, B. (1997). A ceiling or consistency effect for the comprehension of jury instructions. *Psychology, Public Policy, and Law, 3,* 381–401.

Fischer v. Fischer, 142 N. W. 2d 857 (Wis. 1966).

Flango, V. E. (1980). Would jurors do a better job if they could take notes? *Judicature, 63,* 436–443.

Ford, M. C. (1986). The role of extralegal factors in jury verdicts. *Justice System Journal, 11,* 16–39.

ForsterLee, L., & Horowitz, I. (1997). Enhancing juror competence in a complex trial. *Applied Cognitive Psychology, 11,* 305–319.

ForsterLee, L., Horowitz, I., Athaide-Victor, E., & Brown, N. (2000). The bottom line: The effect of written expert witness statements on juror verdicts and information processing. *Law and Human Behavior, 24,* 259–270.

ForsterLee, L., Horowitz, I., & Bourgeois, M. (1994). Effects of notetaking on verdicts and evidence processing in a civil trial. *Law and Human Behavior, 18,* 566–578.

Frank, J. (1949). *Courts on trial.* Princeton, NJ: Princeton University Press.

Galanter, M., & Luban, D. (1993). Poetic justice: Punitive damages and legal pluralism. *American University Law Review, 42,* 1393–1463.

Garber, S. (1998). Product liability, punitive damages, business decisions, and economic outcomes. *Wisconsin Law Review, 1998,* 237–295.

Goodman, J., Greene, E., & Loftus, E. F. (1989). Runaway verdicts or reasoned determinations: Mock juror strategies in awarding damages. *Jurimetrics, 29,* 285–309.

Green, E. (1968). The reasonable man: Legal fiction or psychosocial reality? *Law and Society Review, 2,* 241–257.

Greene, E. (1989). On juries and damage awards: The process of decisionmaking. *Law and Contemporary Problems, 52,* 225–246.

Greene, E., & Bornstein, B. H. (2003). *Determining damages: The psychology of jury awards.* Washington, DC: American Psychological Association.

Greene, E., Chopra, S., Kovera, M. B., Penrod, S., Rose, V. G., Schuller, R., et al. (2002). Jurors and juries: A review of the field. In J. Ogloff (Ed.), *Taking psychology and law into the twenty-first century* (pp. 225–284). New York: Kluwer Academic/Plenum Press.

Greene, E., Goodman, J., & Loftus, E. F. (1991). Jurors' attitudes about civil litigation and the size of damage awards. *American University Law Review, 40,* 805–820.

Greene, E., Johns, M., & Bowman, J. (1999). The effects of injury severity on jury negligence decisions. *Law and Human Behavior, 23,* 675–693.

Greene, E., Johns, M., & Smith, A. (2001). The effects of defendant conduct on jury damage awards. *Journal of Applied Psychology, 86,* 228–237.

Greene, E., Woody, W. D., & Winter, R. (2000). Compensating plaintiffs and punishing defendants: Is bifurcation necessary? *Law and Human Behavior, 24,* 187–205.

Guthrie, C., Rachlinski, J. J., & Wistrich, A. J. (2001). Inside the judicial mind. *Cornell Law Review, 86,* 777–830.

Hannaford, P., Hans, V., & Munsterman, T. (2000). Permitting jury discussions during trial: Impact of the Arizona reform. *Law and Human Behavior, 24,* 359–382.

Hans, V. P., & Ermann, M. D. (1989). Responses to corporate versus individual wrongdoing. *Law and Human Behavior, 13,* 151–166.

Hans, V. P., Hannaford, P., & Munsterman, T. (1999). The Arizona jury reform permitting civil jury trial discussions: The views of trial participants, judges, and jurors. *University of Michigan Journal of Law Reform, 32,* 349–377.

Hans, V. P., & Lofquist, W. S. (1992). Jurors' judgments of business liability in tort cases: Implications for the litigation explosion debate. *Law and Society Review, 26,* 85–115.

Hans, V. P., & Lofquist, W. S. (1994). Perceptions of civil justice: The litigation crisis attitudes of civil jurors. *Behavioral Science and the Law, 12,* 181–196.

Hastie, R. (1983). *Final report to the National Institute for Law Enforcement and Criminal Justice.* Unpublished manuscript, Northwestern University.

Hastie, R., Schkade, D., & Payne, J. (1998). A study of juror and jury judgments in civil cases: Deciding liability for punitive damages. *Law and Human Behavior, 22,* 287–314.

Hastie, R., Schkade, D. A., & Payne, J. W. (1999). Juror judgments in civil cases: Effects of plaintiff's requests and plaintiff's identity on punitive damage awards. *Law and Human Behavior, 23,* 445–470.

Hastie, R., & Viscusi, W. K. (1998). What juries can't do well: The jury's performance as a risk manager. *Arizona Law Review, 40,* 901–921.

Heuer, L., & Penrod, S. D. (1988). Increasing jurors' participation in trials: A field experiment with jury notetaking and question asking. *Law and Human Behavior, 12,* 409–430.

Heuer, L., & Penrod, S. D. (1989). Instructing jurors: A field experiment with written and preliminary instructions. *Law and Human Behavior, 13,* 231–162.

Heuer, L., & Penrod, S. D. (1994a). Juror notetaking and question asking during trial: A national field experiment. *Law and Human Behavior, 18,* 121–150.

Heuer, L., & Penrod, S. D. (1994b). Trial complexity: A field investigation of its meaning and its effects. *Law and Human Behavior, 18,* 29–52.

Hinsz, V. B., & Indahl, K. E. (1995). Assimilation to anchors for damage awards in a mock civil trial. *Journal of Applied Social Psychology, 25,* 991–1026.

Honda Motor Co. v. Oberg, 512 U.S. 415 (1994).

Horowitz, I., & Bordens, K. S. (1990). An experimental investigation of procedural issues in complex tort trials. *Law and Human Behavior, 14,* 269–285.

Horowitz, I., & Bordens, K. (2002). The effects of jury size, evidence complexity, and note taking on jury process and performance in a civil trial. *Journal of Applied Psychology, 87,* 121–130.

Horowitz, I., & ForsterLee, L. (2001). The effects of notetaking and trial transcript access on mock jury decisions in a complex civil trial. *Law and Human Behavior, 25,* 373–391.

Hudson v. Markum, 948 S. W.2d 1 (Tex. App. 1997).

Kahneman, D., Sunstein, C., & Schkade, D. (1998). Shared outrage and erratic awards: The psychology of punitive damages. *Journal of Risk & Uncertainty, 16,* 49–86.

Kalven, H. (1964). The dignity of the civil jury. *Virginia Law Review, 50,* 1055–1075.

Kalven, H., & Zeisel, H. (1966). *The American jury.* Boston: Little, Brown.

Kansas Statutes Annotated § 60–3701 (1994).

Karlovac, M., & Darley, J. M. (1988). Attribution of responsibility for accidents: A negligence law analogy. *Social Cognition, 6,* 287–318.

Kelso, J. C. (1996). Final report of the blue ribbon commission on jury system improvement. *Hastings Law Journal, 47,* 1433–1592.

King, E. M., & Smith, J. P. (1988). *Economic loss and compensation in aviation accidents.* Santa Monica, CA: RAND Corporation.

Kovera, M. B., & McAuliff, B. D. (2000). The effects of peer review and evidence quality on judge evaluations of psychological science: Are judges effective gatekeepers? *Journal of Applied Psychology, 85,* 574–586.

Kovera, M. B., McAuliff, B. D., & Herbert, K. S. (1999). Reasoning about scientific evidence: Effects of juror gender and evidence quality on juror decisions in a hostile work environment case. *Journal of Applied Psychology, 84,* 362–375.

Kozinski, A. (1995, Jan. 19). The case of punitive damages v. democracy. *Wall Street Journal,* p. A-19.

Krause v. State, 132 P.2d 179 (Okla. Crim. App. 1942).

Landes, W. M., & Posner, R. A. (1986, September/October). New light on punitive damages. *Regulation, 10,* 33–36, 54.

Landsman, S., & Rakos, R. F. (1994). A preliminary inquiry into the effects of potentially biasing information on judges and jurors in civil litigation. *Behavioral Science and the Law, 12,* 113–126.

Larsen, S. (1996). Taking and use of trial notes by jury. *American Law Reports, 36,* 1–254.

Lawson v. State, 664 N. E.2d 773 (Ind. Ct. App. 1996).

Lieberman, J., & Sales, B. (1997). What social psychology teaches us about the jury instruction process. *Psychology, Public Policy, and Law, 3,* 589–644.

Litigation Sciences. (1993). Psychological characteristics of punitive damage jurors. In *Jury Research* at 59. (PLI Corp. Law and Prac. Course Handbook Series No. 833) Practising Law Institute.

Louisville Bridge & Terminal Co. v. Brown, 277 S.W. 320 (Ky. 1925).

MacCoun, R. (1993a). Inside the black box: What empirical research tells us about decisionmaking by civil juries. In R. E. Litan (Ed.), *Verdict: Assessing the civil jury system* (pp. 137–180). Washington, DC: Brookings Institution.

MacCoun, R. (1993b). *Is there a "deep-pocket" bias in the tort system? The concern over biases against deep-pocket defendants.* Issue Paper, Santa Monica, CA: RAND Institute for Civil Justice.

MacCoun, R. (1996). Differential treatment of corporate defendants by juries: An examination of the "deep-pockets" hypothesis. *Law and Society Review, 30,* 121–161.

Maggart v. Bell, 2 P.2d 516 (Cal. App. 1931).

Marbley v. State, 461 N. E.2d 110 (Ind. 1984).

Matthews v. Commonwealth Edison Co., WL 478820 (N.D. Ill. 1995).

McLaughlin, M. A. (1982). Questions to witnesses and notetaking by the jury as aids in understanding complex litigation. *New England Law Review, 18,* 687–713.

Missouri Revised Statutes § 538.210.

Moran, G., Cutler, B. L., & De Lisa, A. (1994). Attitudes toward tort reform, scientific jury selection, and juror bias: Verdict inclination in criminal and civil trials. *Law and Psychology Review, 18,* 309–328.

Morrison v. State, 845 S.W.2d 882 (Tex. 1992).

Mott, N. L., Hans, V. P., & Simpson, L. (2000). What's half a lung worth? Civil jurors' accounts of their award decision making. *Law and Human Behavior, 24,* 401–419.

North Dakota Cent. Code § 32-03.2-11.

O'Connor, S. D. (1997). Juries: They may be broken, but we can fix them. *Federal Lawyer, 44,* 20–25.

Owen, D. G. (1994). A punitive damages overview: Functions, problems and reform. *Villanova Law Review, 39,* 363–413.

Pacific Mutual Life Ins. Co. v. Haslip, 498 U.S. 1306 (1991).

Pennington, N., & Hastie, R. (1993). The story model for juror decision making. In R. Hastie (Ed.), *Inside the juror: The psychology of juror decision making* (pp. 192–221). New York: Cambridge University Press.

Penrod, S., Linz, D., & Rios, P. (1983, June). *Allowing jurors to question witnesses: A courtroom experiment.* Paper presented at the Law and Society Association annual meeting, Denver, CO.

Peterson, M. A. (1984). *Compensation of injuries: Civil jury verdicts in Cook County.* Santa Monica, CA: RAND Institute for Civil Justice.

Peterson, M., Sarma, S., & Shanley, M. (1987). *Punitive damages: Empirical findings.* Santa Monica, CA: RAND Institute for Civil Justice.

Posner, R. A. (1995, March 1). Juries on trial. *Commentary, 99,* 49.

Prosser, W. L., & Keeton, P. (1984). *Prosser and Keeton on the law of torts* (5th ed.). St. Paul, MN: West.

Purver, J. M. (1970). Propriety of jurors asking questions in open court during course of trial. *American Law Reports, 31*(Series 3), 872–892.

Quayle, D. (1992). Civil justice reform. *American University Law Review, 41,* 559–569.

Ratton v. Busby, 326 S.W.2d 889 (Ark. 1959).

Reece v. Simpson, 437 So. 2d 68 (Ala. 1983).

Restatement (Second) of Torts, § 908(2).

Robbennolt, J. K. (2000). Outcome severity and judgments of "responsibility": A meta-analytic review. *Journal of Applied Social Psychology, 12,* 2575–2609.

Robbennolt, J. (2002a). Determining punitive damages: Empirical insights and implications for reform. *Buffalo Law Review, 50,* 103–203.

Robbennolt, J. K. (2002b). Punitive damage decision making: The decisions of citizens and trial court judges. *Law and Human Behavior, 26,* 315–341.

Robbennolt, J. K., Darley, J. M., & MacCoun, R. J. (2003). Symbolism and incommensurability in civil sanctioning: Legal decision-makers as goal managers. *Brooklyn Law Review, 68,* 1121–1158.

Robbennolt, J. K., & Studebaker, C. A. (1999). Anchoring in the courtroom: The effects of caps on punitive damages. *Law and Human Behavior, 23,* 353–373.

Robbennolt, J. K., & Studebaker, C. A. (2003). News media reporting on civil litigation and its influence on civil justice decision making. *Law and Human Behavior, 27,* 5–27.

Rosenhan, D. L., Eisner, S. L., & Robinson, R. J. (1994). Notetaking can aid juror recall. *Law and Human Behavior, 18,* 53–61.

Rustad, M. (1991). *Demystifying punitive damages in products liability cases: A survey of a quarter century of trial verdicts.* Washington, DC: Roscoe Pound Foundation.

Rustad, M. (1992). In defense of punitive damages in products liability: Testing tort anecdotes with empirical data. *Iowa Law Review, 78,* 1–88.

Sachdev, A. (2003, March 22). $10 billion smoking judgment: Philip Morris deception found over light cigarettes. *Chicago Tribune,* p. 1.

Saks, M. J. (1992). Do we really know anything about the behavior of the tort litigation system: And why not? *University of Pennsylvania Law Review, 140,* 1147–1289.

Saks, M. J., Hollinger, L. A., Wissler, R. L., Evans, D. L., & Hart, A. J. (1997). Reducing variability in civil jury awards. *Law and Human Behavior, 21,* 243–256.

Sand, L. B., & Reiss, S. A. (1985). A report on seven experiments conducted by district court judges in the Second Circuit. *New York University Law Review, 60,* 423–497.

Schaefer v. St. Louis & Suburban R. Co., 30 S.W. 331 (Mo. 1895).

Scully, J. (1996). Markman and Hilton Davis: The Federal Circuit strikes an awkward balance: The roles of the judge and jury in patent infringement suits. *Hastings Communications and Entertainment Law Journal, 18,* 631–655.

Simpson, J. T. (1996). Discovery of net worth in bifurcated punitive damages cases: A suggested approach after Transportation Insurance Co. v. Moriel. *Southern Texas Law Review, 37,* 193–229.

Sligar v. Bartlett, 916 P.2d 1383 (Okla. 1996).

South Carolina Code Annotated § 15-33-135 (Law Co-op. 1993).

State v. Alexander, 1997 WL 116903 (Ohio App. 1997).

State v. Graves, 907 P.2d 963 (Mont. 1995).

State v. Greer, 948 P.2d 945 (Ariz. Ct. App. 1997).

State v. Howard, 360 S.E.2d 790 (N.C. 1987).

State v. Kendall, 57 S.E. 340 (N.C. 1907).

State v. Sickles, 286 S.W. 432 (Mo. App. 1926).

State v. Triplett, 421 S.E.2d 511 (W. Va. 1992).

State v. Trujillo, 869 S.W.2d 844 (Mo. App. 1994).

State Farm v. Campbell, 538 U.S. 408 (2003).

Tackett, M. (1996, April 20). Dole fires a salvo at Clinton judges. *Chicago Tribune,* p. 1.

Taragin, M. I., Willett, L. R., Wilczek, A. P., Trout, R., & Carson, J. L. (1992). The influence of standard of care and severity of injury on the resolution of medical malpractice claims. *Annals of Internal Medicine, 117,* 780–784.

Texas Civil Practice & Remedies Code § 41.003.

Texas Civil Practice & Remedies Code § 84.003.

Thornton v. Weaber, 112 A.2d 344 (Pa. 1955).

Tift v. Towns, 63 Ga. 237 (1879).

Tripoli, L. (1997). Precipice of change: Professional groups urge striking changes in trial. *Inside Litigation, 3,* 1–6.

Tversky, A., & Kahneman, D. (1982). Availability: A heuristic for judging frequency and probability. In D. Kahneman, P. Slovic, & A. Tversky (Eds.), *Judgment under uncertainty: Heuristics and biases* (pp. 163–178). Cambridge, England: Cambridge University Press.

TXO Production Corp. v. Alliance Resources Corp., 509 U.S. 443 (1993).

United States General Accounting Office. (1989). *Product liability: Verdicts and case resolution in five states.* Washington, DC: Author.

United States v. Ajmal, 67 F.3d 12 (2d Cir. 1995).

United States v. Bush, 47 F.3d 511 (2d Cir. 1995).

United States v. Callahan, 588 F.2d 1078 (5th Cir. 1979).

United States v. Carlisi, 32 F. Supp. 479 (E.D. N.Y. 1940).

United States v. Darden, 70 F.3d 1507 (8th Cir. 1995).

United States v. Davis, 103 F. 457 (W.D. Tenn), aff'd, 107 F. 753 (6th Cir. 1900).

United States v. Douglas, 81 F.3d 324 (2d Cir. 1996).

United States v. Feinberg, 89 F.3d 333 (7th Cir. 1996).

United States v. Johnson, 892 F.2d 707 (8th Cir. 1989).

United States v. Polowichak, 783 F.2d 410 (4th Cir. 1986).

United States v. Richardson, 233 F.3d 1285 (11th Cir. 2000).

United States v. Stierwalt, 16 F.3d 282 (8th Cir. 1994).

United States v. Thompson, 76 F.3d 442 (2d Cir. 1996).

United States v. Wexler, 657 F.Supp. 966 (E.D. Pa. 1987).

Van der Keilen, M., & Garg, R. (1994). Moral realism in adults' judgments of responsibility. *Journal of Psychology, 128,* 149–156.

Vidmar, N. (1995). *Medical malpractice and the American jury: Confronting the myths about jury incompetence, deep pockets, and outrageous damage awards.* Ann Arbor: University of Michigan Press.

Vidmar, N. (1998). The performance of the American civil jury: An empirical perspective. *Arizona Law Review, 40,* 849–899.

Viscusi, W. K. (1998). Why there is no defense of punitive damages. *Georgetown Law Journal, 87,* 381–395.

Viscusi, W. K. (2001a). Jurors, judges, and the mistreatment of risk by the courts. *Journal of Legal Studies, 30,* 107–136.

Viscusi, W. K. (2001b). The challenge of punitive damages mathematics. *Journal of Legal Studies, 30,* 313–350.

Wells, G. L. (1992). Naked statistical evidence of liability: Is subjective probability enough? *Journal of Personality and Social Psychology, 62,* 739–752.

White v. Little, 268 P. 221 (Okla. 1928).

Williams v. Commonwealth, 484 S.E.2d 153 (Va. Ct. App. 1997).

Wissler, R. L., Evans, D. L., Hart, A. J., Morry, M. M., & Saks, M. J. (1997). Explaining "pain and suffering" awards: The role of injury characteristics and fault attributions. *Law and Human Behavior, 21,* 181–207.

Wissler, R. L., Hart, A. J., & Saks, M. J. (1999). Decisionmaking about general damages: A comparison of jurors, judges, and lawyers. *Michigan Law Review, 98,* 751–826.

Wolff, M. A. (1990). Juror questions a survey of theory and use. *Missouri Law Review, 55,* 817–873.

CHAPTER 16

Recommending Probation and Parole

DAVID NUSSBAUM

PROBATION AND parole are two aspects of community corrections. They are often considered jointly because both involve community supervision and, when breached, lead to the real possibility of reincarceration. They differ in that probation is the correctional response to minor crime and a distinct alternative to incarceration, whereas parole involves release to community supervision prior to completion of the entire sentence or mandatory portion of incarceration. Parole has both operational and jurisprudential connotations (Travis & Petersilia, 2001). Operationally, it subsumes the release decision process (parole boards) and a method of community supervision (parole officers). These functions have come under attack in recent years from both left- and right-wing critics for a number of reasons.

This chapter demonstrates the increasing need for probation and parole services, consultation with psychologists, and the changes in philosophy and realities flowing from these shifts. It summarizes current and emerging issues affecting service provision within probation and parole and approaches to address them. Community corrections populations discussed are violent offenders, sexual offenders, substance abusers, young offenders, female offenders, mentally disordered offenders, developmentally delayed offenders, and offenders in domestic violence cases.

In keeping with Gannon's (2004) cogent suggestion to provide numbers to illustrate resource requirements, Table 16.1 portrays the magnitude of specialized services required by the probation and parole populations. All data were obtained from the Bureau of Justice Statistics (BJS) Web site (www.ojp.osdoj.gov/bjs, July 27, 2004, update). These numbers speak to the relevance of, and

Appreciation is expressed to Adam Borgida for comments on a preliminary draft of this chapter. Additionally, the efforts of Jenifer Mulock in searching the literature and locating reference articles is gratefully acknowledged.

Table 16.1

Special Populations on Parole and Probation in the United States

Population	Year	Parole	Probation
Total population	2003	774,588	4,073,987
Females	2002	105,440	918,888
Young offenders	1999	159,400*	677,000
Mentally ill	1999	60,611	547,800
Alcohol-dependent	1999	105,539	712,902
Mentally ill and alcohol-dependent	1999	N/A	190,634
Drugs or alcohol used at time of offense	1999	356,034	1,496,771
Sex offenders	1997	15,866	117,428
Violent offenders	2003	216,885	774,058

Note: *Sentenced to residential placements.
Source: Bureau of Justice Web site, www.ojp.osdoj.gov/bjs, October 4, 2004, update.

need and opportunity for, psychological expertise as an integral part of specialized probation and parole service delivery and planning. Table 16.1 also underlies the choice of topics for this chapter.

ROLE AND SCOPE OF PROBATION AND PAROLE IN THE AMERICAN CRIMINAL JUSTICE SYSTEM

The utility of U.S. probation and parole services is underscored by a dramatic 3.6-fold increase, from an incarceration rate of approximately 175 per 100,000 population in 1980 to 476 per 100,000 in 2002 (BJS, www.ojp.osdoj.gov/bjs, October 4, 2004, update; the interested reader is referred to this site for periodic updates to keep current and to monitor effects of changes in policies relevant to criminal justice systems). Absent community corrections, there would be many more than the 1.3 million individuals currently in prisons, with unsustainable costs required to build new facilities. Nonetheless, by year-end 2000, 16 states had abolished parole boards for releasing all offenders and another 4 no longer utilized parole boards for releasing particular violent offenders (BJS, 2004).

These increasing numbers of community supervisees over the past two decades resulted from a change in emphasis from rehabilitation to lengthier incarcerations via truth in sentencing, mandatory minimums, and abolition or reduction of parole through restrictive parole policies (Austin, 2001). Focusing on the "reentry problem," Travis and Petersilia (2001) note the almost fourfold increase in per capita incarceration rates, disintegration of a unified sentencing philosophy, and weakening of parole as a guiding and organizing principle in current thinking about reintegration.

Austin (2001) illustrates the shortsightedness of this policy since from 1999, approximately 40% of all prison admissions are parole violators and a sizable number are probation violators. Further, over 50% of reincarcerated probationers and 20% of reincarcerated parolees were shunted back into prison for only a technical violation of their release condition. Clearly, then, the number of newly identified criminals has remained stagnant, while repeat business is accelerating. Austin notes the obvious need for more effective preentry preparation and early identification of those individuals for whom standard interventions will not be effective (see Austin, 2001, for additional details and supporting numbers).

Attention is now being shifted to prisoner reentry into the community (Austin, 2001). In the United States, 585,000 individuals exited state and federal prisons in 2000, or about 1,600 per day (Travis & Petersilia, 2001), to provide an equilibrium between those entering and exiting detention facilities. More optimistically, the Office of Justice Programs (with various federal partners; www.ojp.osdoj.gov/reentry/learn.html) has responded by creating "The Serious and Violent Reentry Initiative," a fresh attempt to enhance community safety by coordinating treatment efforts across three locations and presumably readiness to and stage of change. Phase 1, "Protect and Prepare," occurs in the institutions and focuses on education, mental health and substance abuse treatments, job training, mentoring, and full diagnostic and risk assessments. Phase 2, "Control and Restore," begins immediately before release but is primarily a community-based transition program. Depending on need, interventions will cover education, monitoring, mentoring, life skills training, job skills development, and ongoing mental health and substance abuse treatment. Phase 3, "Sustain and Support," connects the parolee/probationer with appropriate services in the community. All of this is now deemed crucial as only about half of released individuals avoid reincarceration for 3 years.

PROBATION AND PAROLE: CHANGING PHILOSOPHIES AND REALITIES

MacKenzie (2001) presents an excellent historical overview of community corrections trends within the general context of sentencing. Briefly, for the century prior to 1970, the American model focused on rehabilitation that was marked by "indeterminate sentencing," allowing the courts broad sentencing discretion to optimize rehabilitation in preparation for eventual community reintegration. The goal was synchrony between societal and offender purposes. Correctional officials tailored programs to maximize the individual's rehabilitation, and parole boards determined the point at which the offender had earned supervised release. President Johnson's Commission on Law Enforcement and Administration of Justice advocated liberal and optimistic recommendations, with an expanded role for community-oriented treatment. Unfortunately, the programs were often poorly implemented, and predictably poor outcomes followed.

In response, Martinson (1974) wrote a scathing critique of the failures of the rehabilitation model that questioned the discretion provided to jurists and prison officials alike. He coined the phrase "Nothing works," symbolic of the trend to negate the rehabilitation model and usher in a more retributive, public safety motif. Judicially, sentencing changed to "flat sentencing," imposing rigid guidelines reflecting specific crime and criminal history. Parole could be eliminated, and "truth in sentencing" would provide justice.

Others argued that the purpose of the criminal justice system was crime control rather than justice. Incapacitation and deterrence were supported by findings that a relatively small proportion of criminals committed a disproportionately large number of crimes. Incapacitation theory held that if these relatively few "career criminals" could be held for lengthy periods, there would be a precipitous drop in crime. What perhaps began as an attempt to focus on and incarcerate a few has mushroomed, as demonstrated by the numbers presented in Table 16.1.

Part of the explanation might be attributed to the 10-fold increase in drug-related incarcerations between 1980 and 1996 (Blumstein & Beck, 1999). Austin (2001) notes that, while new commitments for crimes increased only 1.1%, parole violators increased an alarming 55.6%, partially explained by new surveillance technologies such as mandatory drug testing, which effectively taints the parole process but may not really reflect a worsening of societal safety.

MacKenzie (2001) concludes that although recent research on the topic concurs that a relatively small number of individuals commit a substantial number of crimes, identification of these individuals is far from a simple process. Consequently, there is a renewed interest in identification of career criminals early in their careers, when they might be expected to be more plastic and malleable. Because costs of incarceration and of further crime escalate, there is also a renewed interest in documenting what works, as reflected by Martinson's notable critics, including Gendreau, Andrews, Bonta, and Cullen, among others (Andrews & Bonta, 1994, 1998; Cullen & Gendreau, 2001; Gendreau, Goggin, & Paprozzi, 1996).

Practically, probation and parole provide a different carrot to institutional administrators who continually must deal with increasing demand for beds, crowding, and staffing shortages. Austin (2001) suggests that it is the burgeoning expenses that have recently prompted interest in probation and parole services, rather than an interest in the rehabilitation or welfare of the individual inmate.

Travis and Petersilia (2001) argue that the importance of probation and parole services initially declined somewhat with the changes in sentencing policy. Currently, however, there are many more individuals reentering society from longer and more disruptive incarceration periods. They are rarely better equipped to succeed in society than when they arrived in prison, and at release have a more imposing criminal record. Depriving those reentering society of supervision therefore makes little sense. Interestingly, Travis and Petersilia suggest a decoupling between the percentage of sentence served and the period of supervised reentry, arguing that all returning individuals require supervision for optimal reentry success.

APPROACHES TO PROBATION

Weiss and Wozner (2002) recently provided a conceptual analysis of different trends in community corrections. The authors note that these trends turn on shifting conceptualizations and assigned importance of causes of crime, philosophy of punishment, offender change, victim protection, and, of course, the consequent purpose, basic strategies, and role for probation services and their officers. Weiss and Wosner identify 10 models that they compare and contrast on eight underlying variables: (1) underlying perception of causes of crime, (2) underlying philosophy of punishment, (3) aims of probation, (4) who is the client for change, (5) who is the client for protection, (6) basic (working) strategy, (7) role of probation officers, and (8) other features. These models include the most traditional Individualized Treatment Model, Reintegration Model, Case Management Model, Non-Treatment Assistance Model; the left-wing Radical Socialist Model; the right-wing punitive Deterrence Model; and the four "noncausal" models, Retribution, Justice, Supervision, and Passive-Observation Models. In the latter four models, probation officers exist only to supervise and enforce the probation orders.

One involved in the process might well benefit from considering which model and assumptions one works under. In a recent Toronto case, a probation officer responded to the judge's direction in court by refusing to enact the probation order. Under questioning by the astonished judge, the probation officer explained that with a caseload of 193, he could not in good conscience guarantee what the judge was seeking. Given the daunting demands for service implied by the weight of numbers involved, it is not surprising that individuals charged with implementing and delivering such services would seek an efficient method to meet the system's demands.

WHERE DOES PSYCHOLOGY FIT IN?

Finding this chapter in *The Handbook of Forensic Psychology*, one might realistically ask, "What is the psychologist's role in this vast process?" Given the magnitude of the numbers, coupled with the minimal risk that most returnees pose to the safety of society, it is not surprising that most individuals serviced by probation and parole are supervised by officers without resort to proximal psychological expertise, although many probation and parole programs were developed with psychological consultants or principles developed by forensic/correctional psychologists. Consequently, the psychologist working within the system can wear one of two hats at a time: as a resource for probation and parole officers and, occasionally, as a consultant for thorny individual cases.

The remainder of this chapter highlights recent key developments in the psychological literature where psychologists have developed (or are developing) validated tools to make a positive contribution. This chapter examines both assessment and treatment research that should facilitate hands-on practice and arm's-length consulting. Existing limitations to current techniques are offered where appropriate. Specific subsections describe recent research on psychological involvement with violent offenders, sex offenders, substance abusers, young offenders, female offenders, mentally disordered offenders, intellectually challenged offenders, and domestic offenders. One caveat suggested in reading these sections is that they are artificially subdivided in that many clients share a number of the traits that would qualify them for membership in more than a single group.

RISK ASSESSMENT IN PROBATION AND PAROLE: GENERAL CONSIDERATIONS

The current state of the art accepts that specific, objective, and empirically supported risk assessment tools are more accurate than intrinsic, subjective, and idiosyncratic clinical opinion and intuition. However, Litwack (2001; see Litwack, 2002) has provided a spirited, logical, methodological, and empirical defense of the clinical position, which, at the end of the day, may signal a clear wake-up call for the actuarialists to reexamine the potency of their claims in absolute terms rather than by setting up a straw man in terms of primitive and poorly executed administrative-clinical studies acting as the comparison standard. Nevertheless, clinicians who continue to insist that their unaided professional judgments are superior to existing actuarial risk statements are negligent in not providing peer-reviewed supportive empirical evidence.

There are at least three considerations responsible for the shift from the idiosyncratic clinical to standardized statistical tools for conducting forensic risk assessments. Kemshall (2000) elegantly captures the first consideration in considerable complexity. She notes that decisions about risk are based on far more than a simple calculation of the odds. To illustrate, she notes that people blithely continue to purchase lottery tickets despite full knowledge that their likelihood of winning stands at many millions to one. On the other hand, despite small odds, considerable lengths are traversed to avoid contraction of bovine spongiform encephalopathy (Mad Cow disease).

A second issue (Kemshall, 2000) reflects a trend that society has pursued in light of increasing complexity and the frankly unknowable nature of numerous risks in the modern world: the assignment of blame, which is equally important for administrators and practitioners. Blame for negative outcomes can be reduced if the individual has followed a predetermined, fixed, and empirically defensible procedure. A third consideration involves legal and professional demands for empirical validation to qualify as expert opinion, following landmark cases beginning with *Daubert v. Merrill Dow Pharmaceutical Inc.* (1993) in the United States and *Regina v. Mohan* (1994) in Canada. Barriers to implementation include disenfranchisement felt by front-line staff (Kemshall, 2000) and the fact that many direct service providers are not sufficiently trained in statistical techniques to appreciate the justifications underlying these practices (Corrigan, Steiner, McCracken, & Blaser, 2001).

Inscrutability of risk, liability control, and legal standards themselves do not manufacture validity, nor can an objective standard for validity easily be established to decide how good is good enough. To illustrate, a 75% accuracy level might be acceptable for predicting a slate of baseball game scores. On the other hand, an airline that advertised a 75% successful prediction rate of which destination its flights would arrive at would likely be out of business very shortly. The consequences of being right or wrong may vary considerably from application to application, with no scientific or statistical map to assign the ultimate value of a false positive or false negative outcome. There will always be a divergence of opinion regarding how many nondangerous individuals should remain incarcerated to avoid commission of x numbers of crimes of y severity, assuming that such could be done. Indeed, when writing risk assessment reports for ultimate decision makers or as an aid to probation and parole officers, it would behoove the psychologist to include a statement acknowledging the limitations of existing techniques.

Technical difficulties with actuarial instruments include the fact that they were developed only to aid in calculating group likelihoods. Insurance companies do not care whether Smith, Jones, or Brown is the one member of a risk category to die before age 43; they want to know only how many in a particular risk category will succumb at any particular point in time. This enables them to set insurance premiums for the group and maintain a residual profit at the end of all terms. Criminal justice systems—indeed, the prevailing Western concept of justice itself—do not operate on the basis of group liability.

Many existing actuarial risk instruments are static, which means that they utilize predictor variables that are historical in nature and therefore fixed. They cannot reflect, for example, how an individual might change due to maturational processes at either end of the age spectrum or positive responses to therapy. By dint of their naïve empirical and atheoretical bases, extrapolations beyond tabled values are problematic.

A related number of empirical limitations plague existing static actuarial risk instruments. First, undemonstrated or frank inability to predict severity of a violent incident renders an instrument of dubious utility to a judicial decision maker, as does the inability to predict when the individual might commit an aggressive criminal act. Other consequences of the atheoretical nature of current static risk instruments include an inability to inform intervention planning (beyond incarceration) and missing possible mitigating factors that are not related to risk in their absence.

In light of the focus on actuarial instruments, the role of neurobiological mechanisms underlying psychopathy, violence, and sexual violence have been relatively neglected by researchers in the applied forensic areas. Anomalously, politicians and forensic administrators have expressed little interest in the very control systems that could make ultimate sense of these critically important behaviors, as if the brain only modulated memory, cognition, and psychiatric illnesses, but not type of violence, severity of violence, situations in which the individual would become violent, and the threshold of activation of any neural aggression network. Predictions could be more specific if aggression type, derived from a biological understanding of aggression, was intrinsic to the instrument. Most important, rational, specific, and more effective treatments could then be developed. Research in the general mental health literature is coming to the conclusion that conjoint pharmacological and psychological approaches to behavior and symptom change are optimal.

In summary, then, an ideal risk instrument would have the following properties:

- Demonstrated validity in predicting occurrence of violence.
- Demonstrated validity in predicting severity of violence.
- Demonstrated validity in predicting time to reoffense.
- A theoretical basis and coherence, so it can inform treatment.

- Sensitivity to changes in risk level through maturation and treatment response over time.
- Protective factors that mitigate risk.
- Reducibility to the underlying neurobiology of aggression and violence.

Until our risk assessment tools can satisfy all of these requirements, it is incumbent on us to inform our clients and consumers of our services of these limitations, which should be clearly indicated in reports.

EXISTING APPROACHES TO EFFECTIVE TREATMENT/INTERVENTION FOR PROBATION AND PAROLE

Andrews's (1982) three major principles for effective correctional intervention, *risk, need,* and *responsivity,* are mirrored in most successful attempts at reduction of recidivism. McGuire and Hatcher (2001) summarized components of successful programs as being (1) theory-driven, (2) empirically supported, (3) involving cognitive-behavioral change models, (4) continually evaluated in terms of risk classification levels and empirical success, (5) focused on criminogenic needs (individual characteristics supportive of criminal behavior), (6) employing an interaction style that maximizes individual responsivity, and (7) ensuring fidelity to the intervention model (program integrity) by having well-trained staff who are genuine.

Empirically, community programs report larger effect sizes than institutional programs. McGuire and Hatcher (2001) tentatively attribute this to immediate opportunities for real-life applications of learned principles. Alternatively, community programs primarily deal with more malleable individuals, which may result from decision makers' accuracy in choosing who is shunted into community programs in the first place. Perhaps, too, enhanced efficacy of cognitive programs over more in-depth treatments is due to more limited abstract verbal abilities in offender groups, precluding effectiveness for more in-depth modalities—a violation of the responsivity principle.

As an example of an effective intervention, McGuire and Hatcher (2001) present supportive evidence for a cognitive skills enhancement program called Offense-Focused Problem Solving (OFPS). The program focuses on social interaction problems leading to criminal acts and the requisite skills in effectively negotiating successful resolution of differences. Addressed skills include problem awareness, problem definition, information gathering, differentiating facts from opinion, alternative solution generation, formulating means-ends steps, consequential thinking, decision making, and perspective taking. Cognitive errors are seen to contribute to the confluence of miscognitions that lead to social interaction problems and criminal behavior. OFPS demonstrated impressive pre-post differences, but unfortunately, these were restricted to changes on criminogenic attitudes and their associates. The stated follow-up with violent recidivist data is eagerly awaited. Data were to be available on the Home Office (U.K.) Web site as of October 2004, under "Pathfinder" probation-based interventions (Professor James McGuire, personal communication, September 2004).

To help clarify the status of empirical evidence on treatment effectiveness in recidivism reduction, Pearson, Lipton, Cleland, and Yee (2002) conducted an extensive meta-analysis involving 24 electronic databases and 17 journals. Twenty-five behavioral and 44 cognitive-behavioral studies were included, involving 1,935 and 8,435 cases, respectively. Results for the behavioral analysis barely achieved statistical significance. The more practical statistic, binomial effect size display (BESD) showed a 53% success in behaviorally treated studies versus 46.7% success in controls. Results for the cognitive-behavioral studies demonstrated BESD values of 57% for cognitive-behavioral groups versus only 42.8% success for controls. Pearson et al. note that one difficulty in transporting a behavioral treatment into the community is the change in reinforcement schedules, as trained personnel and intensive monitoring are not typically available. Cognitive-behavioral changes tend to be incorporated into thinking patterns and are therefore more transportable into the community. Pearson et al. conclude that cognitive-behavioral treatments represent the backbone of effective correctional treatments, but they note the need for additional research to examine specific cognitive-behavioral modalities and combinations with other treatment types.

Among cognitive-behavioral variants, the venerable Relapse Prevention (RP) approach has recently undergone a basic conceptual shift (Witkiewitz & Marlatt, 2004), with initial data supportive of this reconceptualization. Initially developed to treat substance abuse, RP has been adapted for application with a number of unwanted behaviors. Briefly, the original conceptualization identified access to a risky environment that was met with poor coping responses, giving rise to decreased self-efficacy and a lapse into the forbidden behavior. This quasi-chance lapse provides both intrinsic reinforcement and knowledge of successful violation that readjusts cognitive schemas to increase the likelihood of future relapse. RP begins with learning an effective coping response (generally through understanding one's offense cycle), leading to increased self-efficacy and reduction in likelihood of relapse. This model represented a linear or unidirectional understanding of the relapse process.

Witkiewitz and Marlatt (2004), responding to a number of criticisms of Marlatt's (1978) original taxonomy, have modified the model into a dynamic, recursive (nonlinear) set of processes operating in the spheres of tonic processes, high-risk situations, and phased responses. Tonic processes include distal risks, cognitive processes, and physical withdrawal. Phased responses include affective state, coping behavior, and the problematic behavior in question. Perceived effects (reinforcement, abstinence, violation effect) operate within the phased response sector and feed back directly on the intensity of the problematic behavior. What is different about this model is that the intensity of the behavior in question also feeds back to phased responses such as affective state and tonic cognitive processes. These continually readjust various parameters that influence subsequent emergence of the problem behavior. Psychologists may want to consider exploring implications of this more comprehensive approach for RP treatment.

Given this general introduction, we now turn to exploration of specifics of assessment and intervention with particular subpopulations in probation and parole services.

CONDUCTING RISK ASSESSMENTS OF FUTURE VIOLENCE

A primary consideration confronting the probation or parole officer for which a consulting psychologist can offer support is deciding which individual is or is not likely to commit another serious violent act over the course of community supervision and beyond. High-risk individuals should have considerably less access to the community, more intensive treatment, or more stringent monitoring at least during initial community exposure. This last point is important because most, but certainly not all, violent recidivists will commit violent crimes relatively shortly after gaining access to the community. A number of instruments currently exist that assess for this risk. Here we will briefly review and update well-known risk instruments and then introduce newer promising approaches.

Psychopathy Check List-Revised: 2nd Edition

Little need be said of the Psychopathy Check List-Revised: 2nd Edition (PCL-R-2; Hare, 2004) to psychologists involved in the forensic area. Initially developed to measure the personality construct called psychopathy, the penultimate version, the PCL-R (Hare, 1991), has been co-opted to greater or lesser extents in different risk assessment tools, such as the Violence Risk Appraisal Guide and the Historical, Clinical and Risk 20, to be described later. The PCL-R is more specific than the *DSM-III-R* or *DSM-IV* conceptualization of Antisocial Personality Disorder (APD) and consequently more specifically predictive of violent offending (Hare, 2004).

Briefly, Hare has argued for a two-factor model for psychopathy (interpersonal/affective, lifestyle/antisocial) and defended his original findings in face of the three-factor model (interpersonal, affective, behavioral/lifestyle) advanced so eloquently by Cooke and Michie (2001). Hare (2004, p. 3) notes that the Cook and Michie factor analysis included only 13 of the 20 items. The PCL-R-2, based on a large number of data sets, replicated the original two factors but fractionates them into four facets. Factor 1 now includes the Interpersonal (4-item) and the Affective (4-item) facets. Factor 2 consists of the Lifestyle (5-item) and Antisocial (5-item) facets. Studies demonstrating cognitive, emotional, neuroanatomical, and neuroactivational differences between psychopaths and nonpsychopaths are contained in the excellent manual accompanying the second edition (Hare, 2004). It is logical to expect that some combinations of facet scores may prove to be more specific of violent offending and its subtypes than total PCL-R scores, and item analysis may even suggest targets for treatment (Loving, 2002).

Violence Risk Appraisal Guide

The Violence Risk Appraisal Guide (VRAG; Harris, Rice, & Quinsey, 1993; Quinsey, Harris, Rice, & Cormier, 1998) is a well-known, 12-item violence risk instrument developed retrospectively on a mixed sample of 648 mentally disordered offenders referred for assessments at the Penetanguishene Mental Health Center. Quinsey et al.'s text provides all the information necessary to produce a VRAG score. The VRAG is likely familiar to forensic mental health practitioners and is not described in detail here, but a few cautions are noted. While the VRAG might be applicable to an initial assessment, by dint of its static nature it has no utility for monitoring possible change in risk. The PCL-R accounted for about 75% of the cumulative explained variance in the multiple discriminant function (regression) analysis. The VRAG score correlated only .18 with severity of recidivist violence and even more modestly (–.13) with latency to recidivate (Quinsey et al., 1998, p. 149). In its development, the authors employed a very liberal alpha to enter and exit of .25 (Harris at al., 1993), possibly resulting in spuriously retained variables. Despite replications by its authors and their colleagues, a number of nonreplications exist at the AUC/R group prediction level (Cooke, Michie, & Ryan, 2001; Loza, Villeneuve, & Loza-Fanous, 2002), clinical application of BIN level (Douglas, Hart, Dempster, & Lyons, 1999; Mills, 2003; Sjostedt & Langstrom, 2002; Tengstrom, 2001), and individual VRAG item-outcome correlations (Mills, 2003; Tengstrom, 2001). Despite these caveats, the VRAG is superior to unaided clinical opinion in evaluating long-term risk.

LEVEL OF SUPERVISION INVENTORY AND LEVEL OF SUPERVISION/CASE MANAGEMENT INVENTORY

The Level of Supervision Inventory (LSI; Andrews, 1982; LSI-R, Andrews & Bonta, 1995) is based on a social-cognitive-psychological model of behavior and behavior change (Andrews & Bonta, 1998). Its original purpose was to aid correctional placements in the community as well as in detention facilities of all types. An immediate advantage for probation and parole application is that it does not have to be imported or adapted from inside to outside the walls. The LSI focused on Andrews's (1982) risk, need, and responsivity principles of effective correctional assessment and intervention. The creators of the LSI series strongly advocate for the assessment and treatment principles and support their contentions with empirical evidence. For example, Bonta (2004) reported recent data from the Canadian federal probation system demonstrating that recidivism was lower in those offered service as opposed to sanctions. Programs that adhered to optimal treatment principles (positive relationships between probation officers and clients and structured guidance) clearly decreased the incidence of recidivism beyond programs where treatment was not optimized and monitored. Prosocial reinforcement was the most powerful behavioral influence technique identified by 72% of the parole officers sampled. Bonta and his colleagues are in the process of examining the recidivism data. Updates to this research effort are available at www.psepc.gc.ca.

The LSI (and offspring LSI-Revised, or LSI-R) transcends pure static risk indicia as it identifies long-term dynamic criminogenic needs, such as education and employment, as potential targets for psychosocial interventions. Its dimensions (with number of items in parentheses) include Criminal History (10), Education/Employment (10), Financial (2), Family/Marital (4), Accommodation (3), Leisure/Recreation (2), Companions (5), Alcohol/Drug Problems (9), Emotional/Personal (5), and Attitudes/Orientation (4).

Illustrative of its utility, a recent Australian study by Ogloff, Lemphers, and Dwyer (2004) found that patients with both major mental illness and a substance abuse disorder possessed extensive criminal histories and presented an increased level of risks and needs when compared with patients with major mental illness alone. Additionally, based on LSI profiles, development and delivery of effective forensic mental health services that address both co-occurring disorders became possible. One might debate the relative merits of the LSI versus the PCL-R in assessing risk of general and possibly violent recidivism (see Gendreau, Goggin, & Smith, 2002, and a rejoinder by Hemphill & Hare, 2004), but there is little debate that the LSI serves a broader set of applied tasks than the PCL-R or the VRAG were intended to provide.

The LSI-R has been recently expanded into the Level of Service/Case Management Inventory (LS/CMI; Andrews, Bonta, & Wormith, 2004), with the explicit intent to link case management to risk assessment. As noted earlier, this is one property of an ideal system. To make it more efficient, the LS/CMI contains only 43 items, and a specific low-frequency, risk-needs section to address violent offending was added, with respectable success ($r = .34$ with violent recidivism). The Emotional/Personal scale has been eliminated, and 3 items were deleted from the Accommodation scale, 2 items from the Criminal History and Financial Scales, and single items were dropped from the Education/Employment, Companions, and Alcohol/Drug Problems scales. A new 4-item scale reflecting Antisocial Pattern was added. Client strengths and unique risk indicators (terrorist activity) are available to help in the professional override section (Wormith, Andrews, & Bonta, 2004).

To address the concern that LSI data were largely collected in Canada and hypothetically nontransferable to U.S. correctional populations, Rzepa, Wormith, Bonta, and Andrews (2004) recently presented normative LS/CMI data on 57,436 U.S. cases, of which 39,118 were being supervised in the community. Additionally, 29,786 of the community inmates were males, with a very sizable number, 9,332, of community supervisees being female. These cases are in addition to 23,721 U.S. cases with the parent LSI-R. The principal finding of this major undertaking was that the earlier Canadian norms generalize to U.S. populations, including probation cases.

A large number of validity studies are contained in the 2003 edition of Andrews and Bonta's *The Psychology of Criminal Conduct.* One regularly updated Web site that displays LSI-R prediction data is www.wsipp.wa.gov, the product of the Washington State Institute for Public Policy.

Another recent predictive validity study of the LSI-Ontario Revision (precursor to the LS/CMI) is that of Girard and Wormith (2004). Specifically with respect to prediction of violent recidivism, Girard and Wormith cogently note that the LSI was originally developed to identify risk and needs of less serious probationary offenders for less serious (i.e., property) offenses in the community. The specific Risk-Needs scale correlated .34 with the Violent Conviction outcome. Perhaps more impressive, Offense Severity (which is not particularly well predicted by the VRAG: $r = .18$, as noted earlier) correlated .41 with the General Risk/Need score and .42 with Criminal History. In the community sample, these associations were not as robust, with Criminal History producing the largest correlation with Violent Recidivism (.25, $p < .001$) but very similar to Severity ($r = .40$, $p = .001$).

Girard and Wormith (2004) perceptively attribute the somewhat lower prediction coefficient in the community sample to the effectiveness of probation officers in ameliorating predicted risk levels. This is an interesting facet to integrating risk and management instruments, in that the better the management/treatment is informed by the risk process, the more effective the treatment regimen can be, which would reduce the predictability if it is simply measured in terms of initial risk level and outcome variable. Perhaps future studies will integrate initial risk levels with treatment success indicators as mediating factors in forecasting outcome. This issue is referred to in coming sections with respect to predictive success in atypical groups (i.e., mentally disordered offenders, domestic violence).

It appears that some of the recent prediction studies with the updated OR/CMS versions can be used to more effectively predict risk levels than earlier versions. The LSI/CM is helpful to probation officers and likely the probation system in its ability to identify psychosocial treatment targets. It presently shows better ability than the VRAG to predict severity of violence. However, it may not be as effective in identifying risk for violence as the PCL-R at present.

Historical, Clinical and Risk-20

The Historical, Clinical and Risk-20 (HCR-20: Version 2; Webster, Douglas, Eaves, & Hart, 1997) represents an attempt to balance risk assessments by anchoring conclusions with static historical factors, but taking into account dynamic clinical variables plus a blend of dynamic and static issues relating to managing risk. Unlike purely actuarial instruments, the HCR-20 was intended to help structure clinical decision making. Consequently, it does not offer norm-referenced or criterion-referenced scores. It affords judgments of low, moderate, or high risk.

All items were selected based on the empirical literature. The items are unweighted, which arguably reduces shrinkage in moving to samples other than the standardization sample (Grann, Belfrage, & Tensgstrom, 2000). The 10 Historical items include previous violence, young age at first violent incident, relationship instability, employment problems, substance use problems, major mental illness, psychopathy, early maladjustment, personality disorder, and prior supervision failure. The 5 dynamic clinician-rated items include lack of insight, negative attitudes, active symptoms of major mental illness, impulsivity, and unresponsiveness to treatment. The risk-related items consist of plans lack feasibility, exposure to destabilizers, lack of personal support, noncompliance with remediation attempts, and stress.

Although it was initially developed for use with mentally disordered offenders, the HCR-20 has been evaluated with correctional populations as well. By dint of its authors' extensive involvement with the international community, the HCR-20 has been tested outside North America. In empirical investigations of predictive validity, the HCR-20 has fared comparably with other static risk instruments such as the VRAG. For example, in a Swedish sample,

Tengstrom (2001) found that the 10 Historical items alone produced an area under the curve (AUC) of .76 and declined marginally to .74 when the PCL-R item was removed. In a Canadian correctional sample, Mills (2003) found an AUC value of the HCR-20 of .72 ($r = .37$), as compared to the VRAG AUC value of .67 ($r = .28$). Numerous other studies report AUC values ranging between .70 and .81. The primary advantage to the HCR-20 is that it is capable of modifying risk levels with changes in the individual's clinical and external risk indicator status. It shows good predictive validity and is clinician-friendly. It does not rely on any particular theory of aggression, but rests on accepted clinical conceptualizations and practices. This makes it more acceptable to front-line staff than instruments that make no utilization of clinical skills.

EMERGING VIOLENCE RISK ASSESSMENT INSTRUMENTS

Having presented the predominant existing instruments for violent risk assessment, we now turn to emerging instruments that have the potential to augment or replace current risk instruments.

SELF-APPRAISAL QUESTIONNAIRE

The Self-Appraisal Questionnaire (SAQ; Loza, 1996) represents a creative departure from the more standard risk assessment tools in that it is a self-report measure. Loza, well aware of inmates' tendencies to attempt impression management, restricted the instrument to those criminogenic content areas that have shown themselves to be reliably reported by inmates. In a sense, the SAQ is more objective than instruments requiring the psychologist to rate numerous items. As a self-report scale, it is more economical and convenient to use than other risk instruments. Instructions can be provided by a paraprofessional, and answers are in a simple yes/no format. Over 50% of items consist of dynamic factors, meaning that they can be used to monitor change over time. The content areas also permit design of individualized cognitive treatment plans. The SAQ can be used for prediction of both violent and nonviolent recidivism, which is an advantage for probation settings.

The SAQ has 72 items divided among 8 subscales reflecting antisocial attitudes, beliefs, behavior, and feeling (Criminal Tendencies). The Antisocial Personality Problems subscale taps issues common to *DSM-IV*'s Axis II APD diagnosis. Childhood misconduct is captured on the Conduct Problems subscale. Other scales include Criminal History, Alcohol and/or Drug Abuse, Anger, and Validity. The 5 Anger scale items are not included in the total SAQ score to predict violence due to the author's previous findings of no relationship in correctional samples between anger and recidivism (Loza & Loza-Fanous, 1999a, 1999b). Validity subscale items serve the dual purposes of testing truthfulness and predicting recidivism.

Loza, Dhaliwal, Kroner, and Loza-Fanous (2000) reported psychometric properties of the SAQ. Highlights include total scale 1-week test-retest reliability of .95. Total scale and subscale correlations raged between .52 and .87. Coefficient alphas for all subscales fell between .42 and .87. Previous studies indicated that the SAQ was statistically equivalent to three (Kroner & Loza, 2001) and four (Loza & Loza-Fanous, 2003) established risk instruments in predicting post-release outcome over 2 years.

More recent predictive validity studies have extended the follow-up to 5 years, which is not surprising in light of an increased base rate from approximately 12% in the Loza and Loza-Fanous (2001) 2-year follow-up study to 18% in their more recent (Loza & Loza-Fanous, 2003) 5-year follow-up report. It should be noted that an 18% base rate for violent recidivism is well below the 31% base rate in the VRAG developmental study. Still, the SAQ correlation with violent recidivism is .34, which is identical to the PCL-R alone in the VRAG developmental study and others. Villeneuve, Oliver, and Loza (2003) have obtained similar results from a sample of 49 psychiatrically treated and 273 nonpsychiatric inmates released from Canadian penitentiaries with correlations of .28 and .33, respectively.

A unique cross-cultural study (Loza et al., 2004) sampled offenders in Australia ($n = 116$), Canada (600), England (75), Singapore (520), and two U.S. states, Pennsylvania (2,730) and North Carolina (86). The sample thus contained individuals of Caucasian, African, Australian Aboriginal, Hispanic, and Asian origins. The SAQ appeared in English, Spanish, Malay, Mandarin, and Spanish, with minor revisions for local references to jail and police. No significant differences were found on SAQ scores for origin and language version, or whether the SAQ was completed for research or release decision purposes. As a postdictive study, the SAQ was able to successfully discriminate between high- and low-frequency offenders in all six sites. It also showed significant group differences between violent and nonviolent offenders in all sites except for North Carolina. The SAQ total score correlated moderately highly with the VRAG, PCL-R, and LSI-R in Canadian offenders. In the Australian sample, the SAQ total score correlated strongly with the PCL-R and VRAG, and highly with the PCL-R in the English sample. (Not all statistical comparisons were done in all samples.)

In light of its recency and need for independent replication, the consulting psychologist may not yet feel comfortable relying entirely on the SAQ for a risk assessment. However, in light of its heuristic values in identifying criminogenic treatment targets, its dynamic nature, and available predictive validity, the SAQ should be strongly considered currently as a screening tool and, pending additional confirmatory evidence, may play a larger role, especially in screening violence risk in future.

Risk and Management Evaluation

The Risk and Management Evaluation (RME; Seifert, 2004) is the adult analogue of the Child and Adolescent Risk Evaluation (CARE; Seifert, 2003; Seifert, Philips, & Parker, 2001), devised to integrate predicting risk of future violence and creating a multifaceted case management plan. As the CARE is described in the later section on young offenders, the structure of the RME is not described further here.

Among adults, correlation coefficients with previous acts of violence are extremely high (AUC = .93), and predictive success with 143 participants is higher than with any other previously published instrument ($R = .65 - .73$).

THE VIOLENCE REDUCTION PROGRAM: INTEGRATING ASSESSMENT AND TREATMENT

Wong and Gordon (2002, 2004) have produced a comprehensive and integrated assessment and treatment program specifically to reduce violent recidivism in highly dangerous, including strongly psychopathic, individuals. Because the program was developed for and supportive data have been collected only from an institutional population, generalizability to high-risk community offenders remains to be demonstrated. However, there is reason to expect transferability to community settings for those cases where a high-risk individual must be released into the community using the Violence Risk Scale (VRS; Wong & Gordon, 2000).

Assessment involves a combination of readiness for change following Prochaska and Declemente's (1992) transtheoretical model and a combination of 6 static and 20 dynamic risk factors that constitute the VRS. The static items include current age, age at first violent conviction, number of juvenile convictions, violence across the life span, prior release failures (including escapes), and stability of family upbringing. Because current age and release failures can change during treatment, these items can be recoded following treatment for an adjusted risk level.

VRS dynamic risk items include items drawn from criminal history (e.g., violent lifestyle, interpersonal aggression, criminal peers, violence cycle, weapon use), personality/cognition (e.g., criminal personality, criminal attitudes, work ethic, emotional control, impulsivity, cognitive distortion, stability of relationships, insight into violence), diagnostic considerations (mental illness, substance abuse), the environment (community support, release into high-risk situations, security level of releasing institution), and behavioral indicators (violence during incarceration and compliance with supervision). Creatively, these factors are rated pretreatment and again during treatment by the stage of change for each item; the number of stages changed is rated, and finally, posttreatment levels are rated. A Total Dynamic Score is calculated and added to the Total Static Score to arrive at a Total Dynamic + Static Score.

Treatment targets are derived from the dynamic items. Treatment itself follows cognitive-behavioral principles and relapse prevention techniques. The model is sufficiently flexible to accommodate a range of responsivity factors, including intelligence, fluctuating mental disorders, culture, and motivation. Appropriate staff training is required, and training manuals and treatment guidelines—the *Violence Reduction Program, Program Management Manual* (Wong & Gordon, 2002) and the *Guidelines for Psychopathy Treatment Program* (Wong & Gordon, in press)—will soon be available for this purpose. The program has been adapted from an inpatient Aggressive Behavior Control (ABC) program delivered at a forensic mental health facility in Canada. The authors were also involved in the development of the ABC program.

For a 5-year follow-up from time of release, reported on 918 offenders, the R2 for Violent Reconviction was extremely high at .92, but even higher (.975) when only the dynamic risk factors were used. This demonstrates two related points. First, dynamic risk indicators aided by statistical methodology can exceed the most optimistic levels reported for static risk indicators. Second, clinically rated variables (including change during treatment) are helpful when done in a theoretically coherent and rigorous manner.

The efficacy of the ABC program is demonstrated by the 35% recidivism rate in treatment completers as compared with 55% recidivism for those who did not complete treatment. An additional, untreated matched control group had a 67% recidivism rate. Combining completers and noncompleters resulted in a 46% recidivism rate. Looked at another way, the mean survival time for completers was over 66 months, as compared to only 37 months for noncompleters.

The publication of this labor-intensive technique could rekindle interest in correctional interventions. Before it becomes a standard of practice, as with all assessment and treatment techniques, replications will have to be reported by nonauthors of the test. For probation and parole psychologists, these techniques will have to demonstrate applicability to community correctional practice. Based on the initial data and the thoroughness of the method, the program will be a welcome entry to the probation and parole roster.

CLASSIFICATION TREE ANALYSIS

While not limited to a particular instrument, a recent methodological trend in analyzing predictive ability is the replacement of multiple regression, discriminant analyses, and logistic regression techniques by classification (or decision) tree analysis (CTA; see Steadman et al., 2000). CTA refers to a family of techniques that approach prediction by creation of smaller subgroups based on sequential identification of variables that optimize classification by branching, in succeeding steps, or iterations, into the most advantageous variables in further discriminating members of a subgroup. Principal advantages of CTA are that it makes no assumptions about the distribution of the data (which is frequently nonnormal and skewed in recidivism studies), and it works in a fashion that is logically similar to clinical reasoning. This results in a third advantage in that once established, a probation officer can easily, quickly, and reliably identify high- and low-risk offenders through a series of yes/no questions following a developed classification tree format (Stalans, Yarnold, Seng, Olson, & Repp, 2004). Stalans et al.'s study with domestic violence is described later as a probation example of CTA.

SUMMARY

Psychologists consulting with probation and parole services have a number of established and emerging instruments with which to inform reentry and community management decisions. No single measure presently possesses all of the ideal qualities enumerated earlier. In keeping with the efficiency demanded by community corrections, one might begin with one or two of the less onerous instruments, such as the SAQ and CTA models (again, pending independent replications). For individuals low on both risk instruments, reentry with low-level supervision would appear appropriate. For those appearing at moderate or higher risk on the screening instruments, or presenting discrepancies between screening instruments, more resource-demanding and established instruments should be utilized. Additionally, instruments that provide direction for treatment recommendations should be utilized. Parole release decisions may warrant a somewhat more conservative track, especially with cases with a more extensive history of moderate and severe community violence. Research is necessary to comprehend the aggression process so that there can be a truly integrated and seamless meshing between assessment and treatment. Additionally, local norms of efficacy of measures used in a particular service are always helpful, especially in dealing with the occasional false negative that should be expected to arise at least rarely, but must be dealt with as openly yet judiciously as possible.

MANAGEMENT/TREATMENT OF VIOLENT TENDENCIES

Although the existing literature neatly dissociates risk management from risk assessment, this state of affairs is less than ideal and stems from the atheoretical nature of many existing risk-evaluation instruments that contain static and generally noncausal variables in their algorithms. Consequently, management and treatment, if suggested at all, is derived from a different perspective. Risk instruments that reflect dynamic change can, at least hypothetically if not definitively, provide explanations for why treatments work.

Perhaps before delving into specifics, it may be best to put one shibboleth of treating violence to rest. It is well recognized that psychopaths commit a disproportionate number of violent crimes, are difficult to treat for a number of reasons, and as a group constitute the highest violence recidivism rates. Some (e.g., Seto & Barbaree, 1999) have argued that it is best not to treat psychopaths because treatment makes them worse. In their empirical study in which they reported worsening of treatment outcome with higher PCL-R scores, Seto and Barbaree used a median split resulting in a cut-score of only 15 on the PCL-R. One cannot meaningfully draw conclusions about psychopathic groups' treatability from this study because, with even the highest cut-score, the group mean did not approach 25, the figure liberally used to identify psychopathic types.

In contrast, in a study of different risk prediction instruments and treatment effects in 468 sex offenders with an average follow-up of 5.9 years, Langton (2003) identified two subgroups of psychopaths: those who did and did not complete treatment. The high PCL-R (>25) treatment-completing group survived longer and exhibited less violent recidivism than the low-scoring non-treatment completing group. Similarly, Skeem, Monahan, and Mulvey (2002) conducted a sophisticated study of the influences of psychopathy and treatment attendance on violence in 871 community-dwelling psychiatric patients. Treatment involvement was measured in terms of the number of treatment sessions during a 10-week follow-up. Psychopathy classification did not moderate the effects of treatment on violence reduction. Indeed, Loving (2002) has suggested that the configuration of the PCL-R should be used to enhance focus of treatment in terms of whether the individual primarily has difficulties with Factor 1 or Factor 2. With the greater specificity given by the PCL-R-2, enhanced treatment specificity may be afforded.

D'Silva, Duggan, and McCarthy (2004) conducted a literature review that uncovered 24 studies purportedly testing psychopaths' nonresponsiveness to treatment. Only three of the studies had designs adequate to address the issue, but were still seriously flawed. D'Silva et al. conclude that the jury is still out on this important question. As more is understood about the neurobiological and cognitive/emotional characteristics of psychopaths, more effective treatments can be expected, as with other behavioral disorders.

TOWARD A BIOPSYCHOLOGICAL INTEGRATION OF RISK ASSESSMENT, TREATMENT, AND MANAGEMENT: A LOOK TO THE FUTURE

To date, few forensic clinicians or researchers have attempted to explore causality of criminal behavior and violence at the neurobiological level. However, this is changing. Numerous authors have come to appreciate that even among forensic patients, those charged with violent crimes disproportionately have histories of brain damage (Leon-Carrion & Ramos, 2003; Filley et al., 2001). The utility of understanding information processing at the neurobiological level is that it may well afford practitioners avenues of treatment previously unconsidered and consequently unexplored.

One attempt to integrate forensics with basic science is based on the well-established animal aggression at both the behavioral and neurobiological levels (Nussbaum, Saint-Cyr, & Bell, 1997), distinguishing three types of aggression most relevant to the criminal justice system: predatory, irritable, and defensive. Each type of aggression in the animal literature shows distinctive behavioral profiles and neuroanatomical and neuropharmacological specificity. Predatory aggression has a specific, identified, tangible goal in mind; is unemotional; and only sufficient violence is delivered to achieve the goal. Once the mugger obtains the purse or wallet, he flees and no further damage is inflicted as the purpose has been accomplished. Genuine remorse is absent after the attack, and success reinforces the behavioral choice. Irritable aggression is a response to a perceived insult or slight, mediated through the emotion of anger. The severity of the attack, reflecting the store of pent-up anger, is often out of proportion to the provocation. The attacker is often remorseful after the assault and at a loss for why he or she did it. Defensive aggression usually is not a concern for the criminal justice system, except when it is based on spurious information such as persecutory delusions or attributions. These attacks promote escape if possible or sufficient incapacitation to alleviate the immediate threat. They are accompanied by a state of extreme fear. Further details of the hypothesized anatomy and pharmacology of these networks is described in Nussbaum et al. Identification of an individual's predominant violent tendency (or tendencies) would help select primary treatment among anger management or possibly minimizing loss of anger control (irritable), monetary/other tangible motivations (predatory), and minimizing delusions (unrealistic defensive).

Advantages to this approach are manifested in terms of risk prediction, and given that a more distinct outcome variable is specified (i.e., predatory or irritable aggression), better prediction should be forthcoming. More precise causal variables would then constitute the predictors themselves. From a research perspective, validation studies utilizing functional neuroimaging become possible to confirm the precise anatomical networks and the principal neurotransmitters subserving the different aggression types. This could lead to targeted cognitive, behavioral, and pharmacological treatments conceptually derived from assessment data. More effective treatment and management of violent behavior would be afforded than is available today.

Supportive neuropsychological and personality data for the model is provided by Levi (2004), who demonstrated good discriminant ability of six psychometric measures in discriminating between predatory and irritable violent inmates at a provincial correctional institute in Ontario. Additionally, use of a quasi-projective, semistructured interview called the Violent Situation Eliciting Inventory (VESI; Nussbaum et al., 1997) was able to improve postdiction of violence density (i.e., number of violent charges corrected for age and access to the community) over criminal history variables (Watson, Nussbaum, & Flett, 2003). Further, different offender subgroups showed different VESI responses that were logically representative of their offense type. Clearly, this line of research is in its infancy but has the promise to enhance risk assessment.

CONDUCTING RISK ASSESSMENTS OF FUTURE SEXUAL VIOLENCE

Perhaps no other type of risk assessment and treatment policy has evoked as much emotion and consequent legislative interest and research funding as sexual offending. Undoubtedly, more than any assault at a remotely comparable level of victim physical injury, sexual violation can lead to long-term affective disturbance and subsequent global dysfunction, quite possibly via mechanisms of stress and resultant glucocorticoid degradation of hippocampal and frontal lobe neurons (Bremner, 1999; McEwen, 2000).

Anecdotally, during testimony on a risk of sexual recidivism assessment for an accused rapist, I reported probability levels from two instruments and described the 25% risk level as low, which was the appropriate descriptor for one of the risk instruments. The judge interrupted and proclaimed that he did not think that 25% represents low risk, because should he release four such individuals, one woman would likely be raped. This is a perspective that academics and researchers might wish to consider before tagging probability levels. Since then, I have chosen to simply report probability levels, leaving the high, medium, or low to the judge's discretion.

Numerous empirical instruments have been devised to aid the parole board or probation officer in deciding on the level of security and scrutiny appropriate for a sex offender. They have typically been formulated to evaluate risk in sex offenders in general, but not discrete categories of either contact sex offenses, such as pedophiles, rapists, or sexual sadists, or noncontact offenders, such as exhibitionists and voyeurs. Among pedophiles, one might attempt to distinguish between homosexual, heterosexual, and bisexual types and familial (i.e., incest) versus extrafamilial offenders. Future research could gain in precision by evaluating these classes separately. In support of greater precision, a number of studies have shown that the age at which sex offending declines differs between rapists (around 40), pedophiles, and sexual sadists (Barbaree, Blanchard, & Langton, 2003; Dickey, Nussbaum, Chevolleau, & Davidson, 2002; Hanson, 2002). Offender's current age could easily be included as a factor to sharpen risk prediction.

A second point for reader caution is whether the outcome variable for the instrument is sexual offending or any violent action in a sex offender population. Pedophiles and rapists likely differ on a number of criminogenic (age of first offense) and personality factors, such as empathy and impulsivity (Nussbaum et al., 2002). An emerging consensus is that the combination of psychopathy with any deviant sexual interest elevates risk to extremely high levels. Perhaps the abiding issues in sex offender assessment remain static versus dynamic risk indicators, integrating an evaluation of change of risk due to treatment or other factors such as maturation.

One does not have to be a psychologist or psychiatrist to administer and interpret most sex offender actuarial instruments, although training in the instrument itself and a good theoretical background of sex offending and offenders is certainly desirable. A good starting place is Hanson and Bussiere's (1998) often-cited meta-analysis of sexual offender recidivism studies. Hanson and Morton-Bourgon (2004) have updated this recently; it is available on the Solicitor General of Canada's Web site at the time of this writing. Here, we will summarize only a few of the many sex offending risk instruments available to psychologists and probation and parole use. Descriptions are relatively brief for derivatives of similar violence assessment instruments.

Sexual Offender Risk Assessment Guide

The Sexual Offender Risk Assessment Guide (SORAG; Rice & Harris, 1995) is a derivative of the VRAG developed to predict any type of violent recidivism, including sexual recidivism in sex offenders. As such, it might more appropriately have been considered in the violent risk predictor section, but is described here because its use is restricted to those with at least one sexual offense in their history.

The SORAG has 14 static items, which are weighted following optimization of the developmental sample. It has four variables not included on the VRAG that provide specificity to the sex offender population: violent criminal history score, number of previous sexual offense convictions, history of sexual offenses against female children only, and phallometric test results. Not surprisingly, the SORAG correlates highly with the VRAG (e.g., .8; Langton, 2003). Unlike the VRAG, the SORAG showed nonlinear increments of violent risk with ascending BINs as BINs 6 and 7 both evidenced violent recidivism rates of .58 over 7-year follow-ups, and BINs 4 and 5 showed identical recidivism rates of .59 with 10-year follow-ups. The greatly higher recidivism rates between 7 and

10 years (see Quinsey et al., 1998, p. 244) also deserves comment as it is agreed that most recidivism occurs within the first year of opportunity, begging the question of why the recidivism rates should increase so dramatically between 7 and 10 years after release.

Structural problems with the SORAG mirror those of the VRAG in terms of insensitivity to change over time, lack of demonstrable ability to predict severity of violent or sexual offending, latency to reoffense or formulate a treatment plan. Langton's (2003) study showed markedly lower (mean = 20%) observed recidivism rates in SORAG BINs 2 through 9 over an average of 5.1-year follow-up than suggested by Quinsey et al.'s (1998) 7-year data.

RAPID RISK ASSESSMENT FOR SEXUAL OFFENDERS AND STATIC-99

The Rapid Risk Assessment for Sexual Offenders (RRASOR; Hanson, 1997) was developed as a quick static actuarial tool for predicting risk of sexual recidivism. It contains only four readily available historical items: history of past sexual offenses, age at first offense, extrafamilial victims, and male victims. Although the initially reported AUC (.68) was promising, it was less than that achieved by other existing instruments. Consequently, Hanson and Thornton (2000) combined the RRASOR variables with others borrowed from the Structured Anchored Clinical Judgment (SACJ; Grubin, 1998), including prior sentencing occasions, current or prior nonsexual violence, unrelated victims, stranger victims, lack of long-term intimate relationship, and age under 25 on release or currently. The result is the Static-99 (Hanson & Thornton, 2000), which is user-friendly and is especially suited to probation and parole settings where time and extensive noncriminal historical data may be lacking. Its typical AUC value in cross-validation studies that have included probation and parole samples is .71 to .76. Nevertheless, it suffers from the shortcomings intrinsic to static instruments.

RISK MATRIX 2000

Developed as an extension of the SAJC-Min, the Risk Matrix 2000 (RM2000; Thornton et al., 2003) is an innovative recent addition to the static risk instrument list. It has the enviable quality of providing separate algorithms for estimating risk of sexual recidivism, nonsexual physical assault, and overall violence. Important for readers of this chapter, the Prison, Probation, and Police Services in England and Wales adopted the RM2000 (Beech, Fisher, & Thornton, 2003). The scale progresses by means of stages. Stage 1 has 3 static items: age at commencement of risk, sexual offense appearances in court, and total number of criminal appearances. Points on Stage 1 factors place the offender in the low, medium, high, or very high category. Stage 2 contains 4 aggravating factors: male victim, stranger victim, lack of a long-term intimate relationship, and noncontact sexual offenses. If 2 aggravating factors exist, the risk category is raised one level. If all 4 are present, the risk level jumps by two. According to Thornton et al., AUC levels range from the low .70s to the low .80s. This scale shows considerable promise for probation and parole applications as it is already used in probation, necessary information is ready available to community corrections, and it is time- and personnel resource-friendly.

Sexual Violence Risk-20

The Sexual Violence Risk-20 (SVR-20; Boer, Hart, Kropp, & Webster, 1997) is an analogue of the HCR-20 in its design as a structured clinical approach to predicting and managing sexual offending. It contains 20 items empirically linked to sexual recidivism. Like the HCR-20, its factors are unweighted in determining final score and a number of them reflect dynamic change. Items are scored on a 3-point (0, 1, 2) scale for absent, somewhat, and definitely present. Items are classified into three groups: Psychosocial Adjustment, Sexual Offenses, and Future Plans. Psychosocial Adjustment factors include a history of sexual deviation, being a victim of child abuse (cf. Pope, 2001, who found this not to be true in 66% of a sex offender sample), PCL-R score over 30, major mental illness (in opposite direction of Schizophrenia in VRAG/SORAG), substance abuse, suicidal/homicidal ideation, relationship problems, employment problems, past nonsexual violent offenses, past nonviolent offenses, and past supervisory failure. Sexual Offenses include high-density sex offenses (i.e., numerous sex offenses in a relatively brief time span), multiple sex offense types, physical harm to victim(s) in sex offenses, use of weapon or death threat in sex offense, escalation of frequency or severity of sex offenses, extreme minimization or denial of sex offenses, and attitudes that support or condone sex offenses. The Future Plans variable includes lacks realistic plans and negative attitude toward intervention (Boer et al., 1997).

The SVR-20 (like the HCR-20) represents an attempt to structure clinically relevant variables into a more valid format. It allows for identification of intervention targets, which is of value to community corrections, but remains atheoretical in terms of understanding sexual offending in its multiple forms and linking treatment based on a theoretical and potentially causal basis. Despite these peccadilloes, the SVR-20 is a clinically relevant instrument that attempts to soften static pronouncements with empirically supported, dynamic clinical factors. As such, it is of definite utility for probation and parole purposes.

Initial Deviance Assessment

Thornton has utilized an implicit theoretically coherent cognitive model of sexual offending in developing a dynamic risk tool to be used in conjunction with a static-historical risk instrument. The Initial Deviance Assessment (IDA; Thornton, 2002) rests on four dynamic risk domains: deviant sexual interests, distorted attitudes, socioaffective functioning, and self-management concerns. Sexual interests include sexual preoccupation, preference for children, sexual violence, and an offense-related fetish. Distorted attitudes supportive of reoffending include adversarial attitudes, hostility to victim group, and women as deserving of rape. Socioaffective functioning indicators include emotional loneliness, aggressive thinking, distorted intimacy balance, and callousness. Self-management includes lifestyle impulsiveness, poor problem-solving skills, and poor emotional control. Repeat sex offenders scored higher than one-time offenders on measures of rape myth, justification of sex with children, emotional congruence, emotional loneliness, self-esteem, anger, and rehearsal of negative emotion, benign control, and aggression control. These variables can be measured psychometrically and are clearly related to identifying treatment targets.

Thornton's (2002) second study was prospective in nature and used both the Static-99 and IDA on 117 adult male sex offenders. He found that even though the Static-99 produced an AUC for sexual recidivism of .92 and was only moderately related to the IDA, the IDA added incremental validity to the Static-99. Most striking, in the group predicted to be high risk by the Static-99, neither of the 2 low IDA members re-offended. Only 1 of the 5 Moderate Deviance (IDA) group reoffended, despite the high-risk Static-99 rating. However, 4 of 6 who rated as high on the Static-99 and scored high on Deviance on the IDA reoffended sexually. This buttresses the utility of including validated dynamic indicators in sex offender assessments. It is especially important for probation and parole consultations to facilitate safe release and suggest clinically meaningful treatments. One problem with the IDA is that the instruments needed for the assessment might not be routinely available to psychologists working in probation and parole, although they appear available from the research literature. This has the added advantage of low cost.

SEXUAL OFFENDER NEEDS ASSESSMENT RATING AND STABLE-2000

Hanson and Harris (2001) distinguished between two types of dynamic factors relevant to sex offenders. First are those that are amenable to change, but over months to years. These stable dynamic factors (e.g., intimacy deficits, attitudes) are differentiated from momentary changes referred to as acute dynamic factors (e.g., substance abuse, anger/hostility). The Sexual Offender Needs Assessment Rating (SONAR; Hanson & Harris, 2001) was intended for both risk assessments and management.

Recently, Thomas, Harris, Forth, and Hanson (2004) reported a prospective study evaluating the relative contributions of the Static-99 and the Stable-2000 in predicting risk in 891 and 726 sex offending probation and parole cases, respectively. The Static-99 produced respectable AUCs of .76 and .75 for sexual and violent recidivism, respectively. More interesting, the Stable-2000 produced AUCs of .76 for sexual recidivism and .73 for violent recidivism. These results are especially encouraging because the sample was diverse, including developmentally delayed, major mental disorders, noncontact sexual, and minor and serious assaults. These data, should they replicate, would further demonstrate the utility of including dynamic risk indicators in any risk assessment.

Another instrument for evaluating stable dynamic factors is the Sex Offender Treatment Evaluation Project test battery by Beech, Fisher, and Beckett (1999). This is specific for child molesters, and for reasons of space and time, is not further explored here.

EVALUATION OF SEXUAL RISK ASSESSMENT INSTRUMENTS

Given the plethora of recently developed static and dynamic risk instruments, a number of studies have attempted to compare their relative predictive validities to inform clinicians. Most find statistical equivalence among these instruments; some individual studies evidence an advantage with one or another that is reversed in other studies. For example, Sjostedt and Langstrom (2002) reported that only the RRASOR appeared to predict sexual recidivism at acceptable levels, whereas the others predicted nonsexual violence. Craig, Browne, and Stringer (2003) recently examined the 12 most widely used instruments for sex offenders. They found that 10 of the 12 were better at predicting general recidivism as opposed to sexual recidivism. They also noted that 10 primarily focus on static indicators and are therefore of limited utility in real life. Seven of the 12 do not consider treatment effects, and few have been independently examined in multisite studies, and, I would add, independent of the test authors. Earlier, Hanson and Thornton (2000) compared the RRASOR, SACJ-Min, and Static-99 on large numbers of correctional releases and found within-site statistics remarkably similar between instruments, although there were differences between sites. For example, the AUC for the SACJ-Min was .74 in HM Prison (England) but only .61 at the Millbrook Penitentiary in Canada.

Bartosh, Garby, Lewis, and Gray (2003) found that the relative efficacy of the Static-99, RRASOR, Minnesota Sex Offender Screening Tool (MnSOST), and SORAG varied depending on the offender type in their cross-validation sample. Overall, the success rate of each measure varied depending on whether the outcome was sexual or violent recidivism. Type of sexual recidivism (rape, noncontact, child molester) also affected predictive ability within and between. This underscores the importance of both the sample in which one is applying the instrument (likely in terms of congruence with the developmental sample) and the specific type of offending used as the outcome variable.

Langton's (2003) PhD thesis also compared a number of popular violence risk instruments for use with sex offenders (including VRAG, SORAG, PCL-R, RRASOR, SVR-20, MnSOST) in a low sexual (11.1%) and general violent (24.4%) sample. There were no statistically reliable differences between these instruments' AUC values, which ranged between .61 for the VRAG, .70 for the MnSOST for sexual reoffending, and .59 for the RRASOR to .70 for the MnSOST and SORAG.

Finally, de Vogel, de Ruiter, van Beek, and Mead (2004) recently reported that the SVR-20 outperformed the Static-99 at predicting sexual recidivism. Their study employed a Dutch sample of 144 sex offenders followed over an average of 140 months. The base rate for sexual recidivism was 39%. AUCs for the SVR-20 and Static-99 were .80 and .66, respectively.

The need for psychologists consulting with probation and parole to carefully consider the generalizability of an instrument is illustrated by Craig, Browne, and Stringer's (2004) finding of different risk scores obtained in a psychiatric facility from those obtained by probationers. Also, there were score reversals between offenders with child and adult victims on RM 2000, Stable-2000, and SACJ-Min on one hand and the RRASOR on the other. Taken collectively, such findings urge extreme caution in considering results from a single test as definitive, even in terms of establishing static risk levels.

Summary

It would appear that the most prudent and practical course for initial risk assessment for community corrections psychologists would be to utilize one or two of the briefer static indicators (Static-99, RM 2000) to screen for a more indepth assessment. Should they indicate moderate to high risk, two disparate instruments drawn from the pool of static-dynamic (e.g., SVR-20) and stable-dynamic (e.g., Stable-2000 or IDA) should be considered. These will allow both identification of intervention targets and baselines for progress in treatment.

MANAGEMENT/TREATMENT OF TENDENCIES TOWARD SEXUAL OFFENDING

Harris and Rice (2003) assert that there are no known effective cognitive-behavioral treatments for sexual recidivism. However, this is certainly not a consensus in the literature. To cite only a few examples from the recent literature available prior to 2002, Aytes, Olsen, Zakrajsek, Murray, and Ireson (2001) reported a 40% reduction in recidivism; Nicholaichuk, Gordon, Deqiang, and Wong (2000) found only a 14.5% sexual recidivism in treated offenders versus a 33.2% rate in matched untreated controls over a 6-year follow-up; and Looman, Abracen, and Nicholaichuk (2000) found a sexual recidivism rate of 51.7% in an untreated sexual offender group versus a 23.6% sexual recidivism rate in a matched and treated group over a 9-year follow-up.

Maletsky and Steinhauer (2002) reported a 25-year follow-up of cognitive-behavioral therapy with 7,275 offenders between 1973 and 1997. A number of different cognitive-behavioral treatments were included with various cohorts that lasted on average for 1 year. Treatments were provided in the community and prisons for the most dangerous offenders. Four outcome variables were employed. Major findings include enhanced success in community treatment settings, and premature termination was a strong indicator of treatment failure (60% to 75% of terminating rapists versus only 10% of completers recidivated sexually). Different offender types showed different treatment success rates with rapists (20%) and homosexual pedophiles (16%) being the highest, and, encouragingly, declining rates for 5-year follow-ups over the life of the study. This was taken to mean that effectiveness is increasing with ongoing CBT refinements.

Wilson, Stewart, Stirpe, Barrett, and Cripps (2000) classified sex offenders into "high risk" ($n = 32$) or "maintenance" ($n = 75$). Treatment consisted of a cognitive-behavioral group format for both groups, differentiated on the basis of the four Fs: feelings, fantasy, future planning, and follow-through (implementation). Over a 3.7-year follow-up, 2.7% of the maintenance group and a marginally higher 6.3% of high-risk offenders committed a further sexual offense. The program was less effective in curbing violent offending (6.7% and

18.8%, respectively). These official recidivism rates are low, especially for federal parolees, and argue for the effectiveness of the program.

Scalora and Garbin (2003), investigating the efficacy of a cognitive-behavior program, found a reduced level of recidivism in successfully treated sex offenders compared to a nontreated and an unsuccessfully treated comparison group. They also found recidivists to be younger, less frequently married, engaged in more victim grooming and less violent offending behavior, but with more nonviolent offenses.

Seager, Jellicoe, and Dhaliwal (2004) have recently challenged this picture of effective reduction of sexual recidivism for successfully treated individuals. Treatment success in their study was multiply determined. The noncompleting group included treatment refusers, dropouts, and a single staff-initiated termination. The researchers followed 109 completers and 37 noncompleters for 2 years. Marking an innovation, Seager et al. statistically removed initial risk levels as estimated by the Static-99. Consistent with earlier reports in the literature, only 4% of successful completers versus 7% of unsuccessful completers were convicted of violent or sexual offenses. The resultant chi-square test was not significant, prompting the authors to conclude that treatment completion/success is confounded with initial static risk level. The authors interpret this finding as implying that resultant success cannot be attributed to treatment, but to preexisting risk level.

Although this identifies a need to remove initial risk as an extraneous variable, in the instant case, the data actually make the counterpoint. The nonsignificant chi-square with 2, 3, 3, and 9 cases suffers from a lack of power. Examining the percentages tells a far different story. In the low-risk group, only 4% of completers versus 27% of noncompleters were convicted. Even more telling was the high-risk group data, where only 5% of completers recidivated compared to 35% of noncompleters. This more realistic evaluation actually demonstrates the efficacy of their program with high-risk sex offenders who complete the program.

A final consideration when psychologically treating sex offenders in a probation and parole framework has been elucidated by Barret, Wilson, and Long (2003). Empirically, motivation to change sexually deviant behavior increased between the intake assessment and termination of institutional treatment. However, for most offenders, this motivation decreased upon release to the community and remained low for the 12-week follow-up. Admission of guilt and acceptance of personal responsibility were both positively related with outcome and should be continually assessed during community treatment.

BIOLOGICAL APPROACHES TO TREATING SEX OFFENDERS IN THE COMMUNITY

Modern psychopharmacology offers a number of approaches to curb sexual arousal to aid in managing sex offenders in the community. As psychopharmacological training becomes more in vogue for psychologists, they will better appreciate when such treatments are likely to be helpful either as an adjunctive or a primary treatment modality. Depending on how contingent sexual offending is on acute sexual arousal, greater or lesser reductions in arousal can be achieved by choice of medications. More specifically, selective serotonin reuptake inhibitors (SSRIs) such as paroxetine (Paxil) and fluoxetine (Prozac) induce a moderate level of sex drive reduction and also help check impulsive decision making. Peripheral hormonal agents such as medroxyprogesterone acetate (Depo-Provera) cause strong reductions in sexual arousal by affecting testicular efficacy in producing testosterone. For the most difficult to manage sex offenders, centrally acting hormonal agents virtually eliminate all traces of testosterone by shutting off the initiating hypothalamic signal to the testis for testosterone synthesis (Maletzky & Field, 2003). Maletzky and Field provide a recent review of this field and present preliminary data from an Oregon study showing that none of the 18 offenders being treated with Depo-Provera have been recharged with a sexual offense. Two comparison offenders (out of 17) who were not treated with Depo-Provera have been recharged with a sexual offense. Bradford (1997) reported similar results in managing a large number of sex offenders in the community. The consulting psychologist may well wish to receive a forensic psychiatric consult around this issue, especially for those sex offenders with violent hands-on histories.

SUMMARY

A number of empirically supported risk assessment tools are available for evaluating risk of sexual and general violent offending in sex offenders. Professional judgment must consider population match, type of predicted sexual offense, and, ideally, responsivity to treatment in choosing the optimal instrument for the individual in context. Community treatments exist as variants under the general cognitive-behavioral umbrella. Ongoing monitoring of treatment effectiveness is necessary, both in terms of compliance and motivation. Psychopharmacological consultations will likely enhance community success, especially in younger sex offenders where a strong sex drive plays a primary role in sexual reoffending.

SUBSTANCE ABUSE IN PAROLE AND PROBATION

There is overwhelming evidence that substance abuse, perhaps most prevalently and seriously involving alcohol, represents one if not the major factor in both violent and nonviolent recidivism among parolees and probationers. Recently released statistics from the Bureau of Justice Web site shows that in 2002, an estimated 1,352,600 adults and 186,200 juveniles were arrested for drug abuse violations (http://www.ojp.usdoj.gov/bjs/glance/tables/rugtab .htm; August 31, 2004). Between 1995 and 1999, the incidence of probationers reporting being under the influence of a substance at the time of the index offense went from 14% to 36%, and a remarkable 49% in mentally ill probationers. In 1999, 105,539 parolees and 712,902 probationers carried diagnoses of alcohol dependence. Substance abuse of alcohol and street drugs is thus a significant problem for the probation and parole systems.

Psychopharmacology of Substance Abuse

The domain of substance abuse covers putative causes of involvement, types of involvement, strategies for combating involvement, and ways in which substance abuse impacts the criminal justice system. As such, a comprehensive treatment of the issues is well beyond the scope of this chapter. However, because substance abuse issues cross all domains of risk assessment, management, and treatment, the interested and motivated reader is referred to *A Primer of Drug Action*, 10th edition (Julien, 2005). For a relatively concise yet sophisticated analysis of the relationships between abusable substances and violence, the reader is encouraged to study Hoaken and Stewart's (2003) recent article. To summarize, they first enumerate four possible associations: accessing drugs or resources to access drugs, resolving disputes within the illicit drug distribution subculture, shared personality characteristics between substance abusers and individuals prone to violence, and the direct actions of the drug on the person. The first two (obtaining and regulating the illicit supply) are most relevant for police intervention, and the latter two (copathology and psychopharmacological effects) are more relevant for informed psychological involvement. Regarding the direct psychopharmacological effects, Hoaken and Stewart cogently note the distinction between the immediate and direct effects of drugs (intoxication), withdrawal effects (abstinence following cessation of intensive use), and neurotoxic effects (damage caused by prolonged use). Different drugs incur different types of aggression through these three time-related aspects of substance abuse.

Mechanistically, psychomotor stimulants (e.g., alcohol, cocaine) enhance excitement and reward and lead to approach behaviors that may include attack in risky situations (Hoaken & Stewart, 2003). Substances with anxiolytic properties may lessen perceptions of fear, threat, or punishment. Absent these informational inhibitors, aggression is more likely to be expressed. Drugs may also alter aggressive tendency by reducing or accentuating sensitivity to pain or disrupting executive functioning, which serves to inhibit aggression.

Details relating to individual drugs and their mechanisms are explicated by Hoaken and Stewart (2003) and are not further described here. In terms of a general mechanism, it should be noted that most abusable drugs produce a relative "high" by the action of dopamine transmission within the ventral tegmentum accumbens (VTA) pathway. Part of this reinforcement mechanism involves focusing attention more strongly on the target. Normally, attending to the immediately reinforcing target is balanced by consideration of long-term costs and mediated by frontal serotonergic pathways that serve to inhibit VTA activity. These principles, hypothesized for decades (see Vogel-Sprott, 1967), have recently been empirically supported by an fMRI study (Vogel-Sprott, Easdon, Fillmore, Finn, & Justus, 2001). This mechanism may be operative in personality disorders (possibly including borderline and psychopathic disorders) for genetic and/or environmental reasons (see Pihl, Assaad, & Hoaken, 2003), substance abuse (Vogel-Sprott et al., 2001), ventromedial prefrontal lobe-amaged patients, and bipolar mood disorders. These seemingly disparate classes share a basic problem: When faced with an immediate reinforcer, they tend to disregard long-term costs in their decision making. The clinical paradox, and perhaps the reason these individuals can be such convincing liars, is that when they are not faced with the reinforcing stimulus, they can access inhibitory material and express a sincere desire to make the correct decision. In real situations, however, the reinforcement pull (dopaminergic VTA activation) overcomes inhibitory considerations (the "serotonergic ventromedial brake") and the troublesome behavior recurs, despite prior reassurances to the contrary. With this theoretical background, we turn to assessment of substance abuse.

ASSESSMENT OF SUBSTANCE ABUSE

Assessment of substance abuse is complicated by the fact that many individuals who abuse substances provide inaccurate information about their involvement, whether for the purposes of easing the punitive response of the criminal justice system, denial of the scope of their problems to themselves, a preexisting personality style, or a true lack of insight into a single area of functioning. The Michigan Alcohol Screening Test (MAST; Selzer, 1971); its derivative, the Brief-MAST (Pokorny, Miller, & Kaplan, 1972); and the Drug Alcohol Screening Test (Skinner, 1982) are self-report scales that work reasonably well, especially with individuals who are seeking treatment. The Cut down, Annoyed, Guilty, Eye opener (CAGE; Ewing, 1984) is a four-item interview asking whether individuals have ever felt that cutting down on their drinking was necessary, whether others have been annoyed by their drinking, whether they felt guilty about drinking, and whether they need a drink first thing in the morning to overcome jitters or a hangover. The CAGE performs surprisingly well as a screen in a walk-in clinic and inpatient settings (Liskow, Campbell, Nickel, & Powel, 1995). In the probation and parole setting, the primary objective for the client is to present well to lessen the intensity or duration of restrictions. These obvious measures may not do as well under forensic conditions.

To avoid this problem, the Substance Abuse Subtle Screening Inventory (SASSI) was developed and is now into its third addition (SASSI-3; Miller, Roberts, Brooks, & Lazowski, 1997). The SASSI-3 has two sides; the first employs questions directly addressing alcohol and drug abuse, and the second side has items reflecting personality traits that have been associated empirically with substance abuse difficulties. Unfortunately, the SASSI was not designed to detect changes in tolerance, dependence, or addictions, but rather indicates a static likelihood of abuse and dependency. Still, this can be useful for spotting the denier of any such difficulties. Multidimensional tests of psychopathology (e.g., the Personality Assessment Inventory [PAI]; Morey, 1991) also have obvious drug and alcohol scales. The computerized reports indicate a warning when these self-report scales are low, but personality correlates of substance abuse are in the ranges where substance abuse is common. These should not be interpreted as necessarily involving defensiveness in individuals either in or recently reentering society after long periods of enforced abstinence, as they may be truthfully responding to their behavior over the past years and not their previous substance abuse. Corroboration by an objective and unintimidated significant other or results of randomized urine screens can be most informative in terms of relapse while in the community. Ashman, Schwartz, Cantor, Hibbard, and Gordon (2004) reported that the SASSI-3 and the CAGE were effective in screening for drug and alcohol abuse, respectively, in a brain-injured sample.

A final note concerns the Addiction Severity Index (ASI; see McLellan et al., 1992, and Fishbein's, 2000, adaptation of that scale). A recent study on a parolee sample by Hanlon, O'Grady, and Bateman (2000) found statistically significant relationships between the ASI and unemployment and drug use. However, the authors note that the effect sizes were too small to use the instrument in making decisions in individual cases. Fishbein's classification of the ASI into five levels was helpful in differentiating among predatory, irritable, and nonviolent offenders (Levi, Nussbaum, & Reimann, 2005) and did correlate with various frontal lobe tasks. These results are preliminary, however, and more study is required to comprehend the complex relationships between substance abuse and preexisting personality, specific neurocognitive processes, and impulsive and violent decision making.

TREATMENT OF SUBSTANCE ABUSE IN PROBATION AND PAROLE SETTINGS

Given the vastness of the treatment literature on substance abuse, this chapter provides only a cursory review of the options. With the large number of probationers and parolees who are returned to custody for technical violations involving substances, it would be easy to conclude that treatment is ineffective and perhaps should be abandoned in light of fiscal restraint in current governmental thinking. However, there is growing evidence that newer drug treatment programs do work in reducing the numbers of parolees and probationers who would otherwise remain stuck in the revolving door. Harrison (2001) provides an excellent discussion with supportive evidence of the efficacy of treatment. She notes that the biggest barrier to expanding treatment options is the belief that treatment does not work. Data from treatment communities in prisons show clear reductions in recidivism rates for those who complete treatment. Effective treatment will have the twin effects of enhancing human quality of life and saving tax dollars.

Biological approaches to treatment have any of three basic goals. One is aimed at punishing the drug-taking behavior itself, as occurs with disulfiram (Antabuse) treatment of alcoholism. Disulfiram disrupts functioning of the enzyme aldehyde dehydrogenase in the second step of alcohol metabolism. This results in a build-up of acetaldehyde that is responsible for flushing and severe noxious subjective sensations similar to an intense hangover. A second approach is for a drug to reduce abstinence symptoms associated with cravings, thereby lessening the urgency prompting drug seeking. Methadone, a synthetic opioid, provides treatment for heroin dependence in this way. Methadone remains in the body longer than heroin, thus reducing the frequency of reinforcing behaviors. Effectively taken by mouth, it helps reduce illness due to needle sharing, significantly reduces illicit drug use, and reduces crime (Julien, 2005, p. 485). The third mechanism involves blocking the reinforcing action of the abused drug, thereby depriving the abuser of the motivating payoff. To that end, naltrexone, an opioid antagonist, helps to reduce the amount of drinking in heavy drinkers (p. 120).

Cornish et al. (1997) found that naltrexone plus counseling resulted in only 80% of positive opioid screens, as compared to 30% in a group receiving only the counseling. Fifty-six percent of the nonnaltrexone group were returned to prison, compared to only 26% of the naltrexone-treated group. Though certainly effective, a difficulty with these treatments is that substance abusers are no more amenable to biological treatments than they are to psychological interventions. Addicts are consumed by their interest in their substance, despite acknowledging its destructive impact on their lives. Anglin, Longshore, and Turner (1999) provided evidence for effective psychosocial community rehabilitation, although the offenders in their study had relatively minor criminal histories and qualified for diversion. Zanis et al. (2003) provide evidence that after statistically removing effects of predisposing criminogenic factors, treatment lessened recidivism by a factor of 1.6 in treated versus untreated parolees.

Summary

Various assessment techniques exist for effective diagnosis of substance-related problems available in probation and parole settings. Some evidence exists that treatment does reduce the amount of substance abuse, official recidivism rates, and returns to incarceration. When treatment is not effective, the problem may be rooted in the individual's personality, for which more effective treatments must be found.

YOUNG OFFENDERS IN PROBATION AND PAROLE

Perhaps the dominant emerging issue regarding young offenders over the past few years has been to distinguish those young offenders who will and those who will not continue with their criminal, especially violent, behavior. As is prominent in the adult literature, the construct of psychopathy is one focus of this matter. Concerns surrounding juvenile psychopathy and its measurement were deemed sufficiently salient that the editor of a leading forensic journal recently assembled a set of papers to explore the matter from a number of perspectives (Wiener, 2002).

Moffitt (1993) and Loeber and Stouthamer-Loeber (1998) and their colleagues have been among the pioneers of these trajectory, or identifiable life span models of criminality and violence. I focus on Moffitt's approach because of the neuropsychological evidence provided in the theory's early development, which accords with an admitted bias of mine toward ultimately understanding explainable behavior in terms of neurally based information processing.

Moffitt, Caspi, Harrington, and Milne (2002) recently provided an extension of their theoretical approach with compelling empirical evidence. Basically, they contend that adolescents can be classified into four groups with respect to life span involvement with the criminal justice system. Their initial two prototypes consisted of life course-persistent (LCP) and adolescent-limited (AL) offenders, who first could be distinguished by the age of onset of antisocial behavior. The LCP group begins in childhood with increasing severity of misconducts developing with increasing age though adolescence and into adulthood. The AL group's antisocial behavior begins after childhood (i.e., in adolescence), and desistence occurs in early adulthood. Important for community interventions, the LCP child's risk is deemed to be from an interaction of different inherited *and/or acquired* neuropsychological variations manifested by such signs as subtle cognitive deficits, difficult temperament, and hyperactivity (Moffitt et al., 2002). Both heredity or acquired brain injury can act or interact to produce long-term antisocial behavior. The environmental risk in childhood includes inadequate parenting, disrupted family bonds, and poverty. As the child ages, this environmental domain expands to include poor relations with other authority figures (teachers, employers), peers, and intimates.

In contrast, the AL antisocial group begins life absent the early problems but experiences dysphoria during the maturation gap, the period between physical maturity and adult opportunity and responsibility. During this period, the LPC delinquent lifestyle is appealing and is mimicked by AL individuals in misplaced efforts to gain autonomy from parents, develop their own identity, affiliate with peers, and gain acceptance as adults. Typically, they desist from this pattern by early adulthood, but if they become subject to snares (criminal record, addiction, educational truncation, teen parenthood, etc.), desistence may be delayed (Moffitt et al., 2002).

Two additional groups have been identified. The first, or low-level chronics (optimistically called the recovery group), begin as behavior-disordered children but exhibit only infrequent antisocial acts persisting during adolescence. The second additional group includes the rare males who had extremely low rates of antisocial and certainly criminal behavior. Moffitt et al. (2002) examined outcomes on these previously identified groups at age 26, thus composing a truly prospective design. Outcomes were based on both self-reports and informant (including court) reports. An unclassified control group was included for comparison purposes. Overall, data supported differences between AL and LCP groups in mean number of various problem behavior indicators (e.g., self-reported and court-convicted drug offenses, self-reports and convictions for violent offenses). Educational and some occupational indices (registered unemployment but not mean past year gross income) also showed differences between the groups. These data support Moffitt's contention that groups identifiable in childhood show different criminal justice involvement and societal contributions. One can also see clear conceptual links between Moffitt et al.'s (2002) theoretical approach and their empirical results and psychopathy. An explanation for why these differences exist remains elusive.

Concerns regarding the utility of the term psychopathy were openly discussed by a number of authors in 2002. Seagrave and Grisso (2002) present an extensive literature review and note that similar troubling behavioral traits might be normal for many youth who pass through stages (much like those reported by Moffitt) but do not go on to criminal careers as adults. Premature use of such instruments could lead to serious consequences, such as withholding of treatment and long-term incarceration. Hart, Watt, and Vincent (2002) amplified these sentiments by noting that construct validity has not yet been established in measurements of adolescent psychopathy.

While agreeing with the preliminary state of risk assessment of juveniles, Frick (2002) argues that qualitatively similar processes occur in "normal" development, but the task of the developmental psychologist is to identify what alters normal processes. The knowledge gaps cited by Seagrave and Grisso (2002) reflect the state of knowledge of psychopathology in general and not only juvenile psychopathy. Frick also notes that what might constitute a true adolescent psychopath is still a subject of debate. The primary goal for research in developmental psychopathology is to facilitate more effective interventions by identifying malleable traits before they have congealed. Similarly, Lynam (2002) argues that psychopathy might be explained in terms of the 5-factor model (Costa & McRae, 1995). Psychopaths are high on all facets suggestive of antagonism, low in different facets of conscientiousness, low in anxiety, high on impulsiveness, and closed to feelings. These qualities make for negative reciprocal relationships with others that reinforce prosocial failures in intimate, educational, and employment settings, further entrenching psychopathic attitudes, emotions, cognitions, and behaviors. Lynam contends that these insights provide targets for effective early intervention. All discussants agree that progress has been made but that more research is needed to allow clinicians to implement valid assessment and treatment techniques with high levels of empirically based confidence. Zhang, Welte, and Weiczorek (2002) provide additional empirical support for psychopathy as a unifying construct underlying different aspects of problem behavior in adolescents.

ASSESSMENT TOOLS FOR YOUNG OFFENDERS

There has been an immediate response to these calls for empirically supported assessment tools for juvenile assessment and resultant treatment and management in community settings. Due to space limitations, only four assessment instruments are outlined here, three of which are relatively well known. The newcomer shows promise in its scope and early successes.

The Structured Assessment of Violence Risk in Youth (SAVRY; Borum, Bartel, & Forth, 2001) focuses exclusively on risk of violence in adolescents. Three categories of predictors are historical, individual, and social/contextual. Twenty-four items are rated by the professional as either high, medium, or low, with specific guidelines provided for each designation. Thus, the SAVRY is unabashedly a structured professional judgment instrument, as opposed to a strictly actuarial tool. Examples of the 10 historical factors include history of violence, exposure to violence in the home, and parental/caregiver criminality. The six social/contextual factors include stress and poor coping and peer rejection. The eight individual/clinical factors include substance abuse, poor compliance, and psychopathic traits. Of importance, the SAVRY also contains six protective factors that are not predictive of risk factors independently, but if present, mitigate risk levels produced by the established risk factors. Protective factors on the SAVRY include strong attachments and bonds and strong commitment to school. Predictive accuracies range from .74

to .80 across studies and are similar for male and female offenders, despite less work with females (Borum, 2003). Advantages over static risk instruments include individual case sensitivity and identification of dynamic targets for intervention.

The Youth Level of Service/Case Management Inventory (YLS/CMI; Hoge & Andrews, 2002)) is an instrument that addresses risk, needs, and management targets for general (as opposed to exclusively violent) criminal involvement by youths. The instrument is a downward extension of the LSI-R (Andrews & Bonta, 1995) described earlier. Coding is less well defined than in actuarial instruments, but decisions are referenced tightly to scores. The YLS/CMI manual (Hoge & Andrews, 2002) contains statistical evaluation of accuracy for different types of reoffending and demonstrates respectable predictive validity. Protective factors are also identified by the YLS/CMI and treatment targets are identified.

Based on the idea that personality disorders are long-standing patterns of responding to internal and external stimuli, the Hare Psychopathy Checklist: Youth Version (PCL:YV; Forth, Kosson, & Hare, 2003) was developed to capture the constellation of psychopathic personality traits in adolescents age 12 to 18. The purposes of its development included both predictive and corrective goals. *DSM-IV* Conduct Disorder as a predictor of extreme lawbreaking and violence overpredicts criminal activity (Lynam, 1996), as does Antisocial Personality Disorder in adults. The PCL:YV retains all 20 PCL-R items but has revised some items to make them more appropriate and relevant to teenagers (Forth et al., 2003), especially attempting to allow for normal adolescent variability.

In a recent study investigating the predictive validity of the PCL:YV, Gretton, Hare, and Catchpole (2004) found that the instrument significantly predicted violent recidivism over a 10-year follow-up ($r_{pb} = .32$) with 82% of individuals in the high ($n = 34$), 73% in the medium ($n = 82$), and 46% in the low ($n = 41$) risk groups recidivating violently.

Corrado, Vincent, Hart, and Cohen (2004) conducted a short-term (average 14.5 months) follow-up study on 182 male adolescents. They compared 2-factor (20 items) and 3-factor (13 items) solutions of the instrument. With the 2-factor model, the AUC for any recidivism was only moderately effective (AUC = .68) and somewhat less so for violent (AUC = .65) and nonviolent (AUC = .63) recidivism. For the 3-factor model, the AUCs were .65 (any), .63 (violent), and only .58 (nonviolent) recidivism. Separating the group into 122 low and 39 high scorers, 51% of high scorers versus only 24.6% of low scorers recidivated violently within the follow-up period. Latency to violent offense was an average of 13.55 as opposed to 18.17 months in the low-scoring group. Perhaps the limiting feature of this study was the relatively brief follow-up, although the base rate of 31% would seem to be typical of adult studies of longer durations. Thus, base-rate is not the culprit in this study.

Regardless of the personality theory issues, it would appear that the PCL:YV shows reasonable predictive validity for identifying youth who, without intervention, have a greater likelihood for committing acts of violence into early adulthood. It remains to be seen whether treatment modalities will be developed to deal with the construct at its factor level.

Work in developing the Child and Adolescent Risk Evaluation (CARE; Seifert, 2003) began in 1996 under the title Child and Adolescent Risk for Violence (Seifert et al., 2001). The CARE is perhaps unique in that it does not make explicit use of the PCL in any form, although there is overlap between some of its items and the PCL. The CARE is premised on the theoretical notion that behavior is at least in part determined by patterns of thinking and feeling about specific issues and topics. Because patterns of thinking and feeling can be changed, if the underlying patterns for an individual can be identified during assessment, there is a clear and achievable target for intervention. The CARE is also unique in that it examines a wide range of empirically established risk factors, scores the individual on them, and scores the individual on resiliency factors, which is then subtracted from the total. The final score relegates the individual into one of five risk categories, ranging from no behavior problems to severe and/or chronic behavior problems and assaultive history. This severity rating, in line with the risk/needs principle, determines the level of intervention intensity, but it is the content of the items themselves that determines both the focus and style of the specific technique and target. A detailed intervention plan is the concluding part of the assessment (Seifert, 2003).

Another unique characteristic of the CARE is that, although it began as an instrument for assessing youth, Seifert (2004) followed the assessees into adult life and constructed an adult version of the instrument (the RME, described earlier), which is undergoing further development. Of particular interest to probation and parole psychologists is that recommendation for placement in the community or residential setting is provided as part of the intervention intensity rating. Sixteen specific intervention modalities follow along with an evaluation of available resources and barriers to success. This thoroughness makes the CARE a turnkey, or stand-alone, operation.

The CARE contains items grouped in five domains: Youth Characteristics (24 items), Peers (4 items), School and Education (5 items), Family (8 items), and Protective (8 items). The CARE contains some items that clinicians believe are important but are not retained on many actuarial instruments because, as rare occurrences, they add insignificantly to the overall prediction afforded by more common predictors. Two examples are "Paranoia or interpretation of benign events as hostile" and "Neurological impairment."

Turning to utility in clinical use, the developmental study included 479 youths. The total CARE score correlated strongly with severity of behavior problems ($r = .78$), reflecting its construct validity. Predictive validity with violent outcome was also excellent ($r = .62$; ROC $= .87$). In light of the excellent predictive ability, clinical acuity, and relevance for intervention and placement in the community, the CARE is an instrument that can be helpful to psychologists in evaluating probation and parole. Additional research is called for to demonstrate the generalizability of Seifert's findings. The CARE adds to the growing list of clinically informed, empirically validated instruments for assessing risk, identifying treatment targets, and thereby informing intervention.

For psychologists using the Minnesota Multiphasic Personality Inventory-Adolescent Version (MMPI-A) in clinical assessments, Glasser, Calhoun, and Petrocelli (2002) have provided at least preliminary evidence that MMPI-A scales can be combined to classify juveniles into offenders against persons, property, or drugs. Seventy-nine percent of the decisions were correct. This study requires replication and clarification but shows promise for extending a clinical instrument into a prediction tool by use of an alternative combination of existing variables.

Treatment of Young Offenders in the Community

Borum (2003) provides a lucid summary of issues and practices regarding community management of young offenders. Regarding treatment, he reiterates the risk, needs, and responsivity principles in providing necessary conditions for successful treatment. Additionally, he stipulates rigor in implementation and follow-up to ensure a successful outcome. Although Borum cites a number of studies that suggest that providing intensive treatment to low-risk young offenders makes them higher-risk, it may be that it is not the intervention per se that provokes the effect, but rather the placement of mildly prone youth within a criminogenic milieu where they are susceptible to peer influence.

As with adults, modalities that appear to work best, even with high-risk youth, are cognitive-behavioral in nature. Tendencies to misperceive hostility and the ability to generate nonaggressive solutions are cited as prime targets for treatment. General programs that demonstrate ability to curb aggressiveness over a 1-year follow-up include multisystemic therapy, functional family therapy, and aggression replacement therapy.

Multisystemic therapy (MST; Henggeler, Melton, & Smith, 1992) is based on the idea that human development occurs as a result of complex influences that social and ecological environments exert on the maturing person (Bronfenbrenner, 1979). It is especially appropriate for community corrections because it is applied in the family setting. It primarily targets high-risk youth and is individualized and intensive, in keeping with both the risk and needs principles. Specific treatment goals were selected from the causal modeling literature, which represents a theoretical shift from strictly associationistic to potentially causal thinking regarding treatment. MST utilizes strategies from family and behavior therapies to intervene directly in systems and processes that are believed to engender antisocial behavior in young people, including family affective relationships, parental discipline, peer associations, and school performance. Interventions follow careful assessments of the strengths and weaknesses of these interacting systems (Henggeler et al., 1992).

The recent literature is supportive of MST in youth at risk for multiple reasons. For example, Letourneau, Schoenwald, and Sheidow (2004) found MST to reduce problem behaviors posttreatment in young offenders regardless of sexual problem behavior status. Henggeler, Clingempeel, Brondino, and Pickrel (2002) compared MST to usual community services in a 4-year follow-up of 80 substance-abusing youth. Aggressive convictions were meaningfully lower for youths who received MST (15% versus 57%), but no differences were found for property crimes. Abstinence rates for marijuana were higher in MST participants (55%) than in alternative treatment controls (28%). MST did not ameliorate psychiatric symptoms, which might be expected because psychotic processes are biologically driven and more amenable to medications obtained by both groups in the study as needed. Finally, Sheidow et al. (2004) found that MST actually reduced costs associated with emergency inpatient psychiatric stays for the average youth by $1,617. This was specific to short-term cost effectiveness in these psychiatrically involved youth. Overall, then, there is good empirical support for involvement of MST in the community treatment of young offenders presenting numerous and serious risk factors for violence and other criminal behavior. The primary difficulty with this therapy is accessing it, as MST requires extensive training and is not yet available in many centers.

Quinn and Van Dyke (2004) have recently provided evidence for the efficacy of multiple-family group intervention (MFGI) in first-time juvenile offenders. The multiple families provide a "community for youths." The model is both theoretically and practically advantageous. By extending group dynamics to a number of families, systems are allowed to interact positively so that parents and professionals can provide multiple sources of insight, encouragement, and positive solutions. Several adults can influence each youth, practically meaning that the (often single) parent does not feel isolated and peer influence does not go unchallenged. Parents and their values are thus validated rather than devalued. Three phases of treatment are (1) group formation, trust, and emotional relief; (2) resistance to treatment; and (3) group involvement and growth.

Quinn and Van Dyke (2004) note that critics of intensive treatment with delinquent groups propose that interactions with antisocial peers induces iatrogenic boosts to criminal thinking and behaviors, also known as "peer contagion." Noting that mixing nondelinquent and delinquent youth for therapeutic purposes is impractical, Quinn and van Dyke contend that having the additional adults present counteracts potential negative peer influence. In their study, they compared official recidivism rates among 95 probation, 267 MFGI, and 93 youths referred for MFGI but who dropped out after fewer than 10 sessions. The usual list of demographic variables examined in the whole group (age, gender, race, family criminal history) did not predict recidivism, but the treatment group did. Specifically, those placed on standard probation were 9.3 times more likely to reoffend than were treatment completers, and dropouts from the treatment program were 4.4 times as likely as treatment completers to recidivate. Combining the completers and dropouts (to counter a self-selection interpretation), standard probationers are 8.1 times more likely than all participants (completers and noncompleters) to recidivate.

Other examples of a community-based programs for serious young offenders include the recent family-centered Growing Up Fast program (Gavazzi, Yarchek, Rhine, & Partridge, 2003) and self-management training, which helps aggression replacement control transfer to the community (Ninness, Ellis, Miller, Baker, & Rutherford, 1995).

SUMMARY

Numerous empirically supported tools are now available for assessing risk in young offenders having contact with the probation system. Effective and specific community-based treatments for young offenders exist, although far more empirical validation is needed across the board to support widespread implementation of these practices. For this to occur, more professionals will have to be trained in these applications, and concerted and widespread evaluations must be instituted as part of assessment and treatment programs. Cooperation between clinicians and researchers will enhance public safety as well as the lives of our troubled youth in a win-win solution to the problem. Cooperation from administrators at various levels of community corrections and government should be aided by emerging reports of the financial as well as the social advantages to effective innovation in community corrections (e.g., Robertson, Grimes, & Rogers, 2001). Implementation of innovative programs will succeed only with administrative support so that existing personnel are (1) able to train adequately for their new duties, (2) do not feel that they are having a host of new duties imposed beyond their already taxing tasks ("mission creep"), and (3) are not confused regarding the purpose, focus, and philosophy of the program ("mission distortion"; Corbett, 1998). Clearly, the means exist to greatly enhance the service delivery within community juvenile justice, and psychologists are in the best position to spearhead this movement. Advancement will be aided by paying attention to dynamic changes in young offenders' neuropsychological and neurobiological development, or lack thereof, with reference to specific types of violent and nonviolent offending.

FEMALE OFFENDERS IN PROBATION AND PAROLE

It has long been accepted that female offenders are fundamentally different from their male counterparts (e.g., Martin, Cloninger, & Guze, 1978). Martin et al. found that prolonged parole or probation supervision had therapeutic benefit, and that the three most powerful predictors of female recidivism were diagnosis of drug dependence, APD, and a history of homosexuality. Serious recidivism was also associated with within-family crime and "maternal hysteria," likely in response to ongoing domestic issues.

More recently, Bloom, Owen, Deschenes, and Rosenbaum (2002) rank-ordered risk and protective categories for juvenile females based on responses to surveys conducted with officials from various state agencies, professionals serving female young offenders, and female youth. These data do not reflect correlates of outcome studies. The surveys identified as risk and protective factors in the following categories: family issues, individual problems, peer group problems, school-related problems, and community-related difficulties. Looking at this list, one is struck by the overlap with many of the risk factors identified in males, such as delinquency, gang involvement, academic failure, substance abusing peers, and availability of firearms.

Comparing risk factors in males and females with respect to offending outcome trajectories, Fergusson and Horwood (2002) found that the sexes did not differ appreciably. Following a large cohort (896) of New Zealand children from birth to 21 years, they found five identical trajectories for both sexes, composed of (1) low risk; (2) early onset, adolescent-limited; (3) intermediate onset, adolescent-limited; (4) late onset, adolescent-limited; and (5) chronic. Mean number of offenses over follow-up was virtually equivalent for the four less serious groups (1.5 versus 1.7, 1.9 versus 6.5, 48.4 versus 49.8, and 23.7 versus 33.8 for males and females, respectively). However, males were more highly represented in the chronic category (43 of 435 males versus 8 of 461 females) and in mean number of offenses, with 159.8 for males and 47.6 for females. Despite proportional and frequency intersex differences, the identified factors predictive of criminal tendencies were the same for both sexes: parental criminality, parental conflict, tendencies toward novelty seeking, low intelligence, and low self-esteem. These factors predicted both property and violent crimes virtually identically. The only emerging difference between males and females from Fergusson and Horwood's (2002) study is membership in the chronic group. Obviously, the issue of specific developmental and criminogenic risk factors for females requires considerably more work.

ASSESSMENT INSTRUMENTS FOR FEMALE OFFENDERS

Some existing instruments originally developed for use in estimating risk in male offenders have been investigated for use with females. As noted earlier, the LSI in its various forms has been normed on a large number of female offenders and is appropriate for applied use. Lowenkamp, Holsinger, and Latessa (2001) conducted a study on 317 males and 125 females using the LSI-R and found similar validity in prediction of reincarceration for males and females. This held despite a greater percentage of females in the moderate-risk category (60.6% versus 47.2%) and fewer in the high-risk category (28.8 versus 18.6), making prediction more difficult. Additionally, Lowenkamp et al. found no incremental validity for adding childhood abuse as a predictor, as it does not add statistically to the predictability afforded by the LSI-R.

Hare (2004, p. 52) notes that although significantly more research is needed, existing studies report that the descriptive properties and criminal justice correlates of the PCL-R found in males are similar for females. In this regard, Salekin, Rogers, and Sewell (1997) concluded from a multitrait-multimethod matrix analysis in 105 females that the construct validity of the PCL-R held for females, although the results of their preliminary ($n = 105$) factor analysis suggested a different factor structure from that in males. Similarly, in a recent study of 589 females, Vitale, Smith, Brinkley, and Newman (2002) found that the PCL-R operated similarly in female offenders, but they noted that a correlation between the PCL-R and anxiety that was not found in males.

Despite these beginnings, clearly more work is necessary before female offenders can be assessed for risk, needs, and treatment in the community with the confidence currently evident with males. In future, an instrument speaking exclusively to female offenders' risk levels should be developed taking into account special needs related to being female, such as teen pregnancy and motherhood, that simply have no counterpart in males but could realistically give rise to other forms of aggression, such as maternal and defensive, arising from situations foreign to male offenders.

TREATMENT OF FEMALE OFFENDERS

Richie (2001) eloquently describes the unique challenges faced by females attempting reentry. In summary, only a minority of women (14.5%) are incarcerated for violent crimes, with more being held for property (~32%) or drug-related (~27%) offenses. Substance abuse and abusive relationships characterize a large proportion of these women. Not surprisingly, they also tend to be young and poor. Perhaps most poignantly for the odds of successful reentry, they overwhelmingly return to the same neighborhood from whence they came.

Richie (2001) identifies a matrix of interacting factors that need to be addressed for a successful transition to the community: substance abuse treatment; health care; treatment of mental health issues, including emotional instability, violence prevention, and treatment for Posttraumatic Stress Disorder from prior abusive relationships; education and employment upgrading; safe, secure, and affordable housing; and child advocacy and family reunification. Given the competing demands placed on a mother on her return, focusing on even a few of these would be intimidating. The reader might consider the daunting task faced by of a woman simultaneously attempting to regain custody of her children, looking for a place to live and a job, and trying to be admitted into a substance abuse program as a condition of probation or parole.

Comprehensive wrap-around programs, according to Richie (2001), will provide for all of these needs in an integrated and individualistic fashion. Communities must be strengthened to be able to accommodate those attempting reentry. She suggests a consciousness-raising or empowerment approach that will educate such women about the factors that negatively impact their lives and how they can more effectively respond. Finally, there is the need for community-peer mentoring to allow the nondefensive assimilation of helpful cognitions to change behavior. Psychologists can act as advocates to help increase the availability of sufficient resources to meet female probationer and parolee needs. Sorbello, Eccleston, Ward, and Jones (2002) suggest a related model that emphasizes offender skills and capabilities to better their satisfaction with life. Implicit is the belief that women come to crime for different reasons from men.

Peugh and Belenko (1999) express similar observations and sentiments. They note the increased likelihood of domestic abuse and subsequent substance abuse with attendant increases in HIV, family repercussions, poverty, and family dissolution. They provided a comprehensive gender-specific treatment program for substance-abusing women, over half of whom had abused some drug in the month prior to their index offense. They note that women differ from male substance abusers in that they have lower self-esteem and more partner-initiated ill treatment, and initiation into drugs is more a reflection of their intimate relationships than is true for males. Their comprehensive program addressed issues that predated substance abuse and would appear independent of substance abuse in male populations. These include (1) parenting, hygiene, nutrition, and empowerment; (2) family planning; (3) vocational/educational counseling; (4) mental health counseling, especially for victims of abuse; (5) HIV/AIDS education and prevention programs; and (6) comprehensive medical care. Important is the need to continue treatment and support after the woman has returned to the community for a sufficient period. Supportive data for continuing care in the community were provided by results from their "Forever Free Program" between 6 and 14 months' post–community release. The relative recidivism rates were 62% for those who dropped out of the program, 28% for program graduates with some community treatment, and only 10% for program graduates who received 5 or more months of community treatment.

SUMMARY

As with most other areas having a microfocus, more work is needed to substantiate these findings in other locales and by other researchers. However, these ground rules can be seen as an ideal to be attempted and evaluated in an effort to both increase public safety and reentry. Additional refinements are required to assess and treat females who are violent and abuse substances. Perhaps the Borderline Personality Disorder construct, although politically incorrect, might serve useful in conceptualizing more serious female offender cases.

MENTALLY DISORDERED OFFENDERS IN PROBATION AND PAROLE

As noted in 2002 figures, approximately 60,611 mentally disordered offenders (MDOs) were on probation and 677,000 are on parole. The trend for a significant proportion of prison inmates being mentally ill (16%; Blumstein & Beck, 1999) suggests that their prevalence on probation and parole rosters will not diminish in the near future. This significant minority within the system likely absorbs a major part of the system's workload because they have multiple needs that have to be coordinated with mental health professionals in the community, who already are stretched. Many community professionals are reluctant to work with MDOs for justifiable concerns of involvement with criminal justice system red tape and fears for personal safety that are perhaps exaggerated.

First-line treatment for most MDOs, especially those suffering from Axis I conditions such as Schizophrenia, Schizoaffective Disorder, Bipolar Mood Disorder, depression, delusional disorders, and some types of anxiety disorders, is appropriate pharmacological intervention (Julien, 2005). For this, psychiatrists or, more recently, advanced clinical nurse practitioners, will have to be intricately involved in the individual's ongoing treatment. The day may come when psychologists will routinely prescribe psychotropic medication (Julien, 2005, p. 527), but that is not yet the case. Perhaps best practice guidelines for antiaggressive psychotropics (serenics) will be included in the next version of this *Handbook*.

Medication is important to public safety with MDOs because a major portion of violence, and some serious violence, results from delusional beliefs of being persecuted. The aggression is defensive, but the context of the attack is delusional and therefore subtyped as unrealistic defensive aggression (Nussbaum et al., 1997). This does not in any way imply that MDOs cannot become assaultive in predatory contexts or when frustrated by goals being blocked.

ASSESSMENT OF RISK IN MENTALLY DISORDERED OFFENDERS

Many of the previously described violence and sexual risk instruments are appropriate for MDO assessment as these individuals represented a significant portion of their developmental samples and were so noted. The HCR-20 and VRAG are examples. The MacArthur Study of Mental Disorder and Violence (Monahan et al., 2001) has produced an innovative instrument to assess violence in briefly hospitalized psychiatric patients over a 1-year community follow-up. Monahan et al. described the classification tree technique, and the interested reader is referred to Steadman et al. (2000) for more details. What is appealing is that it acts as a clinician might approach an assessment, differentiating the entire group first, on the basis of the single best predictor, and then recursively within succeeding subgroups, always seeking the best predictor within smaller emerging subgroups. An algorithm for performing the analysis is forthcoming on the group's Web site to facilitate use of the instrument. The major limitation to adoption by those in corrections is that the MacArthur sample consisted of civilly committed individuals. If extended to the criminally committed population, the MacArthur approach could become a dominant model for assessing MDOs.

Gagliardi, Lovell, Peterson, and Jemelka (2004) recently reported a relatively straightforward risk instrument tool specifically designed for MDOs released to the community from prison. Their final stepwise regression model resulted in six predictors (past felonies, past drug felonies, low infraction rate [–], prison mental health unit [–], old age at first offense [–], and first-time sex offender [–]) and resulted in a respectable AUC of .828. Factors with negative coefficients were interpreted as protective factors. Gagliardi et al. note that results were gleaned from existing correctional department files and not in-depth individual assessments, possibly limiting their accuracy. Also, they have not cross-validated their findings, and because all data were derived form the same state, bootstrapping methods would not solve the sampling problem. They also argue heuristically for using the least resource-intensive prediction tool, provided validities of potential alternatives are essentially equivalent. They note (p. 149, n. 15) that the time investments for the PCL-R (3 hours) and the VRAG (2.5 days) render it impossible to conduct risk assessments routinely in their programs.

TREATMENT OF MENTALLY DISORDERED OFFENDERS

As noted, the primary treatment for individuals with major mental (psychotic) disorders remains medication. However, medication is a resource, like money, and if money is simply thrown at a problem, the problem will not go away: It is important to spend the currency wisely. Similarly, with mental disorders, it is important to embed the newfound pharmacological currency within informational networks that bias thinking and feeling in prosocial streams. Thus, adjunctive treatment in terms of being a listening post, providing motivation for treatment compliance, and shepherding community resources for the MDO client are probably understudied protective factors in helping clients not only avoid recidivating but also enhancing their lives. To this end, Lurigio (2001) has argued that effective community correctional service is maximized if all of the MDO's needs are attended to. He recognizes the array of specialized knowledge and skills necessitating a team approach, including prison discharge staff, parole agents, mental health and substance abuse professionals, and those who can teach housing and life skills. On-site distribution of medications is also identified as helpful.

SUMMARY

The psychologist has a pivotal role to play in integrating the MDO client with appropriate community-based team members and the services they provide. With their assessment, treatment, and research training, psychologists should be placed centrally in this process as they have expertise to keep abreast of new assessment and treatment developments for MDOs. A particular void exists in terms of assessment and treatment outcome studies to show which aspects of intervention are most significant with MDOs in the community. New techniques are also most likely to be pioneered by psychologists.

PROBATION AND PAROLE WITH INDIVIDUALS WITH INTELLECTUAL DISABILITY

It is difficult to estimate the numbers of probation and parole populations suffering from what is currently termed intellectual disability (ID), because there is no universal screening. In England, the ID population appears to be a relatively small percentage because the vast majority of those on parole and probation seems to be dealt with differently at the arrest stage or at initial remand and diverted to appropriate services (Mason & Murphy, 2002). Different studies in the United States arrive at dissimilar estimates, likely based on local conditions.

The ID group represents a special challenge for resource-challenged community corrections for three reasons. First, classification depends on both a formal and comprehensive (read time-consuming) psychometric test result requiring qualified psychology personnel to administer. Qualification for special services in many jurisdictions requires a supplemental requirement of impaired skills of daily living. Second, as this group is verbally challenged, many cognitively based community offender programs are ineffective and inappropriate for them. Third, their numbers, noncorrectional resource drain, and the lack of political interest in them make them a less than compelling group for resource allotment. There are relatively few recent publications available on the topic, and although intellectual level does enter consideration in some of the prediction schemes noted earlier, I could find no empirically supported risk tool developed specifically for this group.

Individuals in this category are particularly unsuited for standard incarceration because they are taken advantage of and brutalized by the regular prison cohorts, do not fit in with standard regimens, and consequently, they rarely accumulate the credits necessary for early release and other reinforcements, despite not having especially high rates of violent or other recidivism compared to others in the system.

EMPIRICAL STUDIES ON PREVALENCE AND COMMUNITY SUCCESS

Among the few available recent studies on prevalence and outcome of ID and probation, Mason and Murphy (2002) found a 7% prevalence rate (defined as 1.6 standard deviations below the mean, or IQ of 76 or below) in 90 probationers in southeast England, based on two screening tools developed especially for probation services: the Quick Test and the Clock Drawing Test, used by the Learning Disabilities in Probation Services. Mason and Murphy found no differences between the identified ID group and others in terms of probation outcome, although they suggest that additional supports might contract the amount of time these individuals spend on probation.

Linhorst, McCutchen, and Bennett (2003) described a specialized private nonprofit probation program, Opportunities for Justice for Persons with Developmental Disabilities. Other disabilities must be manifested in at least two domains of functioning for program access. Case coordinators provide links to required services, typically including vocational rehabilitation, mental health services, substance abuse, social security, and transportation. Program entrance criteria include either mental retardation or a developmental disability resulting in at least two functional limitations.

In evaluating program efficacy, Linhorst et al. (2003) examined arrests among 252 developmentally disabled clients in a probation case management program. Interestingly, only 60% were classified as mentally retarded (although the assessment technique is not described). They report outcome data for both the supervisory period and 6-month postsupervisory period. During the supervisory period, 10.9% were arrested for felonies against persons. Index offense, type of developmental disability, and whether one had a prior conviction were not predictors of felony arrests. However, not being a high school graduate or possessing grade equivalent, being on welfare, or having no income (42.9% and 32.9%, respectively, versus 0% for the 29 employed individuals) and referral source (private or criminal justice but not social service agency) did predict subsequent felony. During the 6-month follow-up, no variables predicted felony arrests, although their prevalence fell, especially for those completing the offered services within the supervisory period. The authors argue for the carryover effects of the program in light of this latter finding, although one might also attribute the result to greater attention and reduced opportunity during the follow-up period. In light of older studies with reported better outcomes, the authors note both discrepancies in outcome variables as well as the mandated nature of probation services in earlier studies.

Taylor, Novaco, Gillmer, and Thorne (2002) provide a more focal report on community treatment of anger intensity for ID offender groups. Their modest statistical findings may well be due to the relatively low power afforded by the small sample size (9 and 10 participants in experimental and control conditions, respectively). Guidelines for treating community-dwelling sexual offending in ID offenders are offered by Lindsay et al. (2002). Sexual reoffending rates increased from 4% after the first year to 21% by the end of the 4-year follow-up. However, an unspecified number of these included hands-off offenses. Unplanned discharge was also significantly related to reoffending ($x^2 = 6.6$; $p < .05$).

SUMMARY

Obviously, significant lacunae exist in the area of effective assessment, treatment, and management of intellectually challenged probationers and parolees. Measures of disability must be more precise in terms of both cognitive and functional domain and severity of impairment. Outcome measures must specify type of aggressive outcome. The preliminary cited findings of monetary source, sexual offending, and anger are suggestive at least in part of the typology described earlier with predatory and irritable subtypes. Additionally, some intellectually challenged individuals are dually diagnosed, and their mental disorders can induce unrealistic defensive aggression as well. Finally, treatment studies with this group must expand to the point where ID offenders can be safely managed in the community, as they are not suited for typical incarceration structure, nor do they improve from standard interventions.

DOMESTIC OFFENDERS

Domestic violence, or battering, is a politically charged issue because women are typically physically vulnerable to stronger male partners. The relationship is also often imbalanced by economic disparities and dependency, especially for minimally educated mothers who are home raising children. This is not to say that females never batter male partners, but most often, female attacks on partners are defensive in nature. Battering by females may be underreported because of the additional shame a male feels reporting that his female partner has beaten him up. Nevertheless, males inflict the preponderance of spousal violence, and numerous explanatory frameworks exist to understand this complex phenomenon. Relationship counseling for important issues less central to probation and parole concerns can be outsourced. Consequently, this section focuses on violent spousal abuse.

Scott (2004) recently summarized theoretical models and empirical findings regarding remediation. Explanatory approaches include feminist, family systems, personality trait, and attachment theories. Scott identifies three basic batterer typologies: family-only (low-level antisocial), dysphoric-borderline, and generally violent/antisocial. These have different trajectories, batter for different reasons (frustration, identity, and domination, respectively), and consequently respond to different intervention approaches. Scott urges consideration of broader than dichotomous outcome measures along with incorporation of stages of change when evaluating intervention success.

Assessment Issues

There exists some question as to whether domestic offenders and stalkers can be assessed (and treated) like other violent individuals. Dutton and Kropp (2000), implicitly favoring specially designed instruments, reviewed specifically constructed spousal violence risk instruments for which at least preliminary validity data existed at the time of their writing. They note limitations with the Danger Assessment but add that the criterion employs women's perception of the danger of being killed by their partner. Despite this dubious criterion, an increase of a single standard deviation on the instrument was associated with a fourfold increase in repeat abuse with a base rate of only 22%. Obviously, the victims know something about their partner.

Dutton's (1995) own instrument is known as the Propensity for Abusiveness Scale (PAS). The PAS was developed using female partners' reports of past abuse as the outcome variable, which is reasonable as male batterers often deny recurrences and official records often underreport domestic (as well as other) violence. The PAS items do not relate to abusive acts but to historical features with clinical relevance, such as parental treatment, attachment style, anger, trauma symptoms, and stability of self-concept (Dutton & Kropp, 2000). Not surprisingly, subsequent studies have found the PAS to best serve in noncriminal populations as it correlates more highly with threats toward victim (.76), borderline personality organization (.70), and anger (.64) and only .30 with actual spousal violence (although this is still respectable).

Perhaps the most investigated example of a risk instrument developed specifically for predicting domestic violence is the Spousal Assault Risk Assessment (SARA; Kropp, Hart, Webster, & Eaves, 1994, 1995). It consists of 20 items, with the first 10 (Part 1) relating to general violence risk factors (e.g., past assault of family and nonfamily members; recent substance abuse/dependence; personality disorder with anger, impulsivity, or behavioral instability); and 10 factors specific to risk of spousal violence (past sexual assault/sexual jealousy, past violation of no-contact orders, minimization or denial of spousal assault, attitudes supportive of or condoning spousal assault). Also calculated was the number of factors (Parts 1 and 2) present and critical items identified in each case by independent pairs of observers.

Kropp and Hart (2000) provide reliability data from 2,309 participants, of whom 1,671 were probationers, making generalizability to community corrections seamless. The SARA demonstrated good interrater reliability. In a subset of the total pool, all calculated scores differentiated between individuals with (638) and without (372) spousal abuse histories at the .0001 level. Of interest, only Part 1 correlated significantly with the VRAG ($r = .50$); the spousal abuse segment (Part 2) did not ($r = .08$). Examining recidivist and nonrecidivist spousal abusers, all Part 2 SARA variables provided excellent separation ($r = .004$, $.008$, and $.001$ for Part 2, Part 2 Factors Present, and Part 2 Critical Items, respectively). None of the historical risk indicators (Part 1) was below .05. The SARA thus represents a reasonable approach to assessing risk of spousal violence, in that it does pay some attention to historical risk factors, but might assign primary weight to dynamic factors that may be amenable to change in some spousal abusers. Certainly, more outcome studies would be useful to substantiate currently available support.

Stalans et al. (2004) recently supplied empirical evidence for differentiating three types of aggressors with relevance to probation and family aggression. These types included 321 family-only aggressors, 717 nonfamily-only aggressors, and 302 generalized aggressors. Use of CTA allows for separation of different classes of offender, with risk factors specific to each type. In other words, interactions are easily dealt with. No rigorous set of assumptions of the data is required by CTA. CTA was able to better discriminate high- and low-risk groups than logistic regression analyses. This appears to be another useful instrument awaiting further refinement.

Williams and Houghton (2004) recently reported performance of the Domestic Violence Screening Instrument (DVSI) in a prospective design, a feature lacking in many of the existing risk instruments. Containing 12 readily available items (e.g., prior nondomestic violence convictions, prior domestic violence treatment, children present during domestic violence), the DVSI is relatively easy to calculate. The sole difficulty with the DVSI is its mediocre predictive validity (AUC for Domestic Violence = .61, r = .18, p = .00). Thus, though promising, it still needs considerable revision before it can be counted on to confidently spot those at high risk for injuring their spouse.

One especially disturbing trend reported in the recent literature involves spousal attacks on pregnant women, occurring in many different cultures. For example, Peedicayil et al. (2004) surveyed 9,938 women in various rural and urban slum and nonslum areas of India and found lifetime prevalence rates of being abused during pregnancy in the following ways and proportions: slapped, 16%; hit, 10%; beaten, 10%; kicked, 9%; hit with weapon, 5%; and assaulted in other way, 5%. Logistic regressions associated the following factors with moderate to severe violence during pregnancy: husband accusing wife of an affair (odds ratio [OR] = 7.1), dowry harassment (OR = 4.1), husband having affair (OR = 3.7%), husband regularly drunk (OR = 3.2), and low education (OR = 2.8). Obviously, dowry harassment is cultural, but all might be explained by beliefs about male/female roles and relationships.

TREATMENT AND MANAGEMENT OF DOMESTIC ABUSERS

As documented by Scott (2004), treatment programs for abusive male partners have existed for approximately 3 decades. She suggests that in appropriate groups, intervention practice and research focus on reduction in anger and other personality-based psychopathology and include stage of change as a gauge of program success.

Wooldredge and Thistlewaite (2002) argue that better results following counseling programs are achieved with high-risk offenders if the courts mandate the treatment. Conversely, there are lower rates of rearrests for low-risk offenders on probation or serving simple jail sentences. This parallels the risk, need, and responsivity principle. Shepard, Falk, and Elliott (2002) argue that wider community involvement is valuable in reducing spousal reoffending. They note that court-ordered programs and program completion favor successful outcome. Their assessment was a component model with police screening 10 different empirically identified risk indicators, while a women's group evaluated a more comprehensive list of 25 spousal risk indicators. Probation officers conducted a more in-depth individual assessment and then categorized offenders as (1) low level (no history of prior violence), (2) batterers with established patterns and of moderate risk, (3) batterers with established patterns of higher risk, or (4) batterers posing a serious risk to their family and community. Court conditions were contingent on risk category. The first two categories involved a matrix of safety measures, stayed jail time, probation conditions, and batterer intervention program, and the two higher-risk categories saw more sanction-oriented sentencing in terms of lengthier jail sentences and probationary periods. Thus, the courts involved the community in relatively specific intervention programs as part of the overall risk reduction effort.

Treatment of batterers remains controversial. Gordon and Moriarty (2003) summarized the 12 national standards for batterer intervention programs (e.g., written contracts with participants, focus on power and control issues, group format, partner contacts) and described results of a program that would appear to comply with these standards. Looking at the efficacy of the program in 248 batterers, Gordon and Moriarty found that program participation per se was not associated with a reduction in recidivism, but (as we have seen before) successful completion of all treatment sessions significantly reduced the likelihood of rearrest and reconviction for spousal violence. This further raises the possibility that the successes are self-selected by dint of their willingness to endure the program to completion, thus rendering any effects of treatment dubious.

Jones, D'Agostino, Gondolf, and Heckert (2004) responded to this general concern by use of "propensity scores" that predict the likelihood of individual attrition, and then employed individual propensities to statistically control for this preexisting tendency in both court-referred and self-referred samples. Based on propensity scores, they were able to identify five groups of participants in terms of likelihood of terminating treatment prematurely. Overall, treatment reduced recidivistic battering by 13%. However, there was only a 1.4% difference in voluntary participants versus 15% in those court-mandated for treatment. More remarkable, when propensity group was taken into consideration, the most likely and third most likely court-ordered groups showed 38.1% and 30% reductions in treatment completers relative to noncompleters. Overall, program completion reduced probability of spousal reassault by 33% over 15 months of follow-up in the complete sample and by 50% in court-mandated batterers. Jones et al.'s sophisticated study (which this necessarily brief synopsis does not do justice to) presents an innovative method to realistically estimate treatment effects and may well be incorporated in future treatment studies across specific domains.

A NOTE ON STALKERS

Occasionally, probation or parole may have a stalker or stalking suspect referred for assessment. Almost invariably, the expert is in the uncomfortable situation of being asked whether the individual is a good or poor risk for release to the community, usually, but not always, with an accompanying restraining order. Rosenfeld (2003) has examined 148 cases for factors that differentiate unrelenting offenders from desisters. Of the 49% who reoffended, 80% reoffended within 12 months. The strongest identified predictor of recidivism was a Cluster B Axis II (personality disorder) diagnosis, exacerbated by concurrent substance abuse. Within this sample, presence of Delusional Disorder (erotomania) was a low-risk indicator, although survival times for Delusional Disorders were virtually identical to the Axis II cluster. Others have identified ever having had an intimate relationship with the target and type of threat as high-risk indicators.

The Ontario Provincial Police have an excellent stalking unit with specially trained officers intimately familiar with the literature and experienced in conducting thorough risk assessments in stalkers. It is likely that local state or FBI officers have similar training and can be called on to assist in a comprehensive assessment, monitoring, and treatment plan. It is entirely fitting to enlist the help of these police services in areas where they are available.

CONCLUSIONS

Psychologist have played a large part in developing state-of-the-art instruments for assessing various types of risk that confront probation and parole decision making. Similarly, psychologists have developed and evaluated many carefully crafted interventions to help reduce risk of serious reoffending that apply to probation and parole contexts. We should not be shy about the profession's prior accomplishments. At the same time, we must be realistic in terms of where we would like to go from here. Consequently, it is mandatory that psychologists continue to think about, develop, evaluate, and report more comprehensive evaluation and intervention techniques so that we move forward. Ultimately, deeper understanding at the neurobehavioral level will facilitate a conceptual integration to energize both streams of advancement. Within the traditional ambit of correctional and forensic psychologists, considerably more research is needed on the responsivity principle. More specifically, the effect of the relationship between probation and parole officers and outcome must be delineated, taking into account the preexisting personalities of the parties and how they affect readiness to change and ability to form a therapeutic alliance. Indeed, research continues to show that a good client-professional relationship is necessary for ongoing client success. Despite all the technical and empirical advances, a good relationship between the probation or parole officers, psychologists, and their clients may be the most important variable in ensuring the success of the program.

One must also keep in mind the special challenge faced by forensic and correctional psychologists in dealing with our clients. It is relatively straightforward to solve an equation with one unknown, more difficult with two unknowns, and the difficulty rises with the number of unknown elements. Many probation and parole clients have multiple problems encompassing the various domains alluded to in this chapter. With increasing foci of difficulty, complexity grows, perhaps exponentially. Behavioral science is still a relatively young discipline and few scientific explanations exist for even simple phenomena, much less complex and interacting systems. As such, we must acknowledge the relatively noteworthy improvements we have brought to a resource-poor enterprise, but modestly yet confidently look to increasing our scope and depth of future understanding and application.

REFERENCES

Andrews, D. A. (1982). *The Level of Supervision Inventory (LSI): The first follow-up.* Toronto: Ontario Ministry of Correctional Services.

Andrews, D. A., & Bonta, J. (1994). *The psychology of criminal conduct.* Cincinnati, OH: Anderson.

Andrews, D. A., & Bonta, J. (1995). *The Level of Supervision Inventory-Revised.* Toronto: Multi-Health Systems.

Andrews, D. A., & Bonta, J. (1998). *The psychology of criminal conduct* (3rd ed.). Cincinnati, OH: Anderson.

Andrews, D. A., & Bonta, J. (2003). *The psychology of criminal conduct* (4th ed.). Cincinnati, OH: Anderson.

Andrews, D. A., Bonta, J., & Wormith, S. (2004). *Level of supervision and case management.* Toronto: Multihelth Systems.

Anglin, M. D., Longshore, D., & Turner, S. (1999). Treatment alternatives to street crime: An evaluation of five programs. *Criminal Justice and Behavior, 26*(2), 168–195.

Ashman, T. A., Schwartz, M. E., Cantor, J. B., Hibbard, M. R., & Gordon, W. A. (2004). Screening for substance abuse in individuals with traumatic brain injury. *Brain Injury, 18*(2), 191–202.

Austin, J. (2001). Prisoner reentry: Current trends, practices, and issues. *Crime and Delinquency, 47,* 314–334.

Aytes, K. E., Olsen, S. S., Zakrajsek, T., Murray, P., & Ireson, R. (2001). Cognitive-behavioural treatment for sexual offenders: An examination of recidivism. *Sexual Abuse: A Journal of Research and Treatment, 13*(4), 223–231.

Barbaree, H. E., Blanchard, R., & Langton, C. (2003). The development of sexual aggression through the lifespan: The effect of age on sexual arousal and sexual recidivism among sex offenders. *Annals of the New York Academy of Sciences, 989,* 59–71.

Barret, M., Wilson, R. J., & Long, C. (2003). Measuring motivation to change in sexual offenders from institutional intake to community treatment. *Sexual Abuse: A Journal of Research and Treatment, 15*(4), 269–283.

Bartosh, D. L., Garby, T., Lewis, D., & Gray, S. (2003). Differences in the predictive validity of actuarial risk assessments in relation to sex offender type. *International Journal of Offender Therapy and Comparative Criminology, 47*(4), 422–438.

Beech, A. R., Fisher, D. D., & Beckett, R. C. (1999). *An evaluation of the prison sex offender treatment programme.* London: Home Office Information Publications Group, Development and Statistics Directorate. Available from www.homeoffice.gov.uk/rds/pdfs/occ-step3.pdf.

Beech, A. R., Fisher, D. D., & Thornton, D. (2003). Risk assessment of sex offenders. *Professional Psychology: Research and Practice, 34*(4), 339–352.

Bloom, B., Owen, B., Deschenes, E. P., & Rosenbaum, J. (2002). Moving toward justice for female juvenile offenders in the new millenium. *Journal of Contemporary Clinical Justice, 18*(1), 37–56.

Blumstein, A., & Beck, A. J. (1999). Population growth in U.S. prisons, 1990–1996. In M. T. J. Petersilia (Ed.), *Prisons* (pp. 17–61). Chicago: University of Chicago Press.

Boer, D. P., Hart, S. D., Kropp, P. R., & Webster, C. D. (1997). *Manual for the Sexual Violence Risk-20: Professional guidelines for assessing risk of sexual violence.* Vancouver, Canada: British Columbia Institute Against Family Violence.

Bonta, J. (2004, July). *Behavioral assessment of case management practices in corrections.* Paper presented at the APA annual convention, Honolulu, HI.

Borum, R. (2003). Managing at-risk juvenile offenders in the community. *Journal of Contemporary Criminal Justice, 19*(1), 114–137.

Borum, R., Bartel, P., & Forth, A. (2001). *Manual for the Structured Assessment for Violence Risk in Youth (SAVRY)* (Consultation Ed.). Tampa: University of South Florida.

Bradford, J. (1997). Medical intervention in sexual deviance. In D. R Laws (Ed.), *Sexual deviance: Theory, assessment and treatment* (pp. 449–464). New York: Guilford Press.

Bremner, J. D. (1999). Does stress damage the brain? *Biological Psychiatry, 45*(7), 797–805.

Bronfenbrenner, U. (1979). *The ecology of human development: Experiments by nature and design.* Cambridge, MA: Harvard University Press.

Bureau of Justice Statistics (BJS), www.ojp.osdoj.gov/bjs, October 4, 2004.

Bureau of Justice Statistics (BJS), www.ojp.osdoj.gov/bjs/glance/tables/rugtab.htm, August 31, 2004.

Cooke, D. J., & Michie, C. (2001). Refining the concept of psychopathy: Towards a hierarchical model. *Psychological Assessment, 13,* 171–188.

Cooke, D. J., Michie C., & Ryan, J. (2001). *Evaluating risk for violence: A preliminary study of the HCR-20, PCL-R and VRAG in a Scottish prison sample* (Occasional paper Series 5/2001). Glasgow, Scotland: Department of Psychology, Glasgow Caledonian University and Douglas Inch Centre.

Cornish, J. W., Woody, G. E., Wilson, D., McLellan, A. T., Vandergrift, B., & O'Brien, C. P. (1997). Naltrexone pharmacotherapy for opioid dependent federal probationers. *Journal of Substance Abuse Treatment, 14,* 529–534.

Corrado, R. R., Vincent, G. M., Hart, S. D., & Cohen, I. M. 92004). Predictive validity of the Psychopathy Checklist: Youth Version for general and violent recidivism. *Behavioral Sciences and the Law, 22,* 5–22.

Corrigan, P. W., Steiner, L., McCracken, S. G., & Blaser, B. B. (2001). Strategies for disseminating evidence-based practices to staff who treat people with serious mental illness. *Psychiatric Services, 52*(12), 1598–1606.

Costa, P., & McRae, R. (1995). Domains and facets: Hierarchical personality assessment using the revised NEO Personality Inventory. *Journal of Personality Assessment, 64,* 21–50.

Corbett, R. P. (1998). Probation blue? The promise (and perils) of probation-police partnerships. *Corrections Management Quarterly, 2,* 31–39.

Craig, L. A., Browne, K. D., & Stringer, I. (2003). Risk scales and factors predictive of sexual offence recidivism. *Trauma, Violence, & Abuse, 4*(1), 45–69.

Craig, L. A., Browne, K. D., & Stringer, I. (2004). Comparing sex offender risk assessment measures on a U.K. sample. *International Journal of Offender Therapy and Comparative Criminology, 48*(1), 7–27.

Cullen, F. T., & Gendreau, P. (2001). From nothing works to what works: Changing professional ideology in the 21st century. *Prison Journal, 81*(3), 313–338.

Daubert v. Merrill Dow Pharmaceutical Inc. 113 S. Ct. 2786. (1993).

de Vogel, V., de Ruiter, C., van Beek, D., & Mead, G. (2004). Predictive validity of the SVR-20 and Static-99 in a Dutch sample of treated sex offenders. *Law and Human Behavior, 28*(3), 235–251.

Dickey, R., Nussbaum, D., Chevolleau, K., & Davidson, H. (2002). Age as a differential characteristic of rapists, pedophiles, and sexual sadists. *Journal of Sex and Marital Therapy, 28*(3), 211–218.

Douglas, K. S., Hart, S. D., Dempster, R. J., & Lyons, D. (1999, July). *Violence Risk Appraisal Guide (VRAG): Attempt at validation in a maximum-security forensic psychiatric sample.* Paper presented at the joint meeting of the American Psychology-Law Society and the European Association of Psychology and Law, Dublin, Ireland.

D'Silva, K., Duggan, C., & McCarthy, L. (2004). Does treatment really make psychopaths worse? A review of the evidence. *Journal of Personality Disorders, 18*(2), 163–177.

Dutton, D. G. (1995). A scale for measuring propensity for abusiveness. *Journal of Family Violence, 10*(2), 203–221.

Dutton, D. G., & Kropp, P. R. (2000). A review of domestic violence risk instruments. *Trauma, Violence, and Abuse, 1*(2), 171–181.

Ewing, J. A. (1984). Detecting alcoholism: The CAGE questionnaire. *Journal of the American Medical Association, 252,* 1905–1907.

Fergusson, D. M., & Horwood, L. J. (2002). Male and female offending trajectories. *Development and Psychopathology, 14,* 159–177.

Filley, P., Nell, B. H., Nell, V., Antoinette, T., Morgan, A. S., Bresnahan, J. F., et al. (2001). Toward an understanding of violence: Neurobehavioral aspects of unwanted physical aggression: Aspen Neurobehavioral Conference consensus statement. *Journal of Neuropsychiatry, Neuropsychology and Behavioral Neurology, 14,* 1–14.

Fishbein, D. (2000). Neuropsychological function, drug abuse, and violence: A conceptual framework. *Criminal Justice and Behavior, 27,* 139–159.

Forth, A. E., Kosson, D. S., & Hare, R. D. (2003). *Hare Psychopathy Checklist: Youth version.* Toronto, Ontario, Canada: Multi-Health Systems.

Frick, P. J. (2002). Juvenile psychopathy from a developmental perspective: Implications for construct development and use in forensic assessment. *Law and Human Behavior, 26*(2), 247–254.

Gagliardi, G. J., Lovell, D., Peterson, P. D., & Jemelka, R. (2004). Forecasting recidivism in mentally ill offenders released from prison. *Law and Human Behavior, 28*(2), 133–155.

Gannon, J. L. (2004). Reentry-AACP project of the year 2004. *Correctional Psychologist, 36*(1), 12–14.

Gavazzi, S. M., Yarcheck, C. M., Rhine, E. E., & Partridge, C. R. (2003). Building bridges between the parole officer and the families of serious juvenile offenders: A preliminary report on a family-based parole program. *International Journal of Offender Therapy and Comparative Criminology, 47*(3), 291–308.

Gendreau, P., Goggin, C., & Paparozzi, M. (1996). Principles of effective assessment for community corrections. *Federal Probation, 60*(3), 64–70.

Gendreau, P., Goggin, C., & Smith, P. (2002). Is the PCL-R really the "unparalleled" measure of offender risk? A lesson in knowledge cumulation. *Criminal Justice and Behavior, 29,* 397–426.

Girard, L., & Wormith, S. (2004). The predictive validity of the Level of Service Inventory: Ontario revision on general and violent recidivism among various offender groups. *Criminal Justice and Behavior, 31,* 150–181.

Glasser, B. A., Calhoun, G. B., & Pertocelli, J. V. (2002). Personality characteristics of male juvenile offenders by adjudicated offences as indicated by the MMPI-A. *Criminal Justice and Behavior, 29*(2), 183–201.

Gordon, J. A., & Moriarty, L. J. (2003). The effects of domestic batterer treatment on domestic violence recidivism: The Chesterfield County experience. *Criminal Justice and Behavior, 30*(1), 118–134.

Grann, M., Belfrage, H., & Tengstrom, A. (2000). Actuarial assessment of risk of violence: Predictive validity of the VRAG and the historical part of the HCR–20. *Criminal Justice and Behavior, 27*(1), 97–114.

Gretton, H. M., Hare, R. D., & Catchpole, R. E. H. (2004). Psychopathy and offending from adolescence to adulthood: A 10-year follow-up. *Journal of Consulting and Clinical Psychology, 72*(4), 636–645.

Grubin, D. (1998). *Sex offending against children: Understanding the risk.* (Paper 99). London: Home Office, Policing and Crime Reducing Unit, Research, Development and Statistics Directorate.

Hanlon, T. E., O'Grady, K. E., & Bateman, R. W. (2000). Using the Addiction Severity Index to predict treatment outcome among substance abusing parolees. *Journal of Offender Rehabilitation, 31*, 67–79.

Hanson, R. K. (1997). *The development of a brief actuarial risk scale for sexual offence recidivism* (User Report No. 1997-04). Ottawa, Canada: Department of the Solicitor General of Canada.

Hanson, R. K. (2002). Recidivism and age: Follow-up data on 4,673 sexual offenders. *Journal of Interpersonal Violence, 17*, 1046–1062.

Hanson, R. K., & Bussiere, M. T. (1998). Predicting relapse: A meta-analysis of sexual offender recidivism studies. *Journal of Consulting and Clinical Psychology, 66*(2), 348–362.

Hanson, R. K., & Harris, A. J. R. (2001). A structured approach to evaluating change among sexual offenders. *Sexual Abuse: A Journal of Assessment and Treatment, 13*(2), 105–122.

Hanson, R. K., & Morton-Bourgon, K. (2004). *Predictors of sexual recidivism: An updated meta-analysis.* Ottawa: Department of Public Safety and Emergency Preparedness Canada.

Hanson, R. K., & Thornton, D. (2000). Improving risk assessments for sex offenders: A comparison of three actuarial scales. *Law and Human Behavior, 24*(1), 119–136.

Hare, R. D. (1991). *The revised Psychopathy Checklist.* Toronto, Ontario, Canada: Multi-Health Systems.

Hare, R. D. (2004). *Hare Psychopathy Checklist-Revised (PCL-R): Technical manual* (2nd ed.).Toronto, Ontario, Canada: Multi-Health Systems.

Harris, G. T., & Rice, M. E. (2003). Actuarial assessment of risk among sex offenders. *Annals of the New York Academy of Sciences, 989*, 198–210.

Harris, G. T., Rice, M. E., & Quinsey, V. L. (1993). Violent recidivism of mentally disordered offenders: The development of a statistical prediction instrument. *Criminal Justice and Behavior, 20*, 315–335.

Hart, S. D., Watt, K. A., & Vincent, G. M. (2002). Commentary on Seagraves and Grisso: Impressions on the state of the art. *Law and Human Behavior, 26*(2), 241–246.

Hemphill, J. F., & Hare, R. D. (2004). Some misconceptions about the Hare PCL-R and risk assessment. *Criminal Justice and Behavior, 31*, 203–243.

Henggeler, S. W., Melton, G. B., & Smith, L. A. (1992). Family preservation using multisystemic therapy: An effective alternative to incarcerating serious juvenile offenders. *Journal of Consulting and Clinical Psychology, 60*(6), 953–961.

Henggeler, S. W., Clingempeel, W. G., Brondino, M. J., & Pickrel, S. G. (2002). Four-year follow-up of multisystemic therapy with substance-abusing and substance-dependent juvenile offenders. *Journal of the American Academy of Child and Adolescent Psychiatry, 41*(7), 868–874.

Hoaken, P. N. S., & Stewart, S. H. (2003). Drugs of abuse and the elicitation of human aggressive behavior. *Addictive Behaviors, 28*, 1533–1554.

Hoge, R., & Andrews, D. A. (2002). *The youth Level of Service/Case Management Inventory manual and scoring key.* Toronto, Canada: Multi-Health Systems.

Hollin, C. R., Palmer, E., McGuire, J., Hounsome, J., Hatcher, R., Bilby, C., et al. (2004). Pathfinder Programmes in the Probation Service: A Retrospective Analysis. Home Office On-Line Report 66/04. http://www.homeoffice.gov.uk/rds/pdfs04/rdsolr6604.pdf.

Jones, S. A., D'Agostino, R. B., Gondolf, E. W., & Heckert, A. (2004). Assessing the effect of batterer program completion on reassault using propensity scores. *Journal of Interpersonal Violence, 19*(9), 1002–1020.

Julien, R. (2005). *A primer of drug action: A concise, nontechnical guide to the actions, uses and side effects of psychoactive drugs* (10th ed.). New York: Worth.

Kemshall, H. (2000). Conflicting knowledges on risk: The case of risk knowledge in the probation service. *Health, Risk & Society, 2*(2), 143–158.

Kroner, D. G., & Loza, W. (2001). Evidence for the efficacy of self-report in predicting nonviolent and violent criminal recidivism. *Journal of Interpersonal Violence, 16*(2), 168–177.

Kropp, P. R., & Hart, S. D. (2000). The Spousal Assault Risk Assessment (SARA) guide: Reliability and validity in adult male offenders. *Law and Human Behavior, 24*(1), 101–118.

Kropp, P. R., Hart, S. D., Webster, C. D., & Eaves, D. (1994). *Manual for the Spousal Assault Risk Assessment.* Vancouver, British Columbia, Canada: British Columbia Institute Against Family Violence.

Kropp, P. R., Hart, S. D., Webster, C. D., & Eaves, D. (1995). *Manual for the Spousal Assault Risk Assessment* (2nd ed.). Vancouver, British Columbia, Canada: British Columbia Institute Against Family Violence.

Langton, C. M. (2003). *Contrasting approaches to risk assessment with adult male sexual offenders: An evaluation of recidivism prediction schemes and the utility of supplemental clinical information for evaluating predictive accuracy.* Unpublished doctoral dissertation, Institute for Medical Science, University of Toronto, Ontario, Canada.

Leon-Carrion, R., & Ramos, F. J. (2003). Blows to the head during development can predispose to violent criminal behaviour: Rehabilitation of consequences of head injury is a measure for crime prevention. *Brain Injury, 17*(3), 207–216.

Letourneau, E. J., Schoenwald, S. K., & Sheidow, A. J. (2004). Children and adolescents with sexual behavior problems. *Child Maltreatment, 9*(1), 49–61.

Levi, M. D. (2004). *Aggression subtypes: The role of neuropsychological functioning and personality.* Unpublished doctoral dissertation, Department of Psychology, York University, Toronto, Ontario, Canada.

Levi, M. D., Nussbaum, D., & Reimann, B. J. (2005, June). *Fishbein's modified ASI ratings and aggression types: Possible underlying psychopharmacology and neuropsychological mechanisms.* Paper presented to the Canadian Psychological Association annual convention, Montreal.

Lindsay, W. R., Smith, A. H. W., Law, J., Quinn, K., Anderson, A., Smith, A., et al. (2002). A treatment service for sex offenders and abusers with intellectual disability: Characteristics of referrals and evaluation. *Journal of Applied Research in Intellectual Disabilities, 15*(2), 166–174.

Linhorst, D. M., McCutchen, T. A., & Bennett, L. (2003). Recidivism among offenders with developmental disabilities participating in a case management program. *Research in Developmental Disabilities, 24,* 210–230.

Liskow, B., Campbell, J., Nickel, E. J., & Powel, B. J. (1995). Validity of the CAGE questionnaire in screening for alcohol dependence in a walk-in (triage) clinic. *Journal of Studies on Alcohol, 56*(3), 277–281.

Litwack, T. (2001). Actuarial versus clinical assessments of dangerousness. *Psychology, Public Policy, and Law, 7*(2), 409–443.

Litwack, T. R. (2002). Some questions for the field of violence risk assessment and forensic mental health: Or, "back to basics" revisited. *International Journal of Forensic Mental Health, 1*(2), 171–179.

Loeber, R., & Stouthamer-Loeber, M. (1998). Development of juvenile aggression and violence: Some common misconceptions and controversies. *American Psychologist, 53*(2), 242–259.

Looman, J., Abracen, J., & Nicholaichuk, T. P. (2000). Recidivism among treated sexual offenders and matched controls: Data from the regional treatment centre (Ontario). *Journal of Interpersonal Violence, 15*(3), 279–290.

Loving, J. L. (2002). Treatment planning with the PCL.-R. *International Journal of Offender Therapy and Comparative Criminology, 46*(3), 281–293.

Lowenkamp, C. T., Holsinger, A. M., & Latessa, E. J. (2001). Risk/need assessment, offender classification, and the role of childhood abuse. *Criminal Justice and Behavior, 28*(5), 543–563.

Loza, W. (1996). *Self-Appraisal Questionnaire (SAQ): A tool for assessing violent and non-violent recidivism.* Unpublished manuscript.

Loza, W. F., Cumberton, A., Shahinfar, A., Neo, H., Evans, M., Conley, M., et al. (2004). Cross-validation of the Self-Appraisal Questionnaire (SAQ): An offender risk and need assessment measure on Australian, British, Canadian, Singaporian and American offenders. *Journal of Interpersonal Violence, 19*(10), 1172–1190.

Loza, W., Dhaliwal, G., Kroner, D. G., & Loza-Fanous, A. (2000). Reliability, construct, and concurrent validities of the Self-Appraisal Questionnaire for assessing violent and non-violent recidivism. *Criminal Justice and Behavior, 27*(3), 356–374.

Loza, W., & Loza-Fanous, A. (1999a). Anger and prediction of violent and non-violent offenders' recidivism. *Journal of Interpersonal Violence, 14,* 1014–1029.

Loza, W., & Loza-Fanous, A. (1999b). The fallacy of reducing rape and violent recidivism by treating anger. *International Journal of Offender Therapy and Comparative Criminology, 43*(4), 492–502.

Loza, W., & Loza-Fanous, A. (2001). The effectiveness of the Self-Appraisal Questionnaire in predicting offender's post-release outcome: A comparison study. *Criminal Justice and Behavior, 28,* 105–121.

Loza, W., & Loza-Fanous, A. (2003). More evidence for the validity of the Self-Appraisal Questionnaire predicitng violent and nonviolent recidivism: A 5-year follow-up. *Criminal Justice and Behavior, 30*(6), 709–721.

Loza, W., Villeneuve, D. B., & Loza-Fanous, A. (2002). Predictive validity of the Violence Risk Appraisal Guide: A tool for assessing violent offender's recidivism. *International Journal of Law and Psychiatry, 25,* 85–92.

Lurigio, A. J. (2001). Effective services for parolees with mental illnesses. *Crime and Delinquency, 47*(3), 446–461.

Lynam, D. R. (1996). Early identification of chronic offenders: Who is the fledgling psychopath? *Psychological Bulletin, 120,* 209–234.

Lynam, D. R. (2002). Fledgling psychopathy: A view from personality theory. *Law and Human Behavior, 26*(2), 255–259.

MacKenzie, D. L. (2001). Corrections and sentencing in the 21st century: Evidence-based corrections and sentencing. *Prison Journal, 81*(3), 299–312.

Maletzky, B. M., & Field, G. (2003). The biological treatment of dangerous sexual offenders: A review and preliminary report of the Oregon pilot Depo-Provera program. *Aggression and Violent Behavior, 8,* 391–412.

Maletzky, B. M., & Steinhauser, C. (2002). A 25-year follow-up of cognitive/behavioral therapy with 7,275 sexual offenders. *Behavior Modification, 26*(2), 123–147.

Marlatt, G. A. (1978). Craving for alcohol, loss of control and relapse: A cognitive-behavioral analysis. In P. E. Nathan, G. A. Marlatt, & T. Loberg (Eds.), *New directions in behavioral research and treatment* (pp. 271–314). New York: Plenum Press.

Martin, R. L., Cloninger, R., & Guze, S. B. (1978). Female criminality and the prediction of recidivism: A prospective six-year follow-up. *Archives of General Psychiatry, 35,* 207–214.

Martinson, R. (1974). What works? Questions and answers about prison reform. *Public Interest, 35,* 22–54.

Mason, J., & Murphy, G. (2002). Intellectual disability amongst people on probation: Prevalence and outcome. *Journal of Intellectual Disability Research, 46*(3), 230–238.

McEwen, B. S. (2000). Allostasis and allostatic load: Implications for neuropsychopharmacology. *Neuropsychopharmacology, 22*(2), 108–124.

McGuire, J., & Hatcher, R. (2001). Offense-focused problem solving: Preliminary evaluation of a cognitive skills program. *Criminal Justice and Behavior, 28*(5), 564–587.

McLellan, A. T., Kushner, H., Metzger, D., Peters, R., Griossom, G., Pwettinati, H., et al. (1992). The fifth edition of the Addiction Severity Index: Historical critique and normative data. *Journal of Substance Abuse and Treatment, 9,* 199–213.

Miller, F. G., Roberts, J., Brooks, M. K., & Lazowski, L. E. (1997). *SASSI-3 user's guide: A quick reference for administration and scoring.* Bloomington, IN: Baugh Enterprises.

Mills, J. F. (2003, August). *Predictive accuracy of risk categories.* Paper presented at the American Psychological Association annual convention, Toronto, Ontario, Canada.

Moffitt, T. E. (1993). "Life-course persistent" and "adolescent-limited" antisocial behavior: A developmental taxonomy. *Psychological Review, 100,* 674–701.

Moffitt, T. E., Caspi, A., Harrington, H., & Milne, B. (2002). Males on the life-course persistence and adolescence-limited antisocial pathways: Follow-up at age 26 years. *Development and Psychopathology, 14,* 179–207.

Monahan, J., Steadman, H. J., Silver, E., Appelbaum, P. S., Robbins, P. C., Mulvey, E., et al. (2001). *Rethinking risk assessment: The MacArthur study of mental disorder and violence.* New York: Oxford University Press.

Morey, L. C. (1991). *Personality Assessment Inventory manual.* Odessa, FL: Psychological Associates Resources.

Nicholaichuk, T., Gordon, A., Deqiang, G., & Wong, S. (2000). Outcome of an institutional sexual offender treatment program: A comparison between treated and matched untreated offenders. *Sexual Abuse: A Journal of Research and Treatment, 12*(2), 139–153.

Ninness, H. A., Ellis, J., Miller, W. B., Baker, D., & Rutherford, R. (1995). The effect of a self-management training package on the transfer of aggression control procedures in the absence of supervision. *Behavior Modification, 19*(4), 464–490.

Nussbaum, D., Collins, M., Cutler, J., Zimmerman, W., Farguson, B., & Jacques, I. (2002). Crime type and specific personality indicia: Cloninger's TCI impulsivity, empathy and attachment subscales in non-violent, violent and sexual offenders. *American Journal of Forensic Psychology, 20*(1), 23–56.

Nussbaum, D., Saint-Cyr, J., & Bell, E. (1997). A biologically derived psychometric model for understanding, predicting and treating tendencies toward future violence. *American Journal of Forensic Psychiatry, 18*(4), 35–51.

Office of Justice Programs, www.ojp.osdoj.gov/reentry/learn.html.

Ogloff, J. R., Lemphers, A., & Dwyer, C. (2004). Dual diagnosis in an Australian forensic psychiatric population: Prevalence and implications for service. *Behavioral Sciences and the Law, 22*(4), 543–562.

Pearson, F. S., Lipton, D. S., Cleland, C. M., & Yee, D. S. (2002). The effects of behavioral/cognitive-behavioral programs on recidivism. *Crime and Delinquency, 48*(3), 476–496.

Peedicayil, A., Sadowski, L. S., Shanker, V., Jain, D., Suresh, S., & Bangdiwala, S. I. (2004). Spousal physical violence against women during pregnancy. *International Journal of Obstetrics and Gynecology, 111*(7), 682–687.

Peugh, J., & Belenko, S. (1999). Substance-involved women inmates: Challenges to providing effective treatment. *Prison Journal, 79*(1), 23–44.

Pihl, R. O., Assaad, J. M., & Hoaken, P. S. (2003). The alcohol-aggression relationship and differential sensitivity to alcohol. *Aggressive Behavior, 29*, 302–315.

Pokorny, A., Miller, B. A., & Kaplan, H. B. (1972). The brief MAST: A shortened version of the Michigan Alcohol Screening Test. *American Journal of Psychiatry, 129*, 342–345.

Pope, V. T. (2001). Prevalence of childhood and adolescent sexual abuse among sex offenders. *Psychological Reports, 89*, 355–362.

Prochaska, J. O., & Declemente, C. C. (1992). Stages of change in the modification of problem behaviors. *Progressive Behavior Modification, 28*, 183–218.

Quinn, W. H., & Van Dyke, D. J. (2004). A multiple family group intervention for first-time juvenile offenders: Comparisons with probation and dropouts on recidivism. *Journal of Community Psychology, 32*(2), 177–200.

Quinsey, V. L., Harris, G. T., Rice, M. E., & Cormier, C. A. (1998). *Violent offenders: Appraising and managing risk.* Washington, DC: American Psychological Association.

Regina v. Mohan, 2 S.C.R. 9 (1994).

Rice, M. E., & Harris, G. T. (1995). Violent recidivism: Assessing predictive validity. *Journal of Consulting and Clinical Psycholgy, 63*(5), 737–748.

Richie, B. E. (2001). Challenges incarcerated women face as they return to their communities: Findings from life history interviews. *Crime and Delinquency, 47*(3), 368–389.

Robertson, A. A., Grimes, P. W., & Rogers, K. E. (2001). A short-run cost-benefit analysis of community-based interventions for juvenile offenders. *Crime and Delinquency, 47*(2), 265–284.

Rosenfeld, B. (2003). Recidivism in stalking and obsessional harassment. *Law and Human Behavior, 27*(3), 251–265.

Rzepa, S., Wormith, S., Bonta, J., & Andrews, D. A. (2004, July). *Generalizability of the LSI-R (LS/CMI) to U.S. offenders.* Paper presented at the APA annual convention, Honolulu, HI.

Salekin, R. T., Rogers, R., & Sewell, K. W. (1997). Construct validity of psychopathy in a female offender sample: A multitrait-multimethod evaluation. *Journal of Abnormal Psychology, 106*(4), 576–585.

Scalora, M. J., & Garbin, C. (2003). A multivariate analysis of sex offender recidivism. *International Journal of Offender Therapy and Comparative Criminology, 47*(3), 309–323.

Scott, K. L. (2004). Predictors of change among male batterers: Applications of theory and review of empirical findings. *Trauma, Violence and Abuse, 5*(3), 260–284.

Seager, J. A., Jellicoe, D., & Dhaliwal, G. K. (2004). Refusers, dropouts, and completers: Measuring sex offender treatment efficacy. *International Journal of Offender Therapy and Comparative Criminology, 48*(5), 600–612.

Seagrave, D., & Grisso, T. (2002). Adolescent development and measurement of juvenile psychopathy. *Law and Human Behavior, 26*(2), 219–240.

Seifert, K. (2003). *CARE: Child and Adolescent Risk Evaluation.* Champaign, IL: Research Press.

Seifert, K. (2004). *RME: Risk Management Evaluation.* Salisbury, MD: Soulight Publishing.

Seifert, K., Philips, S., & Parker, S. (2001). Child and adolescent risk for violence. *Journal of Psychiatry and Law, 29*, 329–344.

Selzer, M. L. (1971). The Michigan Alcohol Screening Test: The quest for a new diagnostic instrument. *American Journal of Psychiatry, 127*, 1653–1658.

Seto, M. C., & Barbaree, H. E. (1999). Psychopathy, treatment behavior and sex offender recidivism. *Journal of Interpersonal Violence, 14*(12), 1235–1248.

Sheidow, A. J., Bradford, W. D., Henggeler, S. W., Rowland, M. D., Halliday-Boykins, C., Schoenwald, S. K., et al. (2004). Treatment costs for youths receiving multisystemic therapy or hospitalization after a psychiatric crisis. *Psychiatric Services, 55*(5), 548–554.

Shepard, M. F., Falk, D. R., & Elliott, B. A. (2002). Enhancing coordinated community responses to reduce recidivism in cases of domestic violence. *Journal of Interpersonal Violence, 17*(5), 551–569.

Sjostedt, G., & Langstrom, N. (2002). Assessment of risk for criminal recidivism among rapists: A comparison of four different measures. *Psychology, Crime, & Law, 8*(1), 25–40.

Skeem, J. L., Monahan, J., & Mulvey, E. P. (2002). Psychopathy, treatment involvement, and subsequent violence among civil psychiatric patients. *Law and Human Behavior, 26*(6), 577–603.

Skinner, H. A. (1982). The Drug Abuse Screening Test. *Addictive Behaviors, 7*, 363–371.

Sorbello, L., Eccleston, L., Ward, T., & Jones, R. (2002). Treatment needs of female offenders: A review. *Australian Psychologist, 37*(3), 198–205.

Stalans, L. J., Yarnold, P. R., Seng, M., Olson, D. E., & Repp, M. (2004). Identifying three types of violent offenders and predicting violent recidivism while on probation: A classification tree analysis. *Law and Human Behavior, 28*(3), 253–271.

Steadman, H. J., Silver, E., Monahan, J., Appelbaum, P. S., Robbins, P. C., Mulvey, E. P., et al. (2000). A classification tree approach to the development of actuarial risk assessment tools. *Law and Human Behavior, 24*(1), 83–100.

Taylor, J. L., Novaco, R. W., Gillmer, B., & Thorne, I. (2002). Cognitive-behavioral treatment of anger intensity among offenders with intellectual disabilities. *Journal of Applied Research in Intellectual Disabilities, 15*(2), 151–165.

Tengstrom, A. (2001). Long-term predictive validity of historical factors in 2 risk assessment instruments in a group of violent offenders with schizophrenia. *Nordic Journal of Psychiatry, 55*, 243–249.

Thomas, T. L., Harris, A. J. R., Forth, A., & Hanson, R. K. (2004, June). *Stable and dynamic factors: Predicting recidivism in adult sexual offenders.* Paper presented at the Canadian Psychological Association, St. John's, Newfoundland.

Thornton, D. (2002). Constructing and testing a framework for dynamic risk assessment. *Sexual Abuse: A Journal of Research and Treatment, 14*(2), 139–153.

Thornton, D., Mann, R., Webster, S., Blud, L., Travers, R., Friendship, C., et al. (2003). Distinguishing and combining risks for sexual and violent recidivism. In E. J. R. Prentky, M. Seto, & A. Burgess (Eds.), *Sexually coercive behavior: Understanding and management* (pp. 225–235). New York: New York Academy of Sciences.

Travis, J., & Petersilia, J. (2001). Reentry reconsidered: A new look at an old question. *Crime and Delinquency, 47*, 291–313.

Villeneuve, D. B., Oliver, N., & Loza, W. (2003). Cross-validation of the Self-Appraisal Questionnaire with a maximum-security psychiatric population. *Journal of Interpersonal Violence, 18*(11), 1325–1334.

Vitale, J. E., Smith, S. S., Brinkley, C. A., & Newman, J. P. (2002). The reliability and validity of the Psychopathy Checklist-Revised in a sample of female offenders. *Criminal Justice and Behavior, 29*(2), 202–231.

Vogel-Sprott, M. (1967). Alcohol effects on human behavior under reward and punishment conditions. *Psychopharmacologia, 11*, 337–344.

Vogel-Sprott, M., Easdon, G., Fillmore, M., Finn, P., & Justus, A. (2001). Alcohol and behavioral control: Cognitive and neural mechanisms. *Alcoholism: Clinical and Experimental Research, 25*, 117–121.

Watson, M., Nussbaum, D., & Flett, G. (2003, April). *Some criminogenic and clinical correlates of the VESI.* Paper presented to the International Association of Forensic Mental Health Services, Miami, FL.

Webster, C. D., Douglas, K. S., Eaves, D., & Hart, S. D. (1997). *HCR-20: Assessing risk for violence, version 2.* Burnaby, British Columbia, Canada: Simon Fraser University.

Weiss, I., & Wozner, Y. (2002). Ten models for probation supervision compared across eight dimensions. *Journal of Offender Rehabilitation, 34*(3), 85–105.

Wiener, R. L. (2002). Adversarial forum: Issues concerning the assessment of juvenile psychopathy. *Law and Human Behavior, 26*(2), 217–218.

Williams, K. R., & Houghton, A. B. (2004). Assessing the risk of domestic violence reoffending: A validation study. *Law and Human Behavior, 28*(4), 437–455.

Wilson, R. J., Stewart, L., Stirpe, T., Barrett, M., & Cripps, J. E. (2000). Community-based sex of-fender management: Combining parole supervision and treatment to reduce recidivism. *Canadian Journal of Criminology, 42*(2), 177–188.

Witkiewitz, K., & Marlatt, G. A. (2004). Relapse prevention for alcohol and drug problems: That was zen, this is tao. *American Psychologist, 59*(4), 224–235.

Wong, S. G., & Gordon, A. (2000). *The Violence Prediction Scale.* Unpublished manuscript.

Wong, S. G., & Gordon, A. (2004). *Assessment and treatment of forensic clients: An integrated approach.* Unpublished manuscript.

Wong, S. G., & Gordon, A. (2004). *Training in the use of the Violence Risk Scale: (VRS).* Unpublished manuscript.

Wong, S. G., & Gordon, A. (in press). The risk-readiness model of post-treatment risk management. *Bulletin of the British Psychological Society.*

Wooldredge, J., & Thistlewaite, A. (2002). Reconsidering domestic violence recidivism: Conditioned effects of legal controls by individual and aggregate levels of stake in conformity. *Journal of Quantitative Criminology, 18*(1), 45–70.

Wormith, S. W., Andrews, D. A., & Bonta, J. (2004, August). *Building a link between risk assessment and case management.* Paper presented at the APA annual convention, Honolulu, HI.

Zanis, D. A., Mulvaney, F., Coviello, D., Alterman, A. I., Savitz, B., & Thompson, W. (2003). The effectiveness of early parole to substance abuse facilities on 24-month criminal rcidivism. *Journal of Drug Issues, 33*(1), 223–236.

Zhang, L., Welte, J. W., & Wieczorek, W. W. (2002). The role of aggression-related alcohol expectancies in explaining the link between alcohol and violent behavior. *Substance Use & Misuse, 37*(4), 457–471.

PART FOUR

SPECIAL APPLICATIONS

CHAPTER 17

Violence Risk Assessment: Research, Legal, and Clinical Considerations

THOMAS R. LITWACK, PATRICIA A. ZAPF,
JENNIFER L. GROSCUP, and STEPHEN D. HART

IN A variety of contexts, our legal system allows for and even expects assessments of the dangerousness of certain individuals, that is, assessments of the probability, or risk, that those individuals will cause certain types of harm under particular conditions within particular periods of time (*Schall v. Martin*, 1984; Shah, 1978). Such assessments, currently most commonly labeled violence risk assessments, can significantly affect the lives of those individuals (*Barefoot v. Estelle*, 1983; *Kansas v. Hendricks*, 1997; *United States v. Salerno*, 1987) and, if a serious proclivity toward violence goes undetected, perhaps other individuals—that is, potential victims—as well (Monahan, 1993; Schlesinger, 1996, p. 314). Mental health professionals are often called on, and may even be obliged, to participate in these decisions (*Addington v. Texas*, 1979; Buckner & Firestone, 2000; Felthous & Kachigian, 2001; *Tarasoff v. Regents of the University of California*, 1976; VandeCreek & Knapp, 2001; Walcott, Cerundolo, & Beck, 2001). As Borum (1996, p. 954) has observed:

> The assessment and the management of violence risk are critical issues, not just for psychologists and psychiatrists in forensic settings but for all practicing clinicians. Despite a long-standing controversy about the ability of mental health professionals to predict violence, the courts continue to rely on them for advice on these issues and in many cases have imposed on them a legal duty to take action when they know or should know that a patient poses a risk of serious danger to others.

This chapter addresses, primarily, assessments of dangerousness, or violence risk assessments, concerning mentally disordered individuals possibly at risk for violence in the community. First, we survey the research regarding such assessments by mental health professionals, actuarial instruments, and structured assessment guides. Then we survey recent developments in the law that concern the admissibility in court of such assessments and the legal standards for depriving individuals of their liberty based on such assessments. Finally, we consider some of the primary factors and procedures that leading forensic clinicians and our own experience suggest should be a part of proper and comprehensive clinical assessments of dangerousness.

THE RESEARCH

The first comprehensive review of the research literature regarding assessments of dangerousness by mental health professionals was John Monahan's influential monograph *Predicting Violent Behavior: An Assessment of Clinical Techniques,* which appeared in 1981. (An earlier, less extensive, review by Dix, 1980, was also quite useful.) Monahan updated his 1981 review in another prominent article published in 1984 (see also Wettstein, 1984). Litwack and Schlesinger (1987) reviewed the research literature through 1985 for the first edition of the present volume and arrived at conclusions somewhat different from those of Monahan. Litwack, Kirschner, and Wack (1993) reviewed the relevant studies from 1985 to 1990 and concluded, echoing both Monahan (1981, 1984) and Litwack and Schlesinger, that "research had *not* negated the possibility that clinical evaluations of dangerousness *can* have a unique and useful role to play in making determinations of dangerousness that our society has decided should be made" (p. 269; emphasis in original). Litwack and Schlesinger (1999) updated their review of the literature (through 1997) for the second edition of this *Handbook* and echoed this sentiment.

However, in 1999, Quinsey, Harris, Rice, and Cormier proposed the "complete replacement" of clinical assessments of dangerousness with actuarial methods (p. 171). In response, Litwack (2001, p. 409, emphasis added) reviewed the studies directly comparing clinical with actuarial risk assessments and concluded that "research to date has *not* demonstrated that actuarial methods of risk assessment are superior to clinical methods." Rather, he proposed, "it seems that much more research is needed to determine the relative merits of clinical versus actuarial assessments of dangerousness and that such research should be conducted in as meaningful a manner as possible" (p. 424). (The actuarial versus clinical distinction, and debate, is discussed further in this chapter.)

Readers are referred to these works for more complete reviews of the research literature than space allows for here. In addition, there have been other, fairly extensive, reviews of the research literature by Borum (1996), Brooks (1992), Monahan (1996, 1997, 2003), Monahan and Steadman (1994), Otto (1992, 1994), Bjørkly (1995), and Mossman (1994a). (Regarding Otto's 1992 review, see also the commentaries by Hart, Webster, & Menzies, 1993, and Mossman, 1994b.) In addition, Beech, Fisher, and Thornton (2003) and Conroy (2003) have published extensive reviews of the literature regarding risk assessments of sex offenders. Here we review, first, some of the most prominent early studies of violence risk assessments both because of their continuing notoriety and because they illustrate important points that need to be considered in evaluating most research studies regarding assessments of dangerousness and/or the assessments themselves. Then we consider major research studies published in recent years to evaluate the current state of research findings concerning vio lence risk assessments—and some needs for research in the future.

KOZOL, BOUCHER, AND GARAFOLO (1972)

The most widely cited study for the often-stated proposition that predictions of violence by mental health professionals are wrong at least two times out of three, even when based on a known history of violence and extensive clinical examinations (*Barefoot v. Estelle,* 1983, dissenting opinion; Monahan, 1984), is a study by Kozol, Boucher, and Garafolo (1972). A close examination of this study illustrates, however, how cautious one should be before drawing firm conclusions from most, if not all, studies of assessments of dangerousness.

Using clinical examinations, extensive life histories, and psychological tests, a team of mental health professionals evaluated 592 males convicted of assaultive offenses (usually sexual in nature) and sentenced to a special facility for continued evaluation and treatment. Of these men, 386 were eventually diagnosed as *not* dangerous by the evaluating team and eventually released. In addition, 49 men diagnosed as still dangerous were also released by judicial or parole authorities *against the advice* of the professional staff.

The released individuals were followed up in the community. At the end of the follow-up period of up to 5 years, 8% of the patients considered by the evaluating teams to be *non*dangerous were found to have committed a serious assaultive crime. By contrast, 34.7% of the patients viewed as dangerous by clinicians, but nevertheless released, were discovered to have committed a serious crime.

On the surface, the clinicians studied here did appear to do much better than chance in their evaluations because the recidivism rate of offender patients released against the advice of the evaluating teams was much higher than the recidivism rate of patients evaluated to be no longer dangerous. However, it appears from the report that the evaluees deemed dangerous but nevertheless released were, on average, at risk for recidivism in the community for a significantly longer period than those released after clinical judgments of nondangerousness. Thus, it cannot be definitively concluded from this study that the clinicians at issue demonstrated at least *some* ability to assess dangerousness. However, for the reasons that follow, neither can it be legitimately concluded from this study that "predictions of violence" by mental health professionals are wrong at least two-thirds of the time.

To begin with, Kozol, Boucher, and Garofalo (1973) reported subsequently that at least 14 of their 49 patients diagnosed as dangerous and yet released were patients who had been committed and studied during the early years of their program and who would *not* have been diagnosed as dangerous in the later years of their study (when, presumably, their diagnostic techniques and judgments were more refined). Thus, Kozol et al. may eventually have developed a diagnostic system that was able to predict which of their sample of patients would be dangerous if released with at least 50% accuracy.

Second, the recidivism rate reported by Kozol et al. (1972) for the patients deemed dangerous—be it 35% or 50%—may have been far less than the actual recidivism rate. Hall (1982) has pointed out that there is good reason to believe that only 20% of serious crimes lead to an arrest. Thus, many seeming false positives (especially among individuals with a history of serious violence) may, in fact, be undiscovered true positives.

Third, and important, the 49 patients released despite clinical judgments of dangerousness were *not a representative sample* of patients judged to be dangerous by the clinicians in this study. Because these 49 individuals were released by judicial or parole authorities against professional advice, they were almost certainly borderline patients in terms of their dangerousness who presented much evidence of being no longer dangerous (despite some evidence to the contrary). Why else, in the main, would they have been released? However, if the far larger number of patients diagnosed as dangerous by the teams and legal authorities and not released had been released, their rate of recidivism—and the apparent accuracy of the clinical assessments of dangerousness—might have been far higher than it appeared to be for the borderline patients. Thus, this study simply does not demonstrate that predictions of violence by mental health professionals are likely to be wrong two-thirds of the time regardless of the sample of individuals being evaluated (Litwack, 1996), the circumstances involved, or the confidence of the clinicians in their judgments (McNiel, Sandberg, & Binder, 1998; see also Douglas & Ogloff, 2003a, for a discussion of confidence and accuracy).

Finally, and most crucially, the judgments of dangerousness at issue in this study, like most judgments of dangerousness, were never predictions of violence to begin with. The patients supposedly predicted to be violent were actually, and more conservatively, simply *"not recommended* for release" (Kozol et al., 1972, p. 390). Clinical concerns regarding a patient's potential dangerousness that lead to a conclusion that the patient cannot be recommended for release do not equate with a prediction that a patient will definitely be violent if released (Mulvey & Lidz, 1995). A clinical judgment that a patient is dangerous, even a judgment that an individual is sufficiently dangerous to warrant confinement, is rarely, if ever, a prediction that a patient unquestionably will be violent if at liberty or, at least, if unsupervised. Rather, almost always, it is a judgment that the assessee poses a *significant risk* of acting violently in certain circumstances. Indeed, in forensic settings, patients with a history of serious violence may well be deemed still dangerous by clinicians and judges even if it clearly could not be concluded with confidence that those patients would recidivate if released, as long as it is determined that the patients are still significantly *at risk* for serious recidivism (Litwack, 1996, pp. 108–115; Monahan & Silver, 2003). That is, a clinical conclusion that a patient cannot be recommended for release—or even a conclusion that a patient remains dangerous— may simply be a determination that the patient remains prone to violence *under certain circumstances* (e.g., if the patient stops taking certain prescribed medications, or reengages in substance abuse, or enters into a certain type of relationship), which, it is recognized, may not occur but which also might well occur, given the totality of the clinical picture. Thus, if a patient deemed by a clinician to be too dangerous to be recommended for release is nevertheless released and does not recidivate, it is simply incorrect to conclude that the clinician made a prediction that turned out to be wrong. To the contrary, although the clinician may have concluded that the risk of causing harm still posed by the patient was too great to recommend the patient for release, the clinician may also have concluded that the patient might well not recidivate. This fact poses serious difficulties for attempts to evaluate the validity of clinical assessments of dangerousness (Litwack, 2002b) or the relative merits of clinical versus actuarial assessments (Litwack, 2001, pp. 425–426).

THE *BAXSTROM* AND *DIXON* STUDIES

Other historically important studies of assessments of dangerousness by mental health professionals are the well-known *Baxstrom* studies (*Baxstrom v. Herold,* 1966; Steadman & Cocozza, 1974) and the similar study of the *Dixon* patients by Thornberry and Jacoby (1979; *Dixon v. Attorney General,* 1971 reviewed in detail by Litwack, 1996, pp. 116–118). Briefly stated, these studies concerned hundreds of individuals (usually convicted offenders) confined for many years in hospitals for the criminally insane because they were considered to be too dangerous to be released to civil mental hospitals, much less to the community. Yet, as a result of judicial decisions, these patients were nevertheless transferred to civil hospitals. Follow-up studies determined that only a small percentage had to be returned to secure facilities, and that only a small minority of patients ultimately released to the community were rearrested for violent offenses. (The great majority of the *Baxstrom* patients, many of whom were quite elderly, did require continued confinement in civil facilities, and of the 65% of Thornberry and Jacoby's sample who were ultimately discharged, 11% were rearrested for violent offenses.)

The findings of these studies indicate that in the past, many mentally ill individuals were wrongfully confined in unduly restrictive facilities because of erroneous assumptions or claims that they were too dangerous to live in less restrictive conditions; therefore, determinations of dangerousness for the purpose of preventive detention warrant careful judicial scrutiny. But it is equally clear that the determinations of dangerousness on which the unnecessarily severe confinements were grounded were not based on careful, individualized assessments but on what have been described as administrative decisions (*Baxstrom v. Herald,* 1966, n.3), global assessments (Steadman & Cocozza, 1980, p. 212), and "political predictions" (Thornberry & Jacoby, 1979, p. 26). Nor is there any evidence that the psychiatrists who made those determinations were anything like a representative sample of psychiatrists. Indeed, given the fact that many of these patients had grown old it is hard to believe that a representative sample of mental health professionals would have determined so many of them to be seriously dangerous.

Litwack (1996) described a representative sample of patients confined on the grounds of dangerousness (and mental disorder) in a secure forensic facility and compared his sample to Thornberry and Jacoby's (1979) sample. Litwack concluded that the samples and means of assessment employed were so different that "the validity, or invalidity, of the 'predictions' of dangerousness at issue in the study of the *Dixon* patients [were] utterly irrelevant to evaluating the validity and/or legitimacy of the assessments of dangerousness" he surveyed (p. 118). Moreover, Litwack pointed out, "once even a semblance of an individualized examination was performed . . . on the Dixon patients, only a distinct minority were still deemed to be dangerous" (p. 118). In short, it is wrong to draw conclusions about assessments of dangerousness in other—much less all—circumstances from findings regarding such assessments in particular (and perhaps highly unrepresentative) circumstances.

ASSESSMENTS OF DANGEROUSNESS BASED ON THREATS OF VIOLENCE

Most studies of assessments of dangerousness do not specify whether any of the assessees were threatening violence at the time. Therefore, these studies are simply irrelevant to determining how well mental health professionals can assess dangerousness regarding individuals (particularly psychotic individuals) who *are* threatening to commit violence. By contrast, MacDonald (1963, 1967) studied the postrelease behavior of a cohort of patients hospitalized because they had made threats to kill. Of 77 (out of 100) such patients about whom follow-up information was obtainable, three had later taken the lives of others, and four had committed suicide. However, *because all the individuals in MacDonald's cohort were hospitalized—and presumably treated—it is impossible to know how many would have acted violently without the imposition of hospitalization.* Most likely, though, the patients in MacDonald's cohort would not have been released unless they apparently no longer had active intentions to kill.

MacDonald's (1963, 1967) study raises important related questions: How can we determine what percentage of mentally ill people who are threatening to kill will actually do so without refraining from confining such individuals even when it appears, to mental health professionals, that their threats should be taken seriously? And how can we determine the accuracy of predictions of violence (much less assessments of dangerousness) in such circumstances? The answer is, of course, we can't! That is, and more generally, *ethical and legal constraints make it impossible to determine the actual dangerousness of many of those individuals who are most definitely assessed to be dangerous by mental health professionals.*

LIDZ, MULVEY, AND GARDNER (1993); GARDNER, LIDZ, MULVEY, AND SHAW (1996A, 1996B)

In 1993, Lidz, Mulvey, and Gardner published a study on dangerousness assessments that was deemed by Monahan in 1996 to be, until that time, "surely the most sophisticated study published on the clinical prediction of violence" (p. 111). That study concluded that mental health professionals can do better than chance in evaluating dangerousness. This study was also particularly noteworthy for determining postassessment patient violence in the community not solely from official records but also via community interviews with the patients and significant collaterals (Mulvey & Lidz, 1993; Mulvey, Shaw, & Lidz, 1994). Still, a close examination of this study demonstrates how difficult it is to study assessments of dangerousness in a way that does justice to the issues involved.

Pairs of clinicians were asked to independently rate hundreds of psychiatric emergency department patients on a scale from 1 to 5 regarding the patients' "potential . . . violence toward others during the next 6 months." Patients who received a summed rating of at least 3 out of a possible score of 10 were included in the "predicted violent" group. Each of these patients was then matched for sex, race, and age with another emergency room patient who had elicited less staff concern about future violence to others.

Ultimately, 357 matched pairs were followed up for 6 months after their discharge from the hospital. Violent incidents were reported in 36% of the comparison cases and 53% of the predicted cases, a statistically significant difference. Even when the patients' preadmission history of violence was controlled for, the clinicians still did statistically better than chance, leading the authors to conclude that "this study . . . show[s] that clinical judgment has been undervalued in previous research" (Lidz, Mulvey, & Gardner, 1993, p. 1010). However, because a significant percentage of the patients who did act violently in the community were not identified as dangerous by the clinicians (a measure of the sensitivity of the clinical judgments) and because a considerable percentage of patients who did not act violently in the community were in the predicted violent group (a measure of the specificity of the judgments), the authors also concluded that "the low sensitivity and specificity of these judgments show that clinicians are relatively inaccurate predictors of violence" (p. 1010).

In fact, the picture is more complex and less definitive. To begin with, the clinicians in this study were not predicting violence but, rather, rating their patients' *potential* for violence. It is simply incorrect to conclude that a patient who elicited some clinical concern regarding future dangerousness (e.g., summed ratings of 3 or 4 out of a possible 10) has been predicted to be violent (cf. Mulvey & Lidz, 1995). Lidz et al. (1993) did find that patients about whom clinicians expressed serious concern, those who had a summed score of 6 or above, were no more likely to commit violence than patients regarding whom the clinicians had expressed some, but less concern. But a high clinical rating of potential violence does not necessarily mean a judgment that the patient is very *likely* to commit violence. Such a concern may instead reflect a judgment that the patient is at risk for committing *serious* violence, even if the risk of occurrence is not high.

That is, the concept of risk is not equivalent to the concept of probability or likelihood. According to the law (see the next section), as well as social science, the concept of risk includes consideration of the nature, severity, imminence, and frequency or duration of harm—as well as its likelihood. Thus, a clinical opinion of high risk could reflect a belief that the patient poses (1) some significant possibility of serious violence, (2) a high probability of minor violence, or (3) a moderate probability of imminent violence. Even if one specifically asks clinicians to rate the probability of the violence they are assessing, there is no single, clearly correct definition of probability. Rather, as Gigerenzer (2004) points out, subjectivist definitions of probability may reflect one's confidence in one's judgments rather than long-run frequencies.

Moreover, the studied judgments were made *prior* to hospitalization or treatment, which may well have modified the original assessments, and the patients who elicited the greatest clinical concern regarding future dangerousness may well have received the most intensive treatment! Thus, the false positive rate of 47% in this study might have been substantially lower if the predicted violent patients were not hospitalized or otherwise treated. And if minor acts of violence were excluded from the follow-up analysis, only 25% of the not predicted violent group were discovered to have committed violent acts, compared to 46% of the predicted violent group, an even stronger showing for clinical judgment.

On the other hand, even though the clinicians in this study did demonstrate a better-than-chance ability to assess future dangerousness, because their judgments were not compared with judgments by laypersons the study did not demonstrate that mental health professionals have any *special* ability to assess dangerousness. And this study certainly does not demonstrate (or refute the idea) that psychiatric emergency room clinicians have sufficient ability to assess future dangerousness to justify emergency commitments based on their assessments of dangerousness. This is because the follow-up measures and analysis, however much a step forward from past efforts, did not assess a crucial variable: *whether the patients' violence in the community, when it occurred, was sufficiently serious, and occurred sufficiently soon after their return to the community, that it would have justified continued confinement had it been foreseen!* Even if clinicians can "do better than chance" when they assess dangerousness, that is a far cry from determining that they can assess dangerousness sufficiently well to justify depriving a person of his or her liberty based on such an assessment.

As is discussed in more detail later, "clear and convincing evidence" of dangerousness is required to justify an extended civil commitment (*Addington v. Texas*, 1979). That a clinical determination of dangerousness can be shown to be likely to be somewhat better than a random judgment, that is, better than chance, does not render that judgment, in and of itself, "clear and convincing evidence" of dangerousness. To put it another way, statistical significance may not amount to legal significance.

Responding in some degree to this concern, Gardner et al. (1996b), in a follow-up analysis of the data compiled from the previously discussed study, compared actuarial and clinical predictions of future violence for their accuracy in predicting *any* community violence versus predicting *serious* community violence. Actuarial predictions had lower rates of false-positive and false-negative errors than the clinical predictions for any violence. But the actuarial instruments were not superior to clinical judgments in predicting serious violence—the issue of practical concern.

Even more important, *data regarding three of the most critical variables in the actuarial prediction equation were collected from patients not in the emergency room, but in the community after their discharge from the hospital.* These variables were the patient's score on the Hostility subscale of the Brief Symptom Inventory (BSI), the patient's recent history of drug abuse, and the patient's recent history of violence. Gardner et al. (1996a) reported that a simple decision tree relying on these three variables (a BSI Hostility score greater than 2, more than three prior violent acts, and heavy drug use) and age less than 18 predicted future violence as well as a regression-based method using those and other variables. However, it is questionable, at best, whether the data required for the decision

tree could be validly and reliably collected in the emergency room given patients' clinical conditions (and other practical considerations) at that time. At
the least, therefore, it has not yet been demonstrated that actuarial methods
are superior to clinical methods in determining which patients evaluated in
psychiatric emergency rooms should or should not be hospitalized involuntarily. To the contrary, because the clinicians in Gardner et al.'s studies did as well
as the actuarial scheme in predicting future *serious* violence, and because there
is every reason to believe that the necessary actuarial data would not have been
nearly as valid if collected in the emergency room—if it could have been collected there at all—there is every reason to suppose that clinicians are *superior*
to actuarial methods in determining short-term serious dangerousness (the
only decision that is actually called for) regarding individuals brought for
evaluation to psychiatric emergency rooms.

Before proceeding to further studies, consideration should be given at this
point to the definition of "actuarial" and "clinical" risk assessments. We define
the distinction as follows: Actuarial assessments are based on previously
demonstrated associations between measurable and specified predictors and
outcome variables and ultimately determined by fixed, or mechanical, and explicit rules. Clinical assessments are ultimately determined by human judgment (beyond a human judgment to rely solely on a particular actuarial
instrument). As discussed further in this chapter, good clinical practice may
well entail, or even require, considering the results of an appropriate actuarial
instrument; in any event, clinicians may well take into account on their own the
same or similar predictive data (e.g., history of arrests) as relevant actuarial instruments. But clinicians may and do take into account whatever available (or
obtainable) data they deem relevant to their assessments, including data that
can be obtained only through clinical methods (e.g., a patient's fantasies or
level of insight). Thus, although clinicians undoubtedly vary in their knowledge of which factors to consider when evaluating dangerousness and in their
ability to properly assess and weigh those factors, we do not accept the notion,
suggested by others (e.g., Grove & Meehl, 1996), that clinical judgments are
merely "subjective" or "impressionistic." Rather, as Holt (1970, p. 348) has written, "Disciplined analytical judgment is generally better than global, diffuse
judgment; but it is not any the less clinical." (For a further discussion of the distinctions between actuarial and clinical assessments and between actuarial and
clinical variables, see Litwack, 2001, pp. 412–414.)

THE VIOLENCE RISK APPRAISAL GUIDE

Quinsey et al. (1999) reported on an extensive effort to derive an actuarial
scheme for assessing future dangerousness with mentally disordered offenders, resulting in the development of the Violence Risk Appraisal Guide (the
VRAG). In brief, the authors obtained important information from the files of
618 mentally disordered offenders released from secure confinement, followed
them up for an average of 7 years (later for 10 years), and then determined how
the variables they had measured related to recidivism. They found that the
best predictor of subsequent recidivism, or lack thereof, was the subject's score

on Hare's (1991) Psychopathy Checklist-Revised (PCL-R), the score having been derived from file data. Also contributing to the final regression equation were elementary school maladjustment, separation from a parent before the age of 16, never having been married, and failure on prior conditional release, among 12 factors. After developing a means for obtaining a total VRAG score that was based on a weighted rating of the significant predictor variables, the authors found, through a series of studies, that VRAG scores correlated significantly with recidivism in the studied population.

In one respect, it should be noted, these figures may have underestimated the actual predictive power of the VRAG. Most of the VRAG subjects were institutionalized in nonsecure facilities following their release from secure facilities (Quinsey et al., 1999, p. 142), and approximately 10% of the total sample were housed in nonsecure facilities throughout the follow-up period (Marnie Rice, personal communication, January 22, 1997), yet they were considered to be at risk for recidivism. However, many forensic patients who would otherwise be dangerous may be relatively nondangerous as long as they are closely monitored (e.g., for compliance with medication). Therefore, at least some of the civilly hospitalized subjects predicted to be violent by the VRAG who did not recidivate might well have recidivated if they were simply at liberty. On the other hand, because violence committed in a hospital setting might be more likely to be detected than violence committed in the community, the VRAG might evidence greater predictive power with hospitalized subjects.

More important, and more problematic, however, is the definition of recidivism in these studies and the length of the follow-up periods. The basic VRAG score predicts the likelihood of *any* violence, including simple assaults, *over a 7-year period at risk*. These factors significantly limit the legal utility of the VRAG. Even if it could be predicted with relative certainty that a subject who scored high on the VRAG would commit a simple assault within the next 7 years, it is questionable if that would then justify the subject's continued detention on either moral or economic grounds. Indeed, Rice and Harris (1995, p. 744) observed that "most violent failures were fairly minor (many were a single common assault, for example)," and the base rate for *severe* violent recidivism after an average of 10 years at risk was 29%. (Of course, the *actual* rate of recidivism, including undetected recidivism, may have been significantly higher.)

Regardless of the length of the follow-up period, and even when only severe violent recidivism was considered over a mean of 10 years, the VRAG performed equally well in that the *relative* likelihood of offending was equally well predicted by the VRAG score. But, granting that the VRAG "can be used to assign persons from different but similar populations to *relative* risk categories with some confidence" (Webster, Harris, Rice, Cormier, & Quinsey, 1994, p. 64; emphasis in the original), the crucial legal issue may be not how well a test differentiates the relative degrees of risk posed by members of a group of previous offenders being considered for release, but how well the test determines the *specific* degree of risk posed by individual offenders—in terms of their likelihood of recidivism, the likely imminence of their recidivism if they fail, and, not least, the probable (or even plausible) severity of their violence if they fail (Villeneuve & Quinsey, 1995, pp. 408–409; Sjostedt & Grann, 2002).

Given the absence of evidence that high VRAG scores are strongly correlated with the commission of serious violence within a few years after release from secure confinement, it remains very questionable whether the VRAG should be used for individualized assessment to determine that a potential releasee should be confined—although it should also be noted that individuals scoring very high on the VRAG (although relatively few in number) were virtually certain to recidivate with at least some violence within 7 years, and nearly 50% of offenders considered to be sexually deviant psychopaths recidivated with some violence within a year of release from secure detention.

On the other hand, the VRAG appears to be a useful determinant of when offenders who have been mentally disordered are *safe* to be released from secure confinement: Subjects who scored in the lower half of all subjects on the VRAG had an average recidivism rate of only slightly over 10% *after an average of 7 years at risk*. Taking into account the additional fact that most of that recidivism was due to fairly minor acts of violence, it seems fair to conclude that mentally disordered offenders falling within that range on the VRAG (and deemed suitable for release from secure confinement by clinicians) almost certainly do *not* require secure detention to protect the public (though they may still require nonsecure hospitalization or intensive community supervision; Webster et al., 1994, p. 65).

However, as the authors of the VRAG fully recognized, it can legitimately be applied only to members of populations similar to those in the study populations. Thus, the VRAG cannot be legitimately used (for other than research purposes) to estimate the risk of recidivism for mentally disordered offenders committed to mental institutions but not released with clinical or judicial consent. For example, a history of homicide was negatively related to recidivism in the studied sample, but it might well be positively related to recidivism in the sample of patients who were seriously mentally disturbed and not released (Litwack et al., 1993, pp. 251–252).

That serious attention should be paid to clinical judgments, and even clinical instincts, that a long-term forensic patient remains seriously dangerous and in need of continued secure confinement is further made clear by a subsidiary finding of a study by Quinsey and Maguire (1986). This study determined the factors that experienced forensic clinicians used to classify patients in a maximum security psychiatric institution as dangerous and compared those factors with the ones that were in fact associated with reoffending in a group of patients who had been released from the institution. The factors emphasized by the clinicians did not appear to predict violence in the released patients, leading Quinsey and Maguire to express "despair" about the clinical judgments they studied (p. 168). Litwack et al. (1993, pp. 248–252) reviewed this study in detail and concluded that Quinsey and Maguire's despair was not justified by their results. Quinsey and Maguire reported another, truly significant finding:

> It has been argued . . . that a group of patients who are passed over repeatedly for release under conditions of indeterminate confinement will eventually come to contain a very high proportion of truly dangerous persons if only a proportion of the clinical assessments have any validity at all. . . . A group of 28 long-term patients [who were] assigned maximal dangerousness ratings . . . should, according

to this argument, be a very dangerous group of individuals. Of these individuals, 20 were [ultimately released] or transferred to a less secure facility; of these, 6 [had] been returned to [the maximum security institution] from less secure institutions . . . and 6 others were convicted of new offenses. Of these latter, one committed a serious sexual assault on a child using a weapon, one received life imprisonment for a series of aggressive sexual crimes against children, one received life for a sadistic rape, two were given life for attempted murder, and one was convicted of mischief and theft. Given the very short follow-up period [for these patients], these results unambiguously confirm the dangerousness of this group. (p. 168; cf. the long-term forensic patients described by Litwack, 1996)

As Litwack et al. (1993, p. 251) observed, "One wonders how dangerous these patients would have been had they been released [to the community] when they were still 'assigned maximally dangerous ratings'!" Moreover, Quinsey and Maguire (1986) did not provide an explanation of why these patients were released. It would be instructive to know. Were they confined under sentences that expired? Did judges release or transfer them against clinical advice? Or did the clinicians ultimately lose sight of the patients' dangerousness? The answer, apparently, is that all these reasons applied to one or more of the cases (personal communication from Vernon Quinsey via Marnie Rice, February 25, 1997). "Are there lessons to be learned [from these outcomes] for future assessments of dangerousness? These are [among] the types of questions . . . that future studies of assessments of dangerousness should focus upon" (Litwack et al., 1993, pp. 251–252).

As noted earlier, in his review of studies of actuarial versus clinical risk assessments, Litwack (2001) concluded that research had not demonstrated the superiority of either method; he observed specifically that no direct comparisons between the VRAG and clinical judgments had been reported to that point. In response, Harris, Rice, and Cormier (2002) conducted a study that purported to demonstrate the superiority of the VRAG over clinical judgments. However, Litwack and Hart (2004) have pointed out that the clinical judgments surveyed (and evaluated) by Harris et al. were not long-term risk assessments (as were the VRAG scores) but, rather, were judgments of the patients' immediate supervisory needs; further, the validity of clinical judgments to override VRAG predictions was not assessed. In short, Litwack and Hart argued, the results reported by Harris et al. should not be considered as evidence of the superiority of actuarial predictions of violence, much less as evidence for relying solely on actuarial methods. Moreover, Gagliardi, Lovell, Peterson, and Jemelka (2004) have reported that a few "ordinary," easily obtainable, correctional variables were as accurate in predicting recidivism among mentally ill offenders as the VRAG has been reported to be. Their study, however, did not involve a direct comparison with the VRAG, and their findings were not cross validated.

THE MACARTHUR STUDY OF MENTAL DISORDER AND VIOLENCE

The MacArthur Violence Risk Assessment Study (Monahan et al., 2001) entailed evaluating nearly 1,000 mentally disordered individuals while they were civilly hospitalized regarding the degree to which they exhibited a wide vari-

ety of presumed risk factors for violence. These individuals were then followed up in the community for up to a year after their departure from the hospital to determine the degree to which these risk factors, and combinations of
risk factors, actually did predict violence. The results led to the development
of a series of decision trees, and combinations thereof, that maximized the accuracy of violence predictions. More specifically, a "clinically feasible" iterative classification tree (ICT), relying only on information readily obtainable by
hospital personnel, was able to classify all but 257 of 939 patients as high risk
or low risk depending on whether patients within their classification exhibited, respectively, more than twice or less than half of the rate of posthospital
violence of the subject population as a whole. Moreover, by using a series of
five ICTs, each beginning with a different risk factor, and determining how
often a patient fit into the high- or low-risk category throughout all these ICTs,
patients could be placed into five risk classes, ranging from the lowest-risk
class (343 cases, of whom 1% were violent after release) to a highest-risk class
(63 patients, 76% of whom exhibited posthospitalization violence. For clinical
practice, using multiple ICTs would require computer-assisted computation.)
The authors further found that among risk factors for violence that were
amenable to treatment, "substance abuse, anger, and violent fantasies stand
out as candidates for being targets of violence risk reduction efforts" (p. 139).
Unfortunately, a potentially important risk factor, patients' insight into their
conditions, was not formally evaluated.

Thus, as with the VRAG findings (for mentally disordered offenders), the
results of the MacArthur Study of Mental Disorder and Violence indicate that,
for civilly hospitalized patients, proper risk assessment tools can classify individuals in forensic populations into widely differing categories of relative risk
for future violence and that, with proper assessment tools, risk assessments
for violence can be made at a level far, far better than chance. And, as just
noted, and of importance, the MacArthur study provided empirical information to guide risk reduction efforts. Moreover, the study produced many other
intriguing findings (summarized, in part, by Litwack, 2002a) with respect to
the relationship between violence and such risk factors as gender, prior violence and criminality, childhood experiences, neighborhood context, diagnosis, psychopathy, delusions, hallucinations, violent thoughts, and anger (see
Monahan, 2002, for a summary of the results of this study). However, the limitations of the MacArthur study must also be kept in mind.

First, the study has little, if anything, to say about the legitimacy of the hospitalization decisions themselves or, more generally, about the validity of clinical assessments leading to or continuing civil hospitalizations. Second, as the
authors recognized, the findings of the study, in terms of risk factors, might
not generalize to emergency admission decisions. Indeed, it would be virtually
impossible to collect the data necessary for use of the "clinically feasible" decision tree under emergency room conditions, and the hierarchy of risk factors
for patients in acute distress might be different from those no longer in that
state. Third, and most important for the purposes of this chapter, the findings
of the MacArthur study should be used with the greatest of caution in making
commitment decisions, that is, to confine, rather than release, individuals.

According to the authors of the MacArthur study, "The mean number of days to a first violent act [after hospitalization] among subjects who engaged in violence during the 1 year follow-up period was 130; the median was 106" (Monahan et al., 2001, p. 31). In addition, even in the highest-risk class, only 36.5 subjects had two or more violent acts during the first 20 weeks after discharge, and only 15.7% of violent incidents led to an arrest. And the degree of violence necessary to count as a violent act was not necessarily great: It could include hitting (or kicking) someone hard enough to cause a bruise or cut (p. 20; personal communication from John Monahan, October 30, 2000). In short, even among the highest-risk class of patients in this study, it is unclear whether any patients committed sufficiently serious violence soon enough after their release from the hospital to have justified further retention *had their violence been foreseen*; or, even more important, what the primary risk factors— or optimal decision trees—would be for truly serious (and sufficiently imminent) violence. In addition, it appears from the data (see Litwack, 2002a, p. 5) that many of the most violent patients in the MacArthur sample were antisocial substance abusers who may have had a brief psychotic reaction to their substance abuse, leading to their hospitalization, but who would have to be released from civil commitment *regardless of their dangerousness* once they were no longer mentally ill. Indeed, only 20% of the MacArthur sample had an admission diagnosis of Schizophrenia (Monahan et al., 2001, p. 160).

STUDIES OF STRUCTURED PROFESSIONAL JUDGMENT APPROACHES TO VIOLENCE RISK ASSESSMENT

A new approach to violence risk assessment emerged in the 1990s, known as structured professional judgment (SPJ) or empirically guided clinical judgment (e.g., Douglas & Kropp, 2002; Douglas & Ogloff, 2003b; Hanson, 1998; Hart, 1998, 2001). Its origins can be traced to the Violence Prediction Scheme (VPS; Webster et al., 1994), a procedure that combined information about dynamic risk factors with information about static risk obtained using the VRAG. Ultimately, the authors were unhappy with their attempt to mix the oil and water of clinical and actuarial risk assessments and abandoned the VPS. While his coauthors went on to pursue pure actuarial approaches to risk assessment, Webster began to explore ways to systematize clinical decisions about violence. His work influenced the development of structured professional guidelines for evaluating risk for various kinds of violence risk, including, for example, risk for general violence in adults (HCR-20; Webster, Douglas, Eaves, & Hart, 1997), adolescents (Borum, 2000, 2003), and children (Augimeri, Koegl, Webster, & Levene, 2001); risk for spousal violence (Kropp, Hart, Webster, & Eaves, 1994, 1995, 1999); and risk for sexual violence (Boer, Wilson, & Gauthier, 1997).

The defining feature of SPJ is the development of a set of guidelines concerning critical risk factors to assess, as well as recommendations concerning how the risk factors should be defined and what kinds of assessment information should be gathered. The selection of SPJ risk factors is based on a comprehensive review of the scientific and professional literatures. Final decisions about violence risk are discretionary, based on the evaluator's perception of both the presence and the relevance of risk factors given the evaluee's current and anticipated living situation rather than on a fixed and explicit algorithm.

The reliability and validity of SPJ risk assessments has been evaluated in various studies. For example, the interrater reliability of judgments concerning the presence of risk factors is good to excellent (e.g., Belfrage, 1998; Dernevik, 1998; Kropp & Hart, 2000), as is the interrater reliability of judgments concerning overall risk, sometimes called summary risk ratings (e.g., Douglas, Hart, & Ogloff, 2003; Kropp & Hart, 2000). In both retrospective and prospective studies, SPJ risk assessments have discriminated significantly between recidivists and nonrecidivists (e.g., Belfrage, Fransson, & Strand, 2000; Douglas et al., 2003; Douglas & Ogloff, 2003a, 2003b; Douglas, Ogloff, Nicholls, & Grant, 1999; Kropp & Hart, 2000).

The major conclusion to be drawn from this research at the present time is that SPJ offers a viable alternative to actuarial procedures; SPJ risk assessments may have even better validity than purely actuarial judgments (de Vogel, de Ruiter, van Beek, & Mead, 2004), and SPJ risk assessments have a greater potential for guiding risk management decisions (Hart, 1998, 2001). Another conclusion is that SPJ approaches appear to have good generalizability: They have been evaluated across diverse groups of psychiatric patients (civil and forensic) and correctional offenders by researchers with diverse cultural and linguistic backgrounds. It remains to be seen, however, how much incremental validity SPJ risk assessments have relative to actuarial assessments; their relative cost-benefit ratios; and, ultimately, the degree to which SPJ assessments can actually be used to guide intervention in a way that prevents violence.

Summary Observations

1. Progress is being made in defining and validating variables that are risk factors for violence (Douglas & Skeem, 2004; Monahan, 2003; Rosenfeld, 2004). A particularly important risk factor, high psychopathy, is discussed further later and in the section on clinical assessment. Based on such findings, actuarial schemes are being developed that may prove to be quite useful in making dangerousness risk assessments in certain cases. But two related and important points that we have already stressed must be kept in mind: (a) The most important and most certain clinical assessments of dangerousness cannot be tested for their accuracy without releasing from confinement precisely those individuals who most clearly pose a risk of committing serious violence if released. No number of studies showing a high rate of false positives for predictions made regarding marginally dangerous individuals (e.g., Kozol et al., 1972) or regarding patients without a serious history of violence (e.g., Mulvey & Lidz, 1993) can change this essential fact. Similarly, (b) it is unlikely that we will ever have meaningful actuarial data to inform us about the statistical risk of violence of confineable individuals seriously at risk for violence, because if such individuals are confined, it will be impossible to validate the possible predictive power of the actuarial variables. (But see Fagan & Guggenheim, 1996, for an interesting study of the validity of judicial assessments of dangerousness regarding juveniles who were released against judicial advice.)

2. The focus on false-positive rates and false-negative rates that has dominated much of the discussion regarding the legitimacy of clinical assessments of dangerousness is fundamentally misplaced—as is the argument that false-positive rates are too high to justify detentions based on such assessments. As noted earlier, an assessment that a person is dangerous (and even in need of confinement) is not necessarily (or even usually) a prediction that the person will become violent unless certain steps are taken (Monahan & Silver, 2003). Rather, it is usually only a conclusion that the person poses a certain risk of a certain degree of violence that (it is recognized in many cases) may or may not eventuate depending on not wholly foreseeable future circumstances. Similarly, a clinical decision or recommendation to release a hospitalized patient does not mean that a prediction has been made that the patient will no longer be violent. Rather, it usually represents a judgment that, taking into account the perceived risk of future violence and the patient's legitimate liberty interests (and perhaps other factors as well, such as population pressures in the institution), the risk is one that should be taken. Indeed, even if it was foreseeable, based on the patient's history, that a patient would be likely to commit additional acts of relatively minor violence some months in the future, a clinical or judicial decision might well be reasonably made to release the patient. If such a patient did later act violently, as was expected, should the patient be considered a false negative?

In recent years, Mossman (1994a, 1994b) and others (e.g., Quinsey et al., 1999) have advocated the use of receiver operating characteristics (ROC) analysis as a means for portraying the accuracy of dangerousness assessments. This analytic tool may well allow researchers to better evaluate the relative validity and utility of various assessment tools and techniques. However, ROC analyses can be as misleading as false-positive and false-negative rates if they view and rate assessments as if they were predictions. Moreover, it is not clear that ROC analyses can adequately take into account different time periods involved in reoffending (as can survival curves) or whether ROC analyses can adequately take into account the relative seriousness of different instances of recidivism.

3. It follows that an important question that has not received sufficient attention is: How can the legitimacy and utility of clinical assessments of dangerousness best be evaluated if clinical determinations of dangerousness, or clinical recommendations of confinement or release cannot properly be viewed as predictions and if, in any event, many assessments of dangerousness cannot be tested without releasing possibly dangerous individuals? There may be no easy answer to this question, but Mulvey and Lidz's observation in 1985 may still be apt:

> It is only by knowing "how" the process [of dangerousness assessment] occurs that we can determine both the potential and strategy for improvement in [such assessments]. . . . Detailed description of these decisions as they actually occur (using either participant observation or coded transcripts) could provide a systematic way to limit [the] presently broad range of potential explanatory variables by isolating those case, clinician, and context variables that appear most

central to the decision-making process. In short, the initial stage of description, so critical to the development of grounded theory, has been largely sidestepped in research on the prediction of dangerousness. It is necessary to go back to basics and to do the work that ideally would have been the first step to systematic inquiry. (pp. 215–216)

4. In part in response to Mulvey and Lidz's (1985) call, Litwack (1996) observed and described in considerable detail the bases for assessments of dangerousness regarding each patient among a representative sample of insanity acquittees confined, on the grounds of their dangerousness, in a forensic hospital. To the best of our knowledge, however, there are no other such reports in the entire literature on assessments of dangerousness. For example, there has not been a single description of the precise bases for commitment decisions on the grounds of dangerousness regarding a representative sample of patients evaluated in psychiatric emergency rooms, or regarding a representative sample of patients recommitted after their emergency commitments (Litwack, 2002b). Pfohl (1978) did observe a large number of assessments of dangerousness regarding inmates of a hospital for the criminally insane, and he described a number of biases that he believed seriously infected many of those assessments. However, he provided no data regarding the frequency of the alleged lapses in diagnostic objectivity or the bases for the ultimate judgments of dangerousness concerning a representative sample of the evaluations he studied. The presence of even the best-validated risk factors does not necessarily indicate that the person exhibiting such factors is likely to be seriously (or even minimally) violent in the future, or that preventive action should or must be taken. In addition, certain putative risk factors need to be studied further to confirm their status as a risk factor, to better determine their temporal relationship to violence, and to determine the extent to which they are risk factors independent of other, often co-occurring risk factors. Nevertheless, we briefly list here certain combinations of variables that have recently received empirical support for their status as risk factors for violence and that may be of particular interest to practicing clinicians:

- Active psychotic symptoms + substance abuse + a history of violence or current hostile attitudes (Mulvey, 1994; Swanson, Borum, Swartz, & Hiday, 1999; Swanson, Borum, Swartz, & Monahan, 1996; Swanson et al., 1997; Torrey, 1994).
- The presence of delusional beliefs about significant others and specific personal targets, especially that a significant other has been replaced by an imposter (Nestor, Haycock, Doiron, Kelly, & Kelly, 1995; Silva, Leong, Garza-Trevino, & Le-Grand, 1994; Silva, Leong, Weinstock, & Kaushal, 1994; Silva, Leong, Weinstock, & Klein, 1995).
- Severe and chronic self-destructiveness (Hillbrand, 1995; cf. Malmquist, 1995).
- Command hallucinations to commit violence when the hallucinated voice is identified or when there is also a delusion related to the hallucination

(Junginger, 1995), or when the content of the hallucination includes references to self-harm (Kasper, Rogers, & Adams, 1996).

- Erotomania with multiple delusional objects and a history of serious antisocial behavior unrelated to delusions (Menzies, Fedoroff, Green, & Isaacson, 1995).
- Recent and currently active narcissistic injury; isolation of affect or grossly inappropriate affect; threatening or provocative behavior, which is usually minimized by the patient; and the availability of a weapon (Schulte, Hall, & Crosby, 1994).

5. The relative merits of clinical versus actuarial assessments need to be approached much more open-mindedly than has sometimes been the case (Litwack, 2001; Webster, Hucker, & Bloom, 2002). First of all, as detailed by Litwack, there are few if any studies comparing the validity of actuarial and clinical assessments of dangerousness regarding a representative sample of clinical assessments in actual practice or regarding the most important clinical assessments (e.g., emergency room assessments or assessments of long-term forensic patients who have a history of serious criminality). Indeed, as we argued earlier, it is far from clear how the validity of an assessment of dangerousness can or should best be measured.

Second, as illustrated by the VRAG and MacArthur studies, if actuarial assessment instruments are to have meaningful and fair utility, they will have to be validated according to outcome criteria that are more relevant to actual (and legitimate) decision making than is currently the case. After all, individuals should not be deprived of their liberty simply because they pose a relatively greater risk of violence than members of some other group, or simply because they pose a specified risk of committing future violence without regard to the likely seriousness and imminence of that violence. Rather, proper assessments of dangerousness for the purpose of possible detention should always take into account and specify the potential seriousness and imminence, as well as the likelihood, of future harm.

Third, the distinction between actuarial and clinical assessments is blurring to the point where there is often no meaningful distinction. For example, as we will see more clearly in a later section of this chapter, good clinical assessment routinely takes into account such actuarial predictors as a history of violence; conversely, the most powerful actuarial predictor in the VRAG studies, the PCL-R, is essentially a clinical variable. Even when using file data to obtain a PCL-R score, an evaluator must make a clinical judgment regarding the extent to which the person being evaluated manifests such traits as "superficial charm," "a grandiose sense of self-worth," a lack of remorse or empathy, and "conning" and being manipulative. Ideally, according to Hare and Hart (1993), the developer and one of the leading proponents of the PCL-R, respectively, "psychopathy should be assessed using expert observer (i.e., clinical) ratings. The ratings should be based on a review of case history materials . . . supplemented with interviews or behavioral observations whenever possible" (Hart & Hare, 1997). Indeed, the VRAG has power in part because it takes clinical variables into account.

6. After reviewing the research literature for the previous editions of this *Handbook,* Litwack and Schlesinger (1987, 1999) arrived at the following conclusions:

- There is no research that contradicts the commonsense notion that when an individual has clearly exhibited a recent history of repeated violence, it is reasonable to assume that the individual is likely to act violently again in the foreseeable future unless there has been a significant change in the attitudes or circumstances that have repeatedly led to violence in the recent past.
- There is no research that contradicts the notion that even when an individual's history of violence is a somewhat distant history of serious violence—which led to a continuing confinement—it can reasonably be assumed that the individual remains at risk for violence if released from confinement, if it can be shown that he or she maintains the same complex of attitudes and personality traits (and physical abilities) that led to violence in the past and that, if released, the individual would confront circumstances quite similar to those that led to violence in the past.
- There is no evidence regarding the validity of predictions of violence in the community that are based on threats, or statements of intention, to commit violence. Thus, serious dangerousness may reasonably be said to exist when psychotic individuals make serious threats or statements of intention to commit violence (at least in the absence of evidence that such threats have frequently been made in the past *without* resulting violence).
- Even in the absence of a history of threats of violence, there may be occasions (e.g., when an individual is clearly on the brink of violence) when preventive action is justified based on an assessment of dangerousness.
- Although mental health professionals have yet to demonstrate any special ability, not shared equally by laypersons, to assess dangerousness, they may well demonstrate such ability, at least in certain circumstances. At least, they may possess special techniques or knowledge or abilities to articulate the meaning of their findings, which can meaningfully and legitimately aid in making determinations of dangerousness.

We believe these conclusions are still valid, or at least unchallenged by actual research findings.

7. Future research in the area of violence risk assessment should focus on the following issues and areas (among others):

- Risk assessment instruments should be validated according to the most meaningful outcome data obtainable.
- More descriptive studies of actual assessments of dangerousness need to be undertaken.
- Clinical decisions to override actuarial assessments should be studied to evaluate the empirical and logical bases for those decisions (Litwack, 2002b, p. 175; cf. Douglas et al., 2003).

- Risk factors should be studied for their amenability to treatment as well as for their predictive power (Sturidsson, Haggard-Grann, Lotterberg, Dernevik, & Grann, 2004).

VIOLENCE RISK ASSESSMENTS AND THE LAW

In this section, we review certain important legal developments concerning assessments of dangerousness by mental health professionals.

ASSESSMENTS OF DANGEROUSNESS AND THE SUPREME COURT

Despite qualms expressed by various professional organizations and legal commentators, and some of their own brethren (all well summarized by Faigman, Kaye, Saks, & Sanders, 1997, pp. 283–295), the Supreme Court of the United States has been receptive to assessments of dangerousness (and even predictions of violence) by mental health professionals in a variety of circumstances. Most notable, perhaps (and perhaps most notorious), in *Barefoot v. Estelle* (1983), by a 6–3 vote, the Supreme Court upheld the constitutionality of a sentence of death that was based, in part, on the prediction of a testifying psychiatrist (who had not interviewed the defendant) that the "probability" that the defendant would commit additional crimes of violence in prison if not executed was "one hundred percent and absolute" (*Texas v. Barefoot*, Record at 2131; quoted by Appelbaum, 1984, at p. 169).

Although not unmindful of the questions that existed regarding the validity of predictions of violence by mental health professionals, in *Barefoot* the majority opined that such questions could adequately be dealt with by the trier of fact: "We are not persuaded," stated the Court, "that such testimony is almost entirely unreliable [i.e., invalid] and that the factfinder and the adversary system will not be competent to uncover, recognize and take due account of its shortcomings" (463 U.S. at 899). In *Schall v. Martin* (1984), the Supreme Court observed that "from a legal point of view there is nothing inherently unattainable about a prediction of future criminal conduct" and that the lower court had "specifically rejected the contention, based on . . . sociological data . . . , 'that it is impossible to predict future violent behavior . . .'" (467 U.S. at 278–279).

Similarly, in *Kansas v. Hendricks* (1997) and *Kansas v. Crane* (2002), the Court voiced approval of risk assessment in the sexual predator context. In *Hendricks*, the Supreme Court determined the constitutionality of a sexually violent predator statute, permitting the postincarceration civil commitment of sexual offenders. The intent of the statute was to civilly detain people who presented a risk to public safety due to tendencies to perpetrate sexual violence. As with other types of civil commitment, a determination of future dangerousness was required by the statute. Future dangerousness could be determined by past sexually violent behavior, such as the crime for which the individual was incarcerated, and a connection between that behavior and a mental "abnormality" reducing the individual's control over the dangerous behavior. The Supreme

Court determined that postconviction civil commitment in this manner did not violate substantive due process rights under the Constitution.

In *Kansas v. Crane* (2002), the Court further interpreted this statute and held that the lack of control over the sexually violent behavior did not have to be absolute. In its reasoning, the Court continued to demonstrate amenability toward risk assessment and a reliance on mental health professionals in stating that the lack of behavioral control

> when viewed in light of such features of the case as *the nature of the psychiatric diagnosis,* and the severity of the mental abnormality itself, must be sufficient to distinguish the dangerous sexual offender whose serious mental illness, abnormality, or disorder subjects him to civil commitment from the dangerous by typical recidivist convicted in an ordinary criminal case. (p. 413, emphasis added)

RECENT DEVELOPMENTS CONCERNING THE ADMISSIBILITY IN COURT OF VIOLENCE RISK ASSESSMENTS BY MENTAL HEALTH PROFESSIONALS

The Supreme Court has also ruled, in *Daubert v. Merrell Dow Pharmaceuticals* (1993), that under the Federal Rules of Evidence, which govern civil trials in federal court, witnesses should be allowed to testify as experts only if the subject of their testimony is "scientific knowledge," and that "in order to qualify as 'scientific knowledge,' an inference or assertion must be derived by the scientific method" (113 S. Ct. 2795). The Court added, "This entails a preliminary assessment of whether the reasoning or methodology underlying the testimony is valid" and that "ordinarily, a key question to be answered in determining whether a theory or technique is scientific knowledge that will assist the trier of fact will be whether it can be (and has been) tested" (p. 2796). In particular, the Court suggested that lower courts focus on whether there was a known *or potential* rate of error regarding the use of the technique at issue.

Questions arose concerning whether psychological testimony was derived from the scientific method and thus subject to a *Daubert*-type evaluation, which would make scientific reliability a requirement for admissibility. However, the requirement of scientific reliability was later extended to all expert testimony by the Supreme Court in *Kumho Tire Co. v. Carmichael* (1999). After *Kumho,* lower courts were required to determine if all types of expert testimony were reliable, as part of its admission under the Federal Rules of Evidence.

Given that mental health professionals have yet to demonstrate that they have any special ability (not shared by laypersons) to assess dangerousness, and given that mental health professionals will not know the error rates of their assessments in many contexts (especially if they rely on clinical methods of assessment), it could be argued that mental health professionals should not be allowed to testify as experts under the *Daubert* standard. However, (1) historically, the Supreme Court has been receptive to professional assessments of dangerousness; (2) in almost any case in which such assessments are made they will be based, at least in part, on validated risk factors; (3) mental health professionals could well make the point that they cannot validate their expertise in many circumstances without releasing dangerous individuals; (4) throughout ᴏᴜʀ society mental health professionals are expected by the law to make professional assessments of dangerousness when patients pose a serious risk of harm to others (see, e.g., *Tarasoff v. Regents of the University of California*, 1976); (5) the Supreme Court also stated in *Daubert* that, still, "widespread acceptance can be an important factor in ruling particular evidence admissible" (p. 2797)—and clinical assessments of dangerousness are widely accepted by the clinical community and increasingly by the academic community; (6) if nothing else, it is likely that mental health professionals will be better able than laypersons to articulate, highlight, and analyze the factors that go into a dangerousness risk assessment (cf. Litwack, Gerber, & Fenster, 1980); and (7) lower federal courts have been receptive to expert testimony, even when relevant error rates are not available, when that testimony is perceived by the court as being helpful to the trier of fact (*Bocanegra v. Vicmar Services, Inc.*, 2003; *United States v. Perez*, 2002; *United States v. Romero*, 1999; but cf. *United States v. Fitzgerald*, 2003). Therefore, it is highly unlikely that the *Daubert* decision will lead to a general exclusion of professional assessments of dangerousness in federal courts or states that follow the *Daubert* decision.

Indeed, our own survey of state and federal cases considering the admissibility of expert testimony on risk assessment after the *Daubert* decision reveals that it is rarely excluded, and the *Daubert* and *Kumho* decisions appear to have exerted little effect on its admission. Testimony on risk assessment can be based on clinical interviewing techniques, reliance on results from actuarial instruments, or a combination of these techniques. Clinical assessments of dangerousness have long been admissible under the *Frye* test (*Frye v. United States*, 1923), which still prevails in many states and which allows for expert testimony regarding the results of professional procedures when those procedures have gained "general acceptance" in their field. When testimony is based on the results of a clinical interview alone, courts typically admit the testimony, stating that clinical interviewing techniques are generally accepted (*Meirhofer v. State*, 2001; *People v. Ward*, 1999). When the testimony is based in part on the results of actuarial instruments, it is also typically admitted. Many courts have indicated that testimony based in part on actuarial instruments is admissible because it is combined with clinical opinion (*Lee v. State*, 2003). Courts have not specifically stated that testimony based solely on the results of actuarial instruments would be excluded. However, this has been implied by court arguments that the testimony is admissible only because combined with clinical judgment. For example, one court stated:

> By this ruling, we are not concluding that actuarial risk assessment instruments are reliable per se or have our approval when used alone and not in conjunction with a full clinical evaluation. We note this was not the situation or issue presented in the instant case. The instruments *were* used in conjunction with a full clinical evaluation and their limitations were clearly made known to the jury. (*In re* Detention of Holtz, 2002, p. 619, emphasis in original; see also *People v. Stevens*, 2004)

Regardless of the basis for the testimony, courts have rarely given substantive consideration to the reliability of risk assessment in their admission decisions, even after the *Daubert* and *Kumho* opinions. In their assessment of relia bility, courts have taken several approaches. Typically, courts argue that a *Frye* or *Daubert* evaluation of the evidence is inappropriate. Many courts draw a distinction between clinical observations, which have a medical basis, and the use of actuarial instruments, which have a scientific basis (*People v. Ward,* 1999). When this distinction is made, it is reasoned that a reliability analysis does not apply to the clinical observations because they are not scientific or novel (*In re* Commitment of R.S., 2001; *Westerheide v. State,* 2000).

The application of *Frye* or *Daubert* to actuarial instruments varies across jurisdictions. As noted, some courts have argued that *Frye* and *Daubert* do not apply to the scientifically based actuarial instruments when they are combined with clinical interviewing, but that they would be if presented alone. They reason that the instruments do not act as a source of "infallible truth" or "scientific infallibility" when combined with clinical judgment (*People v. Stevens,* 2004; *People v. Therrian,* 2003; *State ex rel. Romley v. Fields,* 2001).

Other courts have argued that a *Frye* or *Daubert* analysis must be conducted when any part of the testimony is based on the actuarial instruments because they are scientific (*In re* Commitment of R.S., 2001; *In re* Detention of Hargett, 2003). These courts have largely determined that the use of actuarial instruments in risk assessment is generally accepted, and the testimony is admitted (*In re* Commitment of R.S., 2001; *In re* Detention of Campbell, 1999; *In re* Detention of Thorell, 2003; *People v. Stevens,* 2004). Some courts have pronounced the instruments generally accepted and their results admissible even without a *Frye* hearing (*In re* Detention of Strauss, 2001). Regarding the actuarial instruments, one court stated that they were "at least as good, if not in most cases better, in terms of reliability and predictability than clinical interviews" (*In the Matter of Registrant C. A.,* 1996, p. 106). However, at least one court determined that testimony based on actuarial instruments was subject to a *Frye* analysis and found it inadmissible because the instruments were not generally accepted. The court reasoned that the instruments were still in an experimental phase; their reliability and validity was not yet established, as evidenced by validation on a limited sample, lack of replication, lack of peer review, and scoring inconsistencies (*People v. Taylor,* 2002). Most of these decisions have arisen from *Frye* jurisdictions, but reasoning about these cases in *Daubert* jurisdictions does not differ substantially. The *Daubert* factors are rarely applied to this type of testimony—or are applied loosely (see, e.g., *United States v. Barnette,* 2000, admitting testimony based, in part, on the PCL-R and actuarial data under *Daubert*). In short, whether in *Frye* or in *Daubert* jurisdictions, courts have been receptive to the admissibility of violence risk assessments, whether clinical or actuarial, by mental health professionals. (For an argument in favor of the admissibility of actuarial risk assessments, and for a review of other relevant cases, see Janus & Prentky, 2003.)

CIVIL COMMITMENT DECISIONS

In *Addington v. Texas* (1979), the U.S. Supreme Court ruled that individuals could be involuntarily committed to a mental hospital for an *extended* period of time only if there was "clear and convincing evidence" that they met a legitimate legal standard for confinement. Therefore, to the extent that dangerousness as well as mental illness is required by law to justify an extended commitment, *Addington* requires that such dangerousness be proven by "clear and convincing evidence" (more than a "preponderance of the evidence" but less evidence than is required for proof "beyond a reasonable doubt"). The Court in *Addington* also observed, "Whether the individual is mentally ill and dangerous to either himself or others and is in need of confined therapy turns on the meaning of the facts which *must be interpreted by expert psychiatrists and psychologists*" (441 U.S. at 429, emphasis added).

There are two points to note about the *Addington* decision. First, it applied only to extended confinements. Therefore, presumably (and as is current practice), less than "clear and convincing evidence" of mental illness and dangerousness could justify a relatively brief commitment for the purpose of further evaluation. Second, it is important to recognize that the requirement of "clear and convincing evidence" of dangerousness, when it exists, is not a requirement of proof that the individual is more likely than not to be violent if not hospitalized. Rather, it is a requirement for "clear and convincing evidence" *of enough risk of enough harm to justify the confinement at issue* (see, e.g., Monahan & Silver, 2003; *Rogers v. Okin,* 1980).

Indeed, in a 1990 decision, the Ninth Circuit Court of Appeals ruled that "a finding of [a] 'substantial risk' [of violence sufficient to justify an extended civil commitment] may be based on any activity that evinces a *genuine possibility* of future harm to persons or property" (*United States v. Sahhar,* 1990, 917 F.2d at 1207, emphasis added). And the court also rejected the notion that, to be constitutional, a civil commitment must be based on a *recent* overt act or threat of violence. Rather, the court stated, "Whether [worrisome] activity occurred recently is but one factor . . . to consider in weighing the evidence" (p. 1207; see also *United States v. Evanoff,* 1993).

The decision in the *Sahhar* case is emblematic of a recent trend away from the strict standards for civil commitments that were established in some jurisdictions in the 1970s to more flexible (and perhaps more realistic) criteria. This trend can best be appreciated by comparing more recent decisions with the rulings in *Lessard v. Schmidt* (1972), an often-cited federal court decision of a generation ago that strictly limited the government's power to civilly commit mentally ill individuals. In *Lessard,* the court ruled that a commitment could be justified only by proof of "an *extreme likelihood* that if the person is not confined he will do *immediate harm* to himself or others" (349 F. Supp. 1078, emphasis added). Moreover, the *Lessard* court held that the necessary determination of dangerousness had to be "based upon a finding of a *recent* overt act, attempt, or threat to do substantial harm to oneself or another" (p. 1078, emphasis added).

In addition to rejecting the notion that violence must be likely or based on a recent overt act or threat in order to justify a commitment, other court decisions have rejected the notion that future dangerousness must be "imminent" to justify confinement. For example, in 1991, the Supreme Court of Massachusetts held that "to the degree that the anticipated harm is serious . . . some lessening of a requirement of imminence seems justified" (*Commonwealth v.*

Rosenberg, 1991, 573 N.E. 2d at 958); in *Seltzer v. Hogue* (1993), a New York State appellate court upheld the continued confinement of a mentally ill person who in the past had "invariably" become violent following his release from hospitalization, even though he had not been "imminently" violent upon release. Thus, as one of us has written elsewhere:

> It appears that as the earlier abuses of the civil commitment system (see, e.g., *O'Connor v. Donaldson*, 1975) are supplanted in judicial and public concern by concern about potential violence by mentally ill persons who perhaps could not be committed under a strict reading of earlier and more libertarian oriented decisions, the judicial pendulum is swinging toward a greater willingness to allow civil commitments to protect the public from potential danger, and to allow that danger to be assessed broadly, rather than by rigid, impractical rules. (Litwack, 1993, p. 363)

Moreover, it should be pointed out, the U.S. Supreme Court has ruled that insanity acquittees may be required to prove that they are no longer dangerous before being released from confinement (*Jones v. United States*, 1983). In the case of *In the Matter of George L.* (1995), the New York Court of Appeals approvingly quoted from an earlier decision regarding insanity acquittees that "compliance or lack of dangerousness in a facility does not necessarily mean that an individual does not suffer from a dangerous mental disorder" (624 N.Y.S. 2d at 103). The court went on to observe that "neither the nature of [the acquittee's] criminal act *nor the statistical probability of relapse standing alone* is sufficient to establish current dangerousness" (p. 105). Even more recently, regarding the retention of insanity acquittees, the New York Court of Appeals opined:

> In addition to recent acts of violence . . . a court may consider the nature of the conduct that resulted in the initial commitment, the likelihood of relapse or cure, history of substance or alcohol abuse, the effects of medication, the likelihood that the patient will discontinue medication without supervision, the length of confinement and treatment, the lapse of time since the underlying criminal acts *and any other relevant factors that form a part of an insanity acquittee's psychological profile.* (*In the Matter of David B.*, 2002, p. 279, emphasis added)

Of course, it is ultimately for the courts, rather than clinicians, to decide when mentally disordered individuals pose a sufficient risk of causing significant harm to justify depriving them of their liberty. But emergency room clinicians must make such decisions regarding emergency admissions, and judges frequently look to clinicians for their input and insights before making their decisions. Therefore, before clinicians deem a patient to be dangerous for commitment purposes, they should be mindful of the fact that they are, indeed, making a *risk* assessment—and that, just as a sufficient risk (rather than a certainty) of future violence may justify a patient's confinement, so, too, a patient's right to liberty should be weighed in the balance.

THE *TARASOFF* CASE AND THE DUTY TO PROTECT

In the well-known case of *Tarasoff v. Regents of the University of California* (1976), the supreme court of California ruled:

> Once a therapist does in fact determine, or under applicable professional stan-
> dards reasonably should have determined, that a patient poses a serious danger
> of violence to others, he bears a duty to exercise reasonable care to protect the
> foreseeable victim of that danger. (17 Cal. 3d at 439)

The *Tarasoff* ruling has been followed in most states (though with significant
variations from state to state) and, as Monahan (1993, p. 242) observed in a
seminal article:

> In jurisdictions in which appellate courts [or legislatures] have not yet ruled on
> the question, the prudent clinician is well advised to proceed under the assump-
> tion that some version of *Tarasoff* liability will be imposed. . . . The duty to pro-
> tect, in short, is now a fact of professional life for nearly all American clinicians
> and, potentially, for clinical researchers as well.

The case law, research, and voluminous commentary that has followed from
the *Tarasoff* decision cannot be reviewed here, or the various laws and professional regulations defining *Tarasoff*-like duties that have been adopted in many
states, or the differing responsibilities held by inpatient and outpatient clinicians. For recent examples, see Binder and McNiel (1996); *Emmerich v. Philadelphia Center for Human Development* (1998); *Fraser v. U.S.* (1996); and N.J. Stat. §
21:62A-16 (2001); for recent commentary, see Borum and Reddy (2001); Buckner
and Firestone (2000); Felthous and Kachigan (2001); Tolman (2001); VandeCreek
and Knapp (2001); and Walcott, Cerunddo, and Beck (2001). Suffice it to say for
the purposes of this chapter that clearly one component of the duty to protect is
the duty to conduct a professionally adequate risk assessment when such an assessment is called for.

We now turn to a review of current thinking regarding the major components of professional risk assessments of dangerousness.

THE CLINICAL ASSESSMENT OF DANGEROUSNESS

In 1981, in his still useful monograph, Monahan surveyed much of the research
and clinical literature up to that point regarding the assessment of dangerousness and ultimately derived an excellent list of 14 "questions for the clinician
in predicting violent behavior." Later, Prins (1996, pp. 54–56) and Webster and
Polvi (1995) also provided thoughtful lists of such questions that can serve as
excellent reminders and guides for clinicians. Monahan emphasized the important point that, in assessing dangerousness, "focusing on a limited number
of *relevant* and *valid* predictor items . . . is more important than an exhaustive
examination that yields much irrelevant and ultimately confusing information" (p. 126). He also pointed out a number of perhaps common clinical errors
that may interfere with proper assessment.

In 1972, Kozol et al. published an article titled "The Diagnosis and Treatment of Dangerousness," which remains one of the most substantial articles to
date on the subject. Their article also included an excellent (and somewhat different) list of questions for clinicians to consider when assessing dangerousness. Kozol et al. were concerned with evaluating the dangerousness of serious
offenders being considered for release from confinement; with such a popula-

tion, they emphasized the importance of understanding the precise details of the patient's history of violence. "Of paramount importance," they wrote, "is a meticulous description of the actual assault. . . . The description of the aggressor in action is often the most valuable single source of information" (p. 384).

Still, despite these earlier contributions (and those of Cox, 1982; Scott, 1977), when Litwack and Schlesinger (1999) reviewed the literature on clinical assessments of dangerousness for the first edition of this *Handbook,* they found "a relative lack of published guidance on the topic in comparison to its importance" (Litwack & Schlesinger, 1999, p. 195). By contrast, the previous 2 decades have seen the publication of many excellent guides to the clinical assessment of dangerousness in a variety of situations, including contributions by Appelbaum and Gutheil (1991), Beck (1990), Bednar, Bednar, Lambert, and Waite (1991), Borum (2000), Borum and Reddy (2001), Borum, Swartz, and Swanson (1996), Hall (2002), Heilbrun (in press), Lewis (1987), Lion (1987), Madden (1987), McNiel (1998), Monahan (1993), Pollack, McBain, and Webster (1989), Pollack and Webster (1990), Prins (1988, 1996), Schlesinger (2004), Tardiff (1996, 2001), Wack (1993), Webster et al. (1994), and Webster and Hucker (2003). (See also Heilbrun, 2001, and Meloy, 1989, for good accounts of general principles of forensic evaluation, and Bonta, 2002, for principles of risk assessments relying on actuarial tools. Regarding the assessment of possible *organic* violence risk factors, see Lewis, 1987; Lion, 1987; McNiel, 1998; Tardiff, 1996.) We cannot recount here all of the suggestions made by all of these authors. Instead, we highlight what we believe to be some of the primary themes and ideas that flow from the literature regarding the clinical assessment of dangerousness.

To begin with, it is important to make the obvious observation that what would be considered an adequate or proper assessment of dangerousness depends crucially on the circumstances. Emergency room clinicians do not have the information or the time available to gather information that clinicians typically have in long-term forensic facilities. Clinicians in private practice may, understandably, be hesitant about asking a potentially dangerous client possibly stressful questions or challenging the client in certain ways, because of reasonable fears for their own safety. Tardiff (1996, p. 117) has emphasized that "the safety of the therapist is a prime consideration, because even a feeling that one is unsafe will impair evaluation and treatment" (see also Beck, 1990, pp. 198–199; Borum et al., 1996, p. 211). Therefore, the suggestions that follow should all be considered with the understanding that clinicians cannot be expected to do more than is reasonable *under the circumstances.*

Four Basic Points

At the risk of oversimplification, it appears that four key themes consistently emerge from both the literature and court decisions regarding what a reasonably competent assessment of dangerousness entails when circumstances suggest that a dangerousness assessment is in order. That is, virtually all experienced commentators emphasize these themes. When *Tarasoff* liability has been imposed on clinicians (at least in reported cases), it has usually been because of the *failure* of the clinician to abide by one or more of these themes (see, e.g., Monahan, 1993; *Peck v. The Counseling Service of Addison County,* 1985).

1. All reasonable efforts should be made to obtain details of the patient's past history of violence and response to treatment for violence. For any reasonably comprehensive assessment, "the painstaking assembling of facts and the checking of information from a variety of sources are essential" (Prins, 1988, p. 600). Scott (1977, p. 129) observed:

> Before factors can be considered, they must be gathered. It is patience, thoroughness and persistence in this process, rather than diagnostic or interviewing brilliance that produces results. In this sense the telephone, written requests for records, and the checking of information against other informants are the important diagnostic devices [and can also be used to check the veracity of the patient's own accounts].

Kozol et al. (1972, p. 384) emphasized that an offender's versions of events should be "compared with the victim's version [and other sources of information]. . . . Our most serious errors in diagnosis," they wrote, "have been made when we ignored the details in the description of the assault." Tardiff (1996, p. 62) emphasized that it is also important to determine the *intended* injury. When a patient's level of dangerousness depends crucially on his or her willingness to take prescribed medications or to avoid abusing substances, the patient's history of treatment compliance is also important to consider.

2. Clinicians must be alert to their own tendencies to avoid, deny, or wishfully minimize violent (or violence-related) themes and affects (Kutzer & Lion, 1984, p. 71). Correspondingly, clinicians should be on guard against assuming that violent thoughts or affects, or even a history of violence, is indicative of current dangerousness. However, if necessary for an informed judgment (and if consistent with the clinician's safety), ultimately the patient should be asked direct questions about his or her history of, *and inclinations toward,* violent behavior.

Kozol et al. (1972, p. 383) observed, "The problem for the examiner is to elicit information relevant to [dangerousness], and this can best be done by informality and astute indirection." Ultimately, however, if necessary to obtain the relevant information, patients being assessed for dangerousness should be asked direct and specific questions about the following:

- History of violence (as both perpetrator and victim).
- Fantasies of violence.
- Level of anger.
- Plans to commit violence.
- Familiarity with and access to weapons.
- Techniques of self-control and stress management (and how successful or unsuccessful those techniques have been in the past).
- Motivation for self-control.
- Empathy toward others (especially potential victims).
- Insight into the nature, causes, and seriousness of their problems with violence.

Perhaps crucially, evaluators should also inquire into assessees' *attitudes* toward violence, particularly toward their own acts of violence in the past (Garbarino,

1999, chap. 5). One should also inquire into the presence of substance abuse and possible organically based dyscontrol syndromes.

When patients appear to be at risk for violence, they should be asked if they are thinking of harming anyone and, if so, how they have dealt with such thoughts and feelings in the past (Beck, 1990, p. 194). Appelbaum and Gutheil (1991) suggest that it is often useful to ask the following question: "Have you ever, for any reason, accidentally or otherwise, caused death or serious injury to another human being?" Borum et al. (1996) suggest: "Are you the sort of person who has trouble controlling your temper?" and "Have you found yourself hitting people or damaging things when you are angry?" (See also Mulvey et al., 1994.) Monahan (1993, p. 244) observed:

> Directly asking patients about violent behavior and possible indices of violent behavior (e.g., arrest or hospitalization as "dangerous to others") is surely the easiest and quickest way to obtain this essential information. Open-ended questions such as "What is the most violent thing you have ever done?" or "What is the closest you have ever come to being violent?" may be useful probes, as might "Do you ever worry that you might physically hurt somebody?" The obvious problem, of course, is that patients may lie or distort their history or their current thoughts. . . . Quite often, however, patients are remarkably forthcoming about violence.

Even when a risk assessment is not the focus of an evaluation, any comprehensive mental health assessment should include posing questions like these.

McNiel (1998) suggests that it can be useful to ask patients feeling threatened by others what they would do if they came into contact with those they perceive as tormenting or persecuting them. He also observes, "One approach to facilitating patients' self-disclosure about their violent behavior is to precede such questions by inquiring about whether that patient has been the victim of such behavior" (p. 4). Borum et al. (1996, p. 212) suggest that questions about a patient's history of and inclinations toward violence "should be asked as neutrally as possible, as if inquiring about routine symptoms."

> When patients are seriously violent, their actions are rarely entirely ego-syntonic or conflict free. The [mental health professional] is most likely to prevent future violence if he or she treats the proposed violence as a therapeutic issue. This means *discuss it with the patient*. Discussion is not a substitute for action, when action is judged to be necessary. But, whatever one does or contemplates, one should try to involve the patient in a discussion of the issue and the proposed course of action. (Beck, 1990, p. 194)

Even when patients distort, deny, or minimize their history of violence, comparing the patient's account with what can be derived from records and conversations with significant others, including past victims, can provide useful information. So can questioning the patient about noteworthy discrepancies. It can also be useful to assess the reasons for a patient's minimization or denial of significant violent actions in the past.

3. Consider the circumstances the evaluee may be facing in the future (including whether the evaluee will be in secure confinement). Are these

circumstances similar to those that have led to violence in the past (e.g., a discordant family situation)? Or are these circumstances that have *reduced* the risk of violence in the past (e.g., a supportive family environment or social network or protective conditions of confinement)? If the evaluee will be returning to a less restrictive environment, does he or she demonstrate a meaningful understanding of how to avoid violence in the future? Has the evaluee demonstrated a commitment to avoiding violence in the future? In general, it is worth noting Lion's (1987, p. 5) observation that an "appearance of tranquility in a [recently] violent person can be deceptive. Discharging the patient can be an error when the problem has not been really resolved. The clinician must consider whether anything has really changed."

4. When in doubt, consult! Indeed, when and where feasible, even when not in doubt, consult.

Simply put, it is both ethically and legally advisable to obtain a second, knowledgeable opinion about what to do when one is uncertain whether a patient poses a serious risk of causing serious harm to another person or persons (or self) or when one's course of action is not clear (Monahan, 1993, pp. 245–246). Assessments of dangerousness are more likely to be correct when they are arrived at by more than one clinician (Fuller & Cowan, 1999; McNiel & Binder, 1993; Werner, Rose, & Yesavage, 1990; see also Schwartz & Pinsker, 1987, regarding the possible use of outside evaluators to mediate disputes between staff members or between staff members and patients regarding assessments of dangerousness). Thus, if any reasonable doubt about a risk assessment exists, and time permits, it may be advisable to consult with thoughtful colleagues. (In general, it may be good to remember the biblical observation, "Wisdom belongs to those who seek advice"; Proverbs 13:10.)

MORE COMPREHENSIVE DANGEROUSNESS ASSESSMENTS

In addition to the preceding points, which apply to some degree to all assessments of dangerousness, a number of experienced forensic clinicians have written about the requirements for *comprehensive* dangerousness assessments, particularly regarding individuals who have been seriously violent in the past and who are currently being assessed for dangerousness in institutional settings or who are under supervision in outpatient settings. Here, we highlight some of the major points regarding comprehensive assessments that emerge from these writings and from our own experience.

1. When evaluating individuals who belong to a class of offenders, or potential offenders, for whom specialized risk assessment instruments have been developed, consideration should be given to employing those instruments to guide and structure the ultimate assessment. The ultimate opinions of mental health professionals regarding violence risk should be based on the totality of circumstances in the case at hand, that is, on an integration of all the information collected and considered. To this end, evaluators should consider using specialized violence risk assessment instruments as decision aids or decision supports. As discussed earlier, a variety of such instruments exist, including

actuarial tools and structured professional guidelines. Instruments should be used if they are relevant to the hazard being considered (e.g., imminent risk for lethal intimate partner violence, long-term risk for sexual violence) and the demographic characteristics of the evaluee (e.g., age, sex, ethnicity). The relevance of an instrument can be determined by reviewing its technical manual, as well as any available research reports or independent evaluations. Evaluators should keep in mind that all instruments have limitations; each is optimal for use only in specific assessment contexts and may be entirely inappropriate for use in other contexts. Evaluators should also keep in mind that they are responsible for ensuring that they use the most relevant instruments for a given case; administer, score, and interpret the instruments correctly; and make proper use of information obtained when they make final decisions. Indeed, Douglas et al. (2003, p. 1372) found, in an empirical study, that "clinical judgment, if made within a structured context, can contribute in meaningful ways to the assessment of violence risk."

2. An assessment of the patient's capacity for empathy—and degree of psychopathy—may be crucial. Kozol et al. (1972, p. 379) observed, "The essence of dangerousness appears to be a paucity of feeling-concern for others. . . . The potential for injuring another is compounded when this lack of concern is coupled with anger." Scott (1977) observed: "Unless there is some recognizable sympathy for others, and revulsion at causing suffering, there is always a vulnerability to situational aggressive impulses which are bound to recur." Of course, although lack of empathy is a risk factor for recidivism, some patients without empathy do learn to control their aggressive impulses out of self-interest. And when a patient's previous violence has stemmed from the combination of psychopathic character pathology and either substance abuse or a psychotic episode, successful treatment of the patient's substance abusing tendencies or, if necessary, the patient's vulnerability to psychotic episodes can significantly reduce the risk of recidivism even if the character pathology remains.

In evaluating an offender's level of empathy, stress interviews, group therapy, and projective testing may be useful (Revitch & Schlesinger, 1978, pp. 142–144; 1981, pp. 24–46). Because the PCL-R appears to be the most direct and best-validated test available for evaluating psychopathy, which is closely related to the variable of empathy, serious consideration should be given to administering the PCL-R or its screening version, the PCL-SV (Hemphill & Hart, 2003, pp. 94–95; Monahan et al., 2001, p. 71) to help clarify an assessee's proclivity toward antisocial behavior. It should be kept in mind, however, that only high PCL-R scores (generally > 29) are a good sign of the existence of the possible taxon of psychopathy (Harris, Rice, & Quinsey, 1994), and only low scores indicate a low risk of recidivism. Midrange scores are of little predictive value.

3. As the violent history of the assessee becomes more distant in time, more effort may be required to accurately reconstruct the details, but such efforts should be made. At the same time, *all* potential sources of information regarding the assessee's former violence, current behavior, and mental status should be considered (Mullen, 1992, p. 314; Prins, 1996, p. 57; Scott, 1977, p. 138; Webster & Polvi, 1995, pp. 1380, 1386; Wiest, 1981, p. 274). It is necessary to understand not only the details of previous violent acts (Pollack & Webster, 1990,

p. 495; Wiest, 1981, p. 273) but also the offender's behavior before and after those acts (Wack, 1993, p. 281) and what the triggers were (including unconscious triggers) for the patient's violence (Glasser, 1996).

4. In institutional contexts, it is generally sensible to have patients assessed by clinicians not attached to the patient's ward before final decisions or recommendations are made. Treating clinicians, and ward staff in general, may become so invested in believing that particular patients under their care have made adequate progress, or may so want to avoid disrupting the relative equilibrium achieved by a formerly more disorganized patient, or may so want to support the aspirations of a well-liked patient, that they avoid seeing negative signs and confronting the patient with difficult but necessary questions (Prins, 1988, p. 608–609; 1996, p. 54). Conversely, a patient who is uncooperative or challenging toward staff on the ward may be viewed as more dangerous than he or she really is. Therefore, except in obvious cases, a more detached evaluator may be called for.

5. When inpatients pose a possible risk of serious violence, recommendations for release should not be made without subjecting the patient to stressful questions regarding the sources of his or her previous violence and what the patient needs to do to avoid violence in the future. As Borum et al. (1996, p. 211) have observed:

> Many potentially violent patients can and will appear calm and nonthreatening when not challenged, frustrated, or irritated. The clinician needs to be able to gingerly increase the frustration or challenge in the interview to test the frustration tolerance and impulse control of the patient without precipitating a dangerous outburst. A highly structured, unchallenging interview can dull the examiner into underestimating the violent potential of the patient.

In certain circumstances, with certain patients, we would make the point even more strongly: Sometimes it is precisely the question or challenge that *will* precipitate a "dangerous outburst" that must be posed! (although, as Borum et al. emphasize, always in conditions of safety for the clinician). Indeed, sometimes the clinician's inner sense that certain areas should be avoided lest the patient become overly disturbed is the best guide to determining what areas *require* further exploration (Glasser, 1996, p. 279).

Of course, there is no legitimate reason to provoke a patient needlessly. Thus, there may be no reason to subject a patient to a stressful interview if it is clear from other information that less secure supervision is not in order in any event. But when a patient with a history of serious violence is being considered for transfer to a less secure setting, it is hard to imagine concluding that transfer is in order without at least determining how the patient reacts to stressful questions regarding the circumstances he or she is likely to face in a new setting. If a patient's stability in the community depends on regularly taking prescribed psychiatric medication, the depth of the patient's understanding of the need for medication and the patient's commitment to taking that medication must be tested via challenging questions.

It is well for the clinician to remember that *no* question or challenge he or she might pose is likely to be as stressful to the patient as reality itself, and that, regardless of the patient's expressed wishes, it does the patient no favor to transfer him or her to a less secure—and probably more stressful—setting only to have the patient regress into violent or otherwise seriously disturbed behavior. However, even when stressful questions are indicated, clinicians should be careful not to be excessively or needlessly aggressive in their manner or confrontations. And clinicians should take reasonable steps to calm a disturbed patient once a stressful interview has ended.

On the other hand, because of their understandable desire to retain a therapeutic and supportive stance with their patients—and because of their perhaps justifiable fear of retaliation from a frustrated or provoked patient—it may be unrealistic to expect ward clinicians to conduct sufficiently stressful interviews with certain patients. Thus, once again, it may be advisable, even necessary, in certain cases to have an assessment performed by an off-ward evaluator. But this possibility raises an additional potential problem: To pose suitably stressful questions to the patient, the assessor must be knowledgeable beforehand about the particular vulnerabilities of the patient. That is, to conduct an adequate stress interview, the clinician must first thoroughly inform himself or herself about what has led to and triggered violence or regressions in the patient in the past.

Indeed, it cannot be overly stressed that comprehensive dangerousness evaluations can be accomplished only if the assessor is, first, well versed about the patient's history. It has often been said of legal trial practice that "preparation is the key to cross-examination." Equally so, preparation is the key to a fully comprehensive dangerousness evaluation.

6. Group therapy may be a useful assessment tool, both to discover underlying feelings and concerns and to evaluate whether a previously violent offender still lacks genuine empathy for others. Cox (1982, pp. 83, 87) has observed:

> The mercurial flashpoint(s) of a dynamic group [may] provide [a] disclosure of the patient's inner world [before the patient] had time to reflect upon the consequences. The dynamics of the situation are far removed from those of a formal assessment session, in which [the patient] may well be asking himself about the wisdom of making a particular reply to a question. . . . [The] spontaneity [of the group] offers us insight in to ways in which the patient deals with unknown situations. . . .
>
> [Moreover], a patient who is in a therapeutic group with its spontaneously evolving, unpredictable emotional life, tending to mobilize disclosure potential may, for the first time, declare within such a group that [there] is unfinished business which preoccupies him.

Whether in group therapy or in individual therapy, a patient's *unwillingness* to openly discuss his or her problems with violence should be a worrisome sign. "Mere attendance [in treatment] does not suffice. . . . Programmes are apt to be especially beneficial if they induce some degree of psychological or emotional discomfort. Willingness, or lack thereof, to disclose painful information may be an important consideration" (Webster et al., 1994, p. 56).

7. Determining the patient's level of insight regarding the genesis and dynamics of his or her previous violence and his or her need to comply with

treatment recommendations can provide important information regarding the patient's vulnerability to regression in response to stress. To the extent that an individual's violence in the past stemmed from and was a defense against psychic pain, evidence that the individual can now confront and appropriately deal with such feelings is a positive prognostic sign. However, it must equally be borne in mind that insight is no guarantee against regression and that some offenders, particularly psychopathic and compulsive offenders, may well be able to give the appearance of having considerable insight into their past difficulties while still retaining their most deep-seated and most dangerous pathologies (Cox, 1982). However, if the patient cannot achieve a meaningful (i.e., seemingly accurate and affect-laden) understanding of the psychological forces, defects, and vulnerabilities that led to his or her previous violence, or how to realistically deal with such problems in the future, that would suggest that the patient is still unable to deal with these forces without special assistance, for example, close supervision and/or medication.

Moreover, as Meloy (1987, p. 41) observed, it is important to determine the patient's level of insight regarding his or her

> thoughts and feelings before, during, and after previous violent acts. . . . The unwillingness or inability to evoke memories of intrapsychic experience concurrent with violent behavior is a poor prognostic indicator, and suggests a borderline personality organization with either psychopathic or histrionic traits, respectively. If the patient is able to evoke his thought-affect experience, its evaluation as catalytic or noncatalytic in relation to violence should be determined and clinically documented. The assessment of aggressive thought-affect complexes when actual violence did *not* occur is also critical to prevent systematic bias in the direction of overpredicting violence.

8. When a patient's history of violence has been, at least in part, in response to delusions or fantasies, it is important to search for the continued, even if hidden, existence of delusions or fantasies or preoccupations related to violence (Meloy, 1988; Webster et al., 1994, p. 56). Both extended interviews and projective tests may be useful in this regard, as may carefully monitoring the patient's behavior and activities for signs that he or she is still preoccupied with concerns that led to violence in the past. It should be noted, in any event, that *the discovery of unspoken delusions or fantasies or preoccupations related to violence can be accomplished only by clinical methods.*

9. A comprehensive dangerousness assessment should include an evaluation of the patient's level of self-esteem and susceptibility to narcissistic injury and his or her ability to relate to other people well enough to maintain self-esteem and to tolerate personal losses, should they occur. Cox's (1982, p. 82) observation on the subject is noteworthy:

> I have rarely seen a patient from any diagnostic category in whom self-esteem regulation was not closely related in one way or another to his core psychopathology and, ipso facto, to his deviant behavior. . . . The recovery of lost self-esteem, or the establishment of hitherto negligible or precarious self-esteem, features repeatedly in psychiatric histories [of violent individuals], ranging from those of the inadequate recidivist to the catastrophic homicidal activity of a

patient with previously overcontrolled personality characteristics, or the psychotically disturbed patient . . . or to the narcissistic psychopath's intense delight that everyone was looking for him when he was on the run.

See also Gilligan (1996, p. 110): "I have yet to see a serious act of violence that was not provoked by the experience of feeling shamed and humiliated . . . and that did not represent the attempt to prevent or undo this 'loss of face.'" Thus, indications that a patient with a history of violence remains highly susceptible to overwhelming feelings of worthlessness, humiliation, or emptiness should be worrisome signs (Wishnie, 1977), even if the patient understands having these feeling and that they led to violence in the past. Similarly, the persistence of severe interpersonal difficulties may suggest that the patient has yet to overcome a major source of low self-esteem and that away from a protective environment that patient will be vulnerable to suffering from loneliness and rejection.

Lion (1987, p. 11) has suggested that "patients' vulnerability to object loss can often be obtained from their histories." Schulte et al. (1994) described a group of violent or potentially violent individuals whose dangerousness was intimately related to their susceptibility to narcissistic injury. Madden (1987, p. 61) observed that "violent behavior is [often] a screen that . . . serves to protect a fragile individual who is very afraid." Therefore, he suggests, a good question for the assessor to consider is: "What makes the patient afraid?" (cf. Swanson et al., 1999).

10. Patients with a history of serious violence on supervised outpatient status should be monitored closely for signs of regression toward violent behavior.

> Good follow-up is the key to good assessment in all aspects of medicine, particularly with patients who are prone to impulsiveness and aggressiveness. The clinician needs to ascertain whether a particular patient seeks help in times of stress. . . . [Moreover,] the existence of violence in the thoughts and lives of [potentially dangerous] patients must be monitored as closely as depression. (Lion, 1987, pp. 15–16)

Wack (1993) has described in detail many of the requirements for a comprehensive risk assessment regarding forensic patients on conditional release status. And it is worth noting Prins's (1996, p. 60) observation that "the price that supervisors pay for ensuring the liberty of the [patient] to live safely in the community is that of 'eternal vigilance.' Supervisors must therefore be willing to ask 'unthinkable' and 'unaskable' questions if they are to engage effectively in this work."

Two Special Problems: Catathymic Offenders and Compulsive Offenders

Schlesinger (2004) has written in detail about the concept of catathymic violence, and of the distinction between acute and chronic catathymic processes.[1] In brief, acute catathymic violence involves a sudden act of violence triggered by a sudden, overwhelming affect. Many times, the perpetrator of the assault cannot give an explanation for it. Certain episodes of seemingly senseless violence may be acute catathymic episodes. In the case of chronic catathymia, on the other hand, the buildup of tension takes place over time, and the offender ruminates about committing violence as a means of discharging the tension.

Implications for Risk Assessment

Acute catathymic episodes are essentially unpredictable. However, many chronic catathymic homicides and attacks could possibly have been prevented if the existence of a building catathymic crisis had been recognized and treated with sufficient urgency. Many chronic catathymic processes present themselves initially as cases of depression, but if there is any reason to suspect that the patient is considering a violent solution to his or her problem, further inquiry must be made.

An important sign that should alert the clinician to a serious risk of catathymic violence is indication that the patient has come to the conclusion that the only way out of this state of built-up frustration, tension, and depression is to commit an act of violence. If such an idea is not reported directly by the patient, the examiner should question the patient carefully to see if such an idea has ever occurred to him or her. The clinician should not be overly concerned that by questioning in such a direct fashion such an idea will be implanted; on the contrary, it is often experienced by prospective offenders as comforting to know that someone, at least, understands their plight and the depth of their inner disturbance.

In some cases, however, the catathymic patient's growing obsession with violence may not be recognized at all because warning signs are ignored or because of a failure to elicit sufficient information from the client, perhaps because the clinician is uncomfortable with or frightened by violent ideation. Kutzer and Lion (1984, p. 71) have observed, "The biggest obstacle to assessment is the clinician's denial."

However, eliciting the patient's feelings is only a first step in evaluation and treatment. Some cases of catathymic violence probably could have been prevented if the perpetrator's *stated* concerns about losing control were taken sufficiently seriously, that is, if it was recognized that the patient's preoccupation with violence was the outgrowth of a severe and building catathymic crisis, or if it was recognized that treatment was not yet defusing the crisis. It is important to bear in mind that *the mere fact that the patient is expressing concerns about violence does not necessarily mean that he or she is discharging the underlying tension.*

Schlesinger (2004) has also surveyed, in detail, the phenomenon of compulsive violence. Some individuals experience an extreme internal pressure to commit an act of violence, illegal sexual contact, or some other criminal act that may lead to violence. Such cases have been described in the literature as far back as 1886 by Krafft-Ebing (1934).

Individuals who have a history of serious violence of a seemingly compulsive nature are obviously powerfully disposed to violence and may act violently again even after lengthy prison terms or hospital stays. Indeed, there are numerous accounts of individuals who committed bizarre murders after having served lengthy prison sentences for similar homicides (e.g., Guttmacher, 1963; Kozol et al., 1972; Schlesinger & Revitch, 1990). High intelligence, good adjustment in prison, and a good work record are useless prognostic indicators when a dangerous sexually motivated compulsion is present.

Careful examination of the patient's fantasy life is thus particularly important when a compulsive process is suspected (whether or not the patient has yet acted violently). Especially in cases of gynocide and sexual assault, there is frequently a history of sadistic fantasies. To elicit such dangerous fantasies, there is no substitute for a thorough, unhurried interview. Some projective psychological tests, most notably the thematic techniques, may also be helpful.

However, the patient often will not reveal such fantasies even though he or she is harboring them. Moreover, compulsive offenders may sometimes evidence considerable insight into their condition and yet retain their compulsive tendencies. Thus, compulsive offenders who have been in confinement for some period of time may evidence few signs of continued dangerousness, and their continued dangerousness may easily escape detection, especially if insufficient weight is given to the details of their compulsive history. But, given the severity of the compulsive disorder, especially when there is a history of repeated violence or violence mixed with sexual impulses, extreme caution should be exercised before any presumption of nondangerousness is arrived at in such cases.

AVOIDING ASSESSMENT ERRORS

A number of commentators have suggested that assessments of dangerousness can be improved if assessors avoid making errors that have frequently been observed to pertain to dangerousness evaluations (Ennis & Litwack, 1974, pp. 719–734; Hall, 2002; Monahan, 1981, pp. 57–65; Pfohl, 1978; Webster & Menzies, 1989; Webster & Polvi, 1995). Among the relevant recommendations are the following:

1. Make judgments based on adequate information. Dietz has observed, "The most remediable error in the clinical prediction of crime is the making of a prediction without sufficient data to provide a basis for informed judgment" (quoted in Pollack & Webster, 1990, p. 495). In certain cases, it is essential to review available victim statements, police reports, trial transcripts, or recordings of prior confessions (Mullen, 1992, p. 314; Scott, 1977, p. 138). It is equally important to fully evaluate an offender's ability and desire to *avoid* violence in the future. In any event, all pertinent information should be reviewed, *and reviewed for accuracy*, as circumstances permit or require. Webster and Polvi (1995, p. 1380) have also made the important point that "if this review is undertaken early in the assessment, as it should be, it may be possible to arrange for the recovery of missing items of information."

2. Focus on those variables that are most relevant to determining dangerousness and the *specific question* regarding dangerousness at issue.

3. Always consider the nature of the situations offenders are likely to find themselves in if released from their current level of confinement or supervision, and whether the previous violence was due more to circumstances that have now changed, or can change, than "dispositional variables or personal

traits" (Monahan, 1981, p. 64; Pfohl, 1978, p. 212). Of course, in almost all cases, the offender's previous violence will be due to some combination of personal and situational factors. The task of the evaluator is to weigh how those factors interacted in the past and the chances of similar interactions in the future.

4. Recognize one's own legitimate doubts and legitimate disagreements between evaluators and among staff regarding an assessee's dangerousness to avoid unjustifiably confident determinations of dangerousness in either direction. Avoid a judgmental perspective or aligning oneself too much with the patient's wishes and desires. Be open to information that contradicts one's initial, or even stated, opinion. Indeed, as Appelbaum and Gutheil (1991, p. 350) stressed, it may be useful in many forensic evaluations to imagine that one was retained as an expert by the "other side" of the case, and to imagine how one's evaluation or conclusions might be different if that were so. Moreover, it is ethically required of forensic psychologists that they "maintain professional integrity by examining the issue at hand from all reasonable perspectives, actively seeking information that will differentially test plausible rival hypotheses" (Committee on Ethical Guidelines for Forensic Psychologists, 1991, p. 661).

5. Be as knowledgeable as possible about documented risk factors for violence and look for risk factors. For example, in emergency room contexts, it will often be appropriate to question patients regarding the possible presence of anger and suspiciousness (Monahan et al., 2001, p. 77) or command hallucinations to harm themselves or others. In most contexts in which a dangerousness evaluation is required, it will be necessary to inquire about the possibility of substance abuse.

6. Be careful not to *under*estimate the potential for violence in female patients who have a history of violence. It is true that, on the whole in our society, women have a much lower rate of violence than men, yet recent research indicates that women *who evidence risk factors for violence* are about as likely as men to commit violence (Newhill, Mulvey, & Lidz, 1995) and that, relative to their estimations regarding men, clinicians tend to underestimate the risk of future violence with women (Coontz, Lidz, & Mulvey, 1994; McNiel & Binder, 1995). As Taylor and Monahan (1996) have observed, factors that mitigate against risk in a general offender population (e.g., female gender, nonyoung age) may not necessarily mitigate against risk among people with serious mental disorders (or with a history of violence).

Whereas the majority of research previously conducted with respect to violence and women focused on violence *against* women (especially in domestic situations), recent years have seen somewhat of a proliferation of research conducted on issues related to violence *in* women (i.e., violent women; see Busch & Rosenberg, 2004; Henning & Feder, 2004; Koons-Witt & Schram, 2003; Monahan et al., 2001; Stuart, Moore, & Ramsey, 2003; see also Moretti, Odgers, & Jackson, 2004, for discussions of contributing factors for violence in young girls). Results of the MacArthur risk assessment study indicate that the presence of violence over the course of a 1-year follow-up was equivalent for males and females but that situational and contextual variables differed by gender. Males were more likely to be violent when they had been drinking or using drugs and were not adhering to prescribed psychotropic medications. Violence committed by men was more likely to result in serious injury, and men were more likely to be arrested after a violent incident. Women were more likely to be violent toward family members and to commit violence in the home (see Robbins, Monahan, & Silver, 2003, for a complete discussion of gender-related results).

7. Consider base rate information, if available, regarding the statistical likelihood that patients similar to the one being evaluated will act violently if preventive action is not taken. This is an often-stated and often-emphasized recommendation. Indeed, in his 1981 monograph, Monahan stated, *"knowledge of the appropriate base rate is the most important single piece of information necessary to make an accurate prediction"* (p. 60, emphasis in the original). The base rate of violence for a given group is the proportion of individuals in that group who commit violence under certain circumstances within a given period of time (pp. 59, 66). Actuarial assessments of dangerousness, if validated, in a sense provide the base rates of violence (at least of detected violence) for individuals who obtain various scores, or combinations of scores, on the actuarial index.

However, as Monahan (1981, p. 152) recognized and as we have repeatedly noted, "In many circumstances . . . base rates are neither available nor readily obtainable." We simply have no meaningful base rate information regarding many types of patients who are continually confined because of their complex of symptoms. Even if the risk of violence pertaining to isolated characteristics (e.g., a history of violence, gender, age, active psychotic symptoms) could be attained, the risk associated with the interaction of such factors cannot be obtained without refraining from confining many apparently dangerous individuals (Litwack, 1993, 1996).

Moreover, as discussed earlier, actuarial studies that do exist often do not provide adequate data regarding the probable imminence or seriousness of potential violence to allow those studies to be meaningfully applicable to individual cases. Thus, arguments that "clinical predictions of dangerousness unsupported by actuarial studies should rarely be relied on" (Miller & Morris, 1988; cf. Grisso & Appelbaum, 1992)—much less statements that clinical assessments should be totally forgone in favor of actuarial assessments (Quinsey et al., 1999)—simply ignore the realities involved in many necessary assessments of dangerousness. On the other hand, to repeat what we said earlier, when a confined individual being considered for release appears to belong to a class of offenders with a low rate of recidivism, clinicians should question recommending retention on the grounds of dangerousness unless they can explain why this individual is likely to be different from the class of offenders to which he or she appears to belong. Conversely, when a patient appears to belong to a class of individuals with a high rate of serious recidivism, even if the patient superficially appears to be no longer dangerous (e.g., based on behavior in the institution), caution should be exercised before concluding that the patient poses a substantially lesser threat of recidivism than other members of that class.

CONCLUSION

The field of violence risk assessments has made considerable strides in recent years in terms of (1) advances in research methodology, (2) the identification of risk factors for violence, (3) the development of actuarial risk assessment instruments, and (4) the explication of formal, structured, and experience-based guidelines for clinical assessment. More refined developments remain necessary in each of these areas. It is hoped that the future will evidence increasing recognition of the advantages and disadvantages of various means and methods of violence risk assessment and increasing reliance on various methods in combination to produce the best possible violence risk assessments in individual cases.

NOTE

1. The section "Two Special Problems: Catathymic Offenders and Compulsive Offenders" was written in collaboration with Louis B. Schlesinger.

REFERENCES

Addington v. Texas, 441 U.S. 418 (1979).

Appelbaum, P. S. (1984). Hypothetical, psychiatric testimony, and the death sentence. *Bulletin of the American Academy of Psychiatry and the Law, 12,* 169–177.

Appelbaum, P. S., & Gutheil, T. G. (1991). *Clinical handbook of psychiatry and the law* (2nd ed.). Baltimore: Williams & Wilkins.

Augimeri, L. K., Koegl, C. J., Webster, C. D., & Levene, K. S. (2001). Early assessment risk list for boys: Version 2. Toronto, Canada: Earlscourt Child and Family Centre.

Barefoot v. Estelle, 463 U.S. 880 (1983).

Baxstrom v. Herald, 383 U.S. 107 (1966).

Beck, J. C. (1990). Clinical aspects of the duty to warn or protect. In R. Simon (Ed.), *Review of clinical psychiatry and the law* (Vol. 1, pp. 191–204). Washington, DC: American Psychiatric Press.

Bednar, R. L., Bednar, S. C., Lambert, M. J., & Waite, D. R. (1991). *Psychotherapy with high risk clients: Legal and professional standards.* Pacific Grove, CA: Brooks/Cole.

Beech, A. R., Fisher, D. D., & Thornton, D. (2003). Risk assessment of sex offenders. *Professional Psychology: Research and Practice, 34,* 339–352.

Belfrage, H. (1998). Implementing the HCR-20 scheme for risk assessment in a forensic psychiatric hospital: Integrating research and clinical practice. *Journal of Forensic Psychiatry, 9,* 328–338.

Belfrage, H., Fransson, G., & Strand, S. (2000). Prediction of violence using the HCR-20: A prospective study in two maximum-security correctional institutions. *Journal of Forensic Psychiatry, 11,* 167–175.

Binder, R. L., & McNiel, D. E. (1996). Application of the Tarasoff ruling and its effect on the victims and the therapeutic relationship. *Psychiatric Services, 47,* 1212–1215.

Bjørkly, S. (1995). Prediction of aggression in psychiatric patients: A review of prospective prediction studies. *Clinical Psychology Review, 15,* 475–502.

Bocanegra v. Vicmar Services Inc., 320 F. 3d 581 (2003).

Boer, D. P., Wilson, R. J., & Gauthier, C. M. (1997). Assessing risk of sexual violence: Guidelines for clinical practice. In C. D. Webster & M. A. Jackson (Eds.), *Impulsivity: Theory, assessment, and treatment* (pp. 326–342). New York: Guilford Press.

Bonta, J. (2002). Offender risk assessment: Guidelines for selection and use. *Criminal Justice and Behavior, 29,* 355–379.

Borum, R. (1996). Improving the clinical practice of violence risk assessment: Technology, guidelines, and training. *American Psychologist, 51,* 945–956.

Borum, R. (2000). Assessing violence risk among youth. *Journal of Clinical Psychology, 56,* 1263–1288.

Borum, R. (2003). Managing at-risk juvenile offenders in the community: Putting evidence-based principles into practice. *Journal of Contemporary Criminal Justice, 19,* 114–137.

Borum, R., & Reddy, M. (2001). Assessing violence risk in *Tarasoff* situations: A fact-based model of inquiry. *Behavioral Sciences and the Law, 19,* 375–385.

Borum, R., Swartz, M., & Swanson, J. (1996, July). Assessing and managing violence risk in clinical practice. *Journal of Practical Psychiatry and Behavioral Health, 2*(4), 205–215.

Brooks, A. D. (1992). The constitutionality and morality of civilly committing violent sexual predators. *University of Puget Sound Law Review, 15,* 709–754.

Buckner, F., & Firestone, M. (2000). "Where the public peril begins": 25 years after *Tarasoff. Journal of Legal Medicine, 21,* 187–222.

Busch, A. L., & Rosenberg, M. S. (2004). Comparing women and men arrested for domestic violence: A preliminary report. *Journal of Family Violence, 19,* 49–57.

Committee on Ethical Guidelines for Forensic Psychologists. (1991). Specialty guidelines for forensic psychologists. *Law and Human Behavior, 15,* 655–665.

Commonwealth v. Rosenberg, 410 Mass. 347, 573 N.E. 2d 949 (1991).

Conroy, M. A. (2003). Evaluation of sexual predators. In A. Goldstein (Ed.), *Forensic psychology* (pp. 463–484). Vol. 11 in I. B. Weiner (Editor-in-Chief), *Handbook of psychology.* Hoboken, NJ: Wiley.

Coontz, P. D., Lidz, C. W., & Mulvey, E. P. (1994). Gender and the assessment of dangerousness in the psychiatric emergency room. *International Journal of Law and Psychiatry, 17,* 369–376.

Cox, M. (1982). The psychotherapist as assessor of dangerousness. In J. R. Hamilton & H. Freeman (Eds.), *Dangerousness: Psychiatric assessment and management* (pp. 81–87). London: Gaskell.

Daubert v. Merrell Dow Pharmaceuticals, Inc., 113 S. Ct. 2786 (1993).

Dernevik, M. (1998). Preliminary findings on reliability and validity of the Historical-Clinical-Risk assessment in a forensic psychiatry setting. *Psychology, Crime, and Law, 4,* 127–137.

Developments in the law: Civil commitment of the mentally ill. (1974). *Harvard Law Review, 87,* 1190–1406.

de Vogel, V., de Ruiter, C., van Beek, D., & Mead, G. (2004). Predictive validity of the SVR-20 and Static 99 in a Dutch sample of treated sex offenders. *Law and Human Behavior, 28,* 235–251.

Dix, G. E. (1980). Clinical evaluation of the "dangerousness" of "normal" criminal defendants. *Virginia Law Review, 66,* 523–581.

Dixon v. Attorney General of the Commonwealth of Pennsylvania, 325 F.Supp. 966 (1971).

Douglas, K. D., Hart, S. D., & Ogloff, J. R. P. (2003). Evaluation of a model of violence risk assessment among forensic psychiatric patients. *Psychiatric Services, 54,* 1372–1379.

Douglas, K. D., & Kropp, P. R. (2002). A prevention-based paradigm for violence risk assessment: Clinical and research applications. *Criminal Justice and Behavior, 29,* 617–658.

Douglas, K. D., & Ogloff, J. R. P. (2003a). The impact of confidence on the accuracy of structured professional and actuarial violence risk judgments in a sample of forensic psychiatric patients. *Law and Human Behavior, 27,* 573–587.

Douglas, K. D., & Ogloff, J. R. P. (2003b). Multiple facets of risk for violence: The impact of judgmental specificity on structured decisions about violence risk. *International Journal of Forensic Mental Health, 2,* 19–34.

Douglas, K. D., Ogloff, J. R. P., Nicholls, T. L., & Grant, I. (1999). Assessing risk for violence among psychiatric patients: The HCR-20 violence risk assessment scheme and the Psychopathy Checklist: Screening version. *Journal of Consulting and Clinical Psychology, 67,* 917–930.

Douglas, K. D., & Skeem, J. L. (2004). Violence risk assessment: Getting specific about being dynamic. Manuscript under review.

Emmerich v. Philadelphia Center for Human Development, 720 A. 2d 1032 (1998).

Ennis, B. J., & Litwack, T. R. (1974). Psychiatry and the presumption of expertise: Flipping coins in the courtroom. *California Law Review, 62,* 693–752.

Fagan, J., & Guggenheim, M. (1996). Preventive detention and the judicial prediction of dangerousness for juveniles: A natural experiment. *Journal of Criminal Law and Criminology, 86,* 415–448.

Faigman, D., Kaye, D., Saks, M., & Sanders, J. (1997). *Modern scientific evidence: The law and science of expert testimony.* St. Paul, MN: West Company.

Felthous, A. R., & Kachigian, C. (2001). To warn and to control: Two distinct legal obligations or variations of a single duty to protect? *Behavioral Sciences and the Law, 19,* 355–373.

Fraser v. U.S., 674 A. 2d 811 (Conn., 1996).

Frye v. United States, 293 F. 1013 (D.C. Cir., 1923).

Fuller, J., & Cowan, J. (1999). Risk assessment in a multi-disciplinary forensic setting: Clinical judgment revisited. *Journal of Forensic Psychiatry, 10,* 276–289.

Gagliardi, G. J., Lovell, D., Peterson, P. D., & Jemelka, R. (2004). Forecasting recidivism in mentally ill offenders released from prison. *Law and Human Behavior, 28,* 133–155.

Garbarino, J. (1999). *Lost boys: Why our sons turn violent and how we can save them.* New York: Free Press.

Gardner, W., Lidz, C. W., Mulvey, E. P., & Shaw, E. C. (1996a). Clinical versus actuarial predictions of violence in patients with mental illness. *Journal of Consulting and Clinical Psychology, 64,* 602–609.

Gardner, W., Lidz, C. W., Mulvey, E. P., & Shaw, E. C. (1996b). A comparison of actuarial methods for identifying repetitively violent patients with mental illness. *Law and Human Behavior, 20,* 35–48.

Gigerenzer, G. (2004). Dread risk, September 11, and fatal traffic accidents. *Psychological Science, 15,* 286–287.

Gilligan, J. (1996). *Violence: Our deadly epidemic and its causes.* New York: G. P. Putnam's Sons.

Glasser, M. (1996). The management of dangerousness: The psychoanalytic contribution. *Journal of Forensic Psychiatry, 7,* 271–283.

Grisso, T., & Appelbaum, P. S. (1992). Is it unethical to offer predictions of future violence? *Law and Human Behavior, 16,* 621–633.

Grove, W. M., & Meehl, P. E. (1996). Comparative efficiency of informal (subjective, impressionistic) and formal (mechanical, algorithmic) prediction procedures: The clinical-statistical controversy. *Psychology, Public Policy, and Law, 2,* 293–323.

Guttmacher, M. (1963). Dangerous offenders. *Crime and Delinquency, 9,* 381–390.

Hall, H. V. (1982). Dangerous predictions and the maligned forensic professional: Suggestions for detecting distortions of true basal violence. *Criminal Justice and Behavior, 9,* 3–12.

Hall, H. V. (2002). *Violence prediction: Guidelines for the forensic practitioner.* Springfield, IL: Charles C Thomas.

Hanson, R. K. (1998). What do we know about sex offender risk assessment? *Psychology, Public Policy, and Law, 4,* 50–72.

Hare, R. D. (1991). *Manual for the Hare Psychopathy Checklist-Revised.* Toronto, Canada: Multi-Health Systems.

Hare, R. D., & Hart, S. D. (1993). Psychopathy, mental disorder, and crime. In S. Hodgins (Ed.), *Mental disorder and crime* (pp. 104–115). Newbury Park, CA: Sage.

Harris, G. T., Rice, M. E., & Cormier, C. A. (2002). Prospective replication of the Violence Risk Appraisal Guide in predicting violent recidivism among forensic patients. *Law and Human Behavior, 26,* 377–394.

Harris, G. T., Rice, M. E., & Quinsey, V. L. (1994). Psychopathy as a taxon: Evidence that psychopaths are a discrete class. *Journal of Consulting and Clinical Psychology, 62,* 387–397.

Hart, S. D. (1998). The role of psychopathy in assessing risk for violence: Conceptual and methodological issues. *Legal and Criminological Psychology, 3,* 121–137.

Hart, S. D. (2001). Forensic issues. In J. W. Livesley (Ed.), *Handbook of personality disorders: Theory, research, and treatment* (pp. 555–569). New York: Guilford Press.

Hart, S. D., & Hare, R. D. (1997). Psychopathy: Assessment and association with criminal conduct. In D. M. Stoff, J. Brieling, & J. Maser (Eds.), *Handbook of antisocial behavior* (pp. 22–35). New York: Wiley.

Hart, S. D., Webster, C. D., & Menzies, R. J. (1993). A note on portraying the accuracy of violence predictions. *Law and Human Behavior, 17,* 695–700.

Heilbrun, K. (2001). *Principles of forensic mental health assessment.* New York: Kluwer Academic/Plenum Press.

Heilbrun, K. (in press). Principles of forensic mental health assessment: Implications for the forensic assessment of sexual offenders.

Hemphill, J. F., & Hart, S. D. (2003). Forensic and clinical issues in the assessment of psychopathy. In A. Goldstein (Ed.), *Forensic psychology* (pp. 87–107). Vol. 11 in I. B. Weiner (Editor-in-chief), *Handbook of psychology.* Hoboken, NJ: Wiley.

Henning, K., & Feder, L. (2004). A comparison of men and women arrested for domestic violence: Who presents the greater threat? *Journal of Family Violence, 19,* 69–80.

Hillbrand, M. (1995). Aggression against self and aggression against others in violent psychiatric patients. *Journal of Consulting and Clinical Psychology, 63,* 668–671.

Holt, R. R. (1970). Yet another look at clinical and statistical prediction: Or, is clinical psychology worthwhile? *American Psychologist, 25,* 337–349.

In re Commitment of R. S., 773 A. 2d 72 (N.J. Super. A.D., 2001).

In re Detention of Campbell, 986 P. 2d 771 (Wash., 1999).

In re Detention of Hargett, 786 N.E. 2d 557 (Ill. App. 3 Dist., 2003).

In re Detention of Holtz, 653 N.W. 2d 613 (Iowa, App., 2002).

In re Detention of Strauss, 20 P. 3d 1022 (Wash., App. Div. 1, 2001).

In re Detention of Thorell, 72 P. 3d 708 (Wash., 2003).

In the Matter of David B., 97 N.Y. 2d 267 (2002).

In the Matter of George L., 85 N.Y. 2d 295, 624 N.Y.S. 2d 99, 648 N.E. 2d 475 (1995).

In the Matter of Registrant C. A., 679 A. 2d 1153 (1996).

Janus, E. S., & Prentky, R. A. (2003). Forensic use of actuarial risk assessment with sex offenders: Accuracy, admissibility and accountability. *American Criminal Law Review, 40,* 1443–1499.

Jones v. United States, 463 U.S. 354 (1983).

Junginger, J. (1995). Command hallucinations and the prediction of dangerousness. *Psychiatric Services, 46,* 911–914.

Kansas v. Crane, 122 S. Ct. 867 (2002).

Kansas v. Hendricks, 117 S. Ct. 2072 (1997).

Kasper, M. E., Rogers, R., & Adams, P. A. (1996). Dangerousness and command hallucinations: An investigation of psychotic inpatients. *Bulletin of the American Academy of Psychiatry and Law, 24,* 219–224.

Koons-Witt, B. A., & Schram, P. J. (2003). The prevalence and nature of violent offending by females. *Journal of Criminal Justice, 31,* 361–371.

Kozol, H. L., Boucher, R. J., & Garofalo, R. F. (1972). The diagnosis and treatment of dangerousness. *Crime and Delinquency, 19,* 371–392.

Kozol, H. L., Boucher, R. J., & Garofalo, R. F. (1973). Dangerousness: A reply to Monahan. *Crime and Delinquency, 19,* 554 –555.

Krafft-Ebing, R. von (1934). *Psychopathia sexualis.* (F. J. Redman, Trans.). New York: Physicians and Surgeons Book.

Kropp, P. R., & Hart, S. D. (2000). The Spousal Assault Risk Assessment (SARA) guide: Reliability and validity in adult male offenders. *Law and Human Behavior, 24,* 101–118.

Kropp, P. R., Hart, S. D., Webster, C. D., & Eaves, D. (1994). *Manual for the Spousal Assault Risk Assessment guide.* Vancouver, Canada: British Columbia Institute on Family Violence.

Kropp, P. R., Hart, S. D., Webster, C. D., & Eaves, D. (1995). *Manual for the Spousal Assault Risk Assessment guide* (2nd ed.). Vancouver, Canada: British Columbia Institute on Family Violence.

Kropp, P. R., Hart, S. D., Webster, C. D., & Eaves, D. (1999). *Spousal Assault Risk Assessment guide user's manual.* Toronto, Canada: Multi-Health Systems/British Columbia Institute on Family Violence.

Kumho Tire Co. v. Carmichael, 119 S. Ct. 1167 (1999).

Kutzer, D., & Lion, J. R. (1984). The violent patient: Assessment and intervention. In S. Saunders, A. M. Anderson, C. A. Hart, & G. M. Rubenstein (Eds.), *Violent individuals and families: A handbook for practitioners* (pp. 69–86). Springfield, IL: Charles C Thomas.

Lee v. State, 854 So. 2d 709 (Fla. App. 2 Dist., 2003).

Lessard v. Schmidt (1972) 349 F. Supp. 1978, vacated on other grounds, 414 U.S. 473 (1974).

Lewis, D. O. (1987). Special diagnostic and treatment issues concerning violent juveniles. In L. Roth (Ed.), *Clinical treatment of the violent person* (pp. 138–155). New York: Guilford Press.

Lidz, C. W., Mulvey, E. P., & Gardner, W. (1993). The accuracy of predictions of violence to others. *Journal of the American Medical Association, 269,* 1007–1011.

Lion, J. R. (1987). Clinical assessment of violent patients. In L. Roth (Ed.), *Clinical treatment of the violent person* (pp. 1–19). New York: Guilford Press.

Litwack, T. R. (1993). On the ethics of dangerousness assessments. *Law and Human Behavior, 17,* 479–482.

Litwack, T. R. (1996). "Dangerous" patients: A survey of one forensic facility and review of the issue. *Aggression and Violent Behavior, 1,* 97–122.

Litwack, T. R. (2001). Actuarial versus clinical assessments of dangerousness. *Psychology, Public Policy and Law, 7,* 409–443.

Litwack, T. R. (2002a). Book review: Rethinking risk assessment: The MacArthur Study of Mental Disorder and Violence. *AP-LS News, 22,* 4–5.

Litwack, T. R. (2002b). Some questions for the field of violence risk assessment and forensic mental health: Or, "back to basics" revisited. *International Journal of Forensic Mental Health, 1,* 171–178.

Litwack, T. R., Gerber, G. L., & Fenster, C. A. (1980). The proper role of psychology in child custody disputes. *Journal of Family Law, 18,* 269–300.

Litwack, T. R., & Hart, S. (2004). The horse ain't dead yet: Illusions of actuarial superiority in Harris, Rice, and Cormier (2002). Manuscript under submission.

Litwack, T. R., Kirschner, S. M., & Wack, R. C. (1993). The assessment of dangerousness and predictions of violence: Recent research and future prospects. *Psychiatric Quarterly, 64,* 245–273.

Litwack, T. R., & Schlesinger, L. B. (1987). Assessing and predicting violence: Research, law, and applications. In I. B. Weiner & A. K. Hess (Eds.), *Handbook of forensic psychology* (pp. 205–207). New York: Wiley.

Litwack, T. R., & Schlesinger, L. B. (1999). Dangerousness risk assessments: Research, legal, and clinical considerations. In A. K. Hess & I. B. Weiner (Eds.), *Handbook of forensic psychology* (2nd ed., pp. 171–217). New York: Wiley.

MacDonald, J. M. (1963). The threat to kill. *American Journal of Psychiatry, 120,* 125–130.

MacDonald, J. M. (1967). Homicidal threats. *American Journal of Psychiatry, 124,* 475–482.

Madden, D. J. (1987). Psychotherapeutic approaches in the treatment of violent persons. In L. Roth (Ed.), *Clinical treatment of the violent person* (pp. 54–75). New York: Guilford Press.

Malmquist, C. P. (1995). Depression and homicidal violence. *International Journal of Law and Psychiatry, 18,* 145–162.

McNiel, D. E. (1998). Empirically-based clinical evaluation and management of the potentially violent patient. In P. M. Kleespies (Ed.), *Emergencies in mental health practice: Evaluation and management* (pp. 95–116). New York: Guilford Press.

McNiel, D. E., & Binder, R. L. (1993, August). *Inter-rater agreement: A strategy for improving violence risk assessment.* Paper presented at the annual convention of the American Psychological Association, Toronto, Ontario, Canada.

McNiel, D. E., & Binder, R. L. (1995). Correlates of accuracy in the assessment of psychiatric inpatients' risk of violence. *American Journal of Psychiatry, 152,* 901–906.

McNiel, D. E., Sandberg, D. A., & Binder, R. L. (1998). The relationship between confidence and accuracy in clinical assessment of psychiatric patients' potential for violence. *Law and Human Behavior, 22,* 655–669.

Meirhofer v. State, 109 Wash. App. 1057 (Wash. App. Div. 1, 2001).

Meloy, J. R. (1987). The prediction of violence in outpatient psychotherapy. *American Journal of Psychotherapy, 41,* 38–45.

Meloy, J. R. (1988). Violence and homicidal behavior in primitive mental states. *Journal of the American Academy of Psychoanalysis, 16,* 381–394.

Meloy, J. R. (1989). The forensic interview. In R. J. Craig (Ed.), *Clinical and diagnostic interviewing* (pp. 322–343). Northvale, NJ: Aronson.

Menzies, R. P. D., Fedoroff, J. P., Green, C. M., & Isaacson, K. (1995). Prediction of dangerous behavior in male erotomania. *British Journal of Psychiatry, 166,* 529–536.

Miller, M., & Morris, N. (1988). Predictions of dangerousness: An argument for limited use. *Violence and Victims, 3,* 263–283.

Monahan, J. (1981). *Predicting violent behavior: An assessment of clinical techniques.* Beverly Hills, CA: Sage.

Monahan, J. (1984). The prediction of violence behavior: Toward a second generation of theory and policy. *American Journal of Psychiatry, 141,* 10–15.

Monahan, J. (1993). Limiting therapist exposure to *Tarasoff* liability. *American Psychologist, 48,* 242–250.

Monahan, J. (1996). Violence prediction: The past twenty years and the next twenty years. *Criminal Justice and Behavior, 23,* 107–120.

Monahan, J. (1997). The scientific status of research on clinical and actuarial predictions of violence. In D. Faigman, D. Kaye, M. Saks, & J. Sanders (Eds.), *Modern scientific evidence: The law and science of expert testimony* (pp. 423–445). St. Paul, MN: West Company.

Monahan, J. (2002). The MacArthur studies of violence risk. *Criminal Behavior and Mental Health, 12,* S67–S72.

Monahan, J. (2003). Violence risk assessment. In A. Goldstein (Ed.), *Forensic psychology* (pp. 527–542). Vol. 11 in I. B. Weiner (Editor-in-Chief), *Handbook of psychology.* Hoboken, NJ: Wiley.

Monahan, J., & Silver, E. (2003). Judicial decision thresholds for violence risk management. *International Journal of Forensic Mental Health, 2,* 1–6.

Monahan, J., & Steadman, H. J. (1994). Toward a rejuvenation of risk assessment research. In J. Monahan & H. J. Steadman (Eds.), *Violence and mental disorder: Developments in risk assessment* (pp. 1–17). Chicago: University of Chicago Press.

Monahan, J., Steadman, H. J., Silver, E., Appelbaum, P. S., Robbins, P. C., Mulvey, E. P., et al. (2001). *Rethinking risk assessment: The MacArthur study of mental disorder and violence.* New York: Oxford University Press.

Moretti, M. M., Odgers, C. L., & Jackson, M. A. (2004). Girls and aggression: Contributing factors and intervention principles. New York: Kluwer Academic/Plenum Press.

Mossman, D. (1994a). Assessing predictions of violence: Being accurate about accuracy. *Journal of Consulting and Clinical Psychology, 62,* 783–792.

Mossman, D. (1994b). Further comments on portraying the accuracy of violence predictions. *Law and Human Behavior, 18,* 587–593.

Mullen, P. E. (1992). The clinical prediction of dangerousness. In D. J. Kavanagh (Ed.), *Schizophrenia: An overview and practical handbook* (pp. 309–319). London: Chapman Hall.

Mulvey, E. P. (1994). Assessing the evidence of a link between mental illness and violence. *Hospital and Community Psychiatry, 45,* 663–668.

Mulvey, E. P., & Lidz, C. W. (1985). Back to basics: A critical analysis of dangerousness research in a new legal environment. *Law and Human Behavior, 9,* 209–219.

Mulvey, E. P., & Lidz, C. W. (1993). Measuring patient violence in dangerousness research. *Law and Human Behavior, 17,* 277–288.

Mulvey, E. P., & Lidz, C. W. (1995). Conditional prediction: A model for research on dangerousness to others in a new era. *International Journal of Law and Psychiatry, 18,* 129–143.

Mulvey, E. P., Shaw, E., & Lidz, C. W. (1994). Editorial: Why use multiple sources in research on patient violence in the community? *Criminal Behaviour and Mental Health, 4,* 253–258.

Nestor, P. G., Haycock, J., Doiron, S., Kelly, J., & Kelly, D. (1995). Lethal violence and psychosis: A clinical profile. *Bulletin of the American Academy of Psychiatry and Law, 23,* 331–341.

Newhill, C. E., Mulvey, E. P., & Lidz, C. W. (1995). Characteristics of violence in the community by female patients seen in a psychiatric emergency service. *Psychiatric Services, 46,* 785–789.

N.J. Stat § 21:62A-16 (2001).

O'Connor v. Donaldson, 422 U.S. 563 (1975).

Otto, R. K. (1992). Prediction of dangerous behavior: A review and analysis of "second generation" research. *Forensic Reports, 5,* 103–133.

Otto, R. K. (1994). On the ability of mental health professionals to "predict dangerousness": A commentary and interpretation of the "dangerousness" literature. *Law and Psychology Review, 18,* 43–68.

Peck v. The Counseling Service of Addison County. 499 A. 2d 422 (VT, 1985).

People v. Stevens (*In re* Stevens), 803 N.E. 2d 1036 (2004).

People v. Taylor, 782 N.E. 2d 920 (Ill. App. 2 Dist., 2002).

People v. Therrien, 113 Cal. App. 4th 609, 6 Cal. Rptr. 3d 415 (2003).

People v. Ward, 71 Cal. App. 4th 368, 6 Cal. Rptr. 2d 828 (1999).

Pfohl, S. J. (1978). *Predicting dangerousness.* Lexington, MA: Heath.

Pollack, N., McBain, I., & Webster, C. (1989). Clinical decision making and the assessment of dangerousness. In K. Howells & C. R. Hollen (Eds.), *Clinical approaches to violence.* New York: Wiley.

Pollack, N., & Webster, C. (1990). The clinical assessment of dangerousness. In R. Bluglass & P. Bowden (Eds.), *Principles and practice of forensic psychiatry* (pp. 489–497). London: Churchill Livingston.

Prins, H. (1988). Dangerous clients: Further observations on the limitation of mayhem. *British Journal of Social Work, 18,* 593–609.

Prins, H. (1996). Risk assessment and management in criminal justice and psychiatry. *Journal of Forensic Psychiatry, 7,* 42–62.

Quinsey, V. L., Harris, G. T., Rice, M. E., & Cormier, C. A. (1999). *Violent offenders: Appraising and managing risk.* Washington, DC: American Psychological Association.

Quinsey, V., & Maguire, A. (1986). Maximum security psychiatric patients: Actuarial and clinical predictions of dangerousness. *Journal of Interpersonal Violence, 1,* 143–171.

Revitch, E., & Schlesinger, L. B. (1978). Murder: Evaluation, classification, and prediction. In I. L. Kutash, S. B. Kutash, & L. B. Schlesinger (Eds.), *Violence: Perspectives on murder and aggression* (pp. 138–164). San Francisco: Jossey-Bass.

Revitch, E., & Schlesinger, L. B. (1981). *Psychopathology of Homicide.* Springfield, IL: Charles C. Thomas.

Rice, M. E., & Harris, G. T. (1995). Violent recidivism: Assessing predictive validity. *Journal of Consulting and Clinical Psychology, 63,* 737–748.

Robbins, P. C., Monahan, J., & Silver, E. (2003). Mental disorder, violence, and gender. *Law and Human Behavior, 27,* 561–571.

Rogers v. Okin, 634 F. 2d 650 (1st Cir., 1980).

Rosenfeld, B. (2004). Violence risk factors in stalking and obsessional harassment: A review and preliminary meta-analysis. *Criminal Justice and Behavior, 31,* 9–36.

Schall v. Martin, 467 U.S. 253 (1984).

Schlesinger, L. B. (1996). The catathymic crisis (1912–present): A review and clinical study. *Aggression and Violent Behavior, 1,* 307–316.

Schlesinger, L. B. (2004). *Sexual murder: Catathymic and compulsive homicides.* New York: CRC Press.

Schlesinger, L. B., & Revitch, E. (1990). Outpatient treatment of the sex murderer and potential sex murderer. *Journal of Offender Counseling Services, and Rehabilitation, 15,* 163–178.

Schulte, H. M., Hall, M. J., & Crosby, R. (1994). Violence in patients with narcissistic personality pathology: Observations of a clinical series. *American Journal of Psychotherapy, 48,* 610–623.

Schwartz, H. I., & Pinsker, H. (1987). Mediating retention or release of the potentially dangerous patient. *Hospital and Community Psychiatry, 38,* 75–77.

Scott, P. D. (1977). Assessing dangerousness in criminals. *British Journal of Psychiatry, 131,* 127–142.

Seltzer v. Hogue, 594 N.Y.S. 2d 781 (1993).

Shah, S. A. (1978). Dangerousness: A paradigm for exploring some issues in law and psychology. *American Psychologist, 33,* 224–238.

Silva, J. A., Leong, G. B., Garza-Trevino, E. S., & Le-Grand, J. (1994). A cognitive model of dangerous delusional misidentification syndromes. *Journal of Forensic Sciences, 39,* 1455–1467.

Silva, J. A., Leong, G. B., Weinstock, P. S., & Kaushal, K. (1994). Delusional misidentification syndromes and dangerousness. *Psychopathology, 27,* 215–219.

Silva, J. A., Leong, G. B., Weinstock, R., & Klein, R. L. (1995). Psychiatric factors associated with dangerous mis-identification delusions. *Bulletin of the American Academy of Psychiatry and Law, 23,* 53–61.

Sjostedt, G., & Grann, M. (2002). Risk assessment: What is being predicted by actuarial prediction instruments? *International Journal of Forensic Mental Health, 1,* 179–183.

State ex rel. Romley v. Fields, 35 P. 3d 82 (Ariz. App. Div. 1, 2001).

Steadman, H. J., & Cocozza, J. (1974). *Careers of the criminally insane.* Lexington, MA: Heath.

Steadman, H. J., & Cocozza, J. (1980). The prediction of dangerousness—Baxstrom: A case study. In G. Cooke (Ed.), *The role of the forensic psychologist* (pp. 204–215). Springfield, IL: Charles C. Thomas.

Stuart, G. L., Moore, T. M., & Ramsey, S. E. (2003). Relationship aggression and substance use among women court-referred to domestic violence intervention programs. *Addictive Behaviors, 28,* 1603–1610.

Sturidsson, K., Haggard-Grann, U., Lotterberg, M., Dernevik, M., & Grann, M. (2004). Clinicians' perceptions of which factors increase or decrease the risk of violence among forensic out-patients. *International Journal of Forensic Mental Health, 3,* 23–36.

Swanson, J. W., Borum, R., Swartz, M., & Hiday, V. (1999). Violent behavior preceding hospitalization among persons with severe mental illness. *Law and Human Behavior, 23,* 185–204.

Swanson, J. W., Borum, R., Swartz, M., & Monahan, J. (1996). Psychotic symptoms and disorders and the risk of violent behavior in the community. *Criminal Behaviour and Mental Health, 6,* 317–338.

Swanson, J., Estroff, S., Swartz, M., Borum, R., Lachicotte, W., Zimmer, C., et al. (1997). Violence and severe mental disorder in clinical and community populations: The effects of psychotic symptoms, comorbidity, and lack of treatment. *Psychiatry: Interpersonal and Biological Processes, 60,* 1–22.

Tarasoff v. Regents of the University of California, 17 Cal. 3d 425, 551 P. 2d 334 (1976).

Tardiff, K. (1996). *Concise guide to assessment and management of violent patients* (2nd ed.). Washington, DC: American Psychiatric Press.

Tardiff, K. (2001). Axis II disorders and dangerousness. In G. Pinard & L. Pagani (Eds.), *Clinical assessment of dangerousness: Empirical contributions* (pp. 103–120). New York: Cambridge University Press.

Taylor, P. J., & Monahan, J. (1996). Commentary: Dangerous patients or dangerous diseases? *British Medical Journal, 312,* 967–969.

Thornberry, T. P., & Jacoby, J. E. (1979). *The criminally insane: A community follow-up of mentally ill offenders.* Chicago: University of Chicago Press.

Tolman, A. O. (2001). Clinical training and the duty to protect. *Behavioral Sciences and the Law, 19,* 387–404.

Torrey, E. F. (1994). Violent behavior by individuals with serious mental illness. *Hospital and Community Psychiatry, 45,* 653–662.

United States v. Barnette, 212 F. 3d 803 (2000).

United States v. Evanoff, 10 F. 3d 559 (8th Cir., 1993).

United States v. Fitzgerald, 80 Fed. Appx. 857 (2003).

United States v. Perez, 280 F. 3d 318 (2002).

United States v. Romero, 189 F. 3d 576 (1999).

United States v. Sahhar, 917 F. 2d 1197 (1990); cert. denied, 111 S. Ct. 1591 (1991).

United States v. Salerno, 481 U.S. 739 (1987).

VandeCreek, L., & Knapp, S. (2001). *Tarasoff and beyond: Legal and clinical considerations in the treatment of life-endangering patients* (3rd ed.). Sarasota, FL: Professional Resource Press/Professional Resource Exchange.

Villeneuve, D. B., & Quinsey, V. L. (1995). Predictors of general and violent recidivism among mentally disordered inmates. *Criminal Justice and Behavior, 22,* 397–410.

Wack, R. C. (1993). The ongoing risk assessment in the treatment of forensic patients on conditional release status. *Psychiatric Quarterly, 64,* 275–293.

Walcott, D. M., Cerundolo, P., & Beck, J. C. (2001). Current analysis of the Tarasoff duty: An evolution towards the limitation of the duty to protect. *Behavioral Sciences and the Law, 19,* 325–343.

Webster, C. D., Douglas, K. S., Eaves, D., & Hart, S. D. (1997). *The HCR-20 scheme: The assessment of dangerousness and risk (Version 2).* Burnaby, British Columbia, Canada: Mental Health, Law, and Policy Institute, Simon Fraser University.

Webster, C. D., Harris, G. T., Rice, M. E., Cormier, C., & Quinsey, V. L. (1994). *The violence prediction scheme: Assessing dangerousness in high risk men.* Toronto, Canada: University of Toronto Press.

Webster, C. D., & Hucker, S. J. (2003). *Release decision making.* Hamilton, Canada: St. Joseph's Healthcare.

Webster, C. D., Hucker, S. J., & Bloom, H. (2002). Transcending the actuarial versus clinical polemic in assessing risk for violence. *Criminal Justice and Behavior, 29,* 659–665.

Webster, C. D., & Menzies, R. J. (1989). The clinical prediction of dangerousness. In D. N. Weisstaub (Ed.), *Law and mental health: International perspectives* (Vol. 3). Toronto: Pergamun.

Webster, C. D., & Polvi, N. H. (1995). Challenging assessments of dangerousness and risk. In J. Ziskin (Ed.), *Coping with psychiatric and psychological testimony* (5th ed., pp. 22–38). Los Angeles: Law and Psychology Press.

Werner, P. D., Rose, T. L., & Yesavage, J. A. (1990). Aspects of consensus in clinical predictions of violence. *Journal of Clinical Psychology, 46,* 534–538.

Westerheide v. State, 767 So. 2d 637 (Fla. App. 5 Dist., 2000).

Wettstein, R. M. (1984). The prediction of violent behavior and the duty to protect third parties. *Behavioral Sciences and the Law, 2,* 291–317.

Wiest, J. (1981). Treatment of violent offenders. *Clinical Social Work Journal, 9,* 271–281.

Wishnie, H. (1977). *The impulsive personality.* New York: Plenum Press.

CHAPTER 18

Psychology and Law Enforcement

ELLEN SCRIVNER

THE APPLICATION of psychology to law enforcement has created opportunities for psychologists to contribute to the shaping of public safety in the nation's communities. In some respects, the development of the psychology-law enforcement relationship parallels the forensic collaboration between the larger law and psychology enterprise, as reflected in similar developmental trends and the growing numbers of psychologists involved in these activities. At one time, the disciplines of psychology and law enforcement seemed mutually exclusive, yet, over the past few decades, fruitful collaboration has occurred and the outcomes reflect an expanding body of knowledge that demonstrates how psychology adds value to the operation of law enforcement systems.

Relatively unheard of until the 1960s (Reese, 1987; Reiser, 1972), the practice of applying psychology in law enforcement evolved as forward-thinking public safety executives came to recognize that repeated exposure to a difficult environment can take a toll on human beings. Acknowledging the unique culture of law enforcement, many sought proactive approaches to optimize the psychological functioning and personal adjustment of officers and to reduce occupational stress. Others viewed the services of psychologists as a way to reduce risk and to protect departments from liability claims; they viewed psychological services as a type of cover. Still, their response could be considered tempered when compared to those who resisted these efforts and believed that psychological services were of little value. Consequently, there were significant hurdles that needed to be carefully negotiated by psychologists who were trying to practice in this unique environment.

Notwithstanding the varied initial reasons responsible for bringing psychology into law enforcement, over time psychologists have established a presence in law enforcement agencies and now deliver a range of direct psychological services to individual officers as well as to their respective departments. There is little question today that psychologists have made a difference and have had an impact on the delivery of law enforcement services across the country.

This chapter addresses those differences and how they translate into professional activity. I summarize the evolution of law enforcement psychology and the core technologies that are generally accepted as the basic framework of law enforcement psychological services. Also, I address issues that psychologists encounter when they attempt to practice in this unique setting as well as new trends that are evolving as this partnership continues to grow. Some, but not all, of these trends are responses to the range of public safety issues that have emerged following September 11, 2001.

EVOLUTION AND GAINING ACCEPTANCE

Law enforcement is a highly structured occupation that has been characterized as tight-knit, paramilitary, and rigid and as a hidebound bureaucracy not given to innovation. Although organizational changes have occurred in relation to the increasing presence of more highly educated law enforcement executives and through reforms such as community policing, this clearly was not the atmosphere when psychologists first started working with law enforcement.

Initially, the tradition-clad agencies were uncertain about the need for psychological services, and psychologists had an uphill battle to gain credibility and to develop an understanding of the law enforcement culture. In addition, there was an immediate need to respond to professional practice issues that emerged when trying to establish services in this environment. Questions surfaced about the overall integrity of services and specific activities raised distinct issues. An overarching question was *Who was the client*—the applicants that psychologists screened for police department jobs or the police organizations that wanted to hire them? In the context of providing clinical services, was the client the officer seeking treatment or the organization that referred the officer because of concern about his or her capacity to enforce the law?

The client question drove the confidentiality of communications, the cornerstone of psychological services and a fundamental concern of law enforcement officers. However, confidentiality was not fully understood in nonhealth organizations, and particularly so in those that operated as closed systems. Therefore, limiting feedback to the purpose of evaluations, safeguarding privileged information, and maintaining privacy of records in a system that expects definite answers and is known for reacting quickly to solve problems presented challenges. All too often, psychologists were confronted with statements such as "Tell us who has a problem and we'll fire them."

Fortunately, many of these issues were resolved by state laws and the professional standards that govern the practice and licensure of psychologists. However, for psychologists providing services in a law enforcement setting, practice issues continue to require ongoing and careful monitoring. One misstep that raises questions about professional practices could undo a well-functioning program, and any breach of confidentiality could undermine the years of work it took to build credible services.

Overcoming the initial resistance and resolving professional issues, psychologists went on to make significant inroads into improving psychological functioning in the tradition-clad occupations that are responsible for community public safety. Results of two national surveys (Delprino & Bahn, 1988; Scrivner, 1994) and a comparative analysis of survey findings (1988 to 1998) from large law enforcement organizations (VerHelst, Delprino, & O'Regan, 2001) confirmed trends showing an increase in law enforcement's use of psychologists and related availability of services. These data suggest that psychologists have been able to overcome numerous hurdles and have developed credibility with the rank and file. They also illustrate how psychological service mission(s) have expanded since first introduced in the late 1960s. Further, findings from a more recent national survey (Delprino, O'Quin, & Kennedy, 1997) demonstrate that psychologists opened doors for the involvement of mental health service providers from other disciplines, including police chaplains, to become involved in delivering services to law enforcement, particularly those directed to families.

Overall, it appears that the concept of psychological services has been institutionalized in law enforcement agencies and that psychology has played a major role in breaking down barriers and expanding the use of mental health services in this specialized environment. In essence, psychology has been instrumental in facilitating a major shift in the culture of law enforcement.

KEY EVENTS SIGNIFYING A CULTURE SHIFT

Broad-based use and acceptance of psychologists and other mental health service providers in law enforcement have been supported by a series of key events that represent the building blocks of professional development and signify a major shift in the culture. These events are as follows:

- Five police psychology conferences were hosted by the Federal Bureau of Investigation Training Academy (1984 to 2001). These meetings brought psychologists together to discuss issues relative to providing services in law enforcement agencies. In addition to general practice issues, topics included critical incident stress, organizational issues, the impact on families, and suicide in law enforcement.
- Professional organizations acknowledged the work of psychologists in law enforcement and developed sections in their organizations to shape policy and guide the development of professional procedures. Division 18 (Psychologists in Public Service) of the American Psychological Association (APA) developed a section on Police and Public Safety Psychology, and the International Association of Chiefs of Police developed the Police Psychology Section. These sections continue to provide a venue for peer exchange directed at resolving the unique professional issues faced by law enforcement psychologists.
- Congressional testimony on police stress and family well-being (1991) was the impetus for an amendment to the 1994 Omnibus Crime Act that provided for the development of the federally funded Corrections and Law Enforcement Family Support Program managed by the National Institute of Justice (NIJ). From 1996 to 2003, NIJ funded approximately 30 innovative programs to treat stress, deliver training, and conduct survey research to help understand the needs of law enforcement and corrections

officers. These programs supported partnerships with law enforcement agencies, labor unions, and professional organizations and were designed to address law enforcement stress and the related impact on families.

- In an APA Police Chiefs Roundtable Series, 15 years after establishing a public safety presence in Division 18, police chiefs sought input from the APA Committee on Urban Initiatives on strategies to manage a range of problems that affect the quality of American policing.
- From 2000 to 2002, the *APA Monitor on Psychology* periodically published articles about the breadth of the activities of psychologists working with law enforcement and showcased their professional work.
- There has been a growing literature on law enforcement psychology (Blau, 1994; Kurke & Scrivner, 1995; Toch, 2002), including the compilation of papers from the FBI conference series and articles in peer-reviewed journals.
- Following September 11, the FBI Academy and APA convened a meeting on terrorism. This latest conference represents a significant benchmark for law enforcement and psychology. In contrast to the applied and clinical focus of other conferences, this one brought operational and theoretical viewpoints together to address how psychology could assist in antiterrorism initiatives. Conference participants included psychologists representing the APA Science Directorate, federal agents, and police officers (Smith, 2002).

These developments have strengthened the professional dimensions of the field. They have facilitated a growing law enforcement-psychology literature, presentations at professional conferences, and scholarly research, including a body of work devoted to police stress. Consequently, a more comprehensive and multifaceted role has been established for an active presence of law enforcement psychology in the nation's law enforcement agencies. Further, most of the major law enforcement agencies now provide some level of mental health services for employees.

WHAT DO LAW ENFORCEMENT PSYCHOLOGISTS DO?

The introduction of psychologists into law enforcement brought new sets of skills to these agencies, and these skills defined the core technologies used by law enforcement psychology. With some exceptions, they are the competencies that psychologists provide in other settings and include evaluation activities, clinical services, training, organizational consulting, and operational and investigation support. The last brings psychologists into closer contact with enforcement and also provides an opportunity for psychology to contribute to the broader world of criminal justice.

EVALUATION

In the early 1900s, Terman, and then Thurstone, used psychological tests to try to identify successful candidates for law enforcement (Super, 1999). However, it was the availability of federal discretionary funds from the Law Enforcement Assistance Administration (1967) that encouraged law enforcement agencies to seek the expertise of psychologists to help them select emotionally stable candidates with personal characteristics suitable for law enforcement work. The awarding of these funds also supported recommendations from the 1968 National Advisory Commission on Civil Disorder and subsequently created a law enforcement psychological preemployment screening specialization (Kurke & Scrivner, 1995).

Psychological screening of job candidates was a fairly traditional responsibility for psychologists, but it was quite new to the police personnel function. It has now grown to the point that a 1994 study showed that almost all of the 50 largest cities participating in the Major City Chiefs Association used psychological tests as part of their preemployment applicant screening process (Scrivner, 1994). This area of specialization has positioned psychologists to have a major impact on the quality of law enforcement services.

Critical issues affecting preemployment evaluation activities are well known and involve using tests that can be justified in personnel decision making, communicating test results appropriately, engaging in ongoing validation of the process, and conforming to civil rights legislation and Equal Employment Opportunity Commission requirements. In addition, preemployment evaluation procedures have been influenced by the Americans with Disabilities Act. In fact, the latter has had a major impact on the sequencing of psychological evaluations in preemployment assessment and affects decisions on when to use some psychological tests that have been traditionally administered in evaluation activities, particularly those that screen for mental impairment.

Preemployment applicant evaluations also raised questions about *screening in* viable candidates versus *screening out* those with problems that reflect some level of mental impairment. While it might seem obvious that one would be concerned with both screening in and screening out, much of the early validation work used test instruments that were developed and normed with clinical populations. As such, they were more appropriate to screening-out decisions. Gradually, psychological tests were developed specifically for preemployment screening of police candidates, namely, the Hilson Profile/Success Quotient (Inwald & Brobst, 1988), which measures dimensions such as work ethic and social skills, and a specialized use of the California Personality Inventory known as the Police and Public Safety Selection Report (Roberts, 1995). These instruments examine candidates for suitability to perform law enforcement functions and compare candidate scale scores to norms developed from large samples of incumbent officers.

Another argument related to preemployment screening questions the use of the clinical judgment paradigm to make job-related decisions, in contrast to predictive statistical models, even though the latter have not shown particularly robust validities. More recently, new models are being advanced. One, the Matrix-Psychological Uniform Law Enforcement Selection Evaluation, uses actuarial models to forecast specific law enforcement outcomes that are undesirable, such as use of excessive force (Davis & Rostow, 2002). Another model uses the Behavioral Personnel Assessment Device, which involves having candidates view content-valid police scenarios and then answering questions based on what they saw (Corey, MacAlpine, Rand, Rand, & Wolf, 1996).

Validation studies are critical to this type of evaluation activity, however, validation data remain somewhat limited. Hough (2002) assessed characteristics needed for effective community policing and provided an as-yet unpublished review of the literature that is quite comprehensive. Her review incorporates research done in other jobs where similar performance dimensions were important for successful performance, and she documents assessment scales that are not directed exclusively at eliminating mental impairment. Hough contends that validity of the predictors she cites could be expected to generalize and would be useful for predicting law enforcement performance, particularly community policing. This review of the literature provides a thorough assessment of a wide range of promising selection measures as well as recommendations for criterion validation studies. Her research also is relevant to the screening-in issue and is consistent with current work of the California Police Office Standards and Training Commission (POST). The POST approach to preemployment law enforcement assessment has been broadened to include a range of suitability criteria that are related to effective law enforcement performance. These developments make clear distinctions between mental impairment and the critical traits or characteristics that are necessary to perform the essential functions of the law enforcement job, such as ability to communicate with diverse groups of people, manage conflict, and tolerate stress. Consequently, they are not driven by models based on psychopathology. This changing focus on preemployment psychological evaluations is expanding the utility of screening and adds value to current preemployment evaluation processes.

Fitness-for-Duty Evaluations

Although preemployment screening has dominated the assessment conversation, psychologists subsequently were asked the question, Once hired, do these individuals continue to be psychologically fit for duty? Consequently, evaluation activities expanded into other areas and psychologists became involved in conducting assessments to evaluate fitness for duty and assessing the psychological implications of work-related injury. These activities are highly sensitive and present a different set of issues from those raised by preemployment screening. They involve incumbent officers who are ordered to see the psychologist for an assessment of their psychological fitness to continue in their position. In this context, there is a critical need to differentiate the fitness evaluation from other forms of psychological services and to ensure that the officers understand these differences. These evaluations are the result of mandatory referrals, and verbal or written information is provided to the client agency. Under these conditions, confidentiality is limited.

There is relevant case law pertaining to this type of evaluation that confirms a police chief's right to order an evaluation, to take reasonable steps to assure the psychological suitability of employees, and to ensure that communications regarding fitness evaluations are not confidential (see Flanagan, 1995; Ostrov, 1995). However, a related issue involves the potential for conflict of interest. Ideally, psychologists who see officers as clinical clients or who may have screened them when hired should avoid fitness evaluations because of the inherent conflict in roles as well as dual relationship concerns. Similar issues pertain when evaluating officers for work-related disabilities. There is federal legislation that needs to be considered in disability evaluations and also in other core activities, specifically the Civil Rights Act of 1964, the Rehabilitation Act of 1973, and the Americans with Disability Act of 1991.

CLINICAL SERVICES

As preemployment screening gained some measure of success, law enforcement agencies began to request clinical services. By 1980, both applicant screening and clinical interventions designed to help officers cope with the stressful nature of policing had been identified as primary activities of psychologists working with law enforcement (Stratton, 1980). Responding to an array of personal problems believed to be intensified by this line of work, psychologists developed services to assist officers in dealing with a range of problems, including marital conflict and family problems, substance abuse, depression and anxiety, and suicidal tendencies (Reese & Scrivner, 1994).

More recently, there has been a concentrated focus on preventing police suicide (Sheehan & Warren, 2001), which may have been stimulated by New York City statistics reflecting 26 police suicides in the 2-year period from 1995 through 1996. Finn, Talucci, and Wood (2000) report that negative press coverage and allegations of corruption may have been responsible for these high numbers. Volanti (1996) advances a role constriction theory that is based on the premise that as the police role begins to dominate work life, officers' cognitive coping style becomes constricted and affects how they cope with psychological issues in their personal lives. He contends that with time on the job, law enforcement officers risk becoming overly constricted and that their options to change, such as getting help for a problem, become limited. The interaction of the nature of the job and the socialization into the police culture generally creates the constricted environment, but Volanti also identifies specific factors that drive the constriction, such as law enforcement selection procedures, training experiences, job stress, and department and public expectations.

The focus on suicide also addresses a phenomenon highly unique to law enforcement, termed "suicide by cop," which is a form of victim-precipitated homicide (Kennedy, Homant, & Hupp, 1998). Suicide by cop refers to a situation in which a person with suicidal intent uses deadly force to threaten a law enforcement officer, with the intention that the officer will use fatal force against him or her. This is a difficult phenomenon for the general public to understand, much less accept, and it usually ends up in headlines about "trigger-happy" cops and costly lawsuits. This phenomenon occurs with some frequency and plays a significant role in police shootings (Kennedy et al., 1998). Moreover, it has a strong impact on an officer's mental state.

Law Enforcement Trauma

A significant component of clinical service includes providing a crisis response to help officers adjust to on-duty traumatic incidents, a situation that occurs with some frequency in public safety occupations and at rates that exceed those in the general population. Consequently, psychologists developed focused interventions designed for officers involved in traumatic incidents. Initially developed as a response to potential trauma following an on-duty shooting incident and labeled "postshooting trauma" (Reese, Horn, & Dunning, 1991), this reaction soon became known as "critical incident stress" in order to incorporate other traumatic incidents unrelated to police shootings (Bohl, 1995). Unfortunately, a growing number of incidents have required intervention. Psychologists were active at the Oklahoma City bombing, the TWA airliner crash on Long Island, the 1993 World Trade Center bombing, the 2001 WTC Twin Towers collapse, and the airliner crash into the Pentagon.

Traumatic incident interventions are initiated to reduce immediate stress and to prevent Posttraumatic Stress Disorder (PTSD). From the prevention perspective, they also seek to identify officers who may require further treatment. The process that is used is based on a short-term, crisis intervention response that involves critical incident stress management. Frequently, it is delivered in an individual or group defusing/debriefing format, and it is considered to be a type of emotional first-aid, in contrast to psychotherapy.

The effectiveness of posttraumatic incident debriefings for victims of trauma, not just law enforcement officers, recently has come under question, and the questioning has intensified since the horrific events of September 11, 2001. Several studies are being reported that question their effectiveness in preventing PTSD (McNally, Bryant, & Ehlers, 2003). McNally et al. conclude that although most of the research is faulty, the preponderance of evidence suggests that debriefings do not prevent PTSD and in some instances could be harmful. Given the sensitivity of responding appropriately to those exposed to trauma, it is clear that further research is needed to resolve some of these issues.

FAMILY SERVICES

Niederhoffer and Niederhoffer (1977) discussed the potential negative impact that law enforcement work has on marriages and families. The development of the federally funded CLEF program subsequently intensified the focus on family issues and funded the development of a number of family programs. To provide guidance to CLEF, Finn and Tomz (1997) interviewed mental health practitioners, law enforcement and corrections officers, and family members in selected sites. Their results suggest that job-related stress affects families, who undergo the following behavioral changes:

- Increased cynicism and suspiciousness.
- Increased emotional detachment from various aspects of daily life.
- Reduced efficiency, with absenteeism and early retirement.
- Excessive aggressiveness, resulting in an increase in citizen complaints.
- Increased alcoholism and other substance abuse problems.
- Marital and family problems, compounded by extramarital affairs or domestic violence.
- PTSD.
- Health problems such as ulcers, weight gain, and cardiac problems.
- Suicide.

However, in a "lessons learned" study of the CLEF program, Delprino (2001) found that, although sources of stress for officers and their family members had been identified, typically the actual use of many of these programs was somewhat limited.

Stress in Law Enforcement

Law enforcement officers are daily witnesses to man's inhumanity to man and sustain continued exposure to the dark side of life, such as murder, rape, hostage taking, and other violent acts. Yet, a fairly common finding in studies is that the major negative stressors experienced by law enforcement are related more to administrative or routine work factors. In fact, Liberman et al. (2002) found that routine work stressors were more stressful to law enforcement officers than exposure to danger and critical incidents. Routine stressors can range from work schedules and lack of advancement, to media exposure of negative police events and concerns about liability, to a hardening of the emotions that creates communication and attitudinal problems. Several researchers show how routine stress starts early in a career and subsequently fuels marital conflict (Delprino, 2001; Eisenberg, 1975; Finn & Tomz, 1997; Toch, 2002). Other consistent findings confirm that seeing a partner or fellow officer killed and responding to abused children and to victims of serious accidents also are major stressors.

Even the summary of the NIJ/CLEF research portfolio that documented the causes and effects of job-related stress, as applied to officers and their families, indicated that although exposure to violence, suffering, and death is inherent to the profession, other sources of stress have greater impact on officers; these include light sentences for offenders, unfavorable public opinion of police performance, irregular work hours and shift work, dealing with abused children and child homicides, and ministering to survivors of vehicle crashes. Within the organization, the research cites the nature of the organization, limited advancement potential, and excessive paperwork as being stressful. In contrast to many other occupations, law enforcement personnel view stress as a normal part of their job but also see themselves as being under more pressure in today's environment than what they experienced 10 to 20 years ago (Finn et al., 2000).

Gershon (1999) discussed police stress from the perspective of implications for public health. In a video developed by the NIJ, Gershon presented findings from Project SHIELD, which examined incidence and prevalence of police occupational stress and the related psychological and physical health outcomes in a specific police department. Gershon found that high scores on a stress inventory were related to self-reports of poor health and spouse abuse. More specifically, her results documented the most stressful events as identified by police officers: attending a police funeral (the most stressful event), being a target of an internal investigation, sustaining a needle stick injury, making a violent arrest, and having personal knowledge of a victim. These stressors contributed to low energy, headaches, family abuse of both spouse and children, depression, and anxiety. Further, Gershon reports that 1% of the participants admitted to frequent thoughts about suicide.

These findings confirm that although the job is inherently difficult, law enforcement stress comes from both internal and external sources. However, it is the impact of these issues that typically send law enforcement personnel, and frequently their loved ones, to the psychologist. Moreover, they drive a training agenda that calls for the involvement of psychologists who understand law enforcement issues.

Law Enforcement Training

Psychologists have used the knowledge base of psychology to develop a variety of training programs but have placed strong emphasis on training officers to use stress management tools. The goal has been to make law enforcement officers more resilient and better able to manage the stress in their jobs and to acquaint them with a variety of prevention and stress reduction strategies. In addition to a focus on coping techniques, other training programs have been developed to help supervisors identify signs of stress in their employees and to make appropriate and timely referrals for services.

Although training in stress management is critical, White and Honig (1995) discuss how psychologists also apply their expertise to develop training on other subject matters within the domain of psychology. Some examples include enhancing communication skills, responding to the mentally ill, cross-cultural awareness, hostage negotiations, use of force, domestic violence, dynamics of sexual assault, responding to hate crimes, and practical issues relative to child-rearing practices and preparing for retirement.

Over time, psychologists also brought adult learning models into law enforcement training and made greater use of role play and simulation techniques, in contrast to the "talking head" lecture approach of prior years. In this context, they created an approach to training that is less academic and instructor centered in favor of one that focuses on developing competencies in the adult learner. Currently, these methods are being used to develop health-related competencies that use disease prevention and wellness methods as appropriate models for responding to police stress (Harpold & Feemster, 2002).

Organizational Consulting

Organizational consulting activities go beyond the delivery of traditional mental health services and focus, instead, on strengthening the organization. This can be done by building resiliency from within or by acting as a change agent with a goal of improving agency performance. These are newer roles for psychologists in law enforcement, but they can have a substantial impact on the operation of an organization. Sewell (2002) contends that law enforcement agencies are in an era of change because of technological advances, environmental and economic factors, and new political influences expressed through grassroots, community-based criminal justice (policing, prosecutors, courts, corrections, and victim services). In his view, these changes affect the structure and policies of organizations and create considerable stress, suggesting that the organizations need as much help as the individual officers.

Schmuckler (1995) takes a similar position and suggests that law enforcement agencies need help in directing change efforts. He discusses the potential for psychology to help with organizational activities that range from team building to facilitating strategic management. This type of activity was illustrated in an *APA Monitor on Psychology* article about an organizational psychologist working with a large urban department to implement a significant and long-term systemic change effort. Her work included a focus on systemic change, on integrating adult learning models into management training, and on designing and implementing a strategic planning initiative to address crime, quality of life, and management issues. This project resulted in new internal and external partnerships, something of a sea change for law enforcement, and structural changes within the agency have evolved due to her work (DeAngelis, 2002).

These types of activities suggest that psychology has moved far beyond traditional models of clinical services. They also show that law enforcement organizations are fertile ground for the type of expertise that can help them create and adapt to change.

SUPPORT FOR POLICE OPERATIONS

To a lesser extent, psychologists have become involved in operational areas such as assisting in criminal investigations and developing a hostage negotiation capacity and barricade call-out consultation in police departments. The success of this practical application of psychology to law enforcement operations clearly helped build credibility for psychology in law enforcement. It also strengthened support for developing other niches of specialized services that contributed to investigating and apprehending criminals.

The evolving investigative competency incorporated work with victims and witnesses to crime through the use of forensic hypnosis or cognitive interviewing as methods to access greater details about specific crimes, as well as developing criminal profiles and psychological autopsies. Some of this work has stirred controversy; many consider it more art than science (Super, 1999). Moreover, these processes can result in inaccurate information that could impede an investigation. One only has to recall the profiles that were circulated via national television but that misidentified the snipers who terrorized the Washington, D.C., area for three weeks in 2002.

Hibler (1995) concludes that despite only a 12% rate of success for forensic hypnosis, that level of enhancement could be a serious consideration when a criminal case is stalemated. He argues that it is a potentially valuable tool for law enforcement provided it is used correctly and with the appropriate controls. The same cautions are set forth when discussing the even more controversial area of psychological autopsies, or what is sometimes referred to as an "equivocal death analysis." This process is used as an adjunctive investigative aid and as a tool to help clarify manner of death. It presents a model to assess an individual's behavior and personality to develop a better understanding of his or her death. Cautions similar to those advanced for forensic hypnosis also apply to this area (Gelles, 1995).

MODELS OF SERVICE DELIVERY

How services are actually delivered in law enforcement agencies vary. Because law enforcement is not a 9-to-5 job, there may be an expectation that a psychologist will provide 24/7 on-call availability. Although the frequency of being called out varies with the size of the agency, it is a responsibility that must be factored into the service delivery model because it complicates being able to deliver services within the traditional framework of client-driven schedules.

To meet service delivery goals, some models have become more prevalent than others. All have advantages and disadvantages. One of the more commonly used models appears to be the professional services contract (Finn & Tomz, 1997; Scrivner, 1994). Using contracts, departments can hire consultants either to provide a range of services or to contract for a specific expertise, such as psychological screening or fitness-for-duty evaluation. Other models include developing a link to an employee assistance program, use of a network of clinical referrals, and peer support services. A model that is more prevalent in large departments provides a full range of psychological services to officers and the organization through in-house psychological service units. In 1995, 61 service activities were identified that are now provided by police psychologists. They were categorized into three general areas: individual service activities, program/technical support, and organizational support. These data are another measure of the growth of psychology in law enforcement (Kurke & Scrivner, 1995).

The survey research of Finn and Tomz (1997) laid out a blueprint for how to establish a program of services for law enforcement. Although their survey primarily addressed how law enforcement stress affects families, and included mental health professionals and service providers other than psychologists, the crosscutting issues they defined are critical to establishing and delivering effective services. They are as follows:

- Ensure that services are accessible and private.
- Develop clear guidelines for confidentiality and statements of informed consent that are consistent with state law.
- Develop a record-keeping system that includes procedures for safeguarding privileged information.
- Develop and circulate written policies and procedures that include clear distinctions between mandatory and voluntary referrals.
- Ensure that monitoring systems are in place.
- Educate the user community through training, brochures, or publicity.
- Engage in program planning that includes relevant stakeholders, such as key law enforcement administrators, labor representatives, officers, and family members.
- Avail yourself of ongoing consultation with the jurisdiction's legal counsel.

Their data provide a reasonable protocol for establishing psychological services. To be consistent with most recent practices, however, when providing health services, an additional element is recommended: assuring that all procedures are HIPPA compliant.

ISSUES FACING LAW ENFORCEMENT PSYCHOLOGISTS

As previously referenced, the major issue faced by any psychologist who sets out to work with law enforcement is the need to develop credibility with the rank and file and avoid being seen as a shill for management. There is also a need to overcome significant skepticism about the value and credibility of psychology. Law enforcement officers spend considerable time in court and have had numerous experiences hearing expert witness testimony. It is not unusual for many to have developed a somewhat cynical perception that expert witness testimony can be bought, including that of psychologists. Were these two hurdles not enough, psychologists also need to deal with the stigma attached to making contact with psychological services as well as addressing the fear that services will not be confidential. In the few departments where management actually is the client, this becomes a reality and not a fear, as confidentiality cannot be guaranteed under those conditions. Fortunately, most law enforcement agencies realize that if the services are to be effective, they must be confidential, and therefore respect the need to ensure confidentiality.

Psychologists working with law enforcement also need to be cautious that they do not cross ethical lines through out-of-office contact. Conversations when meeting in the hallway or parking lot may be construed as expert psychological opinion and end up affecting a law enforcement officer's private life or, in some instances, his or her career. The same holds true for socializing with the client base, such as attending retirement dinners and promotion celebrations that take place at the local law enforcement hangout. In any of these situations, casual comments can be misconstrued and ethical standards that govern the practice of psychology can be compromised. To avoid this type of compromise, many psychologists take the position that it is safer to treat all conversations as clinical contacts regardless of where they occur.

Other ethical dilemmas include restricting practice to what you are trained to do and avoiding exceeding your competence by becoming all things to all people. Law enforcement personnel cannot be expected to understand all the specializations in psychology and often believe that the psychologist they hire is trained to do anything classified as a domain within psychology. Consequently, the psychologist must help staff understand the limits of their training and experience and educate the staff as to what they can and cannot do.

NEW AND EMERGING TRENDS

As the presence of psychology in law enforcement continues to expand, some in leadership positions are using psychologists to assist them in addressing significant national law enforcement issues, such as acrimonious interactions between law enforcement officers and citizens. In the series of Police Chief

Roundtables that were conducted in conjunction with the APA annual meetings (1998 to 2000), the police chiefs who met with psychologists identified needs for assistance to end racial profiling, to intervene in police brutality, to strengthen police integrity, and to develop greater understanding of police officer fear. They also examined alternatives to arresting the homeless, the prevalence of hate crime, and skill development for officers in the areas of mediation and anger management. The Roundtables generated ideas for research on psychological issues such as studying how observing violence affects police officers, particularly in relationship to police officer domestic violence, and how psychological research on self-fulfilling prophecies and stereotype-change processes could be helpful in designing interventions to deter ethnic profiling. Race and gender bias also were discussed (Rabasca, 2000).

Some of the issues identified in the Roundtables are consistent with a federally funded project, "Hiring in the Spirit of Service," that is currently under way at five test sites. This project is designed to aggressively market the service characteristics of law enforcement to recruit and identify law enforcement candidates who show a strong service orientation, in contrast to those who are more interested in the spirit of adventure. Moreover, it is examining the psychological screening instruments that have the greatest capacity to accomplish this goal; some of the sites are pilot-testing instruments developed from job-task analyses that include input from community members. This project merits watching as it has promise for developing new methods to screen in applicants for law enforcement.

In yet another venue, the Los Angeles Police Department (LAPD) has moved its psychologists from the consulting rooms into the precincts. Recently, the department psychologists were assigned to operational divisions in an effort to make them more accessible and less intimidating and to enhance their capacity to reach department personnel in a proactive manner. It is believed that this newest development in the psychological services provided to LAPD personnel will provide opportunities for interventions in the field with personnel who would otherwise have little or no contact with department psychologists and will ensure better follow-up with clients (Gelber, 2003). As with any innovation, this process will need to be carefully monitored to ensure that the psychologists' roles are clearly understood.

The blending of law enforcement experience and advanced degrees in psychology is producing what are known as "cop docs," psychologists who have the distinction of also having been law enforcement officers. In fact, as of 2004, the unit chief of the Behavioral Sciences Unit of the FBI Training Academy, a prestigious law enforcement training facility, is an FBI agent who also holds a doctorate in psychology.

The "cop doc" influence has stimulated interest in peer programs that are based on the belief that officers are more comfortable discussing problems with peers who understand the culture, in contrast to professionals. Moreover, some of the labor unions support the peer process provided that peer support officers are well trained. Many psychologists support the notion of peer support but encourage strong supervision of these programs as well as strong familiarity with referral networks.

The measurement of stress has long been wanting in law enforcement. Beyond survey data, there has been little sophisticated analysis that identifies how stress affects behavior and health. Sheehan and Van Hasselt (2003) are attempting to develop a reliable and valid assessment tool, the Law Enforcement Officer Stress Survey, which is a scenario-based assessment tool designed to provide early detection of stress-related problems. They had law enforcement officers identify the major stress issues in each scenario and then rate the scenarios on two dimensions: the likelihood of encountering the situation described, and how difficult each situation would be. Currently, they are developing a scoring system and norms for each scenario. This is a good start, but there is need for more in-depth work in this area in order to develop meaningful conclusions.

Rather than concentrate only on sources of stress, other psychologists are placing greater emphasis on being proactive, developing resilience, and using prevention models that are designed to better prepare law enforcement officers and their families for what to expect. By providing an orientation to police work and to the changing attitudes and behaviors that start to develop early in the career, they hope to prepare family and friends to understand the transition into law enforcement and how it will impact the new officers and their families (Torres, Maggard, & Torres, 2003).

Family orientation programs are examples of the proactive approach advocated by Delprino (2001), who found that many of the programs developed with CLEF funds that were intended to help with family stress actually were diverted to services for law enforcement officers. In his evaluation of the program, he expressed concern that family services may not be prioritized, and he advocates for a more holistic approach that would use resources to develop healthy workplaces that minimize the potential negative effects on the officer and family. Others, such as Artwohl and Christenson (1997), encourage law enforcement officers to develop personal resilience by making healthy lifestyle choices, developing support systems, avoiding overcommitment to the job, retaining a positive focus, and determining what is meaningful in their lives. These trends are compatible with the research on the stress hardiness skills and attitudes that promote transformational coping (Maddi, 2002). This line of research could inform proactive approaches to helping officers and their families tolerate both internal and external stress.

The information age presents other vehicles for proactive responses, including, but not limited to, a proliferation of Web sites that are designed to bring health-related information to officers and their families. Examples include a site developed by the Metropolitan Nashville Police Department (www.policefamilies.com) and the police stress and health program (PSHP) affiliated with the University of California, San Francisco (www.policestressandhealth.net). The policefamilies.com site initially was funded by the U.S. Department of Justice and provides families of law enforcement officers with mental health information and access to a wide variety of online family support services. The PSHP is funded through grants from the National Institute of Mental Health and focuses primarily on duty-related stress and improving quality of life. These federally funded Web sites are harbingers of how mental health information and psychological knowledge can be managed electronically to reach greater numbers of law enforcement consumers.

CONCLUSIONS

The trends outlined in this chapter are only a small sample of all that is happening in this field, but they demonstrate a level of growth and impact that would have been unbelievable when the collaboration between psychology and law enforcement was first initiated. They also bring an increase in legal challenges by those adversely affected by the decisions of psychologists, and there is a body of case law developing, particularly on selection and clinical issues.

As the events and aftermath of 9/11 place new demands on law enforcement, and as new stressors emerge, in all likelihood psychologists will face new challenges. Psychologists will become more involved in assisting officers who are working in the threat-sensitive environment to prevent and deter terrorism, a major feature in today's law enforcement executive portfolio. This has implications for the emergence of new issues, such as dealing with bioterrorism and weapons of mass destruction and understanding how the Patriot Act can be applied without compromising civil liberties. With psychological services better institutionalized, law enforcement agencies now have a capacity to meet the changing psychological needs of officers, and psychology has an opportunity to contribute its knowledge base, professional expertise, and research capacity to help solve real-world problems that make a difference in ensuring public safety.

REFERENCES

Artwohl, A., & Christensen, L. (1997). *Deadly force encounters: What cops need to know to mentally and physically prepare for and survive a gunfight.* Boulder, CO: Paladin Press.

Blau, T. (1994). *Psychological services for law enforcement.* New York: Wiley.

Bohl, N. (1995). Professionally administered critical incident debriefing for police officers. In Martin I. Kurke & Ellen M. Scrivner (Eds.), *Police psychology into the 21st century* (pp. 169–188). Hillsdale, NJ: Lawrence Erlbaum.

Corey, D., MacAlpine, D., Rand, D., Rand, R., & Wolf, G. (1996). *B-PAD technical reports.* Napa, CA: B-PAD Group.

Davis, R. D., & Rostow, C. D. (2002, December). M-PULSE: Matrix-psychological uniform law enforcement selection evaluation. *Forensic Examiner,* Winter, 19–24.

DeAngelis, T. (2002). Revitalizing Boston's police force. *Monitor on psychology, 33*(6), 62.

Delprino, R. P. (2001). *Lessons learned from early corrections and law enforcement family support (CLEFS) programs.* (NCJ 192287). Washington, DC: National Institute of Justice.

Delprino, R. P., & Bahn, C. (1988). National survey of the extent and nature of psychological services in police departments. *Professional Psychology: Research and Practice, 19*(4), 421–425.

Delprino, R. P., O'Quin, K., & Kennedy, C. (1997). *Identification of work and family services for law enforcement personnel.* (171645). Washington, DC: National Institute of Justice, U.S. Department of Justice.

Eisenberg, T. (1975). Labor management relations and psychological stress: View from the bottom. *Police Chief,* 54–58.

Finn, P., Talucci, V., & Wood, J. (2000, January). On-the-job stress in policing—Reducing it, preventing it. *National Institute of Justice Journal,* 19–24.

Finn, P., & Tomz, J. E. (1997, March). *Developing a law enforcement stress program for officers and their families.* (NCJ 163175). Washington, DC: U.S. Department of Justice, National Institute of Justice.

Flanagan, C. L. (1995). Legal issues regarding police psychology. In M. Kurke & E. M. Scrivner (Eds.), *Police psychology into the 21st century* (pp. 93–107). Hillsdale, NJ: Erlbaum.

Gelber, C. (2003, September). LAPD bureau psychologists to hit the streets. *Police Chief, 70*(9), 29–31.

Gelles, M. G. (1995). Psychological autopsy: An investigative aid. In M. Kurke & E. M. Scrivner (Eds.), *Police psychology into the 21st century* (pp. 337–355). Hillsdale, NJ: Lawrence Erlbaum.

Gershon, R. (1999). *Public health implications of law enforcement stress.* Video presentation. Washington, DC: National Institute of Justice, U.S. Department of Justice.

Harpold, J. A., & Feemster, S. L. (2002). Negative influences of police stress. *Law Enforcement Bulletin, 71*(9), 1–6.

Hibler, N. S. (1995). Using hypnosis for investigative purposes. In M. Kurke & E. M. Scrivner (Eds.), *Police psychology into the 21st century* (pp. 319–336). Hillsdale, NJ: Lawrence Erlbaum.

Hough, L. M. (2000). *Hiring in the spirit of service: Definitions, possibilities, evidence and recommendations.* Unpublished report, available through The Dunnette Group, Ltd., St. Paul, MN.

Inwald, R. E., & Brobst, K. E. (1988). *Hilson personnel profile/success quotient manual.* Kew Gardens, NY: Hilson Research.

Kennedy, D. B., Homant, R. J., & Hupp, R. T. (1998). Suicide by cop. *Law Enforcement Bulletin, 67*(8), 21–27.

Kurke, M. I., & Scrivner, E. M. (Eds.) (1995). *Police psychology into the 21st century.* Hillsdale, NJ: Lawrence Erlbaum.

Liberman, A. M., Best, S. R., Metzler, T. J., Fagan, J. A. Weiss, D. S., & Marmar, C. R. (2002). Routine occupational stress and psychological distress in police. *Policing: An International Journal of Police Strategies and Management, 25*(2), 421–439.

Maddi, S. R. (2002). The story of hardiness: Twenty years of theorizing, research and practice. *Consulting Psychology Journal, 54*(3), 173–185.

McNally, R. J., Bryant, R. A., & Ehlers, A. (2003). Does early psychological intervention promote recovery from posttraumatic stress? *American Psychological Society, 4*(2), 45–70.

National Advisory Commission on Civil Disorder. (1968). *Kerner commission report.* New York: Dutton.

Niederhoffer, A., & Niederhoffer, E. (1977). *The police family: From station house to ranch house.* Lexington, MA: Heath.

On the front lines: Police stress and family well-being. (1991, May). Select Committee on Children, Youth and Families, U.S. House of Representatives, 102nd Congress. Washington, DC: U.S. Government Printing Office.

Ostrov, E. (1995). Legal, psychological, and ethical issues in police-related forensic psychology evaluations. In M. Kurke & E. M. Scrivner (Eds.), *Police psychology into the 21st century* (pp. 133–145). Hillsdale, NJ: Erlbaum.

President's Commission on Law Enforcement and Administration of Justice. (1967). *Task force report: The police.* Washington, DC: U.S. Government Printing Office.

Rabasca, L. (2000). Psychologist, police chiefs forge an alliance. *Monitor on Psychology, 50.*

Reese, J. T. (1987). *A history of police psychological services.* Washington, DC: U.S. Department of Justice, Federal Bureau of Investigation.

Reese, J. T., Horn, J. M., & Dunning, C. (Eds.). (1991). *Critical incidents in policing.* Washington, DC: U.S. Department of Justice, Federal Bureau of Investigation.

Reese, J. T., & Scrivner, E. (Eds.). (1994). *Law enforcement families: Issues and answers.* Washington, DC: U.S. Department of Justice, Federal Bureau of Investigation.

Reiser, M. (1972). *The police department psychologist.* Springfield, IL: Charles Thomas.

Roberts, M. (1995). *CPI Form 434 Police and Public Safety Selection Report interpreter's guide: Interim edition.* Palo Alto, CA: Consulting Psychologists Press.

Schmuckler, E. (1995). Strategic planning. In M. I. Kurke & Ellen M. Scrivner (Eds.), *Police psychology into the 21st century* (pp. 497–510). Hillsdale, NJ: Lawrence Erlbaum.

Scrivner, E. M. (1994). *The role of police psychology in controlling excessive force.* Washington, DC: National Institute of Justice Research Report, U.S. Department of Justice.

Sewell, J. D. (2002, March). Managing the stress of organizational change. *FBI Law Enforcement Bulletin, 71*(3), 14–20.

Shcehan, D. C., & Van Hasselt, V. B. (2003, September). Identifying law enforcement stress reactions early. *FBI Law Enforcement Bulletin, 72,* 12–19.

Sheehan, D. C., & Warren, J. I. (Eds.). (2001). *Suicide and law enforcement.* Washington, DC: U.S. Department of Justice, Federal Bureau of Investigation.

Smith, D. (2002, June). Improving the tools to fight terrorism. *Monitor on Psychology, 33*(6).

Stratton, J. G. (1980). Psychological services for police. *Journal of Police Science and Administration, 8,* 38.

Super, J. T. (1999). Forensic psychology and law enforcement. In A. K. Hess & I. B. Weiner (Eds.), *The handbook of forensic psychology* (2nd ed., pp. 409–439). New York: Wiley.

Toch, H. (2002). *Stress in policing.* Washington, DC: American Psychological Association.

Torres, S., Maggard, D. L., & Torres, C. (2003, October). Preparing families for the hazards of police work. *Police Chief, 70*(10), 108–114.

VerHelst, R. A., Delprino, R. P., & O'Regan, J. (2001). *Law enforcement psychological services: A longitudinal study.* Paper presented at the annual convention of the American Psychological Association, San Francisco.

Volanti, J. (1996). *Police suicide: Epidemic in blue.* Springfield, IL: Charles C Thomas.

White, E. K., & Honig, A. L. (1995). The role of the police psychologist in training. In M. Kurke & E. M. Scrivner (Eds.), *Police psychology into the 21st century* (pp. 257–277). Hillsdale, NJ: Erlbaum.

CHAPTER 19

Polygraph ("Lie Detector") Testing: Current Status and Emerging Trends

WILLIAM G. IACONO and CHRISTOPHER J. PATRICK

POLYGRAPH OPERATORS, including those with scientific training, claim that polygraph tests have greater than 90% accuracy, that this claim is supported by the scientific literature, that their techniques are based on sound scientific principles, and that scientists agree with these claims (e.g., Honts, Raskin, & Kircher, 2002; Raskin & Honts, 2002). They further argue that these techniques have great evidentiary value and advocate using them in criminal and civil court proceedings as well as to screen out undesirable employees (e.g., Horvath, 1985, 1993). Despite many critical reviews of polygraph testing that forcefully challenge these assertions (e.g., Fiedler, Schmid, & Stahl, 2002; Iacono & Lykken, 2002; Oksol & O'Donohue, 2003; Saxe & Ben-Shakar, 1999), including a recent volume published by the National Research Council (NRC; 2003) of the National Academy of Sciences, polygraph testing continues to be strongly promoted by the polygraph profession and the U.S. government. Against this backdrop of controversy, we critically examine the current state of polygraph testing as well as future possible applications of deception detection techniques.

APPLICATIONS

Conventional polygraph tests are typically used when the question at hand cannot be easily resolved by the available evidence. When the investigation reaches an evidentiary dead end, police may rely on a polygraph test of a known suspect as the means of last resort to resolve the case. Sometimes those who fail these tests, pressured to own up to their misdeeds, confess, thereby providing the police with incriminating evidence they otherwise would not have. In the absence of a confession, a failed test may lead the police to cease the investigation, believing the suspect at hand is guilty even if the evidence is insufficient for successful prosecution. By contrast, a passed test provides incentive to continue the investigation and look for new suspects.

Polygraph tests are used by psychologists in sex offender treatment programs to ensure that offenders are fully disclosing their offenses and fantasies; by insurance agencies to verify the claims of those insured; in family court to help resolve charges of misbehavior parents level at each other in their effort to obtain custody of their children; by the police to verify victims' charges; by controversial people in the public eye, such as Jeffrey Skilling, former Enron Corporation CEO charged with fraud and insider trading, who wish to sway public opinion in their favor by advertising the fact that they passed a "lie detector" test; by the government to protect national security by requiring those with access to classified information, such as Los Alamos nuclear scientist Wen Ho Lee, to pass tests confirming that they are not spies; and even by those running fishing contests to verify that winners actually followed contest rules rather than purchasing their lunker from the local supermarket.

The Employee Polygraph Protection Act (EPPA) of 1988 (Public Law 100-347) eliminated much of the most widespread application of polygraph testing, the periodic screening of employees to verify their good behavior and the preemployment screening of potential hires to see if they possess the qualities desired by the employer. Ironically, the government exempted itself from coverage by this law, and in fact has been expanding polygraph testing programs in light of concerns about terrorism and national security. For instance, since the passage of EPPA, Public Law 106-65, passed as part of the National Defense Authorization Act of 2000, requires scientists at nuclear weapons laboratories to submit to polygraph tests to maintain their security clearance. In addition, the FBI introduced a preemployment polygraph screening program in 1994 and has administered approximately 27,000 tests through 2001 (NRC, 2003, p. 62). Besides many state and local law enforcement agencies and polygraphers in private practice, there are over two dozen federal agencies that routinely use polygraph tests, including those that are part of the Departments of Defense, Energy, Homeland Security, Justice, and Treasury.

THE POLYGRAPH AND THE POLYGRAPHER

Traditional polygraphs are briefcase-size instruments that use moving chart paper to record the autonomic responses elicited by the subject's answers to test questions. Although these devices are still in widespread use, portable computers that digitally record autonomic activity, displaying and storing it in a manner that mimics the appearance of paper chart recordings, are now in common use. Expandable pneumatic belts positioned around the upper thorax and abdomen provide two separate recordings of the chest movements associated with inspiration and expiration. Changes in palmar sweating (the galvanic skin response, or GSR) are detected by electrodes attached to the fingertips. For the "cardio" channel, a partly inflated blood pressure cuff attached to the arm reflects relative changes in blood pressure and provides an index of pulse. Occasionally, a fifth channel monitoring blood flow to the fingertip is included. Although this instrumentation is relatively simple, it produces records of physiological reactivity that are comparable to those obtained by sophisticated laboratory equipment (Patrick & Iacono, 1991a).

Training in polygraphy is provided by free-standing polygraph schools, most of which are accredited by the American Polygraph Association. The most prestigious of these is at the Department of Defense Polygraph Institute (DoDPI; formerly the U.S. Army Military Police School) located at Fort Jackson, South Carolina. This school offers a one-semester, intensive, hands-on course in polygraphy that covers the various techniques and interview practices employed by examiners. DoDPI also has an in-house research program staffed by doctoral-level psychologists, some of whom share in the teaching of students with polygraph examiners and law enforcement agents. Graduates of the program are typically apprenticed to practicing examiners before becoming fully certified to administer tests on their own. DoDPI offers training for many state and city police departments and most federal government agencies, including the military police, the FBI, the IRS, and all of the government security agencies (except the CIA, which trains its own examiners). DoDPI represents the best training the profession of polygraphy has to offer. Most accredited schools do not offer as rigorous a program as DoDPI; not all practicing polygraph examiners are graduates of approved schools; and because polygraphy is not regulated in most states, polygraphers are not necessarily licensed to practice their trade.

POLYGRAPH TECHNIQUES

The polygraph instrument is not capable of detecting lies, and there is no pattern of physiological response that is unique to lying. Consequently, all polygraph techniques involve asking different types of questions, with differential responding to those pertinent to the issue at hand determining outcome. The techniques, all of which have multiple variants, fall into two categories involving either specific incident or personnel screening applications.

SPECIFIC INCIDENT INVESTIGATIONS

There are three types of specific incident investigations: the control question test (now often called the comparison question test), an offshoot of this procedure called the directed lie technique, and the guilty knowledge test (also called the concealed information test). Each technique has its own distinctive format and is based on different types of psychological assumptions.

The Control Question Technique

The so-called control or comparison question technique (CQT) remains the procedure of choice among polygraphers who conduct specific incident investigations like those concerned with known criminal acts. The CQT typically consists of about 10 questions. The two types of questions that are important to the determination of guilt or innocence are referred to as relevant and control questions. The relevant questions deal directly with the incident under investigation (e.g., Did you shoot Bill Birditsman on the night of March 18?). Control items cover past behaviors that one might associate with "the kind of person" who is capable of killing (e.g., Before the age of 24 did you ever deliberately hurt someone you were close to?). It is assumed that guilty suspects will be more concerned with the relevant than with the control questions. The reverse pattern is expected with innocent people.

The typical CQT has three parts: (1) a pretest interview (lasting from about 30 minutes to perhaps 2 hours in some cases) during which the question list is formulated; (2) the presentation of the question list (usually repeated three times, with the question order varied for each of the three charts) while physiological responses are recorded; and (3) a posttest interrogation.

The pretest phase of the CQT is critical to the successful administration of the test. It is during this interview that the polygrapher creates the circumstances that lead the innocent person to be more disturbed by the possibly trivial issues raised by the control items than by the relevant questions that have to do with the matter under investigation. A common criticism of the CQT is that it is biased against truthful persons because the relevant questions may be just as arousing to innocent suspects, who may view their freedom or livelihood as dependent on their physiological response to these items, as they are to the guilty (Lykken, 1974). To reduce the likelihood of this occurrence, polygraphers use the pretest interview to focus the subject's "psychological set" on the control questions if the examinee is innocent or on the relevant questions if he or she is guilty.

Two tactics are used to accomplish this objective. The first is to convince the subject that lies will be detected. One way to achieve this goal is to demonstrate that the polygraph can detect a known lie. In a typical scenario, the examiner connects the subject to the polygraph and says, "I'm going to ask you to pick a number from 1 to 10, write it down, and then show it to me. Both of us will know which number you've picked. After that, I will say a number and ask you if it is yours. I want you to answer no to each number I say, including the one you picked." The polygrapher then records the subject's responses to each number and tells the subject afterward that his or her largest reaction occurred when he or she lied; if this was indeed the case, the examiner may point it out on the chart. If it was not the case, the examiner may say that it was anyway or mechanically alter the subject's response to the target number to create the impression that it elicited a clearly detectable reaction. Some achieve the desired result by having the subject pick a card from a stacked deck and then relying on the physiological record to "determine" which one he or she picked. Some variant of this type of demonstration procedure, often called a "stim" or "acquaintance" test, is used routinely by most polygraphers.

A second tactic for establishing the correct psychological set is to continually emphasize the importance of being truthful at all times. No distinction is made between the relevant and the control questions regarding the burden of truthfulness. Consequently, innocent individuals are led to believe that lying to control questions will lead to a failed test outcome. How it is that they should reach this conclusion is explained for a case of theft by one of polygraphy's leading proponents, David Raskin (1989, pp. 254–255), as follows:

"Since this is a matter of a theft, I need to ask you some general questions about yourself in order to assess your basic honesty and trustworthiness. I need to make sure that you have never done anything of a similar nature in the past and that you are not the type of person who would do something like stealing that ring and then would lie about it. . . . So if I ask you, 'Before the age of 23, did you ever lie to get out of trouble . . . ?' you could answer that no, couldn't you?" Most subjects initially answer no to the control questions. If the subject answers yes, the examiner asks for an explanation . . . [and] leads the subject to believe that admissions will cause the examiner to form the opinion that the subject is dishonest and therefore guilty. This discourages admissions and maximizes the likelihood that the negative answer is untruthful. However, the manner of introducing and explaining the control questions also causes the subject to believe that deceptive answers to them will result in strong physiological reactions during the test and will lead the examiner to conclude that the subject was deceptive with respect to the relevant issues concerning the theft. In fact, the converse is true. Stronger reactions to the control questions will be interpreted as indicating that the subject's denials to the relevant questions are truthful.

Charts are scored using one or a combination of three approaches. With global scoring, all the information available to the examiner is used to make the diagnosis. Hence, in addition to inspection of the physiological data, the plausibility of the subject's account of the facts, his or her demeanor during the examination, and information from the investigative file may all figure into the evaluation.

With numerical scoring, which is now favored by most polygraphers, the examiner derives a score from the physiological recordings. The magnitude of the response to pairs of control and relevant questions is estimated for each separate physiological channel. In the most commonly employed method, a score from +1 to +3 is assigned if the response to the control item is larger, with the magnitude of the score determined by how large a difference is observed. Likewise, a score from −1 to −3 is assigned if the relevant member of the question pair elicited the stronger response. A total score is obtained by summing these values over all channels and charts, with a negative score less than −5 prompting a deceptive verdict, a positive score exceeding +5 a truthful verdict, and scores between −5 and +5 considered inconclusive and therefore warranting further testing. In our experience with government examiners, about 10% of CQTs end with inconclusive outcomes.

Both global and numerical chart evaluation have high interscorer reliability. Studies in which examiners blind to case facts evaluate the original examiners' charts typically report reliabilities around .90 (e.g., Honts, 1996; Horvath, 1977; Patrick & Iacono, 1991a, 1991b). The retest reliability of polygraph testing has not been evaluated. The absence of such data is unfortunate because often questions about the possible increment in validity gained by retesting a defendant arise in legal proceedings.

The third approach to chart scoring derives from computerized recording systems. Typically, the computer provides a verdict in the form of a probability statement as to the likelihood that the person was truthful when responding to the questions. Because these systems are marketed commercially, the nature of the algorithms and data used to justify the probability statements is proprietary. Although computer scoring is reliable, little is known about the validity of the outputted probability statements, and few polygraphers rely exclusively on computer scoring of charts.

Directed Lie Technique

The directed lie technique (DLT) is often considered a subtype of the CQT. The chief difference lies in the nature of the control questions. For a DLT, the "probable lie" control questions of the CQT are replaced with "directed lie" questions. Directed lies are statements that the subject admits involve a lie before the test begins. In fact, the polygrapher specifically instructs the subject to answer the question deceptively and to think of a particular time when he or she has done whatever the directed lie question covers. Examples of directed lies are "Have you ever done something that hurt or upset someone?" and "Have you ever made even one mistake?" As with the CQT, guilty subjects are expected to respond more strongly to the relevant questions and innocent subjects should react more strongly to the directed lies.

Guilty Knowledge Test

An alternative to the CQT for specific incident investigations is the guilty knowledge test (GKT; Lykken, 1959, 1960), sometimes referred to as a concealed information or knowledge test. Rather than asking directly whether the examinee was responsible for the crime under investigation, the GKT probes for knowledge indicative of guilt: details regarding a crime or incident that only the person who did it would know about. The GKT consists of a series of questions about the crime posed in multiple-choice format. Each question asks about one specific detail of the crime and is followed by a series of alternative answers, including the correct answer as well as other plausible but incorrect options. The following is an example of a GKT question concerning one detail of a homicide: "If you were the one who beat Donna Fisbee to death, then you will know what was used to kill her. Was she beaten with (1) a brick? (2) a crowbar? (3) a pipe? (4) a baseball bat? (5) a hammer?" When presented with a question of this type, the true culprit would be expected to emit a larger physiological reaction to the correct alternative, whereas an innocent person, knowing nothing about the incident, would respond more or less at random.

The simple premise underlying the GKT is that a person will exhibit larger orienting reactions to key information only if he or she recognizes it as distinctive or important. The GKT tests for knowledge of information rather than for deceptiveness, and the irrelevant alternatives are true controls rather than pseudo-controls. In the CQT, deceptiveness is inferred from a pattern of enhanced reactions to relevant questions, but the possibility that "innocent concern" rather than deception is responsible for this outcome can never be ruled out. A pattern of consistent reactions to critical items on a GKT can (within a small, estimable probability) mean only that the examinee possesses guilty knowledge. On a GKT question with five alternative answers, the odds that an innocent person with no knowledge of the crime would react most intensely to the key (relevant) alternative are 1 in 5. On a GKT that included 10 such questions, the odds are vanishingly small (<1 in 10,000,000) that an innocent person would react differentially to the key alternative on each and every test question.

The first study of the GKT (Lykken, 1959) and most others conducted since have relied on peripheral response measures such as skin conductance to index recognition memory. More recently, EEG brain potentials have been used for this purpose.

PERSONNEL SCREENING

Modern screening tests differ from specific incident tests in that it is not known whether any particular transgression has taken place. Consequently, the relevant questions typically cover extended periods of time and many topics, leaving ambiguous what form an adequate control question should have. While there are many different types of screening tests, these procedures are historically linked to the relevant/irrelevant technique (RIT), a polygraphic interrogation method that preceded the development of the CQT and that was used originally in criminal investigations.

Relevant/Irrelevant Technique

In the original RIT, relevant questions (like those used on the CQT) were each preceded and followed by an irrelevant question (e.g., "Is your name Ralph?" or "Is today Tuesday?"). Consistently greater reactions to the relevant items of the test were interpreted as evidence of deceptiveness. However, because of the obvious confound posed by the differential potency of the two categories of questions, the traditional RIT has been roundly criticized and thus is only occasionally used in forensic investigations. However, for purposes of employment screening, polygraph examiners now commonly use a variant of the RIT procedure that might more appropriately be called the relevant/relevant technique because interpretation of test outcome depends on the pattern of responses across all of the relevant questions.

In contrast to specific incident tests, screening examinations contain relevant questions of the form "Have you ever . . . ?" or "During the period in question, did you . . . ?" These questions, which may tap themes related to drug use, trustworthiness, and rule violations, are alternated with innocuous or irrelevant questions (also called "norms"). Law enforcement and security agencies use these types of tests with both prospective and current employees. Although government secrecy makes it difficult to determine how these two types of subjects fare on these tests, it is clear that prospective employees are much more likely to fail such tests than those already screened, trained, and employed.

In a screening test of this type, three or more question sequences are typically presented covering the same topics, but with the form of the questions and their order varied. The irrelevant items are included mainly to provide a rest period or return to baseline rather than a norm for comparison purposes. The test can more accurately be characterized as a polygraph-assisted interview where the development of questions is guided both by the polygrapher's impressions of the examinee's truthfulness as well as the comparative reactions to the various relevant items: "The cardinal rule in chart interpretation is, any change from normal requires an explanation" (Ferguson, 1966, p. 161). If the subject shows persistently strong reactions to one or more content areas in relation to the rest, the examiner concludes that the subject lied or was particularly sensitive about these issues for some hidden reason. In this case, the examiner will probe the examinee for an explanation of what might have provoked these responses and will administer additional question sequences focusing on these specific issues. Examinees who are adept at explaining away their reactions are thus likely to avoid incrimination. Thurber (1981) reported that among applicants for a police training academy, those who scored highest on a questionnaire measure of impression management were most likely to pass a polygraph screening test.

National security organizations use both periodic and aperiodic screening tests. Periodic screening tests are conducted at regular intervals to determine whether existing employees have been honest in their work and whether they remain loyal to the agency. Aperiodic screenings are conducted less frequently and with minimal advance warning. Besides being more economical, this practice is thought to produce a more powerful deterrent to malfeasance. The knowledge that they may be asked to submit to a polygraph test at any time is believed to dissuade existing employees from engaging in misconduct. In effect, the polygraph establishes a climate of fear in which employees are presumably less inclined to be dishonest because they fear detection (NRC, 2003; Samuels, 1983).

Test for Espionage and Sabotage

In addition to RIT-derived tests, national security agencies have recently introduced a type of directed lie test called the Test for Espionage and Sabotage (TES), a procedure that has been used extensively with scientists at nuclear weapons laboratories. With the TES, questions such as "Have you given classified information to any unauthorized person?" are paired with directed lies such as "Did you ever violate a traffic law?" Unlike other types of screening tests, the TES can be scored using the same procedures followed for the CQT.

DETERMINING VALIDITY

There are hundreds of papers pertaining to the validity of polygraph testing. Much of this work is unpublished, and much that is published appears in poor quality or trade journals. Because there are so many studies that touch on the accuracy issue, and because much of the research conducted in this field is not carried out by scientists or published in scientific, peer-review journals, we preface our evaluation of the literature with a summary of the important methodological issues that a serious investigation of polygraph validity must address.

EVALUATION OF POLYGRAPH CHARTS

Although currently semi-objective numerical scoring is the preferred technique for chart evaluation among professional polygraphers, the global approach to chart interpretation is still used. For CQTs conducted using either procedure, the field examiner is exposed to extrapolygraphic cues, such as the case facts, the behavior of the suspect during the examination, and sometimes inculpatory admissions from the examinee. For a validity study to provide a meaningful estimate of the accuracy of the psychophysiological test, the original examiner's charts must be reinterpreted by blind evaluators who have no knowledge of the suspect or case facts. Even though those trained in numerical scoring are specifically taught to ignore extrapolygraphic cues, Patrick and Iacono (1991b), in their field study of Royal Canadian Mounted Police (RCMP) polygraph practices, showed that even these elite examiners nevertheless attend to them. In 21% of the 279 examinations investigated, the original examiners contradicted the conclusions dictated by their own numerical scores by offering written verdicts that were not supported by the charts. We also found that original examiner opinions were likely to be more accurate than their numerical scores, indicating that examiners improved their accuracy when they relied on case facts and other extraneous information. Although one may be tempted to use such data to argue that blind chart scoring underestimates the accuracy of polygraph verdicts (e.g., see Honts et al., 2002), the probative value of the CQT derives from the possibility that the psychophysiological measurements provide a scientifically valid method for detecting liars. No court of law would accept as evidence the opinion of a human "truth verifier," a skilled interviewer who can use the available evidence to reach a correct judgment. The fact that our RCMP data showed that the original examiner was more accurate when he overrode the charts speaks to the invalidity of the psychophysiological test when used to determine truthfulness.

FIELD VERSUS LABORATORY INVESTIGATIONS

Field studies, like our study with the RCMP, involve real-life cases and circumstances. The subjects are actual criminal suspects. Laboratory studies require naïve volunteers to simulate criminal behavior by enacting a mock crime. The latter approach provides unambiguous criteria for establishing ground truth but cannot be used to establish the accuracy of the procedure because the motivational and emotional concerns of the suspects are too dissimilar from those involved in real-life examinations. Unlike those faced with an actual criminal investigation, guilty subjects in the laboratory have little incentive to try to beat the test, and both guilty and innocent subjects have little to fear if they are diagnosed deceptive. Administering the CQT to laboratory subjects is especially likely to lead to overestimates of accuracy for the innocent. Innocent subjects can reasonably be expected to respond more strongly to the potentially embarrassing control questions concerning their personal integrity and honesty than to the relevant questions dealing with a simulated crime they carried out only to satisfy experimental requirements. On the other hand, laboratory research does permit efficient investigation of the influence of factors that may affect test outcome (e.g., effects of countermeasures or personality traits).

It is interesting that two laboratory studies that used mock circumstances designed to approximate some of those found in real life produced error rates that were different from the low rates reported in many studies. Patrick and Iacono (1989) used prison inmates who were led to believe that failing a CQT could possibly lead to reprisals from other inmates who were counting on them to appear innocent on their tests. Forman and McCauley (1986) had their participants choose to be either innocent or guilty, the latter choice leading to a larger monetary reward if they passed the CQT. In these two studies, the average accuracy for the CQT was 73%, considerably lower than the 88% reported for laboratory studies without such verisimilitude (Kircher, Horowitz, & Raskin, 1988). It is unlikely that any laboratory study will ever successfully simulate all the aspects of a real-life investigation. However, by illustrating that simple adjustments to study methods can produce profound shifts in hit rates, these reports point to the difficulty in relying on a typical mock crime study to estimate real-life accuracy.

Laboratory studies of the GKT are also likely to overestimate its accuracy, more so for guilty than innocent individuals. Well-designed laboratory experiments construct a scenario in which guilty participants must attend to details of the crime that the examiner expects perpetrators to know and that can be used to construct the GKT. In real life, a criminal may not attend to the aspects of a crime that an investigator views as salient, and many details may be forgotten. For example, there is evidence that psychopathic individuals are less able to process incidental details when focusing on a primary task (Kosson, 1996), and such individuals may thus be less detectable on a GKT (Lykken, 1955; Waid, Orne, & Wilson, 1979). On the other hand, if a person does remember the details of a real-life crime, he or she should evoke greater physiological reactions, thereby making it easier to detect the guilty.

Although the GKT is used in Israel and exclusively in Japan, there are two reasons it is seldom used in real-life investigations in North America. First, there is a prevailing belief among field examiners that the CQT is virtually infallible (Patrick & Iacono, 1991b). Thus, there is no need to develop an alternative procedure, especially one that is more complicated to administer than the CQT. Second, to construct a valid GKT, there must be salient details of the crime known only to the perpetrator. Not all crimes meet this criterion. For example, alleged sexual assaults in which the question of force versus consent is the only issue to be resolved by the polygraph test would not be amenable to a GKT. However, DNA and fingerprint evidence are not available or necessarily relevant for many crimes, but this has not diminished their evidentiary value for those crimes where such evidence exists.

The problems with laboratory studies dictate that real-life applications must be used to evaluate polygraph tests. Although the CQT has been subjected to field research, there are no field studies of personnel screening tests, and only two of the GKT, facts that limit efforts to evaluate these techniques.

PROBLEMS ESTABLISHING GROUND TRUTH

The advantage of field investigations, that they are based on actual crimes, is also a significant drawback because prima facie evidence of innocence or guilt is often lacking. Proponents of polygraphy have argued that confessions provide the best method for operationalizing ground truth. Confessions identify the culpable and clear the innocent. Although occasionally confessions are false, and those who confess may differ in important ways from those who do not, the major problem with this strategy concerns the likelihood that the confession is not independent of the original polygraph examiner's assessment. For reasons that are unrelated to test accuracy, confessions are associated almost exclusively with charts that indicate a deceptive outcome. When this occurs, the verified cases selected for a validity study will be biased in favor of demonstrating high accuracy for the technique.

To make this point clear, consider the following example. Ten women are suspects in a criminal investigation. A polygrapher tests them one by one until a deceptive outcome is obtained, say on the sixth suspect tested. (Under these circumstances, the remaining four women typically would not be tested unless the crime was believed to involve more than one perpetrator.) According to usual practice, the examiner then attempts to extract a confession from the sixth suspect. If the examinee fails to confess, her guilt or innocence cannot be confirmed. It is possible that the polygrapher committed two errors in testing these six cases: The person with the deceptive chart may have been innocent, and one of those tested before her could have been guilty. In the absence of confession-backed verification, however, the polygraph records from these six cases will never be included as part of a sample in a validity study. On the other hand, if the sixth suspect does confess, these six charts, all of which confirm the original examiner's assessment, will be included. The resulting sample of cases would consist entirely of charts the original examiner judged correctly and would never include cases in which an error was made. As Iacono (1991) has shown, if polygraph testing actually had no-better-than-chance accuracy, by basing validity studies on confession-verified charts selected in this manner, a study could misleadingly conclude that the technique was virtually infallible. Given how cases are selected in confession studies of validity, it should not be surprising that field validity studies typically report that the original examiner was 100% correct (or nearly so; see Honts et al., 2002) for the cases chosen for study. The case selection method assures this result.

Polygraph proponents have asserted that, because it is the original examiners who testify in court, it is the accuracy of the original examiners in these field confession studies that constitutes "the true figure of merit" to determine how accurate polygraph tests would be in legal proceedings (Honts et al., 2002). Despite the fact that the hit rate of the original examiner in these studies is entirely misleading given how cases are selected for study inclusion, this argument also ignores the contribution of extrapolygraph information to the original examiner's opinion and the resulting necessity of blind chart scoring to determine how useful the psychophysiological data are for deciding guilt.

OBTAINING INDEPENDENT EVIDENCE OF GUILT AND INNOCENCE

Although confessions that follow a failed polygraph cannot be used for verification because they are confounded with test outcome, confessions that arise outside the context of the polygraph examination do not suffer from this problem and could be used to establish ground truth. Iacono and Lykken (2002; Iacono, 1998) have outlined how a field study of CQT validity could be executed that would accomplish this result. To eliminate the contamination that arises when confessions are used to establish ground truth, all willing criminal suspects brought in for questioning would take a CQT, but there would be no posttest interrogation, chart scoring, or communication of test results to anyone. The charts would be sealed and stored awaiting resolution of the case. At the time a case was to be closed, an independent panel would review the available evidence to see if it could be used to verify the issues covered by the CQT relevant questions presented to suspects. In this manner, the ground truth criterion, which could still be confession-based (because now whatever confession arose would have been independent of the results of the sealed polygraph exam), would be obtained independently of the outcome of the CQT. The polygraph charts from those cases where the panel was unanimous in its determination of who was guilty and innocent (cases where the confession was retracted, contradicted by other evidence, or was otherwise unconvincing could be discarded by the panel) would then be scored blindly and compared with the criterion judgments. As long as no study such as this exists, it will not be possible to determine the field accuracy of any polygraph technique.

WHAT CAN BE CONCLUDED ABOUT POLYGRAPH VALIDITY?

The degree to which different types of polygraph examinations have been evaluated in the scientific literature varies considerably across techniques. Unfortunately, none of the techniques has received the type of thorough evaluation one would hope given that polygraph test outcomes may have major life-altering effects on examinees.

CONTROL QUESTION TECHNIQUE

The literature relevant to the validity of CQT polygraph testing has been reviewed repeatedly, including in the two prior editions of this *Handbook* (Iacono & Patrick, 1987, 1999) as well as in more recent publications (Ben-Shakar, 2002; Honts et al., 2002; Iacono, 2000; Iacono & Lykken, 2002; NRC, 2003). Because only one study to date has tackled directly the confession-bias problem that characterizes field research (Patrick & Iacono, 1991b), we focus on the results of that investigation here. In this RCMP field study involving over 400 cases, we attempted to circumvent the confession-bias confound by reviewing police files for evidence of ground truth that was collected outside of the context of the polygraph examination (e.g., a confession by someone who did not take a polygraph test, a statement that no crime was committed because items believed stolen were actually misplaced). Independent evidence of ground truth was uncovered for 1 criterion-guilty and 24 criterion-innocent suspects. The fact that it was easier to come by independent evidence of the innocence rather than the guilt of someone taking a CQT stemmed from how the police use polygraph tests to assist their investigations. Polygraph tests are typically administered in cases where the evidence is ambiguous and the police have exhaustively explored available leads to no avail. When a case reaches this point, the investigating officer is hoping that polygraph testing will help close out the case. Ideally, the suspect will fail and confess, thus giving the investigating officer incriminating evidence that can be used to prosecute the suspect. However, if the suspect merely fails, with no new evidentiary leads to follow, the case is effectively closed, with the police concluding that the individual who failed is guilty. On the other hand, if the suspect passes, the case is often left open, and the search for new suspects and evidence continues.

For those independently confirmed as innocent, the blind rescoring of their polygraph charts produced a hit rate of 57%. Because chance accuracy is 50%, this result indicates that the CQT has little better than chance accuracy with the innocent. It also indicates that innocent people are indeed often more disturbed by relevant than control questions. Because only one criterion-guilty person was identified in this investigation, it was not possible to estimate the accuracy of the CQT with persons independently confirmed as guilty.

Although there are no scientifically credible data regarding the accuracy of the CQT with guilty people, there is reason to doubt the validity of truthful polygraph verdicts. Honts, Raskin, and Kircher (1994) showed that with less than a half-hour of instruction on CQT theory and how to recognize control and relevant questions, guilty subjects in a mock crime study could learn to escape detection by augmenting their autonomic responses to control questions. They were able to do this using both physical and mental countermeasures, such as biting the tongue or subtracting 7 serially from a number over 200 when the control question was asked. Moreover, experienced examiners were unable to identify those subjects who employed countermeasures successfully. The information contained in the instructions given to those escaping detection in this study is widely available in various publications (including in Honts et al., 1994, as well as Lykken, 1998) and on the Web (e.g., antipolygraph.org), making it relatively easy for those so motivated to learn both how the CQT works and how to augment responses to control questions. Subsequent studies by Honts and colleagues (reviewed in Honts & Amato, 2002) have explored how easy it is for naïve volunteers to determine on their own how to use countermeasures, and have concluded that uninformed individuals resort to countermeasure strategies that are often ineffective. However, in these studies, the guilty volunteers are typically given little incentive to use countermeasures effectively, thus leaving their generalizability to real-life settings questionable.

The Directed Lie Technique

Little is known about the validity of the directed lie technique (DLT). Although one field study involving the DLT has been published (Honts & Raskin, 1988), this study was also subject to the confession-bias problem. In addition, only a single directed lie question was used, and this question was embedded in a conventional CQT, making it difficult to determine how the test would have fared had directed lie controls been used exclusively. The DLT appears especially susceptible to countermeasures. When the examiner introduces the directed lies to the subject, they are explained as questions designed to elicit a response pattern indicative of lying. Hence, their purpose is made transparent to subjects who may understand that a strong response to these questions will help them pass the test. In addition, the examiner has no idea what issues are covered by the directed lies and how strong an emotional response they are capable of eliciting. For instance, if the directed lie was "Have you ever done something that you later regretted?" and the subject had an abortion or killed someone in a drunk driving incident, might not the emotions elicited by the directed lie elicit stronger autonomic responses than the material covered by a relevant question related to theft or fraud?

GUILTY KNOWLEDGE TEST

Of the three classes of polygraph tests considered in this review, only the guilty knowledge test (GKT) is spurned by practicing polygraphers. Because of this, there is little data available from real-life GKT applications that can be used to evaluate validity. There are many laboratory simulations of the GKT, and Lykken (1998, pp. 288–290) has outlined the criteria that define a well-conceived GKT and reviewed studies that use GKTs meeting these criteria. For instance, Lykken noted that a good test might have 10 items, each with five alternatives, and the person taking the test would be asked to repeat each alternative rather than merely responding no to each to ensure that he or she was paying attention. The alternatives for each item should be distinctly different from each other so the examinee can readily recognize the guilty alternative. Lykken's review of eight studies with well-constructed GKTs found accuracy rates of 88% and 97% for guilty and innocent study subjects, respectively.

A meta-analysis of 22 studies by MacLaren (2001) that used less selective criteria for study inclusion reported somewhat lower accuracies (76% for guilty and 83% for innocent subjects). In a comprehensive meta-analytic review, Ben-Shakar and Elaad (2003) examined 80 studies and included moderator analyses that pointed to several factors that enhanced validity. Studies that used mock crime simulations, motivational incentives to succeed, verbal responses to item alternatives, and five or more questions produced better hit rates than those without these features. These authors concluded that "the GKT may turn out to be one of the most valid applications [of a test based on] psychological principles" (p. 145). Another study by Ben-Shakar and Elaad (2002) showed that a GKT composed of many different questions has better detection efficiency than a test of identical length composed of a few or several questions. This finding is important because in field applications, it is often difficult to develop questions, so it is easier to generate a test composed of one or a few items presented repeatedly than a test composed of many different items.

Because the test is virtually never used in North America, no field studies of the GKT have yet been conducted here. However, the GKT is routinely used in Japan (Nakayama, 2002), and two studies have been reported by investigators in Israel. Elaad (1990) and Elaad, Ginton, and Jungman (1992) examined the GKT records of 178 criminal suspects, tested by examiners from the Israel Police Scientific Interrogation Unit, whose criterion status had been established via confession. In all but one instance, the GKT was administered following a

CQT and included from one to six questions repeated from 2 to 4 times. Using blind chart evaluation and predefined score classification criteria (cf. Lykken, 1959) and excluding inconclusive outcomes, innocent examinees were identified with high accuracy (error rate 2% to 3%). Guilty people were less accurately identified, with hit rates varying from 42% to 75% depending on the choice of scoring criteria.

Consistent with a substantial body of laboratory research, the results of these two studies indicate that the guilty knowledge test is highly accurate with innocent suspects. These data also suggest that the GKT may have a substantial false-negative error rate in real-life cases. However, there are several limitations to these studies that constrain the conclusions that can be drawn, some of which have been acknowledged by Elaad in subsequent papers (Ben-Shakar & Elaad, 2002, 2003). The GKTs in these studies contained an average of only two questions. This compromises test sensitivity by lowering the odds that information uniquely salient to the perpetrator would be represented on the test. A further problem is that the GKTs in these field studies followed a full-length CQT. The physiological response habituation resulting from repeated presentations of the accusatory relevant and control questions on the initial test would almost certainly have the effect of diminishing response differentiation between critical and noncritical GKT items among guilty examinees (see, e.g., O'Toole, Yuille, Patrick, & Iacono, 1994). In addition, the GKT question sets in the Elaad et al. (1992) studies were presented repeatedly to examinees (i.e., an average of 3 times), and item repetition has been shown to diminish accuracy (Ben-Shakar & Elaad, 2002).

PERSONNEL SCREENING

Because almost everyone recognizes that the RIT is biased against the innocent (e.g., Horowitz, Kircher, Honts, & Raskin, 1997), it has been replaced by the CQT for specific incident investigations. However, RIT variants and the TES are nevertheless commonly used with government employees despite their lack of empirical foundation.

Although personnel screening tests that require responses of consistently similar magnitude across many relevant questions to identify truthfulness may appear more credible than the traditional RIT, their premises and implementation have also been challenged. Heightened reactions to certain specific questions may occur for reasons other than deceptiveness due to, for example, indignation about being asked that question, exposure to some related issue through the media, or knowledge of someone else who has engaged in the sort of activity covered by that question. Moreover, there is no reason to assume that enhanced reactions to an evocative question will subside once the examinee has offered an explanation for those enhanced reactions to the examiner. In fact, the CQT rests on the opposing (also unproven) assumption that truthful subjects will remain worried about control questions even after these items have been modified to accommodate their admissions. These criticisms give rise to the concern that personnel screening is likely to be associated with a high false-positive error rate. In fact, however, as applied by government agents, the false-negative error rate seems to be a much more substantial concern because out of the thousands of personnel screening tests given every year, only a handful of individuals fail (NRC, 2003).

Research conducted at DoDPI offers some insight into why few individuals fail polygraph screening tests. In their unpublished government report, Barland, Honts, and Barger (1989) described the results of a large analogue study that was designed to assess the validity of periodic espionage screening tests administered by experienced government examiners from multiple federal government agencies. The 207 study participants were government military and civilian employees. "Guilty" subjects went through complex simulations in which they met with an agent purportedly engaged in espionage who recruited them to collaborate in this activity. Consequent to their recruitment, these "spies" committed acts of mock espionage in which they copied or stole classified documents—that is, activities that periodic screening tests were designed to detect.

The results of this study indicated a high rate of correct classification for innocent participants (94%), but a low hit rate for guilty participants (34%). The high false-negative rate could be related to several factors, but the most likely is related to the fact that the examiners in this study, who were unaware of the base rate of guilt (about 50%), were following the established field practice of passing most everyone who took the test. Because periodic screening in real life is in a sense a fishing expedition in which the base rate of spying is presumably negligible, and because examiners are likely to be discouraged from falsely accusing innocent people, many of whom are high-ranking, well-educated, and trained government officials with many years of government service, testing and decision-making practices in the screening context are likely to be biased toward finding few examinees deceptive (Barland et al., 1989; Honts, 1994).

This prediction is borne out in real-life applications of security screening tests. The most recent statistics available from the U.S. Department of Defense (DoD; 2002) indicate that of about 11,500 tests administered by DoD, approximately 74% (8,245) were security screening tests, 97% of which were passed. Of the remaining 3% (267), 247 failed or made admissions relevant to the issues raised on their tests and had a "favorable adjudication," signifying that they could explain their failures in a manner that led the relevant issues to be "resolved favorably to the individual." All of the remaining 20 cases were still under investigation. These data, which are not unlike those reported in past years by DoD, tell us nothing about either the true-negative or false-negative rates of this testing program, leaving unanswered how often employees who are serious security risks pass these tests. In addition, given the small number of positive outcomes and the absence of even one case of an individual who both failed the polygraph test and was adjudicated unfavorably, it is not clear that this testing program identifies true positives of any significance.

Apparently in part because of findings like these, the TES was developed and subjected to two laboratory studies (U.S. Department of Defense, Polygraph Institute, Research Division Staff, 1997, 1998) that reported relatively low rates of both false-positive (12.5%) and false-negative (17%) errors. As noted previously, classification rates observed in analogue studies cannot be expected to generalize to the field, where one could expect many innocent government employees with top secret security clearances to be more bothered by loyalty-challenging questions about espionage and sabotage than by directed lie questions about traffic violations. Moreover, because even a 12.5% false-positive rate among highly trained weapons lab scientists would wreak havoc on the ability of the United States to carry out its nuclear weapons program, field examiners adjust the threshold for failing the TES so that virtually no one fails. The National Research Council (2003) analysis of the TES, which included additional unpublished government studies not available to the public, reached the conclusion that "these studies do not provide strong evidence for the validity or utility of polygraph screening" (p. 133).

The National Research Council's Conclusion Regarding Lie Detection Accuracy

As noted in the introduction to this chapter, a recent report from the National Academy of Sciences provides a comprehensive review of the evidence for polygraph test accuracy (NRC, 2003). This review, which was requested by the Department of Energy, was launched in part because of concerns regarding the desirability of expanding the government's personnel screening program to include scientists working in the Department of Energy's weapons laboratories. However, the review covered polygraph testing in its entirety, focusing on specific incident polygraph tests because, as we have noted, there are no scientifically peer-reviewed, published studies on the validity of screening tests. The review was carried out by a panel of 14 distinguished scientists, with no connection to polygraphy, who represented a variety of disciplines and types of scientific expertise. Many of the conclusions of this committee are presented in our section "Scientific Opinion." Here, however, we consider how this panel evaluated validity.

The panel did not attempt to estimate precisely polygraph accuracy, nor did they distinguish among types of tests (e.g., CQT versus GKT) or how hit rates may vary for guilty and innocent subjects. Instead they identified a set of 57 specific incident studies that met "minimal criteria" (NRC, 2003, p. 107) for consideration, noting that the selected studies "do not generally reach the high levels of research quality desired in science" (p. 108). Using the data from these studies, they plotted receiver operating curves (ROC), thus borrowing a method from signal detection theory. The primary statistic derived from this analysis was an "accuracy index" (A) corresponding to the area under the ROC curve. A takes on a value between .5 and 1.00, and though similar to percentage correct, does not translate directly to the types of percentage estimates reported in the studies analyzed or to those typically reported in reviews of this literature, in part because the ROC analysis takes into account inconclusive outcomes as well as the differences across studies in the rules followed to determine how the outcome of a polygraph test was classified. Because none of the analyzed studies showed the polygraph to have accuracy at or below chance and these studies indicate well below perfect accuracy, the panel concluded that for naïve examinees untrained in countermeasures, specific incident polygraph tests have hit rates "well above chance, though well below perfection" (p. 214).

BRAIN-BASED METHODS FOR DETECTING DECEPTION

A growing area of interest concerns alternatives to conventional polygraph techniques, including reliance on thermal and functional magnetic resonance imaging. However, the most promising line of inquiry has focused on components of the brain event-related potential (ERP), in particular the P300 component, a positive voltage wave that occurs about 300 ms after presentation of significant, infrequent stimuli (so-called oddball stimuli; Donchin, 1981). In *Harrington v. State of Iowa* (2001), an ERP-based GKT was admitted as evidence in the appeal of Terry Harrington, a man who consistently maintained his innocence despite being convicted of murder more than 20 years earlier. Using the procedures similar to those outlined in Farwell and Donchin (1991), Harrington was found to have passed an ERP-GKT related to his knowledge of the crime scene by showing no brain recognition (P300) response to stimuli involving crime details that were identified by Farwell. In addition, Harrington showed a brain recognition response to stimuli involving his alleged alibi that were developed independently by Farwell without the knowledge or participation of Harrington. Harrington's conviction was ultimately overturned. The momentum gained from the national attention this case received has stimulated interest in this application, leading to a U.S. General Accounting Office (GAO; 2001) review of "brain fingerprinting," the catchphrase adopted by Farwell to describe the ERP-GKT. In addition, Farwell has formed a company that is pushing the development of this technology for more routine forensic applications and reportedly has a waiting list of hundreds of cases involving convicted felons. Early in 2004, Oklahoma death row inmate Jimmy Ray Slaughter passed Farwell's test, a fact that was prominently featured by the media as Slaughter's appeal was pending before the U.S. Supreme Court. Against this backdrop of mounting interest, and because memory-based measures derived from brain electrocortical activity have a strong scientific foundation, we devote special attention to them in this section.

In a P300-based GKT procedure, the crime-relevant keys constitute the rare, meaningful stimuli. When interspersed with the crime-irrelevant multiple-choice alternatives, none of these key alternatives appears odd to the person without guilty knowledge, so they elicit minimal P300 response. For the guilty person, the crime-relevant keys are far fewer in number than irrelevant alternatives and are recognized as special, and thus they elicit enhanced P300 reactions.

The first documented report of a GKT study involving brainwave measurement was a conference abstract by Farwell and Donchin (1986), which described the use of a P300-based "brain detector." Participants (4 guilty, 4 innocent) viewed a series of stimuli consisting of crime-irrelevant nontargets (two-thirds of trials) interspersed with crime-relevant "probes" and crime-irrelevant targets (one-sixth each). Participants were instructed to count the crime-irrelevant targets and ignore all other stimuli in the series. P300 responses to the three categories of stimuli were compared. The hypothesis was that responses to crime-relevant probes and irrelevant stimuli would not differ for innocent individuals, but that participants with guilty knowledge would show enhanced reactions to the probes, akin to those for the target stimuli. This hypothesis was supported: Farwell and Donchin reported that "The Brain Detector was 100% accurate in detecting both 'guilty knowledge' and lack of same" (p. 434), although the criteria for classifying participants were not specified.

The first regular article reporting use of P300 in the detection of guilty knowledge was by Rosenfeld, Nasman, Whalen, Cantwell, and Mazzeri (1987). In this study, participants were shown a box containing nine items (e.g., camera, film, coins) and were asked to identify the item they would most want to keep. Each then wrote a 100-word essay describing reasons for this specific choice. Afterward, participants viewed a series of words on a monitor, each repeated several times, with instructions to attend carefully to all words. For "guilty" participants ($n = 10$), one of the words (the key) corresponded to the chosen item, with the rest consisting of words for novel items of commensurate value (e.g., radio, cassette, medal). For "innocent" participants ($n = 6$), all of the words consisted of labels for novel items; one of these was arbitrarily designated the key. Statistical analysis of ERP amplitude within 400 to 700 ms window following word onset revealed significantly larger P300 for the key versus the irrelevant words in the guilty group; statistics were not presented for the innocent group. A practical limitation of this study was that no criteria were presented for classifying individuals as guilty versus innocent. Nevertheless, based on a visual inspection of the waveforms for each individual, the authors concluded that all but one of the guilty participants showed distinct P300 differentiation between key and irrelevant words.

A further limitation of this study was that participants were explicitly instructed to attempt deception by thinking "no" whenever the key word appeared, which may have contributed to enhanced P300 responses. This feature of the procedure also limits external validity, insofar as real-life guilty suspects could not reasonably be expected to comply with such an instruction. Rosenfeld et al. (1988) addressed this issue with a revised protocol in which attention to test words was ensured by instructing participants to look for and count occurrences of one of the novel irrelevant words whenever it appeared on the screen. Results paralleled those of the initial study. Participants in the guilty group ($n = 7$) showed significantly larger P300 responses to the key nontarget word than to irrelevant nontarget words, and for all individuals, responses to the key word exceeded those to irrelevant nontargets (i.e., in no case did amplitude of response to the 7 irrelevant nontargets exceed 75% of the amplitude for the key word). A procedural limitation in terms of realism was that participants, as in Rosenfeld et al. (1987), were required to compose an essay regarding the chosen item prior to testing. Other limitations were: (1) Statistics were not presented for innocent participants ($n = 5$), (2) no quantitative criteria were provided for categorizing participants as guilty versus innocent based on their test responses, and (3) data from 3 additional guilty participants were excluded from the report due to excessive eye movements or P300 nonresponding.

A third published article on the use of P300 to detect guilty knowledge was by Farwell and Donchin (1991). The two experiments described in this report were innovative in several respects. First, the crime scenarios were quite realistic. In Experiment 1, participants underwent one of two espionage role plays involving the exchange of information with a foreign agent, in which they were exposed to six critical details included as probes on the guilty knowledge test. In Experiment 2, participants were tested about details of minor offenses they had committed in real life. In both experiments, guilt versus innocence was manipulated within subjects (i.e., in Experiment 1, each individual was tested concerning details of the role play in which he or she participated [guilty condition], as well as the other scenario [innocent condition]; in Experiment 2, each participant was tested regarding the offense he or she had committed [guilty], along with details of another offense committed by a different study participant [innocent]). Another notable feature of these experiments was that the GKT protocol, which paralleled that described by Farwell and Donchin (1986), required participants to respond to all test stimuli: Irrelevant targets (one-sixth of trials) prompted a left button press, irrelevant nontargets (two-thirds of trials) and crime-relevant nontargets (probes; one-sixth of trials) a right button press. This ensured that participants attended to all stimuli and classified them in a manner that optimized P300 responses.

A further innovation of this study was that it introduced a statistical criterion for classifying participants as innocent or guilty based on comparative P300 responses to irrelevant nontargets and crime-relevant probes. The technique, known as "bootstrapping" (Efron, 1979), yields an estimate of the sampling distribution for a parameter under circumstances of limited data, by randomly and iteratively sampling from available scores and computing values of the parameter for each subsample. In the Farwell and Donchin (1991) study, bootstrapping was used to estimate, for each individual participant, correlations between (1) the average P300 response to probes and the average response to irrelevant nontargets and (2) the average response to probes and the average to irrelevant targets. If the estimated correlation between probe and target values significantly exceeded that between probe and nontarget values, it was concluded that the participant had recognized the probes as rare and distinctive compared with nontargets, and that guilty knowledge was present. Conversely, if the correlation between values for probe and nontarget trials exceeded that between probe and target trials, it was concluded that guilty knowledge was not present.

Results were impressive. In Experiment 1, 18 of 20 participants were classified correctly in the guilty condition, with two cases inconclusive (i.e., the correlations did not differ significantly), and 17 of 20 were correctly classified in the innocent condition, with three inconclusives. In Experiment 2, all 4 participants were classified correctly in the guilty condition, and 3 of 4 were correctly classified in the innocent condition, with one inconclusive. Thus, in cases for which the bootstrap classification analysis yielded a conclusive outcome, 100% accuracy was achieved.

Nevertheless, there were some notable limitations in this study. Sample sizes were small, particularly in Experiment 2. The accuracy of the test in the guilty conditions was almost certainly enhanced by the fact that in both experiments, participants explicitly reviewed the crime-relevant details (probe items) prior to taking the test—in contrast to real life, where crime-relevant details are encoded ad hoc and unlikely to be rehearsed prior to testing. Also, no adverse consequences were contingent on test performance, as is typically true in real life. Although the presence of threat could augment reactions to critical items among suspects with guilty knowledge, it is also possible that high negative affect might impair memory retrieval and brain response differentiation. A further point is that a simple reaction time (RT) measure (i.e., latency to press the designated button following the stimulus) also differentiated clearly between criterion conditions in Experiment 1: Participants in the guilty condition showed reliably longer RTs to probes versus irrelevant nontargets, whereas in the innocent condition they did not. The authors dismissed RT as a viable index of guilt status on the grounds that it can easily be manipulated, but it remains to be determined empirically whether behavioral responses are more dissimulable than brain responses in this context—particularly in view of recent data indicating that simple countermeasures can be used to defeat a P300-based GKT (Rosenfeld, Soskins, Bosh, & Ryan, 2004; see later discussion) and that an RT-based GKT may be resistant to countermeasures (Seymour, Seifert, Shafto, & Mosmann, 2000).

A subsequent study was published by Allen, Iacono, and Danielson (1992). Although framed more as a study of memory than of deception, this study nonetheless employed a test protocol similar to that of Farwell and Donchin (1991) to assess for the presence of guilty knowledge. Findings were reported for three experiments involving a common protocol. Participants learned two lists of category words, one at the beginning of the experimental session (delayed list) and the other just prior to the P300-based memory test (immediate list), after completing a series of intervening tasks. In the memory test, participants pressed a *yes* button whenever they saw a word from the immediate category list (one-seventh of trials), and a *no* button whenever they saw a word from either the delayed list (one-seventh of trials) or from one of five non-learned category lists (five-sevenths of trials). Thus, on the test, participants had to inhibit a tendency to respond to previously learned words in the same way as words they had just learned. Recognition of words from the delayed list was predicted to yield enhanced P300 response in comparison with non-learned words.

A key feature of this study was that it relied on a novel statistical technique for classifying individual participants as knowledgeable or not with regard to specific word lists, a Bayesian classification strategy. This involved selecting various parameters of the ERP waveform that differentiated learned from unlearned words (e.g., P300 amplitude; area under the curve within 200 ms on either side of the P300 peak), and then using information about the discriminability of these parameters and the relative frequencies of learned and unlearned trials to compute a probability for each participant that an ERP average for a given word list reflected one or the other condition. The discrimination parameters and Bayesian classification algorithm were developed using data from 20 participants in Experiment 1 and then cross-validated on two new samples of 20 participants each in Experiments 2 and 3. Procedures were identical across experiments except that (1) instructions differed slightly in Experiments 2 and 3 (i.e., participants were told to press *yes* for words they had learned and *no* for words they had not, but to deliberately lie about words from the initial learned list by pressing the no button to these words); and (2) participants in Experiment 3 were promised $5 if they could control their brain responses so as to prevent detection of words they had lied about.

Using the Bayesian algorithm and cutpoints developed in Experiment 1, the sensitivities (probability of correctly classifying a learned list as learned; cf. true positive rate) in Experiments 2 and 3 were .925 and .95, respectively, compared with .95 in Experiment 1. The specificities (probability of correctly classifying an unlearned list as unlearned; cf. true negative rate) were .94 and .98, respectively, compared with .96 in Experiment 1. (In a reanalysis of data from this study, Allen & Iacono, 1997, found that the use of Farwell & Donchin's, 1991, bootstrapping method to classify lists as learned versus unlearned yielded no incorrect classifications; however, it yielded inconclusive results for learned lists in 13% of cases, and for unlearned lists in 28% of cases.) Allen et al. (1992) also examined the accuracy of classifications based on two indicators of behavioral response to words from each list (RT, response errors); sensitivities were .95 and .95 in Experiments 2 and 3, respectively, and specificities were .95 and .98 (versus .975 and 1.0, respectively, in Experiment 1). Thus, classification accuracies based on behavioral response indices were commensurate with those based on ERP parameters (cf. Farwell & Donchin, 1991). They were also in line with the findings of Seymour et al. (2000), who found that RTs to probe stimuli could be used to separate guilty from innocent individuals in an RT-based GKT, even when subjects were instructed to modify their responses to escape detection.

These results indicate that concealed information can be detected with very high accuracy in individual cases using a probabilistic analysis of ERP response parameters. Some limitations of the Allen et al. (1992) study should be noted vis-à-vis detection of deception in real-life cases. In particular, the word-learning task has limited external validity in a real-world crime situation. Simple category words are obviously very different from crime-relevant details. Also, as in other work cited, participants in this study explicitly learned the relevant words as opposed to encountering them incidentally in a dynamic real-world context. Furthermore, the Bayesian classification algorithm developed in Experiment 1 capitalized on information that may not readily be available in real-life cases, namely, the ground-truth status of previously learned lists. ERP parameters were selected in part because they discriminated words on these "concealed" lists from words on the unlearned lists. With real-world suspects, the status of information as concealed or not is normally indeterminate. Although a parallel algorithm could be developed using ERP data from real-life cases in which a solid ground-truth criterion (e.g., a corroborated confession, DNA evidence) became available after testing, the generalizability of this algorithm to cases different from those included in the development sample (e.g., in terms of type of crime, latency since commission, suspect characteristics) would be open to question. This is potentially an issue with any test procedure that involves empirically derived decision criteria based on multiple response parameters. With regard to these points, it should be reiterated that the Allen et al. study was framed as an investigation of memory rather than of deception. Nevertheless, issues such as these are important to consider in applying the findings of this study to the problem of detecting deception.

A number of additional papers on the topic of ERP and detection of deception have been published by Rosenfeld and colleagues. The majority of these, following Allen et al. (1992), have focused on P300 as an index of dissimulated ("malingered") amnesia for simple types of learned material such as words, numbers, and basic autobiographical facts rather than details of an enacted "crime" (Ellwanger, Rosenfeld, Hankin, & Sweet, 1999; Ellwanger, Rosenfeld, Sweet, & Bhat, 1996; Ellwanger, Tenhula, Rosenfeld, & Sweet, 2000; Miller, Rosenfeld, Soskins, & Jhee, 2002; Rosenfeld et al., 1999; Rosenfeld, Ellwanger, & Sweet, 1995; Rosenfeld, Rao, Soskins, & Miller, 2003; Rosenfeld et al., 1998; Rosenfeld, Sweet, Chuang, Ellwanger, & Song, 1996; Soskins, Rosenfeld, & Niendem, 2001; for reviews of this work, see Rosenfeld, 2002, and Rosenfeld & Ellwanger, 1999); other investigations of this type have also been published by Allen and colleagues (Allen, Iacono, Laravuso, & Dunn, 1995; Allen & Movius, 2000; van Hooff, Brunia, & Allen, 1996; for a review of this work, see Allen, 2002, and Allen & Iacono, 2001). However, a recent study by Rosenfeld et al. (2004) tested for guilty knowledge arising from participation in crime scenarios akin to those employed by Farwell and Donchin (1991). This report merits special consideration because it evaluated the impact of countermeasures on P300-based detection of deception in a design involving realistic crime conditions.

Data from two experiments were reported in Rosenfeld et al. (2004). Because procedures and results were similar, only the first is detailed here. Guilty participants ($n = 22$) participated in one of two mock crime scenarios (cf. Farwell & Donchin, 1991), one involving the theft of a ring from a desk drawer and the other involving the removal of an official university grade roster from its posted location. Innocent participants ($n = 11$) did not participate in either scenario. To ensure encoding of crime details, guilty participants rehearsed the instructions for their scenario several times and were required to pass a test pertaining to the critical details before undergoing the ERP-based GKT procedure. The test stimuli were a series of single words from various categories, some representing crime-relevant details (probes; 17% of trials) and others irrelevant category words, with some of these designated targets (17% of trials) and the remainder nontargets (66% of trials). As in Farwell and Donchin, participants were instructed to press one button whenever a target word appeared and a different button whenever a nontarget word (whether crime-relevant or -irrelevant) appeared. Half of the guilty participants received training in countermeasure use prior to the GKT, and the others did not. Countermeasures entailed specific covert responses (e.g., pressing a finger against a leg, wiggling a big toe, imagining being slapped) following the appearance of irrelevant nontarget words in order to enhance brain responses to these stimuli.

Two bootstrap techniques were used to classify participants as guilty or innocent on the basis of ERP responses. One of these involved comparing the estimated correlation between probe and target response with that between probe and nontarget response (cf. Farwell & Donchin, 1991). The other involved comparing the difference in mean amplitude of response to probes versus irrelevant nontargets for each individual participant against a distribution of difference scores formed by iterative resampling of the available data. (Differences were evaluated in terms of both base-to-peak and peak-to-peak amplitude, but only results for the more effective, peak-to-peak score analysis are presented here.) Within each analysis, participants were classified as innocent if a significant difference in the direction indicating guilt was not obtained. Using the correlation-difference method, 10 of 11 innocent participants were correctly classified, but only 6 of 11 participants in each of the simple-guilty and guilty-countermeasures groups were correctly classified. For the amplitude-difference method, 10 of 11 innocent participants and 8 of 11 simple-guilty participants were correctly classified, but only 2 of 11 guilty-countermeasures participants were correctly classified. In Experiment 2, hit rates for guilty-countermeasures participants were as follows: correlation difference method, 3/12; amplitude-difference method, 6/12.

Some interpretive difficulties are evident in this study. No inconclusive category was employed in classifications, making it difficult to compare the findings of this study with those of Farwell and Donchin (1991). This is a potentially important omission because countermeasures are likely to blur differences between the nontarget and other stimuli, rather than yielding similar P300s for nontarget stimuli and probes while preserving the nontarget/target difference in P300. In other words, the Farwell-Donchin method has a built-in validity check: Any given test that does not show sharp differentiation between the target and the nontargets is invalid (inconclusive); under these circumstances, it would be no surprise if the probes and nontargets produced misleading associations. Another issue is that the hit rate for simple-guilty participants based on the correlation-difference method (6/11 = 55%) was substantially lower than the rate for guilty participants in the Farwell and Donchin study: Even with inconclusives considered as incorrect, the hit rate across the two experiments in this earlier study was 22/24 = 91.7%. In any case, the results of the Rosenfeld et al. (2004) study raise concerns about the possibility that deliberate countermeasures might be used to beat an ERP-based GKT.

Two other ERP-based studies by Rosenfeld and colleagues warrant mention. One of these (Rosenfeld, Angell, Johnson, & Qian, 1991) examined the accuracy of P300 as an index of deception in a procedure analogous to the standard control question test. Rather than testing for knowledge of specific crime details, the test included "Did you do it?" questions pertaining to a specific offense under investigation, along with control questions pertaining to other accusations. Based on a complex, four-step classification algorithm, hit rates for guilty and innocent participants in this study were 92% and 86.6%, respectively. Another study (M. M. Johnson & Rosenfeld, 1992) employed a test procedure modeled after a preemployment screening examination. Brain responses were recorded to phrases describing various antisocial acts, presented one at a time on a computer monitor, interspersed with a target phrase to which participants responded with a button press. Upon completion of the test, ground truth was evaluated by having participants complete a checklist under ostensibly anonymous conditions, on which they indicated whether they had committed any of the antisocial acts listed in the ERP test. Hit rates for guilty and innocent participants, based on a three-step classification algorithm, were 100% and 76%, respectively. These results appear fairly impressive, yet these studies are subject to the same sorts of criticisms described earlier with regard to other laboratory investigations of the control question and employee screening tests.

A more recent study of the use of P300 in detection of deception that merits mention is one by Farwell and Smith (2001). This study focused on what the authors termed MERMERs ("memory and encoding related multifaceted electroencephalographic responses"), corresponding to various parameters of the ERP response to a test stimulus, including P300. Six participants were tested, 3 of them regarding known biographical details from their own lives and the other 3 regarding unfamiliar biographical details. Hit rates for both groups (guilty-informed, innocent-uninformed) were reported as 3/3 (100%). One serious limitation of this work from the standpoint of scientific evaluation is that the actual brain response (MERMER) criteria are not described in the published report because they are listed as patented, and thus proprietary. Other limitations include issues mentioned in relation to other studies of this kind (e.g., small samples, use of mock crime scenarios, unrealistic rehearsal of crime details prior to testing).

All of the studies on P300 and detection of deception described up to this point have been laboratory analogue investigations. We are aware of only one published field study of the oddball-P300 test protocol in detecting guilty knowledge among criminal suspects (Miyake, Mizutani, & Yamahura, 1993). The study involved the testing of 18 suspects (16 male) in real-life cases involving theft, cannabis possession, and attempted murder, using a 3-stimulus procedure (i.e., infrequent target, infrequent relevant nontarget, and frequent irrelevant nontarget) akin to that of Farwell and Donchin (1986, 1991). Stimuli were presented either visually (on a monitor; 8 cases), or acoustically (through headphones; 10 cases). Tests were ruled incomplete if excessive eye movement or blink contamination occurred in the EEG data. The acoustic presentation method yielded a much higher proportion of incomplete outcomes (4/10 = 40%) than the visual presentation method (1/8 = 12.5%). Although no criteria were reported for inconclusive decisions, outcomes of this sort were comparatively rare for either presentation modality (i.e., 1/10 and 1/8, respectively).

Excluding incomplete and inconclusive test outcomes, the authors reported 100% (5/5) correct classifications for suspects identified on the basis of later case facts as innocent, but only 50% (3/6) correct classification for suspects subsequently identified as guilty. Unfortunately, this sole field study contains numerous fundamental flaws that seriously undermine the credibility of its reported findings. Chief among these are (1) questionable criteria for ground truth (i.e., judicial verdicts were used in some cases rather than confessions); (2) target stimuli (a tone in the acoustic condition, a circle in the visual condition) that were so distinctively different from relevant items that examinees could easily have responded to targets while ignoring other stimuli; (3) failure to report ERP recording parameters, procedures for scoring ERP responses, and the method for comparing responses across stimulus conditions; and (4) criteria for classifying test results as truthful, deceptive, or inconclusive were not reported. In addition, various other elements of the report are unclear or inconsistent (e.g., the nature of irrelevant nontarget stimuli is unspecified; the types of crime details used as relevant nontargets are not clearly described; interstimulus intervals are reported inconsistently across different sections of the report). Although the weaknesses of this report prevent firm conclusions, this study nevertheless demonstrates the feasibility of utilizing P300-based detection in real-life criminal cases and evaluating the validity of this technique within the field. Credible research along these lines is clearly needed.

In addition to P300, there are other components of brain potential response that have been applied to the detection of deception. One is the N400 response that reliably occurs in response to semantic incongruity (i.e., words that complete a sentence in an unexpected fashion; Kutas & Hillyard, 1980). Boaz, Perry, Raney, Fischler, and Shuman (1991) developed an N400-based GKT procedure in which participants, after viewing either a tape of an enacted burglary or a noncrime control tape, were presented with crime-relevant phrases that concluded with either true or false endings. Hit rates in this study (73.2% overall in cross-validation samples) were markedly lower than in most P300-based GKT studies to date. More recently, Fang, Liu, and Shen (2003) explored the use of contingent negative variation (CNV) in detection of deception. The CNV is a slow negative shift in EEG potential that develops during anticipation of a target stimulus following presentation of a warning cue. Fang et al. examined CNV in a task in which participants were first presented with face stimuli, and then upon presentation of a follow-up signal indicated whether the face was familiar to them or not. These authors reported significantly enhanced CNV on trials in which participants prepared to enact a false response compared with trials on which they responded truthfully. The comparative promise of this method for detecting deception is difficult to evaluate because no effort was made to classify individual participants as truthful or deceptive on the basis of brain response. Nevertheless, these intriguing findings merit follow-up.

Two other recent trends in the use of brain response measures to detect deception are noteworthy. One consists of studies designed to link different components of the ERP to specific cognitive *processes* underlying deception (cf. Furedy, Davis, & Gurevich, 1988). For example, R. Johnson, Barnhardt, and Zhu (2003) reported evidence for two distinct components of the ERP connected with the act of deception, one reflecting inhibition of the prepotent (truthful) response and the other reflecting monitoring of past truthful and deceptive responses (see also R. Johnson, Barnhardt, & Zhu, in press). In contrast to prior ERP studies reviewed, the focus of this newer work is on gaining insights into the dynamics of neurocognitive processing associated with deception rather than on classifying individuals as truthful or deceptive based on ERP parameters that discriminate these conditions empirically.

A second, related development is the use of neuroimaging to identify brain regions associated with deception (Ganis, Kosslyn, Stose, Thompson, & Yurgelun-Todd, 2003; Langleben et al., 2002; Lee et al., 2002; Spence et al., 2001). These investigations all utilize the technique of functional magnetic resonance imaging (fMRI), in which changes in blood flow within specific regions of the brain are indexed by perturbations in a magnetic field surrounding the head. The focus of these experiments, like those of Johnson and colleagues, was on investigating underlying processes associated with deception (and affiliated brain regions) rather than on classifying participants as deceptive or truthful.

The first of these studies (Spence et al., 2001) reported enhanced activation in the ventrolateral prefrontal cortex (Brodmann area 47) bilaterally when participants lied about activities they had performed earlier in the day. This activation was interpreted as reflecting an inhibitory process associated with the effort to withhold the truth. Two subsequent studies reported increased activity in a wider array of brain regions (including frontal/prefrontal, parietal, and temporal cortices) when participants lied to critical items on a GKT (Langleben et al., 2002) or GKT-like memory test (Lee et al., 2002). The fourth and most recent study (Ganis et al., 2003) examined activations associated with two distinct parameters of a lie: (1) whether it is spontaneous or rehearsed and (2) whether it is isolated or part of a broader story the participant is telling. Well-rehearsed lies connected to a broader narrative evoked greater activation in right anterior frontal cortex than spontaneous isolated lies, whereas spontaneous isolated lies elicited greater activation in anterior cingulate and posterior visual cortices. Lies of both types evoked greater activation (versus truth telling) in right and left anterior prefrontal cortex and parahippocampal gyrus, right precuneus, and left cerebellum. The findings of this study indicate that different brain regions are recruited in the context of different forms of lying.

Thermal imaging has also been used to detect deception (Pavlidis, Eberhardt, & Levine, 2002). This method uses a high-speed motion picture camera sensitive to rapid changes in facial regional blood flow. In a mock crime study, after excluding 10 subjects without explanation (Knight, 2004), 6/8 guilty and 11/12 innocent subjects were correctly identified based on an undescribed "thermal signature," apparently involving changes in blood flow around the eyes, when they lied about stealing $20. This procedure is intriguing because it may be possible to use it without the subject's knowledge. However, considerably more research is needed to demonstrate that this technique is not vulnerable to many of the same criticisms leveled at conventional polygraph tests. In particular, in real life, it must be demonstrated that falsely accused innocent people do not show heightened facial blood flow when asked a threatening question they answer honestly.

One technique unlikely to be of any value in the detection of deception is voice stress analysis. Recent heightened concerns about security have led to an increase in interest in this technique, which involves analyzing a sample of human speech for effects presumed due to inaudible microtremors of the vocal muscles associated with the stress of lying. The advantage of voice stress analysis is that it can be used unknowingly with recorded or broadcast speech. The disadvantage is that despite 30 years of research, there is virtually no evidence for its scientific basis or that it accurately detects lying (NRC, 2003).

In summary, the use of brain response measurement in the analysis of deception has emerged as an exciting new area of investigation with many intriguing preliminary findings. Two features of this work are worth highlighting. One is that most brain-based studies of deception have utilized

GKT or GKT-like test procedures. The reason is that the GKT involves a clear-cut critical/noncritical item manipulation that provides for a well-controlled evaluation of memory, in contrast to traditional lie detection methods like the CQT and personnel screening tests. We anticipate that interest in field use of the GKT will grow as research of this kind continues to appear. A second point is that brain-based approaches hold great promise for elucidating neurocognitive processes underlying deception. Particularly exciting in this regard are the recent brain-imaging investigations noted earlier. Although the possibilities brain-based methods hold for enhancing classification accuracy in real-life examinations remain uncertain, this is clearly an important area of research with the potential to elucidate underlying mechanisms important to lying and deception. Insights gained from such work may provide a much-needed theoretical foundation for the development of scientifically sound methods of lie detection.

THE POLYGRAPH IN COURT

Although there is one instance of the outcome of an event-related potential GKT finding its way into court (*Harrington v. State of Iowa,* 2003), only the CQT and occasionally its cousin, the DLT, are typically considered for courtroom admission. This state of affairs reflects the fact that the CQT is by far the most common technique used by law enforcement agencies and the polygraph operators in private practice who were once employed by them.

THE ADMISSION OF POLYGRAPH TESTIMONY

Polygraph tests often find their way into criminal court through one of two routes. One involves the stipulated test in which polygraph examinations are administered with the prior agreement of prosecuting and defense attorneys. Often, the prosecution will agree to a stipulated test when the case against the defendant is weak. In these circumstances, if the suspect passes the test, the charges are dropped. If the test is failed, the prosecution reserves the right to submit the polygraph findings to the court. About half of U.S. states endorse the use of stipulated tests, but Canadian courts refuse them.

Another way that polygraph results may enter a courtroom is over the objection of the prosecution in cases where it can "advance the cause of the defense." This practice is allowed by law in New Mexico (although this law underwent review in 2004 by the New Mexico Supreme Court, which, as of this writing, had not made a ruling), provided the polygraph test administration satisfies certain standards. It is also a strategy increasingly adopted by defense attorneys who wish to determine if current circumstances favor the admission of polygraph tests that they have arranged for a client who subsequently passed. Often, a hearing is requested before a judge, who is asked to determine if polygraph tests satisfy standards for scientific evidence in light of new laws, recent rulings, and/or novel developments in the field (e.g., computerization) that may indicate polygraphy has been improved significantly since the last time the court considered admitting such evidence.

In 1923, in *Frye v. United States,* the U.S. Supreme Court established the rules for what constituted acceptable scientific evidence. In this case, James Frye was denied the opportunity to have considered as evidence the results of a polygraph test administered by psychologist William Marston, the "father" of modern polygraphy. Although the *Frye* ruling is no longer relevant to federal courts, it is still influential to the laws of many states that followed the *Frye* precedent of requiring "general acceptance" of a technique by the relevant scientific community before its results can be admitted as evidence. With the current federal criteria for scientific evidence, laid out in *Daubert v. Merrell Dow Pharmaceuticals* (1993), the general acceptance of a technique among scientists remains important along with other considerations, such as whether the technique is based on sound scientific principles and methods or has been the subject of scientific peer review. Hence, following motions submitted by defense attorneys, many courts hold hearings based on principles outlined in *Frye* or *Daubert* to determine if a defendant's passed polygraph test should be admitted as evidence (see Faigman, Kaye, Saks, & Sanders, 2002, for a more thorough review of the legal status of polygraph testing in the United States). Such hearings are likely to be influenced by *United States v. Scheffer* (1998). In this case, the Supreme Court ruled that defendants in military court martial proceedings do not have a right to admit as evidence the results of exculpatory polygraph tests, and the justices noted that there is no consensus in the scientific community that polygraph evidence is valid.

When a defense attorney arranges for a client to take a polygraph test, the results of the test are protected by attorney-client privilege. If the defendant fails the test, the results would not be divulged, because doing so would only serve to undermine the defendant's credibility. A test administered under these circumstances is considered to be "friendly." Such a test stands in contrast to an "adversarial" test administered by the police, the results of which would be known to the prosecution. Because fear of the consequences of being detected is considered to be important to the valid outcome of a test, and there appears to be less to lose and therefore less to fear with a friendly test, it seems likely that friendly tests would be easier to pass than adversarial tests. Moreover, because the defendant is paying the polygrapher with the hope of passing the test, the examiner is being pressured, at least by the defendant, to produce the desired outcome. In a procedure that is as subjective and unstandardized as the CQT, it is easy to imagine how subtle adjustments to the procedure could increase the likelihood of friendly tests being passed. Unfortunately, there are no data attesting to the validity of friendly tests. All the existing field studies deal with adversarial tests.

HOW JURIES EVALUATE POLYGRAPH EVIDENCE

An important issue surrounding the use of polygraph evidence in court is the weight that is likely to be attached to this evidence by juries. This concern derives in part from Federal Rule of Evidence 403 (and its state court equivalents; see Daniels, 2002), which allows courts to exclude evidence if its probative value is substantially outweighed by the prejudicial impact it may have on the jury. Unlike other types of evidence a jury may hear, polygraph evidence has the potential to usurp the jury's constitutionally mandated task of deciding guilt. Because of the scientific and technical aura that surrounds the practice of polygraph testing coupled with concerns that juries may assign excessive probative weight to this evidence, courts have excluded polygraph testimony (see, e.g., *United States v. Alexander*, 1975).

Since our review of how juries consider polygraph evidence in the previous edition of this *Handbook*, no new published studies on this topic have appeared. Unfortunately, the existing literature, consisting of seven studies published between 1939 and 1997, does not adequately address this question. For instance, no study published since 1980 has examined how juries are influenced by passed polygraph tests being presented as evidence, yet federal and state court proceedings regarding the admissibility of polygraph evidence based on *Daubert* and *Frye* considerations involve motions from defense attorneys to admit passed tests.

SCIENTIFIC OPINION

The opinions of scientists regarding polygraphy are obviously important. Conventional polygraph tests have a weak conceptual foundation. Moreover, serious methodological problems that may not be easily overcome make it unlikely that any line of research will yield findings that resolve concerns about accuracy. Given this state of affairs, there is considerable value in the broad-based sampling of the opinions of scientists with sufficient background to evaluate polygraph tests. In addition, the courts, in *Frye* and again in *Daubert*, have made the views of the scientific community about the general acceptance of a technique important to its admission as evidence.

Only one investigation of scientific opinion regarding polygraph techniques has been published in a scientific peer-review journal (Iacono & Lykken, 1997). This study polled members of the Society for Psychophysiological Research and fellows in Division 1 (General Psychology) of the American Psychological Association (APA). High response rates (> 74%) were obtained from those in both organizations, and there was remarkable agreement across groups regarding CQT polygraphy. These scientists expressed a high level of skepticism regarding the claims of polygraph proponents. They did not find the theory of the CQT to be scientifically sound or the accuracy claims of polygraph proponents to be credible. In addition, they expressed opinions indicating that friendly tests have little value and that countermeasures pose a significant threat to the validity of passed tests. Members of neither group would recommend the results of CQTs be admitted in court. Only APA members were asked about directed lie tests, and they did not agree that these tests are scientifically sound. In contrast to these negative opinions about conventional specific incident tests, those polled had favorable opinions about the GKT. The contrast in the scientific credibility of the CQT and GKT is important because it indicates that respondents were not generally skeptical about detection of deception techniques, but have doubts that are specific to the CQT.

The results of these surveys parallel the opinions of the NRC (2003) committee that reviewed polygraph test validity. This distinguished panel of 14 scientists and four NRC staff are broadly representative of those with the skills and now the knowledge to evaluate polygraph testing. This group conducted one of the most thorough and far-reaching analyses of polygraph testing ever undertaken, spanning 19 months of meetings and visits to polygraph facilities at several government agencies. They also reviewed unpublished studies, classified material, and information gathered at public hearings. Their main conclusions, listed here, probably best reflect the current state of the art of polygraph testing in this country:

- Polygraph theory
  —"The theoretical rationale for the polygraph is quite weak, especially in terms of differential fear, arousal, or other emotional states that are triggered in response to relevant and comparison questions" (p. 213).
  —"The situation is somewhat different with research on concealed information [GKT] polygraph testing, which has consistently drawn on the theory of the orienting response" (p. 93).
- Standardization
  —"We have some concern that in practice, polygraph programs and examiners . . . [alter] the test conditions to affect the strength of the examinee's autonomic response. That examiners can do so is reflected in their own claims to the committee about their ability to influence examinees' physiological reactions and by the small worth typically assigned to a polygraph chart collected under circumstances friendly to an examinee. Test conditions may vary systematically according to such factors as expectancies of guilt about individuals and expected base rates of guilt in a population of examinees" (p. 42).
  —"There is virtually no standardization of protocols; the polygraph tests conducted in the field depend greatly on the presumed skill of individual examiners" (p. 204).
- Laboratory studies
  —"The existing validation studies have serious limitations. Laboratory test findings on polygraph validity are not a good guide to accuracy in field settings. They are likely to overestimate accuracy in field practice, but by an unknown amount" (p. 210).
- Field studies
  —"Virtually all of the observational field studies have been focused on specific incidents and have been plagued by measurement biases that favor overestimation of accuracy, such as examiner contamination, as well as biases created by the lack of a clear and independent measure of truth" (p. 214).
  —"In summary, we were unable to find any field experiments, field quasi-experiments, or prospective research-oriented data collection specifically designed to assess polygraph validity and satisfying minimal standards of research quality" (p. 115).

- Accuracy
  —"The evidence does not allow any precise quantitative estimate of polygraph accuracy or provide confidence that accuracy is stable across personality types, sociodemographic groups, psychological and medical conditions, examiner and examinee expectancies, or ways of administering the test and selecting questions" (p. 214).
  —"What is remarkable, given the large body of relevant research, is that claims about the accuracy of the polygraph made today parallel those made throughout the history of the polygraph: practitioners have always claimed extremely high levels of accuracy, and these claims have rarely been reflected in empirical research" (p. 107).
- Personnel screening
  —"Because the studies of acceptable quality all focus on specific incidents, generalizations from them to uses for screening is not justified" (p. 215).
  —"Because actual screening applications involve considerably more ambiguity for the examinee and in determining truth than arises in specific-incident studies, polygraph accuracy for screening purposes is almost certainly lower than what can be achieved by specific-incident polygraph tests in the field" (p. 215).
  —"[Polygraph test] accuracy in distinguishing actual or potential security violators from innocent test takers is insufficient to justify reliance on its use in employee security screening in federal agencies" (p. 219).
- Countermeasures
  —"All of the physiological indicators measured on the polygraph can be altered by conscious efforts through cognitive or physical means, and there is enough empirical research to justify concern that successful countermeasures may be learnable" (p. 216).

The Iacono and Lykken (1997) survey data and NRC panel conclusions clearly document that polygraph testing is not generally accepted by the relevant scientific community. Subsequent to the publication of the NRC report, three members of the panel published an extension of their findings further elaborating the poor opinion they hold of polygraph testing (Faigman, Fienberg, & Stern, 2003).

CONCLUSION

Despite this scientific skepticism, the use of polygraph tests continues unabated, presumably reflecting beliefs among law enforcement and national security policymakers that their utility benefits outweigh concerns regarding costs associated with their misuse. There appears to be little dispute about the utility of polygraph testing, although only anecdotal, not scientific evidence exists to support this contention (NRC, 2003). Nevertheless, many criminal suspects confess following failed tests, providing a means to resolve criminal investigations that otherwise would go unprosecuted. In employee screening, the admissions employees make about their alcohol use, sex lives, and colleagues' suspect behavior provide the government with what is considered to be valuable information that would be virtually impossible to obtain via any other (legal) means. Likewise, those administering sex offender treatment programs have come to rely on polygraph tests to encourage offenders to divulge fully their past sexual misdeeds, so much so that the use of polygraph tests in these programs appears to have at least doubled between 1992 and 2002, with from 36% to 70% of residential treatment and community outpatient programs, respectively, relying on the polygraph (McGrath, Cumming, & Burchard, 2003). When used in such contexts, the polygraph is little more than a prop intended to encourage socially undesirable self-disclosure among those who believe it genuinely works, a phenomenon established over 30 years ago as the "bogus pipeline" effect (Jones & Sigall, 1971; Roese & Jamieson, 1993). However, in the long run, evidence that a technique lacks validity will eventually undercut its utility (NRC, 2003). As Oksol and O'Donohue (2003) noted when pointing out the many ethical problems associated with polygraph testing, if examinees were given true informed consent regarding the fallibility of lie detection and how it is used to extract confessions at the time they are asked to sign the release for their test, few would agree to testing.

For many decades, polygraph testing has been part of the fabric of our institutions of law enforcement and national security. Consequently, reliance on polygraphy as an investigative tool is unlikely to diminish in the future. While it remains possible that the CQT will become accepted as credible scientific evidence, courts have not shown a readiness to embrace the admission of specific incident tests in the decade following *Daubert* (Faigman et al., 2002). As our review indicates, there is little evidence to support their admission, and what evidence does exist, coupled with the obvious weaknesses in CQT theory, indicates that the CQT has little more than chance accuracy with innocent people and can be easily defeated by guilty people by deliberately augmenting responses to control questions.

The GKT, by contrast, is scientifically sound, and ERP adaptations of the GKT are likely to be presented before the court in *Daubert* hearings. The weakness of the GKT and its ERP equivalents lies in our lack of knowledge regarding how to design real-life tests composed of items that guilty people are almost certain to remember. In the absence of such knowledge, it is difficult to be certain that a passed GKT reflects innocence rather than poor item selection or the inadequate memory of a guilty person. However, because the GKT is technically sound, it is possible for a jury to weigh evidence regarding the adequacy of a properly conducted but failed GKT. Consider, for instance, that suspect John Fisbee is asked to preapprove the questions on a 12-item GKT by indicating whether he knows the answer to any of the questions, and he claims no knowledge. In addition, after the test is administered, he is asked if he can guess the answers to any of the items, and the two items he "guesses" the correct answer to are eliminated from further consideration. The test is given by an examiner who is unaware of the correct answers. On the GKT, Fisbee shows the strongest physiological response to all of the guilty alternatives for the remaining questions. When the same test was given to 10 individuals, none of whom could be involved in the crime, they responded to the guilty alternatives at chance levels. Because it is difficult to understand how such an outcome could come about in the absence of Fisbee's guilty knowledge, such a test result provides relatively strong prima facie evidence of guilt. One can alter aspects of this hypothetical scenario in various ways (e.g., Fisbee fails 8 of the remaining 10 items), but with each alteration, it is possible to make a scientifically informed appraisal regarding the level of confidence one can have in the outcome.

REFERENCES

Allen, J. J. B. (2002). The role of psychophysiology in clinical assessment: ERPs in the evaluation of memory. *Psychophysiology, 39,* 261–280.

Allen, J. J. B., & Iacono, W. G. (1997). A comparison of methods for the analysis of event-related potentials in deception detection. *Psychophysiology, 34,* 234–240.

Allen, J. J. B., & Iacono, W. G. (2001). Assessing the validity of amnesia in dissociative identity disorder: A dilemma for the DSM and the courts. *Psychology, Public Policy, and Law, 7,* 311–344.

Allen, J. J. B., Iacono, W. G., & Danielson, K. D. (1992). The identification of concealed memories using the event-related potential and implicit behavioral measures: A methodology for prediction in the face of individual differences. *Psychophysiology, 29,* 504–522.

Allen, J. J. B., Iacono, W. G., Laravuso, J. J., & Dunn, L. A. (1995). An event-related potential investigation of posthypnotic recognition amnesia. *Journal of Abnormal Psychology, 104,* 421–430.

Allen, J. J. B., & Movius, H. L. (2000). The objective assessment of amnesia in dissociative identity disorder using event-related potentials. *International Journal of Psychophysiology, 38,* 21–41.

Barland, G. H., Honts, C. R., & Barger, S. D. (1989). *Studies of the accuracy of security screening polygraph examinations.* Fort McClellan, AL: Department of Defense Polygraph Institute.

Ben-Shakar, G. (2002). A critical review of the control questions test (CQT). In M. Kleiner (Ed.), *Handbook of polygraph testing* (pp. 103–126). San Diego: Academic Press.

Ben-Shakar, G., & Elaad, E. (2002). Effects of questions' repetition and variation on the efficiency of the guilty knowledge test: A reexamination. *Journal of Applied Psychology, 87,* 972–977.

Ben-Shakar, G., & Elaad, E. (2003). The validity of psychophysiological detection of information with the guilty knowledge test: A meta-analytic review. *Journal of Applied Psychology, 88,* 131–151.

Boaz, T. L., Perry, N. W., Raney, G., Fischler, I. S., & Shuman, D. (1991). Detection of guilty knowledge with event related potentials. *Journal of Applied Psychology, 76,* 788–795.

Daniels, C. W. (2002). Legal aspects of polygraph admissibility in the United States. In M. Kleiner (Ed.), *Handbook of polygraph testing* (pp. 327–338). San Diego: Academic Press.

Daubert v. Merrell Dow Pharmaceuticals, 509 U.S. 579 (1993).

Donchin, E. (1981). Surprise! . . . Surprise? *Psychophysiology, 18,* 493–513.

Efron, B. (1979). Bootstrap methods: Another look at the jackknife. *Annals of Statistics, 7,* 1–26.

Elaad, E. (1990). Detection of guilty knowledge in real-life criminal applications. *Journal of Applied Psychology, 75,* 521–529.

Elaad, E., Ginton, A., & Jungman, N. (1992). Detection measures in real-life criminal guilty knowledge tests. *Journal of Applied Psychology, 77,* 757–767.

Ellwanger, J., Rosenfeld, J. P., Hankin, B. L., & Sweet, J. J. (1999). P300 as an index of recognition in a standard and difficult match-to-sample test: A model of amnesia in normal adults. *Clinical Neuropsychologist, 13,* 101–109.

Ellwanger, J., Rosenfeld, J. P., Sweet, J. J., & Bhat, M. (1996). Detecting simulated amnesia for autobiographical and recently learned information using the P300 event-related potential. *International Journal of Psychophysiology, 23,* 9–23.

Ellwanger, J. W., Tenhula, W., Rosenfeld, J. P., & Sweet, J. J. (2000). Identifying simulators of cognitive deficit through combined use of neuropsychological test performance and event-related potentials. *Journal of Clinical and Experimental Neuropsychology, 21,* 866–879.

Employee Polygraph Protection Act, 29 USC 2001 (1988).

Faigman, D. L., Fienberg, S. E., & Stern, P. C. (2003). The limits of the polygraph. *Issues in Science & Technology, 20,* 40–46.

Faigman, D. L., Kaye, D. H., Saks, M. J., & Sanders, J. (2002). The legal relevance of scientific research on polygraph tests. In D. L. Faigman, D. Kaye, M. J. Saks, & J. Sanders (Eds.), *Modern scientific evidence: The law and science of expert testimony* (Vol. 2, pp. 427–446). St. Paul, MN: West.

Fang, F., Liu, Y., & Shen, Z. (2003). Lie detection with contingent negative variation. *International Journal of Psychophysiology, 50,* 247–255.

Farwell, L. A., & Donchin, E. (1986). The "brain detector": P300 in the detection of deception. *Psychophysiology, 24,* 434.

Farwell, L. A., & Donchin, E. (1991). The truth will out: Interrogative polygraphy ("lie detection") with event related brain potentials. *Psychophysiology, 28,* 531–547.

Farwell, L. A., & Smith, S. S. (2001). Using brain MERMER testing to detect knowledge despite efforts to conceal. *Journal of Forensic Sciences, 46,* 1–9.

Ferguson, R. J. (1966). *The polygraph in private industry.* Springfield, IL: Charles C Thomas.

Fiedler, K., Schmid, J., & Stahl, T. (2002). What is the current truth about polygraph lie detection? *Basic and Applied Social Psychology, 24,* 313–324.

Forman, R. F., & McCauley, C. (1986). Validity of the positive control test using the field practice model. *Journal of Applied Psychology, 71,* 691–698.

Frye v. United States, 293 F. 1013 (D.C. Cir. 1923).

Furedy, J. J., Davis, C., & Gurevich, M. (1988). Differentiation of deception as a psychological process: A psychophysiological approach. *Psychophysiology, 25,* 683–688.

Ganis, G., Kosslyn, S. M., Stose, S., Thompson, W. L., & Yurgelun-Todd, D. A. (2003). Neural correlates of different types of deception: An fMRI investigation. *Cerebral Cortex, 13,* 830–836.

Harrington v. State of Iowa, No. 122/01-0653 (Iowa S. Ct. 2003).

Honts, C. R. (1994). Psychophysiological detection of deception. *Current Directions, 3,* 77–82.

Honts, C. R. (1996). Criterion development and validity of the CQT in field application. *Journal of General Psychology, 123,* 309–324.

Honts, C. R., & Amato, S. (2002). Countermeasures. In M. Kleiner (Ed.), *Handbook of polygraph testing* (pp. 251–264). London: Academic Press.

Honts, C. R., & Raskin, D. C. (1988). A field study of the validity of the directed lie control question. *Journal of Police Science and Administration, 16,* 56–61.

Honts, C. R., Raskin, D., & Kircher, J. (1994). Mental and physical countermeasures reduce the accuracy of polygraph tests. *Journal of Applied Psychology, 79,* 252–259.

Honts, C. R., Raskin, D., & Kircher, J. (2002). The scientific status of research on polygraph techniques: The case for polygraph tests. In D. L. Faigman, D. H. Kaye, M. J. Saks, & J. Sanders (Eds.), *Modern scientific evidence: The law and science of expert testimony* (Vol. 2, pp. 446–483). St. Paul, MN: West.

Horowitz, S. W., Kircher, J. C., Honts, C. R., & Raskin, D. C. (1997). The role of comparison questions in physiological detection of deception. *Psychophysiology, 34,* 108–115.

Horvath, F. (1977). The effect of selected variables on the interpretation of polygraph records. *Journal of Applied Psychology, 62,* 127–136.

Horvath, F. S. (1985). Job screening. *Society, 22,* 43–46.

Horvath, F. (1993). Polygraph screening of candidates for police work in large police agencies in the United States: A survey of practices, policies, and evaluative comments. *American Journal of Police, 12,* 67–86.

Iacono, W. G. (1991). Can we determine the accuracy of polygraph tests? In J. R. Jennings, P. K. Ackles, & M. G. H. Coles (Eds.), *Advances in psychophysiology* (Vol. 4, pp. 201–207). London: Jessica Kingsley.

Iacono, W. G. (1998). The detection of deception. In L. G. Tassinary, J. T. Cacioppo, & G. Berntson (Eds.), *Handbook of psychophysiology* (pp. 772–793). New York: Cambridge University Press.

Iacono, W. G. (2000). The detection of deception. In J. T. Cacioppo, L. G. Tassinary, & G. Berntson (Eds.), *Handbook of psychophysiology* (2nd ed., pp. 772–793). New York: Cambridge University Press.

Iacono, W. G., & Lykken, D. T. (1997). The validity of the lie detector: Two surveys of scientific opinion. *Journal of Applied Psychology, 82,* 426–433.

Iacono, W. G., & Lykken, D. T. (2002). The scientific status of research on polygraph techniques: The case against polygraph tests. In D. L. Faigman, D. H. Kaye, M. J. Saks, & J. Sanders (Eds.), *Modern scientific evidence: The law and science of expert testimony* (Vol. 2, pp. 483–538). St. Paul, MN: West.

Iacono, W. G., & Patrick, C. J. (1987). What psychologists should know about lie detection. In I. B. Weiner & A. K. Hess (Eds.), *Handbook of forensic psychology* (pp. 460–489). New York: Wiley.

Iacono, W. G., & Patrick, C. J. (1999). Polygraph ("lie detector") testing: The state of the art. In A. K. Hess & I. B. Weiner (Eds.), *The handbook of forensic psychology* (2nd ed., pp. 440–473). New York: Wiley.

Johnson, M. M., & Rosenfeld, J. P. (1992). Oddball-evoked P300-based method of deception detection in the laboratory II: Utilization of non-selective activation of relevant knowledge. *International Journal of Psychophysiology, 12,* 289–306.

Johnson, R., Jr., Barnhardt, J., & Zhu, J. (2003). The deceptive response: Effects of response conflict and strategic monitoring on the late positive component and episodic memory-related brain activity. *Biological Psychology, 64,* 217–253.

Johnson, R., Jr., Barnhardt, J., & Zhu, J. (in press). The contribution of executive processes to deceptive responding. *Neuropsychologia, 42,* 878–901.

Jones, E. E., & Sigall, H. (1971). The bogus pipeline: A new paradigm for measuring affect and attitude. *Psychological Bulletin, 76,* 349–364.

Kircher, J. C., Horowitz, S. W., & Raskin, D. C. (1988). Meta-analysis of mock crime studies of the control question polygraph technique. *Law and Human Behavior, 12,* 79–90.

Knight, J. (2004). The truth about lying. *Nature, 428,* 692–694.

Kosson, D. S. (1996). Psychopathy and dual-task performance under focusing conditions. *Journal of Abnormal Psychology, 105,* 391–400.

Kutas, M., & Hillyard, S. A. (1980). Reading senseless sentences: Brain potentials reflect semantic incongruity. *Science, 207,* 203–205.

Langleben, D. D., Schroeder, L., Maldjian, J. A., Gur, R. C., McDonald, S., Ragland, J. D., et al. (2002). Brain activity during simulated deception: An event-related functional magnetic resonance study. *Neuroimage, 15,* 727–732.

Lee, T. M., Liu, H. L., Tan, L. H., Chan, C. C., Mahankali, S., Feng, C. M., et al. (2002). Lie detection by functional magnetic resonance imaging. *Human Brain Mapping, 15,* 157–164.

Lykken, D. T. (1955). *A study of anxiety in the sociopathic personality.* Unpublished doctoral dissertation, University of Minnesota.

Lykken, D. T. (1959). The GSR in the detection of guilt. *Journal of Applied Psychology, 43,* 385–388.

Lykken, D. T. (1960). The validity of the guilty knowledge technique: The effects of faking. *Journal of Applied Psychology, 44,* 258–262.

Lykken, D. T. (1974). Psychology and the lie detector industry. *American Psychologist, 29,* 725–739.

Lykken, D. T. (1998). *A tremor in the blood: Uses and abuses of the lie detector* (2nd ed.). New York: Plenum Press.

MacLaren, V. V. (2001). A quantitative review of the guilty knowledge test. *Journal of Applied Psychology, 86,* 674–683.

McGrath, R. J., Cumming, G. F., & Burchard, B. L. (2003). *Current practices and trends in sexual abuser management.* Brandon, VT: Safer Society Press.

Miller, A. R., Rosenfeld, J. P., Soskins, M., & Jhee, M. (2002). P300 amplitude and topography in an autobiographical oddball paradigm involving simulated amnesia. *Journal of Psychophysiology, 16,* 1–11.

Miyake, Y., Mizutani, M., & Yamahura, T. (1993). Event related potentials as an indicator of detecting information in field polygraph examinations. *Polygraph, 22,* 131–149.

Nakayama, M. (2002). Practical use of the concealed information test for criminal investigation in Japan. In M. Kleiner (Ed.), *Handbook of polygraph testing* (pp. 49–86). San Diego: Academic Press.

National Defense Authorization Act, Public Law 106-65, S. 1059 (2000).

National Research Council. (2003). *The polygraph and lie detection.* Washington, DC: National Academies Press.

Oksol, E. M., & O'Donohue, W. T. (2003). A critical analysis of the polygraph. In W. T. O'Donohue & E. Levensky (Eds.), *Handbook of forensic psychology* (pp. 601–634). San Diego: Academic Press.

O'Toole, D., Yuille, J. C., Patrick, C. J., & Iacono, W. G. (1994). Alcohol and the physiological detection of deception: Arousal and memory influences. *Psychophysiology, 31,* 253–263.

Patrick, C. J., & Iacono, W. G. (1989). Psychopathy, threat, and polygraph test accuracy. *Journal of Applied Psychology, 74,* 347–355.

Patrick, C. J., & Iacono, W. G. (1991a). A comparison of field and laboratory polygraphs in the detection of deception. *Psychophysiology, 28,* 632–638.

Patrick, C. J., & Iacono, W. G. (1991b). Validity of the control question polygraph test: The problem of sampling bias. *Journal of Applied Psychology, 76,* 229–238.

Pavlidis, I., Eberhardt, N. L., & Levine, J. A. (2002). Seeing through the face of deception: Thermal imaging offers a promising hands-off approach to mass security screening. *Nature, 415,* 35.

Raskin, D. (1989). Polygraph techniques for the detection of deception. In D. Raskin (Ed.), *Psychological methods in criminal investigation and evidence* (pp. 247–296). New York: Springer.

Raskin, D. C., & Honts, C. R. (2002). The comparison question test. In M. Kleiner (Ed.), *Handbook of polygraph testing* (pp. 1–47). San Diego: Academic Press.

Roese, N. J., & Jamieson, D. W. (1993). Twenty years of bogus pipeline research: A critical review and meta-analysis. *Psychological Bulletin, 114,* 363–375.

Rosenfeld, J. P. (2002). Event-related potentials in the detection of deception, malingering, and false memories. In M. Kleiner (Ed.), *Handbook of polygraph testing* (pp. 265–286). New York: Academic Press.

Rosenfeld, J. P., Angell, A., Johnson, M., & Qian, J. (1991). An ERP-based, control-question lie detector analog: Algorithms for discriminating effects within individuals' average waveforms. *Psychophysiology, 38*, 319–335.

Rosenfeld, J. P., Cantwell, B., Nasman, V. T., Wodjdac, V., Ivanov, S., & Mazzeri, L. (1988). A modified, event-related potential based guilty knowledge test. *International Journal of Neuroscience, 42*, 157–161.

Rosenfeld, J. P., & Ellwanger, J. W. (1999). Cognitive psychophysiology in detection of malingered cognitive deficit. In J. J. Sweet (Ed.), *Forensic neuropsychology: Fundamentals and practice* (pp. 287–312). Lisse, The Netherlands: Swets & Zeitlinger.

Rosenfeld, J. P., Ellwanger, J. W., Nolan, K., Wu, S., Bermann, R. G., & Sweet, J. (1999). P300 scalp amplitude distribution as an index of deception in a simulated cognitive deficit model. *International Journal of Psychophysiology, 33*, 3–19.

Rosenfeld, J. P., Ellwanger, J., & Sweet, J. (1995). Detecting simulated amnesia with event-related brain potentials. *International Journal of Psychophysiology, 19*, 1–11.

Rosenfeld, J. P., Nasman, V. T., Whalen, R., Cantwell, B., & Mazzeri, L. (1987). Late vertex positivity in event-related potentials as a guilty knowledge indicator: A new method of lie detection. *Polygraph, 16*, 258–263.

Rosenfeld, J. P., Rao, A., Soskins, M., & Miller, A. R. (2003). Scaled P300 scalp distribution correlates of verbal deception in an autobiographical oddball paradigm: Control for task demand. *Journal of Psychophysiology, 17*, 14–22.

Rosenfeld, J. P., Reinhart, A. M., Bhatt, M., Ellwanger, J., Gora, K., Sekera, M., et al. (1998). P300 correlates of simulated amnesia in a matching-to-sample task: Topographic analyses of deception versus truthtelling responses. *International Journal of Psychophysiology, 28*, 233–247.

Rosenfeld, J. P., Soskins, M., Bosh, G., & Ryan, A. (2004). Simple, effective countermeasures to P300-based tests of detection of concealed information. *Psychophysiology, 41*, 205–219.

Rosenfeld, J. P., Sweet, J. J., Chuang, J., Ellwanger, J., & Song, L. (1996). Detection of simulated malingering using forced choice recognition enhanced with event-related potential recording. *Clinical Neuropsychologist, 10*, 163–179.

Samuels, D. J. (1983). What if the lie detector lies? *Nation, 237*, 566–567.

Saxe, L., & Ben-Shakar, G. (1999). Admissability of polygraph tests: The application of scientific standards post-Daubert. *Psychology, Public Policy, and Law, 5*, 203–223.

Seymour, T. L., Seifert, C. M., Shafto, M. G., & Mosmann, A. L. (2000). Using response time measures to assess "guilty knowledge." *Journal of Applied Psychology, 85*, 30–37.

Soskins, M., Rosenfeld, J. P., & Niendam, T. (2001). Peak-to-peak measurement of P300 recorded at 0.3 Hz high pass filter settings in intraindividual diagnosis: Complex vs. simple paradigms. *International Journal of Psychophysiology, 40*, 173–180.

Spence, S. A., Farrow, T. F. D., Herford, A. E., Wilkinson, I. D., Zheng, Y., & Woodruff, P. W. R. (2001). Behavioural and functional anatomical correlates of deception in humans. *NeuroReport, 12*, 2433–2438.

Thurber, S. (1981). CPI variables in relation to the polygraph performance of police officer candidates. *Journal of Social Psychology, 113*, 145–146.

U.S. Department of Defense. (2002). *Polygraph program annual report to Congress*. Washington, DC: Author.

U.S. Department of Defense, Polygraph Institute, Research Division Staff. (1997). A comparison of psychophysiological detection of deception accuracy rates obtained using the counterintelligence scope polygraph and the test for espionage and sabotage. *Polygraph, 26*, 79–106.

U.S. Department of Defense, Polygraph Institute, Research Division Staff. (1998). Psychophysiological detection of deception accuracy rates using the test for espionage and sabotage. *Polygraph, 27*, 68–73.

U.S. General Accounting Office. (2001). *Investigative techniques: Federal agency views on the potential application of "brain fingerprinting."* Washington, DC: Author.

United States v. Alexander, 526 F.2d 161. 168 (8th Cir. 1975).

United States v. Scheffer, 1998, WL 141-151 U.S.

van Hooff, J. C., Brunia, C. H. M., & Allen, C. J. (1996). Event-related potentials as indirect measures of recognition memory. *International Journal of Psychophysiology, 21*, 15–31.

Waid, W. M., Orne, M. T., & Wilson, S. K. (1979). Effects of level of socialization on electrodermal detection of deception. *Psychophysiology, 16*, 15–22.

CHAPTER 20

Forensic Uses of Hypnosis

ALAN W. SCHEFLIN

THERE ARE five different situations where the law takes notice of hypnosis. First are the fundamental questions of *who* may practice hypnosis and *how* hypnosis may be practiced. These issues involve *the regulation of hypnosis* and they generally concern articulating the dividing line between licensed professionals and lay practitioners. The second area of forensic interest involves *hypnosis and antisocial conduct.* In this category are the fascinating questions about the abuse and misuse of hypnosis for the purpose of seduction or other criminal conduct (Laurence & Perry, 1988; Scheflin & Opton, 1978). The focus here is on the legal responsibility of hypnotizing influencers and of their hypnotized subjects who commit criminal acts.

The third and most heavily litigated intersection between law and hypnosis concerns *hypnosis for memory recall* or, more accurately, the issue of whether a person who has previously been hypnotized is permitted to testify as a witness in court. Before 1969, there were 39 cases decided by appellate courts involving hypnosis issues (Scheflin & Shapiro, 1989), but only two of them involved hypnosis with memory. By contrast, since 1970, approximately 1,000 cases have appeared, almost all of which have dealt with the issue of the admissibility of hypnotically refreshed recollection (Scheflin, 1994a, 1994b). Although Kihlstrom (1985) barely mentioned forensic issues in his review of trends in hypnosis research, a decade later Sheehan (1996) observed that forensic hypnosis had become one of the fastest growing areas of specialization.

The court rulings involving the admissibility of hypnotically refreshed recollection have had an impact on the practice of therapists using hypnosis with patients (Scheflin, 1993). How licensed mental health professionals use hypnosis in therapy is the fourth area of intersection: *hypnosis and the legal standard of mental health care* (Scheflin, 1997a). Lawyers for patients suing their therapists have been attempting to persuade courts, legislatures, and insurance carriers that hypnosis is an experimental modality. They argue that patients should be given special informed consent forms explaining that hypnosis is "experimental and dangerous." Some even argue that hypnosis should never be used with memory because of the danger of creating false memories.

The fifth area where the law takes cognizance of hypnosis is the use of hypnotic techniques for *courtroom advocacy* (Scheflin, 1998). May lawyers who have training in hypnosis use the skills they learned to influence judges, jurors, and witnesses?

In deciding cases, courts have rarely found it necessary to define hypnosis, which itself is a formidable task considering the diversity of opinion in the scientific community (Lynn & Rhue, 1991). The American Society of Clinical Hypnosis Task Force (Hammond et al., 1994) considers hypnosis to be a congruence of three components: dissociation, absorption, and suggestibility. In addition, situational or context factors play an important part in determining whether hypnosis is present. Hypnosis is a complex alteration in consciousness that can be understood as attentive, receptive concentration characterized by parallel, or dissociated, awareness. This shift in concentration may result in intensely absorbing perceptual and sensory experiences, similar to that of being so engrossed in a good novel, movie, or play that one temporarily suspends awareness of the surrounding circumstances. The interaction between focal attention and peripheral awareness is a constant theme in human consciousness, but with hypnosis there appears to be a relative diminution of peripheral awareness to facilitate the enhancement of focal concentration, although at no time does peripheral awareness disappear entirely. Some people in a trance are capable of experiencing profound sensory alterations such as tingling, lightness, or heaviness in extremities; perceptual alterations such as negative and positive hallucinations; and alterations in motor control (e.g., letting an arm float up in the air with a feeling that they cannot control it, although, in fact, they can). They also experience changes in temporal orientation, such as reliving the past as though it were the present, and dissociation, which is defined as the compartmentalization of mental processes that are otherwise integrated (e.g., feeling a part of the body or a part of their awareness as being separate from the rest).

As the American Society of Clinical Hypnosis Task Force (Hammond et al., 1994, p. 3) has pointed out:

> The courts have leaned toward defining hypnosis in terms of its antecedents, i.e., whether or not a hypnotic induction ceremony was administered. . . . Unfortunately, this has downplayed the importance of defining hypnosis by its consequences (i.e., hypnotizability). . . . We believe that it should be demonstrated that both a hypnotic induction was administered, and that the subject was responsive to such a procedure (e.g., through the elicitation of phenomena either informally, or formally through the administration of a hypnotizability scale).

Some people are not at all hypnotizable, a few are extremely hypnotizable, and the majority of the population has some moderate capacity to experience hypnosis. Court decisions on forensic hypnosis, however, almost never discuss the hypnotizability of the witness, and lawyers in these cases rarely have the witness tested for responsiveness to hypnosis or suggestion.

THE REGULATION OF HYPNOSIS

Hypnosis did not receive professional recognition until the 1950s, when the British Medical Association (1955), the American Medical Association (1958), and the American Psychiatric Association (1961) officially approved hypnosis as a therapeutic modality. Today, statutes in 31 states include hypnosis or hypnotherapy in the definition of psychology or counseling, and two states list hypnosis in the definition of the practice of medicine (Appendix 1). Only a few states, however, including California and Florida, have specific regulations concerning who may practice hypnosis (Appendix 1).

Two modern appellate judicial decisions have dealt with regulating the conduct of lay hypnotists who provide treatment to their clients. In *Masters v. State* (1960), Masters placed an advertisement in the newspaper offering his hypnosis services for a variety of ailments. An inspector employed by the Better Business Bureau posed as a client and was told during a hypnosis session that his problem stemmed from his hatred of his father. At trial, a medical doctor testified that the use of hypnosis required a knowledge of medicine and specialized training. The doctor further testified that

> he never used hypnosis until he had made a complete physical examination of the patient and that he considered such an absolute necessity and that it was not safe for anyone to use hypnosis in an effort to cure unless such person had a background of medicine because by the improper use of hypnosis a patient might be made worse off than he had been before and might resort to suicide. (p. 474)

Masters did not testify on his own behalf. After the jury convicted him for the unauthorized practice of medicine, the appellate court upheld the conviction.

In *People v. Cantor* (1961), Cantor was convicted on two counts of practicing medicine without a license. He advertised himself to be the director of the National Hypnosis Institute of Los Angeles, and he guaranteed results in cases involving weight loss. The appellate court, noting that the question "whether practicing hypnotism is practicing medicine" (p. 849) was one that had not previously been addressed by California court decisions, upheld the conviction. According to the judges:

> It is our considered opinion that . . . the practice of hypnotism as a curative measure or mode of procedure by one not licensed to practice medicine, amounts to the unlawful practice of medicine. . . . To the extent that [Cantor] employed or attempted to practice his hypnotic powers, he was practicing medicine within the meaning of [the statute]. (p. 850)

California has a unique piece of legislation concerning lay hypnotists. Business & Professions Code section 2908 provides two exemptions from the unauthorized practice laws that permit lay practitioners to use hypnosis: (1) if there is referral from a person licensed to practice "medicine, dentistry or psychology"; or (2) if the hypnosis is for "avocational or vocational self-improvement." Each of the exemptions from the general licensing requirement raises as yet unanswered questions because this law has never been interpreted by the courts. The first exemption appears to permit a lay hypnotist to practice psychology if the client is referred by a duly licensed person. It is not clear why a licensed professional would refer a client to a lay hypnotist for treatment. Indeed, it might be malpractice to do so. Because many professional societies have regulations against working with or training lay practitioners, it would violate the ethical code of these associations to refer a patient to a lay practitioner.

The second exemption leaves the crucial phrase "avocational or vocational self-improvement" undefined. Do weight loss or smoking cessation hypnotic treatments fall within this language, or are they medical and/or psychological problems?

Even if the law permits the lay practice of hypnosis under certain circumstances, serious unresolved questions arise concerning the appropriate standard of care (*Johnson v. Gerrish*, 1986), despite the fact that dangers have been reported when lay hypnotists treat patients (Haberman, 1987). Furthermore, clients of nonlicensed hypnotists are not afforded the protection of confidentiality and privilege, and they have no recourse to a disciplinary mechanism whereby improper conduct can result in suspension of practice.

In addition to the legal issue of the unauthorized practice of psychology or medicine, lay hypnotists may face liability if harm occurs as a result of a hypnosis performance. Dangers with stage hypnosis have frequently been reported (Echterling & Emmerling, 1987; Erickson, 1962; Finkelstein, 1989; Harding, 1978; Kleinhauz, Dreyfuss, Beran, Goldberg, & Azikri, 1979). In *Hohe v. San Diego Unified School District* (1990), a high school junior (Hohe) who was injured during a hypnotism show at the school brought an action to recover damages. She had been selected by the hypnotist as a volunteer to participate in his "Magic of the Mind Show." Hohe had seen the prior year's hypnotism show and told her father about a "stunt where a subject was suspended between two objects while another person stood on the subject's stomach" (p. 1563). During the course of the show, Hohe slid from her chair and fell to the floor several times. The appellate court held that a fact issue existed as to whether the wording of the release signed by Hohe and her father barred them from recovering for her personal injuries, thereby allowing the case to go to trial.

Kansas Statutes section 21-4007 makes it a misdemeanor to engage in a "hypnotic exhibition" involving a demonstration of hypnosis, including participation as a subject, for purposes of entertainment.

HYPNOSIS AND ANTISOCIAL CONDUCT

The alleged power of hypnosis to override a person's will has been the subject of many works of fiction and quite a few films. The image of Svengali, with his absolute power to bend his victims to his will, still looms large in the public perception of hypnosis (DuMaurier, 1894). Judges, too, have considered whether hypnosis dilutes criminal or civil responsibility. Cases involving the antisocial aspects of hypnosis fall into two categories: crimes committed *on* hypnotized subjects, usually sexual seduction or undue influence for economic gain, and crimes committed *by* subjects claiming to be in a trance.

CRIMES COMMITTED ON HYPNOTIZED SUBJECTS

The power of hypnosis to override a person's will was a source of great concern to the public and the courts in the late nineteenth century (Laurence & Perry, 1988). Since the mid-1800s, appellate and federal district courts in the United States have dealt with hypnotic seduction in fewer than 25 cases.

Nevertheless, allegations of hypnotic seduction continue to appear against professional and lay hypnotists, though not in great numbers (Venn, 1988). In general, courts have been receptive to the claim that criminal charges may be brought, and convictions upheld, against a defendant accused of hypnotic seduction (*McIlwain v. State,* 1981; *Mirowitz v. State,* 1969; *People v. Sorscher,* 1986; *State v. Donovan,* 1905).

CRIMES COMMITTED BY HYPNOTIZED SUBJECTS

In these cases, defendants charged with criminal conduct plead that they should not be punished because they were acting under the hypnotic instructions of another. The claim that "the hypnotist made me do it" became quite prevalent in the late nineteenth century. Several sensational trials in Europe in the 1880s and 1890s about the possibility of using hypnosis to induce criminal conduct, and the publicity given to these cases, had an immediate influence on defense lawyers. As noted by Brodie-Innes (1891, p. 51):

> Recently the public mind has been startled by accounts of strange new powers, with mysterious and unknown possibilities, and by alarming hints of crimes of an entirely new class, more obscure, more terrible, and more difficult of detection than any yet known to medical jurisprudence.

An article in a British legal journal ("Hypnotism in Criminal Defence," 1894, p. 249) observed that whereas insanity had been a favored plea of criminal suspects, "today hypnotism is the fashionable defense."

Expert opinion on the ability of hypnotists to control their subjects was far from consistent. Some experts contended that the uncontrolled and unscrupulous use of hypnosis could threaten "the national defense and civil society" (Harris, 1985, p. 209). Other experts claimed that a highly hypnotizable subject

> obeyed all the commands of the magnetizer and would execute acts upon waking without any conscious awareness or subsequent memory. [However,] deep inside this human marionette a consciousness of "self" continued to subsist, so that a truly pure hypnotic subject would fail to realize commands that were repugnant to his or her inner nature. (p. 207)

The hypnosis defense faded from the courts shortly thereafter and rarely appears in cases today. Eight appellate cases discuss hypnosis as a criminal defense. In *People v. Worthington* (1894), the first opinion dealing with the topic, a mother convicted of murdering her lover claimed she committed the act under her husband's hypnotic power. The California Supreme Court, in rejecting her argument, said "there was no evidence [that the] defendant was subject to the disease, if it be such. Merely showing that she was told to kill the deceased and that she did it does not prove hypnotism, or, at least, does not tend to establish a defense to a charge of murder" (p. 172). In *Denis v. Commonwealth* (1926), the defendant, a Roman Catholic priest, was convicted of forgery and uttering false financial instruments. He claimed that he was under the influence of a frail woman who was, in fact, insane. However, the defendant admitted that he could not say that he was hypnotized, only that "I was under her influence to the extent that I did a lot of foolish things; whether that is hypnotism, I cannot tell" (p. 576). Not surprisingly, his conviction was affirmed. In *People v. Marsh* (1959), after Marsh escaped from prison and was recaptured, he claimed he had left prison under the influence of a posthypnotic suggestion given to him by his friend, an amateur hypnotist, who told him, while inducing trance, to "go back where he . . . was having a good time" (p. 285). Marsh said he took the words literally and, at the first opportunity, escaped and went home. The court-appointed psychiatrist did not believe the story, the jury did not believe the story, and the court of appeal did not believe the story.

Other cases also strain one's sense of credulity. Indeed, these cases appear to utilize hypnosis as a defense of last resort. In *People v. Baldi* (1974), the defendant's counsel claimed that his client committed murder in a self-induced trance brought about by defendant's fixation on pictures of women with a "prominent bust" (p. 122). *Barfield v. State* (1974) involved a claim that the victim had instructed her to kill him by hypnotizing her using "Vishanti" as a trigger word. The legitimacy of her defense was put into question when she simultaneously argued that she did not commit the crime and could prove that she was 20 miles away, and that she did commit the crime, but only because she was under the hypnotic influence of the deceased. In *U.S. v. Phillips* (1981), the trial judge commented that the case "was one of the most spellbinding that this writer has ever seen enacted on the forensic stage" (p. 758). The defendant claimed that she was a hypnotic slave of her Svengali-like husband. Interestingly, her husband bragged about his influence over his wife and testified that he had been hypnotizing her 10 or 15 times a day ever since she was 15 years old. He told her he was "her mother and her father, and her Lord and God" (p. 760), and he implanted memories of his having held her immediately after she was born and of saving her from drowning when she was 9. Despite the intrigue of the case, there was no direct ruling by the court on the hypnosis issue. Other cases raising the defense (*United States v. McCollum*, 1984; *Tyrone v. State*, 1915) discuss hypnosis only briefly.

Indeed, no case has upheld the validity of the hypnosis defense. A defendant who seeks to convince a court that he or she committed a crime while in trance, or under a posthypnotic suggestion, will face an uphill struggle (Bonnema, 1993).

Despite the absence of a successful plea of hypnotic coercion, many states recognize that actions under hypnosis are not voluntary (Dressler, 2001; *People v. Dunigan*, 1981; *Rogers v. State*, 2003). Montana Crimes Code section 45-2-101(32)(c) defines an "involuntary act" to include "conduct during hypnosis or resulting from hypnotic suggestion." The influential Model Penal Code, in section 2.01(2)(c), lists "conduct during hypnosis or resulting from hypnotic suggestion" as involuntary (American Law Institute, 1985).

The possibility that subjects may be hypnotized into committing antisocial acts has been much debated in the hypnosis scientific community (Deyoub, 1984; Perry, 1979; Watkins, 1972). Significant issues concerning the voluntariness of the hypnosis subject and the ability to resist hypnotic suggestions remain the subject of substantial disagreement (Vingoe, 1997). Several schools of thought exist concerning hypnotic involuntariness. Those who believe hypnosis is a special state assert that executive control is actually altered during trance. According to Hilgard (1977, p. 229), "Hypnosis is a condition in which the normal functioning of the executive ego is temporarily modified so that executive control is divided between the hypnotist and the person being hypnotized." Sociocognitive theorists assert that executive control does not *actually* diminish; rather, the hypnotic subject comes to perceive the hypnotic situation *as if* there is a loss of voluntary control. According to Lynn and Rhue (1991), there have been at least three different schools of thought regarding hypnotic involuntariness:

> The term "involuntary" can be defined in at least three ways. . . . An action can be termed involuntary if it is beyond one's control, so that one cannot act otherwise even if one wishes to. Since the so-called "golden age" of hypnotism (the 1880s and 1890s), the view of the hypnotized subject as a passive automaton under the sway of a powerful hypnotist had faded in popularity. . . .
>
> A second meaning of the term "involuntary" can be that the suggested response occurs automatically, without effort or activity to make it occur, even if the subject is able to prevent it from occurring if he or she so desires. . . .
>
> A third sense in which a response can be classified as "involuntary" is that the subject simple has the *experience* of an action as occurring without direct volitional effort. . . .
>
> Whatever their theoretical persuasion, workers in the field are in agreement that the experience of involuntariness frequently accompanies hypnotic responses. (pp. 606–610)

The idea that hypnotic crime could also include programmed assassins was raised in Richard Condon's (1959) novel *The Manchurian Candidate.* Although a work of fiction, it finds support in documents detailing Central Intelligence Agency experiments with hypnosis (Marks, 1978; Scheflin & Opton, 1978). The CIA's efforts to develop hypnotically programmed agents who could be induced to violate their moral codes without remorse and with amnesia for the circumstances predated Condon's novel, and there is veiled evidence that their efforts met with some success.

These old controversies concerning the outer limits and dark side of hypnotic influence, though occasionally addressed by courts, have not yet reemerged as an important topic of forensic concern.

HYPNOSIS FOR MEMORY RECALL

Although some aspects of hypnosis can trace their history back to the most ancient of civilizations (Kroger, 1977), there is little evidence that hypnosis was used before the 1880s to refresh the recollection of victims, witnesses, or culprits in criminal or civil cases. The first recorded use of hypnosis to solve a crime appeared in 1845 (Gravitz 1983). A local clairvoyant in a mesmeric sleep identified a teenager as the person who had stolen money from a shopkeeper. When confronted with this accusation, the teenager confessed. The first recorded admission in court of hypnotically facilitated memory occurred in

1848 (Gravitz, 1995). A witness in a murder case was hypnotized by the victim's husband to assist her recollection. At trial, the defense called Amariah Bingham, a pioneer in American psychiatry, as an expert to testify that the witness was a hysteric. Hysterical women, he said, often create stories that are false although they believe them to be true. The jury may have accepted this testimony because the defendant was acquitted.

Medical professionals first began systematically examining the relationship between hypnosis and memory for forensic purposes in the closing two decades of the nineteenth century (Ellenberger, 1970). French and German hypnosis specialists were aware of potential problems with hypnotically refreshed recollection. Albert Moll (1889/1958, pp. 345–346) noted that *retroactive hallucinations*, his name for *false memories*, "are of great importance in law. They can be used to falsify testimony. People can be made to believe that they have witnessed certain scenes, or even crimes."

The great French hypnosis pioneer, Hippolyte Bernheim (1891/1980, p. 92), penned similar concerns: "I have shown how a false memory can cause *false testimony given in good faith*, and how examining magistrates can unwittingly cause false testimony by suggestion." Bernheim provided a dramatic example of his point by suggesting to a subject in trance that he had been awakened in the middle of the night by a raucous neighbor's singing and coughing. After the hypnosis, the subject not only reported the implanted incident of the loud neighbor, but also supplied details of the event not suggested by Bernheim, thereby adding confabulation to the false report.

Despite this recognition of the use of hypnosis to refresh recollection, and the potential dangers, there is little evidence that hypnosis was used regularly by police or others for memory refreshment of victims or witnesses of crimes. When police were tempted to use hypnosis, they sought to obtain confessions from criminal defendants. In 1893, Dutch police captured a vicious serial killer and sought to discover the location of the buried bodies of some of his victims. A statute prohibited hypnotically refreshed recollection from being introduced into evidence, but the Dutch police were concerned only with obtaining information about the crimes. When word of the police plans to hypnotize the killer became public, a multinational outcry forced them to back down ("Hypnotism and the Law," 1893). Although several European countries in the late 1800s and early 1900s conducted major trials involving hypnosis, none of these trials appears to concern hypnosis and memory (Harris, 1989).

The first American appellate case to consider hypnosis is *People v. Ebanks* (1897). The hypnosis issue, which was discussed in a single paragraph, involved the defendant's attempt to have an expert who had hypnotized him testify that while he was in trance, he made a statement professing his innocence and that the expert believed him. The trial judge refused to permit this testimony, saying, "The law of the United States does not recognize hypnotism. It would be an illegal defense, and I cannot admit it" (p. 665). The California Supreme Court quoted this statement and held that the trial judge was correct in his ruling.

Although *Ebanks* is cited for the proposition that the court held hypnotically refreshed recollection is inadmissible (Giannelli & Imwinkelried, 1999), the case cannot, for several reasons, be used to support this view. First, hypnosis was not the central concern in *Ebanks,* and it was summarily dealt with by the court. Second, it is clear that the issue involved was *not* the admissibility of hypnotically refreshed memory at all, but whether an expert could testify that the defendant was not guilty and that the defendant in trance denied his guilt. Courts continue to recognize that testimony by an expert as to the truthfulness of a witness invades the province of the jury to decide the credibility of witnesses. Also, an expert may not testify about what a person said in trance if the purpose of that testimony, as it was in *Ebanks,* is to prove the truth of the statements (*People v. Smith,* 1983; *State v. Harris,* 1965). In addition, permitting an expert to testify about whether the defendant committed the crime, or what the defendant said in trance, would allow the defendant to avoid taking the witness stand and being cross-examined (*United States v. Mest,* 1986). As noted by the Ninth Circuit Court of Appeals in *United States v. McCollum* (1984, p. 1423), "The attempt to introduce [a tape recording of the defendant in France] essentially amounted to an effort to put the defendant's testimony directly before the jury without subjecting him to the cross-examination and impeachment that would have followed had he taken the witness stand."

JUDICIAL RULINGS ON HYPNOTICALLY REFRESHED RECOLLECTION

After hypnosis received official professional approval in the United States as a therapeutic procedure in the 1950s, police departments began to express a renewed interest in it to help solve crimes. Lay hypnotists openly began training police officials in the 1950s (Arons, 1967), as did some licensed mental health professionals (Bryan, 1962). By the 1970s, police departments were using hypnosis with increasing fervor (Block, 1976; Diggett & Mulligan, 1982; Hibbard & Worring, 1981; Kuhns, 1981; Monaghan, 1980; Reiser, 1980).

Police use of hypnosis to solve crimes sent hundreds of cases into court, raising the legitimacy of this method of assisting memory. Not surprisingly, the hypnosis community and defense lawyers began to take an interest in this development. The modern era of interest in hypnotically refreshed recollection began in 1968 (Scheflin & Frischholz, 1999).

The Open Admissibility Rule

In 1968, the first appellate opinion on hypnosis used to facilitate recall was decided. In *Harding v. State* (1968), the court held that a person who had been hypnotized to remember the details of a crime could testify in court. The twin engines of truth—cross-examination and the use of expert testimony—were sufficient to test the credibility of the testimony given by the witness. Thus, *Harding* took the position that the issue of whether the witness's memory may have been impaired by hypnosis or suggestion is a matter affecting *credibility,* not *admissibility.* This judicial viewpoint, that refreshing memory with hypnosis was no different from refreshing memory by any other method, is known as the *open admissibility* rule.

Harding inaugurated a decade of court decisions that followed its reasoning. From 1968 to 1978, every appellate court in the United States that addressed the issue of hypnotically refreshed recollection adopted *Harding*'s open admissibility approach. During this decade, courts did not discuss any potential dangers attendant to the use of hypnosis and did not discuss the relevant scientific literature on this topic.

The Per Se Exclusion Rule

As might be expected, judicial acceptance of hypnotically refreshed recollection invited its increased use. Police officers by the thousands received training in hypnosis. To counter these developments, defense attorneys teamed up with some hypnosis experts to turn the tide of cases involving hypnotically refreshed recollection. In 1978, the Ninth Circuit Court of Appeals in *United States v. Adams* sounded a warning that the use of hypnosis to refresh memory may contain special dangers. That warning led to the development of two rules, each of which restricted the admission of hypnotically refreshed testimony. The most restrictive rule is the opposite of the *Harding* open admissibility approach. Known as the per se exclusion rule, it automatically prohibits hypnotically refreshed testimony in all cases. The Minnesota Supreme Court, in *State v. Mack* (1980), became the first court to prohibit the admissibility of hypnotically refreshed recollection into evidence. It was soon followed by the California Supreme Court in its important decision in *People v. Shirley* (1982).

The California Supreme Court, heavily influenced by Diamond's (1980) belief that hypnosis inevitably causes memory hardening ("concreting"), resulting in increased confidence in hypnotically refreshed recollection, expressed concern that previously hypnotized subjects could not effectively be cross-examined, thereby depriving a defendant in a criminal case of the constitutional right to confront adverse witnesses. Consequently, the testimony of these witnesses must be excluded. The Minnesota and California courts concluded that hypnosis lacked reliability, created undue suggestibility, increased confidence in the accuracy of false memories, and led to confabulated testimony.

Interestingly, both *Mack* and *Shirley* based their reasoning on *Frye v. United States* (1923), a case that set the test for the admissibility of *expert* testimony when that testimony is based on a *new* or *novel* scientific device, instrument, or procedure. According to *Frye*, such expert testimony is admissible if the device, instrument, or procedure has *gained general acceptance* for reliability in the relevant scientific community. Technically, *Frye* had no application to the testimony of witnesses, nor to the use of hypnosis, a procedure which was hardly new or novel (D. Spiegel, 1987).

In *People v. Williams* (1982), Judge Gardner strongly objected to the reasoning of *Shirley*, which he described as "really more of a polemic than an opinion":

> I am troubled by the concept that the testimony of a percipient witness as to relevant facts be deemed inadmissible simply because he has undergone hypnosis.
>
> What next? Once we begin to rule evidence inadmissible because of our dissatisfaction with the witness' credibility based on improper memory jogging, where do we stop? What about witnesses who have been brainwashed, coached, coerced, bribed or intimidated? Are we going to reject all this testimony because it is suspect? I have no doubt that a corrupt polygraph operator could convince a witness of limited intelligence that his accurate memory is actually faulty and

thus persuade him to testify to an untruth. The same is true with the so-called truth serums, hallucinogenic drugs or other exotic drugs only hinted at in CIA suspense fiction. I have no doubt that through the misuse of these drugs a witness' testimony may become faulty and even suspect. Once having undergone exposure to something of this nature is the witness still going to be allowed to give his best recollection, or be precluded from testifying?

I am firmly of the belief that jurors are quite capable of seeing through flaky testimony and pseudo-scientific clap-trap. I quite agree that we should not waste our valuable court time watching witch doctors, voo-doo practitioners or brujas go through the entrails of dead chickens in a fruitless search for the truth. However this is only because the practice is too time consuming and its probative value is zilch. I like the rule established in *Frye v. United States* . . . on the basis that it is a good pragmatic tool to keep out unnecessary, time consuming and nonproductive evidence. . . . However, the idea that an eyeball witness to a transaction be denied the opportunity to tell a jury his recollections of what he saw is disturbing to me whether that recollection has been refreshed by hypnosis, truth serum, drugs, intimidation, coercion, coaching, brainwashing or impaired by the plain old passage of time. (pp. 926–928)

The per se exclusion rule prohibits anything remembered during or after a hypnosis session from being admitted into evidence. The *Shirley* rule was actually even more severe. In its initial opinion, the *Shirley* court held that any witness or victim who had been hypnotized for forensic purposes would not be allowed to testify *at all* regarding *any* of the facts of the case. Once a person was hypnotized, that person was disqualified from testifying even about matters remembered and recorded *before* hypnosis was used. Thus, this initial ruling disqualified the witness, not just the posthypnotic testimony. However, the Supreme Court of California modified its *Shirley* ruling to indicate that memories that had been recorded before the hypnosis session would be admissible. Thus, a witness or victim who has given a recorded prehypnosis statement is permitted to testify about memories revealed in this statement. However, the per se exclusion rule bars all testimony that is recalled during or after the hypnosis session, and it prevents the witness or victim from testifying about a posthypnotic identification of the defendant (McConkey & Sheehan, 1995).

The initial *Shirley* opinion was also modified with regard to defendants. The court said that a defendant in a criminal case would be permitted to testify about matters remembered during or after hypnosis. This modification later achieved constitutional status in the U.S. Supreme Court decision in *Rock v. Arkansas* (1987), where the Court held that the Sixth Amendment prohibited a state from automatically excluding, by way of a per se inadmissibility rule, a criminal defendant's testimony.

Commentators who support the per se exclusion rule cite *Shirley* as an example of why the hypnotically refreshed recollection should be prohibited. They claim that hypnosis substantially altered the victim's testimony and was used successfully to get her to tell a coherent story. For example, Karlin and Orne (1996, p. 57) have stated that after Catherine, the alleged victim, was hypnotized, she stopped telling multiple versions of her story; instead, her testimony "did not waver from her final version, which she told in court with considerable certainty." The implication here is that the hypnosis solidified a now consistent, but completely false, story, which was told with confidence and coherence.

Although it is true that Catherine did not tell a consistent and coherent story before hypnosis and was probably hypnotized by the prosecutor to get her to do so, the opposite of what Karlin and Orne report is true (Scheflin, 1997b). According to the California Supreme Court recitation of what actually occurred:

> The jury believed part of Catherine's story, as it convicted the defendant of rape; but it also apparently found that she was lying when she described in detail the alleged act of oral copulation, as it acquitted the defendant of that charge. The jury doubtless had a difficult task, since Catherine's performance as a witness was far from exemplary: the record is replete with instances in which her testimony was vague, changeable, self-contradictory, or prone to unexplained lapses of memory. Indeed, on occasion she professed to be unable to remember assertions that she had herself made on the witness stand only the previous day. (p. 245)

Thus, the hypnosis was *ineffective* in fabricating a coherent, consistent, and false story. Furthermore, the jury was not awed by the use of hypnosis—the jurors reached a reasoned approach that accepted some parts of the hypnotically refreshed testimony and rejected other parts of it, as juries do with testimony that was not hypnotically refreshed.

For many reasons, *Shirley* was a poor vehicle for articulating a per se exclusion rule. First, Catherine had been drinking and using drugs, suggesting that her memory storage at the time of the alleged assault was impaired by the intoxication. Hypnosis is not effective under this condition. Second, the prosecutor, who was hardly neutral, performed the hypnosis and did so on the eve of Catherine's testimony. Third, the hypnosis was not for the purpose of solving a crime, but for the purpose of enhancing Catherine's credibility as a witness. It can be argued that the misuse of hypnosis in *Shirley* did not require a per se exclusion rule in *all* cases, any more than the fact that the police unfairly question a witness in one case should lead to a rule that no witness may be questioned. It should be noted that none of the alleged dangers of using hypnosis to refresh memory were present in *Shirley* because Catherine, before and after the hypnosis, had a slippery memory and lacked confidence in her recollections.

By the time *Shirley* was decided, police across the country were being trained by the thousands in hypnosis. The inadequacy of this training began to alarm the courts and became the subject of frequent media stories. The California Supreme Court was clearly influenced by the expanding use of police hypnotists, especially considering that the country's leading training school was in Los Angeles (Reiser, 1980). The growing number of police hypnotists, coupled with the improper use of hypnosis in the *Shirley* case, shaped the law far more than did the science of hypnosis used with memory.

The Guidelines Test and the "Totality of the Circumstances" Test

In between the *Mack* and *Shirley* cases, in time and in decision, the New Jersey Supreme Court in 1981 rejected the wide-open *Harding* ruling and the completely closed per se rule of *Mack*. Instead, the justices in *State v. Hurd* (1981) permitted hypnotically refreshed recollection to be admissible in court provided the following guidelines had been followed:

First, a psychiatrist or psychologist experienced in the use of hypnosis must conduct the session. . . .

Second, the professional conducting the hypnotic session should be independent of and not regularly employed by the prosecutor, investigator or defense. . . .

Third, any information given to the hypnotist by law enforcement personnel or the defense prior to the hypnotic session must be recorded, either in writing or another suitable form. . . .

Fourth, before inducing hypnosis the hypnotist should obtain from the subject a detailed description of the facts as the subject remembers them. . . .

Fifth, all contacts between the hypnotist and the subject must be recorded. . . .

Sixth, only the hypnotist and the subject should be present during any phase of the hypnotic session, including the prehypnotic testing and the post-hypnotic interview. . . . (p. 533)

This "admissibility with guidelines" test required courts to hold a pretrial hearing to ascertain whether the guidelines had been met, which in turn provided support that the hypnotically refreshed recollection was reliable enough to be admitted into evidence. At trial, experts and cross-examination could further test the memory's reliability.

But what if all of the guidelines had not been scrupulously followed? Should courts strictly adhere to the guidelines, or should they use them more flexibly? Adopting the latter approach, most courts articulated the "totality of the circumstances" test, whereby the reliability of the hypnotically refreshed memory is evaluated pretrial by examining whether, under the totality of the circumstances surrounding the hypnosis sessions, the hypnotically refreshed testimony appears sufficiently free of undue suggestion or other taint so that its reliability should be tested in court rather than excluded in its entirety (*Borawick v. Shay*, 1995; Clemens, 1991).

The main difference between the per se exclusion rule and the totality of the circumstances test is the former's rejection of *every* case in which hypnosis has been performed, compared to the latter's requirement that every case have a pretrial hearing to determine if the hypnosis sessions were likely to be unduly suggestive (Scheflin, 1994a, 1994b).

HYPNOSIS WITH DEFENDANTS

The three rules discussed deal with the admissibility of the hypnotically refreshed recollection of witnesses and victims of crimes. What rule should be applied when the hypnosis is used with persons accused of committing the crime?

In several cases, hypnosis has been misused by the police in an effort to obtain information from a defendant about a crime. For example, in *Leyra v. Denno* (1954), hypnosis was used in an attempt to coerce a confession from Leyra, who was accused of killing his parents. After hours of intense interrogation shortly after the murders, a doctor offered to treat Leyra for a headache. The doctor covertly hypnotized Leyra and told him that he might as well confess to the murders. The doctor assured the defendant that he would see to it that the police would "go easy" on him. Leyra confessed to the doctor, and then to the police.

He was found guilty and sentenced to the electric chair, but this conviction was reversed on appeal because the confession had been coerced by the hypnosis. At the next trial, Leyra was again found guilty based on a second confession, but the U.S. Supreme Court reversed. The majority opinion held that the second confession should be considered part of a continuum clearly related to the first confession and thereby similarly coerced. By the time a third trial was brought, the remaining evidence was largely circumstantial and inadequate. Despite this fact, Leyra was again found guilty but, because of the sparse evidence, the case again was reversed on appeal. Leyra was eventually freed of all charges because of the coercive misuse of hypnosis to elicit his confessions. The law is clear that hypnosis may be used by the police with criminal defendants, but only with their informed consent and only if proper guidelines have been followed to avoid undue influence or impermissible suggestion.

Apart from the police use of hypnosis with suspects, defendants may volunteer to be hypnotized to assist their own defense. In *State v. Papp* (1978; Orne, 1979), a defendant who claimed amnesia for parts of the crime underwent hypnosis. His performance during hypnotic age regression suggested his own exoneration. Expert witnesses for the prosecution testified, however, that his behavior was typical of someone simulating, rather than experiencing, hypnosis. On the strength of this testimony, the hypnosis session was interpreted as self-serving and was not introduced in court. In another case, *People v. Ritchie* (1977; Orne, 1979), a defendant undergoing hypnosis implicated his wife rather than himself, but the court eventually decided to exclude the hypnotic evidence. On the other hand, Mutter (1984, 1990) has reported cases where hypnosis with the defendant produced exonerating statements that were later independently corroborated. In *Rock v. Arkansas* (1987), the U.S. Supreme Court dealt with exactly this situation.

May a per se exclusion rule be applied to criminal defendants to prohibit them from testifying after their memories were hypnotically refreshed? In *Rock v. Arkansas* (1987), a wife and her husband began an argument that eventually led to a physical struggle. A gun was produced and the husband was shot and killed. The wife, charged with his death, could not remember the actual shooting, though she did remember that they were arguing. Limited amnesia (Schacter, 1986), or situation-specific amnesia (Gudjonsson, 1992), following traumatic events has been well documented (E. L. Loftus & Burns, 1982; Scheflin, 2004). Defense counsel sent his client to a mental health professional for hypnosis. During the hypnosis session, the wife remembered that her finger was never on the trigger. As a result of her statement under hypnosis, defense counsel had the gun tested at a laboratory. The results showed that the gun was defective and could discharge even though the trigger had not been pulled. Thus, the wife's exculpatory testimony was at least partially corroborated. However, Arkansas followed a per se exclusion rule which prevented the wife from testifying about her hypnotically refreshed recollection. After being convicted, she appealed on the grounds that the per se exclusion violated her constitutional right to testify. The U.S. Supreme Court held that application of a per se rule of inadmissibility "does not extend to *per se* exclusions that may be reliable in an individual case. Wholesale inadmissibility of a defendant's testimony is an arbitrary restriction on the right to testify in the absence of clear evidence by the State repudiating the validity of all posthypnosis recollections" (p. 61).

The *Rock* ruling was reaffirmed in *United States v. Scheffer* (1998), which upheld a per se exclusion rule where the defendant in a court-martial proceeding sought admission of polygraph results to support his testimony that he had not knowingly used drugs. The Court specifically distinguished *Rock* because in that case, the exclusion of evidence significantly undermined fundamental elements of the defense. The defendant was unable to testify that the killing was accidental because this memory had been refreshed by hypnosis. Thus, the per se rule "deprived the jury of the testimony of the only witness who was at the scene and had firsthand knowledge of the facts. . . . Moreover, the rule infringed upon the accused's interest in testifying in her own defense—an interest that we deemed particularly significant, as it is the defendant who is the target of any criminal prosecution" (pp. 315–316). By contrast, in *Scheffer*, the exclusion of the polygraph results did "not implicate any significant interest of the accused"(pp. 316–317), nor did it significantly impair the defense's presentation of its case. As noted by the Court, the members of the general court-martial "heard all the relevant details of the charged offense from the perspective of the accused, and the [per se] Rule did not preclude him from introducing any factual evidence. Rather, [defendant] was barred merely from introducing expert opinion testimony to bolster his own credibility." (p. 317). Thus, a per se exclusion rule is unconstitutional if it undermines the ability of an accused to present a defense (*Paxton v. Ward*, 1999).

In *Newman v. Hopkins* (2001), a woman who had been sexually assaulted provided police with a description of her assailant, who she claimed spoke with a Hispanic accent. The defendant wanted permission to read a neutral statement aloud in court to demonstrate to the jury that he did not speak with an accent. However, under Nebraska's evidentiary rulings, such voice exemplars were per se inadmissible because they were unreliable for the reason that an accent could be easily manipulated and the circumstances under which the victim heard her attacker's voice could not be replicated. The federal court overruled the defendant's conviction holding that a per se exclusion of such evidence was unreasonable because "the reliability determination was based not on an individualized inquiry into the facts and circumstances of [defendant's] proposed voice exemplar but rather on characteristics common to all voice exemplars" (p. 852). The categorical bar on voice exemplar evidence "prevented [the defendant] from offering factual evidence and significantly undermined his ability to establish the essential elements of his defense" (p. 853). According to the court:

> We recognize full well that the state of Nebraska has a legitimate interest in the reliability of evidence, and if the facts and circumstances surrounding a particular voice exemplar make it so unreliable as to render it inadmissible under Nebraska's evidentiary rules, a defendant would have no absolute right to introduce it. . . . Rather than balancing the state's concern with the defendant's Sixth Amendment rights, however, Nebraska's *per se* rule bars not only unreliable evidence but also evidence that may, in individual cases, be reliable. This the state

may not constitutionally do, for "[a] State's legitimate interest in barring unreliable evidence does not extend to *per se* exclusions that may be reliable in an individual case." *Rock*, 483 U.S. at 61, 107 S.Ct. 2704. . . . The decisions of the Supreme Court clearly establish that such a *per se* rule is unconstitutional. *Rock*, 483 U.S. at 61, 107 S.Ct. 2704. (p. 853)

Thus, even after *Rock*, trial judges may still rule that a defendant's hypnotically refreshed recollection is inadmissible if such testimony is deemed to be unreliable (*State v. Butterworth*, 1990; *State v. L.K.*, 1990; *Tumlinson v. State*, 1988), provided there has been a pretrial hearing on this issue.

Orne (1982, cited in Perry and Laurence, 1990, p. 267) has pointed out that "the risk to the legal system that a defendant's memory be distorted by hypnosis in his favor is probably disproportionately small. Thus, judges and juries expect defendants' statements to be self-serving and designed to present him in the best possible light." Consequently, he supported the *Rock* opinion and argued in favor of a "double standard" whereby defendants are permitted to have access to hypnosis for their defense, but the hypnotically refreshed recollection of witnesses and victims should be excluded (Orne, Dinges, & Orne, 1990). Perry and Laurence (1990, p. 281) have expressed concern that permitting defendants to testify about their hypnotically refreshed memories "may ultimately reverse the trend in American courts to proscribe the admission of testimony derived from hypnosis"; so far, however, courts have not been so inclined.

If the per se exclusion rule is to be altered in states that follow it, it will be for reasons other than the fact that defendants may testify about their hypnotically refreshed recollection. For example, in *Daubert v. Merrell Dow Pharmaceuticals, Inc.* (1993), the U.S. Supreme Court rejected the *Frye* rule and changed the test for the admissibility of scientific evidence in all federal courts. According to *Daubert*, the admissibility of expert testimony in all cases is determined by the trial judge according to a flexibly applied test involving four factors concerning the expert's opinions: (1) whether they are "verifiable or falsifiable," or otherwise derived by a scientific method; (2) whether they have been published or peer-reviewed; (3) whether they have a known or potential error rate; and (4) whether they are generally accepted in the scientific community.

The *Daubert* test has been adopted by most state courts. Because it is based on flexibility, some courts have held that per se exclusion rules are no longer defensible. In two cases involving polygraphs, federal courts have held that evidence obtained from a lie detector cannot automatically be excluded (*United States v. Pettigrew*, 1996; *United States v. Posado*, 1995). In another polygraph case (*United States v. Cordoba*, 1996), the court held that its per se exclusion rule against the admission of polygraph evidence was "effectively overruled" by the 'flexible inquiry' assigned to the trial judge by *Daubert*" (p. 227). The court further noted that other per se rules were equally vulnerable to abolition and had already been overthrown.

More directly on point, in *Rowland v. Commonwealth* (1995), a stepmother saw her stepson shoot her and her daughter in the back. The stepmother's physician diagnosed her as having Posttraumatic Stress Disorder and recommended she see Dr. William Wester, a psychologist. Wester agreed with the diagnosis and decided to treat her with hypnosis. Before beginning the hypnosis treatment,

Wester, a former president of the American Society of Clinical Hypnosis with extensive forensic hypnosis experience, took complete statements from the stepmother about the shooting incident. The first statement was audiotaped and the second statement was videotaped. Following the videotaping, Wester used hypnosis for the first time. The stepmother's statement while in trance was virtually identical to her recorded prehypnotic statements. After the defendant was convicted, on appeal he argued for a rule of per se inadmissibility. In a 4–3 decision, the Supreme Court of Kentucky held that a per se inadmissibility rule was no longer appropriate and might violate *Daubert*.

SUPPORT FOR THE PER SE EXCLUSION RULE

No commentator has defended the application of the open admissibility rule, which is still followed in three states (North Dakota, Oregon, Wyoming). The hypnosis literature debates whether the per se exclusion rule or the totality of the circumstances rule is preferable. Faigman, Kaye, Saks, and Sanders (2002, p. 272), following the lead of other commentators (Giannelli, 1995; Karlin & Orne, 1996; Laurence and Perry, 1988), assert that the "majority of courts employ a per se rule of inadmissibility for hypnotically refreshed testimony." Scoboria, Kirsch, Mazzoni, and Milling (2002, p. 26) state that the per se exclusion rule "is presently applied to hypnotically refreshed testimony in approximately two thirds of the states." However, these claims are not accurate. Most jurisdictions do *not* follow the per se exclusion rule. As of 2004, 23 states have adopted the per se exclusion rule; 15 states and 11 federal courts of appeals have adopted the totality of the circumstances test; and 9 states plus the District of Columbia and the District of Columbia Circuit Court of Appeals have no definitive court rulings (Appendix 2). Thus, the per se exclusion rule applies in 23 of the 63 jurisdictions in the U.S. legal system.

Proponents of the per se exclusion rule (Karlin & Orne, 1997; Laurence & Perry, 1988) point out that it is economical because it saves court time and judicial resources, and they argue that hypnosis *inevitably* contaminates memory, thereby constituting a tampering with evidence. Based on the claims of experts who support automatic exclusion of hypnotically refreshed recollection, courts have identified the following dangers associated with hypnotically refreshed recollection:

A. Suggestibility
   1. The subject becomes "suggestible" and may try to please the hypnotist with answers the subject thinks will be met with approval.
   2. The subject is highly responsive to the creation ("implantation") of pseudomemories.
B. Reliability
   3. The subject is likely to "confabulate," that is, to fill in details from the imagination, in order to make an answer more coherent and complete.
   4. The subject experiences "memory hardening," which gives him or her great confidence in both true and false memories, making effective cross-examination more difficult.
   5. The subject has source amnesia which prevents properly identifying whether a memory occurred before or during hypnosis, or whether the memory is real or suggested.

      6. The subject experiences a loss of critical judgment.
  C. Believability
      7. Juries will disproportionately believe testimony that is the product of hypnosis.
      8. The subject can easily feign hypnosis and can be deceptive in trance. (Scheflin & Frischholz, 1999, p. 93–94)

Two additional arguments against the use of hypnosis with memory have surfaced. First, Perry (1995) has claimed that even when hypnosis is not being utilized directly, its contaminating effects occur with techniques that are actually "disguised" hypnosis. Disguised techniques, which are prevalent in stage hypnosis shows, have been learned and used by "recovered memory" therapists who have added their "New Age ideology which argues that insight into the cause of symptoms leads to their alleviation" (p. 196). For Perry, disguised hypnosis is any use of guided imagery, relaxation, imagination, or visualization. Perry describes a student who discussed with her mother whether she should participate in a hypnosis experiment. On the morning of the experiment, the mother said that maybe the daughter should not participate because "you might never come out of it." Perry claims that this statement acted as a prehypnotic suggestion and the student had great difficulty coming out of the trance. By contrast, H. Spiegel (1997) classified the mother's behavior as a "nocebo," a negative message that inhibits healing. Thus, according to Perry's argument, *even therapists or police who do not use hypnosis are using hypnosis.*

The second objection to hypnosis states that hypnotic consequences may affect people who are not responsive to hypnotic suggestion. In two articles, Orne and his colleagues (Orne, Whitehouse, Dinges, & Orne, 1996; Orne, Whitehouse, Orne, & Dinges, 1996), based on retrospective analyses of earlier research, argued that low and medium hypnotizables are vulnerable to contamination from the inherently corrupting influence of hypnosis. Thus, *even those who are not affected by hypnosis are affected by hypnosis.* Brown, Scheflin, and Hammond (1998) analyze and reject this position based on methodological flaws in the Orne research design. No court has yet dealt with these two additional objections to the admissibility of hypnotically refreshed recollection.

SUPPORT FOR THE TOTALITY OF THE CIRCUMSTANCES RULE

Proponents of the totality of the circumstances test reject the view that hypnotically refreshed testimony should never be admitted in court. Their position has four dimensions: (1) Objections to hypnosis are based on logical errors; (2) a per se exclusion rule is unfair in general, and to real victims of crime in particular; (3) a per se exclusion rule is not practical; and (4) the relevant science fails to support the claim that hypnosis inevitably contaminates memory or makes the hypnotized subject unduly confident, or that hypnotically refreshed recollection is necessarily unreliable.

Logical Errors

Proponents of the totality of the circumstances test argue that experts who support the per se exclusion rule commit four major logical errors. First, they confuse the *use* of hypnosis with the *misuse* of hypnosis. The fact that a police officer may use undue suggestion during a particular interrogation does not mean that all police interrogations are improperly suggestive and should be prohibited. The same argument applies to the use of hypnosis. When the hypnotist follows strict guidelines to prevent undue suggestion or influence, memory is not contaminated. When hypnosis is used improperly (Coons, 1988; *State v. Zimmerman*, 2003), the reliability of resulting memories is subject to question, just as they should be with any other retrieval method not properly applied. Lynn, Neuschatz, Fite, and Kirsch (2001, p. 120) are correct in pointing out that "it would be wrong to scapegoat hypnosis while ignoring or minimizing the potentially misleading and hazardous effects of a variety of nonhypnotic memory enhancement techniques (e.g., leading questions, reinforcement for recall)."

Second, experts supporting the per se exclusion rule mistakenly attribute to hypnosis phenomena that are really aspects of memory. Thus, confabulation, memory hardening, and postevent misinformation are all attributes of *memory;* they are not created solely by hypnosis, and they occur without the use of hypnosis. Memory research has shown that confabulation is a natural way that memory works, rather than a by-product of hypnotic trance (E. F. Loftus, 1980). Experiments with eyewitness testimony have conclusively demonstrated confabulation in nonhypnotic settings and have also demonstrated that hypnotically refreshed recollection is not necessarily confabulated (Brown et al., 1998; Hammond et al., 1995: E. F. Loftus, 1975, 1979a, 1979b, 1979c). Scientific studies demonstrate that the inherent memory problems of confabulation and postevent misinformation effects are not enhanced by hypnosis if appropriate guidelines have been followed (Hammond et al., 1995). Furthermore, memory hardening without hypnosis may be achieved by repetition and rehearsal, as trial lawyers demonstrate on a daily basis.

Third, proponents of the per se exclusion rule mistakenly assume that phenomena that may be more prevalent in high hypnotizables are equally plausible in those who are moderate to low hypnotizables (Diamond, 1980). Most of the scientific studies reporting memory distortion with hypnosis have involved high-hypnotizable subjects, the population most vulnerable to memory distortion. The problems of confabulation and an artificial sense of confidence are especially applicable to the small subgroup of the population who measure as highly hypnotizable, *whether or not hypnosis formally has been used* (D. Spiegel & Spiegel, 1984). An intense, structured, and leading police interrogation or preparation for testimony by an attorney can have a more powerful effect than any formal hypnotic ceremony would ever have in producing a false confession (Connery, 1977; Gudjonsson, 1992) or false memory (Gudjonsson, 2003). Some studies have concluded that high hypnotizability may be a factor equal to or more important than the formal use of the hypnotic ceremony (Zelig & Beidleman, 1981). Barnier and McConkey (1992) showed 30 high- and 30 low-hypnotizable subjects slides of a purse snatching; the subjects then imagined seeing the slides in hypnosis or waking conditions. The experimenter suggested that the offender had a moustache (true), wore a scarf (false), and picked up flowers (false). Memory was tested by the experimenter after the suggestion, by another experimenter during an inquiry session, and again by the second experimenter after the experimenter appeared to have ended the session. Hypnotizability, but not hypnosis, was associated with false memory reports; more high- than low-hypnotizable subjects reported false memories.

Other studies have argued that both high hypnotizability and a formal induction of hypnosis are necessary to produce an alteration in the recall of information (Dywan & Bowers, 1983). Courts have generally overlooked the significance of individual differences in evaluating hypnotically refreshed memory. Using one of the standardized hypnotizability scales, such as the Hypnotic Induction Profile (H. Spiegel & Spiegel, 1978), the Stanford Hypnotic Susceptibility Scales (Weitzenhoffer & Hilgard, 1959), the Stanford Hypnotic Clinical Scale (Hilgard & Hilgard, 1975), the Harvard Group Scale (Perry, Nadon, & Button, 1992), or the Barber Creative Imagination Scale (Barber & Wilson, 1978–1979), to document the subject's degree of hypnotic responsivity, if any, should be an essential part of the forensic use of hypnosis. Indeed, if a subject fails to demonstrate any hypnotic responsivity on formal testing, the person conducting the session would be well advised to forgo any further hypnotic ceremonies as the subject is unlikely to respond, and the problems inherent with the appearance of having induced hypnosis can be avoided.

Fourth, experts who seek to ban hypnotically refreshed recollection from courtrooms overgeneralize the dangers of hypnotically created false memories. The claim that hypnosis always contaminates memory is disproved by the many cases in which hypnosis did not alter the memory of a witness or victim. The fact that memory can be distorted with hypnosis does not mean that it will be so distorted. Furthermore, the fact that an interviewing procedure may be tainted does not mean that the witness is tainted.

Fairness

Scheflin (1997b) has offered the following true case as an example of the way a total exclusion of hypnotically refreshed recollection is unfair to true victims:

> A 4-year-old girl went to her mother and said, "Daddy's touching me in my private parts." The mother had a breakdown and was hospitalized. The child, now in the custody of daddy, learned not to talk about this—Look what happened to mommy when she was told. Several years pass and the molestings continued. Medical records of the child were consistent with molesting, but the child would not talk when asked. After a year of therapy, hypnosis was used and the child talked about the molesting. New York courts would not admit her posthypnotic testimony despite the fact that there was independent medical corroborating evidence that she was molested. Without her evidence, there was no proof that daddy was the molester. Daddy retained custody. (p. 269)

Where is the justice in telling that little girl that the courts will not hear her story?

Fundamental fairness demands that each case be heard on its own merits, at least at a preliminary hearing where the quality of the evidence can be judicially assessed. The per se exclusion rule prohibits posthypnotic memories from being admitted into evidence even though it can be shown that the hypnosis procedures were scrupulously neutral and that the memories can be independently corroborated as true.

The per se exclusion rule has been defended on the grounds that it saves money because it avoids court hearings, but trading judicial economy for a lesser form of justice is a poor bargain. Furthermore, because most trials have preliminary hearings anyway, the cost savings, if any, would not be substantial.

Every area of the law dealing with undue influence or suggestion, including the assessment of police lineups and interrogations, uses a totality of the circumstances test—except the issue of the admissibility of hypnotically refreshed recollection.

As Scheflin (1997b, p. 207) has noted, use of a per se exclusion rule in cases involving forensic hypnosis may appear quite odd:

> According to the . . . *per se* exclusion rule for hypnotized witnesses, a person who has been lobotomized can testify in court, a person who has received massive electroshock treatments can testify in court, a person who has taken enormous dosages of mind-altering psychiatric drugs or psychedelics can testify in court, a person who has suffered substantial organic brain damage can testify in court; but a person who had been competently hypnotized by an experienced licensed professional who carefully followed strict guidelines to avoid undue suggestions, cannot testify in court.

While a per se rule will eliminate some false memories from evidence, it will also eliminate 100% of the true memories.

Practicality

Application of the per se rule creates several complications and undesirable consequences. Scheflin (1994a, pp. 26–32, 1994b, pp. 30–36) has criticized the per se exclusion rule on the following grounds:

- *Sexual seduction:* Under the *per se* rule, an unethical hypnotist who uses trance to facilitate seduction will have committed the perfect crime. The subject-victim will be unable to testify because all his or her memories are posthypnotic. Even the supporters of the *per se* rule have acknowledged that an exception must be made for illegal or unethical conduct committed while the subject was in trance (Giannelli, 1995).
- *Time delays:* Suppose an individual is hypnotized and has no new memories. Five years later, with no intervening hypnosis, additional memories surface. Is the witness disqualified to testify in regard to them simply because of the hypnosis five years earlier? Is there any time limit after which the memories cannot be attributed to the hypnosis?
- *Self-hypnosis:* Suppose a subject is taught self-hypnosis and practices the technique regularly. Are all memories now contaminated?
- *Audiotapes:* The market is flooded with "self-hypnosis/subliminal message" audiotapes. Does listening to such a tape disqualify a person from testifying?
- *Therapeutic hypnosis:* Suppose a patient arrives at therapy and the therapist decides hypnosis would be beneficial. The hypnosis is not conducted for the purpose of retrieving memories. During the trance, however, memories

are revealed. Should the *per se* rule disqualify the witness from testifying about them?

- *Nonhypnotizable subjects:* A person who is nonhypnotizable may be subjected to an hypnotic induction ceremony, but will not experience hypnosis. Opposing counsel, however, will move to block the person's testimony on the basis of the attempted hypnosis. The *per se* rule may thus bar testimony even though no hypnosis actually occurred. For this reason, measurement of hypnotizability is extremely important. Because hypnotizability is a stable and measurable trait, and because people vary in their hypnotic capacity from no responsivity to high responsivity, it is important to determine whether hypnosis has indeed occurred. The California Supreme Court accepted this argument in *People v. Caro* (1988) where an expert, Dr. David Spiegel, was able to show that the witness was not hypnotizable despite police efforts to induce a trance. The court held that the witness could testify fully because the attempt to hypnotize had not succeeded. Similarly, a person who is highly hypnotizable may be susceptible to memory errors even if no hypnosis is used. For this reason, Beahrs (1988) has argued that hypnosis can never be excluded from the legal setting—even if everyone agreed that it was a good idea to do so.

Lynn et al. (2001, p. 119), who conclude that "as a general rule, hypnosis should not be used to assist recall in forensic situations," nevertheless have suggested two other situations in which hypnosis is warranted: where "desperate" circumstances are involved, such as an ongoing kidnapping, and as a "last resort" when "other recall methods have tried and have failed to elicit useful material." A fully documented instance of the latter situation is reported by Raginsky (1969), who used hypnosis to restore a repressed memory of an airline pilot for the events surrounding a major airline crash. In the previous 2 years, the pilot had undergone psychoanalytic interviews, directive interviews, intravenous pentothal, and psychological interviews, all of which were conducted by highly qualified professionals, including a past president of the American Psychiatric Association, a past president of the American Psychoanalytic Association, and a world-famous psychologist. In addition, the pilot had interviews with leading airline safety investigators, all of which were focused on the goal of memory recovery and all of whom were unsuccessful in restoring details of his memory. The hypnotically refreshed recollection led safety investigators to reexamine specific portions the plane wreckage. When they did so, they found a defective part they had previously overlooked, thereby confirming the hypnotically retrieved repressed memory.

Studies of Hypnotic Memory Enhancement

Hypnosis has lent itself to mystification, even in forensic settings. The dramatic and compelling examples of previously amnesic material unearthed with hypnosis, especially in a traumatized witness or victim, led to hopes that hypnosis could be used as a kind of truth serum and that the material elicited with it had some higher order of veracity than ordinary memories. Indeed, many police officers were taught that memory acts like a tape recorder and hypnosis facilitated the replaying of the tape. It has been known for some time, however, that memory is reconstructive (Münsterberg, 1908). Gardner (1932–1933, pp. 400–401) put it quite eloquently when he wrote:

> What memory does not recall, the imagination tends to supply—unconsciously as a rule, half-consciously where bias or suggestion exists, and consciously in whole-cloth perjury. As memory fades, imagination retouches the details; where this is done unconsciously, therefore honestly, we are apt to recall what we *think* should have normally occurred, or, if personally involved, what we *wish* had occurred, or what, from suggestions now half-forgotten, we *believe* occurred. . . . The merest skeleton of fact, repeatedly told, bodies forth as a complete, truthful narrative, "ere long fiction expels reality from memory and reigns in its stead alone" and "unconscious impressions" blend with "conscious realities," playing havoc with objective truth. This "filling-in" of memory occurs so unconsciously that it does not even affect the positive belief or manner of the witness. . . . Memory is more than the re-instatement of the original perception; it involves the interpretation of details, judgment, estimates, and the correlation of related incidents. Imagination and suggestion are twin-artists ever ready to retouch the fading daguerreotype of memory. Just as "Nature abhors a vacuum," the mind abhors an uncompleted picture, and paints in the details, careless indeed as to whether the old picture is reproduced faithfully.

The question of what rule to adopt for the admission of hypnotically refreshed recollection is a policy issue, but the question of what impact hypnosis has on memory retrieval is a question of science. What does the science say about the accuracy of memories recollected with the assistance of hypnosis?

The experimental literature has attempted to answer some of the questions of the effectiveness of hypnosis on improving recall, but these studies are limited by the problem of ecological validity—the strained analogy between the laboratory and the forensic setting, especially when the topic to be studied is the effect of hypnosis on the memory of *traumatized* witnesses and victims. As an expert witness in *United States v. Hall* (1997, p. 1204) correctly noted, "People think of experiments as the be all and end all of science. . . . That is simply not the case. . . . I'm simply saying that . . . given the problems that arise in doing particularly social science research, we cannot do the things to people that we can even do to animals." It is neither legal nor ethical to traumatize people for the purpose of conducting laboratory research, and it is not clear that nontraumatized subjects will behave the way traumatized subjects will behave. There is a difference between watching a carefully crafted film about a crime, and being a witness to or a victim of an actual crime as it occurs. Thus, while the laboratory permits controlled studies to be conducted, there is some question as to whether the results from the laboratory generalize to real-life crime settings.

Even in experiments that attempt to replicate the kind of emotional arousal that may occur in a rape, an assault, a staged mock assassination (Timm, 1981), or a gory film (Putnam, 1979), such artificial settings cannot reproduce the sense of fear, pain, and helplessness that real victims and witnesses may experience during a crime. The intertwined roles of emotion and content in memory retrieval cannot be adequately replicated in a laboratory.

Another confounding effect involves the motivation involved in testimony (McConkey & Sheehan, 1995). It is far different for a college student to attempt to recall information as part of an experiment than for a witness or victim to provide information about a traumatic event that may lead to someone's incarceration. Misidentification of the perpetrator could send an innocent person to prison and expose the public to further harm from the real criminal. These motivational factors are crucial, especially when they affect the response criterion (i.e., the willingness of the subject to report something as a memory), and it cannot be assumed that factors that influence the response criterion in a laboratory experiment are the same as those that affect a witness's willingness to testify. Furthermore, there is always the problem of demand characteristics when evaluating laboratory experiments (Kihlstrom, 2002; Orne, 1959; Perry, 2002).

Finally, none of the laboratory studies deals with amnesia for an event and the spontaneous recovery of memory by hypnosis.

On the other hand, clinical studies, though they have real-world validity, lack scientific rigor. Furthermore, as pointed out by McConkey and Sheehan (1995), in cases involving crimes, excessive motivation to remember details may actually hinder accurate recall. It is possible for a subject to come up with material that is responsive to internal needs or external factors rather than the truth. A number of reports illustrate either self-serving and feigned stories elicited under hypnosis (Orne, 1979; D. Spiegel & Spiegel, 1984) or an artificially induced experimental confabulation in a highly hypnotizable subject instructed to stick by an invented story (H. Spiegel, 1980). Thus, it is clear from the clinical literature that it is possible for hypnotized individuals to come up with compelling stories that are not necessarily true.

When faced with hypnotically refreshed recollection, courts have primarily been concerned that hypnosis inevitably produces confabulation, produces pseudomemories, and increases self-confidence, which inhibits cross-examination. Studies fail to support this view, although the danger of confabulation, pseudomemories, and self-confidence is always present when testimony is presented in court.

Confabulation

Memory research has shown that confabulation is a function of many complex variables, including a personality trait of responsiveness to confabulation, the nature of the social context, and the strength of the memory. Confabulation is not a by-product of hypnotic trance (Brown et al., 1998; E. F. Loftus, 1980). Experiments with eyewitness testimony have conclusively demonstrated confabulation in nonhypnotic settings and have also demonstrated that hypnotically refreshed recollection is not necessarily confabulated (E. F. Loftus, 1975, 1979a, 1979b, 1979c).

Pseudomemories

The judicial belief that hypnosis itself produces pseudomemories is erroneous (Brown et al., 1998; McConkey, Barnier, & Sheehan, 1998). As noted by Lynn and Kirsch (1996, p. 151):

False memories can be created with or without hypnosis, and the role of hypnosis in their creation is likely to be quite small. Similarly, the available data suggest that the trait of fantasy proneness is not likely to be of great importance. . . . Hypnosis does not reliably produce more false memories than are produced in a variety of nonhypnotic situations in which misleading information is conveyed to participants.

Similarly, Beahrs, Cannell, and Gutheil (1996, p. 50) concluded that "false memories are more likely to arise from social influence, either inside or outside of hypnosis or psychotherapy; intrinsic suggestibility (especially interrogative) and dissociative potential; and less so, simply from being hypnotized." Lynn et al. (2001, p. 120) accurately conclude:

The effects of leading or suggestive questions is probably much greater than the effects of the administration of a hypnotic induction which, in general, increases suggestibility to only a small degree. After all, nonhypnotic suggestive procedures can result in the production of very unlikely or false memories that equal or exceed those elicited by hypnosis.

Self-Confidence

Many courts have accepted the view expressed by the Minnesota Supreme Court that "effective cross-examination of a previously hypnotized witness is virtually impossible" (*State v. Ture*, 1984). This has been labeled the "concreting" or "hardening" effect (Diamond, 1980). The only forensic studies on point, however, directly contradict the assertion that hypnotically enhanced pseudomemories are more resistant to cross-examination than are pseudomemories produced by skillful, suggestive interrogation techniques (Spanos, Gwynn, Comer, Baltruweit, & de Groh, 1989; Spanos, Quigley, Gwynn, Glatt, & Perlini, 1991). In *State v. Dreher* (1991, pp. 220–221), the court correctly observed:

The defendant's argument that, because of the hypnosis session, [the hypnotized subject's] trial testimony was delivered with an aura of confidence which it would not otherwise have had is not persuasive. The memory-hardening process is an intrinsic part of a witness's preparation for trial. While ordinarily it takes the form of numerous pretrial interviews and interrogations by counsel, the result is the same as that which defendant claims occurred here: a witness who testifies with conviction and believability. The fact that the witness has been prepped to testify effectively does not disqualify his evidence so long as it has not been falsified.

As correctly noted by Lynn and Kirsch (1996, p. 152), "The role of hypnosis in enhancing confidence in false memories is also exaggerated."

OPINIONS IN THE SCIENTIFIC COMMUNITY

The *legal* question of the admissibility of hypnotically refreshed memory depends in part on the *scientific* question of whether hypnosis is a reliable procedure for facilitating accurate recall. Courts for decades have been influenced by the general acceptance in the relevant scientific community of a method, technique, or procedure under judicial scrutiny. What do experts in the field of hypnosis believe about the science of hypnotically refreshed recollection and the admissibility in court of hypnotically retrieved memories?

The Report of the American Medical Association

The Council on Scientific Affairs of the American Medical Association (AMA) convened an eight-member panel to prepare a report on the scientific status of refreshing recollection by the use of hypnosis. This report was approved by the House of Delegates (AMA, 1985). The panel concluded that there is no evidence that hypnosis enhances recall of meaningless or nonsense material (Barber & Calverley, 1966; Dhanens & Lundy, 1975; Rosenhan & London, 1963), and there is no enhancement of the *recognition* of meaningful material, such as a photo identification (Timm, 1981).

The more interesting, and more significant, area of research for the evaluation of investigative hypnosis is the study of enhancement of *recall* of *meaningful* material. Indeed, "the AMA Report noted that the effectiveness of the use of hypnosis to uncover emotionally arousing memories had not been scientifically proven or disproven" (D. Speigel, personal communication, November 16, 2004). Some early studies indicate greater recall of meaningful material under hypnosis, but the price paid is an increase in incorrect recall and an increased sense of confidence (Steblay & Bothwell, 1994) not justified by the ratio of incorrect to correct new material. However, these studies did not attempt to control response bias. This is important because it is clear that repeated trials, even without hypnosis, can result in an increase in the reporting of new correct and incorrect information (Erdelyi, 1970, 1996). Indeed, the proportion of correct-incorrect responses is similar in hypnosis and nonhypnosis recall conditions; there is simply more productivity in the hypnosis condition (Dywan & Bowers, 1983). However, the research strategy that has been used to control for productivity encourages the subjects to guess; therefore, the significant increase in inaccurate responses in research using that paradigm is likely to be, in part, an artifact of the research design. The Dywan and Bowers study is particularly interesting because it demonstrates that low hypnotizables in the hypnotic condition perform no differently from high or low hypnotizables who are not hypnotized. It was only the high hypnotizables in the hypnosis condition who showed an increase in productivity and confidence. However, even with this group, no follow-ups were conducted to determine whether the reports were actually believed to be memories.

A study by Laurence and Perry (1983) relied on by the panel concluded that hypnotized individuals, told that they heard something while they were sleeping that in fact they did not hear, tended to report as real memories this hypnotically induced memory 7 days later. This study is identical to the experiment conducted by Bernheim a century ago and by Orne in 1982 (Barnes, 1982). It is also reminiscent of the "honest liar" experiment reported by H. Spiegel (1980). But even in the Laurence and Perry study, only a minority of the highly hypnotizable subjects were affected 7 days later. McCann and Sheehan (1988) criticized the study on methodological grounds, and the results have been overgeneralized in media accounts and in courtroom testimony by experts who report that hypnosis inevitably contaminates memory by causing implanted false memories. Similar studies of postevent misinformation that did not use hypnosis and did not use only highly suggestible subjects yield the same percentage of memory distortion. Even these results of memory distortion, however, shrink substantially when the research design is not a forced choice and when demand characteristics are controlled (Brown et al., 1998; Orne, 1962).

In 1994, the AMA reaffirmed its 1985 report, but it did so without a single citation to the post-1985 scientific literature.

Frischholz (1996) has presented an effective critique of the AMA report, noting that it used an outmoded definition of hypnosis and relied primarily on memory research using nonsense material in laboratory settings and on anecdotal reports in legal cases. Furthermore, the report failed to recognize the distinction between memory and hypnotically assisted memory. Precisely the same contaminations the experts cautioned against—confabulation, undue self-confidence, increased responsiveness to suggestion and/or social influences, and demand characteristics—may be produced in memory without hypnosis, as memory researchers have repeatedly demonstrated. Sheehan (1996, p. 13) is correct in observing that "an important conclusion that has emerged from the literature is that memory contamination is a function of memory and influence and not a danger specific to the use of hypnosis."

EXPERT OPINION

In 1995, the American Society of Clinical Hypnosis, after thoroughly examining the research literature and canvassing the opinions of approximately 80 experts on hypnosis, suggestion, and memory, concluded that a per se rule was not scientifically warranted (Hammond et al., 1995). The Society for Clinical and Experimental Hypnosis gave this publication the Arthur Shapiro Award. Brown et al. (1998) conducted a subsequent and more detailed examination of the scientific literature and also concluded that the per se exclusion rule was unnecessarily harsh. This book received many awards, including the American Psychiatric Association's prestigious Manfred S. Guttmacher Award.

Although a minority of experts continue to support the per se exclusion rule (Karlin, 1997; Karlin & Orne, 1996, 1997; Perry, Orne, London, & Orne, 1996), most forensic hypnosis authorities favor the totality of the circumstances test (Brown et al., 1998; Hammond et al., 1995; McConkey & Sheehan, 1995; Scheflin, 1996, 1997b; Scheflin & Shapiro, 1989). As Australian researcher Peter Sheehan (1996, p. 13) noted, the consensus "appears to be that, 'the courts must decide on a case by case basis the admissibility of hypnotically recalled material.'" Sheehan and McConkey (1993, p. 720) concluded, "It seems extreme to take the view that all hypnotically obtained information should be ignored"; 2 years later they expressly rejected the per se exclusion rule in favor of the "admissibility with safeguards" approach (McConkey & Sheehan, 1995). Sadoff and Dubin (1990, p. 121) reached the same conclusion: "The court must decide on a case by case basis about the admissibility of the hypnotic recall. We are opposed to the admissibility per se and the exclusion per se rules." Wagstaff (1996, p. 189), one of Britain's foremost forensic experts, concluded:

> Instead of a blanket rejection of anything said by the witness in such cases, we must judge each case individually. Perhaps we might more usefully ask, what might be the effect of this *particular* hypnosis session, on *particular* statements, made by this *particular* witness?

Some apparent supporters of a per se exclusion rule nevertheless recognize that hypnotically refreshed recollection may be accurate. According to Lynn et al. (2001, p. 120): "Although we argue against the use of hypnosis to bolster recall, it does not necessarily follow that all hypnotically elicited testimony is, by its very nature, inaccurate, and that hypnosis inevitably corrupts a person's memory."

Significantly, four members (Gravitz, Mutter, D. Spiegel, and H. Spiegel) of the original eight-member committee that drafted the AMA report now conclude that their report should not be used by courts to support a per se exclusion rule (Hammond et al., 1995; D. Spiegel, personal communication, November 16, 2004).

HYPNOSIS AND THE LEGAL STANDARD OF MENTAL HEALTH CARE

Hypnosis currently is facing legal challenges in the therapeutic setting in three different ways. First, per se rules serve as a threat to therapists using hypnosis because the therapist may be depriving the patient of the ability to testify in court (Scheflin, 1993). Thus, the rules developed in forensic settings to govern the admissibility of testimony find application in therapy settings to govern the treatment provided to the patient. For example, suppose a patient during a hypnosis session reports memories of child abuse that occurred years earlier. The patient now wants to sue the alleged perpetrator. Even though the hypnosis was competently conducted for therapeutic purposes, and even though memory retrieval was not the purpose for the hypnosis, and even though leading and suggestive questions were not used, the patient in states following a per se rule might be held disqualified from testifying about those memories. These patients may then decide to sue their therapists for disenfranchising them of their legal rights.

Scheflin and Shapiro (1989) first raised this issue and suggested the use of informed consent forms, which protect the patient and the therapist (Scheflin, 1993). The *Guidelines* for forensic and clinical hypnosis developed by the American Society of Clinical Hypnosis (Hammond et al., 1995) now strongly urge the use of informed consent forms. Failure to obtain informed consent before hypnosis is used in a forensic setting could invalidate the procedure, thereby preventing a witness who had been hypnotized from testifying. Failure to obtain informed consent in a therapy setting provides an opportunity for a lawsuit claiming malpractice liability. The difficulty of obtaining an informed consent to hypnosis in therapy is explored by Zeig (1985). The manner in which therapists utilize informed consent (the "event" model versus the "process" model) is discussed in Berg, Appelbaum, Lidz, and Parker (2001).

Second, beginning in the early 1990s, hundreds of lawsuits challenged the validity of repressed memories (Taub, 1996). In recent years, lawyers suing therapists have questioned the legitimacy of using hypnosis to retrieve memories. In other cases, lawyers have defended alleged perpetrators by claiming that the memories of their accusers were tainted by the hypnosis used in the course of the therapy. In essence, it is argued that because hypnosis involves suggestion, hypnotic sessions must inevitably be *unduly* suggestive and memories must be the product of suggestion. A variant of this argument states that hypnosis is always an exercise in fantasy and imagination and therefore cannot result in historically accurate recollection. This challenge is limited to the use of hypnosis with memory.

Third, lawyers have extended the argument against hypnosis beyond the confines of its use to facilitate memory recall. In these cases, the attack is on hypnosis as a form of treatment (*Storm v. Legion Insurance Company*, 2003). These novel legal theories have their basis in *Daubert* (1993), where the U.S. Supreme Court suggested trial judges utilize the previously discussed four factors in evaluating the expert's proposed testimony.

Although *Daubert* was intended to address only the admissibility of expert scientific testimony, lawyers have attempted to extend its four factors to challenge the use of any treatment or therapeutic technique that fails to satisfy each factor. The argument is that any treatment or therapy that cannot be empirically proven to be effective is an "experimental" or "dangerous" procedure. In most cases, proper informed consent may serve as an adequate defense. In addition, therapists are well advised to follow current standards of care (Hammond et al., 1995; Scheflin & Spiegel, 1998). However, it is not unlikely that the legal challenge to hypnosis will eventually claim that it should not be used at all, even when the patient has given informed consent. This more drastic legal challenge should ultimately be resolved by an evaluation of the studies measuring the efficacy, or lack thereof, of hypnotic procedures. Ultimately, science should determine whether hypnosis should be used in therapy and, if so, for what conditions and under what circumstances.

HYPNOSIS AND ADVOCACY

The fifth area of intersection between law and hypnosis concerns hypnosis and advocacy. Should attorneys be permitted to use hypnotic techniques in the courtroom to persuade judges and juries? Little has been written on this intriguing subject (Scheflin, 1998).

The first formal relationship between hypnotists and lawyers seems to have occurred in the 1950s, when Harry Arons (1967), a lay hypnotist based on the East Coast, began teaching hypnosis to doctors, psychologists, police officials, and then attorneys. Meanwhile, on the West Coast, famed attorney Melvin Belli (1976) invited Dr. William J. Bryan Jr. to speak at the 1961 annual Belli Seminars being held that year in St. Louis. Bryan, the only American physician to limit his practice exclusively to hypnosis cases, explained how trial lawyers could benefit from hypnosis training.

Attorney F. Lee Bailey (1971) met Bryan at the Belli Seminar. Bryan hypnotized Bailey, and the next thing Bailey knew there was a hypodermic needle sticking through his hand. Bailey then enrolled in Bryan's American Institute of Hypnosis as a student, graduating from the advanced class in 1964 (*Hypnosis Quarterly*, 1965).

Reference to the use of hypnosis or hypnotic technique makes an occasional appearance, usually unflattering, in court opinions. In *Mason v. Underwood* (1992), after the plaintiff was awarded a sum of money for her claim that the defendant had falsely imprisoned her, a concurring judge complained that the verdict was

> so grossly excessive that it must have been given under some evil influence. Quite possible the plaintiff cast a spell over the jurors; quite possibly her skillful counsel made some passionate, unfair, hypnotic, and prejudicial appeal to the jurors, asking them for smart money, while he posed as a disinterested minister of justice. (p. 950)

In *State v. Rameau* (1996), after a jury acquitted the defendant on the charge of unlawful sexual contact, the trial judge off-handedly commented that defense counsel "had hypnotized the jury" (p. 762).

The possibility that a lawyer might actually possess and use hypnotic powers arose in the case of *Wilburn v. Reitman* (1939), where plaintiff's counsel claimed that the attorney for the defense dominated the court by "will power and by the power of suggestion" (p. 34). Noting that this argument raised "a most serious question," Chief Justice Ross responded:

> It is perfectly ethical for an attorney to use logic, oratorical skill, persuasive power and magnetism to gain his point, but according to the accusations of counsel the opposing counsel employed hypnosis to win his case, that is, he put the judge in "a state resembling normal sleep, differing in being induced by the suggestions and operations of the hypnotizer, with whom the hypnotized subject remains in rapport, responsive to his suggestions." (Webster's New Int'l Dict.) It is true that the law is a social mechanism that grows and expands to keep pace with social progress and needs, but we feel that the practice of hypnotism, at least for the present, should not be permitted in a court of justice. (p. 35)

How realistic is it to believe that skills used by hypnotists would find no place in trials? Is it possible, or desirable, to keep the practice of hypnotism out of the courtroom? Bryan (1962) argued that hypnotic techniques can be used to influence jurors. After noting that this subject had not previously been discussed in hypnosis or legal publications because "it has been considered unthinkable that an ethical lawyer would employ 'hypnotic techniques' in order to influence a jury" (p. 215–216), Bryan make a distinction between "hypnotizing the jury and the use of hypnotic techniques in [an attorney's] courtroom presentation" (p. 216). While the former is clearly unthinkable, the latter is in fact inevitable. Bryan (1971) later explained his techniques of jury selection, which he applied in several high-visibility trials handled by attorney F. Lee Bailey.

If hypnosis is understood as an aspect of persuasive communication, techniques used by hypnotists are relevant to the courtroom tasks that lawyers perform. Thus, lawyers may learn the following from hypnotists: (1) assessing the suggestibility of the audience (jurors, judges, witnesses); (2) attracting attention; (3) concentrating the mind; (4) reducing peripheral awareness; (5) lowering critical thinking to increase reception to suggestion; (6) using metaphors and sensory language; (7) giving positive or negative suggestions; (8) building unconscious associations; (9) motivating posthypnotic action; and (10) facilitating selective amnesia.

Bryan (1962, p. 193)) also suggested that hypnosis might be used to relax a nervous witness before that witness takes the stand to testify:

> There comes a time in the life of every trial lawyer when he has at his disposal a witness who knows the truth, understands the truth, but is simply too nervous and full of stage-fright to give an acceptable performance upon the witness stand. It is in such cases that a qualified medical hypnotist can be of great value to the attorney.

Although Bryan assumed the attorney would hire the services of a licensed hypnotist, he provided no reason why the lawyer with hypnosis training could not use relaxation inductions and techniques without professional assistance. However, there are problems with this use of hypnosis to relax witnesses: Judges might conclude that hypnosis used for relaxation unduly interferes with the cross-examination of the witness.

Related to the issue of lawyers utilizing hypnotic techniques in advocacy is the question of whether hypnotists should teach these skills to attorneys. Codes of ethics of hypnosis associations generally prohibit instructing or training laypersons in the use of hypnosis, with self-help techniques taught to patients constituting the major exception. In the Code of Conduct of the American Society of Clinical Hypnosis (2003), Ethical Standard IV.C. states, "Members do not provide hypnosis training to laypersons." The Code of Ethics of the Society for Clinical and Experimental Hypnosis (1993), Principle III-1, states that a member "shall not give courses in hypnosis to laypeople." The Code of Ethics of the International Society of Hypnosis (1979), Section A Guideline 5(b), states, "A member of ISH shall not give courses involving the teaching of hypnotic techniques to lay individuals who lack training in a relevant science or profession."

CONCLUSION

Hypnosis remains a subject of interest to the law, in part because it engenders much fascination, and in part because it involves issues of central importance to the law: memory, free will, choice, voluntariness, and responsibility. There is every reason to believe that legal cases involving hypnosis will continue to invite judicial and legislative attention. Although the legal rules involving hypnotically refreshed recollection were largely formulated in the 1980s, most of the scientific literature on hypnosis and memory has appeared since that time. The Minnesota Supreme Court, in *State v. Blanchard* (1982, p. 430), wrote, "We are, of course, willing to consider future developments in this area." However, no modern court has carefully examined the recent scientific literature. Lawyers will undoubtedly seek judicial review of evidentiary rules adopted long before science had spoken. Indeed, such cases are already in their preliminary stages.

Hypnosis will continue to be used by therapists, and some patients will continue to insist that they have been harmed by it. Lawyers have been crafting new theories to challenge the use of hypnosis in therapy settings, and it is a safe bet they will find additional opportunities to test them in court. Informed consent is one line of attack; the argument that hypnosis, and any therapeutic technique, should meet an evidence-based standard for efficacy is another. The therapeutic value of hypnosis is itself now being examined in studies responding to the need for scientific validation.

Questions concerning the antisocial use of hypnosis, which have been somewhat dormant, have been the subject of several recent trial proceedings. Some of these cases are apt to get an appellate hearing, again raising significant issues of the criminal and civil culpability of the hypnotizer and the hypnotized subject.

As it has in the past, forensic hypnosis will remain a subject of complication and fascination for jurists.

APPENDIX 1

PRACTICE OF PSYCHOLOGY OR COUNSELING

Alaska Business and Professions Statute § 08.86.230(6)(B)

Arkansas Professions, Occupations, and Businesses Code § 17-97-102 (a)(2)(B)(ii)(g)

Colorado Professions and Occupations Statute § 12-43-303(2)(c)

Delaware Professions and Occupations Code Title 24, § 3502(6)

District of Columbia Code § 3-1201.02(16)(A)

Hawaii Professions and Occupations Code § 465-1

Illinois Professions and Occupations Health Statute Chapter 225, § 15/2(5)

Louisiana Professions and Occupations Code, Title 37, § 2352(5)

Maine Professions and Occupations Statute Title 32, § 3811(2)

Maryland Health Occupations Code § 18-101(e)(1)(ii)

Massachusetts Public Health Law Title 112 § 118

Michigan Public Health Code § 333.18201(b)

Minnesota Health Statute § 148.89, subdivision 5(4)

Mississippi Professions and Vocations Code § 73-31-3(d)

Missouri Occupations and Professions Code, Chapter 337, § 337.015

Montana Professions and Occupations Code § 37-17-102(4)(b)

Nebraska Public Health and Welfare Statute § 71-1,206.08

Nevada Professions, Occupations, and Business Statute § 641.025.5

New Mexico Professional and Occupational Licenses Statute § 61-9-3(H)

North Carolina Statutes § 90-270.2(8)

Ohio Occupations-Professions Code § 4732.01(C)

Rhode Island Business and Professions Statutes § 5-44-1(5)(iv)

South Carolina Professions and Occupations Code §   40-55-50(A)(2); South Carolina Statutes § 40-75-20(16)

South Dakota Professions and Occupations Statute § 36-27A-1(3)

Tennessee Professions of the Healing Arts Code § 63-11-203

Texas Occupations Code §   501.003(c)(3)(A)

Utah Occupations and Professions Code §   58-61-102(9)(a)(iv)

Virginia Professions and Occupations Code § 54.1-3600

Washington Business and Professions Code § 18.19.020(2), §   18.19.020(3)

Wyoming Professions and Occupations Statute § 33-27-113(a)(iii)(B)

Practice of Medicine

Hawaii Professions and Occupations Statute §   453-1

Minnesota Health Statute §   147.081 subdivision 3(5)

APPENDIX 2: STATE AND FEDERAL HYPNOSIS RULES

Per Se Exclusion Rule

Alaska	Michigan
Arizona	Minnesota
California	Missouri
Connecticut	Nebraska
Florida	New York
Georgia	North Carolina
Hawaii	Oklahoma
Illinois	Pennsylvania
Indiana	Utah
Kansas	Virginia
Maryland	Washington
Massachusetts	

Open Admissibility Rule

North Dakota

Oregon (Oregon Revised Statutes §§ 136.675 and 136.675 require that the entire hypnosis procedure be recorded, a copy of the recording must be furnished to the adverse party, and informed consent must be obtained.)

Wyoming

GUIDELINES/TOTALITY OF THE CIRCUMSTANCES RULE

Alabama	Texas
Colorado	Wisconsin
Idaho	First Circuit Court of Appeals
Iowa	Second Circuit Court of Appeals
Kentucky	Third Circuit Court of Appeals
Louisiana	Fourth Circuit Court of Appeals
Mississippi	Fifth Circuit Court of Appeals
New Jersey	Sixth Circuit Court of Appeals
New Mexico	Seventh Circuit Court of Appeals
Ohio	Eighth Circuit Court of Appeals
South Carolina	Ninth Circuit Court of Appeals
South Dakota	Tenth Circuit Court of Appeals
Tennessee	Eleventh Circuit Court of Appeals

NO DEFINITIVE COURT RULING

Arkansas	New Hampshire
Delaware	Rhode Island
District of Columbia	Vermont
Maine	West Virginia
Montana	District of Columbia Circuit Court of Appeals
Nevada	

TOTAL

Per Se Exclusion Rule—23 states

Open Admissibility Rule—3 states

Guidelines/Totality Rule—15 states + 11 federal courts of appeals

No Definitive Rule—9 states + the District of Columbia + the District of Columbia Circuit Court of Appeals

REFERENCES

American Law Institute. (1985). *Model penal code and commentaries*. Philadelphia: PA American Law Institute.

American Medical Association, Council on Mental Health. (1958, September 13). Medical use of hypnosis. *Journal of the American Medical Association, 168,* 186–189.

American Medical Association, Council on Scientific Affairs. (1985). Scientific status of refreshing recollection by the use of hypnosis. *Journal of the American Medical Association, 253,* 1918–1923.

American Medical Association, Council on Scientific Affairs. (1994). Memories of childhood abuse. CSA Report 5-A-94.

American Psychiatric Association. (1961, February). *Regarding hypnosis: Statement of position.* Washington, DC: American Psychiatric Association.

American Society of Clinical Hypnosis. (2003). Code of Conduct. Bloomingdale, IL: Author.

Arons, H. (1967). *Hypnosis in criminal investigation.* Springfield, IL: Charles C Thomas.

Bailey, F. L. (1971). *The defense never rests.* New York: New American Library.

Barber, T. X., & Calverley, D. S. (1966). Effects of recall of hypnotic induction, motivational suggestions, and suggested regression: A methodological and experimental analysis. *Journal of Abnormal Psychology, 71,* 169–180.

Barber, T. X., & Wilson, S. C. (1978–1979). The Barber Suggestibility Scale and the Creative Imagination Scale: Experimental and clinical applications. *American Journal of Clinical Hypnosis, 21,* 84–96.

Barfield v. State, 54 Ala.App. 15, 304 So.2d 257 (1974).

Barnes, M. (1982). (Producer and Director). *Hypnosis on trial.* Television documentary. London: British Broadcasting Company.

Barnier, A. J., & McConkey, K. M. (1992). Reports of real and false memories: The relevance of hypnosis, hypnotizability, and context of memory test. *Journal of Abnormal Psychology, 101*(3), 521–527.

Beahrs, J. O. (1988). Hypnosis cannot be fully nor reliably excluded from the courtroom. *American Journal of Clinical Hypnosis, 31,* 18–27.

Beahrs, J. O., Cannell, J. J., & Gutheil, T. G. (1996). Delayed traumatic recall in adults: A synthesis with legal, clinical, and forensic recommendations. *Bulletin of the American Academy of Psychiatry and Law, 24,* 45–55.

Belli, M. M. (1976). *My life on trial.* New York: Popular Library.

Berg, J. W., Applebaum, P. S., Lidz, C. W., & Parker, L. S. (2001). *Informed consent: Legal theory and clinical practice* (2nd ed.). Oxford: Oxford University Press.

Bernheim, H. (1980). *New studies in hypnotism.* (R. S. Sandor, Trans.). New York: International Universities Press. (Original work published 1891)

Block, E. B. (1976). *Hypnosis: A new tool in crime detection.* New York: David McKay.

Bonnema, M. C. (1993). "Trance on trial": An exegesis of hypnotism and criminal responsibility. *Wayne Law Review, 39,* 1299–1334.

Borawick v. Shay, 68 F.3d 597 (2nd Cir. 1995), *cert. denied,* 517 U.S. 1229, 116 S.Ct. 1869, 134 L.Ed.2d 966 (1996).

British Medical Association. (1955, April 23). Supplementary annual report of council, 1954–5. *British Medical Journal* (Suppl.). 190–193.

Brodie-Innes, J. W. (1891). Legal aspects of hypnotism. *Juridical Review, 3,* 51–61.

Brown, D., Scheflin, A. W., & Hammond, D. C. (1998). *Memory, trauma treatment, and the law.* New York: Norton.

Bryan, W. J., Jr. (1962). *The legal aspects of hypnosis.* Springfield, IL: Charles C Thomas.

Bryan, W. J., Jr. (1971). *The chosen ones: The psychology of jury selection.* New York: Vantage Press.

California Business and Professions Code § 2908.

Clemens, B. (1991). Hypnotically enhanced testimony: Has it lost its charm? *Southern Illinois University Law Journal, 15,* 289–320.

Coons, P. M. (1988). Misuse of forensic hypnosis: A hypnotically elicited false confession with the apparent creation of a multiple personality. *International Journal of Clinical and Experimental Hypnosis, 36*(1), 1–11.

Condon, R. (1959). *The Manchurian candidate.* New York: McGraw-Hill.

Connery, D. S. (1977). *Guilty until proven innocent.* New York: Putnam.

Daubert v. Merrell Dow Pharmaceuticals, Inc., 509 U.S. 579, 113 S.Ct. 2786, 125 L.Ed.2d 469 (1993).

Denis v. Commonwealth, 144 Va. 559, 131 S. E. 131 (1926).

Deyoub, P. L. (1984). Hypnotic stimulation of antisocial behavior: A case report. *International Journal of Clinical and Experimental Hypnosis, 33,* 301–306.

Dhanens, T. P., & Lundy, R. M. (1975). Hypnotic and waking suggestions and recall. *International Journal of Clinical and Experimental Hypnosis, 23,* 68–79.

Diamond, B. L. (1980). Inherent problems in the use of pretrial hypnosis on a prospective witness. *California Law Review, 68,* 313–349.

Diggett, C., & Mulligan, W. C. (1982). *Hypno-Cop.* Garden City, NY: Doubleday.

Dressler, J. (2001). *Understanding criminal law* (3rd ed.). New York: Lexis.

DuMaurier, G. (1894). *Trilby.* New York: Harper & Row.

Dywan, J., & Bowers, K. S. (1983). The use of hypnosis to enhance recall. *Science, 222,* 184–185.

Echterling, L. G., & Emmerling, D. A. (1987). Impact of stage hypnosis. *American Journal of Clinical Hypnosis, 29,* 149–154.

Ellenberger, H. F. (1970). *Discovery of the unconscious: The history and evolution of dynamic psychiatry.* New York: Basic Books.

Erdelyi, M. H. (1970). Recovery of unavailable perceptual input. *Cognitive Psychology, 1,* 99–113.

Erdelyi, M. H. (1996). *The recovery of unconscious memories: Hypermnesia and reminiscence.* Chicago: University of Chicago Press.

Erickson, M. H. (1962). Stage hypnotist back syndrome. *American Journal of Clinical Hypnosis, 3,* 141–142.

Faigman, D. L., Kaye, D. H., Saks, M. J., & Sanders, J. (2002). *Modern scientific evidence: The law and science of expert testimony.* St. Paul, MN: West.

Finkelstein, S. (1989). Adverse effects after exposure to lay hypnosis in a group setting: A case report. *American Journal of Clinical Hypnosis, 32*(2), 107–109.

Frischholz, E. J. (1996, November 11). *Latest developments in forensic hypnosis and memory.* Paper presented at the 47th annual workshops and scientific program of the Society for Clinical and Experimental Hypnosis, Tampa, FL.

Frye v. United States, 54 App.D.C. 46, 293 F. 1013 (1923).

Gardner, D. S. (1932–33). The perception and memory of witnesses. *Cornell Law Quarterly, 18,* 391–409.

Giannelli, P. C. (1995). The admissibility of hypnotic evidence in U.S. courts. *International Journal of Clinical and Experimental Hypnosis, 43,* 212–233.

Giannelli, P. C., & Imwinkelried, E. J. (1999). *Scientific evidence* (3rd ed.). Charlottesville, VA: Lexis Law Publishing.

Gravitz, M. A. (1983). An early case of hypnosis used in the investigation of a crime. *International Journal of Clinical and Experimental Hypnosis, 31,* 224–226.

Gravitz, M. A. (1995). First admission (1846) of hypnotic testimony in court. *American Journal of Clinical Hypnosis, 37*(4), 326–330.

Gudjonsson, G. H. (1992). *The psychology of interrogations, confessions and testimony.* New York: Wiley.

Gudjonsson, G. H. (2003). *The psychology of interrogations and confessions: A handbook.* West Sussex, England: Wiley.

Haberman, M. A. (1987). Complications following hypnosis in a psychotic patient with sexual dysfunction treated by a lay hypnotist. *American Journal of Clinical Hypnosis, 29*(3), 166–170.

Hammond, D. C., Garver, R. B., Mutter, C. B., Crasilneck, H. B., Frischholz, E., Gravitz, M. A., et al. (1994). *Clinical hypnosis and memory: Guidelines for clinicians and for forensic hypnosis.* Des Plaines, IL: American Society of Clinical Hypnosis Press.

Harding, E. C. (1978). Complications arising from hypnosis for entertainment. In F. H. Frankel & H. S. Zamansky (Eds.), *Hypnosis at its bicentennial* (pp. 163–167). New York: Plenum Press.

Harding v. State, 5 Md. App. 230, 246 A.2d 302 (1968), cert. denied, Harding v. Maryland, 395 U.S. 949, 89 S. Ct. 2030, 23 L.Ed.2d 468 (1969), overruled by State v. Collins, 296 Md. 670, 464 A.2d 1028 (1983).

Harris, R. (1985). Murder under hypnosis in the case of Gabrielle Bompard: Psychiatry in the courtroom in belle epoque Paris. In W. F. Bynum, R. Porter, & M. Shepherd (Eds.), *The anatomy of madness: Essays in the history of psychiatry: Vol. II. Institutions and society* (pp. 197–241). London: Tavistock Publications.

Harris, R. (1989). *Murder and madness: Medicine, law, and society in the fin de siecle.* Oxford: Clarendon Press.

Hibbard, W. S., & Worring, R. W. (1981). *Forensic hypnosis.* Springfield, IL: Charles C. Thomas.

Hilgard, E. R. (1977). Divided consciousness: Multiple controls in human thought and action. New York: Wiley.

Hilgard, E. R., & Hilgard, J. R. (1975). *Hypnosis in the relief of pain.* Los Altos, CA: Kaufmann.

Hypnotism and the law. (1893, October 14). *Law Times,* 500.

Hohe v. San Diego Unified School District, 224 Cal.App.3d 1559, 274 Cal.Rptr. 647 (4th Dist. 1990).

Hypnosis Quarterly [Photograph]. (1965). *10*(1), 40.

Hypnotism in criminal defence. (1894). *Barrister,* 249–251.

International Society of Hypnosis. (1979). Code of ethics. West Heidelberg, Victoria, Australia: Author.

Johnson v. Gerrish, 518 A.2d 721 (Me. 1986).

Kansas Statutes §21-4007, repealed 2004 Kansas Laws Ch. 175 (H.B. 2271)(May 20, 2004).

Karlin, R. A. (1997). Illusory safeguards: Legitimizing distortion in recall with guidelines for forensic hypnosis—Two case reports. *International Journal of Clinical and Experimental Hypnosis, 45*(1), 18–40.

Karlin, R. A., & Orne, M. T. (1996). Commentary on *Borawick v. Shay:* Hypnosis, social influence, incestuous child abuse, and satanic ritual abuse: The Iatrogenic creation of horrific memories for the remote past. *Cultic Studies Journal, 13,* 42–94.

Karlin, R. A., & Orne, M. T. (1997). Hypnosis and the iatrogenic creation of memory: On the need for a *per se* exclusion of testimony based on hypnotically influenced memory. *Cultic Studies Journal, 14*(2), 172–206.

Kihlstrom, J. F. (1985). Hypnosis. *Annual Review of Psychology, 36,* 385–418.

Kihlstrom, J. F. (2002, October). Demand characteristics in the laboratory and the clinic: Conversations and collaborations with subjects and patients. *Prevention and Treatment, 5.* Retrieved from http://www.journals.apa.org/prevention/volume5/pre0050036c.html on May 30, 2005.

Kleinhauz, M., Dreyfuss, D. A., Beran, B., Goldberg, T., & Azikri, D. (1979). Some after-effects of stage hypnosis. *International Journal of Clinical and Experimental Hypnosis, 27,* 219–226.

Kroger, W. (1977). *Clinical and experimental hypnosis* (2nd ed.). Philadelphia: J. B. Lippincott.

Kuhns, B. W. (1981). *Hypnosis and the law.* Glendale, CA: Westwood Publishing Co.

Laurence, J.-R., & Perry, C. (1983). Hypnotically created memory among highly hypnotizable subjects. *Science, 222,* 523–524.

Laurence, J.-R., & Perry, C. (1988). *Hypnosis, will, and memory: A psycho-legal history.* New York: Guilford Press.

Leyra v. Denno, 347 U.S. 556, 74 S.Ct. 716, 98 L.Ed. 948 (1954).

Loftus, E. F. (1975). Leading questions and the eyewitness report. *Cognitive Psychology, 7,* 560–572.

Loftus, E. F. (1979a). *Eyewitness testimony.* Cambridge, MA: Harvard University Press.

Loftus, E. F. (1979b). The malleability of memory. *American Scientist, 67,* 312–320.

Loftus, E. F. (1979c). The manipulative uses of language. Audiotape No. 20234, A., Psychology Today Cassette. New York: Ziff-Davis Publishing.

Loftus, E. F. (1980). *Memory.* Reading, MA: Addison-Wesley.

Loftus, E. L., & Burns, T. E. (1982). Mental shock can produce retrograde amnesia. *Memory and Cognition, 10*(4), 318–323.

Lynn, S. J., & Kirsch, I. (1996). Alleged alien abductions: False memories, hypnosis, and fantasy proneness. *Psychological Inquiry, 7,* 151–155.

Lynn, S. J., Neuschatz, J., Fite, R., & Kirsch, I. (2001). Hypnosis in the forensic arena. *Journal of Forensic Psychology Practice, 1*(1), 113–122.

Lynn, S. J., & Rhue, J. (Eds.). (1991). *Theories of hypnosis: Current models and perspectives.* New York: Guilford Press.

Marks, J. (1978). *The search for the Manchurian candidate.* New York: New York Times.

Mason v. Underwood, 49 N. D. 243, 191 N. W. 949 (1992).

Masters v. State, 170 Tex. Crim. 471, 341 S. W.2d 938 (Crim.App. 1960).

McCann, T., & Sheehan, P. W. (1988). Hypnotically induced pseudomemories—Sampling their conditions among hypnotizable subjects. *Journal of Personality and Social Psychology, 54,* 339–346.

McConkey, K. M., Barnier, A. J., & Sheehan, P. W. (1998). Hypnosis and pseudomemory: Understanding the findings and their implications. In S. J. Lynn & K. M. McConkey (Eds.), *Truth in memory* (pp. 227–259). New York: Guilford Press.

McConkey, K. M., & Sheehan, P. W. (1995). *Hypnosis, memory, and behavior in criminal investigation.* New York: Guilford Press.

McIlwain v. State, 402 So.2d 1194 (Fla.App. 5th Dist. 1981), *rehearing denied,* Aug. 25, 1981, *petition for review denied* 412 So.2d 467 (1982).

Mirowitz v. State, 449 S. W.2d 475 (Tex.Crim.App. 1969).

Moll, A. (1958). *The study of hypnosis.* New York: Julian Press (Original work published in 1889).

Monaghan, J. (1980). *Hypnosis in criminal investigation.* Dubuque, IA: Kendall/Hunt Publishing Company.

Montana Crimes Code, § 45-2-101(32)(c).

Münsterberg, H. (1908). *On the witness stand.* New York: Doubleday.

Mutter, C. B. (1984). The use of hypnosis with defendants. *American Journal of Clinical Hypnosis, 27,* 42–51.

Mutter, C. B. (1990). The use of hypnosis with defendants: Does it really work? *American Journal of Clinical Hypnosis, 32,* 257–262.

Newman v. Hopkins, 247 F.3d 848 (8th Cir. 2001).

Orne, M. T. (1959). The nature of hypnosis: Artifact and essence. *Journal of Abnormal and Social Psychology, 58,* 277–299.

Orne, M. T. (1962). On the social psychology of the psychology experiment: With particular reference to demand characteristics and their manipulation. *American Psychologist, 17,* 776–783.

Orne, M. T. (1979). The use and misuse of hypnosis in court. *International Journal of Clinical and Experimental Hypnosis, 27,* 311–341.

Orne, M. T. (1982). Affidavit to *People v. Shirley,* April 28, 1982, quoted in C. Perry and J.-R. Laurence (1990): "Hypnosis with a criminal defendant and a crime witness: Two recent cases." *International Journal of Clinical and Experimental Hypnosis, 38*(4), 266–281.

Orne, M. T., Dinges, D. F., & Orne, E. C. (1990). *Rock v. Arkansas:* Hypnosis, the defendant's privilege. *International Journal of Clinical and Experimental Hypnosis, 38*(1), 250–265.

Orne, M. T., Whitehouse, W. G., Dinges, D. F., & Orne, E. C. (1996). Memory liabilities associated with hypnosis: Does low hypnotizability confer immunity? *International Journal of Clinical and Experimental Hypnosis, 44,* 354–367.

Orne, M. T., Whitehouse, W. G., Orne, E. C., & Dinges, D. F. (1996). "Memories" of anomalous and traumatic autobiographical experiences: Validation and consolidation of fantasy through hypnosis. *Psychological Inquiry, 7*(2), 168–172.

Paxton v. Ward, 199 F.3d 1197 (10th Cir. 1999).

People v. Baldi, 80 Misc.2d 118, 362 N. Y. S.2d 927 (1974).

People v. Cantor, 188 Cal.App.2d Supp. 843, 18 Cal. Rptr. 363 (App.Dept.,Super.Ct., L. A. County, 1961).

People v. Caro, 46 Cal.3d 1035, 251 Cal.Rptr. 757, 761 P.2d 680 (1988).

People v. Dunigan, 52 Ill. Dec. 247, 96 Ill.App.3d 799, 421 N. E.2d 1319 (1st Dist.1981).

People v. Ebanks, 117 Cal. 652, 49 P. 1049 (1897).

People v. Marsh, 170 Cal.App.2d 284, 338 P.2d 495 (4th Dist. 1959).

People v. Ritchie, No. C-36932. Super.Ct. Orange Co., California (April 7, 1977) (unreported).

People v. Shirley, 31 Cal. 3d 18, 723 P.2d 1354, 181 Cal.Rptr. 243, *stay denied California v. Shirley,* 458 U.S. 1125, 103 S.Ct. 13, 73 L.Ed.2d 1400, *cert. denied California v. Shirley,* 459 U.S. 860, 103 S.Ct. 133, 74 L.Ed.2d 114 (1982).

People v. Smith, 117 Misc.2d 737, 459 N. Y. S.2d 528 (1983).

People v. Sorscher, 151 Mich.App.122, 391 N. W.2d 365 (1986).

People v. Williams, 132 Cal.App.3d 920, 183 Cal.Rptr. 498 (4th Dist. 1982).

People v. Worthington, 105 Cal. 166, 38 P. 689 (1894).

Perry, C. (1979). Hypnotic coercion and compliance to act: A review of evidence presented in a legal case. *International Journal of Clinical and Experimental Hypnosis, 36,* 187–218.

Perry, C. (1995). The false memory syndrome (FMS) and "disguised" hypnosis. *Hypnos, 22,* 189–197.

Perry, C. (2002, October). Hypnosis, demand characteristics, and "recovered memory" therapy. *Prevention and Treatment, 5.* Retrieved from http://www.journals.apa.org/prevention/volume5/pre0050040c.html on May 30, 2005.

Perry, C., & Laurence, J.-R. (1990). Hypnosis with a criminal defendant and a crime witness: Two recent cases. *International Journal of Clinical and Experimental Hypnosis, 38*(4), 266–281.

Perry, C., Nadon, R., & Button, J. (1992). The measurement of hypnotic ability. In E. Fromm & M. R. Nash (Eds.), *Contemporary hypnosis research* (pp. 459–490). New York: Guilford Press.

Perry, C., Orne, M. T., London, R. W., & Orne, E. C. (1996). Rethinking per se exclusions of hypnotically elicited recall as legal testimony. *International Journal of Clinical and Experimental Hypnosis, 44,* 66–80.

Putnam, W. H. (1979). Hypnosis and distortions in eyewitness memory. *International Journal of Clinical and Experimental Hypnosis, 27,* 437–448.

Raginsky, B. B. (1969). Hypnotic recall of aircrash cause. *International Journal of Clinical and Experimental Hypnosis, 17,* 1–19.

Reiser, M. (1980). *Handbook of investigative hypnosis.* Los Angeles: LEHI Publishing.

Rock v. Arkansas, 483 U.S.44, 107 S.Ct. 2704, 97 L.Ed. 2d 37 (1987).

Rogers v. State, 105 S. W.3d 630 (Crim.App.Tex. 2003).

Rosenhan, D., & London, P. (1963). Hypnosis in the unhypnotizable: A study in rote learning. *Journal of Experimental Psychology, 65,* 30–34.

Rowland v. Commonwealth, 901 S. W.2d 871 (Ky. 1995).

Sadoff, R., & Dubin, L. (1990). The use of hypnosis as a pretrial discovery tool in civil and criminal lawsuits. In C. H. Wecht (Ed.), *Legal medicine* (pp. 105–124). Dayton, OH: Butterworth-Heinemann.

Schacter, D. L. (1986). Amnesia and crime: How much do we really know? *American Psychologist, 41*(3): 286–295.

Scheflin, A. W. (1993). Avoiding malpractice liability. *American Society of Clinical Hypnosis Newsletter, 34*(1), 6.

Scheflin, A. W. (1994a). Forensic hypnosis: Unanswered questions. *Australian Journal of Clinical and Experimental Hypnosis, 22,* 23–34.

Scheflin, A. W. (1994b). Forensic hypnosis and the law: The current situation in the United States. In B. J. Evans & R. O. Stanley (Eds.), *Hypnosis and the law: Principles and practice* (pp. 25–48). Heideleberg, Victoria, Australia: Australian Society of Hypnosis.

Scheflin, A. W. (1996). Commentary on *Borawick v. Shay:* The fate of hypnotically retrieved memories. *Cultic Studies Journal, 13,* 26–41.

Scheflin, A. W. (1997a). Ethics and hypnosis: Unorthodox or innovative therapies and the legal standard of care. In W. Matthews & J. Edgette (Eds.), *Current thinking and research in brief therapy: Solutions, strategies, narratives* (Vol. 1, pp. 41–62). New York: Brunner/Mazel.

Scheflin, A. W. (1997b). False memory and Buridan's ass: A response to Karlin and Orne. *Cultic Studies Journal, 14,* 207–289.

Scheflin, A. W. (1998). Ethics and hypnosis: A preliminary inquiry into hypnotic advocacy. In W. Matthews & J. Edgette (Eds.), *Current thinking and research in brief therapy: Solutions, strategies, narratives* (Vol. 2, pp. 307–328). New York: Brunner/Mazel.

Scheflin, A. W. (2004, January). *Amnesia and homicide—Do killers forget their crimes?* Talk presented at the 2004 Association of American Law Schools annual meeting, Atlanta, GA.

Scheflin, A. W., & Frischholz, E. J. (1999, October). Significant dates in the history of forensic hypnosis. *American Journal of Clinical Hypnosis, 42*(2), 84–107.

Scheflin, A. W., & Opton, E., Jr. (1978). *The mind manipulators.* London: Paddington Press.

Scheflin, A. W., & Shapiro, L. (1989). *Trance on trial.* New York: Guilford Press.

Scheflin, A. W., & Spiegel, D. (1998). From courtroom to couch: Working with repressed memory and avoiding lawsuits. *Psychiatric Clinics of North America: Diagnostic Dilemmas, Part II, 21*(4), 847–867.

Scoboria, A., Mazzoni, G., Kirsch, I., & Milling, L. S. (2002). Immediate and persisting effects of misleading questions and hypnosis on memory reports. *Journal of experimental psychology: Applied, 8*(1), 26–32.

Sheehan, P. W. (1996, August 17). *Contemporary trends in hypnosis research.* State-of-the-art address presented at the 26th International Congress of Psychology, Montreal, Canada.

Sheehan, P. W., & McConkey, K. M. (1993). Forensic hypnosis: The application of ethical guidelines. In J. W. Rhue, S. J. Lynn, & I. Kirsch (Eds.), *Handbook of clinical hypnosis* (pp. 719–738). Washington, DC: American Psychological Association.

Society for Clinical and Experimental Hypnosis. (1993). Code of ethics. Boston: Author.

Spanos, N. P., Gwynn, M. I., Comer, S. L., Baltruweit, W. J., & de Groh, M. (1989). Are hypnotically-induced pseudomemories resistant to cross-examination? *Law and Human Behavior, 13,* 271–289.

Spanos, N. P., Quigley, C. A., Gwynn, M. I., Glatt, R. L., & Perlini, A. H. (1991). Hypnotic interrogation, pretrial preparation, and witness testimony during direct and cross-examination. *Law and Human Behavior, 15,* 639–653.

Spiegel, D. (1987). The. *Shirley* decision: The cure is worse than the disease. In R. W. Rieber (Ed.), *Advances in forensic psychology and psychiatry* (Vol. 2, pp. 101–118). Norwood, NJ: Ablex.

Spiegel, D., & Spiegel, H. (1984). Hypnosis in psychotherapy. In the *Psychiatric Therapies: Report of the American Psychiatric Association Commission on Psychiatric Therapies* (pp. 701–737). Washington: American Psychiatric Association.

Spiegel, H. (1980). Hypnosis and evidence: Help or hindrance? *Annals of New York Academy of Science, 347,* 73–85.

Spiegel, H. (1997). Nocebo: The power of suggestibility. *Preventive Medicine, 26*(5), 616–621.

Spiegel, H., & Spiegel, D. (1978). *Trance and treatment: Clinical uses of hypnosis.* New York: Basic Books.

State v. Blanchard, 315 N. W.2d 427 (Minn. 1982).

State v. Butterworth, 246 Kan. 541, 792 P.2d 1049 (1990).

State v. Donovan, 128 Iowa 44, 102 N. W. 791 (1905).

State v. Dreher, 251 N. J. Super 300, 598 A 2d 216 (1991).

State v. Harris, 241 Or. 224, 405 P.2d 492 (1965).

State v. Hurd, 86 N. J. 525, 432 A.2d 86 (1981).

State v. L.K., 244 N. J. Super. 261, 582 A.2d 297 (1990).

State v. Mack, 292 N. W.2d 764 (Minn. 1980).

State v. Papp. (1978). No. 78-02-00229. C. P. Summit Co., OH; Lorain Co. No. 16862, March 23, 1978; unrep.; app'd U.S.Sup.Ct. No. 79-5091, *cert. denied* October 27, 1979.

State v. Rameau, 685 A.2d 761 (Me. 1996).

State v. Ture, 353 N. W. 2d 502 (Minn. 1984).

State v. Zimmerman, 266 Wis.2d 1003, 669 N. W.2d 762 (2003).

Steblay, N. M., & Bothwell, R. K. (1994). Evidence for hypnotically refreshed testimony: A view from the laboratory. *Human Behavior, 18*(6): 635–651.

Storm v. Legion Insurance Company, 265 Wis.2d 169, 665 N. W.2d 353 (2003).

Taub, S. (1996). The legal treatment of recovered memories of child sexual abuse. *Journal of Legal Medicine, 17,* 183–214.

Timm, H. W. (1981). The effect of forensic hypnosis techniques on eyewitness recall and recognition. *Journal of Police Science and Administration, 9,* 188–194.

Tumlinson v. State, 757 S. W.2d 440 (Tex.App. 1988).

Tyrone v. State, 77 Tex.Crim. 493, 180 S. W. 125 (1915).

United States v. Adams, 581 F.2d 193 (9th Cir. 1978), cert. denied, 439 U.S. 1006, 99 S.Ct. 621, 58 L.Ed.2d 683 (1978).

United States v. Cordoba, 104 F.3d 225 (9th Cir. 1996).

United States v. Hall, 974 F.Supp. 1198 (C. D.Ill. 1997).

United States v. McCollum, 732 F.2d 1419 (9th Cir.), cert. denied McCollum v. United States, 469 U.S. 920, 105 S.Ct. 301, 83 L.Ed.2d 236 (1984).

United States v. Mest, 789 F.2d 1069 (4th Cir. 1986).

United States v. Pettigrew, 77 F.3d 1500 (5th Cir. 1996).

U.S. v. Phillips, 515 F.Supp. 758 (E. D.Ky. 1981).

United States v. Posado, 57 F.3d 428 (5th Cir. 1995).

United States v. Scheffer, 523 U.S. 303, 118 S.Ct. 1261, 140 L.Ed.2d 413 (1998).

Venn, J. (1988). Misuse of hypnosis in sexual contexts: Two case reports. *International Journal of Clinical and Experimental Hypnosis, 36*(1), 12–18.

Vingoe, F. J. (1997). A note on "experts" in forensic hypnosis. *Contemporary Hypnosis, 14*(1), 48–52.

Wagstaff, G. F. (1996). Should "hypnotized" witnesses be banned from testifying in court? Hypnosis and the M50 murder case. *Contemporary Hypnosis, 13,* 186–190.

Watkins, J. G. (1972). Antisocial behavior under hypnosis: Possible or impossible? *International Journal of Clinical and Experimental Hypnosis, 20,* 95–100.

Weitzenhoffer, A. M., & Hilgard, E. R. (1959). *Stanford Hypnotic Susceptibility Scales: Forms A and B.* Palo Alto, CA: Consulting Psychologists Press.

Wilburn v. Reitman, 54 Ariz. 31, 91 P.2d 865 (1939).

Zeig, J. K. (1985). Ethical issues in hypnosis: Informed consent and training standards. In J. K. Zeig (Ed.), *Ericksonian psychotherapy: Vol. 1. Structures* (pp. 459–473). New York: Brunner/Mazel.

Zelig, M., & Beidleman, W. B. (1981). The investigative use of hypnosis: A word of caution. *International Journal of Clinical and Experimental Hypnosis, 24,* 401–412.

PART FIVE

COMMUNICATING EXPERT OPINIONS

CHAPTER 21

Writing Forensic Reports

IRVING B. WEINER

EFFECTIVE CONSULTATION flows from effective communication. Applied psychologists have usually learned this lesson well from their training and professional experience. They know that their opinions and recommendations are valuable only to the extent that they can be meaningfully conveyed to others.

No matter how sharply they have honed their communications skills as consultants in other contexts, however, most psychologists must learn some new ground rules when they enter the forensic area. As helping professionals, they have been accustomed to working on the behalf of all parties involved in their cases, and not knowingly or intentionally to anyone's disadvantage. The administration of civil and criminal justice marches to a different drummer, however, known as the *adversarial system.* As exemplified by typical courtroom proceedings, the adversarial system pits verbal combatants against each other to produce a winner and a loser. Clinicians provide help in their cases; litigating attorneys win or lose when they take on a case. They air opposing views before the bench, and the arguments that hold sway result in a judgment that gratifies some parties to the case and dismays others.

The adversarial system calls on attorneys to promote the interests of their clients while intentionally trying to prevent opposing attorneys' clients from keeping or getting something they want to have, such as a sum of money or an adjudication of innocence. The concerns of the judge rest not with who gets what or which party feels better or worse, but with safeguarding due process and strict adherence to the rules of evidence. Impartial judicial oversight ensures a full and equal hearing before the bench—every person's "day in court"—whatever the outcome. The familiar statue of the blindfolded goddess of justice, allowing the scales to balance as they may, vividly portrays this feature of the judicial process (see Barrett & Morris, 1993).

Given the nature of the adversarial system, psychologists beginning in forensic work are likely to be what Brodsky and Robey (1972) described many years ago as "courtroom-unfamiliar." To become effective consultants, they need to familiarize themselves with the adversarial system and become comfortable with offering opinions that may contribute to severe penalties and crushing disappointments on the losing side of a case.

In addition, psychologists undertaking forensic consulting must learn to deal with *impersonal clients.* Forensic clients are not individuals seeking service directly on their own behalf. In some cases, they are an entity, such as a court seeking advice, a prosecutor's office seeking a conviction, or a company seeking to defend itself against charges of negligence or malfeasance. In other cases, they are attorneys acting on behalf of a person they are representing in a litigation. Forensic psychologists usually have some direct contact with the plaintiff or defendant in a case on which they are consulting, especially for purposes of conducting a formal evaluation. However, this will not be the person with whom they make arrangements for the evaluation or discuss the nature and import of their findings. Instead, such matters are discussed with the entity or attorney who constitutes the psychologist's client.

The general implications of identifying impersonal clients accurately and working with them appropriately were nicely elaborated by Monahan (1980) in a monograph with which all forensic psychologists should be conversant. Greenberg and Shuman (1997) and Heilbrun (2001, chap. 3) have more recently discussed the distinctly different roles and responsibilities that characterize the conduct of forensic evaluations, as opposed to practicing psychotherapy. The present chapter addresses specific implications that working within the adversarial system and with impersonal clients have for the writing of forensic reports. Especially important in this regard are decisions concerning whether a report should be written at all, should this be an option, and how a written report should be focused. After discussing guidelines for making such decisions, the chapter concludes with some suggestions for writing forensic reports in a clear, relevant, informative, and defensible manner.

DECIDING WHETHER A REPORT SHOULD BE WRITTEN

Deciding whether to write a report may seem to be a frivolous consideration. Psychologists are accustomed to writing reports as a necessary and expected culmination of providing consultative services. In forensic work, however, the inevitability of a written report is tempered by rules concerning the nature of evidence. Expert opinions become evidence not when they are formulated in a consultant's mind, but only when they are stated orally under oath or written down, whether in formal reports that are voluntarily submitted in evidence or informal notes that are subpoenaed during a discovery process. For this reason, attorneys typically advise persons involved in litigation to think whatever they wish but write down only what they are prepared to justify in testimony.

As an exception in this regard, communications to an attorney about the psychologist's arrangements for their work together may be considered part of the attorney's "work product" and therefore privileged, which means that they are protected against disclosure. A psychologist's findings and opinions in a case likewise remain privileged, so long as the psychologist is not identified to the court as an expert witness who might be called to give testimony. Once psychologists are named as a potential witness, however, they may be required to submit a written report for purposes of discovery, which allows opposing counsel an opportunity to ferret out the likely content of their testimony.

When the option is available, deciding whether to write a report should be based on the preferences of the client and certain ethical principles and professional realities that shape the practice of law and psychology.

RESPECTING THE PREFERENCES OF THE CLIENT

Most commonly in forensic cases, the psychologist's client is the court or an attorney. Even when the fees are being paid by other agencies or by private parties, judges and lawyers are the persons to whom forensic psychologists are most directly responsible and with whom they communicate most directly (see Monahan, 1980). These two types of forensic clients typically differ in the kinds of information they seek. Judges, who request psychological evaluations to help them reach decisions, usually want as much relevant information as possible and invite any opinion, whatever its implications, that might be useful to them. Hence, in court-ordered evaluations, a written report typically is expected, and a thorough elaboration of the nature and significance of the psychologist's findings is welcome.

By contrast, attorneys trying a case are looking only for facts and opinions that will strengthen their arguments on a client's behalf. If they consider the psychologist's conclusions damaging to their case, attorneys may prefer not to have a report written and not to include the psychologist on their witness list. The following three cases, each of a type common in the practice of forensic psychology, illustrate circumstances in which the attorney exercised these options.

Case 21.1

Mr. A was a 33-year-old systems analyst who had undergone surgery in connection with an accurately diagnosed medical condition. Apparently as a consequence of some careless surgical procedures, he suffered some unanticipated postoperative complications. Although not permanently disabling, these complications had prolonged Mr. A's recovery, delayed his return to work, and required him to undergo physical rehabilitation. His attorney believed that medical malpractice could be demonstrated and that Mr. A was entitled to compensatory and punitive damages. He believed further that his client must have suffered psychological as well as physical distress, which would warrant a larger damage award than if his iatrogenic problems were only physical.

The psychologist's evaluation suggested that Mr. A was an emotionally resourceful individual who was coping effectively with his unfortunate medical situation. Compared to most people with his illness who had required surgery, he seemed to be adjusting well psychologically. He was, in fact, the kind of patient one hopes to see on a rehabilitation service, for whom an optimistic prognosis for full recovery without emotional setbacks seems indicated.

* * *

As a compassionate individual, the attorney was pleased to receive an oral report to this effect. As Mr. A's representative in a personal injury suit, however, he recognized that the psychologist's opinion, if introduced as evidence, would be more likely to reduce than increase the amount of the damages that would be awarded. Hence, he did not request a written report or any further services from the psychologist.

Case 21.2

An attorney sought a psychologist's opinion while preparing to defend Mr. B, a 37-year-old elementary school teacher accused of sexually molesting several girls in his 5th-grade class. Mr. B had allegedly fondled these girls during class sessions by reaching into their underclothes while he was sitting at his desk and they approached him to ask a question or turn in an assignment. Aside from doubting that his client would have committed such acts so publicly, the attorney was puzzled by the manner in which the complaints had emerged. The initial allegation of molestation was made by just one girl, who spoke to her parents about it. Later, after this girl's parents had talked with the school principal and the police had been called in to investigate, several other girls in Mr. B's class told their parents that they had been fondled by him also.

Interestingly, reports from the school indicated that the girl who had complained first was socially popular and a leader among her peers. Also of note was the impression of several interviewers that none of the girls seemed particularly upset while talking about having been molested. To the contrary, they told their stories as if they were pleased and proud to relate them. As for Mr. B, he had for many years been a highly admired teacher in this school, known especially for a warm and caring attitude toward his students.

*   *   *

The attorney wondered whether there was any reason to think that a group of girls who had not been molested would say that they had been. Some possibilities will come quickly to the minds of psychologists familiar with the romantic fantasies and peer-group interactions that commonly characterize prepubescent development in 10- and 11-year-old girls.

Consider, for example, the possibility of a young girl first fantasizing about an appealing, perhaps paternal male teacher making a sexual overture toward her, and then fabricating such a story as a way of feeling attractive and grown up and impressing her parents and peers in certain ways. Consider further the possibility of other girls in the class, having heard this story from a popular trendsetter, deciding to claim, "He did it to me, too." This is the well-known stuff of which mass hysteria is made, as described in such classical papers as "The Phantom Anesthetist of Matoon" (Johnson, 1945) and in the recounting of the Salem witch trials (Starkey, 1949) and their dramatization in Arthur Miller's play *The Crucible.*

In mentioning these possibilities to the attorney, the psychologist identified them as clinical formulations that could not be substantiated with solid empirical evidence. Having a possible explanation that child specialists would find plausible is far different from having a line of defense that will stand up in court. The psychologist advised the attorney that many of the compelling speculations in this case, if offered in testimony, could be made to look foolish under skillful cross-examination and might thereby detract from other aspects of the defense he was preparing. Hence, a report was not written, and the psychologist did not participate further in the case, which resulted in Mr. B's being convicted and sent to prison.

Case 21.3

This third illustration, because of publicity surrounding it, must be presented in bare outline only. An attorney representing a young man charged with a serious crime was planning to file a plea of incompetence to stand trial. The attorney had been struck by his client's strange and disturbed behavior and expected that a formal psychological examination would provide supporting evidence for claiming incompetence. An examination led the psychologist to conclude that the young man was indeed acting strangely, but was in fact malingering. When he conveyed this opinion to the attorney in a telephone conversation, the attorney indicated that the psychologist would be paid for his time but would not be asked to submit a report.

ETHICAL PRINCIPLES AND PROFESSIONAL REALITIES

For psychologists unfamiliar with forensic consulting, the preceding three illustrations of being dismissed from a case prior to preparing a written report could raise some disturbing questions about proper practice. One might be especially concerned about Case 21.3, in which the psychologist provided an expert opinion that a man accused of committing a felony was attempting to fake mental disturbance. How could the attorney ignore this finding and continue constructing a case for incompetency, and should the psychologist allow this to happen? The answers to these questions touch on some ethical and realistic considerations in the practice of law and psychology.

The Quality of Expert Opinions

To prepare themselves for sometimes unenthusiastic responses to their opinions, forensic consultants need to remain sufficiently humble to recognize that they may at times be in error, or at least not possessed of all the answers. Clinicians must appreciate in particular that their skill and judgment do not transcend all of the imperfections in their assessment tools. As Shapiro (1991, chap. 4) reminds forensic consultants, expert psychological opinions are not statements of fact, but only reasonable conclusions based on the information that is available and has been carefully analyzed.

The psychologist in Case 21.3 was reasonably certain that the defendant was malingering, but he would not have been prepared to testify that he was absolutely certain—nor indeed should he have been, given the difficulty of establishing malingering with absolute certainty (see Berry, Wetter, & Baer, 2002; Rogers, 1997; Rogers & Bender, 2003). From the attorney's point of view, then, the opinion concerning malingering could be taken as a possibility, but not as the only possibility. The attorney might also have had in hand information unknown to the psychologist, perhaps even another expert opinion that in his view argued strongly against malingering.

Like the imperfections of assessment methods, the existence of multiple, contradictory expert opinions brings a sobering measure of reality into forensic consulting. One expert's opinion is neither the only nor the last word. There are no obligations that would have prevented the attorney in Case 21.3 from listening to the psychologist's opinion concerning malingering and then turning to a different consultant, or perhaps a string of consultants, until a qualified psychologist was found in whose opinion the defendant was truly incapable of understanding the proceedings against him and consulting effectively with his attorney, which would make him incompetent to stand trial according to the *Dusky* standard (see Zapf & Roesch, Chapter 12, in this volume; see also Grisso, 2003; Skeem, Golding, Cohn, & Berge, 1988; Stafford, 2003).

Learning of such an outcome, the first consultant could feel strongly that this last expert lacked sufficient experience or diagnostic acumen to recognize a clear case of malingering. However, the court in such a case would ordinarily accept a licensed psychologist with some experience in assessing competence in criminal defendants as qualified to offer such an opinion. To be sure, issues of competency and criminal responsibility commonly feature expert witness testimony on both sides of the case, and arguments may ensue concerning which of several qualified professionals is best qualified to give reliable testimony. The point remains, however, that it is entirely appropriate and consistent with prevailing practice for attorneys to challenge or reject the opinions of a consultant they have retained and to seek other consultants whose opinions will provide better support for their case.

Considerations in Practicing Law

Instead of questioning the quality of expert opinions that fail to meet their needs, attorneys may decide on the basis of a consultant's conclusions to change their approach to a case or consider withdrawing from it. For example, becoming convinced that a client in a criminal case has been faking emotional disturbance, is lying about his or her guilt, or has in other ways behaved in a reprehensible manner may lead an attorney to decline to represent that person further or, if court-appointed, to ask to be excused from the case.

Yet, our system of criminal justice entitles everyone to a defense, no matter how barbarous the offense, how despicable the alleged offender, or how guilty the accused appears to be. Regardless of how many attorneys choose not to represent certain kinds of clients, every defendant in a criminal case will in the end have the right to be represented by a member of the bar. Furthermore, the attorney eventually retained or appointed to provide this representation will be ethically responsible for presenting the strongest possible case on behalf of the defendant. A weak or half-hearted defense of a defendant whom an attorney regards as guilty or as having few redeemable qualities can result in the attorney's appearing inept or unethical in the eyes of the legal community. Ineffective or unprepared trial lawyers may even risk being publicly chastened by the bench for having done a poor job in their client's behalf. Moreover, a decision reached in such an instance could well be reversed on appeal to a higher court on the basis of the defendant having had ineffective counsel.

In addition to preventing such negative consequences, a strong case presented on behalf of a client considered difficult to defend can enhance an attorney's professional reputation. Hence, trial attorneys may enjoy or even seek out opportunities to take on challenging cases and construct convincing briefs in them, especially in trials that capture media attention. Such recent media events as the O. J. Simpson, Timothy McVeigh (Oklahoma bomber), Theodore Kaczinski (Unabomber), and Lee Boyd Malvo (D.C. sniper) murder trials are cases in point.

Forensic psychologists need to appreciate these realistic motivations for attorneys to continue quite properly to build cases that expert consultants think are flawed. Moreover, there are instances in which attorneys have no choice but to continue with a case, regardless of reservations about the worthiness of the client or the weight of the evidence. For example, defense attorneys appointed by the court are in fact rarely given an option to withdraw from the case and can expect the court to be especially intolerant of a lackluster effort on their part. Likewise, prosecuting attorneys may be assigned cases by the office for which they work, without being given much latitude to choose which ones they would prefer to try. These various considerations provide ample basis for conscientious and ethical attorneys to decline to have their consultants furnish evidence that would be damaging to their case.

Considerations in Practicing Psychology

Turning now to the second troublesome question raised by Case 21.3, how could the psychologist allow pertinent information to be suppressed? Being reasonably certain from his data that the accused was malingering psychosis, how could he sit silently by while a competency hearing was taking place? To make matters worse, suppose that daily newspaper accounts of the hearing were predicting that the defendant would be found incompetent to stand trial because of emotional disturbance.

Psychologists struggling with this kind of question need to recognize that their dismay derives from their professional experience with the case conference model. In the case conference model, all relevant information is sought and a wide range of opinions is considered in arriving at a diagnostic formulation and treatment plan. This model is seldom approximated in forensic consultation, except when the client is the court. Then, as noted earlier, any testimony that helps the court reach its decisions will be welcome.

For attorneys, however, who in conformance with the adversarial system are pleading just one side of a case, the only welcome testimony comprises evidence and opinions that support their arguments. If expert opinions exist that would support the other side of the case, it is up to opposing counsel to discover and produce these opinions. Confronted with such realities on cases in which they have consulted, psychologists may experience disappointment, anger, or perhaps even a sense of outrage. They may feel that, in situations like Case 21.3, their findings should be brought to light to prevent a malingering criminal from escaping justice. They may even feel tempted to "blow the whistle," that is, to call the prosecuting attorney or the judge and volunteer their opinion, or to inform the media that critical information concerning the case is being suppressed.

Except in extraordinary circumstances, responsible psychologists must resist any such temptations. To do otherwise would abuse the defendant's right to confidentiality and violate the Ethical Principles of Psychologists and Code of Conduct adopted by the American Psychological Association (2002, 4.01 & 4.05, p. 1066), which state the following:

> Psychologists have a primary obligation and take reasonable precautions to protect confidential information obtained through or stored in any medium, recognizing that the extent and limits of confidentiality may be regulated by law or established by institutional rules or professional or scientific relationship. . . . Psychologists disclose confidential information without the consent of the individual only as mandated by law, or where permitted by law for a valid purpose such as (1) to provide needed professional services; (2) obtain appropriate professional consultations; (3) protect the client/patient, psychologist, or others from harm; or (4) obtain payment for services from a client/patient, in which instance disclosure is limited to the minimum that is necessary to achieve the purpose.

Finally, with respect to deciding whether a report should be written following a forensic consultation, psychologists should be sufficiently aware of applicable case and statutory law and the implications of their findings to advise their attorney clients concerning whether a report is likely to be helpful to them. In addition to being much appreciated, informed opinions of this kind can even result in attorneys requesting a report of findings that would appear to weaken their position, as in the following case.

Case 21.4

An attorney representing Ms. C requested an evaluation of the extent to which she was suffering from Posttraumatic Stress Disorder or any other psychological problems as a consequence of an automobile accident in which she had been involved. On the basis of ample historical data, a detailed clinical interview, and findings from a comprehensive battery of psychological tests, the psychologist concluded that this woman was not displaying any emotional difficulties or behavior problems that were attributable to the accident.

*   *   *

Discussing his impressions in an informal conversation with his attorney client, the psychologist told him, "I don't think I can help you." Surprisingly, however, the attorney responded that he could put the psychologist's negative findings to good use. He went on to say that Ms. C had been pressing him to seek compensation for psychic damage and disability as well as for her well-documented physical injuries. An unambiguous written statement from the psychologist concerning the negative results of the examination would help him convince his client to drop this part of her claim, he said, thereby sparing him from having to pursue a weak part of his case and allowing him to focus on the strong part. A written report was accordingly prepared.

DETERMINING THE FOCUS OF FORENSIC REPORTS

Once a decision has been made that a report will be written, the forensic psychologist must then decide what to say in this report. Now is the time to keep in mind that whatever is written down is discoverable and may become entered into evidence. Moreover, when psychologists are called to testify in a legal proceeding, their testimony on direct examination will ordinarily be based on their written report, which means that everything in the report will be subject to question on cross-examination. As a basic principle, then, forensic psychologists should limit their written reports to statements they will feel comfortable hearing read aloud in the courtroom and to conclusions they feel able to defend against reasonable challenge.

Beyond this preliminary consideration, the appropriate focus of forensic reports varies from one case to the next in relation to the needs of the client. As in providing other kinds of psychological services, forensic consultants should be guided by the familiar principle of giving clients what they want, within appropriate limits dictated by their professional judgment and ethical standards. This guideline does not imply that psychologists should provide attorneys whatever opinions or conclusions the attorneys would like to have to bolster their case. Meeting the client's needs refers to providing the desired services, not the desired findings.

Reports should accordingly focus on matters of concern to the client without including all of the psychological observations that could be made about a person or situation being evaluated. This aspect of focusing forensic reports is embodied in the American Psychological Association (2002, 4.04, p. 1066) Code of Conduct as follows: "Psychologists include in written and oral reports and consultations only information germane to the purpose for which the communication is made."

More specific guidelines in this regard appear in the Specialty Guidelines for Forensic Psychologists:

> With respect to evidence of any type, forensic psychologists avoid offering information from their investigations or evaluations that does not bear directly upon the legal purpose of their professional services and is not critical as support for their product, evidence, or testimony, except where such disclosure is required by law. (Committee on Ethical Guidelines for Forensic Psychologists, 1991, p. 662)

As a further note concerning propriety in this regard, it is helpful to distinguish between acts of *commission* and acts of *omission* in writing reports. Regarding commission, forensic psychologists should under no circumstances compromise their integrity by knowingly making inaccurate or misleading statements. Regarding omission, on the other hand, it is rarely warranted or necessary to answer questions that the client has not asked. Forensic reports focused within the limits described thus far will nevertheless vary in breadth as a function of the nature of the case and the line of attack or defense the client is intending to pursue.

PROVIDING NARROWLY FOCUSED CONSULTATIONS

In some forensic cases, the questions being asked by the client call for fairly limited data collection and a rather narrowly focused written report. The following two cases illustrate such circumstances.

Case 21.5

A young man accused of burglarizing some homes in his neighborhood had signed a confession. His attorney felt that he had been frightened into signing a confession that he was incapable of understanding. The psychologist asked to assess this possibility administered the Wechsler Adult Intelligence Scale (WAIS) and the Shipley Institute of Living Scale. The accused appeared unfamiliar with many of the vocabulary items in these two tests, including several that are listed in the Thorndike-Lorge index as being more frequently used than some of the key words in the confession he had signed. The psychologist's report consisted of stating this finding and indicating its implications for a reasonably certain conclusion that the young man did not fully understand the text of his confession.

Case 21.6

An attorney preparing to plead diminished capacity in defending a man charged with attempted murder had received some divergent reports from several consultants concerning her client's mental status. As one step in trying to resolve this discrepancy, she asked a psychologist experienced in the Rorschach assessment of Schizophrenia if he would review the defendant's Rorschach protocol and answer two questions: Was the record taken properly, and is it consistent with a *DSM-IV* diagnosis of Schizophrenia? In the consultant's opinion, the answers to these two questions were yes and no, respectively, and this is what was communicated to the attorney in a relatively brief and narrowly focused report.

* * *

These examples of narrowly focused forensic consultations may appear to incorporate some undesirable clinical practices. In the first place, the psychologist in both cases based his opinion on just one or two specialized tests, whereas psychodiagnostic assessment as commonly practiced involves a multifaceted test battery. Second, in Case 21.6 the psychologist conducted a blind analysis of the test protocol without seeing the accused or knowing anything about him except his age and sex. Most clinicians regard such blind analysis as appropriate only for didactic or research purposes. Moreover, most clinicians agree that diagnoses should be made by them, not by their tests, and only following thoughtful integration of test findings with relevant information about a person's history and circumstances (Beutler & Groth-Marnat, 2003; Weiner, 2003a, 2005).

Psychologists concerned about such matters might be understandably reluctant to provide the narrow kind of consultation requested in Cases 21.5 and 21.6. From the perspective of attorneys attempting to muster bits of evidence in support of their case, however, the request in both cases for a narrowly focused consultation is entirely appropriate. It was likewise appropriate for the psychologist to respond just to the questions being raised, provided that he felt confident of his ability to do so. Moreover, submitting a narrowly focused report did not prevent the psychologist in Case 21.6 from also assuming an educative function and pointing out to the attorney that an informed psychodiagnostic opinion concerning her client's mental status would have to be based on results of a test battery and contextual information, not just blind evaluation of a single test protocol.

BROADENING THE FOCUS OF FORENSIC CONSULTATION

Although instances of narrowly focused consultation are important to identify and put in perspective, they seldom occur in the practice of most forensic psychologists. Instead, consultative requests are likely to require attention to multiple sources of information in the preparation of reports. Even when psychologists are consulted primarily as experts in psychological test evaluation, they should conduct themselves as broadly knowledgeable mental health professionals who integrate interview data, background information, and test findings into comprehensive opinions and conclusions concerning the case. Psychologists who testify on the basis of a written report that deals solely with test findings, and who must plead ignorance when asked about other elements of the case, are poorly prepared to present themselves effectively. They weaken their client's arguments by being exposed as an expert who has only a superficial grasp of the case, and they demean their own professional status by failing to present themselves as anything more than a tester.

Adequate attention to the context of a forensic case does not always call for extensive data collection or record review, however. Sometimes just a few bits of background information suffice for preparing an effectively focused report, as in the following case.

Case 21.7

Mr. D was a 34-year-old man who had suffered a closed head injury in an accident for which there was alleged liability. He had been rehabilitated on a neurological service to the point where he was considered to have achieved his maximum recovery. His attorney wanted to establish how much permanent loss of function remained as a consequence of the accident. A Wechsler, administered as part of an extensive test battery, yielded a Full-Scale Intelligence Quotient (FSIQ) of 103.

Although no preaccident IQ score was on record in Mr. D's case to provide a baseline, his history revealed that he had received a PhD in chemical engineering from a prestigious university and had had a successful career up to the time of his accident. This fact alone, given the considerable unlikelihood of such accomplishment by a person with an IQ of 103, established a solid basis for arguing that at least some loss of mental capacity could be attributed to the accident, probably too much to allow him to resume his career. The written report was accordingly focused on these particular findings.

*   *   *

Turning to more general guidelines in determining the scope of a report, the previously noted difference between the typical expectations of attorneys and those of judges influences the amount of information a forensic consultant gathers and reports. To recapitulate this difference, attorneys are operating as adversaries on their clients' behalf and are interested in expert opinions that support the case they are making, whereas judges are neutral to both sides of a case and are interested in as many relevant opinions as they can obtain. Hence, reports prepared for attorneys will ordinarily be more limited in scope and more narrowly focused on conclusions pointing in one particular direction than reports prepared for the court. The breadth of the psychologist's focus will additionally be influenced by the *time frame* of the inquiry, with specific respect to whether attention must be paid to present, past, or future circumstances.

Addressing Present Circumstances

When forensic psychological opinions must address primarily the present status of a plaintiff or defendant, the data that needs to be collected are relatively limited, and the task of interpreting them is correspondingly uncomplicated. As previously noted, for example, questions of whether defendants are competent to stand trial concern mainly whether they are currently able to understand the charges against them and participate effectively in their defense. Consultants may struggle with translating these legal criteria for competency into psychological terms, and they may encounter cases of marginal competency that are difficult to call one way or the other. Whatever the difficulty of the task in these evaluations, however, the critical data for determining a defendant's present functioning capacity will be available from currently obtainable interview, test, and observational data.

Assessment of personal injury also focuses mainly on current mental or emotional state and functioning capacity. Evaluations of allegedly reactive psychological conditions or loss of functioning capacity are a bit more complicated than determining competency, because current capacity must ordinarily be compared to some baseline of previous functioning, prior to an allegedly harmful incident (see Greenberg, Otto, & Long, 2003). In most cases, verifiable records of past events provide a baseline for such comparisons. These records may include previously obtained intelligence, neuropsychological, or personality test findings; documentation of a claimant's educational and occupational history (as in Case 21.7); clinicians' and hospital notes concerning prior medical problems and mental health services; and testimony from relatives and long-time acquaintances concerning the injured person's earlier patterns of behavior and adjustment.

Addressing Past Circumstances

Opinions that must address the past status of an individual ordinarily require more extensive data collection than present status evaluations and a more broadly focused report in which the conclusions are less certain (see Weiner, 2003b). The most commonly encountered cases of this kind involve questions of criminal responsibility. As elaborated in Chapter 13, criminal responsibility is determined by the nature of a defendant's mental state at the time of an offense and whether this mental state contributed to the commission of the offense. Efforts to establish a prior mental state and its likely consequences require forensic psychologists to seek out information and confront uncertainties that stretch their capacities well beyond the relatively modest demands of conducting a present status evaluation.

For example, suppose an adult male defendant whose attorney is pleading him not guilty by reason of insanity to a felonious assault committed 3 months earlier shows substantial evidence on psychological examination of a long-standing schizophrenic disorder. This may constitute good reason to believe that the accused was psychologically disturbed 3 months earlier and probably long before that. Even if uncontested, however, this conclusion would not necessarily demonstrate that the defendant's disorder was responsible for his having committed his offense.

Case 21.8

Just prior to the 1984 Summer Olympics in Los Angeles, a man named Daniel Lee Young drove his car recklessly onto a crowded sidewalk, killing one pedestrian and injuring fifty-four others. In his subsequent trial he was identified as having a chronic paranoid schizophrenic disorder. It was nevertheless found that his Schizophrenia was not a contributing factor in his assaultive and homicidal behavior. He was considered to have been legally sane at the time of the crime and was sentenced to a prison term of 106 years and 4 months to life on one count of first-degree murder and forty-eight counts of attempted murder.

* * *

Suppose, as a contrasting example, that an offender pleading temporary insanity or diminished capacity appears at present to be psychologically capable and well-functioning, making it doubtful that he or she was seriously disturbed just a few months earlier, when the crime was committed. Could it nevertheless be argued that any person, no matter how well functioning at the moment, could fall prey to an acute psychotic or dissociative episode during a period of duress? Or, on the other hand, could it be concluded from currently obtained interview and test data that a defendant is not the kind of person who is likely to show psychotic or dissociative reactions to stress? Neither conclusion, whatever its psychological justification, would carry much evidentiary weight, unless it could be convincingly amplified with respect to (1) the nature and amount of stress the defendant was actually likely to have been experiencing shortly before or at the time of the criminal act and (2) how he or she was actually behaving prior to and while committing it.

With this in mind, forensic psychologists addressing questions of criminal responsibility need to investigate carefully and report clearly the events leading up to and occurring during the commission of a crime. The defendant's own recollections, the police arrest report, and statements given by eyewitnesses and other informants should be integrated with current personality evaluations to yield informed opinions concerning whether the stresses in a defendant's life and his or her behavior while committing a crime seem consistent with applicable criteria for reduced criminal responsibility (see Goldstein, Morse, & Shapiro, 2003; Shapiro, 1991, chap. 3; see also Zapf, Golding & Roesch, Chapter 13, in this volume).

Addressing Future Circumstances

In three other types of forensic cases the questions being asked challenge psychologists not to reconstruct the past, but to predict the future. Two of these types of cases involve requests for aid in sentencing convicted criminal offenders, sometimes with respect to whether they should initially be sent to prison or placed on probation, and at other times with respect to whether an incarcerated offender should be granted parole. As noted in Chapter 16, being able to offer reasonable opinions concerning probation and parole depends on being able to estimate how likely the offender is to commit further crimes, especially violent ones; how responsive the person will be to counseling, psychotherapy, job training, or other rehabilitative efforts attempted outside of prison; and how adequate the available services are for providing the kinds of nonprison interventions that offer promise of a successful outcome.

These are usually difficult estimates to make on the basis of currently available information, and forensic reports addressed to future possibilities must typically be more complicated, detailed, and tentative than reports addressing present functioning alone. To extrapolate accurately from current assessment data to future expectations bearing on the advisability of probation or parole, forensic consultants need to muster whatever clinical and empirical knowledge can be obtained concerning recidivism, violence risk, treatment response, and available resources and relate this information to the case at hand.

The other type of forensic case that touches on future circumstances involves the contested child custody and visitation rights between parents who are separated or divorced. What arrangements will be in the best interests of the children? Which parent is likely to provide better child care and supervision? When and under what circumstances should the noncustodial parent have access to his or her children? Like estimating the advisability of probation or parole, these child custody questions are difficult to answer with certainty from presently available data.

Among other demands faced by forensic psychologists in family law cases, their examinations and reports must almost always embrace all members of the family who will be affected by a custody decision, including both parents, all dependent children, and other significant figures in the home or in a child's life. Should a remarried parent be seeking to gain primary residential custody, the stepparent may also need to be evaluated. In addition, to lend some reasonable certainty to their efforts to predict the future, psychologists offering opinions in custody cases need to draw on relevant research findings and clinical wisdom concerning developmental aspects of child-parent relationships and the impact of divorce on children and their parents (see American Psychological Association, 1994; O'Donohue & Bradley, 1999; Otto, Buffington-Vollum, & Edens, 2003; see also K. D. Hess, Chapters 4 and 5, in this volume).

ON BEING CLEAR, RELEVANT, INFORMATIVE, AND DEFENSIBLE

The present chapter has indicated to this point that writing useful and effective forensic reports requires psychologists (1) to have a good grasp of the legal and behavioral issues surrounding a case, (2) to determine what kinds of information will best help to resolve these issues, and then (3) to gather and evaluate such information. Once these tasks are accomplished, what remains is for consultants to express their impressions and conclusions in a clear, relevant, informative, and defensible manner.

BEING CLEAR

Forensic consultants should ordinarily begin their reports by indicating when, by whom, and for what purposes they were appointed or retained to offer their opinions in the particular case. They should then identify the sources of information they have utilized. When, where, for what reason, and in what fashion were parties to the case directly evaluated? What records were examined, such as depositions, police reports, medical charts, and school or military files? What collateral persons were interviewed? To what extent were other discussions, reviews of psychological literature, or examinations of case law undertaken to further the consultant's knowledge and understanding of the case? Explicit answers to these questions in the introduction to a forensic report promote clarity by minimizing uncertainty concerning the basis on which consultants have formed the opinions they are about to state in their report.

In stating their findings and conclusions, forensic psychologists should strive to write in plain English and to limit their use of technical jargon. As previously mentioned, a written report may be gone over word for word by opposing counsel during a deposition or read aloud in its entirety in the courtroom. Some attorneys may even prefer on direct examination to have a consultant's report entered verbatim, to avoid having imprecise or poorly worded statements slip into the consultant's extemporaneous presentation. Hence, consultants should not plan on writing a formal, somewhat technical report for the record and then giving their courtroom testimony in an informal, conversational manner that is easy to follow and understand. Instead, the written report itself should be as clear and conversational as the psychologist can make it. This means using unstilted and uncomplicated language that will be comfortable for consultants to repeat on the witness stand, that will be comprehensible to judge and jury, and that will limit a cross-examining attorney's opportunities to badger them with questions about what their statements mean.

Along with using ordinary language in reports, except where technical terms may be required (e.g., a formal diagnosis), psychologists should concentrate on writing about the person they have evaluated, rather than about psychological processes. A statement like "Coping capacities are good" does not communicate as clearly as "Ms. E has good capacities for coping with stressful experiences without becoming unduly upset by them." When psychologists fail to guard adequately against being murky, impersonal descriptions of psychological processes often go hand in hand with jargon. Compare, for example,

"Homophobia is pronounced" with "This man tends to avoid people because he is unusually fearful of being harmed or taken advantage of by others." Sometimes consultants may not realize that certain expressions commonly used by professionals are not generally understood by the public. For example, "Reality testing is poor" reads better as "Mr. F's reality testing is poor" but even better as "Mr. F often forms distorted or inaccurate impressions of people and events, and he is consequently likely to show poor judgment and fail to anticipate correctly the consequences of his actions." Similar recommendations are elaborated by Brenner (2003), Harvey (1997), Heilbrun (2001, chap. 10), and Nicholson and Norwood (2000) for improving the readability, utility, and communication value of psychological reports.

BEING RELEVANT

As in responding to consultation requests in other areas of practice, psychologists achieve relevance in forensic reports by addressing and attempting to answer the referral question. Being relevant means omitting much of what could be said about an individual's psychological characteristics and probable ways of responding in various circumstances and instead providing a distillate of those features of the individual that bear directly on the issues in the case and the client's questions about these issues.

But what are the client's questions? To some extent, relevance is achieved by adhering to the previously noted ethical guidelines concerning appropriately focused forensic reports. However, to translate this concept into practice—and thereby conduct an adequate evaluation and write a relevant report—forensic psychologists need to be pursuing some specifically stated question, such as whether an accused is competent to stand trial or an allegedly brain-injured person has suffered demonstrable loss of intellectual or cognitive function. If no such question has been framed, one must be elicited from the client by asking, "Why do you want to have this person evaluated?" or "What is it that you would like to learn from me?"

In addition to identifying what information to obtain and how best to organize and report it, specific referral questions also help psychologists anticipate at least in part how well they will be able to respond to consultative requests. Expectations concerning how useful or how powerful the psychological data will be can often be shared with clients to good effect. For example, alerting an attorney that evaluations of possible future behavior generate less certain results than evaluations of present status can enhance the effectiveness of an eventual report by minimizing any unwarranted expectations on the attorney's part. Cases 21.2 and 21.4 presented earlier also illustrate how working with a clear referral question can make it possible to provide a relevant consultation based on the anticipated impact of one's impressions.

Forensic psychologists can increase the relevance of their consultations further by drawing on familiarity with statutory and case law applicable to a case in the particular jurisdiction in which it is being processed. Cognizance of applicable legal standards is an ethical responsibility in forensic practice (Committee on Ethical Guidelines for Forensic Psychologists, 1991, p. 658), and judicious integration of such knowledge into a report, especially with respect to appropriate terminology, will usually enhance its relevance.

Thus, for example, psychologists preparing reports in personal injury cases should address in specific terms the issue of "proximate cause," as spelled out in tort law (see Walfish, Chapter 6, in this volume), and those preparing reports in custody cases should devote specific attention to the "best interests of the child" doctrine, which is a prominent theme in family law (see K. D. Hess, Chapter 4, in this volume). The differing criteria employed in various state and federal jurisdictions for what constitute mitigating mental circumstances in criminal behavior also illustrate the necessity of adequate legal knowledge (see Goldstein et al., 2003; Zapf, Golding, & Roesch, Chapter 13, in this volume). To express a relevant opinion concerning criminal responsibility, forensic psychologists must appreciate how their findings fit with applicable ways of defining it and express themselves accordingly. In a jurisdiction in which the M'Naghten rule applies, for example, the utility of the consultant's report is enhanced by the following kind of statement:

> Mr. G frequently has difficulty perceiving events in his life realistically, and as a result he often misjudges how his behavior affects other people. The severity of this problem and strong indications that he has had it for a long time make it reasonable to think that he was not fully capable of appreciating the wrongfulness of his actions at the time of the crime. Significant in this regard, when asked directly if he thought he was doing anything wrong, he said, "I had every right to do it."

BEING INFORMATIVE

Like clinical reports, forensic reports should be written in an informative manner that educates the nonpsychologist reader. This informational objective can usually be achieved by relating psychological data and impressions to benchmarks that the audience will recognize. For example, saying that a respondent has received a WAIS-III FSIQ of 100 communicates adequately to other psychologists about the person's overall IQ level, but this statement becomes intelligible to most laypeople only when it is amplified with some additional information: for example, that the WAIS-III is currently the most widely used measure of adult intelligence; that it comprises several subtests sampling different kinds of abilities; that, although there is some measurement error associated with a Wechsler IQ, an obtained score of 100 gives a 95% probability that the respondent's true IQ is between 95 and 105; and that about half of all people receive an IQ score higher than 100 on this test, and about half a lower score.

Similarly with respect to impressions of psychological disorder, consultants should indicate how the findings compare with the diagnostic criteria of widely used nomenclatures, as was done in Case 21.6; for example, "The way this person is thinking and feeling, as reflected in the interview and test findings, is consistent with a *DSM-IV-TR* diagnosis of Major Depressive Disorder." There are also instances in which consultants may find it useful to draw on textbook information to summarize a set of circumstances that point to a particular conclusion. For example, a psychologist consulting on a criminal case in which the court was considering a suspended sentence wrote the following informative opinion:

> I am concerned about having this man return without supervision to his previous place of residence. Being a white male in his late 50s, who would be living alone in a run-down section of town, and who has previously attempted to take his own life, he would be in a very high risk group for suicidal behavior.

An informative educational approach of this kind, in a report that is easy to understand and speaks explicitly to the issues at hand, promotes effective communication. Combined with good judgment concerning when reports should be written and how narrowly or broadly they should be focused, skills in being clear, relevant, and informative in writing reports contribute substantially to providing effective forensic consultation. What remains to be considered are some ways in which forensic reports can be written to enhance their defensibility in the face of challenge.

BEING DEFENSIBLE

Unlike clinical reports, which are commonly either praised or ignored but are rarely demeaned, at least not publicly, forensic reports are fair game to opposing counsels. Their duty to their client calls for them to challenge what consulting psychologists on the other side have written, while making them as uneasy, uncertain, and unbelievable as possible on the witness stand. Forensic psychologists accordingly can spare themselves grief by writing reports that say what needs to be said in as defensible a manner as possible. As elaborated elsewhere (Weiner, 2002), there are various ways psychologists can minimize legal and ethical jeopardy in conducting personality assessments. With respect to writing forensic reports, four considerations can help consultants avoid potential pitfalls in giving expert witness testimony.

First, in offering conclusions about people they have evaluated, forensic psychologists are well advised to favor description over categorization. The ground underfoot is safer when describing how a respondent resembles certain types of people who have had certain kinds of experiences than it is when categorizing a respondent as being a particular type of person who has had particular experiences. The following pairs of statements illustrate the difference between describing and categorizing people:

> "This woman shows many features in common with people who have developed a stress disorder subsequent to a traumatic experience" versus "This woman has a Posttraumatic Stress Disorder."

> "Often, children with the kinds of personality characteristics I found in Suzie have not had the benefit of receiving much nurturance from their parents" versus "Suzie has not been adequately nurtured by her parents."

> "Mr. H's attitudes and dispositions closely resemble those often seen in persons who act violently toward others" versus "Mr. H is likely to act violently toward others."

The second part of each of the preceding pairs seldom causes problems when it appears in clinical reports as statements of what the psychologist believes. In forensic reports, however, categorization exposes consultants to thorny questions concerning how they know for sure that people have certain conditions being attributed to them, and whether the consultant was actually present to observe the experiences, events, and action tendencies being alleged to have occurred. By describing rather than categorizing, psychologists can blunt the thrust of such challenges. Thus, in the example of Suzie, the consultant who describes does not say that she was inadequately nurtured by her parents, but only that she shows characteristics in common with children who have not been adequately nurtured.

Second, in similar fashion, relative statements about people usually create fewer difficulties for forensic consultants than absolute statements. In this instance, there is some interprofessional convergence between psychologists' familiarity with uncertainty, on the one hand, and attorneys' attention to matters like "reasonable certainty" and "preponderance of evidence" on the other hand. Statements about persons examined in forensic cases that are couched in terms of conditions they are more or less likely to have and in terms of behavior they probably showed in the past or may be inclined to show in the future will typically stand the consultant in good stead, as will statements about reasonable alternative implications of their findings for the legal issues in a case.

Likewise, statements that paint people in relative and conjectural terms as being more or less likely than other people to show certain characteristics invite fewer challenges than pictures painted only in black-and-white certainty. Thus, for example, it is much easier to justify having written "Ms. I appears to be more self-centered than most people" than "Ms. I is a very self-centered person."

Third, consistent with what psychologists know about the imperfect nature of their assessment tools and about false-negative findings in particular, forensic consultants should avoid writing statements that rule out conditions or events. The fact that certain conditions (e.g., some disorder) or events (e.g., having been sexually abused or abusive) are not suggested by a psychologist's data does not eliminate the possibility of their existing. To minimize their exposure to being challenged and possibly embarrassed as a result of having overstated the findings, forensic psychologists should place the emphasis in their reports on what their findings demonstrate as probably being present (e.g., "There is substantial indication in the available data that Mr. J is a psychologically stable, well-organized, and capable person"; "The evidence at hand suggests that Ms. K is quite depressed and possibly suicidal at the present time").

On those occasions when reporting of negative findings seems called for or is mandated, consultants will do well to exercise caution in drawing conclusions from these findings. Consider, for example, the following statement: "Although it is not possible on the basis of the test findings to rule out closed head injury, the data obtained in the examination do not contain any evidence of neuropsychological impairment."

Fourth, forensic psychologists are well advised to avoid including illustrative test responses in their reports. Knowledgeable examiners are often tempted to illustrate their points with critical items from self-report inventories and rich content themes from the Rorschach. Even when certain repetitive self-reports and pervasive contents have compelling face validity, however, their presentation can cause examiners considerable grief by opening the door to questions about what individual test responses mean. With a foot in this door, skilled cross-examining attorneys can make most psychologists and their tests look foolish by questioning the interpretive significance of subtle test items or responses. A helpful reply to courtroom questions about the meaning of individual items and responses is that they have little significance by themselves and acquire interpretive value only when combined into various multiple-item scales and configurations. Psychologists who have already identified individual responses in their written reports and given interpretive weight to them are poorly positioned to give this answer in the courtroom.

In summary, then, writing effective forensic reports begins with deciding whether a report should be written, a decision that should be based jointly on the preferences of the client and the obligation of the consultant to certain ethical principles and professional realities that govern the practice of forensic psychology. When a written report is expected or required, as is usually the case in forensic work, consulting psychologists need to determine whether their report should be focused in a relatively narrow or relatively broad manner. This determination will be guided by the kinds of questions they are being asked in a particular case and will have implications for how much information they collect, from what sources they collect this information, and how much of what kinds of information they include in their report. Good judgment concerning when reports should be written and how narrowly or broadly they should be focused, when combined with skill in writing clear, relevant, and informative reports that can be defended on the witness stand, are building blocks of providing effective forensic consultation.

REFERENCES

American Psychological Association. (1994). Guidlelines for child custody evaluations in divorce proceedings. *American Psychologist, 47,* 1597–1611.

American Psychological Association. (2002). Ethical principles of psychologists and code of conduct. *American Psychologist, 57,* 1060–1073.

Barrett, G. V., & Morris, S. B. (1993). The American Psychological Association's amicus curiae brief in Price Waterhouse v. Hopkins: The values of science versus the values of the law. *Law and Human Behavior, 17,* 201–216.

Berry, D. T. R., Wetter, M. W., & Baer, R. A. (2002). Assessment of malingering. In J. N. Butcher (Ed.), *Clinical personality assessment* (2nd ed., pp. 269–302). New York: Guilford Press.

Beutler, L. E., & Groth-Marnat, G. (Eds.). (2003). *Integrative assessment of adult personality.* New York: Guilford Press.

Brenner, E. (2003). Consumer-focused psychological assessment. *Professional Psychology, 34,* 240–247.

Brodsky, S. L., & Robey, A. (1972). On becoming an expert witness: Issues of orientation and effectiveness. *Professional Psychology, 3,* 173–176.

Committee on Ethical Guidelines for Forensic Psychologists. (1991). Specialty guidelines for forensic psychologists. *Law and Human Behavior, 15,* 655–665.

Goldstein, A. M., Morse, S. J., & Shapiro, D. L. (2003). Evaluation of criminal responsibility. In A. M. Goldstein (Ed.), *Forensic psychology* (pp. 381–406). Vol. 11 in I. B. Weiner (Editor-in-Chief), *Handbook of psychology.* Hoboken, NJ: Wiley.

Greenberg, S. A., Otto, R. K., & Long, A. C. (2003). The utility of psychological testing in assessing emotional damages in personal injury litigation. *Assessment, 10,* 411–419.

Greenberg, S. A., & Shuman, D. W. (1997). Irreconcilable conflict between therapeutic and forensic roles. *Professional Psychology, 28,* 50–57.

Grisso, T. (2003). *Evaluating competencies: Forensic assessment and instruments* (2nd ed.). New York: Kluwer Academic/Plenum Press.

Harvey, V. S. (1997). Improving the readability of psychological reports. *Professional Psychology, 28,* 271–274.

Heilbrun, K. (2001). *Principles of forensic mental health assessment.* New York: Kluwer Academic/Plenum Press.

Johnson, D. M. (1945). The "phantom anesthetist" of Mattoon: A field study of mass hysteria. *Journal of Abnormal and Social Psychology, 40,* 175–186.

Monahan, J. (Ed.). (1980). *Who is the client?* Washington, DC: American Psychological Association.

Nicholson, R. A., & Norwood, S. (2000). The quality of forensic psychological assessments, reports, and testimony. *Law and Human Behavior, 24,* 9–44.

O'Donohue, W., & Bradley, A. R. (1999). Conceptual and empirical issues in child custody evaluations. *Clinical Psychology: Science and Practice, 6,* 310–322.

Otto, R. K., Buffington-Vollum, J. K., & Edens, J. F. (2003). Child custody evaluation. In A. M. Goldstein (Ed.), *Forensic psychology* (pp. 179–208). Volume 11 in I. B. Weiner (Editor-in-Chief), *Handbook of psychology.* Hoboken, NJ; Wiley.

Rogers, R. (Ed.). (1997). *Clinical assessment of malingering and deception* (2nd ed.). New York: Guilford Press.

Rogers, R., & Bender, S., D. (2003). Evaluation of malingering and deception. In A. M. Goldstein (Ed.), *Forensic psychology (pp. 109–129).* Volume 11 in I. B. Weiner (Editor-in-Chief), *Handbook of psychology.* Hoboken, NJ: Wiley.

Shapiro, D. L. (1991). *Forensic psychological assessment.* Boston: Allyn & Bacon.

Skeem, J., Golding, S. L., Cohn, N., & Berge, G. (1998). Logic and reliability of evaluations of competence to stand trial. *Law and Human Behavior, 22,* 519–547.

Stafford, K. P. (2003). Assessment of competence to stand trial. In A. M. Goldstein (Ed.), *Forensic psychology* (pp. 359–380). Volume 11 in I. B. Weiner (Editor-in-Chief), *Handbook of psychology.* Hoboken, NJ: Wiley.

Starkey, M. L. (1949). *The devil in Massachusetts.* New York: Knopf.

Weiner, I. B. (2002). How to anticipate ethical and legal challenges in personality assessments. In J. Butcher (Ed.), *Clinical personality assessment: Practical applications* (2nd ed., pp. 126–134). New York: Oxford University Press.

Weiner, I. B. (2003a). The assessment process. In J. R. Graham & J. A. Naglieri (Eds.), *Assessment psychology* (pp. 3–26). Vol. 10 in I. B. Weiner (Editor-in-Chief), *Handbook of psychology.* Hoboken, NJ: Wiley.

Weiner, I. B. (2003b). Prediction and postdiction in clinical decision making. *Clinical Psychology: Science and Practice, 10,* 335–338.

Weiner, I. B. (2005). Integrative personality assessment with self-report and performance-based measures. In S. Strack (Ed.), *Personality and psychopathology* (pp. 317–331). Hoboken, NJ: Wiley.

CHAPTER 22

Serving as an Expert Witness

ALLEN K. HESS

No one will deny that the law should in some way effectively use expert knowledge wherever it will aid in settling disputes. The only question is as to *how* it can do so best.

—Judge Learned Hand, 1901

THE ROLE of the expert witness has become increasingly important in the courts and in the practice of many psychologists. This chapter introduces the jurisprudential basis for admitting the expert to the courts, reviews several landmark court decisions and the rules of the evidence that govern the admission and use of the expert in court, and provides a step-by-step guide for the expert witness preparing for court testimony.

THE CONCEPT OF THE EXPERT WITNESS

Often, we can trace a concept or practice back to antiquity and find biblical sources that can guide us in understanding the necessity and origins of the concept or practice. However, the history of the expert witness and expert testimony begins in the more recent past of the thirteenth century (Blau, 1998), at which time physicians and surgeons were called on by the court to consult with judges. The tale of the expert witness takes an evil turn when, during the fifteenth century, the ecclesiastical courts used the services of Johann Sprenger and Heinrich Kraemer. They responded to Pope Innocent VIII's call to attack witchcraft and the Devil (who appeared, in the diagnosticians' eyes, in mentally ill, female, and Jewish forms in disproportionate numbers) by writing the divinely inspired text, *The Malleus Malificarum* or *Witches' Hammer* (Millon, 1969). This allowed the more inquisitionally minded to divine the signs and symptoms of witchcraft and sentenced more than 100,000 poor souls to punishment and death during the next two centuries. Only when the source of knowledge shifted from religion, God, and divinely inspired prophets to the rationality of an enlightened age did we see progress in science, arts, and society. Still, in the twenty-first century, the perennial threat that prejudicial influences have on professional testimony remains a concern.

In earlier centuries, juries were composed of people who had firsthand knowledge of the events before the court. By the mid-1850s a shift toward our current lay juror system took hold. This shift, accompanied by the flood of technical knowledge from the Industrial Revolution, posed increasingly complex questions to the courts. When professions consisted of clergy, military, lawyers, and physicians, juries were permanent and professional, with little need for expert witnesses. But with the explosive development of professions and specialists, vast amounts of knowledge accumulated and formed the basis for law suits. Pursuit or defense of law suits required hiring experts to explain the basis for the allegations or the defenses. Today there is even a specialization within psychology concerning leisure, wherein behaviorists help design gambling settings to maximally extract money from casino patrons. One can easily envision dueling experts when the issue arises as to whether the gambler or the casino is responsible for the gambler's loses (the theory being that the gambler's free will was compromised by the compelling environmental engineering).

Lawyers are specifically enjoined to provide the best and most vigorous advocacy, which can range into inventive defenses or creative civil complaints, buttressed by expert testimony. Thus, attorneys who do not use expert witnesses in actively pursuing their client's interests fail in their professional duties and risk sanctions. This profusion of specialists generally and in psychology in particular began accelerating during the last quarter of the nineteenth century. Briefly tracing this history can be instructive in understanding how the current use of expert testimony evolved.

Sporer (1997) notes psychological arguments cited in Brauer in 1841 to limit testimony by women and children; Binet's experiments in 1900 explore the way questions are posed on the error rate in schoolchildren's answers; and the Sterns' work in 1902 focused on reliability of testimony. (The reader might note that the law uses the term "reliability" as social scientists use the word "validity." In psychology, reliability refers to consistency in measurement, whereas validity refers to whether the measurement assesses what it purports to measure.) Blau (1998) cites such early use of expert witnesses as Godofski in 1904, Jaffe in 1903, and Lobstein in 1904. This marked the beginning a century ago of a gathering momentum of applying psychological knowledge and methods to legal problems. These efforts reached a crescendo with Münsterberg's (1908) championing of applied psychology, but his efforts were defeated for several reasons. His acerbic personality, overreaching claims, and advocacy of the United States entering World War I on Germany's side made him highly unpopular in both academic and public circles. With the exception of his student Marston, who introduced lie detection to the courts, Münsterberg's loss of credibility also marked a decline in legal psychology that lasted decades.

THE DEVELOPMENT OF THE
EXPERT WITNESS

This section examines the development of the legal standing of the expert witness. Several key cases are reviewed, relevant parts of the Federal Rules of Evidence (FRE; 2003) are presented, and literature on the effects of the critical cases and the application of the FRE are reviewed.

FRYE V. UNITED STATES (1923)

One of Münsterberg's students, Marston, earned a law degree and a psychology doctorate, during which he studied physiological responses. Marston thought the systolic blood pressure would spike when a person lied. This early version of the lie detector became the issue at the heart of the *Frye* test in 1923. In this case, Marston offered lie detection evidence, even offering to conduct the test before a jury, to support Frye's second-degree murder appeal. The scientific basis for Marston's work was not generally accepted by the scientific community (Table 22.1).

As the decades ensued, psychologists offering expert testimony were subjugated to working under psychiatrists' purview, much as a psychometric technician whose findings were presented by the psychiatrist. Two cases changed this practice.

BROWN V. BOARD OF EDUCATION (1954)

Brown was concerned that his daughter and her peers were receiving an inferior education in the "separate but equal" school system in Topeka, Kansas. A variety of social scientists issued briefs in support of Brown's quest to challenge the doctrine that kept major sectors of our society segregated. Mamie and Kenneth Clark conducted research with dolls, asking both Black and White children for their playmate preferences. The gist of their testimony is that both preferred White dolls and that segregation, with its wholly unequal distribution of resources, fed this devaluation of Blacks. This testimony and supporting amicus curiae briefs were persuasive to the court in finding the separate but equal doctrine a flawed law.

Table 22.1
The *Frye* Test

General Acceptance Test: "Between experimental and well-recognized scientific principles or discoveries lies a twilight zone, and . . . the thing from which the deduction is made [by the expert witness] must be sufficiently established to have gained general acceptance in the particular field in which it belongs." (*Frye v. United States*, 1923)

Jenkins v. United States (1962)

Up until 1962, the practice in insanity defenses was to have a psychiatrist testify, even if the examination was conducted by psychologists. Psychologists were the handmaidens of the psychiatrist.

Accused of housebreaking, Jenkins saw his experts rebuffed by the court. However, the District of Columbia Court of Appeals granted Jenkins an appeal on his conviction for a variety of charges attached to housebreaking (assault, assault with intent to rape, assault with a deadly weapon). The testimony of three psychologists that Jenkins was incompetent at the time of his trial due to Schizophrenia had been disallowed by the trial judge, creating grounds for an appeal. In *Jenkins* (1962), the court held that

> the determination of a psychologist's competence to render an expert opinion based on his findings as to presence or absence of mental disease or defect must depend upon the nature and extent of his knowledge. It does not depend upon his claim to the title "psychologist." That determination, after a hearing, must be left in each case to traditional discretion of trial court subject to appellate review.

Further, the *Jenkins* court defined the expert witness (see Table 22.2).

The Federal Rules of Evidence

During the next decade, the FRE were codified by the Supreme Court and passed by Congress, and then rewritten in 2002. The FRE or a facsimile govern nonjury cases, criminal and civil cases, worker's compensation cases, and proceedings in probate court whether a judge or a magistrate presides. The FRE are further followed, though in a more relaxed manner due to their nonadversarial nature, in grand jury proceedings, extradition proceedings, preliminary hearings in criminal cases, in sentencing and probation hearings, in issuing search and arrest warrants and criminal summonses, and in contempt proceedings (Bailey, 1995). The FRE merit our attention as it is the vehicle by which expert witness testimony will be admitted or excluded in federal and many state jurisdictions.

Table 22.2
The *Jenkins* Decision

The expert witness is defined as "qualified to testify because he has firsthand knowledge that the jury does not have of the situation or transaction at issue. The expert has something different to contribute. This is the power to draw inferences from the facts that a jury would not be competent to draw. To warrant the use of expert testimony, then, two elements are required. First, the subject of the inference must be so distinctively beyond the ken of the average layman. Second, the witness must have such skill, knowledge or experience in that field or calling as to make it appear that his opinion or inference will probably aid the trier of fact in his search for truth. The knowledge may in some fields be derived from reading alone, in some from practice alone, or as is more commonly the case, from both" (Beis, 1984, p. 234).

From FRE Rule 702 we learn that scientific, technical, or other specialized knowledge is covered. As we shall see, this issue is again visited in *Joiner* to specifically not limit expert testimony to scientists. Second, the criteria by which experts are to be qualified are enumerated as knowledge, education, experience, skills, and training. Thus, an 8th-grade dropout who runs a summer fishing camp with 500 children might be found more qualified to provide evidence in a custody case than the most published child clinical or developmental psychologist, by virtue of his or her experience. Anyone able to keep 500 children on task merits our attention for his or her expertise. The expert should also have a sufficient fact base, with some rational procedure by which the facts were gathered and analyzed, to proffer testimony.

Rule 703 provides several tools for the expert witness. If unable to examine the individual beforehand, the expert may observe the person in question during a hearing and form an opinion on that basis. This is noteworthy because witnesses customarily and by statute are excluded from hearings except for their own appearance so that their testimony is not tainted by what they might hear. Moreover, the expert witness need not have his or her fact base admitted in order for the testimony to be admitted. Here care must be exercised because the fact base should not be slipped in if it is not admitted, if the court determines that the inflammatory and prejudicial parts of the evidence outweigh its probative value. For example, if the prior criminal history of the accused is inadmissible, then the expert should not acknowledge the history as part of the basis for forming his or her opinion about the accused.

This rule allows for three sources of data: (1) firsthand observation by the witness, as in an examination of a patient; (2) presentation of evidence at trial, which may have been presented by another witness, by another expert witness, or by the hypothetical question route; and (3) information from sources other than the expert's direct perception. This last might include hospital records, reports from nurses, police, or family members, public opinion surveys (as in assessing bias in the potential jury pool in change of venue motions), or computer-generated psychological test profiles and reports. The balance for the court is between opening the door to hearsay, as in the case of public opinion surveys composed of thirdhand data (from the court's perspective), versus the value of the findings and the use of an accepted technique (survey methodology) that is "of a type reasonably relied upon by experts in the particular field" (L. T. Perrin, 1997, p. 939).

Rule 704 allows the expert to offer an opinion on the ultimate issue, or the issue before the judge or jury, with one exception. The issue of mental condition in criminal cases, or insanity, as applied to the ultimate question of guilt, is reserved for the fact finder.

Rule 705 allows the expert witness to proffer an opinion without revealing the underlying facts. However, the basis or facts must be revealed if asked on cross-examination. This becomes a thorny issue in the case where the accused has an expectation of confidentiality but either the accused or his or her attorney raised mental conditions as part of the defense. Both parties need to know from the psychologist that raising that defense will lift the lid of privilege on mental issues, as the adversarial side has the right and even the obligation to fully explore mental conditions once they have been raised. Thus, the adversary might bring in issues such as domestic abuse that would have been shielded but for the raising of an insanity plea. The domestic abuse issue might be prejudicial, not probative, and even barely relevant to the charge in dispute, but the domestic abuse issue is now in play in the fact finder's decision making. For example, the prosecutor could bring in child abuse concerns as related to chronically or episodically violent tendencies if an alleged assaulter or murderer presents an insanity plea. The psychologist is now obliged to respond as privilege has been waived by virtue of raising mental conditions as an issue.

Rules 704 and 705 help avoid the introduction of evidence by the circuitous route of the hypothetical question. While the hypothetical question remains a route by which attorneys can introduce testimony, Rules 704 and 705 diminish the need for this circumlocution. For example, consider that an attorney wants to introduce the defendant's low intelligence or intoxicated state as a reason to plea that a meaningful Miranda warning was not given. Prior to the establishment of Rules 704 and 705, the attorney had to ask the expert witness a hypothetical question: whether someone with an IQ of 61 or a blood alcohol level (BAL) of .18 can process information such as the four-pronged Miranda warning. Then the attorney would introduce, or tie the hypothetical inquiry to, evidence that the defendant recorded an IQ of 61 or had a BAL of .18. Under Rules 704 and 705, the witness can testify directly to these issues. Nonetheless, the expert witness will meet the hypothetical question for various technical and tactical reasons, and we discuss how to meet the hypothetical question in the second part of this chapter (Table 22.3 on p. 658).

These cases and rules are the most relevant ones for the expert witness to master. The interested reader would be well served to read the rest of the FRE, as some will be quite informative (e.g., Rule 401, which defines relevant evidence; Rule 403, which defines grounds for excluding evidence; and Rule 404, which outlines grounds for including or excluding character evidence). The Rules are available on a variety of Web sites (cf. www2.law.cornell.edu, which provides online law research), along with commentary that is most informing. The point is not to make the psychologist a junior lawyer but to know the ground rules of the game in which you will be immersed.

THE *DAUBERT-JOINER-KUMHO* TRILOGY

Over the decades there have been periodic outbursts about phony, sham, or junk science. As science gains status, people with political agendas drape their causes in the cloak of science. They are given to justify their agenda with scientific claims and may overstate the scientific grounds for this support. This leads to a counterreaction that caustically examines science and results in pejorative terms, the latest of which is junk science. I recall the great cranberry scare of the 1950s; Paul Ehrlich's jeremiads that we would face world hunger and subsequent food riots by 1990 (recently, the World Health Organization declared a worldwide obesity problem); the alarm about apples soaked in toxic alar of the 1980s; and the "heart attack on a platter" scare regarding linguine Alfredo (and the Chinese and Mexican food scares of the 1990s). Some have alleged that asbestos

Table 22.3
Federal Rules of Evidence 702–705

Rules	Definition
Rule 702	If scientific, technical or other specialized knowledge will assist the trier of fact to understand the evidence or to determine a fact in issue, a witness qualified as an expert by knowledge, skill, experience, training, or education, may testify thereto in the form of an opinion or otherwise, if (1) the testimony is based upon sufficient facts or data, (2) the testimony is the product of reliable principles and methods, and (3) the witness has applied the principles and methods reliably to the facts of the case.
Rule 703	The facts or data in the particular case upon which an expert bases an opinion or inference may be those perceived by or made known to the expert at or before the hearing. If of a type reasonably relied upon by experts in the particular field in forming opinions or inferences upon the subject, the fact or data need not be admissible in evidence in order for the opinion or inference to be admitted. Facts or data otherwise inadmissible shall not be disclosed to the jury by the proponent of the opinion or inference unless the court determines that their probative value in assisting the jury to evaluate the expert's opinion substantially outweighs their prejudicial effect.
Rule 704	(a) Except as provided in subdivision (b), testimony in the form of an opinion of inference otherwise admissible is not objectionable because it embraces an ultimate issue to be decided by the trier of fact. (b) No expert witness testifying with respect to the mental state or condition of a defendant in a criminal case may state an opinion or inference as to whether the defendant did or did not have the mental state or condition constituting an element of the crime charged or of a defense thereto. Such ultimate issues are matters for the trier of fact alone.
Rule 705	The expert may testify in terms of opinion or inference and give reasons therefor without first testifying to the underlying facts or data, unless the court requires otherwise. The expert may in any event be required to disclose the underlying facts or data on cross-examination.

Source: Federal Rules of Evidence (2003).

and the breast implant scares were wildly overstated (see Worthington, Stallard, Price, & Goss, 2002, for an analysis of the latter vis-à-vis *Daubert*).

As psychology increasingly entered the courts in the past three decades, there arose a reaction. Ziskin (1981) and later Ziskin and Faust (1995) wrote guides by which attorneys could take to task psychologist and psychiatrist experts and make them look foolish. Huber's (1991) *Galileo's Revenge* and Hagen's (1997) *Whores of the Court* scathingly critique scientists and mental health professionals, respectively. Public concerns reached the point at which the court deemed it timely to delineate the status of expert testimony. Their examination came by way of *Daubert v. Merrill Dow Pharmaceuticals, Inc.* (1993).

Daubert v. Merrill Dow Pharmaceuticals *(1993)*

The FRE are a vehicle for getting the expert witness to court. But the answers to what was science, who was qualified as an expert, and what could be introduced as evidence by the expert still relied on the 1923 criteria enunciated by

Table 22.4
The Four Prongs of the *Daubert* Test

Standard	Definition
Testability of a theory or technique	The theory's hypotheses or the technique used can be tested, falsified, and refuted.
Scrutiny of the scientific community	The theory or technique has been subjected to peer review and publication.
Known or potential error rate	The theory or technique has or may have standards controlling the technique's operation (allowing us to know how confident we may be in its conclusions, such as the standard error of measurement or standard error of estimate).
General acceptance	The theory or technique is generally accepted within a relevant scientific community [*Frye* test].

Source: Daubert v. Merrill Dow Pharmaceuticals (1993).

Frye. That changed in 1993. Mrs. Daubert used Bendictin to alleviate morning sickness during her pregnancy with her son, Jason. Unfortunately, he was born with limb reduction birth defects. On behalf of their child, the Dauberts sued the manufacturer of Bendictin, Merrill Dow Pharmaceuticals, Inc. The district court upheld the defendant's motion to dismiss. The U.S. Supreme Court heard the case, articulated what has become known as the *Daubert* factors or test, and remanded the case for review in district court (Table 22.4).

Daubert unleashed a flood of concerns. Whereas *Frye* was criticized as not allowing new scientific developments to enter court, *Daubert* was seen as lowering the bar to the degree that there would be a scientific free-for-all in court (Capra, 1998). Others (e.g., Goodman-Delahunty, 1997; Goodman-Delahunty & Foote, 1995) were concerned with the opposite: That is, with four prongs or tests to satisfy, who could meet the new, presumably stringent standards? The court might have responded to the junk science criticisms by overreacting with *Daubert*. These concerns are addressed later; first, we take up the considerations of who is a scientific expert and who decides who is an expert, which became more urgent concerns of the court raised by *Daubert*.

The use of the term "scientific" leads to the question of whether *Daubert* applies to scientists but not to other expert witnesses. That is, would a wine taster, art historian, accountant, rare coin evaluator, economist, handwriting expert, or real estate appraiser be subject to *Daubert*'s criteria? Can their theories be falsified? Do they have standard measurements that they have collected on their appraisals? The possibility loomed that a scientist, who might have a stronger basis to testify, would be excluded but a host of experts with shaky empirical foundations for their testimony would be admitted. Also, the question remained about who is to decide whether a particular expert or a field was admissible or whether the field was not well enough developed or relevant to be admitted. These issues were resolved in two cases that, with *Daubert*, are sometimes referred to as the *Daubert-Joiner-Kumho* trilogy.

General Electric Company v. Joiner *(1997)*

Joiner was an electrician who had to make repairs with his hands and arms immersed in fluids containing polychlorinated biphenyls (PCBs). PCBs had been banned by Congress in 1978 as hazardous to human health. Joiner contracted small cell cancer and sued the manufacturers of PCBs, including General Electric Company. Expert witnesses on behalf of Joiner introduced animal research that was excluded by the district court judge because the evidence "did not rise above subjective belief of unsupported speculation" (*General Electric Company v. Joiner* 1997, p. 136). The U.S. Supreme Court reviewed the case and found that the appropriate standard for reversing the judge's rulings concerning the admissibility of scientific evidence is the "abuse of discretion" standard. That is, to have abused his or her discretion, a judge must have ignored logic, settled law, relevance (relevance is a legal term referring to the logical relationship between testimony and the issue at hand), or reliability. The move from the *Frye* standard to *Daubert* did not diminish the judge's gatekeeping role regarding expert evidence (Table 22.5).

Kumho Tire Co. v. Carmichael *(1999)*

In 1993, Patrick Carmichael's right rear tire blew out in the minivan he was driving. In the subsequent accident, one passenger died and several were injured. Claiming a defective tire as the cause, the Carmichaels and the decedent's representative brought suit against the tire's manufacturer and distributor, collectively known as Kumho Tire. Dennis Carson Jr. was retained as a tire inflation expert. He found upon visual and tactile inspection at least two of four specific physical symptoms of tire failure due to a defect (manufacturer's fault) rather than overdeflection due to inflation irregularities (owner's fault). The crux of appeals concerned whether expert testimony, which was excluded by the lower courts, should be judged by the *Daubert* criteria, aimed at scientific testimony. Essentially, as Hess (1999) asked before *Kumho* reached the U.S. Supreme Court, is the court holding scientists to much higher standards, because science was more advanced, than other experts, who could proffer court testimony meeting minimal standards? Could this technical testimony enter the court, absent the scientific bases in *Daubert*?

Table 22.5
The *Joiner* Decision

Abuse of discretion: "The standard ordinarily applicable to review of evidentiary rulings is the proper standard by which to review a district court's decision to admit or exclude expert scientific evidence Thus, while the Federal Rules of Evidence allow district courts to admit a somewhat broader range of scientific testimony than would have been admissible under Frye, they leave in place the 'gatekeeper' role of the trial judge in screening such evidence neither the difficulty of the task nor any comparative lack of expertise can excuse the judge from exercising the 'gatekeeper' duties that the Federal Rules impose—determining, for example, whether particular expert testimony is reliable and 'will assist the trier of fact,' Fed. Rule Evid. 702, or whether the 'probative value' of testimony is substantially outweighed by risks of prejudice, confusion or waste of time."

Source: General Electric Company v. Joiner (1997).

Table 22.6
The *Kumho* Decsion

Gatekeeper function: "The Daubert factors may apply to the testimony of engineers and other experts who are not scientists. The Daubert 'gatekeeping' obligation applies not only to 'scientific' testimony, but to all expert testimony. Rule 702 does not distinguish between 'scientific' knowledge and 'technical' or 'other specialized' knowledge, but makes clear that any such knowledge might become the subject of expert testimony. It is the Rule's word 'knowledge,' not the words (like 'scientific') that modify that word, that establishes a standard of evidentiary reliability. A trial judge determining the admissibility of an engineering expert's testimony may consider one or more of the specific Daubert factors. The emphasis on the word 'may' reflects Daubert's description of the Rule 702 inquiry as 'a flexible one.' The court of appeals must apply an abuse-of-discretion standard when it reviews the trial court's decision to admit or exclude expert testimony.

Source: Kumho Tire Co. v. Carmichael (1999).

The Supreme Court concluded that Rule 702 does not distinguish between scientists and other technical experts inasmuch as the court used "scientific" in its *Daubert* language because that was the nature of the case before it; that Rules 702 and 703 grant latitude to all expert witnesses; and that it would be impossible to distinguish between scientific and other knowledge. Hence, it is up to the trial judge to determine whether the testimony has "a reliable basis in the knowledge and experience of [the relevant] discipline" (*Daubert*, 1993, p. 592). Note, too, that the Court is consistent in its concern about expert witness testimony in the particular case: "whether the expert could reliably determine the cause of *this* tire's separation" (p. 15; emphasis in the original), not whether there is good science in general. Furthermore, *Daubert* is to be applied "flexibly," as a guide rather than as mandatory criteria. The Court emphasized "knowledge" rather than "science" and its application to a particular case. Greater focus is then placed on the expert and the soundness of the proffered testimony (Table 22.6).

CHALLENGING EXPERT TESTIMONY

The court has a number of tools to counteract dubious expert testimony. The law relies heavily on cross-examination as a prophylactic against misleading testimony. The adversarial side can always produce other experts and contradictory evidence to dispel the evidence of the other side's experts. The judge can issue careful jury instruction on the burden of proof. Finally, the judge can exclude testimony found not relevant or whose relevance is outweighed by its emotional inflammation, or as stated before, whose probative value is outweighed by its prejudicial value.

However, each of these tools has costs. Cross-examination relies on the attorney to be sufficiently knowledgeable to detect junk testimony. As most attorneys cannot be expected to be as knowledgeable in the area in question as is the retained expert, the attorney can retain his or her own expert to help develop lines of questioning. The expert can help determine when such testimony is being "spun," when the expert is incorrect, or whether the expert is simply lying.

These conferrals with the expert can be awkward and break up the rhythm of cross-examination. Producing one's own experts to counteract the adversary's experts can lead to increased costs and to the infamous dueling experts, leaving the fact finder with the task of deciding which expert to believe.

A judge's instructions rely on the judge being sufficiently conversant with the technicalities of science to instruct the jury, or to shift such responsibility to the jury. The decision to bar an expert's testimony again depends on the judge's scientific acumen and, as we shall see, may not allow one side or another to fully present their case (Slobogin, 1999).

Over a decade has elapsed since *Daubert*, allowing us to examine some of the effects of the application of the *Daubert-Joiner-Kumho* trilogy. Our examination focuses on the trilogy as it relates to the practice of the expert witness, rather than survey in any comprehensive fashion the burgeoning legal and psychological literature.

Emanations of Daubert

Daubert—*Strict or Lax?* *Daubert* has been adopted in more than a third of the states. Because the more populous states adopted it, more than half of the U.S. population live in state and local jurisdictions that are governed by *Daubert*.

As alluded to earlier, *Daubert* unleashed speculations about how much more or less restrictive it will be for experts to gain entry to the courtrooms. Taking into account the temper of the times that wondered about "excuse abuse," or the entering of a bewildering variety of criminal defenses and syndromes brought in by expert witnesses, and by the concerns about junk science, it is reasonable to see *Daubert* as the Court's attempt to put some strictures on the expert witness. Two scholars opined:

> The Daubert decision imposes what we believe is a higher standard upon the testimony of forensic psychology than did the Frye "general acceptance" standard . . . the emphasis in Daubert is on requirements for validity and reliability which may be more technically stringent than a general acceptance test, particularly the requirement that the methods be "falsifiable." (Goodman-Delahunty & Foote, 1995, p. 198)

Reed (1996) viewed *Chapple v. Granger* (1994) as portending a tougher time in court for the unprepared expert witness. *Chapple v. Granger* was an odd case in which Ralph Reitan, one of our foremost neuropsychologists, used a flexible battery, but the courts found more compelling a fixed standard battery. Reitan lamented that the courts, not the scientists, were deciding the scientific merits of psychological test procedures. Others (Hess, 1999) thought *Daubert* provided a balancing test by which the totality of the criteria would determine what testimony is admissible, so the celebrations that *Daubert-Joiner-Kumho* would weed out sham science were premature.

While there has been a flood of legal treatises speculating about *Daubert-Joiner-Kumho*, there is also an emerging empirical literature that allows us to follow what effects the trilogy had. These effects are important for the expert to understand in best serving a forensic client. The expert needs to know the lay of the land or what considerations the court will use in allowing or disallowing the expert's testimony.

Daubert's *Effect on the Flow of Cases.* Dixon and Gill (2002) assessed *Daubert*'s impact on federal civil cases in the decade following the decision. They culled 4,097 cases from the 315,000 cases resulting in federal district court opinions. From those, they studied the 30% that concerned substantive challenges to expert testimony. From 1980 through 1987, the number of cases employing expert witnesses held even. The next 6 years saw a rise in such cases. This trend continued in the 2 or so years following *Daubert.* Then the number of cases leveled off from 1995 to 1997, and then rose again. Challenges to testimonial reliability dropped pre-*Daubert*, then rose in the 3 years following *Daubert*, only to drop in the years after 1997. Dixon and Gill suggest that attorneys began to be more careful in presenting experts but then adapted to the courts' interpretations and again used experts. They suggest, too, that at first judges evaluated expert testimony by *Daubert* but then became comfortable enough to use other factors in flexibly applying *Daubert-Joiner-Kumho.* They would justify examinations of testimony on grounds of reliability and of qualifications of the expert.

Whether any of the challenges resulted in more just outcomes to cases is an unanswered but crucial question as to whether *Daubert-Joiner-Kumho* wrought positive changes. But perhaps just raising the court's awareness about better and poorer experts and sound versus sham science is prophylactic in itself. It might be instructive for the expert to know what the judge is considering in qualifying the expert's testimony. These Dixon and Gill (2002) factors are as follows:

1–4. The four *Daubert* factors.
   5. Standards or controls in measurement.
   6. Clarity and coherence of expert's presentation.
   7. Proper extrapolation (generalization).
   8. Breadth of supporting data.
   9. Verifiability of data.
  10. Control or consideration of confounding variables.
  11. Standard data or facts for the discipline.
  12. Consistency of findings with other studies and experts.
  13. Statistical significance.
  14. Real-world data consistent with findings.
  15. Neutral court-appointed expert's agreement.
  16. Purpose for which research was conducted.
  17. Reputation of the expert.

Groscup, Penrod, Studebaker, and Huss (2002) studied 693 appellate cases involving expert witnesses; half the cases were heard 5.5 years before *Daubert* and the other half from the 5.5 years following *Daubert*. These investigators provide a trove of insights: (1) no differences were found regarding admissibility of experts over the time period; (2) admission of technical experts met greater success than admission of scientific experts; and (3) prosecution experts are more likely to be admitted than defense experts. Groscup et al. found statistically significant data that the courts adopting *Daubert* tended to use its criteria, though the practical effects are minor. The data highlight that courts still use "assist the trier of fact" as the most compelling admission criterion, followed by expert qualifications, relevance of testimony, and whether the testimony is prejudicial rather than probative. In terms of expert's qualifications, experience then education were the two chief qualifying attributes, though many experts have more than one source of expertise. These differences were even more evident in cases calling for technical rather than other (scientific, medical/mental health, and business) testimony.

Groscup et al. (2002) find these latter results perplexing. They suggest that the expert's credentials rather than his or her methods are the court's chief concern, in contrast to *Daubert*'s emphasis, and that there seems to be a decrease in the importance of research as a source of testimony. To this writer, it seems clear that the courts, as seen in Chapter 2, are concerned not with adjudicating science, but with providing due process in the just disposition of the case at hand. Consequently, a qualified expert who can help with the case at trial will be useful and relevant. Further, as judges are not trained in the scientific method and may not have scientific talents nor be interested in becoming scientists, they may be more comfortable relying on Rule 702 than applying *Daubert,* conclusions that fit Groscup et al.'s findings. For example, it is difficult enough to teach undergraduates the nuances of Type I and Type II errors when teaching statistical techniques or how to assess incremental validity in psychometric methods. These concepts escape many of our graduate students' nomological network, too. Why do we think justices can bone up on these methods in a week of summer judicial camp so that they can make instant determinations in the court when the same questions baffle some of the finer talents in our profession? Buttressing this opinion, Groscup et al. find that judges reasonably rely more on Rule 104, calling for pretrial determinations about the soundness of expert testimony.

Daubert *in Complex and Class Action Cases.* Worthington et al. (2002) confront another aspect of expert testimony, that of the effects of experts in mitigating hindsight bias. In both civil and criminal cases, a party is harmed. Merely the presence of a harmed person leads us to seek a cause or a responsible party, even if there is no proximate cause or the defendant is not guilty; this is referred to as hindsight bias. A murder victim, a lung cancer patient, a comatose victim of anesthesia call for someone to blame. Junk science can exacerbate hindsight bias when the testimony is complex. For example, Kovera, Russano, and McAuliff (2002) conclude that experts can help increase damage awards, though defense experts did not decrease damage awards. Still, they cite research that opposing experts can sensitize jurors to problems, for example, in expert testimony in a criminal case concerning eyewitness testimony.

In complex cases, the jury may focus on the expert's appearance and paralanguage (McLeod & Rosenthal, 1983) and on stereotypes of the expert's profession (Champagne, Shuman, & Whitaker, 1996). Worthington et al. (2002) trace silicon breast implant litigation to see how complex medical and scientific testimony can be de-biased. They conclude that the judicially appointed scientific panels, as used by Justices Jones, Pointer, and Weinstein, help debride the scientific evidence of hindsight bias. It is tempting, then, to call for panels. But we must recognize that panels are costly, that panels are only as good as those appointed to them, and that science still does not rest on majority votes, though justice in class action lawsuits may rest on precisely that mechanism.

Can Daubert *Make Scientists of Fact Finders?*   Kovera et al. (2002) found that attorneys do not rely on the soundness of the experimental design in deciding whether to object to expert testimony. There is no reason to expect that judges will be any more skilled than attorneys in understanding the threats to internal validity of a research design or to make any of the other fine determinations in assessing the validity of scientific testimony, though jurists are a bit more attuned to matters of external validity (generalizability of findings). Kovera et al. suggest that jurist training in scientific methods may help with their spotting errors in proffered testimony. But they also are realistic in wondering how judges hearing dueling experts will be able to recognize fatal flaws in the evidence and render directed verdicts or summary judgments. Yet, ever the optimists, they suggest that reference manuals for justices (e.g., the Federal Judicial Center's *Reference Manual on Scientific Evidence,* 2000) or scientific methods texts will inculcate in weeks the scientific sophistication that takes years to hone in graduate school.

My university department requires a two-course sequence in research methods and statistical analysis. As part of our quality control, we assess what the students learn. We present two studies to the students, one correlational article and one experimental article, and ask them a set of simple questions. We found mixed results about what a year's training and education has wrought. With training, students can identify the type of study (correlational or experimental) and the variables employed but have trouble identifying populations, threats to validity (9.7% correct in identifying threats to external validity in the experimental article), and constructs and their operational definitions. The students also had trouble knowing which statistical test to employ, determining statistical significance, and interpreting results. Although these data are specific to a two-course sequence in one university at one time, extrapolating these findings leads to several questions: What is the state of scientific knowledge in the general population from which our jury pools are drawn? What is the scientific literacy quotient among our college population from which our future attorneys and judges will be drawn? We invite readers to replicate these findings at their universities, exploring the state of scientific literacy, and to candidly ask themselves how long it took to gain some measure of research sophistication in their own undergraduate, graduate, and postgraduate education. The answers to these questions are the linchpin to the issue: How can expert and scientific testimony enter the courts in the decades to come in a helpful and probative fashion?

The Defendant's Voice Should Be Heard.   Slobogin (1999) argues that even if the *Daubert* criteria are not well met in a case, other jurisprudential considerations may weigh more heavily than purely scientific methodology concerns. If evidence lacks control groups or counterbalancing treatment effects, might the fact finders still find helpful what data are forthcoming? Should not the criminal defense, for example, have available all the help possible in mounting the best and most spirited defense available, which is afforded in a more flexible approach to admissibility? In a post-*Daubert* analysis, Slobogin argues that the defendant deserves a "voice" or "presence" in his or her defense for the system to exercise fairness and appear just.

Considering the inadequate research base supporting syndromes such as the battered woman syndrome (BWS), Slobogin (1999) advocates "flexible" admission of state-of-mind testimony, testimony-based theories and methods of a relevant professional community, and testimony in an area with still unsettled scientific bases. Without these criteria, the syndrome defenses, such as BWS, would have no entry into the court whatsoever. Just how many controlled studies are there of the BWS or other syndromes? Are there any experimental studies on BWS? There is nonexperimental evidence that is compelling. Nonetheless, shouldn't the parties to criminal cases have the right to present whatever evidence they can muster, and see whether it is compelling to the fact finder? Voice counts.

What Prevails in Court: Daubert *or the Federal Rules of Evidence?*   Krafka, Dunn, Johnson, Cecil, and Miletich (2002) surveyed attorneys in 1999 and judges in 1991 and again in 1998 to assess their experiences with *Daubert*. Judges reported rejecting expert testimony in the 1991 survey most often for not assisting the trier of fact (40%); the second most frequent reason was questions about the expert's qualifications (36%). Judges in the later survey most often limited or excluded expert testimony because it was not relevant (47%), the witness was not qualified (42%), and the proffered testimony would not assist the trier of fact (36%). The judges report relying on the 1975 FRE in the cause for their limiting or excluding expert testimony.

Krafka et al. (2002) further find that both judges and attorneys see two key problems needing attention: experts becoming advocates for the side that hired them and the expense incurred in hiring experts (though they seem not to see attorney fees as a problem). Attorneys are paying attention to *Daubert* when hiring experts. Most recently, a firm retaining me went over the *Daubert* criteria as applied to a branch of psychology for which they sought expert testimony, something that had not occurred before. This type of prescreening is carrying over to the courts, as we have seen in more *in limine* (pretrial) hearings and in judges encouraging the exchange of written reports by the experts (sent to the opposing side's attorneys) well before the trial to allow for full preparation and challenge. The challenge may take the form of pretrial motions to exclude or limit testimony, of securing opposing experts, or of a full and vigorous cross-examination in court. Judges report that such procedures reduced the eventual inadmissible rulings during the trial.

A sizable number (35%) of attorneys report that they saw little effect from *Daubert*. Perhaps this is because, in civil cases, Rule 26(a) provides that written reports be furnished to the other side at least 90 days before trial. Further, it requires experts to furnish a list of cases in which they served during the 4 pre-

Table 22.7
Federal Rule of Civil Procedure 26(a)(2)(a)

"(A) . . . A party shall disclose to other parties the identity of any person who may be used at trial to present evidence under Rules 702, 703, or 705 of the Federal Rules of Evidence. (B) . . . This disclosure shall be accompanied by a written report prepared and signed by the witness. The report shall contain a complete statement of all opinions to be expressed and the basis and reasons therefor; the data or other information considered by the witness in forming the opinions; any exhibits to be used as a summary of or support for the opinions; the qualifications of the witness, including a list of all publications authored by the witness within the preceding ten years; the compensation to be paid for the study and testimony; and a listing of any other cases in which the witness has testified as an expert at trial or by deposition within the preceding four years. (C) . . . The disclosures shall be made at least 90 days before the trial date or the date the case is to be ready for trial or, if the evidence is intended solely to contradict or rebut evidence . . . within 30 days after the disclosure made by the other party."

Source: Federal Rules of Code Procedures (2004).

vious years. Rule 26 makes transparency of the expert and his or her testimony the order of the day (Table 22.7).

Answering the question posed at the section's beginning, both the FRE and *Daubert-Joiner-Kumho* count. The FRE provide both the structure for moving the expert into the court and two key elements in evaluating the expert: relevance and helpfulness. *Daubert* provides the grounds for further weighing of the probity or soundness of the evidence brought to the fact finder. The effects of *Daubert-Joiner-Kumho* will continue to echo for years as the courts wrestle with the increasing need to use expert testimony. The legal and psychological literature concerning *Daubert* is burgeoning. Our review necessarily is selective, but it has outlined the concept of the expert witness and described the legal provisions bounding the use of experts.

THE PRAGMATICS OF SERVING AS AN EXPERT WITNESS

This section suggests how the psychologist can bring his or her expertise into the court in an effective fashion. It offers a sequence from the initiation of a case through working with attorneys to the effective presentation of the case in court.

INITIATING THE CASE

Problems in the forensic case in all likelihood originate at the initiation of the case, when a neglected issue or an improperly decided question lays the foundation for later trouble. What may seem to be an inconsequential issue that could easily be handled during the first telephone contact could grow into a major problem jeopardizing the psychologist's well-being if left unattended. Examining these decision points is invaluable for the potential expert witness.

Who Calls You?

In many arenas, such as research, teaching, and practice, the psychologist's performance, while relying on the collaboration of others, is largely a matter of his or her competence and initiative. In the court, the psychologist's testimonial effectiveness is directly tied to the abilities and skills of the attorney or legal team retaining him or her. The psychologist depends on the attorney's ability to understand and use the psychologist's findings, on the attorney's attitudes about psychological phenomena, and on the attorney's willingness to develop strategy and lines of questions that are the vehicles by which the psychologist brings forth his or her findings in depositions and in the courtroom.

The typical case begins with a telephone call from an attorney. The attorney's initial manner will tell the psychologist how the attorney creates a first impression with others, such as a jury. The attorney usually will describe the issues in the case, providing a basis for assessing his or her conceptual and oratorical skills. The attorney will describe the services he or she is seeking from the psychologist. This allows the psychologist to see (1) the degree to which the attorney understands psychological approaches, including the kinds of questions the psychologist can and cannot answer, and the time it may take to perform the requested services; (2) the construct system the attorney is using in both the legal and psychological domains; and (3) the degree to which the attorney is interested in finding the answer to a question or merely wants to hire an expert opinion to support the case, often termed a "hired gun" (M. T. Singer & Nievod, 1987). Hired guns will mouth the words and opinions that the attorney thinks will benefit the client, no matter what the truth is or what probative value the opinions might have. Serving as a hired gun will not serve the truth, will quickly erode the psychologist's reputation, can result in legal and ethical actions, and is simply professionally unfulfilling.

Certainly the attorney did not call the psychologist to worsen the case at hand, so he or she will naturally want to know how the psychologist can help. The attorney will outline the case, beginning a give-and-take with the psychologist. It is the psychologist's turn to create a first impression and begin to structure the working collaboration. The psychologist now has the opportunity to ask about the pertinent facts in the case and the theory the attorney is using to support the complaint or the defense. This allows the psychologist to assess the way the attorney conceives and presents the issues in the case, the degree to which the attorney understands the capabilities of and the limits to psychology, and how the attorney will regard the psychologist's questions and opinions both now and as the case proceeds. Understanding some of the issues in the case, at least those involving psychology, the psychologist may offer a few suggestions about how he or she may help in the case. Two issues gain bold relief here.

First, the psychologist can assess the degree to which the attorney is able and willing to understand the psychological theory and procedures as an indicator of whether the attorney is seeking the expert help of the psychologist or just seeking a hired gun. A second and central issue is the degree to which the psychologist functions as an expert in a narrow sense or a consultant in a broader fashion. Some feel the psychologist's role is narrow; others see effective expert help as necessarily involving the psychologist in understanding the legal theory and suggesting ways of furthering the case. The latter might be seen by proponents of the narrow approach as jeopardizing the objectivity of the expert. As with many ethical questions, it depends on the type of case, the complexity of both the legal and psychological materials, the abilities of the psychologist to understand law and the lawyer to understand psychology, and the degree to which the area is settled or involves novel approaches. During the first phone call, the psychologist can err by getting too specific about the complexities of the case, but the seeds of these issues are sown during the first phone call. If they are not broached then, they should be discussed soon afterward. It is critical to see the role the attorney has in mind for the psychologist and the way the attorney regards psychology in general and the psychologist in particular. Case 22.1 describes how a second-chair attorney retained a psychologist, but the lead attorney harbored a history that was undisclosed until the end of the case.

Case 22.1

The father's legal team decides that a child custody case requires a psychologist to tell the court about the dangers of a manic-depressive mother. The mother had acted erratically, including several incidents during which she had taken her four children and several nieces and nephews on 90-mile-per-hour joy rides on country roads. Also, she had walked up the railroad tracks with her children in her arms or holding her dress, singing hymns for 15 minutes. While they shrieked, she told them it was God's will that the train either take them to their glory or spare them.

The attorney who retained the psychologist had him sit in court, contrary to the judge's ruling, spoiling the witness's ability to testify. Later, the witness, a target of the lead attorney's hostility during the legal team's conferences, learned that the lead attorney's father blew his head off with a shotgun while under treatment by a psychiatrist years earlier. The attorney harbored malice toward all mental health professionals and could not work with any. Custody was awarded to the mother, absent the expert testimony and the introduction of the dangerous and erratic actions by the mother.

Psychologists must know the attorney who retains them, including his or her attitudes and experiences with psychologists. As this may be hard to determine, one must pay particular attention to attitudes influencing the forming of the case.

Does the Psychologist Have the Personal Skill for Courtroom Testimony?

When courtroom testimony is integral to the case, psychologists must assess their own personal skills. Depending on their personality structure, psychologists may have to deal with one or both of two perilous attitudes: being utterly skeptical about what psychology could possible contribute to the case, and being conflict-avoidant. The former attitude is being nurtured by skeptics in our field, often under the rubric of the "clinical science" model. For them, psychologists have not yet developed a sound enough scientific basis, barring solely actuarial data, for the courts. The expert may face an attorney who has consulted with this type of psychologist and should prepare for a staunch *voir dire* (the qualifying procedure for the expert, discussed in a later section) and a withering cross-examination.

This brings us to the conflict-avoidant type. Courtroom combat is not for the faint of heart, nor for those who like to argue but cannot cope with the rules of the court, which allow the attorney to attack but limits the expert's ability to retaliate. The psychologist on the witness stand can expect rough treatment from opposing counsel. If the psychologist either questions the worth of psychology as applied to the case at hand or does not enjoy the verbal combat of the court, he or she may best serve the case and profession by declining forensic referrals.

The psychologist interested in self-assessment regarding courtroom attitude or personality may benefit from reading Ziskin and Faust (1995). They unrelentingly attack psychological testimony, claiming that such testimony does not belong in the court. Their arguments provide a good measure for the reader to see whether he or she can withstand such attacks. Other articles attack both testing (e.g., the dispute about the scientific basis of the Rorschach) and psychotherapy (e.g., attacks on any therapy that does not meet some psychologists' criteria of being empirically based). Some might find such combat distasteful. C. C. Wang, originally trained in law, left that profession to become an artist and art connoisseur; he explained his decision this way: "I hated [the law]. I like everything beautiful and peaceful. I don't want to fight with people." He correctly described courtroom litigation and wisely chose an immensely successful career creating and collecting art:

> Psychologists should critically examine themselves for potential biases. The psychologist who testified only for defendants or only for plaintiffs in case after case should reveal this bias to the attorney. Similarly, any ethical, professional or legal charges that have been raised about the psychologist should be revealed, or the psychologist should politely decline involvement in the case. (Quoted in Lawrence, 1997, p. A16)

Case 22.2

The attorney needed an expert witness in a complex drug offense case. He was delighted to find a psychiatrist-lawyer who was the head of mental health services in a major state penal facility. In the car after the attorney met him at the airport, the expert casually mentioned that he was under indictment of running an illicit drug ring in the state prison. The attorney made a U-turn and deposited the expert at the airport. The attorney told this story to the psychologist who was replacing the other expert, while explaining the perjury penalties for those who misrepresented themselves before the court.

Does the Psychologist Have the Qualifications to Testify?

Both the American Psychological Association (APA) Code of Ethical Conduct (see Chapter 27, in this volume, for a more extended treatment of forensic ethical dilemmas) and the Specialty Guidelines for Forensic Psychologist (Committee on Ethical Guidelines for Forensic Psychologists, 1991) call for the service provider to have competence in the area in which the service is provided. Moreover, testifying about state of mind for an insanity defense might involve a different knowledge base than providing child custody evaluations or psycholinguistics consultation skills. A doctorate does not confer blanket-level expertise, the emanations of which will enlighten any case. The FRE calls for five criteria or prongs for the test of whether one qualifies as an expert: knowledge, skills, education, experience, and training.

As the attorney is describing the case at hand, the psychologist will want to assess what services he or she can provide. In some cases, the services might be fairly standard; in other cases, the psychologist may serve more as a consultant in developing strategy. At the outset, the sensitive forensic psychologist will keep these options in mind in communicating with the attorney. Also, as a matter of course, the expert should furnish his or her curriculum vitae so that a frank discussion can ensue about the psychologist's role in the case. The attorney can view the expert's qualifications, and together they can discuss the scientific basis for subsequent testimony (e.g., research conducted, publication record in the area, offices held in learned societies). Attorneys are increasingly asking at the outset how the expert will measure his or her testimony against the *Daubert* criteria; the expert psychologist should do no less in being careful to anticipate challenges to his or her testimony.

What Legal Knowledge Does the Psychologist Need?

A psychologist should contribute psychological expertise to a case. While that seems self-evident, the psychologist should keep in mind that he or she does not need to know the law as the lawyer does. The cognitive psychologist brings a knowledge of how people process information quickly and under pressure when consulting about whether highway signs were correctly placed so motorists will avoid accidents. Similarly, a clinical psychologist determines the test instruments in best assessing how emotions might interfere with intellectual processes. Neither needs to know the vicissitudes of the hearsay rule, its exceptions, and the exceptions to those exceptions. There is some peril in the experienced expert showing signs of delusions of legal grandeur in overstepping one's role boundaries. Nonetheless, the psychologist can hardly function without knowing the standards used in the state for the insanity defense or for child custody.

The attorney has a role and a duty to furnish basic legal information in helping the psychologist articulate psychological findings into legally meaningful terms. The standard court instructions to the jury are most helpful in knowing the types of terms and decisions the jury will hear before they enter the jury room for deliberations. The cross-education of the lawyer and the psychologist in the first one or two phone calls will provide the information about how they will be able to work together or not.

Does the Psychologist Have the Time to Devote to the Case?

When working with attorneys and courts, psychologists will confront seemingly impossible deadlines that could compromise their services. They need to be clear about what can and cannot be provided in the time frame available. Often, an evaluation will be requested later in a case than it should have been, with an impending hearing date earlier than the psychologist would prefer. The psychologist needs to determine the pertinent dates in the case, the time needed to provide the services requested, and the degree to which competent professional services can be provided in the time allotted. Forensic work is time-consuming and can be inconvenient, with hearings and conferences called at inopportune times and with witnesses who may be available only when the psychologist has other commitments. The psychologist may hurry to meet these demands only to learn that the case has been continued for weeks or even months; then more record review and preparations of materials already mastered will be required.

If demands cannot be met, or if the psychologist will be unavailable at certain times, the psychologist needs to state this as soon as possible. If the attorney or court needs the testimony, they will make scheduling allowances if possible. But the psychologist needs to know that the law and lawyers use a different time frame than do psychologists.

When budgeting time for the case, the psychologist should be aware that the three most important aspects of expert testimony are preparation, preparation, and preparation. There is no recorded instance of a psychologist getting in trouble by overpreparing for a case. However, insufficient preparation can be humiliating and even professionally devastating.

What Role Do the Attorney and Psychologist Envision for the Psychologist?

Standard 7-1.1 of the American Bar Association (ABA; 1989) Criminal Justice Mental Health Standards describes three roles for mental health professionals: the scientific and evaluator role, the consultant role, and the treatment or rehabilitation role. It is common for an attorney to ask the psychologist to administer one or another intelligence or personality test, rather than simply pose the question so the psychologist can determine the best data collection method. The psychologist will necessarily become a consultant in clarifying the legal question at hand, finding the best psychological test or evidence that addresses the legal question, and then helping the attorney understand how the psychological evidence addresses the legal question.

In some cases, such as public advocacy cases, the psychologist's role may become almost wholly one of advocacy. In these instances, the psychologist may use the pronoun "we" in referring to the case. However, most other forums call for objectivity; if the psychologist has personalized the case so that he or she feels a ruling by the court as a personal gain or loss, the psychologist's objectivity should be questioned. In such a case, the psychologist may be better off suggesting another professional to serve as the expert witness, as his or her objectivity may have been compromised in fact and in appearance.

The practice of forensic psychological consultation has grown considerably with the emphasis on applying social psychology to jury selection, to attitude assessment, and to witness preparation. The expert and consultant roles can be seen as being on a continuum. Because an attorney necessarily must consult with the expert on the issues, findings, and deposition and courtroom presentations, the expert serves to some minimal extent as a consultant. Yet, there are significant differences between the roles. Perhaps the principal difference involves emotional commitments. Simply put, the expert's commitment is and should be to the truth, whereas the consultant's commitment may be to the cause or issue at hand. For example, the psychologists involved with the jury selection in the Chicago 7 trial were committed to the protest against the Vietnam War and committed to the civil rights movement of the 1960s. The consultant's efforts can become collaborative to the extent that the psychologist uses the pronoun "we" and may form countertransferences, or personally based emotional allegiances, to the attorney and clients identified with the cause (R. Singer, 1995). Identifying with and supporting political and social causes raises ethical concerns, but this identification may be consonant with aspects of the consultant role. However, when the psychologist as an expert witness identifies with the cause of the attorney's client, the expert's role is compromised and psychological science is in danger of being sold, rightfully provoking the criticism that experts are hired guns. This complex issue is addressed again in a later section. Suffice it to say that at the outset, the psychologist needs to be aware of the type of role the lawyer intends the psychologist to fill and of the emotions and allegiances the psychologist both brings to the case and develops as the case progresses.

On less idealistic grounds, the psychologist may face countertransferential feelings about pleasing the attorney and wanting to be retained in future cases. Usually hefty fees are charged, raising additional grounds for loss of objectivity.

While the psychologist will be an admixture of a consultant and an expert, he or she should abjure from the treatment role completely. When meeting the attorney's client, the psychologist must be mindful of the client's viewing the psychologist in the third or therapeutic role, a situation that can lead to conflict. This conflict involves evaluating a client who, despite being warned of the limits to privilege and confidentiality, relates to the psychologist as if the psychologist were serving as a psychotherapist (G. I. Perrin & Sales, 1994). Being held in police custody can shake a person. The detainee under police interrogation can feel an alliance with the psychologist who, in street clothes, is the first friendly face the detainee sees; the individual may interpret the relationship as therapeutic rather than as part of the investigation. The psychologist may intentionally use reflexive empathy, or "communicating the 'quality of felt awareness' of the experience of another person," as opposed to receptive empathy, or "the perception and understanding of the experiences of another person" (Shuman, 1993, p. 298), to maneuver the client to reveal more information than is in his or her best interest to disclose, raising serious ethical and legal questions. Some hold that once detainees are warned of their rights against self-incrimination, any method is fair in eliciting as much information as possible, even if it involves manipulating the interviewee's vulnerabilities. Others maintain that psychologists have a duty to honor the welfare of the interviewee and not exploit his or her vulnerabilities. The question arises as to the differentiation of the clinical and forensic psychology roles and whether the interviewee or the side hiring the psychologist has sole claim to the psychologist's allegiances. Given an interviewee who cannot monitor the situation for his or her own interests, the ethical psychologist may alert appropriate parties to the case that the interviewee needs assistance, be it psychological or legal. The ethical professional psychologist should try to define the role or roles he or she will play and be aware of shifts in the roles as the case proceeds.

Greenberg and Shuman (1997) raise questions about the inherent conflict between therapeutic and forensic roles in which the psychologist may become enmeshed. If a witness as to fact, the therapist may become involved in a case where therapist-client privilege is an important question. This conundrum can easily arise in marital cases, when one party files for divorce intending to use grounds established though the course of marital therapy. Therapists should avoid the conflict of becoming an expert witness in such cases. On the other hand, the expert witness should not engage a party to the case in psychotherapy subsequent to the case. The peril in this case involves hopelessly confounding the transference, or client's perception of the therapist, as well as compromising subsequent legal events such as an appeal or a countersuit.

Who Is the Attorney?

Because a practicing psychologist's core professional identity and reputation are based on performing a service professionally and successfully, and because the psychologist's performance is dependent in part on the attorney, it is important to assess the attorney's reputation when considering accepting a forensic referral. The psychologist involved in forensic work can learn of the attorney's character and abilities by following cases in the media, visiting courtrooms, calling on a few trusted colleagues for their opinions, and trusting his or her own experience if the psychologist worked with the attorney on a prior case. Yet, the attorney's reputation is not conclusive in determining how he or she may be currently functioning. Case 22.3 presents such an example.

Case 22.3

A psychologist worked with an attorney who was excellent in using psychological assessment to exclude incriminating statements his client made to police investigators. The psychologist's testimony was used adeptly to show how the client did not have the requisite mental capacity to understand his Miranda warning. The psychologist welcomed the attorney's invitation to work on another case, one concerning self-defense.

The attorney seemed distracted and was vague in articulating the theory of defense he intended to use and how the psychologist's testimony would help. He deferred scheduling conferences to review test results, abruptly left in the middle of the only pretrial conference he scheduled, and used the psychological evidence poorly in court. The client lost the homicide case. Several months later, the psychologist read in the newspapers that the attorney lost his license shortly after the case due to drug use.

*   *   *

Because the psychologist's performance is dependent on the competence and character of the attorney in charge of the case, it is essential to assess the attorney's character and competence.

Who Are the Opposing Parties, the Opposing Parties' Attorneys, and the Judge?

As soon as the psychologist picks up the telephone, he or she must be alert as to whether the case is one on which he or she is already working. As the conversation proceeds and the attorney presents the main aspects of the case, the psychologist should ask who are the parties in the case, who are the attorneys that will be working on both sides of the case, and who is the judge. If the psychologist has been retained by the other side, he or she can politely decline the case without revealing that he or she is working on the case, end the phone call quickly but gracefully, and report the contact to the attorney who has retained the psychologist.

Case 22.4

Deleray (1988) reports a case in which an attorney called on a psychologist to review records and give an opinion in a child custody case. The psychologist complied. Some time later, one of the psychologist's psychotherapy clients began to talk about a lawsuit. It became clear to the psychologist that the attorney who had retained the psychologist's consulting services was the counsel for the party opposing the psychologist's psychotherapy client.

*   *   *

The psychologist was serving competing parties and in quite a role conflict. These conflicts are preventable by discussing the involved parties. Just how close a relationship must be before a conflict arises has no clear demarcation line. However, we may be guided by Camus, who wrote, "I love justice but I love my mother before justice."

The psychologist should reveal to the attorney any social, political, financial, or other relationship that he or she may have with anyone involved in the case. Such relationships include those where there is any possibility of conflicting interests or those that may cast the psychologist's testimony in a biased light. These relationships extend to those the psychologist's family might have with a party or with the party's relatives or friends. A relationship does not necessarily prevent the psychologist's involvement in a case. Both the psychologist and the attorney must weigh the degree to which there are any interests that can compromise the psychologist's ability to either keep a confidence, work without competing motives, or appear to others to have such a conflict and thereby compromise his or her testimony. By raising such a question at this point, major problems can be averted, and the attorney can gain confidence in the psychologist's awareness of ethical and legal concerns.

Naturally, the smaller the town, the more likely people will relate to each other in various and sundry roles (Schank & Skovholt, 1997; Sonne, 1994). There are three seemingly ironclad principles that are tested to their limits in small communities: confidentiality, competence, and conflicting interests. It is easier to adopt these principles in urban centers; however, in a town of a few thousand people, it may be impossible to have attorneys, parties in the case, bailiff and clerks, and jurors who are not someone's Little League coach, schoolteacher, or banker. It remains the responsibility of the psychologist to avoid ethical dilemmas, but consultation with the attorney regarding how the law may view conflicting interests and with esteemed colleagues who are experienced in legal and ethical issues will help avoid problems.

However, there is a risk in seeking consultation on cases. If the psychologist who seeks consultation reveals information sufficient to identify the parties in the case, the professional providing consultation to the psychologist may feel ethically compelled to intervene. This would usurp the psychologist's decision making, shifting responsibility to the consultant. Consultation regarding ethics should be conducted in a way that gives the consultant enough information to help clarify ethical and professional issues but not enough to take away decision making from the psychologist who is seeking the consultation. For example, a clinician may not be sure whether to report a child abuse case because of uncertainties in the clinical data. The clinician may then seek consultation and, in sharing the data, may find that the colleague has a lower threshold regarding reporting the possibility of child abuse and feels compelled to report the case to authorities. The colleague, responding to his or her own perceived duty, has usurped the clinician's decision making and duty of confidentiality and privilege to the client.

Who, Besides the Attorney, May Call the Psychologist?

A variety of people may call seeking a psychologist's assistance to help resolve their legal troubles. Asking them to have their attorney call is advisable so the psychologist can determine that his or her involvement in a case will be welcomed by the attorney and be consistent with whatever legal strategy is being considered.

Case 22.5

A father called to ask the psychologist to schedule time to test his 15-year-old son. The son was visiting Alabama from North Carolina over the winter holidays. The father revealed that the son had been diagnosed with Bipolar Disorder by a psychiatrist retained by the mother. A custody hearing was scheduled for the next month in North Carolina, and the father wanted to show how the son regressed under the mother's care, with the hope that this presumed regression would result in his gaining custody. The psychologist suggested to the father that he contact his attorney in North Carolina to determine whether (1) the father's strategy was consistent with the attorney's strategy, (2) a psychologist in the attorney's locale and the case's venue may have an existing working relationship with the attorney and the court, and (3) a psychologist who lived where the son and attorney lived might be more suitable. Such a psychologist can see the son for several sessions separated in time; this would produce a better time-sampled diagnostic picture, be more compelling to the court, and incur fewer expenses for the father when travel is considered.

*   *   *

Another case illustrates the potential for role conflict once the psychologist is working on a case.

Case 22.6

A third-year law student in a clerkship in the district attorney's office sought to interview the psychologist posing as a student who was researching a term paper on the role of the psychologist as an expert witness. It became readily apparent that the intern was trying to gather data to impugn the psychologist's credentials. The psychologist abruptly ended the interview, made notes of the discussion, and called the attorney who had retained him.

A few weeks later, the clerk was seated at the district attorney's side during the psychologist's qualification as an expert witness and during his testimony. The district attorney's office tried to subvert the discovery process and put the psychologist in a role conflict, one that pitted being helpful to a "student" and against that of revealing information only through the process of discovery.

Who Referred the Psychologist to the Attorney?

This question allows the psychologist to learn about possible unstated expectations that the caller may harbor. The person who referred the psychologist undoubtedly did so as a function of some prior contact and will have described the psychologist's skills, abilities, and character to the caller. Knowing the referral source may help clarify the caller's expectations. Also, it is good to know the type of informal referral network operating in one's professional milieu so one can anticipate future referrals. Finally, if the psychologist had a particular fee structure or other working relationship with the referral source, the psychologist can prevent potential misunderstandings with the caller by clarifying the current terms of employment.

Who Pays the Psychologist?

The most satisfactory financial arrangement is through a written agreement with the attorney. Attorneys are more likely to understand why a professional will bill for time spent on the telephone, on scoring test protocols, and on report writing and research time and court preparation time. Also, this arrangement allows the attorney to have privilege regarding the psychologist because the attorney is then the client of the psychologist. If the attorney's client owned privilege, the psychologist could be placed in a position in which the client could invoke privilege. Then the psychologist would be at risk for violating the client's privilege by communicating with the attorney unless a signed waiver is obtained beforehand. Without exception, psychologists should tell individuals who seek their forensic services to have their attorney contact them.

If the psychologist is involved with the client before a forensic contact arises, perhaps in a marital or child psychotherapy case, the relationship operating before the forensic involvement is considered the controlling or regnant relationship. While the psychotherapist may be an expert in other contexts, he or she would have a factual witness role. While the psychologist serving as a psychotherapist may feel pressures of loyalty and empathy toward his or her client, serving in the expert witness or consultant role will complicate the case at the least and subject the psychologist to role conflict and its deleterious consequences. If the client loses, questions about the adequacy of the psychologist's testimony will likely arise, leaving him or her open to more charges than we can consider here.

The pressures to serve the psychotherapy client may come from one or another of the patients, the attorneys, or the psychologist's sense of obligation or identification to the psychotherapy clients. For example, in a custody case, the psychologist may empathize with the parent or the child who is caught in a legal vise constructed by the other spouse or a parent. Nonetheless, the expert witness role may be best served by an independent psychologist, not the one providing clinical services to the client. As Monahan (1980) advises, know who your client is and what role to play.

How Does the Psychologist Determine and Bill Fees?   Some psychologists are copying the ways of attorneys by asking for retainers, which is a reasonable practice. However, a psychologist should never copy the attorney's practice of working on a contingent fee basis. The Specialty Guidelines for Forensic Psychologists states:

> Forensic psychologists do not provide professional services to parties to a legal proceeding on the basis of "contingent fees," when those services involve the offering of expert testimony to a court or administrative body, or when they call upon the psychologist to make affirmations or representations intended to be relied on by third parties. (Committee on Ethical Guidelines for Forensic Psychologists, 1991, IV. B)

The conflict of interest and the appearance of such a conflict for the expert witness is inescapable in a contingent fee arrangement. This arrangement means that the psychologist is or appears to be working to win the case to garner a paycheck rather than providing the court or jury with unbiased scientific guidance that the expert witness role demands.

Psychologists should find out about the prevailing local and regional fee schedules and the degree of specialization called for in the case, realistically assess their own expertise and level of experience, then set up their own fee schedule. Blau and Alberts (2004) present forms for the forensic practitioner for billing clients. In fact, they present forms that help through the whole of the forensic case. The psychologist should bill promptly and periodically. Thus, the psychologist who has tested an attorney's client may want to furnish a bill for services along with the report if there is no set arrangement for services beyond the testing and report. Failure to be accurate and timely in billing can present problems. In a pair of related cases, the attorneys, who were not known for their integrity, and the psychologist had an understanding that the psychologist would bill when the cases were concluded. The two attorneys kept telling the psychologist, who had provided case reviews and reports, that the psychologist would soon be called for the next hearing. They never informed the psychologist when the case and appeals were exhausted. More than a year later, the psychologist found out in the law reporter that the appeal was lost. The attorneys had little incentive to call the psychologist as they would be paying the fee from their own pocket, not from a client's award.

What Records Should the Psychologist Keep and Where Should the Records Be Kept?

The record begins with the first telephone call or conversation. Keep records of all meetings, with dates and times and the parties attending the meetings listed on the records. This should include the times a person left a meeting or joined a meeting in progress or left for a break or telephone call. This allows the psychologist to know what information others may or may not have. All clinical notes taken and test protocols collected as part of a forensic practitioner's interviews, interventions, or assessments form part of the case's record.

A brief set of guidelines for record keeping are available (APA, 1993), and samples of various record forms can be found in Blau and Alberts (2004). One's record-keeping practices need to be in substantial compliance with state statutes. Good practice includes keeping the records in a secure place, with access limited to staff working on the case. The staff should have been taught about safeguarding clinical and forensic materials and are covered under the cloak of the licensed psychologist's privilege.

The expert witness in deposition and court often is asked when certain facts were made known, by whom, and in what context. Notes become invaluable when a case is heard months after meetings have occurred. A corrections dictum holds that if it is not documented, it did not occur. Although one can use recall or oral testimony, written records are so much more reliable, substantial, and difficult to dispute. In one case, a company asked a psychologist to perform a fitness-to-return-to-duty evaluation of an employee who was described by coworkers and supervisors as paranoic and dangerous. The psychologist called the employee, explained the limits of confidentiality, the purpose of the examination, and the fact that, though the company hired the psychologist, the psychologist's opinions were not predetermined. The employee scheduled a meeting later in the week. Five minutes after the appointment time, the employee called to cancel the appointment. The record of the attempted evaluation forms part of the evidence the company intends to use in the coming years when the case comes to trial.

The psychologist needs to understand that his or her notes in the clinical arena may be seen as helpful and even necessary in providing clinical services to the client. In the legal arena, the notes, test data, testing, and research protocols are governed by the rules of evidence in the court's jurisdiction. Subject to certain privileges, the entirety of the records in the case can be discovered. The psychologist is advised to consult closely with the attorney concerning communications and conveyance of case materials to the courts or any third party. How does the psychologist proceed in the case?

THE MIDDLE PHASE

Decades ago, there were no forensic psychology programs or workshops, few journal articles, and no psychology and law journals. The only place to learn about the courts was by going to court. Regular visits to the courtroom each week for several months allow one to see how decisions are made, how witnesses impeach their own cause, how attorneys either muff their opportunities or brilliantly parlay them into a winning hand for their clients. The rhythms of the court can be felt in the marrow of one's bones. The psychologist wishing to become courtwise now can read books, take courses, subscribe to psychology and law journals, attend workshops, and watch the steady diet of televised court trials, proceedings, and the flood of legal analysts deluging the airwaves. Notwithstanding this fare, none of these resources replaces the real-time feel of watching a witness under direct examination, then undergoing a skilled attorney's cross-examination, watching the judge make rulings and the jury's studied inscrutability—in short, attending court. What happens after the retaining of the expert but before the trial is the subject of this section.

Data Gathering

The gathering and organizing of data pose certain problems. Also, the presenting of data in various venues is considered.

Securing Records. After agreeing to serve as an expert witness, the courtwise psychologist will want all the records regarding the case, including the attorney's information, the opposing attorney's evidence, and other records that can bear on psychological aspects of the case (e.g., employment and medical records). The psychologist will want access to parties whom the psychologist needs to assess for a complete evaluation. The attorney has an interest in seeing that the psychologist's expertise is fully exercised or the whole point of contracting for the psychologist's service is compromised. The attorney may say he or she has tried to obtain records or access to informants under the other side's control but has been stymied. The psychologist's reply should be that the attorney needs to relay the psychologist's request nonetheless. If the requested materials are then sent, the psychologist has been useful to the attorney. If the materials are not sent, then when the trial occurs, the attorney can bring into evidence what materials the psychologist requested and the fate of the requests and evidence of the lack of a forthcoming attitude by the other side in their withholding information and informants from the psychologist.

If the attorney says he or she read the records and can provide a synopsis, saving time for all and money for the client, the psychologist should request all records nonetheless. In one case, the psychologist read a stack of mental health records in a jail suicide case that was nearly 3 inches thick. Wading through hundreds of pages of charts, the psychologist noticed that the tone of the psychologist's and social worker's entries in the record changed two days before the inmate committed suicide. The entries changed from being cursory and matter of fact to becoming highly detailed and correct in grammar, form, and content. The copy also had a shadow that was suspicious. The psychologist asked the attorney to examine the original sheets because something seemed irregular. The attorney discovered that the records were pasted over the usual cursory and boilerplate entries and had been doctored. The psychologist can read reports with a different set of lenses than an attorney and should not gainsay the skills he or she brings to the case.

Case 22.7

A teenager accused her father of prolonged incest, describing some specific sodomy practices. The hospital records seemed to be in good shape to the attorney. However, the psychologist realized that some of the sexual activities the teenager described and some of her claimed symptoms were described in clinical detail with highly specific or signature terms. These same terms and idiosyncratic wordings were found in the records when the other members of the teenager's group psychotherapy were recounting their histories. She listened to her fellow group members, but she did not participate in the discussions nor claim any of the same complaints, symptoms, or activities. Yet the same details discussed in the group therapy appeared later in her report to the police, as if she had appropriated their stories. Other aspects of her personality fit this pattern, including descriptions by her schoolmates of the teenager's speaking about her classmates' experiences and boyfriends as her own. Thus, the basis for uncovering the factitious nature of the patient's complaints became obvious by examining progress notes of the therapy group and the police and child care worker's reports.

Scheduling Sessions with Sources. The psychologist should develop a plan with the attorney about whom the psychologist needs to interview or test, the reasons for the session, and the order of people to be interviewed or tested. This allows the attorney to learn the psychologist's reasoning and should help inform the attorney's evolving strategy.

Just as in the search for relevant records, the psychologist should ask to assess those reasonably involved in a case even if it is unlikely that the parties will agree to meet with the psychologist. When the psychologist is asked in court how well he or she prepared the case, the psychologist can mention whom he or she tested (or met with in whatever fact-finding procedure is pertinent to the case). When asked whether the psychologist tested the opposing attorney's client, the psychologist can say that he or she asked the attorney who retained the psychologist to request such a meeting but the attorney reported that such attempts were rebuffed. This tack should be taken only with the approval of the attorney retaining the psychologist because under certain circumstances, such a denial of a request to be examined is prejudicial unless the issue is brought up by the attorney representing the party refusing the examination.

Constructing the Forensic Psychology Record. The courtwise psychologist will note the time, date, and duration of all telephone calls and other electronic communications, the parties on the telephone as reported to him or her, and whether the call was recorded and by whom. Similarly, a record of all meetings with the parties and particulars should be kept. Once the attorney retains the psychologist and so informs the court, records, test protocols, electronic recordings, and notes are subject to discovery. The meetings with the attorney retaining the psychologist are probable exceptions to this practice because there are communications concerning case strategy that may be part of the "work product" privilege, a part of the attorney-client privilege (McCormick, Elliott, & Sutton, 1981; Rothstein, 1981). The meetings are probably discoverable, but the contents of the meeting are probably privileged, though the law in this area changes rapidly.

In developing the evidentiary materials, the interviews, reviews of records and of pertinent literature, test protocols, and interpretations, the courtwise psychologist will review the judicial instructions the judge will use to instruct the jury. Psychologists who practice in a particular jurisdiction, be it federal, state, or municipal, should consider adding to their library the set of instructions the judges use to tell the jury what the specific elements of the charges are that they are to use in their determinations. The responsible psychologist will use the instructions to inform the selection of strategy and the data needed to address the issues raised in the instructions. The attorney should be able to provide the psychologist with jury instructions that he or she expects the court to use.

Courtwise psychologists will keep their records, test protocols, reports, and other materials indexed in a way that allows easy access to critical findings. The greater the amount of material, the greater the need to index. There is nothing so awkward as the expert witness saying, "I recall reading that person X said something like that. Wait a minute while I go through the records to see whether I can find what I am looking for."

Uninvited Contacts from Others.   From time to time there will be an illicit contact from others. In all cases, immediately report the contact to the attorney who retained you and keep a record of the contact and the report to the attorney. A telephone log is indispensable, as are records of electronic mail.

Case 22.8

During a recess at a deposition regarding the rights of a student to special education, the attractive school administrator approached the student's expert witness and marveled at his brilliance. Playing with her necklace and skirt while licking her lips and fluttering her eyes, she said it sure would be nice to hire him as a consultant, given his skills and charm. She said that the school system and his children, who were students in the school system (was there a veiled threat of retaliation against his children?), sure could benefit from his services and the consultant fees that would be forthcoming. This blatant attempt to influence (bribe? intimidate? seduce?) was witnessed by no one but reported to the student's attorney. The psychologist responded to the school administrator as if she were a terrific person, saying that they needed to talk after the case was settled because he was sure they could do a wonderful job together providing services to the school. He knew the ploy, and when the deposition continued he was not surprised at the hostile, pointed, and personal attack by the administrator and her attorney. Of course, there was no consulting contract afterward.

Subpoenas.   Expect to be subpoenaed. The subpoena is part of the discovery process. In preparing for a courtroom appearance, both sides want all the pertinent information they can secure. To do less is irresponsible and could subject an attorney to charges of ineffective counsel. Each side may make their experts available for discovery without a subpoena. The notion of last-minute surprise witnesses is largely a television fiction. Such witnesses would not allow for opposing counsel to fully discover the strengths and weaknesses of the witness and his or her testimony. This would not serve justice.

M. T. Singer and Nievod (1987) point out that the court-naïve psychologist panics, while the courtwise psychologist reviews the request, calls the attorney retaining him or her, and understands what the attorney issuing the subpoena seeks. In areas where the attorney's need to discover conflicts with the psychologist's need to protect a client's confidential and even privileged information or the security of a psychological test, understanding the attorney's needs can result in a compromise by which the interests of the various parties are served. Divulging needed information that is not confidential or part of a confidential record rather than the wholesale revelation may be most appropriate. Also, divulging a third party's information, for example, in records of family or group psychotherapy, may raise a host of issues about the third party's rights.

The Committee on Legal Issues (COLI; 1996) raised a set of helpful issues, beginning with whether the request for information carries the force of law. The client whose records are at issue should be informed about the requested material because he or she may have some claims against revealing the information. COLI suggests a number of ways to partially protect subpoenaed information, including revealing it only to another qualified psychologist retained by the adversary, limiting the information to the court's use by way of a seal or gag, and ensuring that only the relevant parts of the record be entered into the proceedings. The courtwise psychologist would do well to refer to the COLI suggestions.

Regardless of the existence or success of the claim against a subpoena, the client, having been informed, can be psychologically prepared to encounter the impact of revealing the subpoenaed information. Thus, the psychologist would have acted in an ethical and caring manner. When the subpoena clashes with rights and privileges to the point that the conflict resists the negotiations suggested earlier, the court can provide guidance to the parties. From a legal perspective, the court provides protection from the legal consequences of revealing records. However, damage to the client's humanity and to the integrity of one's professional practice caused by revealing information are stresses for the psychologist to resolve. The ethical and caring psychologist earns, by way of experiencing moral angst, the generous forensic fees he or she charges.

Strategy Meeting.   At some point, usually after data have been gathered, the attorney and expert witness should review and interpret the materials. The attorney may find the data unsupportive or even antithetical to his or her strategy. If the attorney does not like what was found, the attorney can pay the psychologist's fee up to that point and not call the psychologist. An attorney may not like it, but the responsible attorney will want to hear the truth as the expert found it. To the extent that the attorney has not listed the psychologist on a witness roster, his or her work on the case may never be known if the other attorney does not ask about anyone who was consulted about the case. In one case, an attorney spoke with the psychologist for a few minutes on the telephone, sent him a check, and never called again; the attorney was assuring that the other side could not retain the psychologist in the case. Other than this instance, once attorneys retain the expert they tend to use the expert.

The psychologist will review the data that support the attorney's theory of the case, the evidence that makes the theory vulnerable, and the data that may support an alternative and sometimes a stronger theory. For example, in Case 22.7, the alleged perpetrator took the child to a clinic on a number of occasions. He signed the clinic's consent forms, paid for the psychotherapy, and had gasoline receipts on clinic session dates from a service station near the clinic but distant from his home, verifying his taking the child to the clinic. This is inconsistent with a child abuse perpetrator. Although not conclusive in itself, the evidence was compelling that in the experience of several of the expert witnesses there was never a case in which the perpetrator took the victim to a clinic, risking and even inviting discovery of the crime. The attorney did not have the experience that would have allowed him to pursue this line of evidence, so the pretrial conference was vital in this case.

In this case, too, there were several expert witnesses. A productive strategy was developed about which expert would cover the various areas to be presented. Because the other side also had several experts, it was decided that the academic department head would be the last witness. From this vantage, he could explain all the witnesses' testimonies for both sides. His role as a teacher, who could be above the fray or parade of experts and hired guns, could give him the ability to complement the work of witnesses from both sides but point out limitations in their work in a way that used the expert testimony from both sides to bolster the theory the attorney proposed. Strategies based on social psychological findings regarding primacy and recency effects of a message and how arguments can be co-opted were relied on to win this case.

At the pretrial meeting, one should learn about the personal style of the opposing attorneys and the judge. According to the attorney in one case, the judge was an avid fisherman and allotted just a few minutes per witness to clear his calendar to go fishing. The attorney advised one-sentence answers instead of paragraph-long explanations, and where a sentence might otherwise work, he advised one-word answers. While this seemed to give justice short shrift, this is the judge with whom both sides had to work. Appeals are expensive and need a basis; the judge was a federal lifetime appointment and was known as efficient and one who cleared his calendar. Better to know what one is facing and adjust to it than to fail gloriously and justly. At this point, one should learn what to expect of the attorneys who may be examining and cross-examining the expert witness. There is no way one can overestimate the value of predeposition and pretrial conferences.

The Deposition.   Depositions are part of the process by which attorneys discover the other side's evidence so each side may prepare as complete a case presentation as possible in the interest of serving their respective clients and serving justice. Before a deposition, the wise psychologist and attorney will meet to decide strategy. Attorneys face a choice at this point. If they feel there is an advantage in presenting a powerful case in the deposition, the witness may be quite detailed in revealing the evidence. In cases that seem sure to be tried, the witness should be responsive but need not be expansive. While the witness should produce all legitimately requested evidence and honestly answer all questions, the degree of detail offered by the expert witness can vary with the attorney's strategy. A good working relationship between the psychologist and the attorney involves both an agreement on strategy and respect for the psychologist's position on telling the truth, the whole truth, and nothing but the truth. Any attorney not respecting this position is an attorney from whom the psychologist should part company (see the ABA, 1989, standards for prosecuting and defense attorneys cited earlier). Nonetheless, the expert is not obliged to tell all but only to be responsive to the specific question.

One example of negotiating the Scylla of revelation and the Charybdis of being spare in one's testimony involves a case concerning whether the conditions on death row were so abysmal as to violate the prisoners' rights to be free from cruel and unusual punishment. The psychologist hired by the state interviewed 12 death row prisoners, three inmates serving life without parole, three sentenced to life, and four guards (correctional officers) assigned to death row over a 3-day period. The plaintiff's psychologist had spent a day and part of another interviewing eight prisoners. The state decided to let the plaintiff know all that their evidence consisted of and see about settling the case without a trial. The plaintiff's attorney hammered away at the state's psychologist. During such attacks, an expert witness may be induced to reveal more than is required, ignore data that conflict with evidence he or she developed, lose sight of the case strategy, or make statements beyond what the data support. In this case, the attorney wore down and the psychologist simply remained responsive to the attorney's questions without revealing more information than was asked.

One further feature of this case is worth noting. The psychologist found some extralegal punitive measures that the guards were taking on their own. He let the assistant attorney general know that if he were asked about using pitchforks to pin prisoners against the wall, among other practices, he would reveal what he found. Neither he nor the assistant attorney general should be put in a position to defend indefensible and abhorrent correctional practices. Why the plaintiff's expert witness did not ferret out the information about these practices is another matter. After some 6 hours of spirited deposition, the plaintiff's attorney asked, "Well, is there anything you did not say that is relevant and that you want to say or that I should know or should ask?" The psychologist replied, "I would be happy to answer any specific question that you may have." The deposition ended in the seventh hour. The case was settled without a trial shortly after the deposition.

Some may say the psychologist should have told about the guards' conduct, but the rules of engagement allow and even require vigorous, penetrating inquiry by the attorneys in discovery by which information is elicited. Stonewalling is inappropriate, unethical, and illegal. The truth, whole truth, and nothing but the truth are required of us in everyday life and just as much when we are under oath, as is the case on deposition and in court. But the rules require the attorney to ask specific questions and the deponent to be responsive, not to be a raconteur.

One must remember that the deposition should be treated as seriously as one treats the court appearance. The deposition is an extension of the court, and the oath plus the record are part of the judge's domain. Even if the setting is a hotel room and the attorneys are fairly casual, the deposition forms part of the court record. What the witness says on deposition can appear at the trial when the opposing attorney spots an inconsistency between what is said at the trial and on deposition. One should be just as practiced and careful in deposition as on trial. In a case of jail suicide, the five sets of defendants had about a dozen attorneys present. They were particularly critical of their opponent, who entered the room with an insult to those assembled. The psychologist who was retained by the county sheriff in charge of the jail was deposed in a particularly hostile way, starting with a withering review of his qualifications. After an unrelenting attack, he was asked where he had gained knowledge of a particular clinical technique. He replied, "Detroit." When the attorney asked, "Detroit, Michigan?" the expert sarcastically replied, "I am not a qualified geographer so I cannot answer that definitively, but when I last checked, Detroit was some 70 miles north of Toledo, Ohio" to the guffaws of the dozen attorneys. Later, when the psychologist read the transcript of the deposition, the humor looked mean-spirited and prejudicial. Generally, humor ill befits the dignity of a competent expert witness. Be careful with humor. It can be useful, as is illustrated later, but use it with care.

When the deposition is taken, often the attorneys and the court reporter suggest that the witness stipulate or waive the right to review the transcription. This is rarely a good idea. On several occasions, I caught errors in the transcription of test scores and of what for psychologists are technical terms, though they may appear to be common terms to nonpsychologists. The terms "cluster" and "factor" have specific meanings in statistical analysis, as does "base rate," "reliability," and "face validity" for the psychometrician, as does "observing ego" and "superego lacunae" for the psychoanalyst. The court reporter can misunderstand and misrecord technical terms, so waiving a proofreading of the transcript can result in a record of the psychologist's words that the psychologist did not say. The psychologist is then in the awkward position of having approved an incorrect transcript of his or her testimony that can be read back at trial.

THE END GAME: THE COURTROOM APPEARANCE

All one's efforts can go for naught unless the expert witness presents the evidence effectively. Before the court appearance, the expert needs to prepare with the attorney, needs to plan the presentation of evidence, and needs to understand the dynamics of the courtroom.

The Pretrial Meeting

If the case is straightforward and the attorney and psychologist have been in contact during the data-gathering stage, the pretrial meeting should be a rehearsal of a set of important questions already reviewed in earlier conferences. These questions include what the psychologist found, how the findings may help the case, how the findings may be vulnerable on cross-examination, what information the judge or jury will already know and what information they will learn subsequent to the psychologist's testimony from other fact or expert witnesses, what is the examining style of the opposing counsel, and what style the judge affects. In a case with other expert witnesses, the conference will involve coordination of findings and developing a common strategy. If the psychologist and attorney work well together and the psychologist understands the attorney's theory and strategy, the psychologist may be able to suggest an order of presentation that will make the materials more effective. For example, in an incest case, several psychiatrists and psychologists testified for the prosecution about the extensive damage that seemed posttraumatic to them. The defense retained two psychologists, one of whom tested the members of the family except for the alleged victim. The other psychologist, who had impressive academic as well as clinical credentials, was used to explain how the mental health professionals' testimony fit together and could most parsimoniously and compellingly support a not-guilty conclusion. He was used to tie up loose ends that the previous witnesses on both sides left dangling.

Preparing Materials

The expert witness should review all the materials to be used in court and have a copy of any other materials about which he or she may be questioned. For example, if a psychiatric report, hospital records, or another psychologist's test report may be at issue, the testifying psychologist should have a copy that he or she has reviewed beforehand. The expert witness should never examine a document for the first time on the stand. Being blindsided will result in a poor performance. Index and tabulate the materials that will be introduced and discussed in court. Fumbling through papers will detract from the psychologist's appearance.

The more material the psychologist can commit to memory, the more impressive will be the appearance. The expert witness should be thoroughly familiar with the tests and techniques employed. For example, when using the Wechsler or Stanford-Binet intelligence scales, I will review the psychometric properties of the instrument, including the most and the least reliable subtests, the literature that may qualify the client's results due to his or her age, gender, race or ethnicity, and the standard error of differences in cases where subtest score differences may be an issue. Be sure no materials are included in what you bring to court that are not relevant to the case; on more than one occasion expert witnesses have brought materials from another case to court. Their credibility suffered. The expert witness should bring at least five copies of his or her curriculum vitae: One copy should be kept by the witness for reference when an attorney discusses a particular entry, and one each should be given to the judge, the court reporter, and each counsel to review during qualification of the witness. This helps the expert witness look prepared and evenhanded. The expert witness should review the vitae before the trial. Also, he or she should review pertinent clinical experience not documented on the vitae and let the attorney have a listing of these at one of the pretrial meetings. For example, in a case concerning jail suicide, the psychologist listed the number of institutions that he visited and worked in and the number and type of inmates he interviewed, diagnosed, and treated. Similarly, he listed the number of times he was retained by the plaintiff and the defendant sides in similar cases so the attorney would know whether the psychologist was vulnerable to an attack as a plaintiff's or a defendant's witness. One psychologist on the jail suicide case, for philosophical and political reasons, has never been a defendant's witness in about 100 civil cases. If a witness has this kind of a skew in his or her history, the witness should be prepared to explain this apparent bias. As mentioned earlier, this should have been disclosed to the attorney when the attorney was first retaining the psychologist. The courtwise psychologist prepares questions for the attorney to ask in court so the psychologist's testimony will be focused for the specific case.

All that has transpired so far should have occurred with the courtroom testimony in mind. Many cases are settled as the trial date approaches. But in some, where the sides cannot reconcile, the expert will next need to consider his or her court appearance. In the trial, the parties will have their day in court with often dramatic and life-altering consequences in the balance.

Some Pragmatics about the Courtroom Appearance

There are workshops, articles, chapters, and entire books concerning pragmatics, gambits, and tricks attorneys use in confronting the other side's experts and an equal number of resources for expert witnesses to counter these maneuvers with tricks of their own. This section provides a framework to understand the courtroom appearance and to make the psychologist's presentation effective.

The expert witness will usually be more at ease if he or she has visited the actual courtroom beforehand. Locating the courthouse and courtroom and finding out about parking will avoid needless problems on the court day. The courtwise psychologist will become familiar with the acoustics, the lighting, the physical layout of the court, the position of the witness stand in relation to the judge, jury, and counsel tables, and the spacing needed for people to see any visual aids that might be used. Walking around the room and the witness stand may avoid problems that one dignified expert witness experienced. She walked into the courtroom dressed in an elegantly understated suit, carried her briefcase with her as she ascended the three steps to the witness stand, gracefully sat in the chair, and, as she repositioned the chair, somersaulted backward into a heap when the chair's back legs went off the stand.

Dressing for Court

The role of the expert witness is to present a set of findings clearly and persuasively. The highest-paid persuaders in our society are in the media. The news anchors usually dress in a way that projects authority and honesty. Expert witnesses should consider wearing a dark blue or a gray suit. Men should wear ties that are not garish and do not "make a statement." Women should consider a modest scarf or a simple necklace, lapel pin, or brooch. Lapel pins that make partisan statements, political buttons, and showy jewelry should be avoided; they distract jurors at best and could antagonize them at worst. Plaids, bow ties, umbrellas, and shoes that squeak can draw attention away from what the witness has to say and render him or her less effective. In recent years, shirts in formal situations often are colored, sometimes intensely, in contrast to what had been the court uniform for attorneys, the white shirt. Because judges may be slightly older and used to the respect that a white shirt or blouse implies, the expert cannot go wrong wearing a white shirt or blouse.

These rules of thumb may be relaxed in the less formal family and child court settings and when the proceedings are in the judge's chambers, when the judge is more casually attired and when the parties are not antagonistic. Also, the expert witness should be aware of local customs; overdressing before a blue-collar jury can invoke resentment.

Court Decorum

Unless specifically instructed otherwise, the expert witness should not be in the courtroom during the trial except for his or her own appearance. Exceptions include a case where the attorney wants the witness to observe a party to the case who was unavailable to the expert. Otherwise, experts may be disqualified by their own violation of FRE Rule 615, or a variant of "The Rule." Rule 615 states:

> At the request of a party the court shall order witnesses excluded so that they cannot hear the testimony of other witnesses, and it may make the order of its own motion. This rule does not authorize exclusion of (1) a party who is a natural person is a living, breathing human individual perceptible through the senses and subject to physical laws, as opposed to a functionary or corporate or juridical or legal person, or (2) an officer or employee of a party which is not a natural person designated as its representative by its attorney, or (3) a person whose presence is shown by a party to be essential to the presentation of his cause.

This rule codifies a long-standing practice that discourages and exposes fabrication, inaccuracy, and collusion. If the expert hangs around the trial before and after, jurors may infer that the expert is personally invested in the case.

Before being seated, the expert is sworn in. Then the attorney retaining the expert will review the expert's credentials. At this point, the expert should have the copies of his or her curriculum vitae (often called a resume to avoid distancing from the jury) and be prepared to review education, training, experiences, skills, and specialized knowledge that make the witness qualified to understand the issues in the case. This is no time for modesty, false or otherwise. Without being boastful or arrogant, the expert witness, who worked hard to attain his or her credentials, should be confident in sharing these with the court. Occasionally, the other side's attorney may stipulate or agree to accept the expert without examining the credentials, but the retaining attorney often wants the judge and jury to hear all the outstanding accomplishments of this expert.

Some experts may be limited in their expertise. One case concerned the understanding of the Miranda warning by an accused murderer with an IQ of 63 who had been drinking. The judge determined that although the expert was an instructor in the DUI (driving under the influence) school, that was not a qualification equal to having clinical or research experience in giving people measured amounts of intoxicants and testing their cognitive functioning. However, as an instructor and practitioner of psychodiagnostics for 20 years, the witness was qualified to discuss the cognitive inability of the accused to understand Miranda with his level of intelligence, regardless of levels of intoxication.

Order of Presentations

The following is the order of presentations:

1. The plaintiff's or state's attorney makes an opening statement.
2. The defendant's attorney makes an opening statement.
3. The plaintiff's side presents direct evidence.
4. The defendant's attorney cross-examines.
5. The defendant's attorney presents direct evidence.
6. The state's or plaintiff's attorney cross-examines.
7. The plaintiff's side presents rebuttal evidence.
8. The defendant's side presents rebuttal evidence.
9. The state's or plaintiff's attorney makes the opening final argument.
10. The defendants' attorney makes the final argument.
11. The state's or plaintiff's attorney makes the closing final argument.
12. The judge instructs the jury.

The expert witness is typically involved in the presentation of direct evidence but may sometimes be recalled at the rebuttal stage. The expert may appear before the trial, too, in such events as a pretrial hearing to exclude evidence. In one case, the expert testified about the inability of a witness to have identified the defendant due to the lighting conditions when the crime occurred, combined with the misuse of hypnosis and a tainted lineup procedure that virtually assured that the victim would identify the accused. With that evidence excluded by the judge, there was no other evidence on which to proceed with the case.

The attorney retaining the expert will ask the witness questions by way of placing before the court the evidence that they have reviewed in pretrial meetings. The effective expert articulates the evidence with the legal standards that the judge will instruct the jury to follow when the jury deliberates. In a non-jury trial, the judge will refer to the legal standards in rendering a decision. This is the focal point of all of the attorneys' and the expert's efforts. The keys to success are to establish credibility, to teach, to tell a compelling story that integrates the facts, and to use words almost in a magical way that graphically illustrates the points, that draws the jurors into the story. The key point for the expert to remember is that the jurors and judge want to make the right decision for the right reason.

Credibility is established by one's being retained (obviously, the attorney and his or her client value the expert, although jurors and judges may have a natural bias against the stereotype of the hired gun) and by the review of credentials, but, most important, by the mastery of the materials weighing in on the issues before the court presented clearly and compellingly. The effective expert listens to the questions carefully, formulates an answer consistent with the evidence gathered, and makes eye contact with the jury. No one likes a windbag, and the court has many witnesses and many cases, so the expert does not have the luxury of 50-minute blocks, as he or she might have when teaching college classes. The concepts of standard error, convergent validity, base rate, and transference are complex; however, it is a poor expert who tells the attorney or the court that an issue is complex. In one case, the expert was confronted with explaining why the jailers should not have been alerted that the 25-year-old male with marital troubles and a few prior arrests who was intoxicated and would be in jail for a day or two was a suicide risk. The opposing counsel thundered that most jail suicides fit that pattern. The expert knew that the modal or most frequently occurring person in jail fits that pattern, making the profile of the suicidal inmate no different from the modal prisoner. The witness referred to a public service advertisement for seat belts popular at that time claiming that the majority of traffic accidents occurred within 25 miles of one's home. However, what the ad did not say was that most driving occurs within 25 miles of one's home. While we should buckle up in any event, the same faulty statistical reasoning was being applied in the case; that is, the majority of people in jail were about 25, male, intoxicated, had marital trouble, had one or two encounters with the law, and would be out in a day or two. Thus, there was no profile that the jailers could use to pick out this person as particularly suicidal. As the ad was mentioned, the jurors' heads bobbed in recognition, they carefully listened and understood the concept of base rates, and they rejected the claims of the victim's family.

The key is to use 25 cent words to explain 25 dollar concepts. Berne's (1964) *Games People Play* and Erikson's (1950) *Childhood and Society* are models in explaining complicated concepts simply. McElhaney (1997) advises avoiding words like "elucidate," "illuminate," "discern," "explicate," and "expound," instead using "teach," "tell," "explain," "help us understand," "show us," and "untangle." Demonstrative words such as "show," "see," "watch," "picture," "view," and "look at" will draw the listener into the expert's story.

Although speaking plainly will carry the day, the expert should avoid being too homey or down-to-earth. After all, the expert is in the courtroom because he or she has specialized knowledge to share. The expert may use technical terms, then explain them graphically. For example, when test results are presented, the opposing attorney may ask how these results can be relied on when the test has an error rate that could easily miss the "real IQ" by 5, 10, or even 15 points in either direction! The expert should mention that every measurement device has an error rate. For example, the local weather report may show that the temperature at the airport, at city hall, and in various parts of the city or town differ by a few degrees; taking the temperature yields a range of figures. So it is with human measurements: Our weight, blood sugar, cholesterol, and libido fluctuate, just as our intelligence and personality test scores vary. However, the scientific basis of psychology allows us to know the error range (the standard error of the instrument used). The expert can use a technical term that establishes expertise, but then should explain the term as the juror's favorite teacher would explain a new concept.

Attorneys will raise objections about qualifying the expert, about hearsay evidence, and about anything else they can contest. The courtwise expert will wait for the judge to hear the arguments and give direction to the witness. The expert witness need not be an attorney and know the vicissitudes of the hearsay rule to appreciate the drama. The hearsay rule is interesting and relevant to the psychologist. A good deal of our evidence is based on statements that are not the declarant's (the person declaring the statement in court, or us; Binder, 1975). The hearsay rule allows the mental health professional to use what otherwise would be hearsay to form a professional opinion. The expert is seen as having the experience and ability to determine the veracity of the statement, and the experience and training of the expert adds more than just the weight of the data or statements that would accrue for the layperson (Binder, 1975).

There are 40 exceptions to the hearsay rule. What gets admitted as evidence that will determine the trial's outcome may well hinge on the decisions made by a judge who has but seconds to decide whether statements are hearsay. Legal knowledge is not necessary for expert witnesses, and certainly they should stay within their role, not participating in the lawyerly deliberations. However, knowing the relevant procedural and substantive law makes the courtroom drama more meaningful and can help shape a more effective response by the expert witness.

Cross-Examination

An old legal adage goes, "If the attorney has the facts, pound on the facts. Lacking the facts, he or she should pound on the law. Lacking either, the attorney should pound on the table." An opposing expert witness is an inviting target to pound, too. Attacking the expert is consistent with the opposing attorney's job to discredit the expert's testimony. There are a number of ways to attack testimony. The attorney may ask, "Doctor, are you aware of the many criticisms of the *DSM* [or intelligence and personality tests, or violence prediction, or psychotherapy, or whatever procedure is the basis for testimony]?" If the expert answers no, then he or she is vulnerable for lacking knowledge of the literature. If the expert answers yes, then the witness is open to the question "Why in the world would you use a flawed technique in a case that could destroy people's lives?!" To further confuse the expert, the attorney may use a double negative and a suggestive question, as in, "You are not telling us that you did not use the best devices available, are you?" The expert should answer, "Every technique is subject to criticism. It is that critical attitude by which we make progress in refining techniques. The techniques used in this case are reliable and shed light on the issues we are facing" (if in fact this is true, and it should be true if the expert did his or her homework in reading the literature and selecting appropriate methodologies).

Misquoting deposition materials and using generalizations and vague terms are ways an attorney can lead a witness astray. The best tactic for the witness is to have the deposition at hand so the correct quote may be reread, and to answer vagueness with an open and specific response. Thus, in response to the query, "I would guess you are pretty confident in what you said today since you say you interviewed Mr. X for a long, long time," the appropriate response would be, "I interviewed Mr. X for two and a half hours, from 9:40 A.M. to 12:10 P.M. on March 23, 1998 and for another hour from 1:05 to 2:05 P.M. on the same date." The attorney can ask, "Would you agree that people lie? Now, you say you interviewed Mr. X for several hours. How do you know he did not lie to you?" Of course the witness would have to answer that people do lie. The witness should anticipate this sort of question. If the psychologist used techniques that have validity indicators, such as addressing questions with known answers to the interviewer, circular lines of questioning that ask similar questions at different points in the interview to determine consistency of responses, and psychometric instruments with dissimulation detection indices built in, then the witness can answer that precautions were taken to determine the truthfulness of the interviewee's responses.

A parallel line of inquiry may be phrased as, "Doctor, have you ever made a mistake? How do you know you are not making a mistake today?" Of course the expert will have made mistakes. (If the expert says "No, I never made a mistake," he or she will lose credibility and appear arrogant.) The appropriate response might be, "I am sure I have made errors. In this case, the evidence is correct. The scores reflect the intelligence [or whatever the issue is at hand], and the tests are consistent both with each other and with the clinical interview materials, as we have reviewed earlier today." In all cases, the expert should be forthcoming and say "I do not know" when he or she has no answer to a question. This is a stronger position than trying to bluff the attorney who is skilled in forensics.

While the list of trick questions can go on and is quite entertaining, the best way to hone one's skills is to read Ziskin and Faust's (1995) *Coping with Psychiatric and Psychological Testimony.* Their express purpose is to embarrass mental health professionals out of the courtroom. They provide an excellent compendium of lines of attacking expert psychological testimony. Years ago, I would read Ziskin the week before going to court because I knew that nothing the attorneys could throw at me would be the equal of Ziskin and none of the attorneys had read Ziskin. Now Ziskin and Faust, though still not commonly known, is on attorneys' reading lists. It is the vulnerable expert witness who does not hone his or her skills on Ziskin and Faust.

The attorney may insult the expert, his or her credentials, or the field of psychology. The expert should monitor his or her emotional reaction. If the expert's voice rises above the attorney's voice, the expert is losing. Juries can live with and even expect a vigorous argument from the attorneys, but the expert witness should not lose poise and the appearance of objectivity. It is curious how professionals trained not to react in kind to a patient's hostility will react to an attorney's attacks. Some witnesses will buckle under and meekly answer any way the attorney moves them. Others will respond hostilely. Both reactions are ineffective at the least. The judge is not insensitive, nor are jurors stupid. The judge will let attacks proceed because both sides are entitled to make as vigorous a presentation of their case as possible. The most vicious cross-examination I have seen was in the Libby Zion case on Court TV, in which Tom Moore screamed at expert and fact witness physician after physician. He usually broke the witnesses down within 15 to 30 seconds, with a few holding out for a minute or two. One cross-examining prosecuting attorney whispered to me, "Hess, Hess. Rudolf Hess, Nazi," attempting to get me to lose my train of thought and my temper while presenting expert testimony. The best recourse for the witness is to take one's time, compose oneself, and answer questions in a factual way. If there is no question, then wait for one. If there seemed to be a question in the tirade, ask that it be repeated or restated.

We cannot cover every courtroom gambit, but the interested reader can refer to Blau (1998), Brodsky (1991), Merenbach and Stephen (1993), Matson (1994), and Wellman (1936), among other materials with court dialogue and gambits. Although it takes time and Court TV is now available, nothing replaces the feel of being in court and witnessing the dialogue.

Humor

Humor is tricky. Generally, the gravity of the court and the issue preclude levity. Therefore, do not joke. However, in the tense atmosphere of a trial, the well-placed response can score points. After an intense cross-examination in a 3-day-long child rape case, the attorney dismissed the expert witness with, "Doctor, I think the jury has heard about as much psychological and psychiatric mumbo jumbo and jargon from all of you expert psychiatrists and psychologists that they can stomach." The psychologist responded in a soft tone, "I bet they heard about enough legal terms, too," at which point jury members nodded to the expert witness, started laughing, and stated, "Ain't that the truth," "We sure have," and "You said it." Apparently the hostility toward the attorneys may have been greater than toward the mental health experts, or at least the jury felt the expert was in touch with the trial and their feelings.

Using humor can backfire. It can detract from the issues, can cast the witness as a smart aleck who may be seen as hostile, and can elicit sympathy for others whom the witness might not want portrayed sympathetically. The expert should be cautious in using humor, though its use can be devastatingly effective. In the case just cited, the attorney was an unsympathetic and belittling person. The interchange came at the end of the presentation of evidence for both sides and before the final arguments. There was no chance for the attorney to respond effectively.

Leaving the Scene

The expert, having been dismissed by the judge after examination, cross-examination, and any redirect examination and recross-examination, should gather up any materials he or she brought to court that have not been attached, smile and nod to the judge for the courtesy of appearing in the court, nod and smile to the jury briefly for their attentiveness, and leave the courtroom. In certain circumstances, the expert may stop by the retaining counsel's table to see whether the witness should remain in the court building should he or she need to be recalled. If the expert witness stays in the court, the jury may wonder whether the witness has nothing else to do (whether his or her practice is not thriving) and has an interest in the case beyond a professional one. Any query to the attorney about how the case is going can be made later. The attorney still has the rest of the case to manage.

DOES THE PSYCHOLOGIST HAVE A ROLE IN THE COURTROOM?

The psychologist can contribute to the welfare of individuals seeking justice and to our courts in providing assistance in understanding technical issues. The mental health expert witness has been described sardonically as "someone who wasn't there when it happened, but who for a fee will gladly imagine what it must have been like" (Sampson, 1993, p. 69).

Wigmore (1909, p. 445) satirized Münsterberg's grand claims for psychology's role in the courtroom and challenged psychology: "Whenever the Psychologist is ready for the Courts, the Courts are ready for him." But the past decades have demonstrated that psychology does have contributions to make in the judicial arena. In entering forensic practice we must be sure that we are not just doing well for ourselves, as Bazelon (1973) criticized, but are helping the court sort through an increasingly complex technical and scientific knowledge in seeking truth. In doing so, we are fulfilling the command "Justice, justice, thou shalt pursue" (Deuteronomy 16:20).

> How can the jury judge between two statements each founded upon an experience confessedly foreign in kind to their own? It is just because they are incompetent for such a task that the expert is necessary at all. (Judge Learned Hand, 1901, p. 54)

REFERENCES

American Bar Association. (1989). *ABA criminal justice mental health standards.* Washington, DC: Author.

American Psychological Association. (1993). Record keeping guidelines. *American Psychologist, 48,* 984–986.

Bailey, C. S. (1995). Hearsay changes under the proposed Alabama Rules of Evidence. *Journal of the Alabama Academy of Science, 66,* 137–147.

Bazelon, D. L. (1973). Psychologists in corrections: Are they doing good for the offender or well for themselves? In S. L. Brodsky (Ed.), *Psychologists in the criminal justice system* (pp. 149–154). Urbana: University of Illinois Press.

Berne, E. (1964). *Games people play.* New York: Penguin.

Binder, D. F. (1975). *The hearsay handbook: The hearsay rule and its 40 exceptions.* New York: McGraw-Hill/Shephard's Citations.

Blau, T. H. (1987). *The psychologist as expert witness.* New York: Wiley.

Blau, T. H. (1998). *The psychologist as expert witness* (2nd ed.). New York: Wiley.

Blau, T. H., & Alberts, F. L., Jr. (2004). *The forensic documentation sourcebook.* Hoboken, NJ: Wiley.

Brodsky, S. L. (1991). *Testifying in court: Guidelines and maxims for the expert.* Washington, DC: American Psychological Association.

Brown v. Board of Education, 347 U.S. 483 (1954).

Capra, D. J. (1998). The Daubert puzzle. *Georgia Law Review, 32,* 699–782.

Champagne, A., Shuman, D. W., & Whitaker, E. (1996). The problem with empirical examination of the use of court appointed experts: A report of non-findings. *Behavioral Sciences and the Law, 14,* 361–365.

Chapple v. Granger, 851 F. Supp. 1481 [E.D. Wash, 1994].

Committee on Ethical Guidelines for Forensic Psychologists. (1991). Specialty guidelines for forensic psychologists. *Law and Human Behavior, 15,* 655–665.

Committee on Legal Issues. (1996). Strategies for private practitioners coping with subpoenas of compelled testimony for client records or test data. *Professional Psychology, 27,* 245–251.

Daubert v. Merrill Dow Pharmaceuticals. 509 U.S. 579 (1993).

Deleray, J. E. (1988, Summer/Spring). The right choice! *Consulting Psychology Bulletin, 40,* 9–10.

Dixon, L., & Gill, B. (2002). Changes in the standards for admitting expert evidence in federal civil cases since the Daubert decision. *Psychology, Public Policy, and Law, 8,* 251–308.

Erikson, E. H. (1950). *Childhood and society.* New York: Norton.

Federal Judicial Center. (2000). *Reference manual on scientific evidence* (2nd ed.). Washington, DC.

Federal Rules of Civil Procedure. (2003). *Title 28 United States Code the committee on judiciary, House of Representatives, 109th Congress.*

Frye v. United States, 293 F.1013 (D.C. Cir. 1923).

General Electric Company v. Joiner, 522 U.S. 136, 118 S. Ct. 512 (1997).

Godofski, O. B. (1904). *The psychology of testimony.*

Goodman-Delahunty, J. (1997). Forensic psychological expertise in the wake of Daubert. *Law and Human Behavior, 21,* 121–140.

Goodman-Delahunty, J., & Foote, W. E. (1995). Compensation for pain, suffering and other psychological injuries: The impact of Daubert on employment discrimination claims. *Behavioral Sciences and the Law, 13,* 183–206.

Greenberg, S. A., & Shuman, D. W. (1997). Irreconcilable conflict between therapeutic and forensic roles. *Professional Psychology: Research and Practice, 28,* 50–57.

Groscup, J. L., Penrod, S. D., Studebaker, C. A., & Huss, M. T. (2002). The effect of Daubert on the admissibility of expert testimony in state and federal criminal cases. *Psychology, Public Policy and Law, 8,* 339–372.

Hagen, M. A. (1997). *Whores of the court: The fraud of psychiatric testimony and the rape of American justice.* New York: HarperCollins.

Hand, L. (1901). Historical and practical considerations regarding expert testimony. *Harvard Law Review, 15*(40), 42–49.

Hess, A. K. (1999). Serving as an expert witness. In A. K. Hess & I. B. Weiner (Eds.), *The handbook of forensic psychology* (2nd ed., pp. 521–555). New York: Wiley.

Huber, P. W. (1991). *Galileo's revenge: Junk science in the courtroom.* New York: Basic Books.

Jenkins v. United States 307 F.2d 637 (D.C. App. 1962).

Kovera, M. B., Russano, M. B., & McAuliff, B. D. (2002). Assessment of the commonsense psychology underlying Daubert: Legal decision-makers' ability to evaluate expert evidence in hostile work environment cases. *Psychology, Public Policy and Law, 8,* 180–200.

Krafka, C., Dunn, M. A., Johnson, M. T., Cecil, J., & Miletich, D. (2002). Judge and attorney experiences, practices, and concerns regarding expert testimony in federal civil trials. *Psychology, Public Policy, and Law, 8,* 309–332.

Kumho Tire Co. v. Carmichael, 526 U.S., 119 S. Ct. 1167 (1999).

Lawrence, L. (1997, July 24). C. C. Wang: The painter as supercollector. *Wall Street Journal,* p. A16.

Matson, J. V. (1994). *Effective expert witnessing* (2nd ed.). Boca Raton, FL: Lewis.

McCormick, C. T., Elliott, F. W., & Sutton, Jr., J. F. (1981). *Cases and materials on evidence* (5th ed.). St. Paul, MN: West.

McElhaney, J. W. (1997, May). Terms of enlightenment: Articulate expert witnesses help jurors visualize facts. *American Bar Association Journal,* 82–83.

McLeod, P. L., & Rosenthal, R. (1983). Micromonentary movement and the decoding of face and body cues. *Journal of Nonverbal Behavior, 8,* 83–90.

Merenbach, D. G., & Stephen, A. (1993). *How to be an expert witness: Credibility in oral testimony.* Santa Barbara, CA: Fithian Press.

Millon, T. (1969). *Modern psychopathology.* Philadelphia: Saunders.

Monahan, J. (Ed.). (1980). *Who is the client?* Washington, DC: American Psychological Association.

Münsterberg, H. (1908). *On the witness stand.* New York: Doubleday.

Perrin, G. I., & Sales, B. D. (1994). Forensic standards in the American Psychological Association's new ethics code. *Professional Psychology, 25,* 376–381.

Perrin, L. T. (1997). Expert witnesses under Rules 703 and 803(4) of the Federal Rules of Evidence: Separating the wheat from the chaff. *Indiana Law Journal, 72,* 939–1014.

Reed, J. E. (1996). Fixed vs. flexible neuropsychological test batteries under the Daubert standard for the admissibility of scientific evidence. *Behavioral Sciences and the Law, 14,* 315–322.

Rothstein, P. F. (1981). *Evidence in a nutshell: State and federal rules.* St. Paul, MN: West.

Sampson, K. (1993). The use and misuse of expert evidence in the courts. *Judicature, 77,* 68–76.

Schank, J. A., & Skovholt, T. M. (1997). Dual-relationship dilemmas of rural and small-community psychologists. *Professional Psychology, 28,* 44–49.

Shuman, D. W. (1993). The use of empathy in forensic examinations. *Ethics and Behavior, 3*, 289–302.

Singer, M. T., & Nievod, A. (1987). Consulting and testifying in court. In I. B. Weiner & A. K. Hess (Eds.), *The handbook of forensic psychology* (pp. 529–554). New York: Wiley.

Singer, R. (1995, August). Overcoming expert witness codependency. In A. M. Horton, Jr. (Chair), *Forensic neuropsychology: Detecting malingering and coping with cross-examination.* Symposium conducted at the annual convention of the American Psychological Association, New York.

Slobogin, C. (1999). The admissibility of behavioral science information in criminal trials: From primitivism to Daubert to voice. *Psychology, Public Policy, and Law, 5*, 100–110.

Sonne, J. L. (1994). Multiple relationships: Does the new ethics code answer the right questions? *Professional Psychology, 25*, 336–343.

Sporer, S. L. (1997). The origins of the psychology of testimony. In W. G. Bringmann, H. E. Luck, R. Miller, & C. E. Early (Eds.), *A pictorial history of psychology* (pp. 476–479). Chicago: Quintessence Publishing.

Wellman, F. L. (1936). *The art of cross-examination* (4th ed., rev. and enlarged). New York: Macmillan.

Wigmore, J. (1909). Professor Münsterberg and the psychology of testimony: Being a report of the case of Cokestone v. Münsterberg. *Illinois Law Review, 3*, 399–445.

Worthington, D. L., Stallard, M. J., Price, J. M., & Goss, P. M. (2002). Hindsight bias, Daubert, and the silicone breast implant litigation: Making the case for court-appointed experts in complex medical and scientific limitation. *Psychology, Public Policy and Law, 8*, 154–179.

Ziskin, J. (1981). *Coping with psychiatric and psychological testimony.* Beverly Hills, CA: Law and Psychology Press.

Ziskin, J., & Faust, D. (1995). *Coping with psychiatric and psychological testimony.* Beverly Hills, CA: Law and Psychology Press.

PART SIX

INTERVENING WITH OFFENDERS

CHAPTER 23

Punishments and Alternate Routes to Crime Prevention

JOAN McCORD

THREE DEVELOPMENTS have contributed to the appearance of a new face in crime prevention over the past decade. The first has been a noticeable increase in the public's willingness to punish juveniles with increasing severity. Some countries that had considered juveniles as typically in need of treatment, rather than punishment, began to respond to juvenile crime with specified punishments that included incarceration (Pfeiffer, 1998). England and Wales, for example, enacted the U.K. Criminal Justice and Public Order Act of 1984, which, augmented by the U.K. Crime and Disorder Act of 1998, placed juveniles at risk for long-term incarceration. In the United States, with the exception of Nebraska, every state has made it easier to transfer juveniles to adult court or increased the punitive element of juvenile justice (McCord, Widom, & Crowell, 2001).

The second development has been the advent of the Campbell Collaboration, an international group of researchers who link results of studies regarding particular forms of intervention to a general assessment of results that could be useful in making policy. The Campbell Collaboration was officially launched in February 2000 to "prepare, maintain and make accessible systematic reviews of research on the effects of social and educational interventions." Named in honor of the influential psychologist Donald T. Campbell, who wrote effectively about the need for sound evidence to inform policy and practice decisions, the Campbell Collaboration is an outgrowth of the Cochrane Collaboration, a reviewing organization for medical practice. The Crime and Justice Group, one of three substantive groups under the Campbell Collaboration rubric (the others being Social Welfare and Education), has commissioned systematic reviews on such topics as street lighting and "scared straight" approaches to crime prevention. When appropriately carried out, systematic reviews overcome biases produced by relying only on published studies. They provide a broader picture of the evidence than would be given by relying on single studies and, because they focus on combining results, can build general results from smaller studies. Thus, systematic reviews are expected to provide reasonable bases for estimating probable effects in a variety of environments (Farrington & Petrosino, 2001).

The third development has been recognition that interventions to reduce crime have had some adverse effects, particularly when these bring young misbehaving teenagers together (McCord, 2003). Adverse effects have been found in counseling programs, in programs that attempt to target lack of social skills among delinquents, in programs that provide after school activities for youth, and in programs that have sought to deal specific messages to youth that might inspire them to avoid further misbehavior.

These three developments have not radically altered the general picture of crime reduction policies as requiring, at the individual level, either punishments or treatments in order to deter crime. These approaches, those that are punitive and those oriented toward treatment, have been based on a conception of crime as developing from a flawed character—one for which the flaws have probably been of long standing.

Indeed, contemporary research appears to feed a view that character flaws account for much of the crime that troubles our society. That research has shown that misbehaving children often become adolescent delinquents, and adolescent delinquents tend to become adult criminals. Evidence for this generalization comes from longitudinal studies in London (Farrington, 1986), Finland (Pulkkinen, 1983), St. Louis (Robins & Ratcliff, 1979), Massachusetts (McCord, 1994), Chicago (McCord & Ensminger, 2003), and New Zealand (Moffitt & Caspi, 2001).

The evidence of continuity seems to support conflicting intervention strategies. On the one hand, strategists have argued that juvenile delinquents have continued their criminal activities because they have not sufficiently understood the negative consequences of crime. On the other hand, if crime is a result of personality deficiencies based on faulty socialization, reformative practices might be justified. Crime reduction, according to this second view, might depend on both avoiding setting in motion self-fulfilling prophecies and training parents or their offspring to behave better.

This review first considers evidence about the effectiveness of punishment as a deterrent to further crimes. It then considers evidence about diversion as a deterrent. After showing that neither increases in punishments nor diversion programs show much promise for decreasing crime, this chapter considers evidence about effects of several types of approaches to crime prevention before concluding that it is time to reconsider what we know and need to learn about crime prevention.

PUNISHMENT AS PREVENTION

The view that fear of punishment reduces crime is as old as Western thought. Plato (Plato, 1956) attributed to Protagoras the argument:

> He who desires to inflict rational punishment does not retaliate for a past wrong which cannot be undone; he has regard to the future, and is desirous that the

man who is punished and he who sees him punished may be deterred from doing wrong again.

During the eighteenth century, Beccaria (1764/1963) and Bentham (1789/1988) placed this view at the foundation of criminology.

If fear of punishment deters crime, increasing sanctions should reduce criminality. So obvious had the link between pain and motivation appeared that its scientific scrutiny awaited the second half of the twentieth century. Measures of the relationship between criminal activities and indices of the certainty and severity of punishment therefore offered promise for testing the role of hedonic calculations in motivations for crime.

Criminologists have bifurcated expected effects of punishment: Those that influence the punished are considered to be specific deterrents; those that influence others who might commit crimes are considered to be general deterrents. As a specific deterrent, punishment is expected to prevent repetitions. When repetition occurs, theory suggests that punishment has been too lenient. This view has a deceptively obvious appearance. Yet, several studies show that severity of sanction is not monotonically related to rates of recidivism (e.g., Crowther, 1969; Glaser & Gordon, 1990; McCord, 1985; Sherman, 1992; Wolfgang, Figlio, & Sellin, 1972). Indeed, Doob and Webster (2003) conclude their review of the deterrence literature with the suggestion that varying sentence severity within plausible limits simply has no effect on crime rates.

Possibly, criminals who receive long sentences learn to accept the procriminal values expressed by convicts (Glaser, 1969). Possibly, longer sentences increase resentment or decrease the socializing values that could control aggressive desires, driving further antisocial development. Possibly, as the opponent process theory suggests, punishments or the rewards of criminality acquire positive incentive value through time (Rosellini & Lashley, 1992; Solomon, 1980). Or, perhaps, punishments are irrelevant, serving only to endorse the image of "hardman" that many criminals find desirable (Katz, 1988).

Although severe punishments seem no more effective as crime deterrents than mild ones, the fear of pain continues to be thought of as an essential motivator. This belief may account for the widespread acceptance of a program in New Jersey that received publicity under the title Scared Straight (Heeren & Shichor, 1984; J. G. Miller & Hoelter, 1979). In that program, lifers dramatically showed young delinquents about life in prison. Despite its popularity, however, careful evaluations have shown the Scared Straight approach to be ineffective in preventing crime (Buchner & Chesney-Lind, 1983; R. V. Lewis, 1983). In fact, when Scared Straight programs were subjected to meta-analysis in the Cochrane and Campbell Collaboration process, Petrosino and his colleagues concluded that the approach created more harm than good (Petrosino, Turpin-Petrosino, & Buehler, 2003). Nevertheless, such programs continue to be popular, and, partly because of the ubiquitous assumption that punishment will deter crime, a further review of the evidence follows.

If street crimes are committed by youngsters proving their courage, perhaps confirming the risks they are taking should not be expected to deter them. Perhaps, too, when people consider whether to commit a crime, they ignore potential sanctions. Although the latter hypothesis cannot be tested directly, Carroll (1982) tested it indirectly. He asked both offenders and nonoffenders to evaluate "crime opportunities" that varied in relation to amount of potential gain, severity of possible punishment, probability of gain, and probability of punishment. The results suggest that most people consider only one of the four features when evaluating opportunities. Participants in the study were, within the ranges considered, more likely to consider the amount or probability of gain than the amount or probability of punishment.

Effective punishments would seem to require that the individual at risk for punishment knows what would be punished. Studies of young children suggest that the timing of punishment as well as its regularity influence this knowledge (Bandura & Walters, 1963; Parke, 1969). The criminal justice system does not lend itself to providing clear and consistent signals for learning what society considers wrong. In an interesting discussion of this issue, Moffitt (1983) suggests that court delays, rewards for successfully executing crimes, and the sporadic nature of apprehension reduce the likelihood that legal sanctions can influence recidivism.

Fear of punishment could be ineffective in deterring further crime among criminals and nevertheless effectively reduce the probability that others would commit crimes. The Uniform Crime Reports seemed to provide a means for testing this general deterrence effect. In 1969, Tittle reported the results of an analysis of the Uniform Crime Reports for the years 1959 to 1963. He showed strong negative correlations between crime rates and his measure of the certainty of punishment, the ratio of convictions to crime rates. Using average length of sentence to measure severity, Tittle found a weak but positive correlation between severity of sanction and crime rate. Chiricos and Waldo (1970), however, reanalyzed the data and contested the conclusion that anything other than chance relationships between crime rates and either certainty or severity had been discovered.

A rash of studies followed. Many, like the one by Antunes and Hunt (1973), used data from the Uniform Crime Reports. Antunes and Hunt defined the ratio of prison admissions to crimes known to the police in the prior year as their measure of certainty. Median length of prison sentence provided their measures of severity. Using data for 1959 to 1960 as evidence of homicide, sex crimes, robbery, assault, burglary, larceny, and auto theft, they tested five linear models. Models predicting crime rates from certainty of punishment supported the hypothesis that a threat of punishment reduces crime. Models based on severity, however, suggested that increases in severity of punishment increased crime rates. As possible explanations for these increases, Antunes and Hunt suggested stigmatization, alienation, and a heightened sense of injustice.

Uses of official records of crime to study the effects of punishment have three major problems. First, official crime rates do not accurately measure crime. At a minimum, the records reflect the behavior of victims, police, and judges as well as the behavior of criminals (Ebbesen & Konecni, 1982; Goldkamp & Gottfredson, 1985; M. S. Greenberg, Wilson, & Mills, 1982; McCord, 1997). Second, correlational approaches to causality cannot uncover essential linkages between events. The direction and size of correlations between crime rates and other social factors depend on the statistical conditions under which the correlations are assessed (D. F. Greenberg & Kessler, 1982b). Third, motivation may have no relation to the reality being measured through official statistics. Motivation depends, at least in part, on how individuals perceive their opportunities. These problems and research generated in attempts to deal with them are discussed later in this chapter.

Crime and clearance rates are used to assess police and prosecutor efficiency. Not surprisingly, they are subject to manipulation for political purposes. Nagin (1978) illustrated this by comparing recorded crimes, clearances, and clearance rates before and after a change of administration in New York City. His computations show that although the number of robberies cleared increased 9% between 1965 and 1966, the clearance rate declined 58% over that period of time. Police discretion and plea bargaining add further noise to what might appear to be objective measures of deterrence.

Researchers have used records of fatal automobile crashes as indirect measures of drunken driving. Ross (1982) used interrupted time series analyses to detect effects of changes in laws related to driving under the influence of alcohol. He reviewed effects of such changes in Norway, Sweden, Great Britain, Canada, Holland, France, New Zealand, Australia, Finland, and the United States. That review failed to show a reduction in accidents attributable to increasing the severity of punishment. In a more recent review of the effects of laws against drunk driving, Ross (1992, p. 59) concluded: "The increasing popularity of mandatory jailing laws in the United States offers a broad and diverse field on which to look for deterrent impacts, and the findings are in general unfavorable." Increasing the perceived certainty of punishment (e.g., through campaigns to enforce laws against driving while intoxicated and checkpoints to identify the intoxicated), however, appears to have some deterrent value.

Changes in the social climate lead to changes in the law. These social changes may, of course, account for either presence or absence of apparent effects of changes in the law. Sadly, few studies have succeeded in providing adequate control groups and appropriate measures of crime (Sherman et al., 1997; Zimring, 1978). To avoid contamination among measures, one would like to manipulate threats of punishment experimentally, using random assignment or matched controls. Then, if crime could be measured accurately before and after the manipulation, it might be possible to discern effects of changes in celerity, certainty, or severity of punishment.

Among the problems encountered in learning how to prevent crime is convincing relevant authorities that they do not already know how best to handle crime. Sherman and Berk (1984), for example, planned a study of misdemeanor domestic violence in which police were expected to arrest, provide advice, or separate couples according to a random assignment. Only a few officers were willing to participate in the study, and even those few sometimes failed to follow the random assignments.

Critical of correlational studies for their failure to produce reliable evidence, Cook (1977) cited "natural experiments" that tended to support a view that increasing the probability of punishment would decrease crime. Crimes decreased on New York subways during 1965 when police increased their presence. Also, crime rates remained constant in a precinct that increased police patrols by 40% while rising in the rest of the city. A 25% reduction in accidents followed closely upon advertisement of new rules regarding arrests for drunken driving embodied in the British Road Safety Act of 1967, as well.

After Chaiken (1978) discovered that police records inflated evidence of effectiveness of the patrolling policies on New York subways, Cook (1980) reviewed 11 studies based on natural experiments, concluding that they justify only modest claims. Acknowledging that identifying causal conditions in a nonexperimental setting can be extremely difficult, Cook suggested that police presence may increase the likelihood for people to report crimes.

D. F. Greenberg and Kessler (1982a) attempted the task of detecting a causal relationship between crime rates and clearance rates, as a measure of certainty, among 98 cities with populations over 25,000 in the United States. As in other studies, simple correlations based on cross-sectional rates produced evidence that could be interpreted as support for a deterrence hypothesis. Zero-order analyses showed negative correlations between clearance rates and murder, assault, robbery, and larceny. The data also suggested that crime rates might be influenced by population density, unemployment, and poverty. Because crime rates might be affecting clearance rates, Greenberg and Kessler also calculated 2- and 3-year lags between crime rates and clearance rates. Consistent effects from certainty of punishment disappeared when population, population density, unemployment, income, skewness of income, and proportion of households headed by women were taken into account.

Some of those who argue that fear of punishment will deter crime justifiably criticize the use of clearance rates to measure certainty and the use of changes in sentencing practices to measure severity. Fear depends on perceptions, and these measures of certainty and severity may be unrelated to perceived certainty or perceived severity of punishment.

Studies based on perceptions have typically asked people to estimate their likelihood of being caught and the severity of anticipated punishments. In one study, for example, students estimated penalties for two crimes: theft and smoking marijuana (Waldo & Chiricos, 1972). They also estimated the probability of arrest for these crimes. Then the students reported on their own thefts of less than $100 and their own use of marijuana. The students who reported smoking pot gave lower estimates of the likelihood of being caught and lower estimates of the likelihood of receiving a maximum penalty should they be caught. Students who reported having stolen also gave lower estimates of the likelihood of being arrested, but their estimates for penalties were not lower than those made by students who reported no thefts. The authors suggested that severity and certainty of punishment have a greater influence on crimes considered *mala prohibita* (wrong because of prohibitions) than on those considered *mala in se* (wrong in themselves).

Doubts that perceived penalties influenced use of marijuana were raised, however, when Meier and Johnson (1977) reported results from a national probability sample of adults. In the national sample, those most likely to use marijuana were also likely to perceive punishment for its use as most severe.

The data showed no relationship between perceived certainty of punishment and marijuana use.

Attempting to account for some of the inconsistencies and to specify more clearly how fear of punishment should influence crime, Grasmick and Bryjak (1980) explained the interactions that an adequate test would involve: Only if apprehension is viewed as a cost should one expect certainty of arrest to influence behavior, and only if arrest is perceived as reasonably likely should one expect estimates of severity to influence behavior. To test their refined propositions, Grasmick and Bryjak asked 400 randomly selected people to report whether they had participated in eight types of illegal activities: petty theft, theft of something worth at least $20, illegal gambling, intentional physical injury of another, income tax evasion, littering, illegal use of fireworks, and driving under the influence of alcohol. For each of these crimes, respondents estimated the probability that they would be arrested if they participated, estimated the chance they would be put in jail if arrested, and reported on the severity of problems that would be created by whatever punishment they considered a plausible consequence for participation.

As in the Meier and Johnson (1977) study, some of the evidence adduced by Grasmick and Bryjak (1980) seemed to show that more severe punishments increased criminal behavior: Those who gave larger estimates of the likelihood of being put in jail if arrested reported participating in more crimes. Analyses taking into account the severity of problems that would be encountered by probable punishments yielded a different picture. Among those whose scores for perceived certainty of punishment were in the highest quartile, subjective estimates of severity were significantly negatively correlated with participation. That is, the data supported the authors' interpretation that those who believed they were likely to be arrested if they committed crimes were influenced by their estimates of the effects of probable punishments. And, except for those who reported little anticipated inconvenience from the plausible outcome of arrest, criminal behavior appeared to be influenced by estimates of the certainty of punishment.

Estimates of the likelihood for punishment have been based on hypothetical situations in which respondents are asked to assume that they have broken the law. Jensen and Stitt (1982) added a dimension to understanding such estimates by asking respondents to report the likelihood that they would commit certain types of crimes. High school students reported their past misbehavior, their probable future misbehavior, and the probabilities of punitive responses under hypothetical conditions of misbehavior. With prior misbehavior controlled statistically, perceived risk of punitive response was related to the students' hypothetical choice to use marijuana, to become drunk, to use more serious drugs, to truant, to participate in shoplifting, to commit vandalism, and to participate in burglary.

These studies of deterrence based on perceived penalties shared a bias that attributed reported behavior to expressed beliefs. Yet none of them could show whether the respondents' behavior had influenced their beliefs about punishment or whether their beliefs about punishment had influenced their behavior. Longitudinal studies could shed light on the direction of impact.

Reasoning that prior experience would affect estimates of punishment, Paternoster, Saltzman, Chiricos, and Waldo (1982; Paternoster, Saltzman, Waldo, & Chiricos, 1982) collected data from 300 college students at two interviews. During each interview, the students reported whether they had stolen something worth less than $10 and whether they had used marijuana or hashish during the prior year. Also during each interview, the students estimated the likelihood of being caught, being arrested, and being convicted for these acts. The investigators considered correlations between time-1 reports of behavior and time-2 perceptions of punishment to be experiential effects; they considered negative correlations between time-1 perceptions of punishment and time-2 reports of behavior to be deterrent effects. Correlations of the first type were stronger than those of the second. The authors concluded that experience influences judgments about punishment and that perceptions of punishment do not influence theft or drug use.

Bishop (1984), too, used a longitudinal design to study effects of perceived sanctions. More than 2,000 high school students responded to two questionnaires asking about participation in 13 types of crimes and about three types of constraints. As measures of the constraints, students were asked to estimate the risk of legal sanctions, the risk of losing their friends if they got into trouble with the law, and the degree to which they believed in the rightness of the law. Bishop analyzed responses to the constraint questions from the first questionnaire as predictors of responses to the delinquent-involvement questions in the second questionnaire. Using multivariable linear regression, she found that all three types of constraints appeared to reduce criminality. Bishop interpreted the data as showing deterrent effects, but because she did not control for prior delinquency, the evidence does not distinguish experiential from deterrent effects.

Although not without problems, the studies based on subjective evaluations of penalties vindicated some of the assumptions of those utilitarians who believe that behavior is a consequence of attempts to maximize self-interest. These studies showed that a rational model of the relationship between perceived pain and intentional choice could give an account of some forms of criminal behavior. Yet, these studies failed to link actual punishments with motivations for crime. Unless subjective estimates of severity and certainty could be shown to be systematically related to objectively defined severity and certainty, a deterrent model of intervention would have no practical value.

In one of the few experimental studies of effects of punishment, Buikhuisen (1974) included measures of perception and an objective measure of illegal activity. He arranged to have an enforcement campaign against driving dangerous vehicles in one town. As a control, he arranged to have no enforcement campaign in a similar town. Using before and after measures based on random selection of automobiles, Buikhuisen discovered increased compliance with the law only in the town that had introduced the campaign of enforcement. There, a majority of both those who did and those who did not comply with the law were aware of the police campaign and knew of potential penalties. Those who disregarded the law were among the group most likely to appear in court for other offenses. They were younger, poorer, and less well-educated.

DIVERSION AS PREVENTION

During the first half of the twentieth century, sociologists began to notice how frequently behavior could be conceived as the playing of roles assigned by associates (Cooley, 1902/1956; Mead, 1918; Tannenbaum, 1938; Thomas, 1923). This way of portraying behavior became known as interaction theory or labeling theory. To many, it seemed reasonable that actions of the criminal justice system provided a role that could lead to further criminal behavior (Ageton & Elliott, 1974; Becker, 1963; Erikson, 1962; Garfinkel, 1956; Kitsuse, 1962; Lemert, 1951; Schur, 1971). To avoid increasing crime through expectations imposed when a youngster was adjudicated delinquent, courts were urged to avoid using a stigmatizing label, and police departments instituted a variety of crime prevention strategies that were designed to give children another chance.

Until recently, the belief that the probability for further delinquency was reduced by diverting youngsters away from the courts seemed too obvious to require evaluation. Indirectly, however, some of the studies that evaluated the deterrence model had also tested the theory that the criminal justice system increases crime through imposing expectations for misbehavior. Positive correlations between severity of sanction and crime rates could be interpreted as evidence of such a labeling process. Klein (1974) tested the theory more directly through looking at recidivism rates as a function of diversion from the criminal justice system.

In 1969, the proportions of arrested youths released by the police in Los Angeles County ranged from 2% to 82% in different departments. Klein (1974) selected the eight departments with the highest and the five departments with the lowest "diversion" rates. These 13 departments had roughly comparable recording procedures. Overall comparisons failed to show a pattern related to differences in diversion rates. When the delinquents were divided into first offenders and multiple offenders, however, a pattern emerged. For first offenders, those arrested in districts with high diversion rates were less likely to commit additional crimes during the 2-year follow-up period. For multiple offenders, those arrested in districts with low diversion rates were less likely to commit additional crimes during the 2-year follow-up period. On this evidence, it would be reasonable to conclude that a labeling effect is more likely to influence first-time offenders.

To test the generality of such a conclusion, McCord (1985) examined the criminal careers of 197 men who, as juveniles, had committed minor crimes that brought them to the attention of the police. In 1938, the police established a Crime Prevention Bureau to deflect juveniles from the courts. The Crime Prevention Bureau had processed and then released 163 of the juveniles at the time of their first encounter with the police; only 34 had been sent to court for a misdemeanor first offense. Comparison of those sent to court with those diverted through the Crime Prevention Bureau indicated neither racial nor social class bias. About half of both groups were from broken homes. Although both groups ranged in age from 7 to 17, those sent to court tended to be the older boys.

More than 30 years later, McCord (1985) gathered criminal records for the men. These records did not support the hypothesis that a court appearance would increase crime. More than half of the boys who had been given a break through the Crime Prevention Bureau (51%) were subsequently convicted for at least one index crime. Fewer than a quarter (23%) of the 26 boys who had been convicted and fined, released, or placed on probation subsequently were convicted for any index crimes. Of the 8 sent to reform school, 3 (38%) were later convicted for index crimes. The diversion project had failed to decrease criminality. But the data also offered no support for a deterrence model.

Similar results were found when Glaser and Gordon (1990) retraced 1,121 people sentenced in 1984 for assault, burglary, drug crimes, driving under the influence, theft, or indecent exposure. They compared outcomes for those given probation only, probation with financial penalties, probation with jail time, and probation with jail time as well as financial penalties. For all the crimes studied, probation with fines resulted in fewer rearrests and revocations of probation than did probation alone or with jail time. This remained true even after taking into account effects of prior arrests, prior convictions, and prior drug problems.

A movement to avoid labeling by diverting youths from the juvenile courts became popular in the United States after World War II. Studies of these projects show that many of their clients would never have appeared on court dockets. Typically, these studies report that the diversion programs tend to bring new groups of people into the criminal justice system. The Children and Young Persons' Act of 1969 reflected concern over possible effects from court processing in Great Britain. This act introduced cautioning, a formal warning procedure believed to be less serious and less stigmatizing than court processing. Farrington and Bennett (1981) studied effects of the new law by examining files of juveniles who were younger than 15 when first arrested. Their sample included 202 who had been sent to court and 705 who had been issued a police caution. Disposition appeared to have been strongly influenced by age and seriousness of the offense. Even after statistically controlling effects of sex, age, race, social class, area, and seriousness of crime, those who received police cautions were less likely than those sent to court to have been rearrested during a 34-month follow-up period. Farrington and Bennett scrutinized the records of 47 cases to learn more about the delinquents. These records included information about family size, attitudes of the parents and the juvenile, academic performance, and school behavior. Analyses indicated that the juvenile's attitude predicted both disposition and rearrest. After statistically controlling effects of these attitudes, rearrest rates following cautions appeared to be greater than those following court appearance.

Probably the most coherent study of how labeling affects juveniles has come from the West and Farrington (1977) study of 411 youths reared in London. These youngsters were interviewed about delinquent acts at ages 14 to 15, 16 to 17, and 18 to 19. When the youths turned 21, West and Farrington reviewed their court records. Farrington (1977) coordinated the court records with the self-reports of delinquency for the 383 youths who had been interviewed all three times. As measured through their own reports of crime, in agreement with the hypothesis of negative labeling effects, the convicted boys had actually committed more crimes.

To discover how the label of delinquent affected self-reported delinquency, Farrington (1977) matched 27 boys who had been first convicted between the ages of 14 and 16 to 27 boys who reported similar crimes at the age of 14 but had not been convicted. At age 16, the convicted group admitted to committing 84 more crimes. Their reports at age 16 included 251 crimes to which they had confessed at age 14 and an additional 65 crimes committed prior to age 14. At age 16, the unconvicted group confessed to 232 crimes they had previously acknowledged and added 43 to the earlier confessions. Because 41 of the 84 crimes that differentiated their self-reports at the age of 16 could be attributed to reporting errors, Farrington concluded that about half the effects of convictions were due to reduced concealment and half to increased criminal behavior.

The longitudinal study of London youths shows that effects of encounters with the court depend on the nature of these encounters. Delinquency reports of those first convicted between the ages of 18 and 21 showed practically no increase among those who had been fined as a penalty; among those who had been discharged without penalty, however, the self-reports showed marked increases (Farrington, Osborn, & West, 1978).

Data from several perspectives suggest that neither increasing the severity of punishment nor avoiding labeling youngsters has a beneficial influence on criminal behavior. In sum, the evidence has failed to support either punitive or diversionary strategies.

COUNSELING AS PREVENTION

Intervention programs have been designed with knowledge that delinquents typically have rejecting, aggressive parents (Dinitz, Scarpitti, & Reckless, 1962; Farrington, 1978; Glueck & Glueck, 1950; Gorman-Smith, Tolan, Zelli, & Huesmann, 1996; Hirschi, 1969; D. O. Lewis, Shanok, Pincus, & Glaser, 1979; McCord, 1979, 1991; Pulkkinen, 1983; Rutter, 1978). Not unreasonably, therefore, some programs have tried to provide substitutes for parental care.

One such project, the Cambridge-Somerville Youth Study, randomly assigned boys to either a treatment or a control group. The program included both "difficult" and "average" youngsters between the ages of 5 and 13. From 1939 to 1945, social workers tutored and counseled 253 boys from 232 families, assisting the boys and their families in a variety of ways (Powers & Witmer, 1951). In 1975, when the boys had become middle-aged men, their names and pseudonyms were checked through vital statistics, court and mental hospital records, and centers for treatment of alcoholism. When interviewed, many of the men in the treatment program recalled their counselors with affection, and a majority believed the program had helped them lead better lives. Yet, when compared with their matched controls who had not received help through the program, those in the treatment group fared poorly: They were more likely to have serious criminal records; to have been diagnosed manic-depressive, schizophrenic, or alcoholic; and to have died at a young age (McCord, 1978, 1992).

Other counseling programs, too, seem to have had detrimental effects. Adults who had received clinic treatment as children in St. Louis (Cass & Thomas, 1979) and in Hawaii (Werner & Smith, 1977) were less well-adjusted than their untreated peers. Discouragingly, Gersten, Langner, and Simcha-Fagan (1979) discovered that delinquents in New York were more likely to sustain delinquent activities if they had been referred for treatment. Because those referred for treatment had not been randomly selected, results of most of the negative evaluations have been treated as anomalies.

A handful of carefully designed evaluations of counseling programs suggest that such results may not be accidental. Many courts in the United States have volunteer programs to provide adult guidance to probationers. One of these, the Volunteers in Probation program, agreed to an evaluation in which consenting probationers were randomly assigned to the volunteer program or to a control group (Berger, Crowley, Gold, Gray, & Arnold, 1975). Two out of three (randomly selected) probationers received the special services of group counseling, individual counseling, and tutoring given by the volunteers. Those in the control group received the ordinary services of the court. Evaluations occurred after 6 months and again after 12 months.

Both self-reports and official records showed that participation in the program had iatrogenic effects. Those assigned to the control group and those who had been assigned to the volunteer program but had not participated in it decreased their rates of crime. Those who participated in the volunteer program, however, increased the number of crimes they reported, and their records showed increases in the number of their police contacts.

SOCIAL SKILLS TRAINING AS PREVENTION

Because of apparent deficiencies in the social skills of delinquents, many schools developed programs designed to increase self-confidence by giving students practice in discussing issues with well-adjusted peers. Typically, adult leaders guide the discussions. The programs have been called Positive Peer Culture, Peer Culture Development, and Peer Group Counseling as well as Guided Group Interaction. Gottfredson (1987) arranged to have students in public elementary and high schools randomly selected for inclusion in either the treatment or the control group of a Guided Group Interaction program. Overall, the results for elementary school children showed no effects. For the high school students, however, the Guided Group Interaction program tended to increase misbehavior and delinquency.

Negative effects from social skills training are not isolated. Nevertheless, when Lösel and Beelmann (2003) considered only those studies using a random assignment to treatment or control group for evaluating the impact of child skills training (in isolation from other types of treatment), they found a generally positive effect in terms of reducing antisocial behavior. Yet, the authors point out that they were able to find only a handful of adequate studies, and the follow-up period for which they had to settle was less than 1 year after treatment for most of the studies.

A spate of therapies have been devised in the attempt to reduce antisocial behavior. Reality therapy (Glasser, 1965) seems to be best known among them. Kaltenbach and Gazda (1975) claimed success for the approach in group practice; Yochelson and Samenow (1977) claimed success with hard-core criminals. Unfortunately, because the approach has not yet been used in a well-controlled study, conclusions about its effectiveness appear premature.

ENVIRONMENTAL MANIPULATIONS AS PREVENTION

Use of random assignment has permitted evaluation of several programs designed to affect criminality through manipulating the environment of people at high risk for crime. In one program (Reckless & Dinitz, 1972), educational environments were manipulated to provide "vulnerable" boys with programs designed to improve their self-esteem. Sixth-grade teachers in Columbus, Ohio, nominated "good" and "bad" boys. The latter were randomly assigned either to experimental or control classes in the 7th grade. The program lasted for 3 years. The experimental group received special help in reading; their discipline was based on "mutual respect"; and special lessons using role model techniques were introduced to teach them how to act. Ratings made by their teachers at the end of 9th grade suggested that the experimental boys were more cooperative, comfortable, and honest and less delinquent. However, no differences were found in the proportions who had police contacts or in the proportions committing serious index offenses. Nor were there differences in school performance, dropout rates, or school attendance.

Boys in the Ohio experiment designed by Reckless and Dinitz (1972) had been assigned to homogeneous groups of "bad" boys for their experimental treatment. Perhaps this feature of the experiment accounted for failure to show benefits—at least by objective measures. Klein (1971) discovered that programs providing gang members with group activities tended to be particularly damaging for 12- to 15-year-olds. Program activities increased cohesiveness of the gangs but also increased delinquency of the members. So clear was the evidence that Klein concluded, "There is good reason to doubt the desirability of continuing such programs or mounting new ones" (p. 119).

Dishion and Andrews (1995) used a random-assignment design to evaluate the impact of teaching techniques of family management and of focusing on peer relations and interactions. For the study, 83 boys and 75 girls, 10 to 14 years old, participated in 12 weekly 90-minute sessions focusing on their families, the teen interaction, both, or a self-directed change program. The two interventions with teen focus increased smoking and aggressive types of behavior (as measured by their teachers). Yet the family focus group improved in terms of aggressive behavior and smoking.

The U.S. Department of Labor sponsored a program testing effects of altering the social environment (Lenihan, 1977). A randomly selected group of men were given $60 a week for 13 weeks after release from prison. The men eligible for this program had committed property crimes, were under 45 years of age, had spent less than 3 months on work release, had less than $400 in savings, and were not first-time offenders. After release, those who received money were more likely to help pay for household expenses and to help support their family. The money appeared to delay return to theft. Through the 2 years of the study, fewer men who received the $780 had been arrested for theft. The beneficial effects increased with increasing age and were most dramatic among the poorest risks: those discharged without parole and poorly educated. Reports by participants suggest that the money enabled them to buy clothes, helped them feel better, and allowed them time to find a decent job. Timing of the help may have been important to its effectiveness. Evidence from a pilot project conducted by A. D. Miller and Ohlin (1985) suggests that experiences after release have a greater impact on recidivism than either background or program experiences.

One of the most promising approaches to intervention combined educating mothers in skills related to child rearing with intellectual stimulation of their young children. In 1962, a project known both as High Scope and as the Perry Preschool Program began with a random assignment of children from low-income neighborhoods to either a preschool or a no-preschool group (Berrueta-Clement, Schweinhart, Barnett, Epstein, & Weikart, 1984). Home visits where parents were taught how to augment the school program were included in the interventions for the preschool group. The two groups have been traced both in school and as young adults. Those in the preschool program were more satisfied with their experiences in school and more likely to have graduated from high school. A higher proportion of those who attended preschool were employed, and a higher proportion reported that they were self-supporting at age 19. The preschool program, including home visits, seems also to have reduced crime up to the age of 32: Those in the program had significantly fewer arrests as juveniles and as adults. Criminal records showed that the intervention group had fewer adult felony arrests and that they were less likely to have been arrested more than four times (Schweinhart, Barnes, & Weikart, 1993).

Similar benefits have been shown when parent training has been combined with child training in early primary school (McCord, Tremblay, Vitaro, & Desmarais-Gervais, 1994; Tremblay, Pagani-Kurtz, Masse, Vitaro, & Pihl, 1995; Webster-Stratton & Hammond, 1997) and in the homes of 12- to 17-year-old delinquents (Borduin, Henggeler, Hanson, & Pruitt, 1995). Tremblay and his colleagues worked with Francophone boys in Montreal whose kindergarten teachers had identified them as among the most disruptive. A randomly selected group was assigned to a 2-year treatment program in which the parents received training in family management and their children were assisted in improving their social skills. At the time of treatment, the boys were between the ages of 7 and 9. Treatment was evaluated against two control groups: One, a placebo, received attention through extensive biannual evaluations; the other received only whatever interventions were already available in the community. By age 15, the boys who had received treatment were more likely than those in either control group to be in regular school classes and less likely to have committed crimes. The program evaluated by Borduin and his colleagues attempted to empower parents by giving them skills to help address their adolescent's problems. Two hundred delinquents between the ages of 12 and 17 were randomly assigned to the treatment group or to a control group that was given individual counseling. A follow-up 4 years later indicated that the empowerment program was more successful: Fewer had been arrested, and they were less likely to have committed violent crimes.

In their preliminary systematic review of early childhood interventions that involve family management training, under the guidelines of the Campbell Collaboration, Bernazzani, Côté, and Tremblay (2001) found seven studies suitable for meta-analysis. Of those seven, four failed to demonstrate effectiveness, and only two were clearly beneficial. The authors point to the heterogeneity of training and to the general lack of adequate information regarding effective parent training.

A related approach that promises to have multiple benefits in terms of health, school performance, and employment as well as delinquency and crime has focused on intervention through home visits that help to educate mothers in child health and development while also providing educational stimulation to the infants. Although the children are still young, analyses have shown benefits in terms of behavior (Brooks-Gunn, Klebanov, Liaw, & Spiker, 1993).

An advantage of training parents in skills that improve their socializing practices is that the training may be beneficial to subsequent offspring. It is wise to remember, however, that many parent training programs fail. It is difficult to get parents who need help to participate in the programs, and, even when they do participate, many return to their old habits after a short period of time. These difficulties seem to have been overcome by some promising programs that include home visits from the time the mother is pregnant through the first 2 years of the infant's life (Olds et al., 1998; Olds, Henderson, Tatelbaum, & Chamberlin, 1986; Olds & Kitzmann, 1990; Rauh, Achenbach, Nurcombe, Howell, & Teti, 1988).

COGNITIVE APPROACHES AS PREVENTION

Several short-term evaluations have provided evidence that teaching children special skills, even without parent training, may be a valuable tool for reducing their criminality. Guerra and Slaby (1990) taught incarcerated violent offenders that aggression was often counterproductive. As compared with both a group tutored in reading and mathematics who received the same amount of attention and a no-attention control group, those who received the training regarding the counterproductivity of aggression were rated by their supervisors (who were blind regarding the treatment condition of those they rated) as less aggressive, impulsive, and inflexible.

Experiments have shown that training children to view television critically can reduce imitative aggression (Eron, 1986) and that academic tutoring can have social consequences for low-achieving children (Coie & Krehbiel, 1984). The results of experiments with such children indicate, however, that not all such training is beneficial.

Hudley and Graham (1993) taught unpopular, aggressive children how to recognize the intentions of others so that they would be less likely to attribute the intention to injure. They used role-playing techniques with nonaggressive, popular peers as teachers. Boys in 4th to 6th grade were assigned to one of three groups: the treatment group; a group having the same number of meetings, but these devoted to nonsocial problems; or a no-attention control group. Treatment lasted 6 weeks, with meetings two times a week. A month after treatment ended, an experimental session showed that the boys taught to recognize nonaggressive cues among their peers were less likely to complain about or criticize a partner whose actions frustrated them. Additionally, the teachers were more likely to recognize reduced aggressiveness among the boys trained to recognize nonaggressive cues.

Kazdin and colleagues (Kazdin, Esveldt-Dawson, French, & Unis, 1987) found that teaching problem-solving skills to hospitalized antisocial children between the ages of 7 and 13 was more effective in reducing dysfunctional behavior than was helping such children express themselves or than providing them with an equivalent amount of attention through games and talking. Although differences continued for a year posttreatment, few of the children maintained behavior within a normal range of problems.

Lipsey, Chapman, and Landenberger (2001) grouped together those approaches that aimed to correct dysfunctional and criminogenic thinking among delinquents into a meta-analysis of cognitive-behavioral programs for offenders. They were able to find 14 programs that met criteria for experimental or strong quasi-experimental designs. These studies demonstrated potential effectiveness of a cognitive-behavioral approach, but as the authors caution: "The best available research evidence supports the concept of CBT [cognitive-behavioral therapy] as an effective intervention for offenders, at least for juvenile offenders. Whether that concept can be translated into effective routine practice, however, is an open question" (p. 155).

SUMMARY

The evidence suggests that when a delinquent fails to receive penalties supporting the law, delinquency is likely to continue. Yet, the evidence does not show that serious penalties have more potent effects than mild penalties. It seems reasonable to interpret the receipt of penalties as a type of information from which youths can learn how society expects them to act.

Although a labeling effect seems to account for some criminal behavior, diversion programs have had only minor success. A recent intervention that may be particularly appropriate for reducing recidivism among juveniles has been developed from the work of Braithwaite (1989). Known both as reintegrative shaming and restorative justice, the program seeks to find a way for the guilty person to admit wrongdoing and yet to avoid being an outcast. The program is being evaluated through experimental designs in Canberra, Australia (Sherman

& Strang, 1997), and in Great Britain (personal communication). The philosophic as well as practical issues involved with this movement are described in Strang and Braithwaite (2000).

Too little is known about how to produce socialized behavior. Counseling programs have typically been ineffective or damaging. Family training may be helpful, though keeping families in programs long enough to change parental behavior is a problem. Some, but not all, educational programs have had beneficial results. Those that seem effective should be replicated. New programs, designed for appropriate evaluation, should be started. Perhaps more important, new ways of thinking about how people become criminals and how they turn from crime to more socially accepted forms of behavior need to be considered (Laub & Sampson, 2003; McCord, 2004; Messner & Rosenfeld, 2004; Wikstrom, 2004). As a consequence, it may become possible to regard intervention as crime prevention.

REFERENCES

Ageton, S., & Elliott, D. S. (1974). The effects of legal processing on delinquent orientations. *Social Problems, 22,* 87–100.

Antunes, G., & Hunt, A. L. (1973). The impact of certainty and severity of punishment on levels of crime in American states: An extended analysis. *Journal of Criminal Law and Criminology, 64,* 489–493.

Bandura, A., & Walters, R. H. (1963). *Social learning and personality development.* New York: Holt, Rinehart and Winston.

Beccaria, C. B. (1764/1963). *On crimes and punishments.* Indianapolis: Bobbs-Merrill.

Becker, H. S. (1963). *Outsiders.* Glencoe, IL: Free Press.

Bentham, J. (1789/1988). *The principles of morals and legislation.* Buffalo, NY: Prometheus.

Berger, R. J., Crowley, J. E., Gold, M., Gray, J., & Arnold, M. S. (1975). *Experiment in a juvenile court: A study of a program of volunteers working with juvenile probationers.* Ann Arbor, MI: Institute for Social Research the University of Michigan.

Bernazzani, O., Côté, C., & Tremblay, R. E. (2001, November). Early parent training to prevent disruptive behavior problems and delinquency in children. *Annals of the American Academy of Political and Social Sciences, 578,* 90–103.

Berrueta-Clement, J. R., Schweinhart, L. J., Barnett, W. S., Epstein, A. S., & Weikart, D. P. (1984). *Changed lives: The effects of the Perry Preschool Program on youths through age 19.* Ypsilanti, MI: High/Scope Press.

Bishop, D. M. (1984). Legal and extralegal barriers to delinquency. *Criminology, 22*(3), 403–419.

Borduin, C. M., Henggeler, S. W., Hanson, C. L., & Pruitt, J. A. (1985). Verbal problem solving in families of father-absent and father-present delinquent boys. *Child and Family Behavior Therapy, 7*(2), 51–63.

Braithwaite, J. (1989). *Crime, shame and reintegration.* Cambridge, England: Cambridge University Press.

Brooks-Gunn, J., Klebanov, P. K., Liaw, F. R., & Spiker, D. (1993). Enhancing the development of low-birthweight, premature infants: Changes in cognition and behavior over the first 3 years. *Child Development, 64*(3), 736–753.

Buchner, J. C., & Chesney-Lind, M. (1983). Dramatic cures for juvenile crime: An evaluation of a prisoner-run delinquency prevention program. *Criminal Justice and Behavior, 10*(2), 227–247.

Buikhuisen, W. (1974). General deterrence: Research and theory. *Abstracts on Criminology and Penology, 14*(3), 285–298.

Carroll, J. S. (1982). The decision to commit the crime. In J. Konecni & E. B. Ebbesen (Eds.), *The criminal justice system* (pp. 49–67). San Francisco: Freeman.

Cass, L. K., & Thomas, C. B. (1979). *Childhood pathology and later adjustment.* New York: Wiley.

Chaiken, J. M. (1978). What is known about deterrent effects of police activities. In J. A. Cramer (Ed.), *Preventing crime.* Beverly Hills, CA: Sage.

Chiricos, T. G., & Waldo, G. P. (1970). Punishment and crime: An examination of some empirical evidence. *Social Problems, 18*(2), 200–217.

Coie, J. D., & Krehbiel, G. (1984). Effects of academic tutoring on the social status of low-achieving, socially rejected children. *Child Development, 55,* 1465–1478.

Cook, P. J. (1977). Punishment and crime: A critique of current findings concerning the preventive effects of punishment. *Law and Contemporary Problems, 41,* 164–204.

Cook, P. J. (1980). The clearance rate as a measure of criminal justice system effectiveness. In E. Bittner & S. L. Messinger (Eds.), *Criminology review yearbook* (Vol. 2, pp. 669–676). Beverly Hills, CA: Sage.

Cooley, C. H. (1902/1956). *Human nature and the social order.* New York: Schocken.

Crowther, C. (1969). Crimes, penalties, and legislatures. *Annals of the American Academy of Political and Social Science, 381,* 147–158.

Dinitz, S., Scarpitti, F. R., & Reckless, W. C. (1962). Delinquency vulnerability: A cross group and longitudinal analysis. *American Sociological Review, 37*(4), 515–517.

Dishion, T. J., & Andrews, D. W. (1995). Preventing escalation in problem behaviors with high-risk young adolescents: Immediate and 1-year outcomes. *Journal of Consulting and Clinical Psychology, 63*(4), 538–548.

Doob, A., & Webster, C. M. (2003). Sentence severity and crime: Accepting the Null hypothesis. In M. Tonry (Ed.), *Crime and justice: A review of research* (Vol. 30, pp. 143–195). Chicago: University of Chicago Press.

Ebbesen, E. B., & Konecni, V. J. (1982). Social psychology and the law: A decision-making approach to the criminal justice system. In J. Konecni & E. B. Ebbesen (Eds.), *The criminal justice system* (pp. 3–23). San Francisco: Freeman.

Erikson, K. T. (1962). Notes on the sociology of deviance. *Social Problems, 9*(3), 307–314.

Eron, L. D. (1986). Interventions to mitigate the psychological effects of media violence on aggressive behavior. *Journal of Social Issues, 42*(3), 155–169.

Farrington, D. P. (1977). The effects of public labeling. *British Journal of Criminology, 17,* 112–125.

Farrington, D. P. (1978). The family backgrounds of aggressive youths. In L. A. Hersov & M. Berger (Eds.), *Aggression and antisocial behaviour in childhood and adolescence* (pp. 73–93). Oxford: Pergamon Press.

Farrington, D. P. (1986). Stepping stones to adult criminal careers. In D. Olweus, J. Block, & M. Radke-Yarrow (Eds.), *Development of antisocial and prosocial behavior* (pp. 359–384). New York: Academic Press.

Farrington, D. P., & Bennett, T. (1981). Police cautioning of juveniles in London. *British Journal of Criminology, 21,* 123–135.

Farrington, D. P., Osborn, S. G., & West, D. J. (1978). The persistence of labeling effects. *British Journal of Criminology, 18,* 277–284.

Farrington, D. P., & Petrosino, A. (2001, November). The Campbell collaboration crime and justice group. *Annals of the American Academy of Political and Social Science, 578,* 35–49.

Garfinkel, H. (1956). Conditions of successful degradation ceremonies. *American Journal of Sociology, 61,* 420–424.

Gersten, J. C., Langner, T. S., & Simcha-Fagan, O. (1979). Developmental patterns of types of behavioral disturbance and secondary prevention. *International Journal of Mental Health, 7,* 132–149.

Glaser, D. (1969). *The effectiveness of a prison and parole system.* New York: Bobbs-Merrill.

Glaser, D., & Gordon, M. A. (1990). Profitable penalties for lower level courts. *Judicature, 73*(5), 248–252.

Glasser, W. (1965). *Reality therapy.* New York: Harper & Row.

Glueck, S., & Glueck, E. T. (1950). *Unraveling juvenile delinquency.* New York: Commonwealth Fund.

Goldkamp, J. S., & Gottfredson, M. R. (1985). *Policy guidelines for bail.* Philadelphia: Temple University Press.

Gorman-Smith, D., Tolan, P. H., Zelli, A., & Huesmann, L. R. (1996). The relation of family functioning to violence among inner-city minority youths. *Journal of Family Psychology, 10*(2), 115–129.

Gottfredson, G. D. (1987). Peer group interventions to reduce the risk of delinquent behavior: A selective review and a new evaluation. *Criminology, 25*(3), 671–714.

Grasmick, H. G., & Bryjak, G. J. (1980). The deterrent effect of perceived severity of punishment. *Social Forces, 59*(2), 471–491.

Greenberg, D. F., & Kessler, R. C. (1982a). The effect of arrests on crime: A multivariate panel analysis. *Social Forces, 60*(3), 771–790.

Greenberg, D. F., & Kessler, R. C. (1982b). Model specification in dynamic analyses of crime deterrence. In J. Hagan (Ed.), *Deterrence reconsidered* (pp. 15–32). Beverly Hills, CA: Sage.

Greenberg, M. S., Wilson, C. E., & Mills, M. K. (1982). Victim decision-making: An experimental approach. In J. Konecni & E. B. Ebbesen (Eds.), *The criminal justice system* (pp. 73–94). San Francisco: Freeman.

Guerra, N. G., & Slaby, R. G. (1990). Cognitive mediators of aggression in adolescent offenders: 2. Intervention. *Developmental Psychology, 26*(2), 269–277.

Heeren, J., & Shichor, D. (1984). Mass media and delinquency prevention: The case of "scared straight." *Deviant Behavior, 5,* 375–386.

Hirschi, T. (1969). *Causes of delinquency.* Berkeley: University of California Press.

Hudley, C., & Graham, S. (1993). An attributional intervention to reduce peer-directed aggression among African-American boys. *Child Development, 64*(1), 124–138.

Jensen, G. F., & Stitt, B. G. (1982). Words and misdeeds. In J. Hagan (Ed.), *Deterrence reconsidered* (pp. 33–54). Beverly Hills, CA: Sage.

Kaltenbach, R. F., & Gazda, G. M. (1975). Reality therapy in groups. In G. M. Gazda (Ed.), *Basic approaches to group psychotherapy and group counseling* (pp. 196–233). Springfield, IL: Charles C. Thomas.

Katz, J. (1988). *Seductions of crimes.* New York: Basil Blackwell.

Kazdin, A. E., Esveldt-Dawson, K., French, N. H., & Unis, A. L. (1987). Problem-solving skills training and relationship therapy in the treatment of antisocial child behavior. *Journal of Consulting and Clinical Psychology, 55*(1), 76–85.

Kitsuse, J. I. (1962). Societal reaction to deviant behavior. *Social Problems, 9,* 247–256.

Klein, M. W. (1971). *Street gangs and street workers.* Englewood Cliffs, NJ: Prentice-Hall.

Klein, M. W. (1974). Labeling, deterrence and recidivism: A study of police dispositions of juvenile offenders. *Social Problems, 22,* 292–303.

Laub, J. H., & Sampson, R. J. (2003). *Shared beginnings, divergent lives: Delinquent boys to age 70.* Cambridge, MA: Harvard University Press.

Lemert, E. (1951). *Social pathology.* New York: McGraw-Hill.

Lenihan, K. J. (1977). *Unlocking the second gate: The role of financial assistance in reducing recidivism among ex-prisoners* (Monograph 45). Washington, DC: U.S. Department of Labor Relations and Development.

Lewis, D. O., Shanok, S. S., Pincus, J., & Glaser, G. H. (1979). Violent juvenile delinquents. *Journal of the American Academy of Child Psychiatry, 18,* 307–319.

Lewis, R. V. (1983). Scared straight: California style. *Criminal Justice and Behavior, 10*(2), 284–289.

Lipsey, M. W., Chapman, G. L., & Landenberger, N. A. (2001, November). Cognitive-behavioral programs for offenders. *Annals of the American Academy of Political and Social Science, 578,* 144–157.

Lösel, F., & Beelmann, A. (2003, May). Effects of child skills training in preventing antisocial behavior: A systematic review of randomized evaluations. *Annals of the American Academy of Political and Social Sciences, 587,* 84–109.

McCord, J. (1978). A thirty-year follow-up of treatment effects. *American Psychologist, 33*(3), 284–289.

McCord, J. (1979). Some child-rearing antecedents of criminal behavior in adult men. *Journal of Personality and Social Psychology, 37,* 1477–1486.

McCord, J. (1985). Deterrence and the light touch of the law. In D. P. Farrington & J. Gunn (Eds.), *Reactions to crime: The public, the police, courts, and prisons* (pp. 73–85). London: Wiley.

McCord, J. (1991). Family relationships, juvenile delinquency, and adult criminality. *Criminology, 29*(3), 397–417.

McCord, J. (1992). The Cambridge-Somerville study: A pioneering longitudinal-experimental study of delinquency prevention. In J. McCord & R. E. Tremblay (Eds.), *Preventing antisocial behavior: Interventions from birth through adolescence* (pp. 196–206). New York: Guilford Press.

McCord, J. (1994). Family socialization and antisocial behavior: Searching for causal relationships in longitudinal research. In E. G. M. Weitekamp & H.-J. Kerner (Eds.), *Cross-national longitudinal research on human development and criminal behavior* (pp. 177–188). Dordrecht, The Netherlands: Kluwer Press.

McCord, J. (1997). Placing American urban violence in context. In J. McCord (Ed.), *Violence and childhood in the inner city.* New York: Cambridge University Press.

McCord, J. (2003, May). Cures that harm: Unanticipated outcomes of crime prevention programs. *Annals of the American Academy of Political and Social Sciences, 587,* 16–30.

McCord, J. (2004). Toward a theory of criminal responsibility. In J. McCord (Ed.), *Beyond empiricism: Institutions and intentions in the study of crime—Advances in criminological theory* (Vol. 13). Picataway, NJ: Transaction Publishers.

McCord, J., & Ensminger, P. (2003). Racial discrimination and violence: A longitudinal perspective. In D. Hawkins (Ed.), *Violent crime: Assessing race and ethnic differences* (pp. 319–330). New York: Cambridge University Press.

McCord, J., Tremblay, R. E., Vitaro, F., & Desmarais-Gervais, L. (1994). Boys' disruptive behavior, school adjustment, and delinquency: The Montreal prevention experiment. *International Journal of Behavioral Development, 17*(4), 739–752.

McCord, J., Widom, C. S., & Crowell, N. A. (Eds.). (2001). *Juvenile crime, juvenile justice.* Washington, DC: National Academy Press.

Mead, G. H. (1918). The psychology of punitive justice. *American Journal of Sociology, 23,* 577–602.

Meier, R. F., & Johnson, W. T. (1977). Deterrence as social control: The legal and extralegal production of conformity. *American Sociological Review, 42,* 292–304.

Messner, S. F., & Rosenfeld, R. (2004). Institutionalizing criminological theory. In J. McCord (Ed.), *Beyond empiricism: Institutions and intentions in the study of crime—Advances in criminological theory* (Vol. 13). Picataway, NJ: Transaction Publishers.

Miller, A. D., & Ohlin, L. E. (1985). *Delinquency and community: Creating opportunities and controls.* Beverly Hills, CA: Sage.

Miller, J. G., & Hoelter, H. H. (1979). *Oversight on scared straight* (Prepared testimony). Washington, DC: U.S. Government Printing Office.

Moffitt, T. E. (1983). The learning theory model of punishment: Implications for delinquency deterrence. *Criminal Justice and Behavior, 10*(2), 131–158.

Moffitt, T. E., & Caspi, A. (2001). Childhood predictors differentiate life-course-persistent and adolescent-limited antisocial pathways, among males and females. *Development and Psychopathology, 13,* 335–375.

Nagin, D. (1978). General deterrence: A review of the empirical evidence. In A. Blumstein, J. Cohen, & D. Nagin (Eds.), *Deterrence and incapacitation: Estimating the effects of criminal sanctions on crime rates* (pp. 95–139). Washington, DC: National Academy of Sciences.

Olds, D., Henderson, C. R., Jr., Cole, R., Eckenrode, J., Kitzman, H., Luckey, D., et al. (1998). Long-term effects of nurse home visitation on children's criminal and anti-social behavior: 15 year follow-up of a randomized controlled trial. *Journal of the American Medical Association, 280*(14), 1238–1244.

Olds, D. L., Henderson, C. R., Tatelbaum, R., & Chamberlin, R. (1986, January). Improving delivery of prenatal care and outcomes of pregnancy: A randomized trial of nurse home visitation. *Pediatrics, 77*(1), 16–28.

Olds, D. L., & Kitzmann, H. (1990, July). Can home visitation improve the health of women and children at environmental risk? *Pediatrics, 86*(1), 108–116.

Parke, R. D. (1969). Effectiveness of punishment as an interaction of intensity, timing, agent nurturance, and cognitive structuring. *Child Development, 40,* 213–235.

Paternoster, R., Saltzman, L. E., Chiricos, T. G., & Waldo, G. P. (1982). Perceived risk and deterrence: Methodological artifacts in perceptual deterrence research. *Journal of Criminal Law and Criminology, 73*(3), 1238–1258.

Paternoster, R., Saltzman, L. E., Waldo, G. P., & Chiricos, T. G. (1982). Causal ordering in deterrence research. In J. Hagan (Ed.), *Deterrence reconsidered* (pp. 55–70). Beverly Hills, CA: Sage.

Petrosino, A., Turpin-Petrosino, C., & Buehler, J. (2003, September). Scared straight and other juvenile awareness programs for preventing juvenile delinquency: A systematic review of the randomized experimental evidence. *Annals of the American Academy of Political and Social Science, 589,* 41–62.

Pfeiffer, C. (1998). Juvenile crime and violence in Europe. In M. Tonry (Ed.), *Crime and justice: A review of research* (Vol. 23, pp. 255–328). Chicago: University of Chicago Press.

Plato. (1956). *Protagoras* (B. Jowett, Trans.; revised by M. Ostwald). Indianapolis: Bobbs-Merrill.

Powers, E., & Witmer, H. (1951). *An experiment in the prevention of delinquency: The Cambridge-Somerville youth study.* New York: Columbia University Press.

Pulkkinen, L. (1983). Search for alternatives to aggression in Finland. In A. P. Goldstein & M. H. Segall (Eds.), *Aggression in global perspective* (pp. 104–144). Elmsford, NY: Pergamon Press.

Rauh, V. A., Achenbach, T. M., Nurcombe, B., Howell, C. T., & Teti, D. M. (1988). Minimizing adverse effects of low birthweight: Four-year results of an early intervention program. *Child Development, 59,* 544–553.

Reckless, W. C., & Dinitz, S. (1972). *The prevention of juvenile delinquency: An experiment.* Columbus: Ohio State University Press.

Robins, L. N., & Ratcliff, K. S. (1979). Risk factors in the continuation of childhood antisocial behavior into adulthood. *International Journal of Mental Health, 7,* 96–116.

Rosellini, R. A., & Lashley, R. L. (1992). Opponent-process theory: Implications for criminality. In J. McCord (Ed.), *Facts, frameworks, and forecasts: Advances in criminological theory* (Vol. 3, pp. 47–62). New Brunswick, NJ: Transaction Press.

Ross, H. L. (1982). Interrupted time series studies of deterrence of drinking and driving. In J. Hagan (Ed.), *Deterrence reconsidered* (pp. 71–97). Beverly Hills, CA: Sage.

Ross, H. L. (1992). *Confronting drunk driving social policy for saving lives.* New Haven, CT: Yale University Press.

Rutter, M. (1978). Family, area and school influences in the genesis of conduct disorders. In L. A. Hersov & M. Berger (Eds.), *Aggression and anti-social behaviour in childhood and adolescence* (pp. 95–113). Oxford: Pergamon Press.

Schur, E. M. (1971). *Labeling deviant behavior: Its sociological implications.* New York: Harper & Row.

Schweinhart, L. J., Barnes, H. V., & Weikart, D. P. (1993). *Significant benefits: The High/Scope Perry Preschool study through age 27.* Ypsilanti, MI: High/Scope Press.

Sherman, L. W. (1992). *Policing domestic violence: Experiments and dilemmas.* New York: Free Press.

Sherman, L. W., & Berk, R. A. (1984). The specific deterrent effects of arrest for domestic assault. *American Sociological Review, 49*(2), 261–272.

Sherman, L. W., Gottfredson, D., MacKenzie, D., Eck, J., Reuter, P., & Bushway, S. (1997). *Preventing crime: What works, what doesn't, what's promising.* A report to the United States Congress.

Sherman, L. W., & Strang, H. (1997, April 21). *The right kind of shame for crime prevention.* RISE Working Papers.

Solomon, R. L. (1980). The opponent-process theory of acquired motivation: The costs of pleasure and the benefits of pain. *American Psychologist, 35*(8), 691–712.

Strang, H., & Braithwaite, J. (Eds.). (2000). *Restorative justice: Philosophy to practice.* Burlington, VT: Ashgate.

Tannenbaum, F. (1938). *Crime and the community.* Boston: Ginn.

Thomas, W. I. (1923). *The unadjusted girl.* Boston: Little, Brown.

Tittle, C. R. (1969). Crime rates and legal sanctions. *Social Problems, 14,* 409–422.

Tremblay, R. E., Pagani-Kurtz, L., Masse, L. C., Vitaro, F., & Pihl, R. O. (1995). A bimodal preventive intervention for disruptive kindergarten boys: Its impact through mid-adolescence. *Journal of Consulting and Clinical Psychology, 63*(4), 560–568.

Waldo, G. P., & Chiricos, T. G. (1972). Perceived penal sanction and self-reported criminality: A neglected approach to deterrence research. *Social Problems, 19,* 522–540.

Webster-Stratton, C., & Hammond, M. (1997). Treating children with early-onset conduct problems: A comparison of child and parent training interventions. *Journal of Consulting and Clinical Psychology, 65*(1), 93–109.

Werner, E. E., & Smith, R. S. (1977). *Kauai's children come of age.* Honolulu: University Press of Hawaii.

West, D. J., & Farrington, D. P. (1977). *The delinquent way of life.* London: Heinemann.

Wikstrom, P.-O. (2004). Crime as alternative: Towards a cross-level action theory of crime causation. In J. McCord (Ed.), *Beyond empiricism: Institutions and intentions in the study of crime—Advances in criminological theory (Vol. 13).* Picataway, NJ: Transaction Publishers.

Wolfgang, M. E., Figlio, R. M., & Sellin, T. (1972). *Delinquency in a birth cohort.* Chicago: University of Chicago Press.

Yochelson, S., & Samenow, S. E. (1977). *The criminal personality: Vol. 2. The change process.* New York: Aronson.

Zimring, F. E. (1978). Policy experiments in general deterrence: 1970–1975. In A. Blumstein, J. Cohen, & D. Nagin (Eds.), *Deterrence and incapacitation: Estimating the effects of criminal sanctions on crime rates* (pp. 140–186). Washington, DC: National Academy of Sciences.

CHAPTER 24

Practicing Psychology in Correctional Settings

PAUL GENDREAU, CLAIRE GOGGIN,
SHEILA FRENCH, and PAULA SMITH

THE PURPOSE of this chapter is to familiarize forensic psychologists with some of the exciting developments regarding what works in reducing offenders' criminal behavior, arguably the primary goal of psychologists who provide treatment and related services to offenders (Gendreau, 1996b). The evidence we present, commonly known under the rubric "principles of effective correctional rehabilitation" (Andrews, 1995; Gendreau, 1996a), applies equally to offenders sentenced to community supervision (e.g., parole) and those in prison.

Before proceeding, a definition of terms is in order. In the correctional rehabilitation literature, the catch phrase "what works" refers broadly to the rehabilitative ideal (Cullen & Gilbert, 1982), which, in addition to promoting pragmatic goals such as reducing offender recidivism, encompasses a host of legal, political, philosophical, and social issues. Our concern in this chapter is with the former, specifically, correctional rehabilitation, or the effectiveness of planned treatment interventions in reducing criminal behavior. A planned intervention is a treatment program that (1) targets malleable criminogenic offender characteristics (e.g., personality and life circumstances) and (2) does so using treatment techniques (e.g., various psychotherapeutic modalities) designed to develop and reinforce pro-social attitudes, behaviors, and skills. Typically, treatments incorporated within the rehabilitative agenda do not include specific deterrence or "get tough" strategies such as incarceration, boot camps, or intermediate sanctions (i.e., intensive surveillance, electronic or otherwise, drug testing, threats of any sort) that are intended to punish or suppress future criminal behavior (Cullen & Gendreau, 2000). Finally, the criterion of interest, criminal behavior, is defined as an official record of recidivism (e.g., reconviction for community-based studies or misconduct in prison-based studies).

The degree to which any attempt at social engineering gains acceptance among policymakers is contingent on not only the amount and quality of the evidence generated, but also on the contemporary social context. It is our view that psychologists must become more sensitized in this regard, as have their counterparts in criminology and sociology. It is delusional to postulate that an "experimenting society," one that generates empirically derived and beneficial social policies (Campbell, 1969), is at work in the criminal justice research field (Gendreau & Ross, 1987). We have previously documented the conditions under which hard-won scientific evidence in the rehabilitative arena has been readily trumped by commonsense ideological panaceas (Gendreau, Goggin, Cullen, & Paparozzi, 2002). These conditions, in turn, place serious restrictions on the capacity of forensic/correctional psychologists, among others, to "do good."

The framework for our presentation is as follows. First, we provide a concise history of the social context that originally gave succor to the rehabilitative ideal and, most recently, has jeopardized its progress, particularly in the United States. Second, lest readers accuse us of viewing the glass as half-empty, we engage in some "bibliotherapy for cynics" (Gendreau & Ross, 1979). We take pains to note the impressive body of evidence that exists and is available to clinicians involved in developing effective services for offenders. In this regard, we offer a brief summary of the offender treatment literature published since 1970, paying particular attention to the findings of several meta-analyses supportive of the principles of effective intervention among treatment programs whose goal is the reduction of recidivism and prison misconducts. Third, we present some recent evidence that further confirms the validity of the principles derived from these meta-analyses. Fourth, we draw attention to three issues that continue to bedevil the viability of the rehabilitative enterprise: the disturbing proliferation of treatments based on correctional quackery, the failure to assess changes in offenders' criminogenic risk factors over time, and the faulty knowledge cumulation practices that have historically been employed in summarizing this literature.

THE REHABILITATIVE IDEAL: IN ASCENDANCE OR IN DECLINE?

Until the 1970s, the rehabilitative ideal had been the preeminent corrections philosophy in North America for approximately 100 years (Cullen & Gendreau, 2000). The belief that offenders should be reformed rather than punished dates back to the beginnings of the penitentiary system in North America in the early 1800s (de Beaumont & de Tocqueville, 1833/1970). One of the period's leading reformers stated in no uncertain terms:

> If punishment, suffering, degradation are deemed deterrent, if they are the best means to reform the criminal and prevent crime, then let prison reform go backward to the pillory, the whipping-post, the gallows, the stake; to corporal violence and extermination! But if the dawn of Christianity has reached us, if we have learned the lesson that *evil is to be overcome with good,* then let prisons and prison systems be lighted by this law of love. Let us leave, for the present, the thought of inflicting punishment upon prisoners to satisfy the so-called justice, and turn toward the two grand divisions of our subject, the real objects of the system, viz: *the protection of society by the prevention of crime and reformation of criminals.* (Brockway, 1871, p. 42)

The language used by the early reformers was prescient. They talked of instilling hope and emphasized reinforcement over punishment, concepts that later resonated in twentieth-century learning theory and behavior modification (Mowrer, 1960; Spiegler & Guevremont, 1998).

The treatment paradigm that evolved from the work of the late nineteenth-century reformers remained inviolate during the succeeding decades (Allen, 1981) and had a significant impact on latter-day rehabilitative practices. It was presumed that psychological and social factors accounted for offender criminality. The role of the rehabilitative enterprise was to identify the factors that led offenders into crime and then design treatment programs that addressed their specific needs.

By the mid-1950s, the rehabilitative ideal underwent further modifications, which were enthusiastically embraced by correctional professionals. In 1954, the American Prison Association, originally founded in 1870 as the National Prison Association of the United States of America, adopted a new focus and new name, the American Correctional Association (Travisono & Hawkes, 1995). Prisons became known as correctional institutions. Sophisticated offender classification systems were introduced (e.g., Warren, 1969). Prison-based treatment programs were actively pursued (i.e., Patuxent Institution, Maryland), ranging from individual and group counseling to therapeutic milieux, behavior modification, and vocational and educational programming. With the emergence of community corrections in the 1960s, the granting of parole was often contingent on the offender making satisfactory progress in institutional treatment programs. As a consequence, treatment professionals had virtually absolute discretion. By 1975, when the American Probation and Parole Association was established, some parole/probation settings had developed innovative treatment programs reporting sizable reductions in offender recidivism (Ross & Gendreau, 1980).

It appeared at the time that the rehabilitative ideal's intellectual hegemony would prevail for the foreseeable future (Menninger, 1968; Task Force on Corrections, 1967; Toby, 1964). But this was not to be. Its foundations were actually much more fragile than most observers in the area had reckoned. In 1974, Robert Martinson published an article entitled "What Works? Questions and Answers about Prison Reform," which was a précis of a more comprehensive review that was published a year later (Lipton, Martinson, & Wilks, 1975). Martinson (1974) analyzed the outcomes from 231 studies of offender treatment programs published between 1945 and 1967 and reasoned ". . . that with few and isolated exceptions the rehabilitative efforts that have been reported so far have had no appreciable effect on recidivism . . ." (p. 25). He concluded, ". . . we haven't the faintest clue about how to rehabilitate offenders and reduce recidivism" (Martinson, 1974, p. 48). From the perspective of knowledge cumulation, however, his conclusions were somewhat suspect (Cullen & Gendreau, 2000). Of the 286 effect sizes reported, only 138 employed recidivism as an outcome. Among these, just 73 outcomes were based on recognizable treatment categories such as counseling or milieu therapy, in contrast to parole, physical custody, or medical methods. The number of outcomes per category was limited (often *k*s < 10), with tremendous heterogeneity among treatment types (i.e., Rogerian nondirective to Thorne directive counseling methods to psychodynamic approaches). Surprisingly, no behavioral treatment category was included, despite its growing contemporary popularity!

We opine that few gave Martinson's (1974) article a thorough reading, for his "nothing works" pronouncement "became an instant *cliché* and exerted an enormous influence on both popular and professional thinking" (Walker, 1985, p. 168). Many scholars and policymakers, Martinson included, advocated a new epoch in criminal justice policy: The punishment of offenders should be pursued much more vigorously (for a review, see Gendreau & Ross, 1981a; Wilks & Martinson, 1976).

Why was Martinson's (1974) declaration so eagerly received when those of others (i.e., Bailey, 1966; Kirby, 1954; Logan, 1972) who had previously expressed similar views were ignored? Some researchers have contended that it was not so much the quality of Martinson's analysis but that his message was propitious, delivered during a period of increasing social tension, especially in the United States (Cullen & Gendreau, 1989). Beginning in the mid-1960s, the United States experienced a decade of significant sociopolitical upheaval (e.g., Kent State, Vietnam, campus unrest, civil disobedience, Watergate), which led many observers to seriously question the ethics, let alone the ability, of government to act as a competent, trustworthy civil administrator (Cullen & Gendreau, 1989). This challenging of the role of government in the lives of its citizens also reverberated in the criminal justice arena. Prison unrest became commonplace (e.g., Attica), and controversy arose over the sentencing and release decisions of judges and parole authorities (Cullen & Gendreau, 2000; Useem & Kimball, 1991).

Not surprisingly, neither side of the political spectrum was impressed with the impact of the rehabilitative ideal on the criminal justice system. Conservative policymakers viewed prison disturbances and the fact that the courts and parole boards allowed offenders to serve only fractions of their sentences as signs of the system's weakness. Like parents wishing to punish disrespectful, wayward children, the conservative response to crime was to "get tough" on criminals. They championed the abolition of parole and the imposition of mandatory minimum or fixed schedules of lengthier sentences (i.e., "three strikes and you're out" legislation). At the same time, they advocated more severe living conditions in prisons and harsher sentences for offenders under community supervision (Erwin, 1986; cf. Johnson, Bennett, & Flanagan, 1997). Only then would order be restored in the criminal justice system.

Curiously, liberals also felt that the justice system was lurching out of control, but not because it was too soft on criminals. Rather, they characterized the rehabilitative model as too lax, affording carte blanche to correctional professionals who were characterized as agents of social control, discriminating against the downtrodden by exercising their professional discretion in an inequitable and coercive fashion (Rothman, 1980). Liberals championed the "justice model," which minimized the goal of crime control. Treatment programs were scathingly described as "degradation ceremonies" that simply widened the net and did more harm than good (see Binder & Geis, 1984). In terms of policy, liberals felt undue discretion would best be reined in by abolishing parole and imposing fixed sentences. Rehabilitation, where it was available at all, was strictly voluntary and seen as a filler to enable offenders to better "do their time." With the establishment of appropriate legal mechanisms, offenders would be protected from a capricious criminal justice system (Conrad, 1981).

Martinson's (1974) message was accepted as the judgment of science: The rehabilitative model had no empirical support, and its claims were exposed as fraudulent. Consequently, both the conservative and the liberal constituencies were revitalized by the task of bringing order to the chaos that ensued from the rehabilitative ideal's misguided policies.

In fairness to Martinson (1974), his conclusions were not entirely misplaced. The National Academy of Science reevaluated his data and came to a similar conclusion (Sechrest, White, & Brown, 1979). The die, therefore, was cast, and any attempts to revivify rehabilitation were regarded with scorn. Ted Palmer (1975), a respected scientist-practitioner known for his innovative juvenile offender treatment programs in California, was vilified when he remarked that about half of all treatment programs were successful and there was probably a sound rationale for their reported success. Martinson (1976) characterized Palmer's analysis as indecipherable rubbish, not worth the price of a cup of coffee (and these were among the more moderate examples of the vitriol!). Then, surprisingly, Martinson (1979, p. 254) updated his initial review by affirming, "I have often said that treatment added to the networks of criminal justice is impotent . . . the conclusion is not correct . . . treatments will be found to be 'impotent' under certain conditions, beneficial under others, and detrimental under still others." Unfortunately, his recantation was ignored by everyone but a few academics, once again demonstrating the potent effect that social context can have on the receptivity of a message.

Obviously, these developments represented an ominous portent for the future viability of the rehabilitation agenda, but, as we later document, the consequences were not immediately felt by policymakers or practitioners. In the interim, a counterattack was launched, led primarily by psychologists working in corrections who, unlike criminologists, were, for a variety of reasons, not opposed to offender treatment (see Cullen & Gendreau, 2001). In this regard, Martinson was an unlikely catalyst as his statements led correctional psychologists of the 1960s and 1970s to the grudging realization that the rehabilitative ideal had been taken for granted (Palmer, 1992; Ross & McKay, 1978). A more substantive knowledge base in support of the usefulness of offender treatment programs was urgently required.

Essentially, the attempted revivification of rehabilitation was accomplished by locating studies published after 1967 (the closing date of the literature search for Martinson's review), conducting additional narrative literature reviews, and gathering insights from the clinical experience of colleagues who had run successful programs, an initiative that collectively became known as "bibliotherapy for cynics" (Gendreau & Ross, 1979).

BIBLIOTHERAPY FOR CYNICS

This initiative was, at one level, an elementary vote-counting exercise. It represented a simple tabulation of the "greatest hits" among offender treatment programs, generated in an effort to counter the prevailing miasma of "nothing works" (e.g., Andrews, 1979; Gendreau & Ross, 1979, 1981b, 1983–1984, 1987; Ross & Gendreau, 1980). But it was also more than that, for among these earliest narrative reviews and various demonstration projects (Andrews, 1980; Andrews & Kiessling, 1980; Gendreau & Andrews, 1979) were planted the seeds to advance the literature in significant ways. Recall that both Martinson (1979) and Palmer (1975) had commented that some treatment programs work while others do not. From that, two questions emerged. The first, following the lead of Martinson and Palmer, was later summarized by Gendreau (1996a, p. 118):

> Unlike Martinson and his followers, we believe it is not sufficient just to sum across studies or file them into general categories. The salient question is what are the principles that distinguish between effective and ineffective programs?—what exactly was accomplished under the name of "employment . . ."?

The framing of the second question was derived from the research of Quay (1977). He reassessed Kassebaum, Ward, and Wilner's (1971) famous prison counseling program—oft-cited as a prime example of a methodologically rigorous evaluation—which demonstrated that treatment was ineffective. Quay discovered that the program had, in fact, little therapeutic integrity. It had a weak conceptual base, used counseling groups that were unstable, and employed unqualified, poorly trained counselors, some of whom did not believe in the efficacy of the program! Additional support came from an examination of 27 empirical investigations of applied behavioral programs for delinquency prevention (Emery & Marholin, 1977). These authors found that in only 30% of studies were the behaviors for which delinquent youth were referred to the program identified as targets for treatment (e.g., a client referred for stealing cars was treated for tardiness).

Gendreau and Ross (1979, p. 467) defined this problem as one of therapeutic integrity and questioned:

> To what extent do treatment personnel actually adhere to the principles and employ the techniques of the therapy they purport to provide? To what extent are the treatment staff competent? How hard do they work? How much is treatment diluted in the correctional environment so that it becomes treatment in name only?

With these two guiding tenets at the forefront, supplemented by evolving theory in the area (e.g., Andrews, 1980), the principles of effective treatment were developed and further articulated in narrative reviews (Andrews, 1995; Gendreau 1996a, 1996b; Gendreau & Ross, 1987; Ross & Fabiano, 1985) and, more convincingly in our view, via a series of meta-analyses.

Why meta-analysis? Even 20 years ago, it was apparent within the psychological literature that the application of narrative review techniques to research summaries was compromised by a host of attendant problems (Beaman,

1991; Glass, McGaw, & Smith, 1981; Rosenthal, 1991), not the least of which was a lack of numerical precision. The offender treatment literature was awash in testimonials, with supporters and detractors engaged in a fruitless shouting contest fueled by a great deal of colorful invective (Gendreau & Ross, 1979). If ever a research literature was in need of "therapy", this was a prime example. Despite opposition from some quarters (Logan & Gaes, 1993; Logan et al., 1991), much of it, in our view, ethnocentric (i.e., meta-analytic conclusions favoring rehabilitation were disputable as they came from the "Canadian" school; see also Cullen, 2002), meta-analysis became the new "gold standard" for arbitrating the "what works" debate.

META-ANALYSIS: WHAT WORKS

Meta-analyses of offender rehabilitation programs began to appear in the mid-1980s (Davidson, Gottschalk, Gensheimer, & Mayer, 1984, also reported in more detail in Apter & Goldstein, 1986; Garrett, 1985). At this writing, there are at least 34 meta-analyses of correctional treatment effectiveness, whose findings have been nicely summarized by McGuire (2002). As space does not permit a detailed review of all of these highly useful contributions, we will focus on key contributions from two broad and somewhat overlapping categories of meta-analyses: (1) those that nominate some general principles of "what works" and affirm that, overall, treatment programs reduce recidivism; and (2) those that search for more specific criteria along clinically and psychologically relevant dimensions.

META-ANALYSES: GENERAL PRINCIPLES AND OVERALL EFFECTS

The first published meta-analyses were produced by Garrett (1985) and the Davidson research group (Davidson et al., 1984; see Apter & Goldstein, 1986, for the published reports). Garrett accumulated 433 effect sizes (ES) from studies of 13,000 juvenile offenders and reported an average reduction of $r = .12$[1] among well-designed studies, albeit recidivism was the criterion of choice for only 43% of ES. She identified cognitive-behavioral therapies as having the highest mean effect ($r = .22$ for more rigorous designs and studies with more than 10 ES). The results from the Davidson group were similar to those of Garrett in that behavioral interventions (i.e., positive reinforcement, token economies, behavioral contracting) proved to be the most effective. As well, the type of professional training (e.g., psychology, education) and the degree of involvement of the evaluators in the design of the therapy were also important.

The gist of these findings has consistently been replicated. Consider Lipsey's (1992) noteworthy research contributions in this area. He summarized the results of a huge database of juvenile interventions (443 ES), 64% of which were positive (i.e., reduced recidivism) and represented a noticeable improvement over the ≈ 50% baseline reported by Martinson and Palmer almost 20 years previously. The average reduction in recidivism in the Lipsey sample varied from 5% to 9%, depending on the statistical adjustments made to the ES. Subsequently, Lösel (1995) provided a comprehensive assessment of 13 meta-analyses of juvenile and adult offenders published between 1985 and

1995 and found that mean ES ranged from .05 to .18, with an overall mean of about $r = .10$. This pattern of results remained after controlling for the effects of factors such as subject attrition, quality of research design, length of follow-up, and study publication status (Lipsey, 1999).

The robust replication of positive results in these meta-analyses is also impressive given the variety of study samples, coding schemes, and research teams involved. Additionally, Lösel (1995) and Lipsey (1992) have suggested that the overall treatment ES is likely underestimated, as treatment studies, by design, often use comparison groups that receive some modicum of treatment as well and tend to include dichotomous criterion measures that are not overly sensitive to detecting differences in outcome (i.e., recidivism).

Cynics may counter that a 10% reduction in recidivism is of little practical value, but nothing could be further from the truth (see Lipsey & Wilson, 1998). Lipsey and Wilson (1993) and Rosenthal and DiMatteo (2001) documented that many medical treatments have proven to be cost-effective when the incidence of serious illness is reduced by even small percentage magnitudes (i.e., 3% to 10%). Cohen (1998) has calculated the cost-effectiveness of saving high-risk juvenile offenders and found that, during the course of a criminal career, an average high-risk youth incurs costs of $1.7 to $2.3 million. Admittedly, crime cost-benefit analyses are imprecise as they are based on estimates of the rate of criminal participation and sometimes include categories such as "prison" and "suffering" along with "property loss" and "lost wages." Notwithstanding these caveats, treatment programs can be highly cost-effective when even small to modest reductions in recidivism result, depending on the interval in which the intervention occurs and its attendant costs (see also Aos, Phipps, Barnoski, & Lieb, 1999; Cohen, 2001; Welsh & Farrington, 2000).

The meta-analyses included in this category have consistently identified the most effective treatment programs ($r = .10$ to .25) as those that are cognitive-behavioral in design, have a high degree of structure, are demonstration programs rather than "real world" programs, and are delivered in the community versus an institutional setting (Cleland, Pearson, Lipton, & Yee, 1997; Izzo & Ross, 1990; Lipsey, 1999; Lipsey, Chapman, & Landenberger, 2001; Lösel, 1995; Redondo, Sanchez-Meca, & Garrido, 1999).

META-ANALYSIS: CLINICALLY AND PSYCHOLOGICALLY RELEVANT PRINCIPLES

In contrast to the meta-analyses just discussed, those included in this section characterize a more aggressive search for additional principles of clinical and psychological relevance to offender treatment. The search for principles in this regard began in earnest in 1990, when Andrews, Zinger, et al. coded the treatment literature along a variety of dimensions, the most important of which was the "appropriateness" of treatment services. Appropriate services were defined as those that are behavioral in nature (general responsivity) and target the criminogenic needs of higher-risk offenders. Behavioral treatments that are standard in the offender literature are well-known to psychologists (see Gendreau, 1996a, pp. 120–122). It should be noted that Andrews and Bonta (2003) also generated a specific responsivity principle (i.e., the matching of offender, therapist, and program characteristics). For example, offenders with lower IQs might function better in token economy-type programs run by staff who are effective in relating to their style of thinking (e.g., Cullen, Gendreau, Jarjoura, & Wright, 1997). Regrettably, very few outcome studies assessing this potentially useful principle have been published to date (see Andrews & Bonta, 2003, p. 263).

Principles 2 and 3 require further elaboration. The second, targeting criminogenic needs, underlies the assumption that effective treatments target attributes that have been empirically validated as reliable predictors of recidivism. There are two classes of predictors in this regard: static (e.g., criminal history) and dynamic (e.g., antisocial values). The latter are typically referred to as criminogenic needs and, given their mutable nature, are optimal treatment targets. Examples include antisocial attitudes and cognitions, pro-criminal associates, and personality factors such as impulsiveness and poor self-control. Subsequent meta-analyses (Bonta, Law, & Hanson, 1998; Gendreau, Little, & Goggin, 1996) demonstrated that these types of criminogenic needs are strong predictors of recidivism and confirmed the negligible predictive validity of attributes once regarded as important treatment targets (e.g., low self-esteem, depression, anxiety). In fact, addressing these latter factors in treatment, historically commonplace in corrections, effects little change in offender recidivism (Gendreau, Little, et al., 1996).

The third principle speaks to the need to distinguish among offenders on the basis of risk, as those rated as higher risk are the primary target population for behavioral intervention, given that they represent the greatest risk to the public (Bonta, 1996). In contrast, lower-risk offenders require much less intervention as they typically have fewer criminogenic needs. Subjecting them to intensive services, therefore, is simply not cost-effective, and some studies have shown increased posttreatment recidivism rates among low-risk offenders (Andrews, Bonta, & Hoge, 1990).

The Andrews, Zinger, et al. (1990) meta-analysis encompassed 154 ES, reporting an overall ES of $r = .10$; more importantly, they found that appropriate treatments reduced recidivism by $r = .30$, or 30%. Meanwhile, inappropriate treatments (e.g., services to lower-risk offenders, nondirective and unstructured psychodynamic or milieux therapies, services based on threats of sanctions) produced an increase in recidivism ($r = -.06$). Appropriate treatments delivered in community settings yielded better results than did prison-based programs ($r = .35$ versus $r = .17$).

Subsequently, this research group increased the number of ES to 374 and assessed several other principles of effectiveness (see Andrews & Bonta, 2003; Andrews, Dowden, & Gendreau, 1999). We have abstracted and rearranged data from Tables 7.1.1 and 7.1.2 of Andrews and Bonta (2003, p. 310). The ES for treatment programs that adhered to all of the aforementioned principles (i.e., risk/need/responsivity) was $r = .28$, as compared to $r = .05$ for those that did not. This represents a 23% improvement in effectiveness (i.e., reduction in recidivism; composite variable, Table 24.1). Inspection of Table 24.1 also reveals that targeting criminogenic needs has robust effects ($r = .20$), as does the use of behavioral treatments ($r = .19$). The best results were found for community-

Table 24.1
Relationship of the Principles of Effective
Correctional Programming with Recidivism

Adherence to the Principle	Reduction in Recidivism (*r*)
1. Risk	.07
2. Criminogenic need*	.20
a. Individual antisocial beliefs and skills	.17
b. Family/peers antisocial beliefs and skills	.15
3. General responsivity (behavioral treatment)	.19
4. Composite (1 to –3)	.23
a. Community-based treatment	.29
b. Residential treatment	.19

Note: *If the need principle is not followed, that is, if *non*criminogenic needs (e.g., personal distress) are targeted for treatment, then recidivism *increases* by 7%.
Source: The Psychology of Criminal Conduct, third edition, by D. A. Andrews and J. Bonta, 2003, Cincinnati, OH: Anderson.

based programs (*r* = .29). Of note, the weakest effects were found for the risk principle (*r* = .07). One possible reason is that, when one cumulates risk scores across studies (see Smith, Goggin, & Gendreau, 2002), definitions of risk level may be wildly inconsistent. They may be based on diverse actuarial measures with variable cutoff scores, different risk criteria, comparison group recidivism rates at follow-up, or simply the study authors' or sponsoring agency's unsubstantiated designation of the sample's risk status (i.e., low, medium).

The Andrews research group has pushed the envelope even further by examining the therapeutic integrity of offender treatment programs and its impact on recidivism. This encompasses the program implementation process

Table 24.2
Relationship of Therapeutic Integrity and
Implementation Processes with Recidivism

Program Characteristic	Reduction in Recidivism (*r*)
Therapeutic Integrity	
1. Relationship skills	.27
2. Effective reinforcement	.24
3. Structuring skills	.24
4. Effective disapproval	.22
5. Effective modeling	.22
6. Structured skill learning	.21
7. Problem solving	.19
8. Effective use of authority	.19
Implementation	
1. Involved evaluator	.19
2. Staff: composite of selection, training, and supervision factors	.15
3. Manuals	15

Source: The Psychology of Criminal Conduct, third edition, by D. A. Andrews and J. Bonta, 2003, Cincinnati, OH: Anderson.

as well as the nature of the therapeutic practices employed by facilitators. One should note that, as the number of programs that adhered to the program standards outlined in Table 24.2 was somewhat limited, the magnitude of reported ES may well change with the addition of more data. In Table 24.2, we present the essence of Andrews and Bonta's (2003) findings from their Table 7.1.3 (p. 311) and encourage readers to explore the original source material.

As indicated in Table 24.2, programs that employ therapists who have adequate relationship skills show lower offender recidivism rates ($r = .27$) than programs that do not. The results from programs with involved evaluators, whose direct participation, one presumes, ensures greater control over therapeutic and evaluative components, indicate reductions in recidivism of $r = .19$.

It has been empirically demonstrated with remarkable consistency that the principles of effective intervention are valid for a variety of unique corrections populations, such as female offenders, minority groups, youthful offenders, mentally disordered offenders, sex offenders (Andrews, Dowden, & Rettinger, 2001), and violent offenders (Dowden & Andrews, 2000), as well as within distinct therapeutic domains (e.g., family interventions; Dowden & Andrews, 2003). Most recently, Dowden and Andrews (2004) have updated the therapeutic integrity data presented in Table 24.2 and assessed the contribution of relapse prevention strategies to effective treatment (Dowden, Antonowicz, & Andrews, 2003). The authors indicated that the greatest reductions in recidivism were associated with programs that help offenders to recognize the sequence of events that precipitate their criminal behavior through relapse rehearsal training for themselves and their significant others.

The final meta-analysis to be discussed here examined the special case of the effectiveness of correctional treatment in reducing criminal behavior in prison (i.e., misconducts). Although managing prisons in a safe and humane fashion is of uppermost concern for correctional managers and policymakers, this area has not been the subject of rigorous empirical attention. The prison management literature is enormous and has generated a multitude of constructive suggestions in this matter, most of it, however, of a case study or qualitative nature. Gendreau and Keyes (2001) conducted a vote-count analysis of the literature and found more than 500 recommendations generated by experts in the field, the majority of whom nominated treatment as the most effective means of reducing misconduct-type behaviors (e.g., assault, theft).

How accurate is the experts' intuitive reckoning? Tentative steps have been taken to address this issue empirically. Keyes (1996; see also Gendreau & Keyes, 2001) and Morgan and Flora (2002) have conducted two meta-analyses that examined the effects of prison treatment programs on misconducts. The mean effect across 46 ES was $r = .10$, with behavioral programs producing an $r \approx .20$.

Most recently, French and Gendreau (2004) updated these literature reviews and, in addition, tested several of the principles of effective treatment with a sample of 105 ESs involving 23,000 prisoners. The results were uncannily similar to those of the community-based treatment meta-analyses. French and Gendreau reported an overall effect of $r = .14$, with the behavioral program category recording the strongest result ($r = .26$). Among programs that targeted 3 to 8 criminogenic needs, the ES was $r = .29$ versus $r = .06$ for those that targeted none. Programs rated high on therapeutic integrity, as measured by the Correctional Program Assessment Inventory-2000 (CPAI-2000; Gendreau & Andrews, 2001), produced an ES of $r = .38$. (The CPAI-2000 is described in the following section.) Programs that were rated low on that dimension had an ES of $r = .13$.

Such results are impressive in that they may translate into significant cost savings for prison systems. Sampling a large medium-security prison, Lovell and Jemelka (1996) calculated an average cost of $920 per misconduct, although this figure is likely an underestimate as the authors did not include the value of related medical costs for serious injuries. These findings were also encouraging in that those programs that were most effective in reducing prison misconducts were also among those associated with lower postrelease recidivism rates ($r = .13$), suggesting that, in measuring the effectiveness of prison-based rehabilitation programs, it may be reasonable to regard prison misconduct as an equivalent criterion to community-based recidivism (Gendreau, Goggin, & Law, 1997; Hill, 1985).

TESTING THE PRINCIPLES

The emergence of the principles of effective correctional treatment was not universally heralded, notably among some criminologists (Cullen & Applegate, 1997). One of the recurring objections was that proponents of rehabilitation may be magically transforming spurious relationships through tautological wizardry (Logan & Gaes, 1993). Despite the fact that the Andrews, Zinger, et al. (1990) meta-analysis was predicated on a theoretical framework espoused 10 years previously (see Gendreau, 1989), there was some merit to the challenge. As a literature review technique, meta-analysis is not foolproof. Researcher biases can affect retrieval and coding decisions, where the latter are often hampered by the relative inconsistency with which descriptive information is included in individual studies. (One need only conduct a meta-analysis of the offender treatment literature to recognize the enormity of the problem.)

Fortunately, a means of empirically testing the principles of effective treatment has been developed. The idea of codifying the principles in an assessment inventory first came about during a 1988 conference presentation on prisons in Nags Head, North Carolina, where most of the attendees were antirehabilitation criminologists. Doris McKenzie, a well-known criminologist and one of the few at the time who was sympathetic to rehabilitation, suggested that the first author develop an inventory of principles; from this the CPAI-2000 was born. It has since undergone several revisions, the latest of which includes 131 items measuring therapeutic integrity or program quality (CPAI-2000; Gendreau & Andrews, 2001). The instrument captures all of the principles elucidated by Andrews (1995), Andrews and Bonta (2003), Gendreau (1996a), and others (see Gendreau & Andrews, 2001). The current version of the measure consists of eight domains: organizational culture, program implementation/maintenance, management/staff characteristics, client risk-need practices, program characteristics, several dimensions of core correctional practice, interagency communication, and evaluation. To date, it has been used to evaluate almost 400 offender treatment programs (Gendreau, Goggin, & Smith, 2001; Lowenkamp,

2004), the majority ($\approx$ 70%) of which have failed to achieve a passing grade. Recall Lipsey's (1999) finding that "real world" programs are sometimes lacking in therapeutic integrity.

Two investigators have recently used the 1997 version of the CPAI-2000 (CPAI; 70 items across 6 domains) to assess its predictive validity. Given that the measure represents a state-of-the-art compilation of what is known about the characteristics of effective treatment, one might expect it could be used to predict offender treatment outcome (i.e., recidivism). On the other hand, should it fail to do so, it would seriously undermine the validity of the rehabilitative agenda, notwithstanding the findings of the meta-analyses reviewed previously.

In the first study, a meta-analysis, Nesovic (2003) gathered 173 studies from the offender treatment literature and reported a mean effect of $r = .12$ with recidivism across 266 ES. Using program descriptions provided by each of the studies, Nesovic assessed their quality using the CPAI and then correlated CPAI scores with ES for each program (some studies described more than one program and, therefore, produced more than one ES). Overall, the CPAI program scores correlated well with reductions in recidivism ($r = .46$), with the "program implementation" domain having the weakest validity ($r = .10$). In contrast, the "client assessment" and "program characteristics" domains were among the most robust ($r = .41$ and $r = .43$, respectively). Nesovic also examined correlations between individual scale items and ES. The following were included among the strongest items (i.e., $r \geq .25$): The program receives appropriate clients; offenders' dynamic risk factors are assessed; the program has a written manual; relapse prevention is practiced; staff are trained and hired based on their knowledge of effective relationship and therapeutic skills; and evaluators are involved in the program. Finally, Nesovic categorized treatment programs in terms of quality (i.e., high, medium, or low) based on their CPAI scores and reported mean effects with recidivism of $r = .20$, $r = .11$, and $r = .01$, respectively.

Subsequently, Lowenkamp (2004) used the CPAI to conduct 38 in situ reviews of Ohio-based offender treatment programs that included treatment and matched comparison groups (i.e., gender, race, actuarial risk measure score) and used reincarceration as the criterion. Even though many of the programs proved to be ineffective—it was not uncommon to find lower recidivism rates in the comparison group—the predictive validity of the CPAI total scores was supported. Across all offenders, the correlation with outcome was $r = .41$; among a sample of program completers, it was $r = .32$. In contrast to Nesovic (2003), Lowenkamp found the "program implementation" domain was a powerful predictor of recidivism ($r = .54$ and $r = .46$ for his two samples), whereas the "staff characteristics" domain was not. Consistent with Nesovic's findings, Lowenkamp reported robust correlations for the "client assessment" and "program characteristics" domains (rs from .30 to .52 for each study). He also isolated those items from the CPAI that correlated with treatment outcome and reported a mean ES of $r = .60$ for all offenders and $r = .47$ among program completers.

With respect to individual items, potent correlations (i.e., $r \geq .25$) with outcome were reported across all offenders for the following: qualifications of program designer; staff trained by program director; program valued by criminal justice stakeholders and communities at large; offenders' risk level and dynamic needs assessed; offenders closely monitored; offenders spend at least 40% of time in therapeutic activities; program and staff matched; program has external quality controls; assessment of in-program progress and community follow-up provided; program has ethical guidelines and defined completion criteria.

Lastly, when programs were categorized as high, medium, low, or very low based on their CPAI scores, Lowenkamp (2004) reported reductions in recidivism of 22%, 10%, and 5% for the first three, respectively, with those rated very low actually increasing recidivism by 19%.

In summary, we believe the evidence reviewed in the previous two sections is convincing. Well-founded principles now exist with which to guide the development and administration of offender treatment programs, whether situated in prison or the community, and such programs can generate meaningful reductions in offender recidivism, resulting in sizable cost-saving benefits.

But is bibliotherapy sufficient for cynical policymakers and academics (see Gendreau & Ross, 1979)? The answer is an equivocal yes and no. It may be for those academics and clinicians who carefully examine the issues. But it may not be if one considers the broader social context and its potential impact on the clinical practices of future forensic/correctional psychologists. We now turn our attention to this critical issue.

FACTORS AFFECTING THE VIABILITY OF THE REHABILITATIVE IDEAL

CORRECTIONAL QUACKERY

At the outset, we alluded to the possibility that the rehabilitative ideal may be under pressure from social context factors. We remarked that after Martinson's (1974) "nothing works" pronouncement it took some time for the anti-rehabilitation forces to prevail. Although reports of successful treatment programs continued to appear in the literature even a decade or so after Martinson's declaration (e.g., Davidson, Redner, Blakely, Mitchell, & Emshoff, 1987; Gibbs, Potter, & Goldstein, 1995; Gordon, Arbuthnot, Gustafson, & McGreen, 1988; Wexler, Falkin, & Lipton, 1990), they were not in the majority. As testament to this, Andrews et al. (1999) discovered that among the 374 ESs in their meta-analysis, a miniscule 13% conformed to the principles of effective treatment, and this represented a 7% decline since their 1990 review (see Andrews, Zinger, et al., 1990).

Should one take this trend as an omen? We hope not, but caution that correctional quackery is clearly de rigueur in today's context (Cullen, Blevins, Trager, & Gendreau, in press; Latessa, Cullen, & Gendreau, 2002). Table 24.3 outlines some examples of such quackery that Ed Latessa and the first author have encountered in the past several years when surveying correctional programs. During this period it has been disquieting to note that such programs may represent only the tip of the iceberg.

What are the reasons for this proclivity? It is apparent that, compared with other Western countries, the United States has crafted distinctly punitive

Table 24.3

Examples of Correctional Quackery

1. Acupuncture
2. Angel in You program
3. Aura focus
4. Baby treatment (dress them in diapers)
5. Been there, done that therapy
6. Cross-dressing humiliation
7. Drama therapy (the "Cyrano" method)
8. Drum circles
9. Dunce cap therapy
10. Ecumenical christianity
11. Haircuts and diets
12. Heart mapping
13. Healing lodges
14. Horticulture therapy
15. John T.V.
16. Plastic surgery
17. Pet therapy
18. Sage smudging
19. Sandwich board justice
20. Yoga

Sources: Kainos Community in Prisons: Report of an Evaluation, by J. Burnside, J. Adler, N. Loucks, and G. Rose, 2001, London: HM Prison Service, Research Development and Statistics Directorate; *The Cyrano Method: Using Theatre in Offender Treatment,* Regional Research Project (R1-1995), by J. Duhame, 1995, Laval, Québec, Canada: Regional Research Committee, Correctional Service of Canada; "The Common Sense Revolution and Correctional Policy" (pp. 359–386), by P. Gendreau, C. Goggin, F. Cullen, and M. Paparozzi, in *Offender Rehabilitation and Treatment: Effective Programmes and Policies to Reduce Reoffending* J. McGuire (Ed.), 2002, Chichester, England: Wiley; "Beyond Correctional Quackery: Professionalism and the Possibility of Effective Treatment," by E. J. Latessa, F. T. Cullen, and P. Gendreau, 2002, *Federal Probation, 66,* pp. 43–49; "Animals and Inmates: A Sharing Companionship behind Bars," by J. M. Moneymaker, and E. O. Strimple, 1991, *Journal of Offender Rehabilitation, 16,* pp. 133–152; "Drama Therapy for Mentally Disordered Offenders: Changes in Levels of Anger," by D. Reiss, M. Quayle, T. Brett, and C. Meux, 1998, *Criminal Behaviour and Mental Health, 8,* pp. 139–153; "Evaluating Horticultural Therapy: The Ecological Context of Urban Jail Inmates" (pp. 203–224), by J. S. Rice and L. L. Remy, (1994), in *People-Plant Relationships: Setting Research Priorities,* J. Flagler and R. P. Poincelot (Eds.), Binghamton, NY: Food Products Press; *Results of an Evaluation of the Pawsitive Directions Canine Program at Nova Institute for Women* (Report No. R-108), by K. Richardson-Taylor and K. Blanchette, (2001), Ottawa, Ontario, Canada: Correctional Service of Canada; "Florida Puts Felons in God's Big House," by D. Saunders, March 17, 2004, *Globe and Mail,* pp. A-1, A-12; and "Man's Sentence: Probation, Yoga," by A. Tilghman, January 22, 2004, *Houston Chronicle,* pp. A-17, A-26.

policies with regard to offenders and criminal behavior. Observe the dramatic increase in U.S. incarceration rates since the 1980s (Cullen, Van Voorhis, & Sundt, 2000; U.S. Department of Justice, 2003) and the U.S. predilection for "get tough" responses in community corrections by "turning up the heat on probationers" (Erwin, 1986, p. 17; cf. Cullen, Wright, & Applegate, 1996). None of these programs (e.g., intensive surveillance, drug testing, electronic monitoring) has any empirical justification in the punishment literature (Gendreau, 1996b). Support for treatment programs fueled by commonsense ideologies has also increased (Gendreau, Goggin, Cullen, et al., 2002). Witness the proliferation of faith-based correctional programming in the United States (Saunders, 2004) and, more generally, the concerns raised by the American scientific community regarding what is considered to be the blatant politicization of the scientific process (Shulman, 2004).

Gendreau, Goggin, Cullen, et al. (2002) also highlighted other factors specific to the criminal justice arena. One is the role of the media in presenting a skewed picture of crime issues. The authors go on to claim that academic turf wars and the revisionist forces (e.g., postmodernists) within antipositivist disciplines are contributing factors in the production of a new generation of policymakers, at least some of whom have gravitated to corrections, who are not *sympathique* to empirically driven best-practice policies.

A second issue of concern is that cultural trends in the United States since the early 1990s paint a bleak picture (Gendreau, 2003). That is, one should not anticipate that the next generation of psychologists will be unconditionally motivated to "do good" for offenders. According to comparative cross-cultural attitude surveys (Adams, 2003), American society is changing, particularly relative to other Western democracies. It is in retreat from idealism and fulfillment, civic engagement, and social and ecological issues. By way of illustration, several years ago the first author gave a colloquium to one of the leading clinical doctoral programs in the United States (Gendreau, Latessa, & Cullen, 2004), fully expecting that the students in such a program would favor an egalitarian, helping orientation. Instead, students questioned devoting one's career to providing services to people who are not deserving of care and who, perhaps more importantly, do not pay as well as does a yuppie clientele.

Adams' (2003) research also reports less empathy, concern, and spiritual quest in American society. The two most rapidly growing constituencies in the United States are adherents of fundamentalist sects, who are inclined to rigidity, exclusion, and deference to authority, and young adults who prize monetary status, thrill-seeking, supremacy in a Darwinian mold, and tend to be nihilistic, alienated, and accepting of violence and sexism. Who is left? According to Adams, the remaining 20% of the population, those who embrace values of autonomy, flexibility, tolerance, diversity, change, generosity, and the helping ethos, and are, logically, among the potential recruits for helping professions, represent a group in decline and one whose influence is rapidly decreasing.

In summary, we are confident that psychologists have played only a minor role in promoting correctional quackery. Forensic psychologists, however, have not been, on the whole, among the vanguard in promoting effective services for offenders. Consider some recent comments by Stanley Brodsky (2000), one of the doyens of forensic psychology, who bemoaned the nature of psychologists' recent contributions to service delivery systems in corrections. He recalled the halcyon days of the 1970s, when powerful government agencies such as the National Institute of Mental Health, the Office of Juvenile Justice and Delinquency Prevention, and the Law Enforcement Assistance Administration sponsored a renowned conference on Psychology in the Criminal Justice System, which advocated a level of interest and support for funding and social action that would be "unthinkable" in today's climate (p. 142). Brodsky is now of the opinion that the latest generation of psychologists have little interest in what goes on in prisons or whether prison treatment and correctional counseling are effective. They have become more management-oriented, which, in itself, is not a bad thing, except that many of the current breed of prison managers seem to care little about individual offender's needs and the obligation to address them with effective programs (Feeley & Simon, 1992). Furthermore, Brodsky deplores forensic psychologists' enthusiasm for churning out yet another MMPI or psychopathy study or antisocial personality diagnostic schema.

While some readers may regard such colorful speculation as idle fancy, our view is that the measurable impact of such trends on offender treatment policy warrants discussion. No doubt, a combination of factors has contributed to the rise of the correctional quackery phenomenon and the scarcity of correctional program data based on sound principles of effective treatment (Andrews et al., 1999). Of course, it is equally possible that our perspective has been adversely influenced by the availability heuristic. It may be that the era in which rehabilitation flourished acted as a deceptive foil and that reality is, in fact, much more grim (Gendreau, 1996a). A pragmatist might argue that one should consider it a success if even 20% of correctional policies are based on sound evidence (Gendreau, 2000). On a more encouraging note, some large correctional organizations—Indiana's is one of the few in the United States—are presently engaged in establishing rigorous treatment program accreditation standards based on best practices (Gendreau, Goggin, Cullen, et al., 2002; Rex, Lieb, Bottoms, & Wilson, 2003). Some contend that evidence-based government policies are indeed attainable (e.g., the United Kingdom; Davies, 2004).

Admittedly, wrestling with the vagaries of social context in an attempt to expose the root causes of facile solutions to complex issues (i.e., offender treatment policy) may be a fool's errand. A more focused approach might yield better results. As such, we turn our attention to two issues whose constructive remediation would help a great deal to vitiate the rehabilitative agenda.

Assessing Changes in Offender Risk

The assessment of changes in risk to reoffend is a key prediction issue. Given the complexity of this literature, space permits only a succinct review; readers are advised to consult Bonta (1996, 2002), Gendreau, Little, et al. (1996), Gendreau, Goggin, and Paparozzi (1996), Simourd (2004), and Wormith (2001) for more detailed summaries.

Historically, the field of corrections has emphasized the use of risk instruments (e.g., Salient Factor Score; Hoffman & Beck, 1974) that consist of a few (<10) items, the majority of which are static in nature (e.g., criminal history; Gendreau, Little, et al., 1996). Measures of personality have also been employed to predict recidivism, but with much less frequency (Gendreau, Little, et al., 1996). Regardless, the assessment of changes in risk, focusing as it must on dynamic risk factors or criminogenic needs (e.g., antisocial attitudes) that can change over time, has been overlooked. The traditional reluctance of criminologists to incorporate dynamic items in risk measures has been credited to an antipathy in that discipline toward individual differences of a psychological nature (Andrews & Wormith, 1989; Cullen & Gendreau, 2001). The new penology, referred to previously (Feeley & Simon, 1992), as well as the view that variables that change must perforce be unreliable for prediction purposes (Jones, 1996), represent additional obstacles.

An extensive survey of 73 public sector correctional agencies in the United States by the National Institute of Corrections has revealed that, although progress has been made in the past several years, there are relatively few jurisdictions using measures that allow for a comprehensive assessment of change (U.S. Department of Justice, 2003). Only 16 of the agencies reported using a measure such as the Level of Service Inventory-Revised (LSI-R; Andrews & Bonta, 1995), which includes a representative sample of dynamic predictors. Twenty-five of those surveyed indicated that they were using the Wisconsin risk scale. Although the Wisconsin can also be used to measure change, one finds that, most often, only its static risk items are scored (Bonta, 1996).

Forensic psychologists, by contrast, have generally been more predisposed to individual differences, albeit they have tended to concentrate on constructs that are relatively immutable (e.g., psychopathy) or else have favored one-shot assessments using general personality tests (e.g., MCMI, MMPI-2, projective tests) that have not been developed specifically for offender samples (Bonta, 2002). Very few (<5%) use a measure like the LSI-R, which is specifically designed to assess change in offenders (Boothby & Clements, 2000; Gallagher, Somwaru, & Ben-Porath, 1999).

Consider for a moment the implications of such practices. Acknowledging that risk level may remain stable over time for some offenders, it is equally true that many offenders exhibit significant increases or decreases in risk level in response to life course changes, situational factors, or treatment interventions. Such undocumented fluctuations can escalate the potential for inaccurate classification regarding (1) security-appropriate inmate assignment and transfer decisions, (2) suitability for parole, (3) parameters for probation/parole supervision, (4) pretreatment identification of criminogenic needs, or (5) monitoring the effectiveness of interventions. The hallmark of a viable correctional system must be flexibility; that is, it must incorporate case management policies that are empirically founded and evaluate the effectiveness of program interventions through ongoing tracking of outcome (i.e., recidivism), making revisions as required per newly generated data. Failing to do so results in a system that is neither cost-effective nor serves the interests of any of its constituents—the kept, the keepers, or the general public—particularly well.

On a more positive note, of late there has been growing support for the utility of dynamic domains as offender risk predictors. In 1996, a meta-analysis by Gendreau, Little, et al. demonstrated the comparable predictive validity of dynamic and static risk factors. Since then, these findings have been further supported and refined with general offender samples (Brown, 2002; Kroner & Mills, 2001; Zamble & Quinsey, 1997) as well as specialized groups such as sex offenders (Hanson & Harris, 2000; Hanson & Morton-Bourgon, 2004). Fortuitously, the measurement of change has also garnered somewhat more interest of late. Whereas, in 1996 Gendreau, Little, et al. (p. 586) reported only a handful of studies that examined change as a predictor of recidivism, the subject is now being vigorously pursued by some psychologists (Miles & Raynor, 2004; Walters, 2003; Walters, Trgovac, Rychlec, Di Fazio, & Olson, 2002). The Miles and Raynor study is a good illustration of just how valuable the assessment of change can be. They reported that low-risk probationers who increased in risk level over time had a 30% higher recidivism rate. In contrast, high-risk offenders whose risk level decreased during the same period produced a 23% lower recidivism rate. By any correctional program standards, such results represent meaningful changes in recidivism rates, changes that would not have been predictable in the absence of interval assessments.

Among the risk measures that report the best predictive validities in assessing change, we recommend the LSI-R (Andrews & Bonta, 1995; see the meta-analysis by Gendreau, Goggin, & Smith, 2002, and the recent primary studies by Girard & Wormith, 2004, and Simourd, 2004). Its predictive validities are in the range of $r \geq .35$ and it covers almost all of the salient offender risk domains.

There are other measures worthy of recommendation, although in most cases only a limited number of ES have been reported and sample sizes have been modest. For example, the Self-Appraisal Questionnaire is a user-friendly self-report scale that includes a number of criminogenic need items and has reported predictive validities equal to other measures over a 5-year follow-up (Loza & Loza-Fanous, 2001, 2003). Although the reliability of self-report measures may be regarded with skepticism in some quarters (e.g., literacy and dissimulation issues), a forthcoming meta-analysis by Walters (in press) verifies that self-report measures do perform well for prediction purposes.

KNOWLEDGE CUMULATION

Having come to the realization that small effects can have meaningful consequences, it is questionable whether significance testing (i.e., $p < .05$) has any useful role to play in knowledge cumulation, particularly in the social sciences (Harlow, Mulaik, & Steiger, 1997). The problem is clear-cut: psychologists pay far more attention to significance testing than they do to estimating the magnitude of an ES, its replicability, or what it means in practical terms. We present three compelling examples in support of our thesis.

One often reads that, because an obtained result is significant at the $p < .05$ level, the result is de facto replicable. Rather, such a result might well be an outlier and not likely replicable, especially if the sample involved is small (see Schmidt, 1992; 1996, Table 2, p. 121). Or, in the event of such a finding with huge samples, as has been the case in some of our recent work (e.g., Smith et al., 2002), the results, albeit statistically significant, may be of little practical import, exemplifying what Meehl (1991) calls "the crud factor."

A second fallacious claim is that significance levels imply a measure of certitude about the findings (i.e., $p < .01$ is superior to $p < .05$). But the probability of an obtained result (i.e., $r = .20$) being less than .05 or .01 is obviously dependent on sample size. Ultimately, the only satisfactory means of determining the accuracy of an estimate is through successive replications or approximations therein (i.e., meta-analysis). A case in point centers on the famous Multisystemic Therapy program, which has been promoted as an exemplary treatment (Cullen & Gendreau, 2000). It is one of the few programs whose effectiveness has been evaluated over time and the robustness of the initial findings (Bourduin et al., 1995) has now been tempered considerably (Littell, 2003).

The third, and in our opinion the most malignant among the deleterious effects of significance testing vis-à-vis sound policy development, is the view that if $p > .05$, then there is no effect and the results are simply due to chance. In truth, this is rarely the case. An equally plausible interpretation might be that a useful effect has been obtained using a sample size inadequate to label it as significant. This could easily be addressed through an increase in power, but in the "real world" of applied corrections research, sample sizes tend to be relatively modest ($n \approx 80$ to 150). Type II error rates, in such instances, occur about 50% of the time (Schmidt, 1996). Frankly, it is clear that, as researchers, we have been shooting ourselves in the foot! The dustbin of offender treatment research is replete with $p > .05$ findings which, we must now belatedly acknowledge, could be of considerable practical importance. The prison treatment literature is also rife with *n.s.* conclusions where so-called null or marginal findings (i.e., $rs \geq .05 \leq .20$), which might be of considerable value to prison managers, have been cavalierly discarded (French & Gendreau, 2004).

Remarkably, a means of statistically clarifying this apparent conundrum has been available for decades. Although out of fashion for years, the utility of the confidence interval (*CI*) has become increasingly apparent of late. Even defenders of significance testing accede to the usefulness of this technique (Abelson, 1997), and the American Psychological Association has also moved in this direction (i.e., Task Force on Statistical Inference; Wilkinson, 1999). Why does the *CI* make such a useful contribution to knowledge cumulation? It holds the overall error rate at 5%; that is, in 95% of *CI*s, one would expect to locate the "true" ES. The *CI* can be used to demonstrate that there is actually more uniformity in literatures than has heretofore been documented (for other examples specific to corrections, see Gendreau, Goggin, & Smith, 2000).

This singular focus on significance testing has had profound implications for offender treatment policy development. The following is a commonplace scenario that the authors have encountered on more than one occasion. At a presentation addressing the issue of pretreatment needs assessment for offenders, a subject with major implications for case management strategies with probationers, one of the reported risk measures predicted recidivism at the $p < .05$ level ($r = .30$, $n = 50$, $CI = .05$ to $.55$), while the other did not ($r = .25$, $n = 30$, $CI = -.09$ to $.59$). The conclusion: Only the former was a useful scale. This, despite the considerable degree of overlap in the respective *CI*s suggesting that, in fact, both measures were sampling from the same population parameter. Erroneous conclusions such as these are often repeated in the literature, resulting in a great deal of angst among researchers when, as was the case here, a useful scale is deemed nonsignificant. The typical response: attempts to explain the unexpected findings using a variety of ad hoc rationalizations or dismissal of potentially useful results.

The *CI* is also a useful estimate of the relative certainty of the magnitude of an effect (Gendreau et al., 2000). Where the *CI* is wide, clinicians and policymakers are forewarned that more primary research (or additional summaries of existing studies through meta-analysis) is needed before choosing a course of action. Again, replication should be given priority.

In addition to the *CI*, other "new" statistics have been developed that also advance our cause in determining the practical significance of research results (Kirk, 1996), that is, results useful in the "real world" of policymakers (Gendreau, 2002). We favor the common language effect size statistic (*CL*; McGraw & Wong, 1992) that is easily understood and so simple to calculate that it can be done manually. (The idea behind it is not novel; we have located an article published by Tilton in 1937 that, for all intents and purposes, was getting at the same idea.) Essentially, the *CL* converts an ES into the probability that a score sampled at random from one distribution will be greater than that sampled at random from a second distribution.

As a case in point, in a recent meta-analysis comparing the predictive validities of two well-known offender risk scales, we found that the LSI-R (Andrews & Bonta, 1995) produced an $r = .37$ ($SD = .12$) with general recidivism, while the Psychopathy Checklist-Revised (PCL-R; Hare, 1991) generated an $r = .24$ ($SD = .15$; Gendreau, Goggin, Smith, et al., 2002). The *CI*s did not overlap, which in itself was telling, but, in our view, that was not a precise enough estimate of how much better a predictor of recidivism one measure was than the other. The *CL* determined that the LSI-R was, on average, 77% more accurate in predicting offender recidivism than was the PCL-R. Is this interpretation not infinitely more useful than a simple report that both measures predict recidivism significantly and one does so significantly better than the other?

As a final note, the development of fail-safe statistics, or what we prefer to call "credibility" statistics (e.g., Gendreau, 2002; Orwin, 1987; Rosenthal, 1991), can assist in determining when the knowledge cumulation process may take a well-deserved siesta. One frequently hears never-say-die types of comments from advocates of various treatments or assessment protocols, à la "Just a few more studies and the results will refute your position and substantiate ours." Using one such index (see Gendreau, 2002), French and Gendreau (2004) found incontrovertible support for prison-based behavioral treatment programs, reporting that 64 additional ES with an average $r = .00$ would be required to reduce the obtained result to that of nonbehavioral treatment programs. (And how credible is that scenario?)

Researchers interested in empirically establishing the stability of their findings (i.e., the likelihood of a result being overturned) and contributing to the development of useful correctional policies and practices based on defensible research practices may find such statistics helpful.

CONCLUSION

This chapter offers a brief summary of the recent history of the rehabilitative ideal, its early ascendance, apparent decline, and ultimate revivification during the second half of the twentieth century. We document the impact of variable sociopolitical forces on its progress toward establishing "what works" in correctional treatment for offenders. We summarize the preponderance of meta-analytic data that have contributed to the development of the three principles regarded as key to reducing offender recidivism: the use of appropriate treatments in targeting and reducing the criminogenic needs of higher-risk offenders. We also present some recent evidence that confirms the predictive validity of these empirically derived principles. Finally, we address three issues with the potential to substantively retard the rehabilitative ideal's future progress: the increasing popularity of offender treatments rooted in correctional quackery, the failure to measure ongoing changes in offender risk, and the historic affection among forensic/correctional psychologists for faulty knowledge cumulation practices.

Given the evidence presented, it is clear that correctional treatments founded on sound empirical principles do work in reducing antisocial behavior. With remarkable consistency, the effectiveness of correctional treatments has been empirically demonstrated among a variety of offender populations across diverse community and institutional contexts, translating into meaningful improvements in public safety and significant cost savings. The requisite characteristics of effective treatment programs for offenders have also been empirically documented, and a mechanism for their evaluation (the CPAI-2000) has been developed.

Why, then, do we caution that the continued ascendancy of the rehabilitative ideal is not guaranteed? There are a number of potential limiters. As arduous as the scientific process can be, its product—knowledge—is still much more easily generated than it is promulgated. Its progress is invariably buffeted by a plethora of factors at play in the dynamic sociopolitical contexts in which we live. History affords us the example of Martinson's (1974) "nothing works" message and how persuasive it was despite having relatively meager empirical support. In the absence of an ongoing commitment to the principles of effective correctional programming, a systematic and quantitatively sophisticated approach to empirical inquiry, and a diligent regard for the application of its fruits, a resurgence of the Martinson ethos among a new generation of forensic/correctional psychologists is not inconceivable.

NOTE

1. Using Rosenthal's (1991) BESD statistic, the *r* value can be taken at face value. Recidivism rates for the treatment and comparison groups are computed from a base rate of 50%. Thus,

with a correlation of $r = .20$ between treatment and reoffending, one can conclude that the recidivism rate in the treatment group is 40% (50% *minus* 10%), as compared with 60% in the comparison group (50% *plus* 10%). Moreover, when summarizing a number of studies or in instances where recidivism base rates are not extreme (i.e., >20% and <80%) and treatment and comparison group sample sizes are within a 3:1 ratio, the r value closely approximates, or is identical to, the recidivism percentage difference between the two groups (Cullen & Gendreau, 2000; French & Gendreau, 2004).

REFERENCES

Abelson, R. P. (1997). On the surprising longevity of flogged horses: Why there is a case for the significance test. *Psychological Science, 8,* 12–15.

Adams, M. (2003). *Fire and ice: The United States, Canada, and the myth of converging values.* Toronto, Ontario, Canada: Penguin.

Allen, F. A. (1981). *The decline of the rehabilitative ideal: Penal policy and social purpose.* New Haven, CT: Yale University Press.

Andrews, D. A. (1979). *The dimensions of correctional counseling and supervision process in probation and parole.* Toronto, Ontario, Canada: Ontario Ministry of Correctional Services.

Andrews, D. A. (1980). Some experimental investigations of the principles of differential association through deliberate manipulations of the structure of service systems. *American Sociological Review, 45,* 448–462.

Andrews, D. A. (1995). The psychology of criminal conduct and effective treatment. In J. McGuire (Ed.), *What works: Reducing reoffending* (pp. 35–62). West Sussex, England: Wiley.

Andrews, D. A., & Bonta, J. (1995). *The Level of Service Inventory-Revised.* Toronto, Ontario, Canada: Multi-Health Systems.

Andrews, D. A., & Bonta, J. (2003). *The psychology of criminal conduct* (3rd ed.). Cincinnati, OH: Anderson.

Andrews, D. A., Bonta, J., & Hoge, R. D. (1990). Classification for effective rehabilitation: Rediscovering psychology. *Criminal Justice and Behavior, 17,* 19–52.

Andrews, D. A., Dowden, C., & Gendreau, P. (1999). *Clinically relevant and psychologically informed approaches to reduced re-offending: A meta-analytic study of human service, risk, need, responsivity, and other concerns in justice contexts.* Unpublished manuscript, Carleton University.

Andrews, D. A., Dowden, C., & Rettinger, L. J. (2001). Special populations within corrections. In J. A. Winterdyk (Ed.), *Corrections in Canada* (pp. 170–212). Toronto, Ontario, Canada: Prentice-Hall.

Andrews, D. A., & Kiessling, J. J. (1980). Program structure and effective correctional practices: A summary of the CaVIC research. In R. R. Ross & P. Gendreau (Eds.), *Effective correctional treatment* (pp. 441–463). Toronto, Ontario, Canada: Butterworths.

Andrews, D. A., & Wormith, J. S. (1989). Personality and crime: Knowledge destruction and construction in criminology. *Justice Quarterly, 6,* 289–309.

Andrews, D. A., Zinger, I., Hoge, R. D., Bonta, J., Gendreau, P., & Cullen, F. T. (1990). Does correctional treatment work? A clinically-relevant and psychologically informed meta-analysis. *Criminology, 28,* 369–404.

Aos, S., Phipps, P., Barnoski, R., & Lieb, R. (1999). *The comparative costs and benefits of programs to reduce crime: A review of national research findings with implications for Washington State.* Olympia: Washington State Institute for Public Safety.

Apter, S. J., & Goldstein, A. P. (1986). *Youth violence: Program and prospects.* New York: Pergamon Press.

Bailey, W. C. (1966). Correctional outcome: An evaluation of 100 reports. *Journal of Criminal Law, Criminology and Police Science, 57,* 153–160.

Beaman, A. L. (1991). An empirical comparison of meta-analytic and traditional reviews. *Personality and Social Psychology Bulletin, 17,* 252–257.

Binder, A., & Geis, G. (1984). Ad populum argumentation in criminology: Juvenile diversion as rhetoric. *Crime and Delinquency, 30,* 624–647.

Bonta, J. (1996). Risk-needs assessment and treatment. In A. T. Harland (Ed.), *Choosing correctional options that work* (pp. 18–32). Thousand Oaks, CA: Sage.

Bonta, J. (2002). Offender risk assessment: Guidelines for selection and use. *Criminal Justice and Behavior, 29,* 355–379.

Bonta, J., Law, M., & Hanson, K. (1998). The prediction of criminal and violent recidivism among mentally disordered offenders: A meta-analysis. *Psychological Bulletin, 123,* 123–142.

Boothby, J. L., & Clements, C. B. (2000). A national survey of correctional psychologists. *Criminal Justice and Behavior, 27,* 715–731.

Bourduin, C. M., Mann, B. J., Cone, L. T., Henggeler, S. W., Fucci, B. R., & Williams, R. A. (1995). Multisystemic treatment of serious juvenile offenders: Long-term prevention of criminality and violence. *Journal of Consulting and Clinical Psychology, 63,* 569–578.

Brockway, Z. R. (1871). The ideal of a true prison system for a state. In E. C. Wines (Ed.), *Transactions of the National Congress on Penitentiary and Reformatory Discipline* (pp. 38–65). Albany, NY: Weed, Parsons.

Brodsky, S. (2000). Guest editorial: Judging the progress of psychology in corrections: The verdict is not good. *International Journal of Offender Therapy and Comparative Criminology, 44,* 141–145.

Brown, S. L. (2002). The dynamic prediction of criminal recidivism: A three-wave prospective study. *Forum on Corrections Research, 14,* 24–27.

Burnside, J., Adler, J., Loucks, N., & Rose, G. (2001). *Kainos community in prisons: Report of an evaluation.* London: HM Prison Service, Research Development and Statistics Directorate.

Campbell, T. D. (1969). Reforms as experiments. *American Psychologist, 24,* 409–429.

Cleland, C. M., Pearson, F. S., Lipton, D. S., & Yee, D. (1997, November). *Does age make a difference? A meta-analytic approach to reductions in criminal offending for juveniles and adults.* Paper presented at the annual meeting of the American Society of Criminology, San Diego, CA.

Cohen, M. A. (1998). The monetary value of saving a high-risk youth. *Journal of Quantitative Criminology, 14,* 5–32.

Cohen, M. A. (2001). To treat or not to treat? A financial perspective. In C. R. Hollin (Ed.), *Handbook of offender assessment and treatment* (pp. 35–49). Rexdale, Ontario, Canada: Wiley.

Conrad, J. P. (1981). Where there's hope there's life. In D. Fogel & J. Hudson (Eds.), *Justice as fairness: Perspectives of the justice model* (pp. 3–21). Cincinnati, OH: Anderson.

Cullen, F. T. (2002). Rehabilitation and treatment programs. In J. Q. Wilson & J. Petersilia (Eds.), *Crime: Public policies for crime control* (pp. 253–289). Oakland, CA: ICS Press.

Cullen, F. T., & Applegate, B. (1997). *Offender rehabilitation: Effective correctional intervention.* Aldershot, England: Ashgate/Dartmouth.

Cullen, F. T., Blevins, K. R., Trager, J. S., & Gendreau, P. (in press). The rise and fall of boot camps: A case study in common-sense corrections. *Journal of Offender Rehabilitation.*

Cullen, F. T., & Gendreau, P. (1989). The effectiveness of correctional treatment: Reconsidering the "nothing works" debate. In L. Goodstein & D. L. MacKenzie (Eds.), *The American prison: Issues in research and policy* (pp. 23–44). New York: Plenum Press.

Cullen, F. T., & Gendreau, P. (2000). Assessing correctional rehabilitation: Policy, practice, and prospects. In J. Horney (Ed.), *National Institute of Justice criminal justice 2000: Changes in decision making and discretion in the criminal justice system* (pp. 109–175). Washington, DC: Department of Justice, National Institute of Justice.

Cullen, F. T., & Gendreau, P. (2001). From nothing works to what works: Changing professional ideology in the 21st century. *The Prison Journal, 81,* 313–338.

Cullen, F. T., Gendreau, P., Jarjoura, G. R., & Wright, J. P. (1997). Crime and the bell curve: Lessons from intelligent criminology. *Crime and Delinquency, 43,* 387–411.

Cullen, F. T., & Gilbert, K. E. (1982). *Reaffirming rehabilitation.* Cincinnati, OH: Anderson.

Cullen, F. T., Van Voorhis, P., & Sundt, J. L. (2000). Prisons in crisis: The American experience. In R. Matthews & P. Francis (Eds.), *Prisons 2000: An international perspective on the current state and future of imprisonment* (pp. 21–52). New York: Macmillan.

Cullen, F. T., Wright, J. P., & Applegate, B. K. (1996). Control in the community: The limits of reform? In A. T. Harland (Ed.), *Choosing correctional interventions that work: Defining the demand and evaluating the supply* (pp. 69–116). Newbury Park, CA: Sage.

Davidson, W., Gottschalk, R., Gensheimer, L., & Mayer, J. (1984). *Interventions with juvenile delinquents: A meta-analysis of treatment efficacy.* Washington, DC: National Institute of Juvenile Justice and Delinquency Prevention.

Davidson, W., Redner, R., Blakely, C., Mitchell, C., & Emshoff, J. (1987). Diversion of juvenile offender: An experimental comparison. *Journal of Consulting and Clinical Psychology, 55,* 68–75.

Davies, P. D. (2004, February). *Is evidence-based government possible? Jerry Lee Lecture 2004.* Paper presented at the Campbell Collaboration Colloquium, Washington, DC.

de Beaumont, G., & de Tocqueville, A. (1970). *On the penitentiary system in the United States and its application in France* (F. Lieber, Trans.). New York: Augustus M. Kelley. (Original work published 1833)

Dowden, C., & Andrews, D. A. (2000). Effective correctional treatment and violent reoffending: A meta-analysis. *Canadian Journal of Criminology, 42,* 449–467.

Dowden, C., & Andrews, D. A. (2003). Does family intervention work for delinquents? Results of a meta-analysis. *Canadian Journal of Criminology and Criminal Justice, 45,* 327–342.

Dowden, C., & Andrews, D. A. (2004). The importance of staff practice in delivering effective correctional treatment: A meta-analytic review of core correctional practice. *International Journal of Offender Therapy and Comparative Criminology, 48,* 203–214.

Dowden, C., Antonowicz, D., & Andrews, D. A. (2003). The effectiveness of relapse prevention with offenders: A meta-analysis. *International Journal of Offender Therapy and Comparative Criminology, 47,* 516–528.

Duhame, J. (1995). *The Cyrano method: Using theatre in offender treatment.* Regional Research Project (R1-1995). Laval, Québec, Canada: Regional Research Committee, Correctional Service of Canada.

Emery, R. E., & Marholin, D. (1977). An applied behavior analysis of delinquency: The irrelevancy of relevant behavior. *American Psychologist, 32,* 860–873.

Erwin, B. J. (1986). Turning up the heat on probationers in Georgia. *Federal Probation, 50,* 17–24.

Feeley, M., & Simon, J. (1992). The new penology: Notes on the emerging strategy of corrections and its implications. *Criminology, 30,* 449–474.

French, S. A., & Gendreau, P. (2004). *Reducing prison misconducts: What works!* Manuscript submitted for publication.

Gallagher, R. W., Somwaru, D. P., & Ben-Porath, Y. S. (1999). Current usage of psychological tests in state correctional settings. *Corrections Compendium, 24,* 1–3, 20.

Garrett, C. J. (1985). Effects of residential treatment of adjudicated delinquents: A meta-analysis. *Journal of Research in Crime and Delinquency, 22,* 287–308.

Gendreau, P. (1989). Programs that do not work: A brief comment on Brodeur and Doob. *Canadian Journal of Criminology, 31,* 133–135.

Gendreau, P. (1996a). Offender rehabilitation: What we know and what needs to be done. *Criminal Justice and Behavior, 23,* 144–161.

Gendreau, P. (1996b). The principles of effective intervention with offenders. In A. T. Harland (Ed.), *Choosing correctional interventions that work: Defining the demand and evaluating the supply* (pp. 117–130). Newbury Park, CA: Sage.

Gendreau, P. (2000). 1998 Margaret Mead award address: Rational policies for reforming offenders. In M. McMahon (Ed.), *Assessment to assistance: Programs for women in community corrections* (pp. 177–212). New York: Grune & Stratton.

Gendreau, P. (2002). We must do a better job of cumulating knowledge. *Canadian Psychology, 43,* 205–210.

Gendreau, P. (2003, August). *Context is crucial: Correctional psychology in the United States and Canada.* Paper presented at the meeting of the American Psychological Association, Toronto, Ontario, Canada.

Gendreau, P., & Andrews, D. A. (1979). Psychological consultation in correctional agencies: Case studies and general issues. In J. J. Platt & R. Wicks (Eds.), *The psychological consultant* (pp. 177–212). New York: Grune & Stratton.

Gendreau, P., & Andrews, D. A. (2001). *Correctional Program Assessment Inventory-2000 (CPAI-2000).* Saint John, New Brunswick, Canada: University of New Brunswick.

Gendreau, P., Goggin, C., Cullen, F., & Paparozzi, M. (2002). The common sense revolution and correctional policy. In J. McGuire (Ed.), *Offender rehabilitation and treatment: Effective programmes and policies to reduce reoffending* (pp. 359–386). Chichester, England: Wiley.

Gendreau, P., Goggin, C., & Law, M. A. (1997). Predicting prison misconducts. *Criminal Justice and Behavior, 24,* 414–431.

Gendreau, P., Goggin, C., & Paparozzi, M. (1996). Principles of effective assessment for community corrections. *Federal Probation, 60,* 64–70.

Gendreau, P., Goggin, C., & Smith, P. (2000). Generating rational correctional policies: An introduction to advances in cumulating knowledge. *Corrections Management Quarterly, 4,* 52–60.

Gendreau, P., Goggin, C., & Smith, P. (2001). Implementation guidelines for correctional programs in the "real world." In G. A. Bernfeld, D. P. Farrington, & A. W. Leschied (Eds.), *Offender rehabilitation in practice* (pp. 247–268). Chichester, England: Wiley.

Gendreau, P., Goggin, C., & Smith, P. (2002). Is the PCL-R really the "unparalleled" measure of offender risk? *Criminal Justice and Behavior, 29,* 397–426.

Gendreau, P., & Keyes, D. (2001). Making prisons safer and more humane environments. *Canadian Journal of Criminology, 43,* 123–130.

Gendreau, P., Latessa, E. J., & Cullen, F. T. (2004). *A comment on Shearer's what doesn't work in the "what works" approach.* Manuscript submitted for publication.

Gendreau, P., Little, T., & Goggin, C. (1996). A meta-analysis of the predictors of adult offender recidivism: What works! *Criminology, 34,* 575–607.

Gendreau, P., & Ross, R. R. (1979). Effective correctional treatment: Bibliotherapy for cynics. *Crime and Delinquency, 25,* 463–489.

Gendreau, P., & Ross, R. R. (1981a). Correctional potency: Treatment and deterrence on trial. In R. Roesch & R. Corrado (Eds.), *Evaluation and criminal justice policy* (pp. 29–57). Beverly Hills, CA: Sage.

Gendreau, P., & Ross, R. R. (1981b). Offender rehabilitation: The appeal of success. *Federal Probation, 45,* 45–48.

Gendreau, P., & Ross, R. R. (1983–1984). Correctional treatment: Some recommendations for successful intervention. *Juvenile and Family Court, 34,* 31–40.

Gendreau, P., & Ross, R. R. (1987). Revivification of rehabilitation: Evidence from the 1980s. *Justice Quarterly, 4,* 349–407.

Gibbs, J. C., Potter, G. B., & Goldstein, A. P. (1995). *The EQUIP program: Teaching youth to think and act responsibly through a peer-helping approach.* Champaign, IL: Research Press.

Girard, L., & Wormith, J. S. (2004). The predictive validity of the Level of Service Inventory-Ontario Revision on general and violent recidivism among various offender groups. *Criminal Justice and Behavior, 31,* 150–181.

Glass, G., McGaw, B., & Smith, M. L. (1981). *Meta-analysis in social research.* Beverly Hills, CA: Sage.

Gordon, D. A., Arbuthnot, J., Gustafson, K. E., & McGreen, P. (1988). Home-based behavioral-systems family therapy with disadvantaged juvenile delinquents. *American Journal of Family Therapy, 16,* 243–255.

Hanson, R. K., & Harris, A. J. R. (2000). Where should we intervene? Dynamic predictors of sexual offender recidivism. *Criminal Justice and Behaviour, 27,* 6–35.

Hanson, R. K., & Morton-Bourgon, K. (2004). *Predictors of sexual recidivism: An updated meta-analysis* (Report 2004–02). Ottawa, Ontario, Canada: Public Safety and Emergency Preparedness Canada.

Hare, R. D. (1991). *Manual for the Hare Psychopathy Checklist-Revised.* Toronto, Ontario, Canada: Multi-Health Systems.

Harlow, L. L., Mulaik, S. A., & Steiger, J. H. (1997). *What if there were no significance tests.* Mahwah, NJ: Erlbaum.

Hill, G. (1985). Predicting recidivism using institutional measures. In D. P. Farrington & R. Tarling (Eds.), *Prediction in criminology* (pp. 96–118). Albany: State University of New York Press.

Hoffman, P. B., & Beck, J. L. (1974). *Parole decision-making: A Salient Factor Score.* Washington, DC: National Institute of Justice.

Izzo, R. L., & Ross, R. R. (1990). Meta-analysis of rehabilitation programs for juvenile delinquents. *Criminal Justice and Behavior, 17,* 134–142.

Johnson, W. W., Bennett, K., & Flanagan, T. J. (1997). Getting tough on prisoners: Results from the National Corrections Executive Survey, 1995. *Crime and Delinquency, 43,* 24–41.

Jones, P. R. (1996). Risk prediction in criminal justice. In A. T. Harland (Ed.), *Choosing correctional options that work: Defining the demand and evaluating the supply* (pp. 33–68). Thousand Oaks, CA: Sage.

Kassebaum, G., Ward, D. A., & Wilner, D. M. (1971). *Prison treatment and parole survival: An empirical assessment.* New York: Wiley.

Keyes, D. (1996). *Preventing prison misconduct behavior: A quantitative review of the literature.* Unpublished manuscript, Centre for Criminal Justice Studies, University of New Brunswick at Saint John, New Brunswick, Canada.

Kirby, B. C. (1954). Measuring effects of treatment of criminals and delinquents. *Sociology and Social Research, 38,* 368–374.

Kirk, R. E. (1996). Practical significance: A concept whose time has come. *Educational and Psychological Measurement, 56,* 746–759.

Kroner, D. G., & Mills, J. F. (2001). The accuracy of five risk appraisal instruments in predicting institutional misconduct and new convictions. *Criminal Justice and Behavior, 28,* 471–489.

Latessa, E. J., Cullen, F. T., & Gendreau, P. (2002). Beyond correctional quackery: Professionalism and the possibility of effective treatment. *Federal Probation, 66,* 43–49.

Lipsey, M. W. (1992). Juvenile delinquency treatment: A meta-analytic inquiry into the variability of effects. In T. D. Cook, H. Cooper, D. S. Cordray, H. Hartmann, L. V. Hedges, R. J. Light, et al. (Eds.), *Meta-analysis for explanation: A casebook* (pp. 83–127). New York: Russell Sage.

Lipsey, M. W. (1999). Can rehabilitative programs reduce the recidivism of juvenile offenders? An inquiry into the effectiveness of practical programs. *Virginia Journal of Social Policy and Law, 6,* 611–641.

Lipsey, M. W., Chapman, G. L., & Landenberger, N. A. (2001). Cognitive-behavioral programs for offenders. *Annals of the American Academy of Political and Social Science, 578,* 144–157.

Lipsey, M. W., & Wilson, D. B. (1993). The efficacy of psychological, educational and behavioral treatment. *American Psychologist, 48,* 1181–1209.

Lipsey, M. W., & Wilson, D. B. (1998). Effective interventions for serious juvenile offenders: A synthesis of research. In R. Loeber & David P. Farrington (Eds.), *Serious and violent juvenile offenders: Risk factors and successful interventions* (pp. 313–366). Thousand Oaks, CA: Sage.

Lipton, D., Martinson, R., & Wilks, J. (1975). *The effectiveness of correctional treatment: A survey of treatment evaluation studies.* New York: Praeger.

Littell, J. H. (2003, November). *Systematic and nonsystematic reviews of empirical evidence on the outcomes of multisystemic treatment.* Paper presented at the Seminar on Evidence-based Policy and Practice, Nordic Campbell Center, Copenhagen, Denmark.

Logan, C. H. (1972). Evaluation research in crime and delinquency: A reappraisal. *Journal of Criminal Law, Criminology and Police Science, 63,* 378–387.

Logan, C. H., & Gaes, G. (1993). Meta-analysis and the rehabilitation of punishment. *Justice Quarterly, 10,* 245–263.

Logan, C. H., Gaes, G. G., Harer, M., Innes, C. A., Karacki, L., & Saylor, W. G. (1991). *Can meta-analysis save correctional rehabilitation?* Washington, DC: Department of Justice, Federal Bureau of Prisons.

Lösel, F. (1995). The efficacy of correctional treatment: A review and synthesis of meta-evaluations. In J. McGuire (Ed.), *What works: Reducing reoffending* (pp. 79–111). West Sussex, England: Wiley.

Lovell, D., & Jemelka, R. (1996). When inmates misbehave: The costs of discipline. *Prison Journal, 76,* 165–179.

Lowenkamp, C. T. (2004). *A program level analysis of the relationship between correctional program integrity and treatment effectiveness.* Unpublished doctoral dissertation, University of Cincinnati, OH.

Loza, W., & Loza-Fanous, A. (2001). Effectiveness of the Self-Appraisal Questionnaire in predicting offenders' postrelease outcome: A comparison study. *Criminal Justice and Behavior, 28,* 105–121.

Loza, W., & Loza-Fanous, A. (2003). More evidence for the validity of the Self-Appraisal Questionnaire for predicting violent and nonviolent recidivism. *Criminal Justice and Behavior, 30,* 709–721.

Martinson, R. (1974). What works? Questions and answers about prison reform. *The Public Interest, 35,* 22–54.

Martinson, R. (1976). California and the crossroads. In R. Martinson, T. Palmer, & S. Adams (Eds.), *Rehabilitation, recidivism and research* (pp. 63–74). Hackensack, NJ: National Council on Crime and Delinquency.

Martinson, R. (1979). New findings, new views: A note of caution regarding sentencing reform. *Hofstra Law Review, 7,* 243–258.

McGraw, K. O., & Wong, S. P. (1992). A common language effect size statistic. *Psychological Bulletin, 111,* 361–365.

McGuire, J. (2002). *Evidence-based programming today.* Draft paper for the International Community Corrections Association (ICCA) annual conference 2002, Boston.

Meehl, P. E. (1991). Why summaries on psychological theories are often uninterpretable. In R. E. Snow & D. E. Wiley (Eds.), *Improving inquiry in social science: A volume in honor of Lee J. Cronbach* (pp. 13–59). Hillsdale, NJ: Erlbaum.

Menninger, K. (1968). *The crime of punishment.* New York: Penguin.

Miles, H., & Raynor, P. (2004). *Community sentences in Jersey: Risk, needs, and rehabilitation.* Jersey, England: Jersey Probation and After Care Service.

Moneymaker, J. M., & Strimple, E. O. (1991). Animals and inmates: A sharing companionship behind bars. *Journal of Offender Rehabilitation, 16,* 133–152.

Morgan, R. D., & Flora, D. B. (2002). Group psychotherapy with incarcerated offenders: A research synthesis. *Group Dynamics, 6,* 203–218.

Mowrer, O. H. (1960). *Learning theory and behavior.* New York: Wiley.

Nesovic, A. (2003). Psychometric evaluation of the Correctional Program Assessment Inventory. *Dissertation Abstracts International, 64*(09), 4674B. (UMI No. AAT NQ83525).

Orwin, R. G. (1987). A fail-safe N for effect size in meta-analysis. *Journal of Educational Statistics, 8,* 157–159.

Palmer, T. (1975). Martinson revisited. *Journal of Research in Crime and Delinquency, 12,* 133–152.

Palmer, T. (1992). *The re-emergence of correctional intervention.* Newbury Park, CA: Sage.

Quay, H. C. (1977). The three faces of evaluation: What can be expected to work. *Criminal Justice and Behaviour, 4,* 21–25.

Redondo, S., Sánchez-Meca, J., & Garrido, V. (1999). The influence of treatment programmes on the recidivism of juvenile and adult offenders: A European meta-analytic review. *Psychology, Crime and Law, 5,* 251–278.

Reiss, D., Quayle, M., Brett, T., & Meux, C. (1998). Drama therapy for mentally disordered offenders: Changes in levels of anger. *Criminal Behaviour and Mental Health, 8,* 139–153.

Rex, S., Lieb, R., Bottoms, A., & Wilson, L. (2003). *Accrediting offender programs: A process-based evaluation of the Joint Prison/Probation Services Accreditation panel.* Home Office Research Study 273. London: Development and Statistics Directorate, Home Office.

Rice, J. S., & Remy, L. L. (1994). Evaluating horticultural therapy: The ecological context of urban jail inmates. In J. Flagler & R. P. Poincelot (Eds.), *People-plant relationships: Setting research priorities* (pp. 203–224). Binghamton, NY: Food Products Press.

Richardson-Taylor, K., & Blanchette, K. (2001). *Results of an evaluation of the Pawsitive Directions Canine Program at Nova Institute for Women* (Report No. R-108). Ottawa, Ontario, Canada: Correctional Service of Canada.

Rosenthal, R. (1991). *Meta-analytic procedures for social research.* Beverly Hills, CA: Sage.

Rosenthal, R., & DiMatteo, M. R. (2001). Meta-analysis: Recent developments in quantitative methods for literature reviews. *Annual Review of Psychology, 52,* 59–82.

Ross, R. R., & Fabiano, E. A. (1985). *Time to think: A cognitive model of delinquency prevention and offender rehabilitation.* Johnson City, TN: Institute of Social Science and Arts.

Ross, R. R., & Gendreau, P. (1980). *Effective correctional treatment.* Toronto, Ontario, Canada: Butterworths.

Ross, R. R., & McKay, B. (1978). Treatment in corrections: Requiem for a panacea. *Canadian Journal of Criminology, 20,* 279–295.

Rothman, D. J. (1980). *Conscience and convenience: The asylum and its alternatives in progressive America.* Boston: Little, Brown.

Saunders, D. (2004, March 17). Florida puts felons in God's big house. *Globe and Mail,* pp. A-1, A-12.

Schmidt, F. (1992). What do data really mean? Research findings, meta-analysis, and cumulative knowledge in psychology. *American Psychologist, 47,* 1173–1181.

Schmidt, F. (1996). Statistical significance testing and cumulative knowledge in psychology: Implications for training of researchers. *Psychological Methods, 1,* 115–129.

Sechrest, L., White, S. O., & Brown, E. D. (1979). *The rehabilitation of criminal offenders: Problems and prospects.* Washington, DC: National Academy of Sciences.

Shulman, S. (2004). *Scientific integrity in policymaking: An investigation into the Bush administration's misuse of science.* Washington, DC: Union of Concerned Scientists.

Simourd, D. J. (2004). Use of dynamic risk/need assessment instruments among long-term incarcerated offenders. *Criminal Justice and Behavior, 31,* 306–323.

Smith, P., Goggin, C., & Gendreau, P. (2002). The effects of prison sentences and intermediate sanctions on recidivism: General effects and individual differences. (Report 2002-01). Ottawa, Ontario, Canada: Solicitor General of Canada.

Spiegler, M. D., & Guevremont, D. C. (1998). *Contemporary behavior therapy* (3rd ed.). Pacific Grove, CA: Brooks/Cole.

Task Force on Corrections, President's Commission on Law Enforcement and Administration of Justice. (1967). *Task force report: Corrections.* Washington, DC: U.S. Government Printing Office.

Tilghman, A. (2004, January 22). Man's sentence: Probation, yoga. *Houston Chronicle,* pp. A-17, A-26.

Tilton, J. W. (1937). The measurement of overlapping. *Journal of Educational Psychology, 28,* 656–662.

Toby, J. (1964). Is punishment necessary? *Journal of Criminal Law, Criminology and Police Science, 55,* 332–337.

Travisono, A. P., & Hawkes, A. F. (1995). *Building a voice: 125 years of history.* Washington, DC: American Correctional Association.

U.S. Department of Justice. (2003). *Prisoners in 2002* (NCJ-200248). Washington, DC: U.S. Department of Justice, Bureau of Justice Statistics.

Useem, B., & Kimball, P. (1991). *States of siege: U.S. Prison Riots, 1971–1986.* New York: Oxford University Press.

Walker, S. (1985). *Sense and nonsense about crime: A policy guide.* Monterey, CA: Brooks/Cole.

Walters, G. D. (2003). Changes in criminal thinking and identity in novice and experienced inmates: Prisonization revisited. *Criminal Justice and Behavior, 30,* 399–421.

Walters, G. D. (in press). Risk-appraisal versus self-report in the prediction of criminal justice outcomes: A meta-analysis. *Criminal Justice and Behavior.*

Walters, G. D., Trgovac, M., Rychlec, M., Di Fazio, R., & Olson, J. R. (2002). Assessing change with the Psychological Inventory of Criminal Thinking Styles: A controlled analysis and multisite cross-validation. *Criminal Justice and Behavior, 29,* 308–331.

Warren, M. Q. (1969). The case for differential treatment of delinquents. *Annals of the American Academy of Political and Social Science, 62,* 239–258.

Welsh, B. C., & Farrington, D. P. (2000). Correctional intervention programs and cost-benefit analysis. *Criminal Justice and Behavior, 27,* 115–133.

Wexler, H. K., Falkin, G. P., & Lipton, D. S. (1990). Outcome evaluation of a prison therapeutic community for substance abuse treatment. *Criminal Justice and Behavior, 17,* 71–92.

Wilkinson, L. (1999). Statistical methods in psychology journals: Guidelines and explanations. *American Psychologist, 54,* 594–604.

Wilks, J., & Martinson, R. (1976). Is the treatment of criminal offenders really necessary? *Federal Probation, 40,* 3–8.

Wormith, J. S. (2001). Assessing offender assessment: Contributing to effective correctional treatment. *ICCA Journal on Community Corrections, 7,* 12–22.

Zamble, E., & Quinsey, V. L. (1997). *Criminal recidivism process.* New York: Cambridge University Press.

CHAPTER 25

Psychotherapy with Criminal Offenders

MAX J. MOBLEY

ONE OF the questions asked to test the intelligence of schoolchildren is "Why are criminals locked up?" The answers given by Wechsler (1974) are clear: deterrence, protection for society, example to others, punishment or revenge, rehabilitation, and segregation. Society itself seems much more conflicted about some of the reasons. Protection for society is clearly a major reason, as demonstrated by the willingness to increase total state and federal prison budgets to $36,426,670,701 in fiscal year 2002.

State correctional populations increased by 71.7%, while the population of the Federal Bureau of Prisons increased by 148.1% from 1990 to 2000 (Bureau of Justice Statistics, 2004). The number of state and federal prison inmates reached 1,310,190 at the end of 2000 (Bureau of Justice Statistics, 2004). This number was managed by state systems operating at 89% to 216% of capacity and the Federal Bureau of Prisons operating at 133% of capacity at the end of 2002 (Bureau of Justice Statistics, 2002). Pressure on correctional systems continues, with 74,633 state and federal prisoners being held in jails at the end of 2002. National incarceration rates have increased from 180 per 100,000 in 1980, to 297 in 1990, and to 478 in 2000. However, the national rate of incarceration seems to have reached a plateau, remaining at 482 per 100,000 at the end of 2003 (Bureau of Justice Statistics, 2004).

Crime Index Offense rates have decreased about 30% from a high of 5,898 per 100,000 in 1990 to 4,118.8 in 2002 (Federal Bureau of Investigation, 2003), suggesting that prisons have been successful in their goal of protecting society by incapacitating offenders. The rates in 2003 and 2004 continue to show decreases (Table 25.1 on p. 752).

Correlations between the incarceration rates for the past 20 years and Uniform Crime Reports (Federal Bureau of Investigation, 2003) and Victimization Reports (Bureau of Justice Statistics, 2003b), are rather impressive. Although

Table 25.1
Relation of Incarceration Rate to Crime and Victimization Rates

Year	Incarceration Rate[a]	UCR Total Index Crimes Reported[b]	BJS Violent Victimization[b]	BJS Property Victimization[b]
1982	171	5,600.5	50.7	468.3
1992	332	5,661.4	47.9	325.3
2002	476	4,118.8	22.8	159.0
Correlation with incarceration rate		0.69	0.70	0.96

Notes: BJS = Bureau of Justice Statistics; UCR = Uniform Crime Report.
[a]*The Corrections Yearbook,* by C. Camp and G. Camp, 1985, 1989, 1997, 2000, South Salem, NY: Criminal Justice Institute; *The Corrections Yearbook,* by G. Camp and C. Camp, 2002, South Salem, NY: Criminal Justice Institute
[b]*2002 Uniform Crime Reports,* by Federal Bureau of Investigation, 2003, Washington, D.C.: U.S. Department of Justice.

this correlation does not demonstrate causality, it does appear that increased incarceration has made us all safer, at least in the short run.

What about the long run? Most prisoners will be released at some point. Will corrections have "corrected" them? Or are we simply increasing the size of the "convict culture" by incarcerating an increasing percentage of the population? The bottom-line standard for success in corrections has long been recidivism. The rate of felons returning to prison (new commitments with prior felonies) has not changed substantially, from 32.6% in 1989 to 32.7% in 1999 (Camp & Camp, 1989, 1999). Rearrest rates within 3 years of release have tended to increase, from 62.5% in 1983 to 67.5% of those released in 1994 (Bureau of Justice Statistics, 2003a). Success on parole, about 41%, remains unchanged since 1990 (Bureau of Justices Statistics, 2003b). Given an increase in the number of releasees from 108,580 in 1983 to 272,111 between 1983 and 1994, almost twice as many people returned to prison with new crimes.

It appears that, while prison systems have shown considerable success with incapacitation, they have not shown progress in the goals of primary (first criminal offense) and secondary (returning to incarceration) deterrence. Yet, construction continues, with 58,422 new beds under construction at the beginning of 2002.

The corrections system has had increasing difficulty retaining prisoners with overcrowding and budget crunches that once again raise the specter of conditions of confinement lawsuits. Although sentence lengths have dropped from an average of 79 months in 1992 (Bureau of Justice Statistics, 1996) to 56.7 months in 2000 (Bureau of Justice Statistics, 2003c), truth-in-sentencing laws and abolishment of discretionary parole have actually kept inmates in prison longer in many jurisdictions.

The bottom line is that incarceration alone does not seem to have the desired effect of correcting behavior (Zamble & Porporino, 1990). In fact, a Canadian study (Smith, Goggin, & Gendreau, 2002, p. ii) concludes, "Prisons and intermediate sanctions should not be used with the expectation of reducing criminal behavior."

What, then, can we say about prison's success in the goal of rehabilitation? Indicators of the success of treatment programs have increasingly appeared in the literature (see the special issue of *Criminal Justice and Behavior*, Gendreau, 1990; Hanson et al., 2002; Harrison, Cappello, Alazewski, Appleton, & Cooke, 2003). These successes have usually impacted a small segment of the inmate population and have had only a small, local impact on recidivism statistics, but they do provide valuable clues as to what works. Hope has not been lost. People continue to believe that our prisons should rehabilitate. F. T. Cullen, Skovon, Scott, and Burton (1990) found that, of people surveyed in two cities, the percentage indicating that the main emphasis of prisons should be rehabilitation was higher than for punishment or protection of society. This is less encouraging than it would seem for correctional psychology, for it appears that most citizens define rehabilitation in terms of education and job preparation rather than psychotherapy.

Budgets for corrections have soared, but this has been primarily due to increasing populations. While the budgets have nearly doubled, from $18 billion in 1991 to $35 billion in 2001, inmate cost per day has increased about 28%, from $48.51 in 1991 to $62.22 in 2001 (Camp & Camp, 2002).

As this only marginally tracks inflation (about 30.9% based on Consumer Price Index [CPI] for those years), it is likely that programs have not increased and probably have suffered in most systems. Priority is usually given to psychological treatment of the diagnosed mentally ill: 4.8% of the correctional population was involved in treatment programs for the mentally ill on January 1, 2002, up from 3.3% in January 1991 (Camp & Camp, 2002). As of January 1, 2002, 2.6% of inmates were in sex offender programs, almost twice the 1.2% involved in January 1991. Chemical dependency treatment, which peaked at 200,980 inmates in 1993, dropped to 117,945 (about 12.9% of the inmate population) as of January 1, 2002.

Where does this leave the considerable influx of psychologists, the result of consent decrees signed in the 1980s by many state departments of correction? It leaves us doing what is necessary (care of individuals with *DSM-IV-TR* Axis I diagnoses), doing what shows promise of working (treatment of drug- and sex-related compulsions), and probing areas where we may help the offender develop controls over other specifically targeted behaviors that people fear from criminals. We have increasingly come to understand that prisoners differ in their motivation from the clients who usually seek mental health services. Their clinical problems show more subtle thought distortion and striking disinhibition with much underlying personality disorder. In addition, the settings in which we work are less supportive, warm, and empathic than the settings in which most of us trained and developed our skills.

This chapter is intended to provide the trained therapist with some insights into treatment of offenders. It begins with a discussion of estimates of treatment needs and then breaks down the tasks of the therapist into crisis intervention, long-term management, short-term therapy, and therapeutic programs. Each task is presented in terms of the characteristics of the client, therapist, and system that have a bearing on its success or failure.

MENTAL DISORDER IN OFFENDER POPULATIONS

How serious a problem is mental disorder in the offender population? In preparation for the first edition of this chapter almost 20 years ago, I asked administrators of mental health programs in several states to estimate the percentage of inmates in their systems who were "mentally disordered to the point of needing to be housed in special facilities." Their estimates showed considerable variation, ranging from less than 1% to 25% of the inmate population. Previously published estimates of psychiatric disorder have ranged from less than 5% (Petrich, 1976) to over 60% (Kal, 1977). Gibbs (1982) pointed out the problems related to sampling and inconsistent definitions that have contributed to the confusion.

Mental health professionals cited as early as 1972 by Abramson and reviewed by Teplin (1983) speculated that mentally ill behavior has been "criminalized" and that many individuals who would formerly have been in mental hospitals are currently being dumped on "The system that cannot say no" (Levinson, 1984). This has almost certainly happened, but so has the reverse: psychologists and psychiatrists providing Get-Out-of-Jail-Free cards to offenders they believe would be better diverted to the mental health system.

Teplin (1984) cites National Institute of Mental Health statistics showing that between 1969 and 1980, the mental hospital inpatient census declined by 66%, and the average length of stay decreased by about 45% between 1969 and 1978. During an overlapping period, 1970 to 1980, the number of prisoners increased by about 61% (Travisono, 1984). The symmetry of these figures has suggested to some that the burden of caring for the chronically mentally ill may have shifted from mental health to the criminal justice system. The correlation here may also be largely coincidental. The rate of incarceration per 100,000 of the population has continued on about the same vector long after deinstitutionalization of mental hospitals was completed.

Studies of arrests suggest that mentally disordered individuals are likely to find their way into the criminal justice system. Sosowsky's (1980) data suggest that mental status is causally related to the increased arrest rate. Teplin (1984) looked at individuals at the point of arrest and concluded that the mentally disordered had a significantly greater chance of being arrested than nonmentally disordered persons for similar offenses. A longitudinal study of a Swedish cohort (Crocker & Hodgins, 1997) suggests that noninstitutionalized mentally retarded individuals are more likely than members of the general population to be arrested for criminal acts. Given this apparently higher arrest rate, it is reasonable to hypothesize that the number of mentally disordered individuals in jails has probably also increased. The hypothesis is difficult to test, however, because information is not collected uniformly on representative samples nor analyzed to give proper epidemiological estimates (Gibbs, 1982). Past estimates suggest that 6% to 7% of men (Teplin, 1994; Torrey et al., 1992) and a higher percentage of women (Teplin, 1996) in jail have severe mental illness.

A study conducted in Ontario (Allodi, Kedward, & Robertson, 1977) did find an increased number and proportion of psychiatrically disordered individuals in jails during the period of reduction in hospital beds, although the jail census did not increase disproportionately. Many law enforcement officials will admit, off the record, that the needs of their communities may be better served by pressing criminal charges against individuals whom the community would prefer to do without than by taking them to a mental health facility. The individual may not be any more "cured" on release, but at least the sheriff and the community get a little longer breathing space.

Steadman and Ribner (1980) found that the percentage of inmates in a county jail who had prior inpatient hospitalization increased from 9% in 1968 to 12% in 1975. Although a prevalence increase of 3% sounds like only a bit more of a nuisance, the number of individuals in county jails also increased by 225% from 1968 to 1975; thus, the 3% increase in prevalence represented a 300% increase in the actual number of offenders with a history of prior inpatient hospitalization in the study. A study of jail detainees (Fisher et al., 2002) suggested that access to mental hospitals might not be the problem, as 52% of mentally ill jail detainees had at least one hospitalization. This was about three times the rate for an unincarcerated comparison group. Thus, if there is a problem, it appears to be with long-term retention or efficacy of the treatment, rather than access.

The percentage or number of offenders in jail or prison with prior inpatient hospitalization does not necessarily provide a clear picture of mental disorder among incarcerated offenders. Often, hospitalization may be a legal maneuver rather than the treatment modality chosen by a mental health professional. Lawyers who have not had time to prepare their cases may request a court-ordered evaluation to get their clients out of jail and give themselves more time. State law for certain felonies may mandate psychiatric assessment. Lacking a solid defense, a lawyer has little to lose by sending a client to the state hospital for a 30-day evaluation and hoping that the doctors can come up with something that the defense can use. Thus, many offenders with a prior history of hospitalization may have been hospitalized for court-ordered evaluations rather than for treatment of a mental disorder.

A survey of women prisoners in England and Wales found a prevalence rate of 13% for any functional psychosis (O'Brien, Mortimer, Singleton, Meltzer, & Goodman, 2003), and half of the women incarcerated were on one or more psychotropic medications. This seems to have been overdiagnosis, as a methodologically similar survey of adolescent psychiatric disorder found that 95% had one or more disorders and about 80% had more than one (Lader, Singleton, & Meltzer, 2003). The difference that diagnostic techniques made in these survey results is pointed out by Fazel and Danesh (2002b). This difference is further shown in research by Corrado, Cohen, Hart, and Roesch (2000) comparing prevalence rates across six different definitions. Fazel and Danesh (2002) reviewed 62 surveys for prevalence of mental disorder within the previous 6 months. These authors found that 3.7% of male and 4.0% of female prisoners had psychotic illness; 10% of males and 12% of females had Major Depression; 47% of males and 21% of females had Antisocial Personality Disorder. It is important to keep in mind that this is prevalence within the previous 6 months, not lifetime incidence. A New Zealand study (Brinded, Stevens, Mulder, Fairley, Malcom, et al., 1999) found prevalence rates in the previous month to be 2.2% for Schizophrenia and related disorders, 1.1% for Bipolar Disorder, and 1.1% for Major Depression among sentenced men, and 4.2% for Schizophrenic Disorder, 1.2% for Bipolar Disorder, and 11.1% for Major Depression among women.

A recent survey of psychiatric disorders in older prisoners of both genders in Tennessee found a prevalence rate of about 16% (Regan, Alderson, & Regan, 2002). Given the increasing appearance of dementia in this age group, it is not surprising that this rate runs higher than those mentioned earlier.

These percentages are important because they provide one type of needs assessment for treatment services. The percentages themselves can be argued. As Collins and Schlenger (1983) note, the prevalence of Antisocial Personality Disorder diagnosed by *DSM-III* rules in their study is lower than that found by James, Gregory, Jones, and Rundell (1980) using *DSM-III* criteria and lower than that diagnosed by judges in Hare (1983). In addition, there are great differences in the treatability of various disorders and the impact they have on the operations of correctional systems and vice versa.

One of the reasons given for a higher rate of mental disorder in prison (Toch, Adams, & Greene, 1987) is based on the assumption of a more restricted and self-defeating response repertoire of the mentally disordered, leading to punitive sanctions and more time served on their sentences. McCorkle (1995) tested this hypothesis and found that a history of being on psychiatric medications or previously hospitalized did not predict disciplinary infraction rate in prison. Some relationship was found between currently being on medication and disciplinary infraction rate, but only for females. Further, this effect was smaller than the effect of age on disciplinary infraction rate.

Rates of mental retardation determined from screening tests have often been estimated to run three to five times the rates found by Denkowski and Denkowski (1985). These researchers found rates of mental retardation to be about 2% in state prison systems when more reliable individual batteries of tests were used. A Florida study (Spruill & May, 1988) had similar findings when more rigorous tests and definitions of mental retardation were used.

It does appear that a number of mentally disordered individuals do better in the predictable, structured environment of prisons. As Toch, Adams, and Grant (1989) note, prisons do seem to have beneficial effects for some offenders. Nevertheless, anyone who has worked in corrections has numerous horror stories of the inability of particular prisoner clients to adapt to incarceration. As noted earlier, over 5.5% of the mentally disordered are in programs; this allows some behaviors that could be considered rule infractions to be treated as symptoms instead.

The seriousness of an individual's problem may also be exacerbated by incarceration. The individual is separated from previously established support systems. Methods of escaping from or dealing with problems that worked for the individual in the past may not be feasible in prison. The new stresses of adapting to the prison environment are added. The individual's self-confidence and ego strength are further undermined by concrete evidence of again being a "loser." In brief, treatment of emotional disorders is needed by a proportionately greater percentage of the population and is needed more intensely in a correctional setting than anywhere else outside a psychiatric hospital.

An example from my experience is an individual who was incarcerated after several hospitalizations. His hospitalizations were usually short term, as his hypersexuality often placed other patients at risk. There was no problem in making criminal charges against him because he tended to walk into other people's houses, undeterred by closed doors, helping himself to clothes and food. Law enforcement was pleased with his incarceration, claiming the individual often got home from the state hospital before they returned from taking him.

He had no income in prison but traded sexual favors for cookies, cigarettes, and pieces of paper on which he drew cryptic designs and wrote biblical quotes and words that had five letters. At times, he would get overloaded by the sexual demands of other inmates and become blatantly psychotic. This was usually easy to detect because he would not enter the office unless all recording devices and my briefcase, which he believed was a direct link to the FBI, had been removed. However, once stabilized, he adamantly refused medication. He did improve enough to make parole, but was back at the prison gate 2 days later, saying that he could not make it "out there."

His mother called after about a week asking that he be let back in because she could not work and keep him from sexually abusing her other children while she was gone. She was informed that we could not take him back unless he committed a crime or violated probation. He was back a short time later for stealing a pair of pants from a clothesline. He flattened his time (completed his sentence without parole) and was discharged. He was not welcome back in his hometown. He drifted until he was struck and killed by a car while panhandling quarters by flagging down cars on a bridge.

This case is not intended to illustrate what happens to all mentally ill persons in prison, nor is it an isolated instance. The interface between correctional and community systems has often ranged from nonexistent to erratic. Correctional psychologists (and their clients) would benefit from visiting (networking) with community service providers. The situation has improved somewhat with the development of programs through state hospitals that provide supervised living arrangements for such individuals. The ability to mandate medications for such individuals also improved after *Washington v. Harper* (1990). That ruling allows a special committee to order the involuntary medication of inmates who suffer mental disorder and are gravely disabled or pose a likelihood of serious harm to self or others.

Asking how large a problem the mentally disordered offender is to the correctional system is much like asking how big a problem a toothache is to an individual. If viewed as a percentage of the mass of a human body, a toothache is insignificant. However, a severe toothache can significantly reduce the functioning of the whole individual. The fact that hundreds of individuals are confined together greatly increases the impact of the problems of any one person on the others. This may well account for the tendency of correctional professionals, even mental health professionals, to overestimate the prevalence of mental disorders in correctional settings.

TYPES OF TREATMENT

Diagnosis seems to interact with the characteristics of the setting to produce four types of treatment for offenders: management, maintenance, outpatient psychotherapy, and programs. These types are outlined in Table 25.2, but are much more vague and interdependent than described. The typology is intended primarily to conceptualize the three-way interaction of therapist, client, and system.

Steadman, McCarty, and Morrisey (1986) provide a conceptual guide to developing jail mental health services. Jail services are not discussed separately in this chapter, as much of what is discussed about prisons is applicable to jails. Differences relate primarily to the higher incidence of mental illness and drug withdrawal in jail, the higher risk of suicide in jail, the short length of many jail stays, and the fact that many smaller jails are unequipped to handle mentally disordered offenders.

Management usually means crisis management. Crises may occur concurrently with or independently of the other three treatment tasks. In prison settings, crises most commonly occur in conjunction with marital or child custody problems, failure to gain parole or after a setback in appeals or other legal action, disciplinary action that the individual considers unfair, threats by fellow inmates, sexual abuse or homosexual panic, or inability to tolerate conditions of incarceration, particularly punitive segregation. Management problems tend to subside with age and adaptation to incarceration as both stress effects and disciplinary problems decrease (Zamble, 1992).

Crises may also be manufactured to create an "out" when the individual has run up gambling debts, been labeled a "rat" or "snitch," provoked individuals willing to resort to violence, or in some way needs help and sees weakness or futility in asking for it directly. Such crises cannot simply be dismissed as malingering as they are associated with emotional states resulting from the crises mentioned earlier. Transient situational crises that are trivialized or ignored often lead to escalation of maladaptive behaviors. More clear-cut malingering occurs when the individual wants a cell change, wants to move to a more comfortable setting in a mental health program, or is trying to join an associate in a particular housing unit. It is necessary for the therapist to recall that instrumental behavior is labeled "malingering" when others find it offensive or "coping" when others approve of that manner of manipulating the system. Whether poor coping evolves from mental disorder or poor judgment, the therapeutic task is to teach appropriate coping skills. Regardless of the source of the management task, there are factors in a correctional setting that often lead to rapid escalation of crises.

An offender is made more vulnerable to crisis by the feeling of being alone. The family may be disrupted or dysfunctional, unable to visit, or may

Table 25.2
Therapy Tasks in a Correctional Setting

	Management	Maintenance	Outpatient Psychotherapy	Programs
Problem type	Self-mutilation Suicidal threat Violence/PTSD Acute psychosis	Chronic psychosis Mental retardation Major affective disorder Dementia	Fear/passivity Adjustment problems Family problems Coping/social skills Depression/ anxiety	Substance abuse Sex offender Anger management Criminal thinking
Referral source	Intake assessment Staff referral Inmate referral Self-referral Event involvement	Intake assessment Pre- incarceration history Segregation rounds Event involvement Staff referral	Lawyer/family/ court/outside clinic referral Intake assessment Institutional history	Intake assessment Self-referral Court-ordered Family request
Precipitated by	Stress/loss of control Loss of support system Victimization Terminal illness Malingering Etiology unknown	Decompen- sation Bizarre behavior Inability to cope Danger to self or others Age/medical status Deteriorating self-care	Inmate reported symptoms Family or personal loss Desire to self- improve Family pressure Impress parole board	Penological requirement Hits bottom Escape situation Impress parole board Regain family acceptance
Treatment goal	Crisis resolution Self-harm prevention Provide safety/ structure Plan/contract treatment Symptom reduction	Stabilization Remission Minimize deterioration Improve coping Symptom control	Increase options/skills/ controls Reduce cognitive distortion Symptom management	Accept responsibility Control deviance Relapse prevention Develop life- long plan Develop better options

have given up on the offender. Inmates usually do not have friends in prison; rather, they have associates. These associates are usually viewed with only slightly more trust than the correctional officers. Associates may create or exacerbate a crisis by increasing pressure to react in a way that is consistent with convict code.

The very fact that a person is an offender suggests poor coping mechanisms. Experiences of having gone through several agencies, therapists, and programs that never worked only serve to prove to the offender the impossibility of getting help. This tends to lead to demands for the therapist to "do me something." If this hooks into the therapist's own power or control needs, the therapist then becomes part of the problem.

Many offenders view admission of problems, expression of feelings other than anger, and compromise as signs of weakness that invite victimization and abuse. These beliefs and experiences further shut down options for dealing with the crisis.

Mental health workers employed by the correctional facility are likely to be thought of as part of the system. This may mean that the professional is seen by offenders as being on the wrong side of the we/they dichotomy and either not caring or likely to "snitch them off to the cops." Mental health workers may also be viewed as being there for the "crazies," thus making contact with them stigmatizing. Such views shut the inmate off from resources for dealing with the problem.

MANAGEMENT OF SELF-DESTRUCTIVE BEHAVIOR

Scarred wrists are a common sight in prison. The majority of these come from gestures intended to call attention to emotional pain or intended to obtain reassignment. But it is never safe to bet that any of these actions are solely "manipulative." Ivanoff (1992) found that psychiatric history and having a model for parasuicide were the strongest predictors of parasuicide in a sample of state prison inmates.

There were 117 suicides in U.S. prisons in 1984. This rate (26.3 per 100,000) was more than twice the U.S. population rate (12.4 per 100,000; Camp & Camp, 1985). The number of prison suicides was 177 during 2002, or about 12.5 per 100,000. This is getting closer to the national rate, which has also been dropping, to 11.0 in 2002 (Kochanek, Murphy, Anderson, & Scott, 2004). These improving rates are probably attributable to better training of staff and improved protocols for suicide prevention.

Suicide has traditionally been a bigger problem in jails than in prisons, with 293 jail suicides in 1983 (U.S. Department of Justice, 1984). This has led to production of a sizable volume of information and training aids. The best single source of information is the *Jail Suicide/Mental Health Update,* published quarterly as a joint project of the National Center on Institutions and Alternatives and the National Institute of Corrections of the U.S. Department of Justice. It is available by mail from Lindsay M. Hayes, Project Director, National Center on Institutions and Alternatives, 40 Lantern Lane, Mansfield, MA 02048, or online at http://ncia.igc.org/ncia/suicide.html. The Training Curriculum on Suicide Detection and Prevention in Jails and Lockups (National Center on Institutions and Alternatives [NCIA], 1995) provides intake screening forms and visual aids for training. This is also available through the NCIA at the address given earlier. A more extensive treatment of the subject is *Suicide behind*

Bars: Prediction and Prevention (Lester & Danto, 1993). The American Correctional Association (1988) markets a *Suicide in Custody* video, along with a leader's guide that can be used for regular training of correctional staff. The American Correctional Association and the National Commission on Correctional Health Care have both issued standards on suicide prevention. Any policy written should heed these standards.

Screening for suicidal ideation or intent should be done with all intakes and intrasystem transfers. Prediction of low-frequency events like suicide is not highly accurate but is getting better and can help prevent the professional from missing signs. A screening instrument using static factors and built on study of inmate suicides is described by Cox (2003). A version developed in Canada (Wichman, Serin, & Motiuk, 2000) is available online at http://www.csc-scc.gc.ca/text/public_e.shtml. Kobylinska and Taylor (2003) found differences in the psychological and institutional factors of inmates in maximum security who had made non-life-threatening attempts from those who made life-threatening attempts.

Any offender returned from escape or experiencing another life crisis with which he or she is coping poorly or counterproductively should be considered a suicide risk (Blaauw, Arensman, Kraaij, Winkel, & Bout, 2002; Holden & Kroner, 2003). Any offender not coping well with the pressures of incarceration or being bullied (Blaauw, Winkel, & Kerhoff, 2001) should also be checked. Offenders who are incarcerated because of domestic violence or who have been disowned by their families are also at high risk. Inmates with histories of mental illness (Goss, Peterson, Smith, Kalb, & Brodey, 2002) and those coming off of recent drug and alcohol use also tend to be at higher risk.

The techniques of crisis intervention taught to most psychologists and counselors (e.g., L. H. Cohen, Claiborn, & Specter, 1983) are usable in corrections settings if the therapist takes the characteristics of the environment into account. Ensure that as little positive reinforcement as possible is given for self-destructive behavior. Inmates who feel that they have nothing else to bargain with may, in effect, hold themselves hostage. If their demands are acceded to, the technique works, and their threats against themselves are likely to increase. However, frustration of the use of suicidal gestures as a coping mechanism has its own risks; a gruesome demonstration of the offender's determination may follow.

Several years ago, adolescents at one unit began swallowing razor blades embedded in cheese or wrapped carefully in toilet paper; the blades could be swallowed without harm but still showed up clearly on X-rays. The consulting physician, seeing a life-threatening situation, performed immediate surgery. When one of the inmates was presented for the fourth time for this surgery, the physician determined that he was at greater risk from repeated incisions through the abdominal wall than from the razor blade. The inmate was locked up, given a bedpan, and told to present evidence when he passed the razor blade. Vital signs were monitored regularly, but no trip to the hospital or other extra attention was provided. Subsequent cases were treated in much the same fashion without incident. The frequency of razor blade swallowing and, with it, the risk of death or serious injury declined drastically. In the boredom and perceived oppressiveness of incarceration, some individuals go to great, and potentially fatal, lengths to produce a change in their circumstances.

This technique of nonintervention obviously raises some ethical and legal questions. It also illustrates the tightrope that therapists walk between suppressing dangerous behavior and seeming to withhold treatment. It is all too easy to engage in treatment that seems appropriate and effective at the time, but even minor attention from the media can produce shock and outrage in the community and lure lawyers into the arena.

Offenders accurately perceive that the correctional system operates on management by crisis. Thus, they do not hesitate to manufacture a crisis when their needs are strong enough. This is not to say that any suicide attempt by an offender can safely be dismissed as manipulative. There is often an element of excitement in gambling with death that can turn a manipulative gesture into a lethal action. The real question involved is often "Does anybody care?" An answer perceived by the offender to be in the negative can lead to either genuine despair or, among younger offenders in particular, see-what-you-made-me-do demonstrations. Finally, coping skills clearly need to be addressed whenever an offender sees suicidal threats or gestures as the method of choice in dealing with any stressful situation.

There is a small but troublesome subgroup of offenders who seem to have a compulsive need to engage in self-harm. Some are male sex offenders who engage in mutilation of their genitals; some are females with major histories of domestic abuse or who have abused their own children and seem to continue the violence cycles independently of other perpetrators or victims. Some are offenders of either gender, often with a borderline personality disorder, who seem to need the stimulation of cutting their own flesh or inserting objects into various body parts. These offenders tend to be relatively refractory to treatment and very frustrating to staff. Still others are inmates who simply thrive on the attention that self-mutilation brings. When I asked one offender who had little skin on his body unscarred from frequent cuttings why he kept doing it, he answered, "I know mental health will always show up to talk to me."

Suicide precautions that isolate can increase the risk. Keep individuals prone to suicide around other people; this keeps them from obsessing about problems and prevents the privacy needed to carry out the suicidal act. Most suicide attempts occur in single cells, or double cells when the cellmate is absent. One rather effective, if unethical, technique from the dark ages of corrections was to put an inmate in the cell with a suicidal inmate and threaten to punish him or her if the suicidal inmate hurt himself or herself. A more modern and ethical version of this is to train volunteer inmates as helpers/companions to provide some support and a reality base for the suicidal individual. In no case should this volunteer be given responsibility for prevention of action or authority over the other inmate.

At the same time, other inmates may provide motivation, encouragement, and actual help in carrying out a suicide attempt. Fellow inmates have been known to provide pieces of glass, sharpened metal, hoarded medications, insecticides, syringes, and other potentially lethal objects to inmates who requested them for attempting suicide. They have even been known to cover for other inmates during a suicide attempt. Some have watched with interest and called other inmates to watch a suicide attempt, making no effort to notify anyone in authority. Asked what they did when a recent suicide was observed hanging from a knotted sheet, cellmates indicated that they had "helped" him by pulling on his feet.

One individual with no record of prior suicide attempts and no suicide threats committed suicide by hanging himself. It was later learned that other inmates in the intake barracks had discovered that he was exceptionally fearful of being abused sexually. Although the inmate was in a single cell, the others played on his fears to the point that, apparently, death seemed preferable. He was a middle-aged White male with a history of depression and alcoholism, sentenced on a drug-related crime. His suicide generally fit the pattern described in an article by Hayes (1983) on jail suicides.

As in the case just described, most jail and prison suicides occur in single cells; therefore, it is essential to ensure continuous observation and appropriate interpersonal support. The therapist should train correctional officers, counselors, chaplains, and others that deal with the suicidal offender to ensure that a consistent plan is being consistently followed.

The "no-suicide contract" is a risky business. Many offenders with antisocial characteristics tend to place heavy emphasis on giving their word. A no-suicide contract may be reliable if the individual is not psychotic and the therapist can get the offender's "convict word" (the promise offenders usually give to cops may be part of the cops-and-robbers game and carry no real obligation for them). It is usually worthwhile to spend some time exploring what an offender's word means to him or her. The other side of this is that anything the therapist seems willing to do is likely to be interpreted by the offender as a promise. A nonjudgmental "hmmm" can be read as agreement to comply with what the offender is requesting. Nothing destroys a therapist's credibility quicker than not doing what was "promised." It is therefore imperative that the therapist have a clear understanding of the available options within the system. This must be followed by clear verbalization of what the therapist has and has not agreed to do.

There is a tendency for a novel type of suicidal gesture to be copied by other inmates. Thus, a fourth technique is to have an action plan ready for a repetition after a novel suicidal gesture. This plan needs to be developed jointly with medical, security, and administrative staff to avoid confusion and missed signals.

Because the individuals most likely to be aware of situations leading to crisis are the jailers or correctional officers, preservice and in-service training must be provided to officers so that they recognize and properly respond to this type of crisis. Proper anticipation and early intervention can keep most problems from growing to crisis proportions. Otherwise, officers' responses may range from ignoring what they consider to be manipulation, to trying to make jokes to get the individual to see how ridiculous the situation is, to actually offering advice about how to "do it right." One officer who was busy unpacking some cleaning supplies was asked by an inmate porter assigned to help him if a piece of baling twine from one of the boxes was strong enough to hang somebody. The officer, thinking that the inmate was joking, said he thought it would do. A few minutes later, the officer was holding up the inmate waiting for someone to cut the twine from the stair railing.

Not all management cases involve suicidal ideation. Offenders tend to have an external locus of control that is further nurtured by the authoritarian and restrictive atmosphere of correctional facilities. This results in professionals being besieged with pleas for help, many of which are manifestations of learned helplessness and the manipulative tendencies of offenders. This can easily become a trap for any professional who needs to be needed and who finds it easier and more gratifying to "fix" problems about mail, classification, or the parole department than to confront dependency, teach problem solving, and risk being confronted for being uncaring and "just like the rest of them."

It is doubtful that 100% prevention of successful suicides will ever be possible. Suicides, executions, homicides, and unexpected deaths from natural causes in custody can have a devastating effect on staff and on fellow inmates. Many systems have gone to techniques of critical incident debriefing to assist staff and, in some jurisdictions, inmates with the emotional and cognitive aftermath. Critical incident debriefing may be available through employee assistance programs. Some jurisdictions train their own multidisciplinary teams of mental health staff, chaplains, and security officers.

Management of Violent Behavior

Mental health workers may also be called on to manage the violent, disruptive, acting-out individual. There are several subtypes of what Toch (1982) calls the DDIs (disturbed disruptive inmates). Some are clearly mentally disordered individuals in a manic or schizophrenic episode. Some tend to be limited intellectually, or at least their repertoire of responses is limited, and they see no option other than to fight back against any limits. Some do "crazy" things to earn admiration, be left alone, mess with the guards, or for a variety of objectives that are neither clearly seen nor articulated. Some simply appear to take pleasure in disrupting the system. Regardless of cause, dysfunctional behavior is being presented for analysis and treatment.

The mentally disordered individuals can usually be handled well by clinically trained staff. There may be an element of fear in their agitation, which is exacerbated and converted to anger by orders and threats and allayed by calm reassurance that the situation is under control and the therapist is neither anxious nor afraid. Once these inmates have been given a chance to talk over whatever precipitated the outburst and been given a clear idea of what will happen next, they usually cooperate.

I was once called to a city jail where a manic individual was housed following arrest for alleged parole violation. The individual had seriously damaged the steel fixtures of his cell and was so loud and convincing in his threats that six parole officers, the city police, and transport officers from the department of correction had chosen discretion as the better part of valor. The parolee was known to have fears about being beaten and was quite good at standing off authority figures with his ferocity and tremendous strength. But after being told twice about the sequence of events he could expect and given the assurance that I would stay with him until he was returned to prison, he submitted to handcuffing and transport.

It takes some experience to recognize when it is time to talk and when it is time to step back and let security officers do their job. I have used (and violated) this rule of thumb: If the offender keeps me talking while making no concessions for more than 15 minutes in a cell-extraction situation, I am probably being used and should step back.

Occasionally, correctional psychologists will encounter individuals whose lack of social control and verbal skills require physical intervention to keep them from hurting themselves or someone else. Often, these individuals have either slipped through the cracks in the mental health system or the developmental disabilities system or have been ejected from these systems as too dangerous to staff.

Where do developmentally disabled persons get sent when their sexually aggressive and destructive behaviors are so extreme that they endanger staff and other clients in a residential treatment setting? Usually back to their families, who have had no success in controlling them either. After a brief stay, they tend to get arrested and sent to the department of corrections.

In my experience, some of these offenders regress to infantile tactics, such as holding their breath, biting themselves, banging their arms or heads, and lying on the floor kicking and screaming. They tend to recycle an anger-producing event for hours, keeping others upset with their temper tantrums. Though these behaviors are usually self-limiting, ignoring these outbursts may not work in a setting where their behavior can produce severe agitation in others who share their confinement.

One such individual developed a pattern of spitting at, throwing urine on, and physically attacking the officers assigned to meet his needs. In addition, he would scream and kick the door of his cell for much of the night, falling asleep out of exhaustion in the early morning. At some point, his screaming began to affect the mental stability of the other offenders. The officers were so angered by his abuse that they feared losing control and hurting him. At that point, "danger to self and others" takes on a new dimension. The ethical question of using medication in the absence of a treatable illness wanes in importance. The inmate slept for some hours after an injection of Thorazine and awoke calm and puzzled over why everybody had been so upset.

Inmates who "intentionally" do "crazy" things tax the resources and skills of the entire system. The inmate who forgoes personal hygiene and engages in bizarre behavior to make himself unattractive as a sex object may be indistinguishable to most officers from the chronic schizophrenic. Although correctional officers tend to be highly skilled at spotting mentally disordered behavior, effective management of instrumental "crazy" behavior may take considerable explanation and in-service training. It is also essential that the correctional psychologist work with the system to help avoid the establishment of contingencies that reinforce "crazy" behavior.

An inmate who injected saliva into his foot, knowing that one of his peers lost a leg with the same technique, was definitely viewed as abnormal by officers and administration. Yet, when mental health staff talked to him, he stated that he did it because he did not want to work. Asked why he did not simply refuse to turn out to work, he replied that he did not want to get sent to punitive segregation. His past experience showed that the disciplinary report usually got lost in the urgency of responding to his medical needs. Thus, instead of going to punitive isolation, he spent a week in the hospital and two or three more weeks in the department's aftercare facility.

Members of security staff are justifiably nervous when dealing with inmates who are willing to use their own bodies as weapons. Mental health staff members are justifiably reluctant to reinforce such behavior by removing inmates from the circumstances they were trying to escape. Correctional officers tend to see behavior that differs from their norms as "crazy." Psychologists may see the same behavior as being manipulative and kick it back to security as a management problem in an effort not to reinforce the "crazy" behavior with attention. This creates a dilemma for security personnel, who are liable for charges of negligence or failure to protect if they ignore the "crazy" behavior. The therapist may be seen as sidestepping obligations to the system to avoid dealing with a frightening or undesirable client. In other words, management problems must be handled cooperatively; neither security nor treatment staff has the skills and resources to handle them alone.

It is easy to avoid setting up groups and programs for violent offenders. After all, violence is not defined as a mental disorder in *DSM-IV*. It usually appears to be a manifestation or symptom of an Axis II disorder. The tough façade of the violent offender usually precludes any interest in therapy. Past treatment has shown little consistent effect. And the offenders can hurt you. But the problem will not go away.

There have been marked increases in prison violence over the years. The average number of assaults per agency has risen from 252 to 350 in the 10 years from 1991 to 2001. There were 16,435 assaults on staff in 2002. Inmate-to-inmate violence is far more prevalent, with 28,827 assaults and 49 inmate homicides in 2002 (Camp & Camp, 2002). The statistics on inmate-to-inmate violence probably grossly underestimate the true prevalence. Most inmates do not report assaults for fear of making themselves the targets of further and often escalated violence.

There are increasing numbers of people making the effort to reduce violence behind bars, and more and more materials are being developed. Tate, Reppucci, and Mulvey (1995) provide a good review of efforts with violent juveniles. The American Correctional Association markets a program that evolved from *Cage Your Rage* (M. Cullen, 1992) that includes a leader's guide, an offender workbook in English and Spanish, and videotapes. The series has been expanded (M. Cullen & Bradley, 2001) to accommodate transition into the community. Roth (1987) edited a book that provides an overview of assessment and various modalities of treatment of violent behavior. A publication on anger management published by the Correctional Services of Canada (Dowden, Blanchette, & Serin, 1999) provides insight into that country's program. Sonkin (1995) provides counselors with a guide to a cognitive-behavioral approach to treating violent individuals. A later work is available from Kassinove and Tafrate (2002). M. Cullen and Freeman-Longo (1996) provide treatment materials applying the techniques of relapse prevention to anger control.

The traditional correctional reaction to violence is to return violence or lock the offender in a smaller, tighter cage. Supermaximum and very high security prisons were intended to make staff and inmates safer. However, there are some indications that the violence level is not impacted by placement in a supermax environment (Briggs, Sundt, & Castellano, 2003). If psychotherapists are to make a difference, here is fertile, albeit stony, ground.

POSTTRAUMATIC STRESS MANAGEMENT

Many inmates bring with them to prison emotional baggage from childhood trauma and neglect. This leads to lifetime and current rates of Posttraumatic Stress Disorder (PTSD) among male inmates that are several times higher than those usually found in epidemiological studies (Guthrie, 1999). The problem may be even more severe among female inmates due to battering and sexual abuse (Battle, Zlotnick, Najavits, Gutierrez, Winsor, et al., 2002; O'Keefe, 1997). Prevalence also seems high among offenders with low psychopathy who have committed homicide or extreme violence (Pollock, 1999). In any case, PTSD can be related to self-injurious behavior or acting-out violently (Collins & Bailey, 1990).

The basis for PTSD may not have been present prior to arrest or incarceration. The experience of being caught, detoxified cold turkey, tried, and sent to prison can be traumatic for both those experiencing it the first time and those returning who were victimized in the course of prior visits. It is not unusual to hear a releasee say, "I'd rather die than come back here." Nor is it unusual for trauma to be experienced during incarceration.

Cuttings and killings in prison most often center around sexual matters, gang matters, snitching, debt collection, and drug deals, or otherwise being "dissed" (disrespected). Anyone who is dissed and does not respond effectively is "not a man," which translates into being a potential victim. According to convict code, if you are a man and want to have respect, you have to react; more often than not, a therapist sees only the aftermath of crises generated in this fashion.

Another primary source of trauma is sexual. Being "hit on" or harassed for sexual favors can be highly traumatic. Often, this is a power play (as are most rapes) rather than an invitation to sexual satisfaction. Targets are most often young, slightly built, "pretty White boys." Aggressors are often Black individuals who were not homosexual on the street. Most male rapes are not reported, though individuals detected in consensual sexual behavior often cry rape. This is a messy and unclear area that therapists too often dodge as a security or medical problem. The aftermath of rape can be devastating to self-esteem, confidence in one's own masculinity, and one's whole identity. This can lead to isolation from family and girlfriends, depression, and, on occasion, suicide attempts. It may be helpful to establish a protocol of interviewing any offender who has been involved in a sexual or violent incident that comes to official attention. Few offenders seek counseling after such trauma. However, a devastating psychological aftermath and a dangerous cycle of retribution may be avoided if the mental health staff team up with the medical staff in dealing with these incidents.

A recent survey of seven states (Struckman-Johnson & Struckman-Johnson, 2000) found that 21% of inmates reported experiencing at least one incident of pressured sexual behavior and 7% reported being raped. There are definite problems with self-report research in this area, but case anecdotes can have huge emotional impact. Human Rights Watch has taken it on as an issue and made recommendations to Congress. Legislative action has resulted in the Prisoner Rape Elimination Act of 2003 (HR 1707). This has led to conferences, development of training materials, and other resources that are available through the National Institute for Corrections, 1860 Industrial Circle, Suite A, Longmont, Colorado 80501.

Some caution needs to be exercised in dealing with PTSD to ensure that it does not become the rationale and excuse for bad choices and behavior. A careful therapist can lead an offender into dealing with the issues of PTSD while pointing out past ineffective coping strategies.

HOSPICE CARE

There has always been a need for counseling of inmates facing terminal illness. The percentage of the inmate population over age 50 has increased from 4.9% in 1990 to 6.8% in 1996 to 8.6% in 2000 (Camp & Camp, 2000). Death from natural causes, other than AIDS-related, accounted for 69.9% of deaths in 1996. Another 10.1% of deaths were related to impairment of the immune system due to AIDS (Camp & Camp, 2000). Thus, counseling related to terminal illness has gained importance.

A book by Anno, Graham, Lawrence, and Shansky (2004) provides information on caring for elderly and infirm inmates, including hospice care for the terminally ill. The newsletters of National Prison Hospice Association up until 1998 may still be available online at www.npha.org.

MANAGEMENT OF INMATES IN ISOLATION

It is arguable (Grassian, 1983), though a fairly well-supported conclusion, that short-term isolation does not place most inmates at serious risk of psychological damage (Gendreau & Bonta, 1984; Zinger, Wichman, & Andrews, 2001). At the same time, there is evidence (Andersen, Sestoft, Lillebaek, Gabrielsen, & Hemmingsen, 2003) that prisoners in isolation do not show as much improvement in psychopathology as prisoners not confined in isolated conditions.

Those inmates who are continuous disciplinary problems and spend extended periods of time on punitive segregation pose a more serious problem. These inmates need to be reviewed frequently, to examine both the causes of their misbehavior and whether psychological deterioration or decompensation is occurring. American Correctional Association (2003) standards (4-4256) require that a written report be prepared by a qualified mental health professional on any inmate remaining in segregation for more than 30 days, and at least quarterly thereafter.

The bad behavior of inmates has been the ball in a Ping-Pong game between mental health and security. Security personnel tend to see violent, unpredictable, erratic behavior as reflecting mental illness, and want mental health services to fix it. Mental health services personnel often view the same behavior as not being the product of an Axis I diagnosis, but as Axis II, and want security to handle the problem administratively. It is incumbent upon mental health staff to build and nurture a working relationship with security staff for the benefit of all concerned.

The increase in supermaximum prisons has led to long-term isolation for an estimated 2% to 3% of the prison population. These inmates spend most of their day in their cell, receiving their food through a trap door and having reduced contact through solid doors. Correctional staff maintain that this is the appropriate use of hardware to protect staff and other inmates from the most violent inmates. Outside groups (Human Rights Watch, 2000; United Nations, 2000) question this use of long-term isolation, seeing it as inhumane and in violation of various international treaties and standards.

The number of individuals with mental illness who get pulled into supermaximum security settings is not known, but it is probable that the percentage is sizable. An early study of two Canadian high-maximum security units found that 29% to 31% of the inmates housed there had severe mental disorders, primarily Schizophrenia and Bipolar Disorder (Hodgins & Cote, 1991). It is hoped that screening and the impact of mandated psychological reviews have more recently ensured that mentally disordered individuals are being diverted from supermax prisons. The question then becomes: Diverted to what? Most mental health services are understaffed and ill-equipped to handle violent high-security inmates without putting their own client load at risk.

Doing assessments and providing services to supermax inmates is a challenge. Most jurisdictions require two officers for movement of any supermax inmate, plus handcuffs, belly chains, and leg irons. Security staff are uncomfortable allowing these inmates the privacy that most mental health professionals believe to be necessary for assessment and treatment. However, these challenges must be worked out, often on a case-by-case basis. Without adequate assessment and treatment, the whole system of supermaximum prisons is subject to litigation (MacArthur Justice Center, 2000).

MAINTENANCE

As discussed earlier, psychosis and mental retardation appear to be somewhat more prevalent among offender populations than in the community. As in the broader community, many of these individuals are able to integrate themselves into the prison community; to do so, they may require special education and additional supervision and structure. Others cannot reach a level of adaptive behavior that allows them to be on their own in either the community or the correctional facility.

All departments of correction and larger jails now have either mental health areas within correctional facilities, designated health service facilities, or access to forensic facilities in state hospitals. The majority view among correctional administrators, though with notable reluctance, appears to be that these problems are best handled within the secure confines of correctional facilities. Based on the average from reporting agencies, 5.5% of inmates were in specialized facilities or programs for mental illness in 1999, up from 4.2% in 1996 (Camp & Camp, 1997, 2000).

Although mentally disordered offenders represent 6% to 16% or so of the offender population, they typically receive the bulk of the available mental health resources. Even if their adaptive behavior reaches a level allowing reintegration into the broader population, they often require extensive long-term aftercare. And some mentally disordered offenders will spend most, if not all, of their incarceration in mental health housing. This is as it should be. However, most systems do not have sufficient resources to both care for mentally disordered offenders and offer programs needed for meaningful correction.

One individual with a history of Schizophrenia was being taken to the county courthouse for involuntary commitment proceedings by his family. While walking down the hall in the courthouse, he broke free. He then grabbed a woman who worked in the courthouse and dragged her into an elevator. He stopped the elevator between floors and attempted to rape his captive. The man was found competent to stand trial, sentenced to 40 years, and sent to prison. Soon after his arrival, while apparently trying to flee from the voices he commonly hears, he ran from his assigned area and refused all orders to return. He backed into a corner and held several correctional officers at bay for some time. (This individual was 6 feet 9 inches tall, and his weight exceeded the scale's limit of 350 pounds.) For the next 8 years, this man lived in a mental health management area of the department. At no time had he been completely clear of psychosis, despite massive doses of psychotropic drugs. He had a work assignment, attended group therapy, and was generally involved in the activities of the mental health unit. He was instructed to open his mouth wide when hearing voices. He complied for a while and found that he did not hear the voices when he was gaping widely. Unfortunately, he was not willing to stay compliant with this procedure. By the terms of his behavioral contract, when the voices got to be overpowering, he would put on a headset radio turned to the maximum volume he could stand. His fellow inmates tended to be reliable about reminding him to do this and, if they doubted its efficacy, retired quickly to their rooms. He frequently incorporated staff into delusions in which they tried to hurt him or make him perform sexual acts against his will. He occasionally became loud and agitated in response to delusions and confronted staff with the fact that he was going to stop them from doing "it" to him. Once the episode was over, he was usually docile and tearful, begging for help not to be that way again. Had he not been in a specialized setting, some other offender would probably have picked the wrong moment to tease him and gotten hurt. In the mental health unit, he never hurt anyone during the term of his incarceration, which was over 15 years, though he definitely made several staff and offenders nervous. He was later released, stayed on his medication, held a job, lived with his family, and adjusted to the community. Unfortunately, he died from heat stroke related probably to the combination of working at his job of building fences in the summer heat and side effects of his medication.

The elderly are also an increasing proportion of most correctional populations. Some of these individuals function well in the general population. Others need the protection of a sheltered unit with more intensive nursing and mental health coverage. Debility and attitude are usually greater factors than chronological age in determining placement needs.

THE SETTING

The techniques that would be used in a Veterans Administration or state hospital inpatient setting are largely applicable to a mental health unit within a correctional setting. However, there are some differences related to the setting and others related to the fact that the patients are also offenders.

A major problem with the correctional setting is that, in an effort to maintain consistency, little accommodation is available for individual differences and needs. Any individual in a setting that is, by definition, punishing can be expected to try to escape that setting. Many inmates request placement in a mental health unit, though most do not get there. Once placed in a mental health unit, nobody in his or her "right mind" would want to leave its relative safety, quiet, and sanity to be with regular inmates in a more oppressive setting. Some patients pretend to work on their problems to stay in the unit but are careful to not show rapid improvement. They maintain a careful balance between need and progress to assure their stay in the unit.

The perceived desirability of being in a mental health unit also creates problems for staff in screening out malingerers. One individual had been told in county jail that being "crazy" or "queer" would cause him to be placed in housing apart from the other inmates. He was well coached by another offender who had spent much of his time in mental health units and had firsthand knowledge of what symptoms impressed the shrinks. This particular inmate took no chances and claimed to be both queer and crazy. But he overplayed the crazy and was put on a sizable dose of a neuroleptic, which had the effect of making him think that he really was going crazy. In a panic, he admitted the whole scheme.

Malingering is usually detectable either because the individual gets carried away with the act and overplays the role or because the individual gets tired of maintaining the role. However, some inmates are highly skilled in playing mentally ill (Yochelson & Samenow, 1976). Cavanaugh and Rogers (1984) provide some techniques for identifying these inmates. The most difficult manipulation to detect is that presented by inmates who have a real psychological disorder and have learned to continue or exaggerate their symptoms for secondary gain.

The second problem relating to the setting has to do with the fact that mentally disordered individuals are confined with offenders who model antisocial behaviors. Most mentally disordered offenders already have some degree of personality disorder, which may be minimal during an acute episode of psychopathology but emerge as the individual is stabilized. When those who have not previously shown antisocial personality characteristics see others using those characteristics, apparently gaining possessions and status, it does not take long for them to model and adopt the manipulative, sexual, and aggressive behaviors.

The third problem is that the mental health unit is often a small part of a much larger institutional system. Necessarily, the needs of the larger unit dictate schedules such as meals, movie availability, pill calls, head counts, doctor and dental calls, and so on. Shared facilities such as infirmaries, gyms, and mess halls may not be available at desirable times. Movement may be limited by other activities going on in the larger unit. Security concerns may become acute when inmates of different security levels are mixed or when a particularly high-security-risk inmate is seen as being in need of inpatient treatment. These problems can usually be resolved or other options developed with the cooperation of the warden but must be considered in setting up any programming.

Fourth, correctional settings often require the management of an individual for years rather than allowing for transition to another support system when the therapist and client believe the client is ready. It is usually not feasible or at least not responsible to drop inmates from treatment or urge them to find another therapist. Failures and dropouts remain to haunt the therapist on a daily basis.

The long-term presence of many of these clients raises issues of transference and countertransference to breadths and intensities that are seldom encountered outside of psychoanalysis proper. This creates a burnout danger for the therapist, who takes on a task that almost amounts to reparenting or, at least, involves long-term services to a highly demanding and sometimes psychologically primitive population. There is also a potential for physical danger as the therapist becomes incorporated into delusional systems of individuals with a record of hurting others. One female inmate with a history of chronic Schizophrenia became aware of feeling "different." She hypothesized that these strange feelings were drug-induced. She stripped and searched her body for needle marks. When she found what she interpreted to be needle marks and was unaware of having been given an injection, she concluded that she was being injected while she slept. She began staying awake several days at a stretch, but would inevitably succumb to sleep. Upon awakening, she always found more needle marks. She concluded that I, her therapist, was living in a nearby closet and sneaking out to inject her whenever she fell asleep. She filed a cogent writ that was accepted for trial by the federal court. Ultimately, her court-appointed attorney withdrew, complaining that the offender was crazy. She was sent to the state hospital for one day of staffing and medication review.

The problems of inclusion in delusional systems, transference, and counter-transference tend to be insidious and are often recognized only in hindsight, yet there are several methods for prevention. A staffing committee rather than the individual therapist should make or at least confirm treatment decisions. Community meetings with the offenders and staff involved in residential treatment can expose covert relationships among the staff and the offenders or between staff and individual offenders. The use of outside therapists to consult, review programs, monitor staffing, do quality assurance, and generally be involved also serves to maintain proper perspective.

Finally, like most institutions, correctional facilities operate on rules and expectations of consistent treatment. It becomes problematic at best to deal with offenders who do not fit the mold. If the policy of the department is that all offenders who are able to work do so, should offenders housed in a mental health unit be required to work? If a mentally disordered offender runs for the fence, should the officer in the tower shoot? One offender being strip-searched prior to transport to a facility with a mental health unit was asked to "bend over and spread 'em." He apparently "goosed" himself in the process and ran screaming, naked, out a door immediately under a gun tower. The officer in the tower tracked the inmate with his weapon, but fortunately concluded that because the inmate was running in circles, he was not attempting to escape.

If a "crazy" breaks a rule in the hall, should the correctional officer write a disciplinary report? Correctional officers, unless they have had specialized training and experience, have difficulty responding normally to the abnormal. Similarly, psychologists have difficulty helping their clients adapt to a system that challenges their ethics and expectations about how people should be treated (for a discussion of ethical issues, see Ashford, Sales, & Reid, 2000; for a discussion of legal issues, see F. Cohen, 1985; for a discussion of applicable standards, see F. Cohen & Griset, 1985).

When our mental health unit was moved to a new parent unit, a number of officers assigned to the parent unit avoided the area unless ordered to enter it. Officers who worked for mental health were asked, "How can you work with them?" Conversely, inmates who had progressed to a more mentally stable state and had begun limit-testing were cut extra slack by sympathetic officers assigned to the unit. Generally, the mental health inmates were seen as unpredictable and dangerous or as incompetent and not to be held responsible. This set of issues is one of the more difficult to resolve because the cognitive impairment of the inmate fluctuates, thus altering what can reasonably be expected from him or her. Even professional staff members have problems determining levels of control and responsibility as inmates learn to use their symptoms to avoid responsibility for their actions.

The issue of expectations and rules is further complicated by the interactions of the custody and treatment environments. The psychologist may see the prison environment as not only failing to correct but, in many cases, doing harm; the harshness and oppressiveness may be seen as meeting the needs of the staff but having little to do with correcting inmates. Alternatively, security staff may see the treatment environment as overly permissive, undermining inmates with pity instead of making them get on with life, or as irrelevant to the real problems of convicts; some security staff may even see treatment as undermining the authority of officers and the order of the institution.

The conflict here is powerful and attractive to cynics. It is easy to say, "Therapy is impossible in such a punitive environment." This makes it easy to form an unhelpful psychological alliance with prisoners around their perceived mistreatment. Therapists, being human, inevitably get hooked by this conflict from time to time. At such times, it may help the therapist to recall the levels of brutality and destruction that have occurred when the system has broken down (e.g., Attica, New Mexico Penitentiary) and look for ways to improve rather than undermine it. All correctional psychologists should receive security training and should, in turn, provide correctional officers training related to managing human behavior.

The inequities and negative aspects of the system, both real and imagined, can and should be brought into treatment. It is possible to use misperceptions to teach reality-based thinking and to use real unfairness to teach frustration tolerance and empathy for victims. Some therapists in private practice seek "creative anxiety" to move their patients. Correctional psychologists may find this task already done for them.

OUTPATIENT PSYCHOTHERAPY

Outpatient therapy is an elective rather than a required service in most correctional settings. As long as crisis management keeps incidents from happening that would produce liability or bad press for the system, as long as security staff do not have to deal with the mentally ill and retarded offenders, and as long as there are some programs that betoken rehabilitation opportunities, there may be little or no administrative emphasis placed on treatment services for the bulk of the offender population (Lombardo, 1985). This leaves the field fairly clear to offer elective treatment and to be eclectic in approach. The real limit is lack of staff resources.

There is no point in listing all of the approaches. Suffice it to say that they have run the gamut from assertiveness training to Zen. Each approach has claimed some measure of success. Usually, this success has been in terms of improvement on some psychometric device or adaptation to incarceration rather than lasting changes in socially significant behavior. Most approaches have been attacked: the more humanistic for coddling criminals, the more behavior-oriented for brainwashing or depriving offenders of constitutional rights. Attempts have been made to stamp them all null and void under the "nothing works" blanket (Martinson, Lipton, & Wilks, 1975).

It is, in fact, easy to believe that nothing works when the therapist daily encounters offenders who have not benefited from treatment. In mental health centers and private practice, a therapist can at least fantasize that the client who dropped out or was terminated has undergone a healthy transformation. In a correctional setting, the failures tend to stay on while the successes leave and get on with their lives. Nor does the therapist in a correctional setting have the opportunity to select cases, as therapists do in other settings. Mental health centers and private practitioners can transfer responsibility for non-treatment, premature terminations, and failures with a mere wave of the not-motivated-for-treatment wand, and the miscreant disappears. The therapist in a correctional setting may refuse to treat or may terminate treatment because of the client's behavior and still be held responsible for the treatment of all those whom the court has seen fit to incarcerate.

There are also factors that can work to the advantage of the therapist: Correctional clients by virtue of their sentences have time to put into treatment; environmental factors are mostly known and maintained at an unusually stable level; external observation and reporting are system requirements; and the potential for follow-up is high. In brief, correctional facilities offer the possibility of greatly expanding the frontiers of psychotherapy, provided that the trailblazers are a hardy enough breed to survive severe trials.

Therapy in a correctional setting encounters many of the same problems that therapy encounters in any setting. Some problems are more prevalent; most problems are intensified, echoing off the walls. Even so, therapy seems to work as well (Gendreau, 1996) and fail as sadly in prison as it does anywhere else. The mistakes are just more difficult to keep buried.

PROGRAMS

Programs have increasingly become the focus of treatment efforts in corrections. Regardless of the focus, programs have a number of advantages that seem to raise the chances of success over those seen in outpatient therapy. Programs provide opportunities for many more contact hours than would be feasible in outpatient treatment. Alcohol and drug programs originally adopted the community model of 28-day intensive treatment programs. This has been found to be insufficient, and emphasis is shifting toward treatment lasting 6 months to a year (Wexler, Falkin, & Lipton, 1990). Programs for sex offenders commonly are more than a year in duration. Therapeutic communities treating personality disorder usually involve the individual for more than 6 months and up to several years. Treatment programs are usually designed around separation from the general population. This simultaneously lessens the impact of the inmate culture and sets up an environment that offers psychological protection and permission to try new behaviors, along with positive role models and pro-social group norms.

Few programs have sufficient free-world staff. Many rely to varying degrees on inmate peer counselors. These individuals do not generate the automatic resistance that authority figures do. They are usually also adept at translating psychobabble into a language that speaks to the needs of offenders. They often have the zeal and energy of the new convert and can greatly extend the effectiveness of a therapist. At the same time, they are no more immune from corruption or abuse of power than anyone else and require careful supervision.

Programs are costly, both in terms of dollars and in terms of stress on the correctional system. That, together with the amount of staff time invested in programs, has usually led to clear mission statements and task definition. This makes it likely that the therapist and the clients, having plans and blueprints, can build a better house together than by going where the mood takes them.

Therapy programs tend to process a group of people through emotionally loaded shared experiences toward a common goal. This may produce a powerful conversion-like experience and a vehement renunciation of old deviant or self-destructive behaviors. However, the types of behaviors (drug use, deviant sex, and the constellation of antisocial personality behaviors) have such habit strength and such powerful reinforcers tied to them that short-term treatment can be expected to have only short-term effects. Treatment effects are likely to be sustained only if the individual participates in ongoing support groups, which may require a waiver of the rules limiting contacts among parolees.

The difficulties attendant in operating programs in a correctional setting are in proportion to their potential for producing real and relevant change. A program usually has the irritant effect in a correctional system that a foreign substance has in the human body. The fact that a program is good does not guarantee its success or even its survival. The following are some considerations that need to be taken into account for a program to continue to function.

It helps if the program is mandated by the federal court, state law, or strongly felt administrative needs. Programs are costly in terms of space, staff resources, and offender time. In a period of prison overcrowding, limited budgets, and doubt and cynicism about the efficacy of treatment, it is much easier to close a program than to start or expand one.

Access to offenders needs to be built into the classification system of the facility. "Good convicts" are much in demand for institutional needs. "Screwups" (jargon modified somewhat) are seen as needing straightening out (i.e., through punishment and hard work), not some soft assignment to a treatment unit. Some offenders do not have sentences long enough to allow them to complete treatment; others have sentences so long that the opportunity for them to apply some types of treatment will be years in coming.

There is a tendency for prison-based programs to get "dirty." Individuals in programs are usually involved in them over a substantial period of time. It is to be expected that, once offenders learn the program, they will try to manipulate it to their own ends and inject their value system into it. Periodic house cleanings are required to ensure that the program stays on track and that the participants stay on task. The changes that lead to a program's getting dirty tend to be mild and insidious; thus, it usually requires a therapist not connected with the day-to-day operations to detect them.

Programs tend to have two major effects on staff: They provide excellent training in therapy, and they produce burnout in record time. Wherever possible, programs should provide for staff rotation or relief. Staff rotation can provide quality therapists for the other treatment areas; staff relief can be built in either by having other therapists who can cover or by closing down the program periodically to allow brief sabbaticals. These shutdown periods can be used to provide staff training and rejuvenation and allow time for program evaluation and changes.

The program must be carefully explained to correctional staff. Nobody questions the number of years it takes to earn a high school diploma or learn a professional skill, but immediate results are expected in treatment programs. Officers become suspicious of the length of time offenders are expected to stay in the program. In addition, the type of open, trusting relationship considered by therapists to form the basis for treatment is antithetical to what officers have been taught about handling convicts. The therapist who fails to address these and similar concerns is likely to spend more time trying to overcome obstacles than doing treatment.

Public relations are essential. The political entity whose resources enable the programs to exist needs to be told frequently about the good being done by the program. It is much easier politically to allocate resources for children and the elderly than for convicts. Other agents of the criminal justice system need accurate information about the program; these are the individuals who refer the clients, explain to offenders and their families what is going to happen in prison, and make decisions about sentencing, revocation of parole, probation, and the handling of offenders in general. Judges who hear about a program may assume that they can sentence offenders to it. Parole boards may decide to withhold parole pending completion of a program by an offender who is unmotivated or inappropriate for the program.

Three types of programs have seen fairly wide use with offenders. These are sex offender treatment, substance abuse treatment, and therapeutic communities for treating personality disorders with characteristics including anger control and criminal thinking. These programs are dealt with by other contributors to this volume and will not be further described here.

THERAPISTS

I have told all applicants for therapist positions in my department that they would have to work at least 6 months before they could expect to become effective, but if they stayed in the system for 3 years, they might find themselves getting crazy. If they stayed for much longer, they might find themselves becoming institutionalized. This was based on my own experience and was usually laughed off by new staff. However, those staff members who have stayed, and many who have left, indicated that what they had taken as a joke turned out to be a fairly accurate prediction. Therapists who have remained and become effective share some common characteristics. Therapists most likely to succeed in therapy with offenders are those who can empathize without sympathy, confront without demeaning, care without carrying, direct without controlling, see manipulation as a poor coping strategy rather than a personal assault, find satisfaction in erratic progress toward limited and clearly defined goals, tolerate the ambiguities and conflicts of the setting, and accept their own limits.

Therapists who sympathize will find no shortage of offenders who love them and need a great deal of their time. Nor will they find any shortage of life events among the offender population deserving of their sympathy. They will receive much flattery and many demands for their services. In the long run, they will find themselves being used up, working instead of rather than with the offender, feeling used, being disappointed, and becoming angry with their clients.

Therapists who have difficulty confronting will be seen as sympathetic and receive much the same payoffs as just described. Therapists who confront in anger or with put-downs may effectively shape the way the offender interacts with the therapist and the group. However, the change that occurs may not be generalizable progress. For some offenders, confrontive therapy may simply represent a new external locus of control. Unless it is followed by techniques for developing internal controls and learning and practicing prosocial behaviors, what it does accomplish may be lost. Angry, demeaning confrontation may have its place, like the proverbial 2-by-4 to get the mule's attention. But it is a poor mule trainer who does not know when to put down the 2-by-4.

Caring is likely to be seen by the offender as a weakness that makes a person a good mark for a con. The natural response of most offenders to caring is "Do me something, prove that you really care." A demonstration of good faith is likely to lead to demands for further demonstrations. Rescue is a severe temptation in a correctional setting, as relatively solvable problems take on epic proportions and offer the therapist an easy route to heroic stature. The therapist who sees rescue as necessary should remember to throw a line rather than a lifeboat and avoid crushing the drowning victim.

The therapist who refuses to be directive with offender clients may never progress beyond the level of small talk or silence. Verbal interaction was more likely used in the offender's past to ask for things than in self-disclosure, problem solving, or conflict resolution. The offender is likely to see the purpose of talking about problems as an effort to find out who is to blame. On the other hand, direction must take the shape of coaching, not controlling. Many offenders have no desire to take responsibility for their lives and would be only too happy to give control to the therapist. The best outcome of giving control over to the therapist is likely to be that the offender has someone new to blame for how screwed up things are.

In a setting in which one has no power, one is going to look for the nearest outlet and attempt to plug into it. Offenders can be counted on to attempt to manipulate the therapist to do the things they lack the energy or perceived power to do for themselves. This is not only normative behavior for a correctional setting, it is necessary for survival. The therapist can monitor this by checking what feelings are being hooked, what beliefs are being played to, and what obligations generate resentments. It may be appropriate to pull the plug. However, if the therapist is close to being as effective a manipulator as the offender is, it may be feasible to bill for the power. It usually only wastes energy to get angry over manipulation, although at times it may work well to act angry.

OFFENDERS

There are characteristics in any offender group that lend themselves to the therapy process. Therapy may proceed efficiently and effectively if the therapist understands these characteristics and how to make them work for the therapeutic process.

A free-world person seeks therapy to alleviate emotional distress, to learn to control a troublesome behavior, to deal with conflicts in a relationship, to straighten out confusion and misperceptions, and for a variety of other problems. The offender usually seeks therapy to avoid or escape the external forces of society's reaction to the offensive behavior. Therapists often think that therapy can be effective only if the person volunteers for treatment and genuinely wants to change. Actually, all therapy is probably coerced by internal discomfort, family discomfort, or societal discomfort with some set of behaviors. The fact that the leverage for treatment for offenders is external more often than not makes it no less useful as a starting point. Horses do sometimes drink when led to water. "Not motivated for treatment" is more often a therapist's excuse than a real reason for not treating an offender.

The majority of offenders have written off school early in their academic careers. Although the average claimed education level of offenders entering the Arkansas Department of Correction in 1996 was 8th to 11th grade, depending on local pressure to stay in school, academic attainment as measured by achievement tests was more likely to be 6th or 7th grade. Over a third of the offenders coming into many departments of correction are functionally illiterate (Wilson & Herrnstein, 1985). Thus, didactic techniques are likely to be written off as "just words," unless activities, participation, role playing, and the like are built into the lessons. Pretraining can also be helpful in teaching these individuals to use therapy services effectively (Hilkey, Wilhelm, & Home, 1982). Mentoring or tutoring is often used in programs to help the less skilled participants and to get the more skilled participants to learn by teaching.

Many offenders have great need for excitement and drama in their lives. These individuals can often be hooked by psychodrama (Schranski & Harvey, 1983) and confrontational therapies (Dies & Hess, 1971). Much energy can be directed into and appropriately released through role play. But unless these are properly planned and directed toward clear goals, they tend to become entertaining pastimes with little therapeutic gain.

Many offenders lack self-discipline and frustration tolerance; they want to see immediate results and may quickly lose interest in programs that require them to practice on their own. Thus, relaxation techniques, self-hypnosis, and meditation may produce dramatic effects initially but be dropped as the newness wears off. Therefore, it is usually necessary to build in a support group, strengthening or feedback sessions, or some other method of sustaining interest.

Offenders are often astute observers who are quick to see the games, faults, and weaknesses of others. They may be much quicker to identify some negative behavior patterns than a trained therapist. Thus, group therapy tends to be the modality of choice. Carefully supervised peer counselors may develop better therapy skills in dealing with offender clients than the supervising therapist.

These skills as astute social observers can also become liabilities. Most offenders have long histories of finding fault with others, which they use to justify their own behavior or to shift attention from their own misdeeds. These skills can also be used to find the vulnerabilities of therapists and become their ego support and reality check. It is crucial that therapists check their relationships and perspectives frequently to ensure that they are still seeing through their own eyes.

Many offenders, despite some highly romanticized and largely fictional tales, have a history of poor relationships. The interaction usually starts off with high intensity and crashes when the other person finally recognizes that his or her role is more that of a victim than a partner in a relationship. The offender then feels betrayed and concludes that people are "no damn good." This pattern then transfers to therapy but can be modulated somewhat by damping the intensity of the highs and lows. This is difficult when the therapist is alternately invited to be a hero, a punisher, and a righteously angered victim.

Cognitive distortions common to offenders act as landmines in the treatment field. A good general source for exploring these is the two-volume set of books by Yochelson and Samenow (1976, 1977). Samenow and Bussard (1994) have published a guide and workbook with accompanying videos. These materials are brief enough to use in an outpatient program and meaty enough to be a module in a more extended treatment program. *The Criminal Lifestyle* (Walters, 1990) provides an experienced practitioner's insight into offender dynamics.

A more detailed picture of the individual offender can often be developed from reviewing facility records such as disciplinary reports and seeking reality-based information from the staff who work with the offender on a daily basis. Many correctional officers hesitate to share their opinions and observations with professionals, but a little mining of these resources is usually well worth the effort.

When confronted about a particular action, offenders usually do not know why they did it, or they indicate that it was the fault of the victim, a third party, or a psychoactive drug. Wherever the causes of criminal behavior are to be found, they are usually not in the explanations offered by offenders. Similarly, having an offender recount past history, though often moving enough to be the basis of a soap opera, may provide little more than an opportunity for the offender to control the session.

CORRECTIONAL ENVIRONMENT

The correctional environment is, in some ways, a reflection of the offender. Planning occurs, but the system is mostly reactive. It has a strong tendency to victimize all who come into contact with it, staff and offender alike, with an almost total lack of empathy. Its goals, other than security, are usually unclear and often conflicting. Its means can be self-defeating. It sometimes creates high drama and excitement as the staff play cops to the offenders' robbers. And the correctional system, like the offenders it holds, usually gets public notice only by messing up.

The prison often seems an alien, frightening, and hostile environment to newly arrived treatment staff, just as it does to new commitments. On the other hand, the injection of treatment staff, in many systems by court order, has probably been equally traumatic for some correctional systems. The tension between security and treatment generates a dialectic that ultimately benefits

both systems, achieving a balance between support and opportunities for rehabilitation on the one hand, and security and discipline on the other.

Corrections departments usually operate on paramilitary models, with
sergeants, lieutenants, a chain of command, and the assumption of absolute
loyalty and blind obedience. Correctional officers tend to assume that psychologists are naïve and unaware of the nature of offenders, likely to believe any allegation against them that an offender makes, and likely to take the offender's
side in we/they controversies. The offender, on the other hand, knows who
pays the psychologist's salary and may see the therapist as just another part of
the system that must be avoided or manipulated. The psychologist must avoid
overidentification with either side of we/they controversies while remaining
acceptable to both. This often requires clear, firm, and frequent communication as to the roles (and there are multiple roles) the psychologist is prepared to
play in a correctional system.

Zimbardo's classic experiment in setting up a mock prison (Zimbardo,
Haney, Banks, & Jaffe, 1975) gave some insight into the effects that pronounced
differences in power have on people in a prison environment. The only ana-
logues of such discrepancies in power seem to be found in the parent-child and
master-slave relationships. These levels of paternalism and authoritarianism
may not be desirable, but they are real and must be taken into consideration.
This may require that the offender be taught social discrimination skills along
with any other new skills. The offender who tries assertiveness training with
an officer in the hall or problem-solving skills with the classification committee may be in for a difficult time.

The powerlessness of the offenders exists only in a formal, positional-power
sense. Any therapist who hopes to facilitate changes for individuals must
reckon with the psychological power of the offender culture. Security officers
manage behavior largely by focusing on rule violations and removing reinforcers, usually for a set period of time, during which positive behavior on the
part of the offender cannot earn them back. Those items and behaviors that are
positive reinforcers but are not guaranteed by law or policy are more likely to
be dispensed by inmates than by staff. Thus, for many offenders, the influence
of the inmate culture may outweigh that wielded by the staff. The therapist
may need to inoculate the client to resist the temptations of the inmate culture
and persist in the face of ridicule, scorn, or negative attitudes of peers.

Correction departments generally remove an offender's right to privacy
along with the offender's clothing at the point of intake. Most psychologists believe that therapy requires a modicum of privacy, though privacy may be more
a luxury than a necessity at times. Ethics do require that an offender be told
the limits of confidentiality that can be maintained in a correctional environment; usually, these include the duty to warn of planned or threatened actions
that could harm self or others. In a group setting, there is often one member
who will put other members' business "on the street." Most offenders who
have been around know this already, and frank discussion of the problems of
confidentiality may support rather than limit openness. For some offenders,
confidentiality may most clearly be conceptualized in terms of respect and
their feelings about snitching.

A more important issue in confidentiality is the degree to which the actions of the therapist affect the liberty interests of the offenders. Often, offenders want the fact that they have been in treatment to go into their records, hoping that the parole board will be duly impressed by their seeking rehabilitation. Other offenders may feel stigmatized by the same treatment. Even more crucial are the psychological assessments that are done at various times during incarceration. Ethics require that the offenders be informed of the purpose and intended distribution of such assessments and their right to refuse assessment.

THE SYSTEM AS THE CLIENT

Monahan (1980) asks an astute question in the title of the volume he edited: "Who is the client?" It seems plausible that the therapist may ultimately do more good by helping the system become more effective than by helping the offender deal with the system. Several factors should be considered before taking on the system as a client.

Efforts to change the system should be kept separate from therapy. The offender may believe that the psychologist is allied with him or her against the system, setting up a let's-you-and-him-fight situation. At the same time, the therapist may be seen by the administration as a loose cannon or not a team player or as choosing sides. It is difficult to improve a system that views one with distrust. There is an old maxim in prison systems: If you can't get the man, get his inmate. This can lead to disciplinary action, undesirable reassignment, and the like for inmates with whom the therapist is working.

Efforts to change the system should not be undertaken unless both the aspect needing change and the direction of the change are clear. The therapist may need to spend a good deal of time diagnosing the problems before undertaking to "fix" them. "Facts," whether presented by staff or offenders, tend to be better reflections of those individuals' perceptions and expectations than reality. Never assume the first version you hear accurately portrays the situation; situations are usually much more ambiguous than they first appear. If easy fixes were available, there would be no problem to solve. Affixing blame fixes nothing.

Offenders and correctional officers tend to see themselves as highly dissimilar, and their differences often get so polarized that no resolution seems possible. The therapist who chooses sides only serves to heighten the conflict. All parties in corrections—inmates, officers, and even treatment staff—tend to wear gray hats. It is possible to empathize with all of them and work with the system as one would with a troubled family.

Efforts to change the system should follow good psychological techniques. In a setting where the dominant feeling is anger, it is easy to give rein to righteous indignation and condemnation. This is useful with the system about as often as it is with an individual client. The therapist who tries to punish the system for punishing the offender will seldom find the method to be corrective. The therapist who is willing to participate fully in an imperfect system and model positive methods of dealing with people and problems can have a therapeutic impact considerably broader than his or her caseload alone. An effective therapist is quickly recognized by administrators and correctional officers as a powerful resource and can exercise considerable leverage in changing the system. A therapist seen as ineffective or undermining the safety and good order will be shut out of essential communication loops and not last long in isolation.

There are also expectations of omniscience that systems tend to place on correctional psychologists: Is it safe to move this offender to a lower security level within the institution? Is this offender that we are considering for parole safe to be back in society? The area of risk prediction is evolving (Monahan & Steadman, 1994; Webster, Harris, Rice, Corimer, & Quinsey, 1994). Some of the best work (Andrews & Bonta, 1995) has been done in Canada with the Level of Service Index (LSI-R). But it is still wise to just say no to invitations to predict the future behavior of individuals with Axis II diagnoses. If addressing the question cannot be avoided, it may be necessary to do the hedging in which mental health professionals are so well trained. It is also wise to try to shift the responsibility for competency evaluations outside the jail or prison. Competency to be executed can become a real ethical and practical issue for a therapist whose professional life is "in the back" (of the facility, where offenders are housed).

DEFINING SUCCESS

Those who indicate that therapy with personality disorders usually fails often neglect to indicate the criteria for success. If failure is defined as failure to restructure an individual's personality, then certainly psychotherapy, as it is legally and ethically practiced, must fail. Anyone who has ever tried to lose weight can attest to failures to restructure even this well-defined, circumscribed behavior. Eating and drinking behaviors, having their built-in reinforcers, may be appropriate models for many of the behaviors that characterize the antisocial personality. It is patently absurd to say, "A house can't be built; I know because I tried all day and didn't build one." Success in any task requires understanding what the task is, selecting proper tools, and using them correctly over a sufficient period of time to accomplish specified goals.

The benchmark in corrections is the recidivism statistic. It is at best a poor standard in a society where fewer than 1% of illegal acts result in incarceration. But it is the political reality that determines funding and the standard against which the desirability of programs is measured. Thus, all therapists are to some degree held accountable for what their treatments contribute to the offender's probability of staying out of prison.

Recidivism is usually measured over a 3-year period, yet few nonlethal interventions have sustained impact over that long a time. The therapist who wishes to show treatment success should make sure that community follow-up is occurring. A strong emphasis on community corrections may well be the most effective action a correctional psychologist can take. Lurigio (1996) addresses many of the linkage issues with community corrections.

The therapist who wishes to continue employment must include treatment that has face validity for reducing recidivism. This is usually measured in terms of skills for "making it" and controls over deviant impulses that keep the offender from making it. There is also a heavy element of mobilizing motivation for making it. No matter how good the tools the therapist provides, making it depends on whether or not the offender chooses to use them. An active criminal with better self-esteem, more rationalizations for deviant behavior, or a more integrated personality is not an acceptable treatment product.

CONCLUSIONS (SO FAR)

Motivation need not be a problem for most offenders. The wreckage of their lives and past endeavors can be called up to provide enough angst to motivate change. The problem for the inmate is a mixture of healthy and unhealthy skepticism that anything can really change.

The situation need not be a problem. One of my former professors angered me at the time by denying my request to provide a better site for an experiment. He said, "If you can demonstrate the effect only under perfect conditions, the effect is probably too trivial to be worth fooling with."

Therapists, or rather, the lack of them is a problem. There are too few universities training therapists to work with offenders (Ogloff, Tomkins, & Bersoff, 1996). There is still the stigma of correctional psychology being for those who cannot handle real jobs. And it takes an astute therapist 6 months or more to discover that some of the techniques learned in graduate school do not work or are iatrogenic.

Realistic success criteria need to be explained to therapists, judges, offenders, families, and all who have an interest in the criminal justice system. Antisocial personality characteristics cannot be cured. The offender can learn controls but not quickly, easily, or cheaply. The offender, having learned these controls, continues to have the option to use them or not.

Because success is measured in terms of control, not cure, aftercare and the ongoing availability of a support group is essential for offenders with personality disorders to continue to exercise their controls in the face of so much temptation.

Independent outcome research is essential. We must find out what works, who it works on, and the factors that can enhance its effectiveness. But if all our outcome research comes from people who have a financial interest in the process, credibility is going to be a long time coming.

Psychotherapy has not failed because it has not been adequately tried. We simply thought we could run a steeplechase while we were still in our toddler stage. We must clarify our goals, refine our techniques, and accept and publicly acknowledge realistic limits. We must do this quickly. The trend now is to incarcerate longer rather than correct more effectively. With longer sentences, the three strikes rule, the push to build more prisons and require a higher percentage of sentences to be served in prison, we are moving increasingly toward corrections as incapacitation and away from the notion that corrections can correct behavior. Though incapacitation is the surer bet in the short term, it is likely to have a long-term cost that our society cannot afford.

REFERENCES

Abramson, M. F. (1972). The criminalization of mentally disordered behavior: Possible side effect of a new mental health law. *Hospital and Community Psychiatry, 23,* 101–105.

Allodi, F. A., Kedward, H. B., & Robertson, M. (1977). "Insane but guilty": Psychiatric patients in jail. *Canada's Mental Health, 25,* 3–7.

American Correctional Association. (1988). *Suicide prevention in custody.* Videotape. (Available from American Correctional Association, 4380 Forbes Blvd., Lanham, MD 20706-4322).

American Correctional Association. (2003). *Standards for adult correctional institutions* (4th ed.). (Available from American Correctional Association, 4380 Forbes Blvd., Lanham, MD 20706-4322).

Andersen, H., Sestoft, D., Lillebaek, T., Gabrielsen, G., & Hemmingsen, R. A. (2003). Longitudinal study of prisoners on remand: Repeated measures of psychopathology in the initial phase of solitary versus nonsolitary confinement. *International Journal of Law and Psychiatry, 26*(2), 165–177.

Andrews, D., & Bonta, J. (1995). *LSI-R: The Level of Service Inventory-Revised.* Toronto, Canada: Multi-Health Systems.

Anno, B., Graham, C., Lawrence, J., & Shansky, R. (2004). *Correctional health care: Addressing the needs of elderly, chronically ill, and terminally ill inmates.* Washington D.C. National Institute of Corrections.

Ashford, J., Sales, B., & Reid, W. (Eds.). (2000). *Treating adult and juvenile offenders with special needs.* Washington DC: American Psychological Association.

Battle, C., Zlotnick, C., Najavits, L., Gutierrez, M., & Winsor, C. (2002). Posttraumatic stress disorder and substance use disorder among incarcerated women. In P. Ouimette & P. Brown (Eds.), *Trauma and substance abuse: Causes consequences, and treatment of comorbid disorders* (pp. 209–225). Washington, DC: American Psychological Association.

Blaauw, E., Arensman, E., Kraaij, V., Winkel, F., & Bout, R. (2002). Traumatic life events and suicide risk among jail inmates: The influence of types of events, time period and significant others. *Journal of Traumatic Stress, 15*(1), 9–16.

Blaauw, E., Winkel, F., & Kerhoff, A. (2001). Bullying and suicidal behavior in jails. *Criminal Justice and Behavior, 28*(3), 279–299.

Briggs, C., Sundt, J., & Castellano, C. (2003). The impact of opening a supermaximum prison on level of institutional violence. *Criminology and Public Policy, 41*(4), 1341–1376.

Brinded, P. M. J., Stevens, I., Mulder, R. T., Fairley, N., Malcom, F., & Wells, J. E. (1999). The Christchurch prisons psychiatric epidemiology study: Methodology and prevalence rates for psychiatric disorders. *Criminal Behaviour and Mental Health, 9,* 131–143.

Bureau of Justice Statistics. (1996). *Felony sentences in the United States: 1992.* Washington, DC: U.S. Department of Justice.

Bureau of Justice Statistics. (2002). *Compendium of federal justice statistics: 2000.* Washington, DC: U.S. Department of Justice.

Bureau of Justice Statistics. (2003a). *National Crime Victimization Survey: 1973–2003.* BJS Web site, Washington, DC: U.S. Department of Justice. http://www.ojp.usdoj.gov/bjs/cvictgen.htm.

Bureau of Justice Statistics. (2003b). *Reentry trends in the United States.* U.S. Department of Justice Web site: http://www.ojp.usdoj.gov/bjs/reentry/reentry.htm.

Bureau of Justice Statistics. (2003c). *State court sentencing of convicted felons: 2000.* Washington, DC: U.S. Department of Justice.

Bureau of Justice Statistics. (2004). *Prisoners in 2003.* Washington, DC: U.S. Department of Justice.

Camp, C., & Camp, G. (1985). *The corrections yearbook.* South Salem, NY: Criminal Justice Institute.

Camp, C., & Camp, G. (1989). *The corrections yearbook.* South Salem, NY: Criminal Justice Institute.

Camp, C., & Camp, G. (1997). *The corrections yearbook.* South Salem, NY: Criminal Justice Institute.

Camp, C., & Camp, G. (2000). *The corrections yearbook.* South Salem, NY: Criminal Justice Institute.

Camp, G., & Camp, C. (2002). *The corrections yearbook.* South Salem, NY: Criminal Justice Institute.

Cavanaugh, J. L., & Rogers, R. (Eds.). (1984). Malingering and deception. *Behavioral Sciences and the Law, 2,* 3–168.

Cohen, F. (Ed.). (2000 with 2003 supplement). Kingston, NJ: Civic Research Institute.

Cohen, F., & Griset, P. (1985). *Standards by legal topic. In Source book on the mentally disordered prisoner* (pp. 91–121). Washington, DC: National Institute of Corrections.

Cohen, L. H., Claiborn, W. L., & Specter, C. A. (1983). *Crisis intervention* (2nd ed.). New York: Human Sciences Press.

Coid, J. (1984). How many psychiatric patients in prison? *British Journal of Psychiatry, 145,* 78–86.

Collins, J. J., & Bailey, S. (1990). Traumatic stress disorder and violent behavior. *Journal of Traumatic Stress, 3*(2), 203–220.

Collins, J. J., & Schlenger, W. E. (1983, November). *The prevalence of psychiatric disorder among admissions to prison.* Paper presented at the American Society of Criminology, Denver, CO.

Corrado, R., Cohen, I., Hart, S., & Roesch, R. (2000). Diagnosing mental disorders in offenders: Conceptual and methodological issues. *Criminal Behavior and Mental Health, 10*(1), 29–39.

Cox, G. (2003). Screening inmates for suicide using static risk factors. *Behavior Therapist, 26*(1), 212–214.

Crocker, A. G., & Hodgins, S. (1997). The criminality of noninstitutionalized mental retarded persons. *Criminal Justice and Behavior, 24*(4) 432–454.

Cullen, F. T., Skovon, S. E., Scott, J. E., & Burton, V. S., Jr. (1990). Public support for correctional treatment: The tenacity of rehabilitative ideology. *Criminal Justice and Behavior, 17,* 6–18.

Cullen, M. (1992). *Cage your rage.* Lanham, MD: American Correctional Association.

Cullen, M., & Bradley, M. (2001). *Inside/out: Continuing to cage your rage.* Lanham, MD: American Correctional Association.

Cullen, M., & Freeman-Longo, R. E. (1996). *Men and anger: Understanding and managing your anger for a much better life.* Brandon, VT: Safer Society Press.

Denkowski, G. C., & Denkowski, K. M. (1985). The mentally retarded offender in the state prison system: Identification, prevalence, adjustment, and rehabilitation. *Criminal Justice and Behavior, 12,* 55–70.

Dies, R., & Hess, A. K. (1971). An experimental investigation of cohesiveness in marathon and conventional group psychotherapy. *Journal of Abnormal Behavior, 77,* 258–262.

Dowden, C., Blanchette, K., & Serin, R. (1999). *Anger management programming for federal male inmates: An effective intervention.* Ottawa, Ontario, Canada: Correctional Service Canada, Research Branch.

Fazel, S., & Danesh, J. (2002). Serious mental disorder in 23,000 prisoners: A systematic review of 62 surveys: Reply. *Lancet, 360,* 573.

Federal Bureau of Investigation. (2003). 2002 Uniform Crime Reports. Washington, DC: U.S. Department of Justice.

Fisher, W., Packer, I., Banks, S., Smith, D., Simon, L., & Roy-Bujnowski, K. (2002). Self-reported lifetime psychiatric hospitalization histories of jail detainees with mental disorders: Comparison with a non-incarcerated national sample. *Journal of Behavioral Health Services and Research, 29*(4), 458–465.

Gendreau, P. (Guest Ed.). (1990). Reaffirming rehabilitation [Special issue]. *Criminal Justice and Behavior, 17.*

Gendreau, P. (1996). Offender rehabilitation: What we know and what needs to be done. *Criminal Justice and Behavior, 23,* 144–161.

Gendreau, P., & Bonta, J. (1984). Solitary confinement is not cruel and unusual punishment: People sometimes are. *Canadian Journal of Criminology, 26*(4), 467–478.

Gibbs, I. I. (1982). On "demons" and "gaols": A summary and review of investigations concerning the psychological problems of jail prisoners. In C. S. Dunn & H. J. Steadman (Eds.), *Mental health services in local jails: Report of a special national workshop* (pp. 14–33). Rockville, MD: National Institute of Mental Health.

Goss, R., Peterson, K., Smith, L., Kalb, K., & Brodey, B. (2002). Characteristics of suicide attempts in a large urban jail system with an established suicide prevention program. *Psychiatric Services, 53*(5), 574–579.

Grassian, S. (1983). Psychopathological effects of solitary confinement. *American Journal of Psychiatry, 140*(11), 1450–1454.

Guthrie, R. (1999). The prevalence of posttraumatic stress disorder among federal prison inmates. *Dissertation Abstracts International, 60*(6B), 2943.

Hanson, R. K., Gordon, A., Harris, A. J. R., Marques, J. K., Murphy, W., Quinsey, V. L., et al. (2002). First report on the Collaborative Outcome Data Project on the effectiveness of psychological treatment for sexual offenders. *Sexual Abuse: A Journal for Research and Treatment, 14*(2), 169–194.

Hare, R. D. (1983). Diagnosis of antisocial personality disorder in two prison populations. *American Journal of Psychiatry, 140,* 887–890.

Harrison, L., Cappello, R., Alazewski, A., Appleton, S., & Cooke, G. (2003). *The effectiveness of treatment of substance dependence within the prison system in England: A review.* University of Kent at Canterbury.

Hayes, L. M. (1983). And darkness closes in: A national study of jail suicides. *Criminal Justice and Behavior, 10,* 461–484.

Hilkey, J. H., Wilhelm, C. L., & Home, A. M. (1982). Comparative effectiveness of video tape pretraining versus no pretraining on selected process and outcome variables in group therapy. *Psychological Reports, 50*(3, Pt. 2), 1151–1159.

Hodgins, S., & Cote, G. (1991). The mental health of penitentiary inmates in isolation. *Canadian Journal of Criminology, 33*(2), 175–182.

Holden, R., & Kroner, D. (2003). Differentiating suicidal motivations and manifestations in a forensic sample. *Canadian Journal of Behavioural Science, 35*(1), 35–44.

Human Rights Watch. (2000). *Out of sight: HRW briefing paper on supermaximum prisons, 12*(1). Available at: http://www.hrw.org/reports/2000/supermax/Sprmx002.htm.

Ivanoff, A. (1992). Background factors associated with parasuicide among male prison inmates. *Criminal Justice and Behavior, 4,* 426–436.

James, J. F., Gregory, D., Jones, R. K., & Rundell, O. H. (1980). Psychiatric morbidity in prisons. *Hospital and Community Psychiatry, 31,* 674–677.

Kal, E. (1977). Mental health in jail. *American Journal of Psychiatry, 134,* 463.

Kassinove, H., & Tafrate, R. (2002). *Anger management.* Atascadero, CA: Impact Publishers.

Kobylinska, E., & Taylor, A. (2003). Characteristics of recent suicide attempts by inmates in maximum security. *Archives of Suicide Research, 6*(3), 227–236.

Kochanek, K. D., Murphy, S. L., Anderson, R. N., & Scott, C. (2004). Deaths: final data for 2002. *National Vital Statistics Reports, 53*(5). Hyattsville, MD: National Center for Health Statistics. DHHS Publication No. (PHS) 2005-1120.

Lader, D., Singleton, N., & Meltzer, H. (2003). Psychiatric morbidity among young offenders in England and Wales. *International Review of Psychiatry, 15*(1/2), 144–147.

Lester, D., & Danto, B. L. (1993). *Suicide behind bars: Prediction and prevention.* Philadelphia: Charles Press.

Levinson, R. (1984). The system that cannot say no. *American Psychologist, 39,* 811–812.

Lombardo, L. X. (1985). Mental health work in prisons and jails: Inmate adjustment and indigenous correctional personnel. *Criminal Justice and Behavior, 12,* 17–28.

Lurigio, A. J. (1996). *Community corrections in America: New directions and sounder investments for person with mental illness and codisorders.* U.S. Department of Health and Human Services, Substance Abuse and Mental Health Services Administration. (Call 800-877-1461 for copies.)

MacArthur Justice Center. (2000). *MacArthur Justice Center: Response concerning the housing of the mentally ill in supermaximum prisons.* Chicago: University of Chicago Law School.

Martinson, R., Lipton, D., & Wilks, I. (1975). *The effectiveness of correctional treatment: A survey of treatment evaluation studies.* New York: Praeger.

McCorkle, R. C. (1995). Gender, psychopathology, and institutional behavior: A comparison of male and female mentally ill prison inmates. *Journal of Criminal Justice, 25,* 53–61.

Monahan, J. (Ed.). (1980). *Who is the client?* Washington, DC: American Psychological Association.

Monahan, J., & Steadman, H. (Eds.). (1994). *Violence and mental disorder: Developments in risk assessment.* Chicago: University of Chicago Press.

National Center on Institutions and Alternatives. (1995). *Training curriculum on suicide detection and prevention in jail and lockups.* Mansfield, MA: Author.

National Prison Hospice Association. (1998). Newsletter. (Available from P.O. Box 4623, Boulder, CO 80306-4623 or online at www.npha.org).

O'Brien, M., Mortimer, L., Singleton, N., Meltzer, H., & Goodman, R. (2003). Psychiatric morbidity among women prisoners in England and Wales. *International Review of Psychiatry, 15*(1/2), 153–157.

Ogloff, J. R. P., Tomkins, A. J., & Bersoff, D. N. (1996). Education and training in psychology and law/criminal justice. *Criminal Justice and Behavior, 23,* 200–235.

O'Keefe, M. (1997). Posttraumatic stress disorder among incarcerated battered women: A comparison of battered women who killed their abusers and those incarcerated for other offenses. *Journal of Traumatic Stress, 11*(1), 71–85.

Petrich, J. (1976). Rate of psychiatric morbidity in a metropolitan county jail population. *American Journal of Psychiatry, 133,* 1439–1444.

Pollock, P. (1999). When the killer suffers: Post-traumatic stress reactions following homicide. *Legal and Criminological Psychology, 4*(Pt. 2), 185–202.

Regan, J., Alderson, A., & Regan, W. (2002). Psychiatric disorders in aging prisoners. *Clinical Gerontologist, 26*(1/2), 117–124.

Roth, L. H. (Ed.). (1987). *Clinical treatment of the violent person.* New York: Guilford Press.

Samenow, S. E., & Bussard, R. W. (1994). *Commitment to change: Overcoming errors in thinking.* Carpenteria, CA: FMS Productions.

Schranski, I. G., & Harvey, D. R. (1983). The impact of psychodrama and role playing in the correctional environment. *International Journal of Offender Therapy and Comparative Criminology, 27,* 243–254.

Smith, P., Goggin, C., & Gendreau, P. (2002). *The effects of prison sentences and intermediate sanctions on recidivism: General effects and individual differences.* Ottawa, Ontario. Government of Canada Publications.

Sonkin, D. I. (1995). *The counselor's guide to learning to live without violence.* Volcano, CA: Volcano Press.

Sosowsky, L. (1980). Explaining increased arrest rate among mental patients. *American Journal of Psychiatry, 137,* 1602–1605.

Spruill, J., & May, J. (1988). The mentally retarded offender: Prevalence rates based on individual versus group intelligence tests. *Criminal Justice and Behavior, 15*(4), 484–491.

Steadman, H. J., McCarty, D. W., & Morrisey, I. P. (1986). *Developing jail mental health services: Practice and principles.* Rockville, MD: National Institute of Mental Health.

Steadman, H. J., & Ribner, S. A. (1980). Changing perceptions of the mental health needs of inmates in local jails. *American Journal of Psychiatry, 137,* 1115–1116.

Struckman-Johnson, C., & Struckman-Johnson, D. (2000). Sexual coercion rates in seven midwestern prison facilities for men. *Prison Journal, 80,* 379–390.

Tate, D. C., Reppucci, N. D., & Mulvey, E. P. (1995). Violent delinquents: Treatment effectiveness and implications for future action. *American Psychologist, 50,* 777–781.

Teplin, L. A. (1983). The criminalization of the mentally ill: Speculation in search of data. *Psychological Bulletin, 94,* 54–67.

Teplin, L. A. (1984). Criminalizing mental disorder: The comparative arrest rate of the mentally ill. *American Psychologist, 39,* 794–803.

Teplin, L. A. (1994). Psychiatric and substance abuse disorders among male urban inmates. *American Journal of Public Health, 84,* 290–293.

Teplin, L. A. (1996). Prevalence of psychiatric disorders among incarcerated women. *Archives of General Psychiatry, 53,* 505–512.

Toch, H. (1982). The disturbed disruptive inmate: Where does the bus stop? *Journal of Psychiatry and Law, 10,* 327–349.

Toch, H., Adams, K., & Grant, J. D. (1989). *Coping: Maladaptation in prisons.* New Brunswick, NJ: Transaction.

Toch, H., Adams, K., & Greene, R. (1987). Ethnicity, disruptiveness and emotional disorder among prison inmates. *Criminal Justice and Behavior, 14,* 93–109.

Torrey, E. F., Stieber, J., Ezekiel, J., Wolfe, S. M., Sharfstein, J., Noble, J. H., et al. (1992). *Criminalizing the seriously mentally ill: The abuse of jails as mental hospitals.* Washington, DC: Public Citizen's Health Research Group and the National Alliance for the Mentally Ill.

Travisono, D. N. (1984). *Directory of juvenile and adult correctional departments, institutions, agencies and paroling authorities.* College Park, MD: American Correctional Association.

United Nations. (2000). *Conclusions and recommendation of the Committee Against Torture.* A/55/44, paras. 179–180. New York, United Nations http://daccessdds.un.org/doc/UNDOC/GEN/G00/434/06/PDF/G0043406.pdf?OpenElement.

U.S. Department of Justice. (1984). *The 1983 jail census.* Washington, DC: Bureau of Justice Statistics.

U.S. Department of Justice, Federal Bureau of Investigation. (2003). *Crimes in the United States.* Clarksburg, WV.

Walters, G. D. (1990). *The criminal lifestyle.* Newbury Park, CA: Sage.

Washington v. Harper, 494 US 210 (1990).

Webster, C. D., Harris, G. T., Rice, M. E., Corimer, C., & Quinsey, V. L. (1994). *The violence prediction scheme: Assessing dangerousness in high-risk men.* Toronto, Canada: University of Toronto Centre of Criminology.

Wechsler, D. (1974). *Wechsler Scales: Wechsler Intelligence Scale for Children—revised.* New York, The Psychological Corporation.

Wexler, H., Falkin, G., & Lipton, D. (1990). Outcome evaluation of a prison therapeutic community for substance abuse treatment. *Criminal Justice and Behavior, 17*, pp. 71–92.

Wichman, C., Serin, R., & Motiuk, L. L. (2001). *Predicting suicide attempts among male offenders in federal penitentiaries.* Ottawa, Ontario, Canada: Correctional Service of Canada 17.

Wilson, J. Q., & Herrnstein, R. J. (1985). *Crime and human nature.* New York: Simon & Schuster.

Yochelson, S., & Samenow, S. (1976). *The criminal personality: Vol. I. A profile for change.* New York: Aronson.

Yochelson, S., & Samenow, S. (1977). *The criminal personality: Vol. II. The change process.* New York: Aronson.

Zamble, E. (1992). Behavior and adaptation in long-term prison inmates: Descriptive longitudinal results. *Criminal Justice and Behavior, 19*, 409–425.

Zamble, E., & Porporino, F. (1990). Coping, imprisonment and rehabilitation: Some data and their implications. *Criminal Justice and Behavior, 17*, 53–70.

Zimbardo, P. G., Haney, C., Banks, W. C., & Jaffe, D. (1975). The psychology of imprisonment: Privation, power, and pathology. In D. Rosenhan & P. London (Eds.), *Theory and research in abnormal psychology* (2nd ed., pp. 270–287). New York: Holt, Rinehart and Winston.

Zinger, I., Wichmann, C., & Andrews, D. (2001). The psychological effects of 60 days in administrative segregation. *Canadian Journal of Criminology, 43*(1), 47–83.

CHAPTER 26

Diagnosis and Treatment
of Sexual Offenders

WILLIAM L. MARSHALL

SEXUAL OFFENDING is a significant social problem affecting the lives of many innocent victims (W. L. Marshall, 1998a). Depending on the source of the data, up to 50% of adult women will report having been sexually abused on at least one occasion (Di Vasto et al., 1984), and a similar number of children also appear to have been abused (W. L. Marshall & Marshall, 2000). Even when quite restrictive definitions of abuse are applied, the number of people victimized by sexual offenders remains alarmingly high. This is, then, an important social issue calling for a systematic and comprehensive response. Of course, such a response is most effective when it is based on carefully collected evidence. The present chapter addresses some of the available evidence, but it is not possible to provide a comprehensive appraisal. In particular, it is not possible to provide a detailed account of the effects on the victims, except to say that in most cases, they suffer both immediate and long-term consequences that can be quite disruptive. Accordingly, the focus is on limited aspects of the offenders and what can be done to identify their problems, their threat to reoffend, and how we can reduce that threat.

Because the diagnosis and assessment of these offenders is the critical first step in dealing with them, the greatest emphasis in what follows is on these issues. A brief overview of treatment is given, and the interested reader will be able to pursue this in the references provided in that section. Two major issues omitted from this chapter concern theoretical accounts of the etiology and maintenance of sexual offending and attempts to reduce the variability apparent in these offenders by classification systems. Theories of sexual offending are provided in Laws and O'Donohue (1997) and Ward, Laws, and Hudson (2003), and the best classification system presently available is described by Knight and Prentky (1990).

DIAGNOSTIC ISSUES

Many clinicians working with sexual offenders are required to provide a diagnosis to be paid for their services. Those who provide reports to Sexually Violent Predator hearings must indicate which diagnostic category applies to the offender. Also, diagnoses influence decisions by most Parole Boards when dealing with sexual offenders, However, there are problems with the application of diagnostic criteria to sexual offenders. The following sections address these difficulties.

CHILD MOLESTERS

The American Psychiatric Association's *Diagnostic and Statistical Manual of Mental Disorders* (*DSM*) first used the term "pedophilia" in *DSM-III* (American Psychiatric Association, 1980) to describe a specific subset of child molesters. Until the publication of *DSM-IV* (American Psychiatric Association, 1994), the manual defined pedophilia in such a way that it excluded a substantial number of child molesters. Although this is not an unreasonable position, unfortunately many clinicians and researchers used the term more generically to include all child molesters, thereby causing considerable confusion. Given that most clinicians consider it necessary to evaluate and treat all child molesters, it is no wonder many have chosen to disregard *DSM* criteria. In this regard, it would have been preferable if the more diagnostically neutral term child molesters had been used as the generic descriptor rather than pedophiles. Abel, Mittelman, and Becker (1985) declared that 100% of child molesters could be diagnosed as pedophiles, but they did not make clear the basis for their diagnosis, and it does not appear that all child molesters would meet even *DSM-IV*, or its successor *DSM-IV-TR* (American Psychiatric Association, 2000), criteria.

DSM III-R defined pedophilia as involving "recurrent intense sexual urges and sexually arousing fantasies involving sexual activity with a prepubescent child or children" (American Psychiatric Association, 1987, p. 285). Because these criteria did not include actually engaging in sexual activities with a child, a *DSM-III-R* diagnosis of pedophilia could be applied to persons who had never committed an offense. On the other hand, unfortunately, it could not be applied to those persons who had molested a child but who were not plagued by deviant urges and fantasies. As reported earlier (W. L. Marshall, 1998a), an examination of my clinical files revealed no clear evidence of *recurrent* urges or fantasies in almost 60% of our nonfamilial child molesters and in over 75% of our incest offenders. Apparently, recurrent urges and fantasies are not diagnostic of all child molesters. Obviously, then, a *DSM-III-R* diagnosis of pedophilia did not have relevance for treatment, for clinicians have been treating all child molesters regardless of their diagnostic status. Fortunately, current versions of *DSM* (i.e., *DSM-IV* and *DSM-IV-TR*) have added to the criteria for pedophilia. It now reads "recurrent, intense sexually arousing fantasies, sexual urges, *or behaviors* involving sexual activity with a prepubescent child or children" (*DSM-IV-TR*, American Psychiatric Association, 2000, p. 572, emphasis added). The addition of "behaviors" along with the amendment to criterion B to read "the person has acted on these sexual urges, or the sexual urges or fantasies cause marked distress or personal difficulty" (p. 572), clearly suggest that if a person has sexually abused a child, then he or she is a pedophile. These changes would seem to imply that all child molesters are now to be considered pedophiles. Whether or not clinicians will change their diagnostic practices in this way remains to be seen, but so far it seems most are still distinguishing pedophiles from other child molesters.

Of course, it may be that pedophiles (diagnosed as a distinct subgroup of child molesters) are more or less responsive to treatment than are other child molesters. Again, a detailed examination of my records over 27 years (over 1,000 child molesters) revealed no differences in the reoffense rates for those offenders who could be classified as pedophiles versus those who could not (W. L. Marshall, 1998b). It is important to note here that offenders treated in our programs were significantly less likely to reoffend than were untreated comparison subjects (W. L. Marshall & Anderson, 1996; W. L. Marshall & Barbaree, 1988; W. L. Marshall & Fernandez, 1997). I prefer the term "child molesters" rather than "pedophiles" because my view is that all child molesters need treatment and that diagnosing someone as a pedophile appears to have no implications for treatment response (see previous discussion) or for future risk (Wilson, Abracen, Picheca, Malcolm, & Prinzo, 2003).

A significant difficulty facing diagnosticians is that child molesters are understandably reluctant to admit having deviant thoughts or feelings even when they have admitted to committing an offense. Faced with this, many clinicians and researchers have for many years employed phallometry, which is presumed to produce an assessment of sexual preferences. It is assumed that if a man displays deviant arousal to children during phallometric testing, then he almost certainly has deviant urges or fantasies; accordingly, he is judged to meet the criteria for a diagnosis of pedophilia (Freund & Blanchard, 1989; Freund & Watson, 1991). Pedophiles, according to this view, are those child molesters, and only those child molesters, who display sexual preferences for children at phallometric evaluation. The results of phallometric assessments, then, are seen as relevant not only to diagnosis but also to the identification of treatment targets (W. L. Marshall & Fernandez, 1997) and risk assessment (Quinsey, Harris, & Rice, 1995; Quinsey, Lalumière, Rice, & Harris, 1995).

The evidence bearing on the value of phallometrics has been reviewed by numerous authors, with almost all coming to positive conclusions (Abel & Blanchard, 1976; Freund, 1981; Murphy & Barbaree, 1994; O'Donohue & Letourneau, 1992; Rosen & Beck, 1988). However, in our recent comprehensive review (W. L. Marshall & Fernandez, 2003a), we were unable to find convincing evidence that the procedures were reliable, which is an essential first step in establishing the utility of any measure. It has been found that phallometric assessments differentiate nonfamilial child molesters as a group from nonoffenders (Abel, Becker, Murphy, & Flanagan, 1981; Frenzel & Lang, 1989; Freund, 1967; Freund & Blanchard, 1989; W. L. Marshall, Barbaree, & Butt, 1988; W. L. Marshall, Barbaree, & Christophe, 1986; Quinsey & Chaplin, 1988; Quinsey, Chaplin, & Carrigan, 1979), but only when the child molesters admit their problems and have multiple victims. Child molesters who are in denial or who have only a single victim display normative sexual preferences (Freund,

Chan, & Coulthard, 1979; Freund & Watson, 1991), and yet these are just the clients for whom diagnostic issues are the most problematic. Even when group differences have been found between nonfamilial child molesters and comparison groups, there is clear heterogeneity among the child molesters. Indeed, we found five clearly different sets of phallometric responses among our nonfamilial offenders (Barbaree & Marshall, 1989). Familial child molesters, according to most studies, do not differ in their phallometric responses from normal males (Frenzel & Lang, 1989; Freund, Watson, & Dickey, 1991; W. L. Marshall et al., 1986; Quinsey et al., 1979).

Clearly, then, phallometric procedures will not answer all our diagnostic questions, despite the fact that *DSM* criteria continue to identify "intense sexual arousing fantasies, [and] sexual urges" (*DSM-IV-TR,* American Psychiatric Association, 2000, p. 572) as critical to the diagnosis of pedophilia. The addition of "behaviors" to the diagnostic criteria of *DSM-IV* and *DSM-IV-TR* represents a sensible change and allows for all child molesters (at least those who molest prepubescent children) to be diagnosed as pedophiles. This and other changes over the years, however, cause serious problems in integrating research over time. In addition to the habit that some researchers have of using the term pedophilia as a generic descriptor, these changes make it hard to compare different studies, as it is not clear that the samples of child molesters are comparable.

There are two particular problems facing the clinician who wishes to rely on *DSM-IV-TR* to diagnose child molester clients. According to *DSM-IV-TR,* pedophilia can be diagnosed if "the sexual urges or fantasies cause marked distress or interpersonal difficulty" (American Psychiatric Association, 2000, p. 572). Presumably this is to allow the diagnosis to be applied to someone who complains of having unwanted sexual fantasies about children but who has not yet acted on them. The criterion that specifies the child must be prepubescent, with the indication that this typically means under age 13 years, seems arbitrary and may be difficult to determine. In many cases, clinicians have no information independent of the offender as to the victim's age, and my experience is that child molesters characteristically report the child to be older at the time of the offending than the victim claims. Even with available official information, when the victim reports the offending some time after it commenced, clinicians are often faced with discrepant claims from the offender and the victim about the child's age at the time of abuse. More detailed and thorough criticisms of *DSM* criteria for pedophilia are provided by W. L. Marshall (1997a, in press) and O'Donohue, Regev, and Hagstrom (2000).

RAPISTS

Absurdly, the diagnostic manual does not deem rapists (or, for that matter, child molesters who offend against postpubescent children) to have a diagnosable problem. Just why it is that a homosexual who feels uncomfortable about his or her sexual orientation should be said to have a disorder, whereas a man who repeatedly rapes women does not, is difficult to understand. The only rapists who would meet diagnostic criteria for a disorder according to *DSM-IV-TR* are those who are sexual sadists, although some clinicians diagnose rapists in the category "paraphilia NOS" (see Doren, 2002, for a discussion). This decision seems arbitrary at best and contradicts the decisions of the *DSM* committee.

In a recent series of articles, we have examined the meaning, application, and reliability of the diagnosis of sexual sadism. Our review of the literature (W. L. Marshall & Kennedy, 2003) revealed remarkably variable criteria employed by researchers and quite variable evidence used to determine whether or not an individual met these criteria. When we examined the information available to experienced diagnosticians applying *DSM* criteria in a prison setting, we found serious problems. Those offenders who were diagnosed as sexually sadistic had engaged in less brutal, less cruel, and less torturous acts than were those to whom the diagnosis was not applied (W. L. Marshall, Kennedy, & Yates, 2002). Finally, 15 internationally renowned experts on sadism were asked to identify sexual sadists from detailed accounts (including life history, offense history, offense details, psychological and phallometric test results, and offenders' self-reports) extracted from the information made available to the diagnosticians in the earlier study by Marshall, Kennedy, and Yates. The classifications made by these experts (is or is not a sexual sadist) appeared almost random (W. L. Marshall, Kennedy, Yates, & Serran, 2002). Using the kappa statistic as an index, considerable disagreement was evident (kappa = .14, where the required minimum level of agreement should have been in excess of kappa = .80 for such an important decision). These three reports clearly suggest that sexual sadism is, at best, a diagnosis in desperate need of clarification.

Unfortunately, phallometry does not appear to be helpful with rapists. Early small-sample studies employing phallometry did find differences between rapists and nonrapists (Abel, Barlow, Blanchard, & Guild, 1977; Barbaree, Marshall, & Lanthier, 1979; Quinsey, Chaplin, & Upfold, 1984). More recent large-sample studies, however, have not found differences (Baxter, Barbaree, & Marshall, 1986; Fernandez & Marshall, 2003b; Hall, 1989; Langevin, Paitich, & Russon, 1985; Looman & Marshall, 2001; Murphy, Krisak, Stalgaitis, & Anderson, 1984; Wormith, Bradford, Pawlak, Borzecki, & Zohar, 1988). In addition, the reliability of phallometric assessments with rapists is far too low to justify these evaluations (Barbaree, Baxter, & Marshall, 1989; Fernandez & Marshall, 2003c).

Despite these problems, clinicians consider that all rapists are in need of treatment, and programs have been designed and implemented accordingly.

EXHIBITIONISTS

The diagnostic manual is quite clear about exhibitionists, indicating that to meet the diagnostic criteria for this disorder, a person (typically a male) must have "recurrent, intense sexually arousing fantasies, sexual urges, or behaviors involving the exposure of one's genitals to an unsuspecting stranger" (*DSM-IV-TR*, American Psychiatric Association, 2000, p. 569). Because all exhibitionists, by definition, engage in behaviors involving the exposure of their genitals to unsuspecting strangers, they all appear to meet the diagnostic criteria of a paraphilia. On the other hand, few exhibitionists report fantasies involving exposure; almost all indicate that their fantasies are of their victims consenting to have sex with them (W. L. Marshall, Payne, Barbaree, & Eccles, 1991). Clinicians have always considered such offenders to need treatment, particularly because this behavior is persistent. W. L. Marshall, Eccles, and Barbaree (1991), for example, report that 57% of their untreated exhibitionists reoffended within 4 years of initial identification, and Maletzky (1991) found that his 770 exhibitionists averaged almost three exposures per week over an average period of 7.5 years. Unlike the problems raised in this chapter about pedophilia and sexual sadism, the diagnosis of exhibitionism appears uncomplicated. All these offenders presumably are paraphilic, as the criteria from *DSM-IV* has included behavioral acts of exhibitionism. With exhibitionism, then, diagnosis leads to treatment because all such offenders meet diagnostic criteria and all are deemed to need treatment.

An Alternative to Diagnosis

As noted earlier, most clinicians working with sexual offenders consider them all to be in need of treatment regardless of whether or not they meet diagnostic criteria for a disorder. Given the remarkably damaging effects of these offensive behaviors, and the limitations of the diagnostic manual, this is a sensible strategy. In their work with sexual offenders, clinicians are faced with a number of issues they either must address or are asked to address. To meet these demands, clinicians must come to some conclusion regarding the nature of the problem the offender presents, and to do this, they must complete a thorough evaluation.

It is not possible in this chapter to cover all the questions asked of those who deal with sexual offenders, but one issue can be dismissed right away. There is no basis in evidence for a clinician to offer assistance in the determination of the guilt or innocence of an alleged sexual offender. Several reviews have considered the potential problems that arise when such an appraisal is attempted (Barbaree & Peacock, 1995; W. L. Marshall, 1996b; W. L. Marshall & Fernandez, 2000; Peters & Murphy, 1992; Simon & Schouten, 1992). These reviews have examined the empirical bases of a variety of procedures and have concluded that none of them is adequate to the task of determining whether an accused did or did not actually commit an offense. It was noted earlier that phallometric evaluations of nonadmitters (presumably, the only cases where the question of guilt or innocence would be raised) do not distinguish them from nonoffenders, and the same is essentially true for personality measures (W. L. Marshall, 1996b; W. L. Marshall & Hall, 1995). Responsible clinicians, therefore, will refuse to conduct appraisals aimed at determining culpability in accused sexual offenders.

Perhaps the three most important reasons to conduct a thorough assessment of sexual offenders are to (1) determine future risk to reoffend, (2) determine treatment needs, and (3) evaluate whether or not treatment has produced the desired changes. In many states of the United States, assessors are also required to conduct thorough assessments of convicted sexual offenders to assist the courts in determining whether or not they meet criteria for civil commitment (Doren, 2002). The goals of assessment are essentially the same across these four different reasons for assessment, although higher standards are usually expected in civil commitment proceedings (see Doren, 2002).

Assessing Treatment Needs and Treatment-Induced Changes

The targets in these assessments should, of course, match the targets addressed in treatment. Treatment, as we will see, typically includes the following components: acceptance of responsibility; identification of cognitive distortions; identification of victim harm; development of victim empathy; modification of deviant sexual interests; enhancement of social, relational, and coping skills; dealing with substance abuse; and developing relapse-prevention plans. Assessments, therefore, characteristically target each of these areas, although other, rather obvious features are also appraised; for example, whether or not the offender has another serious disorder (e.g., brain damage, psychosis, or depression) may affect his or her ability to participate in treatment, as might the offender's intellectual ability and educational attainment. Several test procedures are available that can be used to evaluate these various issues; however, interviews remain a primary source of information with these offenders. Interview strategies with sexual offenders have not been clearly defined or subjected to empirical evaluation, but they remain a crucial source of information.

Acceptance of Responsibility

Interviews appear to be the only way at present of evaluating the degree to which an offender accepts responsibility for the offenses. Rarely does a sexual offender accept full responsibility, typically deflecting responsibility onto someone else (e.g., "The victim wanted me to have sex with her"; "His mother should not have left us alone") or to some set of circumstances (e.g., "I was drunk and didn't know what I was doing"; "I hadn't had sex for a long time so I couldn't control myself"). Barbaree (1991) used Nichols and Molinder's (1984) Multiphasic Sex Inventory to identify aspects of the acceptance of responsibility; this proved to be of some value, but it is rather limited in assessing responsibility taking. A more specific instrument should be developed for this purpose.

Cognitive Distortions

It is apparent that there is considerable disagreement about what constitutes cognitive distortions. Basically, this descriptor refers to distorted perceptions or memories that are self-serving and protect offenders from taking full responsibility for their offenses. These distortions take a multitude of forms and are directed by various inappropriate attitudes, beliefs, and schemas, most particularly those concerned with women or children in general and their sexuality in particular. Langton and Marshall (2000, 2001) have outlined a model of cognitive distortions in sexual offenders that suggests more detailed ways to evaluate these aspects of offenders. Although there are female sexual offenders and juveniles who sexually abuse, the focus of this chapter is on adult male sexual offenders.

Although the evidence is not convincing that sexual offenders have problems in all these areas, most clinicians remain convinced that these issues must be addressed in treatment. Also, the instruments that have been used to evaluate cognitive distortions are quite transparent, so it is presumed that sexual offenders simply present themselves in a positive light on these measures by endorsing only the evidently prosocial alternatives.

Abel et al. (1989) developed and provided data on the value of a measure of cognitive distortions in child molesters. However, others have not found it to be as useful as the initial data promised (Ward, Hudson, Johnston, & Marshall, 1997). Similarly, although the measures of attitudes and beliefs about women and rape, originally described by Burt (1980), appeared to initially differentiate rapists (Burt, 1983) and rape-prone nonoffenders (Malamuth, 1984) from other males, overall, the results of such studies have not encouraged confidence in these measures (Segal & Stermac, 1990). More recently, two studies reported the development of measures that appear to reliably identify these cognitive distortions. Bumby (1996) described a MOLEST Scale (for child molesters) and a RAPE Scale (for rapists), and he provides data on their psychometric properties. Subsequent use of these scales by others appears to support their value. A Justifications Scale to evaluate the distortions of child molesters developed by W. L. Marshall (1991) has been appraised by S. Webster, Wakeling, Milner, and Marshall (2003). These researchers, using large samples of sexual offenders and nonoffenders, demonstrated the reliability and criterion validity of this Justifications Scale. Nevertheless, most clinicians rely on clinical interviews to infer the attitudes, beliefs, and distortions of sexual offenders.

Victim Harm/Victim Empathy

It has typically been thought that the capacity to identify victim harm is a prerequisite to the development of victim empathy (Pithers, 1994). As a consequence, measurement procedures have focused on empathy, although some items on Abel et al.'s (1989) cognitive distortions scale reveal the ability to discern victim harm. Our review of the evidence on sexual offenders' capacity for empathy suggested that they do not have a general deficit, but rather are specifically deficient in empathy toward their own victims (W. L. Marshall, Hudson, Jones, & Fernandez, 1995). Our subsequent research (Fernandez & Marshall, 2003d; Fernandez, Marshall, Lightbody, & O'Sullivan, 1999) has confirmed this view with both child molesters and rapists. We take this lack of empathy for their victims to mean that sexual offenders distort their perception of the harm they have done and, as a consequence, do not feel any empathy toward their victim. This means that measures of victim harm, rather than measures of empathic responding, are critical to the evaluation of sexual offenders. Unfortunately, there are no available instruments (other than the few items on Abel's scale) that directly assess the offender's understanding of the harm he has done. Once again, interviews seem the only recourse.

Deviant Sexual Interests

The most popular way to evaluate the strength of sexual offenders' interests in their deviant acts is to phallometrically evaluate their sexual responses to various sexual and nonsexual stimuli. This procedure measures the client's erectile responses to these stimuli. While visual images remain the most popular stimuli used in these evaluations, they present ethical and legal problems. Fortunately, audiotaped descriptions of sexual acts involving either consenting adults, children, or nonconsenting adults who are forced to submit sexually generate as much arousal, and in some cases more arousal, than do visual stimuli (Fernandez & Marshall, 2003a, 2003b).

The value of phallometric assessments in determining the sexual preferences of sexual offenders has already been considered and found wanting. Additionally, it is important to note that more than 20% of all sexual offenders fail to show any arousal at phallometric testing and that most offenders can fake their arousal patterns to look normal (W. L. Marshall & Fernandez, 2003a).

Over the past 12 years, Abel and his colleagues (Abel, 1995; Abel, Huffman, Warberg, & Holland, 1998; Abel, Lawry, Karlstrom, Osborn, & Gillespie, 1994) have developed what they call a Visual Reaction Time test. Actually, it is a viewing-time task where subjects are asked to make judgments of visual images of clothed adults and children, while the time they take to make the appraisal is recorded. A subject who views a stimulus for either shorter or longer than average is, along with other evidence, deemed to have a problem. Although criticisms of this measure have been made (Fischer, 2000; Fischer & Smith, 1999), a recent study by Letourneau (2002) offers some independent support for its value.

The basic question here is not so much the availability of reliable measures of sexual interests, but rather, whether sexual interests should be targets of assessment and treatment with sexual offenders. W. L. Marshall and Fernandez (2003b) have challenged the value of addressing sexual preferences. They suggest that deviant sexual interests arise as distorted attempts to meet the same range of needs all people seek in intimate and sexual relationships. Marshall and Fernandez propose that it is the lack of the skills and self-confidence necessary to meet these needs in prosocial ways that leads some men to turn to sexual offending. As a result of offending or of fantasizing such offending, some of these men develop sexually deviant interests, but many who offend do not develop such interests (W. L. Marshall & Eccles, 1993). Among those offenders who do develop deviant interest, Marshall and Fernandez suggest that these interests are epiphenomenal to their deficient skills and confidence. These deviant interests not only serve to meet thwarted needs, but also serve to reassure these low-self-esteem males of their masculinity. Marshall and Fernandez suggest that treating the deficiencies in social and relationship skills, and the associated lack of confidence, along with providing them with the attitudes and empathy necessary to meet their needs appropriately, should resolve all their problems, including the elimination of their deviant interests. In support of this viewpoint, W. L. Marshall (1997b) provided evidence that effective treatment of all these other aspects of sexual offenders' functioning has the ef-

fect of reducing deviant interests without the necessity of specifically targeting them in treatment.

Social Skills

This is a broad descriptor that covers all aspects of social functioning, but of
course, it is impossible to assess every feature of social competence. Early interest among behavior therapists concerned conversational skills (Barlow,
1973), but most clinicians working with sexual offenders today appear to all
but neglect this aspect of functioning. Recent interest has focused on clients'
self-confidence in personal relations, their capacity for intimacy, their assertiveness, and their problems with anger.

Sexual offenders have been found to lack self-esteem in dealing with other
people (W. L. Marshall, Anderson, & Champagne, 1996). The Social Self-
Esteem Inventory (Lawson, Marshall, & McGrath, 1979) is a reliable and valid
measure of these deficiencies. Whether self-confidence has anything to do
with the origins of sexual offending or with its maintenance has yet to be determined, although it appears as an etiologic feature in several theories (e.g.,
Marshall & Barbaree, 1990; Williams & Finkelhor, 1990). The importance of
self-confidence has more to do with effectively engaging the client in treatment
(W. L. Marshall, 1996c), and so it is in that light that evaluations of self-esteem
are relevant. It is quite important to have an understanding of an offender's
self-confidence prior to treatment, and this is not always evident at interview.

Although concerns about sexual offenders' capacity for intimacy have been
noted by several authors over the years, it was not formally addressed until
1989 (W. L. Marshall, 1989). The suggestion in Marshall's paper was that a lack
of intimacy might be due to deficient relationship skills, which might in turn
encourage the man to seek sexual contacts in circumstances that do not demand these skills (e.g., by raping a woman or molesting a child). It is important
to keep in mind that the reciprocal of intimacy is loneliness, which has been
shown to facilitate aggression in males (Check, Perlman, & Malamuth, 1985).
Subsequent research has confirmed that sexual offenders do indeed lack intimacy and experience loneliness (Bumby & Hansen, 1997; Garlick, Marshall, &
Thornton, 1996; Seidman, Marshall, Hudson, & Robertson, 1994) and that they
have inadequate attachment styles (Ward, Hudson, & Marshall, 1996). Fortunately, good measures of intimacy (Miller & Lefcourt, 1982) and loneliness
(Russell, Peplau, & Cutrona, 1980) are available.

There have been numerous suggestions that sexual offenders have problems
with assertiveness (Abel et al., 1984; Barnard, Fuller, Robbins, & Shaw, 1989;
Finkelhor, 1984), although in contrast, it has also been claimed that they are
angry and aggressive (e.g., Groth, 1979). The evidence on the pervasive underassertiveness and anger among sexual offenders has not presented an entirely
clear picture (Stermac, Segal, & Gillis, 1990). What few studies there are have
found rapists to be angry (Levine & Koenig, 1980), and nonfamilial child molesters (Knight & Prentky, 1990) and incest fathers to have problems with anger
control (Paveza, 1987). Similarly, research has shown that sexual offenders
tend to be underassertive (Overholser & Beck, 1986; Stermac & Quinsey, 1985),

although it has been found that all sexual offenders displayed overassertiveness in some situations, underassertiveness in others, and appropriate assertiveness in yet other situations (W. L. Marshall, Barbaree, & Fernandez, 1995). The measure used by Marshall, Barbaree, et al., the Social Response Inventory (P. G. Marshall, Keltner, & Marshall, 1981), allows clients to select one of five possible responses (ranging from extremely underassertive to blatantly aggressive responses) to over 40 different situations. In the W. L. Marshall, Barbaree, et al. (1995) study, subjects also rated the appropriateness of the behaviors, depicted in videotapes, of three males responding to a demanding acquaintance whose requests they wished to refuse. Neither the child molesters nor the rapists rated the socially appropriate response (i.e., polite but firm denial) as the most appropriate. The child molesters thought the unassertive man was the most appropriate, whereas the rapists considered the aggressive male to be the most appropriate. Sexual offenders, therefore, may have problems with assertiveness (i.e., be underassertive or underaggressive), not necessarily because of lack of skill but perhaps because they have mistaken ideas of what constitutes appropriate social behavior.

Coping Skills

Since the early 1980s (Marques, 1982; Pithers, Marques, Gibat, & Marlatt, 1983), relapse prevention advocates have claimed that sexual offenders typically fail to cope effectively with numerous problems in their lives and that this failure to cope leads to distress, which in turn leads to offending. From this one would assume that training in appropriate coping styles and strategies would be a prominent feature of sexual offender treatment. However, there are few descriptions of such a component in treatment programs. Recent research (Cortoni & Marshall, 1995; W. L. Marshall, Serran, & Cortoni, 2000) has shown that sexual offenders, particularly child molesters, characteristically adopt maladaptive copying styles by typically either becoming absorbed in their own emotional distress or avoiding attending to the problem. Endler and Parker (1990) have developed a sound measure of coping styles that allows a determination of the type of response people consistently make to the problems life presents to them. This permits the identification of maladaptive coping from which a treatment approach can be defined.

Substance Abuse

Numerous reports indicate significant abuse or misuse of alcohol and other substances among sexual offenders (Apfelberg, Sugar, & Pfeff, 1944; Araji & Finkelhor, 1985; Lightfoot & Barbaree, 1993; Marques & Nelson, 1989; Rada, 1978). In most of these reports, however, no distinction is made between chronic substance use and the specific use of intoxicants in the context of offending. For example, it may be that chronic use erodes the offender's concerns about society's rules in a more general sense, and this may allow him to begin offending without giving thought to the consequences. On the other hand, a person who carefully premeditates sexual offending may deliberately use alcohol (or some other substance) to disinhibit social constraints. In a reanalysis of data on alcohol use by sexual offenders collected in 1979 (Christie, Marshall,

& Lanthier, 1979), W. L. Marshall (1996a) found that some 70% of offenders were at least mildly intoxicated at the time of the offense, with slightly more than 60% having a clear and persistent drinking problem. For the most part, however, it appears that few sexual offenders are intoxicated to dysfunctional levels while they are actually engaged in their abusive behaviors. Most appear to use an intoxicant simply to facilitate offending by reducing their inhibitions, whether or not they are at other times substance users, abusers, or substance dependent.

Adequate measures of problems with alcohol or other drugs are available, although an extensive history of use is essential to get a complete picture of the problem. The Michigan Alcoholism Screening Test (Selzer, 1971) and the Drug Abuse Screening Test (Skinner, 1982) are both quite satisfactory measures.

Relapse Prevention

There are, in fact, few measures to assess the relevant facets of relapse prevention. To protect against the potential for reoffending, sexual offenders need to be able to identify both the situations that put them at risk and their offense cycle (including those emotional states and stress factors that put them at risk, as well as their typical victim-seeking and grooming strategies). This is necessary in order to assist offenders to develop sensible plans for avoiding these problems or dealing with them should they arise in the future.

Noting that high-risk situations are essentially those in which offenders are at risk because they do not have the skills to deal with them, Miner, Day, and Nafpaktitis (1989) designed a situational competency test that measures these potential skills. The utility of this test, however, has not been convincingly demonstrated, and recently Serran (2003) found that this measure was not responsive to treatment-induced changes.

Other Issues

No doubt, there are many idiosyncratic features or factors that may be relevant to the full assessment of particular sexual offenders. Two that seem to be frequently salient are the offenders' own history of being abused and his hormonal functioning.

A history of sexual, physical, or emotional abuse may have left the offender with many personal deficits and unresolved emotional conflicts, or it may have persuaded him that sexual abuse is normative and is not that bad after all (Starzyk & Marshall, 2003). Obviously, a therapist would need to know this. Perhaps the best way to determine the incidence of abuse is by interview. There appears to be no doubt that a disproportionate number of sexual offenders report being sexually abused as children (see Hanson & Slater, 1988, for a review of this literature), but there is no way to independently verify their reports and there are obvious self-serving reasons why they may exaggerate or fabricate incidents of abuse.

Hormonal evaluations are costly, and, unless the facilities are readily available, it would be impractical and likely not useful to assess every sexual offender to determine whether his sex steroid system was functioning normally. There are reports (Bradford, 1990; Hucker & Bain, 1990; Land, 1995) clearly indicating that some, but few, sexual offenders have elevated levels of one or another of the sex steroids (not always testosterone). Well-controlled studies have demonstrated that reducing these abnormal levels has a positive therapeutic effect (Bradford, 1990, 1993), so these problems cannot be dismissed.

PREDICTING RECIDIVISM

Early attempts to identify the factors that might predict the likelihood of a sexual offense were based on clinical judgments that proved to be unsound (see reviews by Quinsey, Lalumière, et al., 1995; C. D. Webster, Harris, Rice, Cormier, & Quinsey, 1994). Quinsey and Maguire (1986) showed that actuarial approaches provided far more accurate bases for predicting future reoffending among dangerous offenders; as a result, they developed actuarial measures for their work with sexual offenders. The Sex Offender Risk Appraisal Guide described by Quinsey, Harris, Rice, and Cormier (1998) was an adapted version of their Violence Risk Appraisal Guide (C. D. Webster et al., 1994), which had been shown to accurately predict subsequent violent offenses.

On the basis of a meta-analysis (Hanson & Bussière, 1998) of all available recidivism studies of sexual offenders, Hanson (1997) extracted features that were significantly related to later offending. These features then entered an actuarial risk prediction scale, called the Rapid Risk Assessment for Sexual Offense Recidivism. This instrument was subjected to repeated revisions to generate the STATIC-99 (Hanson & Thornton, 2000). The reliability of this later instrument has been established (Barbaree, Seto, Langton, & Peacock, 2001), and it has proved popular in correctional settings. There are other actuarial risk instruments for predicting the likelihood of sexual reoffending (e.g., MnSOST, developed by Epperson, Kaul, & Huot, 1995) that have also generated supportive data.

Comprehensive evaluations of the potential future risk of sexual offenders generally incorporate both sexual offender-specific measures (such as the STATIC-99 and the MnSOST) and actuarially based instruments for determining the likelihood of more general offenses (e.g., the Level of Service Inventory by Andrews & Bonta, 1995) and for violence (the Violence Risk Appraisal Guide by C. D. Webster et al., 1994). In his comprehensive appraisal of evaluating risk among sexual offenders, Doren (2002) makes a case for the clinical adjustment of actuarially determined risk based on risk features unique to the individual that would not otherwise be considered. In addition, there are efforts under way to go beyond the static information (e.g., offense and life histories) considered in actuarial methods to include dynamic factors that may be responsive to treatment or may be managed by supervision in the community (Hanson & Harris, 2000).

TREATMENT

As our understanding of the range of problems that characterize sexual offenders has increased, so have the targets in treatment been expanded. In the late 1960s, behavior therapists, for example, assumed that sexual offending was motivated by deviant sexual preferences. Accordingly, the modification of deviant arousal was the prime, if not the only, focus of treatment (Bond & Evans, 1967). From the beginning of the 1970s, several authors suggested that social skills also need to be increased (Barlow, 1973; W. L. Marshall, 1971); shortly thereafter, treatment providers added cognitive distortions (Abel, Blanchard, & Becker, 1978) and a broad range of other targets for treatment (W. L. Marshall, Earls, Segal, & Darke, 1983). While treatment providers typically expose sexual offenders to most, if not all, components of their programs, treatment is adjusted to meet each offender's specific needs. Today, the most common psychological approach to the treatment of sexual offenders involves cognitive-behavioral group therapy aimed at a comprehensive range of targets and guided by a relapse-prevention approach. It is important to note, however, that the use of pharmacological interventions is generally considered an essential adjunct to these cognitive-behavioral programs. More about that in a moment.

What follows is a brief description of the usual targets in treatment and some typical approaches to producing changes in these targets. First, however, a comment about the processes of treatment.

PROCESS VERSUS PROCEDURES

One advantage that resulted from the early challenges of behavior therapists to established approaches to treatment was the demand that all therapists make explicit the procedures they used to produce change. This had definite benefits, but over time it also had the drawback of convincing most behavior therapists and their progeny (i.e., cognitive-behavior therapists) that procedures were all that mattered. The skill of a therapist and client-therapist relationship features were set aside in research that focused exclusively on examining the value of particular procedures. In terms of actual practice, this led to a neglect of concern about process. As a result, a substantial number of treatment approaches with sexual offenders evolved into and remain as psychoeducational programs, where the therapist is essentially construed as, and acts as, a teacher (Green, 1995; Smith, 1995). The group leader in the most extreme form of these programs may do little more than lecture to the clients. Such a highly structured approach has been encouraged by the production of treatment manuals that do little more than specify the procedural aspects of treatment, as if to imply that good procedures in the hands of any therapist will be effective. Though this may be true, there is no evidence available to support the idea that procedures alone have powerful effects, and most therapists behave as though the manner in which therapeutic interventions are presented is quite important.

Over the years, numerous writers (e.g., Frank, 1971; Kleinke, 1994; Rogers, 1957) have stressed the important role of the therapist in generating benefits from psychotherapy, and research has demonstrated the influence of the therapists' behavior on long-term changes (Horvath & Symonds, 1991; Lambert, 1989; Luborsky, McLellan, Woody, O'Brien & Auerbach, 1985; Martin, Garske, & Davis, 2000; Orlinsky & Howard, 1986). Some cognitive-behavioral therapists working in various fields have also stressed the importance of process variables in treatment and have provided evidence of their value (see Schaap, Bennum, Schindler, & Hoogduin, 1993, for a summary of this research).

On the basis of a review of the general literature on the influence of process variables (W. L. Marshall, Fernandez, et al., 2003), W. L. Marshall and his colleagues conducted a series of studies examining the role of the therapist in generating the sought-after treatment changes in sexual offenders. A large sample of videotapes of treatment supplied by the English Prison Service provided the bases for these studies. In the first study, trained judges were shown to be able to reliably identify various features of the therapists' behaviors (W. L. Marshall, Serran, et al., 2002). These researchers then evaluated a new set of videotapes from several prisons where treatment was conducted in the early to mid-1990s by the English Prison Service. It was found that several features of the therapists' behaviors were significantly related to beneficial changes displayed at posttreatment (W. L. Marshall, Serran, et al., 2003). Among these positive therapist characteristics were empathy, warmth, rewardingness, and directiveness. One feature that was consistently displayed by these therapists, however, had a negative effect. Confrontation, which in this study was defined as harsh and aggressive challenges that were somewhat denigrating of the offender, was significantly but negatively related to changes in treatment targets. As a result of this study, the English Prison Service modified its therapist training program, and confrontation of this kind all but disappeared.

A final study (W. L. Marshall, Serran, et al., 2002) involved a more detailed examination of the features identified in the earlier study as particularly influential when employed by the more recently trained therapists. Empathy, warmth, rewardingness, and directiveness were even more powerfully related to beneficial changes in the behaviors, attitudes, and cognitive products of the sexual offenders. Not only do these features clearly influence change over and above the simple implementation of procedures, but the results of this final study suggest that the revised therapist training program is effective in producing changes in the targets of treatment (attitudes, skills, self-confidence, etc.). To date these features of therapists have not been examined in relation to long-term reductions in offending behavior. The role of the therapist in sexual offender treatment, then, appears to be quite important, and the features of an effective therapist can be readily trained.

Treatment Components

The following sections identify the targets that are addressed in sexual offender treatment and outline the procedures used to modify each of these targets.

Acceptance of Responsibility

The majority of sexual offenders either deny any responsibility for their offending (i.e., they either claim they did not do it, or they attribute responsibility to persons or factors outside their control), or they minimize their responsibility in one way or another (Barbaree, 1991). Some treatment providers exclude from entry to treatment those sexual offenders who do not accept full, or at least substantial, responsibility. Our observations suggest that this will lead to the exclusion of many high-risk offenders; we therefore consider it to be our job to motivate these offenders (W. L. Marshall, 1998a; W. L. Marshall, Anderson, & Fernandez, 1999). For the most part, we appear to be successful in securing the full participation in treatment of these men, and the evidence we have collected indicates that we are also successful in persuading them to accept full responsibility (W. L. Marshall, 1994; W. L. Marshall, Anderson, & Fernandez, 2001; W. L. Marshall & Redondo, 2002).

As the first step in treatment, each offender has to provide a disclosure detailing all aspects of his abusive behavior, including the thoughts and feelings he had prior to, during, and after the offense(s). All group members (usually 8 to 10 in total) are asked to challenge the offender who is giving his disclosure, and the therapist models appropriately supportive but firm challenges. In this, the therapist is assisted by having available the official police account of the offense, the victim's description of what happened, and the transcript of the trial in which the offender was convicted. These challenges are meant not only to diminish denial and minimizations, but also to correct faulty thinking, distorted perceptions, and inappropriate attitudes that were functionally linked to offending. Until the client changes his negative attitudes and his distorted thinking and perceptions, he cannot be said to have accepted full responsibility. This, then, is a critical and rather extensive initial component in treatment.

Empathy

Our investigations of empathy deficits (W. L. Marshall, Hudson, et al., 1995), as noted earlier, suggest that sexual offenders lack empathy primarily for their own victims rather than having a more generalized deficit. We take this to mean that they are simply distorting their view of the harm they have done. In this view, empathy training as it has typically been done with sexual offenders (see W. L. Marshall & Fernandez, 2001, and Hildebran & Pithers, 1989, for descriptions of the typical treatment procedures aimed at enhancing empathy) is misplaced. It is certainly true that these procedures seem to enhance empathy (W. L. Marshall, O'Sullivan, & Fernandez, 1996; Pithers, 1994), but it may be that they are not essential to effective treatment. For instance, if it is the case that the apparent deficits in empathy toward their victims are due to distorted perceptions of harm, then the initial part of treatment that attempts to correct distortions may be all that is necessary, so long as it includes identification of harm. We are presently evaluating this possibility, and the data so far look encouraging.

Social Functioning

The targets in this component vary considerably across programs. For example, the Vermont Treatment Program (Pithers, Martin, & Cumming, 1989) includes components that address anger, communication skills, and emotional recognition but no explicit training in conversational or relationship skills. Maletzky (1991) targets heterosocial and heterosexual behaviors to increase success in consenting relationships; he also includes training to reduce anxiety and to increase assertiveness.

In our treatment programs (W. L. Marshall et al., 1999), we make the acquisition of behavioral skills and appropriate attitudes, thoughts, perceptions, and feelings about adult relationships the central focus of our social skills component. In this context, it is necessary for clients to learn the features of relationships that maximize satisfaction for both partners, and then acquire the skills (behavioral, cognitive, and affective) necessary to achieve the goal of forming effective relationships. This includes enhancement of self-confidence, overcoming blocks to intimacy (e.g., fear or avoidance of intimacy, distrust of others, poor communication), anger control, problem solving, assertiveness, and sex education.

We have described in detail elsewhere these various elements (e.g., self-esteem, relationship skills, general interpersonal skills, anger control, empathy) and the procedures and processes we employ to achieve changes on these features (W. L. Marshall, 2001; W. L. Marshall, Bryce, Hudson, Ward, & Moth, 1996; W. L. Marshall, Champagne, Sturgeon, & Bryce, 1997). Our appraisals, as reported in these articles, have revealed positive benefits for these interventions.

Deviant Sexual Interests

We have shifted our focus over the years to markedly de-emphasize the importance of deviant sexuality in treatment (W. L. Marshall & Fernandez, 2003b). We do this for several reasons, not the least of which is that this reduces the likelihood that the offenders will think of their behaviors as driven exclusively, or even primarily, by deviant sexual desires. No doubt, deviant desires play some part in their offending, but we, along with most clinicians, believe that other motives (e.g., power, control over others, desire for physical contact, desire to be admired) are more salient. Certainly, what offenders think seems to have more to do with offending than does genital arousal. As noted earlier, our position (W. L. Marshall & Fernandez, 2003b) is essentially that if we can have our clients develop the skills, attitudes, and feelings necessary to meet their needs in prosocial ways, they will have no need for deviant acts or fantasies. In most cases, this approach seems to produce the changes we expected (W. L. Marshall, 1997b), but some offenders who display deviant arousal do need direct interventions aimed at reducing their deviance.

Most programs do, in fact, target deviant arousal. Behavioral techniques are used to individually train offenders to eliminate deviant thoughts and increase the frequency and attractiveness of appropriate sexual fantasies. Covert sensitization (Cautela, 1967), masturbatory reconditioning (Marquis, 1970), satiation therapy (W. L. Marshall, 1979), and aversion therapy (Abel, Levis, & Clancy, 1970) have all been used to achieve the goal of altering sexual interests. Unfortunately, the evidence bearing on the value of specific procedures remains somewhat limited (Laws & Marshall, 1991; Quinsey & Earls, 1990; Quinsey & Marshall, 1983).

Pharmacological interventions appear to be effective in eliminating deviant desires and, when properly administered, may leave appropriate sexual interests intact (Bradford, 1990, 1993; Land, 1995). Antiandrogens, such as medroxyprogesterone acetate and cyproterone acetate, as well as gonadotropin-releasing hormone, are effective in this regard (Nelson,

Soutullo, DelBello, & McElroy, 2002), so long as the dosage does not so significantly lower testosterone levels that all sexual functioning is eliminated (Bradford & Pawlak, 1993). However, compliance can be a serious problem with the use of these agents (Langevin et al., 1979), so extreme care must be taken to prepare clients for the treatment; the use of injected rather than oral administration may increase compliance. There is also recent evidence supporting the value of serotonin-reuptake inhibitors (such as fluoxetine, buspirone, and clomipramine). Several reports (e.g., Fedoroff & Fedoroff, 1992; Kafka, 1991; Kruesi, Fine, Valladeres, Phillips, & Rapoport, 1992; Perilstein, Lipper, & Friedman, 1991) have demonstrated benefits for these drugs in controlling the intrusiveness of deviant sexual fantasies, and they seem to present fewer problems of compliance than do the antiandrogens. However, in our treatment programs (W. L. Marshall et al., 1999), we have used pharmacological agents with fewer than 6% of our clients in any one year, and it is usually far lower than that. In any case, pharmacological interventions should not be viewed as the sole or even primary treatment agents; they are best viewed as adjunctive to comprehensive psychological treatment.

Substance Abuse

Problems with substance use, abuse, and dependence are best dealt with in specialized additional programs; the sexual offender program can serve to integrate what is learned from these interventions with the client's overall relapse-prevention plans. Substance abuse programs are based on relapse-prevention strategies developed by Marlatt and colleagues (Marlatt, 1982; Marlatt & Gordon, 1985), and the reader is referred to those sources for a more complete understanding. The next section describes the application of Marlatt's principles to the treatment of sexually deviant behavior; this illustrates the general approach of relapse-prevention strategies.

Relapse Prevention

Major treatment programs typically employ a quite comprehensive approach to training sexual offenders in the use of relapse-prevention principles (Jenkins-Hall, Osborn, Anderson, Anderson, & Shockley-Smith, 1989; Marques, Day, Nelson, & Miner, 1989; Pithers, 1990). Typically, these programs train clients to understand the various and complex notions of relapse prevention and assist them in developing sound plans for avoiding future risks; most also have a significant postdischarge supervision component. This latter component may involve frequent, intensive, and extended supervision by a person trained in relapse prevention, and it usually also involves follow-up treatment sessions, again for an extended period. To date, it has not been shown that such extensive postdischarge supervision and treatment adds anything to standard cognitive-behavioral treatment (W. L. Marshall & Anderson, 1996), but it may appeal to the public, politicians, and bureaucrats in the present climate that is so hostile to sexual offenders. Similarly, there is no evidence that elaborate within-treatment training of sexual offenders in the principles and concepts of relapse prevention (e.g., having clients understand notions such as the abstinence violation effect or the problem of immediate gratification) is necessary or has the effect of enhancing treatment benefits (W. L. Marshall & Anderson, 2000).

The theories underlying these relapse-prevention approaches, and most of their procedures, have been appraised, criticized, and revamped by Laws, Hudson, and Ward (2000). They provide a better-integrated theoretical basis of relapse prevention and offer alternative ways to implement this approach. We restrict our use of the approach to having clients identify their offense cycle, develop plans to avoid or deal with unexpected occurrences of risks or precipitating problems, and define a set of warning signs that will alert themselves and others (e.g., friends, family, and probation/parole officers) that they may be moving to higher risk levels. In identifying their offense cycle, clients must generate a set of factors (e.g., anger, low self-esteem, intoxication) that put them at risk for either fantasizing about sexual abuse or enacting it. They must also identify situations or behaviors (e.g., being alone with a child; driving aimlessly, in the case of an exhibitionist or a rapist) that put them at risk and the steps they typically go through to get access to a victim, including, for example, deceiving and manipulating others, grooming a child, and convincing themselves that their preparatory actions are not aimed at offending.

Once they have identified their offense cycle, they must then develop plans for dealing more effectively with problems, for avoiding or escaping from risky situations, and for meeting their needs in prosocial ways. The process of examining in detail the offense cycle yields significant information that is relevant to designing relapse-prevention plans and also to defining the offender's warning signs (i.e., those features that indicate a move to higher risk).

VALUE OF TREATMENT

There are many problems facing researchers who attempt to evaluate the effects of treatment with sexual offenders. Few of these problems arise, of course, when the task is simply to determine whether or not the goals of the treatment components have been achieved (e.g., the enhancement of self-esteem, the acceptance of responsibility, and the attainment of social skills). Difficulties arise when we wish to estimate the effects of treatment on subsequent recidivism.

Accessing official records (records held by police as well as by probation or parole officers) can be difficult, and in the United States, there may be a problem tracing ex-clients outside of the researcher's home state. For researchers working in Canada, this is not a problem, as all crimes are under federal criminal codes, and all countrywide records are kept in a federal recording system accessible to approved researchers.

The primary problem with conducting an evaluation of treatment outcome concerns the difficulty of implementing a controlled study. The ideal requirements for such a study include, among other things, the random allocation of matched offenders, all of whom are seeking treatment, to either treatment or no treatment. These treated and untreated offenders must then be released and followed for several years (at least 4 years, but preferably longer). For most sexual offenders, the failure to participate in treatment has serious implications; for example, they may be kept in prison longer, they may be transferred to a higher-security prison, or they may be refused access to their children. Thus, volunteering for a study that may allocate them to a no-treatment condition may not seem wise to most sexual offenders. More to the point, however, is the concern that sexual offenders are hardly the ones who should be given the right to agree to such a study. The potential victims of sexual offenders are, after all, the ones likely to suffer should an offender's behavior remain unchanged. Therefore, women and children, as the prime victims of sexual abuse, are the ones who should be asked to agree to the implementation of a controlled evaluation that deliberately withholds treatment from some sexual offenders. Even in the absence of any evidence that treatment might reduce reoffending, I suspect that few, if any, women and children would approve of such a controlled treatment trial.

In addition, few organizations funding treatment for sexual offenders are prepared to deliberately withhold treatment from any of these dangerous men for fear of the potential public outcry that likely will follow a reoffense among the untreated men. Related to this is the fact that in most systems, untreated sexual offenders are held in custody longer than those who enter treatment. Thus, the ideal design would be seriously compromised because the treated and untreated men would thereby differ on presumably significant features (namely, the length of time in prison and, no doubt, resentment on the part of untreated offenders). In fact, in any ethically appropriate format, all offenders should be offered the choice of entering the controlled study and thereby run the risk of being left untreated with all its consequences, or simply entering a regular treatment program. To deny offenders this type of choice seems unethical. In California's controlled outcome study of the treatment of sexual offenders (Marques et al., 1989), volunteers were randomly allocated to treatment or no treatment without the option of selecting themselves out of the evaluation in order to enter treatment. Those who did not volunteer were excluded from the possibility of receiving treatment. It is surprising that prisoner advocates and civil rights lawyers did not successfully challenge the procedures of this study.

Finally, there is the problem of low base rates (i.e., the recidivism rates of untreated offenders). Untreated sexual offenders display remarkably variable recidivism rates, but in almost all cases, the rates are quite low for statistical purposes, although this is not how the public perceives it. Barbaree (1997) has calculated the statistical power necessary to discern benefits from treatment with sexual offenders. According to his calculations, with the usual base rates and a reasonably powerful treatment effect, we would need almost 1,000 subjects in an outcome study followed for up to 10 years to demonstrate the effectiveness of treatment. Meta-analysis seems to be the only strategy that is likely to generate these kinds of numbers.

Recently, Hanson et al. (2002) conducted a meta-analysis of 42 outcome studies of sexual offender treatment gathered from around the world. They insisted that to enter the analysis, studies had to have an untreated compari-son group of sexual offenders from the same setting, they had to employ offi-cial recidivism data as the basis for their appraisal, and they had to have a sufficiently long follow-up period after discharge. In this study, cognitive-behavioral programs were shown to be effective in reducing recidivism among the treated sexual offenders ($n = 5,078$) to 9.9%, whereas the untreated subjects ($n = 4,376$) recidivated at a 17.3% rate; these benefits were evident for adult and juvenile offenders and for institutional and community-based pro-grams. Noncognitive behavioral programs were not effective. In addition, as W. L. Marshall and McGuire (2003) have shown, the size of these treatment effects with sexual offenders is comparable to those produced in the treat-ment of other psychological as well as physical disorders. Thus, we can have confidence that treatment, properly conducted, will reduce the risk that sex-ual offenders constitute to the community.

CONCLUSION

Comprehensive assessment and treatment programs for sexual offenders have been developed over the past 30 years, and they appear to effectively achieve their goals of both identifying risk and treatment needs and reducing risk. No doubt, researchers and clinicians will continue to identify additional features of the offenders in need of treatment and refine treatment strategies. The pri-mary focus for the near future, however, should be the development of better approaches to assessment. Current assessment measures are quite transparent, and offenders have little difficulty figuring out what the socially acceptable re-sponses would be. Strategies for circumventing dissimulation in assessment are urgently needed.

REFERENCES

Abel, G. G. (1995). *New technology: The Abel Assessment for Interest in Paraphilias*. Atlanta, GA: Abel Screening Inc.

Abel, G. G., Barlow, D. H., Blanchard, E. B., & Guild, D. (1977). The components of rapists' sex-ual arousal. *Archives of General Psychiatry, 34*, 895–903.

Abel, G. G., Becker, J. V., Cunningham-Rathner, J., Rouleau, J. L., Kaplan, M., & Reich, J. (1984). *Treatment manual: The treatment of child molesters*. Atlanta, GA: Emory University School of Medicine, Department of Psychiatry.

Abel, G. G., Becker, J. V., Murphy, W. D., & Flanagan, B. (1981). Identifying dangerous child mo-lesters. In R. B. Stuart (Ed.), *Violent behavior: Social learning approaches to prediction, manage-ment and treatment* (pp. 116–137). New York: Brunner/Mazel.

Abel, G. G., & Blanchard, E. B. (1976). The measurement and generation of sexual arousal in male sexual deviates. In M. Hersen, R. Eisler, & P. M. Miller (Eds.), *Progress in behavior modi-fication* (Vol. 11, pp. 99–136). New York: Academic Press.

Abel, G. G., Blanchard, E. B., & Becker, J. V. (1978). An integrated treatment program for rapists. In R. T. Rada (Ed.), *Clinical aspects of the rapist* (pp. 161–214). New York: Grune & Stratton.

Abel, G. G., Gore, D. K., Holland, C. L., Camp, N., Becker, J. V., & Rathner, J. (1989). The mea-surement of the cognitive distortions of child molesters. *Annals of Sex Research, 2*, 135–152.

Abel, G. G., Huffman, J., Warberg, B., & Holland, C. L. (1998). Visual reaction time and plethys-mography as measures of sexual interest in child molesters. *Sexual Abuse: A Journal of Re-search and Treatment, 10*, 81–96.

Abel, G. G., Lawry, S. S., Karlstrom, E., Osborn, C. A., & Gillespie, C. F. (1994). Screening tests for pedophiles. *Criminal Justice and Behavior, 21*, 115–131.

Abel, G. G., Levis, D., & Clancy, J. (1970). Aversion therapy applied to taped sequences of deviant behavior in exhibitionists and other sexual deviations: Preliminary report. *Journal of Behavior Therapy and Experimental Psychiatry, 1,* 59–60.

Abel, G. G., Mittelman, M. S., & Becker, J. V. (1985). Sexual offenders: Results of assessments and recommendations for treatment. In M. H. Ben-Aron, S. J. Hucker, & C. D. Webster (Eds.), *Clinical criminology: Current concepts* (pp. 191–205). Toronto, Ontario, Canada: M&M Graphics.

American Psychiatric Association. (1980). *Diagnostic and statistical manual of mental disorders* (3rd ed.). Washington, DC: Author.

American Psychiatric Association. (1987). *Diagnostic and statistical manual of mental disorders* (3rd ed., rev.). Washington, DC: Author.

American Psychiatric Association. (1994). *Diagnostic and statistical manual of mental disorders* (4th ed.). Washington, DC: Author.

American Psychiatric Association. (2000). *Diagnostic and statistical manual of mental disorders* (4th ed., text rev.). Washington, DC: Author.

Andrews, D. A., & Bonta, J. (1995). *LSI-R: The Level of Service Inventory-Revised.* Toronto, Canada: Multi-Health Systems.

Apfelberg, C., Sugar, C., & Pfeff, A. Z. (1944). A psychiatric study of 250 sex offenders. *American Journal of Psychiatry, 100,* 762–769.

Araji, S., & Finkelhor, D. (1985). Explanations of pedophilia: Review of empirical research. *Bulletin of the American Academy of Psychiatry and Law, 13,* 17.

Barbaree, H. E. (1991). Denial and minimization among sex offenders: Assessment and treatment outcome. *Forum on Corrections Research, 3,* 300–333.

Barbaree, H. E. (1997). Evaluating treatment efficacy with sexual offenders: The insensitivity of recidivism studies to treatment effects. *Sexual Abuse: A Journal of Research and Treatment, 9,* 111–128.

Barbaree, H. E., Baxter, D. J., & Marshall, W. L. (1989). The reliability of the rape index in a sample of rapists and nonrapists. *Violence and Victims, 4,* 299–306.

Barbaree, H. E., & Marshall, W. L. (1989). Erectile responses amongst heterosexual child molesters, father-daughter incest offenders, and matched nonoffenders: Five distinct age preference profiles. *Canadian Journal of Behavioural Science, 21,* 70–82.

Barbaree, H. E., Marshall, W. L., & Lanthier, R. D. (1979). Deviant sexual arousal in rapists. *Behaviour Research and Therapy, 14,* 215–222.

Barbaree, H. E., & Peacock, E. J. (1995). Phallometric assessment of sexual preferences as an investigative tool in cases of alleged child sexual abuse. In T. Ney (Ed.), *Allegations of child sexual abuse: Assessment and case management* (pp. 242–259). New York: Brunner/Mazel.

Barbaree, H. E., Seto, M. C., Langton, C., & Peacock, E. (2001). Evaluating the predictive accuracy of six risk assessment instruments with adult sex offenders. *Criminal Justice and Behavior, 28,* 490–521.

Barlow, D. H. (1973). Increasing heterosexual responsiveness in the treatment of sexual deviation: A review of the clinical and experimental evidence. *Behavior Therapy, 4,* 655–671.

Barnard, G. W., Fuller, A. K., Robbins, L., & Shaw, T. (1989). *The child molester: An integrated approach to evaluation and treatment.* New York: Brunner/Mazel.

Baxter, D. J., Barbaree, H. E., & Marshall, W. L. (1986). Sexual responses to consenting and forced sex in a large sample of rapists and nonrapists. *Behaviour Research and Therapy, 24,* 513–520.

Bond, I., & Evans, D. (1967). Avoidance therapy: Its use in two cases of underwear fetishism. *Canadian Medical Association Journal, 96,* 1160–1162.

Bradford, J. M. W. (1990). The antiandrogen and hormonal treatment of sex offenders. In W. L. Marshall, D. R. Laws, & H. E. Barbaree (Eds.), *Handbook of sexual assault: Issues, theories, and treatment of the offender* (pp. 297–310). New York: Plenum Press.

Bradford, J. M. W. (1993). The pharmacological treatment of the adolescent sex offender. In H. E. Barbaree, W. L. Marshall, & S. M. Hudson (Eds.), *The juvenile sex offender* (pp. 278–288). New York: Guilford Press.

Bradford, J. M. W., & Pawlak, A. (1993). Double-blind placebo crossover study of cyproterone acetate in the treatment of the paraphilias. *Archives of Sexual Behavior, 22,* 383–402.

Bumby, K. M. (1996). Assessing the cognitive distortions of child molesters and rapists: Development and validation of the MOLEST and RAPE scales. *Sexual Abuse: A Journal of Research and Treatment, 8,* 37–54.

Bumby, K. M., & Hansen, D. J. (1997). Intimacy deficits, fear of intimacy, and loneliness among sexual offenders. *Criminal Justice and Behavior, 24,* 315–331.

Burt, M. (1980). Cultural myths and supports for rape. *Journal of Personality and Social Psychology, 38,* 217–230.

Burt, M. R. (1983). Justifying personal violence: A comparison of rapists and the general public. *Victimology, 8,* 131–150.

Cautela, J. R. (1967). Covert sensitization. *Psychological Record, 20,* 459–468.

Check, J. V. P., Perlman, D., & Malamuth, N. M. (1985). Loneliness and aggressive behavior. *Journal of Social and Personal Relations, 2,* 243–252.

Christie, M. M., Marshall, W. L., & Lanthier, R. D. (1979). *A descriptive study of incarcerated rapists and pedophiles.* Report to the Solicitor General of Canada, Ottawa.

Cortoni, F. A., & Marshall, W. L. (1995, October). *Childhood attachments, juvenile sexual history and adult coping skills in sexual offenders.* Paper presented at the 14th annual Research and Treatment Conference of the Association for the Treatment of Sexual Abusers, New Orleans, LA.

Di Vasto, P. V., Kaufman, L. R., Jackson, R., Christy, J., Pearson, S., & Burgett, T. (1984). The prevalence of sexually stressful events among females in the general population. *Archives of Sexual Behavior, 13,* 59–67.

Doren, D. M. (2002). *Evaluating sex offenders: A manual for civil commitments and beyond.* Thousand Oaks, CA: Sage.

Endler, N. S., & Parker, J. D. A. (1990). Multidimensional assessment of coping: A critical evaluation. *Journal of Personality and Social Psychology, 58,* 844–854.

Epperson, D. L., Kaul, J. D., & Huot, S. J. (1995, October). *Predicting risk of recidivism for incarcerated sex offenders: Updated development on the Sex Offender Screening Tool (SOST).* Paper presented at the 14th annual Research and Treatment Conference of the Association for the Treatment of Sexual Abusers, New Orleans, LA.

Fedoroff, J. P., & Fedoroff, I. C. (1992). Buspirone and paraphilic sexual behavior. *Journal of Offender Rehabilitation, 18,* 89–108.

Fernandez, Y. M., & Marshall, W. L. (2003a). *Phallometric assessments of child molesters.* Submitted for publication.

Fernandez, Y. M., & Marshall, W. L. (2003b). *Phallometric assessment of rapists.* Submitted for publication.

Fernandez, Y. M., & Marshall, W. L. (2003c). *The reliability of phallometric assessments: Internal consistency and test-retest reliability.* Submitted for publication.

Fernandez, Y. M., & Marshall, W. L. (2003d). Victim empathy, social self-esteem and psychopathy in rapists. *Sexual Abuse: A Journal of Research and Treatment, 15,* 11–26.

Fernandez, Y. M., Marshall, W. L., Lightbody, S., & O'Sullivan, C. (1999). The child molester empathy measure: Description and an examination of its reliability and validity. *Sexual Abuse: A Journal of Research and Treatment, 11,* 17–31.

Finkelhor, D. (1984). *Child sexual abuse: New theory and research.* New York: Free Press.

Fischer, L. (2000). The Abel Screen: A nonintrusive alternative. In D. R. Laws, S. M. Hudson, & T. Ward (Eds.), *Remaking relapse prevention with sex offenders: A sourcebook* (pp. 303–318). Thousand Oaks, CA: Sage.

Fischer, L., & Smith, G. (1999). Statistical adequacy of the Abel Assessment for Interest in Paraphilias. *Sexual Abuse: A Journal of Research and Treatment, 11,* 195–206.

Frank, J. D. (1971). Therapeutic factors in psychotherapy. *American Journal of Psychotherapy, 25,* 350–361.

Frenzel, R. R., & Lang, R. A. (1989). Identifying sexual preferences in intrafamilial and extrafamilial child sexual abusers. *Annals of Sex Research, 2,* 255–275.

Freund, K. (1967). Erotic preference in pedophilia. *Behaviour Research and Therapy, 5,* 339–348.

Freund, K. (1981). Assessment of pedophilia. In M. Cook & K. Howells (Eds.), *Adult sexual interest in children* (pp. 139–179). London: Academic Press.

Freund, K., & Blanchard, R. (1989). Phallometric diagnosis of pedophilia. *Journal of Consulting and Clinical Psychology, 57,* 1–6.

Freund, K., Chan, S., & Coulthard, R. (1979). Phallometric diagnoses with "nonadmitters." *Behaviour Research and Therapy, 17,* 451–457.

Freund, K., & Watson, R. J. (1991). Assessment of the sensitivity and specificity of a phallometric test: An update of phallometric diagnosis of pedophilia. *Psychological Assessment: A Journal of Consulting and Clinical Psychology, 3,* 254–260.

Freund, K., Watson, R. J., & Dickey, R. (1991). Sex offenses against female children perpetrated by men who are not pedophiles. *Journal of Sex Research, 28,* 409–423.

Garlick, Y., Marshall, W. L., & Thornton, D. (1996). Intimacy deficits and attribution of blame among sexual offenders. *Legal and Criminological Psychology, 1,* 251–258.

Green, R. (1995). Psycho-educational modules. In B. K. Schwartz & H. R. Cellini (Eds.), *The sex offender: Corrections, treatment and legal practice* (pp. 13.1–13.10). Kingston, NJ: Civic Research Institute.

Groth, A. N. (1979). *Men who rape: The psychology of the offender.* New York: Plenum Press.

Hall, G. C. N. (1989). Sexual arousal and arousability in a sexual offender population. *Journal of Abnormal Psychology, 98,* 145–149.

Hanson, R. K. (1997). *The development of a brief actuarial risk scale for sexual offense recidivism* (User Report 97-04). Ottawa: Department of the Solicitor General of Canada.

Hanson, R. K., & Bussière, M. T. (1998). Predicting relapse: A meta-analysis of sexual offender recidivism studies. *Journal of Consulting and Clinical Psychology, 66,* 348–362.

Hanson, R. K., Gordon, A., Harris, A. J. R., Marques, J. K., Murphy, W., Quinsey, V. L., et al. (2002). First report of the Collaborative Outcome Data Project on the Effectiveness of Psychological Treatment for Sex Offenders. *Sexual Abuse: A Journal of Research and Treatment, 14,* 169–194.

Hanson, R. K., & Harris, A. J. R. (2000). Where should we intervene? Dynamic predictors of sexual offense recidivism. *Criminal Justice and Behavior, 27,* 6–35.

Hanson, R. K., & Slater, S. (1988). Sexual victimization in the history of child sexual abusers: A review. *Annals of Sex Research, 1,* 485–499.

Hanson, R. K., & Thornton, D. (2000). Improving risk assessments for sex offenders: A comparison of three actuarial scales. *Law and Human Behavior, 24,* 119–136.

Hildebran, D., & Pithers, W. D. (1989). Enhancing offender empathy for sexual-abuse victims. In D. R. Laws (Ed.), *Relapse prevention with sex offenders* (pp. 236–243). New York: Guilford Press.

Horvath, A. O., & Symonds, B. D. (1991). Relation between working alliance and outcome in psychotherapy: A meta-analysis. *Journal of Counseling Psychology, 38,* 139–149.

Hucker, S. J., & Bain, J. (1990). Androgenic hormones and sexual assault. In W. L. Marshall, D. R. Laws, & H. E. Barbaree (Eds.), *Handbook of sexual assault: Issues, theories, and treatment of the offender* (pp. 93–102). New York: Plenum Press.

Jenkins-Hall, K. D., Osborn, C. A., Anderson, C. S., Anderson, K. A., & Shockley-Smith, C. (1989). The Center for Prevention of Child Molestation. In D. R. Laws (Ed.), *Relapse prevention with sex offenders* (pp. 268–291). New York: Guilford Press.

Kafka, M. P. (1991). Successful treatment of paraphilic coercive disorder (a rapist) with fluoxetine hydrochloride. *British Journal of Psychiatry, 158,* 844–847.

Kleinke, C. L. (1994). *Common principles of psychotherapy.* Pacific Grove, CA: Brooks/Cole.

Knight, R. A., & Prentky, R. A. (1990). Classifying sexual offenders: The development and corroboration of taxonomic models. In W. L. Marshall, D. R. Laws, & H. E. Barbaree (Eds.), *Handbook of sexual assault: Issues, theories, and treatment of the offender* (pp. 23–52). New York: Plenum Press.

Kruesi, J. M. P., Fine, S., Valladeres, L., Phillips, R. A., & Rapoport, J. L. (1992). Paraphilias: A double-blind crossover comparison of clomipramine versus dosipramine. *Archives of Sexual Behavior, 21,* 587–593.

Lambert, M. J. (1989). The individual therapist's contribution to psychotherapy process and outcome. *Clinical Psychology Review, 9,* 469–485.

Land, W. B. (1995). Psychopharmacological options for sex offenders. In B. K. Schwartz & H. R. Cellini (Eds.), *The sex offender: Corrections, treatment and legal practice* (pp. 18.1–18.7). Kingston, NJ: Civic Research Institute.

Langevin, R., Paitich, D., Ramsey, G., Anderson, C., Kamrad, J., Pope, S., et al. (1979). Experimental studies in the etiology of genital exhibitionism. *Archives of Sexual Behavior, 8,* 307–331.

Langevin, R., Paitich, D., & Russon, A. E. (1985). Are rapists sexually anomalous, aggressive, or both? In R. Langevin (Ed.), *Erotic preference, gender identity, and aggression in men: New research studies* (pp. 13–38). Hillsdale, NJ: Erlbaum.

Langton, C., & Marshall, W. L. (2000). The role of cognitive distortions in relapse prevention programs. In D. R. Laws, S. M. Hudson, & T. Ward (Eds.), *Remaking relapse prevention with sex offenders: A sourcebook* (pp. 167–186). Thousand Oaks, CA: Sage.

Langton, C., & Marshall, W. L. (2001). Cognition in rapists: Theoretical patterns by typological breakdown. *Aggression and Violent Behavior: A Review Journal, 6,* 499–518.

Laws, D. R., Hudson, S. M., & Ward, T. (Eds.). (2000). *Remaking relapse prevention with sex offenders: A sourcebook.* Thousand Oaks, CA: Sage.

Laws, D. R., & Marshall, W. L. (1991). Masturbatory reconditioning: An evaluative review. *Advances in Behaviour Research and Therapy, 13,* 13–25.

Laws, D. R., & O'Donohue, W. (Eds.). (1997). *Sexual deviance: Theory, assessment, and treatment.* New York: Guilford Press.

Lawson, J. S., Marshall, W. L., & McGrath, P. (1979). The Social Self-Esteem Inventory. *Educational and Psychological Measurement, 39,* 803–811.

Letourneau, E. J. (2002). A comparison of objective measures of sexual arousal and interest: Visual reaction time and penile plethysmography. *Sexual Abuse: A Journal of Research and Treatment, 14,* 207–223.

Levine, S., & Koenig, J. (1980). *Why men rape: Interviews with convicted rapists.* New York: Macmillan.

Lightfoot, L. O., & Barbaree, H. E. (1993). The relationship between substance use and abuse and sexual offending in adolescents. In H. E. Barbaree, W. L. Marshall, & S. M. Hudson (Eds.), *The juvenile sex offender* (pp. 203–224). New York: Guilford Press.

Looman, J., & Marshall, W. L. (2001). Phallometric assessments designed to detect arousal to children: The responses of rapists and child molesters. *Sexual Abuse: A Journal of Research and Treatment, 13,* 3–13.

Luborsky, L., McLellan, T., Woody, G. E., O'Brien, C. P., & Auerbach, A. (1985). Therapist success and its determinants. *Archives of General Psychiatry, 42,* 602–611.

Malamuth, N. M. (1984). Aggression against women: Cultural and individual causes. In N. M. Malamuth & E. Donnerstein (Eds.), *Pornography and sexual aggression* (pp. 19–52). Orlando, FL: Academic Press.

Maletzky, B. M. (1991). *Treating the sexual offender.* Newbury Park, CA: Sage.

Marlatt, G. A. (1982). Relapse prevention: A self-control program for the treatment of addictive behaviors. In R. B. Stuart (Ed.), *Adherence, compliance, and generalization in behavioral medicine* (pp. 329–378). New York: Brunner/Mazel.

Marlatt, G. A., & Gordon, J. R. (Eds.). (1985). *Relapse prevention.* New York: Guilford Press.

Marques, J. K. (1982, March) *Relapse prevention: A self-control model for the treatment of sex offenders.* Paper presented at the 7th annual Forensic Mental Health Conference, Asilomar, CA.

Marques, J. K., Day, D. M., Nelson, C., & Miner, M. H. (1989). The sex offender treatment and evaluation project: California's relapse prevention program. In D. R. Laws (Ed.), *Relapse prevention with sex offenders* (pp. 96–104). New York: Guilford Press.

Marques, J. K., & Nelson, C. (1989). Elements of high-risk situations for sex offenders. In D. R. Laws (Ed.), *Relapse prevention with sex offenders* (pp. 35–46). New York: Guilford Press.

Marquis, J. (1970). Orgasmic reconditioning: Changing sexual object choice through controlling masturbation fantasies. *Journal of Behavior Therapy and Experimental Psychiatry, 1,* 263–270.

Marshall, P. G., Keltner, A., & Marshall, W. L. (1981). Anxiety reduction, assertive training, and enactment of consequences: A comparative study in the modification of nonassertive and social fear. *Behavior Modification, 5,* 85–102.

Marshall, W. L. (1971). A combined treatment method for certain sexual deviations. *Behaviour Research and Therapy, 9,* 292–294.

Marshall, W. L. (1979). Satiation therapy: A procedure for reducing deviant sexual arousal. *Journal of Applied Behavior Analysis, 12,* 10–22.

Marshall, W. L. (1989). Intimacy, loneliness and sexual offenders. *Behaviour Research and Therapy, 27,* 691–503.

Marshall, W. L. (1991). *The Justifications Scale: A measure for assessing cognitive distortions in child molesters.* Unpublished scale, Queen's University, Kingston, Ontario, Canada.

Marshall, W. L. (1994). Treatment effects on denial and minimization in incarcerated sex offenders. *Behaviour Research and Therapy, 32,* 559–564.

Marshall, W. L. (1996a). Assessment, treatment, and theorizing about sex offenders: Developments over the past 20 years and future directions. *Criminal Justice and Behavior, 23,* 162–199.

Marshall, W. L. (1996b). Psychological evaluation in sexual offence cases. *Queen's Law Journal, 21,* 499–514.

Marshall, W. L. (1996c). The sexual offender: Monster, victim, or everyman? *Sexual Abuse: A Journal of Research and Treatment, 8,* 317–335.

Marshall, W. L. (1997a). Pedophilia: Psychopathology and theory. In D. R. Laws & W. O'Donohue (Eds.), *Handbook of sexual deviance: Theory and application* (pp. 152–179). New York: Guilford Press.

Marshall, W. L. (1997b). The relationship between self-esteem and deviant sexual arousal in nonfamilial child molesters. *Behavior Modification, 21,* 86–96.

Marshall, W. L. (1998a). Adult sexual offenders. In A. S. Bellack & M. Hersen (Series Eds.) & N. Singh (Vol. Ed.), *Comprehensive clinical psychology: Vol. 9. Applications in diverse populations* (pp. 407–420). Oxford: Elsevier Science.

Marshall, W. L. (1998b). Diagnosing and treating sexual offenders. In A. K. Hess & I. B. Weiner (Eds.), *The handbook of forensic psychology* (2nd ed., pp. 640–670). New York: Wiley.

Marshall, W. L. (2001). Enhancing social and relationship skills. In M. S. Carich & S. Mussack (Eds.), *Handbook for sexual abuser assessment and treatment* (pp. 149–162). Brandon, VT: Safer Society Press.

Marshall, W. L. (in press). Diagnostic problems with sexual offenders. In W. L. Marshall, L. E. Marshall, & Y. M. Fernandez (Eds.), *Sexual offender treatment and assessment: Issues and controversies.* Chichester, England: Wiley.

Marshall, W. L., & Anderson, D. (1996). An evaluation of the benefits of relapse prevention programs with sexual offenders. *Sexual Abuse: A Journal of Research and Treatment, 8,* 209–221.

Marshall, W. L., & Anderson, D. (2000). Do relapse prevention components enhance treatment effectiveness? In D. R. Laws, S. M. Hudson, & T. Ward (Eds.), *Remaking relapse prevention with sex offenders: A sourcebook* (pp. 39–55). Newbury Park, CA: Sage.

Marshall, W. L., Anderson, D., & Champagne, F. (1996). The importance of self-esteem in sexual offenders. *Psychology, Crime and Law, 3,* 81–106.

Marshall, W. L., Anderson, D., & Fernandez, Y. M. (1999). *Cognitive behavioural treatment of sexual offenders.* Chichester, England: Wiley.

Marshall, W. L., Anderson, D., & Fernandez, Y. M. (2001). *Il trattemento cognitivo-comportamentale degli aggressori sessual?* Torino, Italy: Centro Scientifico Editore.

Marshall, W. L., & Barbaree, H. E. (1988). The long-term evaluation of a behavioral treatment program for child molesters. *Behaviour Research and Therapy, 26,* 499–511.

Marshall, W. L., & Barbaree, H. E. (1990). An integrated theory of sexual offending. In W. L. Marshall, D. R. Laws, & H. E. Barbaree (Eds.), *Handbook of sexual assault: Issues, theories, and treatment of the offender* (pp. 257–275). New York: Plenum Press.

Marshall, W. L., Barbaree, H. E., & Butt, J. (1988). Sexual offenders against male children: Sexual preferences. *Behaviour Research and Therapy, 26,* 383–391.

Marshall, W. L., Barbaree, H. E., & Christophe, D. (1986). Sexual offenders against female children: Sexual preferences for age of victims and type of behaviour. *Canadian Journal of Behavioural Science, 18,* 424–439.

Marshall, W. L., Barbaree, H. E., & Fernandez, Y. M. (1995). Some aspects of social competence in sexual offenders. *Sexual Abuse: A Journal of Research and Treatment, 7,* 113–127.

Marshall, W. L., Bryce, P., Hudson, S. M., Ward, T., & Moth, B. (1996). The enhancement of intimacy and the reduction of loneliness among child molesters. *Journal of Family Violence, 11,* 219–235.

Marshall, W. L., Champagne, F., Sturgeon, C., & Bryce, P. (1997). Increasing the self-esteem of child molesters. *Sexual Abuse: A Journal of Research and Treatment, 9,* 321–333.

Marshall, W. L., Earls, C. M., Segal, Z. V., & Darke, J. (1983). A behavioral program for the assessment and treatment of sexual aggressors. In K. Craig & R. McMahon (Eds.), *Advances in clinical behavior therapy* (pp. 148–174). New York: Brunner/Mazel.

Marshall, W. L., & Eccles, A. (1993). Pavlovian conditioning processes in adolescent sex offenders. In H. E. Barbee, W. L. Marshall, & S. M. Hudson (Eds.), *The juvenile sex offender* (pp. 118–142), New York: Guilford Press.

Marshall, W. L., Eccles, A., & Barbaree, H. E. (1991). Treatment of exhibitionists: A focus on sexual deviance versus cognitive and relationship features. *Behaviour Research and Therapy, 29,* 129–135.

Marshall, W. L., & Fernandez, Y. M. (1997). Enfoques cognitivo-conductuales para las parafilias: El tratameinto de la delincuencia sexual. In V. E. Caballo (Ed.), *Manual para el tratamiento cognitivo-conductual de los trastornos psicológicos: Vol. 1. Trastornos por ansiedad, sexualas, afectivos y psicóticos* (pp. 299–331). Madrid, Spain: Siglio Veintiuno de España Editore, S. A.

Marshall, W. L., & Fernandez, Y. M. (2000). Phallometry in forensic practice. *Journal of Forensic Psychology Practice, 1,* 77–87.

Marshall, W. L., & Fernandez, Y. M. (2001). Empathy training. In M. S. Carich & S. Mussack (Eds.), *Handbook for sexual abuser assessment and treatment* (pp. 141–147). Brandon, VT: Safer Society Press.

Marshall, W. L., & Fernandez, Y. M. (2003a). *Phallometric testing with sexual offenders: Theory, research, and practice.* Brandon, VT: Safer Society Press.

Marshall, W. L., & Fernandez, Y. M. (2003b). Sexual preferences: Are they useful in the assessment and treatment of sexual offenders? *Aggression and Violent Behavior: A Review Journal, 8,* 131–143.

Marshall, W. L., Fernandez, Y. M., Serran, G. A., Mulloy, R., Thornton, D., Mann, R. E., et al. (2003). Process variables in the treatment of sexual offenders: A review of the relevant literature. *Aggression and Violent Behavior: A Review Journal, 8,* 205–234.

Marshall, W. L., & Hall, G. C. N. (1995). The value of the MMPI in deciding forensic issues in accused sexual offenders. *Sexual Abuse: A Journal of Research and Treatment, 7,* 205–219.

Marshall, W. L., Hudson, S. M., Jones, R., & Fernandez, Y. M. (1995). Empathy in sex offenders. *Clinical Psychology Review, 15,* 99–113.

Marshall, W. L., & Kennedy, P. (2003). Sexual sadism in sexual offenders: An elusive diagnosis. *Aggression and Violent Behavior: A Review Journal, 8*, 1–22.

Marshall, W. L., Kennedy, P., & Yates, P. (2002). Issues concerning the reliability and validity of the diagnosis of sexual sadism applied in prison settings. *Sexual Abuse: A Journal of Research and Treatment, 14*, 301–311.

Marshall, W. L., Kennedy, P., Yates, P., & Serran, G. (2002). Diagnosing sexual sadism in sexual offenders: Reliability across diagnosticians. *International Journal of Offender Therapy and Comparative Criminology, 46*, 668–676.

Marshall, W. L., & Marshall, L. E. (2000). Child sexual molestation. In V. B. Van Hasselt & M. Hersen (Eds.), *Aggression and violence: An introductory text* (pp. 67–91). New York: Allyn & Bacon.

Marshall, W. L., & McGuire, J. (2003). Effect sizes in treatment of sexual offenders. *International Journal of Offender Therapy and Comparative Criminology, 46*, 653–663.

Marshall, W. L., O'Sullivan, C., & Fernandez, Y. M. (1996). The enhancement of victim empathy among incarcerated child molesters. *Legal and Criminological Psychology, 1*, 95–102.

Marshall, W. L., Payne, K., Barbaree, H. E., & Eccles, A. (1991). Exhibitionists: Sexual preferences for exposing. *Behaviour Research and Therapy, 29*, 37–40.

Marshall, W. L., & Redondo, S. (2002). Control y tratamiento de la agresion sexual. In S. Redondo (Ed.), *Delincuencia sexual y sociedad*. Barcelona: Ariel.

Marshall, W. L., Serran, G. A., & Cortoni, F. A. (2000). Childhood attachments, sexual abuse, and their relationship to adult coping in child molesters. *Sexual Abuse: A Journal of Research and Treatment, 12*, 17–26.

Marshall, W. L., Serran, G. A., Fernandez, Y. M., Mulloy, R., Mann, R. E., & Thornton, D. (2003). Therapist characteristics in the treatment of sexual offenders: Tentative data on their relationship with indices of behavior change. *Journal of Sexual Aggression, 9*, 25–30.

Marshall, W. L., Serran, G. A., Moulden, H., Mulloy, R., Fernandez, Y. M., Mann, R. E., et al. (2002). Therapist features in sexual offender treatment: Their reliable identification and influence on behavior change. *Clinical Psychology and Psychotherapy, 9*, 395–405.

Martin, D. J., Garske, J. P., & Davis, M. K. (2000). Relation of the therapeutic alliance with outcome and other variables: A meta-analytic review. *Journal of Consulting and Clinical Psychology, 62*, 435–450.

Miller, R. S., & Lefcourt, H. M. (1982). The assessment of social intimacy. *Journal of Personality Assessment, 46*, 514–518.

Miner, M. H., Day, D. M., & Nafpaktitis, M. K. (1989). Assessment of coping skills: Development of a situational competency test. In D. R. Laws (Ed.), *Relapse prevention with sex offenders* (pp. 127–136). New York: Guilford Press.

Murphy, W. D., & Barbaree, H. E. (1994). *Assessments of sex offenders by measures of erectile response: Psychometric properties and decision making*. Brandon, VT: Safer Society Press.

Murphy, W. D., Krisak, J., Stalgaitis, S. J., & Anderson, K. (1984). The use of penile tumescence measures with incarcerated rapists: Further validity issues. *Archives of Sexual Behavior, 13*, 545–554.

Nelson, E. B., Soutullo, C. A., DelBello, M. P., & McElroy, S. L. (2002). The psychopharmacological treatment of sex offenders. In B. K. Schwartz (Ed.), *The sex offender: Current treatment modalities and systems issues* (Vol. 4, pp. 13.1–13.30). Kingston, NJ: Civic Research Institute.

Nichols, H. R., & Molinder, I. (1984). *Multiphasic Sex Inventory manual*. Tacoma, WA: Author.

O'Donohue, W. T., & Letourneau, E. (1992). The psychometric properties of the penile tumescence assessment of child molesters. *Journal of Psychopathology and Behavioral Assessment, 14*, 123–174.

O'Donohue, W. T., Regev, L. G., & Hagstrom, A. (2000). Problems with the DSM-IV diagnosis of pedophilia. *Sexual Abuse: A Journal of Research and Treatment, 12*, 95–105.

Orlinsky, D. E., & Howard, K. I. (1986). Process and outcome in psychotherapy. In S. L. Garfield & A. E. Bergin (Eds.), *Handbook of psychotherapy and behavior change* (3rd ed., pp. 311–384). New York: Wiley.

Overholser, J. C., & Beck, S. (1986). Multimethod assessment of rapists, child molesters, and three control groups on behavioral and psychological measures. *Journal of Consulting and Clinical Psychology, 54*, 682–687.

Paveza, G. (1987, September). *Risk factors in father-daughter child sexual abuse: Findings from a case-control study*. Paper presented at the 3rd annual Family Violence Research Conference, Durham, NC.

Perilstein, R. D., Lipper, S., & Friedman, L. J. (1991). Three cases of paraphilias responsive to fluoxetine treatment. *Journal of Clinical Psychiatry, 52*, 169–170.

Peters, J. M., & Murphy, W. D. (1992). Profiling child sexual abusers: Legal considerations. *Criminal Justice and Behavior, 19*, 38–53.

Pithers, W. D. (1990). Relapse prevention with sexual aggressors: A method for maintaining therapeutic gain and enhancing external supervision. In W. L. Marshall, D. R. Laws, & H. E. Barbaree (Eds.), *Handbook of sexual assault: Issues, theories, and treatment of the offender* (pp. 343–361). New York: Plenum Press.

Pithers, W. D. (1994). Process evaluation of a group therapy component designed to enhance sex offenders' empathy for sexual abuse survivors. *Behaviour Research and Therapy, 32,* 565–570.

Pithers, W. D., Marques, J. K., Gibat, C. C., & Marlatt, G. A. (1983). Relapse prevention with sexual aggressors: A self-control model of treatment and maintenance of change. In J. G. Greer & I. R. Stuart (Eds.), *The sexual aggressor: Current perspectives on treatment* (pp. 214–239). New York: Van Nostrand-Reinhold.

Pithers, W. D., Martin, G. R., & Cumming, G. F. (1989). Vermont treatment program for sexual aggressors. In D. R. Laws (Ed.), *Relapse prevention with sex offenders* (pp. 292–310). New York: Guilford Press.

Quinsey, V. L., & Chaplin, T. C. (1988). Penile responses of child molesters and normals to descriptions of encounters with children involving sex and violence. *Journal of Interpersonal Violence, 3,* 259–274.

Quinsey, V. L., Chaplin, T. C., & Carrigan, W. F. (1979). Sexual preferences among incestuous and nonincestuous child molesters. *Behavior Therapy, 10,* 562–565.

Quinsey, V. L., Chaplin, T. C., & Upfold, D. (1984). Sexual arousal to nonsexual violence and sadomasochistic themes among rapists and non-sex-offenders. *Journal of Consulting and Clinical Psychology, 52,* 651–657.

Quinsey, V. L., & Earls, C. M. (1990). The modification of sexual preferences. In W. L. Marshall, D. R. Laws, & H. E. Barbaree (Eds.), *Handbook of sexual assault: Issues, theories, and treatment of the offender* (pp. 279–295). New York: Plenum Press.

Quinsey, V. L., Harris, G. T., & Rice, M. E. (1995). Actuarial prediction of sexual recidivism. *Journal of Interpersonal Violence, 10,* 85–105.

Quinsey, V. L., Harris, G. T., Rice, M. E., & Cormier, C. (1998). *Violent offenders: Appraising and managing risk.* Washington, DC: American Psychological Association.

Quinsey, V. L., Lalumière, M. L., Rice, M. E., & Harris, G. T. (1995). Predicting sexual offenses. In J. C. Campbell (Ed.), *Assessing dangerousness: Violence by sexual offenders, batterers, and child abusers* (pp. 114–137). Thousand Oaks, CA: Sage.

Quinsey, V. L., & Maguire, A. (1986). Maximum security psychiatry patients: Actuarial and clinical prediction of dangerousness. *Journal of Interpersonal Violence, 1,* 143–171.

Quinsey, V. L., & Marshall, W. L. (1983). Procedures for reducing deviant arousal: An evaluation review. In J. G. Greer & I. R. Stuart (Eds.), *The sexual aggressor: Current perspectives on treatment* (pp. 267–289). New York: Van Nostrand-Reinhold.

Rada, R. T. (1978). *Clinical aspects of the rapist.* New York: Grune & Stratton.

Rogers, C. R. (1957). The necessary and sufficient conditions of therapeutic personality change. *Journal of Consulting Psychology, 21,* 95–103.

Rosen, R. C., & Beck, G. (1988). *Patterns of sexual arousal: Psychophysiological processes and clinical applications.* New York: Guilford Press.

Russell, D., Peplau, L. A., & Cutrona, C. A. (1980). The revised UCLA Loneliness Scale. *Journal of Personality and Social Psychology, 39,* 472–480.

Schaap, C., Bennum, I., Schindler, L., & Hoogduin, K. (1993). *The therapeutic relationship in behavioral psychotherapy.* New York: Wiley.

Segal, Z. V., & Stermac, L. E. (1990). The role of cognition in sexual assault. In W. L. Marshall, D. R. Laws, & H. E. Barbaree (Eds.), *Handbook of sexual assault: Issues, theories, and treatment of the offender* (pp. 161–174). New York: Plenum Press.

Seidman, B. T., Marshall, W. L., Hudson, S. M., & Robertson, P. J. (1994). An examination of intimacy and loneliness in sex offenders. *Journal of Interpersonal Violence, 9,* 518–534.

Selzer, M. L. (1971). The Michigan Alcoholism Screening Test (MAST): The quest for a new diagnostic instrument. *American Journal of Psychiatry, 127,* 1653–1658.

Serran, G. A. (2003). *Coping in sexual offenders: Treatment-induced changes.* Unpublished doctoral thesis, Ottawa University, Canada.

Simon, W. T., & Schouten, P. G. W. (1992). Problems in sexual preference testing in child sexual abuse cases: A legal and community perspective. *Journal of Interpersonal Violence, 7,* 503–516.

Skinner, H. A. (1982). The Drug Abuse Screening Test. *Addictive Behaviors, 7,* 363–371.

Smith, R. C. (1995). Sex offender program planning and implementation. In B. K. Schwartz & H. R. Cellini (Eds.), *The sex offender: Corrections, treatment and legal practice* (pp. 7.1–7.13). Kingston, NJ: Civic Research Institute.

Starzyk, K. B., & Marshall, W. L. (2003). Childhood family and personological risk factors for sexual offending. *Aggression and Violent Behaviors: A Review Journal, 8,* 93–105.

Stermac, L. E., & Quinsey, V. L. (1985). Social competence among rapists. *Behavioral Assessment, 8,* 171–185.

Stermac, L. E., Segal, Z. V., & Gillis, R. (1990). Social and cultural factors in sexual assault. In W. L. Marshall, D. R. Laws, & H. E. Barbaree (Eds.), *Handbook of sexual assault: Issues, theories, and treatment of the offender* (pp. 143–159). New York: Plenum Press.

Ward, T., Hudson, S. M., Johnston, L., & Marshall, W. L. (1997). Cognitive distortions in sex offenders: An integrative review. *Clinical Psychology Review, 17,* 479–507.

Ward, T., Hudson, S. M., & Marshall, W. L. (1996). Attachment style in sex offenders: A preliminary study. *Journal of Sex Research, 33,* 17–26.

Ward, T., Laws, D. R., & Hudson, S. M. (Eds.). (2003). *Sexual deviance: Issues and controversies.* Thousand Oaks, CA: Sage.

Webster, C. D., Harris, G. T., Rice, M. E., Cormier, C., & Quinsey, V. L. (1994). *The violence prediction scheme: Assessing dangerousness in high risk men.* Toronto, Canada: University of Toronto, Centre of Criminology.

Webster, S., Wakeling, H., Milner, R., & Marshall, W. L. (2003). *The Justifications Scale for child molesters: Reliability, discriminant validity, and tracking treatment-induced changes.* Manuscript in preparation. (Available from Rockwood Psychological Services, Suite 403, 303 Bagot Street, Kingston, Ontario K7K 5W7, Canada)

Williams, L. M., & Finkelhor, D. (1990). The characteristics of incestuous fathers: A review of recent studies. In W. L. Marshall, D. R. Laws, & H. E. Barbaree (Eds.), *Handbook of sexual assault: Issues, theories, and treatment of the offender* (pp. 143–159). New York: Plenum Press.

Wilson, R. J., Abracen, J., Picheca, J. E., Malcolm, P. B., & Prinzo, M. (2003, October). *Pedophilia: An evaluation of diagnostic and risk management methods.* Paper presented at the 22nd annual conference of the Association for the Treatment of Sexual Offenders, St. Louis, MO.

Wormith, J. S., Bradford, J. M. W., Pawlak, A., Borzecki, M., & Zohar, A. (1988). The assessment of deviant sexual arousal as a function of intelligence, instructional set and alcohol ingestion. *Canadian Journal of Psychiatry, 33,* 800–808.

PART SEVEN

PROFESSIONAL ISSUES

Practicing Principled Forensic Psychology: Legal, Ethical, and Moral Considerations

ALLEN K. HESS

> The danger for most of us is not that our aim is too high and we miss it,
> but too low and we reach it.
>
> —Attributed to Michelangelo

THIS QUOTE represents two approaches to principled conduct and, by extension, to principled professional practice. One approach indicates that behaving well involves avoiding sin and is analogous to the "push" theories of motivation, called "d-motivation" by Maslow, from the term "deprivation." This view is consistent with a legal approach. The law requires few actions from people. For a person to behave legally, he or she simply needs to avoid committing a wrongful act. Only a few actions, such as filing taxes and caring for dependents, are required by the law.

The second approach to principled conduct is aspirational, called "b-motivation" for "being." It leads us to consider the higher reaches of conduct, immerses principled conduct in an interpersonal matrix, and constantly requires the examination of each act in terms of its implications for the actor and society. Both approaches are legitimate and deserve our attention. However, whereas the avoidance-of-sin approach promotes conduct that is adequate, the aspirational approach sets our sights on the possibility of excellence in our individual practice and for our profession.

This chapter examines ethics codes generically, studies the ethics codes for psychology and for forensic psychology by applying the American Psychological Association (APA) ethics codes and guidelines to particular areas of vulnerability in the practice of forensic psychology, and concludes with recommendations for both the individual and our profession.

ETHICS CODES

When times were simpler, there were four professions: medicine, law, the military, and the clergy. The common factors among these, and perhaps all professions, are that a profession (1) requires extensive study for entry, (2) invokes a testing or initiation process, (3) uses an apprenticeship or mentoring procedure, (4) requires continued, lifelong study, (5) mandates pro bono publico work for the client base, and (6) strives to put itself out of business.

These foundations still serve well. The reader is invited to apply these criteria to psychology and to his or her own practices. However, as time passed, society became more complex, and more formalized ethics codes have evolved. For example, continuing education used to be taken for granted: Good practitioners stayed current as a matter of course, and the half-life of knowledge seemed longer. But with the quickening pace of knowledge and its dissemination, plus the growing complexity of psychology's practice as it interfaces with more public constituencies, most states in the union now mandate formal continuing education hours.

WHY HAVE ETHICS CODES?

Professions use ethics codes to regulate, educate, and inspire their practitioners (Frankel, 1989). When the public grants a trust to a profession, the profession assumes an obligation to practice in a way that serves the public and not merely the individual professional's appetites. Privileged communication is granted to allow the public to consult professionals without fear that their intimate disclosures will be revealed. Surgeons are allowed to cut into human flesh to serve the patient's medical needs. This trust is not granted irrevocably or unconditionally; the conditions are that the profession regulate itself by developing norms, values, standards, and practices that shape the individual practitioner. The profession does not genetically produce the next generation of practitioners, but it does produce its next generation of professionals through socialization (Pavalko, 1979). Although the ultimate responsibility for ethical conduct is and must remain with the individual practitioner, the promotion of ethical conduct is the province of the profession. These norms, values, standards, and practices are embodied in codes of ethical professional conduct, be they as short as the American Medical Association's seven principles stated in 10 sentences (Edge & Groves, 1994) or as lengthy as the American Bar Association's (ABA; 2002) Model Rules of Professional Conduct, or inclusive of the equally lengthy disciplinary procedures nor the separate standards of conduct for prosecutorial, defense, or judicial functions of attorneys (West Publishing Company, 1984).

The more open the process used in developing the code, the more the profession and its practitioners are likely to be morally committed to the values expressed in the code. Similarly, in light of public distrust of professions, more lay involvement in the drafting and implementation has occurred as a prophylactic to further erosion of trust. The more the profession can tolerate publicizing its code violators or publishing casebooks, the more educational and trust inducing will be its ethical procedures.

FUNCTIONS

Frankel (1989) sees ethics codes as serving eight functions:

1. As an enabling document, the *code provides a moral compass* against which the practitioner can guide his or her conduct. No matter how well intentioned a professional, he or she will experience confusion and anxiety without a framework to guide decisions.

2. The code proclaims to the public *a set of standards that the public should expect from the practitioners* in the profession.

3. *Pride, power, prestige, and a sense of allegiance to the shared values and skills of the profession* accompany ethics codes.

4. Codes serve to *educate the public and induce trust in the profession.* By benefiting the public, a profession is granted social and economic rewards and special exemptions, as in the case of holding surgeons harmless for cutting into flesh for medically beneficial purposes. Yet ethics codes can be political devices that thwart adversaries and minimize threats to the profession's autonomy. The monopoly a profession enjoys and the values it espouses are protected by ethics codes. These values typically are in the public's interest, such as the public's granting dentists the right to cut away gum tissue and to drill into teeth, or granting the client the security of privileged communication so the psychologist can delve into the person's private thoughts, feelings, and concerns.

Yet, codes are restrictive and conserve a profession's values. While preserving minimal skill levels to practice, they can be used to stifle creativity and foster greed. One notable neuropsychologist was on a crusade to ban the use of the Bender-Gestalt, given its disputed validity in determining brain dysfunction. He wanted anyone using the Bender to be subject to ethics review and sanctions. Whatever the Bender-Gestalt's usefulness might be, banning it would be nonsensical from a scientific perspective. One would be asserting the null hypothesis and foreclosing any possibility of discovering a future use for the test. In fact, Schretlen, Wilkins, Van Gorp, and Bobholz (1992) found the first five Bender designs were useful in detecting feigned insanity in a group of prisoners, a use unanticipated by the neuropsychologist and undiscoverable if we banned the Bender.

A few critics garnered publicity in claiming that the Rorschach should be banned from both clinical and forensic use because of questions these skeptics raised about the Rorschach's validity. If an instrument is banned, how can we discover its uses? Moreover, it is the use of the instrument in the clinician's hands rather than the instrument that is central to validated use (American Educational Research Association, 1999). The interested reader should refer to Meyer and Archer (2001) regarding the validated use of Rorschach.

Another way an ethics code can be twisted to serve ignoble purposes is illustrated by a state ethics committee that passed a rule holding psychologists to be malpracticing if they did not bill the insurance company their full fee in cases where the client was seen at a reduced rate. The insurance companies apprised the committee of the definitions of fraud and misrepresentation, and the rule vanished.

5. Ethics codes confer a sense of power, prestige, group solidarity, and common purpose that culminate in a *sense of professional identity.* Frankel (1989) describes the public trust placed in a profession's status and autonomy that flows from an ethics code. As mentioned in function 4, this can be a double-edged sword. The profession can use ethics procedures to disarm critics, privatize conflict, and insulate the profession. One antidote to this malady is the addition of lay members to ethics committees and hearing panels. The degree to which the medical and legal professions in many states have only professionals on their boards and hearing panels to the exclusion of respected members of the laity is the degree to which cynicism has met the panels' findings. Another remedy is holding open-air or sunshine meetings, which are open to the public and the press, except when an individual case is being considered that might damage the person's reputation.

6. Ethics codes *deter unethical behavior by the use of sanctions* and by affirming the duty of peers to monitor misbehaving colleagues. Although ethics committees cannot levy jail time and fines on offenders, their findings can lead to letters of reprimand, suspension and revocation of membership in the professional society, and suspension and revocation of a state practitioner's license. These actions are severe. They have implications for practitioners being able to secure liability insurance, to be listed in directories and on panels that insurers reimburse, and, most pointedly for forensic psychologists, to be credible in court. In light of the availability of electronic databases and the growing sophistication of attorneys in challenging expert witnesses, such a sanction could be devastating to an expert witness. This is especially so in domestic relations cases (see Chapters 4 and 5, in this volume), in which the use of ethics complaints against expert witnesses for the other side has become as common or pro forma a tactic as alleging child abuse charges against the opposing parent in child custody cases. In fact, Glassman (1998) found 7% to 10% of the APA ethics complaints concerned custody evaluations. Kirkland and Kirkland (2001) claim child custody cases yield a higher number of ethics complaints against forensic psychologists than any other complaint. In domestic disputes, every tactic one can imagine is used, including intimidating the expert witness by threatened lawsuits and ethics complaints.

All these property interest losses imposed on sanctioned psychologists call for ethics committees to exercise care, fairness, and due process for the professional in hearing complaints and to consider rehabilitative actions for the ethically impaired (Peterson, 2001; Schoenfeld, Hatch, & Gonzalez, 2001; Williams, 2001). In fact, the new APA Ethical Principles were designed to correct the tone of the 1992 version that was used as a cudgel against practitioners (Knapp & VandeCreek, 2003). For example, the 2002 code suspends the adjudicative process when a case is also before a court. This suspension effectively removes a finding by the Ethics Committee from being used as a bludgeon by the plaintiff in the legal proceeding. The introduction specifically states:

> The Ethics Code is not to be used as the basis of civil liability. Whether a psychologist has violated the Ethics Code standards does not by itself determine whether the psychologist is legally liable in a court action, whether a contract is enforceable or whether other legal consequences occur. (APA, 2002, p. 1061)

Further, see Principle 1.08 concerning the strong admonition not to deny any advantage to a psychologist subject to an ethics complaint solely on the basis of the complaint and absent any further information. In prior times, the Ethics Committee finding could be used against the psychologist in the court proceeding. This language naturally cannot prevent Ethics Committee findings from entering court proceedings but does pose an impediment to such entry.

7. Practitioners find that *ethics codes can be supportive.* The profession as well as individuals can use ethical principles against improper claims by clients. One psychologist underestimated his client's maladjustment. He assigned bibliotherapy tasks in addition to regular sessions; she complained to the Ethics Committee of his abandoning and not adequately caring for her. The committee was able to inform the client that bibliotherapy was a legitimate way for the psychologist to help augment their sessions, and the case went no further. Practitioners find codes useful when faced with unreasonable or intrusive demands by employers, bureaucrats, and others in allied professions.

Case 27.1

Consider the prison pastoral counselor who served on disciplinary committees hearing his patients' cases and deciding on punishments. Ethically and psychologically uninformed, he saw no conflict of interest. Furthermore, he wore a prison guard's windbreaker around the prison and, bearing a shotgun, he participated in the armed hunting for escapees. He saw no reason why his clients should not see him as a benevolent, caring, trustworthy psychotherapist. When he became the unit director and told other counselors to "be part of the team" and join in hunts for escapees, the counselors asked the consulting psychologist how to confront the unit director. He advised them to use the ethics codes of their disciplines and then seek guidance from the Department of Corrections central office psychology director.

*   *   *

Correctional psychologists puzzling through the institutional role conflict between treatment and security would benefit from reading Weinberger and Sreenivasan (1994). The interested reader might be surprised to find over 50 different ethics codes concerning rendering psychological services that can provide some guidance. These range from the American Academy of Forensic Psychology and the American Association of Christian Counselors to the National Council of Social Workers and the National Council for Hypnotherapy (see www.kspope.com/ethcodes/ for a listing of at least 60 such codes). While seemingly whimsical, this listing might be useful in helping educate an errant colleague or informing oneself about particular ethical issues in a specialized practice or setting.

8. Ethics codes can help *adjudicate disputes both within the profession and with outside interests.* A psychologist whose testing protocols are subpoenaed can refer to ethics codes and test standards, as well as the copyright laws safeguarding the published tests, to appeal that the protocols that the judge does deem discoverable be restricted in circulation. This may mean that the attorney issuing the subpoena hires a psychologist to read and interpret the records and

that the records do not find their way into a reporter's hands; the attorney can request that the judge issue instructions to try the case in court and not the press. This becomes pressing when the data are psychological and easy to spin or slant. This needs to be done with deftness, as one's own client-attorney may be the one spinning and the judge may not be inclined to counsel by the psychologist on how to run the trial.

Case 27.2

The neuropsychologist was asked to evaluate a judge whose decisions were becoming increasingly disengaged from the cases before him and whose conduct in and outside court began to cause concern among clerks, attorneys, and others. Removal of a judge is fraught with political danger, which is why our society insulates judges from capricious removal and requires a high threshold for cause. The morning after furnishing his report to the attorney, the psychologist came into the professional issues seminar to tell the interns about confidentiality strictures prohibiting him from telling anything but rough contours of the case. The interns asked, "Then why is the psychological test report in the front pages of the newspaper along with an editorial for the judge to resign due to pinpoint hemorrhaging due to chronic alcohol abuse?" The attorney retaining the psychologist had leaked the report.

WHAT GUIDANCE DO OUR CODES PROVIDE?

Ethics codes articulate the values of the profession in a set of principles. *Principles* are rules within an ethical system, such as the principle "First, do no harm." Whatever else physicians do, we expect them to do no harm, notwithstanding that they may cause pain to accomplish a second principle, that of "beneficence," or doing good. *Standards* are patterns of conduct, established by custom or authority, adherence to which fulfills the principles. The authority in psychology refers to scientific canonical knowledge. *Guidelines* are outlines of conduct, protocols, or procedures operationalizing the standards (Bennett, Bryant, VandenBos, & Greenwood, 1990).

PRINCIPLES, CODES, GUIDELINES, AND STANDARDS FOR FORENSIC PSYCHOLOGISTS

There are five principles and 10 standards in the APA (2002) Principles and Code. The five principles are these:

1. *Beneficence and malfeasance:* Safeguard the welfare and rights of others and maintain vigilance in seeing the psychologist's influence is not misused.
2. *Fidelity and responsibility:* Establish trust with clients, clarify roles and obligations, coordinate services with other professionals to the client's benefit, see to the general ethical probity of colleagues, and provide some measure of pro bono service.
3. *Integrity:* Promote truthfulness in research, teaching, and service, avoid dishonesty, deception, subterfuge, and misrepresenting, and where any such activities are necessary, be sure the benefits outweigh the costs and client damage is minimized or repaired.

4. *Justice:* Allow equal access to services by the advantaged and the disadvantaged alike, and take reasonable care that any biases and limitations to competence or expertise do not harm recipients of the services.
5. *Respect for people's rights and dignity:* Respect the dignity, worth, and rights of all people to privacy and autonomy, apply safeguards to protect the vulnerable or impaired, maintain awareness for cultural, individual, and role-driven differences so biases do not adversely affect the client.

When applying the principles to cases, it becomes clear that they have considerable overlap and that cases illustrating one principle frequently have applicability to others. It is only a bit less entangling to see how the ethical standards help guide the forensic psychologist. The reader interested in the general application of the Code and standards may find Koocher and Keith-Spiegel (1998) and Fisher (2003) useful, enlightening, and entertaining. What follows is a look at the Code with specific application of the standards to forensic psychology.

STANDARD 1: RESOLVING ETHICAL ISSUES

This standard advises us about resolution of ethical conflicts. Parts 1.02 and 1.03 concern conflict between the Code and the law or an institution, as mentioned in the case about the unit manager and hunting escapees. Part 1.04 suggests informal contact with the party about whom the psychologist is concerned. Parts 1.05 and 1.06 concern processing the complaint if informal resolution does not work.

There might be occasions when the standards' applicability to forensic matters is limited. In the following case, ethical misconduct was found. Was the practitioner's obligation to report the misdeed to the attorney who retained him rather than to correct his colleague? Because forensic psychology operates in an adversarial arena, finding that the other side's expert made a critical error works to the side that retained the psychologist.

Case 27.3

A psychologist was asked by an attorney retained by one parent to examine a report concerning child custody performed by a psychologist retained by the other parent. He found the psychologist's report to be excellent on its surface, with all the boilerplate language to qualify all the aspersions. On closer inspection, however, he did not like the extensive use of quotes from computer-generated reports, knowing that such reports should be used to generate hypotheses and not be the basis for conclusions. This is so because the progenitor of the report cannot know the particular client and qualify its findings accordingly. He purchased a copy of the report.

He found that the word "not" was omitted in the critical paragraph, which changed the whole substance of the report and the finding as to the suitability of the parent for custody. He took the stand and showed the computer-generated printout. The psychologist who had misrepresented the computer-generated report was found in court to have doctored the report to please the attorney who retained him.

After the case, that attorney and our psychologist discussed what to do. The attorney said he was going to take steps to limit the offending psychologist's practice on such cases in the future in that area of the United States, and he asked the consulting psychologist to help him in this. In this case, would the psychologist who found the misreported data have been in more trouble by correcting his colleague? Was the impugning of the psychologist's ability to testify in future cases already the natural consequence of his misrepresentation? Should the district attorney be referred the case to prosecute for perjury? Whether this psychologist should have taken further steps with the state ethics committee is for the reader to judge.

STANDARD 2: COMPETENCE

The standard of competence bears directly on a number of issues in forensic practice. Part 2.01 of the APA Code concerns the preparation for service provision in both technical areas and personal and cultural competencies. Nowhere is this more apropos than forensic psychology, in which a number of subcultures, ranging from the boardroom to the drug house, require knowledge of specialized argot and concepts. No psychologist can be adequately educated for every exigency, and some degree of judgment is involved as to whether competent service is being provided.

Case 27.4

The psychologist was asked to analyze insurance policies for their readability levels. He had published in this area years ago and had since then spent a quarter of a century assessing intellectual functions. The psychologist did some reading in the literature and consulted with two colleagues who conduct readability studies regularly, both to gather references and to make sure they were available for consultation should the need arise. He described his background to the lawyers, his clients in this case, to be clear about his skills and the services they needed. He provided the required readability analysis. They referred him to an allied firm to assess comprehensibility of insurance policies, a bit farther afield than his usual competencies. The psychologist specified the types of analyses that would be needed, proceeded to secure consultants and began reading treatises in the area, and described his procedures to the new set of attorneys, including the limits of his capabilities and the consultants available.

*   *   *

Part 2.02 loosens the competence requirement in cases of emergency when other qualified help is not available. Part 2.03 tells us to engage in continuing education. Part 2.04 is central to forensic psychology in requiring us to establish firm ties between our practices and the scientific bases for them. The chapter in this volume concerning the expert witness dwells on basing our statements in court activities (consultation, administrative hearings, and depositions as well as on the witness stand) on as firm an empirical basis as possible. Note that there will be tensions between what we know and what we are asked to do. For example, are suicide prevention methods sufficiently established empirically to be defensible in a lawsuit? Are such methods developed in psychiatric facilities generalizable to correctional facilities? Sometimes a best practices basis rather than a method that will satisfy some Platonic ideal of knowledge must suffice in the application of psychology to the instant case. Pepper (1942) calls this "pragmatic ethics," as we might know only that there is a 70% chance of rain but must either take our umbrella or not. That is, we are faced with discrete decisions (insane or not, competent or not) when we might not have evidence beyond the p .05 level. Perhaps the most principled course is to proffer the estimation, such as a 35% chance of reoffending in the case of probation or parole, and let the court or administrative body address the dichotomous question that is properly theirs to decide.

As competence is a critical standard for forensic psychologists, and one that can most easily result in an ethics complaint or a lawsuit, let us consider this standard, and its parallel in the Specialty Guidelines for Forensic Psychologists (Committee on Ethical Guidelines for Forensic Psychologists, 1991), thoroughly. The Guidelines call for psychologists to provide services only in areas in which they have special knowledge, skills, experience, and education; that they explain to the court the factual basis for and the limits to their profferings; that psychologists have knowledge of the substance and procedure of the legal and professional standards in the legal proceedings in which they are participating; that client civil rights are known and respected; and that the psychologist's own values are clear and do not compromise the service being rendered.

The competence standard requires the psychologist to offer services only in areas that he or she has had education, training, supervision, or experience. However, in developing areas, the psychologist may offer services after taking steps to secure appropriate training, education, supervision, or experience as available given the current knowledge base in the field to ensure competence in the skills and knowledge base at issue (Standard 1.04). The Specialty Guidelines for Forensic Psychologists (Committee on Ethical Guidelines for Forensic Psychologists, 1991, currently undergoing revision) adds knowledge and skill to the definition of competence, in keeping with the *Daubert* test (*Daubert v. Merrell Dow Pharmaceuticals*, 1993). A psychologist may be expert in providing competency and insanity evaluations but may not be aware of the literature, techniques, and issues involved with a fitness-for-duty evaluation. Such an evaluation may require expertise in vocational psychology, in confidentiality issues specific to the workplace, and in prediction questions specific to job evaluations (Super, 1997). Or a psychologist may know a great deal about competence to stand trial in a criminal assault case but not know the skills that contribute to probate and estate administration. A civil or criminal fraud case regarding misfeasance by an estate administrator or executor may require knowledge of such skills and competencies that contribute to appropriate probate and estate management.

Golding (1990) describes the testimony of Grigson, a psychiatrist, in *Barefoot v. Estelle* (1983). Without seeing Barefoot, Grigson claimed to be able to "predict future dangerousness of an individual within reasonable medical certainty," that Barefoot was in the "most severe category of sociopaths," and that Grigson was "one hundred % and absolutely [certain that] Barefoot would commit future acts of violence that would constitute a continuing threat to society" (Golding, 1990, p. 291). Cross-examination has been the mechanism that courts traditionally use to confirm or dismiss "junk science." However, cross-examination is inadequate in that it relies on attorneys, judges, and jurors to make a determination concerning epistemological, technical, and statistical matters beyond the ability of any but other experts in the area. Golding suggests that a partial solution is to place an affirmative duty on the potential expert to clarify the basis of his or her testimony, to show the evidence of the specific bases for the testimony rather than to passively react to attorney questions, and to describe the limits of the testimony. This suggestion places responsibility and consequences on the slipshod expert to produce better than junk testimony. However, this may be asking the fox to guard the henhouse because attorneys rarely have the expertise to conduct a telling cross-examination on the technicalities of psychology. Again, the integrity-challenged expert is not about to engage in such self-scrutiny and self-revelation.

Shuman and Greenberg (1998) offer another solution. They decry judges' dismissal of professional ethics codes and assert that many of the problems with expert testimony could be resolved by the judges taking ethics codes seriously. Thus, Grigson's testimony passed judicial review, but it did not pass psychiatric peer review when the American Psychiatric Association's amicus brief asserted that Grigson should not have been permitted to testify in *Barefoot v. Estelle* (1983) because it is "unethical for a psychologist [*sic*; Grigson was a psychiatrist] to offer a professional opinion unless he or she has conducted an examination" (Shuman & Greenberg, 1998, p. 7).

Shuman and Greenberg (1998) review other instances, such as courts accepting expert testimony in custody cases when the psychologist examined only one parent and then offered an opinion about which parent would be best for the child. This practice is unsound both on the face of it, because how can one make a comparative decision when one has seen only one party, and because such practice is countermanded by the professions' guidelines (e. g., APA, 2002). Shuman and Greenberg put it pithily: "It [the opinion] does not lack an adequate foundation because it is unethical, it is unethical because it lacks an adequate foundation" (p. 8).

Case 27.5

Consider both the competence and the integrity of a pair of opposing psychologists in an insanity defense case. The first psychologist testified that a Borderline Personality Disorder led the defendant to lifelong maladaptiveness, including mood fluctuations, inappropriate anger, and poor emotional control. These, he said, prevented the defendant from conforming his conduct to the law and from distinguishing right from wrong when he stabbed to death a 74-year-old grandmother and her 4-year-old granddaughter. The psychologist offered this testimony despite the existence of a letter found in the defendant's former wife's purse outlining the steps she was to take in helping him sustain a defense. (The astute observer will note that the defendant may have been insane at the moments around the stabbings and still be planful afterward in the construction of the defense. The judge ruled the letter inadmissible due to the marital privilege, though the couple had divorced the year before the stabbings.)

Whatever questions the expert's testimony may raise were trumped by the psychologist retained by the prosecutor. The psychologist testified that the defendant knew the nature and quality of the charges against him (a competency issue rather than an insanity issue) and that he could distinguish right from wrong because the voices the defendant heard were not true hallucinations but came from *inside the defendant's head and not outside his head*! True hallucinations came from outside his head, the psychologist opined. Although one may feel the defendant, judge, and both psychologists deserve each other, the public's view of psychology after learning about cases such as this has become increasingly cynical and distrusting of mental health experts or, in S. J. Perelman's term, "head candlers" (after the poultry farmers' practice of judging eggs by holding them up to candlelight).

*   *   *

Did the psychologists know the legal standard for insanity? Did the state law disqualify personality disorders, of which borderline is one, from consideration as a valid insanity defense, as many state laws hold? Did the psychologists select the most appropriate measures (neither proffered any testing, but based their testimonies on their clinical interviews)? Could they articulate their psychological findings to the standard? Was each psychologist inclined to have his expert opinion in mind and work backward to see how the data could be molded to fit a predetermined conclusion rather than allowing the data to drive his testimony? Did their testimonies have adequate foundations? Such displays fuel the distrust and hostility that is expressed in such scathing best sellers as Huber's (1993) *Galileo's Revenge: Junk Science in the Courtroom* and Hagen's (1997) *Whores of the Court*.

LEVELS OF CERTAINTY

Huber (1993) and Hagen (1997) raise a set of important issues regarding the level of knowledge in a field on which experts base their opinions. The two psychologists in the insanity case just described have a well-developed methodology that they use in forming an opinion. For a century, we have refined psychological testing and defined the two components to determine insanity: whether there are sufficient cognitive capacities for the accused to know the nature and quality of the action at issue and, in jurisdictions using both prongs of the insanity definition, whether emotional disruptions were of a magnitude that preempted the accused's cognitive capacities.

There are other areas of practice that have far less developed methodologies. For example, one key problem with jury selection is that we might be able to do a good job understanding a person's opinions regarding the issue at trial but when the jury adjourns to the jury room, the confounding effects of the foreperson's leadership style and the particular group's dynamics might undo the psychologist's work in voir dire, or juror selection. Thus, we might do a decent job with *juror* selection but not *jury* selection. The forensic psychologist might be well advised to have a graded system of levels of confidence in his or her conclusions. These levels can be expressed as "certain, within the bounds of the well-developed knowledge in the discipline," to "highly suggestive," to "indicative but not certain," to "no expert opinion can be offered regarding this question." These levels should be based on both the state of knowledge in the discipline and the degree to which the case has ecological validity or is highly parallel to the knowledge base in the discipline.

Rotgers and Barrett (1996) proposed a two-by-two table, with empirical support on one axis and theory adequacy on the other. They group various areas (e.g., battered woman syndrome, parenting skills) in four quadrants with estimates of confidence by which the expert can regard the field and present the evidence with qualifying statements about the confidence the testimony merits.

Case 27.6

The psychologist was asked to examine a case of Munchausen-by-proxy that a large teaching hospital alleged against a mother. The top medical investigators in this disorder were based at the medical center and were said to be testifying. Upon reviewing the case, the psychologist found that the entire database consisted of 57 cases and that not one case of a Black woman was in this national database. Several other features in the case did not make sense, including the fact that the physician who referred the case had filed the same charges against several other women whose children died under his care. The psychologist wanted to examine the physician as the possible perpetrator. When the attorney who consulted with the psychologist presented this information while deposing one of the experts on Munchausen-by-proxy, the medical center backed away in the case. Their much acclaimed Munchausen-by-proxy database was simply inadequate and irrelevant in this particular case.

*   *   *

Level of certainty is a researchable forensic topic with at least two dimensions: the soundness of the empirical base, and the degree to which the methodology fits the case at hand, or ecological validity. Even our most developed instruments may not be revealing in a particular case, and the psychologist needs to say so. Expressing levels of certainty of a knowledge base to the attorney is important when first encountering a case, and expressing both the knowledge base certainty and the certainty of findings in the particular case are important in rendering testimony, whether legislatively or in a courtroom. Even when we do not have a methodology that reaches a compelling level of certainty, the court may ask for expert guidance:

> It is, of course, not easy to predict future behavior. The fact that such a determination is difficult, however, does not mean that it cannot be made. Indeed, prediction of future criminal conduct is an essential element in many of the decisions rendered throughout our criminal justice system. . . . What is essential is that the jury have before it all possible relevant information about the individual defendant whose fate it must determine. (*Jurek v. Texas*, 1976, 274-276)

The courts require all relevant information, and it is the ethical psychologist's responsibility to describe the weight that such evidence should be accorded (Golding, 1990).

KNOWLEDGE OF LEGAL ISSUES

The Guidelines further oblige forensic psychologists to understand the applicable legal standards that govern the issues and procedures in which they participate and to understand the civil rights of the parties involved. If the psychologist is not knowledgeable about the charges, then an evaluation of competence to stand trial will be compromised because the psychologist cannot adequately assess whether the defendant can understand the charges. Some charges are easily understood on their face, but others can be complex, requiring a higher level of cognitive complexity in helping form a defense. The psychologist must weigh the defendant's cognitive abilities against the complexity of the charges and the case. A simple criminal assault differs in complexity from civil or tort charges arising from that assault, which in turn call for fewer cognitive abilities than would be needed by a defendant in a complex securities fraud case or in a case involving fraudulent administration of estate and probate matters. The psychologist must learn about the legal standards and articulate them with the psychological aspects of the case at hand.

ROLE BOUNDARIES

Regarding the second point, suppose a psychologist interviews a defendant for the prosecutor and in doing so notices the defendant in dire need of psychological support. Instead of again warning the defendant that the information is to be used in court and that the psychologist works for the prosecutor, the psychologist uses reflexive empathy rather than receptive empathy (Greenberg & Shuman, 1997; Shuman, 1993) in eliciting information. The psychologist would be operating legally, having informed the examinee. But he or she may be using a professional advantage in an ethically dubious way to gain for the prosecutor the upper hand at the expense of the defendant's civil liberties and human welfare. The defendant may have been psychologically and legally unable to exercise his or her right to withhold information in the face of the hope for psychological help and so may compromise his or her own case. Besides being unethical, the offending psychologist may have committed a breach of duty and be legally liable.

STANDARD 3: HUMAN RELATIONS

As we shall see in the privacy section later, in forensic cases there are different expectations of privacy. However, in all cases, the well-being of the client must be taken into account, and the people who will find out about test and other findings must be only those who are supposed to be informed and have a need to know.

Case 27.7

The Kelly Flinn case, concerning the B-52 pilot who was separated from the U.S. Air Force charged with adultery and then lying, shows the need to clarify that the psychologist is retained by the attorney, that there will be limitations on the materials gleaned from interviews and tests, that the types of inference are both usable and within the bounds of scientific and professional standards, and that these issues are clear before proceeding in the case. Flinn claims that her attorney told her to see Dr. Ann Duncan, a St. Louis psychologist the attorney knew, so

> we could find out more about Marc's [Zigo, the coadulterer] character and have her draw up a psychological profile of me to convey how someone so successful could get into such a mess. . . . I was mad at everyone in the room. . . . Especially Dr. Duncan. I'd just found out that she had told my mother that I had chosen to fly a B-52 because it was the largest penis I could find. She also revealed to my mother the intimate details of my sex life with Marc and told her I had the social skills of a 12-year-old. I felt betrayed. (Flinn, 1997, pp. 57–58)

Case 27.8

In a case concerning competence to stand trial, the psychologist found the client to be mentally retarded. The psychologist informed the client that he "would be saying some things in court that might make the client feel bad or look bad in terms of his relatives and friends who would be in court. These are not meant to be personal." Also, the psychologist told the client the contours of the results and how intelligence can be measured in different ways and that the results do not say anything about whether the client is a good or bad person. A good rapport was established, so the client's hearing about his diminished intelligence had a framework that deflected harm, to the extent possible.

STANDARD 4: PRIVACY AND CONFIDENTIALITY

Forensic psychologists face a different set of challenges regarding privacy than do other psychologists (see Committee on Ethical Guidelines for Forensic Psychologists, 1991, V). Simply put, the forensic psychologist is *supposed to unearth sensitive findings and report on them.* The key questions are:

- What information is sought?
- To whom does one report?
- From whom does one keep the information?
- How is the information reported?

Case 27.9

The attorney asked the psychologist to examine a 32-year-old woman who was sexually assaulted by an appliance repairman. Discovery found the appliance company had complaints about the alleged offender when he worked in the central office. He was noxious enough in the central office (under supervision) that they sent him alone in a repair truck to people's homes! The task for the psychologist was to determine damages inflicted on the woman. The psychologist provided documentation of damages from the initial assault, and even more damage done by the harsh depositions conducted by corporate attorneys. The woman's attorney went to corporate headquarters to speak with the corporation's ethics officer. Presented with the evidence, the corporation settled. The psychologist was paid and never heard anything about the outcome. Without being told, the psychologist knew there was a nondisclosure agreement included in the settlement. Any use of the case with any identifying information could void the settlement and put the psychologist at enormous risk of actions by the client, her attorneys, and the corporation. Interestingly, the psychologist took his daughter, a graduate student, on the case with the attorney's permission. She, too, is bound by the privilege rights of the client as she was working as an agent of the principal (psychologist), just as secretaries, psychological assistants, and janitors who access sensitive and privileged information are civilly liable for revealing privileged information.

STANDARD 5: ADVERTISING AND OTHER PUBLIC STATEMENTS

Forensic psychologists find their clients among attorneys, so any effective advertising is aimed at media to which the attorneys attend. Most psychologists will find it to their advantage to present a workshop for attorneys offering continuing education unit credits. The local and state bars are usually welcoming of this offering by the psychologist. Naturally, claims should be modest and not guarantee any outcome.

Case 27.10

The psychologist presented a Web page of the International Listing of Forensic Psychologists. He was the only psychologist listed; apparently, the membership is fairly exclusive and meets at breakfast with him each morning. The Web page was exulting of the services he provided and listed cases on which he worked. Is this ethical? Did he lead viewers of his Web site to think he had unique specialties shared by virtually no other professional?

*   *   *

As long as he did not reveal any protected client information and the case listings are a matter of public record, he did not violate any ethical guidelines. He did make his listing seem unique, and the fact that no one else in the country is on his "International" listing seems cheesy and should make a discerning attorney queasy.

STANDARD 6: RECORD KEEPING AND FEES

APA's Record Keeping Guidelines should be consulted. Moreover, in forensic matters, the psychologist should be aware of the statute of limitations relevant for both the cases he or she works on and any appeals process extension of the limitations. Forensic cases pose additional questions regarding record keeping. Some clients have real enemies who might seek out information harmful to the client.

Case 27.11

Elaine came to see the psychologist because of the stresses of her husband's state-wide drug trafficking, in which she helped with the distribution. During the course of psychotherapy, she grew increasingly paranoid that she was being followed to and from the psychotherapist's office. Elaine cautioned the psychologist to alter his routes to his house in case he was being followed. She inquired about who had access to his (university-based) office and offered that the janitors with master keys could be bribed or intimidated. The psychotherapist assured her that her file was hidden. After one such session, the psychologist hid her file behind his textbooks. After the next session he moved them again. Upon the third moving of the files, he realized that Elaine's paranoic state might be contagious. During treatment, some significant materials surfaced regarding her being raped by an uncle and two cousins on a weekend camping trip. She was working through a number of emotional issues when she failed to show up for a session. The following week, she appeared dazed and reported that the week before, her husband and the local sheriff had her committed to an institution at which she underwent a lobotomy. Soon afterward, her husband informed the psychologist that they were moving out of state. Was she correct all the while about their being followed? About the records being a security risk? About both being in some jeopardy?

*   *   *

Fees pose another ethical issue (Committee on Ethical Guidelines for Forensic Psychologists, 1991, IV Relationships). Specifically, the psychologist should obtain a retainer and *never charge on a contingency basis*—that is, based on the outcome of the case. To do so makes the psychologist an interested party who cannot be expected to provide unbiased and objective testimony. To accept a contingency fee means being paid only if the psychologist's side prevails, making him or her an interested party. An ethical psychologist provides a service and charges for the service on a time-based (per hour) and service-based (deposition or trial testimony can have a different rate or fee attached) system of charges.

STANDARD 7: EDUCATION AND TRAINING

Education and training are important issues generally; in forensic arenas, they assume life-and-death proportions. Standard 7.01 holds psychologists responsible for designing appropriate experiences and providing appropriate knowledge to accomplish the goals of the program, which should be clearly stated according to Standard 7.02. These standards and 7.03 (Accuracy in teaching) and 7.06 (Assessing student and supervisee performance) address general concerns. However, the forensic psychologist may face more grave circumstances.

Case 27.12

A local university offered its clinical students to the district attorney's office to evaluate defendants. The students gained unpaid experience, and several faculty were paid consulting fees and were employed as expert witnesses. In a case in which a mother killed her 4-year-old daughter, tests administered by the student helped seal a first-degree murder conviction, according to media reports. However, the student subsequently testified in deposition that she was unsupervised, and it may have been the first such MMPI-2 she ever administered, scored, or interpreted. She said she was told by the professor to change the answers based on the fact that the test was administered in prison. The prosecutor's office, which saved thousands of dollars by using these interns, claimed they did not know until shortly before this incident that the students were sent alone to conduct evaluations on first-degree murder cases. As a result, eight first-degree murder cases are under review, with one attorney claiming that the psychological testing was crucial in her client's accepting a guilty plea instead of contesting the case. The prosecutor's office said it would not use students in first-degree murder cases in the future. (So life-or-death cases would not be affected? But how about the liberty interests of the defendants in second-degree murder cases, or when evaluating any crime that can lead to a three-strikes long-term incarceration, all in the interest of cheap justice and ill-advised "supervision" [author comment]!)

Subsequently, the professor said that it was all a misunderstanding and that the student was sandbagged—that her being surprised on deposition led to misleading statements, though there was no disputing the production of a second answer sheet. The student was awarded an A in the course.

*   *   *

This case cuts across several ethical principles. We offer the reader the exercise of measuring this case against the other principles.

STANDARD 8: RESEARCH AND PUBLICATION

There are a number of potential ethical snares that are awaiting the researcher who focuses on forensic psychology. These include the matter of whether informed consent can be given by incarcerated participants who may not be operating under free will within penal confines. The ethical researcher should be sure data do not compromise the participants by having them testify against themselves. Alternatively, if the researcher does gain incriminating information, can he or she keep the data from authorities, posing a risk of becoming an accessory? Does the researcher have the sophistication to operate in a prison, and even more, has he or she prepared the research assistants to operate within prison confines? This involves educating the assistants about contraband and prisoner games. Once research is completed, its dissemination can be problematic, as can be seen in the following case.

Case 27.13

A prominent forensic psychologist was presenting a paper on ethics and was the expert witness at the annual APA convention. He mentioned that one ought to practice to the highest standards of empiricism and decided to use as one example the testing battery developed by a prominent husband-and-wife team of child clinical psychologists. He assailed the instrument's lack of reliability and validity. After a few minutes, a man rose in the audience, introduced himself as the psychologist being vilified, and asked the presenter if he had read the following studies; he then listed studies in several prominent journals. The speaker began to quake and sweat and mumbled something inaudibly. The presentation was truncated.

* * *

One ought to speak as if the objects of one's speech were in the room. If a person cannot in good conscience say something in another's presence, should he or she be saying it at all? And should this principled forensic psychologist have impugned the other psychologists' work without being exhaustive in his search of the literature? Fairness demands no less.

Standard 9: Assessment

Perhaps more problems can arise in assessment than any other forensic activity. Examples abound in the cases already reviewed. Consider another emerging ethical problem in forensic psychology: Can a psychologist agree to coach a client? Most would agree that if approached by an attorney to help instruct an indigent client to establish eye contact with the judge, prosecutor, and jurors, rather than using avoidant behaviors such as slouching and looking down at his hands, the psychologist might be performing a noble service. If the avoidant behaviors would tend to send cues that the client is guilty, irrespective of the evidence, then the psychologist might well be serving justice. However, if the attorney, serving in his or her client's best interests, asks the psychologist to coach the client on how to appear symptomatic on neuropsychological instruments when facing a competency examination or a disability determination, most psychologists would deem this activity unethical.

What if the psychologist were asked to prepare a shaky client on what he or she faces during an examination? Would the reader's opinion vary if the preparation were conducted by the psychologist and the examination were conducted by another psychologist? Victor and Abeles (2004) describe how malingering measures are compromised by coaching. They determined that coaching has clear and significant effects on test results.

As mentioned in brief earlier, a few critics have taken the Rorschach to task. Perhaps as a product of misguided zeal, at least one Web site was produced that attempted to undermine the Rorschach by publishing a guide on how to defeat it. This included publishing facsimiles of the plates and sample responses for each, as well as suggesting behaviors to avoid during the testing.

In terms of ethics, contributing to the misrepresentation of test results is unethical. Consider the psychologist who helps a police candidate or ship's captain pass an employment test, and the police officer mistakenly and fatally shoots a citizen or the ship's captain causes a tragedy of the kind the test was intended to prevent. How can the psychologist avoid ethical, civil, and, possibly, criminal charges?

STANDARD 10: THERAPY

The principled psychologist must realize the inherent conflicts between zealously guarding a patient's privilege (*Jaffe v. Redmond*, 1996) and the goal of forensic work that typically requires one's findings to be forwarded to some judicial office, administrator, or court. This might confuse the client as well.

Case 27.14

The psychotherapist was assigned a prostitute drug addict in a federal institution for the treatment of the addicted. The federal program was a 6-month program. During her career she had been brutalized and was now wholly untrusting of men, seeing them as either johns or pimps. About halfway through her stay in the program, she casually mentioned returning to her home in Windsor, Canada. A few weeks later, she became furious with the psychologist. Her fury centered around his *not* reporting her to the administration. Shortly thereafter, the institution erupted with teams of lawyers from Washington descending on the institution to investigate. The central concern was how she, a Canadian citizen, was in a program expressly reserved for U.S. citizens. She had so few ego resources to explore the question of trust that she terminated psychotherapy because she could not trust a man who would not betray her.

Case 27.15

In the same facility as in Case 27.14, a client told the psychologist he had "50 cc's of liquid cocaine on the ward." The psychologist realized the conflicting issues between security and privilege concerns: Tell on the client and lose trust or keep the client's secret and appear to collude with the client?

*   *   *

Complicating this inherent conflict between keeping a secret and helping one's client versus revealing information for court or security concerns, a forensic psychologist with feelings and concern for the well-being of clients would be hard-pressed not to provide some help to a client in pain. It cannot be stressed enough that these issues must be clarified before a case is undertaken: To whom are what duties due and under what circumstances (Monahan, 1980)?

Even when the client has been informed about the limits to confidentiality or privilege during a forensic interview, empathy-stimulated responses to the psychologist may remain problematic. Suppose a psychologist interviews a defendant on behalf of the prosecutor and in doing so notices the defendant in dire need of psychological support. Instead of again warning the defendant that the information is to be used in court and the psychologist works for the prosecutor, the psychologist uses reflexive empathy rather than receptive empathy

(Shuman, 1993) in eliciting information. The psychologist would be operating legally, having informed the examinee, but may be using a professional advantage in an ethically dubious way to gain for the prosecutor the upper hand at the expense of the civil liberties of the defendant. If the defendant is psychologically dilapidated, he or she may have been unable to exercise his or her legal rights or good sense to terminate the interview. This clearly was the case in the Central Park rape case, in which a half-dozen youths were intimidated into confessions and spent years in prison before their confessions were found to be false. The investigators assumed poses as helpers who would hear their confessions to their emotional relief. Note bene: None of the interrogators was a psychologist. If a psychologist were involved, then he or she might be found unethical in breaching a duty to safeguard the client's rights.

BACK TO THE PRINCIPLES

As mentioned earlier, the APA principles are broad and overlapping. Nonetheless, there are a few more lessons to be learned by reviewing them here.

Integrity

The principles call for psychologists to be aware of their own belief systems, values, needs, and limitations and the effects of these on their work and to avoid improper and potentially harmful dual relationships. The guidelines anticipate *Daubert v. Merrell Dow Pharmaceuticals,* 1993 and *General Electric v. Joiner,* 1997 in obliging psychologists to show integrity in presenting the factual bases of their findings and the limits or confidence intervals of their data, or in the words of the court, the known or potential error rate of a technique. Knowing one's own values and how they impact a case may be ambiguous but no less serious than competence issues.

The area of child abuse prosecution shows how a truly devastating criminal charge has been politicized by the advocates of the "victim," who say that if a victim claims abuse, it occurred, versus those who say there may be a few child abuse incidents, but the bulk of them are fictional. Contaminating the true believers on each side are the gains that experts garner by virtue of their exalted status as experts, handsome fees, and even some political advantages. Certainly the miscarriages of justice experienced by the Amiraults in Massachusetts, the McMartin-Buckeys in California (cf. Eberle & Eberle, 1993), and the Little Rascals staff in North Carolina necessarily involved expert witnesses who carried a variety of agendas into the investigation. In *Secrets and Lies* (Morrison, 2004), interviews reveal the lasting damages to the children who were intimidated and tricked into testifying against their parents, portraying them as pedophiles and worse. Now adults, the children of the accused and convicted parents had frozen affect and feared their own children's touch, sometimes smacking away a 4-year-old child climbing on her dad's lap.

Perhaps as unsettling as those cases is the case of Margaret Kelly Michaels. She was sentenced to 47 years at age 26 for a crime that involved neither murder nor drugs. Rabinowitz (1990, also see 2003) details her prosecution in a little-known case that involved such ethically questionable procedures as misuse of psychological principles. While some have claimed that a professional is never without his or her values and consequently prejudices, it is qualitatively different to accept a case with some opinion on the issues as opposed to seeking out the role of an expert witness as a way to promote a sociopolitical agenda.

One psychologist has never testified on behalf of the state, often helping those he sees as the underclass to bring forth legal cases for which he serves as the expert witness. His fees often are paid by the court or civil liberties agencies. Clark (1990), Golding (1990), and Hess (1998) identify flashpoints that every expert should attend to before proceeding with a case. These include whether one is using the expert role as a moral advocate or providing objective expertise; whether one is qualified by knowledge, skills, education, experience, or training to provide information helping the fact finders; whether one's involvement is probative (truly informative) or prejudicial; and the degree to which the adversary nature of the legal system will distort one's proffered evidence.

Diamond (1959) argued that there are no professionals who are without values and opinions. Indeed, that is a truism. However, the question is not whether a professional has values but when those become so important to the professional that they become an interest, compromising the objective and putatively neutral position that the expert witness is supposed to bring to the courtroom. Suppose a psychologist involved in child custody cases has lost custody of his own child and subsequently adopts a mission that no other man should lose custody of a child. In each case, the psychologist truly comes to believe that the father should be awarded child custody and the professional's examinations always find for the father. The conflict of interest becomes palpable and damaging to individuals, families, and the legal process. The psychologist does have the right to believe all fathers should be awarded custody, but the correct platform for expressing these views may be as an amicus curiae or testifying to legislative bodies or forming sociopolitical action groups; it is not the platform of the expert witness.

Perhaps the most recent and extreme position that attacks the legal structures directly is that of the legal criticism and deconstructionist views. They would hold that the very structure of our justice system is a product of our society's values that are fundamentally biased and destructive to those not in power. Consequently it would be fitting and proper to use the expert witness role to express ideological positions. For example, in the Woodward au pair trial, one set of experts termed themselves "child abuse experts" and their unit the Child Protection Team at Boston's Children's Hospital. In other cases, members of the False Memory Syndrome Foundation testified. By so identifying themselves, both sides impeach the position of impartiality central to the role of the expert witness.

The deconstructionist position claims that because all people are value driven and the legal process itself is conservative of the prevalent values, using the system to depict the flaws in the system and to level the playing field for the powerless is not merely justified but an affirmative duty. The speciousness of this argument is easily seen if one realizes that it claims the ends justify the means, a teleological argument. Principle-driven or deontological philosophies would hold that telling the truth as we are able is the higher duty. That is what our APA principles hold.

Again, deconstructionists may hold that those are the duties imposed by the dominant culture. However, the deconstructionists may be undone by their not being able to pose alternatives. Everyone has ends they prefer. Some of these ends violate others. How would one propose to develop a value system other than rampant hedonism or the mighty rule? Hedonism is one major system that our legal system tries to curb while also allowing each individual the pursuit of happiness within a system that preserves others' rights to happiness. The expert witness agrees to bring a scientific, or at least discipline-informed, view to evidence beyond the knowledge of the fact finder, that is, the judge or jury. To do otherwise is to invite ethics charges and malpractice claims.

Wettstein, Mulvey, and Rogers (1991) provide another intriguing example of a professional's values affecting judicial proceedings. They investigated the effects of using four standards for the insanity defense and found that even if the law changes standards, the "evaluator's political ideology, professional, personal views about the insanity defense or concern about the outcome of such judgments" are reflected in clinical judgments of criminal responsibility (p. 26). In this case, politically based changes in insanity defense criteria fomented by public demand may be defeated by the inertial effect of customary practice.

The integrity principle enjoins the psychologist to examine third-party relationships. These have been long recognized as important in forensic psychology. Attorneys have a different perspective than do psychologists on what constitutes a conflictual relationship. First, when an attorney hires an expert, the psychologist must be certain that the attorney does not see himself or herself acting as an agent for the attorney's client. That is, as an agent, the attorney can retain help in serving the client, but the client is the principal and as such is the client of the psychologist. The psychologist is advised to be sure that the attorney is the one hiring the psychologist as a principal and not as an agent. Thus, the psychologist will avoid the bind of not being able to communicate with the attorney without the express consent of the client. Most practitioners have assumed that the attorney is the client, and attorneys have operated that way. However, in one case, an attorney retained an expert, then maintained that the $18,000 fee was not his responsibility but that of his principal. The court held otherwise, although note that this ruling so far may be limited to Ohio.

Second, attorneys often see the fact that a psychologist who served as a psychotherapist may be the best person to call on as an expert witness, a conflict of roles that many psychiatrists did not recognize (Weinstock, 1986, 1989). In fact, the ABA Criminal Justice Mental Health Standards (1989, p. 132) hold that a criterion for qualification as an expert in testifying about mental conditions is "a professional therapeutic or habilitative relationship with the person whose mental condition is in question." This is in contradiction with the dual-role relationship dilemma.

Case 27.16

The conflict between providing testimony in a bitter divorce and custody battle versus providing marital therapy was anticipated by a psychologist. He was called by an attorney to counsel the attorney and his wife, whose marriage was on the verge of violence and dissolution. For the sake of their young son, both wanted to see whether there was anything salvageable. The psychologist agreed to see them on condition that whatever was revealed in the course of marital psychotherapy was not accessible for use in subsequent legal proceedings. The reasoning, explained to both parties, is that any other posture would mean either or both might be inclined to look favorable in the psychologist's eyes and to make the other look unfavorable, defeating any psychotherapeutic possibilities. Both said they understood and agreed to the condition.

The ill-fated marriage was not refractory to the treatment. Two months later, the attorney told the psychologist that the psychologist would be subpoenaed as a witness regarding the wife's instability. The psychologist reminded him of the agreement. The attorney said it did not matter. The psychologist intimated that he would speak to the attorney's attorney first to see whether he really wanted the psychologist's testimony because the violation of the condition would be the second of the psychologist's utterances; the first would be an appeal to the judge that the other spouse did not waive privilege. And if she did, then both would not like the testimony forthcoming from the psychologist. The attorney's attorney felt the best course was not to call the psychologist.

*   *   *

Attorneys can understand that the separation of therapeutic role from the expert witness role is essential for the former to work. In fact, *Jaffe v. Redmond* (1996) affirms the necessity of privilege as essential for psychotherapy. Whereas an attorney might call the psychotherapist as a fact witness, perils loom when the attorney presses for expert witness testimony from the psychotherapist. Stasburger, Gutheil, and Brodsky (1997) show the irreconcilability of the two roles and the conflicts waiting for the psychologist broaching the dual-role relationship. Nonetheless, when the roles are joined, special care needs to be exercised.

The psychotherapist role may be confounded with other, nonexpert witness roles. Consider the prison psychologist who conducts sex offender group psychotherapy. The explicit task set forth by the Department of Corrections was to run such groups so they could release successfully treated offenders. Among the ethical dilemmas are violating the offender's privacy by reporting the offender's progress with regard to parole consideration and learning of offenses previously unknown to the authorities. In this case, the psychologist affirmed at the outset that the offenders knew that their general progress and risk of reoffending, but not any specific information, would be reported. Moreover, the psychologist confirmed with the authorities that information gleaned in psychotherapy would not be forwarded nor be useful for prosecution because of the privilege that would remain but for the general progress report. This was carefully explained to the group psychotherapy members, including the advice that should anyone bring up information in the group, including about other group members, it would be shielded. However, should they choose to discuss material outside of group sessions, the shield might no longer hold for them. The psychologist who elicits information in group psychotherapy cannot possibly guarantee confidentiality outside the group or shield the inmate patients from real-world repercussions outside the sanctuary of psychotherapy but behind the prison walls.

Principle C, Justice, enjoines psychologists to ". . . ensure that their potential biases, the boundaries of their competence, and the limitations of their expertise do not lead to or condone unjust practices."

The Justice Principle asserts that "psychologists strive to be aware of their own belief systems, values, needs, and limitations and the effects of these on their work" (APA, 2002, p. 1599). Golding (1990) describes one critique of the expert witness who serves as a moral advocate with a hidden moral agenda rather than a professional, objective expert. Brown (1997) raises the point that because "objectivity" may be simply the subjectivity of the dominant group and that at least by declaiming the "collective professional mythology of pure empiricism and objectivity in which social constructions of reality are denied or minimized" (p. 450) and by declaring what her values are, Brown can foster Tikkun Olam (a world healed, perfected or made whole).

The problems of the expert-as-advocate can be seen by an illustration and by the direct contrast between the advocate and expert roles in the ethical code. Szasz is a distinguished psychiatrist who advocates that mental illness is a myth. One would be hard pressed to call on him as a witness who could assert a defendant as sane, as his well-published position holds the insanity of the insanity defense (Szasz, 1981–1982). Again, all the rules of the game, from the Federal Rules of Evidence to the APA Code of Ethics, call for an objective rendering of professional determinations. Perhaps as amicus curiae, consultant, or plaintiff the psychologist may espouse partisan positions, but as an expert witness a higher standard for suspension of furthering one's own values is crucial in accepting a case. It does make a difference whether a psychologist determining workmen's compensation has a view that we all work with some degree of pain or holds a more sympathetic view that the worker paid for what amounts to insurance and is entitled to relief from work-induced stress (Colbach, 1997). Attorneys are prone to calling on experts who are likely to share the attorney's view of the facts.

Colbach (1997) suggests that constant scrutiny by oneself, by someone like a psychotherapy supervisor, by a data bank recording the type of cases a person takes and turns down is needed. "If objectivity is so elusive in our current adversary system, and if changes aren't forthcoming, we would all be better off doing what I have done and giving up on court appearances" (p. 166). Given that mental health services are being (de)capitated by third-party payers and that the courtroom is providing a livelihood for a growing number of mental health professionals, this question of impartiality demands greater attention. Schlesinger (2003) provides us with his self-scrutiny and the wise observation that when the other expert's findings contradict his own, he tries to understand the other's viewpoint, as well as his own biases. He then describes two other forms of bias: the blatant hired gun and the more subtly influenced practitioner who finds symptoms obliquely suggested by the attorney, a phenomenon Schlesinger calls "malingering by proxy."

PROFESSIONAL AND SCIENTIFIC RESPONSIBILITY

The psychologist serves the best interests of the client(s) while upholding professional standards. Among a plethora of responsibilities, one particular aspect of forensic practice is the fact that experts are called on to provide service across state lines. The popular expert faces the dilemma of practicing in a state where he or she is not licensed.

Interstate Practice

When attorneys seek help, they might find the most fitting expert in a state other than where the case will be tried. Such circuit riding or practicing out of state and possibly without a license in the case's venue can pose problems. Several authors (Drogin, 1999; Reid, 2000; Shuman, Cunningham, Connell, & Reid, 2003; Simon & Shuman, 1999; Tucillo, DeFilippis, Denney, & Dsurney, 2002) address various aspects of this question concerning portability of forensic services. Essentially, this is another aspect of the distinction between clinical and forensic service delivery. A forensic case might involve a brief appearance in the other state. The type of service can vary from providing statistical consultation on an employment discrimination case in which most of the work is done over the telephone and in the expert's office but for the actual delivery of testimony. Thus, the practitioner may construe the work as not psychological service delivery. In other cases, some extended testing over days and weeks might be involved, looking almost indistinguishable from clinical service delivery. In those cases, some practitioners have worked in states without a local license, relying on the court's need for them as exempting them from local licensing. Attorneys working on a case where they are not licensed use pro hoc vice to ally with a local attorney, who vouches to the court to allow the visiting attorney to practice on that case.

Concerned about interstate forensic practice and licensure, Drogin (1999) and Tucillo et al. (2002) surveyed all 50 states, 9 Canadian provinces, and the U.S. territories. They found little uniformity of regulations with regard to time allowed in state, renewal opportunities, application process rigor, standards for exemption, and sponsorship requirements. There was ambiguity concerning the duties of sponsors and generally unavailability of clear guidelines. Finally, some 30% of the states furnished no provisions whatever, resulting in what Shuman et al. (2003) termed "functional prohibition." They propose a uniform model rule for state boards to consider. The principled forensic psychologist should be aware of this issue and make suitable provisions.

Case 27.17

The psychologist was called to testify in federal court in a neighboring state. He contacted the licensing board, making provision for a 10-day practice in that state through a reciprocal license from the Board (no mention by him or the

Board as to whether this was 10 consecutive days or 10 days over the course of the year). As it turned out, the case was settled and his testimony was not needed.

Social Responsibility

Forensic psychologists must prevent misuse of their work. This can take a number of forms. Desperate people seek desperate solutions.

Case 27.18

A psychologist was called by two attorneys from a firm he had helped on an earlier case. One attorney wanted help with defending a student who was found cheating from another student's work. The attorney was working on the theory that the cheater scanned his environment in search of answers due to an innate tendency that caused his eyes to wander. He appealed to the psychologist's vanity in offering to help develop a "wandering eyes syndrome" by which both could achieve some degree of fame (or notoriety).

Case 27.19

The second attorney wanted to know whether the innate threat sensitivity of his client may have justifiably caused him to beat his brother-in-law to death before his brother-in-law beat him to death, in the absence of any evidence that the victim aggressed in a potentially lethal manner to the client.

*   *   *

The psychologist correctly declined participating in either case, costing him several fees but preserving his reputation for cases in which expertise would be responsibly used. Testifying in these contrived defenses would have the psychologist act as a hired gun and harm the profession's reputation. Perhaps the cheater should face the disciplinary committee and the brother-in-law ought to face a jury. Unlike attorneys, psychologists are not obliged as individuals or as a profession to provide defenses or services when it is inadvisable to do so. Even as individuals, attorneys often turn down cases for sundry reasons. So, too, can psychologists.

RECOMMENDATIONS

In distilling some of the materials reviewed here, one can practice principled forensic psychology by attending to the following recommendations:

- Practicing principled psychology involves knowing the ethics codes generally and those principles and standards most applicable to the practice in which the forensic psychologist is engaged.
- The principled psychologist offers services in which he or she has achieved a level of proficiency by virtue of a combination of knowledge, skills, education, training, and experience. Thus, when the psychologist

presents a subtest score difference on psychological tests but does not keep up with testing principles such as the standard error of the differences on the measures used, the psychologist may be malpracticing.

- Just as the psychologist practicing in the medical setting or dental school must know clinical phenomena, the language and concepts, and the professional practices of the setting, the forensic psychologist must be conversant with the concepts, practices, and standards in the correctional and legal arenas. Thus, the psychologist practicing in a setting with patients who may be harmful is knowledgeable about the threshold that triggers the need to warn, the literature concerning the validity of such predictions, and the applicable statutes and reporting authorities concerning required reporting.

- Such knowledge allows the psychologist to anticipate events that would otherwise lead to ethical and legal difficulties. The client or patient has a right to know the limits to confidentiality and to privilege before revealing information in a setting the client may have thought to be inviolate. The forensic psychologist gets in trouble when he or she is not aware of issues and when he or she operates out of a motivation that does not fit the situation. Thus, the principled forensic psychologist has enough training, education, experience, and supervision to anticipate ethical conundrums and to take appropriate steps to inform forensic clients about the limitations to privacy that may differ from the expectations held by clinical clients.

- The principled psychologist is mindful of the corrections dictum that if an event is not documented, it did not occur. Compiling and keeping good records in a secure location is essential.

- Failing to understand and evaluate the various roles the forensic client may expect can lead the psychologist to practice irresponsibly.

- The principled psychologist seeks to understand the positions and motivations of the other parties involved, with a specific sensitivity to conflicts of interest and other circumstances that can compromise the psychologist's principled practice.

- When accepting a case and finding himself or herself in uncharted territory, or when confronted by a dilemma, the principled psychologist seeks the counsel, and possibly the supervision, of esteemed and trusted colleagues. If the psychologist is fair to the colleague and the case, he or she will reveal enough of the facts that the colleague needs to know to help guide the psychologist but will not reveal enough facts sufficient to identify the client or case. To do so would transfer the ethical responsibility posed by the dilemma to the consultant, removing it from the psychologist who sought the consultation.

- The wise psychologist confronting forensic questions develops relationships with a few trusted attorneys so that questions with legal implications may be resolved.

- The principled forensic psychologist ought to participate in helping our profession in several areas:

- Our professional associations need to compile casebooks to guide the practitioner to a better understanding of how the ethical principles are applied in particular instances.
- Our associations need to monitor the relevance and completeness of the ethics codes and update them in this rapidly developing specialty. Just as there has been an initiative to construct a functional forensic psychology database by collecting cases of like issues (Fishman, 1999, 2004), we suggest this database or one like it be compiled of ethics cases to help provide ongoing guidance—just as case law informs judges and attorneys.
- Our associations need to develop guidelines for the forensic psychologist's relationships with the public and the media by way of the practitioner's public statements. This ought to concern both how forensic services are offered and how public relations are handled during a case. The thrust of these efforts ought to be educational rather than fault seeking.

One can try to avoid unethical practices, in one's private life and in professional endeavors, and manage to avoid evil. However, life is not that simple. We are active agents in the world, a world that poses contradictory values in situations. In forensic psychology, we should not merely try to avoid evil but to see our practice as a way to achieve a level of excellence unparalleled by other areas of psychology. The path to principled, ethical action proposed here is that we weigh our actions on an aspirational scale, rather than a defensive one. If the forensic psychologist acts from a basis of wisdom with humility and awe regarding the responsibilities and opportunities to do good rather than doing well, he or she is on the road to principled practice. If the psychologist realizes that he or she will not attain wealth through forensic work and, instead, that a love of truth serves as a nobler motivational base, the forensic psychologist will find the path to ethical practice easier to follow. Finally, forensic psychologists who practice aspirationally will find that they will bring enduring respect to themselves and to our profession. We have a place in the courts, helping to bring justice to those who seek it.

Perhaps it is fitting to recall the words addressed to physicians in years past:

> You are in this profession as a calling, not a business. Once you get down to a purely business level, your influence is gone and the light of your life is dimmed. You must work in this missionary spirit, with breadth of charity that raises you far above the petty jealousies of life. (Attributed to Sir William Osler)

REFERENCES

American Bar Association. (1989). *ABA criminal justice mental health standards*. Washington, DC: Author.

American Bar Association. (2002). *Model rules of professional conduct*, with changes through February 2002, at http://www.abanet.org/cpr/mrpc/mrcp.toc.html.

American Educational Research Association. (1999). *Standards for educational and psychological tests*. Washington, DC: American Psychological Association.

American Psychological Association. (2002). Ethical principles of psychologists and code of conduct. *American Psychologist, 57*, 1060–1073.

Barefoot v. Estelle, 463 U.S. 880 (1983).

Bennett, B. E., Bryant, B. K., VandenBos, G. R., & Greenwood, A. (1990). *Professional liability and risk management.* Washington, DC: American Psychological Association.

Brown, L. S. (1997). The private practice of subversion: Psychology as Tikkun Olam. *American Psychologist, 52,* 449–462.

Clark, C., R. (1990). Agreeing to be an expert witness: Considerations of competence and role integrity. *Register Report, 16,* 4–6.

Colbach, E. M. (1997). The trouble with American forensic psychiatry. *International Journal of Offender Therapy and Comparative Criminology, 41,* 160–167.

Committee on Ethical Guidelines for Forensic Psychologists. (1991). Specialty guidelines for forensic psychologists. *Law and Human Behavior, 15,* 655–665.

Daubert v. Merrell Dow Pharmaceuticals, Inc., 509 U.S. 579 (1993).

Diamond, B. L. (1959). The fallacy of the impartial expert. *Archives of Criminal Psychodynamics, 3,* 221–227.

Drogin, E. Y. (1999). Prophets in another land: Utilizing psychological expertise from foreign jurisdictions. *Mental and Psychological Disabilities Law Reporter, 23,* 767–770.

Eberle, P., & Eberle, S. (1993). *The abuse of innocence: The McMartin Preschool trial.* Buffalo, NY: Prometheus Books.

Edge, R. S., & Groves, J. R. (1994). *The ethics of health care: A guide for clinical practice.* Albany, NY: Delmar.

Fisher, C. B. (2003). *Decoding the ethics code: A practical guide for psychologists.* Thousand Oaks, CA: Sage.

Fishman, D. B. (1999). *The case for pragmatic psychology.* New York: New York University Press.

Fishman, D. B. (2004). Integrative themes: Prospects for developing a "psychological lexis." *Psychology, Public Policy, and Law, 10*(1/2), 178–200.

Flinn, K. (1997, November 24). Excerpted from "Proud to Be" *Newsweek,* pp. 57–58.

Frankel, M. S. (1989). Professional codes: Why, how, and with what impact? *Journal of Business Ethics, 8,* 109–115.

General Electric v. Joiner, 118 U.S. Ct. 512 (1997).

Glassman, J. (1998). Preventing and managing board complaints: The downside risk of custody evaluation. *Professional Psychology, 29,* 121–124.

Golding, S. L. (1990). Mental health professionals and the courts: The ethics of expertise. *International Journal of Law and Psychiatry, 13,* 281–307.

Greenberg, S. A., & Shuman, D. W. (1997). Irreconcilable conflict between therapeutic and forensic roles. *Professional Psychology, 28,* 50–57.

Hagen, M. A. (1997). *Whores of the court: The fraud of psychiatric testimony and the rape of American justice.* New York: HarperCollins.

Hess, A. K. (1998). Accepting forensic case referrals: Ethical and professional considerations. *Professional Psychology, 29,* 109–114.

Huber, P. W. (1993). *Galileo's revenge: Junk science in the courtroom.* New York: Basic Books.

Jaffe v. Redmond, 116 S. Ct. 1923, 135 L.Ed. 2nd 337 (1996).

Jurek v. Texas, 428 U.S. 262 (1976).

Kirkland, K., & Kirkland, K. L. (2001). Frequency of child custody evaluation complaints and related disciplinary action: A survey of the association of state and provincial psychology boards. *Professional Psychology, 32,* 171–174.

Knapp, S., & VandeCreek, L. (2003). An overview of the major changes in the 2002 APA Ethics Code. *Professional Psychology, 34,* 301–308.

Koocher, G. P., & Keith-Spiegel, P. (1998). *Ethics in psychology: Professional standards and cases.* New York: Oxford University Press.

Meyer, G. J., & Archer, R. P. (2001). The hard science of Rorschach research: What do we know and where do we go? *Psychological Assessment, 13,* 486–502.

Monahan, J. (Ed.). (1980). *Who is the client?* Washington, DC: American Psychological Association.

Morrison, J. (Producer). (2004). *Secrets and Lies* [Cover-to-Cover Series]. New York: CNBC.

Pavalko, R. M. (1979). *Sociology of occupations and professions.* Itasca, IL: Peacock.

Pepper, S. C. (1942). *World hypotheses: A study in evidence.* Berkeley: University of California Press.

Peterson, M. B. (2001). Recognizing concerns about how some licensing boards are treating psychologists. *Professional Psychology, 32,* 339–340.

Rabinowitz, D. (1990, May). From the mouths of babes to a jail cell. *Harper's, 280*(1680), 52–63.

Rabinowitz, D. (2003). *No crueler tyrannies: Accusation, false witness, and other terrors of our times.* New York: Free Press.

Reid, W. H. (2000). Licensing requirements for out-of-state forensic examinations. *Journal of the American Academy of Psychiatry and Law, 28,* 433–437.

Rotgers, F., & Barrett, D. (1996). Daubert v. Merrell Dow and expert testimony by clinical psychologists: Implications and recommendations for practice. *Professional Psychology, 27,* 467–474.

Schlesinger, L. B. (2003). A case study involving competency to stand trial: Incompetent defendant, incompetent examiner, or "malingering by proxy"? *Psychology, Public Policy, and Law, 9,* 399–481.

Schoenfeld, L. S., Hatch, J. P., & Gonzalez, J. M. (2001). Responses of psychologists to complaints filed against them with a state licensing board. *Professional Psychology, 32,* 491–495.

Schretlen, D., Wilkins, S. S., Van Gorp, W. G., & Bobholz, J. H. (1992). Cross-validation of a psychological test battery to detect faked insanity. *Psychological Assessment, 4,* 77–83.

Shuman, D. W. (1993). The use of empathy in forensic examinations. *Ethics and Behavior, 3,* 289–302.

Shuman, D. W., Cunningham, M. D., Connell, M. A., & Reid, W. H. (2003). Interstate forensic psychology consultation: A call for reform and proposal of a model rule. *Professional Psychology, 34,* 233–239.

Shuman, D. W., & Greenberg, S. (1998). The role of ethical norms in the admissibility of expert testimony. *The Judges' Journal: A Quarterly of the Judicial Division, 37,* 4–43.

Simon, R. I., & Schuman, D. W. (1999). Conducting forensic evaluation on the road: Are you practicing your profession without a license? *Journal of the American Academy of Psychiatry and Law, 27,* 75–82.

Stasburger, L. H., Gutheil, T. G., & Brodsky, S. L. (1997). On wearing two hats: Role conflict in serving as both psychotherapist and expert witness. *American Journal of Psychiatry, 154,* 448–456.

Super, J. T. (1997). Select legal and ethical aspects of fitness for duty evaluations. *Journal of Criminal Justice, 25,* 223–229.

Szasz, T. (1981–1982). The political use of psychiatry: The case of Dan White. *American Journal of Forensic Psychiatry, 2,* 22–26.

Tucillo, J. A., DeFilippis, N. A., Denney, R. L., & Dsurney, J. (2002). Licensure requirements for interjurisdictional forensic evaluations. *Professional Psychology, 33,* 377–383.

Victor, T. L., & Abeles, N. (2004). Coaching clients to take psychological and neuropsychological tests: A clash of ethical obligations. *Professional Psychology, 35,* 373–379.

Weinberger, L. E., & Sreenivasan, S. (1994). Ethical and professional conflicts in correctional psychology. *Professional Psychology, 25,* 161–167.

Weinstock, R. (1986). Ethical concerns expressed by forensic psychiatrists. *Journal of Forensic Sciences, 31,* 596–602.

Weinstock, R. (1989). Perceptions of ethical problems by forensic psychiatrists. *Bulletin of the American Academy of Psychiatry and Law, 17,* 189–202.

Weissman, H. N., & DeBow, D. (2004). Ethical principles and professional competencies. In I. B. Weiner (Series Ed.) & A. Goldstein (Vol. Ed.), *Handbook of psychology: Vol. 12. Forensic psychology* (pp. 33–53). Hoboken, NJ: Wiley.

West Publishing Company. (1984). *Selected statues, rules and standards on the legal profession.* St. Paul, MN: Author.

Wettstein, R. M., Mulvey, E. P., & Rogers, R. (1991). A prospective comparison of four insanity defense standards. *American Journal of Psychiatry, 148,* 21–27.

Williams, M. H. (2001). The question of psychologists' maltreatment by state licensing boards: Overcoming denial and seeking remedies. *Professional Psychology, 32,* 341–344.

CHAPTER 28

Training in Forensic Psychology: Training for What Goal?

DANIEL A. KRAUSS and BRUCE D. SALES

ALTHOUGH THE beginnings of forensic psychology have their roots in the early twentieth-century works of Hugo Münsterberg and Sigmund Freud (see Bartol & Bartol, Chapter 1, in this volume), it was not until 1973 that the first specific training program in forensic psychology was founded at the University of Nebraska. Since that time, the membership in Division 41, the American Psychology-Law Society (AP-LS) of the American Psychological Association (APA), the division of APA most associated with forensic practice, has increased dramatically (Bersoff, Goodman-Delahunty, Grisso, Hans, Poythress, et al., 1997), nearly doubling in size in the past seven years. In addition, the division has sponsored a national conference on training in psychology and law, including forensic psychology in 1995.

Currently, there are over 30 programs listed on the Division 41 Web site offering some form of graduate training in forensic psychology (AP-LS, 2005). These programs can be classified into subgroups based on the particular type of training they offer. Five programs offer the dual JD-PhD (Juris Doctorate-Doctor of Philosophy or -Doctor of Psychology) degrees (i.e., Drexel University, Pacific Graduate School of Psychology, University of Arizona, University of Nebraska, and Widener University). Of these five, the University of Arizona's and the University of Nebraska's are the only programs that offer the option of either clinical or nonclinical training in their psychology component. These five programs also offer the opportunity for students to pursue the PhD without also pursuing a JD. These five plus 10 additional programs offer a programmatic emphasis in clinical forensic psychology or in clinical psychology with a subspecialty in forensic psychology (Alliant International University, Carlos Albizo University in Miami, Fordham University, John Jay College of Criminal Justice–City University of New York [CUNY], Nova Southeastern University, Sam Houston State University, Simon Fraser University, University of Alabama, University of Florida, West Virginia University).

Fourteen programs allow students to focus on the application of nonclinical psychology areas (e.g., cognitive, social) to forensic issues (Alliant International University, Florida International University, Georgetown University, John Jay College of Criminal Justice-CUNY, Pacific Graduate School of Psychology, Simon Fraser University, University of Arizona, University of Florida, University of Illinois at Chicago, University of Minnesota, University of Nebraska, University of Nevada-Reno, University of Texas at El Paso, University of Wyoming). Finally, forensic training is also offered by some schools at the subdoctoral level. Eight programs offer a master's degree in forensic psychology (Castleton College, Chicago School of Professional Psychology, John Jay College of Criminal Justice-CUNY, Marymount University, Sage Colleges, Tiffin University, University of Denver, University of Nebraska).

To understand the reason for the existing differences in training approaches, it is first necessary to understand the differing skills of forensic scientists and practitioners. It is the breadth of professional duties and the scientific questions associated with forensic practice that necessitate varied types of training approaches. For example, one of the most celebrated uses of expert testimony is for a psychologist to testify about the reliability of the eyewitness testimony against a defendant. The expert witness might testify as to the effect of several factors on perception, including stress and weapon focus. The expert might also offer testimony on the effect of certain factors on accurate identification, such as the forgetting curve and suggestive pretrial identification procedures (see, e.g., *United States v. Norwood*, 1996). Although this type of testimony is well known and may be presented by a forensic clinical psychologist (Contreras, 2001), it is more likely to be the province of someone trained in cognitive or social psychology who studies basic perception, memory, and/or identification accuracy issues.

In contrast, clinical psychologists are more likely to be involved in testifying concerning an assessment they performed on a litigant or other relevant party to a lawsuit (e.g., Melton, Petrila, Poythress, & Slobogin, 1997) or a treatment they performed for a litigant or offender (e.g., Ashford, Sales, & Reid, 2001). For example, they may testify as to the results of their forensic assessment on a variety of topics, such as what is in the best interests of the child for post-divorce custodial placement (e.g., Benjamin & Gollan, 2003); is termination of parental rights in the best interest of the child (e.g., *In re* L. A. M., 2001); did the defendant suffer from a learning disability in a lawsuit alleging that the disability was caused by chemical exposure (e.g., *Mancuso v. Consolidated Edison Co.*, 2000)? In other cases, both clinical and nonclinical forensic psychologists educate the jury about the state of knowledge on some topic (e.g., Rape Trauma Syndrome; causes of eyewitness identification errors) rather than directly focusing on a specific factual question in dispute (e.g., *People v. Wheeler*, 1992).

Although expert testimony is an important part of forensic work, it is by no means exhaustive of forensic practice opportunities. For example, some forensic psychologists work in the administration of forensic correctional facilities (see, e.g., Hafemeister, Hall, & Dvoskin, 2001), in providing treatment services in detention facilities for juveniles or adult offenders, or in policy analysis for a state or the federal government. Finally, whereas these activities are practice related, many psychologists are more interested in producing the research and scholarship that provide the foundation for forensic practice.

What type of education and training is best suited for this diverse set of activities? There is no simple answer. The ideal training options should be varied based on both the trainee's career goals and the educational administrative limits of the existing programs. This chapter considers both the more mundane and more nuanced aspects of training goals, approaches, and issues. The reader is cautioned that although we provide examples of programs offering a specific approach to training, these are examples only and should not be considered an exhaustive list of all programs offering each type of approach. Those interested in learning more about the opportunities offered by each training program should consult the relevant Web sites and contact the program directors. Forensic specialty training programs are listed at www.ap-ls.org/students/graduateIndex.html. Forensic internship programs are listed at www.ap-ls.org/AP-LSAAFPInternshipDir.pdf.

TRAINING GOALS

Training never occurs in a vacuum. We train and pursue educational opportunities to achieve specific career goals. The student interested in working with elderly patients logically seeks training relevant to gerontological issues, and programs interested in attracting students who wish to work with persons with dementia of the Alzheimer's type will create didactic, experiential, and research training opportunities specific to these students' needs. It is no different for students interested in being qualified to work in legal and law-related settings. In this section, we describe the most common training goals in forensic psychology.

CLINICAL SCIENTIST-PRACTITIONER

One of the more common clinical training goals for general clinical psychology programs is the development of scientist-practitioners based on the Boulder model. Under this paradigm, an individual is trained first and foremost as a scientist versed in the critical thinking skills, hypothesis testing, research methodologies, and techniques that are specific to the science of psychology. In addition, these individuals are instructed, trained, and mentored to apply the existing and most current psychological research findings to their work in assessing and treating the clients they see in their clinical practice. Successful completion of this training is recognized by attainment of a doctor of philosophy degree (PhD) in psychology.

The eventual goals for clinical psychologists trained as scientist-practitioners in forensic psychology are for them to be competent to (1) perform their own well-designed research on forensic topics of particular interest; (2) effectively identify, keep abreast of, and evaluate the scientific research and professional literatures specific to various areas of forensic practice; (3) implement the most scientifically appropriate assessment or treatment techniques for a particular case while at the same time be aware of the limitations of the chosen techniques; and (4) recognize when no scientifically valid technique exists for a particular issue or question and use the most promising clinical technique available while being aware of its limitations.

Clinical Practitioner-Scientist

Some PhD and most PsyD programs de-emphasize the scientific research component of their clinical training, replacing it with more practice-focused didactic and experiential training. This description characterizes forensic training opportunities at a number of programs in this country (e.g., Nova Southeastern University, Widener University). These forensic programs are designed primarily to train students to become clinical practitioners and consultants to the courts, and fewer graduates of these programs will likely seek employment in research and/or academic settings. As such, trainees from these programs will often (1) graduate with more hands-on clinical training experiences; (2) have had more classes devoted specifically to clinical practice issues; and (3) have had more opportunities to practice their clinical skills on real-world populations. These students, however, will have spent less time conducting their own empirical research and will have fewer courses directly addressing the design, methodology, analysis, and evaluation of forensic psychology research.

Arguably, individuals receiving this type of training are better prepared to provide clinical services than students who have received less education and training focused on practice issues. Yet, the argument is refutable if the discipline of psychology is to be built on knowledge of the science of human behavior. To respond to this concern, faculty who focus on training practitioners endeavor to teach their students how to be effective consumers of scientific research. To date, little research exists examining how the more practice-oriented training inherent in these programs affects actual practice competence, and no such research exists in the forensic area. As a result, controversy still exists regarding the benefits and limits of professionally focused training, with advocates on both sides suggesting the superiority of their model for training clinical practitioners (Peterson, 2003).

Nonclinical and Clinical Scientist-Scholar

Obviously, not all psychologists are clinically trained and licensure-eligible for clinical practice. Training programs in cognitive, developmental, and social psychology, to name just a few of the subfields of psychology, are also widely available. Through a series of didactic and intensive research experiences, these programs train PhDs to undertake research in academic settings, research laboratories, and industry settings.

It is no different in forensic psychology. Although most forensic psychologists are interested in the assessment and treatment of forensic-clinical populations, there are many nonclinical forensic psychologists who have been trained to pursue a career as a scientist-scholar, constantly trying to expand the boundaries of our forensic knowledge. Given the importance of the scientific foundation for understanding human behavior in legal settings (e.g., jury decision making) and for improving the structure and administration of law (Sales, 1983), this type of forensic training is prominent at many universities.

Similarly, there are clinically trained forensic psychologists who, though able to offer assessment and treatment services, do not focus their career on these practices. These individuals spend the majority of their time critically analyzing and synthesizing existing research and carrying out new research on clinical forensic topics, so that that their colleagues are aware of the state of the science in clinical forensic practice. For example, the most recent advances in risk assessment central to legal decisions on civil commitment, execution (in states that use dangerousness as a criterion), and postconviction confinement of sexual predators have been completed by such scholars (e.g., Monahan et al., 2001). The training goals in this category are not uniform or unitary. Students need to be trained in two very different kinds of academic skills to carry out this type of work.

Scientist

Training for a career as an empirical researcher requires rigorous didactic and experiential training in methodology and data analytic techniques, and these educational experiences are common to all branches of scientific psychology. Although the goal is to allow graduates to design and carry out their own research in the future, the specific types of research that this training prepares one for differ across programs. For example, not all scientists design or carry out their research for forensic purposes. In *United States v. Virginia* (1996), the U.S. Supreme Court had to decide on the constitutionality of the State of Virginia maintaining an all-male military college, the Virginia Military Institute (VMI). As part of its decision, the Court considered research on the psychological effects of females receiving education in a single-gender versus coeducational environment. Although this research was originally conducted because of the researchers' interest in social development and gender studies, its application to the legal question at issue in the VMI case makes this research forensically relevant work (English & Sales, 2005).

Not surprisingly, nonforensic psychological researchers find their work being used in litigation and policy decision making across numerous issues. For example, research on child development can be used in the drafting of educational legislation, while social psychological studies of gender stereotyping can be used in sex harassment lawsuits (e.g., Fiske, Bersoff, Borgida, Deaux, & Heilman, 1993). Training psychologists for a nonforensic scientific career, even though the products of the subsequent research may have unanticipated forensic uses, is a common aspiration of traditional PhD programs.

But increasingly today, some PhD programs are offering students the opportunity to specialize in forensically relevant research. This research training can be categorized as basic or driven by policy, law, or litigation. Basic forensic studies seek to expand our knowledge of forensic phenomena (e.g., cognitive biases in judicial decision making; see Krauss, 2004) or techniques (e.g., research on assessment of dangerousness; see Quinsey, Harris, Rice, & Cormier, 1998). Policy-, law-, or litigation-driven forensic research is designed and carried out to answer specific questions posed by a specific legal or policy question (e.g., death qualification of juries; see *Lockhart v. McCree,* 1986). For example, in *Lockhart v. McCree,* researchers attempted to demonstrate that the process of death-qualifying juries (jurors who were morally opposed and could not sentence a defendant to the death penalty were dismissed from both phases of the trial) in a capital hearing case created an unconstitutionally biased jury in favor of the prosecution for the guilt/innocence phase of the trial. Although the majority of the Supreme Court was unpersuaded by this research for both methodological and legal reasons, the research presented to the Court was undertaken specifically to address these questions that were left open by the Court's decision in *Witherspoon v. Illinois* (1968).

Training for forensic research competency requires more than training in science, however. For forensic psychological research to be useful to the law (e.g., courts) or policymakers (e.g., legislators), it must both be relevant to the legal questions being adjudicated or considered and be sufficiently tied to issues under dispute or consideration in a particular case, statute, or policy. The importance of these considerations has been made explicitly clear with regard to the introduction of scientific evidence in the federal courts and in the majority of state courts (e.g., A. K. Hess, Chapter 27, in this volume; Sales & Shuman, 2004). The U.S. Supreme Court, in *Daubert v. Merrell Dow Pharmaceuticals, Inc.* (1993), adopted relevancy and fit requirements for the admissibility of scientific expert testimony at trial. As the Court in *Daubert* noted, in discussing the importance of the fit between the science being offered and the legal question being asked, "scientific validity for one purpose is not necessarily scientific validity for other, unrelated purposes" (p. 2796). *Daubert* and two subsequent cases (*General Electric Company v. Joiner,* 1997, and *Kumho Tire Company v. Carmichael,* 1999) have held that federal trial court judges must evaluate the reliability, relevancy, and fit of proffered expert testimony and research, and reject evidence that does not meet these criteria (Krauss & Sales, 1999).

Because *Daubert* controls decision making only in the federal courts, it technically is not required to be used in considering the admissibility of expert evidence in state courts, before state and federal legislatures, or in administrative agencies. The *Daubert* logic should be applicable, however, to studying any issue or question in the law (e.g., Schopp, 2001). Indeed, the majority of states have adopted the federal rule concerning the admissibility of expert evidence into their state rules of evidence (Sales & Shuman, 2005). Forensic researchers need to understand the law that provides the issues and questions they wish to study. Not to answer the questions posed by the court will likely result in forensic researchers' or practitioners' findings having little legal relevance and value (for a review the problems inherent in psychological research and expert testimony on child custody determinations, see Krauss & Sales, 1999, 2000).

Scholar

Designing and executing research are only part of the skill set required of individuals who are attempting to influence a field. It is also important that scholars be able to critically evaluate existing theory and research and identify where the field is weak and where theory and research need to be directed. For example, divorce mediation, which is prevalent throughout the United States, is touted as an alternative dispute-resolution system that offers substantial benefits for avoiding common disputes that arise during marital dissolution through the legal system. After critically reviewing the extensive empirical literature on divorce mediation, however, Beck and Sales (2001) concluded that most of the benefits associated with divorce mediation are not yet supported due to a host of legal, theoretical, methodical, and statistical weaknesses in the research literature. And there is research evidence to suggest that some of mediation's touted benefits are false. As this example demonstrates, training scholarly skills is particularly important to produce individuals who can generate a critical understanding of the state of the science on any forensic topic.

APPROACHES TO ACHIEVING TRAINING GOALS

Given that the training and career goals of forensic practitioners and scientists can differ markedly within and across categories, training programs have developed divergent programmatic approaches to educating their students so that they can attain these disparate goals. These programmatic approaches are not solely based on achieving specific training goals, however. They are also subject to administrative factors that affect the type of training a program can offer (e.g., number of faculty lines in forensics). As a result, the existing subtypes of training programs all possess both benefits and limitations that affect their ability to effectively train their students to attain their career goals. In this section, we describe the most common types of training programs and highlight the areas in which they are likely to benefit and limit their students for different types of forensic careers.

FORENSIC CLINICAL PRACTITIONERS

The vast majority of practitioners who currently describe themselves as forensic psychologists were not trained in graduate programs specializing in forensic psychology. This occurred because few such specialty programs existed until recently. As a result, the largest cohort of forensic practitioners received general clinical training in graduate school and later undertook more specialized training through postdoctoral work, continuing education courses, on-the-job training, or some combination of these.

Individuals trained under such a paradigm are likely to benefit in their forensic work from the generalist knowledge gained during clinical training. In addition, these individuals often will have accrued a wide range of clinical experience across a significant range of treatment settings, patient characteristics, and disorders before attempting more forensic-based clinical practice. As these practitioners refine their skills in the forensic arena, this general clinical training can serve as part of the foundation for forensic practice.

Yet, in a variety of ways, such general clinical training is also likely to serve as a constraint on the forensic skills of these professionals. First, general clinical training does not often prepare individuals to understand the clinical and research literature most pertinent to forensic practice. For example, forensic assessment is often predicated on the evaluator's responding to specific legal questions (e.g., Is the person incompetent to stand trial? Which custodial placement would be in the best interests of the child?). Not understanding the governing law can lead to inappropriate assessments. Because general clinical training is unlikely to offer trainees such specific legal training, even if trainees want to access the forensic literature they would be unlikely to know under what circumstances they would need to access it and where to find it. And even if practitioners uncovered the appropriate literature for the legal question at issue, they would be unlikely to understand the legal nuances of these writings.

Consider the case of a practitioner who wishes to perform an insanity evaluation for the first time. Without explicit knowledge of the legal standard governing such an assessment in the jurisdiction prosecuting the defendant, it would be impossible for a practitioner to do an appropriate job. Insanity standards vary markedly from jurisdiction to jurisdiction. For example, the federal system defines an insane individual as a defendant who "at the time of the commission of acts constituting the offense . . . as a result of severe mental disease or defect was unable to appreciate the nature and quality or the wrongfulness of his [or her] acts" (United States Code, 2001, 18 U.S.C. § 17). Other jurisdictions, however, also include a volitional component in their definition that allows for the acquittal of individuals whose mental illness affects the ability to conform their behaviors to the requirements of the law. Furthermore, within these two large subtypes of insanity definitions there are several additional minor jurisdictional variations. As a consequence, the assessment techniques utilized by the practitioner must be based on the idiosyncrasies of the controlling legal definition, or the practitioner will end up answering a question that the legal system is not interested in. Without specialized forensic training, the clinical practitioner is unlikely to know the controlling law or realize that reading relevant to the insanity defense in one jurisdiction may not be informative about the insanity defense in the jurisdiction in which the forensic practitioner currently practices (Zapf, Golding, & Roesch, Chapter 12, in this volume).

In regard to forensic treatment, the practitioner trained as a generalist is also likely to experience problems in forensic practice. Clinical training typically encompasses courses on various major therapeutic modalities, such as cognitive-behavior therapy. But these same programs are unlikely to assign the literatures that address which type of treatment modality will work best with various types of adult and juvenile offenders (e.g., Ashford et al., 2001). Indeed, the research literature on treatment for offenders, or persons otherwise involved with the law, is typically not covered in general courses on clinical treatments and interventions.

A related problem is that forensic services often have different goals from those set for therapy with private clients. Whereas in the latter, the client is seeking to "feel better" mentally and emotionally, the goal for the treatment of forensic patients is set by the law. For example, the most appropriate treatment or intervention for persons found incompetent to stand trial involves making the person competent to return to court, and not necessarily making the person mentally or emotionally healthy (Zapf & Roesch, Chapter 13, in this volume). Similarly, correctional administrators are more concerned about clinical services that reduce inmates' dangerousness and suicidality and are less concerned with programs designed to produce mentally healthy inmates. In general clinical programs, trainees will not receive important information specifically relevant to the needs of and the requirements imposed by various laws and legal systems (e.g., state and federal courts, state or federal Departments of Corrections) that set the standards for the clinicians hired by the government.

The lack of specialized forensic training in general clinical training programs is not limited to forensic treatment outcome research or to legally relevant standards and criteria. Generalized clinical training also suffers because it typically does not include didactic training on the unique ethical problems that forensic practitioners face (A. K. Hess, Chapter 27, in this volume). Shuman and Greenberg (2003), for example, have written on the unique ethical problems that treating therapists confront when they are retained to evaluate and testify about their client. These kinds of unique concerns have led to the publication of the *Specialty Guidelines for Forensic Psychologists* in 1991 (Committee on Ethical Guidelines for Forensic Psychologists, 1991), which is in the process of being revised. These specific ethical issues are unlikely to be adequately covered in general clinical training.

Graduating students from general clinical training programs have relied on several routes to respond to their lack of appropriate forensic training: attending an internship program that focuses on forensics, receiving postdoctoral supervision from a forensic specialist, attending continuing education programs, and engaging in self-directed readings. All are likely to improve one's forensic abilities. Unfortunately, anecdotal evidence suggests that some graduates of general clinical training programs do none of the above, assuming that good clinical practice for other settings will be sufficient in the legal arena.

As a direct solution, some general clinical training programs offer an emphasis in forensics (e.g., University of Alabama). Such training can compensate for the limits in general clinical training, with the caveat that how well a program compensates depends on the comprehensiveness of its forensic emphasis and the training and education opportunities the program provides. Students would be well advised to check the specialty courses and practica that programs of interest offer. For example, many of the existing programs still lack adequate legal training for forensic practice in most areas. Sales, Miller, and Hall (2005) have identified more than 75 areas of law that substantially affect the provision of forensic services.

The most effective form of training for providing forensic clinical services should logically be provided by forensic specialty training programs (e.g., Simon Fraser University). We say "logically" because there are no empirical studies of training outcomes in this area. These programs typically offer comprehensive forensic coursework and externship placements to ensure that the graduates are well prepared for forensic practice after licensure.

FORENSIC NONCLINICAL PRACTITIONERS

Not all forensic practice is related to clinical psychology. For example, training to be a government policy analyst may be best accomplished through focusing on evaluation research and methodology (e.g., Claremont Graduate University). In contrast, training to provide consultation to child protective service agencies may be better accomplished through applied developmental training than clinical training, while individuals interested in providing trial consultation to lawyers are typically best prepared for their occupation through forensic social psychological training.

These programs, because they are organized in ways similar to that of forensic clinical programs, suffer from the same benefits and limitations. Some are general programs, others have a forensic focus (e.g., University of Texas at El Paso), and still others offer forensic nonclinical specialty training (e.g., John Jay College of Criminal Justice-CUNY).

FORENSIC SCIENTISTS

Not all forensic trainees aspire to a practice career. As already noted, a subset of these students will look to academic careers to pursue their research or to other venues that will allow them to work as researchers (e.g., research think tanks, such as the RAND Corporation). Training for these positions is in many ways similar to training scientists in any subfield of psychology, with only the content of the research examined changing. Thus, individuals interested in studying eyewitness identifications often study in a cognitive psychology program, whereas individuals interested in pursuing child suggestibility in interview situations often enroll in a developmental psychology program. Finally, individuals interested in researching forensic assessment could pursue their interests through one of the scientifically driven clinical programs.

Such training has its benefits. Trainees graduate from respected traditional psychology programs, which often opens the door to faculty positions in other respected psychology departments. But there are also costs to attending such programs. Often, these programs do not have a faculty person who is expert on forensic issues beyond his or her own research interests. For the individual interested in broader training in forensic psychological science, the solution is to attend a program that focuses more generally on forensic science and offers the necessary concomitant didactic and experiential opportunities for more expansive forensic scientific training (e.g., Simon Fraser University, University of Arizona, University of Nebraska).

DEGREE AND NONDEGREE
TRAINING OPPORTUNITIES

Given the different approaches to achieving training goals, what are the specific degree and nondegree training opportunities in forensics that are available to trainees? As it turns out, there are quite a few.

PhD Programs

As noted in the prior section, few schools that offer forensic training do so through a program devoted to forensic psychology. Typically, a student enters a clinical psychology program that offers a forensic emphasis (e.g., Nova Southeastern University), but there are schools where training in forensics is accomplished through a specialized forensic program (e.g., Drexel University). As noted earlier, the benefit of such focused training is that it offers an intensive program of study in forensics.

Internship Training

Students in clinical or other professional training programs (e.g., counseling psychology, school psychology), whether they have a forensic emphasis or not, are required to take a year of internship experience, which can be at sites that offer a forensic focus (e.g., Patton State Hospital, California). Because these experiences are focused on patient assessment and/or treatment, the opportunity for experiential learning is substantial. When combined with a forensic specialty predoctoral training program, these internships can substantially broaden a trainee's skills. However, if the student attends a predoctoral program that focuses on training generalists, these internships, although valuable, will not replace the trainee's lack of knowledge about the pertinent forensic literature.

Joint Majors in Psychology and Joint Degree Programs

Some schools allow students to pursue concurrent training in two specialties within one PhD program (e.g., University of Arizona). The benefit of this approach typically is greatest for those seeking academic careers. Training in two majors typically forces students to master a greater array of the psychological literature and allows them to seek employment in departments that have jobs available in either specialty. Clearly, for joint training to substantively benefit trainees, the acquired knowledge should be integrated to enhance forensic research and scholarship. For example, studying social psychology can enhance forensic research on jury decision making (e.g., Lieberman & Arndt, 2000).

When joint training is mentioned, however, it is typically across colleges rather than within a department, with a number of schools offering the opportunity for students to pursue the PhD in combination with the JD degree (e.g., Pacific Graduate School of Psychology, Golden Gate University School of Law), or the PhD and the MLS (master of legal studies) degree (e.g., University of Nebraska). The MLS degree is typically a 1-year intensive training program for individuals not seeking to be licensed as lawyers but who still want to learn a sufficient amount of law to be able to enhance their forensic scholarship or practice.

The benefits of joint degree training include (1) increased proficiency in psychological science and legal research, writing, and thinking; (2) integration of the two fields of study through the course of one's graduate education, so that the individual can both think like a lawyer and perform research and practice like a psychological scientist; (3) greater understanding of legal norms, rules, and standards so that, at the least, forensic practitioners emerging from such programs know the laws that affect their practice and the specifics of the legal questions that the court might ask them to address; and (4) greater understanding of legal norms, rules, and standards so that their forensic research meaningfully addresses relevant legal topics, thereby increasing the likelihood that the research will be accepted by the legal system and policymakers.

Finally, some students who pursue the PhD come to recognize only after graduation that they have an interest in pursuing legal training. This typically takes one of two forms: entering law school to pursue the JD or entering an MLS program (e.g., Yale University) after the doctoral degree is completed. The obvious benefit of taking this route is that the forensic psychologist will obtain valuable legal training. The less obvious deficiency of such an approach is that taking training sequentially increases the chances that the student will not learn how to integrate the two fields. Learning biology and learning chemistry, for example, do not ensure that you will learn the theory, findings, and methods of biochemistry. It is no different when combining psychology with the law.

RESPECIALIZATION AND POSTDOCTORAL TRAINEESHIPS

Two other postdoctoral pathways exist for increasing forensic knowledge. First, students trained in nonclinical programs can reapply after graduation to achieve respecialization in clinical psychology with a forensic emphasis. This type of training may take 2 or 3 years and is a substantial investment of time, and where one does respecialization will affect how competent one becomes in forensics.

The other alternative is for doctoral graduates to seek additional postdoctoral research or practice experience for 1 or 2 years. Postdoctoral training allows intensive work in a given area under direct supervision, in this case, forensic science or practice, and thereby provides an excellent opportunity for doctoral graduates to acquire or increase their forensic knowledge (e.g., the forensic psychology fellowship at the University of Massachusetts Medical School at Worcester).

CONTINUING EDUCATION PROGRAMS

Perhaps the most common means for many practitioners to increase their forensic knowledge in specified areas is to attend continuing education programs focused on forensic practice issues. For example, the American Academy of Forensic Psychology offers continuing education programs on a wide array of forensic topics, which are aimed at practitioners possessing different levels of forensic skills and experience. It is not clear, however, if 1-, 2-, or even 3-day workshops can adequately prepare practitioners to fully understand the complexities of different forensic practice areas without additional supervision by a qualified practitioner, additional self-directed readings, prior training, or attendance at a substantial number of continuing education programs.

FORENSIC PSYCHOLOGICAL TRAINING FOR LAWYERS

It is worth mentioning that some law students and lawyers seek training in psychology to improve their legal practice skills or scholarship. While students in JD-PhD programs automatically have this opportunity, those who do not want a doctorate in psychology can still pursue an MA or MS degree in psychology in a variety of programs (e.g., Castleton College, University of Denver). The benefit of this type of training is that it will enhance the lawyer's or legal scholar's ability to identify and understand the psychological literature. The disadvantage of relying on master's degree training in forensic psychology is that such training rarely makes a graduate competent to critically analyze the extant literature.

DISCUSSION

Understanding the training goals, the approaches to achieving these goals, and the alternative structures used for delivering training, although a good first step for understanding forensic training opportunities, is not sufficient. There are myriad issues that these programs face, and that training raises, that deserve extended discussion. Some of these, such as the importance of the law and ethics, were considered briefly but are worth reconsidering given their importance. The other topics logically extend our prior discussion.

FACULTY EXPERTISE AND STUDENT GOALS

In assessing a forensic program, it is reasonable to ask who are the trainers and faculty and what are their qualifications for training the next generation of forensic psychologists. It is important that programs have faculty who are well qualified to teach and supervise in the areas to which they are assigned (APA, 2002, Standard 2.01). Although this admonition sounds obvious, as the pressure for forensic training increases and new programs are created, it is important that programs critically evaluate the expertise of their faculty for providing forensic training. We should never confuse competence in clinical services with competence in forensic clinical services or nonclinical forensic services or research.

The type and quality of training also will be affected by the administrative structure and financing of the training programs. For example, generalist programs are less likely than forensic specialty programs to have faculty who are broadly trained in forensics. The availability and size of the faculty who are expert in forensics will also impact the type of training available. This is not to argue that having one faculty member is necessarily worse than having five faculty members in a program. The issue is one of fit between the particular career aspirations of the trainee and the skills, abilities, and availability of the faculty at a particular program.

Perhaps the most basic and often overlooked issue in forensic training is that forensic services are broader than simply providing assessment or treatment in legal settings. For example, psychologists serving as policy analysts in a state legislature, serving in an administrative capacity in a governmental agency, or providing expert testimony on a wide variety of psychological topics are all providing forensic services. Trainees need to look critically at what specific training programs offer and how well those programs match their career goals. In addition, programs that focus on clinical assessment or treatment typically limit their focus to particular areas of forensic services in these two domains. Once again, trainees need to understand how these limitations will affect their competence when they graduate. Forensic research programs face the same issue: Not all programs provide training in all areas of forensic research.

Moreover, it is unreasonable to expect a limited number of faculty to competently train students in all areas of forensics. What is reasonable, however, is to expect that training programs will accurately represent what areas of forensics research and services training will be offered to trainees if they choose to attend that program.

FACULTY AS ADVISORS AND MENTORS

No matter what the expertise of the faculty, it is important to consider whether faculty view themselves as advisors or mentors. The former, which is more typical, occurs when faculty perceive their role as only imparting information to students and being available to answer student questions. The latter role involves the faculty taking a personal interest in the growth of the student and in his or her ultimate success after graduation. We have no data to know how individual students will fare under each type of training role, but students ought to be aware of the existing differences in supervision styles and seek information about the faculty approaches to training before making a decision about which program to attend.

NUMBER OF TRAINEES

Much like the size and expertise of the faculty, the number of students currently enrolled in a program is likely to affect the training experiences and education of a trainee. Some forensic training programs admit few students, whereas others admit many more. Being in a program with a small cohort of students is likely to lead to more individualized attention for the trainee, but it will also limit a student's opportunities to interact with, share experiences with, and learn from other graduate students in the field. Programs with a smaller cohort of students may also (but not necessarily) experience a smaller number of experiential and didactic training options. In contrast, larger forensic training programs, while offering less individualized attention, are more likely to offer a wider array of both training opportunities and coursework across a range of forensic topics. This typically occurs because the larger the student body, the more faculty there are likely to be associated with the program. Prospective trainees should obtain a realistic picture of what the programs are like in this regard.

DIDACTIC AND EXPERIENTIAL TRAINING OPPORTUNITIES

Forensic training of necessity needs both didactic and experiential training components. Didactic courses are necessary because they provide the intensive opportunity to acquire the scientific and practice knowledge base underlying forensics. Simply apprenticing under a practitioner might lead to a narrow perception of what forensics entails and a skill set that is limited to what that practitioner knows and does in practice. Experiential training through externships, internships, and other supervised practica can augment the learning that has occurred in the classroom and in directed readings courses.

The important point for the prospective student is to evaluate how well the available courses and experiential learning opportunities match the needs of the trainee to become a forensic psychologist. This is not an easy task. Programs are unlikely to provide training in all areas of forensics. Thus, all trainees by definition will be deficient in some areas of forensic knowledge (e.g., learning about guardianship law and forensic practice). Although not being expert in all forensic areas is a foregone conclusion given the existing training programs, it is not necessarily a problem. Graduate training is the beginning, we hope, of a lifetime of learning and not the end of one's learning about forensic knowledge and skills. To the extent that the trainee is taught how to identify specific legal issues, the scientific knowledge base available to address the legal question, and the forensic skills related to those issues, the trainee can acquire the substantive knowledge after graduation.

Of particular concern in didactic and experiential training is the quality of that training. It is important for the student to be educated regarding the current approaches to forensic practice, but the hallmark of the scientist-practitioner model (i.e., the Boulder model) is that the trainee learn how to think like a scientist and ask whether what is, is what ought to be. The importance of this level of critical analysis in teaching in the classroom, in research settings, and in experiential settings cannot be overemphasized because it fosters critical questioning of forensic skills and services. Externships and internships are particularly vulnerable to not allowing for this analytic process to be learned. Trainees often begin their practice experiences in work settings with professionals who are overworked and claim to have limited time to stay abreast of the current scholarly literature. What they share with the trainees is what they do, rather than presenting the full panoply of approaches that are available for use with different problems and clients. For example, a psychodynamically oriented practitioner may provide excellent training to the extern concerning his or her approach to therapy with particular types of clients, but provide no information about alternative approaches or how one chooses between them given a particular problem, client, and setting. The result is that the trainees can confuse information acquired during apprenticeship with the best available scholarly information in the field, or even the best current clinical practices.

LEARNING THE RELEVANT LAW AND HOW TO FIND IT

Training programs need to be especially cognizant of the legal research and training skills that are a necessary component of effective training. For example, it is one thing for forensic trainees to know the legal standard that governs the specific legal evaluation they are being asked to perform in a jurisdiction. It is quite another thing for students to be trained in the skill set that would allow them to identify the relevant law, fully understand it and its implications for forensic practice, and keep abreast of changes in that law in the future. At a minimum, this entails being able to (1) identify and read the central case law in that jurisdiction on a particular evaluation question; (2) use this case law in a meaningful way so that their evaluation best addresses the legal standard controlling the forensic issue in question; (3) keep current on changes in that law and related evaluation practices; (4) be aware of legal standards in other jurisdictions that may have implications for the forensic work on the identified case; and (5) be aware of legal changes not central to the evaluation standard itself but critical to the success of the forensic work (e.g., changes in admissibility standards) because they will affect both the evaluative procedures utilized and whether the eventual psychological conclusions generated will be accepted by the court as expert testimony. Training programs that do not have extensive legal components risk handicapping their trainees by compromising the quality of their future work.

FORENSIC ETHICS TRAINING

It is also important that forensic training that focuses on practice offer competent training in forensic ethics (A. K. Hess, Chapter 27, in this volume). Ethical challenges in general practice are not always identical to the challenges faced by forensic practitioners, with forensic practice generally raising more and different ethical issues than general practice (Melton et al., 1997). For example, who is the client when a psychologist performs services with a prisoner? Is it the prisoner, the prison, or the Department of Corrections? As noted earlier, to help answer questions such as these, there are specialty ethical guidelines designed specifically for forensic practice (Committee on Ethical Guidelines for Forensic Psychologists, 1991). Although these guidelines are aspirational, all forensic practitioners should be aware of, understand, and strive to follow them, as well as keep abreast of more current forensic ethics scholarship. Due to these unique ethical concerns, not having an expert in ethics teach the ethics sequence, and not having that supplemented by an expert in forensic ethics, is questionable training practice. The reality is that in many schools, this training is provided by practitioners or faculty who are not expert in ethics.

FORENSIC COMPETENCE

Defining forensic competence in one area of practice or research or across several areas is not an easy task. For example, the acceptance of certain types of expert testimony, research, or practice by the legal system is often a poor indicator of the competence of individuals who proffer, engage in, or use such techniques. Consider a jurisdiction that has accepted expert testimony based on pure clinical hunches about a defendant's future dangerousness in death penalty sentencing (*Barefoot v. Estelle*, 1983). Ironically, a practitioner offering such testimony is not forensically competent. A forensically competent practitioner would be aware of the superiority of actuarially based dangerousness predictions over more clinical judgments (Grove & Meehl, 1996; Krauss & Sales, 2001) and recognize the limitations in using an existing actuarial instrument as the basis for expert testimony on dangerousness (Monahan, Steadman, Silver, Appelbaum, Robbins, Mulvey, et al., 2001).

Forensic competence is also not necessarily performing a forensic service in the exact same manner as supervisors did during training. It entails recognizing that advances in the field, differences in the applicable law based on the jurisdiction where the evaluation takes place, and changes in the law over time will have a bearing on how each forensic service should be performed in the future. The key is for forensic training programs to instill in their graduates the necessary intellectual rigor to regularly ask themselves, "Is what I am about to do 'what ought to be done' rather than simply repeating past practices?"

CREDENTIALING IN PSYCHOLOGY

The timing of forensic training raises a fundamental training issue. As previously noted, forensic training can occur predoctorally, during internship, postdoctorally, through continuing education programs, through on-the-job training, or through self-directed reading. All may be perfectly appropriate for providing forensic expertise, but we have no data to know what kind of impact these training methods have on the acquisition of forensic knowledge and skills.

Because the discipline and specialty is uncertain about the merits of the different training approaches, licensure for practice is still dependent on doctoral training that includes an internship component. But after licensure is attained, decisions about whether to engage in a specialty forensic practice is left to the ethics of the individual practitioners. Once again, we have no data to know how well practitioners self-monitor and self-evaluate the competency of their forensic skills. Not surprisingly, some jurisdictions, in response to perceived weaknesses in forensic practitioner competency, now require specialty training for certain types of evaluations (e.g., see California Rules of Court, 2003, 5.225(d)–(i), which specify specific training, education, and continuing education requirements for individuals performing child custody evaluations for the California courts).

The timing, extent, and type of training individuals receive will also affect their ability to obtain board certification in forensic psychology. Board certification as endorsed by the American Board of Professional Psychology allows certification in 11 distinct psychological areas, including forensic psychology, and represents one of the two board certifications listed in the APA directory. To become a board-certified diplomate in forensic psychology, individuals must complete an approved internship, accrue a significant number of hours of general clinical practice experience, obtain a specific number of hours of specialized training in forensic psychology, work within the field of forensic psychology for a number of years, and pass both oral and written examinations (for the specific requirements for board certification in forensic psychology, see http://www.abfp.com/certification.asp). So if forensic practitioners or students are interested in becoming diplomates, they must choose training experiences that will fulfill these requirements. Thus, the timing and adequacy of training need to be carefully addressed by prospective trainees and practitioners interested in specialty certification.

MAINTAINING AND INCREASING FORENSIC COMPETENCE

One measure of the success of forensic training programs is whether graduates are motivated to seek continuing education programs that will maintain and increase their forensic competence. Unfortunately, there are no current data available to address this issue. In addition, although continuing education programs exist in the forensic arena, there has been limited analysis of the variety of topics covered by existing programs, the comprehensiveness of the coverage of the presented topics, the availability of programs in various parts of the country, and whether the covered topics match the wide diversity of forensic training needs. It is hoped that research will address these important issues in the future.

ACCREDITATION OF FORENSIC TRAINING

Forensic training programs are not accredited by APA. When training programs advertise that they are accredited, they are referring to the fact that their generalist clinical, counseling, or school psychology program is APA-accredited. Whether accreditation is something that will increase the quality of forensic practice training is an issue that the field needs to consider. If the consensus is yes, representatives of the field will need to petition and work with the APA Accreditation Office to ensure that forensic training programs come under APA's accreditation umbrella.

CHALLENGES IN TRAINING FORENSIC SCIENTISTS

Programs specializing in the training of forensic scientists must face specific challenges. To perform useful forensic research on a topic, students must be trained to identify the questions that the law needs answered by psychological science. For example, in the case of *McCleskey v. Kemp* (1987), Kemp, an African American, was charged with the murder of a White man. The defense introduced the testimony of an expert to support its claim that the Georgia death penalty statute and process discriminated against the defendant. Although the expert had conducted a social science analysis of 2,000 death penalty decisions in the State of Georgia, the U.S. Supreme Court was not persuaded, noting, among other things, that the case was brought on a challenge to the Georgia death penalty statute under the U.S. Constitution's Fourteenth Amendment Equal Protection Clause. This clause requires not only a showing of discrimination, but also a showing that the discrimination was intentional. Although the social science data demonstrated a relationship between death penalty decisions and defendant and victim race, the data did not address whether the discrimination was intentional. In the end, the Court was unpersuaded by the data because they did not specifically address this latter issue.

Training programs must teach their students how to identify issues that are testable through psychological science techniques and are also important to legal proceedings. To accomplish this goal, students must be taught to operationalize difficult legal constructs in such a way that meaningful empirical examination can occur. Without the ability to effectively operationalize these concepts, it is impossible to measure and study them using available psychological techniques and methodology (Krauss & Sales, 2003).

Some scholars in the field would argue that it is not always possible to operationalize legal concepts using psychological science because legal standards often include moral and normative judgments that are impossible to effectively evaluate with psychological methodology (Grisso, 1986, 2003). This does not suggest, however, that operationalization and empirical investigation of legal questions is inappropriate or unimportant. Rather, it suggests that empirical research must be seen as a means to enhance and inform judicial and legal decision making, rather than as a substitute for it (Krauss & Sales, 2003). Students' awareness and understanding of these issues is thus a necessary precondition to useful forensic research being performed; they must not only understand how to effectively test important legal issues, but also recognize the limitations of empirical research to answer all legal questions.

For example, the law does not always allow for experimentation in legal settings. As a result, researchers often are left with no choice but to use simulated tests in simulated settings. This often is the case, for instance, in jury research, which is typically conducted using college students who are exposed to a brief transcript in a laboratory setting. The result is that the research, although internally valid, lacks ecological validity (i.e., realism) and external validity (i.e., the results lack generalizability to other settings).

It is not only the use of simulations that leads to compromised findings for the implementation of legal policy. Even ecologically valid research can lack external validity. The results of studying mediation in one jurisdiction may not be generalizable to other jurisdictions because of differences in mediators and mediation procedures (Beck & Sales, 2001). Thus, when training forensic scientists and educating the consumers of their research, it is important that training programs include specific educational opportunities that focus on understanding the needs of the law and how research can and cannot address those needs under varying conditions.

EMPIRICAL RESEARCH ON FORENSIC TRAINING

Ultimately, forensic training, like training in all fields, will need to be systematically scrutinized empirically if we are to discern the best pathways to improving forensic competence in practice. This is not a simple task, however, given that the learned professions, including forensic psychology, have never embraced such a research agenda. The problem for forensics is that such research will be confounded by the validity of the knowledge base that is imparted during training. For example, if a training approach is not empirically shown to produce competence in practice, is it the result of the approach or the lack of validity in the treatment method taught? Although a problematic issue for research design, the importance of the larger issue still stands—the need to empirically study the outcomes of different training approaches—and deserves serious scholarly attention in the future.

REFERENCES

American Psychological Association. (2002). Ethical principles of psychologists and code of conduct. *American Psychologist, 57,* 1060–1073.

American Psychology-Law Society. (2005). *Graduate programs in psychology and law related programs.* Retrieved May 17, 2005, from www.ap-ls.org/students/graduateIndex.html.

Ashford, J. B., Sales, B. D., & Reid, W. H. (Eds.). (2001). *Treating adult and juvenile offenders with special needs.* Washington, DC: American Psychological Association.

Barefoot v. Estelle, No. 82-6080, 463 U.S. 880 (1983).

Beck, C. J. A., & Sales, B. D. (2001). *Family mediation: Facts, myths, and future prospects.* Washington, DC: American Psychological Association.

Benjamin, G. A. H., & Gollan, J. K. (2003). *Family evaluation in custody litigation: Reducing risks of ethical infractions and malpractice.* Washington, DC: American Psychological Association.

Bersoff, D. N., Goodman-Delahunty, J., Grisso, T., Hans, V. P., Poythress, N. G., & Roesch, R. G. (1997). Training in law and psychology: Models from the Villanova conference. *American Psychologist, 52,* 1301–1310.

California Rules of Court 5.225(d)–(i) (amended January 1, 2003).

Committee on Ethical Guidelines for Forensic Psychologists. (1991). Specialty guidelines for forensic psychologists. *Law and Human Behavior, 6,* 655–665.

Contreras, R. (2001, August 10). More courts let experts debunk witness accounts, *Wall Street Journal,* p. B-1.

Daubert v. Merrell Dow Pharmaceuticals, Inc., 509 U.S. 579 (1993).

English, P. W., & Sales, B. D. (2005). *More than the law: Social and behavioral knowledge in legal decision-making.* Washington, DC: American Psychological Association.

Fiske, S. T., Bersoff, D. N., Borgida, E., Deaux, K., & Heilman, M. (1993). A brief rejoinder: Accuracy and objectivity on behalf of the APA. *American Psychologist, 48,* 55–56.

General Electric Company v. Joiner, 522 U.S. 136 (1997).

Grisso, T. (1986). *Evaluating competencies: Forensic assessments and instruments.* New York: Plenum Press.

Grisso, T. (2003). *Evaluating competencies: Forensic assessments and instruments* (2nd ed.). New York: Plenum Press.

Grove, W., & Meehl, P. (1996). Comparing the efficiency of informal (impressionistic, subjective) and formal (mechanistic, algorithmic) predictions procedures: The clinical-statistical controversy. *Psychology, Public Policy, and Law, 2,* 293–323.

Hafemeister, T. L., Hall, S. R., & Dvoskin, J. A. (2001). Administrative concerns associated with the treatment of offenders with mental illness. In J. B. Ashford, B. D. Sales, & W. H. Reid (Eds.), *Treating adult and juvenile offenders with special needs* (pp. 419–445). Washington, DC: American Psychological Association.

In re L. A. M., WL 246371, Iowa (2001).

Krauss, D. (2004). *Clinically adjusting risk of recidivism: Do judicial departures worsen or improve recidivism prediction under the Federal Sentencing Guidelines?* Manuscript submitted for review.

Krauss, D., & Sales, B. D. (1999). The problem of helpfulness in applying *Daubert* to expert testimony: Child custody determination in family law as an exemplar. [Special issue: *Daubert* and social science research]. *Psychology, Public Policy, and Law, 5,* 78–100.

Krauss, D., & Sales, B. D. (2000). Legal standards, expertise, and experts in the resolution of contested child custody cases. *Psychology, Public Policy, and Law, 6,* 843–879.

Krauss, D., & Sales, B. D. (2001). The effects of clinical and scientific expert testimony on juror decision-making in capital sentencing. *Psychology, Public Policy, and Law, 7,* 267–310.

Krauss, D., & Sales, B. D. (2003). Forensic psychology, public policy, and the law. In A. M. Goldstein (Ed.), *Forensic psychology* (pp. 543–561). Vol. 11 in I. B. Weiner (Editor-in-Chief), *Handbook of psychology*. Hoboken, NJ: Wiley.

Kumho Tire Company v. Carmichael, 526 U.S. 137 (1999).

Lieberman, J., & Arndt, J. (2000). Understanding the limits of limiting instructions: Social psychological explanations for the failure of instructions to disregard pretrial publicity and other inadmissible evidence. *Psychology, Public Policy, and Law, 6*, 677–711.

Lockhart v. McCree, 476 U.S. 162 (1986).

Mancuso v. Consolidated Edison Co., 2000 U.S. App. LEXIS 20534 (2d. Cir., 2000).

McCleskey v. Kemp, 481 U.S. 279 (1987).

Melton, G. B., Petrila, J., Poythress, N. G., & Slobogin, C. (1997). *Psychological evaluations for the courts: A handbook for mental health professionals and lawyers* (2nd ed.). New York: Guilford Press.

Monahan, J., Steadman, H., Silver, E., Appelbaum, A., Robbins, P., Mulvey, E., et al. (2001). *Rethinking risk assessment: The MacArthur study of mental disorder and violence.* New York: Oxford University Press.

People v. Wheeler, 602 N.E. 2d 826 (Ill., 1992).

Peterson, D. (2003). Unintended consequences: Ventures and misadventures in the education of professional psychologists. *American Psychologist, 58*, 791–800.

Quinsey, V., Harris, G., Rice, M., & Cormier, C. (1998). *Violent offenders: Appraising and managing risk.* Washington, DC: American Psychological Association.

Sales, B. D. (1983). The legal regulation of psychology: Professional and scientific interactions. In C. J. Scheirer & B. L. Hammonds (Eds.), *The master lecture series: Vol. II. Psychology and the law* (pp. 5–36). Washington, DC: American Psychological Association.

Sales, B. D., Miller, M. O., & Hall, S. R. (2005). *Laws affecting clinical practice.* Washington, DC: American Psychological Association.

Sales, B. D., & Shuman, D. W. (2004). *Experts in court: Reconciling law, science, and professional knowledge.* Manuscript submitted for publication.

Schopp, R. F. (2001). *Competence, condemnation, and commitment: An integrated theory of mental health law.* Washington, DC: American Psychological Association.

Shuman, D., & Greenberg, S. (2003). The expert, the adversary system, and the voice of reason: Reconciling objectivity and advocacy. *Professional Psychology: Research and Practice, 34*, 219–224.

United States Code, 18 U.S.C. § 17 (2001).

United States v. Norwood, 939 F. Supp. 1132 (D.N.J. 1996).

United States v. Virginia, 518 U.S. 515 (1996).

Witherspoon v. Illinois, 391 U.S. 510 (1968).

Author Index

Subject Index